1000 VEGETARIAN

RECIPES FROM AROUND THE WORLD

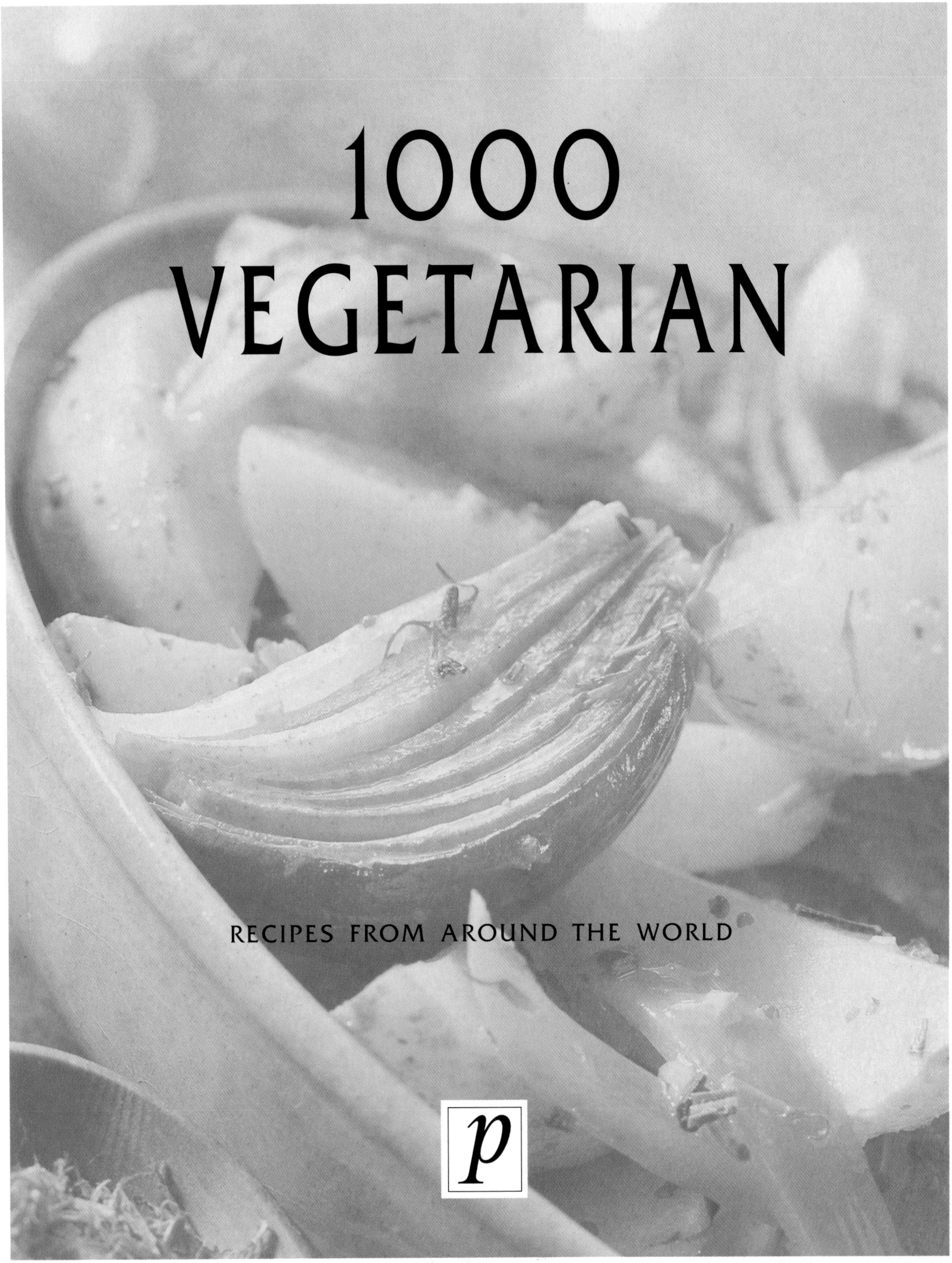

1000 VEGETARIAN

RECIPES FROM AROUND THE WORLD

p

This is a Parragon Book
This edition published in 2003

Parragon
Queen Street House
4 Queen Street
Bath BA1 1HE, UK

ISBN: 1-40541-588-6

Printed in China

NOTE

This book uses metric and imperial measurements. Follow the same units
of measurement throughout; do not mix metric and imperial.
All spoon measurements are level: teaspoons are assumed to be 5 ml and
tablespoons are assumed to be 15 ml. Unless otherwise stated,
milk is assumed to be full fat, eggs and individual vegetables such as potatoes
are medium and pepper is freshly ground black pepper.

The nutritional information provided for each recipe is per serving or per person.
Optional ingredients, variations or serving suggestions have
not been included in the calculations. The times given for each recipe are an approximate
guide only because the preparation times may differ according to the techniques used by
different people and the cooking times may vary as a result of the type of oven used.

Recipes using raw or very lightly cooked eggs should be
avoided by infants, the elderly, pregnant women, convalescents
and anyone suffering from an illness.

contents

INTRODUCTION

This book contains 1,000 vegetarian recipes that have been carefully selected to provide an almost unlimited variety of healthy and delicious meals. Each recipe contains the following information: nutritional calculations, preparation and cooking times, and level of difficulty (one chef's hat for an easy recipe, rising to five chef's hats for a difficult recipe).

basic recipes

Fresh Vegetable Stock

Keep this stock refrigerated for up to 3 days, or frozen for up to 3 months.
makes 1.5 litres/2¾ pints

250 g/9 oz shallots

1 large carrot, diced

1 celery stick, chopped

½ fennel bulb

1 garlic clove

1 bay leaf

4–6 sprigs of fresh parsley and tarragon

2 litres/3½ pints water

pepper

1 Put all the ingredients in a large saucepan and bring to the boil.

2 Skim off the surface scum with a flat spoon and reduce to a gentle simmer. Partially cover and cook for 45 minutes. Leave to cool.

3 Line a sieve with clean muslin and put it over a large jug or bowl. Pour the stock through the sieve. Discard the herbs and vegetables.

4 Cover with clingfilm and store in the refrigerator or freezer until ready to use.

Béchamel Sauce

275 ml/9½ fl oz skimmed milk

4 cloves

1 bay leaf

pinch of freshly grated nutmeg

2 tbsp polyunsaturated margarine

2 tbsp plain flour

pepper and low-sodium salt

1 Put the milk in a saucepan and add the cloves, bay leaf and nutmeg. Gradually bring to the boil. Remove from the heat and leave for 15 minutes.

2 Melt the margarine in another saucepan and stir in the flour to make a roux. Cook gently, stirring, for 1 minute. Remove the pan from the heat.

3 Strain the milk and gradually blend into the roux. Return the pan to the heat and gently bring to the boil, stirring, until the sauce thickens. Season to taste.

VARIATIONS

All sorts of ingredients can be added to the basic Béchamel recipe to make interesting, low-fat sauces which go particularly well with vegetables and fish.

Watercress Sauce

Add 1 small bunch of watercress, finely chopped, to the basic sauce.

Green Herb Sauce

Add 1–2 tablespoon chopped fresh mixed herbs to the sauce just before serving.

Parsley Sauce

Add 2 tablespoons finely chopped fresh parsley to the basic sauce.

Mushroom Sauce

Wash and finely slice 125 g/4 oz button mushrooms, and add them to the basic sauce with 1 tablespoon of finely chopped fresh tarragon.

Lemon Sauce

Add some finely grated lemon rind and juice to the basic sauce.

Mustard Sauce

Add 1 tablespoon French mustard and a squeeze of lemon juice to the basic sauce.

Basic Tomato Sauce

1 tbsp olive oil

1 small onion, chopped

1 garlic clove, chopped

400 g/14 oz canned chopped tomatoes

2 tbsp chopped fresh parsley

1 tsp dried oregano

2 bay leaves

2 tbsp tomato purée

1 tsp sugar

pepper and low-sodium salt

1 Heat the oil in a pan over a medium heat and fry the onion for 2–3 minutes or until translucent. Add the garlic and fry for 1 minute. Stir in the chopped tomatoes, parsley, oregano, bay leaves, tomato purée, and sugar, and season with pepper and a pinch of salt.

2 Bring the sauce to the boil, then lower the heat and simmer, uncovered, for 15–20 minutes, or until the sauce has reduced by half. Discard the bay leaves just before serving.

Red Wine Sauce

425 ml/15 fl oz Vegetable Stock (see page 6)

425 ml/15 fl oz red wine

small piece of onion, peeled

1 garlic clove, peeled and sliced

1 bay leaf

1 sprig fresh thyme

2–3 sprigs fresh parsley

½ tsp black peppercorns

1 tbsp redcurrant jelly

3 tbsp polyunsaturated margarine

1½ tbsp plain flour

pepper and low-sodium salt

1 Put the stock and red wine in a pan with the onion, garlic, bay leaf, thyme and parsley sprigs, and peppercorns. Bring to the boil and boil for 10–15 minutes to reduce the liquid by half.

2 Strain the liquid into a clean pan and mix in the redcurrant jelly, some pepper and a pinch of salt.

3 Mix half the margarine with the flour to make a paste and add to the warm sauce in small pieces. Mix well after each addition.

4 Return the sauce to the heat and stir gently until it thickens slightly. Simmer gently for a few minutes to cook the flour. Beat in the remaining margarine just before serving.

Honey and Yogurt Dressing

makes about 125 ml/4 fl oz

1 tbsp clear honey

6 tbsp low-fat natural yogurt

salt and pepper

Put the honey and yogurt in a glass bowl and beat with a fork until thoroughly combined. Season to taste with salt and pepper.

Mild Mustard Sauce

2 egg yolks

2 tbsp lemon juice

2 garlic cloves, chopped

300 ml/10 fl oz olive oil

1 tbsp Dijon mustard

salt and pepper

Put the egg yolks, lemon juice and garlic in a blender or food processor and process until combined and smooth. With the motor running, gradually add the olive oil through the feeder tube until thick and creamy. Transfer to a bowl, stir in the Dijon mustard and season to taste with salt and pepper.

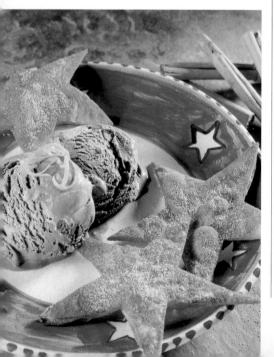

Mayonnaise

makes 300 ml/10 fl oz

2 egg yolks

150 ml/5 fl oz sunflower oil

150 ml/5 fl oz olive oil

1 tbsp white wine vinegar

2 tsp Dijon mustard

salt and pepper

1 Beat the egg yolks with a pinch of salt. Combine the oils in a jug. Gradually add the oil, a drop at a time, beating constantly with a whisk or electric mixer.

2 When a quarter of the oil has been incorporated, beat in the vinegar. Continue adding the oil, in a steady stream, beating constantly.

3 Stir in the mustard and season to taste with salt and pepper.

Chilli Flowers

To make chilli flowers, hold the stem of the chilli and cut down its length several times with a sharp knife. Place in a bowl of chilled water and chill so that the 'petals' turn out. Remove the chilli seeds when the 'petals' have opened.

Home-made Crème Fraîche

225 ml/8 fl oz whipping cream

2 tbsp buttermilk

1 Combine the two ingredients well in a glass container.

2 Cover and let stand at room temperature from 8 to 24 hours or until very thick. Use as required.

Rich Shortcrust Pastry Dough

makes 1 x 23 cm/9 in flan

175 g/6 oz plain flour

85 g/3 oz butter, plus extra for greasing

1 egg yolk

3 tbsp iced water

salt

1 Sift the flour with a pinch of salt into a bowl. Add the butter, cut it into the flour and then rub in with your fingertips until the mixture resembles fine breadcrumbs.

2 Beat the egg yolk with the water in a small bowl. Sprinkle the liquid over the flour mixture and combine with a round-bladed knife or your fingertips.

3 Form the dough into a ball, cover and chill for 30 minutes.

Crêpe Batter

makes 12 crêpes

115 g/4 oz plain flour

1 egg, lightly beaten

300 ml/10 fl oz milk

1 tsp sunflower oil

salt

1 Sift the flour with a pinch of salt into a bowl. Using a wooden spoon, beat in the egg and half the milk. Continue beating until the mixture is smooth and lump free.

2 Stir in the remaining milk and the sunflower oil.

3 Pour the batter into a jug and, if you have time, set aside to rest for 30–60 minutes. Stir the batter before cooking.

Basic Cheesy Rice

60–75 g/2–2¾ oz unsalted butter

1 onion, finely chopped

300 g/10½ oz arborio or carnaroli rice

120 ml/4 fl oz dry white vermouth or white wine

1.2 litres/2 pints vegetable stock, simmering

80 g/3 oz freshly grated Parmesan cheese, plus extra for sprinkling

salt and pepper

1 Heat about 25 g/1 oz of the butter in a large heavy-based saucepan over a medium heat. Add the onion and cook for about 2 minutes until just beginning to soften. Add the rice and cook for about 2 minutes, stirring frequently, until translucent and well coated with the butter.

2 Pour in the vermouth: it will bubble and steam rapidly and evaporate almost immediately. Add a ladleful (about 225 ml/8 fl oz) of the simmering stock and cook, stirring constantly, until the stock is absorbed.

3 Continue adding the stock, about half a ladleful at a time, allowing each addition to be absorbed before adding the next – never allow the rice to cook 'dry'. This should take 20–25 minutes. The mix should have a creamy consistency and the rice grains should be tender, but still firm to the bite.

4 Remove the pan from the heat and stir in the remaining butter and Parmesan. Season with salt and a little pepper, to taste. Cover and stand for about 1 minute, then sprinkle with extra Parmesan.

Cheese Sauce

2 tbsp polyunsaturated margarine

25 g/1 oz plain flour

1 bay leaf

425 ml/15 fl oz skimmed milk

60 g/2¼ oz grated mature half-fat Cheddar cheese

1 tsp English mustard powder

pinch of cayenne pepper

black pepper

1 Melt the margarine in a pan and stir in the flour. Cook, stirring, over a low heat until the roux is light in colour and crumbly in texture. Add the bay leaf. Stir in one-third of the milk, beat until the sauce is thick then repeat twice to use all the milk.

2 Remove the sauce from the heat, remove the bay leaf, and beat in the grated cheese, mustard, a tiny pinch of cayenne pepper and the black pepper. There is no need to add extra salt because the cheese will be salty.

Soups, Starters & Snacks

Home-made soups make an excellent contribution to the vegetarian diet. Try the light and elegant Avocado and Mint Soup, or the more robust Vegetable and Corn Chowder, which is perfect for cheering a midwinter day. Although soups also make excellent starters themselves, there are plenty of recipes here that will make the perfect beginning to any kind of meal. Try the delicious Feta Cheese Tartlets or Mushroom & Garlic Soufflés for a tasty start to a dinner party, or serve up Roasted Cheese with Salsa or Potato Skins with Guacamole to your hungry family at an informal lunch. Whatever the occasion, there are wonderful recipes, flavours and textures to try here.

Asparagus Soup

Fresh asparagus is now available for most of the year, so this soup can be made at any time. It can also be made using canned asparagus.

NUTRITIONAL INFORMATION

Calories	196	Sugars	.........7g
Protein	.........7g	Fat	..........12g
Carbohydrate	...15g	Saturates	.......4g

5–10 mins   55 mins

SERVES 6

INGREDIENTS

1 bunch asparagus, about 350 g/12 oz, or 2 packs mini asparagus, about 150 g/5½ oz each

700 ml/1¼ pints vegetable stock

60 g/2 oz butter or margarine

1 onion, chopped

3 tbsp plain flour

salt and pepper

¼ tsp ground coriander

1 tbsp lemon juice

450 ml/16 fl oz milk

4–6 tbsp double or single cream

COOK'S TIP

If using canned asparagus, drain off the liquid and use as part of the measured stock. Remove a few small asparagus tips for garnish and chop the remainder. Continue as above.

1 Wash and trim the asparagus, discarding the lower, woody part of the stem. Cut the remainder into short lengths, keeping aside a few tips to use as a garnish. Mini asparagus does not need to be trimmed.

2 Cook the tips in the minimum of boiling salted water for 5–10 minutes. Drain and set aside.

3 Put the asparagus in a saucepan with the stock, bring to the boil, cover and simmer for about 20 minutes, until soft. Drain and reserve the stock.

4 Melt the butter or margarine in a saucepan. Add the onion and fry over a low heat until soft, but only barely coloured. Stir in the flour and cook for 1 minute, then gradually whisk in the reserved stock and bring to the boil.

5 Simmer for 2–3 minutes, until thickened, then stir in the cooked asparagus, seasoning, coriander and lemon juice. Simmer for 10 minutes, then cool a little and either press through a sieve with the back of a spoon or process in a blender or food processor until smooth.

6 Pour into a clean pan, add the milk and reserved asparagus tips and bring to the boil. Simmer for 2 minutes. Stir in the cream, reheat gently and serve.

Wild Mushroom Soup

The Calabrian mountains in southern Italy provide large amounts of wild mushrooms. Rich in flavour and colour, they make a wonderful soup.

NUTRITIONAL INFORMATION

Calories ......452 Sugars 5g
Protein ....15g Fat 26g
Carbohydrate ...42g Saturates 12g

 5 mins 🕐 25–30 mins

SERVES 4

INGREDIENTS

2 tbsp olive oil

1 onion, chopped

450g/1 lb mixed mushrooms, such as ceps, oyster and button

300 ml/½ pint milk

850 ml/1½ pints hot vegetable stock

8 slices of granary bread or French stick

50 g/1¾ oz butter, melted

2 garlic cloves, crushed

75 g/2¾ oz Gruyère cheese, finely grated

salt and pepper

1 Heat the oil in a large frying pan and fry the onion for 3–4 minutes, or until soft and golden.

2 Wipe each mushroom with a damp cloth and cut any large mushrooms into smaller, bite-size pieces.

3 Add the mushrooms to the pan, stirring quickly to coat them well in the oil.

4 Add the milk to the pan, bring to the boil, cover and leave to simmer for about 5 minutes. Gradually stir in the hot vegetable stock. Season to taste.

5 Under a preheated grill, toast the bread on both sides until golden.

6 Mix together the melted butter and crushed garlic and then spoon it generously over the toast.

7 Place the slices of buttered toast in the bottom of a large soup tureen or divide them among 4 individual serving bowls. Pour the hot soup over the toast. Top with the grated Gruyère cheese and serve at once.

Pepper & Chilli Soup

This soup has a real Mediterranean flavour, using sweet red peppers, tomato, chilli and basil. It is great served with olive bread.

NUTRITIONAL INFORMATION

Calories	 55	Sugars	. . . . 10g
Protein	. . . . 2g	Fat	. . . . 0.5g
Carbohydrate	. . . . 11g	Saturates	. . . . . 0.1g

 10 mins 25 mins

SERVES 4

INGREDIENTS

225 g/8 oz red peppers, seeded and sliced

1 onion, sliced

2 garlic cloves, crushed

1 green chilli, chopped

300 ml/½ pint passata

600 ml/1 pint vegetable stock

2 tbsp chopped basil

basil sprigs, to garnish

salt and pepper

VARIATION

This soup is also delicious served cold with 150 ml/¼ pint of natural yogurt swirled into it.

1 Put the sliced red peppers in a large saucepan with the onion, garlic and chilli. Add the passata and the vegetable stock and bring to the boil, stirring well.

2 Reduce the heat to a simmer and continue to cook the vegetables for 20 minutes, or until the peppers have softened. Drain, reserving the liquid and vegetables separately.

3 Using the back of a spoon, press the vegetables through a sieve. Alternatively, process in a food processor until smooth.

4 Return the vegetable purée to a clean saucepan with the reserved cooking liquid. Add the basil, season, and heat through until hot. Garnish the soup with fresh basil sprigs and serve immediately.

Sweet Potato & Onion Soup

This simple recipe uses the sweet potato with its distinctive flavour and colour, combined with a hint of orange and coriander.

NUTRITIONAL INFORMATION

Calories 320   Sugars 26g
Protein . . . . .7g   Fat 7g
Carbohydrate . . .62g   Saturates 1g

 15 mins   30 mins

SERVES 4

INGREDIENTS

2 tbsp vegetable oil

900 g/2 lb sweet potatoes, diced

1 carrot, diced

2 onions, sliced

2 garlic cloves, crushed

600 ml/1 pint vegetable stock

300 ml/½ pint orange juice

225 ml/8 fl oz low-fat natural yogurt

2 tbsp chopped fresh coriander

salt and pepper

TO GARNISH

fresh coriander sprigs

orange rind

1 Heat the vegetable oil in a large, heavy-based saucepan and add the sweet potatoes, carrot, onions and garlic. Sauté the vegetables over a low heat, stirring constantly for 5 minutes until they are softened.

2 Pour in the vegetable stock and orange juice and bring to the boil.

3 Reduce the heat to a simmer, cover the saucepan and cook the vegetables for 20 minutes or until the sweet potatoes and carrot are tender.

4 Transfer the mixture to a food processor or blender in batches and process for 1 minute until puréed. Return the purée to the rinsed-out saucepan.

5 Stir in the yogurt and chopped coriander and season to taste with salt and pepper.

6 Serve the soup in warm bowls and garnish with coriander sprigs and orange rind.

VARIATION

This soup can be chilled before serving, if preferred. If chilling, stir the yogurt into the dish just before serving. Serve in chilled bowls.

Carrot, Apple & Celery Soup

For this fresh-tasting soup, use your favourite variety of eating apple rather than a cooking variety, which will give too tart a flavour.

NUTRITIONAL INFORMATION

Calories 153	Sugars 34g
Protein 2g	Fat 1g
Carbohydrate ...36g	Saturates 0.2g

 30 mins 40 mins

SERVES 4

INGREDIENTS

900 g/2 lb carrots, finely diced

1 onion, chopped

3 celery sticks, sliced

1 litre/1¾ pints vegetable stock

3 apples

2 tbsp tomato purée

1 bay leaf

2 tsp caster sugar

¼ large lemon

salt and pepper

celery leaves, shredded, to garnish

1 Place the carrots, onion and celery in a large, heavy-based pan and add the stock. Bring to the boil, lower the heat, cover and simmer for 10 minutes.

2 Peel, core and dice 2 of the apples. Add the apple, the tomato purée, bay leaf and caster sugar to the pan and bring to the boil over a medium heat. Reduce the heat, half-cover with a lid and simmer for 20 minutes. Remove the bay leaf.

3 Meanwhile, wash, core and cut the remaining apple into thin slices, without peeling.

4 Place the apple slices in a small pan and squeeze over the lemon juice. Heat the apple slices gently and simmer for 1–2 minutes until tender.

5 Drain the apple slices and set aside until required.

6 Place the carrot and apple mixture in a blender or food processor and process until smooth. Alternatively, press the mixture through a sieve with the back of a wooden spoon.

7 Gently re-heat the soup if necessary and season with salt and pepper to taste. Ladle the soup into warmed bowls and serve topped with the reserved apple slices and shredded celery leaves.

Parisian Pea Soup

This is one occasion when cooking with just a little butter is worthwhile because of its rich flavour.

NUTRITIONAL INFORMATION

Calories	114	Sugars	.........3g
Protein	.........5g	Fat	..........6g
Carbohydrate	...10g	Saturates	.......4g

10 mins   15 mins

SERVES 4

INGREDIENTS

25 g/1 oz butter

2 shallots, finely chopped

450 g/1 lb peas

2 Little Gem or 1 small cos or Webb's lettuce, shredded

1.2 litres/2 pints vegetable stock

pinch of freshly grated nutmeg

salt and pepper

1 Shell the peas. Melt the butter in a large saucepan. Add the shallots and cook over a medium heat, stirring occasionally, for 5 minutes, until softened.

2 Add the peas, shredded lettuce and stock to the pan and season to taste with nutmeg, salt and pepper. Bring to the boil, cover and simmer for 10–15 minutes until the peas are tender.

3 Remove the pan from the heat and allow to cool slightly. Pour into a blender or food processor and process to a purée. Return the soup to the clean pan and heat through gently before serving.

VARIATION

For a classic side dish, cook as for soup, but add only 150 ml/5 fl oz stock and serve without processing.

Spinach & Ginger Soup

This mildly spiced, rich green soup is delicately scented with ginger and lemongrass. It makes a good light starter or summer lunch dish.

NUTRITIONAL INFORMATION

Calories	38	Sugars	.......0.8g
Protein	........3.2g	Fat	..........1.8g
Carbohydrate	...2.4g	Saturates	.....0.2g

 5–10 mins   25 mins

SERVES 4

INGREDIENTS

2 tbsp sunflower oil

1 onion, chopped

2 garlic cloves, finely chopped

2 tsp finely chopped fresh root ginger

250 g/9 oz young spinach leaves

1 small lemongrass stalk, finely chopped

1 litre/1¾ pints vegetable stock

225 g/8 oz potatoes, chopped

1 tbsp rice wine or dry sherry

salt and pepper

1 tsp sesame oil

1 Heat the oil in a large saucepan. Add the onion, garlic and ginger and fry over a low heat, stirring occasionally, for 3–4 minutes until softened.

2 Reserve 2–3 small spinach leaves. Add the remaining leaves and lemongrass to the saucepan, stirring until the spinach is wilted. Add the stock and potatoes to the pan and bring to the boil. Lower the heat, cover the pan and simmer for about 10 minutes.

3 Remove the pan from the heat and set aside to cool slightly. Then tip the soup into a blender or food processor and process until completely smooth.

4 Return the soup to the pan and add the rice wine or sherry, then adjust the seasoning to taste with salt and pepper. Heat until just about to boil.

5 Finely shred the reserved spinach leaves and sprinkle some over the top. Drizzle a few drops of sesame oil into the soup. Ladle into warmed soup bowls, sprinkle the remaining shredded spinach on each and serve the soup immediately.

COOK'S TIP

To make a creamy-textured spinach and coconut soup, stir in about 4 tablespoons creamed coconut or replace about 300 ml/10 fl oz of the stock with coconut milk. Serve the soup with shavings of fresh coconut scattered over the surface.

Stilton & Walnut Soup

Full of flavour, this rich and creamy soup is very simple to make and utterly delicious to eat.

NUTRITIONAL INFORMATION

Calories 392	Sugars 8g
Protein 15g	Fat 30g
Carbohydrate . . .15g	Saturates 16g

 10 mins   30 mins

SERVES 4

I N G R E D I E N T S

60 g/2 oz butter

2 shallots, chopped

3 celery sticks, chopped

1 garlic clove, crushed

2 tbsp plain flour

600 ml/1 pint vegetable stock

300 ml/½ pint milk

150 g/5½ oz blue Stilton cheese, crumbled, plus extra to garnish

2 tbsp roughly chopped walnut halves

150 ml/¼ pint natural yogurt

salt and pepper

chopped celery leaves, to garnish

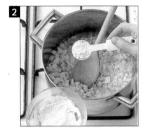

1 Melt the butter in a large, heavy-based saucepan and sauté the shallots, celery and garlic, stirring occasionally, for 2–3 minutes, until they are softened.

2 Lower the heat, add the flour and continue to cook, stirring constantly, for 30 seconds.

3 Gradually stir in the vegetable stock and milk and bring to the boil.

4 Reduce the heat to a gentle simmer and add the crumbled blue Stilton cheese and walnut halves. Cover and simmer for 20 minutes.

5 Stir in the yogurt and heat through for a further 2 minutes, but be careful not to let the soup boil.

6 Season the soup to taste with salt and pepper, then transfer to a warm soup tureen or individual serving bowls, garnish with chopped celery leaves and extra crumbled blue Stilton cheese and serve at once.

COOK'S TIP
As well as adding protein, vitamins and useful fats to the diet, nuts add important flavour and texture to vegetarian meals.

Indian Potato & Pea Soup

A slightly hot and spicy Indian flavour is given to this soup with the use of garam masala, chilli, cumin and coriander.

NUTRITIONAL INFORMATION

Calories 160   Sugars 8g
Protein ....6g   Fat 7g
Carbohydrate ...21g   Saturates 1g

 5 mins   35 mins

SERVES 4

INGREDIENTS

2 tbsp vegetable oil

225 g/8 oz floury potatoes, diced

1 large onion, chopped

2 garlic cloves, crushed

1 tsp garam masala

1 tsp ground coriander

1 tsp ground cumin

850 ml/1½ pints vegetable stock

1 fresh red chilli, deseeded and chopped

100 g/3½ oz frozen peas

4 tbsp natural yogurt

salt and pepper

chopped fresh coriander, to garnish

warm bread, to serve

VARIATION

For slightly less heat, deseed the chilli before adding it to the soup. Always wash your hands after handling chillies because they contain volatile oils that can irritate the skin and make your eyes burn if you touch your face.

1 Heat the vegetable oil in a large saucepan. Add the potatoes, onion and garlic and sauté over a low heat, stirring constantly, for about 5 minutes.

2 Add the garam masala, coriander and cumin and cook, stirring constantly, for 1 minute.

3 Stir in the vegetable stock and red chilli and bring the mixture to the boil. Reduce the heat, cover the pan and simmer for 20 minutes, until the potatoes begin to break down.

4 Add the peas and cook for a further 5 minutes. Stir in the yogurt and season to taste with salt and pepper.

5 Pour into warmed soup bowls, garnish with chopped fresh coriander and serve hot with warm bread.

Spicy Dhal & Carrot Soup

This nutritious soup uses split red lentils and carrots as the two main ingredients and includes a selection of spices to give it a kick.

NUTRITIONAL INFORMATION

Calories . . . . . . .173 Sugars 11g
Protein . . . . .9g Fat 5g
Carbohydrate . . .24g Saturates 1g

15 mins   45 mins

SERVES 6

INGREDIENTS

125 g/4½ oz split red lentils

1.2 litres/2 pints vegetable stock

350 g/12 oz carrots, sliced

2 onions, chopped

225 g/8 oz canned chopped tomatoes

2 garlic cloves, chopped

2 tbsp ghee or oil

1 tsp ground cumin

1 tsp ground coriander

1 fresh green chilli, deseeded and chopped, or 1 tsp minced chilli

½ tsp turmeric

1 tbsp lemon juice

salt

300 ml/½ pint milk

2 tbsp chopped fresh coriander

natural yogurt, to serve

2 Meanwhile, heat the ghee or oil in a small pan. Add the cumin, ground coriander, chilli and turmeric and fry over a low heat for 1 minute. Remove from the heat and stir in the lemon juice. Season with salt to taste.

3 Process the soup in batches in a blender or food processor. Return the soup to the saucepan, add the spice mixture and the remaining 300 ml/ ½ pint stock and simmer over a low heat for 10 minutes.

4 Add the milk, taste and adjust the seasoning, if necessary. Stir in the chopped coriander and reheat gently. Serve hot with a swirl of yogurt.

1 Place the lentils in a sieve and rinse well under cold running water. Drain and place in a large saucepan, together with 900 ml/1½ pints of the stock, the carrots, onions, tomatoes and garlic. Bring the mixture to the boil, reduce the heat, cover and simmer for 30 minutes, or until the vegetables and lentils are tender.

Parsnip Soup with Ginger

The exotic flavours give this simple soup a lift. If you wish, use bought ginger purée instead of grating it; add to taste as the strength varies.

NUTRITIONAL INFORMATION

Calories 151	Sugars 19g	
Protein 4g	Fat 3g	
Carbohydrate . . .29g	Saturates 0g	

 10 mins   55 mins

SERVES 6

INGREDIENTS

2 tsp olive oil

1 large onion, chopped

1 large leek, sliced

800 g/1 lb 12 oz parsnips, sliced

2 carrots, thinly sliced

4 tbsp grated fresh root ginger

2–3 garlic cloves, finely chopped

grated rind of ½ orange

1.4 litres/2½ pints water

225 ml/8 fl oz orange juice

salt and pepper

snipped fresh chives or slivers of spring
  onion, to garnish

1 Heat the olive oil in a large pan over a medium heat. Add the onion and leek and cook, stirring occasionally, for about 5 minutes until softened.

2 Add the parsnips, carrots, ginger, garlic, grated orange rind, water and a pinch of salt. Reduce the heat, cover the pan and simmer, stirring occasionally, for about 40 minutes until the vegetables are soft.

3 Remove from the heat and set aside to cool slightly, then transfer to a blender or food processor and process to a smooth purée, in batches if necessary.

4 Return the soup to the pan and stir in the orange juice. Add a little water or more orange juice, if you prefer a thinner consistency. Taste and adjust the seasoning with salt and pepper.

5 Simmer for about 10 minutes to heat through. Ladle into warmed bowls, garnish with chives or slivers of spring onion and serve immediately.

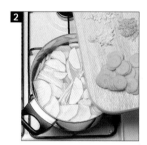

VARIATION
You could make the soup using
equal amounts (450 g/1 lb each)
of carrots and parsnips.

Greek Bean Soup

This is based on a simple soup typical of Greek home cooking.
The artichoke hearts make it fancier, but they are not essential.

NUTRITIONAL INFORMATION

Calories 109	Sugars 7g
Protein 6g	Fat 3g
Carbohydrate . . .16g	Saturates 0g

 10 mins   1¼ hrs

SERVES 6

INGREDIENTS

1 tbsp olive oil

1 large onion, finely chopped

1 large carrot, finely diced

2 celery sticks, finely chopped

4 tomatoes, peeled, deseeded and chopped, or 250 g/9 oz canned tomatoes, drained

2 garlic cloves, finely chopped

800g/1lb 12 oz canned cannellini or haricot beans, drained and rinsed

1.2 litres/2 pints water

1 courgette, finely diced

grated rind of ½ lemon

1 tbsp chopped fresh mint or ¼ tsp dried mint

1 tsp chopped fresh thyme or ⅛ tsp dried thyme

1 bay leaf

salt and pepper

400 g/14 oz canned artichoke hearts, drained

1 Heat 1 teaspoon of the olive oil in a large pan over a medium heat. Add the onion and cook, stirring occasionally, for 3–4 minutes until softened. Add the carrot, celery, tomatoes and garlic and continue cooking for a further 5 minutes, stirring frequently.

2 Add the beans and water. Bring to the boil, reduce the heat, cover and cook gently for about 10 minutes.

3 Add the courgette, lemon rind, mint, thyme and bay leaf and season to taste with salt and pepper. Cover and simmer for about 40 minutes until all the vegetables are tender. Remove the pan from the heat and set aside to cool slightly. Remove the bay leaf and transfer 450 ml/16 fl oz of the soup to a blender or food processor, process to a smooth purée and recombine.

4 Meanwhile, heat the remaining oil in a frying pan over a medium heat. Fry the artichokes, cut side down, until lightly browned. Turn over and fry long enough to heat through. Ladle the soup into warmed bowls and top each with an artichoke heart. Serve immediately.

Celeriac, Leek & Potato Soup

It is hard to imagine that celeriac, a coarse, knobbly vegetable, can taste so sweet. It makes a wonderfully tasty soup.

NUTRITIONAL INFORMATION

Calories 20   Sugars 1.3g
Protein ....0.8g Fat 0.7g
Carbohydrate ...2.7g Saturates 0.4g

 10 mins   35 mins

SERVES 4

INGREDIENTS

1 tbsp butter

1 onion, chopped

2 large leeks, halved lengthways and sliced

1 large celeriac (about 750 g/1 lb 10 oz), peeled and diced

1 potato, diced

1 carrot, quartered and thinly sliced

1.2 litres/2 pints water

⅛ tsp dried marjoram

1 bay leaf

salt and pepper

freshly grated nutmeg

celery leaves, to garnish

1 Melt the butter in a large saucepan over a medium heat. Add the onion and leeks and cook for about 4 minutes, stirring frequently, until just softened; do not allow to colour.

2 Add the celeriac, potato, carrot, water, marjoram and bay leaf, with a large pinch of salt. Bring to the boil, reduce the heat, cover and simmer for about 25 minutes until the vegetables are tender. Remove the bay leaf.

3 Allow the soup to cool slightly. Transfer to a food processor or blender and purée until smooth. (If using a food processor, strain off the cooking liquid and reserve. Purée the soup solids, moistened with a little cooking liquid, then combine with the remaining liquid.)

4 Return the puréed soup to the saucepan and stir to blend. Season with salt, pepper and nutmeg. Stir over a medium heat until reheated.

5 Ladle the soup into warm bowls, garnish with celery leaves and serve.

Plum Tomato Soup

Home-made tomato soup is easy to make and always tastes better than bought varieties. Try this version with its Mediterranean influences.

NUTRITIONAL INFORMATION

Calories . . . . .402 Sugars 14g
Protein . . . . .7g Fat 32g
Carbohydrate . . .16g Saturates 3g

 20 mins   30–35 mins

SERVES 4

I N G R E D I E N T S

2 tbsp olive oil

2 red onions, chopped

2 celery sticks, chopped

1 carrot, chopped

500 g/1 lb 2 oz plum tomatoes, halved

750 ml/1¼ pints vegetable stock

1 tbsp chopped fresh oregano

1 tbsp chopped fresh basil

150 ml/¼ pint dry white wine

2 tsp caster sugar

125 g/4½ oz hazelnuts, toasted

125 g/4½ oz stoned black or green olives

handful of fresh basil leaves

1 tbsp olive oil

1 loaf ciabatta bread

salt and pepper

fresh basil sprigs, to garnish

1 Heat the oil in a large saucepan. Add the onions, celery and carrot and fry over a low heat, stirring frequently, until softened, but not coloured.

2 Add the tomatoes, stock, chopped herbs, wine and sugar. Bring to the boil, cover and simmer for 20 minutes.

3 Place the toasted hazelnuts in a blender or food processor, together with the olives and basil leaves, and process until thoroughly combined, but not too smooth. Alternatively, finely chop the nuts, olives and basil leaves and pound them together in a mortar with a pestle, then turn into a small bowl. Add the olive oil and process or beat thoroughly for a few seconds to combine. Turn the mixture into a serving bowl.

4 Warm the ciabatta bread in a preheated oven, 190°C/375°F/Gas Mark 5, for 3–4 minutes.

5 Process the soup in a blender or a food processor, or press through a sieve, until smooth. Check the seasoning. Ladle into warmed soup bowls and garnish with sprigs of basil. Slice the warm bread and spread with the olive and hazelnut paste. Serve with the soup.

Pumpkin Soup

This is an American classic that has now become popular worldwide.
When pumpkin is out of season, use butternut squash in its place.

NUTRITIONAL INFORMATION

Calories . . . . .112 Sugars 7g
Protein . . . . .4g Fat 7g
Carbohydrate . . . .8g Saturates 2g

  10 mins   30 mins

SERVES 6

I N G R E D I E N T S

about 1 kg/2 lb 4 oz pumpkin

40 g/1½ oz butter or margarine

1 onion, thinly sliced

1 garlic clove, crushed

900 ml/1½ pints vegetable stock

salt and pepper

½ tsp ground ginger

1 tbsp lemon juice

3–4 thinly pared strips of orange rind
(optional)

1–2 bay leaves or 1 bouquet garni

300 ml/½ pint milk

T O   G A R N I S H

4–6 tbsp single or double cream, natural
yogurt or fromage frais

snipped fresh chives

1 Peel the pumpkin, remove the seeds and then cut the flesh into 2.5 cm/1 inch cubes.

2 Melt the butter or margarine in a large, heavy-based saucepan. Add the onion and garlic and fry over a low heat until soft but not coloured.

3 Add the pumpkin and toss with the onion and garlic for 2–3 minutes.

4 Add the stock and bring to the boil over a medium heat. Season to taste with salt and pepper and add the ground ginger and lemon juice, the strips of orange rind, if using, and the bay leaves or bouquet garni.

5 Cover the pan and gently simmer the soup over a low heat for about 20 minutes, stirring occasionally, until the pumpkin is tender.

6 Discard the orange rind, if using, and the bay leaves or bouquet garni. Cool the soup slightly, then press through a sieve with the back of a spoon, or process in a food processor or blender until smooth. Pour into a clean saucepan.

7 Add the milk and reheat gently. Adjust the seasoning. Garnish with a swirl of cream, natural yogurt or fromage frais and snipped chives, and serve.

Pistou

This hearty soup of beans and vegetables is from Nice and gets its name from the fresh basil sauce stirred in at the last minute.

NUTRITIONAL INFORMATION

Calories 55	Sugars 1.2g
Protein 3.8g	Fat 2.6g
Carbohydrate . . .4.2g	Saturates 0.6g

10 mins   25 mins

SERVES 6

INGREDIENTS

2 young carrots

450 g/1 lb potatoes

200 g/7 oz fresh peas in their pods

200 g/7 oz French beans

150 g/5½ oz young courgettes

2 tbsp olive oil

1 garlic clove, crushed

1 large onion, finely chopped

2.5 litres/4½ pints vegetable stock or water

1 bouquet garni of 2 fresh parsley sprigs and 1 bay leaf tied in a 7.5 cm/3 inch piece of celery

85 g/3 oz dried small soup pasta

1 large tomato, peeled, deseeded and chopped or diced

salt and pepper

Parmesan cheese shavings, to serve

PISTOU SAUCE

85 g/3 oz fresh basil leaves

1 garlic clove

5 tbsp extra virgin olive oil

salt and pepper

1 To make the pistou sauce, put the basil leaves, garlic and olive oil in a food processor and process until thoroughly blended. Season with salt and pepper to taste. Scrape the sauce into a bowl, cover with clingfilm and store in the refrigerator until required.

2 Cut the carrots in half lengthways, then slice. Cut the potatoes into quarters lengthways, then slice. Set aside in a bowl of water until ready to use to prevent them from discolouring.

3 Shell the peas. Trim the French beans and cut them into 2.5 cm/1 inch pieces. Cut the courgettes in half lengthways, then slice.

4 Heat the oil in a large saucepan or flameproof casserole. Add the garlic and fry for 2 minutes, stirring constantly. Add the onion and fry for a further 2 minutes until soft. Add the carrots and potatoes and stir for about 30 seconds.

5 Pour in the stock, add the bouquet garni and bring to the boil. Lower the heat, partially cover the pan and simmer for about 8 minutes until the vegetables are starting to become tender.

6 Stir in the peas, beans, courgettes, pasta and tomato. Season and cook for 4 minutes or until the vegetables and pasta are tender. Stir in the pistou sauce and serve with Parmesan shavings.

Minted Pea & Yogurt Soup

A deliciously refreshing, summery soup that is full of goodness. It is also extremely tasty served chilled.

NUTRITIONAL INFORMATION

Calories	208	Sugars	.........9g
Protein	........10g	Fat	...........7g
Carbohydrate	...26g	Saturates	.......2g

 15 mins   25 mins

SERVES 6

INGREDIENTS

2 tbsp ghee or sunflower oil

2 onions, roughly chopped

225 g/8 oz potato, roughly chopped

2 garlic cloves

2.5 cm/1 inch piece fresh root ginger, chopped

1 tsp ground coriander

1 tsp ground cumin

1 tbsp plain flour

900 ml/1½ pints vegetable stock

500 g/1 lb frozen peas

2–3 tbsp chopped fresh mint

salt and pepper

150 ml/¼ pint Greek-style yogurt, plus extra to serve

½ tsp cornflour

300 ml/½ pint milk

fresh mint sprigs, to garnish

1 Heat the vegetable ghee or sunflower oil in a saucepan, add the onions and potato and cook over a low heat, stirring occasionally, for about 3 minutes, until the onion is soft and translucent.

2 Stir in the garlic, ginger, coriander, cumin and flour and cook, stirring constantly, for 1 minute.

3 Add the vegetable stock, peas and half the mint and bring to the boil, stirring. Reduce the heat, cover and simmer gently for 15 minutes, or until the vegetables are tender.

4 Process the soup, in batches, in a blender or food processor. Return the mixture to the pan and season with salt and pepper to taste. Blend the yogurt with the cornflour to a smooth paste and stir into the soup.

5 Add the milk and bring almost to the boil, stirring constantly. Cook very gently for 2 minutes. Serve hot, sprinkled with the remaining mint and a swirl of extra yogurt. Garnish with mint sprigs.

Garlic & Potato Soup

The combination of potato, garlic and onion works brilliantly in soup.
In this recipe the garlic is roasted to give it added depth.

NUTRITIONAL INFORMATION

Calories ....240 Sugars 7g
Protein ....8g Fat 10g
Carbohydrate ...33g Saturates 5g

 10 mins   1 hr

SERVES 4

INGREDIENTS

1 large bulb of garlic with large cloves,
    peeled (about 100 g/3½ oz)

2 tsp olive oil, plus extra for brushing

2 large leeks, thinly sliced

1 large onion, finely chopped

500 g/1 lb 2 oz potatoes, diced

1.2 litres/2 pints vegetable stock

1 bay leaf

salt and pepper

150 ml/5 fl oz single cream

freshly grated nutmeg

lemon juice, optional

snipped fresh chives or parsley, to garnish

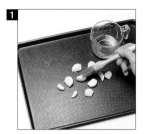

1 Put the garlic cloves in a baking dish, lightly brush with olive oil and bake in a preheated oven at 180°C/350°F/Gas Mark 4 for about 20 minutes until golden.

2 Heat the oil in a large saucepan over a medium heat. Add the leeks and onion, cover and cook for about 3 minutes, stirring frequently, until they begin to soften.

3 Add the potatoes, roasted garlic, stock and bay leaf. Season with salt (unless the stock is salty already) and pepper. Bring to the boil, reduce the heat,

cover and cook gently for about 30 minutes, until the vegetables are tender. Remove the bay leaf.

4 Allow the soup to cool slightly, then transfer to a blender or food processor and purée until smooth, working in batches if necessary. (If using a food processor, strain off the cooking liquid and reserve. Purée the soup solids with enough

cooking liquid to moisten them, then combine with the remaining liquid.)

5 Return the soup to the saucepan and stir in the cream and a generous grating of nutmeg. Taste and adjust the seasoning, if necessary, adding a few drops of lemon juice, if desired. Reheat over a low heat. Ladle into warm soup bowls, garnish with chives or parsley and serve.

Thick Onion Soup

This is a delicious creamy soup with grated carrot and parsley for texture and colour. Serve with crusty cheese scones for a hearty lunch.

NUTRITIONAL INFORMATION

Calories	277	Sugars	........12g
Protein	.........6g	Fat	..........20g
Carbohydrate	...19g	Saturates	.......8g

    20 mins   1hr 10 mins

SERVES 4

I N G R E D I E N T S

75 g/2¾ oz butter

500 g/1 lb 2 oz onions, finely chopped

1 garlic clove, crushed

40 g/1½ oz plain flour

600 ml/1 pint vegetable stock

600 ml/1 pint milk

salt and pepper

2–3 tsp lemon or lime juice

good pinch of ground allspice

1 bay leaf

1 carrot, coarsely grated

4–6 tbsp double cream

2 tbsp chopped fresh parsley

CHEESE SCONES

225 g/8 oz malted wheat or
  wholemeal flour

2 tsp baking powder

salt and pepper

60 g/2 oz butter

4 tbsp grated Parmesan cheese

1 egg, beaten

about 75 ml/3 fl oz milk

1 Melt the butter in a saucepan and fry the onions and garlic over a low heat, stirring frequently, for 10–15 minutes, until soft, but not coloured. Stir in the flour and cook, stirring, for 1 minute, then gradually stir in the stock and bring to the boil, stirring frequently. Add the milk, then bring back to the boil.

2 Season to taste with salt and pepper and add 2 teaspoons of the lemon or lime juice, the allspice and bay leaf. Cover and simmer for about 25 minutes until the vegetables are tender. Discard the bay leaf.

3 Meanwhile, make the scones. Combine the flour, baking powder and seasoning and rub in the butter until the mixture resembles fine breadcrumbs. Stir in 3 tablespoons of the cheese, the egg and enough milk to mix to a soft dough.

4 Shape into a bar about 2 cm/¾ inch thick. Place on a floured baking tray and mark into slices. Sprinkle with the remaining cheese and bake in a preheated oven, 220°C/425°F/Gas Mark 7, for about 20 minutes, until risen and golden brown.

5 Stir the carrot into the soup and simmer for 2–3 minutes. Add more lemon or lime juice, if necessary. Stir in the cream and reheat. Garnish with the chopped parsley and serve with the warm scones.

Chinese Cabbage Soup

This is a piquant soup, which is slightly sweet-and-sour in flavour.
It can be served as a hearty meal or appetizer.

NUTRITIONAL INFORMATION

Calories 65   Sugars 7g
Protein . . . . .3g   Fat 0.5g
Carbohydrate . . . .11g   Saturates 0.1g

 5 mins   30 mins

SERVES 4

INGREDIENTS

450 g/1 lb pak choi

600 ml/1 pint vegetable stock

1 tbsp rice wine vinegar

1 tbsp light soy sauce

1 tbsp caster sugar

1 tbsp dry sherry

1 fresh red chilli, deseeded and thinly sliced

1 tbsp cornflour

2 tbsp water

1 Wash the pak choi thoroughly under cold running water, rinse and drain. Pat dry on kitchen paper.

2 Trim the stems of the pak choi and shred the leaves.

3 Heat the vegetable stock in a large saucepan. Add the pak choi and cook for 10–15 minutes.

4 Mix together the rice wine vinegar, soy sauce, caster sugar and sherry in a small bowl. Add this mixture to the stock, together with the sliced chilli.

5 Bring to the boil, lower the heat and cook for 2–3 minutes.

6 Blend the cornflour with the water to form a smooth paste.

7 Gradually stir the cornflour mixture into the soup and cook, stirring constantly, until it thickens. Cook for a further 4–5 minutes.

8 Ladle the Chinese cabbage soup into individual warm serving bowls and serve immediately.

COOK'S TIP
Pak choi, also known as bok choi or spoon cabbage, has long, white leaf stalks and fleshy, spoon-shaped, shiny green leaves. There are a number of varieties available, which differ mainly in size rather than flavour.

Broccoli Soup

Adding soft cheese to this soup just before serving makes it very special, while the rice and croûtons provide an excellent contrast of textures.

NUTRITIONAL INFORMATION

Calories 384	Sugars 7g
Protein 8g	Fat 30g
Carbohydrate . . .21g	Saturates 18g

 5 mins   40 mins

SERVES 4

INGREDIENTS

400 g/14 oz broccoli (from 1 large head)

2 tsp butter

1 tsp oil

1 onion, finely chopped

1 leek, thinly sliced

1 small carrot, finely chopped

3 tbsp white rice

850 ml/1½ pints water

1 bay leaf

freshly grated nutmeg

4 tbsp double cream

100 g/3½ oz soft cheese

salt and pepper

croûtons, to serve (see Cook's Tip)

COOK'S TIP

To make croûtons, remove the crusts from thick slices of bread, then cut the bread into dice. Fry in vegetable oil, stirring constantly, until evenly browned, then drain on kitchen paper.

1 Divide the broccoli into small florets and cut off the stems. Peel the large stems and then chop all the stems into small pieces.

2 Heat the butter and oil in a large saucepan over a medium heat and add the onion, leek and carrot. Cook for 3–4 minutes, stirring frequently, until the onion is soft.

3 Add the broccoli stems, rice, water, bay leaf and a pinch of salt. Bring just to the boil and reduce the heat to low.

Cover the pan and simmer the soup for 15 minutes. Add the broccoli florets and continue cooking, covered, for 15–20 minutes until the rice and vegetables are tender. Remove the bay leaf.

4 Season the soup with nutmeg, pepper and, if needed, more salt. Stir in the cream and soft cheese. Simmer over a low heat for a few minutes until heated through, stirring occasionally. Taste, and adjust the seasoning if necessary. Ladle the soup into warm bowls and serve sprinkled with the croûtons.

Carrot & Almond Soup

Ground almonds add valuable protein and a rich, luxurious depth to this delicately coloured soup.

NUTRITIONAL INFORMATION

Calories	275	Sugars	........10g
Protein	.........9g	Fat	..........20g
Carbohydrate	...16g	Saturates	.......2g

10 mins   50 mins

SERVES 4–6

I N G R E D I E N T S

2 tsp olive oil

1 onion, finely chopped

1 leek, thinly sliced

500 g/1 lb 2 oz carrots, thinly sliced

1.5 litres/2¾ pints water

salt and pepper

200 g/7 oz ground almonds

50 g/1¾ oz soft white breadcrumbs

1 tbsp fresh lemon juice, or to taste

snipped fresh chives, to garnish

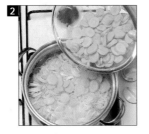

1   Heat the oil in a large saucepan over a medium heat and add the onion and leek. Cover and cook for about 3 minutes, stirring occasionally, until just softened; do not allow them to brown.

2   Add the carrots and water and season with a little salt and pepper. Bring to the boil, reduce the heat and simmer gently, partially covered, for about 45 minutes until the vegetables are tender.

3   Soak the breadcrumbs in cold water to cover for 2–3 minutes, then strain them and press out any excess water.

4   Put the ground almonds and breadcrumbs in a blender or food processor with a ladleful of the carrot cooking water and purée until smooth and paste-like.

5   Transfer the soup vegetables and remaining cooking liquid to the blender or food processor and purée until smooth, working in batches if necessary. (If using a food processor, strain off the cooking liquid and reserve. Purée the soup solids with enough cooking liquid to moisten them, then combine with the remaining liquid.)

6   Return the soup to the saucepan and simmer over a low heat, stirring occasionally, until heated through. Add lemon juice, and salt and pepper to taste. Ladle the soup into warm bowls, garnish with chives and serve.

Fresh Mushroom Soup

When you see mushrooms at a special price, think of this soup. Chestnut, field or horse mushrooms are especially tasty.

NUTRITIONAL INFORMATION

Calories	229	Sugars	.........5g
Protein	.........6g	Fat	..........17g
Carbohydrate	....11g	Saturates	......10g

10 mins   40 mins

SERVES 4

INGREDIENTS

40 g/1½ oz butter

700 g/1 lb 9 oz mushrooms, sliced

salt and pepper

1 onion, finely chopped

1 shallot, finely chopped

25 g/1 oz plain flour

2–3 tbsp dry white wine or sherry

1.4 litres/2½ pints vegetable stock

150 ml/¼ pint single cream

2 tbsp chopped fresh parsley

lemon juice (optional)

4 tbsp soured cream or crème fraîche, to garnish

1 Melt half the butter in a large frying pan over a medium heat. Add the mushrooms and season with salt and pepper. Cook for about 8 minutes until they are golden brown, stirring occasionally at first, then more often after they start to colour. Remove the pan from the heat.

2 Melt the remaining butter in a saucepan over a medium heat, add the onion and shallot and cook for 2–3 minutes until just softened. Stir the flour into the pan and continue cooking for 2 minutes. Add the wine and stock and stir well.

3 Set aside about one-quarter of the mushrooms. Add the remainder to the pan. Reduce the heat, cover and cook gently for 20 minutes, stirring occasionally.

4 Allow the soup to cool slightly, then transfer to a blender or food processor and purée until smooth, working in batches, if necessary. (If using a food processor, strain off the cooking liquid and reserve. Purée the soup solids with enough cooking liquid to moisten them, then combine with the remaining liquid.)

5 Return the soup to the saucepan and stir in the reserved mushrooms, the cream and parsley. Cook for about 5 minutes to heat through. Taste and adjust the seasoning, adding a few drops of lemon juice if wished. Ladle into warm bowls and garnish with soured cream or crème fraîche.

Cauliflower & Cider Soup

Cauliflower can taste rather bland, but using dry cider in this creamy soup gives it an unusual kick.

NUTRITIONAL INFORMATION

Calories	.312	Sugars	.13g
Protein	.7g	Fat	.21g
Carbohydrate	.15g	Saturates	.13g

10 mins   55 mins

SERVES 4

INGREDIENTS

25 g/1 oz butter

1 onion, finely chopped

1 garlic clove, crushed

1 carrot, thinly sliced

500 g/1 lb 2 oz cauliflower florets
   (from 1 head)

600 ml/1 pint dry cider

salt and pepper

freshly grated nutmeg

125 ml/4 fl oz milk

125 ml/4 fl oz double cream

snipped fresh chives, to garnish

1 Melt the butter in a saucepan over a medium heat. Add the onion and garlic and cook for about 5 minutes, stirring occasionally, until just softened.

2 Add the carrot and cauliflower to the pan and pour over the cider. Season with salt, pepper and a generous grating of nutmeg. Bring to the boil, then reduce the heat to low. Cover and cook very gently for about 50 minutes until the vegetables are very soft.

3 Allow the soup to cool slightly, then transfer to a blender or food processor and purée until smooth, working in batches if necessary. (If using a food processor, strain off the cooking liquid and reserve. Purée the soup solids with enough cooking liquid to moisten them, then combine with the remaining liquid.)

4 Return the soup to the saucepan and stir in the milk and cream. Taste and adjust the seasoning, if necessary. Simmer the soup over a low heat, stirring occasionally, until heated through.

5 Ladle the soup into warm bowls, garnish with chives and serve.

COOK'S TIP
If you don't have dry cider, substitute 125 ml/4 fl oz each white wine, apple juice and water.

Vegetable & Corn Chowder

This is a really filling soup, which is best served before a light main course. It is easy to prepare and full of flavour.

NUTRITIONAL INFORMATION

Calories	378	Sugars	........20g
Protein	........16g	Fat	..........13g
Carbohydrate	...52g	Saturates	.......6g

 15 mins   30 mins

SERVES 4

INGREDIENTS

1 tbsp vegetable oil

1 red onion, diced

1 red pepper, deseeded and diced

3 garlic cloves, crushed

300 g/10 oz potatoes, diced

2 tbsp plain flour

600 ml/1 pint milk

300 ml/½ pint vegetable stock

50 g/2 oz broccoli florets

300 g/10 oz canned sweetcorn, drained

75 g/2¾ oz Cheddar cheese, grated

salt and pepper

1 tbsp chopped fresh coriander, to garnish

COOK'S TIP
Vegetarian cheeses are made with rennets of non-animal origin, using microbial or fungal enzymes.

1 Heat the oil in a large saucepan. Add the onion, red pepper, garlic and potatoes and sauté over a low heat, stirring frequently, for 2–3 minutes.

2 Stir in the flour and cook, stirring, for 30 seconds. Gradually stir in the milk and stock.

3 Add the broccoli and sweetcorn. Bring the mixture to the boil, stirring constantly, then reduce the heat and simmer for about 20 minutes, or until all the vegetables are tender.

4 Stir in 50 g/1¾ oz of the cheese until it melts.

5 Season to taste, then spoon the chowder into a warm soup tureen. Garnish with the remaining cheese and the coriander and serve.

Chick Pea & Tomato Soup

This thick vegetable soup is a delicious meal in itself. Serve with Parmesan cheese and warm sun-dried tomato bread.

NUTRITIONAL INFORMATION

Calories ....285 Sugar 11g
Protein ....16g Fats 12g
Carbohydrates ...29g Saturates 3g

 5 mins   15 mins

SERVES 4

I N G R E D I E N T S

2 tbsp olive oil

2 leeks, sliced

2 courgettes, diced

2 garlic cloves, crushed

800 g/1 lb 12 oz canned chopped tomatoes

1 tbsp tomato purée

1 bay leaf

850 ml/1½ pints vegetable stock

400 g/14 oz canned chick peas, drained and rinsed

225 g/8 oz spinach

salt and pepper

T O S E R V E

Parmesan cheese, freshly grated

sun-dried tomato bread

1 Heat the olive oil in a large saucepan, then add the leeks and courgettes and cook them briskly for 5 minutes, stirring constantly.

2 Add the garlic, tomatoes, tomato purée, bay leaf, vegetable stock and chick peas.

3 Bring the soup to the boil and simmer for 5 minutes.

4 Shred the spinach finely, add to the soup and cook for 2 minutes. Season to taste.

5 Discard the bay leaf. Serve the soup immediately with freshly grated Parmesan cheese and warm sun-dried tomato bread.

COOK'S TIP

Chick peas are used extensively in North African cuisine and are also found in Spanish, Middle Eastern and Indian cooking. They have a nutty flavour with a firm texture and are excellent canned.

Lentil & Pasta Soup

Packed with the flavour of garlic, this soup is a filling supper dish when it is served with crusty bread and a crisp salad.

NUTRITIONAL INFORMATION

Calories 390   Sugars 12g
Protein ....20g   Fat 5g
Carbohydrate ....71g   Saturates 1g

 10 mins   55 mins

SERVES 4

INGREDIENTS

1 tbsp olive oil

1 onion, chopped

4 garlic cloves, finely chopped

350 g/12 oz carrot, sliced

1 stick celery, sliced

225 g/8 oz red lentils

600 ml/1 pint vegetable stock

700 ml/1¼ pints boiling water

salt and pepper

150 g/5½ oz dried pasta

150 ml/5 fl oz natural low-fat fromage
   frais, plus extra to serve

2 tbsp chopped fresh parsley, to garnish

COOK'S TIP

Avoid boiling the soup once the fromage frais has been added. Otherwise it will separate and become watery, spoiling the appearance of the soup.

1 Heat the olive oil in a large saucepan and gently fry the prepared onion, garlic, carrot and celery, stirring gently, for about 5 minutes or until the vegetables begin to soften.

2 Add the lentils, stock and boiling water. Season well, stir and bring back to the boil. Simmer, uncovered, for 15 minutes until the lentils are completely tender. Allow to cool for 10 minutes.

3 Meanwhile, bring another saucepan of water to the boil and cook the pasta according to the instructions on the packet. Drain well and set aside.

4 Place the soup in a blender or food processor and process until smooth. Return to a saucepan and add the pasta. Bring back to a simmer and heat for 2–3 minutes until piping hot. Remove from the heat and stir in the fromage frais. Adjust the seasoning if necessary.

5 Serve sprinkled with freshly ground black pepper and chopped parsley and with extra fromage frais if wished.

Sweet Potato & Apple Soup

This soup makes a marvellous late autumn or winter starter. It has a delicious texture and cheerful golden colour.

NUTRITIONAL INFORMATION

Calories 57   Sugars 3.8g
Protein . . . . .0.7g   Fat 2.9g
Carbohydrate . . .7.4g   Saturates 1.8g

 10 mins   45 mins

SERVES 6

I N G R E D I E N T S

1 tbsp butter

3 leeks, thinly sliced

1 large carrot, thinly sliced

600 g/1 lb 5 oz sweet potatoes,
    peeled and diced

2 large Bramley apples, peeled and diced

1.2 litres/2 pints water

salt and pepper

freshly grated nutmeg

225 ml/8 fl oz apple juice

225 ml/8 fl oz single cream

snipped fresh chives or coriander,
    to garnish

1 Melt the butter in a large saucepan over a low–medium heat. Add the leeks, cover and cook for 6–8 minutes, or until softened, stirring frequently.

2 Add the carrot, sweet potatoes, apples and water. Season lightly with salt, pepper and nutmeg to taste. Bring to the boil, reduce the heat and simmer, covered, for about 20 minutes, stirring occasionally, until the vegetables are very tender.

3 Allow the soup to cool slightly, then transfer to a blender or food processor and purée until smooth, working in batches if necessary. (If using a food processor, strain off the cooking liquid and reserve. Purée the soup solids with enough cooking liquid to moisten them, then combine with the remaining liquid.)

4 Return the puréed soup to the saucepan and stir in the apple juice.

Place over a low heat and simmer for about 10 minutes until heated through.

5 Stir in the cream and continue simmering for about 5 minutes, stirring frequently, until heated through. Taste and adjust the seasoning, adding more salt, pepper and nutmeg, if necessary. Ladle the soup into warm bowls, garnish with chives or coriander and serve.

Potato & Chick Pea Soup

This spicy and substantial soup uses ingredients you are likely to have at hand and makes a delicious meal-in-a-bowl.

NUTRITIONAL INFORMATION

Calories	40	Sugars	.......1.6g
Protein	........1.8g	Fat	..........1g
Carbohydrate	...6.5g	Saturates	.....0.1g

5 mins   50 mins

SERVES 4

INGREDIENTS

1 tbsp olive oil

1 large onion, finely chopped

2–3 garlic cloves, finely chopped or crushed

1 carrot, quartered and thinly sliced

350 g/12 oz potatoes, diced

¼ tsp turmeric

¼ tsp garam masala

¼ tsp mild curry powder

400 g/14 oz canned chopped tomatoes

850 ml/1½ pints water

¼ tsp chilli purée, or to taste

salt

400 g/14 oz canned chick peas,
   rinsed and drained

85 g/3 oz fresh or frozen peas

pepper

chopped fresh coriander, to garnish

1 Heat the olive oil in a large saucepan over a medium heat. Add the onion and garlic and cook for 3–4 minutes, stirring occasionally, until the onion is beginning to soften.

2 Add the carrot, potatoes, turmeric, garam masala and curry powder and continue cooking for 1–2 minutes.

3 Add the tomatoes, water and chilli purée with a large pinch of salt. Reduce the heat, cover and simmer for 30 minutes, stirring occasionally.

4 Add the chick peas and peas to the pan, cover and continue cooking for about 15 minutes, or until all the vegetables are tender.

5 Taste the soup and adjust the seasoning, if necessary, adding a little more chilli if desired. Ladle into warm soup bowls and sprinkle with coriander.

Minestrone

This version of the classic Italian soup has chunks of colourful pumpkin as well as all the traditional ingredients.

NUTRITIONAL INFORMATION

Calories . . . . . . .143 Sugars 6g
Protein . . . . .7g Fat 2g
Carbohydrate . . .25g Saturates 0.5g

30 mins   1¼ hrs

SERVES 6–8

I N G R E D I E N T S

1 tbsp olive oil

1 onion, finely chopped

1 leek, halved lengthways and thinly sliced

2 garlic cloves, finely chopped

400 g/14 oz canned chopped tomatoes

1 carrot, finely diced

1 small turnip, finely diced

1 small potato, finely diced

125 g/4½ oz peeled celeriac, finely diced

250 g/9 oz peeled pumpkin, finely diced

700 ml/1¼ pints water

1 litre/1¾ pints vegetable stock

400 g/14 oz canned cannellini or borlotti beans, drained and rinsed

100 g/3½ oz leafy cabbage, such as cavolo nero

salt and pepper

85 g/3 oz small dried pasta shapes or broken spaghetti

freshly grated Parmesan cheese, to serve

1 Heat the olive oil in a large saucepan over a medium heat. Add the onion, leek and garlic to the oil and cook for 3–4 minutes, stirring occasionally, until they are slightly softened.

2 Add the tomatoes, carrot, turnip, potato, celeriac, pumpkin, water and vegetable stock to the pan. Bring to the boil, stirring occasionally.

3 Stir in the beans and cabbage. Season the soup lightly with salt and pepper.

Reduce the heat and simmer, partially covered, for about 50 minutes until all the vegetables are tender.

4 Meanwhile, bring salted water to the boil in a saucepan. Add the pasta and cook until it is just tender. Drain and add the pasta to the cooked soup.

5 Taste the soup and adjust the seasoning. Ladle into warm bowls and serve with the grated Parmesan cheese sprinkled on the top.

Pear and Watercress Soup

This unusual combination of ingredients makes a creamy and sophisticated soup, which may be served hot or chilled.

NUTRITIONAL INFORMATION

Calories 136	Sugars 11g
Protein 1g	Fat 10g
Carbohydrate 11g	Saturates 6g

15 mins, plus chilling (optional) 20 mins

SERVES 6

INGREDIENTS

4 pears

1 bunch of watercress

850 ml/1½ pints vegetable stock

juice of ½ lemon

salt and pepper

125 ml/4 fl oz double cream

CROÛTONS (OPTIONAL)

2–3 slices day-old bread

2 tbsp olive oil

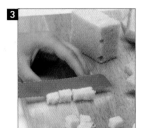

1 Core the pears and slice them lengthways. Set aside about one-third of the watercress leaves. Place the remaining leaves with the stalks in a heavy-based saucepan and add the pears and stock. Bring to the boil, lower the heat and simmer for 15 minutes.

2 Remove the pan from the heat, leave to cool slightly, then add the reserved watercress leaves. Pour into a blender or food processor and process until smooth. Pour the soup through a fine-mesh sieve into a bowl, stir in the lemon juice and season to taste.

3 To make the croûtons, cut the day-old bread into 5 mm/¼ inch squares. Heat the olive oil in a heavy-based frying pan and add the bread cubes. Cook, tossing and stirring constantly until evenly coloured. Drain on kitchen paper.

4 If serving hot, stir in the cream and return the soup to the clean pan. Heat gently until warmed through, then serve immediately, garnished with the croûtons. If serving cold, let the soup cool before you stir in the cream, then cover with clingfilm and chill in the refrigerator.

Gardener's Broth

This hearty soup uses a variety of green vegetables with a flavouring of ground coriander. A finishing touch of thinly sliced leeks adds texture.

NUTRITIONAL INFORMATION

Calories	169	Sugars	........5g
Protein	.........4g	Fat	...........13g
Carbohydrate	....8g	Saturates	.......5g

 10 mins   45 mins

SERVES 6

INGREDIENTS

40 g/1½ oz butter

1 onion, chopped

1–2 garlic cloves, crushed

1 large leek

225 g/8 oz Brussels sprouts

125 g/4½ oz French or runner beans

1.2 litres/2 pints vegetable stock

125 g/4½ oz frozen peas

salt and pepper

1 tbsp lemon juice

½ tsp ground coriander

4 tbsp double cream

MELBA TOAST

4–6 slices white bread

1 Melt the butter in a saucepan. Add the onion and garlic and fry over a low heat, stirring occasionally, until they begin to soften, but not colour.

2 Slice the white part of the leek very thinly and reserve; slice the remaining leek. Slice the Brussels sprouts and thinly slice the beans.

3 Add the green part of the leeks, the Brussels sprouts and beans to the saucepan. Add the stock and bring to the boil. Simmer for 10 minutes.

4 Add the frozen peas, seasoning, lemon juice and coriander and continue to simmer for 10–15 minutes, until the vegetables are tender.

5 Leave the soup to cool a little, then press through a sieve or process in a food processor or blender until smooth. Pour into a clean pan.

6 Add the reserved slices of leek to the soup, bring back to the boil and simmer for about 5 minutes, until the leek is tender. Adjust the seasoning, stir in the cream and reheat gently.

7 To make the melba toast, toast the bread on both sides under a preheated grill. Cut horizontally through the slices, then toast the uncooked sides until they curl up. Serve immediately with the soup.

Tarragon Pea Soup

This soup looks and tastes very sophisticated, but in fact it is very quick and easy to prepare using frozen peas.

NUTRITIONAL INFORMATION

Calories	160	Sugars	.........7g
Protein	.........9g	Fat	...........4g
Carbohydrate	...23g	Saturates	.......2g

 10 mins   55 mins

SERVES 4

INGREDIENTS

2 tsp butter

1 onion, finely chopped

2 leeks, finely chopped

1½ tbsp white rice

500 g/1 lb 2 oz frozen peas

1 litre/1¾ pints water

1 vegetable stock cube

½ tsp dried tarragon

salt and pepper

chopped hard-boiled egg or croûtons (see page 32), to garnish

1 Melt the butter in a large saucepan over a low-medium heat. Add the onion, leeks and rice. Cover and cook for about 10 minutes, stirring occasionally, until the vegetables are soft.

2 Add the peas, water, stock cube and tarragon and bring just to the boil. Season with a little pepper. Cover the pan and simmer the soup for about 35 minutes, stirring occasionally, until the vegetables are very tender.

3 Allow the soup to cool slightly, then transfer to a blender or food processor and purée until smooth, working in batches if necessary. (If using a food processor, strain off the cooking liquid and reserve. Purée the soup solids with enough cooking liquid to moisten them, then combine with the remaining liquid.)

4 Return the puréed soup to the saucepan. Taste and adjust the seasoning, adding plenty of pepper and, if needed, salt. Gently reheat the soup over a low heat for about 10 minutes until hot.

5 Ladle into warm bowls and garnish with hard-boiled egg or croûtons.

COOK'S TIP

The rice gives the soup a little extra body, but a small amount of raw or cooked potato would do the same job.

Roasted Vegetable Soup

Mediterranean vegetables, roasted in olive oil and flavoured with thyme, are the basis for this delicious soup.

NUTRITIONAL INFORMATION

Calories 163	Sugars 13g	
Protein 5g	Fat 10g	
Carbohydrate ...15g	Saturates 3g	

 1 hr 10 mins   15 mins

SERVES 6

I N G R E D I E N T S

2–3 tbsp olive oil

700 g/1 lb 9 oz ripe tomatoes, skinned, cored and halved

3 large yellow peppers, halved, cored and deseeded

3 courgettes, halved lengthways

1 small aubergine, halved lengthways

4 garlic cloves, halved

2 onions, cut into eighths

salt and pepper

pinch of dried thyme

1 litre/1¾ pints vegetable stock

125 ml/4 fl oz single cream

shredded fresh basil leaves, to garnish

1 Brush a large shallow baking dish with olive oil. Laying them cut-side down, arrange the tomatoes, peppers, courgettes and aubergine in one layer (use two dishes, if necessary). Tuck the garlic cloves and onion pieces into the gaps and drizzle the vegetables with olive oil. Season lightly with salt and pepper and sprinkle with the thyme.

2 Place the vegetables in a preheated oven at 190°C/375°F/Gas Mark 5 and bake, uncovered, for 30–35 minutes, or until soft and browned around the edges. Leave to cool, then scrape out the aubergine flesh and remove the skin from the peppers.

3 Working in batches, put the aubergine, pepper flesh, courgettes, tomatoes, garlic and onions into a food processor and chop to the consistency of salsa or pickle; do not purée. Alternatively, place in a bowl and chop together with a knife.

4 Combine the stock with the chopped vegetable mixture in a saucepan and simmer over a medium heat for 20–30 minutes until all the vegetables are tender and the flavours have completely blended.

5 Stir in the cream and heat the soup very gently for about 5 minutes, stirring occasionally, until hot. Taste and adjust the seasoning, if necessary. Ladle the soup into warm bowls, garnish with fresh shredded basil and serve.

Mixed Bean Soup

This thick, satisfying blend of beans and vegetables in a rich red wine and tomato stock, based on an Italian favourite, would make a tasty supper.

NUTRITIONAL INFORMATION

Calories ....192 Sugars 10g
Protein ....10g Fat 5g
Carbohydrate ...23g Saturates 1g

5 mins   25 mins

SERVES 4

INGREDIENTS

1 onion, chopped

1 garlic clove, finely chopped

2 celery sticks, sliced

1 large carrot, diced

400 g/14 oz canned chopped tomatoes

150 ml/¼ pint Italian dry red wine

1.2 litres/2 pints fresh vegetable stock

1 tsp dried oregano

425 g/15 oz canned mixed beans and
   pulses, drained

2 courgettes, diced

1 tbsp tomato purée

salt and pepper

TO SERVE

pesto sauce

crusty bread

COOK'S TIP

Use a jar of good quality pesto sauce from the supermarket as the garnish for this soup.

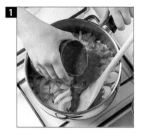

1 Place the prepared onion, garlic, celery and carrot in a large saucepan. Stir in the tomatoes, red wine, vegetable stock and oregano.

2 Bring the vegetable mixture to the boil, cover and leave to simmer for 15 minutes. Stir the mixed beans and pulses into the mixture with the courgettes, and continue to cook, uncovered, for a further 5 minutes.

3 Add the tomato purée to the mixture and season well with salt and pepper to taste. Then heat through, stirring occasionally, for a further 2–3 minutes, but be careful not to allow the mixture to boil again.

4 Ladle the soup into warm bowls and serve with a spoonful of pesto on each portion and accompanied by chunks of crusty bread.

Jerusalem Artichoke Soup

Jerusalem artichokes are native to North America, but are also grown in Europe. They have a nutty flavour which combines well with orange.

NUTRITIONAL INFORMATION

Calories	...211	Sugars	...17g
Protein	...7g	Fat	...8g
Carbohydrate	...29g	Saturates	...4g

10 mins   30 mins

SERVES 4

INGREDIENTS

675 g/1½ lb Jerusalem artichokes

5 tbsp orange juice

2 tbsp butter

1 leek, chopped

1 garlic clove, crushed

300 ml/½ pint vegetable stock

150 ml/¼ pint milk

2 tbsp chopped fresh coriander

150 ml/¼ pint natural yogurt

grated orange rind, to garnish

1 Rinse the Jerusalem artichokes and place in a large saucepan with 2 tablespoons of the orange juice and enough water to cover. Bring to the boil, reduce the heat and cook for 20 minutes, or until the artichokes are tender.

2 Drain the artichokes, reserving 425 ml/¾ pint of the cooking liquid. Leave the artichokes to cool, then peel and place in a large bowl. Mash the flesh with a potato masher.

3 Melt the butter in a large saucepan. Add the leek and garlic and fry over a low heat, stirring frequently, for 2–3 minutes, until the leek is soft.

4 Stir in the mashed artichoke, stock, milk, remaining orange juice and reserved cooking water. Bring to the boil, then simmer for 2–3 minutes.

5 Remove a few pieces of the leek with a slotted spoon and reserve. Process the remainder of the mixture in a food processor or blender for 1 minute until smooth. Alternatively, press through a sieve with the back of a spoon.

6 Return the soup to a clean saucepan and stir in the reserved leeks, coriander and yogurt and heat through. Transfer to individual soup bowls, garnish with orange rind and serve.

Artichoke and Swede Soup

This recipe uses the knobbly Jerusalem artichokes, which are curious to look at but taste delicious in a winter soup.

NUTRITIONAL INFORMATION

Calories	285	Sugars	.........5g
Protein	.........5g	Fat	..........24g
Carbohydrate	...16g	Saturates	.......9g

10 mins   30 mins

SERVES 6

I N G R E D I E N T S

500 g/1 lb 2 oz Jerusalem artichokes

2 tbsp butter

1 onion, finely chopped

115 g/4 oz peeled swede, diced

1 strip lemon rind

700 ml/1¼ pints vegetable stock

salt and pepper

3 tbsp double cream

1 tbsp lemon juice, or to taste

4 tbsp lightly toasted pine nuts, to garnish

1 Peel the Jerusalem artichokes and cut the larger ones into pieces. Drop them into a bowl of cold water to prevent discolouration.

2 Melt the butter in a large saucepan over a medium heat. Add the onion and cook for about 3 minutes, stirring frequently, until just softened.

3 Drain the Jerusalem artichokes and add them to the saucepan with the swede and lemon rind. Pour in the stock, season with a little salt and pepper and stir to combine. Bring just to the boil, reduce the heat and simmer gently for about 20 minutes until the vegetables are tender.

4 Allow the soup to cool slightly, then transfer to a blender or food processor and purée until smooth. (If you are using a food processor, strain off the cooking liquid and reserve. Purée the soup solids with enough cooking liquid to moisten them, then combine with the remaining liquid.)

5 Return the soup to the saucepan, stir in the cream and simmer for about 5 minutes until reheated. Add the lemon juice. Taste and adjust the seasoning, adding more lemon juice if wished. Ladle the soup into warm bowls and very gently place the pine nuts on top, dividing them evenly. Serve at once.

Bean Soup

Beans feature widely in Mexican cooking, and here pinto beans are used to give an interesting texture. Pinto beans require soaking overnight.

NUTRITIONAL INFORMATION

Calories	188	Sugars	........9g
Protein	........13g	Fat	..........1g
Carbohydrate	...33g	Saturates	.....0.3g

 20 mins   3 hrs

SERVES 4

INGREDIENTS

175 g/6 oz pinto beans

1.25 litres/2¼ pints water

175–225 g/6–8 oz carrots, finely chopped

1 large onion, finely chopped

2–3 garlic cloves, crushed

½–1 fresh chilli, deseeded and finely chopped

1 litre /1¾ pints vegetable stock

2 tomatoes, peeled and finely chopped

2 celery sticks, very thinly sliced

salt and pepper

1 tbsp chopped fresh coriander (optional)

CROÛTONS

3 slices white bread, crusts removed

oil, for deep-frying

1–2 garlic cloves, crushed

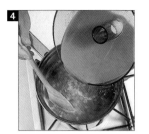

1 Soak the beans overnight in cold water; drain and place in a pan with the water. Bring to the boil and boil vigorously for 10 minutes. Lower the heat, cover and simmer for 2 hours, or until the beans are tender.

2 Add the carrots, onion, garlic, chilli and stock and bring back to the boil. Cover and simmer for a further 30 minutes, until very tender.

3 Remove half the beans and vegetables with the cooking juices and press through a strainer or process in a food processor or blender until smooth.

4 Return the bean purée to the saucepan and add the tomatoes and celery. Simmer for 10–15 minutes, or until the celery is just tender, adding a little more stock or water if necessary.

5 Meanwhile, prepare the croûtons. Dice the bread. Heat the oil with the garlic in a small frying pan and fry the croûtons until golden brown. Drain on kitchen paper.

6 Season the soup and stir in the chopped coriander, if using. Transfer to a warm tureen and serve immediately with the croûtons.

VARIATION

Pinto beans are widely available, but if you cannot find them or you wish to vary the recipe, you can use cannellini beans or black-eyed beans as an alternative.

Split Pea & Parsnip Soup

This soup is surprisingly delicate. The yellow peas give it an appealing light colour, while the parsnips add an aromatic flavour.

NUTRITIONAL INFORMATION

Calories	270	Sugars	........5g
Protein	........16g	Fat	..........7g
Carbohydrate	...39g	Saturates	.......1g

 10 mins   🕐 1 hr

SERVES 4

I N G R E D I E N T S

250 g/9 oz split yellow peas

1 tbsp olive oil

1 onion, finely chopped

1 small leek, finely chopped

3 garlic cloves, finely chopped

2 parsnips, sliced (about 225 g/8 oz)

2 litres/3½ pints water

10 fresh sage leaves or ¼ tsp dried sage

pinch of dried thyme

¼ tsp ground coriander

1 bay leaf

salt and pepper

freshly grated nutmeg

chopped fresh coriander leaves or parsley, to garnish

1 Rinse the peas well under cold running water. Put in a pan and cover generously with water. Bring to the boil and boil for 3 minutes, skimming off the foam from the surface. Drain the peas.

2 Heat the oil in a large pan over a medium heat. Add the onion and leek and cook, stirring occasionally, for about 3 minutes until just softened. Add the garlic and parsnips and continue cooking, stirring occasionally, for 2 minutes.

3 Add the peas, water, sage, thyme, coriander and bay leaf. Bring almost to the boil, reduce the heat, cover and simmer gently for about 40 minutes until the vegetables are very soft. Remove the bay leaf.

4 Remove the pan from the heat and set aside to cool slightly, then transfer to a blender or food processor and process to a smooth purée, in batches if necessary. (If using a food processor, strain off the cooking liquid and reserve. Purée the soup solids with enough cooking liquid to moisten them, then combine with the remaining liquid.)

5 Return the soup to the pan and thin with a little more water, if wished. Season generously with salt, pepper and nutmeg. Place over a low heat and simmer until reheated. Ladle into warmed soup plates and garnish with fresh coriander leaves or parsley.

Bean & Pasta Soup

A dish with proud Mediterranean origins, this soup is a winter warmer.
Serve with warm, crusty bread and, if you like, a slice of cheese.

NUTRITIONAL INFORMATION

Calories	463	Sugars	.........5g
Protein	........13g	Fat	.........33g
Carbohydrate	...30g	Saturates	.......7g

 5–10 mins   1¼ hrs

SERVES 4

INGREDIENTS

225 g/8 oz dried haricot beans, soaked
　overnight, drained and rinsed

4 tbsp olive oil

2 large onions, sliced

3 garlic cloves, chopped

400 g/14 oz canned chopped tomatoes

1 tsp dried oregano

1 tsp tomato purée

850 ml/1½ pints water

90 g/3 oz dried small pasta shapes, such as
　fusilli or conchigliette

salt and pepper

125 g/4½ oz sun-dried tomatoes,
　drained and thinly sliced

1 tbsp chopped fresh coriander or flat-leaf
　parsley

2 tbsp freshly grated Parmesan cheese

1 Put the soaked beans into a large pan,
cover with cold water and bring them
to the boil. Boil rapidly for 15 minutes to
remove any harmful toxins. Drain the
beans in a colander.

2 Heat the oil in a pan over a medium
heat and fry the onions until they
are just beginning to change colour. Stir
in the garlic and cook for 1 further
minute. Stir in the chopped tomatoes,
oregano and the tomato purée and pour
on the water. Add the drained beans, bring
to the boil and cover the pan. Simmer for
about 45 minutes or until the beans are
almost tender.

3 Add the pasta, season the soup with
salt and pepper to taste and stir in
the sun-dried tomatoes. Return the soup
to the boil, partly cover the pan and
continue cooking for 10 minutes, or until
the pasta is nearly tender.

4 Stir in the chopped coriander or
parsley. Taste the soup and adjust the
seasoning if necessary. Transfer to a
warmed soup tureen to serve. Sprinkle
with the Parmesan cheese and serve hot.

Plum Tomato & Pasta Soup

Plum tomatoes are ideal for making soups and sauces as they have denser, less watery flesh than rounder varieties.

NUTRITIONAL INFORMATION

Calories 503	Sugars 16g
Protein 9g	Fat 28g
Carbohydrate ...59g	Saturates 17g

  5 mins   50–55 mins

SERVES 4

INGREDIENTS

60 g/2 oz butter

1 large onion, chopped

600 ml/1 pint vegetable stock

900 g/2 lb Italian plum tomatoes, skinned and roughly chopped

pinch of bicarbonate of soda

225 g/8 oz dried fusilli

salt and pepper

1 tbsp caster sugar

150 ml/¼ pint double cream

fresh basil leaves, to garnish

1 Melt the butter in a large pan, add the onion and fry for 3 minutes, stirring. Add 300 ml/½ pint of vegetable stock to the pan, with the chopped tomatoes and bicarbonate of soda. Bring the soup to the boil and simmer for 20 minutes.

2 Remove the pan from the heat and set aside to cool a little. Purée the soup in a blender or food processor and then pour it through a fine sieve back into the saucepan.

3 Add the remaining vegetable stock and the fusilli to the pan, and season to taste with salt and pepper.

4 Add the sugar to the pan, bring to the boil, then lower the heat and simmer for about 15 minutes.

5 Pour the soup into a warm tureen or individual warmed bowls, swirl the double cream around the surface of the soup and garnish with fresh basil leaves. Serve immediately.

VARIATION

To make orange and tomato soup, simply use half the quantity of vegetable stock, topped up with the same amount of fresh orange juice, and garnish the soup with orange rind.

Yogurt & Spinach Soup

Whole young spinach leaves add vibrant colour to this unusual soup.
Serve with hot, crusty bread for a nutritious light meal.

NUTRITIONAL INFORMATION

Calories ....227 Sugars 13g
Protein ....14g Fat 7g
Carbohydrate ...29g Saturates 2g

15 mins   30 mins

SERVES 4

INGREDIENTS

600 ml/1 pint vegetable stock

salt and pepper

4 tbsp long grain rice, rinsed and drained

4 tbsp water

1 tbsp cornflour

600 ml/1 pint low-fat natural yogurt

3 egg yolks, lightly beaten

juice of 1 lemon

350 g/12 oz young spinach leaves,
   washed and drained

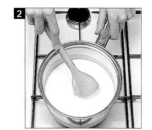

1 Pour the stock into a large pan, season and bring to the boil. Add the rice and simmer for 10 minutes until barely cooked. Remove from the heat.

2 Combine the water and cornflour to a smooth paste. Pour the yogurt into a second pan and stir in the cornflour mixture. Set the pan over a low heat and bring the yogurt to the boil, stirring with a wooden spoon in one direction only. This will stabilise the yogurt and prevent it from separating or curdling on contact with the hot stock. When the yogurt has reached boiling point, stand the pan on a heat diffuser and simmer gently for 10 minutes. Remove the pan from the heat and set the mixture aside to cool slightly before stirring in the beaten egg yolks.

3 Pour the yogurt mixture into the stock, stir in the lemon juice and stir to blend thoroughly. Keep the soup warm, but do not allow it to boil.

4 Blanch the washed and drained spinach leaves in a large pan of boiling, salted water for 2–3 minutes until they begin to soften but have not wilted. Tip the spinach into a colander, drain well and stir it into the soup. Warm through.

5 Taste the soup and adjust the seasoning if necessary. Serve immediately in wide shallow soup plates, with hot, fresh crusty bread.

Spanish Tomato Soup

This Mediterranean tomato soup is thickened with bread, as is traditional in some parts of Spain, and served with garlic bread.

NUTRITIONAL INFORMATION

Calories	297	Sugars	.........7g
Protein	.........8g	Fat	..........13g
Carbohydrate	...39g	Saturates	.......2g

 10 mins   20 mins

SERVES 4

I N G R E D I E N T S

4 tbsp olive oil

1 onion, chopped

3 garlic cloves, crushed

1 green pepper, deseeded and chopped

½ tsp chilli powder

500 g/1 lb 2 oz tomatoes, chopped

225 g/8 oz French or Italian bread, cubed

1 litre/1¾ pints vegetable stock

G A R L I C   B R E A D

4 slices ciabatta or French bread

4 tbsp olive oil

2 garlic cloves, crushed

25 g/1 oz Cheddar cheese, grated

chilli powder, to garnish

VARIATION

Replace the green pepper with red or orange pepper, if you prefer.

1 Heat the olive oil in a large frying pan. Add the onion, garlic and pepper and sauté over a low heat, stirring frequently, for 2–3 minutes, or until the onion has softened.

2 Add the chilli powder and tomatoes and cook over a medium heat until the mixture has thickened.

3 Stir in the bread cubes and stock and cook for 10–15 minutes, until the soup is thick and fairly smooth.

4 Meanwhile, prepare the garlic bread. Toast the bread slices under a medium grill. Drizzle the oil over the top of the bread, rub with the garlic, sprinkle with the grated cheese and return to the grill for a further 2–3 minutes, until the cheese is bubbling and melting. Sprinkle the bread with a little chilli powder.

5 When the garlic bread is ready, ladle the soup into warmed individual soup bowls and serve immediately with generous chunks of the bread.

Tomato & Red Pepper Soup

Sweet red peppers and tangy tomatoes are blended together in a smooth vegetable soup that makes a perfect starter or light lunch.

NUTRITIONAL INFORMATION

Calories	52	Sugars	.........9g
Protein	.........3g	Fat	..........0.4g
Carbohydrate	...10g	Saturates	......0g

15 mins   35 mins

SERVES 4

INGREDIENTS

2 large red peppers

1 large onion, chopped

2 sticks celery, trimmed and chopped

1 garlic clove, crushed

600 ml/1 pint vegetable stock

2 bay leaves

800 g/1lb 12 oz canned plum tomatoes

salt and pepper

2 spring onions, finely shredded,
   to garnish

crusty bread, to serve

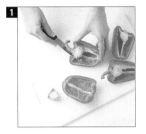

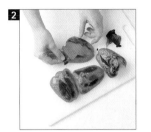

1 Preheat the grill to hot. Halve and deseed the peppers, arrange them on the grill rack and cook, turning occasionally, for 8–10 minutes until softened and charred.

2 Leave the peppers to cool slightly, then carefully peel off the charred skin. Reserving a small piece for garnish, chop the pepper flesh and place it in a large saucepan.

3 Mix in the onion, celery and garlic. Add the stock and the bay leaves. Bring to the boil, cover and simmer for 15 minutes. Remove from the heat.

4 Stir in the tomatoes and transfer to a food processor or blender. Process for a few seconds until the mixture is smooth, then return it to the saucepan.

5 Season the soup with salt and pepper to taste and heat for 3–4 minutes until piping hot. Ladle into warm bowls and garnish with the reserved pepper, cut into strips, and the shredded spring onion. Serve with crusty bread.

COOK'S TIP

If you prefer a coarser, more robust soup, lightly mash the tomatoes with a wooden spoon and omit the blending process in step 4.

Spinach & Tofu Soup

This is a very colourful and delicious soup. If spinach is not in season, watercress or lettuce can be used instead.

NUTRITIONAL INFORMATION

Calories 33   Sugar 1g
Protein . . . . .4g   Fat 2g
Carbohydrate . . . .1g   Saturates 0.2g

15 mins   10 mins

SERVES 4

INGREDIENTS

1 cake of firm tofu

125 g/4½ oz spinach leaves without stems

700 ml/1¼ pints water or vegetable stock

1 tbsp light soy sauce

salt and pepper

1 Using a sharp knife to avoid squashing it, cut the tofu into small cubes about 5 mm/¼ inch thick.

2 Wash the spinach leaves under cold, running water and drain well.

3 Cut the spinach leaves into small pieces or shreds, discarding any discoloured leaves and tough stalks. (If possible, use fresh young spinach leaves, which have not yet developed tough ribs. Otherwise, it is important to cut out all the ribs and stems for this soup.) Set the spinach aside until required.

4 In a preheated wok or large frying pan, bring the water or vegetable stock to a rolling boil.

5 Add the tofu cubes and light soy sauce, bring back to the boil and simmer for about 2 minutes over a medium heat.

6 Add the spinach and simmer for 1 more minute, stirring gently. Skim the surface of the soup to make it clear and season to taste.

7 Transfer the soup into either a warm soup tureen or warmed individual serving bowls, and serve with chopsticks to pick up the spinach and chunks of tofu and a broad, shallow spoon for drinking the soup.

COOK'S TIP

Soup is an integral part of a Chinese meal; it is usually presented in a large bowl placed in the centre of the table, and consumed as the meal progresses. It serves as a refresher between different dishes and as a beverage throughout the meal.

Broccoli and Cheese Soup

This richly flavoured soup is popular with adults and children alike and, served with wholemeal bread, makes a filling lunchtime snack.

NUTRITIONAL INFORMATION

Calories ....249 Sugars 4g
Protein ....14g Fat 15g
Carbohydrate ...16g Saturates 9g

15 mins   20 mins

SERVES 6

INGREDIENTS

25 g/1 oz butter

1 onion, chopped

2 tsp chopped fresh tarragon

450 g/1 lb potatoes, peeled and grated

salt and pepper

1.7 litres/3 pints vegetable stock

700 g/1 lb 9 oz broccoli, cut into
   small florets

175 g/6 oz Cheddar cheese

1 tbsp chopped fresh parsley

wholemeal bread, to serve

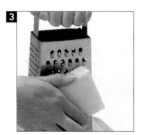

1 Melt the butter in a large, heavy-based saucepan. Add the onion and cook, stirring occasionally, for 5 minutes, until softened. Add the freshly chopped tarragon to the saucepan with the potatoes, season to taste and mix well. Pour in just enough of the stock to cover and bring to the boil. Lower the heat, cover and simmer for 10 minutes.

2 Meanwhile, bring the remaining stock to the boil in another saucepan. Add the broccoli and cook for 6-8 minutes, until just tender.

3 Remove both pans from the heat, leave to cool slightly, then ladle the contents of both pans into a blender or food processor. Process until smooth, then pour the mixture into a clean pan. Grate the cheese, stir into the pan with the parsley and heat gently to warm through, but do not allow the soup to boil. Ladle into warmed soup bowls, garnish with tarragon and serve immediately with chunks of wholemeal bread.

Borscht

This is a lighter, easier version of the original Russian beetroot soup, said to have been created by Antonin Carême, chef to Czar Alexander I.

NUTRITIONAL INFORMATION

Calories 169	Sugars 12g	
Protein 3g	Fat 12g	
Carbohydrate ...13g	Saturates 8g	

 25 mins   1¼ hrs

SERVES 6

INGREDIENTS

1 onion

3 celery sticks

50 g/2 oz butter

350 g/12 oz beetroot, cut into thin batons

1 carrot, cut into thin batons

2 tomatoes, skinned, deseeded and chopped

fresh dill

1.4 litres/2½ pints vegetable stock

1 tbsp white wine vinegar

1 tbsp sugar

salt and pepper

115 g/4 oz white cabbage, shredded

1 beetroot, grated

150 ml/5 fl oz soured cream, to garnish

rye bread, to serve

COOK'S TIP

It is not essential to add extra beetroot towards the end of cooking, but this helps to provide the spectacular colour of the soup and freshens the flavour.

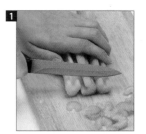
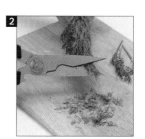

1 Slice the onion into rings and the celery sticks thinly. Melt the butter in a large, heavy-based saucepan. Add the onion and cook over a low heat, stirring occasionally, for 3–5 minutes, until softened. Add the beetroot and carrot batons, sliced celery and chopped tomatoes to the saucepan and cook, stirring frequently, for 4–5 minutes.

2 Snip two tablespoons worth of dill, add half to the saucepan with the stock, vinegar and sugar and season to taste with salt and pepper. Bring to the boil, lower the heat and simmer for 35–40 minutes, until all the vegetables are tender.

3 Stir in the cabbage, cover and simmer for 10 minutes. Stir in the grated beetroot, with any juices, and cook for 10 minutes more. Ladle into warm bowls, garnish with a spoonful of soured cream and the remaining snipped dill and serve immediately with rye bread.

Crécy Soup

The small French towns of Crécy-la-Chapelle and Crécy-en-Ponthieu both claim to be the originators of this classic soup.

NUTRITIONAL INFORMATION

Calories	208	Sugars	.........5g
Protein	.........1g	Fat	..........18g
Carbohydrate	...12g	Saturates	......12g

20 mins   45 mins

SERVES 4

INGREDIENTS

2 shallots

225 g/8 oz carrots

85 g/3 oz butter

pinch of sugar and salt

25 g/1 oz long grain rice

1 fresh thyme sprig

700 ml/1¼ pints vegetable stock

salt and pepper

TO GARNISH

1 tbsp chopped fresh parsley

croûtons (see page 32)

2 Remove the pan from the heat and leave the mixture to cool slightly. Remove and discard the thyme sprig and then pour the soup into a blender or a food processor. Process the mixture to a smooth purée.

3 Return to a clean pan and reheat gently. Season to taste with salt and pepper and whisk in the remaining butter in small pieces. Ladle into warm soup bowls, garnish with the parsley and croûtons and serve immediately.

1 Chop the shallots and slice the carrots. Melt 55 g/2 oz of the butter in a saucepan. Add the shallots, carrots, the sugar and salt, cover and cook over a very low heat, stirring occasionally, for 10 minutes. Stir in the rice and thyme and pour in the stock. Bring to the boil, then lower the heat and simmer for 30 minutes.

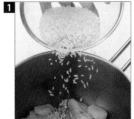
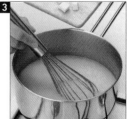

Tomato & Almond Soup

This quick and easy creamy soup has a lovely fresh tomato flavour.
The basil adds a special taste of summer.

NUTRITIONAL INFORMATION

Calories 286   Sugars 9g
Protein ....5g   Fat 25g
Carbohydrate ....9g   Saturates 12g

 10 mins   20 mins

SERVES 4

INGREDIENTS

50 g/1¾ oz butter

700 g/1 lb 9 oz ripe tomatoes, preferably
  plum, roughly chopped

850 ml/1½ pints hot vegetable stock

50 g/1¾ oz ground almonds

150 ml/5 fl oz milk or single cream

1 tsp sugar

2 tbsp shredded fresh basil leaves

salt and pepper

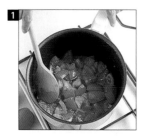

1 Melt the butter in a large saucepan. Add the tomatoes and cook for 5 minutes until the skins start to wrinkle. Season to taste with salt and pepper.

2 Add the stock to the pan, bring to the boil, then cover and simmer for 10 minutes.

3 Meanwhile, under a preheated grill, lightly toast the ground almonds until they are golden brown. This will take only 1–2 minutes, so watch them closely or they may burn.

4 Remove the soup from the heat and place in a food processor or blender and blend the mixture to form a smooth consistency. Alternatively, mash the soup with a potato masher.

5 Pass the soup through a sieve to remove any tomato skin or pips.

6 Place the soup in the pan and return to the heat. Stir in the milk or cream, ground almonds and sugar. Warm the soup through and add the shredded basil just before serving.

7 Transfer the creamy tomato soup to warm soup bowls and serve hot.

VARIATION

Very fine breadcrumbs can be used instead of the ground almonds, if you prefer. Toast them in the same way as the almonds and add with the milk or cream in step 6.

Broccoli & Potato Soup

This creamy soup has a delightful pale green colouring and rich flavour from the blend of tender broccoli and blue cheese.

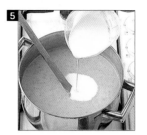

NUTRITIONAL INFORMATION

Calories 452	Sugars 4g	
Protein 14g	Fat 35g	
Carbohydrate ...20g	Saturates 19g	

5–10 mins   35 mins

SERVES 4

INGREDIENTS

2 tbsp olive oil

450 g/1 lb potatoes, diced

1 onion, diced

225 g/8 oz broccoli florets

125 g/4½ oz blue cheese, crumbled

1 litre/1¾ pints vegetable stock

150 m/5 fl oz double cream

pinch of paprika

salt and pepper

1 Heat the oil in a large saucepan. Add the potatoes and onion. Sauté, stirring constantly, for 5 minutes.

2 Reserve a few broccoli florets for the garnish and add the remaining broccoli to the pan. Add the cheese and the vegetable stock.

3 Bring to the boil, then reduce the heat, cover the pan and simmer for 25 minutes, until the potatoes are tender.

4 Transfer the soup to a food processor or blender in batches and process until the mixture is smooth. Alternatively, press the vegetables through a sieve with the back of a wooden spoon.

5 Return the purée to a clean saucepan and stir in the double cream and a pinch of paprika. Season to taste with salt and pepper.

6 Blanch the reserved broccoli florets in a little boiling water for about 2 minutes, then lift them out of the pan with a slotted spoon.

7 Pour the soup into warmed individual bowls and garnish with the broccoli florets and a sprinkling of paprika. Serve the soup immediately.

COOK'S TIP
This soup freezes very successfully. Follow the method described here up to step 4, and freeze the soup after it has been puréed. Add the cream and paprika just before serving. Garnish and serve.

Cream Cheese & Herb Soup

Make the most of home-grown herbs to create this wonderfully creamy soup with its marvellous garden-fresh fragrance.

NUTRITIONAL INFORMATION

Calories 275	Sugars 5g	
Protein 7g	Fat 22g	
Carbohydrate ...14g	Saturates 11g	

 15 mins   35 mins

SERVES 4

I N G R E D I E N T S

25 g/1 oz butter or margarine

2 onions, chopped

850 ml/1½ pints vegetable stock

25 g/1 oz coarsely chopped fresh mixed herbs, such as parsley, chives, thyme, basil and oregano

200 g/7 oz full-fat soft cheese

1 tbsp cornflour

1 tbsp milk

salt and pepper

chopped fresh chives, to garnish

1 Melt the butter or margarine in a large, heavy-based saucepan. Add the onions and fry over a medium heat for 2 minutes, then cover and turn the heat to low. Continue to cook the onions for 5 minutes, then remove the lid.

2 Add the vegetable stock and herbs to the saucepan. Bring to the boil over a moderate heat. Lower the heat, cover and simmer gently for 20 minutes.

3 Remove the saucepan from the heat. Transfer the soup to a food processor or blender and process for about

15 seconds, until smooth. Alternatively, press it through a sieve with the back of a wooden spoon. Return the soup to the saucepan.

4 Reserve a little of the cheese for garnish. Spoon the remaining cheese into the soup and whisk until it has melted and is incorporated.

5 Mix the cornflour with the milk to a paste, then stir the mixture into the soup. Heat, stirring constantly, until thickened and smooth. Season to taste.

6 Pour the soup into warmed individual bowls. Spoon some of the reserved cheese into each bowl and garnish with chives. Serve at once.

Mushroom Noodle Soup

This is a light, refreshing clear soup of mushrooms, cucumber and small pieces of rice noodles, flavoured with soy sauce and a touch of garlic.

NUTRITIONAL INFORMATION

Calories	84	Sugars	.........1g
Protein	.........1g	Fat	..........8g
Carbohydrate	....3g	Saturates	.......1g

 5 mins   10 mins

SERVES 4

INGREDIENTS

125 g/4½ oz flat or open-cap mushrooms

½ cucumber

2 spring onions

1 garlic clove

2 tbsp vegetable oil

600 ml/1 pint water

25 g/1 oz Chinese rice noodles

¾ tsp salt

1 tbsp soy sauce

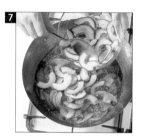

1 Wash the mushrooms and pat them dry on kitchen paper. Slice thinly. Do not remove the mushroom peel as this adds more flavour.

2 Cut the cucumber in half lengthways. Taking care not to damage the flesh, scoop out the seeds, using a teaspoon, and slice the cucumber thinly.

3 Chop the spring onions finely and cut the garlic clove into thin strips.

4 Heat the vegetable oil in a large saucepan or wok.

5 Add the spring onions and garlic to the pan or wok and stir-fry for 30 seconds. Add the mushrooms and stir-fry for a further 2–3 minutes.

6 Stir in the water. Break the noodles into short lengths and add to the soup. Bring to the boil, stirring occasionally.

7 Add the cucumber slices, salt and soy sauce, and simmer for 2–3 minutes.

8 Serve the mushroom noodle soup in warmed bowls, distributing the noodles and vegetables evenly.

COOK'S TIP
Scooping the seeds out from the cucumber gives it a prettier effect when sliced, and also helps to reduce any bitterness, but if you prefer, you can leave them in.

Spinach & Mascarpone Soup

Spinach is the basis for this delicious soup, which has creamy mascarpone cheese stirred through it to give it a wonderful texture.

NUTRITIONAL INFORMATION

Calories 402	Sugars 2g
Protein 11g	Fat 36g
Carbohydrate . . .10g	Saturates 21g

 15 mins   30 mins

SERVES 4

INGREDIENTS

60 g/2 oz butter

1 bunch spring onions, trimmed and chopped

2 celery sticks, chopped

350 g/12 oz spinach or sorrel, or 3 bunches watercress

850 ml /1½ pints vegetable stock

225 g/8 oz mascarpone cheese

salt and pepper

sesame bread sticks, to serve

CROÛTONS

1 tbsp olive oil

2 slices thick-cut bread, cut into cubes

½ tsp caraway seeds

1 Melt half the butter in a very large saucepan. Add the spring onions and celery, and cook them over a medium heat, stirring frequently, for about 5 minutes, until softened.

2 Pack the spinach, sorrel or watercress into the saucepan. Add the stock and bring to the boil, then reduce the heat, cover and simmer for 15–20 minutes.

3 Transfer the soup to a blender or food processor and process until smooth. Alternatively, rub it through a sieve. Return to the saucepan.

4 Add the mascarpone to the soup and heat gently, stirring constantly, until smooth and blended. Season to taste with salt and pepper.

5 To make the croûtons, heat the remaining butter with the oil in a frying pan. Add the bread cubes and fry, turning frequently, until golden brown, adding the caraway seeds towards the end of cooking, so that they do not burn.

6 Ladle the soup into warmed bowls. Sprinkle with the croûtons and seeds and serve with the sesame bread sticks.

VARIATION

Any leafy vegetable can be used to vary the flavour of this soup. For anyone who grows their own vegetables, it is the perfect recipe for experimenting with a glut of produce. Try young beetroot leaves or surplus lettuces for a change.

Lentil and Tomato Soup

This fresh-tasting and colourful soup is substantial enough to serve on its own with some crusty fresh bread for a light lunch or supper.

NUTRITIONAL INFORMATION

Calories ....158 Sugars 6g
Protein ....9g Fat 4g
Carbohydrate ...24g Saturates 1g

20 mins   50 mins

SERVES 4

I N G R E D I E N T S

450 g/1 lb tomatoes

1 tbsp corn or sunflower oil

1 onion, finely chopped

1 garlic glove, crushed

½ tsp ground cumin

½ tsp ground coriander

125 g/4 oz red lentils

1.2 litres/2 pints vegetable stock

salt and pepper

finely chopped fresh coriander, to garnish

1 Using a small, serrated knife make a cross in the tomato skins. Place in boiling water for 20 seconds and then plunge into cold water. Slip off the skins. Halve the tomatoes, remove the seeds and chop the flesh. Heat the oil in a saucepan. Add the onion and cook over a low heat, stirring occasionally, for 5 minutes, until softened. Stir in the garlic, cumin, coriander, tomatoes and lentils and cook, stirring constantly, for 4 minutes more.

2 Pour in the stock, bring to the boil, then simmer gently for 30–40 minutes until the lentils are tender. Season to taste with salt and pepper.

3 Remove the pan from the heat and allow to cool slightly, then process in a blender or food processor to a purée. Return to the clean pan and reheat. Serve the soup immediately, garnished with chopped coriander.

COOK'S TIP
Never season lentils with salt until they have finished cooking, or they will become tough.

Lettuce & Rocket Soup

Rocket has a distinctive flavour that blends well with lettuce in this delicious creamy soup. The rice adds body to the soup.

NUTRITIONAL INFORMATION

Calories	253	Sugars	.........8g
Protein	.........4g	Fat	..........18g
Carbohydrate	...21g	Saturates	......10g

 15 mins   55 mins

SERVES 4–6

INGREDIENTS

1 tbsp butter

1 large sweet onion, such as Vidalia, halved and sliced

2 leeks, sliced

1.5 litres/2¾ pints vegetable stock

85 g/3 oz white rice

2 carrots, thinly sliced

3 garlic cloves

1 bay leaf

2 heads soft round lettuce (about 450 g/ 1 lb), cored and chopped

175 ml/6 fl oz double cream

freshly grated nutmeg

85 g/3 oz rocket leaves, finely chopped

salt and pepper

rocket leaves, to garnish

1 Melt the butter in a large saucepan over a medium heat and add the onion and leeks. Cover and cook for 3–4 minutes, stirring frequently, until the vegetables begin to soften.

2 Add the stock, rice, carrots, garlic and bay leaf with a large pinch of salt. Bring just to the boil. Reduce the heat, cover and simmer for 25–30 minutes, or until the rice and vegetables are tender. Remove the bay leaf.

3 Add the lettuce to the saucepan and cook for 10 minutes, until the leaves are soft, stirring occasionally.

4 Allow the soup to cool slightly, then transfer to a blender or a food processor and purée until smooth, working in batches if necessary. (If using a food processor, strain off the cooking liquid and reserve. Purée the soup solids with enough cooking liquid to moisten them, then combine with the remaining liquid.)

5 Return the soup to the saucepan and place over a low-medium heat. Stir in the cream, reserving a little for the garnish, and the nutmeg. Simmer for 5 minutes, stirring occasionally, until it is reheated.

6 Add the rocket leaves and simmer for 2–3 minutes, stirring occasionally, until wilted. Adjust the seasoning and ladle the soup into warm bowls. Garnish each serving with a swirl of cream and a rocket leaf, and serve immediately.

French Onion Soup

This vegetarian version of the classic French onion soup is flavoured with vegetable stock instead of the traditional beef stock.

NUTRITIONAL INFORMATION

Calories 417   Sugars 10g
Protein . . . . .16g   Fat 19g
Carbohydrate . . .41g   Saturates 9g

15 mins   1 hr 45 mins

SERVES 6

INGREDIENTS

1 tbsp butter

2 tbsp olive oil

1 kg/2 lb 4 oz large yellow onions,
   halved and sliced into half-circles

3 large garlic cloves, finely chopped

salt and pepper

2 tbsp plain flour

200 ml/7 fl oz dry white wine

2 litres/3½ pints vegetable stock

3 tbsp Cognac or brandy

6 slices French bread

200 g/7 oz Gruyère cheese, grated

1 Melt the butter with the olive oil in a large heavy-based saucepan over a medium heat. Add the onions and cook, covered, for 10–12 minutes until they soften, stirring occasionally. Add the garlic and sprinkle with salt and pepper.

2 Reduce the heat a little and continue cooking, uncovered, for 30–35 minutes, or until the onions turn a deep, golden brown, stirring from time to time until they start to colour, then stirring more frequently and scraping the bottom of the pan as they begin to stick.

3 Sprinkle the flour over the onions and stir to blend. Stir in the white wine and bubble for 1 minute. Pour in the vegetable stock and bring to the boil, scraping the bottom of the pan and stirring to combine well. Reduce the heat to low, add the Cognac or brandy and simmer gently, stirring occasionally, for 45 minutes.

4 Put 6 soup bowls to warm. Toast the bread on one side under a preheated hot grill. Turn over and top with the cheese, dividing it evenly between the slices. Grill until the cheese bubbles and melts.

5 Place a piece of cheese toast in each of the 6 warmed bowls, then ladle the hot soup over. Serve at once.

Porcini Soup

This soup has an intense, earthy flavour that brings to mind woodland aromas. It makes a memorable, rich-tasting starter.

NUTRITIONAL INFORMATION

Calories 130   Sugars 5g
Protein . . . . .3g   Fat 9g
Carbohydrate . . . .6g   Saturates 5g

 20 mins   1 hr

SERVES 4

INGREDIENTS

25 g/1 oz dried porcini mushrooms

350 ml/12 fl oz boiling water

125 g/4½ oz fresh porcini mushrooms

2 tsp olive oil

1 celery stick, chopped

1 carrot, chopped

1 onion, chopped

3 garlic cloves, crushed

1.2 litres/2 pints vegetable stock or water

leaves from 2 fresh thyme sprigs

1 tbsp butter

salt and pepper

3 tbsp dry or medium sherry

2–3 tbsp soured cream

chopped fresh parsley, to garnish

1 Put the dried mushrooms in a bowl and pour the boiling water over them. Set aside to soak for 10–15 minutes.

2 Brush or wash the fresh mushrooms. Trim and reserve the stems. Slice any large mushroom caps.

3 Heat the oil in a large saucepan over a medium heat. Add the celery, carrot, onion and mushroom stems. Cook, stirring frequently, for about 8 minutes until the onion begins to colour. Stir in the garlic and continue cooking for 1 minute.

4 Add the vegetable stock or water and thyme leaves with a pinch of salt. Using a draining spoon, transfer the soaked dried mushrooms to the pan. Strain the soaking liquid through a muslin-lined sieve into the pan. Bring to the boil, reduce the heat, partially cover and simmer gently for 30–40 minutes or until the carrots are tender.

5 Remove the pan from the heat and set aside to cool slightly, then transfer the soup solids to a blender or food processor with enough of the cooking liquid to moisten, and purée until smooth. Return it to the pan, combine with the remaining cooking liquid, cover and simmer gently.

6 Meanwhile, melt the butter in a frying pan over a medium heat. Add the fresh mushroom caps and season to taste with salt and pepper. Cook, stirring occasionally, for about 8 minutes until the mushrooms start to colour, stirring more frequently as the liquid evaporates. When the pan becomes dry, add the sherry and cook briefly.

7 Add the mushrooms and sherry to the soup. Taste and adjust the seasoning, if necessary. Ladle into warmed soup bowls, put a spoonful of soured cream in each and garnish with parsley. Serve the soup immediately.

Lettuce & Tofu Soup

This is a delicate, clear soup of shredded lettuce and small chunks of tofu with sliced carrot and spring onion.

NUTRITIONAL INFORMATION

Calories 113   Sugars 2g
Protein . . . . .5g   Fat 8g
Carbohydrate . . . .3g   Saturates 1g

 5 mins   15 mins

SERVES 4

INGREDIENTS

200 g/7 oz tofu

2 tbsp vegetable oil

1 carrot, thinly sliced

1 cm/½ inch piece root ginger, cut into thin shreds

3 spring onions, diagonally sliced

1.2 litres/2 pints vegetable stock

2 tbsp soy sauce

2 tbsp dry sherry

1 tsp sugar

125 g/4½ oz cos lettuce, shredded

salt and pepper

1 Using a sharp knife, cut the tofu into small cubes.

2 Heat the vegetable oil in a preheated wok or large saucepan, then add the tofu and stir-fry until browned. Remove it with a perforated spoon and drain on kitchen paper.

3 Add the carrot, ginger root and spring onions to the wok or saucepan and stir-fry for 2 minutes.

4 Add the vegetable stock, soy sauce, sherry and sugar. Stir well to mix all the ingredients. Bring to the boil and simmer for 1 minute.

5 Add the cos lettuce to the wok or saucepan and stir until it wilts.

6 Return the tofu to the pan to reheat. Season with salt and pepper to taste and serve the soup immediately in warmed bowls.

COOK'S TIP

For a pretty effect, score grooves along the length of the carrot with a sharp knife before slicing. This will create a flower effect as the carrot is cut into rounds. You could also try slicing the carrot on the diagonal to make longer slices.

Celery & Stilton Soup

Crisp, fresh celery and creamy Stilton cheese are a delicious combination, which works equally well in soup.

  15 mins   40 mins

SERVES 4

INGREDIENTS

2 tbsp butter

1 onion, finely chopped

4 large sticks celery, peeled and finely chopped

1 large carrot, finely chopped

salt and pepper

1 litre/1¾ pints vegetable stock

3–4 fresh thyme sprigs

1 bay leaf

125 ml/4 fl oz double cream

150 g/5½ oz Stilton cheese, crumbled

freshly grated nutmeg

celery leaves, to garnish

1 Melt the butter in a large saucepan over a low-medium heat. Add the onion and cook for 3–4 minutes, stirring frequently, until just softened. Add the celery and carrot to the pan and continue cooking for 3 minutes. Season lightly with salt and pepper.

2 Add the stock, thyme and bay leaf and bring to the boil. Reduce the heat, cover and simmer gently for about 25 minutes, stirring occasionally, until the vegetables are very tender.

3 Allow the soup to cool slightly and remove the thyme and bay leaf. Transfer the soup to a blender or food processor and purée until smooth, working in batches, if necessary. (If using a food processor, strain off the cooking liquid and reserve. Purée the soup solids with enough cooking liquid to moisten them, then combine with the remaining liquid.)

4 Return the puréed soup to the saucepan and stir in the cream. Simmer over a low heat for 5 minutes.

5 Add the Stilton slowly, stirring constantly, until smooth (do not allow the soup to boil). Taste and adjust the seasoning, adding salt, if needed, plenty of pepper and nutmeg to taste.

6 Ladle into warm bowls, garnish with celery leaves and serve.

VARIATION
Substitute mature Cheddar or Gruyère for the Stilton.

Broad Bean & Mint Soup

Fresh broad beans are best for this scrumptious soup, but if they are unavailable, use frozen beans instead.

NUTRITIONAL INFORMATION

Calories	224	Sugars	.........4g
Protein	........12g	Fat	...........6g
Carbohydrate	...31g	Saturates	.......1g

 15 mins   40 mins

SERVES 4

I N G R E D I E N T S

2 tbsp olive oil

1 red onion, chopped

2 garlic cloves, crushed

450 g/1 lb potatoes, diced

500 g/1 lb 2 oz broad beans,
  thawed if frozen

850 ml/1½ pints vegetable stock

2 tbsp freshly chopped mint

fresh mint sprigs and natural yogurt,
  to garnish

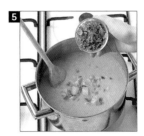

1 Heat the olive oil in a large saucepan. Add the onion and garlic and sauté for 2–3 minutes, until softened.

2 Add the potatoes and cook, stirring constantly, for 5 minutes.

3 Stir in the beans and the stock, then cover the pan and simmer for 30 minutes, or until the beans and potatoes are tender.

4 Remove a few vegetables with a slotted spoon and set aside. Place the remainder of the soup in a food processor or blender and process until smooth.

5 Return the soup to a clean saucepan and add the reserved vegetables and chopped mint. Stir thoroughly and heat through gently.

6 Transfer the soup to a warm tureen or individual serving bowls. Garnish with swirls of yogurt and sprigs of fresh mint and serve immediately.

VARIATION

Use fresh coriander and ½ teaspoon ground cumin as flavourings in the soup, if you prefer.

Green Soup

This fresh-tasting soup with green beans, cucumber and watercress can be served warm, or chilled on a hot summer day.

NUTRITIONAL INFORMATION

Calories	121	Sugars	2g
Protein	2g	Fat	8g
Carbohydrate	10g	Saturates	1g

5 mins   25 mins

SERVES 4

INGREDIENTS

1 tbsp olive oil

1 onion, chopped

1 garlic clove, chopped

200 g/7 oz potatoes, cut into 2.5 cm/
   1 inch cubes

700 ml/1¼ pints vegetable stock

1 small cucumber or ½ large cucumber,
   cut into chunks

85 g/3 oz watercress

125 g/4½ oz French beans, trimmed and
   halved lengthways

salt and pepper

1 Heat the oil in a large pan and cook the onion and garlic over a medium heat for 3–4 minutes or until softened.

2 Add the cubed potato and cook for a further 2–3 minutes. Stir in the stock and bring to the boil. Lower the heat and simmer for 5 minutes.

3 Add the cucumber to the pan and cook for a further 3 minutes or until the potatoes are tender. Test by inserting the tip of a knife into the potato cubes – it should pass through easily.

4 Add the watercress and cook until just wilted. Remove from the heat and set

aside to cool slightly, then transfer to a food processor and process to a smooth purée. Alternatively, before adding the watercress, mash the vegetables with a potato masher and push through a sieve, then chop the watercress finely and stir into the soup.

5 Bring a small pan of water to the boil and steam the beans for 3–4 minutes or until tender. Add the beans to the soup, season to taste with salt and pepper and warm through. Ladle into warmed soup bowls and serve immediately or set aside to cool and then chill.

Beetroot & Potato Soup

A deep red soup makes a stunning first course – and it's easy in the microwave. A swirl of soured cream gives a very pretty effect.

NUTRITIONAL INFORMATION

Calories . . . . . . .120 Sugars 11g
Protein . . . . .4g Fat 2g
Carbohydrate . . .22g Saturates 1g

   20 mins   30 mins

SERVES 6

I N G R E D I E N T S

1 onion, chopped

350 g/12 oz potatoes, diced

1 small Bramley apple, peeled, cored
   and grated

3 tbsp water

1 tsp cumin seeds

500 g/1 lb 2 oz cooked beetroot,
   peeled and diced

1 bay leaf

pinch of dried thyme

1 tsp lemon juice

600 ml/1 pint hot vegetable stock

salt and pepper

6 tbsp soured cream

fresh dill sprigs, to garnish

1 Place the onion, potatoes, apple and water in a large bowl. Cover and cook on HIGH power for 10 minutes.

2 Stir in the cumin seeds and cook on HIGH power for 1 minute.

3 Stir in the beetroot, bay leaf, thyme, lemon juice and stock. Cover and cook on HIGH power for 12 minutes, stirring halfway through. Set aside, uncovered, for 5 minutes.

4 Remove and discard the bay leaf. Strain the vegetables and reserve the liquid in a jug.

5 Place the vegetables with a little of the reserved liquid in a food processor or blender and process to a smooth and creamy purée. Alternatively, either mash the vegetable with a potato masher or press through a sieve.

6 Pour the vegetable purée into a clean bowl with the reserved liquid and mix well. Season with salt and pepper to taste. Cover and cook on HIGH power for 4–5 minutes until piping hot.

7 Serve the soup in warmed bowls. Swirl 1 tablespoon of soured cream into each serving and garnish with a few sprigs of fresh dill.

Cauliflower & Broccoli Soup

Full of flavour, this creamy cauliflower and broccoli soup is simple to make and absolutely delicious to eat.

NUTRITIONAL INFORMATION

Calories	378	Sugars	........14g
Protein	........18g	Fat	..........26g
Carbohydrate	...20g	Saturates	.......7g

 10 mins   35 mins

SERVES 4

INGREDIENTS

3 tbsp vegetable oil

1 red onion, chopped

2 garlic cloves, crushed

300 g/10½ oz cauliflower florets

300 g/10½ oz broccoli florets

1 tbsp plain flour

600 ml/1 pint milk

300 ml/½ pint vegetable stock

75 g/2¾ oz Gruyère cheese, grated

pinch of paprika

150 ml/¼ pint single cream

paprika and Gruyère cheese shavings, to garnish

1 Heat the vegetable oil in a large, heavy-based saucepan. Add the onion, garlic, cauliflower florets and broccoli florets and sauté over a low heat, stirring constantly, for about 3–4 minutes. Sprinkle the flour over the vegetables and cook, stirring constantly, for a further 1 minute.

2 Gradually stir in the milk and stock and bring to the boil, stirring constantly. Reduce the heat and simmer for 20 minutes.

3 Remove about a quarter of the vegetables with a slotted spoon and set aside. Put the remaining soup in a food processor or blender and process for about 30 seconds, until smooth. Alternatively, press the vegetables through a sieve with the back of a wooden spoon. Transfer the soup to a clean saucepan.

4 Return the reserved vegetable pieces to the soup. Stir in the grated cheese, paprika and single cream and heat through over a low heat, without boiling, for about 2–3 minutes, or until the cheese starts to melt.

5 Ladle the soup into warmed individual serving bowls, garnish with shavings of Gruyère and dust with the paprika. Serve immediately.

COOK'S TIP

The soup must not start to boil after the cream has been added, otherwise it will curdle. Use natural yogurt instead of the cream if preferred, but again do not allow it to boil.

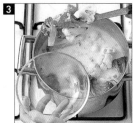

Pumpkin & Orange Soup

This thick, creamy soup has a wonderful, warming golden colour.
It is flavoured with orange and thyme.

NUTRITIONAL INFORMATION

Calories 111   Sugars 4g
Protein . . . . .2g   Fat 6g
Carbohydrate . . . .5g   Saturates 2g

 10 mins   35–40 mins

SERVES 4

INGREDIENTS

2 tbsp olive oil

2 onions, chopped

2 garlic cloves, chopped

900 g/2 lb pumpkin, peeled and cut into
   2.5 cm/1 inch chunks

1.5 litres/2¾ pints boiling vegetable stock

finely grated rind and juice of 1 orange

3 tbsp fresh thyme leaves

150 ml/¼ pint milk

salt and pepper

crusty bread, to serve

1 Heat the olive oil in a large saucepan. Add the onions to the pan and cook for 3–4 minutes or until softened. Add the garlic and pumpkin and cook for a further 2 minutes, stirring well.

2 Add the boiling vegetable stock, the orange rind and juice and 2 tablespoons of the thyme to the pan. Leave to simmer, covered, for 20 minutes or until the pumpkin is tender.

3 Place the mixture in a blender or food processor and blend until smooth. Alternatively, mash the mixture with a potato masher until smooth. Season to taste.

4 Return the soup to the saucepan and add the milk. Reheat the soup for about 3–4 minutes or until it is piping hot but not boiling.

5 Sprinkle with the remaining fresh thyme just before serving.

6 Ladle the soup into 4 warm soup bowls and serve it with plenty of fresh crusty bread.

COOK'S TIP

Pumpkins are usually large vegetables. To make things a little easier, ask the greengrocer to cut a chunk off for you. Alternatively, make double the quantity and freeze the soup for up to 3 months.

Chinese Vegetable Soup

This tasty vegetable broth would make an unusual first course for a dinner party or a delicious light lunch.

NUTRITIONAL INFORMATION

Calories . . . . .117 Sugars 2g
Protein . . . . .6g Fat 8g
Carbohydrate . . . .5g Saturates 1g

 15 mins   10 mins

SERVES 4

INGREDIENTS

225 g/8 oz marinated tofu

2 garlic cloves

4 spring onions

1 carrot

115 g/4 oz Chinese leaves

2 tbsp groundnut oil

1 litre/1¾ pints vegetable stock

1 tbsp Chinese rice wine

2 tbsp light soy sauce

1 tsp sugar

salt and pepper

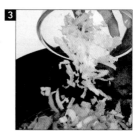

1 Cut the tofu into 1 cm/½ inch cubes. Slice the garlic, spring onion and carrot thinly and shred the Chinese leaves. Set the vegetables aside.

COOK'S TIP

Always use a sharp knife when cutting tofu because it is very easily squashed.

2 Heat the groundnut oil in a large wok or heavy-based frying pan. Add the tofu cubes and stir-fry for 4-5 minutes, until browned. Remove from the wok or pan with a slotted spoon and drain on kitchen paper.

3 Add the garlic, spring onions and carrot to the wok or pan and stir-fry for 2 minutes. Pour in the stock, Chinese rice wine and soy sauce and add the sugar and Chinese leaves. Continue to cook over a medium heat for 1-2 minutes, until heated through.

4 Season to taste with salt and pepper and add the tofu. Ladle the soup into warm bowls and serve immediately.

Chilli & Watercress Soup

This delicious soup is a wonderful blend of colours and flavours. It is very hot, so if you prefer a milder taste, omit the seeds from the chillies.

NUTRITIONAL INFORMATION

Calories ....90 Sugars 1g
Protein ....7g Fat 6g
Carbohydrate ....2g Saturates 1g

10 mins   15 mins

SERVES 4

INGREDIENTS

1 tbsp sunflower oil

250 g/9 oz smoked tofu, sliced

90 g/3 oz shiitake mushrooms, sliced

2 tbsp chopped fresh coriander

125 g/4½ oz watercress

1 fresh red chilli, deseeded and finely
  sliced, to garnish

STOCK

1 tbsp tamarind pulp

2 dried red chillies, chopped

2 kaffir lime leaves, torn in half

2.5 cm/1 inch piece fresh root ginger,
  chopped

5 cm/2 inch piece galangal, chopped

1 stalk lemongrass, chopped

1 onion, quartered

1 litre/1¾ pints cold water

1 Put all the ingredients for the stock into a saucepan and bring to the boil.

2 Simmer the stock for 5 minutes. Remove from the heat and strain, reserving the stock.

3 Heat the sunflower oil in a wok or large, heavy frying pan and cook the tofu over a high heat for about 2 minutes, stirring constantly so that the tofu cooks

evenly on both sides. Add the strained stock to the frying pan.

4 Add the mushrooms and coriander and boil for 3 minutes.

5 Add the watercress and boil for a further 1 minute.

6 Serve immediately, garnished with red chilli slices.

VARIATION
You might like to try a mixture of different types of mushroom. Oyster, button and straw mushrooms are all suitable.

Mushroom & Ginger Soup

Thai soups are very quickly and easily put together, and are cooked so that each ingredient can still be tasted in the finished dish.

NUTRITIONAL INFORMATION

Calories 74   Sugars 1g
Protein . . . . .3g   Fat 3g
Carbohydrate . . . .9g   Saturates 0.4g

30 mins   15 mins

SERVES 4

I N G R E D I E N T S

15 g/½ oz dried Chinese mushrooms or
125 g/4½ oz field or chestnut mushrooms

1 litre/1¾ pints hot vegetable stock

125 g/4½ oz thread egg noodles

2 tsp sunflower oil

3 garlic cloves, crushed

2.5 cm/1 inch piece fresh root ginger,
finely shredded

½ tsp mushroom ketchup

1 tsp light soy sauce

125 g/4½ oz beansprouts

fresh coriander leaves, to garnish

1 Soak the dried Chinese mushrooms (if using) for at least 30 minutes in 300 ml/½ pint of the hot vegetable stock. Remove the stalks and discard, then slice the mushrooms. Reserve the stock.

2 Cook the noodles for 2–3 minutes in boiling water. Drain and rinse. Set them aside.

3 Heat the oil in a wok or large, heavy frying pan over a high heat. Add the garlic and ginger, stir and add the mushrooms. Stir over a high heat for 2 minutes.

4 Add the remaining vegetable stock with the reserved stock and bring to the boil. Add the mushroom ketchup and soy sauce.

5 Stir in the beansprouts and cook until tender. Put some noodles in each bowl and ladle the soup on top. Garnish with coriander leaves and serve immediately.

COOK'S TIP

Rice noodles contain no fat and are ideal for anyone on a low-fat diet.

Beetroot Soup

Here are two variations using the same vegetable: a creamy soup made with puréed cooked beetroot and a traditional clear soup, Borscht.

NUTRITIONAL INFORMATION

Calories 106	Sugars 11g
Protein 3g	Fat 5g
Carbohydrate . . .13g	Saturates 3g

🧊 25 mins   🕐 35–55 mins

SERVES 6

INGREDIENTS

BORSCHT

500 g/1 lb 2 oz raw beetroot, peeled and grated

2 carrots, finely chopped

1 large onion, finely chopped

1 garlic clove, crushed

1 bouquet garni

1 litre/1¾ pints vegetable stock

2–3 tsp lemon juice

salt and pepper

150 ml/¼ pint soured cream, to serve

CREAMED BEETROOT SOUP

60 g/2 oz butter or margarine

2 large onions, finely chopped

1–2 carrots, chopped

2 celery sticks, chopped

500 g/1 lb 2 oz cooked beetroot, diced

1–2 tbsp lemon juice

900 ml/1½ pints vegetable stock

salt and pepper

300 ml/½ pint milk

TO SERVE

grated cooked beetroot or 6 tbsp double cream, lightly whipped

1 To make borscht, place the beetroot, carrots, onion, garlic, bouquet garni, stock and lemon juice in a saucepan and season to taste with salt and pepper. Bring to the boil, cover the pan and simmer for 45 minutes.

2 Press the soup through a fine sieve or a sieve lined with muslin, then pour into a clean pan. Taste and adjust the seasoning and add a little extra lemon juice, if necessary.

3 Bring to the boil and simmer for 1–2 minutes. Serve with a spoonful of soured cream swirled through.

4 To make creamed beetroot soup, melt the butter or margarine in a saucepan. Add the onions, carrots and celery and fry until just beginning to colour.

5 Add the beetroot, 1 tbsp of the lemon juice, the stock and seasoning and bring to the boil. Cover and simmer for 30 minutes, until tender.

6 Cool slightly, then press through a sieve or process in a food processor. Pour into a clean pan. Add the milk and bring to the boil. Adjust the seasoning and add extra lemon juice, if necessary. Top with grated beetroot or double cream.

Curried Parsnip Soup

Parsnips make a delicious soup as they have a slightly sweet flavour. In this recipe, spices are added to complement this sweetness.

NUTRITIONAL INFORMATION

Calories ....152 Sugars 7g
Protein ....3g Fat 8g
Carbohydrate ...18g Saturates 3g

 10 mins   35 mins

SERVES 4

INGREDIENTS

1 tbsp vegetable oil

15 g/½ oz butter

1 red onion, chopped

3 parsnips, chopped

2 garlic cloves, crushed

2 tsp garam masala

½ tsp chilli powder

1 tbsp plain flour

850 ml/1½ pints vegetable stock

grated rind and juice of 1 lemon

salt and pepper

lemon rind, to garnish

1 Heat the oil and butter in a large saucepan until the butter has melted. Add the onion, parsnips and garlic and sauté, stirring frequently, for about 5–7 minutes, until the vegetables have softened, but not coloured.

2 Add the garam masala and chilli powder and cook, stirring constantly, for 30 seconds. Sprinkle in the flour, mixing well, and cook, stirring constantly, for a further 30 seconds.

3 Stir in the stock, lemon rind and juice and bring to the boil. Reduce the heat and simmer for 20 minutes.

4 Remove some of the vegetable pieces with a slotted spoon and reserve until required. Transfer the remaining soup and vegetables to a food processor or blender and process for about 1 minute, or until a smooth purée is formed. Alternatively, press the vegetables through a sieve with the back of a wooden spoon.

5 Return the soup to a clean saucepan and stir in the reserved vegetables. Heat the soup through for 2 minutes until piping hot.

6 Season to taste with salt and pepper, then transfer to soup bowls, garnish with strips of lemon rind and serve.

Hearty Bean Soup

This is a really hearty soup, filled with colour, flavour and goodness, which may be adapted to any vegetables that you have to hand.

NUTRITIONAL INFORMATION

Calories	190	Sugars	9g
Protein	10g	Fat	4g
Carbohydrate	30g	Saturates	0.5g

 10 mins   40 mins

SERVES 4

INGREDIENTS

1 tbsp vegetable oil

1 red onion, halved and sliced

100 g/3½ oz potatoes, diced

1 carrot, diced

1 leek, sliced

1 fresh green chilli, deseeded and sliced

3 garlic cloves, crushed

1 tsp ground coriander

1 tsp chilli powder

1 litre/1¾ pints vegetable stock

450 g/1 lb mixed canned beans, such as red kidney, borlotti, black-eyed or flageolet, drained

salt and pepper

2 tbsp chopped fresh coriander, to garnish

1 Heat the vegetable oil in a large saucepan. Add the onion, potatoes, carrot and leek and sauté, stirring constantly, for about 2 minutes, until the vegetables are slightly softened.

2 Add the chilli and crushed garlic and cook for a further minute.

3 Stir in the ground coriander, chilli powder and vegetable stock.

4 Bring the soup to the boil, reduce the heat and cook for 20 minutes, or until the vegetables are tender.

5 Stir in the beans, season well with salt and pepper and cook, stirring occasionally, for a further 10 minutes.

6 Transfer the soup to a warm tureen or warmed individual bowls, garnish with chopped coriander and serve.

COOK'S TIP
Serve this soup with slices of warm corn bread or a cheese loaf.

Sweet Potato Soup

When there's a chill in the air, this vivid soup is just the thing to serve – it's very warming and comforting.

NUTRITIONAL INFORMATION

Calories	57	Sugars	.......1.5g
Protein	........2.3g	Fat	.........2.5g
Carbohydrate	...6.6g	Saturates	.....0.8g

15 mins   1 hr 15 mins

SERVES 6

INGREDIENTS

350 g/12 oz sweet potatoes

1 acorn squash

4 shallots

olive oil, for brushing

5–6 garlic cloves, unpeeled

850 ml/1½ pints vegetable stock

125 ml/¼ pint single cream

salt and pepper

snipped fresh chives, to garnish

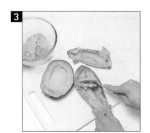

1 Cut the sweet potatoes, squash and shallots in half lengthways. Brush the cut sides with oil.

2 Put the vegetables, cut sides down, in a shallow roasting tin. Add the garlic cloves. Roast in a preheated oven at 190°C/375°F/Gas Mark 5 for about 40 minutes until tender and light brown.

3 When cool, scoop the flesh from the potato and squash halves and put in a saucepan with the shallots. Remove the garlic peel and add the soft insides to the other vegetables.

4 Add the stock and a pinch of salt. Bring just to the boil, reduce the heat and simmer, partially covered, for about 30 minutes, stirring occasionally, until the vegetables are very tender.

5 Allow the soup to cool slightly, then transfer to a blender or food processor and purée until smooth, working in batches, if necessary. (If using a food processor, strain off the cooking liquid and reserve. Purée the soup solids then combine with the remaining liquid.)

6 Return the soup to the saucepan and stir in the cream, reserving a little to garnish. Season to taste, then simmer for 5–10 minutes until completely heated through. Ladle into warm bowls, garnish with chives and a swirl of cream and serve.

Corn & Spinach Soup

Fresh corn-on-the-cob is used in this unusual recipe. The spinach is added at the last minute so that its vibrant colour is retained.

NUTRITIONAL INFORMATION

Calories 347   Sugars 11g
Protein ....9g   Fat 20g
Carbohydrate ...36g   Saturates 10g

20 mins   35 mins

SERVES 4

3 corn-on-the-cobs, cooked

1 tsp butter

1 tsp oil

1 large onion, finely chopped

1 leek, thinly sliced

1 carrot, finely chopped

1 large potato, diced

1.2 litres/2 pints water

125 ml/4 fl oz double cream

125 ml/4 fl oz milk

salt and pepper

freshly grated nutmeg

175 g/6 oz spinach leaves, finely chopped

1 Cut the kernels from the corn, without cutting all the way down to the cob. Using the back of a knife, scrape the cobs to extract the milky liquid, and set it aside.

2 Heat the butter and oil in a large saucepan over a medium heat and add the onion and leek. Cover and cook for 3–4 minutes, stirring frequently, until the vegetables have softened.

3 Add the carrot, potato and water to the pan with a large pinch of salt. Bring just to the boil and stir in the corn kernels and the liquid scraped from the cobs. Reduce the heat to low, cover and simmer for about 25 minutes, or until the carrot and potato are tender.

4 Allow the soup to cool slightly, then transfer about half of it to a blender or food processor and purée until smooth.

5 Return the puréed soup to the saucepan, add the cream and milk and stir to blend. Thin with a little more milk, if preferred. Season with salt, pepper and nutmeg. Simmer over a low heat until reheated, but do not allow to boil.

6 Add the spinach to the soup and cook for 4–5 minutes, stirring frequently, just until the spinach is completely wilted.

Taste and adjust the seasoning, if necessary, then ladle the soup into warm bowls. Serve at once.

COOK'S TIP

To cut corn kernels off the cob, lay on its side on a chopping board and slice lengthways, rotating until all kernels are removed. Then stand on its stem and scrape down to extract the remaining pulp and juice.

Carrot & Cumin Soup

Carrot soups are very popular and here cumin, tomato, potato and celery give the soup both richness and depth.

NUTRITIONAL INFORMATION

Calories 114   Sugars 8g
Protein . . . . .3g   Fat 6g
Carbohydrate . . .12g   Saturates 4g

15 mins   45 mins

SERVES 4–6

INGREDIENTS

3 tbsp butter or margarine

1 large onion, chopped

1–2 garlic cloves, crushed

350 g/12 oz carrots, sliced

900 ml/1½ pints vegetable stock

¾ tsp ground cumin

salt and pepper

2 celery sticks, thinly sliced

115 g/4 oz potato, diced

2 tsp tomato purée

2 tsp lemon juice

2 bay leaves

about 300 ml/½ pint skimmed milk

celery leaves, to garnish

1 Melt the butter or margarine in a large pan. Add the onion and garlic and cook very gently until softened.

2 Add the carrots and cook gently for a further 5 minutes, stirring frequently and taking care they do not brown.

3 Add the stock, cumin, seasoning, celery, potato, tomato purée, lemon juice and bay leaves and bring to the boil. Cover and simmer for about 30 minutes until the vegetables are tender.

4 Remove and discard the bay leaves, cool the soup a little and then press it through a sieve or process in a food processor or blender until smooth.

5 Pour the soup into a clean pan, add the milk and bring to the boil over a low heat. Taste and adjust the seasoning if necessary.

6 Ladle the soup into warmed bowls, garnish each serving with a small celery leaf and serve.

COOK'S TIP

This soup can be frozen for up to 3 months. Add the milk when reheating.

Avocado & Vegetable Soup

Avocado has a rich flavour and colour which makes a creamy-flavoured soup. It is best served chilled, but may also be eaten warm.

NUTRITIONAL INFORMATION

Calories	167	Sugars	.........5g
Protein	.........4g	Fat	..........13g
Carbohydrate	....8g	Saturates	.......3g

 15 mins   10 mins

SERVES 4

INGREDIENTS

1 large avocado

2 tbsp lemon juice

1 tbsp vegetable oil

50 g/2 oz canned sweetcorn, drained

2 tomatoes, peeled and deseeded

1 garlic clove, crushed

1 leek, chopped

1 fresh red chilli, deseeded and chopped

425 ml/¾ pint vegetable stock

150 ml/¼ pint milk

shredded leek, to garnish

1 Peel the avocado and mash the flesh with a fork, stir in the lemon juice and reserve until required.

2 Heat the vegetable oil in a large saucepan. Add the sweetcorn, tomatoes, garlic, leek and chilli and sauté over a low heat for 2–3 minutes, or until the vegetables have softened.

3 Put half the vegetable mixture in a food processor or blender, together with the mashed avocado, and process until smooth. Transfer the mixture to a clean saucepan.

4 Add the vegetable stock, milk and reserved vegetables and cook over a low heat for 3–4 minutes, until hot. Transfer to warmed individual serving bowls, garnish with shredded leek and serve immediately.

COOK'S TIP

If serving chilled, transfer from the food processor to a bowl, stir in the vegetable stock and milk, cover and chill in the refrigerator for at least 4 hours.

Tuscan Bean Soup

This thick and creamy soup is based on a traditional Tuscan recipe.
If you use dried beans, the preparation and cooking times will be longer.

NUTRITIONAL INFORMATION

Calories	250	Sugars	........4g
Protein	........13g	Fat	..........10g
Carbohydrate	...29g	Saturates	.......2g

 5 mins   10 mins

SERVES 4

INGREDIENTS

225 g/8 oz dried butter beans, soaked overnight, or 800 g/1 lb 12 oz canned butter beans

1 tbsp olive oil

2 garlic cloves, crushed

1 vegetable stock cube, crumbled

150 ml/¼ pint milk

salt and pepper

2 tbsp chopped fresh oregano

1 If you are using dried beans that have been soaked overnight, drain them thoroughly. Bring a large pan of water to the boil, add the beans and boil for 10 minutes. Cover the pan and simmer for a further 30 minutes or until the beans are tender. Drain the beans, reserving the cooking liquid. If you are using canned beans, drain them thoroughly and reserve the liquid.

2 Heat the oil in a large frying pan and fry the garlic for 2–3 minutes or until just beginning to brown.

3 Add the beans and 400 ml/14 fl oz of the reserved liquid to the pan, stirring. You may need to add a little water if there is insufficient liquid. Stir in the crumbled stock cube. Bring the mixture to the boil and then remove the pan from the heat.

4 Place the bean mixture in a food processor or blender and process until a smooth purée is formed. Alternatively, mash the bean mixture to a smooth consistency. Season the soup to taste with salt and pepper and stir in the milk.

5 Pour the soup back into the pan and gently heat to just below boiling point. Stir in the chopped fresh oregano just before serving.

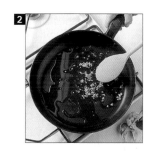

Cream of Artichoke Soup

This creamy soup has the unique, subtle flavouring of Jerusalem artichokes and a garnish of grated carrots for extra crunch.

NUTRITIONAL INFORMATION

Calories 19   Sugars 0g
Protein . . . . .0.4g   Fat 2g
Carbohydrate . . .0.7g   Saturates 0.7g

 10–15 mins   55–60 mins

SERVES 6

I N G R E D I E N T S

750 g/1 lb 10 oz Jerusalem artichokes

1 lemon, thickly sliced

60 g/2 oz butter or margarine

2 onions, chopped

1 garlic clove, crushed

1.25 litres/2¼ pints vegetable stock

salt and pepper

2 bay leaves

¼ tsp ground mace or ground nutmeg

1 tbsp lemon juice

150 ml/¼ pint single cream or natural
    fromage frais

T O   G A R N I S H

coarsely grated carrot

chopped fresh parsley or coriander

1 Peel and slice the artichokes. Put into a bowl of water with the lemon slices.

2 Melt the butter or margarine in a large saucepan. Add the onions and garlic and fry gently for 3–4 minutes until soft but not coloured.

3 Drain the artichokes (discarding the lemon) and add to the pan. Mix well

and cook gently for 2–3 minutes without allowing to colour.

4 Add the stock, seasoning, bay leaves, mace or nutmeg and lemon juice. Bring slowly to the boil, then cover and simmer gently for about 30 minutes until the vegetables are very tender.

5 Discard the bay leaves. Cool the soup slightly then press through a sieve or blend in a food processor until smooth. If

liked, a little of the soup may be only partially puréed and added to the rest of the puréed soup, to give extra texture.

6 Pour into a clean pan and bring to the boil. Adjust the seasoning and stir in the cream or fromage frais. Reheat gently without boiling.

7 Ladle the soup into serving bowls and garnish with grated carrot and chopped parsley or coriander to serve.

Aubergine Soup

The parsnip and carrot bring a balancing sweetness to the aubergines in this delicious soup.

NUTRITIONAL INFORMATION

Calories 130   Sugars 9g
Protein . . . . .3g   Fat 8g
Carbohydrate . . .12g   Saturates 3g

 15 mins   1 hr 15 mins

SERVES 6

INGREDIENTS

1 tbsp olive oil, plus extra for brushing

750 g/1 lb 10 oz aubergines, halved lengthways

1 carrot, halved

1 small parsnip, halved

2 onions, finely chopped

3 garlic cloves, finely chopped

1 litre/1¾ pints vegetable stock

¼ tsp fresh thyme leaves, or a pinch of dried thyme

1 bay leaf

⅛ tsp ground coriander

1 tbsp tomato purée

150 ml/5 fl oz single cream

salt and pepper

lemon juice

LEMON–GARLIC SEASONING

grated rind of ½ lemon

1 garlic clove, finely chopped

3 tbsp chopped fresh parsley

1 Brush a shallow roasting tin with oil and add the aubergine, cut sides down, and the carrot and parsnip. Brush the vegetables with oil. Roast in a preheated oven at 200°C/400°F/Gas Mark 6 for 30 minutes, turning once.

2 When cool enough to handle, scrape the aubergine flesh away from the skin, or scoop it out, then roughly chop. Cut the carrot and parsnip into chunks.

3 Heat the oil in a large saucepan over a medium-low heat. Add the onions and garlic and cook for about 5 minutes, stirring frequently, until softened. Add the aubergine, parsnip, carrot, stock, thyme, bay leaf, coriander and tomato purée, with a little salt. Stir to combine. Cover and simmer for 30 minutes, or until tender.

4 Allow the soup to cool slightly, then transfer to a blender or food processor and purée until smooth, working in batches if necessary. (If using a food processor, strain off the cooking liquid and reserve. Purée the soup solids with enough cooking liquid to moisten them, then combine with the remaining liquid.)

5 Return the puréed soup to the saucepan and stir in the cream. Reheat the soup over a low heat for about 10 minutes until hot. Adjust the seasoning, adding lemon juice to taste.

6 To make the lemon-garlic seasoning, chop together the lemon rind, garlic and parsley until very fine and well mixed. Ladle the soup into warm bowls, then garnish with the lemon-garlic seasoning.

Spicy Vegetable Soup

Wake up the taste buds with a hint of curry spices in this easy-to-prepare vegetable soup. For a light lunch, serve with Indian bread.

NUTRITIONAL INFORMATION

Calories 75	Sugars 5g	
Protein 3g	Fat 4g	
Carbohydrate 8g	Saturates 1g	

 15 mins 15 mins

SERVES 4

I N G R E D I E N T S

280 g/10 oz leeks

2.5 cm/1 inch piece fresh root ginger

1 tbsp sunflower or corn oil

2 garlic cloves, finely chopped

½ tsp ground cumin

½ tsp ground coriander

½ tsp ground turmeric

1.2 litres/2 pints vegetable stock

450 g/1 lb tomatoes, finely diced

2 courgettes, cut into batons

salt and pepper

3 tbsp chopped fresh coriander, to garnish

1 Slice the leeks thinly and grate half a teaspoon of ginger. Heat the oil in a saucepan. Add the leeks, garlic and ginger and cook, stirring occasionally, for 2 minutes. Stir in the ground spices and cook, stirring constantly, for 30 seconds.

2 Pour in the stock and bring to the boil. Cover the pan and simmer for about 5 minutes.

3 Stir in the diced tomatoes and courgette batons. Cover and simmer for a further 3 minutes.

4 Season the soup to taste with salt and pepper, then serve, garnished with the chopped coriander.

COOK'S TIP

If you buy whole cumin and coriander seeds and grind them yourself with a pestle and mortar or spice mill, the flavour and aroma will be stronger.

Sweetcorn & Lentil Soup

This pale-coloured soup is made with sweetcorn and green lentils.
Serve it with wholemeal bread for a perfectly balanced light meal.

NUTRITIONAL INFORMATION

Calories	171	Sugars	. . . . .9g
Protein	. . . . .5g	Fat	. . . . .2g
Carbohydrate	. . .30g	Saturates	. . . . .0.3g

 5 mins   30 mins

SERVES 4

INGREDIENTS

25 g/1 oz green lentils, washed

1 litre/1¾ pints vegetable stock

1-cm/½-inch piece root ginger, finely
chopped

2 tsp soy sauce

1 tsp sugar

1 tbsp cornflour

3 tbsp dry sherry

325 g/11½ oz canned sweetcorn

1 egg white

1 tsp sesame oil

salt and pepper

TO GARNISH

strips of spring onion

strips of red chilli

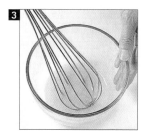

COOK'S TIP

Ginger should be smooth and
fresh looking. Keep unused
ginger in a plastic bag and
store in the refrigerator.

1 Place the lentils in a saucepan with the stock, root ginger, soy sauce and sugar. Boil rapidly, uncovered, for 10 minutes. Skim the liquid. Reduce the heat, cover and simmer for 15 minutes.

2 Mix the cornflour with the sherry in a small bowl and add to the saucepan. Add the sweetcorn and its liquid. Simmer for a further 2 minutes.

3 Whisk the egg white lightly with the sesame oil. Pour the egg mixture into the soup in a thin stream, remove from the heat and stir. The egg white will form white strands.

4 Season the soup to taste with salt and pepper. Pour into 4 warmed soup bowls and garnish with strips of spring onion and chilli before serving.

Saffron Noodle Soup

This soup has everything going for it – it is very low in fat, takes little time to make, looks intriguing and has wonderful flavours and textures.

NUTRITIONAL INFORMATION

Calories	135	Sugars	.........3g
Protein	.........3g	Fat	...........1g
Carbohydrate	...29g	Saturates	.......0g

10 mins   15 mins

SERVES 4

I N G R E D I E N T S

2 courgettes

1.2 litres/2 pints vegetable stock

2 tbsp light soy sauce

1½ tsp saffron threads

4 spring onions, sliced into rings

2 large tomatoes, skinned and chopped

1 garlic clove, finely chopped

115 g/4 oz rice noodles

pepper

finely chopped garlic chives, to garnish

1 Cut the courgettes into batons and set aside. Pour the stock into a large saucepan, add the soy sauce and bring to the boil. Crush the saffron with a mortar and pestle and stir it into the stock.

2 Add the spring onions, courgettes, tomatoes, garlic and noodles to the stock, bring back to the boil, cover and simmer for 5 minutes.

3 Season the soup to taste with pepper and serve, garnished with the chopped garlic chives.

COOK'S TIP
Soy sauce is quite salty, so this soup is unlikely to need any additional salt. In the interests of healthy eating, you may prefer to use low-sodium soy sauce.

Potato & Split Pea Soup

Split green peas are sweeter than other varieties of split pea and reduce down to a purée when cooked, which acts as a thickener in soups.

NUTRITIONAL INFORMATION

Calories 260	Sugars 5g
Protein 11g	Fat 10g
Carbohydrate ...32g	Saturates 3g

 5–10 mins   45 mins

SERVES 4

INGREDIENTS

2 tbsp vegetable oil

2 unpeeled floury potatoes, diced

2 onions, diced

75 g/2¾ oz split green peas

1 litre/1¾ pints vegetable stock

5 tbsp grated Gruyère cheese

salt and pepper

CROÛTONS

40 g/1½ oz butter

1 garlic clove, crushed

1 tbsp chopped fresh parsley

1 thick slice of white bread, cubed

1 Heat the vegetable oil in a large saucepan. Add the potatoes and onions and sauté over a low heat, stirring constantly, for about 5 minutes.

VARIATION

For a richly coloured soup, red lentils could be used instead of split green peas. Add a large pinch of brown sugar to the recipe for extra sweetness if red lentils are used.

2 Add the split green peas to the pan and stir to mix together well.

3 Pour the vegetable stock into the pan and bring it to the boil. Reduce the heat to low and simmer for 35 minutes, until the potatoes are tender and the split peas are cooked.

4 Meanwhile, make the croûtons. Melt the butter in a frying pan. Add the garlic, parsley and bread cubes and cook,

turning over frequently, for about 2 minutes, until the bread cubes are golden brown on all sides.

5 Stir the grated cheese into the soup and season to taste with salt and pepper. Heat gently until the cheese is starting to melt.

6 Pour the soup into warmed individual bowls and sprinkle the croûtons on top. Serve at once.

Curried Lentil Soup

Dhal is a delicious Indian lentil dish. This soup is a variation of the theme — it is made with red lentils and spiced with curry powder.

NUTRITIONAL INFORMATION

Calories . . . . . . .284 Sugars 13g
Protein . . . . .16g Fat 9g
Carbohydrate . . .38g Saturates 5g

  5 mins   35 mins

SERVES 4

I N G R E D I E N T S

25 g/1 oz butter

2 garlic cloves, crushed

1 onion, chopped

½ tsp ground turmeric

1 tsp garam masala

¼ tsp chilli powder

1 tsp ground cumin

1 kg/2 lb 4 oz canned chopped tomatoes, drained

175 g/6 oz red lentils

2 tsp lemon juice

600 ml/1 pint vegetable stock

300 ml/½ pint coconut milk

salt and pepper

chopped fresh coriander and lemon slices, to garnish

naan bread, to serve

1 Melt the butter in a large saucepan and sauté the crushed garlic and onion for 2–3 minutes, stirring. Add the turmeric, garam masala, chilli powder and ground cumin and cook for a further 30 seconds.

2 Stir in the tomatoes, red lentils, lemon juice, vegetable stock and coconut milk and bring to the boil.

3 Reduce the heat and simmer for 25–30 minutes until the lentils are tender and cooked.

4 Season to taste and spoon the soup into a warm tureen. Garnish with the chopped coriander and lemon slices and serve with warm naan bread.

COOK'S TIP
You can buy cans of coconut milk from supermarkets and delicatessens. It can also be made by grating creamed coconut, which comes in the form of a solid bar, and mixing it with water.

Tomato & Rice Soup

This warming, comforting soup is easy to make from store cupboard ingredients. The rice adds a satisfying bite to the blended soup.

NUTRITIONAL INFORMATION

Calories ....253 Sugars 14g
Protein ....5g Fat 14g
Carbohydrate ...30g Saturates 3g

  10 mins   1hr 10 mins

SERVES 4

INGREDIENTS

1 tbsp olive oil

1 large onion, finely chopped

2 garlic cloves, finely chopped or crushed

2 carrots, grated

1 celery stick, thinly sliced

800 g/1 lb 12 oz canned plum tomatoes

1 tsp dark brown sugar, or to taste

850 ml/1½ pints vegetable stock or water

1 bay leaf

175 g/6 oz cooked white rice

2 tbsp chopped fresh dill

salt and pepper

75 ml/ 2½ fl oz double cream,
  plus extra to serve

fresh dill sprigs, to garnish

1 Heat the olive oil in a large saucepan over a medium heat. Add the onion, cover and cook for about 3–4 minutes, stirring occasionally, until the onion is just softened.

2 Add the garlic, carrots, celery, the tomatoes and their juice, brown sugar, stock and the bay leaf to the saucepan. Reduce the heat, cover and simmer the soup for 1 hour, stirring occasionally. Discard the bay leaf.

3 Allow the soup to cool slightly, then transfer it to a blender or food processor and purée until smooth, working in batches if necessary. (If using a food processor, strain off the cooking liquid and reserve. Purée the soup solids with enough cooking liquid to moisten them, then combine with the remaining liquid.)

4 Return the soup to the saucepan and stir in the rice and dill. Season with salt, if needed, and pepper. Cook gently over a low-medium heat for about 5 minutes, or until hot.

5 Stir in the cream. Taste the soup and adjust the seasoning, if necessary. Ladle into warm soup bowls and garnish each serving with a swirl of cream and dill sprigs. Serve at once.

Corn Soup with Chillies

A dried ancho chilli adds a kick to this glowing Mexican corn soup.
The sweetcorn is browned in butter, giving the soup a roasted flavour.

NUTRITIONAL INFORMATION

Calories	824	Sugars	........12g
Protein	.........9g	Fat	..........74g
Carbohydrate	...33g	Saturates	......45g

15 mins
plus 15 mins
standing

1 hr

SERVES 4

I N G R E D I E N T S

1 dried ancho chilli

4 tbsp butter

500 g/1 lb 2 oz frozen sweetcorn, defrosted

1 large onion, finely chopped

1 large garlic clove, finely chopped

1 red pepper, cored, deseeded and
    finely chopped

300 ml/½ pint vegetable stock or water

600 ml/1 pint whipping cream

½ tsp ground cumin

salt

chopped fresh coriander or parsley,
    to garnish

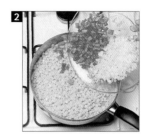

1 Put the chilli in a bowl and cover with boiling water. Stand for about 15 minutes to soften.

2 Melt the butter in a frying pan over a low-medium heat. Add the sweetcorn and turn to coat thoroughly. Cook for about 15 minutes, stirring frequently, until the corn starts to brown slightly. Add the onion, garlic and pepper and cook for about 7–10 minutes, stirring frequently, until the onion is softened and the mixture starts to stick.

3 Transfer the mixture to a blender or food processor, add the stock and purée until smooth.

4 Put the cream in a large saucepan, stir in the puréed vegetables and bring the mixture almost to the boil. Add the cumin. Season with a little salt. Adjust the heat so the soup bubbles very gently and cook until the mixture is reduced by about one-quarter.

5 Remove the ancho chilli from its liquid and discard the core and the seeds. (Wash hands well after touching chillies.) Put the chilli into a blender or food processor with 4–5 tablespoons of the soaking water and purée until smooth. Stir 2–4 tablespoons of the purée into the soup, according to taste, and continue cooking for a further 5 minutes.

6 Taste the soup and adjust the seasoning, if necessary. Ladle the soup into warm bowls, garnish with coriander or parsley and serve.

Indian Bean Soup

This thick and hearty soup is nourishing and substantial enough to serve as a main meal with wholemeal bread.

NUTRITIONAL INFORMATION

Calories	237	Sugars	........9g
Protein	.........9g	Fat	..........9g
Carbohydrate	...33g	Saturates	.......1g

 20 mins   50 mins

SERVES 6

INGREDIENTS

4 tbsp ghee or vegetable oil

2 onions, peeled and chopped

225 g/8 oz potatoes, cut into chunks

225 g/8 oz parsnip, cut into chunks

225 g/8 oz turnip or swede, cut into chunks

2 celery sticks, sliced

2 courgettes, sliced

1 green pepper, deseeded and cut into
    1-cm/½-inch pieces

2 garlic cloves, crushed

2 tsp ground coriander

1 tbsp paprika

1 tbsp mild curry paste

1.2 litres/2 pints vegetable stock

salt

400 g/14 oz canned black-eyed beans,
    drained and rinsed

chopped fresh coriander, to garnish
    (optional)

1 Heat the ghee or oil in a saucepan, add all the prepared vegetables, except the courgettes and green pepper, and cook over a moderate heat, stirring frequently, for 5 minutes. Add the garlic, ground coriander, paprika and curry paste and cook, stirring constantly, for 1 minute.

2 Stir in the stock and season with salt to taste. Bring to the boil, cover and simmer over a low heat, stirring occasionally, for 25 minutes.

3 Stir in the black-eyed beans, sliced courgettes and green pepper, then replace the lid and continue cooking for a further 15 minutes, or until all the vegetables are tender.

4 Process 300 ml/½ pint of the soup mixture (about 2 ladlefuls) in a food processor or blender. Return the puréed mixture to the soup in the saucepan and reheat until piping hot. Sprinkle with chopped coriander if using, and serve hot.

Baked Leek & Cabbage Soup

This unusual baked soup is perfect for lunch on a crisp, cold winter's day – pop it in the oven and enjoy a brisk walk while it is cooking.

NUTRITIONAL INFORMATION

Calories	420	Sugars	.........8g
Protein	........24g	Fat	..........25g
Carbohydrate	...27g	Saturates	......15g

 15 mins   1 hr 20 mins

SERVES 4

INGREDIENTS

2 tbsp butter

2 large leeks, halved lengthways and
  thinly sliced

1 large onion, halved and thinly sliced

3 garlic cloves, finely chopped

250 g/9 oz green cabbage, finely shredded

1 litre/1¾ pints vegetable stock

salt and pepper

4 slices firm bread, cut in half,
  or 8 slices French bread

250 g/9 oz Gruyère cheese, grated

1 Melt the butter in a large saucepan over a medium heat. Add the leeks and onion and cook for 4–5 minutes, stirring frequently, until just softened.

2 Add the garlic and cabbage, stir to combine and continue cooking for about 5 minutes until the cabbage has just wilted.

3 Stir in the stock and simmer the soup for 10 minutes. Taste and season with salt and pepper.

4 Arrange the bread in the base of a large deep 3-litre/5¼-pint ovenproof dish. Sprinkle about half the cheese over the bread.

5 Ladle over the soup and top with the remaining cheese. Bake in a preheated oven at 180°C/350°F/Gas Mark 4 for 1 hour. Serve at once.

COOK'S TIP
A large soufflé dish or earthenware casserole at least 10 cm/4 inches deep, or an enamelled cast-iron casserole, is good for baking the soup. If necessary, put a baking sheet with a rim underneath to catch any overflow.

Curried Courgette Soup

This soup can be frozen, so it is a good way to use up a glut of courgettes from the garden. Adding curry powder gives the flavour a lift.

NUTRITIONAL INFORMATION

Calories ....147 Sugars 8g
Protein ....6g Fat 9g
Carbohydrate ...10g Saturates 5g

 10 mins   30 mins

SERVES 4

INGREDIENTS

2 tsp butter

1 large onion, finely chopped

900 g/2 lb courgettes, sliced

450 ml/16 fl oz vegetable stock

1 tsp curry powder

salt and pepper

125 ml/4 fl oz soured cream

soured cream and croutons (see page 32),
  to garnish

1 Melt the butter in a saucepan over a medium heat. Add the onion and cook for 3 minutes until it begins to soften.

2 Add the courgettes, stock and curry powder, plus salt if using unsalted stock. Bring the soup to the boil, reduce the heat, cover and cook for about 25 minutes until the vegetables are tender.

3 Allow the soup to cool slightly, then transfer it to a blender or food processor, working in batches if necessary. Purée the soup until just smooth, but still with green flecks. (If using a food processor, strain off the cooking liquid and reserve. Purée the soup solids with enough cooking liquid to moisten them, then combine with the remaining liquid.)

4 Return the soup to the saucepan and stir in the soured cream. Reheat gently over a low heat just until hot, but be careful not to allow the soup to boil.

5 Taste and adjust the seasoning, if needed. Ladle the soup into warm bowls and serve, garnished with a swirl of soured cream and croûtons.

COOK'S TIP

Stock made from a cube or liquid stock base is fine for this soup. In this case, you may wish to add a little more soured cream. The soup freezes well, but freeze it without the cream and add before serving.

Roasted Pumpkin & Tomato Soup

This soup is a wonderful way to use autumn harvest vegetables. Make it when tomatoes are still plentiful and pumpkins are in the markets.

NUTRITIONAL INFORMATION

Calories	180	Sugars	........11g
Protein	.........4g	Fat	..........12g
Carbohydrate	...13g	Saturates	.......5g

15 mins   1 hr 5 mins

SERVES 4

INGREDIENTS

2 tbsp olive oil

900 g/2 lb peeled pumpkin flesh, cut into slices 2 cm/¾ inch thick

450 g/1 lb ripe tomatoes, skinned, cored and thickly sliced

1 onion, chopped

2 garlic cloves, finely chopped

4 tbsp white wine

2 tbsp water

salt and pepper

600 ml/1 pint vegetable stock

120 ml/4 fl oz single cream

snipped fresh chives, to garnish

1 Drizzle 1 tablespoon of the olive oil over the base of a large baking dish. Layer the pumpkin, tomatoes, onion and garlic in 2 or 3 layers. Drizzle the top with the remaining olive oil, pour over the wine and water. Season the mixture with a little salt and pepper.

2 Cover the vegetables with kitchen foil and bake in a preheated oven at 190°C/375°F/Gas Mark 5 for about 45 minutes, or until all the vegetables are tender.

3 Allow the vegetables to cool slightly, then transfer to a blender or food processor and add the cooking juices and as much stock as needed to cover the vegetables. Purée the mixture until it is smooth, working in small batches if necessary.

4 Pour the purée into a saucepan and stir in the remaining stock. Cook gently over a medium heat, stirring occasionally, for about 15 minutes, or until heated through. Stir in the cream and continue cooking for 3–4 minutes.

5 Taste and adjust the seasoning, if necessary. Ladle the soup into warm bowls, garnish with chives and serve.

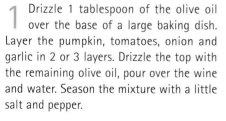

Leek, Potato & Carrot Soup

A quick chunky soup, ideal for a snack or a quick lunch. Save some of the soup and purée it to make a portion of creamed soup for the next day.

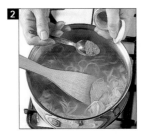

NUTRITIONAL INFORMATION

Calories	156	Sugars	.........7g
Protein	.........4g	Fat	...........6g
Carbohydrate	...22g	Saturates	.....0.7g

10 mins   25 mins

SERVES 2

I N G R E D I E N T S

1 leek, about 175 g/6 oz

1 tbsp sunflower oil

1 garlic clove, crushed

700 ml/1¼ pints vegetable stock

1 bay leaf

¼ tsp ground cumin

salt and pepper

175 g/6 oz potatoes, diced

125 g/4½ oz coarsely grated carrot

chopped fresh parsley, to garnish

P U R E E D   S O U P

5–6 tbsp milk

1–2 tbsp double cream, crème fraîche or soured cream

1 Trim off and discard some of the coarse green part of the leek, then slice thinly and rinse thoroughly in cold water. Drain well.

2 Heat the sunflower oil in a heavy-based saucepan. Add the leek and garlic, and fry over a low heat for about 2–3 minutes, until soft, but barely coloured. Add the vegetable stock, bay leaf and cumin and season to taste with salt and pepper. Bring the mixture to the boil, stirring constantly.

3 Add the diced potato to the saucepan, cover and simmer over a low heat for 10–15 minutes. Keep a careful eye on the soup during the cooking time to make sure the potato cooks until it is just tender, but not broken up.

4 Add the grated carrot to the pan and simmer the soup for a further 2–3 minutes. Adjust the seasoning if necessary, discard the bay leaf and serve the soup in warmed bowls, sprinkled liberally with the chopped parsley.

5 To make a puréed soup, first process the leftovers (about half the original soup) in a blender or food processor, or press through a sieve with the back of a wooden spoon until smooth, and then return to a clean saucepan with the milk. Bring to the boil and simmer for 2–3 minutes.

6 Adjust the seasoning and stir in the cream or crème fraîche before serving the soup in warmed bowls, sprinkled with chopped parsley.

Green Vegetable Soup

This soup takes advantage of summer vegetables bursting with flavour. If you find fresh flageolets or other fresh beans, be sure to include them.

NUTRITIONAL INFORMATION

Calories	...... .260	Sugars	.... .7g
Protein	........12g	Fat	.... .15g
Carbohydrate	...21g	Saturates	.... .4g

15 mins · 45 mins

SERVES 6

INGREDIENTS

1 tbsp olive oil

1 onion, finely chopped

1 large leek, split and thinly sliced

1 celery stick, thinly sliced

1 carrot, quartered and thinly sliced

1 garlic clove, finely chopped

1.4 litres/2½ pints water

1 potato, diced

1 parsnip, finely diced

1 small kohlrabi or turnip, diced

150 g/5½ oz green beans, cut in
  small pieces

150 g/5½ oz fresh or frozen peas

2 small courgettes, quartered lengthways
  and sliced

400 g/14 oz can flageolet beans, drained
  and rinsed

100 g/3½ oz spinach leaves, cut into
  thin ribbons

salt and pepper

PESTO

1 large garlic clove, very finely chopped

15 g/½ oz basil leaves

85 g/3 oz Parmesan cheese, grated

4 tbsp extra virgin olive oil

1 Heat the oil in a large pan. Cook the onion and leek over a low heat, stirring occasionally, for 5 minutes. Add the celery, carrot and garlic, cover and cook for a further 5 minutes.

2 Add the water, potato, parsnip, kohlrabi or turnip and green beans. Bring to the boil, reduce the heat, cover and simmer for 5 minutes.

3 Add the peas, courgettes and flageolet beans and season to taste.

Cover and simmer for about 25 minutes until all the vegetables are tender.

4 Meanwhile, make the pesto. Put all the ingredients in a food processor and process until smooth, scraping down the sides as necessary. Alternatively, pound together using a pestle and mortar.

5 Add the spinach to the soup and simmer for 5 minutes. Stir a spoon of the pesto into the soup. Ladle into bowls and pass the remaining pesto separately.

Vegetable Chilli

This is a hearty and flavourful soup that is good on its own or spooned over cooked rice or baked potatoes for a more substantial meal.

NUTRITIONAL INFORMATION

Calories	.213	Sugars	.11g
Protein	.12g	Fat	.10g
Carbohydrate	.21g	Saturates	.5g

 10 mins   1¼ hrs

SERVES 5–6

INGREDIENTS

1 aubergine, peeled if wished,
  cut into 2.5 cm/1 inch slices

1 tbsp olive oil, plus extra for brushing

1 large red or yellow onion, finely chopped

2 red or yellow peppers, deseeded and
  finely chopped

3–4 garlic cloves, finely chopped or crushed

800 g/1lb 12 oz canned chopped tomatoes

1 tbsp mild chilli powder

½ tsp ground cumin

½ tsp dried oregano

salt and pepper

2 small courgettes, quartered lengthways
  and sliced

400 g/14 oz canned kidney beans, drained
  and rinsed

450 ml/16 fl oz water

1 tbsp tomato purée

6 spring onions, finely chopped

115 g/4 oz Cheddar cheese, grated

1 Brush the aubergine slices on one side with olive oil. Heat half the oil in a large, heavy-based frying pan over a medium-high heat. Add the aubergine slices, oiled side up, and cook for 5–6 minutes until browned on one side. Turn the slices over, cook on the other side until browned and transfer to a plate. Cut into bite-size pieces.

2 Heat the remaining oil in a large saucepan over a medium heat. Add the onion and peppers and cook, stirring occasionally, for 3–4 minutes until the onion is just softened, but not browned. Add the garlic and continue cooking for 2–3 minutes or until the onion is just beginning to colour.

3 Add the tomatoes, chilli powder, cumin and oregano. Season to taste with salt and pepper. Bring just to the boil, reduce the heat, cover and simmer gently for 15 minutes.

4 Add the sliced courgettes, aubergine pieces and kidney beans. Stir in the water and the tomato purée. Bring back to the boil, then cover the pan and continue simmering for about 45 minutes or until the vegetables are tender. Taste and then adjust the seasoning if necessary. If you prefer a hotter dish, stir in a little more chilli powder.

5 Ladle into warmed bowls and top with the spring onions and cheese.

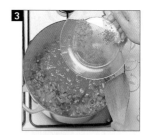

Gazpacho

This Spanish soup is full of chopped and grated vegetables with a puréed tomato base. It requires chilling, so prepare well in advance.

NUTRITIONAL INFORMATION

Calories . . . . . . .140 Sugars 12g

Protein . . . . .3g Fat 9g

Carbohydrate . . .13g Saturates 1g

30 mins, plus chilling 0 mins

SERVES 4

INGREDIENTS

½ small cucumber

½ small green pepper, deseeded and very finely chopped

500 g/1 lb 2 oz ripe tomatoes, peeled, or 400 g/14 oz canned chopped tomatoes

½ onion, roughly chopped

2–3 garlic cloves, crushed

3 tbsp olive oil

2 tbsp white wine vinegar

1–2 tbsp lemon or lime juice

2 tbsp tomato purée

450 ml/16 fl oz tomato juice

salt and pepper

TO SERVE

chopped green pepper

thinly sliced onion rings

croûtons (see page 92)

1 Coarsely grate the cucumber into a large bowl and add the chopped green pepper.

2 Put the tomatoes, onion and garlic in a food processor or blender, add the oil, vinegar, lemon or lime juice and tomato purée, and process until a smooth purée is formed. Alternatively, finely chop the tomatoes and finely grate the onion, then mix together and add the crushed garlic, oil, vinegar, lemon or lime juice and tomato purée.

3 Add the tomato mixture to the bowl and mix well, then add the tomato juice and mix again.

4 Season to taste, cover the bowl with clingfilm and chill for at least 6 hours and preferably longer so that the flavours have time to meld together.

5 Prepare the side dishes of chopped green pepper, thinly sliced onion rings and garlic croûtons, and arrange them in individual serving bowls.

6 Ladle the soup into cold bowls, preferably from a soup tureen set on the table with the side dishes of pepper, onion rings and croûtons placed around it. Hand the dishes around to allow the guests to help themselves.

Barley & Rice Soup

This hearty winter soup makes a warming lunch or supper when served with a crusty loaf of ciabatta.

NUTRITIONAL INFORMATION

Calories . . . . . . .260 Sugars 8g
Protein . . . . .9g Fat 6g
Carbohydrate . . .46g Saturates 1g

 15 mins 1½ hrs

SERVES 4–6

I N G R E D I E N T S

100 g/3½ oz pearl barley

100 g/3½ oz long grain brown rice

450 g/1 lb Swiss chard, trimmed and soaked for 10 minutes

2 tbsp olive oil

1 large onion, finely chopped

2 carrots, finely chopped

2 celery sticks, finely chopped

2 garlic cloves, finely chopped

800 g/1lb 12 oz canned chopped Italian plum tomatoes

1 bay leaf

1 tsp dried thyme

1 tsp herbes de Provence or dried oregano

1 litre/1¾ pints vegetable stock

450 g/1 lb canned cannellini beans, drained

2 tbsp chopped fresh parsley

salt and pepper

freshly grated Parmesan cheese, to serve

1 Bring a large pan of water to the boil. Add the barley and the brown rice and return to the boil. Reduce the heat and simmer gently for 30–35 minutes until just tender. Drain and set aside.

2 Drain the Swiss chard. Cut out the hard white stems. Slice the stems crossways into very thin strips and set aside. Roll the leaves into a long cigar shape, shred thinly and set aside.

3 Heat the oil in a large, heavy-based pan. Add the onion, carrots and celery and cook, stirring frequently, for about 5 minutes until soft and beginning to colour. Add the garlic and cook for a minute longer. Add the tomatoes with their juice, the bay leaf, thyme and herbes de Provence. Reduce the heat, partially cover and simmer for about 7 minutes until all the vegetables are soft.

4 Stir in the sliced white chard stems and the stock. Simmer gently for about 20 minutes. Add the shredded green chard and simmer for a further 15 minutes.

5 Stir in the beans and parsley with the cooked barley and brown rice. Season with salt and pepper. Bring back to the boil and simmer for a further 8–10 minutes. Remove the bay leaf and serve with Parmesan.

Vermicelli & Vegetable Soup

This wonderful combination of beans, vegetables and vermicelli is made even richer by the addition of pesto and dried mushrooms.

NUTRITIONAL INFORMATION

Calories	225	Sugars	.........6g
Protein	........11g	Fat	..........5g
Carbohydrate	...36g	Saturates	.......1g

 15 mins   20 mins

SERVES 4

INGREDIENTS

1 small aubergine

2 large tomatoes

1 potato, peeled

1 carrot, peeled

1 leek

400 g/14 oz canned cannelini beans

850 ml/1½ pints hot vegetable stock

2 tsp dried basil

10 g/¼ oz dried porcini mushrooms, soaked for 10 minutes in enough warm water to cover

50 g/1¾ oz dried vermicelli

3 tbsp pesto

freshly grated Parmesan cheese, to serve (optional)

 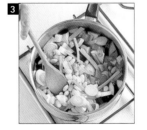 

1 Slice the aubergine into rings about 1 cm/½ inch thick, then cut each ring into 4 pieces.

2 Cut the tomatoes and potato into small dice. Cut the carrot into sticks about 2.5 cm/1 inch long and cut the leek into rings.

3 Place the cannelini beans and their liquid in a large saucepan. Add the aubergine, tomatoes, potatoes, carrot and leek, stirring to mix.

4 Add the stock to the pan and bring to the boil. Reduce the heat and leave to simmer for 15 minutes.

5 Add the basil, dried mushrooms, their soaking liquid and the vermicelli and simmer for 5 minutes, or until all of the vegetables are tender.

6 Remove the pan from the heat and add the pesto. Serve with Parmesan cheese sprinkled on top, if using.

Fresh Tomato Soup

This soup, made with fresh tomatoes, tastes of summer, although it can be made at any time of year as long as the tomatoes are ripe.

NUTRITIONAL INFORMATION

Calories 254	Sugars 13g	
Protein 3g	Fat 21g	
Carbohydrate ...14g	Saturates 10g	

 15 mins   55 mins

SERVES 4

INGREDIENTS

1 kg/2 lb 4 oz ripe plum tomatoes, skinned

2 tsp olive oil

1 large sweet onion, such as Vidalia, finely chopped

1 carrot, finely chopped

1 celery stick, finely chopped

2 garlic cloves, finely chopped or crushed

1 tsp fresh marjoram leaves, or ¼ tsp dried marjoram

450 ml/16 fl oz water

4–5 tbsp double cream, plus extra to garnish

2 tbsp chopped fresh basil leaves

salt and pepper

1 Cut the tomatoes in half and scrape the seeds into a sieve set over a bowl to catch the juice. Reserve the juice and discard the seeds. Chop the tomato flesh into large chunks.

2 Heat the olive oil in a large saucepan. Add the onion, carrot and celery and cook over a low-medium heat for 3–4 minutes, stirring occasionally.

3 Add the tomatoes and their juice, with the garlic and marjoram. Cook for 2 minutes. Stir in the water, reduce the heat and simmer, covered, for about 45 minutes until the vegetables are very soft, stirring occasionally.

4 Allow the soup to cool slightly, then transfer to a blender or food processor and purée until smooth, working in batches if necessary. (If using a food processor, strain off the cooking liquid and reserve. Purée the soup solids with enough cooking liquid to moisten them, then combine with the remaining liquid.)

5 Return the soup to the saucepan and place over a low-medium heat. Add the cream and stir in the basil. Season with salt and pepper and heat through; do not allow to boil.

6 Ladle the soup into warm bowls and swirl a little extra cream into each serving. Serve at once.

COOK'S TIP
For the best flavour, this soup needs to be made with ripe tomatoes. If supermarket tomatoes are pale and hard, leave them to ripen at room temperature for several days.

Cheesy Vegetable Chowder

This hearty soup is wonderful made in the middle of winter with fresh seasonal vegetables. Use a really well-flavoured mature Cheddar cheese.

NUTRITIONAL INFORMATION

Calories	669	Sugars	........13g
Protein	........26g	Fat	..........49g
Carbohydrate	...33g	Saturates	......30g

15 mins   45 mins

SERVES 4

INGREDIENTS

25 g/1 oz butter

1 large onion, finely chopped

1 large leek, split lengthways and thinly sliced

1–2 garlic cloves, crushed

55 g/2 oz plain flour

1.2 litres/2 pints vegetable stock

3 carrots, finely diced

2 celery sticks, finely diced

1 turnip, finely diced

1 large potato, finely diced

3–4 sprigs fresh thyme or ⅛ tsp dried thyme

1 bay leaf

350 ml/12 fl oz single cream

300 g/10½ oz mature Cheddar cheese, grated

salt and pepper

chopped fresh parsley, to garnish

1 Melt the butter in a large heavy-based saucepan over a low-medium heat. Add the onion, leek and garlic. Cover and cook for about 5 minutes, stirring frequently, until the vegetables are starting to soften.

2 Stir the flour into the vegetables and continue cooking for 2 minutes. Add a little of the stock and stir well, scraping the bottom of the pan to mix in the flour. Bring to the boil, stirring frequently, and slowly stir in the rest of the stock.

3 Add the carrots, celery, turnip, potato, thyme and bay leaf. Reduce the heat, cover the pan and cook the soup gently for about 35 minutes, stirring occasionally, until the vegetables are tender. Remove the bay leaf and the thyme sprigs.

4 Stir in the cream and simmer over a very low heat for 5 minutes.

5 Add the cheese a handful at a time, stirring constantly for 1 minute after each addition to make sure it is completely melted. Do not boil. Taste the soup and adjust the seasoning, adding salt if needed, and pepper to taste.

6 Ladle the soup immediately into warm bowls, sprinkle with chopped fresh parsley and serve.

Watermelon & Tomato Soup

Although this chilled soup is not an authentic Indian dish, it is wonderful served as a 'cooler' between hot, spicy courses.

NUTRITIONAL INFORMATION

Calories	73	Sugar	........16g
Protein	.........2g	Fats	..........1g
Carbohydrates	...16g	Saturates	.....0.2g

20 mins, plus chilling | 0 mins

SERVES 6

INGREDIENTS

4 tomatoes, peeled and deseeded

1.5 kg/3 lb 5 oz watermelon, seedless if available

10 cm/4 inch piece cucumber, peeled and deseeded

2 spring onions, green part only, chopped

1 tbsp chopped fresh mint

salt and pepper

fresh mint sprigs, to garnish

1 Using a sharp knife, cut 1 tomato into 1 cm/½ inch dice.

2 Remove the rind from the melon, and remove the seeds if it is not seedless.

3 Put the 3 remaining tomatoes into a blender or food processor and, with the motor running, add the deseeded cucumber, chopped spring onions and watermelon. Blend until smooth.

4 If not using a food processor, push the deseeded watermelon through a sieve. Stir the diced tomatoes and mint into the melon mixture. Adjust the seasoning to taste. Chop the cucumber, spring onions and the 3 remaining tomatoes finely and add to the melon.

5 Chill the watermelon and tomato soup overnight in the refrigerator. Check the seasoning and transfer to a serving dish. Garnish with mint sprigs.

COOK'S TIP

Although this soup does improve if chilled overnight, it is also delicious as a quick appetizer if whipped up just before a meal, and served immediately.

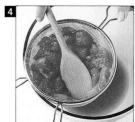

Melon & Ginger Soup

The zingy hot taste of fresh ginger blends perfectly with cool melon in this delicious and intriguing soup.

NUTRITIONAL INFORMATION

Calories . . . . . . .176 Sugars 16g
Protein . . . . .2g Fat 12g
Carbohydrate . . .16g Saturates 7g

 10 mins   0 mins

SERVES 4

I N G R E D I E N T S

1 large ripe melon (about 1 kg/2 lb 4 oz)

¾ tsp grated peeled fresh ginger root, or to taste

1 tbsp fresh lemon juice, or to taste

1 tsp caster sugar

salt

125 ml/4 fl oz whipping cream

snipped fresh chives, to garnish

1 Halve the melon, discard the seeds and scoop the flesh into a blender or food processor. Purée until smooth, stopping to scrape down the sides as necessary to ensure no lumps of melon remain (you may need to work in batches).

2 Add the grated ginger, lemon juice and sugar with a pinch of salt and process to combine. Taste and add a little more ginger, if liked. Scrape into a bowl, cover and chill completely, usually for about 30 minutes, or until cold.

3 Add the cream and stir to combine well. Taste and adjust the seasoning, adding a little extra salt and lemon juice if necessary.

4 To serve, divide the melon purée among 4 chilled bowls and garnish with chives.

COOK'S TIP
To determine the ripeness of melon, gently press the end opposite the stem – it should 'give' a little, and there is usually a characteristic aroma on pressing that helps to confirm the verdict.

Iced Salsa Soup

A chunky mix of colourful vegetables, highlighted with Mexican flavours, this cold soup makes a lively starter to any meal.

NUTRITIONAL INFORMATION

Calories	138	Sugars	........12g
Protein	.........5g	Fat	...........4g
Carbohydrate	...22g	Saturates	.......1g

🍲 10 mins, plus chilling   🕐 12–15 mins

SERVES 4

INGREDIENTS

2 large corn cobs or 225 g/8 oz frozen sweetcorn

1 tbsp olive oil

1 orange or red pepper, deseeded and finely chopped

1 green pepper, deseeded and finely chopped

1 sweet onion, such as Vidalia, finely chopped

3 ripe tomatoes, peeled, deseeded and chopped

½ tsp chilli powder

125 ml/4 fl oz water

450 ml/16 fl oz tomato juice

salt and pepper

chilli purée (optional)

TO GARNISH

3–4 spring onions, finely chopped

fresh coriander leaves, chopped

1 Cut the corn kernels away from the cobs, or thaw and drain frozen sweetcorn, if using.

2 Heat the oil in a pan over a medium-high heat. Add the peppers and cook, stirring briskly, for 3 minutes. Add the onion and continue cooking for about 2 minutes or until it starts to colour slightly.

3 Add the tomatoes, corn and chilli powder. Continue cooking, stirring frequently, for 1 minute. Pour in the water and when it begins to boil, reduce the heat, cover and cook for a further 4–5 minutes or until the peppers are just barely tender.

4 Transfer the mixture to a large container and stir in the tomato juice. Season with salt and pepper to taste and add a little more chilli powder if wished. Cover with clingfilm and chill in the refrigerator until cold.

5 Taste, and adjust the seasoning if necessary. For a spicier soup, stir in a little chilli purée to taste. For a thinner soup, add a small amount of iced water. Ladle the soup into chilled bowls and serve garnished with spring onions and fresh coriander leaves.

Avocado & Mint Soup

A rich and creamy pale green soup made with avocados and enhanced by a touch of chopped mint. Serve chilled in summer or hot in winter.

NUTRITIONAL INFORMATION

Calories 199	Sugars 3g	
Protein 3g	Fat 18g	
Carbohydrate 7g	Saturates 6g	

 15 mins, plus chilling   35 mins

SERVES 6

I N G R E D I E N T S

40 g/1½ oz butter or margarine

6 spring onions, sliced

1 garlic clove, crushed

25 g/1 oz plain flour

600 ml/1 pint vegetable stock

2 avocados

2–3 tsp lemon juice

pinch of grated lemon rind

salt and pepper

150 ml/¼ pint milk

150 ml/¼ pint single cream

1–1½ tbsp chopped fresh mint

fresh mint sprigs, to garnish

MINTED GARLIC BREAD

125 g/4½ oz butter

1–2 tbsp chopped fresh mint

1–2 garlic cloves, crushed

1 wholemeal or white French bread stick

1 Melt the butter or margarine in a large, heavy-based saucepan. Add the spring onions and garlic clove to the pan and fry over a low heat, stirring occasionally, for about 3 minutes, until soft and translucent.

2 Stir in the flour and cook, stirring, for 1–2 minutes. Gradually stir in the stock, then bring to the boil. Simmer gently while preparing the avocados.

3 Peel the avocados, discard the stones and chop coarsely. Add to the soup with the lemon juice and rind and seasoning. Cover and simmer for about 10 minutes, until tender.

4 Cool the soup slightly, then press through a sieve with the back of a spoon or process in a food processor or blender until a smooth purée forms. Pour into a bowl.

5 Stir in the milk and cream, adjust the seasoning, then stir in the mint. Cover and chill thoroughly.

6 To make the minted garlic bread, soften the butter and beat in the mint and garlic. Cut the loaf into slanting slices but leave a hinge on the bottom crust. Spread each slice with the butter and reassemble the loaf. Wrap in foil and place in a preheated oven, 180°C/350°F/Gas Mark 4, for about 15 minutes.

7 Serve the soup garnished with a sprig of mint and accompanied by the minted garlic bread.

Watercress Vichyssoise

Vichyssoise is simply cold leek and potato soup flavoured with chives. The addition of watercress gives it a cool, refreshing flavour and lovely colour.

NUTRITIONAL INFORMATION

Calories	42	Sugars	.......0.8g
Protein	........2.1g	Fat	..........2.2g
Carbohydrate	...3.6g	Saturates	.......1g

15 mins, plus chillling   35 mins

SERVES 6

INGREDIENTS

1 tbsp olive oil

3 large leeks, thinly sliced

350 g/12 oz potatoes, finely diced

600 ml/1 pint vegetable stock

450 ml/16 fl oz water

1 bay leaf

175 g/6 oz watercress, washed and dried

175 ml/6 fl oz single cream

salt and pepper

watercress leaves, to garnish

1 Heat the oil in a heavy-based saucepan over a medium heat. Add the sliced leeks and cook for about 3 minutes, stirring frequently, until they begin to soften.

2 Add the potatoes, stock, water and bay leaf. Add salt if the stock is unsalted. Bring to the boil, then reduce the heat, cover the saucepan and cook gently for about 25 minutes, until the vegetables are tender. Remove the bay leaf and discard it.

3 Add the watercress and continue to cook for a further 2–3 minutes, stirring frequently, until the watercress is completely wilted.

4 Allow the soup to cool slightly, then transfer to a blender or food processor and purée until smooth, working in batches if necessary. (If using a food processor, strain off the cooking liquid and reserve. Purée the soup solids with enough cooking liquid to moisten them, then combine with the remaining liquid.)

5 Put the soup into a large bowl and then stir in half the cream. Season with salt, if needed, and plenty of pepper. Leave to cool to room temperature.

6 Refrigerate until cold. Taste and adjust the seasoning, if necessary.

7 Ladle into chilled bowls, drizzle the remaining cream on top and garnish with watercress leaves. Serve at once.

Wonton Soup

The recipe for the wonton skins makes 24 but the soup requires only half this quantity. The other half can be frozen ready for another time.

NUTRITIONAL INFORMATION

Calories ....278 Sugars 2g
Protein ....10g Fat 5g
Carbohydrate ...50g Saturates 1g

 45 mins   5 mins

SERVES 4

INGREDIENTS

WONTON SKINS

1 egg

6 tbsp water

250 g/9 oz plain flour, plus extra for dusting

FILLING

125 g/4½ oz frozen chopped spinach, defrosted

15 g/½ oz pine kernels, toasted and chopped

25 g/1 oz minced quorn

salt

SOUP

600 ml/1 pint vegetable stock

1 tbsp dry sherry

1 tbsp light soy sauce

2 spring onions, chopped

1 To make the wonton skins, beat the egg lightly in a bowl and mix with the water. Stir in the flour to form a stiff dough. Knead lightly, then cover with a damp cloth and leave to rest for 30 minutes.

2 Roll the dough out into a large sheet about 1.5 mm/ ¼ inch thick. Cut out 24 x 7 cm/3 inch squares and dust each square lightly with flour. Only 12 squares are required for the soup, but the remainder can be frozen to use on another occasion.

3 To make the filling, squeeze out the excess water from the defrosted spinach. Mix the spinach with the pine kernels and quorn until thoroughly combined. Season the mixture with salt.

4 Divide the mixture into 12 equal portions. Using a teaspoon, place one portion in the centre of each square. Seal the wontons by bringing the opposite corners of each square together and squeezing well.

5 To make the soup, bring the vegetable stock, dry sherry and soy sauce to the boil, then add the wontons and boil rapidly for 2–3 minutes. Add the chopped spring onions and serve the soup immediately in warmed bowls, dividing the wontons equally.

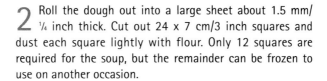

Vichyssoise

This is a classic chilled soup made from potatoes and leeks. To achieve the delicate pale colour, be sure to use only the white parts of the leeks.

NUTRITIONAL INFORMATION

Calories ......208 Sugars 5g
Protein ....5g Fat 12g
Carbohydrate ...20g Saturates 6g

10 mins, plus chilling   40 mins

SERVES 6

I N G R E D I E N T S

3 large leeks

3 tbsp butter or margarine

1 onion, thinly sliced

500 g/1 lb 2 oz potatoes, chopped

850 ml/1½ pints vegetable stock

2 tsp lemon juice

pinch of ground nutmeg

¼ tsp ground coriander

1 bay leaf

salt and pepper

1 egg yolk

150 ml/¼ pint single cream

freshly snipped chives, to garnish

1 Trim the leeks and remove most of the green parts. Slice the white parts of the leeks very finely.

2 Melt the butter or margarine in a saucepan. Add the leeks and onion and fry, stirring occasionally, for about 5 minutes without browning.

3 Add the potatoes, vegetable stock, lemon juice, nutmeg, coriander and bay leaf to the pan, season to taste with salt and pepper and bring to the boil. Cover and simmer for about 30 minutes, until all the vegetables are very soft.

4 Cool the soup a little, remove and discard the bay leaf and then press through a sieve or process in a food processor or blender until smooth. Pour into a clean pan.

5 Blend the egg yolk into the cream, add a little of the soup to the mixture and then whisk it all back into the soup and reheat gently, without boiling. Adjust the seasoning to taste. Leave to cool and then chill thoroughly in the refrigerator.

6 Serve the soup sprinkled with freshly snipped chives.

Iced Gazpacho

This delicious soup, with its brightly coloured garnish of peppers, cucumber and spring onions, is perfect to serve at a summer lunch party.

NUTRITIONAL INFORMATION

Calories	164	Sugars	.........7g
Protein	.........3g	Fat	..........12g
Carbohydrate	...13g	Saturates	.......3g

20 mins, plus chilling

5 mins

SERVES 4–6

INGREDIENTS

2 red peppers

1 cucumber

400 g/14 oz large, juicy tomatoes, skinned, deseeded and roughly chopped

4 tbsp olive oil

2 tbsp sherry vinegar

salt and pepper

GARLIC CROUTONS

2 tbsp olive oil

1 garlic clove, halved

2 slices bread, crusts removed and cut into 5 mm/¼ inch dice

sea salt

TO GARNISH

diced green pepper

diced red pepper

finely diced deseeded cucumber

chopped spring onions

ice cubes

1 Cut the peppers in half and remove the cores and seeds, then coarsely chop. Peel the cucumber, cut it in half lengthways, then cut into quarters. Remove the seeds with a teaspoon, then coarsely chop the flesh.

2 Put the peppers, cucumber, tomatoes, olive oil and sherry vinegar in a food processor or blender and process until smooth. Season with salt and pepper to taste. Transfer to a bowl, cover and chill for at least 4 hours.

3 Meanwhile, make the garlic croûtons. Heat the oil in a frying pan over a medium–high heat. Add the garlic and fry, stirring, for 2 minutes to flavour the oil.

4 Remove the garlic from the oil and discard it. Add the diced bread to the pan and fry until golden on all sides. Drain well on kitchen paper and sprinkle with sea salt. Store the croûtons in an airtight container if not using immediately.

5 To serve, place each of the vegetable garnishes in bowls for guests to add to their soup. Taste the soup and adjust the seasoning if necessary. Put ice cubes into soup bowls and ladle the soup on top. Serve at once.

Onion & Artichoke Soup

This refreshing chilled soup is ideal for al fresco dining. It is very quick to make, but needs several hours in the refrigerator to chill thoroughly.

NUTRITIONAL INFORMATION

Calories 159   Sugars 2g
Protein ....2g   Fat 15g
Carbohydrate ....5g   Saturates 6g

 5 mins, plus chilling   15 mins

SERVES 4

INGREDIENTS

1 tbsp olive oil

1 onion, chopped

1 garlic clove, crushed

800 g/1lb 12oz canned artichoke hearts, drained

600 ml/1 pint hot vegetable stock

150 ml/5 fl oz single cream

2 tbsp fresh thyme, stalks removed

2 sun-dried tomatoes, cut into strips, to garnish

crusty bread, to serve

1 Heat the olive oil in a large saucepan and fry the chopped onion and crushed garlic over a medium heat until just softened.

2 Using a sharp knife, roughly chop the artichoke hearts. Add the artichoke pieces to the onion and garlic mixture in the pan. Add the hot vegetable stock to the pan, stirring constantly.

3 Bring the mixture to the boil, then reduce the heat and leave to simmer, covered, for about 3 minutes.

4 Place the mixture in a food processor or blender and blend until a smooth purée is formed. Alternatively, push the mixture through a sieve with the back of a wooden spoon to purée it.

5 Return the soup to the saucepan. Stir the single cream and fresh thyme into the soup.

6 Transfer the soup to a large bowl, cover and leave to chill in the refrigerator for about 3–4 hours.

7 Transfer the chilled soup to individual soup bowls and garnish with strips of sun-dried tomato. Serve with lots of fresh, crusty bread.

COOK'S TIP

Try adding 2 tablespoons of dry vermouth, such as Martini, to the soup in step 5 if you wish.

Garlic & Almond Soup

This pretty, pale, chilled soup looks beautiful with its unusual garnish of sliced white grapes and a swirl of olive oil.

NUTRITIONAL INFORMATION

Calories	513	Sugars	3g
Protein	15g	Fat	34g
Carbohydrate	40g	Saturates	4g

 30 mins, plus chilling   0 mins

SERVES 4-6

400 g/14 oz day-old French bread, sliced

4 large garlic cloves, peeled

3–4 tbsp sherry vinegar

1 litre/1¾ pints water, chilled

6 tbsp extra virgin olive oil

225 g/8 oz ground almonds

salt and pepper

TO GARNISH

seedless white grapes, chilled and sliced

pepper

extra virgin olive oil

1 Tear the bread into small pieces and put in a bowl. Pour over enough cold water to cover and leave to soak for 10–15 minutes. Using your hands, squeeze the bread dry. Transfer the moist bread to a food processor or blender.

2 Cut the garlic cloves in half lengthways and use the tip of the knife to remove the pale green or white cores. Add to the food processor with 3 tablespoons of sherry vinegar and 225 ml/8 fl oz of water, and process until blended. Add the olive oil and ground almonds and blend.

3 With the motor running, slowly pour in the remaining water until a smooth soup forms. Add extra sherry vinegar to taste and season with salt and pepper. Transfer to a bowl, cover and chill the soup for at least 4 hours.

4 To serve, adjust the seasoning. Ladle into bowls and float grapes on top. Garnish each with a sprinkling of pepper and a swirl of olive oil.

COOK'S TIP

Chilled grapes are the traditional accompaniment for this, but the soup will also look attractive sprinkled lightly with paprika or very finely chopped fresh parsley just before serving.

Cold Coriander Soup

This soup brings together Thai flavours for a cool, refreshing starter.
It highlights fresh coriander, now widely available.

NUTRITIONAL INFORMATION

Calories	79	Sugars	.........5g
Protein	.........3g	Fat	...........3g
Carbohydrate	...13g	Saturates	.......0g

15 mins, plus chilling   30 mins

SERVES 4

INGREDIENTS

2 tsp olive oil

1 large onion, finely chopped

1 leek, thinly sliced

1 garlic clove, thinly sliced

1 litre/1¾ pints water

1 courgette, about 200 g/7 oz, peeled and chopped

4 tbsp long grain white rice

salt and pepper

5 cm/2 inch piece of lemongrass

2 lime leaves

55 g/2 oz fresh coriander leaves and soft stems

chilli purée (optional)

finely chopped red pepper and/or fresh red chillies and coriander leaves, to garnish

1 Heat the oil in a large pan over a medium heat. Add the onion, leek and garlic and cook, stirring occasionally, for 4–5 minutes until the onion is softened, but not browned.

2 Add the water, courgette and rice with a pinch of salt and some pepper. Stir in the lemongrass and lime leaves. Bring just to the boil and reduce the heat to low. Cover and simmer for 15–20 minutes until the rice is soft and tender.

3 Add the fresh coriander leaves and stems, pushing them down into the liquid. Continue cooking over a low heat for 2–3 minutes until the leaves are wilted. Remove and discard the lemongrass and lime leaves.

4 Remove from the heat and set aside to cool slightly, then transfer to a blender or food processor and process to a smooth purée, working in batches if necessary. (If using a food processor, strain off the cooking liquid and reserve. Purée the soup solids with enough cooking liquid to moisten them, then combine with the remaining liquid.)

5 Scrape the soup into a large container. Season to taste with salt and pepper. Cover with clingfilm and chill in the refrigerator until cold.

6 Taste and adjust the seasoning. For a spicier soup, stir in a little chilli purée to taste. For a thinner soup, add a small amount of iced water. Ladle into chilled bowls and garnish with finely chopped red pepper and/or chillies and coriander leaves.

Spiced Fruit Soup

This delicately flavoured apple and apricot soup is gently spiced with ginger and allspice and finished with a swirl of soured cream.

NUTRITIONAL INFORMATION

Calories	147	Sugars	........28g
Protein	.........3g	Fat	..........0.4g
Carbohydrate	...29g	Saturates	.......0g

15 mins, plus chilling   25 mins

SERVES 4–6

INGREDIENTS

125 g/4½ oz dried apricots, soaked overnight, or no-need-to-soak dried apricots

500 g/1 lb 2 oz apples, peeled, cored and chopped

1 small onion, chopped

1 tbsp lemon or lime juice

700 ml/1¼ pints vegetable stock

150 ml/5 fl oz dry white wine

¼ tsp ground ginger

pinch of ground allspice

salt and pepper

TO GARNISH

4–6 tbsp soured cream

ground ginger or ground allspice

1 Drain the apricots, if necessary, and chop coarsely.

2 Put the apricots in a pan and add the apples, onion, lemon or lime juice and stock. Bring to the boil, cover and simmer gently for about 20 minutes.

3 Set the soup aside to cool a little, then press through a sieve or process in a food processor or blender until a smooth purée is formed. Pour the fruit soup into a clean pan.

4 Add the wine and spices and season to taste. Bring back to the boil, then set aside to cool. If it is too thick, add a little more stock or water and then chill in the refrigerator for several hours.

5 Garnish with soured cream and dust lightly with ginger or allspice.

VARIATION

Other fruits can be combined with apples to make fruit soups — try raspberries, blackberries, blackcurrants or cherries. If the fruits have a lot of pips or stones, sieve the soup after puréeing.

Vegetarian Hot & Sour Soup

This popular soup is easy to make and very filling. It can be eaten as a meal on its own or served as an appetizer before a light main course.

NUTRITIONAL INFORMATION

Calories 61	Sugars 1g
Protein 5g	Fat 2g
Carbohydrate 8g	Saturates 0.2g

30 mins

10 mins

SERVES 4

INGREDIENTS

4 Chinese dried mushrooms (if unavailable, use open-cup mushrooms)

125 g/4½ oz firm tofu

60 g/2 oz canned bamboo shoots

600 ml/1 pint vegetable stock or water

60 g/2 oz frozen peas

1 tbsp dark soy sauce

2 tbsp white wine vinegar

2 tbsp cornflour

salt and pepper

sesame oil, to serve

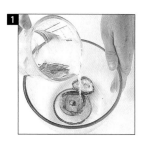

1 Place the Chinese dried mushrooms in a small bowl and cover with warm water. Leave them to soak for about 20–25 minutes.

COOK'S TIP

If you use open-cup mushrooms instead of dried mushrooms, add an extra 150 ml/¼ pint vegetable stock or water to the soup, as these mushrooms do not need soaking.

2 Drain the mushrooms and squeeze out the excess water, reserving this. Remove the tough centres and cut the mushrooms into thin shreds. Shred the tofu and bamboo shoots.

3 Bring the vegetable stock or water to the boil in a large saucepan. Add the mushrooms, tofu, bamboo shoots and peas. Simmer for 2 minutes.

4 Mix together the soy sauce, the white wine vinegar and the cornflour with 2 tablespoons of the liquid reserved from soaking the mushrooms.

5 Stir the soy sauce and cornflour mixture into the soup with the remaining mushroom liquid. Bring the mixture to the boil and season with salt and plenty of pepper. Simmer for a further 2 minutes.

6 Ladle the soup into warmed bowls and serve with a few drops of sesame oil sprinkled over the top of each.

Minestrone with Pesto

This version of minestrone contains cannellini beans – these need to be soaked overnight, so prepare in advance.

NUTRITIONAL INFORMATION

Calories 604	Sugars 3g	
Protein 26g	Fat 45g	
Carbohydrate ...24g	Saturates 11g	

 10–15 mins   1¾ hrs

SERVES 6

I N G R E D I E N T S

175 g/6 oz dried cannellini beans, soaked overnight

2.5 litres/4½ pints water or vegetable stock

1 large onion, chopped

1 leek, trimmed and thinly sliced

2 celery sticks, very thinly sliced

2 carrots, chopped

3 tbsp olive oil

2 tomatoes, peeled and roughly chopped

1 courgette, trimmed and thinly sliced

2 potatoes, diced

90 g/3 oz dried elbow macaroni (or other small macaroni)

salt and pepper

4–6 tbsp freshly grated Parmesan cheese, to serve

P E S T O

2 tbsp pine kernels

5 tbsp olive oil

2 bunches fresh basil, stems removed

4–6 garlic cloves, crushed

90 g/3 oz pecorino or Parmesan cheese, grated

1 Drain the soaked beans, rinse and put in a pan with the water or vegetable stock (avoid using a very salty stock, or the beans will become tough during cooking). Bring to the boil, cover and simmer for 1 hour.

2 Add the onion, leek, celery, carrots and oil. Cover and simmer for 4–5 minutes.

3 Add the tomatoes, courgette, potatoes, macaroni and seasoning. Cover again and continue to simmer for about 30 minutes or until very tender.

4 Meanwhile, make the pesto. Fry the pine kernels in 1 tablespoon of the oil until pale brown, then drain. Put the basil into a food processor or blender with the pine kernels and garlic and process until well chopped. Alternatively, chop the basil finely by hand and pound with the pine kernels and crushed garlic using a pestle and mortar. Gradually add the remaining oil until smooth. Turn into a bowl, add the cheese and seasoning, and mix thoroughly.

5 Add 1½ tablespoons of the pesto to the soup and stir until it is well blended. Simmer the soup for a further 5 minutes and adjust the seasoning if necessary. Serve the soup very hot in warmed bowls, sprinkled with the freshly grated Parmesan cheese.

Cucumber Soup

Parsley tames the pungent garlic flavour of this traditional Balkan soup. The cucumber and yogurt make it a refreshing summer starter.

NUTRITIONAL INFORMATION

Calories	208	Sugars	........10g
Protein	.........8g	Fat	..........15g
Carbohydrate	...10g	Saturates	.......2g

15 mins, plus chilling   0 mins

SERVES 4

INGREDIENTS

1 large cucumber

60 g/2 oz walnut pieces, toasted (see Cook's Tip)

15 g/½ oz fresh parsley leaves

1 small garlic clove, very finely chopped

2 tbsp olive oil

4 tbsp water

1 tbsp lemon juice

300 ml/½ pint Greek-style yogurt

salt and pepper

fresh mint leaves, to garnish

1 Peel the cucumber, slice in two lengthways and scoop out the seeds with a small pointed spoon. Cut the flesh into 2.5 cm/1 inch pieces.

COOK'S TIP

Toasting the walnuts gives them extra flavour. Just heat them in a dry frying pan over a low-medium heat until they begin to colour and smell aromatic.

2 Put the walnuts, parsley leaves, garlic, oil and water in a blender or food processor with half of the cucumber and process to a smooth purée, stopping to scrape down the sides as necessary.

3 Add the remaining cucumber to the blender or processor with a pinch of salt and the lemon juice. Process briefly until smooth.

4 Scrape the purée into a large bowl and stir in the yogurt. Season to taste with salt and pepper and add a little more lemon juice, if wished.

5 Cover with clingfilm and chill in the refrigerator for about 30 minutes or until cold. Taste and adjust the seasoning if necessary. Ladle into chilled bowls and garnish with mint leaves.

Walnut, Egg & Cheese Pâté

This unusual pâté, flavoured with parsley and dill, can be served with crackers, crusty bread or toast. The pâté requires chilling until set.

NUTRITIONAL INFORMATION

Calories 438	Sugars 2g
Protein 21g	Fat 38g
Carbohydrate 2g	Saturates 18g

20 mins | 2 mins

SERVES 4

INGREDIENTS

1 celery stick

1–2 spring onions

25 g/1 oz shelled walnuts

1 tbsp chopped fresh parsley

1 tsp chopped fresh dill or ½ tsp dried dill

1 garlic clove, crushed

dash of vegetarian Worcestershire sauce

115 g/4 oz cottage cheese

55 g/2 oz blue cheese, such as
   Stilton or Danish blue

1 hard-boiled egg

salt and pepper

2 tbsp butter

fresh herbs, to garnish

crackers, toast or crusty bread and
   crudités, to serve

1 Finely chop the celery, slice the spring onions very thinly and chop the walnuts evenly. Place in a bowl.

2 Add the chopped herbs and garlic and vegetarian Worcestershire sauce to taste. Mix well, then stir the cottage cheese evenly through the mixture.

3 Grate the blue cheese finely into the pâté mixture. Finely chop the hard-boiled egg and stir it into the mixture. Season to taste with salt and pepper.

4 Melt the butter and stir it into the pâté, then spoon into 1 serving dish or 4 individual dishes. Smooth the top, but do not press down firmly. Chill until set.

5 Garnish with fresh herbs and serve with crackers, toast or fresh, crusty bread, and a few crudités, if liked.

COOK'S TIP

You can also use this as a stuffing for vegetables. Cut the tops off extra-large tomatoes, scoop out the seeds and fill with the pâté, piling it well up, or spoon into the hollows of celery sticks cut into 5 cm/2 inch pieces.

Lentil Pâté

Red lentils are used in this spicy recipe for speed as they do not require pre-soaking. If you use other lentils, soak and pre-cook them first.

NUTRITIONAL INFORMATION

Calories 267   Sugars 12g
Protein ....14g   Fat 8g
Carbohydrate ...37g   Saturates 1g

  25 mins   1¼ hrs

SERVES 4

INGREDIENTS

1 tbsp vegetable oil, plus extra for greasing

1 onion, chopped

2 garlic cloves, crushed

1 tsp garam masala

½ tsp ground coriander

850 ml/1½ pints vegetable stock

175 g/6 oz red lentils

1 small egg

2 tbsp milk

2 tbsp mango chutney

2 tbsp chopped fresh parsley, plus extra to garnish

salad leaves and warm toast, to serve

1 Heat the vegetable oil in a large saucepan and sauté the onion and garlic for 2–3 minutes, stirring. Add the spices and cook for a further 30 seconds. Stir in the vegetable stock and lentils and bring the mixture to the boil. Reduce the heat and simmer for 20 minutes until the lentils are cooked and softened. Remove the pan from the heat and drain off any excess moisture.

2 Put the mixture in a food processor and add the egg, milk, mango chutney and parsley. Blend until smooth.

3 Grease and line the base of a 450 g/ 1 lb loaf tin and spoon the mixture into the tin. Cover and cook in a preheated oven at 200°C/400°F/Gas Mark 6 for 40–45 minutes or until firm.

4 Allow the pâté to cool in the tin for 20 minutes, then transfer to the refrigerator to cool completely. Slice the pâté and garnish with chopped parsley. Serve with salad leaves and warm toast.

VARIATION

Use other spices, such as chilli powder or Chinese five-spice powder, to flavour the pâté and add tomato relish or chilli relish instead of the mango chutney, if you prefer.

Hummus Toasts with Olives

Hummus is an especially good spread on these garlic toasts for a delicious starter or as part of a light lunch.

NUTRITIONAL INFORMATION

Calories 731   Sugars 2g
Protein . . . . . . .22g   Fat 55g
Carbohydrate . . .39g   Saturates 8g

 10–15 mins   5 mins

SERVES 4

INGREDIENTS

400 g/14 oz canned chick peas

juice of 1 large lemon

6 tbsp tahini

2 tbsp olive oil

2 garlic cloves, crushed

salt and pepper

olive oil, chopped fresh coriander and black olives, to garnish

GARLIC TOASTS

1 ciabatta loaf, sliced

2 garlic cloves, crushed

1 tbsp chopped fresh coriander

4 tbsp olive oil

1 To make the hummus, firstly drain the chick peas, reserving a little of the liquid. Put the chick peas and liquid in a food processor and blend, gradually adding the reserved liquid and lemon juice. Blend well after each addition until smooth.

2 Stir in the tahini and all but 1 teaspoon of the olive oil. Add the garlic, season to taste and blend again until smooth.

3 Spoon the hummus into a serving dish. Drizzle the remaining olive oil over the top, garnish with chopped coriander and olives. Leave to chill in the refrigerator while preparing the toasts.

4 Lay the slices of ciabatta on a grill rack in a single layer.

5 Mix the garlic, coriander and olive oil together and drizzle over the bread slices. Cook under a hot grill for 2–3 minutes until golden brown, turning once. Serve hot with the hummus.

Mushroom & Garlic Soufflés

These individual soufflés are very impressive starters, but must be cooked just before serving to prevent them from sinking.

NUTRITIONAL INFORMATION

Calories	179	Sugars	........3g
Protein	.........6g	Fat	..........14g
Carbohydrate	....8g	Saturates	.......8g

 10 mins ⏱ 20 mins

SERVES 4

INGREDIENTS

50 g/1¾ oz butter, plus extra for greasing

75 g/2¾ oz flat mushrooms, chopped

2 tsp lime juice

2 garlic cloves, crushed

2 tbsp chopped fresh marjoram

25 g/1 oz plain flour

225 ml/8 fl oz milk

salt and pepper

2 eggs, separated

1 Lightly grease the inside of 4 150 ml/¼ pint individual soufflé dishes with a little butter.

2 Melt 25 g/1 oz of the butter in a frying pan. Add the mushrooms, lime juice and garlic and sauté for 2–3 minutes. Remove the mushroom mixture from the frying pan with a slotted spoon and transfer it to a mixing bowl. Stir in the marjoram.

3 Melt the remaining butter in a pan. Add the flour and cook for 1 minute, then remove from the heat. Stir in the milk and return to the heat. Bring to the boil, stirring until thickened.

4 Mix the sauce into the mushroom mixture and beat in the egg yolks.

5 Whisk the egg whites until they form peaks and fold into the mushroom mixture until fully incorporated.

6 Divide the mixture between the prepared soufflé dishes. Place the dishes on a baking tray and cook in a preheated oven, 200°C/400°F/Gas Mark 6, for about 8–10 minutes, or until the soufflés are well risen and cooked through. Serve immediately.

COOK'S TIP

Insert a skewer into the centre of the soufflés to test if they are cooked through – it should come out clean. If not, cook for a few minutes longer, but do not overcook otherwise they will become rubbery.

Stuffed Vine Leaves

These refreshing little parcels with their fragrant filling are a lovely way to start a summer meal. Serve them warm, the way the Greeks do.

NUTRITIONAL INFORMATION

Calories	.407	Sugars	.1g
Protein	.5g	Fat	.32g
Carbohydrate	.27g	Saturates	.4g

20 mins   45 mins

SERVES 6

INGREDIENTS

225 g/8 oz fresh or preserved vine leaves

4 spring onions, finely chopped

2 shallots, finely chopped

25 g/1 oz flaked almonds, toasted

3 tbsp chopped fresh parsley

3 tbsp chopped fresh mint

finely grated rind of 1 lemon

175 g/6 oz long grain rice

125 ml/4 fl oz olive oil

300 ml/½ pint boiling vegetable stock

salt and ground black pepper

FOR THE DRESSING

125 ml/4 fl oz extra virgin olive oil

salt and pepper

3 tbsp lemon juice

1 tbsp chopped fresh mint

1 If using fresh vine leaves, blanch them in boiling water for 5 minutes, then refresh under cold water and pat dry. If using preserved vines leaves, rinse thoroughly and pat dry. Cut off the stalks.

2 Chop the spring onions, shallots and parsley then combine with the mint, lemon rind and rice in a bowl and add half the oil. Season to taste with salt. Spread out a vine leaf on a work surface and place a spoonful of the filling near the stalk end. Fold the stalk end over, fold the sides in and roll up to make a neat parcel. Repeat until all the leaves are used up.

3 Line the base of a large saucepan with any remaining vine leaves and place the parcels on top in a single layer. Sprinkle with the remaining oil and pour in the stock. Place a plate on top of the leaves to keep them submerged, cover the pan and simmer for 45 minutes. To make the dressing, pour the oil into a small serving bowl and season well with salt and pepper. Whisk in the lemon juice and stir in the mint. Serve the vine leaves warm or cold, with the dressing.

Filo Parcels

These crisp pastry parcels can be served as a main course with a potato salad and mixed leaves or on their own as appetizers.

NUTRITIONAL INFORMATION

Calories	410	Sugars	.........5g
Protein	........14g	Fat	..........19g
Carbohydrate	...45g	Saturates	......11g

15 mins, plus chilling   45 mins

SERVES 6

INGREDIENTS

55 g/2 oz butter

1 tbsp sunflower oil

4 leeks, sliced

2 onions, chopped

1 garlic clove, finely chopped

2 tsp chopped fresh thyme

salt and pepper

2 tbsp single cream

140 g/4½ oz Gruyère or Emmenthal cheese, grated

12 sheet filo pastry, thawed if frozen

1 Melt half the butter with the oil in a large, heavy-based frying pan. Add the leeks, onions, garlic and thyme and season to taste with salt and pepper. Cook, stirring frequently, for 10 minutes. Stir in the cream and cook for 2–3 minutes more, until all the liquid has been absorbed. Remove the pan from the heat and set aside to cool. Stir in the cheese, cover with clingfilm and chill in the refrigerator for 30 minutes.

2 Melt the remaining butter and brush a little on to a baking sheet. Brush 2 sheets of filo with butter and place them one on top of the other. Place a heaped spoonful of the leek mixture close to one corner. Fold the corner over the filling, fold in the sides and roll up the parcel. Place the parcel, seam side down, on the baking sheet and make 5 more parcels in the same way.

3 Brush the pastry parcels with the remaining melted butter and bake in a preheated oven, 180°C/350°F/Gas Mark 4, for 30 minutes, until crisp and golden. Serve immediately.

Mixed Bhajis

These small bhajis are often served as accompaniments to a main meal, but they are delicious as a starter with a small salad and yogurt sauce.

NUTRITIONAL INFORMATION

Calories 414   Sugars 7g
Protein . . . . .9g   Fat 26g
Carbohydrate . . .38g   Saturates 3g

25 mins   30 mins

SERVES 4

I N G R E D I E N T S

B H A J I S

175 g/6 oz gram flour (see page 149)

1 tsp bicarbonate of soda

2 tsp ground coriander

1 tsp garam masala

1½ tsp turmeric

1½ tsp chilli powder

2 tbsp chopped fresh coriander

1 small onion, halved and sliced

1 small leek, sliced

100 g/3½ oz cooked cauliflower

135–175 ml/4½–6 fl oz cold water

salt and pepper

vegetable oil, for deep-frying

S A U C E

150 ml/¼ pint natural yogurt

2 tbsp chopped fresh mint

½ tsp turmeric

1 garlic clove, crushed

fresh mint sprigs, to garnish

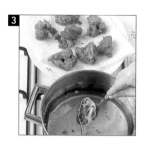

1 Sift the flour, bicarbonate of soda and salt to taste into a mixing bowl and add the spices and fresh coriander. Mix together thoroughly.

2 Divide the mixture into 3 and place in separate bowls. Stir the onion into one bowl, the leek into another and the cauliflower into the third bowl. Add 3–4 tablespoons of water to each bowl and mix each to form a smooth paste.

3 Heat the vegetable oil in a deep-fat fryer to 180°C/350°F or until a cube of bread browns in 30 seconds. Using 2 dessert spoons, form the mixture into rounds and cook each in the oil for 3–4 minutes, until browned.

4 Remove the bhajis with a slotted spoon, drain well on absorbent kitchen paper and keep warm in the oven while cooking the remainder.

5 Mix the sauce ingredients together. Garnish with mint sprigs and serve with the warm bhajis.

Feta Cheese Tartlets

These crisp-baked bread cases, filled with sliced tomatoes, feta cheese, black olives and quail's eggs, are quick to make and taste delicious.

NUTRITIONAL INFORMATION

Calories 570   Sugars 3g
Protein . . . . .14g   Fat 42g
Carbohydrate . . .36g   Saturates 23g

30 mins   10 mins

SERVES 4

INGREDIENTS

8 slices bread from a medium-cut large loaf

125 g/4½ oz butter, melted

125 g/4½ oz feta cheese (drained weight), cut into small cubes

4 cherry tomatoes, cut into wedges

8 stoned black or green olives, halved

8 quail's eggs, hard-boiled

2 tbsp olive oil

1 tbsp white wine vinegar

1 tsp wholegrain mustard

pinch of caster sugar

salt and pepper

fresh parsley sprigs, to garnish

1 Remove the crusts from the bread. Trim the bread into squares and flatten each piece with a rolling pin.

2 Brush the bread squares with melted butter, and then arrange them in bun or muffin tins. Press a piece of crumpled foil into each bread case to secure in place. Bake the cases in a preheated oven, 190°C/375°F/Gas Mark 5, for 10 minutes, or until crisp and browned.

3 Meanwhile, mix together the feta cheese, tomatoes and olives. Shell the eggs and quarter them. Mix together the olive oil, vinegar, mustard and sugar. Season to taste with salt and pepper.

4 Remove the bread cases from the oven and discard the foil. Leave to cool.

5 Just before serving, fill the bread cases with the cheese and tomato mixture. Arrange the eggs on top and spoon over the dressing. Garnish with parsley sprigs.

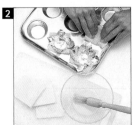

Spinach Filo Baskets

If you use frozen spinach, it only needs to be thawed and drained before being mixed with the cheeses and seasonings.

NUTRITIONAL INFORMATION

Calories	533	Sugars	.........3g
Protein	........24g	Fat	..........38g
Carbohydrate	...26g	Saturates	......22g

55 mins   30 mins

SERVES 2

INGREDIENTS

125 g/4½ oz fresh leaf spinach, washed and chopped roughly, or 90 g/3 oz frozen spinach, thawed

2–4 spring onions, trimmed and chopped, or 1 tbsp onion, finely chopped

1 garlic clove, crushed

2 tbsp grated Parmesan cheese

90 g/3 oz mature Cheddar cheese, grated

pinch of ground allspice

1 egg yolk

salt and pepper

4 sheets filo pastry

25 g/1 oz butter, melted

2 spring onions, to garnish

1 If using fresh spinach, cook it in the minimum of boiling salted water for 3–4 minutes, until tender. Drain very thoroughly, using a potato masher to remove excess liquid, then chop and put into a bowl. If using frozen spinach, simply drain and chop.

2 Add the spring onions or onion, garlic, cheeses, allspice, egg yolk and seasoning, and mix well.

3 Grease 2 individual Yorkshire pudding tins, or alternatively use ovenproof dishes or tins about 12 cm/5 inches in diameter, and 4 cm/1½ inches deep. Cut the filo pastry sheets in half to make 8 pieces and brush each piece lightly with melted butter.

4 Place one piece of filo pastry in a tin or dish and then cover with a second piece at right angles to the first. Add two more pieces at right angles, so that all the corners are in different places. Line the other tin in the same way.

5 Spoon the spinach mixture into the 'baskets' and cook in a preheated oven, 180°C/350°F/Gas Mark 4, for about 20 minutes, or until the pastry is golden brown. Garnish with a spring onion tassel (see below) and serve hot or cold.

6 Make the spring onion tassels about 30 minutes before required. Trim off the root end and cut to a length of 5–7 cm/2–3 inches. Make a series of cuts from the green end to within 2 cm/¾ inch of the other end. Place in a bowl of iced water to open out. Drain well before use.

Leek & Tomato Timbales

Angel-hair pasta, known as cappellini, is mixed with fried leeks, sun-dried tomatoes, fresh oregano and beaten eggs, and baked in ramekins.

NUTRITIONAL INFORMATION

Calories	331	Sugars	........10g
Protein	........10g	Fat	..........21g
Carbohydrate	...26g	Saturates	.......9g

 5-10 mins   🕐 50 mins

SERVES 4

INGREDIENTS

90 g/3 oz dried angel-hair pasta (cappellini)

25 g/1 oz butter

1 tbsp olive oil

1 large leek, finely sliced

60 g/2 oz sun-dried tomatoes in oil, drained and chopped

1 tbsp chopped fresh oregano or 1 tsp dried oregano

2 eggs, beaten

100 ml/3½ fl oz single cream

1 tbsp freshly grated Parmesan cheese

salt and pepper

sprigs of fresh oregano, to garnish

lettuce leaves, to serve

SAUCE

1 small onion, finely chopped

1 small garlic clove, crushed

350 g/12 oz tomatoes, peeled and chopped

1 tsp mixed dried Italian herbs

4 tbsp dry white wine

1 Cook the pasta in plenty of boiling salted water for about 3 minutes until 'al dente' (just tender). Drain and rinse with cold water to cool quickly.

2 Meanwhile, heat half the butter and oil in a frying pan. Gently fry the leek until softened, about 5–6 minutes. Add the sun-dried tomatoes and oregano, and cook for a further 2 minutes. Remove the pan from the heat.

3 Add the leek mixture to the pasta. Stir in the beaten eggs, cream and Parmesan. Season with salt and pepper. Divide between 4 greased ramekin dishes or dariole moulds.

4 Place the dishes in a roasting tin with enough warm water to come halfway up their sides. Bake in a preheated oven,

180°C/350°F/Gas Mark 4, for about 30 minutes, until set.

5 Meanwhile, make the tomato sauce. Fry the onion and garlic in the remaining butter and oil until softened. Add the tomatoes, herbs and wine. Cover and cook gently for about 20 minutes until pulpy. Blend in a food processor until smooth, or press through a sieve.

6 Run a knife or small spatula around the edge of the ramekins, then turn out the timbales on to 4 warm serving plates. Pour over a little sauce and garnish with oregano. Serve with the lettuce leaves.

Vegetable Fritters

These mixed vegetable fritters are coated in a light batter and deep-fried until golden. They are ideal with the sweet and sour dipping sauce.

NUTRITIONAL INFORMATION

Calories	479	Sugars	........18g
Protein	.........8g	Fat	.........32g
Carbohydrate	...42g	Saturates	.......5g

20 mins   20 mins

SERVES 4

INGREDIENTS

100 g/3½ oz wholemeal flour

salt

pinch of cayenne pepper

4 tsp olive oil

175 ml/6 fl oz cold water

100 g/3½ oz broccoli florets

100 g/3½ oz cauliflower florets

50 g/2 oz mangetouts

1 large carrot, cut into batons

1 red pepper, deseeded and sliced

2 egg whites, beaten

oil, for deep-frying

SAUCE

150 ml/¼ pint pineapple juice

150 ml/¼ pint vegetable stock

2 tbsp white wine vinegar

2 tbsp light brown sugar

2 tsp cornflour

2 spring onions, chopped

1 Sift the flour and a pinch of salt into a mixing bowl and add the cayenne pepper. Make a well in the centre and gradually beat in the oil and cold water to make a smooth batter.

2 Cook the vegetables in boiling water for 5 minutes and drain well.

3 Whisk the egg whites until they form peaks and gently fold them into the flour batter.

4 Dip the vegetables into the batter, turning to coat well. Drain off any excess batter. Heat the oil in a deep-fat fryer to 180°C/350°F or until a cube of bread browns in 30 seconds. Fry the vegetables, in batches, for 1–2 minutes, until golden. Remove from the oil with a slotted spoon and drain on kitchen paper.

5 Place all of the sauce ingredients in a pan and bring to the boil, stirring, until the sauce is thickened and clear. Serve with the fritters.

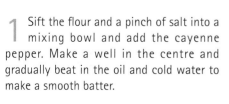

Heavenly Garlic Dip

Anyone who loves garlic will adore this dip – it is very potent! Serve it at a barbecue and dip raw vegetables or chunks of French bread into it.

NUTRITIONAL INFORMATION

Calories 344   Sugars 2g
Protein . . . . .6g   Fat 34g
Carbohydrate . . . .3g   Saturates 5g

 15 mins   20 mins

SERVES 4

I N G R E D I E N T S

2 bulbs garlic

6 tbsp olive oil

1 small onion, finely chopped

2 tbsp lemon juice

3 tbsp tahini

2 tbsp chopped fresh parsley

salt and pepper

TO SERVE

fresh vegetable crudités

French bread or warmed pitta breads

1 Separate the bulbs of garlic into individual cloves. Place them on a baking tray and roast in a preheated oven, 200°C/400°F/Gas Mark 6, for about 8–10 minutes. Set them aside to cool for a few minutes.

2 When they are cool enough to handle, peel the garlic cloves and then chop them finely.

3 Heat the olive oil in a saucepan or frying pan and add the garlic and onion. Fry over a low heat, stirring occasionally, for 8–10 minutes, until softened. Remove the pan from the heat.

4 Mix in the lemon juice, tahini and parsley. Season to taste with salt and pepper. Transfer the dip to a small heatproof bowl and keep warm at one side of the barbecue.

5 Serve with fresh vegetable crudités, or with chunks of French bread or warm pitta breads.

VARIATION
If you come across smoked garlic, use it in this recipe – it tastes wonderful. There is no need to roast the smoked garlic, so omit the first step. This dip can also be used to baste vegetarian burgers.

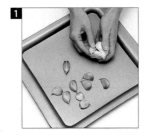

Mixed Bean Pâté

This is a really quick starter to prepare if canned beans are used.
Choose a wide variety of beans for colour and flavour.

NUTRITIONAL INFORMATION

Calories 126	Sugars 3g
Protein 5g	Fat 6g
Carbohydrate . . .13g	Saturates 1g

 1 hr, plus chilling   0 mins

SERVES 4

INGREDIENTS

400 g/14 oz canned mixed beans, drained

2 tbsp olive oil

juice of 1 lemon

2 garlic cloves, crushed

1 tbsp chopped fresh coriander

2 spring onions, chopped

salt and pepper

shredded spring onions, to garnish

1 Rinse the beans thoroughly under cold running water and drain well.

2 Transfer the beans to a food processor or blender and process until smooth. Alternatively, place the beans in a bowl and mash thoroughly by hand with a fork or potato masher.

3 Add the olive oil, lemon juice, garlic, coriander and spring onions and blend until fairly smooth. Season with salt and pepper to taste.

4 Transfer the pâté to a serving bowl, cover and chill in the refrigerator for at least 30 minutes.

5 Garnish with shredded spring onions and serve.

Vegetable Medley

This is a colourful dish of shredded vegetables in a fresh garlic and honey dressing. It is delicious served with crusty bread.

NUTRITIONAL INFORMATION

Calories	209	Sugars	........10g
Protein	.........2g	Fat	..........14g
Carbohydrate	...20g	Saturates	.......2g

🍞 🍞 🍞

🥘 15 mins   🕐 5 mins

SERVES 4

I N G R E D I E N T S

2 tbsp olive oil

1 potato, cut into thin strips

1 fennel bulb, cut into thin strips

2 carrots, grated

1 red onion, cut into thin strips

chopped chives and fennel fronds,
   to garnish

D R E S S I N G

3 tbsp olive oil

1 tbsp garlic wine vinegar

1 garlic clove, crushed

1 tsp Dijon mustard

2 tsp clear honey

salt and pepper

1 Heat the olive oil in a frying pan, add the potato and fennel strips and cook them over a medium heat for about 2–3 minutes, or until they are beginning to brown.

2 Remove the vegetables from the frying pan with a slotted spoon and drain on kitchen paper.

3 Arrange the carrot, red onion, potato and fennel in separate piles on a serving platter.

4 Mix the dressing ingredients together and pour over the vegetables. Toss well and sprinkle with chopped chives and fennel fronds. Serve immediately or leave in the refrigerator until required.

VARIATION

Use mixed, grilled peppers or shredded leeks in this dish for variety, or add bean sprouts and a segmented orange, if you prefer.

Avocado Cream Terrine

The smooth, rich taste of ripe avocados combines well with thick, creamy yogurt and single cream to make this impressive terrine.

NUTRITIONAL INFORMATION

Calories	327	Sugars	.........3g
Protein	.........6g	Fat	..........32g
Carbohydrate	....4g	Saturates	.......8g

15 mins, plus chilling   15 mins

SERVES 4

INGREDIENTS

2 ripe avocados

4 tbsp cold water

2 tsp gelazone (vegetarian gelatine)

1 tbsp lemon juice

4 tbsp low-fat mayonnaise

150 ml/5 fl oz natural yogurt

150 ml/5 fl oz single cream

salt and pepper

mixed salad leaves, to serve

TO GARNISH

cucumber slices

nasturtium flowers

1 Peel the avocados and remove and discard the stones. Put the flesh in a blender or food processor or a large bowl with the water, vegetarian gelatine, lemon juice, mayonnaise, yogurt and cream. Season to taste with salt and pepper.

2 Process for about 10–15 seconds or beat by hand, using a fork or whisk, until smooth.

3 Transfer the mixture to a small, heavy-based pan and heat very gently, stirring constantly, until just beginning to boil.

4 Pour the mixture into a 900 ml/ 1½ pint terrine, non-stick loaf tin or plastic food storage box and smooth the surface. Allow the mixture to cool and set and then chill in the refrigerator for about 1½–2 hours.

5 Turn the terrine out of its container and cut into neat slices. Arrange a bed of salad leaves on 4 serving plates. Place a slice of avocado terrine on top and garnish with cucumber slices and nasturtium flowers.

Artichokes & Sauce Maltaise

Always an elegant starter, globe artichokes are served here with an unusual and deliciously creamy orange-flavoured sauce.

NUTRITIONAL INFORMATION

Calories . . . . .383 Sugars 7g
Protein . . . . .8g Fat 36g
Carbohydrate . . .10g Saturates 24g

20 mins   25 mins

SERVES 4

INGREDIENTS

4 large globe artichokes

2 lemon slices

SAUCE MALTAISE

1 blood orange

175 g/6 oz butter

2–3 tbsp lemon juice

3 tbsp water

salt and pepper

3 egg yolks

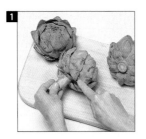
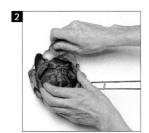

1 To prepare the globe artichokes, bring lightly salted water to the boil in a pan large enough to hold the 4 artichokes upright. Add the lemon slices. Break off the stems and trim the bases of the artichokes so they are flat and will sit upright on a plate.

2 Put the artichokes in the pan and place a heatproof plate on top. Lower the heat and simmer for 20–25 minutes, until you can easily pull out a leaf.

3 Meanwhile, make the sauce. Finely grate the rind from the orange and squeeze 2 tablespoons orange juice. Put the butter in a saucepan over medium heat and melt, skimming the surface.

4 Put 2 tablespoons of the lemon juice, the water, plus salt and pepper, in a bowl. Set it over a pan of simmering water, making sure the base of the bowl does not come into contact with the water. Whisk until heated.

5 Whisk in the egg yolks until they are thoroughly blended and warmed through. Then add the hot butter in a steady stream, whisking constantly, and continue to whisk the mixture until a thick, smooth sauce is formed.

6 Stir the grated orange rind and the orange juice into the sauce. Taste, and adjust the seasoning, adding a little extra lemon juice if necessary. Remove the sauce from the heat.

7 Drain the artichokes well. To serve, place each one on an individual plate with a ramekin of the warm sauce maltaise for dipping.

COOK'S TIP

Pull out the leaves, starting with the outer layer, dip the base of each leaf into the sauce and scrape off the fleshy part with your teeth. Cut off the central core of purple leaves, which are inedible, and the hairy choke to reveal the delicious 'heart'.

Mini Vegetable Puff Pastries

These puff pastries are ideal with a more formal meal – they only take a short time to prepare but they look really impressive.

NUTRITIONAL INFORMATION

Calories 210   Sugars 2.3g
Protein . . . . .3.8g   Fat 12.9g
Carbohydrate . .20.8g   Saturates 1.7g

 15 mins   25 mins

SERVES 4

I N G R E D I E N T S

PASTRY CASES

450 g/1 lb puff pastry

1 egg, beaten

FILLING

225 g/8 oz sweet potatoes, diced

100 g/3½ oz baby asparagus spears

2 tbsp butter or margarine

1 leek, sliced

2 small open-cap mushrooms, sliced

1 tsp lime juice

1 tsp chopped fresh thyme

pinch of dried mustard

salt and pepper

 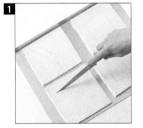 

1 Cut the pastry into 4 equal pieces. Roll each piece out on a lightly floured work surface to form a 13 cm/ 5 inch square. Place on a dampened baking tray and score a smaller 6 cm/2½ inch square inside.

2 Brush with the beaten egg and cook in a preheated oven, 200°C/400°F/ Gas Mark 6, for 20 minutes or until risen and golden brown.

3 While the pastry is cooking, start the filling. Cook the sweet potato in boiling water for 15 minutes, then drain.

Blanch the asparagus in boiling water for 10 minutes or until tender. Drain and reserve.

4 Remove the pastry squares from the oven. Carefully cut out the central square of pastry, lift it out and reserve.

5 Melt the butter in a saucepan and sauté the leek and mushrooms for 2–3 minutes. Add the lime juice, thyme and mustard, season well and stir in the sweet potatoes and asparagus. Spoon into the pastry cases, top with the reserved pastry squares and serve immediately.

COOK'S TIP
Use a colourful selection of any vegetables you have at hand for this recipe.

Buttered Nut & Lentil Dip

This tasty dip is very easy to make. It is perfect to have at barbecues, as it gives your guests something to nibble while they are waiting.

NUTRITIONAL INFORMATION

Calories ....395 Sugars 4g
Protein ....12g Fat 31g
Carbohydrate ...18g Saturates 10g

 5-10 mins 40 mins

SERVES 4

INGREDIENTS

60 g/2 oz butter

1 small onion, chopped

90 g/3 oz red lentils

300 ml/½ pint vegetable stock

60 g/2 oz blanched almonds

60 g/2 oz pine nuts

½ tsp ground coriander

½ tsp ground cumin

½ tsp grated fresh root ginger

1 tsp chopped fresh coriander

salt and pepper

sprigs of fresh coriander, to garnish

TO SERVE

fresh vegetable crudités

bread sticks

VARIATION

Green or brown lentils can be used, but they will take longer to cook than red lentils. If you wish, substitute peanuts for the almonds. Ground ginger can be used instead of fresh – substitute ½ teaspoon and add it with the other spices.

1 Melt half the butter in a saucepan, add the onion and fry over a medium heat, stirring frequently, until it is golden brown in colour.

2 Add the lentils and vegetable stock. Bring to the boil, then reduce the heat and simmer gently, uncovered, for about 25–30 minutes, until the lentils are tender. Drain well.

3 Melt the remaining butter in a small frying pan. Add the almonds and pine nuts and fry them over a low heat, stirring frequently, until golden brown. Remove the pan from the heat.

4 Put the lentils, the almonds and the pine nuts into a food processor or blender, together with any butter remaining in the frying pan. Add the ground coriander, cumin, ginger and fresh coriander. Process for about 15–20 seconds, until the mixture is smooth. Alternatively, press the lentils through a sieve with the back of a wooden spoon to purée them and then mix with the finely chopped nuts, spices and herbs.

5 Season the dip with salt and pepper and garnish with sprigs of fresh coriander. Serve with fresh vegetable crudités and bread sticks.

Onions à la Grecque

This is a well-known method of cooking vegetables and is perfect with shallots or onions, served with a crisp salad.

NUTRITIONAL INFORMATION

Calories 200   Sugars 26g
Protein . . . . .2g   Fat 9g
Carbohydrate . . .28g   Saturates 1g

10 mins   15 mins

SERVES 4

I N G R E D I E N T S

450 g/1 lb shallots

3 tbsp olive oil

3 tbsp clear honey

2 tbsp garlic wine vinegar

3 tbsp dry white wine

1 tbsp tomato purée

2 celery sticks, sliced

2 tomatoes, deseeded and chopped

salt and pepper

chopped celery leaves, to garnish

1 Peel the shallots. Heat the oil in a large saucepan, add the shallots and cook, stirring, for 3–5 minutes, or until they begin to brown.

2 Add the honey and cook over a high heat for a further 30 seconds, then add the garlic wine vinegar and dry white wine, stirring well.

3 Stir in the tomato purée, the celery and the tomatoes, and bring the mixture to the boil. Cook over a high heat for 5–6 minutes. Season to taste and leave to cool slightly.

4 Garnish with chopped celery leaves and serve warm. Alternatively, chill in the refrigerator before serving.

Tofu Tempura

Crispy coated vegetables and tofu, accompanied by a sweet, spicy dip, give a real taste of the Orient in this Japanese-style dish.

NUTRITIONAL INFORMATION

Calories	582	Sugars	........10g
Protein	........16g	Fat	..........27g
Carbohydrate	...65g	Saturates	.......4g

 15 mins   20 mins

SERVES 4

INGREDIENTS

125 g/4½ oz baby courgettes

125 g/4½ oz baby carrots

125 g/4½ oz baby sweetcorn cobs

125 g/4½ oz baby leeks

2 baby aubergines

225 g/8 oz tofu

vegetable oil, for deep-frying

julienne strips of carrot, root ginger and
  baby leek, to garnish

noodles, to serve

BATTER

2 egg yolks

300 ml/½ pint water

225 g/8 oz plain flour

DIPPING SAUCE

5 tbsp mirin or dry sherry

5 tbsp Japanese soy sauce

2 tsp clear honey

1 garlic clove, crushed

1 tsp grated fresh root ginger

1 Cut the courgettes and carrots in half lengthways. Trim the corn. Trim the leeks at both ends. Cut the aubergines into quarters lengthways. Cut the tofu into 2.5 cm/1 inch cubes.

2 To make the batter, mix the egg yolks with the water. Sift in 175 g/6 oz of the flour and beat with a balloon whisk to form a thick batter. Don't worry if there are any lumps. Heat the oil for deep-frying to 180°C/350°F or until a cube of bread browns in 30 seconds.

3 Place the remaining flour on a large plate and toss the vegetables and tofu until lightly coated.

4 Dip the tofu in the batter and deep-fry for 2–3 minutes, until lightly golden. Drain on kitchen paper and keep warm.

5 Dip the vegetables in the batter and deep-fry, a few at a time, for 3–4 minutes, until golden. Drain and place on a warmed serving plate.

6 To make the dipping sauce, mix all the ingredients together. Serve with the vegetables and tofu, accompanied with noodles and garnished with julienne strips of vegetables.

Avocado Margherita

Avocados filled with a classic Italian combination of tomatoes, basil and mozzarella cheese are easy to prepare in this microwave oven recipe.

NUTRITIONAL INFORMATION

Calories 284   Sugars 3g
Protein . . . . .6g   Fat 27g
Carbohydrate . . . .6g   Saturates 7g

10 mins   7 mins

SERVES 4

INGREDIENTS

1 small red onion, sliced

1 garlic clove, crushed

1 tbsp olive oil

2 small tomatoes

2 avocados, halved and stoned

4 fresh basil leaves, torn into shreds

60 g/2 oz mozzarella cheese, thinly sliced

salt and pepper

TO GARNISH

mixed salad

fresh basil leaves

1 Place the onion, garlic and the olive oil in a bowl. Cover and cook on HIGH power for 2 minutes.

2 Meanwhile, peel the tomatoes by cutting a cross in the base of the tomatoes and placing them in a small bowl. Pour on boiling water and leave for about 45 seconds. Drain and then plunge into cold water. The skins will slide off without too much difficulty.

3 Arrange the avocado halves on a plate, narrow ends towards the centre. Spoon the onions into the hollows.

4 Cut the tomatoes into slices. Divide the tomatoes, basil and thin slices of mozzarella between the four avocado halves, and season to taste with salt and pepper.

5 Cook on MEDIUM power for 5 minutes until the avocados are heated through and the cheese has melted. Serve immediately with a mixed salad garnished with basil leaves.

COOK'S TIP
This recipe is ideal for combination microwave ovens with a grill. Arrange the avocados on the low rack of the grill or on the turntable. Cook on combination grill 1 and LOW power for 8 minutes until browned and bubbling.

Hummus with Crudités

Making your own hummus couldn't be simpler and it tastes much better than shop-bought varieties.

NUTRITIONAL INFORMATION

Calories	311	Sugars	.........8g
Protein	........11g	Fat	..........23g
Carbohydrate	...16g	Saturates	.......3g

 15 mins   0 mins

SERVES 4

INGREDIENTS

175 g/6 oz canned chick peas, drained and rinsed

125 ml/4 fl oz tahini

2 garlic cloves

125 ml/4 fl oz lemon juice

salt

2–3 tbsp water

1 tbsp olive oil

1 tbsp chopped fresh parsley

pinch of cayenne pepper

CRUDITES

4 carrots, cut into thin batons

4 celery sticks, cut into thin batons

4 radishes

½ small cauliflower, cut into florets

1 green pepper, deseeded and cut into thin batons

1 red pepper, deseeded and cut into thin batons

1 Place the drained chick peas, the tahini, the garlic and the lemon juice in a blender or food processor and season to taste with salt. Prepare crudités.

2 Process the ingredients, gradually adding water to the mixture as necessary until the consistency becomes smooth and creamy. Taste, and adjust the seasoning if necessary.

3 Transfer the mixture into a serving bowl and make a hollow in the centre with the back of a spoon. Pour the olive oil into the hollow, then sprinkle the hummus with the chopped fresh parsley and the cayenne pepper.

4 Arrange the prepared raw vegetables on a large serving platter and serve immediately with the hummus.

Caponata

This Sicilian speciality varies slightly from one part of the island to the other, but it always contains aubergine, onion, celery, tomato and capers.

NUTRITIONAL INFORMATION

Calories	178	Sugars	........10g
Protein	.........2g	Fat	..........14g
Carbohydrate	...12g	Saturates	.......2g

 10 mins 25 mins

SERVES 4

INGREDIENTS

4 tbsp olive oil

1 onion, sliced

2 celery sticks, sliced

1 aubergine, diced

5 plum tomatoes, chopped

1 garlic clove, finely chopped

3 tbsp red wine vinegar

1 tbsp sugar

12 black olives, stoned

2 tbsp capers, drained and rinsed

salt

3 tbsp chopped fresh flat-leaved parsley, to garnish

1 Heat 2 tablespoons of the oil in a large, heavy-based saucepan. Add the onion and celery and cook over a low heat, stirring frequently, for 5 minutes, until softened. Add the remaining oil with the aubergine and cook, stirring constantly, for 10 minutes.

2 Stir in the tomatoes, garlic, vinegar and sugar. Cover the surface with a circle of greaseproof paper and simmer for 10 minutes.

3 Stir the olives and capers into the mixture and season to taste with salt.

4 Transfer the mixture to a serving dish and leave it to cool to room temperature. Sprinkle with the chopped parsley and serve.

COOK'S TIP

Serve plenty of fresh, crusty bread with this delicious dish to mop up the juices.

Soft Dumplings in Yogurt

These are very light and make a good summer afternoon snack, as well as a good starter to any vegetarian meal.

NUTRITIONAL INFORMATION

Calories . . . . .476 Sugars 29g
Protein . . . . .11g Fat 21g
Carbohydrate . . .64g Saturates 3g

15 mins   20 mins

SERVES 4

I N G R E D I E N T S

200 g/7 oz urid dhal powder

1 tsp baking powder

½ tsp ground ginger

700 ml/1¼ pints water

oil, for deep-frying

400 ml/14 fl oz natural yogurt

75 g/2¾ oz sugar

M A S A L A

50 g/1¾ oz coriander seeds

50 g/1¾ oz white cumin seeds

25 g/1 oz crushed red chillies

100 g/3½ oz citric acid

chopped fresh red chillies, to garnish

1 Place the powdered urid dhal in a large mixing bowl. Add the baking powder and ginger and stir to combine. Add the water and mix to form a batter.

2 Heat the oil in a deep saucepan. Pour in the batter, 1 teaspoon at a time, and deep-fry the dumplings until golden brown, lowering the heat when the oil gets too hot. Set the dumplings aside.

3 Place the yogurt in a separate bowl. Add 400 ml/14 fl oz water and the sugar and mix together with a whisk or fork. Set aside.

4 To make the masala, roast the ground coriander and the white cumin in a saucepan until a little darker in colour and giving off their aroma. Grind coarsely in a food processor or in a mortar with a pestle. Add the crushed red chillies and citric acid and blend well together.

5 Sprinkle about 1 tablespoon of the masala over the dumplings and store the remainder in an airtight jar for future use. Garnish with chopped red chillies. Serve with the reserved yogurt mixture.

Tzatziki & Black Olive Dips

Cool, minty cucumber and yoghurt tzatziki and garlicky black olive dips taste superb with warm pitta bread.

NUTRITIONAL INFORMATION

Calories 381	Sugars 8g	
Protein 11g	Fat 15g	
Carbohydrate ...52g	Saturates 2g	

1 hr   3 mins

SERVES 4

INGREDIENTS

½ cucumber

225 g/8 oz thick natural yogurt

1 tbsp chopped fresh mint

salt and pepper

4 pitta breads

DIP

2 garlic cloves, crushed

125 g/4½ oz black olives, stoned

4 tbsp olive oil

2 tbsp lemon juice

1 tbsp chopped fresh parsley

TO GARNISH

fresh mint sprigs

fresh parsley sprigs

1 To make the tzatziki, peel the cucumber and chop it roughly. Sprinkle with salt and leave to stand for 15–20 minutes. Rinse with cold water and drain well.

2 Mix the cucumber, yogurt and mint together. Season to taste with salt and pepper and transfer to a serving bowl. Cover and chill for 20–30 minutes.

3 To make the black olive dip, put the crushed garlic and olives into a blender or food processor and process for 15–20 seconds. Alternatively, chop them very finely.

4 Add the olive oil, lemon juice and parsley to the blender or food processor and process for a few more seconds. Alternatively, mix with the chopped garlic and olives and mash together. Season with salt and pepper.

5 Wrap the pitta breads in foil and either place over a barbecue for 2–3 minutes, turning once to warm through, or heat in the oven or under the grill. Cut into pieces and serve with the tzatziki and black olive dip, garnished with sprigs of fresh mint and parsley.

COOK'S TIP

Sprinkling the cucumber with salt draws out some of its moisture, making it crisper. If you are in a hurry, you can omit this procedure.

Cheese, Garlic & Herb Pâté

This wonderful soft cheese pâté is fragrant with the aroma of fresh herbs and garlic. Serve with triangles of Melba toast for a perfect starter.

NUTRITIONAL INFORMATION

Calories 392	Sugars 1g	
Protein 17g	Fat 28g	
Carbohydrate ...18g	Saturates 18g	

 20 mins   10 mins

SERVES 4

INGREDIENTS

15 g/½ oz butter

1 garlic clove, crushed

3 spring onions, finely chopped

125 g/4½ oz full-fat soft cheese

2 tbsp chopped fresh mixed herbs, such as parsley, chives, marjoram, oregano and basil

175 g/6 oz mature Cheddar cheese, finely grated

pepper

4–6 slices of white bread from a medium-cut sliced loaf

mixed salad leaves and cherry tomatoes, to serve

TO GARNISH

ground paprika

fresh herb sprigs

1 Melt the butter in a small frying pan and gently fry the garlic and spring onions together for 3–4 minutes, until softened. Allow to cool.

2 Beat the soft cheese in a large mixing bowl until smooth, then add the garlic and spring onions. Stir in the chopped mixed herbs, mixing well.

3 Add the Cheddar and work the mixture together to form a stiff paste. Cover and chill until ready to serve.

4 To make the Melba toast, toast the slices of bread on both sides, and then cut off the crusts. Using a sharp bread knife, cut through the slices horizontally to make very thin slices. Cut into triangles and then lightly grill the untoasted sides until golden.

5 Arrange the mixed salad leaves on 4 serving plates with the cherry tomatoes. Pile the cheese pâté on top and sprinkle with a little paprika. Garnish with sprigs of fresh herbs and serve with the Melba toast.

Garlicky Mushroom Pakoras

Whole mushrooms are dunked in a spiced garlicky batter and deep-fried until golden. They are at their most delicious served piping hot.

NUTRITIONAL INFORMATION

Calories 297   Sugars 3g
Protein . . . . .5g   Fat 21g
Carbohydrate . . .24g   Saturates 2g

20 mins    10–15 mins

SERVES 4

I N G R E D I E N T S

175 g/6 oz gram flour (see Cook's Tip)

½ tsp salt

¼ tsp baking powder

1 tsp cumin seeds

½–1 tsp chilli powder

200 ml/7 fl oz water

2 garlic cloves, crushed

1 small onion, finely chopped

vegetable oil, for deep-frying

500 g/1 lb 2 oz button mushrooms, trimmed and wiped

sea salt, to serve

lemon wedges and fresh coriander sprigs, to garnish

1 Put the gram flour, salt, baking powder, cumin and chilli powder into a bowl and mix well together. Make a well in the centre of the mixture and gradually stir in the water, mixing thoroughly to form a batter.

2 Stir the crushed garlic and the chopped onion into the batter and leave the mixture to infuse for 10 minutes. One-third fill a deep-fat fryer or pan with vegetable oil and heat to 180°C/350°F or until a cube of bread browns in 30 seconds. Lower the basket into the hot oil.

3 Meanwhile, mix the mushrooms into the batter, stirring to coat. Remove a few at a time and place them into the hot oil. Fry for about 2 minutes, or until golden brown.

4 Remove the mushrooms from the pan with a slotted spoon and drain on kitchen paper while you are cooking the remainder in the same way.

5 Serve hot, sprinkled with sea salt and garnished with lemon wedges and coriander sprigs.

COOK'S TIP

Gram flour, also known as besan flour, is a pale yellow flour made from chick peas. It is now readily available from larger supermarkets, as well as Indian food shops and some ethnic delicatessens.

Hyderabad Pickles

This is a very versatile dish that will go with almost anything and can be served warm or cold. It is perfect as a starter for a dinner party.

NUTRITIONAL INFORMATION

Calories	732	Sugars	.........6g
Protein	.........6g	Fat	..........75g
Carbohydrate	....8g	Saturates	......10g

  30 mins, plus cooling   30 mins

SERVES 4

I N G R E D I E N T S

2 tsp ground coriander

2 tsp ground cumin

2 tsp desiccated coconut

2 tsp sesame seeds

1 tsp mixed mustard and onion seeds

300 ml/½ pint vegetable oil

3 medium onions, sliced

1 tsp finely chopped root ginger

1 tsp crushed garlic

½ tsp turmeric

1½ tsp chilli powder

1½ tsp salt

3 medium aubergines, halved lengthways

1 tbsp tamarind paste

300 ml/½ pint water

3 hard-boiled eggs, halved, to garnish

B A G H A A R

1 tsp mixed onion and mustard seeds

1 tsp cumin seeds

4 dried red chillies, chopped

150 ml/¼ pint vegetable oil

fresh coriander leaves

1 green chilli, deseeded and finely chopped

1 Dry-fry the ground coriander, cumin, coconut, sesame seeds and mustard and onion seeds in a pan until lightly coloured and the spices release their aroma. Grind in a pestle and mortar or food processor and set aside.

2 Heat the oil in a frying pan and fry the onions until golden. Reduce the heat and add the ginger, garlic, turmeric, chilli powder and salt, stirring. Leave to cool, then grind this mixture to form a paste.

3 Make 4 cuts across each aubergine half. Blend the prepared spices with the onion paste. Spoon this mixture into the slits in the aubergines.

4 In a bowl, mix the tamarind paste and 3 tablespoons of the water to make a fine paste and set aside.

5 For the baghaar (a seasoned oil dressing), fry the onion and mustard seeds, cumin seeds and chillies in the oil. Reduce the heat, place the aubergines in the baghaar and stir gently. Stir in the tamarind paste and the remaining water and cook over a medium heat for 15–20 minutes. Add the coriander and chopped chilli.

6 When cool, transfer to a serving dish and serve garnished with the hard-boiled eggs.

Vegetable & Nut Samosas

These delicious little fried pastries are really quite simple to make. Serve them hot or cold as a starter to an Indian meal.

NUTRITIONAL INFORMATION

Calories 343	Sugars 2g	
Protein 5g	Fat 26g	
Carbohydrate ...24g	Saturates 5g	

30 mins   40 mins

MAKES 12

INGREDIENTS

350 g/12 oz potatoes, diced

salt

125 g/4½ oz frozen peas

3 tbsp vegetable oil

1 onion, chopped

2.5 cm/1 inch piece of fresh root ginger, chopped

1 garlic clove, crushed

1 tsp garam masala

2 tsp mild curry paste

½ tsp cumin seeds

2 tsp lemon juice

60 g/2 oz unsalted cashews, coarsely chopped

vegetable oil, for shallow frying

fresh coriander sprigs, to garnish

mango chutney, to serve

PASTRY

225 g/8 oz plain flour

60 g/2 oz butter

6 tbsp warm milk

1 Cook the potatoes in a saucepan of boiling, salted water for 5 minutes. Add the peas and cook for a further 4 minutes, or until the potatoes are tender. Drain well. Heat the oil in a frying pan and fry the onion, the potato and pea mixture and the ginger, garlic and spices for 2 minutes. Stir in the lemon juice and cook gently, uncovered, for 2 minutes. Remove from the heat, slightly mash the potato and peas, then add the cashews, mix well and season with salt.

2 To make the pastry, put the flour in a bowl and rub in the butter. Mix in the milk to form a dough. Knead lightly and divide into 6 portions. Form each into a ball and roll out to an 18 cm/7 inch round. Cut each one in half.

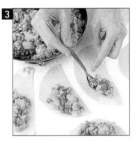

3 Divide the filling equally between the semi-circles of pastry, spreading it out to within 5 mm/¼ inch of the edges. Brush the edges of pastry all the way round with water and fold over to form triangular shapes, sealing the edges well together to enclose the filling completely.

4 Heat the vegetable oil in a frying pan to 180°C/350°F or until a cube of bread browns in 30 seconds. Fry the samosas, a few at a time, turning frequently until golden brown and heated through. Drain on kitchen paper and keep warm while cooking the remainder. Garnish with coriander sprigs and serve hot, with mango chutney.

Vegetable-topped Muffins

Roasted vegetables are delicious and attractive. Served on warm muffins with a herb sauce, they are unbeatable.

NUTRITIONAL INFORMATION

Calories 740	Sugars 27g
Protein 20g	Fat 45g
Carbohydrate ...67g	Saturates 17g

 1¼ hrs   35 mins

SERVES 4

INGREDIENTS

1 red onion, cut into 8 wedges

1 aubergine, halved and sliced

1 yellow pepper, deseeded and sliced

1 courgette, sliced

4 tbsp olive oil

1 tbsp garlic vinegar

2 tbsp vermouth

2 garlic cloves, crushed

1 tbsp chopped fresh thyme

2 tsp light brown sugar

4 muffins

SAUCE

2 tbsp butter

1 tbsp plain flour

150 ml/5 fl oz milk

5 tbsp vegetable stock

85 g/3 oz Cheddar cheese, grated

1 tsp wholegrain mustard

3 tbsp chopped fresh mixed herbs

salt and pepper

and sugar and pour over the vegetables, turning to coat well. Set aside to marinate for 1 hour.

2 Transfer the vegetables to a baking sheet. Roast in a preheated oven, 200°C/400°F/Gas Mark 6, for about 20–25 minutes or until the vegetables have softened.

3 Meanwhile, make the sauce. Melt the butter in a small pan and stir in the flour. Cook, stirring constantly, for

1 minute, then remove from the heat. Gradually stir in the milk and stock and return the pan to the heat. Bring to the boil, stirring constantly until thickened. Stir in the cheese, mustard and mixed herbs and season well.

4 Cut the muffins in half and toast under a preheated grill for 2–3 minutes until golden brown, then transfer to a serving plate. Spoon the roasted vegetables on to the muffins and pour the sauce over the top. Serve immediately.

1 Arrange the onion, aubergine, yellow pepper and courgette in a shallow non-metallic dish. Mix together the olive oil, garlic vinegar, vermouth, garlic, thyme

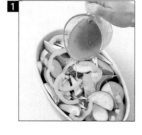

Bruschetta

Traditionally, this Italian savoury is enriched with olive oil. Here, sun-dried tomatoes are a good substitute and only a little oil is used.

NUTRITIONAL INFORMATION

Calories 178	Sugars 2g	
Protein 8g	Fat 6g	
Carbohydrate . . .24g	Saturates 2g	

45 mins   5 mins

SERVES 4

INGREDIENTS

60 g/2 oz dry-pack sun-dried tomatoes

300 ml/½ pint boiling water

35 cm/14 inch long granary or wholemeal stick of French bread

1 large garlic clove, halved

25 g/1 oz black olives in brine, stoned, drained and quartered

2 tsp olive oil

salt and pepper

2 tbsp chopped fresh basil

40 g/1½ oz low-fat mozzarella cheese, grated

fresh basil leaves, to garnish

1 Place the sun-dried tomatoes in a heatproof bowl and pour over the boiling water.

2 Set aside for 30 minutes to allow the tomatoes to soften. Drain well and pat dry with kitchen paper. Slice into thin strips and set aside.

3 Trim and discard the ends from the bread and cut into 12 slices. Arrange on a grill rack and place under a preheated hot grill and cook for 1–2 minutes on each side until lightly golden.

4 Rub both sides of each piece of bread with the cut sides of the garlic. Top with strips of sun-dried tomato and olives.

5 Brush lightly with olive oil and season well. Sprinkle with the basil and mozzarella cheese and return to the grill for 1–2 minutes until the cheese is melted and bubbling.

6 Transfer to a warmed serving platter and garnish with fresh basil leaves.

COOK'S TIP
If you use sun-dried tomatoes packed in oil, drain them, rinse well in warm water and drain again on kitchen paper to remove as much oil as possible. Sun-dried tomatoes give a rich, full flavour to this dish, but thinly sliced fresh tomatoes can be used instead.

Dressed Artichoke Hearts

Artichoke hearts are truly a luxury and taste superb with this warm, nutty dressing. Use the leaves on another occasion, served with citrus vinaigrette.

NUTRITIONAL INFORMATION

Calories 287   Sugars 2g
Protein ....7g   Fat 18g
Carbohydrate ...14g   Saturates 2g

 15 mins   45 mins

SERVES 4

INGREDIENTS

250 g/9 oz mixed salad leaves, such as lollo rosso, escarole and lamb's lettuce

6 tbsp lemon juice

4 globe artichokes

5 tbsp Calvados

1 shallot, very finely chopped

1 tbsp red wine vinegar

3 tbsp walnut oil

salt and pepper

TO GARNISH

55 g/2 oz shelled walnuts, chopped

1 tbsp finely chopped fresh parsley

VARIATION

This recipe also works well with good quality canned or bottled artichoke hearts. Drain and rinse well before using.

1 Place the salad leaves in a bowl and set aside. Fill a bowl with cold water and add 2 tablespoons of the lemon juice. Prepare the artichokes one at a time. Twist off the artichoke stalk, cut the base flat and pull off all the dark outer leaves. Slice the artichoke in half horizontally and discard the top part. Trim around the base to remove the outer dark green layer and place in the acidulated water while you prepare the remainder.

2 Bring a large pan of water to the boil, add the remaining lemon juice, and cook the artichoke bases, covered, for 30–40 minutes or until tender. Drain, refresh under cold water and drain again. Pull off the remaining leaves and scoop out and discard the chokes. Set the artichoke hearts aside.

3 Pour the Calvados into a small saucepan, add the shallot and a pinch of salt and bring to just below boiling point. Lower the heat, carefully ignite the Calvados and continue to cook until the flames have died down. Stir in the vinegar and oil and cook, stirring constantly, for 1 minute. Remove the pan from the heat.

4 Spoon half the dressing over the salad leaves and toss well to coat. Transfer the salad leaves to a serving platter and top with the artichoke hearts. Spoon the remaining dressing over the artichoke hearts, garnish with the walnuts and parsley and serve immediately.

Dolmades

Start a Greek meal with these delicious vine leaves with a vegetarian stuffing of rice, currants, pine kernels and fresh herbs.

NUTRITIONAL INFORMATION

Calories	82	Sugars	.........2g
Protein	.........1g	Fat	...........7g
Carbohydrate	....5g	Saturates	.......1g

1¼ hrs   45 mins

SERVES 4

INGREDIENTS

225 g/8 oz vine leaves preserved in brine, about 40 in total

150 ml/5 fl oz olive oil

4 tbsp lemon juice

300 ml/10 fl oz water

lemon wedges, to serve

FILLING

115 g/4 oz long grain rice, not basmati

350 ml/12 fl oz water

55 g/2 oz currants

55 g/2 oz pine kernels, chopped

2 spring onions, very finely chopped

1 tbsp very finely chopped fresh coriander

1 tbsp very finely chopped fresh parsley

1 tbsp very finely chopped fresh dill

finely grated rind of ½ lemon

salt and pepper

1 Rinse the vine leaves under cold running water and place them in a heatproof bowl. Pour over enough boiling water to cover and set aside to soak for 5 minutes. Drain well.

2 Meanwhile, place the rice and water in a pan with a pinch of salt and bring to the boil. Lower the heat, cover and simmer for 10–12 minutes or until all the liquid is completely absorbed. Drain and set aside to cool.

3 Stir the currants, pine kernels, spring onions, coriander, parsley, dill and lemon rind into the cooled rice. Season to taste with salt and pepper.

4 Line the bottom of a large frying pan with 3 or 4 of the thickest vine leaves or with any that are torn.

5 Put a vine leaf on the work surface, vein side upwards, with the pointed end facing away from you. Put a small, compact roll of the rice stuffing at the base of the leaf. Fold up the bottom end of the leaf.

6 Fold in each side of the leaf to overlap in the centre. Roll up the leaf around the filling and squeeze lightly in your hand to shape and seal it. Continue this process with the remaining vine leaves and stuffing mixture.

7 Place the leaf rolls in a single layer in the pan, seam side down. Combine the olive oil, lemon juice and water and pour into the pan.

8 Fit a heatproof plate over the rolls and cover the pan. Simmer for 30 minutes, then remove the pan from the heat and set the stuffed vine leaves aside to cool in the liquid. Serve chilled with lemon wedges.

Cauliflower Roulade

A light-as-air mixture of eggs and vegetables produces a stylish vegetarian dish that can be enjoyed hot or cold.

NUTRITIONAL INFORMATION

Calories . . . . .271 Sugars 4g
Protein . . . . .15g Fat 20g
Carbohydrate . . . .7g Saturates 11g

 30 mins   40 mins

SERVES 4

I N G R E D I E N T S

1 small cauliflower, divided into florets

4 eggs, separated

90 g/3 oz Cheddar cheese, grated

60 g/2 oz cottage cheese

pinch of grated nutmeg

½ tsp mustard powder

salt and pepper

F I L L I N G

1 bunch watercress, trimmed

60 g/2 oz butter

25 g/1 oz flour

175 ml/6 fl oz natural yogurt

25 g/1 oz Cheddar cheese, grated

60 g/2 oz cottage cheese

1 Line a Swiss roll tin with baking paper.

2 Steam the cauliflower until just tender, then drain under cold water. Process the cauliflower in a food processor or chop and press through a sieve.

3 Beat the egg yolks, then stir in the cauliflower, 60 g/2 oz of the Cheddar and the cottage cheese. Season with nutmeg, mustard, and salt and pepper. Whisk the egg whites until stiff but not dry, then fold them in.

4 Spread the mixture evenly in the tin. Bake the roulade in a preheated oven, 190°C/375°F/Gas Mark 5, for about 20–25 minutes, until risen and golden.

5 Chop the watercress, reserving a few sprigs for garnish. Melt the butter in a small pan. Cook the watercress, stirring, for 3 minutes, until wilted. Blend in the flour, then stir in the yogurt and simmer for 2 minutes. Stir in the cheeses.

6 Turn out the roulade on to a damp tea towel covered with a fresh sheet of baking paper. Peel off the paper and leave for a minute to allow the steam to escape. Using the new sheet of baking parchment to help you, roll up the roulade, starting from one narrow end.

7 Unroll the roulade, spread the filling to within 2.5 cm/1 inch of the edges, and roll it up again. Transfer to a baking tray, sprinkle with the remaining Cheddar cheese and return it to the oven for 5 minutes. Serve immediately if serving hot, or allow to cool completely.

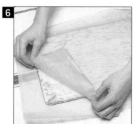

Sicilian Caramelised Onions

This is a typical Sicilian dish, combining honey and vinegar to give a delicate sweet and sour flavour. Serve hot as an accompaniment.

NUTRITIONAL INFORMATION

Calories 131	Sugars 11g	
Protein 2g	Fat 6g	
Carbohydrate ...19g	Saturates 1g	

🍲 2 mins   🕐 15 mins

SERVES 4

INGREDIENTS

350 g/12 oz baby or pickling onions

2 tbsp olive oil

2 fresh bay leaves, torn into strips

thinly pared rind of 1 lemon

1 tbsp soft brown sugar

1 tbsp clear honey

4 tbsp red wine vinegar

1 Soak the onions in a bowl of boiling water – this will make them easier to peel (see Cook's Tip). Using a sharp knife, peel and halve the onions.

2 Heat the oil in a large frying pan. Add the bay leaves and onions to the pan and cook for 5–6 minutes over a medium-high heat, or until the onions are browned all over.

3 Cut the lemon rind into thin matchsticks. Add to the frying pan with the sugar and honey. Cook for 2–3 minutes, stirring occasionally, until the onions are lightly caramelized.

4 Add the red wine vinegar to the frying pan, being careful because it will spit. Cook for about 5 minutes, stirring, or until the onions are tender and the liquid has all but disappeared.

5 Transfer the onions to a serving dish and serve at once.

COOK'S TIP
To make the onions easier to peel, place them in a large bowl, pour over boiling water and leave for 10 minutes. Drain the onions thoroughly, and when they are cool enough to handle, peel them.

Minted Onion Bhajis

Gram flour (also known as besan flour) is a fine yellow flour made from chick peas and is available from supermarkets and Asian food shops.

NUTRITIONAL INFORMATION

Calories 251	Sugars 7g
Protein 7g	Fat 8g
Carbohydrate . . .39g	Saturates 1g

 5 mins   15 mins

MAKES 12

INGREDIENTS

125 g/4½ oz gram flour

¼ tsp cayenne pepper

¼–½ tsp ground coriander

¼–½ tsp ground cumin

1 tbsp chopped fresh mint

4 tbsp Greek style yogurt

65 ml/2½ fl oz cold water

1 large onion, quartered and thinly sliced

vegetable oil, for frying

salt and pepper

sprigs of fresh mint, to garnish

1 Put the gram flour into a bowl, add the cayenne pepper, coriander, cumin and mint and season with salt and pepper to taste. Stir in the yogurt, water and sliced onion and mix well together.

2 One-third fill a large, deep frying pan with oil and heat until very hot. Drop heaped spoonfuls of the mixture, a few at a time, into the hot oil and use two forks to neaten the mixture into rough ball shapes.

3 Fry the bhajis until golden brown and cooked through, turning frequently.

4 Drain the bhajis thoroughly on absorbent kitchen paper and keep them warm while cooking the remainder in the same way.

5 Arrange the bhajis on a platter and garnish with sprigs of fresh mint. Serve hot or warm.

COOK'S TIP

Gram flour is excellent for making batter and is used in India in place of flour. It can be made from ground split peas as well as chick peas.

Roasted Cheese with Salsa

This delicious, warming Mexican dish is very satisfying – the salsa is cooked with the cheese for a wonderful mingling of textures.

NUTRITIONAL INFORMATION

Calories 476   Sugars 4g
Protein . . . . .23g   Fat 13g
Carbohydrate . . .70g   Saturates 7g

 15 mins   5–10 mins

SERVES 4

I N G R E D I E N T S

225 g/8 oz mozzarella cheese, fresh
   pecorino or Mexican queso Oaxaca

175 ml/6 fl oz salsa cruda, or other good
   salsa (see page 830)

½–1 onion, finely chopped

8 tortillas, to serve

1 To warm the tortillas ready for serving, heat a non-stick frying pan, add a tortilla and heat through, sprinkling with a few drops of water as it heats. Wrap in kitchen foil to keep warm. Repeat with the other tortillas.

2 Cut chunks or slabs of the cheese and arrange them in the bottom of a large, shallow ovenproof dish or in individual ovenproof dishes.

3 Spoon the salsa over the cheese to cover and place either in a preheated oven at 200°C/400°F/Gas Mark 6 or under a preheated grill. Cook until the cheese melts and bubbles, becoming lightly browned in places.

4 Sprinkle with chopped onion to taste and serve with the warmed tortillas for dipping. Serve immediately, as the melted cheese turns stringy when cold and becomes difficult to eat.

COOK'S TIP

Queso Oaxaca is the authentic cheese to use, but mozzarella or pecorino make excellent substitutes, since they produce the right effect when melted.

Frijoles

Beans take a starring role in both Mexican cuisine and vegetarian diets. This delicious recipe is known simply as frijoles, that is, beans.

NUTRITIONAL INFORMATION

Calories 213   Sugars 5g
Protein . . . . .14g   Fat 5g
Carbohydrate . . .31g   Saturates 1g

15 mins   2 hrs

SERVES 6

INGREDIENTS

350 g/12 oz dried red kidney beans, soaked in cold water for 3 hours

2 onions, chopped

2 garlic cloves, chopped

2 fresh green chillies, deseeded

1 bay leaf

2 tbsp corn oil

2 tomatoes

salt

1 Chop the chillies, skin and chop the tomatoes. Drain the beans and place in a large, heavy-based saucepan. Add sufficient cold water to cover by about 2.5 cm/1 inch. Add half the onion, half the garlic, the chillies and bay leaf. Bring to the boil and boil vigorously for 15 minutes,

then lower the heat and simmer for 30 minutes, adding more boiling water if the mixture begins to dry out.

2 Add 1 tablespoon of the oil and simmer for 30 minutes more, adding more boiling water if necessary. Season to taste with salt and simmer for another 30 minutes, but do not add any more water.

3 Meanwhile, heat the remaining oil in a frying pan. Add the remaining onion and garlic and cook, stirring occasionally, for 5 minutes, until softened. Stir in the tomatoes and cook for 5 minutes more. Add 3 tablespoons of the cooked beans to the tomato mixture, mash thoroughly to a paste and then stir the paste into the beans. Heat through gently, then serve.

COOK'S TIP

Some dried pulses, including red kidney beans, contain a toxin that is only destroyed by cooking. It is essential to boil the beans vigorously for 15 minutes, before simmering to finish cooking.

Mushroom Bites with Aïoli

These crispy morsels make delicious canapés and are wonderful warm snacks to serve at parties.

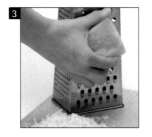

NUTRITIONAL INFORMATION

Calories	504	Sugars	.........1g
Protein	.........8g	Fat	.........46g
Carbohydrate	...15g	Saturates	.......8g

20 mins | 15 mins

SERVES 4

INGREDIENTS

115 g/4 oz fresh white breadcrumbs

2 tbsp freshly grated Parmesan cheese

1 tsp paprika

225 g/8 oz button mushrooms

2 egg whites

FOR THE AIOLI

4 garlic cloves, crushed

2 egg yolks

225 ml/8 fl oz extra virgin olive oil

salt and pepper

1 First make the aïoli. Put the garlic in a bowl, add a pinch of salt and mash with the back of a spoon. Add the egg yolks and beat with a whisk for 30 seconds until creamy. Beat in the oil, one drop at a time. As the mixture begins to thicken, add the oil in a steady stream, beating constantly.

2 Season the aïoli to taste with salt and pepper, cover the bowl with clingfilm and chill in the refrigerator until required.

3 Grate the Parmesan and lightly whisk the egg whites. Combine the bread-crumbs, Parmesan and paprika in a bowl. Dip each mushroom into the egg whites then into the breadcrumbs. Place on a baking sheet lined with baking paper.

4 Bake in a preheated oven, 190°C/375°F/Gas Mark 5, for 15 minutes, until the coating is crisp and golden. Serve immediately with the aïoli.

VARIATION
Instead of aïoli, serve the mushrooms with a herb cream. Combine 4 tbsp chopped, mixed fresh herbs with 200 ml/7 fl oz soured cream or crème fraîche, 1 finely chopped garlic clove and 1 tbsp lemon juice. Season to taste with salt and pepper.

Antipasto Mushrooms

Traditionally, porcini mushrooms, also known as ceps, would be used for this dish, but you can make it with any of your favourite varieties.

NUTRITIONAL INFORMATION

Calories 413   Sugars 2g
Protein . . . . .3g   Fat 9g
Carbohydrate . . . .2g   Saturates 1g

10 mins, plus cooling   30 mins

SERVES 4

INGREDIENTS

225 g/8 oz tomatoes

3 tbsp olive oil

2 garlic cloves, finely chopped

1 tbsp finely chopped fresh oregano

salt and pepper

500 g /1 lb 2 oz porcini or other mushrooms

fresh flat-leaved parsley sprigs, to garnish

1 Skin, deseed and chop the tomatoes. Heat 1 tablespoon of the oil in a saucepan, add the garlic and cook over a low heat for 1 minute, stirring constantly. Add the tomatoes and oregano and season to taste with salt and pepper. Continue to cook over a low heat, stirring frequently, for about 20 minutes, or until pulpy and thickened.

2 Meanwhile, thinly slice the mushrooms. Heat the remaining oil in a frying pan. Add the mushrooms and cook over a medium heat, stirring frequently, for about 5 minutes, or until tender. Stir the mushrooms into the tomato mixture and season with salt. Lower the heat, cover and simmer for 10 minutes more.

3 Transfer the mushroom mixture to a bowl and set aside to cool. Serve the dish at room temperature, garnished with flat-leaved parsley.

COOK'S TIP

Try to find sun-ripened tomatoes for this dish as they have a sweeter, fuller flavour than those ripened under glass.

Cheese & Bean Quesadillas

These bite-size rolls are made from flour tortillas filled with a scrumptious mixture of refried beans, melted cheese, coriander and salsa.

NUTRITIONAL INFORMATION

Calories	452	Sugars	........11g
Protein	........18g	Fat	..........16g
Carbohydrate	...62g	Saturates	.......7g

  10 mins 10 mins

SERVES 4–6

INGREDIENTS

400 g/14 oz canned refried beans

8 flour tortillas

200 g/7 oz Cheddar cheese, grated

1 onion, chopped

½ bunch of fresh coriander leaves, chopped

8 tbsp Salsa Cruda (see page 830)

1 Place the beans in a small pan and set over a low heat to warm through.

2 Meanwhile, make the tortillas pliable by warming them gently in a lightly greased non-stick frying pan.

3 Remove the tortillas from the pan and quickly spread with a layer of warm beans. Top each tortilla with grated cheese, onion, fresh coriander and a spoonful of salsa. Roll up tightly.

4 Just before serving, heat the non-stick frying pan over a medium heat, sprinkling lightly with a couple of drops of water. Add the tortilla rolls, cover the pan and heat through until the cheese melts. Allow to brown lightly, if wished.

5 Remove the tortilla rolls from the pan and slice each roll, on the diagonal, into about 4 bite-size pieces. Serve the quesadillas at once.

Vegetables with Tahini Dip

This tasty dip is great for livening up simply cooked vegetables.
You can vary the vegetables according to the season.

NUTRITIONAL INFORMATION

Calories 126   Sugars 7g
Protein ....11g   Fat 6g
Carbohydrate ....8g   Saturates 1g

  5 mins   20 mins

SERVES 4

INGREDIENTS

225 g/8 oz small broccoli florets

225 g/8 oz small cauliflower florets

225 g/8 oz asparagus, sliced into
   5 cm/2 inch lengths

2 small red onions, quartered

1 tbsp lime juice

2 tsp toasted sesame seeds

1 tbsp chopped fresh chives, to garnish

HOT TAHINI DIP

1 tsp sunflower oil

2 garlic cloves, crushed

½–1 tsp chilli powder

salt and pepper

2 tsp tahini

150 ml/5 fl oz low-fat natural fromage frais

2 tbsp chopped fresh chives

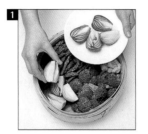

1 Line the base of a steamer with baking parchment and arrange the broccoli florets, cauliflower florets, asparagus and onion pieces on top.

2 Bring a wok or a large saucepan of water to the boil, and place the steamer on the top. Sprinkle the vegetables with lime juice for extra flavour and steam for 10 minutes until they are just tender.

3 Meanwhile, make the dip. Heat the oil in a small non-stick saucepan, add the garlic, chilli powder and seasoning to taste and fry gently for 2–3 minutes until the garlic is softened.

4 Remove the saucepan from the heat and stir in the tahini and fromage frais. Return the pan to the heat and cook gently for 1–2 minutes without boiling. Stir in the chopped chives.

5 Remove the vegetables from the steamer and arrange them on a warmed serving platter.

6 Sprinkle the vegetables with the sesame seeds and garnish with chopped chives. Serve with the hot dip.

Gazpacho Water Ice

Try serving this refreshing appetizer at a dinner party – it's certain to impress and contains virtually no fat.

NUTRITIONAL INFORMATION

Calories 33	Sugars 6g
Protein 1g	Fat 1g
Carbohydrate 6g	Saturates 0.2g

 5½ hrs   0 mins

SERVES 4

INGREDIENTS

500 g/1 lb 2 oz tomatoes

about 600 ml/1 pint boiling water

4 spring onions, chopped

2 celery sticks, chopped

1 small red pepper, deseeded and chopped

1 garlic clove, crushed

1 tbsp tomato purée

1 tbsp chopped fresh parsley

salt and pepper

fresh parsley sprigs, to garnish

TO SERVE

shredded iceberg lettuce

bread sticks

1 Prick the skin of the tomatoes with a fork at the stalk end and place in a large heatproof bowl. Pour over enough boiling water to cover them. Leave for 5–10 minutes. After this time, the skin should start peeling away from the flesh.

2 Skewer the tomatoes with a fork and peel away the skin. Slice the tomatoes in half, scoop out the seeds and discard. Chop the flesh.

3 Place the chopped tomatoes, spring onions, celery, pepper, garlic and tomato purée in a food processor or blender. Blend for a few seconds until smooth. Alternatively, finely chop or mince the vegetables then mix with the tomato purée. Pour into a freezerproof container and freeze until firm.

4 Remove from the freezer and leave at room temperature for 30 minutes. Break up with a fork and place in a blender or food processor. Blend for a few seconds to break up the ice crystals and form a smooth mixture. Alternatively, beat with a wooden spoon until smooth.

5 Transfer the mixture to a mixing bowl and stir in the parsley and seasoning. Return to the freezer container and freeze for a further 30 minutes. Fork through the water ice again and serve immediately, garnished with parsley, with shredded iceberg lettuce and bread sticks.

Potato & Bean Pâté

This pâté is easy to prepare and may be stored in the refrigerator for up to two days. Serve with small toasts; Melba toast or crudités.

NUTRITIONAL INFORMATION

Calories 84   Sugars 3g
Protein . . . . .5.1g   Fat 0.5g
Carbohydrate . .15.7g   Saturates 0.1g

 3 mins   10 mins

SERVES 4

INGREDIENTS

100 g/3½ oz floury potatoes, diced

225 g/8 oz mixed canned beans, such as borlotti, flageolet and kidney beans, drained

1 garlic clove, crushed

2 tsp lime juice

1 tbsp chopped fresh coriander

salt and pepper

2 tbsp natural yogurt

chopped fresh coriander, to garnish

COOK'S TIP
To make Melba toast, toast sliced white or brown bread lightly on both sides under a pre-heated high grill and remove the crusts. Split the toasted bread through horizontally with a sharp knife. Cut into triangles and toast the untoasted sides.

1 Cook the potatoes in a saucepan of boiling water for 10 minutes until tender. Drain well and mash.

2 Transfer the potato to a food processor or blender and add the beans, garlic, lime juice and the fresh coriander. Season the mixture and process for 1 minute to make a smooth purée. Alternatively, mix the beans with the potato, garlic, lime juice and coriander and mash well.

3 Turn the purée into a bowl and add the yogurt. Mix together thoroughly.

4 Spoon the pâté into a serving dish and garnish with the chopped coriander. Serve at once or cover with clingfilm and leave to chill before use.

Potato Skins with Guacamole

Although avocados do contain fat, if they are used in small quantities you can still enjoy their creamy texture.

NUTRITIONAL INFORMATION

Calories 399	Sugars 4g
Protein 10g	Fat 15g
Carbohydrate ...59g	Saturates 4g

45 mins   1¾ hrs

SERVES 4

INGREDIENTS

4 x 225g/8 oz baking potatoes

2 tsp olive oil

sea salt and pepper

chopped fresh chives, to garnish

GUACAMOLE DIP

175 g/6 oz ripe avocado

1 tbsp lemon juice

2 ripe, firm tomatoes, finely chopped

1 tsp grated lemon rind

100 g/3½ oz low-fat soft cheese with herbs and garlic

4 spring onions, finely chopped

a few drops of Tabasco sauce

salt and pepper

1 Bake the potatoes in a preheated oven at 200°C/400°F/Gas Mark 6 for 1¼ hours. Remove from the oven and allow to cool for 30 minutes. Reset the oven to 220°C/425°F/Gas Mark 7.

2 Halve the potatoes lengthways and scoop out 2 tbsp of the flesh, then slice lengthways in half again. Place on a baking tray and brush the flesh side lightly with oil. Sprinkle with salt and pepper. Bake for a further 25 minutes until the potatoes are golden and crisp.

3 To make the guacamole dip, mash the avocado with the lemon juice. Add the remaining ingredients and mix.

4 Drain the potato skins on paper towels and transfer to a warmed serving platter. Garnish with chives. Pile the avocado mixture into a serving bowl.

COOK'S TIP
Mash the left-over potato flesh with natural yogurt and seasoning, and serve as an accompaniment.

Marinated Fennel

Fennel has a wonderful aniseed flavour which is ideal for grilling or barbecuing. This marinated recipe is really delicious.

NUTRITIONAL INFORMATION

Calories	117	Sugars	.........3g
Protein	.........1g	Fat	...........11g
Carbohydrate	....3g	Saturates	.......2g

🥘

🍖 1¼ hrs   🕐 10 mins

SERVES 4

INGREDIENTS

2 fennel bulbs

1 red pepper, deseeded and cut into large dice

1 lime, cut into 8 wedges

MARINADE

2 tbsp lime juice

4 tbsp olive oil

2 garlic cloves, crushed

1 tsp wholegrain mustard

1 tbsp chopped thyme

fennel fronds, to garnish

crisp salad, to serve

1 Cut off and reserve the fennel fronds for the garnish. Cut each of the bulbs into 8 pieces and place in a shallow dish. Add the pepper and mix well.

2 To make the marinade, combine the lime juice, olive oil, garlic, mustard and thyme. Pour the marinade over the fennel and pepper and toss to coat thoroughly. Cover with clingfilm and set aside to marinate for 1 hour.

3 Thread the fennel and pepper on to wooden skewers with the lime wedges. Cook the kebabs under a preheated medium grill, turning and basting frequently with the marinade, for about 10 minutes. Alternatively, cook on a medium hot barbecue, turning and basting frequently, for about 10 minutes.

4 Transfer the kebabs to serving plates, garnish with fennel fronds and serve immediately with a crisp salad.

COOK'S TIP

Soak the skewers in cold water for 20 minutes before using to prevent them from burning during grilling. You could substitute 2 tablespoons orange juice for the lime juice and add 1 tbsp honey, if you prefer.

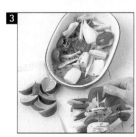

Rosy Melon & Strawberries

The combination of sweet melon and strawberries macerated in rosé wine and a hint of rosewater is a delightful start to a special meal.

NUTRITIONAL INFORMATION

Calories	85	Sugars	14g
Protein	2g	Fat	0g
Carbohydrate	14g	Saturates	0g

10 mins, plus chilling

0 mins

SERVES 4

INGREDIENTS

¼ honeydew melon

½ Charentais or Cantaloupe melon

150 ml/5 fl oz rosé wine

2–3 tsp rosewater

175 g/6 oz small strawberries, washed and hulled

rose petals, to garnish

1 Scoop out the seeds from both melons with a spoon. Then carefully remove the skin, taking care not to remove too much flesh.

2 Cut the melon flesh into thin strips and place in a bowl. Pour over the wine and sufficient rosewater to taste. Stir the melon and the liquid together gently to combine, cover and leave to chill in the refrigerator for at least 2 hours.

3 Halve the strawberries and carefully mix them into the macerated melon. Allow the melon and strawberries to stand at room temperature for about 15 minutes for the flavours to develop before serving – if the melon is too cold, there will be little flavour.

4 Arrange the melon and strawberries on individual serving plates and serve sprinkled with a few rose petals.

COOK'S TIP

Rosewater is generally available from pharmacies and supermarkets as well as from specialist food suppliers.

Paprika Crisps

These wafer-thin potato crisps are great cooked over a barbecue and served with spicy vegetable kebabs.

NUTRITIONAL INFORMATION

Calories 149   Sugars 0.6g
Protein ....2g   Fat 8g
Carbohydrate ...17g   Saturates 1g

5 mins   25 mins

SERVES 4

INGREDIENTS

2 large potatoes

3 tbsp olive oil

½ tsp paprika

salt

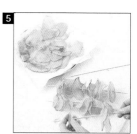

 1 Using a sharp knife, slice the potatoes very thinly so that they are almost transparent. Drain the potato slices thoroughly and pat dry with kitchen paper.

 2 Heat the oil in a large frying pan and add the paprika, stirring constantly to ensure that the paprika doesn't catch and burn.

3 Add the potato slices to the frying pan and cook them in a single layer for about 5 minutes or until the potato slices just begin to curl slightly at the edges.

4 Remove the potato slices from the pan using a slotted spoon and transfer them to kitchen paper to drain thoroughly.

5 Thread the potato slices on to several wooden kebab skewers.

6 Sprinkle the potato slices with a little salt and cook over a medium hot barbecue or under a medium grill, turning frequently, for 10 minutes, until the potato slices begin to go crisp. Sprinkle with a little more salt, if preferred, and serve immediately.

VARIATION

You could use curry powder or any other spice to flavour the crisps instead of the paprika, if you prefer.

Vegetarian Spring Rolls

These crisp little spring rolls are bursting with texture and flavour.
They are excellent served as an appetiser before a Chinese meal.

NUTRITIONAL INFORMATION

Calories	491	Sugars	2g
Protein	7g	Fat	34g
Carbohydrate	40g	Saturates	7g

20 mins   20 mins

SERVES 4

INGREDIENTS

25 g/1 oz fine cellophane noodles

2 tbsp groundnut oil

2 garlic cloves, crushed

½ tsp grated fresh root ginger

55 g/2 oz oyster mushrooms, thinly sliced

2 spring onions, finely chopped

50g/1¾ oz beansprouts

1 small carrot, finely shredded

½ tsp sesame oil

1 tbsp light soy sauce

1 tbsp rice wine or dry sherry

¼ tsp pepper

1 tbsp chopped fresh coriander

1 tbsp chopped fresh mint

24 spring-roll wrappers

½ tsp cornflour

groundnut oil, for deep-frying

fresh mint sprigs, to garnish

2 Heat the groundnut oil in a wok or wide pan over a high heat. Add the garlic, ginger, oyster mushrooms, spring onions, beansprouts and carrot and stir-fry for about 1 minute until just softened.

3 Stir in the sesame oil, soy sauce, rice wine, pepper, chopped coriander and mint, then remove the pan from the heat. Stir in the rice noodles.

4 Arrange the spring-roll wrappers on a work surface, pointing diagonally. Mix the cornflour with 1 tablespoon water to a smooth paste and brush the edges of 1 wrapper with it. Spoon a little filling on to the pointed side of the same wrapper.

5 Roll the point of the wrapper over the filling, then fold the side points inwards over the filling. Continue to roll up the wrapper away from you, moistening the tip with a little more cornflour paste to secure the roll.

6 Heat the oil in a wok or deep frying pan to 180°C/350°F or until a cube of bread browns in 30 seconds. Add the rolls, in batches, and deep-fry for 2–3 minutes each until golden and crisp.

1 Place the noodles in a heatproof bowl, pour over enough boiling water to cover and leave them to stand for 4 minutes. Drain, rinse in cold water, then drain again. Cut or snip the noodles into 5 cm/2 inch lengths.

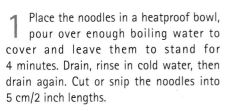 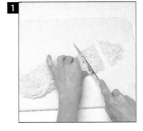  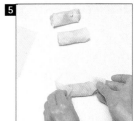

Imam Bayildi

In this Turkish dish, aubergine halves are baked with a deliciously aromatic topping of tomatoes and green pepper, and served chilled.

NUTRITIONAL INFORMATION

Calories	.207	Sugars	.2g
Protein	.3g	Fat	.12g
Carbohydrate	.23g	Saturates	.2g

  15 mins, plus standing and chilling · 45 mins

SERVES 4

INGREDIENTS

2 aubergines

4 tbsp olive oil

2 onions, thinly sliced

2 garlic cloves, finely chopped

1 green pepper, deseeded and sliced

400 g/14 oz canned chopped tomatoes

3 tbsp sugar

1 tsp ground coriander

salt and pepper

2 tbsp chopped fresh coriander

COOK'S TIP

Even after salting, aubergines tend to absorb a lot of oil, so you may need to add a little more before cooking the onions in step 2.

1 Slice the aubergines in half lengthways. Slash the flesh 4 or 5 times and sprinkle with salt. Place in a colander and set aside for 30 minutes. Rinse and pat dry.

2 Heat the oil in a large, heavy-based frying pan. Add the aubergines, cut side down, and cook for 5 minutes. Drain well and place in a casserole. Add the onions, garlic and green pepper to the frying pan and cook, stirring occasionally,

for 10 minutes. Add the tomatoes, sugar and ground coriander and season to taste with salt and pepper. Stir in the chopped fresh coriander.

3 Spoon the onion and tomato mixture on top of the aubergine halves, cover and bake in a preheated oven, 190°C/350°F/Gas Mark 5, for 30 minutes. Remove from the oven and set aside to cool, then chill for 1 hour before serving.

Crispy Wontons

Mushroom-filled crispy wontons are served on skewers with a dipping sauce flavoured with chillies.

NUTRITIONAL INFORMATION

Calories	302	Sugars	.........1g
Protein	.........3g	Fat	25
Carbohydrate	...15g	Saturates	.......6g

 45 mins   20 mins

SERVES 4

INGREDIENTS

8 wooden skewers, soaked in cold water
    for 30 minutes

1 tbsp vegetable oil

1 tbsp chopped onion

1 small garlic clove, chopped

½ tsp chopped fresh root ginger

60 g/2 oz flat mushrooms, chopped

salt

16 wonton skins (see page 113)

vegetable oil, for deep-frying

SAUCE

2 tbsp vegetable oil

2 spring onions, thinly shredded

1 red and 1 green chilli, deseeded and
    thinly shredded

3 tbsp light soy sauce

1 tbsp vinegar

1 tbsp dry sherry

pinch of sugar

1 Heat the vegetable oil in a preheated wok or frying pan.

2 Add the onion, garlic and ginger root to the wok or pan and stir-fry for 2 minutes. Stir in the mushrooms and fry for a further 2 minutes. Season well with salt and leave to cool.

3 Place 1 teaspoon of the cooled mushroom filling in the centre of each wonton skin.

4 Bring two opposite corners of each wonton skin together to cover the mixture and pinch together to seal. Repeat with the remaining corners.

5 Thread 2 wontons on to each skewer. Heat enough oil in a large saucepan to deep-fry the wontons in batches until golden and crisp. Do not overheat the oil or the wontons will brown on the outside before they are properly cooked inside.

Remove the wontons with a perforated spoon and drain thoroughly on absorbent kitchen paper.

6 To make the sauce, heat the vegetable oil in a small saucepan until quite hot or until a small cube of bread dropped in the oil browns in a few seconds. Put the spring onions and chillies in a bowl and pour the hot oil slowly on top. Mix in the remaining ingredients.

7 Transfer the crispy wontons to a serving dish and serve with the dipping sauce.

Gado Gado

This is a well-known and very popular Indonesian salad of mixed vegetables with a peanut dressing.

 10 mins   🕐 25 mins

SERVES 4

INGREDIENTS

100 g/3½ oz white cabbage, shredded

100 g/3½ oz French beans, cut into thirds

100 g/3½ oz carrots, cut into matchsticks

100 g/3½ oz cauliflower florets

100 g/3½ oz beansprouts

DRESSING

100 ml/3½ fl oz vegetable oil

100 g/3½ oz unsalted peanuts

2 garlic cloves, crushed

1 small onion, finely chopped

½ tsp chilli powder

½ tsp light brown sugar

salt

425 ml/¾ pint water

juice of ½ lemon

sliced spring onions, to garnish

1 Cook the vegetables separately in a saucepan of salted boiling water for 4–5 minutes, drain well and chill.

2 To make the dressing, heat the oil in a frying pan and fry the peanuts, tossing frequently, for 3–4 minutes.

3 Remove from the pan with a slotted spoon and drain on kitchen paper. Process in a food processor or crush with a rolling pin until a fine mixture is formed.

4 Leave 1 tablespoon of oil in the pan and fry the garlic and onion for 1 minute. Add the chilli powder, sugar, a pinch of salt and the water and boil.

5 Stir the peanuts into the sauce. Reduce the heat and simmer for 4–5 minutes, until the sauce thickens. Add the lemon juice and set aside to cool.

6 Arrange the vegetables in a serving dish and spoon the peanut dressing into the centre. Garnish with the sliced spring onions and serve.

Thai-spiced Aubergine

This tasty Thai dish is really simple to make, and is perfect served with an authentic spicy chilli dip.

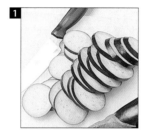  

NUTRITIONAL INFORMATION

Calories 169	Sugars 2g
Protein 2g	Fat 12g
Carbohydrate ...15g	Saturates 1g

35 mins | 20 mins

SERVES 4

INGREDIENTS

450 g/1 lb aubergines, wiped

1 egg white

50 g/1¾ oz cornflour

1 tsp salt

1 tbsp Thai seven-spice seasoning

oil, for deep-frying

1 Using a sharp knife, slice the aubergines into thin rings.

2 Place the egg white in a small bowl and whip until light and foamy.

3 Mix together the cornflour, salt and seven-spice seasoning on a large plate.

4 Heat the oil for deep-frying in a large wok.

5 Dip each piece of aubergine into the beaten egg white then coat in the cornflour and seven-spice mixture.

6 Deep-fry the coated aubergine slices, in batches, for 5 minutes, or until pale golden and crispy.

7 Transfer the aubergines to absorbent kitchen paper and leave to drain. Transfer to serving plates and serve hot.

Son-in-Law Eggs

This recipe is supposedly so called because it is an easy dish for a son-in-law to cook to impress his new mother-in-law!

NUTRITIONAL INFORMATION

Calories 229   Sugars 8g
Protein ....9g   Fat 18g
Carbohydrate ....8g   Saturates 3g

 15 mins   15 mins

SERVES 4

INGREDIENTS

6 eggs, hard-boiled and shelled

4 tbsp sunflower oil

1 onion, thinly sliced

2 fresh red chillies, deseeded and sliced

2 tbsp sugar

1 tbsp water

2 tsp tamarind pulp

1 tbsp liquid seasoning, such as Maggi

rice, to serve

1 Prick the hard-boiled eggs 2 or 3 times with a cocktail stick.

2 Heat the sunflower oil in a wok and fry the eggs until crispy and golden. Drain on absorbent kitchen paper.

3 Halve the eggs lengthways and put on a serving dish.

4 Reserve one tablespoon of the oil, pour off the rest, then heat the tablespoonful in the wok.

5 Cook the onion and chillies over a high heat until golden and slightly crisp. Drain on kitchen paper.

6 Heat the sugar, water, tamarind pulp (or lemon juice – see Cook's Tip) and liquid seasoning in the wok and simmer over a low heat for 5 minutes, until the mixture has thickened.

7 Pour the tamarind sauce over the eggs and spoon over the onion and chilli mix to garnish. Serve immediately with the rice.

COOK'S TIP

Tamarind pulp is sold in Oriental stores, and is quite sour. If it is not available, use twice the amount of lemon juice in its place.

Peppers & Rosemary

The flavour of grilled or roasted peppers is very different from when they are eaten raw, so do try them cooked in this way.

NUTRITIONAL INFORMATION

Calories 201   Sugars 6g
Protein . . . . .2g   Fat 19g
Carbohydrate . . . .6g   Saturates 2g

20 mins   10 mins

SERVES 4

I N G R E D I E N T S

4 tbsp olive oil

finely grated rind of 1 lemon

4 tbsp lemon juice

1 tbsp balsamic vinegar

1 tbsp crushed fresh rosemary,
   or 1 tsp dried rosemary

2 garlic cloves, crushed

salt and pepper

2 red peppers, halved and deseeded

2 yellow peppers, halved and deseeded

2 tbsp pine kernels

fresh rosemary sprigs, to garnish

1 Mix together the olive oil, lemon rind, lemon juice, balsamic vinegar, rosemary and garlic. Season with salt and pepper to taste.

2 Place the red and yellow peppers, skin side up, on the rack of a grill pan, lined with foil. Brush the olive oil mixture over them.

3 Grill the peppers for 3–4 minutes or until the skin begins to char, basting frequently with the olive oil mixture. Remove from the heat, cover with foil to trap the steam and leave for 5 minutes.

4 Meanwhile, scatter the pine kernels on to the grill pan and toast them lightly for 2–3 minutes. Keep a close eye on them, as they tend to burn very quickly.

5 Peel the peppers, slice into strips and place in a warmed serving dish. Sprinkle with the pine kernels and drizzle over any remaining olive oil mixture. Garnish with rosemary sprigs and serve.

COOK'S TIP
A combination of red and yellow peppers looks attractive, but you could use all one colour or substitute an orange pepper. Green peppers, however, are not really sweet enough for this dish.

Little Golden Parcels

These little parcels will draw admiring gasps from your guests, but they are fairly simple to prepare.

NUTRITIONAL INFORMATION

Calories . . . . . . .320 Sugars 1g
Protein . . . . .6g Fat 21g
Carbohydrate . . .28g Saturates 5g

35 mins   35 mins

SERVES 4

INGREDIENTS

1 garlic clove, crushed

1 tsp chopped coriander root

1 tsp pepper

250 g/9 oz boiled mashed potato

175 g/6 oz water chestnuts, finely chopped

1 tsp grated fresh root ginger

2 tbsp ground dry-roasted peanuts

2 tsp light soy sauce

½ tsp salt

½ tsp sugar

30 wonton sheets, defrosted

1 tsp cornflour, made into a paste with a little water

vegetable oil, for deep-frying

fresh chives, to garnish

sweet chilli sauce, to serve

VARIATION

If wonton sheets are not available, use spring-roll sheets or filo pastry, and cut the large squares down to about 10 cm/ 4 inches square.

1 Mix together all the ingredients except the wonton sheets, cornflour paste and vegetable oil.

2 Keeping the remainder of the wonton sheets covered with a damp cloth to prevent them drying out, lay 4 sheets out on a work surface. Put a teaspoonful of the mixture on each. Make a line of the cornflour paste around each sheet, about 1 cm/½ inch from the edge.

3 Bring all four corners to the centre and press together to form little bags. Repeat with all the wonton sheets.

4 Heat 5 cm/2 inches of oil in a pan until a light haze appears on top and fry the parcels, in batches of 3, until golden brown. Remove and drain on kitchen paper. Tie a chive around the neck of each bag to garnish, and serve with sweet chilli sauce for dipping.

Money Bags

These traditional steamed dumplings can be eaten on their own or dipped in a mixture of soy sauce, sherry and slivers of ginger root.

NUTRITIONAL INFORMATION

Calories 315   Sugars 3g
Protein . . . . .8g   Fat 8g
Carbohydrate . . .56g   Saturates 1g

 45 mins   20 mins

SERVES 4

INGREDIENTS

3 Chinese dried mushrooms (if unavailable, use thinly sliced open-cup mushrooms)

250 g/9 oz plain flour

1 egg, beaten

75 ml/3 fl oz water

1 tsp baking powder

¾ tsp salt

2 tbsp vegetable oil

2 spring onions, chopped

90 g/3 oz sweetcorn kernels

½ red chilli, deseeded and chopped

1 tbsp brown bean sauce

1 Place the dried mushrooms in a small bowl, cover with warm water and leave to soak for 20–25 minutes.

2 To make the wrappers, sift the plain flour into a bowl. Add the beaten egg and mix in lightly. Stir in the water, baking powder and salt, and mix together to make a soft dough.

3 Knead the dough lightly on a floured board. Cover with a damp tea towel and set aside for 5–6 minutes. This allows the baking powder time to activate, so that the dumplings swell when steaming.

4 Drain the mushrooms, squeezing them dry. Remove the tough centres and chop the mushrooms.

5 Heat the vegetable oil in a wok or large frying pan and stir-fry the mushrooms, spring onions, sweetcorn and chilli for 2 minutes.

6 Stir in the brown bean sauce and remove from the heat.

7 Roll the dough into a large sausage and cut into 24 even-sized pieces. Roll each piece out into a thin round and place a teaspoonful of the filling in the centre. Gather up the edges to a point, pinch together and twist to seal.

8 Stand the dumplings in an oiled steaming basket. Place over a saucepan of simmering water, cover and steam for 12–14 minutes before serving.

Lentil Balls with Sauce

Crisp golden lentil balls are served in a sweet and sour sauce with peppers and pineapple chunks.

NUTRITIONAL INFORMATION

Calories 384	Sugars 15g
Protein 17g	Fat 14g
Carbohydrate ...49g	Saturates 2g

 15 mins 35 mins

SERVES 4

I N G R E D I E N T S

250 g/9 oz red lentils

425 ml/¾ pint water

½ green chilli, deseeded and chopped

4 spring onions, finely chopped

1 garlic clove, crushed

1 tsp salt

4 tbsp canned pineapple juice

1 egg, beaten

vegetable oil, for deep-frying

rice or noodles, to serve

S A U C E

3 tbsp white wine vinegar

2 tbsp sugar

2 tbsp tomato purée

1 tsp sesame oil

1 tsp cornflour

½ tsp salt

6 tbsp water

2 tbsp vegetable oil

½ red pepper, deseeded and cut into chunks

½ green pepper, deseeded and cut into chunks

2 canned pineapple rings, cut into chunks

1 Wash the lentils, then place them in a saucepan with the water and bring to the boil. Skim and boil rapidly for 10 minutes, uncovered. Reduce the heat to low and cook the lentils for a further 5 minutes, stirring occasionally, until you have a fairly dry mixture.

2 Remove the pan from the heat and stir in the chilli, spring onions, garlic, salt and pineapple juice. Leave to cool for 10 minutes.

3 To make the sauce, mix together the vinegar, sugar, tomato purée, sesame oil, cornflour, salt and water, and set aside.

4 Add the beaten egg to the lentil mixture. Heat the oil in a large pan or wok and deep-fry tablespoonfuls of the mixture in batches until crisp and golden. Remove with a perforated spoon and drain on kitchen paper.

5 Heat the 2 tablespoons of oil in a wok or frying pan. Stir-fry the peppers for 2 minutes. Add the sauce mixture with the pineapple chunks. Bring to the boil, then reduce the heat and simmer for 1 minute, stirring constantly, until the sauce has thickened. Add the lentil balls and heat thoroughly, taking care not to break them up. Serve with rice or noodles.

Deep-fried Chilli Corn Balls

These small corn balls have a wonderful hot and sweet flavour, offset by the pungent coriander.

NUTRITIONAL INFORMATION

Calories	248	Sugars	.........6g
Protein	.........6g	Fat	12
Carbohydrate	...30g	Saturates	.......5g

 15 mins   30 mins

SERVES 4

I N G R E D I E N T S

6 spring onions, sliced

3 tbsp fresh coriander, chopped

225 g/8 oz canned sweetcorn kernels, drained

1 tsp mild chilli powder

1 tbsp sweet chilli sauce

25 g/1 oz desiccated coconut

1 egg

75 g/2¾ oz polenta

oil, for deep-frying

extra-sweet chilli sauce, to serve

1 In a large bowl, mix together the spring onions, coriander, sweetcorn, chilli powder, chilli sauce, coconut, egg and polenta until well blended.

2 Cover the bowl with clingfilm and leave to stand for about 10 minutes.

3 Heat the oil for deep-frying in a large preheated wok or frying pan to 180°C/350°F or until a cube of bread browns in 30 seconds.

4 Carefully drop spoonfuls of the chilli and polenta mixture into the hot oil. Deep-fry the chilli corn balls, in batches, for 4–5 minutes or until crispy and a deep golden brown colour.

5 Remove the chilli corn balls with a slotted spoon, transfer to absorbent kitchen paper and leave to drain thoroughly.

6 Transfer the chilli corn balls to serving plates and serve with an extra-sweet chilli sauce for dipping.

COOK'S TIP

For safe deep-frying in a round-bottomed wok, place it on a wok rack so that it rests securely. Only half-fill the wok with oil. Never leave the wok unattended over a high heat.

Aubergine Satay

Aubergines and mushrooms are grilled on skewers and served with a satay sauce.

NUTRITIONAL INFORMATION

Calories ....155 Sugars 2g
Protein ....4g Fat 14g
Carbohydrate ....3g Saturates 3g

2¼ hours   25 mins

SERVES 4

INGREDIENTS

2 aubergines, cut into 2.5 cm/1 inch pieces

175 g/6 oz small chestnut mushrooms

MARINADE

1 tsp cumin seeds

1 tsp coriander seeds

2.5 cm/1 inch piece fresh root ginger, grated

2 garlic cloves, lightly crushed

½ stalk lemongrass, roughly chopped

4 tbsp light soy sauce

8 tbsp sunflower oil

2 tbsp lemon juice

PEANUT SAUCE

½ tsp cumin seeds

½ tsp coriander seeds

3 garlic cloves

1 small onion, puréed in a food processor or chopped very finely by hand

1 tbsp lemon juice

1 tsp salt

½ red chilli, deseeded and sliced

125 ml/4½ fl oz coconut milk

250 g/9 oz crunchy peanut butter

250 ml/8 fl oz water

1 Thread the vegetables on to eight metal or pre-soaked wooden skewers.

2 For the marinade, grind the cumin and coriander seeds, ginger, garlic and lemongrass. Stir-fry over a high heat until fragrant. Remove from the heat and add the remaining marinade ingredients. Place the skewers in a dish and spoon the marinade over. Leave to marinate for at least 2 hours and up to 8 hours.

3 To make the sauce, grind the cumin and coriander seeds with the garlic. Add all the ingredients except the water. Transfer to a pan and stir in the water. Bring to the boil and cook until thick.

4 Cook the vegetable skewers under a preheated very hot grill for 15–20 minutes. Brush with the marinade frequently and turn once. Serve with the peanut sauce.

Vegetable Rolls

In this recipe a mixed vegetable stuffing is wrapped in Chinese leaves and steamed until tender.

NUTRITIONAL INFORMATION

Calories 69	Sugars 1g
Protein 2g	Fat 5g
Carbohydrate 3g	Saturates 1g

10 mins   20 mins

SERVES 4

INGREDIENTS

8 large Chinese leaves

FILLING

2 baby sweetcorn cobs, sliced

1 carrot, finely chopped

1 celery stick, chopped

4 spring onions, chopped

4 water chestnuts, chopped

2 tbsp unsalted cashews, chopped

1 garlic clove, chopped

1 tsp grated fresh root ginger

25 g/1 oz canned bamboo shoots, drained, rinsed and chopped

1 tsp sesame oil

2 tsp soy sauce

1 Place the Chinese leaves in a large bowl and pour over boiling water to soften them. Leave them to stand for 1 minute and drain thoroughly.

2 Mix together the baby sweetcorn cobs, chopped carrot, celery, spring onions, water chestnuts, cashews, garlic, ginger and bamboo shoots in a large bowl.

3 In a separate bowl, whisk together the sesame oil and soy sauce. Add this to the vegetables, and stir well until all the vegetables are thoroughly coated in the mixture.

4 Spread out the Chinese leaves on a chopping board and divide the filling mixture between them, carefully spooning an equal quantity of the mixture on to each leaf.

5 Roll up the Chinese leaves, folding in the sides, to make neat parcels. Secure the parcels with cocktail sticks.

6 Place in a small heatproof dish in a steamer, cover and cook for 15–20 minutes, until the parcels are cooked.

7 Transfer the vegetable rolls to a warm serving dish and serve with a soy or chilli sauce.

Rice Cubes with Satay Sauce

Plain rice cubes are a good foil to any piquant dipping sauce, and they are often served with satay, to complement the dipping sauce.

NUTRITIONAL INFORMATION

Calories 317	Sugars 3g
Protein 10g	Fat 10g
Carbohydrate . . .49g	Saturates 2g

8¼ hrs   25 mins

SERVES 4

INGREDIENTS

300 g/10½ oz jasmine rice

1.3 litres/2¼ pints water

CORIANDER DIPPING SAUCE

1 garlic clove

2 tsp salt

1 tbsp black peppercorns

60 g/2 oz washed fresh coriander, including roots and stem

3 tbsp lemon juice

175 ml/6 fl oz coconut milk

2 tbsp peanut butter

2 spring onions, roughly chopped

1 red chilli, deseeded and sliced

1 Grease and line a 20 x 10 x 2.5 cm/ 8 x 4 x 1 inch tin.

2 To cook the rice, do not rinse. Bring the water to the boil and add the rice. Stir and return to a medium boil. Cook, uncovered, for 14–16 minutes until very soft. Drain thoroughly.

3 Put 125 g/4½ oz of the cooked rice in a blender or food processor and purée until smooth. Alternatively, grind to a paste in a pestle and mortar.

4 Combine the puréed rice with the remaining cooked rice and spoon into the lined tin. Level the surface and cover with a layer of clingfilm. Compress the rice by using either a slightly smaller-sized tin or a small piece of board, and weigh this down with cans. Chill the rice in the refrigerator for at least 8 hours.

5 Invert the tin on to a board. Cut the rice into cubes with a wet knife.

6 To make the sauce, grind together the garlic, salt, peppercorns, coriander and lemon juice in either a pestle and mortar or a blender.

7 Add the coconut milk, peanut butter, spring onions and chilli. Grind finely. Transfer to a saucepan and bring to the boil. Leave to cool.

Aspagarus Parcels

These small parcels are ideal as part of a main meal and irresistible as a quick snack with extra plum sauce for dipping.

NUTRITIONAL INFORMATION

Calories 194   Sugars 2g
Protein . . . . .3g   Fat 16g
Carbohydrate . . . .11g   Saturates 4g

5 mins   25 mins

SERVES 4

I N G R E D I E N T S

100 g/3½ oz fine tip asparagus

1 red pepper, deseeded and thinly sliced

50 g/1¾ oz beansprouts

2 tbsp plum sauce

1 egg yolk

8 sheets filo pastry

oil, for deep-frying

1 Place the asparagus, pepper and beansprouts in a large mixing bowl.

2 Add the plum sauce to the vegetables and mix until well combined.

3 Beat the egg yolk and set aside until required.

4 Lay the sheets of filo pastry out on to a clean work surface, and cover with a damp cloth to prevent them drying out.

5 Working with one sheet of filo pastry at a time, place a small quantity of the asparagus and red pepper filling at the top end of the sheet. Brush all the edges of the filo pastry with a little of the beaten egg yolk. Roll up the sheet, tucking in the ends to enclose the filling like a spring roll. Continue filling and rolling the remaining filo pastry sheets.

6 Heat the oil for deep-frying in a large preheated wok. Carefully cook the parcels, 2 at a time, in the hot oil for 4–5 minutes or until crispy.

7 Remove the parcels with a slotted spoon and leave them to drain on kitchen paper.

8 Transfer the parcels to warm serving plates and serve immediately.

COOK'S TIP

Be sure to use fine-tipped asparagus as it is more tender than the larger stems.

Thai-style Sweetcorn Fritters

These quick little fritters make a really appetizing first course, served with a spoonful of spicy chilli relish and a squeeze of lime juice.

NUTRITIONAL INFORMATION

Calories 203   Sugars 3g
Protein . . . . .7g   Fat 7g
Carbohydrate . . .29g   Saturates 1g

 15 mins   30 mins

SERVES 4

INGREDIENTS

55 g/2 oz plain flour

1 large egg

2 tsp Thai green curry paste

5 tbsp coconut milk

400 g/14 oz canned or frozen
    sweetcorn kernels

4 spring onions

1 tbsp chopped fresh coriander

1 tbsp chopped fresh basil

salt and pepper

vegetable oil, for frying

TO SERVE

lime wedges

chilli relish

1 Place the flour, egg, curry paste, coconut milk and about half the sweetcorn kernels in a food processor and process until a smooth, thick batter forms. Pour into a bowl.

2 Finely chop the spring onions and stir into the batter with the remaining sweetcorn, chopped coriander and basil. Season to taste with salt and pepper.

3 Heat a small amount of oil in a wide, heavy-based frying pan. Drop in tablespoonfuls of the batter and cook for 2–3 minutes until golden brown.

4 Turn the fritters over and cook for a further 2–3 minutes until golden all over. Fry the batter in batches, making about 12–16 fritters and keeping the cooked fritters hot while you cook the remaining batter.

5 Serve the fritters as soon as they are all cooked, with lime wedges and a chilli relish.

COOK'S TIP

If you prefer to use fresh sweetcorn, strip the kernels from the cobs with a sharp knife, then cook in boiling water for about 4–5 minutes until just tender. Drain well before using.

Aïoli

This garlic mayonnaise features in many traditional Provençal recipes, but also makes a delicious dip, surrounded by a selection of vegetables.

NUTRITIONAL INFORMATION

Calories	239	Sugars 0g
Protein	.........1g	Fat 26g
Carbohydrate	....1g	Saturates 4g

 15 mins   0 mins

SERVES 6

INGREDIENTS

4 large garlic cloves, or to taste

2 large egg yolks

300 ml/10 fl oz extra virgin olive oil

1–2 tbsp lemon juice

1 tbsp fresh white breadcrumbs

sea salt and pepper

TO SERVE (OPTIONAL)

a selection of raw vegetables, such as
    sliced red peppers, courgette slices,
    whole spring onions and tomato wedges

a selection of blanched and cooled
    vegetables, such as baby artichoke
    hearts, cauliflower or broccoli florets or
    French beans

1 Finely chop the garlic on a chopping board. Add a pinch of sea salt to the garlic and use the tip and broad side of a knife to work the garlic and salt into a smooth paste.

2 Transfer the garlic paste to a food processor. Add the egg yolks and process until well blended, scraping down the side of the bowl with a rubber spatula, if necessary.

3 With the motor running, slowly pour in the olive oil in a steady stream through the feeder tube, processing until a thick mayonnaise forms.

4 Add 1 tablespoon of the lemon juice and the breadcrumbs and process again. Taste and add more lemon juice if necessary. Season to taste with sea salt and pepper.

5 Place the aïoli in a bowl, cover and chill until ready to serve. To serve, place the bowl of aïoli on a large platter and surround with a selection of raw and lightly blanched vegetables.

COOK'S TIP
The amount of garlic in a traditional Provençal aïoli is a matter of personal taste. Local cooks use 2 cloves per person as a rule of thumb, but this version is slightly milder, although still bursting with flavour.

Crudités with Coriander Dip

Raw vegetables are the ideal healthy start to a meal, and this dip is the perfect accompaniment – full of flavour, but no fat.

NUTRITIONAL INFORMATION

Calories ....67 Sugars 8g
Protein ....7g Fat 1g
Carbohydrate ....9g Saturates 0g

 10 mins   2 mins

SERVES 4

I N G R E D I E N T S

FOR THE CRUDITES

115 g/4 oz baby sweetcorn cobs

115 g/4 oz young asparagus spears

1 head of chicory, leaves separated

1 red pepper, deseeded and sliced

1 orange pepper, deseeded and sliced

8 radishes, trimmed

FOR THE DIP

1 tbsp hot water

1 tsp saffron threads

225 g/8 oz fat-free fromage frais

3 tbsp chopped fresh coriander

1 tbsp chopped garlic chives

salt and pepper

fresh coriander sprigs, to garnish

COOK'S TIP

Although it is made from skimmed milk, the fat content of fromage frais ranges between zero and 8 per cent and this is reflected in the consistency. Fat-free fromage frais is great for dips because it is soft and easily combined with other ingredients.

1 Blanch the baby sweetcorn cobs and asparagus spears in separate pans of boiling water for 2 minutes. Drain, plunge into iced water and drain again.

2 Arrange all the vegetables on a serving platter and cover with a damp tea towel while you make the dip.

3 Put the tablespoonful of hot water into a small bowl. Lightly crush the saffron threads between your fingers and add them to the bowl. Set aside for about 3-4 minutes, until the water has turned a rich golden colour.

4 Beat the fromage frais until it becomes smooth, then beat in the infused saffron water. Stir in the chopped coriander and chives and season to taste with salt and pepper. Serve the dip immediately with the vegetables.

Courgette & Thyme Fritters

These tasty little fritters, flecked with green, are great to serve at a drinks party or as an appetiser. Dried chillies can be added to spice them up.

NUTRITIONAL INFORMATION

Calories	162	Sugars	........2g
Protein	.........7g	Fat	..........6g
Carbohydrate	...20g	Saturates	.......2g

 5–10 mins   20 mins

MAKES 16–30

INGREDIENTS

100 g/3½ oz self-raising flour

2 eggs, beaten

50 ml/2 fl oz milk

300 g/10½ oz courgettes

2 tbsp fresh thyme

salt and pepper

1 tbsp oil

1 Sift the self-raising flour into a large bowl and make a well in the centre. Add the eggs to the well, and using a wooden spoon, gradually draw in the flour.

2 Slowly add the milk to the mixture, stirring constantly until a thick batter is formed. Set aside.

3 Wash the courgettes then grate them over a sheet of kitchen paper placed in a bowl to absorb some of the juices.

4 Add the courgettes, thyme and salt and pepper to taste to the batter and mix thoroughly.

5 Heat the oil in a large, heavy-based frying pan. Taking a tablespoon of the batter for a medium-sized fritter or half a tablespoon of batter for a smaller-sized fritter, spoon the mixture into the hot oil

and cook the fritters, in batches, for 3–4 minutes on each side.

6 Remove the fritters with a perforated spoon and drain them thoroughly on absorbent kitchen paper. Keep each batch of fritters warm in the oven while making the rest. Transfer to warmed serving plates and serve hot.

VARIATION

Try adding ½ teaspoon of dried, crushed chillies to the batter in step 4 for spicier tasting fritters.

Orange-dressed Asparagus

Try to use locally grown asparagus for this recipe – it is in season only for a short time in late spring and early summer, and the flavour is superb.

NUTRITIONAL INFORMATION

Calories	88	Sugars	.........6g
Protein	.........3g	Fat	...........6g
Carbohydrate	....6g	Saturates	.......1g

10 mins, plus standing   10 mins

SERVES 4

INGREDIENTS

thinly pared rind and juice of 2 oranges

350 g/12 oz asparagus, trimmed

1 tbsp lemon juice

1 spring onion, finely chopped

1 garlic clove, finely chopped

2 tbsp extra virgin olive oil

1 tbsp white wine vinegar

1 Bring a small pan of water to the boil. Cut the orange rind into very thin strips, add to the pan, bring back to the boil and simmer for 1 minute. Drain, refresh under cold water and drain again.

2 Bring water to the boil in an asparagus kettle or a deep saucepan (see Cook's Tip). Add the asparagus and cook for 5 minutes, or until crisp-tender. Drain, refresh under cold water and drain again. Pat dry with kitchen paper.

3 Arrange the asparagus on a serving dish, cover and chill until required.

4 To make the orange dressing, combine 5 tablespoons of the orange juice with the lemon juice, spring onion, garlic and orange rind. Set aside at room temperature for 15 minutes to allow the flavours to mingle. Whisk in the olive oil and vinegar.

5 Pour the orange dressing over the chilled asparagus and serve immediately.

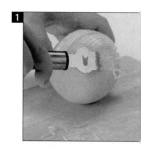

COOK'S TIP

An asparagus kettle is a tall, lidded pan with a basket, designed so that the stems cook in the water while the tips are gently steamed. If you don't have one, tie the asparagus loosely in a bundle and wedge upright in a deep saucepan. Cover with foil if the stems protrude.

Spicy Sweetcorn Fritters

Polenta can be found in most supermarkets or healthfood shops.
Yellow in colour, it acts as a binding agent in this recipe.

NUTRITIONAL INFORMATION

Calories	213	Sugars	.........6g
Protein	.........5g	Fat	...........8g
Carbohydrate	...30g	Saturates	.......1g

5 mins   15 mins

SERVES 4

INGREDIENTS

225 g/8 oz canned or frozen sweetcorn
  kernels

2 red chillies, deseeded and finely chopped

2 cloves garlic, crushed

10 lime leaves, finely chopped

2 tbsp chopped fresh coriander

1 large egg

75 g/2¾ oz polenta

100 g/3½ oz French beans, finely sliced

groundnut oil, for frying

1 Place the sweetcorn, chillies, garlic, lime leaves, coriander, egg and polenta in a large mixing bowl, and stir to combine thoroughly.

2 Add the sliced French beans to the ingredients in the bowl and mix well, using a wooden spoon.

3 Divide the mixture into small, evenly sized balls. Flatten the balls of mixture gently between the palms of your hands to form rounds.

4 Heat a little groundnut oil in a preheated wok or large frying pan until really hot. Cook the fritters in batches, turning occasionally, until brown and crispy on the outside.

5 Leave the fritters to drain on absorbent kitchen paper while frying the remaining fritters.

6 Transfer the drained fritters to warm serving plates and serve immediately.

Spiced Corn & Nut Mix

This is a tasty mixture of buttery-spiced nuts, raisins and popcorn to enjoy as a snack or with pre-dinner drinks.

NUTRITIONAL INFORMATION

Calories . . . . . . .372 Sugars 9g

Protein . . . . .8g Fat 31g

Carbohydrate . . .16g Saturates 9g

🕐 5 mins   🕐 10 mins

SERVES 4

INGREDIENTS

2 tbsp vegetable oil

60 g/2 oz popping corn

60 g/2 oz butter

1 garlic clove, crushed

60 g/2 oz unblanched almonds

60 g/2 oz unsalted cashews

60 g/2 oz unsalted peanuts

1 tsp vegetarian Worcestershire sauce

1 tsp curry powder or paste

¼ tsp chilli powder

60 g/2 oz seedless raisins

salt

1 Heat the oil in a saucepan. Add the popping corn, stir well, then cover and cook over a fairly high heat for 3–5 minutes, holding the saucepan lid firmly and shaking the pan frequently until the popping stops.

2 Turn the popped corn into a dish, discarding any unpopped corn kernels.

3 Melt the butter in a frying pan and add the garlic, almonds, cashews and peanuts, then stir in the Worcestershire sauce, the curry powder or paste and the chilli powder and cook the mixture over a medium heat, stirring frequently, for 2–3 minutes, until the nuts are lightly toasted.

4 Remove the pan from the heat and stir in the raisins and popped corn. Season with salt to taste and mix thoroughly. Transfer to a serving bowl and serve warm or cold.

VARIATION

Use a mixture of any unsalted nuts of your choice – walnuts, pecans, hazelnuts, Brazils, macadamia and pine nuts. For a less fiery flavour, omit the curry and chilli powder and add 1 tsp cumin seeds, 1 tsp ground coriander and ½ tsp paprika.

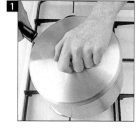

Crispy Seaweed

This tasty Chinese starter is not all that it seems – the 'seaweed' is in fact pak choi which is deep-fried, salted and tossed with pine kernels.

NUTRITIONAL INFORMATION

Calories	214	Sugars	........14g
Protein	.........6g	Fat	..........15g
Carbohydrate	...15g	Saturates	.......2g

 10 mins   5 mins

SERVES 4

INGREDIENTS

1 kg/2 lb 4 oz pak choi

900 ml/1½ pints groundnut oil, for deep-frying

1 tsp salt

1 tbsp caster sugar

2½ tbsp toasted pine kernels

1 Rinse the pak choi leaves under cold running water and then pat dry thoroughly with absorbent kitchen paper.

2 Discarding any tough outer leaves, roll each pak choi leaf up, then slice through thinly so that the leaves are finely shredded. Alternatively, use a food processor to shred the pak choi.

3 Heat the groundnut oil in a large wok or heavy-based frying pan.

4 Carefully add the shredded pak choi leaves to the wok or frying pan and fry for about 30 seconds or until they shrivel up and become crispy, resembling seaweed (you will probably need to do this in several batches, depending on the size of your wok).

5 Remove the crispy seaweed from the wok with a slotted spoon and drain on absorbent kitchen paper.

6 Transfer the crispy seaweed to a large bowl and toss with the salt, sugar and pine kernels. Serve immediately on warm serving plates.

COOK'S TIP

The tough, outer leaves of pak choi are discarded as these will spoil the overall taste and texture of the dish. Use Savoy cabbage instead of the pak choi if it is unavailable, drying the leaves thoroughly before frying.

Mixed Peppers with Thyme

These peppers are wonderful served as an antipasto, but they can also be used as an interesting side dish.

NUTRITIONAL INFORMATION

Calories	103	Sugars	14g
Protein	3g	Fat	4g
Carbohydrate	16g	Saturates	1g

 15 mins   35 mins

SERVES 4

INGREDIENTS

2 each, red, yellow and orange peppers

4 tomatoes, halved

1 tbsp olive oil

3 garlic cloves, chopped

1 onion, sliced in rings

2 tbsp fresh thyme

salt and pepper

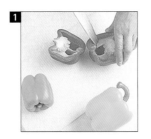

1 Halve and deseed the peppers. Place them, cut side down, on a baking tray and cook under a preheated grill for 10 minutes.

2 Add the tomatoes to the baking tray and grill for 5 minutes, or until the pepper and tomato skins are charred.

3 Put the peppers into a polythene bag for 10 minutes to sweat, which will make the skin easier to peel. Remove the tomato skins and roughly chop the flesh.

4 Peel the skins from the peppers and slice the flesh into strips.

5 Heat the oil in a large frying pan and fry the garlic and onion for 3–4 minutes, or until softened. Then add the peppers and tomatoes to the frying pan and continue to cook the mixture for a further 5 minutes.

6 Stir in the fresh thyme and season to taste with salt and pepper.

7 Transfer to serving bowls and serve warm or chilled.

COOK'S TIP

You can preserve the peppers in the refrigerator by placing them in a sterilized jar and pouring olive oil over the top to seal.

Roman Artichokes

This is a traditional Roman dish. The artichokes are stewed in olive oil with fresh herbs.

NUTRITIONAL INFORMATION

Calories 190   Sugars 0g
Protein ....6g   Fat 11g
Carbohydrate ...16g   Saturates 2g

10 mins   40 mins

SERVES 4

I N G R E D I E N T S

4 small globe artichokes

olive oil

4 garlic cloves, peeled

2 bay leaves

finely grated rind and juice of 1 lemon

2 tbsp fresh marjoram

lemon wedges, to serve

1 Using a sharp knife, carefully peel away the tough outer leaves surrounding the artichokes. Trim the stems to about 2.5 cm/1 inch.

2 Using a knife, cut each artichoke in half and scoop out the choke.

3 Place the artichokes in a large heavy-based pan. Pour over enough olive oil to half cover the artichokes in the pan.

4 Add the garlic cloves, bay leaves and half of the grated lemon rind.

5 Start to heat the artichokes gently, cover the pan and continue to cook over a low heat for about 40 minutes. It is important that the artichokes should be stewed in the oil, not fried.

6 Once the artichokes are tender, remove them from the oil with a perforated spoon and drain thoroughly. Remove the bay leaves.

7 Transfer the artichokes to warm serving plates. Serve the artichokes immediately, sprinkled with the remaining grated lemon rind and the fresh marjoram and garnished with lemon wedges.

COOK'S TIP
Use the oil used for cooking the artichokes to make salad dressings – it will impart a lovely lemon and herb flavour.

Rice & Cheese Balls

The Italian name for this dish translates as 'telephone wires', which refers to the strings of melted mozzarella cheese hidden inside the risotto balls.

NUTRITIONAL INFORMATION

Calories 282	Sugars 2g
Protein 8g	Fat 11g
Carbohydrate ...36g	Saturates 1g

 30 mins 25 mins

SERVES 4

I N G R E D I E N T S

2 tbsp olive oil

1 onion, finely chopped

1 garlic clove, chopped

½ red pepper, deseeded and diced

150 g/5 oz arborio rice, washed

1 tsp dried oregano

400 ml/14 fl oz hot vegetable stock

100 ml/3½ fl oz dry white wine

75 g/2¾ oz mozzarella cheese

oil, for deep-frying

fresh basil sprig, to garnish

1 Heat the oil in a frying pan and cook the onion and garlic for 3–4 minutes, or until just softened.

2 Add the pepper, rice and oregano to the pan. Cook for 2–3 minutes, stirring to coat the rice in the oil.

3 Mix the stock together with the wine and add to the pan a ladleful at a time, waiting for the liquid to be absorbed by the rice before you add the next ladleful of liquid.

4 Once all of the liquid has been absorbed and the rice is tender (it should take about 15 minutes in total), remove the pan from the heat. Leave until the mixture is cool enough to handle.

5 Cut the cheese into 12 pieces. Taking about a tablespoon of risotto, shape the mixture around the cheese pieces to make 12 balls.

6 Heat the oil until a piece of bread browns in 30 seconds. Cook the risotto balls in batches of 4 for 2 minutes, or until golden.

7 Remove the risotto balls with a perforated spoon and drain thoroughly on absorbent kitchen paper. Garnish with a sprig of basil and serve hot.

COOK'S TIP

Although mozzarella is the traditional cheese for this recipe and creates the stringy 'telephone wire' effect, other cheeses, such as Cheddar, may be used if you prefer.

Vegetable Spring Rolls

This version of vegetarian spring rolls is very quick and easy to make, using filo pastry to make the crisp cases.

NUTRITIONAL INFORMATION

Calories	189	Sugars	.........4g
Protein	.........2g	Fat	..........16g
Carbohydrate	....11g	Saturates	.......5g

 10 mins   15 mins

SERVES 4

I N G R E D I E N T S

225 g/8 oz carrots

1 red pepper

1 tbsp sunflower oil, plus extra for frying

75 g/2¾ oz beansprouts

finely grated rind and juice of 1 lime

1 red chilli, deseeded and finely chopped

1 tbsp soy sauce

½ tsp arrowroot

2 tbsp chopped fresh coriander

8 sheets filo pastry

25 g/1 oz butter

2 tsp sesame oil

TO SERVE

chilli sauce

spring onion tassels (see page 131)

1 Using a sharp knife, cut the carrots into thin sticks. Seed the pepper and cut into thin slices.

2 Heat the sunflower oil in a large preheated wok.

3 Add the carrot, red pepper and beansprouts and cook, stirring, for 2 minutes, or until softened. Remove the wok from the heat and toss in the lime zest and juice, and the red chilli.

4 Mix the soy sauce with the arrowroot. Stir the mixture into the wok, return to the heat and cook for 2 minutes or until the juices thicken.

5 Add the chopped fresh coriander to the wok and mix well.

6 Lay the sheets of filo pastry out on a board. Melt the butter and sesame oil and brush each sheet with the mixture.

7 Spoon a little of the vegetable filling at the top of each sheet, fold over each long side, and roll up.

8 Clean the wok, add a little oil and cook the spring rolls in batches, for 2–3 minutes, or until crisp and golden.

9 Transfer the spring rolls to a serving dish, garnish and serve hot with chilli dipping sauce.

Tuscan Ciabatta

Using ripe tomatoes and the best extra virgin olive oil will make this Tuscan dish absolutely delicious.

NUTRITIONAL INFORMATION

Calories ....308 Sugars 3g
Protein ....7g Fat 15g
Carbohydrate ...37g Saturates 2g

10 mins   5 mins

SERVES 4

I N G R E D I E N T S

300 g/10½ oz cherry tomatoes

4 sun-dried tomatoes

4 tbsp extra virgin olive oil

16 fresh basil leaves, shredded

salt and pepper

8 slices ciabatta

2 garlic cloves, peeled

1 Using a sharp knife, cut the cherry tomatoes in half.

2 Using a sharp knife, slice the sun-dried tomatoes into strips.

3 Place the cherry tomatoes and sun-dried tomatoes in a bowl. Add the

olive oil and the shredded basil leaves and toss to mix well. Season to taste with a little salt and pepper.

4 Lightly toast the ciabatta bread on both sides. Using a sharp knife, cut the garlic cloves in half.

5 Rub the garlic, with the cut side down, over both sides of the toasted ciabatta bread.

6 Top the ciabatta bread with the tomato mixture and serve at once on warmed plates.

COOK'S TIP

Ciabatta is an Italian rustic bread which is slightly holey and quite chewy. It is very good in this recipe as it absorbs the full flavour of the garlic and extra virgin olive oil.

Bite-sized Bhajis

Don't be surprised at the shape these form – they are odd but look lovely when arranged on a tray with the yogurt dipping sauce.

NUTRITIONAL INFORMATION

Calories ....122 Sugars 2g
Protein ....2g Fat 10g
Carbohydrate ....6g Saturates 1g

15 mins   15 mins

MAKES 20

INGREDIENTS

2 heaped tbsp gram flour (see page 149)

½ tsp turmeric

½ tsp cumin seeds, ground

1 tsp garam masala

pinch of cayenne pepper

1 egg

1 large onion, quartered and sliced

salt

1 tbsp chopped fresh coriander

3 tbsp breadcrumbs, optional

vegetable oil, for deep-frying

SAUCE

1 tsp coriander seeds, ground

1½ tsp cumin seeds, ground

225 ml/8 fl oz natural yogurt

salt and pepper

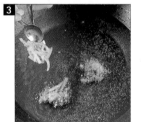

1 Put the gram flour into a large bowl and mix in the turmeric, cumin, garam masala and cayenne. Make a well in the centre and add the egg. Stir to form a gluey mixture. Add the onion and sprinkle in a little salt. Add the coriander and stir. If the mixture is not stiff enough, stir in the breadcrumbs.

2 Heat the oil for deep-frying over a medium heat until fairly hot – it should just be starting to smoke.

3 Push a teaspoonful of the mixture into the oil with a second teaspoon to form fairly round balls. The bhajis should firm up quite quickly. Cook in batches of 8–10, stirring so that they brown evenly. Drain on kitchen paper and keep them warm in the oven until ready to serve.

4 To make the sauce, roast the spices in a frying pan. Remove from the heat and stir in the yogurt. Season well.

COOK'S TIP

Make sure that the pan and all the utensils are properly dried before use. Do not let any water come into contact with the hot oil or the oil will spit and splutter, which could be dangerous.

Crispy-fried Vegetables

A hot and sweet dipping sauce makes the perfect accompaniment to fresh vegetables coated in a light batter and deep-fried.

NUTRITIONAL INFORMATION

Calories	258	Sugars	........11g
Protein	.........6g	Fat	...........9g
Carbohydrate	...39g	Saturates	......11g

 40 mins   10 mins

SERVES 4

INGREDIENTS

vegetable oil, for deep-frying

500 g/1 lb 2 oz selection of vegetables, such as cauliflower, broccoli, mushrooms, courgettes, peppers and baby sweetcorn, cut into even-sized pieces

BATTER

125 g/4½ oz plain flour

½ tsp salt

1 tsp caster sugar

1 tsp baking powder

3 tbsp vegetable oil

200 ml/7 fl oz warm water

SAUCE

6 tbsp light malt vinegar

2 tbsp light soy sauce

2 tbsp water

1 tbsp soft brown sugar

pinch of salt

2 garlic cloves, crushed

2 tsp grated fresh ginger root

2 red chillies, deseeded and finely chopped

2 tbsp chopped fresh coriander

1 To make the batter, sift the flour, salt, sugar and baking powder into a bowl. Add the oil and most of the water. Whisk together to make a smooth batter, adding extra water to give it the consistency of single cream. Chill for 20–30 minutes.

2 Meanwhile, make the sauce. Heat the vinegar, soy sauce, water, sugar and salt until boiling. Remove from the heat and leave to cool.

3 Mix together the garlic, ginger, chillies and coriander. Add the cooled vinegar mixture and stir well to combine.

4 Heat the oil for deep-frying in a wok. Dip the vegetables in the batter and fry, in batches, until crisp and golden – about 2 minutes. Drain on kitchen paper.

5 Serve the vegetables accompanied by the dipping sauce.

Celeriac Rémoulade

Celeriac served with a rémoulade sauce - a mustard-flavoured mayonnaise - is a classically simple French dish.

NUTRITIONAL INFORMATION

Calories 236   Sugars 3g
Protein ....3g   Fat 24g
Carbohydrate ....4g   Saturates 3g

10 mins   0 mins

SERVES 4

INGREDIENTS

225 ml/8 fl oz mayonnaise (see page 8)

2 tsp lemon juice

1 tbsp Dijon mustard

salt and pepper

225 g/8 oz celeriac

1 shallot, grated

6 lettuce leaves

snipped fresh chives, to garnish

1 Combine the mayonnaise, lemon juice and mustard in a large bowl and season to taste with salt and pepper. Peel and grate the celeriac into the mixture.

2 Stir in the shallot and mix thoroughly, making sure the celeriac is well coated in the dressing.

3 Line a salad bowl with the lettuce leaves and spoon the celeriac mixture into the centre. Sprinkle with the snipped chives and serve.

COOK'S TIP

Do not grate the celeriac in advance, as it will discolour quickly on exposure to air.

Pear & Roquefort Salad

The sweetness of the pear is a perfect partner to the peppery 'bite' of the radicchio and the piquancy of the cheese.

NUTRITIONAL INFORMATION

Calories ....94 Sugars 10g
Protein ....5g Fat 4g
Carbohydrate ...10g Saturates 3g

 10 mins   0 mins

SERVES 4

I N G R E D I E N T S

55 g/2 oz Roquefort cheese

150 ml/5 fl oz low-fat natural yogurt

2 tbsp snipped fresh chives

pepper

few leaves of lollo rosso

few leaves of radicchio

few leaves of lamb's lettuce

2 ripe pears

whole fresh chives, to garnish

1 Place the cheese in a bowl and mash with a fork. Gradually blend the yogurt into the cheese to make a smooth dressing. Add the chives and season with pepper to taste.

2 Tear the lollo rosso, radicchio and lamb's lettuce leaves into manageable pieces. Arrange the salad leaves on a large serving platter or divide them between individual serving plates.

3 Cut the pears into quarters and remove the cores. Cut the quarters into slices. Arrange the pear slices over the salad leaves.

4 Drizzle the Roquefort dressing over the pears and garnish with a few whole chives.

COOK'S TIP

Look out for bags of mixed salad leaves as these are generally more economical than buying lots of different leaves separately.

Cress & Cheese Tartlets

These tasty and attractive individual tartlets are great served hot at lunchtime or cool for picnic food.

NUTRITIONAL INFORMATION

Calories 410	Sugars 4g
Protein 15g	Fat 29g
Carbohydrate . . .24g	Saturates 19g

20 mins 　 25 mins

SERVES 4

INGREDIENTS

100 g/4 oz plain flour, plus extra
　for dusting

pinch of salt

85 g/3 oz butter or margarine

2–3 tbsp cold water

2 bunches of watercress

2 garlic cloves, crushed

1 shallot, chopped

150 g/5½ oz Cheddar cheese, grated

4 tbsp natural yogurt

½ tsp paprika

1 Sift the flour into a mixing bowl and add the salt. Rub 60 g/2 oz of the butter or margarine into the flour until the mixture resembles breadcrumbs. Stir in enough of the cold water to make a smooth dough.

2 Roll the dough out on a lightly floured surface and use to line 4 x 10 cm/4 inch tartlet tins. Prick the bases with a fork and set aside to chill in the refrigerator.

3 Heat the remaining butter or margarine in a frying pan. Discard the stems from the watercress. Add the leaves to the pan with the garlic and shallot and cook for 1–2 minutes until wilted.

4 Remove the pan from the heat and stir in the grated Cheddar cheese, yogurt and paprika.

5 Spoon the mixture into the pastry cases and cook in a preheated oven, 180°C/350°F/Gas Mark 4, for 20 minutes or until the filling is just firm. Turn out the tartlets and serve immediately, if serving hot, or place on a wire rack to cool, if serving cold.

VARIATION
Use spinach instead of the watercress, making sure it is well drained before mixing with the remaining filling ingredients.

Spanish Tortilla

This classic Spanish dish is often served as part of a tapas selection. A variety of cooked vegetables can be added to this recipe.

NUTRITIONAL INFORMATION

Calories ....430 Sugars 6g
Protein ....16g Fat 20g
Carbohydrate ...50g Saturates 4g

  10 mins   35 mins

SERVES 4

I N G R E D I E N T S

1 kg/2 lb 4 oz waxy potatoes, thinly sliced

4 tbsp vegetable oil

1 onion, sliced

2 garlic cloves, crushed

1 green pepper, deseeded and diced

2 tomatoes, deseeded and chopped

25 g/1 oz canned sweetcorn, drained

6 large eggs, beaten

2 tbsp chopped fresh parsley

salt and pepper

1 Parboil the potatoes in a saucepan of lightly salted boiling water for 5 minutes. Drain well.

2 Heat the oil in a large frying pan, add the potatoes and onion and then sauté over a low heat, stirring constantly, for 5 minutes until the potatoes have browned.

3 Add the garlic, green pepper, tomatoes and sweetcorn, mixing well.

4 Pour in the eggs and add the parsley. Season to taste with salt and pepper. Cook for 10–12 minutes until the underside is cooked.

5 Remove the frying pan from the heat and continue to cook the tortilla under a preheated medium grill for 5–7 minutes or until the tortilla is set and the top is golden brown.

6 Cut the tortilla into wedges or cubes, depending on your preference, and transfer to serving dishes. Serve with salad. Tortillas are also delicious eaten cold, so they are excellent for packed lunches.

COOK'S TIP

Ensure that the handle of your pan is heatproof before placing it under the grill and be sure to use an oven glove when removing it because it will be very hot.

Baked Potatoes with Salsa

This is a great way to eat a baked potato. Once cooked, the flesh is flavoured with avocado, piled back into the shell and served with salsa.

NUTRITIONAL INFORMATION

Calories 71	Sugars 1.4g	
Protein 2.3g	Fat 2.7g	
Carbohydrate . . .10g	Saturates 0.5g	

 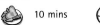

10 mins   1 hr

SERVES 4

INGREDIENTS

4 baking potatoes

1 large avocado

1 tsp lemon juice

175 g/6 oz smoked tofu, diced

2 garlic cloves, crushed

1 onion, finely chopped

1 tomato, finely chopped

125 g/4½ oz mixed salad leaves

fresh coriander sprigs, to garnish

SALSA

2 ripe tomatoes, deseeded and diced

1 tbsp chopped coriander

1 shallot, finely diced

1 green chilli, deseeded and diced

1 tbsp lemon juice

salt and pepper

1 Scrub the potatoes and prick the skins with a fork. Rub a little salt into the skins and place them on a baking tray.

2 Cook in a preheated oven, 190°C/ 375°F/Gas Mark 5, for 1 hour or until cooked through and the skins are crisp.

3 Cut the potatoes in half lengthways and scoop most of the flesh into a bowl, leaving a thin layer of potato inside the shells.

4 Halve and stone the avocado. Using a spoon, scoop out the avocado flesh and add to the bowl containing the potato. Stir in the lemon juice and mash the mixture together with a fork. Mix in the tofu, garlic, onion and tomato. Spoon the mixture into one half of the potato shells.

5 Arrange the salad leaves on top of the guacamole mixture and place the other half of the potato shell on top.

6 To make the salsa, mix the tomatoes, coriander, shallots, chilli, lemon juice and salt and pepper to taste in a mixing bowl.

7 Garnish the potatoes with the sprigs of fresh coriander and serve with a spoonful of the salsa.

Dumplings in Yogurt Sauce

Adding a baghaar (seasoned oil dressing) just before serving makes this a mouth-watering accompaniment to any meal.

NUTRITIONAL INFORMATION

Calories . . . . .719 Sugars 9g
Protein . . . . .9g Fat 60g
Carbohydrate . . .38g Saturates 7g

 35 mins   35 mins

SERVES 4

INGREDIENTS

DUMPLINGS

100 g/3½ oz gram flour (see page 149)

1 tsp chilli powder

salt

½ tsp bicarbonate of soda

1 onion, finely chopped

2 green chillies, deseeded and sliced

fresh coriander leaves

150 ml/¼ pint water

300 ml/½ pint vegetable oil

YOGURT SAUCE

300 ml/½ pint natural yogurt

3 tbsp gram flour

150 ml/¼ pint water

1 tsp chopped fresh root ginger

1 tsp crushed garlic

1½ tsp chilli powder

½ tsp turmeric

1 tsp ground coriander

1 tsp ground cumin

SEASONED DRESSING

150 ml/¼ pint vegetable oil

1 tsp white cumin seeds

6 dried red chillies, diced

1 To make the dumplings, sift the gram flour into a large bowl. Add the chilli powder, ½ teaspoon salt, bicarbonate of soda, onion, green chillies and coriander and mix. Add the water and mix thoroughly to form a thick paste. Heat the oil in a frying pan. Place teaspoonfuls of the paste in the oil and fry over a medium heat, turning once, until a crisp golden brown. Set aside.

2 To make the sauce, place the yogurt in a bowl and whisk in the gram flour and the water. Add all of the spices and 1½ teaspoons salt and mix well.

3 Press this mixture through a large sieve into a saucepan. Bring to the boil over a low heat, stirring constantly. If the yogurt sauce becomes too thick, add a little extra water.

4 Pour the sauce into a deep serving dish and arrange all the dumplings on top. Set aside and keep warm.

5 To make the dressing, heat the oil in a frying pan. Add the cumin seeds and the chillies and fry until darker in colour and giving off their aroma. Pour the dressing over the dumplings and serve hot.

Samosas

Samosas, which are a sort of Indian Cornish pasty, make excellent snacks. In India, they are popular snacks at roadside stalls.

NUTRITIONAL INFORMATION

Calories	261	Sugars	.......0.4g
Protein	.........2g	Fat	.........23g
Carbohydrate	...13g	Saturates	.......4g

40 mins   40 mins

MAKES 12

INGREDIENTS

PASTRY

100 g/3½ oz self-raising flour

½ tsp salt

40 g/1½ oz butter, cut into small pieces

4 tbsp water

FILLING

3 potatoes, boiled

1 tsp finely chopped root ginger

1 tsp crushed garlic

½ tsp white cumin seeds

½ tsp mixed onion and mustard seeds

1 tsp salt

½ tsp crushed red chillies

2 tbsp lemon juice

2 small green chillies, finely chopped

ghee or oil, for deep-frying

3 To make the filling, mash the boiled potatoes gently and mix with the ginger, garlic, white cumin seeds, onion and mustard seeds, salt, crushed red chillies, lemon juice and green chillies.

4 Form the dough into 12 small balls and roll out very thinly to form a round. Cut in half, dampen the edges and shape into cones. Fill the cones with a little of the filling, dampen the top and bottom edges of the cones and pinch together to seal. Set aside.

5 Fill a deep pan one-third full with oil and heat to 180°C/350°F or until a small cube of bread browns in 30 seconds. Carefully lower the samosas into the oil, a few at a time, and fry for 2–3 minutes, or until golden brown. Remove from the oil and drain thoroughly on kitchen paper. Serve hot or cold.

1 Sift the flour and salt into a bowl. Add the butter and rub into the flour until the mixture resembles fine breadcrumbs.

2 Pour in the water and mix with a fork to form a dough. Pat it into a ball and knead for 5 minutes, or until smooth. Cover and leave to rise.

Potato Fritters with Relish

These are incredibly simple to make and sure to be popular served as a tempting snack or as an accompaniment to almost any Indian meal.

NUTRITIONAL INFORMATION

Calories 294   Sugars 4g
Protein . . . . .4g   Fat 24g
Carbohydrate . . .18g   Saturates 3g

 40 mins   15 mins

SERVES 8

INGREDIENTS

60 g/2 oz wholemeal flour

½ tsp ground coriander

½ tsp cumin seeds

¼ tsp chilli powder

½ tsp turmeric

¼ tsp salt

1 egg

3 tbsp milk

350 g/12 oz potatoes, peeled

1–2 garlic cloves, crushed

4 spring onions, chopped

60 g/2 oz sweetcorn kernels

vegetable oil, for shallow frying

ONION & TOMATO RELISH

1 onion, peeled

225 g/8 oz tomatoes

2 tbsp chopped fresh coriander

2 tbsp chopped fresh mint

2 tbsp lemon juice

½ tsp roasted cumin seeds

¼ tsp salt

pinch of cayenne pepper

 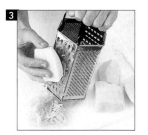 

1 First make the relish. Cut the onion and tomatoes into small dice and place in a bowl with the remaining ingredients. Mix together well and leave to stand for at least 15 minutes before serving to allow the flavours to blend.

2 Place the flour in a bowl, stir in the spices and salt and make a well in the centre. Add the egg and milk and mix to form a fairly thick batter.

3 Coarsely grate the potatoes, place them in a sieve and rinse well under cold running water. Drain and squeeze dry, then stir them into the batter with the garlic, spring onions and corn and mix to combine thoroughly.

4 Heat about 5 mm/¼ inch of vegetable oil in a large frying pan and add a few tablespoonfuls of the mixture at a time, flattening each one to form a thin cake. Fry over a low heat, turning frequently, for 2–3 minutes, or until golden brown and cooked through.

5 Drain the fritters on absorbent kitchen paper and keep them hot while frying the remaining mixture in the same way. Serve the potato fritters hot with the onion and tomato relish.

Falafel

These are a very tasty, well-known Middle Eastern dish of small chick pea-based balls, spiced and deep-fried.

NUTRITIONAL INFORMATION

Calories . . . . .491 Sugars 3g
Protein . . . . .15g Fat 30g
Carbohydrate . . .43g Saturates 3g

25 mins   10–15 mins

SERVES 4

I N G R E D I E N T S

675 g/1½ lb canned chick peas, drained

1 red onion, chopped

3 garlic cloves, crushed

100 g/3½ oz wholemeal bread

2 small fresh red chillies

1 tsp ground cumin

1 tsp ground coriander

½ tsp turmeric

1 tbsp chopped fresh coriander, plus extra
   to garnish

salt and pepper

1 egg, beaten

100 g/3½ oz wholemeal breadcrumbs

vegetable oil, for deep-frying

tomato and cucumber salad and lemon
   wedges, to serve

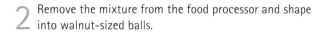

1 Put the chick peas, onion, garlic, wholemeal bread, chillies, spices and fresh coriander in a food processor or blender and process for 30 seconds. Stir the mixture and season to taste with salt and pepper.

2 Remove the mixture from the food processor and shape into walnut-sized balls.

3 Place the beaten egg in a shallow bowl and place the wholemeal breadcrumbs on a plate. First dip the chick pea balls into the egg to coat them thoroughly and then roll them in the breadcrumbs, shaking off any excess.

4 Heat the oil for deep-frying to 180°C/350°F or until a cube of bread browns in 30 seconds. Fry the falafel, in batches if necessary, for 2–3 minutes, until crisp and browned. Carefully remove them from the oil with a slotted spoon and dry on absorbent kitchen paper.

5 Garnish the falafel with the reserved chopped coriander and serve with a tomato and cucumber salad and lemon wedges.

Gnocchi with Tomato Sauce

These gnocchi, or small dumplings, are made with potato, flavoured with spinach and served in a delicious tomato and basil sauce.

NUTRITIONAL INFORMATION

Calories 337   Sugars 4g
Protein . . . . .9g   Fat 10g
Carbohydrate . . .52g   Saturates 4g

 25 mins   1 hr

SERVES 4

I N G R E D I E N T S

450 g/1 lb baking potatoes

75 g/2¾ oz fresh spinach

1 tsp water

3 tbsp butter or margarine

1 small egg, beaten

150 g/5½ oz plain flour

fresh basil leaves, to garnish

T O M A T O   S A U C E

1 tbsp olive oil

1 shallot, chopped

1 tbsp tomato purée

225 g/8 oz canned chopped tomatoes

2 tbsp chopped fresh basil

6 tbsp red wine

1 tsp caster sugar

salt and pepper

1 Cook the potatoes in their skins in a pan of boiling salted water for 20 minutes. Drain well and press through a sieve into a bowl.

2 Cook the spinach in the water for 5 minutes or until wilted. Drain and pat dry with kitchen paper, then chop and stir into the potatoes.

3 Add the butter or margarine, egg and half of the flour to the spinach and potato mixture, mixing well. Turn out on to a floured surface, gradually kneading in the remaining flour to form a soft dough.

4 With floured hands, roll the dough into thin ropes and cut off 2 cm/¾ inch pieces. Press the centre of each dumpling with your finger, drawing it towards you to curl the sides of the gnocchi. Cover the gnocchi with clingfilm and leave to chill.

5 Heat the oil for the sauce in a pan and sauté the chopped shallot for 5 minutes. Add the tomato purée, tomatoes, basil, red wine and sugar and season well. Bring to the boil and then simmer for 20 minutes.

6 Bring a pan of salted water to the boil and cook the gnocchi for 2–3 minutes or until they rise to the top of the pan. Drain well and transfer to serving dishes. Spoon the tomato sauce over the gnocchi. Garnish with basil and serve.

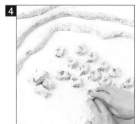
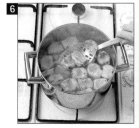

Indian-style Omelette

Omelettes are very versatile: they go with almost anything and you can also serve them at any time of the day.

NUTRITIONAL INFORMATION

Calories	132	Sugars	.........1g
Protein	.........7g	Fat	...........11g
Carbohydrate	....2g	Saturates	.......2g

  10 mins   20 mins

SERVES 4

INGREDIENTS

1 small onion, very finely chopped

2 fresh green chillies, deseeded and finely chopped

2 tbsp finely chopped fresh coriander leaves

4 eggs

1 tsp salt

4 tbsp vegetable oil

fresh basil sprigs, to garnish

toasted bread or crisp green salad, to serve

1 Place the chopped onion, chillies and coriander in a large mixing bowl and mix together.

2 Whisk the eggs in a separate bowl. Stir the onion mixture into the eggs. Add the salt and whisk again.

3 Heat 1 tbsp of the oil in a large, heavy-based frying pan over a medium heat. Place a ladleful of the omelette batter in the pan. Cook the omelette, turning once and pressing down with a flat spoon to make sure that the egg is cooked right through, until the omelette is just firm and golden brown.

4 Repeat the same process with the remaining batter. Set the omelettes aside as you make them and keep them warm while you cook the remaining batter.

5 Serve the omelettes hot, garnished with the fresh basil sprigs and accompanied by toasted bread. Alternatively, simply serve the omelettes with a crisp green salad for a light lunch.

COOK'S TIP
Whether free-range or intensively farmed, eggs are susceptible to bacteria. Store them in the refrigerator, with the pointed end downwards, for up to 2 weeks, and never use cracked or dirty eggs. Bring them to room temperature about 30 minutes before using.

Creamy Stuffed Mushrooms

These oven-baked mushrooms are covered with a creamy potato and mushroom filling topped with melted cheese.

NUTRITIONAL INFORMATION

Calories 214   Sugars 1g
Protein . . . . .5g   Fat 17g
Carbohydrate . . . .11g   Saturates 11g

20 mins, plus soaking time

40 mins

SERVES 4

INGREDIENTS

25 g/1 oz dried ceps

225 g/8 oz floury potatoes, diced

2 tbsp butter, melted

4 tbsp double cream

2 tbsp chopped fresh chives

salt and pepper

8 large open-cap mushrooms

25 g/1 oz Emmenthal cheese, grated

150 ml/5 fl oz vegetable stock

fresh chives, to garnish

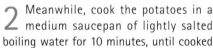

1 Place the dried ceps in a small bowl. Add sufficient boiling water to cover and set aside to soak for 20 minutes.

2 Meanwhile, cook the potatoes in a medium saucepan of lightly salted boiling water for 10 minutes, until cooked through and tender. Drain them well and mash until smooth.

3 Drain the soaked ceps and then chop them finely. Mix them into the mashed potato.

4 Thoroughly blend the butter, cream and chives together and pour the mixture into the ceps and potato mixture, stirring well to combine. Season to taste with salt and pepper.

5 Remove the stalks from the open-cap mushrooms. Chop the stalks and stir them into the potato mixture. Spoon the mixture into the open-cap mushrooms and sprinkle the grated cheese over the top.

6 Arrange the filled mushrooms in a shallow ovenproof dish and pour the vegetable stock around them.

7 Cover the dish and cook in a preheated oven, 220°C/425°F/Gas Mark 7, for 20 minutes. Remove the lid and cook for a further 5 minutes until the tops are golden.

8 Garnish the mushrooms with fresh chives and serve at once.

VARIATION

Use fresh mushrooms instead of the dried ceps, if preferred, and stir some chopped mixed nuts into the mushroom stuffing mixture for extra crunch.

Lentils & Mixed Vegetables

The green lentils used in this recipe require soaking but are worth it for the flavour. If time is short, you could use red split peas instead.

NUTRITIONAL INFORMATION

Calories	386	Sugars	........16g
Protein	........12g	Fat	.........23g
Carbohydrate	...35g	Saturates	......12g

 45 mins   40–45 mins

SERVES 4

INGREDIENTS

150 g/5½ oz green lentils

60 g/2 oz butter or margarine

2 garlic cloves, crushed

2 tbsp olive oil

1 tbsp cider vinegar

1 red onion, cut into 8 wedges

50 g/1¾ oz baby sweetcorn cobs, halved lengthways

1 yellow pepper, deseeded and cut into strips

1 red pepper, deseeded and cut into strips

50 g/1¾ oz French beans, halved

125 ml/4 fl oz vegetable stock

2 tbsp clear honey

salt and pepper

crusty bread, to serve

1 Soak the lentils in a large saucepan of cold water for 25 minutes. Bring to the boil, reduce the heat and simmer for 20 minutes. Drain thoroughly.

2 Add 1 tablespoon of the butter or margarine, 1 of the garlic cloves, 1 tablespoon of olive oil and the vinegar to the lentils and mix well.

3 Melt the remaining butter, garlic and olive oil in a frying pan and stir-fry the onion, corn cobs, peppers and beans for 3–4 minutes.

4 Add the vegetable stock and bring to the boil. Boil for about 10 minutes, or until the liquid has evaporated.

5 Add the honey and season with salt and pepper to taste. Stir in the lentil mixture and cook for 1 minute to heat through. Spoon on to warmed serving plates and serve with crusty bread.

VARIATION
This pan-fry is very versatile: you can use a mixture of your favourite vegetables, if you prefer. Try courgettes, carrots or mangetout.

Corn & Potato Fritters

These crisp little fritters make an ideal supper dish for two – topped with a poached egg or two, they are surprisingly filling.

NUTRITIONAL INFORMATION

Calories ....639 Sugars 17g
Protein ....28g Fat 31g
Carbohydrate ...65g Saturates 9g

 20 mins   20 mins

SERVES 2

INGREDIENTS

2 tbsp oil

1 small onion, thinly sliced

1 garlic clove, crushed

350 g/12 oz potatoes

200 g/7 oz canned sweetcorn, drained

½ tsp dried oregano

1 egg, beaten

salt and pepper

60 g/2 oz Edam or Gouda cheese, grated

2–4 eggs

2–4 tomatoes, sliced

fresh parsley sprigs, to garnish

1 Heat 1 tablespoon of the oil in a non-stick frying pan. Add the onion and garlic and fry very gently, stirring frequently, until soft but only lightly coloured. Remove the pan from the heat.

2 Grate the potatoes coarsely into a bowl and mix in the sweetcorn, oregano, beaten egg and salt and pepper to taste. Add the fried onion.

3 Heat the remaining oil in the frying pan. Divide the potato mixture in half and add to the pan to make 2 oval-shaped cakes, levelling and shaping the cakes with a palette knife.

4 Cook the fritters over a low heat for about 10 minutes, until golden brown underneath and almost cooked through, keeping them tidily in shape with the palette knife and loosening so they don't stick.

5 Sprinkle each potato fritter with the grated cheese and place under a preheated moderately hot grill until golden brown.

6 Meanwhile, poach 1 or 2 eggs for each person until just cooked. Transfer the fritters to warmed plates and top with the eggs and sliced tomatoes. Garnish with parsley and serve at once.

Stuffed Onions

Try to find onions that are all about the same size for even cooking and an attractive presentation. Serve this dish with rice and a salad.

NUTRITIONAL INFORMATION

Calories 190   Sugars 21g
Protein ....7g   Fat 6g
Carbohydrate ...28g   Saturates 1g

30 mins   40 mins

SERVES 6

INGREDIENTS

40 g/1½ oz raisins

6 onions

1 tbsp sunflower oil

1 garlic clove, finely chopped

450 g/1 lb spinach, thick stalks removed

salt

125 ml/4 fl oz natural yogurt

25 g/1 oz pine nuts, toasted

pinch of freshly grated nutmeg

2 tbsp fresh wholemeal breadcrumbs

1 Place the raisins in a small bowl, cover with water and set aside. Meanwhile, cut a thin slice off the bases of the onions so that they stand level. Cut off a 1 cm/½ inch slice from the tops. Using a teaspoon or melon baller, carefully scoop out the onion flesh, leaving a shell 1 cm/½ inch thick. Set a steamer over a saucepan of boiling water and arrange the onion shells inside it. Cover tightly and steam for 10–15 minutes, until tender. Remove from the heat and set aside.

2 Finely chop the scooped-out onion flesh. Heat the oil in a heavy-based frying pan. Add the chopped onion and cook, stirring occasionally, for 5 minutes,

until softened. Stir in the garlic and cook for 2 minutes, then add the spinach. Cover and cook for 3 minutes, until the spinach has wilted. Season with salt and cook, uncovered, stirring occasionally, for about 5 minutes, until all the liquid has evaporated. Remove from the heat and set aside to cool.

3 Drain the raisins and add them to the onion and spinach mixture with the

yogurt, pine nuts and nutmeg. Drain the onion shells, then spoon the spinach stuffing into them. Spread the remaining stuffing over the base of an ovenproof dish and stand the stuffed onions on top. Sprinkle the onions with the breadcrumbs and bake in a preheated oven, 180°C/350°F/Gas Mark 4, for 25 minutes. Place the dish under a preheated grill for 3-4 minutes, until the breadcrumbs are crisp. Serve immediately.

Spanish Omelette

This is an incredibly adaptable dish and you can incorporate left-over and fresh vegetables of your choice.

NUTRITIONAL INFORMATION

Calories	376	Sugars	.........7g
Protein	........19g	Fat	.........22g
Carbohydrate	...27g	Saturates	.......8g

20 mins   20 mins

SERVES 4

I N G R E D I E N T S

2 tbsp olive oil

1 Spanish onion, chopped

2 garlic cloves, finely chopped

1 red pepper, deseeded and diced

250 g/9 oz courgettes, thinly sliced

2 tomatoes, skinned and diced

350 g/12 oz boiled potatoes,
  diced (optional)

6 eggs

4 tbsp milk

2 tsp chopped fresh tarragon

salt and pepper

85 g/3 oz Cheddar cheese, grated

1 Heat the oil in a large, heavy-based frying pan with a flameproof handle. Add the onion and cook, stirring occasionally, for 5 minutes, until softened. Add the garlic, red pepper and courgettes and cook, stirring frequently, for 5 minutes more. Add the tomatoes and potatoes and cook, stirring frequently, for 3 minutes.

2 Beat the eggs with the milk and chopped tarragon in a bowl and season to taste with salt and pepper. Pour the egg mixture into the pan and cook, without stirring, until the eggs begin to set and the underside of the omelette is golden brown.

3 Sprinkle the cheese evenly over the surface and place the pan under a preheated grill. Cook for 3-4 minutes, until the cheese has melted and the top is golden brown. Cut into wedges to serve.

COOK'S TIP

If you do not have a frying pan with a heatproof handle, cover the handle with a double layer of foil, but be very careful that the pan doesn't slip out as you lift it.

Garlic Mushrooms on Toast

This is so simple to prepare and looks great if you use a variety of mushrooms for shape and texture.

NUTRITIONAL INFORMATION

Calories 366   Sugars 2g
Protein ....9g   Fat 18g
Carbohydrate ...45g   Saturates 4g

 10 mins   10 mins

SERVES 4

INGREDIENTS

75 g/2¾ oz margarine

2 garlic cloves, crushed

350 g/12 oz mixed mushrooms,
  such as open-cap, button, oyster and
  shiitake, sliced

8 diagonally cut slices French bread

1 tbsp chopped fresh parsley

salt and pepper

1 Melt the margarine in a frying pan. Add the crushed garlic and cook, stirring constantly, for 30 seconds.

2 Add the mushrooms and cook, turning occasionally, for 5 minutes.

3 Toast the French bread slices under a preheated medium grill for 2–3 minutes, turning once. Transfer the toasts to a serving plate.

4 Toss the parsley into the mushrooms, mixing well, and season well with salt and pepper to taste.

5 Spoon the mushroom mixture over the toasts and serve immediately.

COOK'S TIP
Always store mushrooms for a maximum of 24–36 hours in the refrigerator, in paper bags, as they sweat in plastic. Wild mushrooms should be washed but cultivated varieties can simply be wiped clean with kitchen paper.

Pakoras

Pakoras are eaten all over India. They are made in many different ways and with a variety of fillings. Sometimes they are served with yogurt.

NUTRITIONAL INFORMATION

Calories 331	Sugars 5g
Protein 9g	Fat 22g
Carbohydrate . . .27g	Saturates 3g

 15 mins   15–20 mins

SERVES 4

INGREDIENTS

6 tbsp gram flour (see page 149)

½ tsp salt

1 tsp chilli powder

1 tsp baking powder

1½ tsp white cumin seeds

1 tsp pomegranate seeds

300 ml/½ pint water

1 tbsp finely chopped fresh coriander

vegetables of your choice: cauliflower cut into small florets, onions cut into rings, sliced potatoes, sliced aubergines or fresh spinach leaves

vegetable oil, for deep-frying

sprigs of fresh coriander, to garnish

COOK'S TIP

When deep-frying, it is important to use oil at the correct temperature. If the oil is too hot, the outside of the food will burn, as will the spices, before the inside is cooked. If the oil is too cool, the food will be sodden with oil before a crisp batter forms.

1 Sift the gram flour into a large mixing bowl. Add the salt, chilli powder, baking powder, cumin and pomegranate seeds and blend together well. Pour in the water and beat thoroughly to form a smooth batter.

2 Add the chopped coriander and mix. Set the batter aside.

3 Dip the prepared vegetables of your choice into the batter, coat well and shake off any excess batter.

4 Heat the vegetable oil in a large heavy-based pan to 180°C/350°F, when a cube of bread will brown in it in 30 seconds. Place the battered vegetables in the oil and deep-fry them, in batches, turning once. Remove with a slotted spoon when crisp.

5 Transfer the cooked vegetables to absorbent kitchen paper and drain thoroughly. Serve immediately on a warmed plate, with a sprig of fresh coriander to garnish.

Grilled Potatoes with Lime

This dish is ideal with grilled or barbecued foods, because the potatoes themselves may be cooked by either method.

NUTRITIONAL INFORMATION

Calories 253   Sugars 0.7g
Protein . . . . .1.8g   Fat 22.2g
Carbohydrate . .12.4g   Saturates 5.8g

10 mins   15–20 mins

SERVES 4

I N G R E D I E N T S

450 g/1 lb potatoes, unpeeled and scrubbed

3 tbsp butter, melted

2 tbsp chopped fresh thyme

salt and pepper

paprika, for dusting

LIME MAYONNAISE

150 ml/5 fl oz mayonnaise

2 tsp lime juice

finely grated rind of 1 lime

1 garlic clove, crushed

pinch of paprika

salt and pepper

1 Cut the potatoes into 1 cm/½ inch thick slices.

2 Cook the potatoes in a saucepan of boiling water for 5–7 minutes – they should still be quite firm. Remove the potatoes with a perforated spoon and drain thoroughly.

3 Line a grill pan with kitchen foil. Place a layer of potato slices on the foil.

4 Brush the potatoes with the melted butter and sprinkle the thyme on top. Season to taste with salt and pepper.

5 Cook the potatoes under a preheated medium grill for 10 minutes, turning once during cooking.

6 Meanwhile, prepare the lime mayonnaise. In a small bowl, combine the mayonnaise, lime juice, lime rind, garlic and paprika, and season with salt and pepper to taste.

7 Dust the hot potato slices with a little paprika and serve them hot with the lime mayonnaise.

COOK'S TIP

For an impressive side dish, thread the potato slices on to skewers and cook over medium-hot barbecue coals.

Spinach Pancakes

Serve these attractive stuffed pancakes as a light lunch or supper dish, with a tomato and basil salad for a dramatic colour contrast.

NUTRITIONAL INFORMATION

Calories ....663 Sugars 9g
Protein ....32g Fat 48g
Carbohydrate ...28g Saturates 18g

 25 mins   25 mins

SERVES 4

INGREDIENTS

90 g/3 oz wholemeal flour

1 egg

150 ml/5 fl oz natural yogurt

3 tbsp water

1 tbsp vegetable oil, plus extra for brushing

200 g/7 oz frozen leaf spinach, thawed and puréed

pinch of grated nutmeg

salt and pepper

TO GARNISH

lemon wedges

fresh coriander sprigs

FILLING

1 tbsp vegetable oil

3 spring onions, thinly sliced

225 g/8 oz ricotta cheese

4 tbsp natural yogurt

85 g/3 oz Gruyère cheese, grated

1 egg, lightly beaten

115 g/4 oz unsalted cashew nuts

2 tbsp chopped fresh parsley

pinch of cayenne pepper

1 Sift the flour and a pinch of salt into a bowl and tip in any bran left in the sieve. Whisk the egg with the yogurt, water and oil. Gradually pour it on to the flour, beating constantly. Stir in the spinach and season with pepper and nutmeg.

2 To make the filling, heat the oil in a pan and fry the spring onions until translucent. Remove with a slotted spoon and drain on kitchen paper.

3 Beat the ricotta with the yogurt and half the Gruyère. Beat in the egg and stir in the spring onions, the cashew nuts and the parsley. Season with salt and cayenne to taste.

4 Lightly brush a small, heavy frying pan with oil and heat. Pour in 3–4 tablespoons of the pancake batter and tilt the pan so that it covers the base. Cook for about 3 minutes until bubbles appear in the centre. Turn and cook the other side for about 2 minutes until lightly browned. Slide the pancake on to a warmed plate, cover with foil and keep warm while you cook the remainder. The batter should make 8–12 pancakes.

5 Spread a little filling over each pancake and fold in half and then half again, envelope style. Spoon the remaining filling into the opening.

6 Grease a shallow, ovenproof dish and arrange the pancakes in a single layer. Sprinkle on the remaining cheese and cook in a preheated oven, 180°C/350°F/Gas Mark 4, for about 15 minutes. Serve hot, garnished with lemon and coriander.

Sweet Potato Salad

This piquant salad is a meal in itself. Choose a mixture of colourful salad leaves with a range of sweet and bitter flavours.

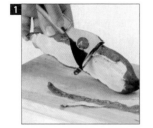  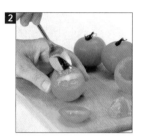

NUTRITIONAL INFORMATION

Calories	143	Sugars	........19g
Protein	.........6g	Fat	...........1g
Carbohydrate	...29g	Saturates	.......1g

 10 mins   10 mins

SERVES 4

INGREDIENTS

1 sweet potato, peeled and diced

4 baby carrots, halved

4 tomatoes

4 celery sticks, chopped

225 g/8 oz canned borlotti beans, drained and rinsed

115 g/4 oz mixed salad leaves, such as frisée, rocket, radicchio and oakleaf lettuce

1 tbsp sultanas

4 spring onions, finely chopped

125 ml/4 fl oz Honey and Yogurt Dressing (see page 8)

1 Cook the sweet potato in a pan of boiling water until just tender. Drain and set aside in a bowl. Cook the carrots in a pan of boiling water for 1 minute. Drain and add to the bowl.

2 Drain and rinse the beans. Cut the tops off the tomatoes and scoop out the seeds. Chop the flesh and add to the bowl, mixing in the celery and beans.

3 Line a serving bowl with the salad leaves. Spoon the sweet potato and bean mixture on top. Sprinkle with the sultanas and spring onions, spoon on the Honey and Yogurt dressing and serve the salad immediately.

COOK'S TIP
Cook the sweet potato until it is just tender, otherwise it will absorb too much water and become unpleasantly soggy.

Hash Browns & Tomato

Hash Browns are a popular American recipe of fried potato squares, often served as brunch. This recipe includes extra vegetables.

NUTRITIONAL INFORMATION

Calories 339   Sugars 9g
Protein . . . . .10g   Fat 21g
Carbohydrate . . .29g   Saturates 7g

 20 mins   45 mins

SERVES 4

INGREDIENTS

500 g/1 lb 2 oz waxy potatoes

1 carrot, diced

1 celery stick, diced

55 g/2 oz button mushrooms, diced

1 onion, diced

2 garlic cloves, crushed

25 g/1 oz frozen peas, thawed

55 g/2 oz Parmesan cheese, freshly grated

salt and pepper

4 tbsp vegetable oil

2 tbsp butter

SAUCE

300 ml/10 fl oz passata

2 tbsp chopped fresh coriander

1 tbsp vegetarian Worcestershire sauce

½ tsp chilli powder

2 tsp brown sugar

2 tsp American mustard

75 ml/2½ fl oz vegetable stock

1 Cook the potatoes in a saucepan of lightly salted boiling water for 10 minutes. Drain and leave to cool. Meanwhile, cook the carrot in lightly salted boiling water for 5 minutes.

2 When the potatoes are cool enough to handle, grate them with a coarse grater.

3 Drain the carrot and add it to the grated potatoes, together with the celery, mushrooms, onion, garlic, peas and cheese. Mix together gently and season to taste with salt and pepper.

4 Put all of the sauce ingredients in a small saucepan and bring to the boil. Reduce the heat to low and simmer for 15 minutes.

5 Divide the potato mixture into 8 portions of equal size and shape into flattened rectangles with your hands.

6 Heat the oil and butter in a frying pan and cook the hash browns in batches over a low heat for 4–5 minutes on each side, until crisp and golden brown.

7 Transfer the hash browns to a serving plate and serve immediately with the tomato sauce.

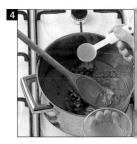

Tofu Burgers

Flavoured with spices and served with a tahini-flavoured relish, these delicious burgers are perfect for vegetarians.

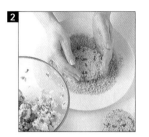

NUTRITIONAL INFORMATION

Calories 471	Sugars 7g
Protein 22g	Fat 12g
Carbohydrate ...74g	Saturates 2g

 15 mins 20 mins

SERVES 4

I N G R E D I E N T S

1 small red onion, finely chopped

1 garlic clove, crushed

1 tsp ground cumin

1 tsp ground coriander

2 tbsp lemon juice

400 g/14 oz canned chick peas, drained and rinsed

75 g/2¾ oz soft silken tofu, drained

115 g/4 oz cooked potato, diced

4 tbsp freshly chopped coriander

salt and pepper

75 g/2¾ oz dry brown breadcrumbs

1 tbsp vegetable oil

burger buns

2 tomatoes, sliced

1 large carrot, grated

R E L I S H

1 tsp tahini

4 tbsp low-fat natural fromage frais

2.5 cm/1 inch piece cucumber, finely chopped

1 tbsp chopped fresh coriander

garlic salt, to season

1 Place the onion, garlic, spices and lemon juice in a pan, bring to the boil, cover and simmer for 5 minutes until the onions are softened.

2 Place the chick peas, tofu and potato in a bowl and mash well. Stir in the onion mixture, the coriander and the seasoning, and mix together. Divide the mixture into 4 equal portions and form into patties 10 cm/4 inch across.

3 Sprinkle the breadcrumbs on to a plate and press the burgers into the crumbs to coat both sides.

4 Heat the oil in a large frying pan and fry the burgers for 5 minutes on each side until golden. Mix the relish ingredients together in a bowl and leave to chill. Place the sliced tomato and grated carrot on the buns and top each with a burger. Serve with the relish.

Vegetable Croquettes

These croquettes, made from a spicy vegetable mixture, are delightfully easy to make and taste delicious.

NUTRITIONAL INFORMATION

Calories 268   Sugars 1g
Protein . . . . .2g   Fat 25g
Carbohydrate . . . .9g   Saturates 3g

20 mins   25 mins

MAKES 12

INGREDIENTS

600 g/1 lb 5 oz potatoes, sliced

1 onion, sliced

½ cauliflower, cut into small florets

50 g/1¾ oz cooked peas

1 tbsp spinach purée

2–3 green chillies

1 tbsp fresh coriander leaves

1 tsp finely chopped fresh root ginger

1 tsp crushed garlic

1 tsp ground coriander

1 pinch turmeric

1 tsp salt

50 g/1¾ oz breadcrumbs

300 ml/10 fl oz vegetable oil

fresh chilli strips, to garnish

1 Place the potatoes, onion and cauliflower florets in a pan of water and bring to the boil. Reduce the heat and simmer until the potatoes are cooked through. Remove the vegetables from the pan with a slotted spoon and drain thoroughly. Set aside.

2 Add the peas and spinach to the vegetables and mix, mashing down thoroughly with a fork.

3 Using a sharp knife, deseed and finely chop the green chillies and the fresh coriander leaves.

4 Mix the chillies and fresh coriander leaves with the ginger, garlic, ground coriander, turmeric and salt.

5 Blend the spice mixture into the vegetables, mixing with a fork to make a paste.

6 Scatter the breadcrumbs on to a large plate.

7 Break off 10–12 small balls from the spice paste. Flatten them with the palm of your hand or with a palette knife to make flat, round shapes.

8 Dip each croquette in the breadcrumbs, coating well.

9 Heat the oil in a heavy-based frying-pan and shallow-fry the croquettes, in batches, until golden brown, turning occasionally. Transfer to warm serving plates and garnish with the fresh chilli strips. Serve hot.

Buck Rarebit

This substantial version of cheese on toast – a creamy cheese sauce topped with a poached egg – makes a tasty, filling snack.

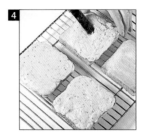

NUTRITIONAL INFORMATION

Calories	478	Sugars	.........2g
Protein	........29g	Fat	..........34g
Carbohydrate	...14g	Saturates	......20g

 10 mins 15-20 mins

SERVES 4

I N G R E D I E N T S

350 g/12 oz mature Cheddar cheese

125 g/4½ oz Gouda, Gruyère or
　　Emmenthal cheese

1 tsp mustard powder

1 tsp wholegrain mustard

salt and pepper

2-4 tbsp brown ale, cider or milk

½ tsp vegetarian Worcestershire sauce

4 thick slices white or brown bread

4 eggs

TO GARNISH

tomato wedges

watercress sprigs

1 Grate the cheeses and place in a non-stick saucepan.

2 Add the mustards, seasoning, brown ale, cider or milk and the vegetarian Worcestershire sauce and mix well.

3 Heat the cheese mixture gently, stirring until it has melted and is completely thick and creamy. Remove from the heat and leave to cool a little.

4 Toast the slices of bread on each side under a preheated grill then spread the rarebit mixture evenly over each piece.

Put under a moderate grill until golden brown and bubbling.

5 Meanwhile, poach the eggs. If using a poacher, grease the cups, heat the water in the pan and, when just boiling, break the eggs into the cups. Cover and simmer for 4–5 minutes until just set. Alternatively, bring about 4 cm/1½ inches of water to the boil in a frying pan or large saucepan and for each egg quickly swirl the water with a knife and drop the egg into the 'hole' created. Cook for about 4 minutes until just set.

6 Top the rarebits with a poached egg and serve garnished with tomato wedges and sprigs of watercress.

VARIATION
For a change, you can use part or all Stilton or other blue cheese; the appearance is not so attractive but the flavour is very good.

Feta and Potato Cakes

Served with a salad, these tasty patties make a satisfying light lunch and they are very easy to prepare, too.

NUTRITIONAL INFORMATION

Calories	269	Sugars	.........1g
Protein	.........9g	Fat	..........16g
Carbohydrate	...24g	Saturates	.......1g

 20 mins, plus chilling 35 mins

SERVES 4

INGREDIENTS

500 g/1 lb 2 oz floury potatoes, unpeeled

4 spring onions, chopped

115 g/4 oz feta cheese (drained weight), crumbled

2 tsp chopped fresh thyme

1 egg, beaten

1 tbsp lemon juice

salt and pepper

plain flour, for dusting

3 tbsp sunflower or corn oil

1 Cook the potatoes in lightly salted boiling water for about 25 minutes, until tender. Drain and peel. Place the potatoes in a bowl and mash well with a potato masher or fork.

2 Add the spring onions, feta, thyme, egg and lemon juice and season to taste with salt and pepper. Mix thoroughly. Cover the bowl with clingfilm and chill for 1 hour.

3 Take small handfuls of the potato mixture and roll into balls about the size of a walnut between the palms of your hands. Flatten each one slightly and dust all over with flour.

4 Heat the oil in a frying pan and fry the potato cakes, in batches if necessary, until golden brown on both sides. Drain on absorbent kitchen paper and serve immediately.

VARIATION
These potato cakes are also delicious made with goat's cheese instead of feta.

Paprika Potatoes

Baked potatoes are an easy and welcome snack on a cold day and here they are given a new twist with an interesting and colourful filling.

NUTRITIONAL INFORMATION

Calories 177	Sugars 6g
Protein 6g	Fat 1g
Carbohydrate . . .38g	Saturates 0g

 15 mins   1 hr 10 mins

SERVES 4

INGREDIENTS

4 baking potatoes

125 ml/4 fl oz vegetable stock

1 onion, finely chopped

1 garlic clove, finely chopped

125 ml/4 fl oz natural yogurt

2 tsp paprika

salt and pepper

1 Prick the potatoes with a fork and bake in a preheated oven, 200°C/400°F/Gas Mark 6, for about 1 hour, until tender.

2 Just before the potatoes are ready, pour the stock into a saucepan and add the onion and garlic. Bring to the boil and simmer for 5 minutes.

3 Remove the potatoes from the oven and cut a lengthways slice from the top of each. Do not switch off the oven. Using a teaspoon, carefully scoop out the flesh, leaving a shell. Stir the potato flesh into the onion mixture, then add half the

yogurt and 1½ teaspoons of the paprika and season to taste with salt and pepper. Mix well and push through a sieve with the back of a wooden spoon.

4 Spoon the potato mixture into the potato shells and return to the oven for 10 minutes, until heated through. Top the potatoes with the remaining yogurt, sprinkle the remaining paprika over it and serve immediately.

COOK'S TIP
If you like a crisp skin on baked potatoes, rub them all over with a little olive oil before baking.

Tofu Toasts

These colourful, healthy open sandwiches take only a few minutes to prepare, but they look and taste very special.

NUTRITIONAL INFORMATION

Calories 392   Sugars 6g
Protein . . . . .16g   Fat 22g
Carbohydrate . . .35g   Saturates 4g

 5–10 mins   5 mins

SERVES 4

INGREDIENTS

75 g/2¾ oz margarine

450 g/1 lb marinated, firm tofu

1 red onion, chopped

1 red pepper, deseeded and chopped

4 ciabatta rolls

2 tbsp chopped mixed fresh herbs

salt and pepper

fresh herbs, to garnish

1 Melt the margarine in a frying pan and crumble the tofu into the pan.

2 Add the onion and pepper and cook for 3–4 minutes, stirring occasionally.

3 Meanwhile, slice the ciabatta rolls in half horizontally and toast them under a hot grill for about 2–3 minutes, turning once, until lightly golden. Remove the toasts and transfer them to a warm serving plate.

4 Add the herbs to the tofu mixture, stir gently to combine and season with salt and pepper.

5 Spoon the tofu mixture on to the toast and garnish with fresh herbs. Serve at once.

COOK'S TIP

Marinated tofu adds extra flavour to this dish. Smoked tofu could be used in its place.

Lentil Croquettes

These mildly spiced croquettes are an ideal light lunch served with a crisp salad and a tahini dip.

NUTRITIONAL INFORMATION

Calories 409	Sugars 5g	
Protein 19g	Fat 17g	
Carbohydrate ...48g	Saturates 2g	

 1¼ hrs 1 hr

SERVES 4

INGREDIENTS

225 g/8 oz split red lentils

1 green pepper, deseeded and finely chopped

1 red onion, finely chopped

2 garlic cloves, crushed

1 tsp garam masala

½ tsp chilli powder

1 tsp ground cumin

2 tsp lemon juice

2 tbsp chopped unsalted peanuts

600 ml/1 pint water

1 egg, beaten

salt and pepper

3 tbsp plain flour

1 tsp turmeric

1 tsp chilli powder

4 tbsp vegetable oil

salad leaves and herbs, to garnish

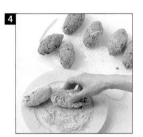

1 Put the lentils in a large pan with the pepper, onion, garlic, garam masala, chilli powder, ground cumin, lemon juice and peanuts. Add the water and bring to the boil. Reduce the heat and simmer gently, stirring occasionally, for about 30 minutes or until all the liquid has been absorbed.

2 Remove the mixture from the heat and set aside to cool slightly. Beat in the egg and season to taste with salt and pepper. Set aside to cool completely.

3 With floured hands, form the mixture into 8 rectangles or ovals.

4 Combine the flour, turmeric and chilli powder on a small plate. Roll the croquettes in the spiced flour mixture to coat thoroughly.

5 Heat the vegetable oil in a large frying pan. Add the croquettes to the pan, cooking them in 2 batches if necessary. Fry for about 10 minutes, turning once carefully to prevent the croquettes breaking up, until they are crisp and lightly coloured on both sides.

6 Transfer the croquettes to warmed serving plates and serve them immediately with a garnish of crisp salad leaves and fresh herbs.

Mixed Mushroom Cakes

These appetising little cakes are packed with creamy potato and a variety of mushrooms, and make a quick and satisfying snack.

NUTRITIONAL INFORMATION

Calories ....298 Sugars 0.8g
Protein ....5g Fat 22g
Carbohydrate ...22g Saturates 5g

 20 mins   25 mins

SERVES 4

INGREDIENTS

500 g/1 lb 2 oz floury potatoes, diced

2 tbsp butter

175 g/6 oz mixed mushrooms, chopped

2 garlic cloves, crushed

1 small egg, beaten

1 tbsp chopped fresh chives, plus extra
  to garnish

flour, for dusting

oil, for frying

salt and pepper

1 Cook the potatoes in a pan of lightly salted boiling water for 10 minutes, or until cooked through.

2 Drain the potatoes well, mash with a potato masher or fork and set aside.

3 Meanwhile, melt the butter in a frying pan. Add the mushrooms and garlic and cook, stirring constantly, for 5 minutes. Drain well.

4 Stir the mushrooms and garlic into the potatoes, together with the beaten egg and chives.

5 Divide the mixture equally into 4 portions and shape them into round

cakes. Toss the cakes in the flour until they are completely coated.

6 Heat the oil in a frying pan. Add the potato cakes and fry over a medium heat for 10 minutes until they are golden brown, turning them over carefully halfway through.

7 Serve the cakes immediately, garnished with chopped chives.

COOK'S TIP

Prepare the cakes in advance, cover and leave to chill in the refrigerator for up to 24 hours, if you wish.

Stuffed Aubergines

In this recipe, aubergines are filled with a spicy bulgur wheat and vegetable stuffing for a delicious light meal.

NUTRITIONAL INFORMATION

Calories .... .360	Sugars 17g	
Protein 9g	Fat 16g	
Carbohydrate ...50g	Saturates 2g	

40 mins   30 mins

SERVES 4

INGREDIENTS

4 aubergines

salt

175 g/6 oz bulgur wheat

300 ml/½ pint boiling water

3 tbsp olive oil

2 garlic cloves, crushed

2 tbsp pine kernels

½ tsp turmeric

1 tsp chilli powder

2 celery sticks, chopped

4 spring onions, chopped

1 carrot, grated

55 g/2 oz button mushrooms, chopped

2 tbsp raisins

2 tbsp chopped fresh coriander

green salad, to serve

1 Cut the aubergines in half lengthways and carefully scoop out the flesh with a teaspoon without piercing the 'shells'. Chop the flesh and set aside. Rub the insides of the aubergines with a little salt and set aside for 20 minutes.

2 Meanwhile, put the bulgur wheat in a large bowl and pour the boiling water over it. Set aside for about 20 minutes or until the bulgur wheat has completely absorbed the water.

3 Heat the oil in a heavy-based frying pan. Add the garlic, pine kernels, turmeric, chilli powder, celery, spring onions, carrot, mushrooms and raisins and cook over a low heat, stirring occasionally, for 2–3 minutes.

4 Stir in the reserved aubergine flesh and cook for a further 2–3 minutes. Add the chopped coriander, mixing well.

5 Remove the pan from the heat and stir in the bulgur wheat. Rinse the aubergine shells under cold water and pat dry with kitchen paper.

6 Spoon the bulgur filling into the aubergines and place in a roasting tin. Pour in a little boiling water and cook in a preheated oven, 180°C/350°F/Gas Mark 4, for about 15–20 minutes until piping hot. Remove from the oven, transfer to a warmed serving plate and serve hot with a green salad.

Spicy Potato Fries

These home-made chips are flavoured with spices and cooked in the oven. They can be served with Lime Mayonnaise (see page 219).

NUTRITIONAL INFORMATION

Calories ...... .328	Sugars 2g	
Protein 5g	Fat .... .11g	
Carbohydrate ...56g	Saturates 7g	

15 mins, plus soaking   40 mins

SERVES 4

I N G R E D I E N T S

4 large waxy potatoes

2 sweet potatoes

4 tbsp butter, melted

½ tsp chilli powder

1 tsp garam masala

salt

1 Cut the potatoes and sweet potatoes into slices about 1 cm/½ inch thick, then cut them into chip shapes.

2 Place the potatoes in a large bowl of cold salted water. Set aside to soak for 20 minutes.

3 Remove the potato slices with a slotted spoon and drain thoroughly. Pat with kitchen paper until they are completely dry.

4 Pour the melted butter on to a baking tray. Transfer the potato slices to the baking tray.

5 Sprinkle with the chilli powder, garam masala and salt (to taste), turning the potato slices to coat them with the mixture.

6 Cook the chips in a preheated oven, 200°C/400°F/Gas Mark 6, turning frequently, for 40 minutes, until browned and cooked through.

7 Drain the chips on kitchen paper to remove the excess oil and serve.

COOK'S TIP

Rinsing potatoes in cold water before cooking removes the starch, thus preventing them from sticking together. Soaking the potatoes in a bowl of cold salted water actually makes the cooked chips crisper.

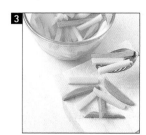

Mexican Refried Beans

Refried beans are a classic Mexican dish. They make a delicious snack served with warm tortillas and a quick onion relish.

NUTRITIONAL INFORMATION

Calories 519   Sugars 14g
Protein . . . . .25g   Fat 28g
Carbohydrate . . .44g   Saturates 9g

15 mins   15 mins

SERVES 4

INGREDIENTS

2 tbsp olive oil

1 onion, finely chopped

3 garlic cloves, crushed

1 green chilli, deseeded and chopped

400 g/14 oz canned red kidney beans, drained

400 g/14 oz canned pinto beans, drained

2 tbsp chopped fresh coriander

150 ml/¼ pint vegetable stock

8 wheat tortillas

25 g/1 oz Cheddar cheese, grated

salt and pepper

RELISH

4 spring onions, chopped

1 red onion, chopped

1 green chilli, deseeded and chopped

1 tbsp garlic wine vinegar

1 tsp caster sugar

1 tomato, chopped

1 Heat the oil in a large frying pan. Add the onion and sauté for 3–5 minutes. Stir in the garlic and chilli and cook for a further 1 minute.

2 Mash the beans with a potato masher and stir them into the pan with the chopped coriander.

3 Stir in the vegetable stock and cook the beans, stirring, for 5 minutes until soft and pulpy. Season well.

4 Place the tortillas on a baking tray and heat through in a warm oven for 1–2 minutes.

5 Mix together the relish ingredients and set aside.

6 Spoon the beans into a serving dish and top with the cheese. Roll up the tortillas and serve them immediately with the beans and relish.

COOK'S TIP
Add a little more liquid to the beans when they are cooking if they begin to catch on the bottom of the frying pan.

Vegetable Enchiladas

This warming Mexican dish consists of tortillas filled with a spicy vegetable mixture and topped with a hot tomato sauce.

NUTRITIONAL INFORMATION

Calories	264	Sugars	.........8g
Protein	........11g	Fat	..........13g
Carbohydrate	...28g	Saturates	.......5g

 20 mins 50 mins

SERVES 4

INGREDIENTS

4 flour tortillas

75 g/2¾ oz Cheddar cheese, grated

FILLING

75 g/2¾ oz spinach

2 tbsp olive oil

8 baby sweetcorn cobs, sliced

25 g/1 oz frozen peas, thawed

1 red pepper, deseeded and diced

1 carrot, diced

1 leek, sliced

2 garlic cloves, crushed

1 red chilli, deseeded and chopped

salt and pepper

SAUCE

300 ml/½ pint passata

2 shallots, chopped

1 garlic clove, crushed

300 ml/½ pint vegetable stock

1 tsp caster sugar

1 tsp chilli powder

1 To make the filling, blanch the spinach in a pan of boiling water for 2 minutes, drain well and chop.

2 Heat the oil in a frying pan and sauté the corn, peas, pepper, carrot, leek, garlic and chilli for 3–4 minutes, stirring briskly. Stir in the spinach and season well with salt and pepper to taste.

3 Put all of the sauce ingredients in a saucepan and bring them to the boil, stirring constantly. Continue to cook over a high heat for a further 20 minutes, stirring, until the sauce has thickened and reduced by a third.

4 Spoon a quarter of the filling along the centre of each tortilla. Roll the tortillas around the filling and place in an ovenproof dish, seam-side down.

5 Pour the tomato sauce over the tortillas and sprinkle the grated cheese on top. Cook in a preheated oven, 180°C/350°F/Gas Mark 4, for 20 minutes or until the cheese has melted and browned. Serve immediately.

Feta Cheese Patties

Grated carrots, courgettes and feta cheese are combined with cumin seeds, poppy seeds, curry powder and fresh parsley in these little patties.

NUTRITIONAL INFORMATION

Calories	217	Sugars	.........6g
Protein	.........6g	Fat	..........16g
Carbohydrate	...12g	Saturates	.......7g

 15 mins   20 mins

SERVES 4

I N G R E D I E N T S

2 large carrots

1 large courgette

1 small onion

55 g/2 oz feta cheese (drained weight)

4 tbsp plain flour

¼ tsp cumin seeds

½ tsp poppy seeds

1 tsp medium curry powder

1 tbsp chopped fresh parsley

salt and pepper

1 egg, beaten

2 tbsp butter

2 tbsp vegetable oil

fresh herb sprigs, to garnish

1 Grate the carrots, courgette, onion and feta cheese coarsely, either by hand or in a food processor.

2 Place the flour, cumin seeds, poppy seeds, curry powder and parsley in a large bowl and stir to combine. Season to taste with salt and pepper.

3 Add the vegetable and cheese mixture to the seasoned flour, tossing well to combine. Stir in the beaten egg.

4 Heat the butter and oil in a large, heavy-based frying pan. Place heaped tablespoonfuls of the patty mixture in the pan, flattening them slightly with the back of the spoon. Cook over a low heat for about 2 minutes on each side until crisp and golden brown. Drain on kitchen paper and keep warm. Cook more patties in the same way until all the mixture is used.

5 Serve immediately, garnished with sprigs of fresh herbs.

Bombay Bowl

You can use dried chick peas for this popular snack, but the canned sort are quick and easy without sacrificing much flavour.

NUTRITIONAL INFORMATION

Calories	183	Sugars	.........6g
Protein	.........9g	Fat	..........3g
Carbohydrate	...33g	Saturates	.....0.3g

 15 mins   15 mins

SERVES 4

I N G R E D I E N T S

400 g/14 oz canned chick peas

2 potatoes

1 onion

2 tbsp tamarind paste

6 tbsp water

1 tsp chilli powder

2 tsp sugar

1 tsp salt

G A R N I S H

1 tomato, sliced

2 fresh green chillies, deseeded and chopped

fresh coriander leaves

1 Drain the can of chick peas and place them in a bowl.

2 Using a sharp knife, cut the potatoes into even-size dice.

3 Place the diced potatoes in a saucepan of water and boil until cooked through. Test by inserting the tip of a knife into the potatoes – they should feel soft and tender. Drain and set the potatoes aside until required.

4 Using a sharp knife, finely chop the onion. Set aside until required.

5 Mix together the tamarind paste and water in a small mixing bowl.

6 Add the chilli powder, sugar and salt to the tamarind paste mixture and stir well to combine. Pour the mixture over the chick peas.

7 Add the chopped onion and the diced potatoes, and stir to mix. Season to taste with a little salt.

8 Transfer the mixture to a serving bowl and garnish with tomato, chillies and coriander leaves.

COOK'S TIP

Cream-coloured and resembling hazelnuts in appearance, chick peas have a distinctive nutty flavour and slightly crunchy texture.

Stuffed Mushrooms

Use large open-cap mushrooms for this recipe, both for their flavour and because they are ideal for stuffing.

NUTRITIONAL INFORMATION

Calories ....273 Sugars 5g
Protein ....13g Fat 18g
Carbohydrate ...15g Saturates 5g

15 mins   25 mins

SERVES 4

I N G R E D I E N T S

8 open-cap mushrooms

1 tbsp olive oil

1 small leek, chopped

1 celery stick, chopped

100 g/3½ oz firm tofu, diced

1 courgette, chopped

1 carrot, chopped

100 g/3½ oz wholemeal breadcrumbs

2 tbsp chopped fresh basil

1 tbsp tomato purée

2 tbsp pine kernels

salt and pepper

85 g/3 oz Cheddar cheese, grated

150 ml/5 fl oz vegetable stock

salad, to serve

1 Carefully remove the stalks from the mushrooms and chop them finely. Set aside the caps.

2 Heat the olive oil in a large, heavy-based frying pan over a medium heat. Add the chopped mushroom stalks, leek, celery, tofu, courgette and carrot and cook, stirring constantly, for 3–4 minutes.

3 Stir in the breadcrumbs, chopped basil, tomato purée and pine kernels. Season with salt and pepper to taste and mix thoroughly.

4 Divide the stuffing mixture evenly between the mushroom caps and sprinkle the grated cheese over the top. Arrange the mushrooms in a shallow ovenproof dish and pour the vegetable stock around them.

5 Cook in a preheated oven, 220°C/ 425°F/Gas Mark 7, for 20 minutes or until the mushrooms are cooked through and the cheese has melted. Remove the mushrooms from the dish and serve immediately with a salad.

Fritters with Garlic Sauce

Chunks of cooked potato are coated first in Parmesan cheese, then in a light batter before being fried until golden for a delicious hot snack.

NUTRITIONAL INFORMATION

Calories	599	Sugars	.........9g
Protein	........22g	Fat	..........39g
Carbohydrate	...42g	Saturates	......13g

 20 mins   20–25 mins

SERVES 4

I N G R E D I E N T S

500 g/1 lb 2 oz waxy potatoes, diced

125 g/4½ oz Parmesan cheese, freshly grated

vegetable oil, for deep-frying

S A U C E

2 tbsp butter

1 onion, halved and sliced

2 garlic cloves, crushed

2½ tbsp plain flour

300 ml/½ pint milk

1 tbsp chopped fresh parsley

B A T T E R

5 tbsp plain flour

1 small egg

150 ml/5 fl oz milk

1 To make the sauce, melt the butter in a saucepan and cook the onion and garlic over a low heat, stirring frequently, for 2–3 minutes. Add the flour and cook, stirring constantly, for 1 minute.

2 Remove from the heat and stir in the milk and parsley. Return to the heat and bring to the boil. Keep warm.

3 Meanwhile, cook the diced potatoes in a saucepan of boiling water for 5–10 minutes, until just firm. Do not overcook or they will fall apart.

4 Drain the potatoes and toss them in the Parmesan cheese. If the potatoes are still slightly wet, the cheese will stick to them and coat them well.

5 To make the batter, place the flour in a mixing bowl and gradually beat in the egg and milk until smooth. Dip the potato cubes into the batter to coat them.

6 In a large saucepan or deep-fryer, heat the oil to 180°C/350°F or until a cube of bread browns in 30 seconds. Add the fritters, in batches if necessary, and cook for 3–4 minutes, or until golden.

7 Remove the fritters with a slotted spoon and drain well. Transfer them to a warm serving bowl and serve immediately with the garlic sauce.

Cheese & Onion Rostis

These grated-potato cakes are also known as straw cakes, because they resemble a straw mat. Serve them with a tomato sauce or salad.

NUTRITIONAL INFORMATION

Calories 307   Sugars 4g
Protein . . . . .8g   Fat 13g
Carbohydrate . . .42g   Saturates 6g

10 mins   40 mins

SERVES 4

I N G R E D I E N T S

900 g/2 lb potatoes

1 onion, grated

50 g/1¾ oz Gruyère cheese, grated

2 tbsp chopped fresh parsley

salt and pepper

1 tbsp olive oil

2 tbsp butter

G A R N I S H

1 spring onion, shredded

1 small tomato, quartered

1 Parboil the potatoes in a pan of lightly salted boiling water for 10 minutes and leave to cool. Peel the potatoes and grate with a coarse grater. Place the grated potatoes in a large mixing bowl.

2 Stir in the onion, cheese and parsley. Season well with salt and pepper. Divide the potato mixture into 4 portions of equal size and form them into cakes.

3 Heat half of the olive oil and butter in a frying pan and cook two of the potato cakes over a high heat for 1 minute, then reduce the heat and cook for 5 minutes, until they are golden underneath. Turn them over and cook for a further 5 minutes. Keep warm.

4 Repeat with the other half of the oil and the remaining butter to cook the remaining 2 cakes. Transfer to warm individual serving plates, garnish and serve immediately.

COOK'S TIP

The potato cakes should be flattened as much as possible during cooking, otherwise the outsides will be cooked before the centres are done.

Aubergine Timbale

This is a great way to serve pasta as a starter, wrapped in an aubergine mould. It looks really impressive, yet it is so easy to make.

NUTRITIONAL INFORMATION

Calories	291	Sugars	11g
Protein	8g	Fat	18g
Carbohydrate	25g	Saturates	4g

25 mins   40 mins

SERVES 4

INGREDIENTS

1 large aubergine

55 g/2 oz dried macaroni

1 tbsp vegetable oil

1 onion, chopped

2 garlic cloves, crushed

2 tbsp drained canned sweetcorn

2 tbsp frozen peas, thawed

100 g/3½ oz spinach

4 tbsp grated Cheddar cheese

1 egg, beaten

225 g/8 oz canned, chopped tomatoes

1 tbsp chopped fresh basil

salt and pepper

SAUCE

4 tbsp olive oil

2 tbsp white wine vinegar

2 garlic cloves, crushed

3 tbsp chopped basil

1 tbsp caster sugar

1 Cut the aubergine lengthways into thin strips, using a potato peeler. Place in a bowl of salted boiling water and leave to stand for 3–4 minutes. Drain well.

2 Grease 4 x 150 ml/5 fl oz ramekin dishes and line with the aubergine strips, leaving 2.5 cm/1 inch overlapping.

3 Bring a pan of lightly salted water to the boil. Add the pasta, bring back to the boil and cook for 8–10 minutes until tender, but still firm to the bite. Drain.

4 Heat the oil in a pan and sauté the onion and garlic for 2–3 minutes. Stir in the sweetcorn and peas and remove the pan from the heat.

5 Blanch the spinach, drain well, chop and reserve. Add the pasta to the onion mixture with the cheese, egg,

tomatoes and basil. Season and mix. Half-fill each ramekin with some of the pasta. Place the spinach on top and then the remaining pasta mixture. Fold the aubergine over the pasta filling to cover. Put the ramekins in a roasting tin half-filled with boiling water, cover and cook in a preheated oven, 180°C/350°F/Gas Mark 4, for 20–25 minutes or until set.

6 Meanwhile, heat all the sauce ingredients in a pan. Turn out the ramekins and serve with the sauce.

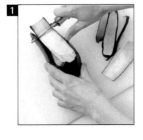
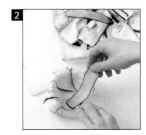

Vegetable Biryani

The Biryani originated in the north of India and was a dish reserved for festivals. The vegetables are marinated in a yogurt-based marinade.

NUTRITIONAL INFORMATION

Calories	449	Sugars	........18g
Protein	........12g	Fat	..........12g
Carbohydrate	...79g	Saturates	.......6g

15 mins, plus marinating   1 hr 5 mins

SERVES 4

I N G R E D I E N T S

300 g/10½ oz potato, diced

100 g/3½ oz baby carrots

50 g/1¾ oz okra, thickly sliced

2 celery sticks, sliced

75 g/2¾ oz baby button mushrooms, halved

1 aubergine, halved and sliced

300 ml/½ pint natural yogurt

1 tbsp grated fresh root ginger

2 large onions, grated

4 garlic cloves, crushed

1 tsp turmeric

1 tbsp curry powder

2 tbsp butter

2 onions, sliced

225 g/8 oz basmati rice

chopped fresh coriander, to garnish

1 Cook the potato cubes, carrots and okra in a pan of boiling salted water for 7–8 minutes. Drain well and place in a large bowl. Mix with the celery, mushrooms and aubergine.

2 Mix the natural yogurt, ginger, grated onions, garlic, turmeric and curry powder and spoon over the vegetables. Set aside in a cool place to marinate for at least 2 hours.

3 Heat the butter in a heavy-based frying pan. Add the sliced onions and cook over a medium heat for 5–6 minutes, until golden brown. Remove a few onions from the pan and reserve to garnish the finished dish.

4 Cook the rice in a large pan of boiling water for 7 minutes. Drain thoroughly and set aside.

5 Add the marinated vegetables to the onions and cook for 10 minutes.

6 Put half of the rice in a 2 litre/3½ pint casserole dish. Spoon the vegetable mixture on top and cover with the remaining rice.

7 Cover the dish and cook the biryani in a preheated oven, 190°C/375°F/ Gas Mark 5, for 20–25 minutes, or until the rice is tender.

8 Spoon the biryani on to a serving plate, garnish with the reserved onions and coriander and serve.

Aloo Gobi

It is not surprising that this vegetable curry is so popular, as it looks attractive, smells wonderful and tastes superb.

NUTRITIONAL INFORMATION

Calories 164	Sugars 2g
Protein 5g	Fat 7g
Carbohydrate . . .22g	Saturates 1g

 20 mins   ⏱ 20 mins

SERVES 4

INGREDIENTS

450 g/1 lb potatoes

2 tbsp groundnut or sunflower oil

1 tsp cumin seeds

2 fresh green chillies, deseeded and finely chopped

1 cauliflower, cut into florets

1 tsp ground cumin

1 tsp ground coriander

½ tsp turmeric

¼ tsp chilli powder

salt

chopped fresh coriander, to garnish

1 Cut the potatoes into 2.5-cm/1-inch pieces. Cook the potatoes in a large saucepan of boiling water for 10 minutes. Drain well.

2 Meanwhile, heat the oil in a large, heavy-based frying pan. Add the cumin seeds and fry, stirring constantly, for about 1½ minutes, until they begin to pop and give off their aroma. Add the chilli and cook, stirring constantly, for a further 1 minute.

3 Add the cauliflower to the pan and cook, stirring constantly, for 5 minutes.

4 Add the potatoes, cumin, coriander, turmeric and chilli powder and season to taste with salt. Cook, stirring frequently, for a further 10 minutes, until all the vegetables are tender.

5 Transfer the aloo gobi to a warm serving dish, garnish with the fresh coriander and serve immediately.

Vegetable-stuffed Parathas

This bread can be quite rich and is usually made for special occasions.
It can be eaten on its own or with a vegetable curry.

NUTRITIONAL INFORMATION

Calories 391	Sugars 2g
Protein 6g	Fat 24g
Carbohydrate . . .40g	Saturates 2.5g

🍞 🍞 🍞

🍲 25 mins   🕐 30–35 mins

SERVES 6

I N G R E D I E N T S

D O U G H

225 g/8 oz wholemeal flour
(ata or chapatti flour)

½ tsp salt

200 ml/7 fl oz water

100 g/3½ oz ghee, plus extra for frying

F I L L I N G

675 g/1½ lb potatoes

½ tsp turmeric

1 tsp garam masala

1 tsp finely chopped fresh root ginger

1 tbsp fresh coriander leaves

3 green chillies, deseeded and finely
chopped

1 tsp salt

1 To make the parathas, mix the flour, salt, water and ghee together in a bowl to form a dough.

2 Divide the dough into 6 equal portions. Roll each portion out on to a floured work surface. Brush the middle of the dough portions with ½ teaspoon of ghee. Fold the dough portions in half, roll into a pipe-like shape, flatten with the palms of your hands, then roll around a finger to form a coil. Roll out again, using flour to dust when necessary, to form a round about 18 cm/7 inches in diameter.

3 Place the potatoes in a saucepan of boiling water and cook until soft enough to be mashed.

4 Blend the turmeric, garam masala, ginger, coriander leaves, chillies and salt together in a bowl.

5 Add the spice mixture to the mashed potato and mix well. Spread about 1 tablespoon of the spicy potato mixture on each dough portion and cover with another rolled-out piece of dough. Seal the edges well.

6 Heat 2 teaspoons of ghee in a heavy-based frying pan. Place the parathas gently in the pan, one by one, and fry, turning and moving them about gently with a spatula, until golden.

7 Remove the parathas from the frying pan, keep hot and serve immediately.

Vegetable Samosas

These Indian snacks are perfect for a quick or light meal, served with a salad. They can be made in advance and frozen for ease of use.

NUTRITIONAL INFORMATION

Calories 291   Sugars 2g
Protein . . . . .4g   Fat 23g
Carbohydrate . . .18g   Saturates 3g

  20 mins   30 mins

MAKES 12

I N G R E D I E N T S

FILLING

2 tbsp vegetable oil

1 onion, chopped

½ tsp ground coriander

½ tsp ground cumin

pinch of turmeric

½ tsp ground ginger

½ tsp garam masala

1 garlic clove, crushed

225 g/8 oz potatoes, diced

100 g/3½ oz frozen peas, thawed

150 g/5½ oz fresh spinach, chopped

PASTRY

350 g/12 oz (12 sheets) filo pastry

oil, for deep-frying

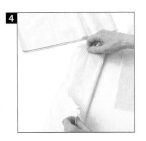

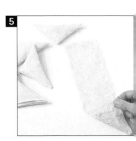

1 To make the filling, heat the oil in a frying pan. Add the onion and sauté, stirring frequently, for 1–2 minutes, until softened. Stir in all of the spices and garlic and cook for 1 minute.

2 Add the potatoes and cook over a low heat, stirring frequently, for 5 minutes, until they begin to soften.

3 Stir in the peas and spinach and cook for a further 3–4 minutes.

4 Lay the filo pastry sheets out on a clean work surface and fold each sheet in half lengthways.

5 Place 2 tablespoons of the vegetable filling at one end of each folded pastry sheet. Fold over one corner to make a triangle. Continue folding in this way to make a triangular package and seal the edges with water.

6 Repeat with the remaining pastry and the remaining filling.

7 Heat the oil for deep-frying to 180°C/350°F or until a cube of bread browns in 30 seconds. Fry the samosas, in batches, for 1–2 minutes until golden. Drain each batch on absorbent kitchen paper and keep warm while cooking the remainder. Serve immediately.

Ciabatta Rolls

Sandwiches are always a welcome snack, but can be mundane.
These crisp rolls filled with roasted peppers and cheese are irresistible.

NUTRITIONAL INFORMATION

Calories 328   Sugars 6g
Protein . . . . .8g   Fat 19g
Carbohydrate . . .34g   Saturates 9g

15 mins   10 mins

SERVES 4

INGREDIENTS

4 ciabatta rolls

2 tbsp olive oil

1 garlic clove, crushed

FILLING

1 red pepper

1 green pepper

1 yellow pepper

4 radishes, sliced

1 bunch of watercress

115 g/4 oz cream cheese

1 Slice the ciabatta rolls in half. Heat the olive oil and garlic in a saucepan. Pour the garlic and oil mixture over the cut surfaces of the rolls and set aside.

2 Halve and deseed the peppers and place, skin side up, on a grill rack. Cook under a preheated hot grill for 8–10 minutes until just beginning to char. Remove the peppers from the grill and place in a polythene bag. When cool enough to handle, peel and slice thinly.

3 Arrange the radish slices on 1 half of each roll with a few watercress leaves. Spoon the cream cheese on top. Pile the roasted peppers on top of the cream cheese and top with the other half of the roll. Serve immediately.

Feta & Spinach Omelette

This quick chunky omelette has pieces of potato cooked into the egg mixture and is then filled with feta cheese and spinach.

NUTRITIONAL INFORMATION

Calories	564	Sugars	.........6g
Protein	........30g	Fat	..........39g
Carbohydrate	...25g	Saturates	......19g

 20 mins   25–30 mins

SERVES 4

INGREDIENTS

75 g/2¾ oz butter

1.3 kg/3 lb waxy potatoes, diced

3 garlic cloves, crushed

1 tsp paprika

2 tomatoes, peeled, deseeded and diced

12 eggs

pepper

FILLING

225 g/8 oz baby spinach

1 tsp fennel seeds

125 g/4½ oz feta cheese, diced
  (drained weight)

4 tbsp natural yogurt

VARIATION
Use any other cheese, such as blue cheese, instead of the feta, and blanched broccoli in place of the baby spinach, if you prefer.

1 Heat 25 g/1 oz of the butter in a frying pan and cook the potatoes over a low heat, stirring constantly, for 7–10 minutes until golden. Transfer to a bowl.

2 Add the garlic, paprika and diced tomatoes to the pan and cook for a further 2 minutes.

3 Whisk the eggs together and season with pepper. Pour the eggs into the potatoes and mix well.

4 Cook the spinach in boiling water for 1 minute, until just wilted. Drain and refresh under cold running water. Pat dry with kitchen paper. Stir in the fennel seeds, feta cheese and yogurt.

5 Heat a quarter of the remaining butter in a 15 cm/6 inch omelette pan. Ladle a quarter of the egg and potato mixture into the pan. Cook, turning over once, for 2 minutes, until set.

6 Transfer the omelette to a serving plate. Spoon a quarter of the spinach mixture on to one half of the omelette, then fold the omelette in half over the filling. Repeat to make 4 omelettes.

Potato & Mushroom Bake

Use any mixture of mushrooms for this creamy layered bake.
It can be served straight from the dish in which it is cooked.

NUTRITIONAL INFORMATION

Calories	304	Sugars	.........2g
Protein	.........4g	Fat	..........24g
Carbohydrate	...20g	Saturates	......15g

 15 mins   1 hr

SERVES 4

I N G R E D I E N T S

2 tbsp butter

500 g/1 lb 2 oz waxy potatoes, thinly sliced

150 g/5½ oz sliced mixed mushrooms

1 tbsp chopped fresh rosemary

4 tbsp chopped fresh chives

2 garlic cloves, crushed

150 ml/5 fl oz double cream

salt and pepper

snipped fresh chives, to garnish

1 Grease a shallow round ovenproof dish with the butter.

2 Parboil the potatoes in a saucepan of boiling water for 10 minutes. Drain well. Layer a quarter of the potatoes in the base of the dish.

3 Arrange one-third of the mushrooms on top of the potatoes and sprinkle with one-third of the rosemary, chives and garlic. Continue making the layers in the same order, and finish with a layer of potatoes on top.

4 Pour the double cream evenly over the top of the potatoes. Season to taste with salt and pepper.

5 Place the dish in a preheated oven, 190°C/375°F/Gas Mark 5, and cook for about 45 minutes, or until the bake is golden brown and piping hot.

6 Garnish with snipped chives and serve at once straight from the dish.

COOK'S TIP
For a special occasion, the bake may be made in a lined cake tin and then turned out to serve.

Three-cheese Fondue

A hot cheese dip made from three different cheeses can be prepared easily and with guaranteed success in the microwave oven.

NUTRITIONAL INFORMATION

Calories ....565 Sugars 1g
Protein ....29g Fat 38g
Carbohydrate ...15g Saturates 24g

 15 mins   10 mins

SERVES 4

INGREDIENTS

1 garlic clove

300 ml/½ pint dry white wine

250 g/8 oz mild Cheddar cheese, grated

125 g/4½ oz Gruyère cheese, grated

125 g/4½ oz mozzarella cheese, grated

2 tbsp cornflour

pepper

TO SERVE

French bread

vegetables, such as courgettes, mushrooms, baby sweetcorn cobs and cauliflower

1 Bruise the garlic by placing the flat side of a knife on top and pressing down with the heel of your hand.

2 Rub the garlic around the inside of a large bowl. Discard the garlic.

3 Pour the wine into the bowl and heat, uncovered, on HIGH power for 3–4 minutes, until hot but not boiling.

4 Gradually add the Cheddar and Gruyère cheeses, stirring well after each addition (see Cook's Tip), then add the mozzarella. Stir until all the cheese is completely melted.

5 Mix the cornflour with a little water to form a smooth paste and stir it into the cheese mixture. Season to taste with pepper.

6 Cover and cook on MEDIUM power for 6 minutes, stirring twice during cooking, until the sauce is smooth.

7 Cut the French bread into bite-sized cubes and the vegetables into batons, slices or florets. To serve, keep the fondue warm over a spirit lamp or reheat as necessary in the microwave oven. Dip in cubes of French bread and batons, slices or florets of vegetables.

COOK'S TIP

Make sure you add the cheese to the wine gradually, mixing well in between each addition, to prevent the mixture from curdling.

Stuffed Tomatoes

These attractive tomatoes, with a mushroom and fresh herb filling, would be wonderful served as part of a light buffet lunch in late summer.

NUTRITIONAL INFORMATION

Calories	78	Sugars	.........5g
Protein	.........3g	Fat	..........6g
Carbohydrate	....6g	Saturates	.......1g

20 mins   35 mins

SERVES 4

INGREDIENTS

4 large tomatoes

2 tbsp finely chopped fresh basil

4 tsp olive oil

280 g/10 oz button mushrooms, very finely chopped

1 small onion, very finely chopped

2 garlic cloves, very finely chopped

1 tbsp chopped fresh parsley

225 ml/8 fl oz vegetable stock

1 tbsp freshly grated Parmesan cheese

salt and pepper

fresh basil sprigs, to garnish

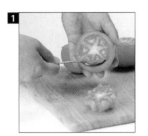

1 Slice a 'lid' from the top of each tomato and reserve. Using a teaspoon, carefully scoop out the flesh from the tomato shells and chop. Place it in a bowl and add 1 teaspoon of the basil. Invert the tomato shells on kitchen paper to drain.

2 Heat 1 tablespoon of the oil in a frying pan. Add the mushrooms, onion, garlic, parsley and remaining basil and season with pepper to taste. Cover and cook over a low heat for 2 minutes, then remove the lid and cook, stirring occasionally, for 8–10 minutes more. Meanwhile, bring the stock to the boil in a saucepan and cook until reduced by about three-quarters. Stir in the chopped tomato mixture and cook for 3–4 minutes more until thickened. Push the mixture through a sieve with a wooden spoon and stir it into the mushroom mixture. Stir in the Parmesan.

3 Stand the tomatoes in an ovenproof dish and season the insides with salt. Fill each tomato with stuffing and replace the 'lids'. Brush with the remaining oil and bake in a preheated oven, 180°C/350°F/ Gas Mark 4, for about 15 minutes, or until tender and cooked through. Serve warm, garnished with basil sprigs.

COOK'S TIP
Check for any seeds remaining in the tomato shells after you have scooped out the flesh and remove them.

Cheese & Potato Slices

This recipe takes some trouble to prepare but it is well worth the effort. The golden potato slices coated in breadcrumbs and cheese are delicious.

NUTRITIONAL INFORMATION

Calories 560	Sugars 3g
Protein 19g	Fat 31g
Carbohydrate ...55g	Saturates 7g

  10 mins 40 mins

SERVES 4

INGREDIENTS

900 g/2 lb waxy potatoes, unpeeled and thickly sliced

70 g/2½ oz fresh white breadcrumbs

40 g/1½ oz Parmesan cheese, freshly grated

1½ tsp chilli powder

2 eggs, beaten

oil, for deep frying

chilli powder, for dusting (optional)

1 Cook the potatoes in a saucepan of boiling water for about 10–15 minutes, or until the potatoes are just tender. Drain thoroughly.

2 Mix the breadcrumbs, cheese and chilli powder together in a bowl, then transfer to a shallow dish. Pour the beaten eggs into a separate shallow dish.

COOK'S TIP

The potato slices may be coated in the cheese and breadcrumb mixture in advance and then stored in the refrigerator until ready to use.

3 Dip the potato slices first in egg and then roll them in the breadcrumbs to coat completely.

4 Heat the oil in a large saucepan or deep-fat fryer to 180°C/350°F or until a cube of bread browns in 30 seconds. Cook the cheese and potato slices, in several batches, for 4–5 minutes or until they turn a golden brown colour.

5 Remove the cheese and potato slices from the oil with a slotted spoon and drain thoroughly on kitchen paper. Keep the cheese and potato slices warm while you cook the remaining batches.

6 Transfer the cheese and potato slices to warm individual serving plates. Dust lightly with chilli powder, if using, and serve immediately.

Corn and Pepper Pancakes

These light-as-air pancakes are very more-ish, so it's fortunate that they are so easy to make. For best results, use a heavy frying pan or griddle.

NUTRITIONAL INFORMATION

Calories 239	Sugars 6g	
Protein 8g	Fat 6g	
Carbohydrate 4g	Saturates 1g	

15 mins   20 mins

SERVES 4

I N G R E D I E N T S

150 g/5½ oz frozen sweetcorn kernels, thawed

4 tbsp cornmeal

4 tbsp plain flour

1 tbsp very finely chopped fresh parsley

1 small red pepper, deseeded and very finely chopped

1 small egg yolk

½ tsp caster sugar

2 egg whites

1 tbsp olive oil

1 Process half the sweetcorn in a food processor until finely chopped. Scrape into a bowl and add the remaining sweetcorn, cornmeal, flour, parsley and chopped pepper. Beat the egg yolk with the sugar in a small bowl, then add it to the sweetcorn mixture and stir thoroughly.

2 Beat the egg whites in a clean bowl until they stand in soft peaks (see Cook's Tip). Gently fold half the egg whites into the sweetcorn mixture, then fold in the remaining egg whites.

3 Heat half the oil in a heavy frying pan. Drop spoonfuls of the batter into the pan, spacing them out well, and cook for 3 minutes, until the undersides are golden brown. Flip the pancakes over carefully with a spatula and cook the other sides for about 3 minutes, until golden brown. Transfer the pancakes to a plate and keep warm while you cook the remaining batter, adding more oil to the pan if necessary. Serve immediately.

COOK'S TIP
Remove the eggs from the refrigerator about 30 minutes before using so that the whites will whisk fully and easily.

Spinach & Cheese Pancakes

Ricotta cheese and spinach are made for each other and feature in many Italian recipes. Here they are combined in a delicious filling for pancakes.

NUTRITIONAL INFORMATION

Calories	630	Sugars	........10g
Protein	........36g	Fat	..........38g
Carbohydrate	...38g	Saturates	.......2g

 25 mins   45 mins

SERVES 4-6

INGREDIENTS

1 tbsp sunflower oil, plus extra for brushing

1 quantity pancake batter (see page 8)

½ quantity hot cheese sauce (see page 9), made with Parmesan cheese

115 g/4 oz mozzarella cheese, thinly sliced

FOR THE FILLING

750 g/1 lb 10 oz spinach, coarse stalks removed

25 g/1 oz butter

225 g/8 oz ricotta cheese

1 egg, lightly beaten

pinch of freshly grated nutmeg

salt and pepper

VARIATION

If you like, substitute 55 g/2 oz buckwheat flour for half the plain flour, when making the pancake batter.

1 Brush a frying pan with oil, cook 12 pancakes, and keep warm. Cook the spinach in a heavy-based saucepan, with just the water clinging to the leaves after washing, for 7 minutes. Drain and squeeze out any excess moisture.

2 Coarsely chop the spinach, place in a blender or food processor with the butter and process to a smooth purée. Add the ricotta cheese and process until blended. Scrape into a bowl, stir in the egg

and season to taste with nutmeg, salt and pepper. Brush an ovenproof dish with a little oil. Divide the spinach mixture between the pancakes, roll up and place, seam side down, in the dish.

3 Pour the cheese sauce over the pancakes and cover with the slices of mozzarella. Bake in a preheated oven, 220°C/425°F/Gas Mark 7, for 15–20 minutes, until the topping is melted and golden. Serve immediately.

Cheesy Sausages & Mash

Cheesy Glamorgan sausages served with sweet potato mash turn 'bangers and mash' into a sophisticated lunch or supper dish.

NUTRITIONAL INFORMATION

Calories	909	Sugars	........15g
Protein	.........2g	Fat	..........65g
Carbohydrate	...63g	Saturates	......36g

30 mins   40 mins

SERVES 4

INGREDIENTS

FOR THE SAUSAGES

115 g/4 oz fresh wholemeal breadcrumbs

175 g/6 oz Caerphilly cheese, grated

1 leek, finely chopped

2 tbsp finely chopped fresh parsley

1 tbsp finely chopped fresh marjoram

1 tbsp wholegrain mustard

2 eggs

55 g/2 oz dried breadcrumbs

corn oil, for deep-frying

FOR THE MASH

700 g/1 lb 9 oz sweet potatoes

115 g/4 oz butter

1 onion, grated

125 ml/4 fl oz double cream

pinch of freshly grated nutmeg

salt and pepper

1 For the mash, cook the unpeeled sweet potatoes in a large pan of lightly salted boiling water for 25–30 minutes, until tender.

2 Meanwhile, make the sausage mix. Combine the fresh breadcrumbs, Caerphilly, leek, parsley, marjoram and mustard in a bowl. Separate 1 egg and add the yolk with the remaining egg to the mixture. Season to taste with pepper and knead lightly until the mixture comes together. Using your fingers, form it into 8 sausage shapes.

3 When the sweet potatoes are tender, drain and leave to cool slightly, then peel and mash well with a potato masher. Heat the butter in a small frying pan. Add the onion and fry over a very low heat for 5 minutes. Pour the onion mixture into the mashed potatoes, add the cream and beat well with a wooden spoon. Season to taste with nutmeg, salt and pepper. Keep warm while you finish the sausages.

4 Heat the oil for deep-frying to 180–190°C/350–375°F or until a cube of bread browns in 30 seconds. Whisk the egg white in a shallow dish until frothy. Place the dried breadcrumbs in another shallow dish. Dip the sausages, first in the egg white, then in the breadcrumbs to coat thoroughly. Shake off any excess. Deep-fry the sausages, in batches, for about 2 minutes. Drain on kitchen paper and keep warm while you cook the remainder.

5 When all the sausages are cooked, serve them immediately on warmed plates with the sweet potato mash.

  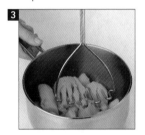

Potato & Mushroom Hash

This is an easy one-pan dish which is ideal for a quick snack. Packed with colour and flavour, you can add any other vegetable you have at hand.

NUTRITIONAL INFORMATION

Calories	378	Sugars	........14g
Protein	........18g	Fat	..........26g
Carbohydrate	...20g	Saturates	......7g

 10 mins   35 mins

SERVES 4

INGREDIENTS

675 g/1½ lb potatoes, diced

1 tbsp olive oil

2 garlic cloves, crushed

1 green pepper, deseeded and diced

1 yellow pepper, deseeded and diced

3 tomatoes, diced

75 g/3 oz button mushrooms, halved

1 tbsp vegetarian Worcestershire sauce

2 tbsp chopped fresh basil

salt and pepper

fresh basil sprigs, to garnish

warm crusty bread, to serve

1 Cook the potatoes in a saucepan of boiling salted water for 7–8 minutes. Drain well and reserve.

2 Heat the oil in a large, heavy-based frying pan and cook the potatoes for 8–10 minutes, stirring until browned.

3 Add the garlic and peppers to the frying pan and cook for 2–3 minutes.

4 Stir the tomatoes and mushrooms into the mixture and continue to cook, stirring, for a further 5–6 minutes.

5 Stir in the Worcestershire sauce and basil and season well.

6 Transfer the hash to a warmed serving dish, garnish with the fresh basil and serve at once with crusty bread.

COOK'S TIP

Most brands of Worcestershire sauce contain anchovies. When cooking for vegetarians, make sure you choose a vegetarian variety.

Vegetable Jambalaya

This spicy rice dish is a vegetarian version of the traditional jambalaya.
Packed with a variety of vegetables, it is both colourful and nutritious.

NUTRITIONAL INFORMATION

Calories	181	Sugars	.........8g
Protein	.........6g	Fat	..........7g
Carbohydrate	...25g	Saturates	.......1g

10 mins   55 mins

SERVES 4

INGREDIENTS

75 g/2¾ oz brown rice (see Cook's Tip)

2 tbsp olive oil

2 garlic cloves, crushed

1 red onion, cut into 8 wedges

1 aubergine, diced

1 green pepper, deseeded and diced

50 g/2 oz baby sweetcorn cobs,
  halved lengthways

50 g/1¾ oz frozen peas

100 g/3½ oz small broccoli florets

150 ml/¼ pint vegetable stock

225 g/8 oz canned chopped tomatoes

1 tbsp tomato purée

1 tsp creole seasoning

½ tsp chilli flakes

salt and pepper

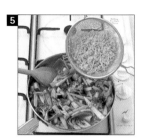

1 Cook the rice in a large saucepan of salted boiling water for 20 minutes, or until cooked through. Drain, rinse with boiling water, drain again and set aside.

2 Heat the oil in a heavy-based frying pan and cook the garlic and onion, stirring constantly, for 2–3 minutes. Add the aubergine, pepper, corn cobs, peas and broccoli to the pan and cook, stirring occasionally, for a further 2–3 minutes.

3 Stir in the vegetable stock and the canned tomatoes, tomato purée, creole seasoning and chilli flakes.

4 Season to taste and cook over a low heat for 15–20 minutes, or until the vegetables are tender.

5 Stir the brown rice into the vegetable mixture and cook, mixing well, for 3–4 minutes, or until hot.

6 Transfer the vegetable jambalaya to a warm serving dish and serve at once.

COOK'S TIP
Use a mixture of different kinds of rice, such as wild or red rice, to add colour and texture to this dish. Cook the rice in advance, following the instructions on the packet, for a speedier recipe.

Potato & Spinach Triangles

These small pasties are made with crisp filo pastry and filled with a tasty spinach and potato mixture flavoured with chilli and tomato.

NUTRITIONAL INFORMATION

Calories	.514	Sugars	.4g
Protein	.9g	Fat	.37g
Carbohydrate	...37g	Saturates	.8g

 25 mins   35 mins

SERVES 4

I N G R E D I E N T S

2 tbsp butter, melted, plus extra for greasing

225 g/8 oz waxy potatoes, finely diced

500 g/1 lb 2 oz baby spinach

2 tbsp water

1 tomato, deseeded and chopped

¼ tsp chilli powder

½ tsp lemon juice

salt and pepper

225 g/8 oz (8 sheets) filo pastry, thawed if frozen

crisp salad, to serve

L E M O N   M A Y O N N A I S E

150 ml/5 fl oz mayonnaise

2 tsp lemon juice

rind of 1 lemon

1 Lightly grease a baking tray with a little butter.

2 Cook the potatoes in a saucepan of lightly salted boiling water for 10 minutes, or until cooked through. Drain thoroughly and place in a mixing bowl.

3 Meanwhile, put the spinach in a large saucepan with 2 tablespoons of water, cover and cook, stirring occasionally, over a low heat for 2 minutes, until wilted. Drain the spinach thoroughly, squeezing out excess moisture, and add to the potatoes.

4 Stir in the tomato, chilli powder and lemon juice. Season to taste with salt and pepper.

5 Lightly brush 8 sheets of filo pastry with melted butter. Spread out four of the sheets and lay a second sheet on top of each. Cut them into rectangles about 20 x 10 cm/8 x 4 inches.

6 Spoon a portion of the potato and spinach mixture on to one end of each rectangle. Fold a corner of the pastry over the filling, fold the pointed end back over the pastry strip, then fold over the remaining pastry to form a triangle.

7 Place the triangles on the baking tray and bake in a preheated oven, 190°C/375°F/Gas Mark 5, for 20 minutes, or until golden brown.

8 To make the mayonnaise, mix the mayonnaise, lemon juice and lemon rind together in a small bowl. Serve the potato and spinach filo triangles either warm or cold with the lemon mayonnaise and a crisp salad.

 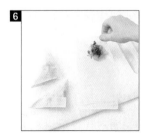 

Red Onion Bruschetta

Garlic-flavoured toast is topped with a melt-in-the-mouth mixture of caramelized onions, olives and melted goat's cheese.

NUTRITIONAL INFORMATION

Calories 418   Sugars 20g
Protein ....11g   Fat 24g
Carbohydrate ...42g   Saturates 6g

10 mins   20 mins

SERVES 4

INGREDIENTS

6 tbsp extra virgin olive oil

4 red onions, thickly sliced

2 tbsp balsamic vinegar

8 black olives, stoned and chopped

1 tsp fresh thyme leaves

115 g/4 oz goat's cheese, sliced

4 thick slices of rustic bread, such as ciabatta

4 garlic cloves, cut lengthways

1 Heat 2 tablespoons of the oil in a large, heavy-based frying pan. Add the onions and cook over a low heat, stirring occasionally, for 5 minutes until softened. Increase the heat to medium and cook, stirring occasionally, until the onions have begun to colour. Add the balsamic vinegar to the pan and cook, stirring constantly, until it has almost completely evaporated. Stir in the olives and thyme leaves.

2 Toast the bread on 1 side only. Rub the toasted sides with the garlic cloves. Place the bread, toasted side down, on the grill rack and drizzle with the remaining olive oil. Toast the second side.

3 Divide the onion mixture among the slices of toast and top with the goat's cheese. Return the toast to the grill for 2 minutes, or until the cheese has melted. Serve immediately.

VARIATION
To make little party snacks, use a slender French stick or 2 sfilatini (thin ciabatta) instead of the rustic bread.

Oeufs au Nid

Soft-baked eggs sitting in a bed of mashed potato look just as if they are resting in a nest, and they taste superb.

NUTRITIONAL INFORMATION

Calories	673	Sugars	.........4g
Protein	........18g	Fat	..........49g
Carbohydrate	...42g	Saturates	......30g

 15 mins 40 mins

SERVES 4

INGREDIENTS

100 g/4 oz Cheddar cheese

900 g/2 lb floury potatoes, unpeeled

175 g/6 oz butter

salt and pepper

about 225 ml/8 fl oz milk

4 eggs

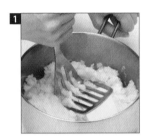

1 Grate the cheese and set aside. Cook the potatoes in lightly salted boiling water for about 25 minutes, until tender. Drain and peel. Mash the potatoes in a bowl with 115 g/4 oz of the butter until no lumps remain. Season to taste with salt and pepper. Pour in half the milk and beat vigorously with a whisk or wooden spoon. Continue whisking, adding more milk if necessary, until the potato is light and smooth.

COOK'S TIP

Don't be tempted to beat the potatoes in a food processor, as this will make them sticky and will fail to incorporate enough air to make a light mash.

2 Use a little of the remaining butter to grease an ovenproof dish. Spoon the mashed potato into the dish and make 4 hollows with the back of a spoon. Dot a little butter in each of the hollows and crack in the eggs. Season the eggs with salt and pepper.

3 Using the tines of a fork, make grooves around each egg to create a 'nest'. Sprinkle the cheese over the eggs and bake them in a preheated oven 200°C/400°F/Gas Mark 6, for 15 minutes or until the whites are set, but the yolks are still runny. Serve immediately.

Carrot & Potato Soufflé

Hot soufflés have a reputation for being difficult to make, but this one is both simple and impressive. Make sure you serve it as soon as it is ready.

NUTRITIONAL INFORMATION

Calories	294	Sugars	.........6g
Protein	........10g	Fat	...........9g
Carbohydrate	...46g	Saturates	.......4g

15 mins

40 mins

SERVES 4

INGREDIENTS

2 tbsp butter, melted

4 tbsp fresh wholemeal breadcrumbs

3 floury potatoes, baked in their skins

2 carrots, grated

2 eggs, separated

2 tbsp orange juice

¼ tsp grated nutmeg

salt and pepper

carrot curls, to garnish

1 Brush the inside of an 850 ml/ 1½ pint soufflé dish with the butter. Sprinkle about three-quarters of the breadcrumbs over the base and sides.

2 Cut the baked potatoes in half and scoop the flesh into a mixing bowl.

3 Add the carrots, egg yolks, orange juice and nutmeg to the potato flesh. Season to taste with salt and pepper.

4 In a separate bowl, whisk the egg whites until soft peaks form, then gently fold into the potato mixture with a metal spoon until well incorporated.

5 Gently spoon the potato and carrot mixture into the prepared soufflé dish. Sprinkle the remaining breadcrumbs over the top of the mixture.

6 Cook in a preheated oven, 200°C/ 400°F/Gas Mark 6, for 40 minutes, until risen and golden. Do not open the oven door during the cooking time, otherwise the soufflé will sink. Serve at once, garnished with carrot curls.

COOK'S TIP
To bake the potatoes, prick the skins and cook in a preheated oven, 180°C/350°F/ Gas Mark 4, for about 1–1¼ hours.

Vegetable Stir-fry

A range of delicious flavours are captured in this simple recipe, which is ideal if you are in a hurry.

NUTRITIONAL INFORMATION

Calories 138   Sugars 5g
Protein ....3g   Fat 12g
Carbohydrate ....5g   Saturates 2g

5 mins   25 mins

SERVES 4

INGREDIENTS

3 tbsp vegetable oil

8 baby onions, halved

1 aubergine, cubed

225 g/8 oz courgettes, sliced

225 g/8 oz open-cap mushrooms, halved

2 cloves garlic, crushed

400 g/14 oz canned chopped tomatoes

2 tbsp sun-dried tomato purée

2 tbsp soy sauce

1 tsp sesame oil

1 tbsp Chinese rice wine or dry sherry

pepper

fresh basil leaves, to garnish

1 Heat the vegetable oil in a large preheated wok or frying pan.

COOK'S TIP

Basil has a very strong flavour which is perfect with vegetables and Chinese flavourings. Instead of using basil simply as a garnish in this dish, try adding a handful of fresh basil leaves to the stir-fry in step 4.

2 Add the baby onions and aubergine to the wok or frying pan and stir-fry for 5 minutes, or until the vegetables are golden and just beginning to soften.

3 Add the courgettes, mushrooms, garlic, chopped tomatoes and sun-dried tomato purée to the wok and stir-fry for about 5 minutes. Reduce the heat and simmer for 10 minutes or until the vegetables are tender.

4 Add the soy sauce, sesame oil and rice wine or sherry to the wok, bring back to the boil and cook for 1 minute.

5 Season the stir-fry with freshly ground black pepper to taste.

6 Transfer the vegetable stir-fry to a warmed serving dish and serve immediately, sprinkled with a garnish of fresh basil leaves.

Stuffed Globe Artichokes

This imaginative and attractive recipe for artichokes stuffed with nuts, tomatoes, olives and mushrooms has been adapted for the microwave.

NUTRITIONAL INFORMATION

Calories	248	Sugars	.........8g
Protein	.........5g	Fat	..........19g
Carbohydrate	...16g	Saturates	.......2g

 30 mins   25 mins

SERVES 4

I N G R E D I E N T S

4 globe artichokes

8 tbsp water

4 tbsp lemon juice

1 onion, chopped

1 garlic clove, crushed

2 tbsp olive oil

225 g/8 oz button mushrooms, chopped

40 g/1½ oz black olives, stoned and sliced

60 g/2 oz sun-dried tomatoes in oil,
    drained and chopped

1 tbsp chopped fresh basil

60 g/2 oz fresh white breadcrumbs

25 g/1 oz pine kernels, toasted

salt and pepper

oil from the jar of sun-dried tomatoes,
    for drizzling

1 Cut the stalks and lower leaves off the artichokes. Snip off the leaf tips with scissors. Place 2 artichokes in a large bowl with half the water and half the lemon juice. Cover and cook on HIGH power for 10 minutes, turning the artichokes over halfway through, until a leaf pulls away easily from the base. Leave to stand, covered, for 3 minutes before draining. Turn the artichokes upside down and leave to cool. Repeat to cook the remaining artichokes.

2 Place the onion, garlic and oil in a bowl. Cover and cook on HIGH power for 2 minutes, stirring once. Add the mushrooms, olives and sun-dried tomatoes. Cover and cook on HIGH power for 2 minutes.

3 Stir in the basil, breadcrumbs and pine kernels. Season the mixture to taste with salt and pepper.

4 Turn the artichokes the right way up and carefully open out the leaves. Remove the purple-tipped central leaves.

Using a teaspoon, scrape out the hairy choke and discard.

5 Divide the stuffing into 4 equal portions and spoon into the centre of each artichoke. Push the leaves back around the stuffing.

6 Arrange the stuffed artichokes in a shallow dish and drizzle over a little oil from the jar of sun-dried tomatoes. Cook on HIGH power for 7–8 minutes to reheat, turning the artichokes around halfway through.

Baked Fennel Gratinati

Fennel is a common ingredient in Italian cooking. In this dish its distinctive flavour is offset by the smooth Béchamel sauce.

NUTRITIONAL INFORMATION

Calories	426	Sugars	.........9g
Protein	.........13g	Fat	..........35g
Carbohydrate	...16g	Saturates	......19g

 5–10 mins   45 mins

SERVES 4

I N G R E D I E N T S

4 fennel bulbs

2 tbsp butter

150 ml/5 fl oz dry white wine

Béchamel sauce (see page 6),
  enriched with 2 egg yolks

salt and pepper

25 g/1 oz fresh white breadcrumbs

3 tbsp freshly grated Parmesan cheese

fennel fronds, to garnish

1 Remove any bruised or tough outer stalks of fennel and cut each bulb in half. Put into a pan of lightly salted boiling water and simmer for 20 minutes until tender, then drain.

2 Butter an ovenproof dish liberally and arrange the drained fennel in it.

3 Stir the wine into the Béchamel sauce and season with salt and pepper to taste. Pour the sauce over the fennel.

4 Sprinkle evenly with the breadcrumbs and then the Parmesan.

5 Bake in a preheated oven, 200°C/ 400°F/Gas Mark 6, for 20 minutes until the top is golden. Serve garnished with fennel fronds.

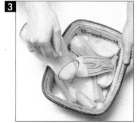

Summer Stir-fry

Not only are stir-fries quick and easy, they are also a great way to cook vegetables, because their flavour, colour and texture are preserved.

NUTRITIONAL INFORMATION

Calories	105	Sugars	5g
Protein	5g	Fat	7g
Carbohydrate	6g	Saturates	1g

15 mins   10 mins

SERVES 4

INGREDIENTS

2 tbsp groundnut or sunflower oil

2.5 cm/1 inch piece fresh root ginger, finely chopped

2 garlic cloves, finely chopped

115 g/4 oz French beans

115 g/4 oz mangetouts

115 g/4 oz broccoli florets

115 g/4 oz carrots, thinly sliced diagonally

115 g/4 oz asparagus spears, thinly sliced diagonally

½ red pepper, deseeded and thinly sliced

½ orange pepper, deseeded and thinly sliced

½ yellow pepper, deseeded and thinly sliced

2 celery sticks, thinly sliced

3 spring onions, thinly sliced diagonally

salt

Chinese chives, to garnish

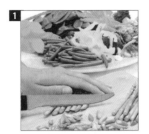

1 Prepare the vegetables. Heat half the oil in a wok or heavy-based frying pan. Add the ginger and garlic and stir-fry for a few seconds, then add the beans and continue to stir-fry for 2 minutes.

2 Add the mangetouts and stir-fry them for 1 minute, then add the broccoli florets, carrots and asparagus and stir-fry for a further 2 minutes.

3 Add the remaining oil to the wok with the peppers, celery and spring onions and stir-fry for 2-3 minutes more, until all the vegetables are crisp-tender.

4 Season the stir-fry to taste with salt and serve immediately, garnished with Chinese chives.

COOK'S TIP
Cutting vegetables into diagonal slices maximizes their surface area so that they cook more rapidly and evenly.

Garlic & Pine Kernel Tarts

A crisp lining of bread is filled with garlic butter and pine kernels to make a delightful and unusual light meal.

NUTRITIONAL INFORMATION

Calories ....435 Sugars 1g
Protein ....6g Fat 39g
Carbohydrate ...17g Saturates 20g

 20 mins   15 mins

SERVES 4

INGREDIENTS

4 slices wholemeal or granary bread

50 g/1¾ oz pine kernels

150 g/5½ oz butter

5 garlic cloves, peeled and halved

2 tbsp chopped fresh oregano, plus extra for garnish

4 stoned black olives, halved

oregano leaves, to garnish

1 Using a rolling pin, flatten the bread slightly. With a pastry cutter, cut out 4 circles of bread to fit your individual tart tins – they should measure about 10 cm/ 4 inches across. Reserve the offcuts of bread and leave them in the refrigerator for 10 minutes or until required.

2 Meanwhile, place the pine kernels on a baking tray and toast them under a preheated grill for 2–3 minutes or until golden. Make sure they do not burn.

3 Put the bread offcuts, pine kernels, butter, garlic and oregano into a food processor and blend for about 20 seconds. Alternatively, pound the ingredients by hand with a mortar and pestle. The mixture should have a rough texture.

4 Spoon the pine kernel and butter mixture into the lined tins and top with the olives. Bake in a preheated oven, 200°C/400°F/Gas Mark 6, for 10–15 minutes or until golden.

5 Transfer the tarts to serving plates and serve warm, garnished with the fresh oregano leaves.

VARIATION

Use 200 g/7oz puff pastry to line 4 tart tins. Leave to chill for 20 minutes then line with foil and bake blind for 10 minutes. Remove the foil and bake for 3–4 minutes or until the pastry is set. Continue from step 2, adding 2 tablespoons breadcrumbs to the mixture.

Mushroom & Onion Quiche

For the best flavour, use a mixture of several different types of mushroom to make this delicious light quiche.

NUTRITIONAL INFORMATION

Calories	640	Sugars	........11g
Protein	.........11g	Fat	..........48g
Carbohydrate	...44g	Saturates	......28g

40 mins, plus chilling and cooling

1¼ hrs

SERVES 4-6

INGREDIENTS

butter, for greasing

plain flour, for dusting

1 quantity rich shortcrust pastry dough (see page 8), chilled

FILLING

50 g/2 oz unsalted butter

3 red onions, halved and sliced

350 g/12 oz mixed wild mushrooms, such as ceps, morels, chanterelles and oyster

2 tsp chopped fresh thyme

1 egg

2 egg yolks

100 ml/3½ fl oz double cream

salt and pepper

1 Lightly grease a 23 cm/9 inch loose-based flan tin with butter. Roll out the dough on a lightly floured surface and line the tin. Prick the base and chill for 30 minutes. Line with foil and baking beans and bake blind in a preheated oven, 190°C/375°F/Gas Mark 5, for 25 minutes. Remove the foil and beans and cool on a wire rack.

2 To make the filling, melt the butter in a large, heavy-based frying pan. Add the onions, cover and cook over a very low heat, stirring occasionally, for 20 minutes. Add the mushrooms and thyme and cook, stirring occasionally, for 10 minutes more. Spoon the mixture into the cooled pastry case and place the tin on a baking sheet.

3 Lightly beat the egg with the egg yolks and cream and season to taste with salt and pepper. Pour the mixture over the mushroom filling and bake in a preheated oven, 180°C/350°F/Gas Mark 4, for 20 minutes, until the filling is set and golden. Serve hot or at room temperature.

COOK'S TIP

You can use ready-prepared shortcrust pastry dough for the quiche. Make sure that you thaw frozen pastry thoroughly before use.

Thai-style Omelette

In Thailand, egg dishes such as this one are eaten as part of a main course or as a snack, depending on the time of day.

NUTRITIONAL INFORMATION

Calories ...... .304   Sugars 7g
Protein ....11g   Fat .... .24g
Carbohydrate ....11g   Saturates 4g

 10 mins   10 mins

SERVES 4

INGREDIENTS

3 tbsp vegetable oil

1 garlic clove, finely chopped

1 small onion, finely chopped

1 small aubergine, diced

½ small green pepper, deseeded and chopped

1 tomato, diced

1 large dried Chinese black mushroom, soaked, drained and sliced

1 tbsp light soy sauce

½ tsp sugar

¼ tsp pepper

2 large eggs

salad leaves, tomato wedges and cucumber slices, to garnish

1 Heat half the vegetable oil in a pan and cook the garlic over a high heat for 30 seconds. Add the onion and aubergine and stir-fry until golden.

2 Add the green pepper and stir-fry for a further minute. Stir in the tomato, mushroom, soy sauce, sugar and pepper. Remove from the pan and keep hot.

3 Beat the eggs lightly. Heat the remaining oil, swirling to coat the pan thoroughly. Pour in the eggs and swirl to set around the pan.

4 When the egg is set, spoon the filling into the centre of the omelette. Fold in the sides to make a neat, square parcel.

5 Slide the omelette carefully on to a warmed dish and then garnish it with a selection of salad leaves and some tomato wedges and cucumber slices. Serve the omelette hot.

COOK'S TIP

If you heat the pan thoroughly before adding the oil, and heat the oil before adding the ingredients, you should not have a problem with ingredients sticking to the pan.

Jacket Potatoes with Beans

Baked jacket potatoes, topped with a tasty mixture of beans in a spicy sauce, provide a deliciously filling, high-fibre dish.

NUTRITIONAL INFORMATION

Calories 378	Sugars 9g
Protein 15g	Fat 9g
Carbohydrate ...64g	Saturates 1g

15 mins

1 hr 15 mins

SERVES 6

INGREDIENTS

1.8 kg/4 lb potatoes

4 tbsp ghee or vegetable oil

1 large onion, chopped

2 garlic cloves, crushed

1 tsp turmeric

1 tbsp cumin seeds

2 tbsp mild or medium curry paste

350 g/12 oz cherry tomatoes

400 g/14 oz canned black-eyed beans,
   drained and rinsed

400 g/14 oz canned red kidney beans,
   drained and rinsed

1 tbsp lemon juice

2 tbsp tomato purée

150 ml/5 fl oz water

2 tbsp chopped fresh mint or coriander

salt and pepper

1 Scrub the potatoes and prick several times with a fork. Place in a preheated oven, 180°C/350°F/Gas Mark 4, and cook for 1–1¼ hours, or until the potatoes feel soft when gently squeezed.

2 About 20 minutes before the end of cooking time, prepare the topping. Heat the ghee or oil in a saucepan, add the onion and cook over a low heat, stirring frequently, for 5 minutes. Add the garlic, turmeric, cumin seeds and curry paste and cook gently for 1 minute.

3 Stir in the tomatoes, black-eyed beans and red kidney beans, lemon juice, tomato purée, water and mint or coriander. Season to taste with salt and pepper, then cover and simmer over a low heat, stirring frequently, for 10 minutes.

4 When the potatoes are cooked, cut them in half and mash the flesh lightly with a fork. Spoon the prepared bean mixture on top, place on warm serving plates and serve immediately.

VARIATION

Instead of cutting the potatoes in half, cut a cross in each and squeeze gently to open out. Spoon some of the prepared filling into the cross and serve any remaining filling on the side.

Thai-style Noodle Röstis

These unusual röstis, flavoured with fresh lemon grass and coconut, look wonderful layered up with beansprouts, red onion and avocado.

NUTRITIONAL INFORMATION

Calories	 365	Sugars	.... 2g
Protein	.... 4g	Fat	.... 25g
Carbohydrate	... 29g	Saturates	.... 5g

 5 mins   10 mins

SERVES 4

INGREDIENTS

125 g/4½ oz vermicelli rice noodles

2 spring onions, finely shredded

1 lemongrass stalk, finely shredded

3 tbsp fresh coconut, finely shredded

salt and pepper

vegetable oil, for frying

fresh whole red chillies, to garnish

TO SERVE

115 g/4 oz beansprouts

1 small red onion, thinly sliced

1 avocado, thinly sliced

2 tbsp lime juice

2 tbsp rice wine

1 tsp chilli sauce

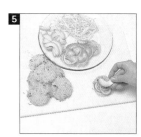

1 Break the rice noodles into short pieces and soak in hot water for about 4 minutes or according to the packet instructions. Drain thoroughly and pat dry with kitchen paper.

2 Stir together the noodles, spring onions, lemongrass and coconut.

3 Heat a small amount of oil in a heavy-based frying pan until very hot.

Brush the inside of a 9 cm/3½ inch round biscuit cutter with oil and place in the pan. Spoon a small amount of noodle mixture into the cutter just to cover the base of the pan, then press down lightly with the back of a spoon.

4 Fry for 30 seconds, then carefully remove the cutter and continue frying the rösti until it is golden brown, turning it over once with a spatula. Remove the

rösti and drain it on absorbent kitchen paper. Repeat with the remaining noodles, to make about 12 röstis.

5 To serve, arrange the noodle röstis in small stacks, with some beansprouts, red onion and avocado between the layers. Mix the lime juice, rice wine and chilli sauce together and spoon a little over each stack of röstis just before serving, garnished with red chillies.

Gnocchi with Tomato Sauce

Freshly made potato gnocchi are delicious, especially when they are topped with a fragrant tomato sauce.

NUTRITIONAL INFORMATION

Calories 216   Sugars 5g
Protein . . . . .5g   Fat 6g
Carbohydrate . . .39g   Saturates 1g

 30 mins   45 mins

SERVES 4

INGREDIENTS

350 g/12 oz floury potatoes, halved

salt and pepper

85 g/3 oz self-raising flour, plus extra for dusting

2 tsp dried oregano

2 tbsp vegetable oil

1 large onion, chopped

2 garlic cloves, chopped

400 g/14 oz canned chopped tomatoes

½ vegetable stock cube dissolved in 100 ml/3½ fl oz boiling water

2 tbsp fresh basil, shredded, plus whole leaves to garnish

Parmesan cheese, freshly grated, to serve

1 Bring a large saucepan of water to the boil. Add the potatoes and cook for 15 minutes or until tender. Drain and set aside to cool.

2 Peel and then mash the potatoes with the salt and pepper, sifted flour and oregano. Mix together with your hands to form a dough.

3 Heat the oil in a pan. Add the onions and garlic and cook for 3–4 minutes. Add the tomatoes and stock and cook, uncovered, for 10 minutes. Season with salt and pepper to taste.

4 Roll the potato dough into a sausage about 2.5 cm/1 inch in diameter. Cut the sausage into 2.5 cm/1 inch lengths. Flour your hands, then press a fork into each piece to create a series of ridges on one side and the indent of your index finger on the other.

5 Bring a large saucepan of water to the boil, add the gnocchi in batches and cook for 2–3 minutes. They should rise to the surface when cooked. Remove from the pan with a draining spoon, drain well and keep warm while you cook the remaining batches.

6 Stir the basil into the tomato sauce and pour over the gnocchi. Garnish with basil leaves and season with pepper to taste. Sprinkle with grated Parmesan and serve immediately.

VARIATION

The gnocchi can also be served with a pesto sauce made from fresh basil leaves, pine kernels, garlic, olive oil and Pecorino or Parmesan cheese.

Mixed Rice, Nuts & Raisins

This is one of the most popular nut mixtures in India and is very tasty. Make a large quantity and store it in an airtight container.

NUTRITIONAL INFORMATION

Calories . . . . . . .568 Sugars 28g
Protein . . . . .6g Fat 39g
Carbohydrate . . .51g Saturates 4g

15 mins,
plus soaking

15–20 mins

SERVES 4

INGREDIENTS

300 ml/½ pint vegetable oil

2 tsp onion seeds

6 curry leaves

200 g/7 oz parva (flaked rice)

2 tbsp peanuts

25 g/1 oz raisins

75 g/2¾ oz sugar

2 tsp salt

2 tsp chilli powder

50 g/1¾ oz sev (optional) (see Cook's Tip)

50 g/1¾ oz chana dhal, soaked in cold water for 3 hours

1 Heat the oil in a saucepan. Add the onion seeds and the curry leaves and fry, stirring constantly, until the onion seeds are crisp and golden.

2 Add the parva (flaked rice) to the mixture in the pan and fry until crisp and golden (do not allow it to burn).

3 Remove the mixture from the pan with a slotted spoon and drain on kitchen paper.

4 Fry the peanuts in the remaining oil, stirring constantly.

5 Add the peanuts to the flaked rice mixture, stirring to mix well.

6 Add the raisins, sugar, salt and chilli powder and mix together. Mix in the sev (if using). Transfer to a serving dish.

7 Re-heat the oil remaining in the pan. Drain the soaked chana dhal, add to the pan and fry until golden. Add to the other ingredients in the serving dish and mix together.

8 This dish can be eaten straight away but will keep well stored in an airtight container until you need it.

COOK'S TIP

Sev are very thin sticks made of gram flour which can be bought in Indian and Pakistani grocers.

Paglia e Fieno

This simple pasta dish, which literally means 'straw and hay', makes a quick and easy, light summer lunch that is surprisingly tasty.

NUTRITIONAL INFORMATION

Calories	823	Sugars	.........7g
Protein	........23g	Fat	..........43g
Carbohydrate	...94g	Saturates	......26g

 15 mins   12 mins

SERVES 4

INGREDIENTS

450 g/1 lb mixed plain and green dried tagliarini or spaghetti

55 g/2 oz unsalted butter

900 g/2 lb fresh peas, shelled

200 ml/7 fl oz double cream

55 g/2 oz freshly grated pecorino cheese, plus extra to serve

pinch of freshly grated nutmeg

salt and pepper

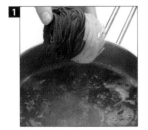

1 Bring a large saucepan of lightly salted water to the boil. Add the pasta, bring back to the boil and simmer for 8–10 minutes, until tender, but still firm to the bite.

2 Meanwhile, melt the butter in a wok or heavy-based saucepan. Add the peas and cook over a low heat, stirring frequently, for 4–5 minutes. Pour in 150 ml/5 fl oz of the cream, bring to the boil and simmer for 1 minute.

3 When the pasta is al dente, drain well and add to the peas. Pour in the extra cream, add the Pecorino and season to taste with nutmeg, salt and pepper. Toss well, then transfer to a warm serving dish and serve immediately.

COOK'S TIP
Although peas freeze exceptionally well, they have neither the flavour nor the texture of fresh peas, so it is really only worth making this dish when fresh peas are in season.

Mediterranean Pancakes

A rich tomato and herb filling makes these pancakes irresistible.
They make an impressive light supper dish served with a crisp salad.

NUTRITIONAL INFORMATION

Calories	376	Sugars	........13g
Protein	........11g	Fat	.........22g
Carbohydrate	...36g	Saturates	.......7g

🔔 25 mins   🕐 about 1¼ hrs

SERVES 4-6

INGREDIENTS

1 tbsp sunflower oil, plus extra for brushing

1 quantity pancake batter (see page 8)

FILLING

2 tbsp olive oil

1 onion, chopped

2 garlic cloves, finely chopped

1 small aubergine, diced

1 red pepper, deseeded and diced

4 tomatoes, skinned and diced

1 tbsp sun-dried tomato purée

1 tbsp chopped fresh parsley

2 tsp chopped fresh thyme

salt and pepper

TOPPING

25 g/1 oz butter, melted

3 tbsp freshly grated Parmesan cheese

1 Brush a frying pan with a little oil and heat well. Add a little of the batter and quickly tilt and rotate the pan to cover the base with a thin layer. Cook for about 1 minute, until the underside is golden. Flip over the pancake with a palette knife and cook the second side for about 30 seconds, until golden. Slide the pancake out on to a warm plate. Cook the

remaining batter in the same way to make 12 pancakes, stacking them on the plate interleaved with greaseproof paper.

2 To make the filling for the pancakes, heat the oil in a heavy-based frying pan. Add the onion and cook, stirring occasionally, for 5 minutes, until softened. Add the garlic, aubergine and red pepper and continue to cook, stirring occasionally, for 10 minutes. Stir in the tomatoes, sun-dried tomato purée, parsley and thyme, season to taste with salt and pepper, cover and simmer for 15 minutes.

3 Lightly brush an ovenproof dish with oil. Divide the filling between the pancakes, roll up and place, seam side down, in the dish.

4 Brush them with melted butter, sprinkle with the Parmesan and bake in a preheated oven, 190°C/ 375°F/Gas Mark 5, for 15 minutes. Serve immediately.

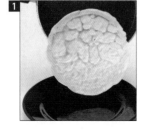

Deep-fried Diamond Pastries

This simple-to-make snack will retain its crispness if stored in an airtight container. Serve with drinks or at coffee time.

NUTRITIONAL INFORMATION

Calories 465	Sugars 0.6g
Protein 4g	Fat 38g
Carbohydrate ...29g	Saturates 4g

15 mins

15–20 mins

SERVES 4

INGREDIENTS

150 g/5½ oz plain flour

1 tsp baking powder

½ tsp salt

1 tbsp black cumin seeds

100 ml/3½ fl oz water

300 ml/½ pint oil

dhal, to serve

1 Place the flour in a large mixing bowl. Add the baking powder, salt and the black cumin seeds and stir to mix.

2 Add the water to the dry ingredients and mix together until combined to form a soft, elastic dough.

3 Roll out the dough on to a clean work surface to about 6 mm/¼ inch thick.

4 Using a sharp knife, score the dough to form diamond shapes. Re-roll the trimmings and cut out more diamond shapes until the dough has been used up.

5 Heat the oil in a large pan to 180°F/350°C or until a cube of bread browns in 30 seconds.

6 Carefully place the pastry diamonds in the oil, in batches if necessary, and deep-fry until golden brown.

7 Remove the diamond pastries with a slotted spoon and drain on kitchen paper. Serve with a dhal for dipping or store and serve when required.

COOK'S TIP

Black cumin seeds are used here for their strong aromatic flavour – do not be tempted to use white cumin seeds as a substitute.

Vegetable Dim Sum

Dim sum are small Chinese parcels which may be filled with any variety of fillings, steamed or fried and served with a dipping sauce.

NUTRITIONAL INFORMATION

Calories	295	Sugars	.........1g
Protein	.........5g	Fat	..........22g
Carbohydrate	...20g	Saturates	.......6g

15 mins   15 mins

SERVES 4

INGREDIENTS

2 spring onions, chopped

25 g/1 oz French beans, chopped

½ small carrot, finely chopped

1 red chilli, deseeded and chopped

25 g/1 oz beansprouts, chopped

25 g/1 oz button mushrooms, chopped

25 g/1 oz unsalted cashew nuts, chopped

1 small egg, beaten

2 tbsp cornflour

1 tsp light soy sauce

1 tsp hoisin sauce

1 tsp sesame oil

32 dim sum wrappers

oil, for deep-frying

1 tbsp sesame seeds

COOK'S TIP

If preferred, arrange the dim sum on a heatproof plate and then steam in a steamer for 5–7 minutes for a healthier cooking method.

1 Mix all of the vegetables together in a bowl. Add the nuts, egg, cornflour, soy sauce, hoisin sauce and sesame oil to the bowl. Mix well.

2 Lay the dim sum wrappers out on a chopping board and spoon small quantities of the mixture into the centre of each. Gather the wrapper around the filling at the top, to make little parcels, leaving the top open.

3 Heat the oil for deep-frying in a wok to 180°C/350°F or until a cube of bread browns in 30 seconds. Fry the dim sum, in batches, for 1–2 minutes or until golden brown. Drain them on kitchen paper and keep warm while frying the remaining wontons.

4 Sprinkle the sesame seeds over the dim sum. Serve the vegetable dim sum with a soy or plum dipping sauce.

Mexican-style Pizzas

Ready-made pizza bases are covered with a chilli-flavoured tomato sauce and topped with kidney beans, cheese and jalapeño chillies.

NUTRITIONAL INFORMATION

Calories 350	Sugars 8g
Protein 18g	Fat 10g
Carbohydrate . . .49g	Saturates 3g

 10 mins   20 mins

SERVES 4

I N G R E D I E N T S

4 ready-made individual pizza bases

1 tbsp olive oil

200 g/7 oz canned chopped tomatoes with garlic and herbs

2 tbsp tomato purée

200 g/7 oz canned kidney beans, drained and rinsed

115 g/4 oz sweetcorn kernels, defrosted if frozen

1–2 tsp chilli sauce

salt and pepper

1 large red onion, shredded

100 g/3½ oz reduced-fat mature Cheddar cheese, grated

1 large green chilli, sliced into rings

1 Arrange the pizza bases on a baking tray and brush the surfaces over lightly with the olive oil.

2 In a bowl, mix together the chopped tomatoes, the tomato purée, the kidney beans and the sweetcorn and add chilli sauce to taste. Season the mixture with salt and pepper.

3 Spread the tomato and kidney bean mixture evenly over each pizza base to cover, leaving a narrow rim.

4 Top each pizza with shredded onion and sprinkle with some grated cheese and a few slices of green chilli to taste.

5 Bake the pizzas in a preheated oven, 220°C/425°F/Gas Mark 7, for about 20 minutes or until the vegetables are tender, the cheese has melted and the base is crisp and golden.

6 Remove the pizzas from the baking tray and transfer to serving plates. Serve immediately.

COOK'S TIP
Serve a Mexican-style salad with this pizza. Arrange sliced tomatoes, fresh coriander leaves and a few slices of a small, ripe avocado on a platter. Sprinkle with fresh lime juice and coarse sea salt.

Cottage Potatoes

Give the humble potato a surprising kick with this spiced cheese filling. Serve with a tomato and onion salad or on a bed of mixed salad leaves.

NUTRITIONAL INFORMATION

Calories	.211	Sugars	.4g
Protein	.11g	Fat	.6g
Carbohydrate	.29g	Saturates	.1g

 10 mins 1 hr

SERVES 4

INGREDIENTS

4 baking potatoes

2 tsp sun-dried tomato purée

½ tsp ground coriander

salt and pepper

1 tbsp olive oil

3–4 spring onions, finely chopped

1–2 fresh green chillies, deseeded and finely chopped

1 tbsp tequila

225 g/8 oz low-fat cottage cheese

1 tbsp finely chopped fresh coriander

lime wedges and fresh coriander sprigs, to garnish

1 Cut a cross in the middle of each potato and prick the skins with a fork. Wrap the potatoes individually in foil and bake in a preheated oven, 200°C/400°F/ Gas Mark 6, for 1 hour, or until soft and cooked through.

2 Meanwhile, combine the sun-dried tomato purée and ground coriander in a small bowl. Season to taste with salt and pepper. Just before the potatoes are ready, heat the oil in a small saucepan and add the spring onions and chopped chillies. Cook, stirring occasionally, for 2–3 minutes until softened. Stir in the sun-dried tomato paste mixture and tequila and cook for 1 minute more. Remove from the heat and stir in the chopped coriander.

3 Place the cottage cheese in a bowl and add the tomato mixture. Stir in to blend thoroughly.

4 Unwrap the potatoes and squeeze gently to open out the cut side. Divide the cottage cheese equally among the potatoes and serve, garnished with lime wedges and coriander sprigs.

COOK'S TIP

Speed up this recipe by cooking the potatoes in the microwave. Prick them all over with a fork and arrange on a piece of kitchen paper in the oven. Cook on HIGH for 6 minutes, turn them over and cook on HIGH for 8 minutes more. Wrap each potato in foil and leave to stand for 5 minutes.

  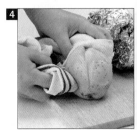

Pasta with Low-fat Pesto

Pesto is a wonderfully versatile sauce but is usually very high in fat. The fat content in this recipe is about a quarter of that of traditional pesto.

NUTRITIONAL INFORMATION

Calories 288	Sugars 3g	
Protein 15g	Fat 7g	
Carbohydrate ...44g	Saturates 1g	

5 mins

8–10 mins

SERVES 4

INGREDIENTS

225 g/8 oz dried linguine or spaghetti

55 g/2 oz fresh basil leaves

25 g/1 oz fresh flat-leaved parsley sprigs

1 garlic clove, roughly chopped

25 g/1 oz pine kernels

115 g/4 oz low-fat curd cheese

2 tbsp freshly grated Parmesan cheese

salt and pepper

fresh basil sprigs, to garnish

1 Bring a large pan of lightly salted water to the boil. Add the pasta, bring back to the boil and cook for 8–10 minutes, until tender but still firm to the bite. Drain and return to the pan.

2 Meanwhile, put half the basil, half the parsley, the garlic, pine kernels and curd cheese into a blender or food processor and process until smooth. Add the remaining basil and parsley. Grate about 2 tablespoons worth of Parmesan, add to the blender and season to taste. Process again briefly.

3 Add the pesto sauce to the pasta and toss thoroughly with 2 forks to combine. Transfer the pasta to 4 warm plates and serve immediately, garnished with basil sprigs.

COOK'S TIP

If the pesto is too thick, you can dilute it with a little of the pasta cooking water – but remember to reserve it when you drain the pasta.

Spanish Potato Omelette

Adding garlic and onions to this dish gives it extra flavour, while the potatoes give it body, making it a very satisfying snack meal.

NUTRITIONAL INFORMATION

Calories	300	Sugars	........3g
Protein	.........9g	Fat	..........21g
Carbohydrate	...20g	Saturates	.......4g

 20 mins   35 mins

SERVES 6

INGREDIENTS

125 ml/4 fl oz olive oil

600 g/1 lb 5 oz potatoes, sliced

1 large onion, sliced

1 large garlic clove, crushed

6 large eggs

salt and pepper

1 Heat a 25 cm/10 inch frying pan, preferably non-stick, over a high heat. Pour in the olive oil and heat. Lower the heat, add the potatoes, onion and garlic and cook for 15–20 minutes, stirring frequently, until the potatoes are tender.

2 Beat the eggs together in a large bowl and season generously with salt and pepper. Using a slotted spoon, transfer the potatoes and onion to the bowl of eggs. Pour the excess oil left in the frying pan into a heatproof jug, then scrape off the crusty bits from the base of the pan.

3 Reheat the pan and add about 2 tablespoons of the oil reserved in the jug. Pour in the potato mixture, smoothing the vegetables into an even layer. Cook for about 5 minutes, shaking the pan occasionally, or until the base is set.

4 Shake the pan and use a spatula to loosen the edge of the omelette. Place a large plate over the pan. Carefully invert the omelette on to the plate.

5 If you are not using a non-stick pan, add 1 tablespoon of the reserved oil to the pan and swirl around. Gently slide the omelette back into the pan, cooked-side up. Use the spatula to 'tuck down' the edge of the omelette. Continue cooking over medium heat for 3–5 minutes until set.

6 Remove the pan from the heat and slide the tortilla on to a serving plate. Leave to stand for at least 5 minutes before cutting. Serve hot, warm or at room temperature with salad.

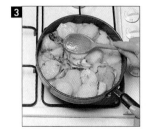

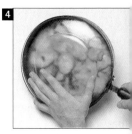

Spinach & Herb Frittata

If you find the prospect of turning over a Spanish tortilla daunting, try this Italian version of a flat omelette – it finishes cooking under a grill.

NUTRITIONAL INFORMATION

Calories 145	Sugars 1g
Protein 8g	Fat 12g
Carbohydrate 1g	Saturates 13g

 15 mins   12 mins

SERVES 6–8

INGREDIENTS

4 tbsp olive oil

6 spring onions, sliced

250 g/9 oz young spinach leaves, any
    coarse stems removed, rinsed

6 large eggs

salt and pepper

3 tbsp finely chopped mixed fresh herbs,
    such as flat-leaved parsley, thyme
    and coriander

2 tbsp freshly grated Parmesan cheese,
    plus extra for garnishing

fresh parsley sprigs, to garnish

1 Heat a 25 cm/10 inch frying pan,
preferably non-stick with a flameproof
handle, over a medium heat. Add the oil
and heat. Add the spring onions and cook
for about 2 minutes.

2 Add the spinach and cook until it is
just wilted.

3 Beat the eggs in a large bowl and
season to taste with salt and pepper.
Using a draining spoon, transfer the
spinach and onions to the bowl of eggs
and stir in the herbs. Pour the excess oil
left in the frying pan into a heatproof jug,
then scrape off the crusty bits from the
base of the pan.

4 Reheat the pan. Add 2 tablespoons of
the reserved oil. Pour in the egg
mixture, smoothing it into an even layer.
Cook, shaking the pan occasionally, for
6 minutes or until the base is set when
you lift up the side with a spatula.

5 Sprinkle the top of the frittata with
the Parmesan. Place the pan under a
preheated grill and cook for about

3 minutes or until the excess liquid is set
and the cheese is golden.

6 Remove the pan from the heat and
slide the frittata out onto a warm
serving plate. Set the frittata aside for at
least 5 minutes before cutting and
garnishing with extra Parmesan and
parsley. The frittata can be served hot,
warm or at room temperature.

Soufflé Omelette

Sweet cherry tomatoes, mushrooms and peppery rocket leaves make a mouthwatering filling for these light, fluffy omelettes.

NUTRITIONAL INFORMATION

Calories 146	Sugars 2g
Protein 10g	Fat 11g
Carbohydrate 2g	Saturates 2g

 1¼ hrs   45 mins

SERVES 4

I N G R E D I E N T S

175 g/6 oz cherry tomatoes

225 g/8 oz mixed mushrooms, such as button, chestnut, shiitake and oyster

4 tbsp vegetable stock

small bunch of fresh thyme, tied with string

4 eggs, separated

125 ml/4 fl oz water

4 egg whites

4 tsp olive oil

25 g/1 oz rocket leaves

fresh thyme sprigs, to garnish

1 Halve the tomatoes and place them in a saucepan. Wipe the mushrooms with kitchen paper, trim if necessary and slice if large. Place the mushrooms in the pan with the tomatoes.

2 Add the stock and the bunch of thyme to the pan. Bring to the boil, cover and simmer for 5–6 minutes until tender. Drain, remove the thyme and discard. Keep the mixture warm.

3 Meanwhile, separate the eggs and whisk the egg yolks with the water until frothy. In a clean, grease-free bowl, whisk the 8 egg whites until stiff and dry.

4 Spoon the egg yolk mixture into the egg whites and, using a metal spoon, fold together until well mixed. Take care not to knock out too much of the air.

5 For each omelette, brush a small omelette pan with 1 teaspoon of the oil and heat until hot. Pour in a quarter of the egg mixture and cook for 4–5 minutes until the mixture has set.

6 Finish cooking the omelette under a preheated medium grill for 2–3 minutes.

7 Transfer the omelette to a warm serving plate. Fill the omelette with a few rocket leaves, and a quarter of the mushroom and tomato mixture. Flip over the top of the omelette, garnish with sprigs of thyme and serve.

Tomato & Onion Bake

This nourishing and flavoursome bake is just the right thing for a weekend lunch on a cold winter's day.

NUTRITIONAL INFORMATION

Calories	307	Sugars	........11g
Protein	........11g	Fat	..........18g
Carbohydrate	...28g	Saturates	.......9g

  10 mins 1 hr

SERVES 4

INGREDIENTS

55 g/2 oz butter, plus extra for greasing

2 large onions, thinly sliced

500 g/1 lb 2 oz tomatoes, skinned and sliced

115 g/4 oz fresh white breadcrumbs

salt and pepper

4 eggs

1 Grease an ovenproof dish with butter. Melt 40 g/1½ oz of the butter in a heavy-based frying pan. Add the onions and cook over a low heat, stirring occasionally, for 5 minutes, until softened.

2 Layer the onions, tomatoes and breadcrumbs in the dish, seasoning each layer with salt and pepper to taste. Dot the remaining butter on top and bake in a preheated oven, 180°C/350°F/Gas Mark 4, for 40 minutes.

3 Make 4 hollows in the mixture with the back of a spoon. Crack 1 egg into each hollow. Return the dish to the oven and bake for 15 minutes more, until the eggs are just set. Serve immediately.

VARIATION

For a more substantial and spicier dish, add 2 deseeded and sliced red peppers to the frying pan once the onions have softened, and cook for 10 minutes more. Stir in a pinch of cayenne pepper before making the layers as above.

Leek and Onion Tartlets

Rather like mini quiches, these flavoursome tartlets are delicious served warm or cold and are an excellent choice for a picnic.

NUTRITIONAL INFORMATION

Calories 575	Sugars 5g
Protein 11g	Fat 47g
Carbohydrate ...28g	Saturates 28g

30 mins, plus chilling and cooling

40 mins

SERVES 6

INGREDIENTS

butter, for greasing

plain flour, for dusting

1 quantity rich shortcrust pastry dough (see page 8)

FILLING

25 g/1 oz unsalted butter

1 onion, thinly sliced

450 g/1 lb leeks, thinly sliced

2 tsp chopped fresh thyme

55 g/2 oz Gruyère cheese, grated

3 eggs

300 ml/½ pint double cream

salt and pepper

1 Lightly grease 6 x 10 cm/4 inch tartlet tins with butter. Roll out the dough on a lightly floured surface and stamp out 6 rounds with a 13 cm/5 inch cutter, re-rolling as necessary. Gently ease the dough into the tartlet tins, prick the bases and chill for 30 minutes. Line the pastry cases with foil or greaseproof paper and baking beans, place them on a baking sheet and bake blind in a preheated oven, 190°C/375°F/Gas Mark 5, for 8 minutes. Remove the foil and beans and bake for a further 2 minutes. Transfer the tins to a wire rack to cool.

2 Meanwhile, make the filling. Melt the butter in a heavy-based frying pan. Add the onion and cook, stirring occasionally, for 5 minutes, until softened. Add the leeks and thyme and cook, stirring occasionally, for 10 minutes, until softened. Divide the leek and onion mixture among the tartlet cases, then sprinkle with Gruyère.

3 Lightly beat the eggs with the cream and season to taste with salt and pepper. Place the tartlet tins on a baking sheet and divide the egg mixture among them. Bake in a preheated oven, 180°C/350°F/Gas Mark 4, for 15 minutes, or until the filling is set and golden brown. Transfer to a wire rack to cool slightly before removing from the tins.

Bean Burgers

These tasty veggie burgers are both delicious and nutritious – good news if you are cooking for children.

NUTRITIONAL INFORMATION

Calories	145	Sugars	.........5g
Protein	.........8g	Fat	...........4g
Carbohydrate	....2g	Saturates	.......1g

15 mins   20 mins

SERVES 4

INGREDIENTS

1 tbsp sunflower oil, plus extra for brushing

1 onion, finely chopped

1 garlic clove, finely chopped

1 tsp ground coriander

1 tsp ground cumin

115 g/5 oz button mushrooms, finely chopped

425 g/15 oz canned pinto or red kidney beans, drained and rinsed

2 tbsp chopped fresh flat-leaved parsley

plain flour, for dusting

salt and pepper

burger buns and salad, to serve

1 Heat the oil in a heavy-based frying pan. Add the onion and cook, stirring occasionally, for 5 minutes, until softened. Add the garlic, coriander and cumin and cook, stirring frequently, for 1 minute more. Add the mushrooms and cook, stirring constantly, for 4–5 minutes until all the liquid has evaporated. Transfer the mixture to a bowl.

2 Place the beans in a small bowl and mash with a potato masher or fork.

Stir the beans into the mushroom mixture with the parsley and season to taste with salt and pepper.

3 Form the mixture into 4 portions and shape each into a round, flat patty. Dust with flour. Brush the patties with oil and cook under a preheated grill for 4–5 minutes on each side. Serve immediately in burger buns with salad.

VARIATION
Substitute 115 g/4 oz mixed, finely chopped courgette and carrot for the mushrooms.

Tomato Soufflés

These individual soufflés are cooked in tomato shells to make an intriguing and attractive dish.

NUTRITIONAL INFORMATION

Calories	179	Sugars 5g
Protein	.........7g	Fat 13g
Carbohydrate	....8g	Saturates 7g

 30 mins 30 mins

SERVES 6

INGREDIENTS

6 beef tomatoes, halved

25 g/1 oz butter

25 g/1 oz flour

2 tbsp double cream

2 tbsp freshly grated Parmesan cheese

½ tsp mustard powder

pinch of grated nutmeg

salt and pepper

5 egg whites

4 egg yolks

1 Scoop out the flesh and seeds of the tomatoes with a teaspoon. Place the shells upside down on kitchen paper to drain. Place the flesh and seeds in a small saucepan and simmer gently for 3 minutes. Rub the mixture through a fine sieve into a small bowl and reserve.

2 Melt the butter in a small saucepan. Stir in the flour and cook, stirring constantly, for 1 minute. Remove the pan from the heat and gradually stir in the reserved tomato and the cream. Return the pan to the heat and cook, stirring constantly, for 2 minutes, until smooth and thickened. Remove the pan from the heat, stir in the cheese and mustard and season to taste with nutmeg, salt and pepper. Set aside to cool for 10 minutes.

3 Whisk the egg whites in a grease-free bowl until they form stiff peaks. Beat the egg yolks into the tomato mixture, 1 at a time. Fold 2 tablespoons of the egg whites into the mixture, then fold in the remainder. If necessary, pat dry the insides of the tomato shells, then divide the soufflé mixture among them.

4 Place on a baking sheet and bake in a preheated oven, 220°C/425°F/Gas Mark 7, for 5 minutes. Lower the oven temperature to 200°C/400°F/Gas Mark 6 and bake for 15–20 minutes more, until golden brown on top. Serve immediately.

Leek & Herb Soufflé

Hot soufflés look very impressive if served as soon as they come out of the oven; otherwise they will sink quite quickly.

NUTRITIONAL INFORMATION

Calories 182   Sugars 4g
Protein ....8g   Fat 15g
Carbohydrate ....5g   Saturates 2g

15 mins

50 mins

SERVES 4

INGREDIENTS

350 g/12 oz baby leeks

1 tbsp olive oil

125 ml/4 fl oz vegetable stock

50 g/1¾ oz walnuts

2 eggs, separated

2 tbsp chopped mixed herbs

2 tbsp natural yogurt

salt and pepper

1 Using a sharp knife, chop the leeks finely. Heat the olive oil in a frying pan. Add the leeks and sauté over a medium heat, stirring occasionally, for 2–3 minutes.

2 Add the vegetable stock to the pan, lower the heat and simmer gently for a further 5 minutes.

3 Place the walnuts in a food processor or blender and process until finely chopped. Add the leek mixture to the nuts and process briefly to form a purée. Transfer to a mixing bowl.

4 Mix together the egg yolks, the herbs and the yogurt until thoroughly combined. Pour the egg mixture into the leek purée. Season with salt and pepper to taste and mix well.

5 In a separate, grease-free mixing bowl, whisk the egg whites until firm peaks form.

6 Fold the egg whites into the leek mixture. Spoon the mixture into a lightly greased 900 ml/1½ pint soufflé dish and place on a warmed baking tray.

7 Cook in a preheated oven, 180°C/ 350°F/Gas Mark 4, for 35–40 minutes, or until well risen and set. Serve the soufflé immediately.

COOK'S TIP

Placing the soufflé dish on a warm baking tray helps to cook the soufflé from the bottom, thus aiding its cooking and lightness.

Fresh Tomato Tarts

These tomato-flavoured tarts should be eaten as fresh as possible to enjoy the flaky and crisp buttery puff pastry.

NUTRITIONAL INFORMATION

Calories 217	Sugars 3g
Protein 5g	Fat 14g
Carbohydrate . . .18g	Saturates 1g

🍲 35 mins   🕐 20 mins

SERVES 6

INGREDIENTS

250 g/9 oz puff pastry, defrosted if frozen

1 egg, beaten

2 tbsp Pesto (see page 121)

6 plum tomatoes, sliced

salt and pepper

fresh thyme leaves, to garnish (optional)

1 On a lightly floured surface, roll out the pastry to a rectangle measuring 30 x 25 cm/12 x 10 inches.

2 Cut the rectangle in half and divide each half into 3 pieces to make 6 even-size rectangles. Leave in the refrigerator to chill for 20 minutes.

3 Lightly score the edges of the pastry rectangles and brush them with the beaten egg.

4 Spread the Pesto over the rectangles, dividing it equally between them, leaving a 2½ cm/1 inch border around each one.

5 Arrange the tomato along the centre of each rectangle on top of the Pesto.

6 Season well with salt and pepper to taste and lightly sprinkle with fresh thyme leaves, if using.

7 Bake in a preheated oven, 200°C/400°F/Gas Mark 6, for 15–20 minutes until well risen and golden brown.

8 Transfer the tomato tarts to warm serving plates, garnish, and serve while they are still piping hot.

VARIATION

Instead of individual tarts, roll the pastry out to form 1 large rectangle. Spoon over the Pesto and arrange the tomatoes over the top.

Hot Chilli Pasta

Chillies are not usually associated with Italian cooking, but some regions of the country grow fiery hot chillies that are nicknamed 'little devils'.

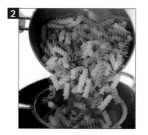

NUTRITIONAL INFORMATION

Calories 320	Sugars 7g
Protein 10g	Fat 4g
Carbohydrate ...61g	Saturates 0g

10 mins   15 mins

SERVES 6

INGREDIENTS

2 garlic cloves, finely chopped

2 fresh red chillies

550 g/1 lb 4 oz passata or crushed plum tomatoes

200 g/7 oz canned chopped plum tomatoes

200 ml/7 fl oz dry white wine

4 tsp sun-dried tomato purée

450 g/1 lb dried gemelli

3 tbsp chopped fresh flat-leaved parsley

salt and pepper

freshly grated Parmesan cheese, to serve (optional)

1 Put the garlic, whole chillies, passata or crushed tomatoes, chopped tomatoes, white wine and sun-dried tomato purée into a large, heavy-based saucepan and bring to the boil, stirring occasionally. Lower the heat, cover and simmer while you cook the pasta.

2 Bring a large pan of lightly salted water to the boil. Add the pasta, bring back to the boil and simmer for 8–10 minutes, until tender, but still firm to the bite. Drain well and place in a large warm serving dish.

3 Remove the chillies from the sauce. If you like a hot spicy flavour, chop 1 or both and return to the sauce. If you prefer a milder flavour, discard them. Season to taste with salt and pepper, then pour the sauce on to the pasta. Toss well and serve immediately, with the Parmesan if you like.

COOK'S TIP
Gemelli, which means 'twins', are made from two short pieces of pasta twisted together. You can use any small pasta shapes for this dish.

Artichoke Heart Soufflé

This exquisite dish is perfect for entertaining, but for maximum impact, be sure to serve it as soon as the dish comes out of the oven.

NUTRITIONAL INFORMATION

Calories	350	Sugars	.........5g
Protein	........18g	Fat	..........24g
Carbohydrate	...18g	Saturates	......13g

 20 mins   40 mins

SERVES 4

INGREDIENTS

55 g/2 oz butter, plus extra for greasing

55 g/2 oz plain flour

300 ml/½ pint milk

pinch of freshly grated nutmeg

salt and pepper

2 tbsp single cream

55 g/2 oz Emmenthal cheese, grated

6 canned artichoke hearts,
    drained and mashed

4 egg yolks

5 egg whites

1 Grease a 1.7 litre/3 pint soufflé dish with butter. Tie a double strip of greaseproof paper around the dish so that it protrudes about 5 cm/2 inches above the rim. Melt the butter in a heavy-based saucepan. Add the flour and cook, stirring constantly, for 2 minutes. Remove the pan from the heat and gradually stir in the milk. Return to the heat and bring to the boil, whisking constantly, for 2 minutes, until thickened and smooth. Remove from the heat, season to taste with nutmeg, salt and pepper and beat in the cream, Emmenthal and mashed artichoke hearts. Beat in the egg yolks, 1 at a time.

2 Whisk the egg whites in a grease-free bowl until they form stiff peaks. Fold 2 tablespoons of the egg whites into the artichoke mixture to loosen, then gently fold in the remainder.

3 Pour the mixture into the soufflé dish and bake in a preheated oven, 190°C/375°F/Gas Mark 5, for 35 minutes, until the soufflé is well risen and the top is golden brown. Serve immediately.

VARIATION

For spinach soufflé, substitute 225 g/8 oz cooked, drained and chopped spinach for the artichoke hearts.

Three-cheese Soufflé

This soufflé is very simple to make, yet it has a delicious flavour and melts in the mouth. Choose three alternative cheeses, if preferred.

NUTRITIONAL INFORMATION

Calories	447	Sugars	.........1g
Protein	........22g	Fat	.........23g
Carbohydrate	...41g	Saturates	......11g

10 mins   55 mins

SERVES 4

INGREDIENTS

2 tbsp butter

2 tsp plain flour

900 g/2 lb floury potatoes

8 eggs, separated

4 tbsp grated Gruyère cheese

4 tbsp crumbled blue cheese

4 tbsp grated mature Cheddar cheese

salt and pepper

1 Butter a 2.25 litre/4 pint soufflé dish and dust with the flour. Set aside.

2 Cook the potatoes in a saucepan of boiling water until tender. Mash until very smooth and then transfer to a mixing bowl to cool.

3 Beat the egg yolks into the potato and stir in the Gruyère cheese, blue cheese and Cheddar, mixing well. Season to taste with salt and pepper.

4 Whisk the egg whites until standing in peaks, then gently fold them into the potato mixture with a metal spoon until fully incorporated.

5 Spoon the potato mixture into the prepared soufflé dish.

6 Cook in a preheated oven, 220°C/ 425°F/Gas Mark 7, for 35–40 minutes until risen and set. Serve immediately.

COOK'S TIP
Insert a fine skewer into the centre of the soufflé; it should come out clean when the soufflé is fully cooked through.

Spicy Vegetable Fritters

These crisp, attractive little vegetable fritters, served with a spicy hot chilli dip, make a fantastic snack.

NUTRITIONAL INFORMATION

Calories	290	Sugars	.........6g
Protein	.........6g	Fat	..........12g
Carbohydrate	...33g	Saturates	......10g

 15 mins   10 mins

SERVES 4–6

I N G R E D I E N T S

150 g/5½ oz plain flour

1 tsp ground coriander

1 tsp cumin

1 tsp turmeric

1 tsp salt

½ tsp pepper

2 garlic cloves, finely chopped

3 cm/1¼ inch piece fresh root ginger, chopped

2 small fresh green chillies, deseeded and finely chopped

1 tbsp chopped fresh coriander

about 225 ml/8 fl oz water

1 onion, chopped

1 potato, roughly grated

85 g/3 oz sweetcorn kernels

1 small aubergine, diced

125 g/4½ oz Chinese broccoli, cut into short lengths

coconut oil, for deep frying

S W E E T   C H I L L I   D I P

2 fresh red bird's-eye chillies, deseeded and finely chopped

4 tbsp caster sugar

4 tbsp rice vinegar

1 tbsp light soy sauce

1 Make the dip by mixing together all the ingredients in a bowl, stirring well until the caster sugar is completely dissolved. Cover the dip and set aside so that the flavours can mingle.

2 To make the fritters, place the flour in a bowl and stir in the ground coriander, cumin, turmeric, salt and pepper. Add the chopped garlic, ginger, chillies and coriander and then stir in just enough cold water to make a thick batter.

3 Add the onion, potato, sweetcorn, aubergine and broccoli to the batter and stir well to distribute the ingredients evenly.

4 Heat the oil in a wok to 180°C/350°F or until a cube of bread browns in 30 seconds. Drop tablespoons of the batter into the hot oil and fry, in batches, until golden and crisp, turning once.

5 Keep the first batches of fried fritters hot in a warm oven while you are cooking the others.

6 Drain the fritters well on absorbent kitchen paper and serve them at once while they are still hot and crispy, accompanied by a bowl of the sweet chilli dip.

Sweet Potato Cakes

These are enticing little tasty mouthfuls of sweet potato, served hot and sizzling from the pan with a delicious fresh soy-tomato sauce.

NUTRITIONAL INFORMATION

Calories 349	Sugars 9g	
Protein 4g	Fat 24g	
Carbohydrate ...32g	Saturates 3g	

15 mins   15 mins

SERVES 4

INGREDIENTS

500 g/1 lb 2 oz sweet potatoes

2 garlic cloves, crushed

1 small fresh green chilli, deseeded and chopped

2 fresh coriander sprigs, chopped

1 tbsp dark soy sauce

plain flour, for shaping

vegetable oil, for frying

sesame seeds, for sprinkling

SOY-TOMATO SAUCE

2 tsp vegetable oil

1 garlic clove, finely chopped

1½ tsp finely chopped fresh root ginger

3 tomatoes, peeled and chopped

2 tbsp dark soy sauce

1 tbsp lime juice

2 tbsp chopped fresh coriander

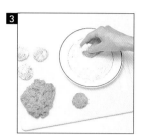

1 To make the soy-tomato sauce, heat the oil in a wok and stir-fry the garlic and ginger for about 1 minute. Add the tomatoes and stir-fry for a further 2 minutes. Remove from the heat and stir in the soy sauce, lime juice and chopped coriander. Set aside and keep warm.

2 Peel the sweet potatoes and grate finely (you can do this quickly with a food processor). Place the garlic, chilli and coriander in a mortar and crush to a smooth paste with a pestle. Stir in the soy sauce and mix with the sweet potatoes.

3 Divide the mixture into 12 equal portions. Dip into flour and pat into a flat, round patty shape.

4 Heat a shallow layer of oil in a wide frying pan. Fry the sweet potato cakes in batches over a high heat until golden, turning once.

5 Drain on kitchen paper and sprinkle with sesame seeds. Serve hot, with a spoonful of the soy-tomato sauce.

COOK'S TIP

Although deeper in colour than light soy sauce, dark soy sauce is not so strongly flavoured and is sweeter.

Spinach Cakes with Fennel

'Nudo' or naked is the word used to describe this mixture, which can also be made into thin pancakes or used as a filling for tortelloni.

NUTRITIONAL INFORMATION

Calories . . . . . . .360 Sugars 3g
Protein . . . . .17g Fat 29g
Carbohydrate . . . .8g Saturates 18g

20 mins

30 mins

SERVES 4

I N G R E D I E N T S

450 g/1 lb fresh spinach

250 g/9 oz ricotta cheese

1 egg, beaten

2 tsp fennel seeds, lightly crushed

salt and pepper

50 g/1¾ oz pecorino or Parmesan cheese,
 finely grated

25 g/1 oz plain flour, mixed with 1 tsp
 dried thyme

75 g/2¾ oz butter

2 garlic cloves, crushed

1 Wash the spinach and trim off any long stalks. Place in a pan, cover and cook for 4–5 minutes, or until wilted. You may need to do this in batches as the volume of spinach is quite large. Place in a colander and leave to drain and cool.

COOK'S TIP

Once it is washed, spinach holds enough water on the leaves to cook without adding any extra liquid. If you use frozen spinach instead of fresh, simply defrost it and squeeze out the excess water.

2 Mash the ricotta and beat in the egg and the fennel seeds. Season with plenty of salt and pepper, then stir in the pecorino or Parmesan cheese.

3 Squeeze as much excess water as possible from the spinach and finely chop the leaves. Stir the spinach into the cheese mixture.

4 Taking about 1 tablespoon of the spinach and cheese mixture, shape it into a ball and flatten it slightly to form a patty. Gently roll in the seasoned flour.

Continue this process until all of the mixture has been used up.

5 Half fill a large frying pan with wate and bring to the boil. Carefully add the patties and cook for 3–4 minutes, o until they rise to the surface. Remove with a perforated spoon.

6 Melt the butter in a pan. Add the crushed garlic and cook for 2–3 minutes. Pour the garlic butter over the patties, season with freshly ground blac pepper and serve at once.

Sweet Potato & Leek Patties

Sweet potatoes have very dense flesh and a delicious, sweet, earthy taste, which contrasts well with the pungent flavour of the ginger.

NUTRITIONAL INFORMATION

Calories	403	Sugars	........34g
Protein	.........8g	Fat	..........12g
Carbohydrate	...67g	Saturates	......2g

🕙 15 mins, plus chilling   🕐 40 mins

SERVES 4

INGREDIENTS

900 g/2 lb sweet potatoes

4 tsp sunflower oil

2 leeks, trimmed and finely chopped

1 garlic clove, crushed

2 tsp finely chopped fresh root ginger

200 g/7 oz canned sweetcorn, drained

salt and pepper

2 tbsp low-fat natural fromage frais

6 tbsp wholemeal flour

GINGER SAUCE

2 tbsp white wine vinegar

2 tsp caster sugar

1 red chilli, deseeded and chopped

2.5 cm/1 inch piece fresh root ginger, cut into thin strips

2 tbsp ginger wine

4 tbsp vegetable stock

1 tsp cornflour

TO SERVE

lettuce leaves

spring onions, shredded

1 Peel the potatoes, cut into thick cubes and boil for 10–15 minutes. Drain well and mash. Leave to cool.

2 Heat 2 teaspoons of the oil and fry the leeks, garlic and ginger for 2–3 minutes. Stir into the potato with the sweetcorn, seasoning and fromage frais. Form into 8 patties and toss in the flour. Chill for 30 minutes. Place the patties on a preheated grill rack and lightly brush with

oil. Grill the patties for 5 minutes, then turn over, brush with oil and grill for a further 5 minutes.

3 To make the sauce, place the vinegar, sugar, chilli and ginger in a pan and simmer for 5 minutes. Stir in the wine. Blend the stock and cornflour and add to the sauce, stirring, until thickened. Serve the patties with lettuce and spring onions, and the sauce.

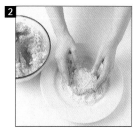

Roast Summer Vegetables

This appetizing and colourful mixture of Mediterranean vegetables makes a sensational summer lunch.

NUTRITIONAL INFORMATION

Calories ....142 Sugars 13g
Protein ....4g Fat 7g
Carbohydrate ...18g Saturates 1g

 10 mins   20-25 mins

SERVES 4

INGREDIENTS

1 fennel bulb

2 red onions

2 beefsteak tomatoes

1 aubergine

2 courgettes

1 yellow pepper, deseeded

1 red pepper, deseeded

1 orange pepper, deseeded

2 tbsp olive oil

4 garlic cloves

4 fresh rosemary sprigs

pepper

crusty bread, to serve (optional)

1 Cut the fennel, onions and tomatoes into wedges. Thickly slice the aubergine and courgettes. Cut the peppers into chunks. Brush a large ovenproof dish with a little of the oil. Arrange the prepared vegetables in the dish and tuck the garlic cloves and rosemary sprigs among them. Drizzle with the remaining oil and season to taste with plenty of freshly ground black pepper.

2 Roast the vegetables in a preheated oven, 200°C/400°F/Gas Mark 6, for 20–25 minutes, turning once until they are tender and beginning to turn golden brown.

3 Serve the vegetables straight from the dish or transfer to a warm serving platter. Serve immediately, with crusty bread, if you like, to mop up the juices.

COOK'S TIP

You can also serve this dish as an accompaniment. This quantity will serve 8 people.

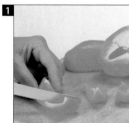

Filled Pitta Breads

Pitta breads are warmed over hot coals, then split and filled with a Greek salad tossed in a warm, fragrant rosemary dressing.

NUTRITIONAL INFORMATION

Calories 456   Sugars 4g
Protein ....13g   Fat 25g
Carbohydrate ...49g   Saturates 7g

15 mins   10 mins

SERVES 4

INGREDIENTS

½ iceberg lettuce, roughly chopped

2 large tomatoes, cut into wedges

7.5 cm/3 inch piece of cucumber, cut into chunks

25 g/1 oz black olives, stoned

115 g/4 oz feta cheese (drained weight)

4 pitta breads

DRESSING

6 tbsp olive oil

3 tbsp red wine vinegar

1 tbsp crushed rosemary

½ tsp caster sugar

salt and pepper

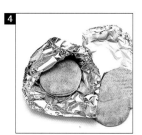

1 To make the salad, combine the lettuce, tomatoes, cucumber and black olives in a bowl.

2 Cut the feta cheese into chunks and add to the salad. Toss gently.

3 To make the dressing, whisk together the olive oil, red wine vinegar, rosemary and sugar. Season to taste with salt and pepper. Place in a small saucepan or heatproof bowl and heat very gently or place on the side of a barbecue to warm through gently.

4 Wrap the individual pitta breads tightly in foil and place on a hot barbecue for 2–3 minutes, turning once, to warm through. Alternatively, wrap in foil and warm through in a hot oven for a few minutes.

5 Unwrap the breads and split them open. Fill with the Greek salad mixture and drizzle over the warm dressing. Serve immediately.

COOK'S TIP

Substitute different herbs for the rosemary – either oregano or basil would make a delicious alternative. Pack plenty of the salad into the pitta breads – they taste much better when they are full to bursting!

Cauliflower Cheese Surprise

The surprise is all the other delicious ingredients cooked with the cauliflower in this version of the well-known family favourite.

NUTRITIONAL INFORMATION

Calories 549	Sugars 20g	
Protein 24g	Fat 32g	
Carbohydrate ...43g	Saturates 17g	

 15 mins   15 mins

SERVES 4

INGREDIENTS

2 tbsp sunflower oil

2 onions, chopped

115 g/4 oz mushrooms, chopped

4 tomatoes, skinned and chopped

200 g/7 oz canned sweetcorn, drained

1 large cauliflower, cut into florets

600 ml/1 pint Cheese Sauce (see page 304), made with 70 g/2½ oz Cheddar and 70 g/2½ oz Gruyère cheese

4 tbsp freshly grated Parmesan cheese

4 tbsp dry breadcrumbs

salt and pepper

1 Heat the oil in a heavy-based frying pan. Add the onions and cook over a low heat, stirring occasionally, for 5 minutes, until softened. Add the mushrooms and cook, stirring occasionally, for 5 minutes. Mix in the tomatoes and sweetcorn, season and heat through.

2 Meanwhile, cook the cauliflower in a pan of lightly salted boiling water for 5–10 minutes, until just tender. Drain well and keep warm.

3 Stir 150 ml/5 fl oz of the cheese sauce into the onion and sweetcorn mixture, then spoon it into a large, flameproof dish. Top with cauliflower and pour the remaining cheese sauce over it.

4 Combine the grated Parmesan and the breadcrumbs and sprinkle them over the top. Place under a preheated grill for 3–5 minutes, until lightly browned. Serve the cauliflower cheese immediately, on warmed plates.

VARIATION

For an attractive effect, use half cauliflower and half broccoli florets.

Lattice Flan

This pretty flan, with its lattice effect revealing the pale green spinach filling, tastes every bit as good as it looks. Serve warm or cold.

NUTRITIONAL INFORMATION

Calories	930	Sugars	.........8g
Protein	........28g	Fat	..........59g
Carbohydrate	...78g	Saturates	......33g

30 mins   1 hr

SERVES 4–6

I N G R E D I E N T S

butter, for greasing

plain flour, for dusting

2 x quantity rich shortcrust pastry dough
(see page 8), chilled

lightly beaten egg, to glaze

FILLING

450 g/1 lb frozen spinach, thawed

2 tbsp olive oil

1 large onion, chopped

2 garlic cloves, finely chopped

2 eggs, lightly beaten

225 g/8 oz ricotta cheese

55 g/2 oz Parmesan cheese, freshly grated

pinch of freshly grated nutmeg

salt and pepper

1 To make the filling, drain the spinach and squeeze out as much moisture as possible and chop finely. Heat the oil in a large, heavy-based frying pan. Add the onion and cook, stirring occasionally, for 5 minutes, until softened. Add the garlic and spinach to the pan and cook, stirring occasionally, for a further 10 minutes.

2 Remove the pan from the heat, leave the mixture to cool slightly, then beat in the eggs, ricotta and Parmesan. Season to taste with nutmeg, salt and pepper.

3 Lightly grease a 23 cm/9 inch loose-based flan tin with butter. Roll out two-thirds of the dough on a lightly floured surface and use to line the flan tin, leaving the dough overhanging the sides. Spoon in the spinach mixture, spreading it evenly over the base.

4 Roll out the remaining dough on a lightly floured surface and cut into 5 mm/¼ inch strips. Arrange the strips in a lattice pattern on top of the flan, pressing the ends securely to seal. Trim any excess pastry. Brush with the egg glaze and bake in a preheated oven, 200°C/400°F/ Gas Mark 6, for about 45 minutes, until golden brown.

5 Transfer the flan to a wire rack to cool slightly before removing from the tin.

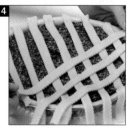

Egg Curry

This curry can be made very quickly. It can either be served as a side dish or, with parathas, as a light lunch.

NUTRITIONAL INFORMATION

Calories 189	Sugars 3g	
Protein 7g	Fat 16g	
Carbohydrate 4g	Saturates 3g	

 10 mins   🕐 15 mins

SERVES 4

I N G R E D I E N T S

4 tbsp vegetable oil

1 onion, sliced

1 fresh red chilli, deseeded and
  finely chopped

½ tsp chilli powder

½ tsp finely chopped fresh root ginger

½ tsp fresh garlic, crushed

4 eggs

1 firm tomato, sliced

fresh coriander leaves

parathas, to serve (optional)

1 Heat the oil in a large heavy-based saucepan. Add the sliced onion to the pan and fry over a medium heat, stirring occasionally, for about 5 minutes, until it is just softened and a light golden colour.

2 Lower the heat. Add the fresh red chilli, the chilli powder, the chopped ginger and the crushed garlic to the pan and fry over a low heat, stirring constantly, for about 1 minute.

3 Add the eggs and tomatoes to the pan and continue cooking, stirring to break up the eggs when they begin to cook, for a further 3–5 minutes.

4 Sprinkle the fresh coriander leaves over the curry and transfer it to warm serving plates.

5 Serve the egg curry immediately, with parathas to accompany it, if you wish.

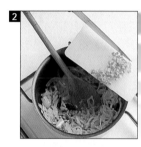

COOK'S TIP

Both the leaves and the finely chopped stems of coriander are used in Indian cooking, to flavour dishes and as edible garnishes. It has a very distinctive and pronounced taste.

Layered Vegetable Bake

Simplicity itself, this tasty bake makes a superb meal in itself, or it can be served as an accompaniment.

NUTRITIONAL INFORMATION

Calories . . . . . . .174 Sugars 4g
Protein . . . . .5g Fat 4g
Carbohydrate . . .33g Saturates 1g

10 mins | 1½ hrs

SERVES 4

INGREDIENTS

1 tbsp olive oil, for brushing

675 g/1½ lb potatoes, thinly sliced

8 fresh basil leaves

2 leeks, sliced

2 beef tomatoes

1 garlic clove, finely chopped

300 ml/10 fl oz vegetable stock

salt and pepper

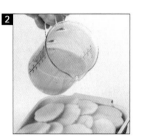

1 Brush a large ovenproof dish with a little of the oil. Place a layer of potato slices in the base, sprinkle with half the basil leaves and cover with a layer of leeks. Cut the tomatoes into thin slices and arrange in a layer on top. Repeat these layers until all the vegetables are used up, ending with a layer of potatoes.

2 Stir the chopped garlic into the stock and season to taste with salt and pepper. Pour the stock over the vegetables and brush the top with the remaining oil.

3 Bake in a preheated oven, 180°C/ 350°F/Gas Mark 4, for 1½ hours, until the vegetables are tender and the topping is golden brown.

COOK'S TIP
Try to find sun-ripened tomatoes, which have a sweeter and fuller flavour than those grown under glass.

Savoury Pepper Bread

This flavoursome bread contains only the minimum amount of fat.
Serve with a bowl of hot soup for a filling and nutritious light meal.

NUTRITIONAL INFORMATION

Calories ....468 Sugars 11g
Protein ....16g Fat 5g
Carbohydrate ...97g Saturates 1g

2 hrs   50 mins

SERVES 4

INGREDIENTS

1 small red pepper

1 small green pepper

1 small yellow pepper

60 g/2 oz dry-pack sun-dried tomatoes

50 ml/2 fl oz boiling water

2 tsp dried yeast

1 tsp caster sugar

150 ml/5 fl oz tepid water

450 g/1 lb strong white bread flour

2 tsp dried rosemary

2 tbsp tomato purée

150 ml/5 fl oz low-fat natural fromage frais

1 tbsp sea salt

1 tbsp olive oil

1 Preheat the oven to 220°C/425°F/Gas Mark 7 and the grill to hot. Halve and deseed the peppers, arrange on the grill rack and cook until the skin is charred. Leave to cool for 10 minutes, peel off the skin and chop the flesh. Slice the tomatoes into strips, place in a bowl and pour over the boiling water. Leave to soak.

2 Place the yeast and sugar in a small jug, pour over the tepid water and leave for 10–15 minutes until frothy. Sift the flour into a bowl and add 1 teaspoon dried rosemary. Make a well in the centre and pour in the yeast mixture.

3 Add the tomato purée, tomatoes and soaking liquid, peppers, fromage frais and half the salt. Mix to form a soft dough. Turn out on to a lightly floured surface and knead for 3–4 minutes until smooth and elastic. Place in a lightly floured bowl, cover and leave in a warm room for 40 minutes until doubled in size.

4 Knead the dough again and place in a lightly greased 23 cm/9 inch round springform cake tin. Using a wooden spoon, form 'dimples' in the surface. Cover and leave for 30 minutes. Brush with the olive oil and sprinkle with the dried rosemary and sea salt. Bake for 35–40 minutes, cool for 10 minutes and release from the tin. Leave to cool on a rack and serve.

COOK'S TIP

For a quick, filling snack, serve the bread with a bowl of hot soup in winter, or a crisp leaf salad in summer.

Onion & Mozzarella Tarts

These individual tarts are delicious hot or cold, so they are great for lunchboxes or picnics as well as a light snack.

NUTRITIONAL INFORMATION

Calories . . . . . . .327 Sugars 3g
Protein . . . . .5g Fat 23g
Carbohydrate . . .25g Saturates 9g

45 mins   45 mins

SERVES 4

I N G R E D I E N T S

250g/9 oz puff pastry,
 defrosted if frozen

2 red onions

1 red pepper

8 cherry tomatoes, halved

100g/3½ oz mozzarella cheese,
 cut into chunks

8 sprigs fresh thyme

1 Roll out the pastry to make 4 x 7.5 cm/3 inch squares. Using a sharp knife, trim the edges of the pastry, reserving the trimmings. Leave the pastry to chill in the refrigerator for 30 minutes.

2 Place the pastry squares on a baking tray. Brush a little water along each edge of the pastry squares and use the reserved pastry trimmings to make a rim around each tart.

3 Cut the red onions into thin wedges and halve and deseed the pepper.

4 Place the onions and pepper in a roasting tin. Cook under a preheated grill for 15 minutes or until charred.

5 Place the roasted pepper halves in a polythene bag and leave to sweat for 10 minutes. When the pepper is cool

enough to handle, peel off the skin and cut the flesh into strips.

6 Line the pastry squares with squares of foil. Bake in a preheated oven, 200°C/400°F/Gas Mark 6, for 10 minutes. Remove and discard the foil squares, return the tart cases to the oven and bake for a further 5 minutes.

7 Place a portion of the onions, pepper strips, tomatoes and cheese in each tart and sprinkle with the fresh thyme.

8 Return the tarts to the oven for 15 minutes or until the pastry is golden and the cheese melted. Transfer to warmed serving plates if serving hot or to a cooling tray if serving cold.

Baked Potatoes with Pesto

This is an easy but very filling meal. The potatoes are baked until fluffy, scooped out and mixed with a tasty pesto filling and baked again.

NUTRITIONAL INFORMATION

Calories 444	Sugars 3g
Protein 10g	Fat 28g
Carbohydrate ...40g	Saturates 13g

 10 mins   1½ hrs

SERVES 4

INGREDIENTS

4 baking potatoes, about 225 g/8 oz each

150 ml/¼ pint double cream

75 ml/3 fl oz vegetable stock

1 tbsp lemon juice

2 garlic cloves, crushed

3 tbsp chopped fresh basil

salt and pepper

2 tbsp pine kernels

2 tbsp grated Parmesan cheese

1 Scrub the potatoes well and prick the skins with a fork. Rub a little salt into the skins and place on a baking tray.

2 Cook in a preheated oven, 190°C/375°F/Gas Mark 5, for 1 hour, or until the potatoes are cooked through and the skins are crisp.

3 Remove the potatoes from the oven and cut them in half lengthways. Using a spoon, scoop the potato flesh into a mixing bowl, leaving a thin shell of potato inside the skins. Mash the potato flesh with a fork.

4 Meanwhile, mix the cream and stock in a saucepan and simmer over a low heat for about 8–10 minutes, or until reduced by half.

5 Stir in the lemon juice, garlic and chopped basil and season to taste with salt and pepper. Stir the mixture into the mashed potato flesh, together with the pine kernels.

6 Spoon the mixture back into the potato shells and sprinkle the Parmesan cheese on top. Return the potatoes to the oven for 10 minutes, or until the cheese has browned, and serve.

VARIATION

Add full-fat soft cheese or thinly sliced mushrooms to the mashed potato flesh in step 5, if you prefer.

Vegetable Calzone

These pizza-base parcels are great for making in advance and freezing – they can be defrosted when required for a quick snack.

NUTRITIONAL INFORMATION

Calories 446	Sugars 10g
Protein 16g	Fat 8g
Carbohydrate ...82g	Saturates 2g

 30 mins, plus rising   30 mins

Makes 4

INGREDIENTS

DOUGH

450 g/1 lb strong white flour

2 tsp easy-blend dried yeast

1 tsp caster sugar

150 ml/¼ pint vegetable stock

150 ml/¼ pint passata

beaten egg

FILLING

1 tbsp vegetable oil

1 onion, chopped

1 garlic clove, crushed

2 tbsp chopped sun-dried tomatoes

100 g/3½ oz spinach, chopped

3 tbsp drained canned sweetcorn kernels

25 g/1 oz French beans, cut into thirds

1 tbsp tomato purée

1 tbsp chopped oregano

salt and pepper

50 g/1¾ oz mozzarella cheese, sliced

1 Sieve the flour into a bowl. Add the dried yeast and sugar and beat in the vegetable stock and passata to make a smooth dough.

2 Knead the dough on a lightly floured surface for 10 minutes, then place in a clean, lightly oiled bowl and leave to rise in a warm place for 1 hour.

3 Heat the oil in a frying pan and sauté the onion for 2–3 minutes. Stir in the garlic, tomatoes, spinach, corn and beans and cook for 3–4 minutes. Add the tomato purée and oregano and season well.

4 Divide the risen dough into 4 equal portions and roll each portion out on a floured surface to form an 18 cm/7 inch circle. Spoon a quarter of the filling mixture on to one half of each circle and top with the sliced mozzarella cheese.

5 Fold the dough over to encase the filling, pressing the edge firmly with a fork to seal. Glaze the dough with the beaten egg.

6 Put the calzone on a lightly greased baking tray and cook in a preheated oven, 220°C/425°F/Gas Mark 7, for 25–30 minutes until risen and golden. Serve warm.

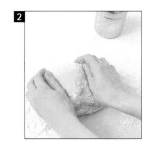

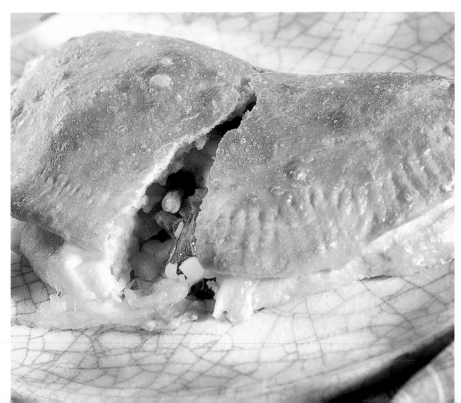

Golden Macaroni Cheese

Always a useful storecupboard stand-by, macaroni cheese can be a little dull, but adding some extra ingredients livens it up.

NUTRITIONAL INFORMATION

Calories 618	Sugars 12g	
Protein 29g	Fat 32g	
Carbohydrate . . .58g	Saturates 18g	

 15 mins   20 mins

SERVES 4

INGREDIENTS

200 g/7 oz dried elbow macaroni

1 onion, sliced

4 cherry tomatoes, halved

4 hard-boiled eggs, quartered

3 tbsp dried breadcrumbs

2 tbsp finely grated red Leicester cheese

salt

CHEESE SAUCE

40 g/1½ oz butter

40 g/1½ oz plain flour

600 ml/1 pint milk

140 g/5 oz red Leicester cheese, grated

pinch of cayenne pepper

salt

1 Bring a large pan of lightly salted water to the boil. Add the macaroni and onion, bring back to the boil and cook for 8–10 minutes, until the pasta is tender, but still firm to the bite. Drain well and tip the macaroni and onion into an ovenproof dish.

2 To make the cheese sauce, melt the butter in a saucepan. Stir in the flour and cook, stirring constantly, for 1–2 minutes. Remove the pan from the heat and gradually whisk in the milk.

3 Return the pan to the heat and bring to the boil, whisking constantly. Simmer for about 2 minutes, until the sauce is thick and glossy.

4 Remove the pan from the heat, stir in the cheese and season to taste with cayenne and salt.

5 Pour the sauce over the macaroni, add the hard-boiled eggs and mix lightly. Arrange the tomato halves on top. Mix together the breadcrumbs and finely grated Red Leicester cheese and sprinkle over the surface.

6 Cook under a preheated grill for 3-4 minutes, until the topping is golden brown and bubbling. Serve the macaroni cheese immediately.

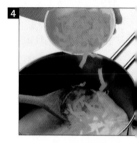

COOK'S TIP

When making cheese sauce, always remove the pan from the heat before stirring in the grated cheese, or the sauce will become rubbery.

Penne with Walnut Sauce

Pasta is wonderfully versatile and goes with a wide range of vegetables. Here it is served in a creamy sauce with courgettes, walnuts and herbs.

NUTRITIONAL INFORMATION

Calories 635	Sugars 8g	
Protein 19g	Fat 29g	
Carbohydrate . . .82g	Saturates 8g	

 15 mins   35 mins

SERVES 4

I N G R E D I E N T S

25 g/1 oz butter

3 tbsp olive oil

2 red onions, thinly sliced

450 g/1 lb courgettes, thinly sliced

375 g/12 oz dried penne

55 g/2 oz chopped walnuts

3 tbsp chopped fresh flat-leaved parsley

2 tbsp crème fraîche

salt and pepper

2 tbsp freshly grated Parmesan cheese

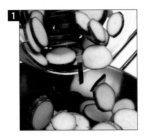

1 Melt the butter with the olive oil in a large, heavy-based frying pan. Add the sliced red onions, cover and cook over a low heat, stirring occasionally, for 5 minutes, until softened. Add the courgettes to the pan, cover and cook, stirring occasionally, for 15–20 minutes, until the vegetables are very tender.

2 Bring a large saucepan of lightly salted water to the boil. Add the pasta, bring back to the boil and simmer for 8–10 minutes, until the pasta is tender, but still firm to the bite.

3 Meanwhile, stir the walnuts, parsley and crème fraîche into the courgette mixture and add salt and pepper to taste.

4 When the pasta is al dente, drain it and tip into a serving dish. Add the courgette mixture and toss well. Sprinkle over the grated Parmesan and serve the pasta immediately.

COOK'S TIP

For perfect pasta, start checking for tenderness by breaking off a small piece and biting it, when it has been cooking for about 7 minutes. As soon as it is ready, turn off the heat and drain.

Spinach & Ricotta Shells

This is a classic combination in which the smooth, creamy cheese balances the sharper taste of the spinach.

NUTRITIONAL INFORMATION

Calories ....672 Sugars 10g
Protein ....23g Fat 26g
Carbohydrate ...93g Saturates 8g

 5 mins   40 mins

SERVES 4

INGREDIENTS

400 g/14 oz dried lumache rigate grande pasta

5 tbsp olive oil

55 g/2 oz fresh white breadcrumbs

125 ml/4 fl oz milk

300 g/10½ oz frozen spinach, defrosted and drained

225 g/8 oz ricotta cheese

pinch of freshly grated nutmeg

salt and pepper

400 g/14 oz canned chopped tomatoes, drained

1 garlic clove, crushed

1 Bring a large saucepan of lightly salted water to the boil. Add the lumache and 1 tablespoon of the olive oil, bring back to the boil and cook for 8–10 minutes until just tender, but still firm to the bite. Drain the pasta, refresh under cold running water, drain again and set aside until required.

2 Place the breadcrumbs, milk and 3 tablespoons of the remaining olive oil in a food processor or blender and process to combine.

3 Add the spinach and ricotta cheese to the food processor and process to a smooth mixture. Transfer to a bowl, stir in the nutmeg and season with salt and pepper to taste.

4 Mix together the tomatoes, garlic and the remaining tablespoon of oil and spoon the mixture into the base of a large ovenproof dish.

5 Using a teaspoon, fill the lumache with the spinach and ricotta mixture and arrange them on top of the tomato mixture in the dish.

6 Cover and bake in a preheated oven, 180°C/350°F/Gas Mark 4, for 20 minutes. Serve the stuffed pasta shells hot, straight from the dish.

COOK'S TIP

Ricotta is a creamy Italian cheese traditionally made from ewes' milk whey. It is soft and white, with a smooth texture and a slightly sweet flavour. It should be used within 2–3 days of purchase.

 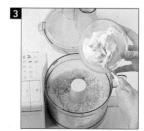 

Aubergine Sandwiches

These unusual and delicious barbecued sandwiches are made from two slices of aubergine with a cheese and tomato filling.

NUTRITIONAL INFORMATION

Calories 270   Sugars 4g
Protein . . . . .10g   Fat 15g
Carbohydrate . . .25g   Saturates 7g

5 mins   10–15 mins

SERVES 2

INGREDIENTS

1 large aubergine

1 tbsp lemon juice

3 tbsp olive oil

salt and pepper

125 g/4½ oz grated mozzarella cheese

2 sun-dried tomatoes, chopped

TO SERVE

Italian bread, such as focaccia or ciabatta

mixed salad leaves

slices of tomato

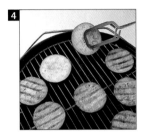

1 Slice the aubergine into thin rounds, using a very sharp knife.

2 Combine the lemon juice and olive oil in a small bowl and season the mixture with salt and pepper to taste.

3 Brush the aubergine slices with the oil and lemon juice mixture and barbecue over medium hot coals for 2–3 minutes, without turning, until they are golden on the underside.

4 Turn half of the aubergine slices over and sprinkle with cheese and chopped sun-dried tomatoes.

5 Place the remaining aubergine slices on top of the cheese and tomatoes, turning them over so that the pale side is now uppermost.

6 Barbecue for 1–2 minutes, then carefully turn the whole sandwich over and barbecue for 1–2 minutes. Baste with the oil mixture.

7 Serve the aubergine sandwiches with Italian bread, mixed salad leaves and a few slices of tomato.

VARIATION
Try feta cheese instead of mozzarella but omit the salt from the basting oil because feta is quite salty. A creamy goat's cheese would be equally delicious.

Sweetcorn Patties

These are a delicious addition to any party buffet, and very simple to prepare. Serve with a sweet chilli sauce.

NUTRITIONAL INFORMATION

Calories 90   Sugars 3g
Protein . . . . .2g   Fat 5g
Carbohydrate . . . .11g   Saturates 0.6g

🥟 🥟

🍲 10 mins   🕐 10 mins

SERVES 6

INGREDIENTS

325 g/11½ oz canned sweetcorn, drained

1 onion, finely chopped

1 tsp curry powder

1 garlic clove, crushed

1 tsp ground coriander

2 spring onions, chopped

3 tbsp plain flour

½ tsp baking powder

1 large egg

4 tbsp sunflower oil

salt

1 spring onion, sliced, to garnish

1 Mash the drained sweetcorn lightly in a medium-sized bowl. Add the onion, curry powder, garlic, ground coriander, spring onions, flour, baking powder and egg. Stir well and season with salt.

2 Heat the sunflower oil in a frying pan. Drop tablespoonfuls of the mixture carefully on to the hot oil, far enough apart for them not to run into each other as they cook.

3 Cook for about 4–5 minutes, turning each patty once, until they are golden brown and firm to the touch. Take care not to turn them too soon, or they will break up in the pan.

4 Remove the patties from the pan with a slice and drain them well on absorbent kitchen paper. Serve at once, garnished with the spring onion.

COOK'S TIP

To make this dish more attractive, you can serve the patties on large leaves, like those shown in the photograph. Be sure to cut the spring onions on the diagonal, as shown, for a more elegant appearance.

Spinach Frittata

This Italian dish may be made with many flavourings. Spinach is used as the main ingredient in this recipe for colour and flavour.

NUTRITIONAL INFORMATION

Calories 307   Sugars 4g
Protein . . . . .15g   Fat 25g
Carbohydrate . . . .6g   Saturates 8g

20 mins   20 mins

SERVES 4

INGREDIENTS

450 g/1 lb fresh spinach

2 tsp water

4 eggs, beaten

2 tbsp single cream

2 garlic cloves, crushed

55 g/2 oz canned sweetcorn, drained

1 celery stick, chopped

1 fresh red chilli, deseeded and chopped

2 tomatoes, deseeded and diced

2 tbsp olive oil

2 tbsp butter

4 tbsp pecan nut halves

2 tbsp grated pecorino cheese

25 g/1 oz Fontina cheese, cubed

a pinch of paprika

1 Cook the spinach in 2 teaspoons of water in a covered pan for 5 minutes. Drain thoroughly and pat dry on absorbent kitchen paper.

2 Beat the eggs in a bowl and stir in the spinach, single cream, garlic, sweetcorn, celery, chilli and tomatoes until the ingredients are well mixed.

3 Heat the oil and butter in a 20 cm/ 8 inch heavy-based frying pan over a medium heat.

4 Spoon the egg mixture into the frying pan and sprinkle with the pecan nut halves, pecorino and Fontina cheeses and paprika. Cook, without stirring, over a medium heat for 5–7 minutes or until the underside of the frittata is brown.

5 Put a large plate over the pan and invert to turn out the frittata. Slide it back into the frying pan and cook the other side for a further 2–3 minutes. Serve the frittata straight from the frying pan or transfer to a serving plate.

COOK'S TIP
Be careful not to burn the underside of the frittata during the initial cooking stage – this is why it is important to use a heavy-based frying pan. Add a little extra oil to the pan when you turn the frittata over, if required.

Potato-filled Naan Breads

This is a filling Indian sandwich. Spicy potatoes fill the naan breads, which are served with a cool cucumber raita and lime pickle.

NUTRITIONAL INFORMATION

Calories	244	Sugars	........7g
Protein	.........8g	Fat	...........8g
Carbohydrate	...37g	Saturates	......1g

 10 mins   25 mins

SERVES 4

INGREDIENTS

225 g/8 oz waxy potatoes, scrubbed and diced

1 tbsp vegetable oil

1 onion, chopped

2 garlic cloves, crushed

1 tsp ground cumin

1 tsp ground coriander

½ tsp chilli powder

1 tbsp tomato purée

3 tbsp vegetable stock

85 g/3 oz baby spinach, shredded

4 small or 2 large naan breads

lime pickle, to serve

RAITA

150 ml/5 fl oz low-fat natural yogurt

4 tbsp diced cucumber

1 tbsp chopped fresh mint

1 Parboil the diced potatoes in a saucepan of boiling water for 10 minutes. Drain thoroughly.

2 Heat the vegetable oil in a separate saucepan and cook the onion and garlic over a low heat, stirring frequently, for 3 minutes. Add the spices to the pan and cook for a further 2 minutes.

3 Stir in the potatoes, tomato purée, vegetable stock and shredded spinach. Cook for 5 minutes until the potatoes are tender.

4 Warm the naan breads through in a preheated oven, 150°C/300°F/Gas Mark 2, for about 2 minutes.

5 To make the raita, mix the low-fat yogurt, the diced cucumber and the chopped mint together in a small bowl (see Cook's Tip).

6 Remove the warm naan breads from the oven. Using a sharp knife, cut a slit into the side of each bread to make a pocket. Spoon a portion of the spicy potato mixture into each pocket.

7 Serve the filled naan breads immediately, accompanied by the raita and lime pickle.

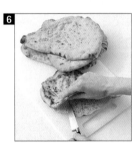

COOK'S TIP

To give the raita a much stronger flavour, make it in advance and chill in the refrigerator until ready to serve.

Mexican Eggs

In this unusual recipe, the eggs are cooked nestling in a spicy tomato, pepper and red wine sauce.

NUTRITIONAL INFORMATION

Calories	156	Sugars	.........6g
Protein	.........8g	Fat	...........8g
Carbohydrate	....7g	Saturates	.......2g

10 mins   50 mins

SERVES 4

INGREDIENTS

1 tbsp corn or sunflower oil

1 red pepper, deseeded and cut into batons

1 yellow pepper, deseeded and cut into batons

1 garlic clove, finely chopped

2 fresh red chillies, deseeded and finely chopped

1 tsp ground coriander

1 tsp ground cumin

125 ml/4 fl oz red wine

800 g/1lb 12 oz canned chopped tomatoes

1 tsp muscovado sugar

4 eggs

salt and pepper

2 tbsp chopped fresh coriander, to garnish

1 Heat the oil in a large frying pan. Add the peppers and garlic and cook over a medium heat, stirring occasionally, for about 2 minutes, until softened.

2 Add the chopped red chillies, the coriander and the cumin to the pan and continue to cook, stirring constantly, for 1 minute more. Pour in the red wine, bring the mixture to the boil and simmer for 3 minutes.

3 Stir in the tomatoes with their can juice and the sugar. Lower the heat and simmer gently for 20–25 minutes. Season to taste with salt and pepper.

4 Using a large spoon, make 4 hollows in the tomato mixture. Break an egg into each hollow, cover the pan and cook for 10–15 minutes, until the eggs are set. Sprinkle with the chopped coriander and serve immediately.

COOK'S TIP
Although chilli seeds themselves contain no capsaicin - the substance that makes chillies hot - it is very concentrated in the flesh surrounding them, so removing the seeds reduces the heat.

Pasta, Grains & Pulses

Pasta, grains and pulses are fantastically

versatile staple foods and a perfect base for

vegetarian recipes – they go wonderfully well

with all sorts of vegetables, cheese and nuts,

so the scope for making colourful, tasty and

highly nutritious dishes is endless. Pasta,

grains such as rice, and pulses – lentils and beans – all

come in a variety of shapes, colours and textures, making

them ideal for all sorts of exciting recipe ideas, from quick

dishes cooked on the hob, such as Vegetable & Pesto

Tagliatelle, to hearty bakes like Brown Rice Gratin, which

are great served hot, straight from the oven, when a

warming supper is called for.

Summertime Tagliatelle

This is a really fresh-tasting dish, made with courgettes and cream, which is ideal with a crisp white wine and some crusty bread.

NUTRITIONAL INFORMATION

Calories 502	Sugars 5g	
Protein 16g	Fat 30g	
Carbohydrate ...44g	Saturates 9g	

10 mins   20 mins

SERVES 4

I N G R E D I E N T S

650 g/1 lb 7 oz courgettes

6 tbsp olive oil

3 garlic cloves, crushed

3 tbsp chopped fresh basil

2 fresh red chillies, deseeded and sliced

juice of 1 large lemon

5 tbsp single cream

4 tbsp grated Parmesan cheese

salt and pepper

225 g/8 oz dried tagliatelle

crusty bread, to serve

1 Using a swivel vegetable peeler, slice the courgettes into thin ribbons.

2 Heat the oil in a frying pan and cook the garlic for 30 seconds.

3 Add the courgette ribbons and cook over a low heat, stirring constantly, for 5–7 minutes.

4 Stir in the basil, chillies, lemon juice, cream and Parmesan cheese and season with salt and pepper to taste. Keep the sauce warm over a very low heat until you are ready to serve it.

5 Meanwhile, bring a large pan of lightly salted water to the boil. Add the pasta, bring back to the boil and cook for 8–10 minutes until tender, but still firm to the bite. Drain thoroughly and put the pasta in a warm serving bowl.

6 Pile the courgette mixture on top of the pasta. Serve hot with crusty bread.

COOK'S TIP

Lime juice could be used instead of the lemon. As limes are usually smaller, squeeze the juice from 2 fruits.

Pasta with Nuts & Cheese

Simple and inexpensive, this tasty dish is fairly quick and easy to prepare, but looks and tastes very impressive.

NUTRITIONAL INFORMATION

Calories 531   Sugars 4g
Protein . . . . .20g   Fat 35g
Carbohydrate . . .35g   Saturates 16g

    10 mins   30 mins

SERVES 4

I N G R E D I E N T S

60 g/2 oz pine kernels

350 g/12 oz dried pasta shapes

2 courgettes, sliced

125 g/4½ oz broccoli, broken into florets

200 g/7 oz full-fat soft cheese

150 ml/¼ pint milk

1 tbsp chopped fresh basil

125 g/4½ oz button mushrooms, sliced

90 g/3 oz blue cheese, crumbled

salt and pepper

sprigs of fresh basil, to garnish

green salad, to serve

3 Meanwhile, cook the courgettes and broccoli in a small amount of boiling, lightly salted water for about 5 minutes or until just tender.

4 Put the soft cheese into a pan and heat gently, stirring constantly. Add the milk and stir to mix. Add the basil and mushrooms and cook gently for 2–3 minutes. Stir in the blue cheese and season to taste.

5 Drain the pasta and the vegetables and mix together. Pour over the cheese and mushroom sauce and add the pine kernels. Toss gently to mix. Garnish with basil sprigs and serve immediately with a green salad.

1 Scatter the pine kernels onto a large baking tray and grill, turning occasionally, until lightly browned all over. Set aside.

2 Cook the pasta in plenty of boiling salted water for 8–10 minutes or until it is just tender.

Tagliatelle with Mushrooms

This dish can be prepared in a moment – the intense flavours are sure to make this a popular recipe.

NUTRITIONAL INFORMATION

Calories . . . . .501 Sugars 3g
Protein . . . . .15g Fat 31g
Carbohydrate . . .43g Saturates 11g

 15 mins   20 mins

SERVES 4

I N G R E D I E N T S

2 tbsp walnut oil

1 bunch spring onions, sliced

2 garlic cloves, thinly sliced

225 g/8 oz mushrooms, sliced

500 g/1 lb 2 oz fresh green and
    white tagliatelle

225 g/8 oz frozen chopped leaf spinach,
    thawed and drained

125 g/4½ oz full-fat soft cheese with
    garlic and herbs

4 tbsp single cream

60 g/2 oz chopped unsalted pistachio nuts

salt and pepper

2 tbsp shredded fresh basil

sprigs of fresh basil, to garnish

Italian bread, to serve

1 Gently heat the oil in a wok or frying pan and fry the spring onions and garlic for 1 minute or until just softened. Add the mushrooms to the pan, stir well, cover and cook gently for 5 minutes or until softened.

2 Meanwhile, bring a large saucepan of lightly salted water to the boil and cook the pasta for 3–5 minutes or until just tender. Drain the pasta thoroughly and return to the saucepan.

3 Add the spinach to the mushrooms and heat through for 1–2 minutes. Add the cheese and allow to melt slightly. Stir in the cream and continue to heat without allowing to boil.

4 Pour the vegetable mixture over the pasta, season to taste and mix well. Heat gently, stirring, for 2–3 minutes.

5 Transfer the pasta to a warmed serving bowl and sprinkle over the pistachio nuts and shredded basil. Garnish with fresh basil sprigs and serve with Italian bread.

Pasta Omelette

This is a superb and unusual way of using up any left-over short pasta, such as penne, macaroni or conchiglie.

NUTRITIONAL INFORMATION

Calories	460	Sugars 3g
Protein	........16g	Fat 34g
Carbohydrate	...23g	Saturates 6g

10 mins   15–20 mins

SERVES 2

INGREDIENTS

4 tbsp olive oil

1 small onion, chopped

1 fennel bulb, thinly sliced

115 g/4 oz potato, diced

1 garlic clove, chopped

4 eggs

1 tbsp chopped fresh flat-leaf parsley

salt and pepper

pinch of chilli powder

100 g/3½ oz cooked short pasta

2 tbsp stuffed green olives, halved

fresh marjoram sprigs, to garnish

tomato salad, to serve

1 Heat half of the oil in a heavy-based frying pan over a low heat. Add the onion, fennel and potato and cook, stirring occasionally, for 8–10 minutes, until the potato is just tender.

2 Stir in the garlic and cook for 1 minute. Remove the pan from the heat, transfer the vegetables to a plate and set aside.

3 Beat the eggs until they are frothy. Stir in the parsley and season with salt, pepper and a pinch of chilli powder.

4 Heat 1 tablespoon of the remaining oil in a clean frying pan. Add half of the egg mixture to the pan, then add the cooked vegetables, pasta and half of the olives. Pour in the remaining egg mixture and cook until the sides begin to set.

5 Lift up the edges of the omelette with a palette knife to allow the uncooked egg to spread underneath. Cook, shaking the pan occasionally, until the underside is a light golden brown colour.

6 Slide the omelette out of the pan on to a large plate. Wipe the pan with kitchen paper and heat the remaining olive oil. Invert the omelette into the pan and cook until the other side is a golden brown colour.

7 Slide the omelette on to a warmed serving dish and garnish with the remaining olives and the marjoram sprigs. Cut the omelette into wedges and serve with a tomato salad.

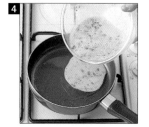  

Penne & Vegetables

The sweet cherry tomatoes in this recipe add colour and flavour and are complemented by the black olives and mixed peppers.

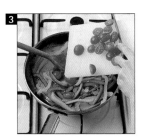

NUTRITIONAL INFORMATION

Calories	380	Sugars	.........6g
Protein	.........8g	Fat	..........16g
Carbohydrate	...48g	Saturates	.......7g

 10 mins   25 mins

SERVES 4

INGREDIENTS

225 g/8 oz dried penne

2 tbsp olive oil

2 tbsp butter

2 garlic cloves, crushed

1 green pepper, deseeded and thinly sliced

1 yellow pepper, deseeded and thinly sliced

16 cherry tomatoes, halved

1 tbsp chopped fresh oregano

125 ml/4 fl oz dry white wine

2 tbsp stoned black olives, quartered

salt and pepper

75 g/2¾ oz rocket

fresh oregano sprigs, to garnish

1 Bring a large pan of lightly salted water to the boil. Add the pasta, bring back to the boil and cook for 8–10 minutes

VARIATION

If rocket is unavailable, spinach makes a good substitute. Follow the same cooking instructions as for rocket.

until tender, but still firm to the bite. Drain thoroughly.

2 Heat the oil and butter in a pan until the butter melts. Sauté the garlic for 30 seconds. Add the peppers and cook, stirring occasionally, for 3–4 minutes.

3 Stir in the cherry tomatoes, oregano, wine and olives and cook for 3–4 minutes. Season with salt and pepper and stir in the rocket until just wilted.

4 Transfer the pasta to a serving dish, spoon over the sauce and garnish.

Spaghetti with Ricotta

This light pasta dish is quickly made and has a delicate flavour, making it ideally suited for a summer lunch.

NUTRITIONAL INFORMATION

Calories	701	Sugars	12g
Protein	17g	Fat	40g
Carbohydrate	73g	Saturates	15g

 5 mins   25 mins

SERVES 4

I N G R E D I E N T S

350 g/12 oz dried spaghetti

3 tbsp butter

2 tbsp chopped fresh flat-leaved parsley

115 g/4 oz almonds, freshly ground

115 g/4 oz ricotta cheese

pinch of freshly grated nutmeg

pinch of ground cinnamon

150 ml/5 fl oz crème fraîche

2 tbsp olive oil

125 ml/4 fl oz hot vegetable stock

salt and pepper

1 tbsp pine kernels

fresh flat-leaved parsley sprigs, to garnish

1 Bring a pan of lightly salted water to the boil. Add the spaghetti, bring back to the boil and cook for 8–10 minutes until tender, but still firm to the bite.

2 Drain the pasta, return to the pan and toss with the butter and chopped parsley. Set aside and keep warm.

3 To make the sauce, combine the ground almonds, ricotta cheese, nutmeg, cinnamon and crème fraîche in a small pan and stir over a low heat to a thick paste. Gradually stir in the oil. When the oil has been fully incorporated, gradually stir in the hot vegetable stock, until smooth. Season to taste with pepper.

4 Transfer the spaghetti to a warm serving dish, pour the sauce over it and toss together well (see Cook's Tip). Sprinkle over the pine kernels, garnish with the sprigs of flat-leaved parsley and serve immediately.

COOK'S TIP

Use 2 large forks to toss spaghetti or other long pasta, so that it is thoroughly coated with the sauce. Special spaghetti forks are available from some cookware departments and kitchen shops.

Spinach & Nut Pasta

Use any pasta shapes that you have for this recipe – fusilli are used here. Multi-coloured pasta is visually the most attractive to use.

NUTRITIONAL INFORMATION

Calories ....603 Sugars 5g
Protein ....12g Fat 41g
Carbohydrate ...46g Saturates 6g

 5 mins   15 mins

SERVES 4

INGREDIENTS

225 g/8 oz dried pasta shapes

125 ml/4 fl oz olive oil

2 garlic cloves, crushed

1 onion, quartered and sliced

3 large flat mushrooms, sliced

225 g/8 oz spinach

2 tbsp pine nuts

5 tbsp dry white wine

salt and pepper

Parmesan shavings, to garnish

1 Bring a large pan of lightly salted water to the boil. Add the pasta, bring back to the boil and cook for 8–10 minutes until tender, but still firm to the bite. Drain well.

2 Meanwhile, heat the oil in a large pan. Add the garlic and onion and cook over a low heat, stirring occasionally, for 1 minute.

3 Add the sliced mushrooms to the pan and cook over a medium heat, stirring occasionally, for 2 minutes.

4 Lower the heat, add the spinach and cook, stirring occasionally, for a further 4–5 minutes or until the spinach has just wilted.

5 Stir in the pine nuts and wine, season to taste with salt and pepper and cook for 1 minute.

6 Transfer the pasta to a warm serving bowl and toss the sauce into it, mixing well. Garnish with shavings of Parmesan cheese and serve immediately.

COOK'S TIP

Grate a little nutmeg over the dish for extra flavour, as this spice has a particular affinity with spinach.

Home-made Tagliatelle

Pasta is not difficult to make yourself, just a little time consuming.
The pasta only takes a couple of minutes to cook and tastes wonderful.

NUTRITIONAL INFORMATION

Calories	642	Sugars	.........2g
Protein	........16g	Fat	..........29g
Carbohydrate	...84g	Saturates	......13g

  45 mins   5 mins

SERVES 4

INGREDIENTS

450 g/1 lb strong white flour, plus extra
    for dredging

2 tsp salt

4 eggs

3 tbsp olive oil

75 g/2¾ oz butter, melted

3 garlic cloves, finely chopped

2 tbsp chopped fresh parsley

pepper

1 Sift the flour into a large bowl and stir in the salt.

2 Make a well in the middle of the dry ingredients and add the eggs and 2 tablespoons of oil. Using a wooden spoon, stir in the eggs, gradually drawing in the flour. After a few minutes the dough will be too stiff to use a spoon and you will need to use your fingers.

3 Turn the dough out on to a floured surface and knead for about 5 minutes, or until smooth and elastic. If you find the dough is too wet, add a little more flour and continue kneading. Cover with clingfilm and leave to rest for at least 15 minutes.

4 The basic dough is now ready; roll out the pasta thinly and create the pasta shapes required. This can be done by hand or using a pasta machine. Results from a machine are usually neater and thinner, but not necessarily better.

5 To make the tagliatelle by hand, fold the thinly rolled pasta sheets into 3 and cut out long, thin strips, about 1 cm/ ½ inch wide.

6 To cook, bring a pan of water to the boil, add the remaining 1 tablespoon of oil and the pasta. It will take 2–3 minutes to cook, and the texture should have a slight bite to it. Drain.

7 Mix together the butter, garlic and parsley. Stir into the pasta, season with a little pepper to taste and serve immediately.

COOK'S TIP

Generally allow about
150 g/5½ oz fresh pasta
or about 100 g/3½ oz
dried pasta per person.

Lemon Spaghetti

Steaming vegetables helps to preserve their nutritional content and allows them to retain their bright, natural colours and crunchy texture.

NUTRITIONAL INFORMATION

Calories ....133 Sugars 8g
Protein ....8g Fat 1g
Carbohydrate ...25g Saturates 0.2g

🍐 10 mins   🕐 25 mins

SERVES 4

INGREDIENTS

225 g/8 oz celeriac

2 carrots

2 leeks

1 small red pepper

1 small yellow pepper

2 garlic cloves

1 tsp celery seeds

1 tbsp lemon juice

300 g/10½ oz dried spaghetti

salt

chopped celery leaves, to garnish

LEMON DRESSING

1 tsp finely grated lemon rind

1 tbsp lemon juice

4 tbsp low-fat natural fromage frais

salt and pepper

2 tbsp snipped fresh chives

1 Peel the celeriac and carrots, cut them into thin batons and place in a bowl. Trim and slice the leeks, rinse them under cold running water to flush out any trapped dirt, then shred finely. Halve, deseed and slice the peppers. Peel and thinly slice the garlic.

2 Add all of the vegetables to the bowl with the celeriac and the carrots. Toss the vegetables with the celery seeds and lemon juice.

3 Bring a large pan of lightly salted water to the boil. Add the pasta, bring back to the boil and cook for 8–10 minutes until tender, but still firm to the bite. Drain and keep warm.

4 Meanwhile, bring another large pan of water to the boil, put the

vegetables in a steamer and place them over the boiling water. Cover and steam for 6–7 minutes or until all the vegetables are just tender.

5 Whisk all of the ingredients for the lemon dressing together until thoroughly blended.

6 Transfer the spaghetti and vegetables to a warmed serving bowl and mix with the dressing. Garnish with chopped celery leaves and serve.

Vegetable Pasta Salad

This combination of vegetables and pasta, tossed in a tomato dressing and served on a bed of assorted salad leaves, makes a tasty main meal.

NUTRITIONAL INFORMATION

Calories 197   Sugars 5g
Protein ....10g   Fat 5g
Carbohydrate ...30g   Saturates 1g

10 mins   15 mins

SERVES 4

INGREDIENTS

225 g/8 oz dried penne

1 tbsp olive oil

25 g/1 oz dry-pack sun-dried tomatoes, soaked, drained and chopped

salt and pepper

400 g/14 oz canned artichoke hearts, drained and halved

115 g/4 oz baby courgettes, trimmed and sliced

115 g/4 oz baby plum tomatoes, halved

25 g/1 oz black olives, drained, stoned and chopped

100 g/3½ oz assorted baby salad leaves

shredded basil leaves, to garnish

DRESSING

4 tbsp passata

2 tbsp low-fat natural fromage frais

1 tbsp unsweetened orange juice

1 small bunch fresh basil, shredded

1 Cook the penne according to the instructions on the packet. Do not overcook – it should still have 'bite'. Drain well and return to the pan. Stir in the olive oil, olives and sun-dried tomatoes. Season with salt and pepper. Leave to cool.

2 Gently mix the artichokes, courgettes and plum tomatoes into the cooked pasta. Arrange the salad leaves in a serving bowl.

3 To make the dressing, mix all the ingredients together and toss into the vegetables and pasta.

4 Spoon the mixture on top of the salad leaves and serve garnished with shredded basil leaves.

VARIATION
Try making this dish with other pasta shapes, or a mixture – look out for farfalle (bows) and rotelle (spoked wheels).

Spicy Pasta Wheels

Wheel-shaped pasta (rotelle) looks attractive, and it tastes great tossed in a basic red wine sauce spiced up with fresh chillies.

NUTRITIONAL INFORMATION

Calories	490	Sugars	........3g
Protein	........13g	Fat	..........16g
Carbohydrate	...77g	Saturates	.......2g

  30 mins   25 mins

SERVES 4

INGREDIENTS

5 tbsp olive oil

3 garlic cloves, crushed

2 fresh red chillies, deseeded and chopped

1 fresh green chilli, deseeded and chopped

200 ml/7 fl oz Red Wine Sauce (see page 7)

salt and pepper

400 g/14 oz dried rotelle

warm Italian bread, to serve

1 Make the Red Wine Sauce (see page 7).

2 Heat 4 tablespoons of the oil in a saucepan. Add the garlic and chillies and fry for 3 minutes.

3 Stir the Red Wine Sauce into the saucepan, season with salt and pepper to taste and simmer gently over a low heat for 20 minutes.

4 Bring a large saucepan of lightly salted water to the boil. Add the rotelle and the remaining oil and cook for 8 minutes, until just tender, but still firm to the bite. Drain the pasta.

5 Toss the rotelle in the spicy sauce, transfer to a warm serving dish and serve with warm Italian bread.

COOK'S TIP

Take care when preparing fresh chillies as they can burn your skin. Wear rubber gloves if necessary, and wash your hands thoroughly afterwards. Remove the seeds before chopping the chillies, as they are the hottest part.

Cream & Sage Tagliarini

This simple, creamy, blue cheese and fresh sage pasta sauce is a classic Italian recipe.

NUTRITIONAL INFORMATION

Calories	880	Sugars	.........3g
Protein	........35g	Fat	..........49g
Carbohydrate	...79g	Saturates	......27g

10 mins   25 mins

SERVES 4

I N G R E D I E N T S

25 g/1 oz butter

225 g/8 oz Gorgonzola cheese, roughly crumbled

150 ml/5 fl oz double cream

30 ml/1 fl oz dry white wine

1 tsp cornflour

4 fresh sage sprigs, finely chopped

salt and white pepper

400 g/14 oz dried tagliarini

2 tbsp olive oil

1 Melt the butter in a heavy-based saucepan. Stir in 175 g/6 oz of the Gorgonzola cheese and melt, over a low heat, for about 2 minutes.

2 Add the cream, wine and cornflour and beat with a whisk until fully incorporated.

3 Stir in the sage and season to taste with salt and white pepper. Bring to the boil over a low heat, whisking constantly, until the sauce thickens. Remove from the heat and set aside while you cook the pasta.

4 Bring a large saucepan of lightly salted water to the boil. Add the tagliarini and 1 tablespoon of the olive oil.

Cook the pasta for 12–14 minutes, or until just tender, then drain thoroughly and toss in the remaining olive oil. Transfer the pasta to a serving dish and keep warm.

5 When the pasta is almost cooked, gently reheat the Gorgonzola sauce over a low heat, whisking constantly. Spoon the sauce over the tagliarini, generously sprinkle over the remaining cheese and serve immediately.

COOK'S TIP
When buying Gorgonzola, always check that it is creamy yellow with delicate green veining. Avoid hard or discoloured cheese. If you find Gorgonzola too strong or rich, you could substitute Danish Blue.

Pasta & Chilli Tomatoes

The pappardelle and vegetables are tossed in an unusual chilli and tomato sauce for a quick and economical meal.

NUTRITIONAL INFORMATION

Calories	353	Sugars	.........7g
Protein	........10g	Fat	..........24g
Carbohydrate	...26g	Saturates	.......4g

 15 mins   20 mins

SERVES 4

I N G R E D I E N T S

280 g/10 oz dried pappardelle

3 tbsp groundnut oil

2 garlic cloves, crushed

2 shallots, sliced

225 g/8 oz French beans, sliced

100 g/3½ oz cherry tomatoes, halved

1 tsp chilli flakes

4 tbsp crunchy peanut butter

150 ml/5 fl oz coconut milk

1 tbsp tomato purée

sliced spring onions, to garnish

1 Bring a large pan of lightly salted water to the boil. Add the pappardelle, bring back to the boil and cook for 8–10 minutes until tender, but still firm to the bite. Drain thoroughly and set aside.

2 Meanwhile, heat the groundnut oil in a large, heavy-based frying pan or preheated wok. Add the garlic and shallots and stir-fry for 1 minute.

3 Add the green beans and the drained pasta to the frying pan or wok and stir-fry for 5 minutes. Add the cherry tomatoes and mix well.

4 Combine the chilli flakes, peanut butter, coconut milk and tomato purée. Pour the chilli mixture into the frying pan or wok, toss well to combine and heat through.

5 Transfer to warm serving dishes and garnish with the spring onion slices. Serve immediately.

VARIATION

Try using egg noodles for this dish, instead of the pappardelle. Follow the instructions on the packet for cooking the noodles, then toss them in the wok with the sauce.

Pasta & Vegetable Sauce

The different shapes and textures of the vegetables make a mouth-watering presentation in this light and summery dish.

NUTRITIONAL INFORMATION

Calories 389	Sugars 4g	
Protein 16g	Fat 20g	
Carbohydrate ...38g	Saturates 11g	

10 mins   30 mins

SERVES 4

INGREDIENTS

225 g/8 oz dried gemelli or other pasta shapes

1 broccoli head, cut into florets

2 courgettes, sliced

225 g/8 oz asparagus spears

115 g/4 oz mangetouts

115 g/4 oz frozen peas

2 tbsp butter

3 tbsp vegetable stock

4 tbsp double cream

salt and pepper

freshly grated nutmeg

2 tbsp chopped fresh parsley

2 tbsp freshly grated Parmesan cheese

1 Bring a large pan of lightly salted water to the boil. Add the pasta, bring back to the boil and cook for 8–10 minutes or until tender, but still firm to the bite. Drain the pasta, return to the pan, cover and keep warm.

2 Steam the broccoli, courgettes, asparagus spears and mangetouts over a pan of boiling salted water until they are just beginning to soften. Remove from the heat and refresh in cold water. Drain and set aside.

3 Bring a small pan of lightly salted water to the boil. Add the frozen peas and cook for 3 minutes. Drain the peas, refresh in cold water and then drain again. Set aside with the other vegetables.

4 Put the butter and the vegetable stock in a pan over a medium heat. Add all of the vegetables, reserving a few of the asparagus spears, and toss them carefully with a wooden spoon until they have heated through, taking care not to break them up.

5 Stir in the double cream and heat the sauce through very gently, without bringing it to the boil. Season to taste with salt, pepper and freshly grated nutmeg.

6 Transfer the pasta to a warmed serving dish and stir in the chopped fresh parsley.

7 Spoon over the vegetable sauce and sprinkle over the Parmesan cheese. Arrange the reserved asparagus spears in a pattern on top and serve.

Pasta & Cheese Puddings

These delicious individual pasta puddings are served with a tasty tomato and bay leaf sauce.

NUTRITIONAL INFORMATION

Calories	517	Sugars	.........8g
Protein	........19g	Fat	..........27g
Carbohydrate	...47g	Saturates	......13g

45 mins   50 mins

SERVES 4

I N G R E D I E N T S

15 g/½ oz butter or margarine, softened

60 g/2 oz dried white breadcrumbs

175 g/6 oz dried tricolour spaghetti

300 ml/½ pint Béchamel sauce
(see page 6)

1 egg yolk

125 g/4½ oz Gruyère cheese, grated

salt and pepper

fresh flat-leaf parsley, to garnish

T O M A T O   S A U C E

2 tsp olive oil

1 onion, finely chopped

1 bay leaf

150 ml/¼ pint dry white wine

150 ml/¼ pint passatta

1 tbsp tomato purée

salt and pepper

1 Grease four 180 ml/6 fl oz cup moulds or ramekins with the butter or margarine. Evenly coat the insides with half of the breadcrumbs.

2 Break the spaghetti into 5 cm/2 inch lengths. Bring a saucepan of lightly salted water to the boil and cook the spaghetti for 5–6 minutes or until just tender. Drain well and put in a bowl.

3 Mix the Béchamel sauce, egg yolk, cheese and seasoning into the cooked pasta and pack into the moulds.

4 Sprinkle the puddings with the remaining breadcrumbs and place the moulds on a baking tray. Bake in a preheated oven, 220°C/425°F/Gas Mark 7, for 20 minutes until golden. Leave to stand for 10 minutes.

5 Meanwhile, make the sauce. Heat the oil in a pan and fry the onion and bay leaf for 2–3 minutes or until just softened.

6 Stir in the wine, passata, tomato purée and seasoning. Bring the sauce to the boil and simmer for 20 minutes or until thickened. Remove from the heat and discard the bay leaf.

7 Run a palette knife around the inside of the moulds. Turn the puddings out on to serving plates, garnish and serve with the tomato sauce.

Vegetable Cannelloni

This dish is made with prepared cannelloni tubes, but may also be made by rolling ready-bought lasagne sheets.

NUTRITIONAL INFORMATION

Calories ....594 Sugars 12g
Protein ....13g Fat 38g
Carbohydrate ...52g Saturates 7g

  10 mins   45 mins

SERVES 4

I N G R E D I E N T S

1 aubergine

125 ml/4 fl oz olive oil

225 g/8 oz spinach

2 garlic cloves, crushed

1 tsp ground cumin

85 g/3 oz mushrooms, chopped

salt and pepper

12 cannelloni tubes

T O M A T O   S A U C E

1 tbsp olive oil

1 onion, chopped

2 garlic cloves, crushed

2 x 400 g/14 oz canned chopped tomatoes

1 tsp caster sugar

2 tbsp chopped fresh basil

55 g/2 oz sliced mozzarella

1 Cut the aubergine into small dice. Heat the oil in a frying pan. Add the aubergine and cook over a moderate heat, stirring frequently, for 2–3 minutes.

2 Add the spinach, garlic, cumin and mushrooms and reduce the heat. Season to taste with salt and pepper and cook, stirring constantly, for 2–3 minutes. Spoon the mixture into the cannelloni tubes and place in an ovenproof dish in a single layer.

3 To make the sauce, heat the olive oil in a pan and cook the onion and garlic for 1 minute. Add the tomatoes, sugar and basil and bring to the boil. Reduce the heat and simmer gently for about 5 minutes. Spoon the sauce over the cannelloni tubes.

4 Arrange the sliced mozzarella on top of the sauce and cook in a preheated oven, 190°C/375°F/Gas Mark 5, for about 30 minutes or until the cheese is bubbling and golden brown. Serve immediately.

Vegetable & Pasta Parcels

These small parcels are very easy to make and can be filled with your favourite mixture of succulent mushrooms.

NUTRITIONAL INFORMATION

Calories ....333 Sugars 1g
Protein ....7g Fat 30g
Carbohydrate ...10g Saturates 13g

 20 mins   20 mins

SERVES 4

INGREDIENTS

FILLING

25 g/1 oz butter or margarine

2 garlic cloves, crushed

1 small leek, chopped

2 celery sticks, chopped

200 g/7 oz open-cap mushrooms, chopped

1 egg, beaten

2 tbsp grated Parmesan cheese

salt and pepper

RAVIOLI

4 sheets filo pastry

25 g/1 oz margarine

oil, for deep-frying

1 To make the filling, melt the butter or margarine in a frying pan and sauté the garlic and leek for 2–3 minutes, or until softened.

2 Add the celery and mushrooms and cook for a further 4–5 minutes until all of the vegetables are tender.

3 Turn off the heat and stir in the egg and grated Parmesan cheese. Season with salt and pepper to taste.

4 Lay the pastry sheets on a chopping board and cut each into nine squares.

5 Spoon a little of the filling into the centre of the squares and brush the edges of the pastry with butter or margarine. Lay another square on top and seal the edges to make a parcel.

6 Heat the oil for deep-frying to 180°C/350°F or until a cube of bread browns in 30 seconds. Fry the ravioli, in batches, for 2–3 minutes or until golden brown. Carefully remove from the oil with a slotted spoon and pat dry on absorbent kitchen paper. Transfer to a warm serving plate and serve.

Filled Aubergines

Combined with tomatoes and melting mozzarella cheese, pasta makes a tasty filling for baked aubergine shells.

NUTRITIONAL INFORMATION

Calories 342	Sugars 6g	
Protein 11g	Fat 16g	
Carbohydrate ...40g	Saturates 4g	

25 mins   55 mins

SERVES 4

INGREDIENTS

225 g/8 oz dried penne or other short
    pasta shapes

4 tbsp olive oil, plus extra for brushing

2 aubergines

1 large onion, chopped

2 garlic cloves, crushed

400 g/14 oz canned chopped tomatoes

2 tsp dried oregano

salt and pepper

55 g/2 oz mozzarella cheese, thinly sliced

25 g/1 oz Parmesan cheese, freshly grated

5 tbsp dry breadcrumbs

salad leaves, to serve

1 Bring a large saucepan of lightly salted water to the boil. Add the pasta and 1 tablespoon of the olive oil, bring back to the boil and cook for 8–10 minutes or until the pasta is just tender, but still firm to the bite. Drain, return to the pan, cover and keep warm.

2 Cut the aubergines in half lengthways and score around the inside with a sharp knife, being careful not to pierce the shells. Scoop out the flesh with a spoon. Brush the insides of the shells with olive oil. Chop the flesh and set aside.

3 Heat the remaining oil in a frying pan. Fry the onion over a low heat for 5 minutes, until softened. Add the garlic and fry for 1 minute. Add the chopped aubergine and fry, stirring frequently, for 5 minutes. Add the tomatoes and oregano and season to taste with salt and pepper. Bring to the boil and simmer for 10 minutes until thickened. Remove the pan from the heat and stir in the pasta.

4 Brush a baking sheet with oil and arrange the aubergine shells in a single layer. Divide half of the tomato and pasta mixture between them. Scatter over the slices of mozzarella, then pile the remaining tomato and pasta mixture on top. Mix the Parmesan cheese and breadcrumbs and sprinkle over the top, patting it lightly into the mixture.

5 Bake in a preheated oven, 200°C/ 400°C/Gas Mark 6, for about 25 minutes or until the topping is golden brown. Serve hot with a selection of mixed salad leaves.

Tomato & Pasta Bake

This pasta dish is baked in a pudding basin and cut into slices for serving. It looks and tastes terrific and is perfect when you want to impress.

NUTRITIONAL INFORMATION

Calories . . . . . . .179 Sugars 6g
Protein . . . . .8g Fat 10g
Carbohydrate . . .16g Saturates 3g

🥗 10 mins   🕐 1 hr 5 mins

SERVES 4

INGREDIENTS

100 g/3½ oz dried pasta shapes, such as penne or casareccia

1 tbsp olive oil

1 leek, chopped

3 garlic cloves, crushed

1 green pepper, deseeded and chopped

400 g/14 oz canned chopped tomatoes

2 tbsp black olives, stoned and chopped

2 eggs, beaten

1 tbsp chopped fresh basil

salt and pepper

TOMATO SAUCE

1 tbsp olive oil

1 onion, chopped

225 g/8 oz canned chopped tomatoes

1 tsp caster sugar

2 tbsp tomato purée

150 ml/¼ pint vegetable stock

salt and pepper

1 Cook the pasta in a saucepan of boiling salted water for 8 minutes. Drain thoroughly.

2 Meanwhile, heat the olive oil in a saucepan and sauté the leek and garlic for 2 minutes, stirring constantly. Add the pepper, tomatoes and olives to the pan and cook for a further 5 minutes.

3 Remove the pan from the heat and stir in the pasta, beaten eggs and basil. Season well, and spoon into a lightly greased 1 litre/2 pint ovenproof pudding basin.

4 Place the pudding basin in a roasting tin and half-fill the tin with boiling water. Cover the pudding and cook in a preheated oven, 180°C/350°F/Gas Mark 4, for 40 minutes until set.

5 To make the sauce, heat the olive oil in a pan and sauté the onion for 2 minutes. Add the remaining ingredients to the pan and cook for a further 10 minutes. Put the sauce in a food processor or blender and blend until smooth. Return to a clean saucepan and heat through again until hot.

6 Turn the pasta out of the pudding basin on to a warm plate. Slice and serve with the tomato sauce.

Aubergine Lasagne

This filling aubergine, courgette and mozzarella lasagne is one of many variations of a classic Italian dish.

NUTRITIONAL INFORMATION

Calories 525	Sugars 14g
Protein 17g	Fat 39g
Carbohydrate ...28g	Saturates 15g

 1¼ hrs   1 hr

SERVES 4

INGREDIENTS

1 kg/2 lb 4 oz aubergines

4 tsp salt

8 tbsp olive oil

25 g/1 oz garlic and herb butter
  or margarine

500 g/1 lb 2 oz courgettes, sliced

225 g/8 oz mozzarella cheese, grated

600 ml/1 pint passata

6 sheets pre-cooked green lasagne

pepper

600 ml/1 pint Béchamel sauce
  (see page 6)

60 g/2 oz Parmesan cheese, grated

1 tsp dried oregano

1 Thinly slice the aubergines. Layer the slices in a bowl, sprinkling with the salt as you go. Set aside for 30 minutes. Rinse well in cold water and pat dry with kitchen paper.

2 Heat 4 tablespoons of olive oil in a frying pan and fry half of the aubergine slices for 6–7 minutes or until they are lightly golden all over. Drain thoroughly on kitchen paper. Repeat with the remaining aubergine slices and oil.

3 Melt the garlic and herb butter or margarine in the frying pan and fry the courgette slices for about 5–6 minutes until golden brown. Drain thoroughly on kitchen paper.

4 Place half of the aubergine and courgette slices in the bottom of a large ovenproof dish. Season to taste with pepper and sprinkle over half of the grated mozzarella. Spoon over half of the passata and top with 3 sheets of lasagne.

5 Arrange the remaining aubergine and courgette slices on top. Season with pepper and top with the remaining grated mozzarella, the passata and another layer of 3 sheets of lasagne.

6 Spoon over the Béchamel sauce and top with the grated Parmesan and a sprinkling of oregano. Place on a baking tray and bake in a preheated oven, 220°C/425°F/Gas Mark 7, for 30–35 minutes or until golden brown.

Aubergine & Linguine

Prepare the marinated aubergines well in advance so that when you are ready to eat all you have to do is cook the pasta.

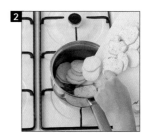

NUTRITIONAL INFORMATION

Calories 378	Sugars 3g
Protein 12g	Fat 30g
Carbohydrate . . .16g	Saturates 3g

15 mins, plus marinating — 15 mins

SERVES 4

I N G R E D I E N T S

150 ml/5 fl oz vegetable stock

150 ml/5 fl oz white wine vinegar

2 tsp balsamic vinegar

3 tbsp olive oil

fresh oregano sprig

450 g/1 lb aubergines, peeled and thinly sliced

400 g/14 oz dried linguine

M A R I N A D E

2 tbsp extra virgin olive oil

2 garlic cloves, crushed

2 tbsp chopped fresh oregano

2 tbsp finely chopped roasted almonds

2 tbsp diced red pepper

2 tbsp lime juice

grated rind and juice of 1 orange

salt and pepper

1 Put the vegetable stock, wine vinegar and balsamic vinegar into a saucepan and bring to the boil over a low heat. Add 2 teaspoons of the olive oil and the sprig of oregano and simmer gently for about 1 minute.

2 Add the aubergine slices to the pan, remove from the heat and set aside for 10 minutes.

3 Meanwhile, make the marinade. Combine the oil, garlic, fresh oregano, almonds, red pepper, lime juice, orange rind and juice in a large bowl and season to taste with salt and pepper.

4 Carefully remove the aubergine from the saucepan with a draining spoon, and drain well. Add the aubergine slices to the marinade, mixing well to coat. Cover with clingfilm and set aside in the refrigerator for about 12 hours.

5 Bring a large saucepan of lightly salted water to the boil. Add half of the remaining olive oil and the linguine. Bring back to the boil and cook for 8–10 minutes until just tender, but still firm to the bite.

6 Drain the pasta thoroughly and toss with the remaining oil while it is still warm. Arrange the pasta on a serving plate with the aubergine slices and the marinade and serve immediately.

Vegetable Pasta Nests

These large pasta nests look impressive filled with grilled mixed vegetables, and taste absolutely delicious.

NUTRITIONAL INFORMATION

Calories	392	Sugars	.........1g
Protein	.........6g	Fat	..........28g
Carbohydrate	...32g	Saturates	.......9g

 25 mins   40 mins

SERVES 4

INGREDIENTS

175 g/6 oz dried spaghetti

1 aubergine, halved and sliced

1 courgette, diced

1 red pepper, deseeded and chopped diagonally

6 tbsp olive oil

2 garlic cloves, crushed

4 tbsp butter or margarine, melted, plus extra for greasing

15 g/½ oz dry white breadcrumbs

salt and pepper

fresh parsley sprigs, to garnish

  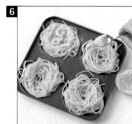

1 Bring a saucepan of lightly salted water to the boil, add the spaghetti, bring back to the boil cook for 8–10 minutes until just tender. Drain well and set aside.

2 Place the aubergine, courgette and pepper on a baking tray.

3 Mix the oil and garlic together and pour over the vegetables, tossing to coat all over.

4 Cook under a preheated hot grill for about 10 minutes, turning occasionally, until tender and lightly charred. Set aside and keep warm.

5 Divide the spaghetti among 4 lightly greased Yorkshire pudding tins. Using 2 forks, curl the spaghetti to form nests.

6 Brush the pasta nests with melted butter or margarine and sprinkle with the breadcrumbs. Bake in a preheated oven, 200°C/400°F/Gas Mark 6, for 15 minutes or until lightly golden. Remove the pasta nests from the tins and transfer to serving plates. Divide the grilled vegetables between the pasta nests, season to taste with salt and pepper and garnish with parsley sprigs.

COOK'S TIP
The Italian term *al dente* means 'to the bite' and describes cooked pasta that is not too soft, but still has a 'bite' to it.

Three-cheese Bake

Serve this dish while the cheese is still hot and melted, because cooked cheese turns very rubbery if it is allowed to cool down.

NUTRITIONAL INFORMATION

Calories 710   Sugars 6g
Protein . . . . .34g   Fat 30g
Carbohydrate . . .80g   Saturates 16g

 5 mins   1 hr

SERVES 4

INGREDIENTS

butter, for greasing

400 g/14 oz dried penne pasta

2 eggs, beaten

350 g/12 oz ricotta cheese

4 fresh basil sprigs

115 g/4 oz mozzarella or halloumi
   cheese, grated

70 g/2½ oz Parmesan cheese,
   freshly grated

fresh basil leaves, to garnish (optional)

selection of cooked vegetables, to serve

1 Lightly grease a large ovenproof dish with butter.

2 Bring a pan of lightly salted water to the boil. Add the pasta, bring back to the boil and cook for 8–10 minutes until just tender, but still firm to the bite. Drain the pasta, set aside and keep warm.

3 Beat the eggs into the ricotta cheese and season to taste.

4 Spoon half of the pasta into the base of the prepared dish and cover with half of the basil leaves.

5 Spoon over half of the ricotta cheese mixture. Sprinkle over the mozzarella or halloumi cheese and top with the remaining basil leaves. Cover with the remaining pasta and then spoon over the remaining ricotta cheese mixture. Lightly sprinkle the freshly grated Parmesan cheese over the top.

6 Bake in a preheated oven, 190°C/ 375°F/Gas Mark 5, for 30–40 minutes until golden brown and the cheese topping is hot and bubbling. Garnish with fresh basil leaves and serve immediately with a selection of cooked vegetables.

Vegetable Lasagne

This colourful and tasty lasagne has layers of vegetables in tomato sauce and aubergines, all topped with a rich cheese sauce.

NUTRITIONAL INFORMATION

Calories	544	Sugars	........18g
Protein	........20g	Fat	.........26g
Carbohydrate	...61g	Saturates	......12g

35 mins   55 mins

SERVES 4

I N G R E D I E N T S

1 aubergine, sliced

salt

3 tbsp olive oil

2 garlic cloves, crushed

1 red onion, halved and sliced

3 mixed peppers, deseeded and diced

225 g/8 oz mixed mushrooms, sliced

2 celery sticks, sliced

1 courgette, diced

½ tsp chilli powder

½ tsp ground cumin

2 tomatoes, chopped

300 ml/½ pint passata

2 tbsp chopped fresh basil

salt and pepper

8 pre-cooked lasagne verdi sheets

CHEESE SAUCE

2 tbsp butter or margarine

1 tbsp flour

150ml/¼ pint vegetable stock

300 ml/½ pint milk

75 g/2¾ oz Cheddar cheese, grated

1 tsp Dijon mustard

1 tbsp chopped fresh basil

1 egg, beaten

1 Place the aubergine slices in a colander, sprinkle them with salt and leave for 20 minutes. Rinse under cold water, drain and reserve.

2 Heat the oil in a pan and sauté the garlic and onion for 1–2 minutes. Add the peppers, mushrooms, celery and courgette and cook, stirring constantly, for 3–4 minutes.

3 Stir in the spices and cook for 1 minute. Mix in the chopped tomatoes, passata and basil and season to taste with salt and pepper.

4 For the sauce, melt the butter in a pan, stir in the flour and cook for 1 minute. Remove from the heat and stir in the stock and milk. Return to the heat and boil, stirring for 3 minutes, or until thickened. Stir in half the cheese, mustard and basil. Remove from the heat, cool slightly and stir in the egg.

5 Place half the lasagne sheets in an ovenproof dish. Top with half the vegetable mixture then half the aubergines. Repeat and spoon the cheese sauce on top.

6 Sprinkle the lasagne with the remaining cheese and cook in a preheated oven, 180°C/350°F/ Gas Mark 4, for 40 minutes, until the top is golden brown.

Aubergine Pasta Cake

This recipe would make a stunning dinner party dish, yet it contains simple ingredients and is easy to make.

NUTRITIONAL INFORMATION

Calories	201	Sugars	. . . . .4g
Protein	. . . . .14g	Fat	. . . . .7g
Carbohydrate	. . .22g	Saturates	. . . . . .4g

 55 mins   35 mins

SERVES 4

I N G R E D I E N T S

butter, for greasing

1 aubergine

300 g/10½ oz dried tricolour pasta shapes

125 g/4½ oz low-fat soft cheese with garlic and herbs

350ml/12 fl oz passata

70 g/2½ oz Parmesan cheese, freshly grated

1½ tsp dried oregano

salt and pepper

25 g/1 oz dry white breadcrumbs

1 Grease and line a 20 cm/8 inch round springform cake tin.

2 Trim the aubergine and cut it lengthways into slices about 5 mm/ ¼ inch thick. Place in a bowl, sprinkle with salt and set aside for 30 minutes to remove any bitter juices. Rinse well under cold running water and drain.

3 Bring a saucepan of water to the boil and blanch the aubergine slices for 1 minute. Drain and pat dry with kitchen paper. Set aside.

4 Bring another large saucepan of lightly salted water to the boil. Add the pasta shapes, return to the boil and cook for 8–10 minutes until tender, but still firm to the bite. Drain well and return to the saucepan. Add the soft cheese and allow it to melt over the pasta.

5 Stir in the passata, Parmesan cheese, oregano and salt and pepper to taste.

6 Arrange the aubergine over the base and sides of the tin, overlapping the slices and making sure there are no gaps.

7 Pile the pasta mixture into the tin, packing it down well, and sprinkle with the breadcrumbs. Bake in a preheated oven, 190°C/375°F/Gas Mark 5, for 20 minutes and then leave to stand for 15 minutes.

8 Loosen the cake round the edge with a palette knife and release from the tin. Turn out the pasta cake, aubergine side uppermost, and serve hot.

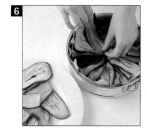

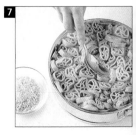

Mushroom & Vermicelli Flan

Lightly cooked vermicelli is pressed into a flan ring and baked with a creamy mushroom filling.

NUTRITIONAL INFORMATION

Calories 557	Sugars 5g
Protein 15g	Fat 36g
Carbohydrate ...47g	Saturates 19g

 10 mins  1 hr 10 mins

SERVES 4

I N G R E D I E N T S

225 g/8 oz dried vermicelli or spaghetti

1 tbsp olive oil

25 g/1 oz butter, plus extra
   for greasing

salt and pepper

tomato and basil salad, to serve

FILLING

60 g/2 oz butter

1 onion, chopped

150 g/5½ oz button mushrooms, trimmed

1 green pepper, cored, deseeded and sliced
   into thin rings

150 ml/¼ pint milk

3 eggs, lightly beaten

2 tbsp double cream

1 tsp dried oregano

pinch of finely grated nutmeg

1 tbsp freshly grated Parmesan cheese

1 Cook the pasta in a large pan of salted boiling water, adding the olive oil, for 8–10 minutes or until tender. Drain the pasta in a colander, return to the pan, add the butter and shake the pan well.

2 Grease a 20 cm/8 inch loose-based flan tin. Press the pasta onto the base and around the sides to form a case.

3 Heat the butter in a frying pan over a medium heat and fry the onion until it is translucent. Remove with a slotted spoon and spread in the flan base.

4 Add the mushrooms and pepper rings to the pan and turn them in the oil until glazed. Fry for 2 minutes on each side, then arrange in the flan base.

5 Beat together the milk, eggs and cream, stir in the dried oregano, and season to taste with nutmeg and pepper. Pour the mixture carefully over the vegetables and sprinkle the grated Parmesan cheese over the top.

6 Bake the flan in the preheated oven, 180°C/350°F/Gas Mark 4, for 40–45 minutes, or until the filling is set.

7 Slide the flan carefully on to a serving plate and serve warm.

Linguine with Pesto Sauce

The basil, olive oil, garlic and pine kernels in this traditional pasta sauce are the essence of Italian cooking.

NUTRITIONAL INFORMATION

Calories 860	Sugars 4g
Protein 30g	Fat 50g
Carbohydrate . . .77g	Saturates 12g

15 mins, plus chilling

10–15 mins

SERVES 4

INGREDIENTS

400 g/14 oz dried or fresh linguine

freshly grated Parmesan cheese,
  to serve (optional)

PESTO SAUCE

150 g/5½ oz Parmesan cheese in a wedge

3 garlic cloves, or to taste

150 g/5½ oz fresh basil leaves

5 tbsp pine kernels

150 ml/5 fl oz fruity extra-virgin olive oil

salt and pepper

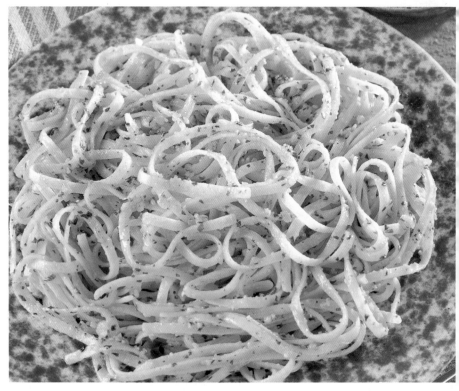

1 To make the pesto sauce, cut the rind off the Parmesan and finely grate the cheese. Set aside. Cut each garlic clove in half lengthways and use the tip of the knife to lift out the green core, which can have a bitter flavour if the cloves are old. Coarsely chop the garlic.

2 Rinse the basil leaves and pat dry with kitchen paper. Put the basil in a food processor and add the pine kernels, grated cheese, chopped garlic and olive oil. Process for about 30 seconds, just until blended.

3 Add pepper and salt to taste, but remember the cheese is already salty. Cover with a sheet of clingfilm and chill for up to 5 days.

4 Bring a large pan of water to the boil. Add ½ teaspoon salt and the linguine and cook according to the packet instructions until al dente. Drain well, reserving a little of the cooking water.

5 Return the linguine to the pan over a low heat and stir in the pesto sauce. Toss until the pasta is well coated and the sauce is heated though. Stir in about 2 tablespoons of the reserved cooking water if the sauce seems too thick.

6 Serve at once with grated Parmesan for sprinkling over the top, if desired.

VARIATION

Use blanched almonds instead of pine kernels. To make a creamy dip to serve with sliced courgettes and pepper strips, stir 4 tablespoons of the pesto sauce into 4 tablespoons natural yogurt.

Italian Pasta Salad

Tomatoes and mozzarella cheese are a classic Italian combination. Here they are combined with pasta and avocado for an extra touch of luxury.

NUTRITIONAL INFORMATION

Calories 541	Sugars 5g	
Protein 12g	Fat 43g	
Carbohydrate . . .29g	Saturates 10g	

15 mins   15 mins

SERVES 4

INGREDIENTS

2 tbsp pine kernels

175 g/6 oz dried fusilli

1 tbsp olive oil

6 tomatoes

225 g/8 oz mozzarella cheese

1 large avocado

2 tbsp lemon juice

3 tbsp chopped fresh basil

salt and pepper

fresh basil sprigs, to garnish

DRESSING

6 tbsp extra virgin olive oil

2 tbsp white wine vinegar

1 tsp wholegrain mustard

pinch of sugar

salt and pepper

1 Spread the pine kernels out on a baking sheet and toast them under a preheated grill for 1–2 minutes. Remove and set aside to cool.

2 Bring a large pan of lightly salted water to the boil. Add the oil and pasta, bring back to the boil and cook for 8–10 minutes or until tender, but still firm to the bite. Drain the pasta and refresh in cold water. Drain again and set aside to cool.

3 Thinly slice the tomatoes and the mozzarella cheese.

4 Cut the avocado in half lengthways, carefully remove the stone, then peel. Cut the flesh into thin slices lengthways and sprinkle with lemon juice to prevent it from turning brown.

5 To make the dressing, whisk together the oil, vinegar, mustard and sugar in a small bowl and season to taste with salt and pepper.

6 Arrange the tomatoes, mozzarella cheese and avocado pear alternately in overlapping slices on a large serving platter, leaving room in the centre.

7 Toss the pasta with half of the dressing and the chopped basil and season to taste with salt and pepper. Spoon the pasta into the centre of the platter and pour over the remaining dressing. Sprinkle over the pine kernels, garnish with fresh sprigs of basil and serve immediately.

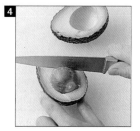

Garlicky Spaghetti

This easy and satisfying Roman dish originated as a cheap meal for the impoverished, but is now a favourite in restaurants and trattorias.

NUTRITIONAL INFORMATION

Calories	669	Sugars	........4g
Protein	........14g	Fat	..........33g
Carbohydrate	...84g	Saturates	.......5g

 5 mins   5–10 mins

SERVES 4

INGREDIENTS

125 ml/4 fl oz olive oil

3 garlic cloves, crushed

450 g/1 lb fresh spaghetti

salt and pepper

3 tbsp roughly chopped fresh parsley

1 Reserve 1 tablespoon of the olive oil and heat the remainder in a medium saucepan. Add the garlic and a pinch of salt and cook over a low heat, stirring constantly, until golden brown, then remove the pan from the heat. Do not allow the garlic to burn as it will taint its flavour. (If it does burn, you will have to start all over again!)

2 Meanwhile, bring a large saucepan of lightly salted water to the boil. Add the spaghetti and remaining olive oil and cook for 2–3 minutes, or until tender but still firm to the bite. Drain the spaghetti thoroughly and return to the pan.

3 Add the oil and garlic mixture to the spaghetti and toss to coat thoroughly.

Season to taste with pepper, add the chopped fresh parsley and toss well to coat again.

4 Transfer the spaghetti to a warm serving dish and serve immediately.

COOK'S TIP

It is worth buying the best-quality olive oil for dishes such as this one which makes a feature of its flavour. Extra-virgin oil is produced from the first pressing and has the lowest acidity. It is more expensive than other types of olive oil, but has the finest flavour.

Three-cheese Macaroni

Based on a traditional family favourite, this pasta bake has plenty of flavour. Serve with a crisp salad for a simple, tasty supper.

NUTRITIONAL INFORMATION

Calories 672	Sugars 10g
Protein 31g	Fat 44g
Carbohydrate . . .40g	Saturates 23g

30 mins   45 mins

SERVES 4

I N G R E D I E N T S

600 ml/1 pint Béchamel sauce
  (see page 6)

225 g/8 oz dried macaroni

1 egg, beaten

125 g/4½ oz mature Cheddar cheese,
  grated

1 tbsp wholegrain mustard

2 tbsp chopped fresh chives

salt and pepper

4 tomatoes, sliced

125 g/4½ oz red Leicester cheese, grated

60 g/2 oz blue cheese, grated

2 tbsp sunflower seeds

snipped fresh chives, to garnish

1 Make the Béchamel sauce, transfer it to a bowl and cover with clingfilm to prevent a skin forming on the surface of the sauce. Set aside.

2 Bring a saucepan of salted water to the boil and cook the macaroni for 8–10 minutes or until just tender. Drain well and place in a lightly greased ovenproof dish.

3 Stir the beaten egg, Cheddar cheese, mustard and chives into the Béchamel sauce and season to taste with salt and pepper.

4 Spoon the sauce over the macaroni, making sure it is well covered. Arrange the sliced tomatoes in a layer over the top.

5 Sprinkle the red Leicester and blue cheeses and the sunflower seeds evenly over the pasta bake. Put the dish on a baking tray and bake in a preheated oven, 190°C/375°F/Gas Mark 5, for 25–30 minutes or until the topping is bubbling and golden.

6 Garnish the pasta bake with snipped chives and serve immediately on warmed plates.

Pear & Walnut Pasta

This is quite an unusual combination of ingredients in a savoury dish, but is absolutely wonderful tossed into a fine pasta, such as spaghetti.

NUTRITIONAL INFORMATION

Calories	508	Sugars	.........9g
Protein	........15g	Fat	..........27g
Carbohydrate	...50g	Saturates	......11g

 10 mins   20 mins

SERVES 4

I N G R E D I E N T S

225 g/8 oz dried spaghetti

2 small ripe pears, peeled and sliced

150 ml/10 fl oz vegetable stock

6 tbsp dry white wine

2 tbsp butter

1 tbsp olive oil

1 red onion, quartered and sliced

1 garlic clove, crushed

55 g/2 oz walnut halves

2 tbsp chopped fresh oregano

1 tbsp lemon juice

85 g/3 oz dolcelatte cheese

salt and pepper

fresh oregano sprigs, to garnish

1 Bring a large pan of lightly salted water to the boil. Add the pasta, bring back to the boil and cook for 8–10 minutes until tender, but still firm to the bite. Drain thoroughly and keep warm until required.

2 Meanwhile, place the pears in a pan and pour in the stock and wine. Poach the pears over a low heat for about 10 minutes until tender. Remove the pears with a draining spoon and reserve the cooking liquid. Set the pears aside.

3 Heat the butter and oil in a pan until the butter melts. Add the onion and garlic and cook over a low heat, stirring frequently, for 2–3 minutes.

4 Stir in the walnut halves, chopped oregano and lemon juice. Stir in the reserved pears with 4 tablespoons of the poaching liquid.

5 Crumble the dolcelatte cheese into the pan and cook over a low heat, stirring occasionally, for 1–2 minutes or until the cheese is just beginning to melt. Season with salt and pepper to taste.

6 Add the pasta and toss in the sauce, using 2 forks. Transfer to a serving dish, garnish with oregano and serve.

Walnut & Olive Pasta

This mouthwatering dish would make an excellent light lunch for four people, or a good starter for six.

NUTRITIONAL INFORMATION

Calories	833	Sugars	.........5g
Protein	........20g	Fat	..........66g
Carbohydrate	...44g	Saturates	......15g

15 mins   10 mins

SERVES 4–6

INGREDIENTS

2 thick slices wholemeal bread, crusts removed

300 ml/½ pint milk

275 g/9½ oz shelled walnuts

2 garlic cloves, crushed

115 g/4 oz black olives, stoned

55 g/2 oz Parmesan cheese, freshly grated

8 tbsp extra-virgin olive oil

salt and pepper

150 ml/5 fl oz double cream

450 g/1 lb fresh fettuccine

2–3 tbsp chopped fresh parsley

  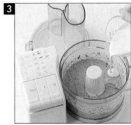

1 Put the bread in a shallow dish, pour over the milk and set aside to soak until the liquid has been absorbed.

2 Spread the walnuts out on a baking tray and toast in a preheated oven at 190°C/375°F/Gas Mark 5 for about 5 minutes until golden. Set aside to cool.

3 Put the soaked bread, walnuts, garlic, olives, Parmesan cheese and 6 tablespoons of the olive oil in a food processor and work to make a purée. Season to taste with salt and black pepper and stir in the cream.

4 Bring a large pan of lightly salted water to the boil. Add the fettuccine and 1 tablespoons of the remaining olive oil and cook for 2–3 minutes, or until tender but still firm to the bite. Drain the fettuccine thoroughly and toss with the remaining olive oil.

5 Divide the fettuccine between individual serving plates and spoon the olive, garlic and walnut sauce on top. Sprinkle over the fresh parsley and serve.

COOK'S TIP

Grated Parmesan quickly loses its pungency. It is better to buy solid cheese and grate it when needed. Wrapped in foil, Parmesan will keep in the refrigerator for several months.

Mozzarella & Broccoli Pasta

This colourful dish provides a mouth-watering contrast in the crisp *al dente* texture of the broccoli and the creamy cheese sauce.

NUTRITIONAL INFORMATION

Calories 472	Sugars 6g
Protein 15g	Fat 24g
Carbohydrate ...52g	Saturates 14g

10 mins   25 mins

SERVES 4

INGREDIENTS

55 g/2 oz butter

1 large onion, finely chopped

450 g/1 lb broccoli, broken into florets

450 g/1 lb dried ribbon pasta

150 ml/¼ pint boiling vegetable stock

salt and white pepper

1 tbsp plain flour

150 ml/¼ pint single cream

55 g/2 oz grated mozzarella cheese

freshly grated nutmeg

fresh apple slices, to garnish

1 Melt half of the butter in a large saucepan over a medium heat. Add the onion and fry for 4 minutes.

2 Add the broccoli and pasta to the pan and continue to cook, stirring constantly, for 2 minutes. Add the vegetable stock, bring back to the boil and simmer for a further 12 minutes. Season well with salt and white pepper.

3 Meanwhile, melt the remaining butter in a saucepan over a medium heat. Sprinkle over the flour and cook, stirring constantly, for 2 minutes. Gradually stir in the cream and bring to simmering point, but do not boil. Add the grated mozzarella cheese and season with salt and a little freshly grated nutmeg.

4 Drain the pasta and broccoli mixture and pour over the cheese sauce. Cook, stirring occasionally, for about 2 minutes. Transfer the pasta and broccoli mixture to a warm, large, deep serving dish and serve garnished with slices of fresh apple.

VARIATION

This dish would also be delicious and look just as colourful made with Cape broccoli, which is actually a purple variety of cauliflower and not broccoli at all.

Macaroni & Corn Pancakes

These vegetable pancakes are tasty and filling, and look very attractive served with a garnish of oyster mushrooms and fried leek rings.

NUTRITIONAL INFORMATION

Calories 702	Sugars 4g	
Protein 13g	Fat 50g	
Carbohydrate . . .55g	Saturates 23g	

15 mins   40 mins

SERVES 4

INGREDIENTS

2 corn cobs

4 tbsp butter

115 g/4 oz red peppers, deseeded and finely diced

285 g/10 oz dried short-cut macaroni

150 ml/5 fl oz double cream

25 g/1 oz plain flour

4 egg yolks

4 tbsp olive oil

salt and pepper

TO SERVE

oyster mushrooms

fried leeks

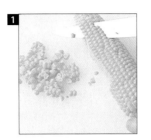

1 Bring a pan of water to the boil, add the corn cobs and cook for about 8 minutes. Drain thoroughly and refresh under cold running water for 3 minutes. Carefully cut away the kernels on to kitchen paper and set aside to dry.

2 Melt 2 tablespoons of the butter in a frying pan. Add the peppers and cook over a low heat for 4 minutes. Drain and pat dry with kitchen paper.

3 Bring a large pan of lightly salted water to the boil. Add the macaroni, bring back to the boil and cook for about 12 minutes or until tender, but still firm to the bite. Drain the macaroni thoroughly and set aside to cool in cold water until required.

4 Beat the cream with the flour, a pinch of salt and the egg yolks in a bowl until smooth. Add the corn and peppers. Drain the macaroni and then toss into the corn and cream mixture. Season with pepper to taste.

5 Heat the remaining butter with the oil in a large frying pan. Drop spoonfuls of the mixture into the pan and press down to form flat pancakes. Fry until golden on both sides. Drain on absorbent paper. Serve immediately with oyster mushrooms and fried leeks.

Macaroni Cheese & Tomato

This is a really simple, family dish which is inexpensive and easy to prepare and cook. Serve with a salad or fresh green vegetables.

NUTRITIONAL INFORMATION

Calories 592   Sugars 6g
Protein ....28g   Fat 29g
Carbohydrate ...57g   Saturates 17g

 15 mins   35–40 mins

SERVES 4

I N G R E D I E N T S

225 g/8 oz dried elbow macaroni

175 g/6 oz grated Cheddar cheese

100 g/3½ oz grated Parmesan cheese

1 tbsp butter or margarine, plus extra for greasing

4 tbsp fresh white breadcrumbs

1 tbsp chopped fresh basil

T O M A T O   S A U C E

1 tbsp olive oil

1 shallot, finely chopped

2 garlic cloves, crushed

500 g/1 lb 2 oz canned chopped tomatoes

1 tbsp chopped fresh basil

salt and pepper

1 To make the tomato sauce, heat the oil in a heavy-based pan. Add the shallots and garlic and cook, stirring constantly, for 1 minute. Add the tomatoes and basil and season with salt and pepper to taste. Cook over a medium heat, stirring constantly, for 10 minutes.

2 Meanwhile, bring a large pan of lightly salted water to the boil. Add the macaroni, bring back to the boil and cook for 8 minutes or until tender, but still firm to the bite. Drain well.

3 Combine the grated Cheddar and Parmesan in a bowl. Grease a deep, ovenproof dish. Spoon one-third of the tomato sauce into the base of the dish, cover with one-third of the macaroni and then top with one-third of the mixed cheeses. Season to taste with salt and pepper. Repeat these layers twice, ending with a layer of grated cheese.

4 Combine the breadcrumbs and basil and sprinkle evenly over the top. Dot the topping with the butter or margarine and cook in a preheated oven, 190°C/375°F/Gas Mark 5, for 25 minutes or until the the topping is golden brown and bubbling. Serve immediately.

Spinach Lasagne

Always check the seasoning of vegetables – you can always add a little more to a recipe, but you cannot take it out once it has been added.

NUTRITIONAL INFORMATION

Calories	720	Sugars	.........9g
Protein	........31g	Fat	.........52g
Carbohydrate	...36g	Saturates	......32g

 20 mins   40 mins

SERVES 4

INGREDIENTS

115 g/4 oz butter, plus extra for greasing

2 garlic cloves, finely chopped

115 g/4 oz shallots, finely chopped

225 g/8 oz wild mushrooms, such as chanterelles, sliced

450 g/1 lb spinach, cooked, drained and finely chopped

225 g/8 oz Cheddar cheese, grated

¼ tsp freshly grated nutmeg

1 tsp chopped fresh basil

salt and pepper

6 tbsp plain flour

600 ml/1 pint hot milk

55 g/2 oz Cheshire cheese, grated

8 sheets pre-cooked lasagne

1 Lightly grease a large, fairly deep, rectangular or square ovenproof dish with a little butter.

2 Melt 55 g/2 oz of the butter in a large frying pan. Add the garlic, shallots and wild mushrooms and fry over a low heat, stirring occasionally, for 3 minutes.

3 Stir in the spinach, Cheddar cheese, nutmeg and basil. Season with salt and pepper to taste, remove from the heat and set aside.

4 Melt the remaining butter in a saucepan over a low heat. Add the flour and cook over a low heat, stirring constantly, for 1 minute. Gradually stir in the hot milk, whisking constantly until smooth and thickened. Remove the pan from the heat, stir in 25 g/1 oz of the Cheshire cheese and season to taste with salt and pepper.

5 Spread half of the mushroom and spinach mixture over the base of the prepared dish. Cover with half the lasagne sheets and then with half of the cheese sauce. Repeat the layers and then sprinkle the remaining grated Cheshire cheese over the top.

6 Bake in a preheated oven, 200°C/400°F/Gas Mark 6, for 30 minutes or until golden brown. Serve hot.

VARIATION

You could substitute 4 peppers for the spinach. Roast them in a preheated oven, 200°C/400°F/Gas Mark 6, for 20 minutes. Rub off the skins under cold water, deseed and chop before using.

Vegetable Ravioli

It is important not to overcook the vegetable filling or it will become sloppy and unexciting, instead of firm to the bite and delicious.

NUTRITIONAL INFORMATION

Calories ....622 Sugars 10g
Protein ....12g Fat 40g
Carbohydrate ...58g Saturates 6g

1½ hrs   55 mins

SERVES 4

INGREDIENTS

450 g/1 lb basic pasta dough
  (see page 321)

1 tbsp olive oil

6 tbsp butter

150 ml/5 fl oz single cream

85 g/3 oz Parmesan cheese, freshly grated

fresh basil sprigs, to garnish

STUFFING

2 large aubergines

3 large courgettes

6 large tomatoes

1 large green pepper

1 large red pepper

3 garlic cloves

1 large onion

125 ml/4 fl oz olive oil

4½ tsp tomato purée

½ tsp chopped fresh basil

salt and pepper

1 To make the stuffing, cut the aubergines and the courgettes into 2.5 cm/1 inch chunks. Layer the aubergine pieces in a colander, sprinkle each layer with salt and set aside for 20 minutes. Rinse and drain, then pat dry on absorbent kitchen paper.

2 Blanch the tomatoes in boiling water for 2 minutes. Drain, peel and chop the flesh. Core and deseed the peppers and cut into 2.5 cm/1 inch dice. Crush the garlic and finely chop the onion.

3 Heat the olive oil in a saucepan. Add the garlic and onion and fry over a low heat, stirring occasionally, for 3 minutes.

4 Stir in the aubergines, courgettes, tomatoes, peppers, tomato purée and basil. Season with salt and pepper to taste, cover and simmer for 20 minutes, stirring frequently.

5 Roll out the pasta dough and cut out 7.5 cm/3 inch rounds with a plain cutter. Put a spoonful of the vegetable stuffing on each round. Dampen the edges slightly and fold the pasta rounds over, pressing together to seal.

6 Bring a saucepan of salted water to the boil. Add the ravioli and the oil and cook for 3–4 minutes. Drain and transfer to a greased ovenproof dish, dotting each layer with butter. Pour over the cream and sprinkle over the Parmesan cheese. Bake in a preheated oven, 200°C/400°F/Gas Mark 6, for 20 minutes. Garnish and serve hot.

Goat's Cheese & Penne Salad

This superb and substantial salad is a delicious combination of goat's cheese with the slightly bitter taste of radicchio.

NUTRITIONAL INFORMATION

Calories ....634 Sugars 13g
Protein ....18g Fat 51g
Carbohydrate ...27g Saturates 13g

 1½ hrs   15 mins

SERVES 4

INGREDIENTS

250 g/9 oz dried penne

1 head radicchio, torn into pieces

1 Webbs lettuce, torn into pieces

7 tbsp chopped walnuts

2 ripe pears, cored and diced

1 fresh basil sprig

1 bunch of watercress, trimmed

2 tbsp lemon juice

4 tbsp olive oil

3 tbsp garlic vinegar

4 tomatoes, quartered

1 small onion, sliced

1 large carrot, grated

250 g/9 oz goat's cheese, diced

salt

1 Bring a large saucepan of lightly salted water to the boil. Add the pasta, bring back to the boil and cook for 8–10 minutes or until tender, but still firm to the bite. Drain the pasta, refresh under cold running water, drain thoroughly again and set aside to cool.

2 Place the radicchio and Webbs lettuce in a large salad bowl and mix together well. Top with the pasta, walnuts, pears, basil and watercress.

3 Mix together the lemon juice, olive oil and the vinegar in a measuring jug. Pour the dressing over the salad ingredients and toss to coat the salad leaves well.

4 Add the tomato quarters, onion slices, grated carrot and diced goat's cheese and toss together, using 2 forks, until well mixed. Cover the salad with clingfilm and chill in the refrigerator for about 1 hour before serving.

COOK'S TIP
Radicchio is a variety of chicory originating in Italy. It has a slightly bitter flavour.

Mushroom Tortelloni

These tasty little squares of pasta stuffed with mushrooms and cheese are surprisingly filling. This recipe makes 36 tortelloni.

NUTRITIONAL INFORMATION

Calories	360	Sugars	.........1g
Protein	.........9g	Fat	..........21g
Carbohydrate	...36g	Saturates	......12g

   1¼ hrs   25 mins

SERVES 4

I N G R E D I E N T S

about 300 g/10½ oz pasta dough (see page 32), rolled out to thin sheets

5 tbsp butter

55 g/2 oz shallots, finely chopped

3 garlic cloves, crushed

55 g/2 oz mushrooms, wiped and finely chopped

½ celery stick, finely chopped

5 tbsp grated pecorino cheese, plus extra to garnish

salt and pepper

1 tbsp vegetable oil

1 Using a serrated pasta cutter, cut 5 cm/2 inch squares from the sheets of fresh pasta. To make 36 tortelloni you will need 72 squares. Once the pasta is cut, cover the squares with clingfilm to prevent them from drying out.

2 Heat 3 tablespoons of the butter in a frying pan. Add the shallots, 1 crushed garlic clove, the mushrooms and celery and cook for 4–5 minutes.

3 Remove the pan from the heat, stir in the cheese and season with salt and pepper to taste.

4 Spoon ½ teaspoon of the mixture on to the middle of 36 pasta squares. Brush the edges of the squares with water and top with the remaining 36 squares. Press the edges together to seal. Set aside to rest for 5 minutes.

5 Bring a large pan of water to the boil, add the oil and cook the tortelloni, in batches, for 2–3 minutes. The tortelloni will rise to the surface when cooked and the pasta should be tender, but still firm to the bite. Remove from the pan with a draining spoon and drain thoroughly.

6 Meanwhile, melt the remaining butter in a pan over a low heat. Add the remaining garlic and plenty of pepper and cook for 1–2 minutes. Transfer the tortelloni to serving plates and pour the garlic butter over them. Garnish with grated pecorino and serve immediately.

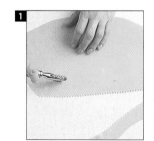

Basil & Tomato Pasta

Roasting the tomatoes gives a sweeter, smoother flavour to the sauce. Italian plum or flavia tomatoes are ideal for this dish.

NUTRITIONAL INFORMATION

Calories 177   Sugars 4g
Protein ....5g   Fat 4g
Carbohydrate ...31g   Saturates 1g

10 mins   25–35 mins

SERVES 4

INGREDIENTS

1 tbsp olive oil, plus extra for drizzling

2 sprigs fresh rosemary

2 garlic cloves, unpeeled

450 g/1 lb tomatoes, halved

1 tbsp sun-dried tomato purée

12 fresh basil leaves, plus extra to garnish

salt and pepper

675 g/1lb 8 oz fresh farfalle or 350 g/12 oz dried

1 Place the oil, rosemary, garlic and tomatoes, skin side up, in a shallow roasting tin.

2 Drizzle with a little oil and cook under a preheated grill for about 20 minutes, or until the tomato skins are becoming slightly charred.

3 Peel the skin from the tomatoes. Roughly chop the tomato flesh and place in a pan.

4 Squeeze the pulp from the garlic cloves and mix with the tomato flesh and sun-dried tomato purée.

5 Roughly tear the fresh basil leaves into smaller pieces and then stir them into the sauce. Season with a little salt and pepper to taste.

6 Cook the farfalle in a saucepan of boiling water according to the instructions on the packet or until it is cooked through, but still has 'bite'. Drain thoroughly.

7 Gently heat the tomato and basil sauce until warmed through.

8 Transfer the farfalle to serving plates and serve at once with the basil and tomato sauce.

COOK'S TIP
This sauce tastes just as good when served cold in a pasta salad.

Chilli Tagliatelle

Pasta with a deliciously fresh and slightly spicy tomato sauce, which is excellent for lunch or a light supper.

NUTRITIONAL INFORMATION

Calories 306   Sugars 7g
Protein ....8g   Fat 12g
Carbohydrate ...45g   Saturates 7g

 15 mins   35 mins

SERVES 4

INGREDIENTS

50 g/1¾ oz butter

1 onion, finely chopped

1 garlic clove, crushed

2 small red chillies, deseeded and diced

450 g/1 lb fresh tomatoes, skinned, deseeded and diced

200 ml/7 fl oz vegetable stock

2 tbsp tomato purée

1 tsp sugar

salt and pepper

675 g/1 lb 8 oz fresh green and white tagliatelle, or 350 g/12 oz dried

1 Melt the butter in a large saucepan. Add the onion and garlic and cook for 3–4 minutes, or until softened.

2 Add the chillies to the pan and continue cooking for about 2 minutes.

3 Add the tomatoes and stock, then reduce the heat and leave to simmer for 10 minutes, stirring.

4 Pour the sauce into a food processor and blend for 1 minute, or until smooth. Alternatively, push the sauce through a sieve.

5 Return the sauce to the pan and add the tomato purée, sugar, and salt and pepper to taste. Gently reheat over a low heat, until piping hot.

6 Cook the tagliatelle in a pan of boiling water according to the instructions on the packet or until it is cooked, but still has 'bite'. Drain the tagliatelle, transfer to warm serving plates and serve with the tomato sauce.

VARIATION

Try using a different shape of pasta, such as penne, for this recipe, then put it in an ovenproof dish, top it with some grated cheese and bake it for a warming winter feast.

Penne & Apple Salad

This gorgeous crisp salad, dressed in garlic mayonnaise, is perfect to serve as part of a summer buffet lunch al fresco.

NUTRITIONAL INFORMATION

Calories 858	Sugars 35g
Protein 11g	Fat 64g
Carbohydrate ...64g	Saturates 8g

20 mins, plus chilling   10–15 mins

SERVES 4

INGREDIENTS

2 large lettuces

250 g/9 oz dried penne

1 tbsp olive oil

8 red apples, diced

juice of 4 lemons

1 head of celery, sliced

115 g/4 oz shelled, halved walnuts

250 ml/9 fl oz fresh garlic mayonnaise (see Cook's Tip, right)

salt

1 Wash, drain and pat dry the lettuce leaves with kitchen paper. Transfer them to the refrigerator for 1 hour, or until crisp.

2 Meanwhile, bring a large saucepan of lightly salted water to the boil. Add the pasta and olive oil and cook until tender, but still firm to the bite. Drain the pasta and refresh under cold running water. Drain thoroughly and cool.

3 Core and dice the apples, place them in a bowl and sprinkle with the lemon juice to coat them thoroughly – this will prevent them turning brown. Mix together the cold pasta, sliced celery, diced apples and walnut halves and toss the mixture in the garlic mayonnaise.

4 Line a salad bowl with the lettuce leaves and spoon the pasta salad on top. Chill until required.

COOK'S TIP
To make garlic mayonnaise, beat 2 egg yolks with a pinch of salt and 6 crushed garlic cloves. Beat in 350 ml/12 fl oz olive oil, 1–2 tsp at a time. When ¼ of the oil has been used, add 1–2 tbsp white wine vinegar. Beat in the rest of the oil in a thin stream. Add 1 tsp Dijon mustard, and season.

Traditional Cannelloni

You can buy ready-made dried pasta tubes for this recipe, or use fresh pasta dough cut into squares and rolled around the filling.

NUTRITIONAL INFORMATION

Calories 342	Sugars 6g
Protein 15g	Fat 15g
Carbohydrate . . .38g	Saturates 8g

 50 mins   30 mins

SERVES 4

INGREDIENTS

20 tubes dried cannelloni (about 200 g/ 7 oz) or 20 square sheets of fresh pasta (about 350 g/12 oz), see page 321

250 g/9 oz ricotta cheese

150 g/5½ oz frozen spinach, thawed

½ small red pepper, deseeded and diced

2 spring onions, chopped

salt and pepper

butter, for greasing

150 ml/5 fl oz hot vegetable stock

1 quantity Tomato Sauce (see page 7), made with 2 tbsp chopped fresh basil instead of parsley

25 g/1 oz Parmesan or pecorino cheese, freshly grated

VARIATION

If you would prefer a creamier version, omit the stock and the tomato sauce and replace with Béchamel sauce.

1 If necessary, pre-cook the dried cannelloni. Bring a large pan of water to the boil, add the pasta, bring back to the boil and cook for 3–4 minutes. Cook in batches if this is easier.

2 Combine the ricotta, spinach, pepper and spring onions in a bowl and season to taste with salt and pepper.

3 Lightly grease an ovenproof dish, large enough to contain all of the pasta tubes in a single layer, with a little butter. Spoon the ricotta mixture into the pasta tubes and place them in the prepared dish. If you are using fresh sheets of pasta, spread the ricotta mixture along one side of each fresh pasta square and roll up to form a tube.

4 Combine the stock and tomato sauce and pour it over the pasta tubes.

5 Sprinkle the Parmesan or pecorino cheese over the cannelloni and bake in a preheated oven, 190°C/375°F/Gas Mark 5, for about 20–25 minutes or until the pasta is cooked through and the topping is golden brown and bubbling. Serve immediately.

Mushroom Lasagne

Layers of pasta, tomatoes and mushrooms are baked in a creamy sauce for a filling, colourful and truly scrumptious supper.

NUTRITIONAL INFORMATION

Calories	628	Sugars	........10g
Protein	24	Fat	..........41g
Carbohydrate	43	Saturates	......23g

45 mins · 40 mins

SERVES 4

INGREDIENTS

1½ oz/40 g dried porcini mushrooms

2 tbsp olive oil

1 onion, finely chopped

400 g/14 oz canned chopped tomatoes

salt and pepper

450 g/1 lb button mushrooms, thinly sliced

55 g/2 oz butter, plus extra for greasing

1 garlic clove, finely chopped

1 tbsp lemon juice

6 sheets ready-to-use lasagne

½ tsp Dijon mustard

¾ quantity Cheese Sauce (see page 304), made with Cheddar cheese

55 g/2 oz freshly grated Parmesan cheese

1 Place the porcini mushrooms in a small bowl, cover with boiling water and set aside for 30 minutes. Meanwhile, heat the olive oil in a small frying pan. Add the onion and cook, stirring occasionally, for 5 minutes, until softened. Add the tomatoes and cook, stirring frequently, for 7–8 minutes. Season the mixture to taste with salt and pepper and set aside.

2 Drain the porcini mushrooms and slice. Melt half the butter in a large, heavy-based frying pan. Add the porcini and button mushrooms and cook until they start to give off their juices. Add the garlic and lemon juice and season to taste with salt and pepper. Cook over a low heat, stirring occasionally, until the liquid has almost evaporated.

3 Lightly grease an ovenproof dish with butter. Stir the mustard into the cheese sauce, then spread one third over the base of the dish. Place half the lasagne on top, cover with the mushrooms, another layer of sauce, another layer of lasagne, the tomato mixture and, finally, another layer of sauce. Sprinkle with the cheese and dot with the remaining butter.

4 Bake in a preheated oven, 200°C/400°F/Gas Mark 6, for 20 minutes. Leave the lasagne to stand for 5 minutes before serving.

Patriotic Pasta

The ingredients of this dish have the same bright colours as the Italian flag: red, white and green – hence its name.

NUTRITIONAL INFORMATION

Calories	325	Sugars	.........5g
Protein	.........8g	Fat	..........13g
Carbohydrate	...48g	Saturates	.......2g

 5 mins   15 mins

SERVES 4

INGREDIENTS

450 g/1 lb dried farfalle

450 g/1 lb cherry tomatoes

85 g/3 oz rocket

3 tbsp olive oil

salt and pepper

pecorino cheese shavings, to garnish

1 Bring a large pan of lightly salted water to the boil. Add the farfalle, bring back to the boil and cook for 8–10 minutes or until tender, but still firm to the bite. Drain the farfalle thoroughly and return to the pan.

2 Cut the cherry tomatoes in half and trim the rocket.

3 Heat the olive oil in a large, heavy-based pan. Add the tomatoes to the pan and cook for 1 minute.

4 Add the farfalle and the rocket to the pan and stir very gently over a low heat until thoroughly mixed and warmed through, but be careful not to overcook – the rocket should just have wilted from the heat. Season the mixture to taste with salt and pepper.

5 Meanwhile, using a vegetable peeler, shave thin slices of pecorino cheese.

6 Transfer the farfalle and vegetables to a warmed serving dish. Garnish with the pecorino cheese shavings and serve the pasta immediately.

COOK'S TIP

Pecorino cheese is a hard sheep's-milk cheese that resembles Parmesan and is often used for grating over a variety of Italian dishes. It has a sharp flavour and is used only in small quantities.

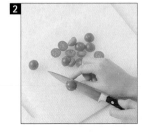

Pasta with Alfredo Sauce

This simple, traditional dish can be made with any long pasta, but is especially good with flat noodles, such as fettuccine or tagliatelle.

NUTRITIONAL INFORMATION

Calories	627	Sugars	.........2g
Protein	........18g	Fat	..........41g
Carbohydrate	...51g	Saturates	......23g

5 mins   10 mins

SERVES 4

INGREDIENTS

25 g/1 oz butter

200 ml/7 fl oz double cream

450 g/1 lb fresh fettuccine

1 tbsp olive oil

85 g/3 oz Parmesan cheese, freshly grated, plus extra to serve

pinch of freshly grated nutmeg

salt and pepper

fresh parsley sprigs, to garnish

1 Put the butter and 150 ml/5 fl oz of the cream in a large saucepan and bring the mixture to the boil over a medium heat. Reduce the heat and then simmer gently for about 1½ minutes, or until slightly thickened.

2 Meanwhile, bring a large pan of lightly salted water to the boil. Add the fettuccine and olive oil and cook for 2–3 minutes, or until tender but still firm to the bite. Drain the fettuccine, then pour over the cream sauce.

3 Toss the fettuccine in the sauce over a low heat until thoroughly coated.

4 Add the remaining cream, the Parmesan cheese and nutmeg to the fettuccine mixture and season to taste with salt and pepper. Toss thoroughly to coat while gently heating through.

5 Transfer the fettucine mixture to a warm serving plate and garnish with the fresh sprigs of parsley. Serve immediately, handing round extra grated Parmesan cheese separately.

VARIATION
This classic Roman dish is delicious served with the addition of fresh peas. Add 225 g/8 oz shelled cooked peas with the Parmesan cheese in step 4.

Macaroni Potato Bake

This warming and satisfying dish would make an excellent supper for a mid-week family meal on a dreary winter's day.

NUTRITIONAL INFORMATION

Calories 728   Sugars 11g
Protein ....17g   Fat 42g
Carbohydrate ...75g   Saturates 23g

    15 mins   45 mins

SERVES 4

INGREDIENTS

450 g/1 lb dried short-cut macaroni

1 tbsp olive oil

4 tbsp butter

450 g/1 lb potatoes, thinly sliced

450 g/1 lb onions, sliced

225 g/8 oz mozzarella cheese, grated

salt and pepper

150 ml/5 fl oz double cream

crusty brown bread and butter, to serve

1 Bring a large saucepan of lightly salted water to the boil. Add the macaroni and olive oil, bring back to the boil and cook for about 12 minutes or until the pasta is just tender but still firm to the bite. Drain the macaroni thoroughly and set aside.

2 Melt the butter in a large flameproof casserole, then remove from the heat.

3 Make alternate layers of potatoes, onions, macaroni and grated mozzarella cheese in the casserole, seasoning well with salt and pepper between each layer and finishing with a layer of cheese on top. Finally, pour the all of the double cream over the top layer of cheese.

4 Bake in a preheated oven, 200°C/ 400°F/Gas Mark 6, for 25 minutes. Remove the casserole from the oven and carefully brown the top of the bake under a hot grill.

5 Serve the bake straight from the casserole with crusty brown bread and butter as a main course. Alternatively, serve as a vegetable accompaniment with your favourite main course.

VARIATION

For a stronger flavour, use mozzarella affumicata, a smoked version of this cheese, or Gruyère cheese, instead of the mozzarella.

Aubergine & Artichoke Pasta

Delicious Mediterranean vegetables, cooked in rich tomato sauce, make an ideal topping for nutty wholemeal pasta.

NUTRITIONAL INFORMATION

Calories	492	Sugars	........13g
Protein	........15g	Fat	..........16g
Carbohydrate	...77g	Saturates	.......5g

10 mins   40 mins

SERVES 4

I N G R E D I E N T S

2 tbsp olive oil

1 large red onion, chopped

2 garlic cloves, crushed

1 tbsp lemon juice

4 baby aubergines, quartered

600 ml/1 pint passata

2 tsp caster sugar

salt and pepper

2 tbsp tomato purée

400 g/14 oz canned artichoke hearts,
    drained and halved

115 g/4 oz black olives, stoned

350 g/12 oz dried spaghetti

25 g/1 oz butter

fresh basil sprigs, to garnish

olive bread, to serve

tomato purée. Bring to the boil, lower the heat and then simmer, stirring occasionally, for 20 minutes.

3 Gently stir in the artichoke hearts and black olives and continue to cook for a further 5 minutes.

4 Meanwhile, bring a large saucepan of lightly salted water to the boil. Add the spaghetti and the remaining oil and

cook for 7–8 minutes, or until tender, but still firm to the bite.

5 Drain the spaghetti thoroughly and toss with the butter. Transfer the spaghetti to a large serving dish.

6 Pour the vegetable sauce over the spaghetti, garnish with the sprigs of fresh basil and serve immediately with olive bread.

1 Heat 1 tablespoon of the olive oil in a large frying pan. Add the onion, garlic, lemon juice and aubergines and cook over a low heat for 4–5 minutes, or until the onion and aubergines are lightly golden.

2 Pour in the passata, season to taste and stir in the caster sugar and

Mushroom Pasta with Port

This easy but impressive dish is ideal for busy people who have little time to spare, but very good taste!

NUTRITIONAL INFORMATION

Calories	763	Sugars	........11g
Protein	........17g	Fat	..........38g
Carbohydrate	...93g	Saturates	......20g

 10 mins   35 mins

SERVES 4

INGREDIENTS

55 g/2 oz butter

2 tbsp olive oil

6 shallots, sliced

450 g/1 lb button mushrooms, sliced

salt and pepper

1 tsp plain flour

150 ml/5 fl oz double cream

2 tbsp port

115 g/4 oz sun-dried tomatoes, chopped

freshly grated nutmeg

450 g /1 lb dried spaghetti

1 tbsp chopped fresh parsley

6 triangles of fried white bread, to serve

VARIATION

If you like the sound of this recipe but don't have any port available, you can use 2 tbsp of dry white wine instead.

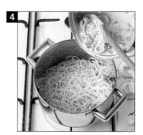

1 Heat the butter and 1 tablespoon of the oil in a large saucepan. Add the shallots and cook over a medium heat for 3 minutes. Add the mushrooms and cook over a low heat for a further 2 minutes. Season to taste with salt and pepper, sprinkle over the flour and cook, stirring constantly, for 1 minute.

2 Gradually stir in the cream and port, add the sun-dried tomatoes and a pinch of grated nutmeg and cook over a low heat for 8 minutes.

3 Meanwhile, bring a large saucepan of lightly salted water to the boil. Add the spaghetti and remaining olive oil and cook for 12–14 minutes, or until tender but still firm to the bite.

4 Drain the spaghetti and return to the pan. Pour over the mushroom sauce and cook for 3 minutes. Transfer the spaghetti and mushroom sauce to a large serving plate and sprinkle over the chopped parsley. Serve with crispy triangles of fried bread.

Beetroot Cannolicchi

Quick and simple, this colourful, warm salad works equally well as a tasty starter or as a main dish for a light lunch.

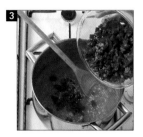

NUTRITIONAL INFORMATION

Calories 449   Sugars 13g
Protein . . . . .13g   Fat 16g
Carbohydrate . . .70g   Saturates 2g

 10 mins   25 mins

SERVES 4

I N G R E D I E N T S

300 g/11 oz dried ditalini rigati

5 tbsp olive oil

2 garlic cloves chopped

400 g/14 oz canned chopped tomatoes

400 g/14 oz cooked beetroot, diced

2 tbsp chopped fresh basil leaves

1 tsp mustard seeds

salt and pepper

TO SERVE

mixed salad leaves, tossed in olive oil

4 Italian plum tomatoes, sliced

1 Bring a large saucepan of lightly salted water to the boil. Add the pasta and 1 tbsp of the oil. Bring back to the boil and cook for 8–10 minutes until tender, but still firm to the bite. Drain and set aside.

2 Heat the remaining olive oil in a large saucepan. Add the garlic and fry over a low heat for 3 minutes. Add the chopped tomatoes and cook for 10 minutes.

3 Remove the pan from the heat and carefully add the beetroot, basil, mustard seeds and pasta and season to taste with salt and pepper.

4 Serve while still warm on a bed of mixed salad leaves, tossed in olive oil, and sliced plum tomatoes.

COOK'S TIP
To cook raw beetroot, trim off the leaves about 5 cm/2 inches above the root and ensure that the skin is not broken. Boil in very lightly salted water for 30–40 minutes, until tender. Set aside to cool and then rub off the skin.

Vegetable & Pesto Tagliatelle

This low-fat version of the traditional rich Italian pesto, combined with pasta and vegetables, makes a healthy and satisfying meal.

NUTRITIONAL INFORMATION

Calories 283	Sugars 5g
Protein 14g	Fat 3g
Carbohydrate ...37g	Saturates 1g

 1 hr   30 mins

SERVES 4

INGREDIENTS

225 g/8 oz chestnut mushrooms, sliced

150 ml/5 fl oz vegetable stock

175 g/6 oz asparagus, trimmed and cut into 5 cm/2 inch lengths

300 g/10½ oz green and white tagliatelle

400 g/14 oz canned artichoke hearts, drained and halved

PESTO

2 large garlic cloves, crushed

15 g/½ oz fresh basil leaves

6 tbsp low-fat natural fromage frais

2 tbsp freshly grated Parmesan cheese

salt and pepper

TO GARNISH

shredded fresh basil leaves

Parmesan shavings

1 Place the mushrooms in a pan with the stock. Bring to the boil, cover and simmer for 3–4 minutes until just tender. Drain and set aside, reserving the cooking liquid to use in soups if wished.

2 Bring a small pan of water to the boil and cook the asparagus for 3–4 minutes until just tender. Drain and set aside until required.

3 Bring a large pan of lightly salted water to the boil. Add the pasta, bring back to the boil and cook until tender, but still firm to the bite: allow about 8–10 minutes for dried pasta or 2–3 minutes for fresh tagliatelle. Drain, return to the pan and keep warm.

4 Meanwhile, make the pesto. Place all of the ingredients in a blender or food processor and process for a few seconds until smooth. Alternatively, finely chop the basil and mix all the ingredients together.

5 Add the mushrooms, asparagus and artichoke hearts to the pasta and cook, stirring, over a low heat for 2–3 minutes. Remove from the heat and mix with the pesto.

6 Transfer to a warm bowl. Garnish with basil and Parmesan and serve.

Vegetable & Pasta Stir-fry

Prepare all the vegetables and cook the pasta in advance, then the dish can be assembled in a few minutes when you are ready to eat.

NUTRITIONAL INFORMATION

Calories	575	Sugars	........13g
Protein	........15g	Fat	..........17g
Carbohydrate	...94g	Saturates	.......2g

15 mins   25 mins

SERVES 4

I N G R E D I E N T S

400 g/14 oz dried wholemeal pasta shells or other short pasta shapes

1 tbsp olive oil

2 carrots, thinly sliced

115 g/4 oz baby sweetcorn

3 tbsp corn oil

2.5 cm/1 inch piece fresh root ginger, thinly sliced

1 large onion, thinly sliced

1 garlic clove, thinly sliced

3 celery sticks, thinly sliced

1 small red pepper, cored, deseeded and cut into matchsticks

1 small green pepper, cored, deseeded and cut into matchsticks

1 tsp cornflour

2 tbsp water

3 tbsp soy sauce

3 tbsp dry sherry

1 tsp clear honey

a dash of hot pepper sauce (optional)

salt

1 Bring a large saucepan of lightly salted water to the boil. Add the pasta and olive oil and cook until tender, but still firm to the bite. Drain, return to the pan and keep warm.

2 Bring a saucepan of lightly salted water to the boil. Add the carrots and sweetcorn and cook for 2 minutes. Drain, then refresh in cold water and drain again.

3 Heat the corn oil in a preheated wok or large frying pan. Add the ginger and stir-fry over a medium heat for 1 minute to flavour the oil. Remove the ginger with a slotted spoon and discard.

4 Add the onion, garlic, celery and peppers to the pan and stir-fry them for 2 minutes. Add the carrots and baby sweetcorn and stir-fry for a further 2 minutes. Stir in the drained pasta.

5 Mix together the cornflour and water to make a smooth paste. Stir in the soy sauce, sherry and honey. Pour the cornflour mixture into the pasta and cook, stirring occasionally, for 2 minutes. Stir in a dash of pepper sauce, if liked.

6 Transfer the stir-fry to a serving dish and serve immediately.

Spicy Fried Noodles

This is a simple idea to add an extra kick to noodles, which accompany many main course dishes in Thailand.

NUTRITIONAL INFORMATION

Calories	568	Sugars	.........3g
Protein	........16g	Fat	..........19g
Carbohydrate	...90g	Saturates	.......4g

15 mins   3-5 mins

SERVES 4

INGREDIENTS

500 g/1 lb 2 oz dried medium egg noodles

60 g/2 oz beansprouts

15 g/½ oz chives

3 tbsp sunflower oil

1 garlic clove, crushed

4 fresh green chillies, deseeded, sliced and soaked in 2 tbsp rice vinegar

salt

1 Place the noodles in a bowl, cover with boiling water and soak for 10 minutes. Drain and set aside.

2 Pick over the beansprouts and soak in cold water while you cut the chives into 2.5 cm/1 inch pieces. Set a few chives aside for the garnish. Drain the beansprouts thoroughly.

3 Heat the oil in a preheated wok or large, heavy-based frying pan. Add the crushed garlic and stir; then add the chillies and vinegar and stir-fry for about 1 minute, until fragrant.

4 Add the beansprouts, stir and then add the noodles. Stir in salt to taste and add the chives. Using 2 spoons or a wok scoop, lift and toss the noodles for 1 minute, until the beansprouts and noodles are heated through.

5 Transfer the noodle mixture to a warm serving dish, garnish with the reserved chives and serve immediately.

COOK'S TIP

Soaking a chilli in rice vinegar has the effect of distributing the hot chilli flavour throughout the dish. To reduce the heat, you can slice the chilli more thickly before soaking.

Chow Mein

Egg noodles are cooked and then fried with a colourful variety of vegetables to make this well-known and ever-popular dish.

NUTRITIONAL INFORMATION

Calories	669	Sugars	.........9g
Protein	........19g	Fat	..........23g
Carbohydrate	..100g	Saturates	.......4g

 15 mins   10 mins

SERVES 4

I N G R E D I E N T S

500 g/1 lb 2 oz dried medium egg noodles

4 tbsp vegetable oil

1 onion, thinly sliced

2 carrots, cut into matchsticks

125 g/4½ oz button mushrooms, quartered

125 g/4½ oz mangetouts

½ cucumber, cut into sticks

125 g/4½ oz spinach, shredded

125 g/4½ oz beansprouts

2 tbsp dark soy sauce

1 tbsp sherry

1 tsp salt

1 tsp sugar

1 tsp cornflour

1 tsp sesame oil

1 Cook the egg noodles according to the instructions on the packet. Drain and rinse under cold running water until cool. Set aside.

2 Heat 3 tablespoons of the vegetable oil in a preheated wok or frying pan. Add the onion and carrots and stir-fry for 1 minute, then add the mushrooms, mangetout and cucumber and stir-fry for a further 1 minute.

3 Stir in the remaining vegetable oil and add the drained noodles, together with the spinach and beansprouts.

4 Blend together all the remaining ingredients and pour over the noodles and vegetables.

5 Stir-fry until the noodle mixture is thoroughly heated through, transfer to a warm serving dish and serve.

COOK'S TIP
For a spicy hot chow mein, add 1 tablespoon chilli sauce or substitute chilli oil for the sesame oil.

Thai-style Stir-fried Noodles

This dish is considered the Thai national dish, as it is made and eaten everywhere – a one-dish fast food for eating on the move.

NUTRITIONAL INFORMATION

Calories 407	Sugars 11g	
Protein 14g	Fat 16g	
Carbohydrate . . .56g	Saturates 3g	

🖐 15 mins   🕐 5 mins

SERVES 4

INGREDIENTS

225 g/8 oz dried rice noodles

2 red chillies, deseeded and finely chopped

2 shallots, finely chopped

2 tbsp sugar

2 tbsp tamarind water

1 tbsp lime juice

2 tbsp light soy sauce

pepper

1 tbsp sunflower oil

1 tsp sesame oil

175 g/6 oz smoked tofu, diced

2 tbsp chopped dry-roasted peanuts, to garnish

COOK'S TIP

Tamarind water is made by soaking tamarind paste in a little boiling water, then pressing it through a sieve.

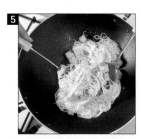

1 Cook the rice noodles as directed on the pack, or soak them in boiling water for 5 minutes.

2 Grind together the chillies, shallots, sugar, tamarind water, lime juice, light soy sauce and pepper to taste.

3 Heat the sunflower and sesame oils together in a preheated wok or large, heavy frying pan over a high heat. Add the tofu and stir-fry for 1 minute.

4 Add the chilli mixture, bring to the boil, and continue to cook, stirring constantly, for about 2 minutes, until the sauce has thickened.

5 Drain the rice noodles and add them to the chilli mixture. Use 2 spoons to lift and stir the noodles until they are no longer steaming.

6 Serve the hot noodles immediately, garnished with the chopped peanuts.

Stir-fried Japanese Noodles

This quick dish is an ideal lunchtime meal, packed with mixed mushrooms in a sweet sauce.

NUTRITIONAL INFORMATION

Calories	379	Sugars	........8g
Protein	........12g	Fat	..........13g
Carbohydrate	...53g	Saturates	.......3g

🍳 15 mins   🕐 15 mins

SERVES 4

I N G R E D I E N T S

250 g/9 oz dried Japanese egg noodles

2 tbsp sunflower oil

1 red onion, sliced

1 clove garlic, crushed

450 g/1 lb mixed mushrooms
   (shiitake, oyster, brown cap)

350 g/12 oz pak choi (or Chinese leaves)

2 tbsp sweet sherry

6 tbsp oyster sauce

4 spring onions, sliced

1 tbsp toasted sesame seeds

1 Place the Japanese egg noodles in a large bowl. Pour over enough boiling water to cover and leave them to soak for 10 minutes.

2 Heat the sunflower oil in a large preheated wok.

3 Add the red onion and garlic to the wok and stir-fry for 2–3 minutes, or until softened.

4 Add the mushrooms to the wok and stir-fry for about 5 minutes, or until the mushrooms have softened.

5 Drain the egg noodles thoroughly and set aside.

6 Add the pak choi (or Chinese leaves), noodles, sweet sherry and oyster sauce to the wok. Toss all of the ingredients together and stir-fry for 2–3 minutes or until the liquid is just beginning to bubble.

7 Transfer the mushroom noodles to warm serving bowls and scatter with sliced spring onions and toasted sesame seeds. Serve immediately.

COOK'S TIP
The variety of mushrooms in supermarkets has greatly improved and a good mixture should be easily obtainable. If not, use the more common button and flat mushrooms.

Hot & Sour Noodles

This simple, fast-food dish is sold from street food stalls in Thailand, with many and varied additions.

NUTRITIONAL INFORMATION

Calories	337	Sugars	.........1g
Protein	........10g	Fat	...........11g
Carbohydrate	...53g	Saturates	.......1g

  5 mins   8 mins

SERVES 4

INGREDIENTS

250 g/9 oz dried medium egg noodles

1 tbsp sesame oil

1 tbsp chilli oil

1 garlic clove, crushed

2 spring onions, finely chopped

55 g/2 oz button mushrooms, sliced

40 g/1½ oz dried Chinese black
mushrooms, soaked, drained and sliced

2 tbsp lime juice

3 tbsp light soy sauce

1 tsp sugar

salt

shredded Chinese leaves, to serve

TO GARNISH

2 tbsp chopped fresh coriander

2 tbsp chopped unsalted, dry-roasted
peanuts

COOK'S TIP

Thai chilli oil is very hot, so if you want a milder flavour, use vegetable oil for the initial cooking instead, then add a final drizzle of chilli oil just for seasoning.

1 Cook the noodles in a large pan of boiling water for 3–4 minutes or according to the packet instructions. Drain well, return to the pan, toss with the sesame oil and set aside.

2 Heat the chilli oil in a large frying pan or wok and quickly stir-fry the garlic, onions and button mushrooms for 2 minutes until just softened.

3 Add the black mushrooms, lime juice, soy sauce and sugar and continue stir-frying until boiling. Add the noodles and toss to mix.

4 Make a bed of shredded Chinese leaves on a serving platter and spoon the noodle mixture on top. Garnish with the fresh coriander and chopped peanuts and serve immediately.

Chilled Noodles & Peppers

This is a convenient dish to serve when you are arriving home just before family or friends. Quick to prepare and assemble, it is ready in minutes.

NUTRITIONAL INFORMATION

Calories	260	Sugars	........4g
Protein	.........4g	Fat	..........21g
Carbohydrate	...15g	Saturates	.......4g

🧊 5 mins   🕐 15 mins

SERVES 4–6

I N G R E D I E N T S

250 g/9 oz fresh ribbon noodles, or Chinese egg noodles

1 tbsp sesame oil

1 red pepper

1 yellow pepper

1 green pepper

6 spring onions, cut into matchsticks

salt

D R E S S I N G

5 tbsp sesame oil

2 tbsp light soy sauce

1 tbsp tahini

4–5 drops hot pepper sauce

1 Preheat the grill to medium. Cook the noodles in a large pan of boiling, salted water until they are almost tender. Drain them in a colander, run cold water through them and drain thoroughly. Tip the noodles into a bowl, stir in the sesame oil, cover and chill.

2 Cook the peppers under the grill, turning them over frequently, until they are blackened on all sides. Plunge into cold water, then skin them. Cut in half, remove the core and seeds and cut the flesh into thick strips. Set them aside in a covered container.

3 To make the dressing, mix together the sesame oil, light soy sauce, tahini and hot pepper sauce until well combined.

4 Pour the dressing on the noodles, reserving 1 tablespoon, and toss well. Turn the noodles into a serving dish, arrange the grilled peppers over the noodles and spoon on the reserved dressing. Scatter on the spring onion strips.

COOK'S TIP

If you have time, another way of skinning peppers is to first grill them, then place in a polythene bag, seal and leave for about 20 minutes. The skins will then peel off easily.

Spicy Japanese Noodles

These noodles are highly spiced with chilli and flavoured with sesame seeds for a nutty taste which is a true delight.

NUTRITIONAL INFORMATION

Calories	381	Sugars	........12g
Protein	.........11g	Fat	..........13g
Carbohydrate	...59g	Saturates	.......2g

 5 mins   15 mins

SERVES 4

I N G R E D I E N T S

450 g/1 lb fresh Japanese noodles

1 tbsp sesame oil

1 tbsp sesame seeds

1 tbsp sunflower oil

1 red onion, sliced

100 g/3½ oz mangetouts

175 g/6 oz carrots, thinly sliced

350 g/12 oz white cabbage, shredded

3 tbsp sweet chilli sauce

2 spring onions, sliced, to garnish

1 Bring a large saucepan of water to the boil. Add the Japanese noodles to the pan and cook for 2–3 minutes. Drain the noodles thoroughly.

2 Toss the noodles with the sesame oil and sesame seeds.

3 Heat the sunflower oil in a large preheated wok.

4 Add the onion slices, mangetouts, carrot slices and shredded cabbage to the wok and stir-fry for about 5 minutes.

5 Add the sweet chilli sauce to the wok and cook, stirring occasionally, for a further 2 minutes.

6 Add the sesame noodles to the wok, toss well to combine and heat through for a further 2–3 minutes.

7 Transfer the Japanese noodles and spicy vegetables to warm serving bowls and garnish with sliced spring onions. Serve immediately. If you prefer, you can serve the noodles separately with the sauce spooned on top.

COOK'S TIP

If fresh Japanese noodles are difficult to get hold of, use dried rice noodles or thin egg noodles instead.

Oriental Vegetable Noodles

This dish has a mild, nutty flavour from the peanut butter and dry-roasted peanuts.

NUTRITIONAL INFORMATION

Calories ....193 Sugars 5g
Protein ....7g Fat 12g
Carbohydrate ...14g Saturates 2g

  10 mins   15 mins

SERVES 4

INGREDIENTS

175 g/6 oz green thread noodles or
  multi-coloured spaghetti

1 tsp sesame oil

2 tbsp crunchy peanut butter

2 tbsp light soy sauce

1 tbsp white wine vinegar

1 tsp clear honey

salt and pepper

125 g/4½ oz mooli, grated

125 g/4½ oz carrot, grated

125 g/4½ oz cucumber, finely shredded

1 bunch spring onions, finely shredded

1 tbsp dry-roasted peanuts, crushed

TO GARNISH

carrot flowers

spring onion tassels (see page 131)

1 Bring a large saucepan of water to the boil, add the noodles or spaghetti and cook according to the packet instructions. Drain well and rinse in cold water. Set aside in a bowl of cold water until required.

2 To make the peanut butter sauce, put the sesame oil, peanut butter, soy sauce, vinegar and honey into a small screw-top jar. Seal tightly and shake well to mix thoroughly.

3 Drain the noodles or spaghetti well, place in a large serving bowl and mix in half the peanut sauce.

4 Using 2 forks, toss in the mooli, carrot, cucumber, and spring onions. Sprinkle with crushed peanuts and garnish with carrot flowers and spring onion tassels.

5 Serve the noodles with the remaining peanut sauce.

COOK'S TIP

There are many varieties of oriental noodles available from oriental markets, delicatessens and supermarkets. Try rice noodles, which contain very little fat and require little cooking; usually soaking in boiling water is sufficient.

Crispy Noodles & Tofu

This dish requires a certain amount of care and attention to get the crispy noodles properly cooked, but it is well worth the effort.

NUTRITIONAL INFORMATION

Calories	242	Sugars	........2g
Protein	........13g	Fat	..........17g
Carbohydrate	...10g	Saturates	.......3g

35 mins   25 mins

SERVES 4

INGREDIENTS

175 g/6 oz dried thread egg noodles

600 ml/1 pint sunflower oil, for deep-frying

2 tsp grated lemon peel

1 tbsp light soy sauce

1 tbsp rice vinegar

1 tbsp lemon juice

1½ tbsp sugar

250 g/9 oz marinated tofu, diced

2 garlic cloves, crushed

1 red chilli, deseeded and finely sliced

1 red pepper, deseeded and diced

4 eggs, beaten

red chilli strips, to garnish

1 Blanch the egg noodles briefly in hot water, to which a little of the oil has been added. Drain the noodles and spread out to dry for at least 30 minutes. Cut into threads about 7 cm/3 inches long.

2 Combine the lemon peel, light soy sauce, rice vinegar, lemon juice and sugar in a small bowl. Set the mixture aside until required.

3 Heat the sunflower oil in a wok or large, heavy frying pan, and test the temperature with a few strands of the noodles. They should swell to many times their original size, but if they do not, wait a little longer until the oil is hot enough; otherwise they will be tough and stringy, not puffy and light.

4 Cook the noodles in batches. As soon as they turn a pale gold colour, scoop them out and drain on plenty of absorbent kitchen paper. Leave to cool.

5 Reserve 2 tablespoons of the oil and pour off the rest. Heat the reserved oil in the wok or pan.

6 Add the marinated tofu to the wok or frying pan and cook quickly over a high heat to seal.

7 Add the crushed garlic cloves, sliced red chilli and diced red pepper to the wok. Stir-fry for 1–2 minutes.

8 Add the reserved vinegar mixture to the wok, stir to mix well and add the beaten eggs, stirring until they are set.

9 Serve the tofu mixture with the crispy fried noodles, garnished with a red chilli 'flower'.

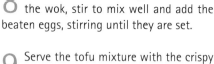
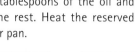

Fried Vegetable Noodles

In this recipe, noodles are first boiled and then deep-fried for a crisply textured dish, and tossed with fried vegetables.

NUTRITIONAL INFORMATION

Calories	229	Sugars	........4g
Protein	.........5g	Fat	..........15g
Carbohydrate	...20g	Saturates	.......2g

5 mins   25 mins

SERVES 4

INGREDIENTS

350 g/12 oz dried egg noodles

2 tbsp peanut oil

2 garlic cloves, crushed

½ tsp ground star anise

1 carrot, cut into matchsticks

1 green pepper, cut into matchsticks

1 onion, quartered and sliced

125 g/4 oz broccoli florets

75 g/3 oz bamboo shoots

1 celery stick, sliced

1 tbsp light soy sauce

150 ml/5 fl oz vegetable stock

oil, for deep-frying

1 tsp cornflour

2 tsp water

1 Cook the noodles in a saucepan of boiling water for 1–2 minutes. Drain well and rinse under cold running water. Leave the noodles to drain thoroughly in a colander until required.

2 Heat the peanut oil in a preheated wok until smoking. Reduce the heat, add the crushed garlic and ground star anise and stir-fry for 30 seconds. Add the remaining vegetables and stir-fry for 1–2 minutes.

3 Add the soy sauce and vegetable stock to the wok and cook over a low heat for 5 minutes.

4 Heat the oil for deep-frying in another wok to 180°C/350°F, or until a cube of bread browns in 30 seconds.

5 Using a fork, twist the drained noodles and form them into rounds. Deep-fry them in batches until crisp, turning once. Leave them to drain on kitchen paper.

6 Blend the cornflour with the water to form a paste and stir into the vegetables. Bring to the boil, stirring until the sauce is thickened and clear.

7 Arrange the noodles on a warm serving plate, spoon the vegetables on top and serve immediately.

Home-made Noodles

These noodles are simple to make; you do not need a pasta-making machine as they are rolled out by hand.

NUTRITIONAL INFORMATION

Calories 294   Sugars 3g
Protein . . . . .7g   Fat 15g
Carbohydrate . . .35g   Saturates 2g

🍠 20 mins   🕐 15 mins

SERVES 2–4

I N G R E D I E N T S

N O O D L E S
125 g/4½ oz plain flour

2 tbsp cornflour

½ tsp salt

125 ml/4 fl oz boiling water

5 tbsp vegetable oil

S T I R – F R Y
1 courgette, cut into matchsticks

1 celery stick, cut into matchsticks

1 carrot, cut into matchsticks

125 g/4½oz open-cap mushrooms, sliced

125 g/4½ oz broccoli florets and stalks, peeled and thinly sliced

1 leek, sliced

125 g/4½ oz beansprouts

1 tbsp soy sauce

2 tsp rice wine vinegar

½ tsp sugar

2 Make the noodles by breaking off small pieces of dough and rolling into balls. Roll each ball across a very lightly oiled work surface with the palm of your hand to form thin noodles. Do not worry if some of the noodles break into shorter lengths. Set the noodles aside.

3 Heat 3 tablespoons of vegetable oil in a wok. Add the noodles in batches and fry over a high heat for 1 minute. Reduce the heat and cook for a further 2 minutes. Remove and drain on absorbent kitchen paper. Set aside.

4 Heat the remaining vegetable oil in the wok. Add the courgette, celery and carrot, and stir-fry for 1 minute. Add the mushrooms, broccoli and leek, and stir-fry for a further minute.

5 Add the beansprouts, soy sauce, rice wine vinegar and sugar to the pan and mix well until thoroughly heated.

6 Add the noodles and continue to cook over a high heat until they are heated through, tossing with 2 forks to mix the ingredients. Serve immediately.

1 To prepare the noodles, sift the flour, cornflour and salt into a bowl. Make a well in the centre and pour in the boiling water and 1 teaspoon of oil. Mix quickly to make a soft dough. Cover and leave for 5–6 minutes.

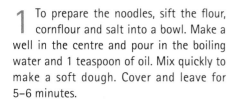

Sesame Hot Noodles

Plain egg noodles are tossed in a dressing made with sesame oil, soy sauce, peanut butter, coriander, lime, chilli and sesame seeds.

NUTRITIONAL INFORMATION

Calories 300   Sugars 1g
Protein ....7g   Fat 21g
Carbohydrate ...21g   Saturates 3g

5 mins   10 mins

SERVES 4

INGREDIENTS

500 g/18 oz dried medium egg noodles

3 tbsp sunflower oil

2 tbsp sesame oil

1 garlic clove, crushed

1 tbsp smooth peanut butter

1 small green chilli, deseeded and very finely chopped

3 tbsp toasted sesame seeds

4 tbsp light soy sauce

½ tbsp lime juice

salt and pepper

4 tbsp chopped fresh coriander

1 Place the noodles in a large pan of boiling water, then immediately remove from the heat. Cover and leave to stand for 6 minutes, stirring once halfway through the time. At the end of 6 minutes the noodles will be perfectly cooked. Alternatively, cook the noodles following the packet instructions.

2 Meanwhile, make the dressing. Mix together the sunflower oil, sesame oil, crushed garlic and peanut butter in a mixing bowl until smooth.

3 Add the chopped green chilli, sesame seeds and light soy sauce to the bowl.

Add the lime juice, according to taste, and mix well. Season to taste with salt and pepper.

4 Drain the noodles thoroughly then place in a heated serving bowl.

5 Add the dressing and chopped fresh coriander to the noodles and toss well to mix. Serve hot as a main meal or as an accompaniment.

COOK'S TIP
If you are cooking the noodles ahead of time, toss the cooked, drained noodles in 2 tsp sesame oil, then turn into a bowl. Cover and keep warm until required.

Noodle & Mango Salad

Fruit combines well with the peanut dressing, peppers and chilli in this delicious hot salad.

NUTRITIONAL INFORMATION

Calories 368   Sugars 11g
Protein ....11g   Fat 26g
Carbohydrate ...24g   Saturates 5g

15 mins   5 mins

SERVES 4

INGREDIENTS

250 g/9 oz dried thread egg noodles

2 tbsp groundnut oil

4 shallots, sliced

2 cloves garlic, crushed

1 red chilli, deseeded and sliced

1 red pepper, deseeded and sliced

1 green pepper, deseeded and sliced

1 ripe mango, sliced into thin strips

25 g/1 oz salted peanuts, chopped

DRESSING

4 tbsp peanut butter

100 ml/3½ fl oz coconut milk

1 tbsp tomato purée

1 Place the egg noodles in a large dish or bowl. Pour over enough boiling water to cover the noodles and leave to stand for 10 minutes.

2 Heat the groundnut oil in a large preheated wok or frying pan.

3 Add the shallots, crushed garlic, chilli and pepper slices to the wok or frying pan and stir-fry for 2–3 minutes.

4 Drain the egg noodles thoroughly in a colander. Add the drained noodles and mango slices to the wok or frying pan and heat through for about 2 minutes.

5 Transfer the noodle and mango salad to warmed serving dishes and scatter with chopped peanuts.

6 To make the dressing, mix together the peanut butter, coconut milk and tomato purée then spoon over the noodle salad. Serve immediately.

COOK'S TIP

If preferred, gently heat the peanut dressing before pouring over the noodle salad.

Courgette & Basil Risotto

An easy way of livening up a simple risotto is to use a flavoured olive oil. Here a basil-flavoured oil heightens the taste of the dish.

NUTRITIONAL INFORMATION

Calories	460	Sugars	.........5g
Protein	........13g	Fat	..........18g
Carbohydrate	...64g	Saturates	.......7g

 5–10 mins 🕐 35 mins

SERVES 4

I N G R E D I E N T S

4 tbsp basil-flavoured extra virgin olive oil, plus extra for drizzling

4 courgettes, diced

1 yellow pepper, deseeded and diced

2 garlic cloves, finely chopped

1 large onion, finely chopped

400 g/14 oz arborio or carnaroli rice

4 tbsp dry white vermouth

1.5 litres/2¾ pints vegetable stock, simmering

2 tbsp unsalted butter, at room temperature

large handful of fresh basil leaves, torn, plus a few leaves to garnish

85 g/3 oz Parmesan cheese, freshly grated

1 Heat half the olive oil in a large frying pan over high heat. When very hot, but not smoking, add the diced courgettes and yellow pepper and stir-fry for 3 minutes until lightly golden. Stir in the chopped garlic and cook for about 30 seconds longer. Transfer to a plate and set aside.

2 Heat the remaining oil in a large heavy-based pan over a medium heat. Add the onion and cook, stirring occasionally, for about 2 minutes until softened. Add the rice and cook, stirring frequently, for about 2 minutes until the rice is translucent and well coated with the olive oil.

3 Pour in the vermouth; it will bubble and steam rapidly and evaporate almost immediately. Add a ladleful (about 225 ml/8 fl oz) of the simmering stock and cook, stirring constantly until the stock is completely absorbed.

4 Continue adding the stock, about half a ladleful at a time, allowing each addition to be absorbed before adding the next. This should take 20–25 minutes. The risotto should have a creamy consistency and the rice should be tender, but still firm to the bite.

5 Stir in the courgette mixture with any juices, the butter, basil and grated Parmesan. Drizzle with a little oil and garnish with basil. Serve hot.

Mooli Curry

This is rather an unusual recipe for a vegetarian curry using mooli, a long white radish. The dish is good served hot with chapatis.

NUTRITIONAL INFORMATION

Calories	384	Sugars	.........4g
Protein	.........3g	Fat	..........38g
Carbohydrate	....9g	Saturates	.......4g

🍴 10 mins 🕐 20 mins

SERVES 4

INGREDIENTS

500 g/1 lb 2 oz mooli, preferably
   with leaves

1 tbsp moong dhal (see page 441)

600 ml/1 pint water

150 ml/¼ pint vegetable oil

1 onion, thinly sliced

1 tsp crushed garlic

1 tsp crushed dried red chillies

1 tsp salt

1 Rinse, peel and roughly slice the mooli, with its leaves, if using.

2 Place the mooli, the leaves, if using, and the moong dhal in a large saucepan and pour over the water. Bring to the boil and cook over a medium heat until the mooli has softened.

3 Drain the mooli mixture thoroughly and squeeze out any excess water, using your hands.

4 Heat the vegetable oil in a heavy-based saucepan. Add the onion, garlic, crushed red chillies and salt and fry over a medium heat, stirring from time to time, for about 5–7 minutes, until the onions have softened and turned light golden brown in colour.

5 Stir the mooli mixture into the spiced onion mixture and combine well. Reduce the heat and continue cooking, stirring frequently, for about 3–5 minutes.

6 Transfer the mooli curry to individual warmed serving plates and serve hot with chapatis.

COOK'S TIP

The vegetable used in this recipe, mooli, looks a bit like a parsnip without the tapering end and is now sold in most supermarkets, as well as in Indian grocers.

Kofta Kebabs

Traditionally, koftas are made from a spicy meat mixture, but this bean and wheat version makes a tasty vegetarian alternative.

NUTRITIONAL INFORMATION

Calories 598	Sugars 7g	
Protein 26g	Fat 17g	
Carbohydrate . . .90g	Saturates 3g	

1 hr 20 mins   1½ hrs

SERVES 4

INGREDIENTS

175 g/6 oz aduki beans

175 g/6 oz bulgur wheat

450 ml/16 fl oz vegetable stock

3 tbsp olive oil, plus extra for brushing

1 onion, finely chopped

2 garlic cloves, crushed

1 tsp ground coriander

1 tsp ground cumin

2 tbsp chopped fresh coriander

salt and pepper

3 eggs, beaten

125 g/4½ oz dried breadcrumbs

TABBOULEH

175 g/6 oz bulgur wheat

2 tbsp lemon juice

1 tbsp olive oil

6 tbsp chopped fresh parsley

4 spring onions, finely chopped

60 g/2 oz cucumber, finely chopped

3 tbsp chopped fresh mint

1 extra-large tomato, finely chopped

TO SERVE

black olives

pitta bread

1 Cook the aduki beans in boiling water for 15 minutes, until tender, then simmer for 20–30 minutes. Drain, rinse and leave to cool. Cook the bulgur wheat in the stock for 10 minutes, until the stock is absorbed. Set aside.

2 Heat 1 tablespoon of the oil in a frying pan and fry the onion, garlic and spices for 4–5 minutes.

3 Transfer to a bowl, together with the beans, spices, seasoning and eggs and mash with a potato masher or fork. Stir in the breadcrumbs and bulgur wheat. Cover and chill for 1 hour, until firm.

4 To make the tabbouleh, soak the bulgur wheat in 425 ml/¾ pint of boiling water for 15 minutes or until all the water has been absorbed. Combine with the remaining ingredients then cover and chill until required.

5 With wet hands, mould the kofta mixture into 32 oval shapes.

6 Press on to skewers, brush with oil and grill for 5–6 minutes until golden. Turn, brush with oil again and cook for 5–6 minutes. Drain on kitchen paper. Garnish and serve with the tabbouleh, black olives and pitta bread.

Deep South Rice & Beans

Cajun spices add a flavour of the American Deep South to this colourful rice and red kidney bean salad.

NUTRITIONAL INFORMATION

Calories	336	Sugars	.........8g
Protein	.........7g	Fat	..........13g
Carbohydrate	...51g	Saturates	.......2g

 10 mins   15 mins

SERVES 4

I N G R E D I E N T S

175 g/6 oz long grain rice

4 tbsp olive oil

1 small green pepper, deseeded and chopped

1 small red pepper, deseeded and chopped

1 onion, finely chopped

1 small red or green chilli, deseeded and finely chopped

2 tomatoes, chopped

125 g/4½ oz canned red kidney beans, rinsed and drained

1 tbsp chopped fresh basil

2 tsp chopped fresh thyme

1 tsp Cajun spice

salt and pepper

fresh basil leaves, to garnish

1 Cook the rice in plenty of boiling, lightly salted water for about 12 minutes, until it is just tender. Rinse under cold water, drain well and set aside.

2 Meanwhile, heat the olive oil in a frying pan, add the green and red peppers and the onion and fry gently for about 5 minutes, until softened.

3 Add the chilli and tomatoes, and cook for a further 2 minutes.

4 Add the vegetable mixture and the drained red kidney beans to the rice. Stir well to combine thoroughly.

5 Stir the chopped fresh herbs and the Cajun spice into the rice mixture.

6 Season the salad to taste with salt and pepper, and serve, garnished with fresh basil leaves.

Milanese Risotto

Italian rice is a round, short-grained variety with a nutty flavour, which is essential for a good risotto. Arborio is a good one to use.

NUTRITIONAL INFORMATION

Calories	631	Sugars	. . . . .1g
Protein	. . . . .16g	Fat	. . . . .29g
Carbohydrate	. . .77g	Saturates	. . . . . .17g

10 mins   35 mins

SERVES 4

INGREDIENTS

2 good pinches of saffron threads

1 large onion, chopped finely

1–2 garlic cloves, crushed

90 g/3 oz butter

350 g/12 oz arborio rice

150 ml/¼ pint dry white wine

1.2 litres/2 pints boiling vegetable stock

90 g/3 oz Parmesan cheese, grated

salt and pepper

1 Put the saffron in a small bowl, cover with 3–4 tablespoons of boiling water and leave to soak while you prepare the risotto.

2 Fry the onion and garlic in 60 g/2 oz of the butter until they are soft but not coloured. Add the rice and continue to cook for 2–3 minutes or until all of the grains are coated in oil and just beginning to colour lightly.

3 Add the wine to the rice and simmer gently, stirring from time to time, until it is all absorbed.

4 Add the boiling stock a little at a time, about 150 ml/¼ pint, cooking until the liquid is fully absorbed before adding more, and stirring frequently.

5 When all the stock has been absorbed (this should take about 20 minutes), the rice should be tender but not soft and soggy. Add the saffron liquid, Parmesan, remaining butter and salt and pepper to taste. Leave to simmer for 2 minutes until piping hot and thoroughly mixed.

6 Cover the pan tightly and leave to stand for 5 minutes off the heat. Give a good stir and serve at once.

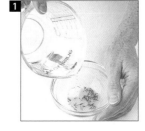

Spiced Basmati Pilau

The whole spices are not meant to be eaten and may be removed before serving. Omit the broccoli and mushrooms for a plain, spiced pilau.

NUTRITIONAL INFORMATION

Calories ....450 Sugars 3g
Protein ....9g Fat 15g
Carbohydrate ...76g Saturates 2g

20 mins   25 mins

SERVES 4

INGREDIENTS

500 g/1 lb 2 oz basmati rice

175 g/6 oz broccoli, trimmed

6 tbsp vegetable oil

2 large onions, chopped

225 g/8 oz mushrooms, sliced

2 garlic cloves, crushed

6 cardamom pods, split

6 whole cloves

8 black peppercorns

1 cinnamon stick or piece of cassia bark

1 tsp turmeric

1.2 litres/2 pints boiling vegetable stock or water

salt and pepper

60 g/2 oz seedless raisins

60 g/2 oz unsalted pistachios, roughly chopped

VARIATION

For added richness, you could stir a spoonful of ghee through the rice mixture just before serving. A little diced red pepper and a few cooked peas forked through at step 4 add a colourful touch.

1 Place the rice in a sieve and wash well under cold running water. Drain. Trim off most of the broccoli stalk and cut into small florets, then quarter the stalk lengthways and cut diagonally into 1 cm/½ inch pieces.

2 Heat the oil in a large saucepan. Add the onions and broccoli stalks and cook over a low heat, stirring frequently, for 3 minutes. Add the mushrooms, rice, garlic and spices and cook for 1 minute, stirring, until the rice is coated in oil.

3 Add the boiling stock and season to taste with salt and pepper. Stir in the broccoli florets and return the mixture to the boil. Cover, reduce the heat and cook over a low heat for 15 minutes without uncovering the pan.

4 Remove the pan from the heat and leave the pilau to stand for 5 minutes without uncovering. Remove the whole spices, add the raisins and pistachios and gently fork through to fluff up the grains. Serve the pilau hot.

Tabbouleh Salad

This kind of salad is eaten widely throughout the Middle East. The flavour improves as it is kept, so it tastes even better on the second day.

NUTRITIONAL INFORMATION

Calories 637	Sugars 8g	
Protein 20g	Fat 41g	
Carbohydrate . . .50g	Saturates 11g	

 1½ hrs   5–10 mins

SERVES 2

I N G R E D I E N T S

125 g/4½ oz bulgur wheat

600 ml/1 pint boiling water

1 red pepper, deseeded and halved

3 tbsp olive oil

1 garlic clove, crushed

grated rind of ½ lime

about 1 tbsp lime juice

salt and pepper

1 tbsp chopped fresh mint

1 tbsp chopped fresh parsley

3–4 spring onions, trimmed and
    thinly sliced

8 stoned black olives, halved

40 g/1½ oz large salted peanuts or
    cashew nuts

1–2 tsp lemon juice

60–90 g/2–3 oz Gruyère cheese

fresh mint sprigs, to garnish

warm pitta bread or crusty rolls, to serve

1 Put the bulgur wheat into a bowl and cover with the boiling water to reach about 2.5 cm/1 inch above the bulgar. Set aside to soak for up to 1 hour, until most of the water is absorbed and is cold.

2 Meanwhile, put the halved red pepper, skin side upwards, on a grill rack and cook under a preheated moderate grill until the skin is thoroughly charred and blistered. Leave to cool slightly.

3 When the pepper is cool enough to handle, peel off the skin and discard the seeds, then cut the pepper flesh into narrow strips.

4 Whisk together the oil, garlic and lime rind and juice. Season to taste with salt and pepper and whisk until thoroughly blended. Add 4½ teaspoons of the dressing to the peppers and mix lightly.

5 Drain the soaked bulgur wheat thoroughly, squeezing it in a dry cloth to make it even drier, then place in a bowl.

6 Add the chopped herbs, spring onions, olives and peanuts or cashew nuts to the bulgar and toss well to combine. Add the lemon juice to the remaining dressing, and stir through the salad. Spoon the salad on to 2 serving plates.

7 Cut the cheese into narrow strips and mix with the pepper strips. Spoon alongside the bulgur salad. Garnish with mint sprigs and serve with warm pitta bread or crusty rolls.

Thai Jasmine Rice

Every Thai meal has as its centrepiece a big bowl of steaming, fluffy Thai jasmine rice, to which salt should not be added.

NUTRITIONAL INFORMATION

Calories	239	Sugars	.........0g
Protein	.........5g	Fat	...........2g
Carbohydrate	...54g	Saturates	.....0.6g

 5 mins   10–15 mins

SERVES 4

INGREDIENTS

OPEN PAN METHOD

225 g/8 oz Thai jasmine rice

1 litre/1¾ pints water

ABSORPTION METHOD

225 g/8 oz Thai jasmine rice

450 ml/16 fl oz water

1 For the open pan method, rinse the rice in a sieve under cold running water and leave to drain.

2 Bring the water to the boil. Add the rice, stir once and return to a medium boil. Cook, uncovered, for 8–10 minutes, until tender.

3 Drain thoroughly and fork through lightly before serving.

4 For the absorption method, rinse the rice under cold running water.

5 Put the rice and water into a saucepan and bring to the boil. Stir once and then cover the pan tightly.

Lower the heat as much as possible. Cook for 10 minutes, and leave to rest for a further 5 minutes.

6 Fork through lightly and serve the rice immediately.

COOK'S TIP

Thai jasmine rice can be frozen. Freeze in a plastic sealed container. Frozen rice is ideal for stir-fry dishes, as the process seems to separate the grains.

Couscous Royale

Serve this stunning dish as a centrepiece for a North African-style feast; it will prove to be a truly memorable meal.

NUTRITIONAL INFORMATION

Calories	329	Sugars	. . . . . . .31g
Protein	. . . . .6g	Fat	. . . . .13g
Carbohydrate	. . .50g	Saturates	. . . . . . .6g

25 mins   45 mins

SERVES 6

I N G R E D I E N T S

3 carrots

3 courgettes

350 g/12 oz pumpkin or squash

1.25 litres/2¼ pints vegetable stock

2 cinnamon sticks, broken in half

2 tsp ground cumin

1 tsp ground coriander

pinch of saffron strands

2 tbsp olive oil

pared rind and juice of 1 lemon

2 tbsp clear honey

500 g/1 lb 2 oz pre-cooked couscous

60 g/2 oz butter, softened

175 g/6 oz large seedless raisins

salt and pepper

fresh coriander, to garnish

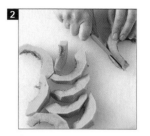

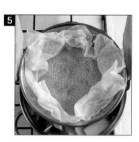

1 Cut the carrots and courgettes into 7 cm/3 inch pieces and cut these in half lengthways.

2 Trim the pumpkin or squash, remove the seeds with a spoon and discard them. Peel and cut into pieces the same size as the carrots and courgettes.

3 Put the stock, spices, saffron and carrots in a large saucepan. Bring to the boil, skim off any scum and add the olive oil. Simmer for 15 minutes.

4 Add the lemon rind and juice to the pan, together with the clear honey, courgettes and pumpkin or squash. Season well. Bring back to the boil and simmer for a further 10 minutes.

5 Meanwhile, soak the couscous according to the packet instructions. Transfer it to a steamer or large sieve lined with muslin and place over the vegetable pan. Cover and steam as directed. Stir in the butter.

6 Pile the couscous on to a warmed serving plate. Drain the vegetables, reserving the stock, lemon rind and cinnamon. Arrange the vegetables on top of the couscous. Put the raisins on top and spoon over 6 tablespoons of the reserved stock. Keep warm.

7 Return the remaining stock to the heat and boil for 5 minutes until it has reduced slightly. Remove the lemon rind and cinnamon stick from the sauce and discard them.

8 Garnish the dish with sprigs of fresh coriander and serve immediately, passing round the sauce separately.

Risotto Verde

Baby spinach and fresh herbs are the basis of this colourful, refreshing and summery risotto.

NUTRITIONAL INFORMATION

Calories 374   Sugars 5g
Protein ....10g   Fat 9g
Carbohydrate ...55g   Saturates 2g

 5 mins   45 mins

SERVES 4

INGREDIENTS

1.7 litres/3 pints vegetable stock

2 tbsp olive oil

2 garlic cloves, crushed

2 leeks, shredded

225 g/8 oz arborio rice

300 ml/10 fl oz dry white wine

4 tbsp chopped fresh mixed herbs

225 g/8 oz baby spinach

salt and pepper

3 tbsp low-fat natural yogurt

shredded leek, to garnish

1 Pour the stock into a large pan and bring it to the boil. Reduce the heat to a simmer.

2 Meanwhile, heat the oil in a separate pan and cook the garlic and leeks, stirring occasionally, for 2–3 minutes until softened, but not browned.

3 Stir in the rice and cook, stirring constantly, until translucent and well coated with oil.

4 Pour in half of the wine and a little of the hot stock; it will bubble and steam rapidly. Cook over a gentle heat until all of the liquid has been absorbed.

5 Add the remaining stock and wine and cook over a low heat for 25 minutes or until the rice is creamy.

6 Stir in the chopped mixed herbs and the baby spinach, season to taste with salt and pepper and cook for a further 2 minutes. Stir in the natural yogurt.

7 Garnish with the shredded leek and serve the risotto immediately.

COOK'S TIP

Do not hurry the process of cooking the risotto as the rice must absorb the liquid slowly in order for it to reach the correct consistency.

Rice with Fruit & Nuts

Here is a tasty and filling rice dish that is nice and spicy and includes fruits for a refreshing flavour and toasted nuts for a crunchy texture.

NUTRITIONAL INFORMATION

Calories ......423 Sugars 19g
Protein ....10g Fat 17g
Carbohydrate ...62g Saturates 2g

20 mins

1 hr

SERVES 6

INGREDIENTS

4 tbsp ghee or vegetable oil

1 large onion, chopped

2 garlic cloves, crushed

2.5 cm/1 inch piece of fresh root ginger, chopped

1 tsp chilli powder

1 tsp cumin seeds

1 tbsp mild or medium curry powder or paste

300 g/10½ oz brown rice

850 ml/1½ pints boiling vegetable stock

400 g/14 oz canned chopped tomatoes

salt and pepper

175 g/6 oz ready-to-eat dried apricots or peaches, cut into slivers

1 red pepper, deseeded and diced

85 g/3 oz frozen peas

1–2 small, slightly green bananas

55–85 g/2–3 oz toasted nuts, such as almonds, cashews and hazelnuts or pine nuts

fresh coriander sprigs, to garnish

1 Heat the ghee or oil in a large pan. Add the onion and cook over a low heat for 3 minutes. Stir in the garlic, ginger, spices and rice and cook gently, stirring constantly, for 2 minutes, until the rice is coated in the spiced oil.

2 Pour in the boiling stock, add the chopped tomatoes and season with salt and pepper to taste. Bring to the boil, then reduce the heat, cover and simmer gently for 40 minutes or until the rice is almost cooked and most of the liquid has been absorbed.

3 Add the slivered apricots or peaches, diced red pepper and peas. Cover and continue cooking for 10 minutes. Remove from the heat and set aside for 5 minutes without uncovering.

4 Peel and slice the bananas. Uncover the rice mixture and fork through to mix the ingredients and fluff up the rice. Add the toasted nuts and sliced bananas and toss together lightly. Transfer the mixture to a warmed serving platter and garnish with the fresh coriander sprigs. Serve immediately.

Fried Rice with Spicy Beans

This rice is really colourful and satisfyingly crunchy with the addition of sweetcorn and red kidney beans.

NUTRITIONAL INFORMATION

Calories	363	Sugars	.........3g
Protein	........10g	Fat	..........11g
Carbohydrate	...61g	Saturates	.......2g

 10 mins   25 mins

SERVES 4

INGREDIENTS

3 tbsp sunflower oil

1 onion, finely chopped

225 g/8 oz long grain rice

1 green pepper, deseeded and diced

1 tsp chilli powder

600 ml/1 pint boiling water

100 g/3½ oz canned sweetcorn drained

225 g/8 oz canned red kidney beans, drained and rinsed

2 tbsp chopped fresh coriander, plus extra for garnish (optional)

1 Heat the sunflower oil in a large preheated wok.

2 Add the onion and stir-fry over a medium heat for about 2 minutes or until softened.

3 Lower the heat, add the rice, green pepper and chilli powder to the wok and stir-fry for 1 minute.

4 Pour in the boiling water. Bring back to the boil, then reduce the heat and simmer for 15 minutes.

5 Stir in the sweetcorn, kidney beans and coriander and heat through, stirring occasionally.

6 Transfer to a warmed serving bowl and serve hot, sprinkled with extra coriander, if wished.

COOK'S TIP

For perfect fried rice, the raw rice should ideally be soaked in a bowl of water for a short time before cooking to remove excess starch. Short grain Oriental rice can be substituted for the long grain rice.

Refried Bean Nachos

A Mexican classic, refried beans and tortilla chips are topped with luscious melted cheese, salsa and assorted toppings.

NUTRITIONAL INFORMATION

Calories	287	Sugars	.........2g
Protein	........15g	Fat	..........15g
Carbohydrate	...22g	Saturates	.......7g

15 mins   15 mins

SERVES 6–8

INGREDIENTS

400 g/14 oz canned refried beans

400 g/14 oz canned pinto beans, drained

large pinch of ground cumin

large pinch of mild chilli powder

175 g/6 oz tortilla chips

225 g/8 oz grated cheese, such as Cheddar

salsa of your choice

1 avocado, stoned, diced and tossed with
lime juice

½ small onion or 3–5 spring
onions, chopped

2 ripe tomatoes, diced

handful of shredded lettuce

3–4 tbsp chopped fresh coriander

soured cream, to serve

1 Place the refried beans in a pan with the pinto beans, cumin and chilli powder. Add enough water to make a thick soup-like consistency, stirring gently so that the beans do not lose their texture.

2 Heat the bean mixture over a medium heat until hot, then reduce the heat and keep the mixture warm while you prepare the rest of the dish.

3 Arrange half the tortilla chips in the bottom of a flameproof casserole or gratin dish and cover with the bean mixture. Sprinkle with the cheese and bake in a preheated oven, 200°C/ 400°F/Gas Mark 6, until the cheese melts.

4 Alternatively, place the casserole under a preheated grill and grill for 5–7 minutes or until the cheese melts and lightly sizzles in places.

5 Arrange the salsa, avocado, onion, tomatoes, lettuce and fresh coriander on top of the melted cheese. Surround with the remaining tortilla chips and serve immediately with soured cream.

VARIATION
Replace the soured cream with Greek-style yogurt as an alternative.

Cashew Nut Paella

This vegetarian version of paella is packed with vegetables and nuts for a truly delicious and simple dish.

NUTRITIONAL INFORMATION

Calories 406   Sugars 8g
Protein ....10g   Fat 22g
Carbohydrate ...44g   Saturates 6g

15 mins   35 mins

SERVES 4

INGREDIENTS

2 tbsp olive oil

1 tbsp butter

1 red onion, chopped

150 g/5½ oz arborio rice

1 tsp turmeric

1 tsp ground cumin

½ tsp chilli powder

3 garlic cloves, crushed

1 fresh green chilli, deseeded and sliced

1 green pepper, deseeded and diced

1 red pepper, deseeded and diced

85 g/3 oz baby sweetcorn cobs,
   halved lengthways

2 tbsp stoned black olives

1 large tomato, deseeded and diced

450 ml/16 fl oz vegetable stock

85 g/3 oz unsalted cashew nuts

55 g/2 oz frozen peas

salt and pepper

2 tbsp chopped fresh parsley

pinch of cayenne pepper

fresh herbs, to garnish

1 Heat the olive oil and butter in a large frying pan or paella pan until the butter has melted.

2 Add the onion and cook over a medium heat, stirring constantly, for 2–3 minutes until softened.

3 Stir in the rice, turmeric, cumin, chilli powder, garlic, sliced chilli, green and red peppers, corn cobs, olives and tomato and cook over a medium heat, stirring occasionally, for 1–2 minutes.

4 Pour in the stock and bring the mixture to the boil. Reduce the heat and cook gently, stirring constantly, for a further 20 minutes.

5 Add the cashew nuts and peas and continue to cook, stirring occasionally, for a further 5 minutes. Season to taste with salt and pepper and add the chopped fresh parsley and a pinch of cayenne pepper. Transfer the paella to warm serving plates, garnish with fresh herbs and serve immediately.

Mushroom & Cheese Risotto

Make this creamy risotto with Italian arborio rice and freshly grated Parmesan cheese for the best results.

NUTRITIONAL INFORMATION

Calories	358	Sugars	.........3g
Protein	........11g	Fat	..........14g
Carbohydrate	...50g	Saturates	.......5g

20 mins   40 mins

SERVES 4

INGREDIENTS

2 tbsp olive or vegetable oil

225 g/8 oz arborio rice

2 garlic cloves, crushed

1 onion, chopped

2 celery sticks, chopped

1 red or green pepper, deseeded and chopped

225 g/8 oz mushrooms, sliced

1 tbsp chopped fresh oregano or 1 tsp dried oregano

1 litre/1¾ pints vegetable stock

55 g /2 oz sun-dried tomatoes in olive oil, drained and chopped (optional)

55 g/2 oz Parmesan cheese, finely grated

salt and pepper

TO GARNISH

fresh flat-leaved parsley sprigs

fresh bay leaves

1 Heat the oil in a wok or large frying pan. Add the rice and cook, stirring constantly, for 5 minutes.

2 Add the garlic, onion, celery and pepper and cook, stirring constantly, for 5 minutes. Add the mushrooms and cook for 3–4 minutes.

3 Stir in the oregano and stock. Heat until just boiling, then reduce the heat, cover and simmer for 20 minutes or until the rice is tender and creamy.

4 Add the sun-dried tomatoes, if using, and season the risotto to taste with salt and pepper. Stir in half of the grated Parmesan cheese.

5 Top with the remaining cheese, garnish with flat-leaved parsley and bay leaves and serve.

Mixed Mushroom Risotto

This creamy risotto is flavoured with a mixture of wild and cultivated mushrooms and fresh thyme.

NUTRITIONAL INFORMATION

Calories	364	Sugars	.........1g
Protein	........15g	Fat	..........16g
Carbohydrate	...44g	Saturates	.......6g

 15 mins   30 mins

SERVES 4

INGREDIENTS

2 tbsp olive oil

1 large onion, finely chopped

1 garlic clove, crushed

200 g/7 oz mixed wild and cultivated mushrooms, such as ceps, oyster, porcini and button, wiped and sliced if large

250 g/9 oz arborio rice, washed

pinch saffron threads

700 ml/1¼ pints hot vegetable stock

60 ml/4 tbsp dry white wine

100 g/3½ oz Parmesan cheese, grated, plus extra for serving

2 tbsp chopped fresh thyme

salt and pepper

COOK'S TIP

Wild mushrooms have their own distinctive flavours and make a change from button mushrooms. However, they can be quite expensive, so you can always use a mixture with chestnut or button mushrooms instead.

1 Heat the olive oil in a large frying pan. Add the onions and garlic and sauté for 3–4 minutes, or until softened.

2 Add the mushrooms to the pan and cook for a further 3 minutes, or until they are just beginning to brown.

3 Add the rice and saffron to the pan and stir to coat the rice in the oil.

4 Mix together the stock and the wine and add to the pan, a ladleful at a time. Stir the rice mixture and allow the liquid to be fully absorbed before adding more liquid, a ladleful at a time.

5 When all of the wine and stock has been incorporated, the rice should be cooked. Test by tasting a grain – it should be soft, but still retain some of its 'bite'. If it is still crunchy, add a little more hot water and continue cooking. It should take about 20 minutes to cook.

6 Stir in the grated Parmesan cheese and the chopped thyme, and season to taste with freshly ground black pepper. Leave to stand for a few minutes.

7 Transfer the risotto to warmed serving plates and serve sprinkled with extra Parmesan cheese.

Green Risotto

A simple rice dish cooked with green vegetables and herbs, this recipe has been adapted for the microwave.

NUTRITIONAL INFORMATION

Calories	344	Sugars 4g
Protein	........13g	Fat 10g
Carbohydrate	...54g	Saturates 4g

🥔 15 mins   🕐 20 mins

SERVES 4

INGREDIENTS

1 onion, chopped

2 tbsp olive oil

225 g/8 oz arborio rice

700 ml/1¼ pints hot vegetable stock

350 g/12 oz mixed green vegetables,
  such as asparagus, French beans,
  mangetouts, courgettes, broccoli florets,
  frozen peas

2 tbsp chopped fresh parsley

salt and pepper

60 g/2 oz fresh Parmesan cheese,
  thinly shaved

1 Place the onion and olive oil in a large bowl. Cover and cook on HIGH power for 2 minutes.

2 Add the rice and stir until thoroughly coated in the oil. Pour in about 75 ml/ 3 fl oz of the hot stock. Cook, uncovered, for 2 minutes, until the liquid has been absorbed. Pour in another 75 ml/3 fl oz of the stock and cook, uncovered, on HIGH power for 2 minutes. Repeat once more.

3 Chop or slice the vegetables into even-sized pieces. Stir into the rice with the remaining stock. Cover and cook

on HIGH power for 8 minutes, stirring occasionally, until most of the liquid has been absorbed and the rice is just tender.

4 Stir in the chopped parsley and season generously with salt and pepper. Leave the risotto to stand, covered, for about 5 minutes. The rice should be tender and creamy.

5 Scatter the Parmesan cheese over the risotto before serving.

COOK'S TIP

For extra texture, stir in a few toasted pine kernels or coarsely chopped cashew nuts at the end of the cooking time.

Rice-stuffed Mushrooms

Flat mushrooms are ideal for baking. They are filled with more strongly flavoured wild mushrooms, although you can use the ordinary varieties.

NUTRITIONAL INFORMATION

Calories 168	Sugars 1g
Protein 7g	Fat 3g
Carbohydrate ...23g	Saturates 1g

 25 mins   35 mins

SERVES 4

INGREDIENTS

4 large flat mushrooms

100 g/3½ oz assorted wild mushrooms, sliced

4 dry-pack sun-dried tomatoes, shredded

150 ml/5 fl oz dry red wine

4 spring onions, trimmed and finely chopped

75 g/2¾ oz cooked red rice

salt and pepper

2 tbsp freshly grated Parmesan cheese

4 thick slices granary bread

spring onion, shredded, to garnish

1 Preheat the oven to 190°C/375°F/Gas Mark 5. Peel the flat mushrooms, pull out the stalks and set aside. Finely chop the stalks and place in a saucepan.

2 Add the wild mushrooms to the saucepan along with the tomatoes and red wine.

3 Bring to the boil, cover and gently simmer the tomatoes and mushrooms for 2–3 minutes until just tender. Drain off and reserve the cooking liquid. Place the mixture in a small bowl.

4 Gently stir in the chopped spring onions and cooked rice. Season well, and spoon into the flat mushrooms, pressing the mixture down gently. Sprinkle with the grated Parmesan.

5 Arrange the mushrooms in an ovenproof baking dish and pour the reserved cooking juices around them. Bake in the oven for 20–25 minutes until they are just cooked.

6 Trim the crusts from the bread and lightly toast each side under a hot grill.

7 Drain the mushrooms and place each one on a piece of toast. Garnish with spring onions and serve.

Pesto Rice with Garlic Bread

Try this combination of two types of rice with the richness of pine kernels, basil and freshly grated Parmesan.

NUTRITIONAL INFORMATION

Calories 918   Sugars 2g
Protein . . . . .18g   Fat 64g
Carbohydrate . . .73g   Saturates 19g

🍲 20 mins   🕐 40 mins

SERVES 4

I N G R E D I E N T S

300 g/10½ oz mixed long-grain and
  wild rice

fresh basil sprigs, to garnish

tomato and orange salad, to serve

P E S T O   D R E S S I N G

15 g/½ oz fresh basil

125 g/4½ oz pine kernels

2 garlic cloves, crushed

6 tbsp olive oil

60 g/2 oz Parmesan cheese, freshly grated

salt and pepper

G A R L I C   B R E A D

2 small granary or wholemeal French bread
  sticks

90 g/3 oz butter or margarine, softened

2 garlic cloves, crushed

1 tsp dried mixed herbs

1 Place the rice in a saucepan and cover with water. Bring to the boil and cook for 15–20 minutes. Drain well and keep warm.

2 Meanwhile, make the pesto dressing. Remove the basil leaves from the stalks and finely chop the leaves. Reserve 25 g/1 oz of the pine kernels and finely chop the remainder. Mix with the chopped basil and the rest of the dressing ingredients. Alternatively, put all the ingredients in a food processor or blender and blend for a few seconds until smooth. Set aside.

3 To make the garlic bread, slice the bread at 2.5 cm/1 inch intervals, taking care not to slice all the way through. Mix the butter or margarine with the garlic and mixed herbs. Spread thickly between each slice.

4 Wrap the bread in foil and bake in a preheated oven, 200°C/400°F/Gas Mark 6, for 10–15 minutes.

5 To serve, toast the reserved pine kernels under a preheated medium grill for 2–3 minutes until golden. Toss the pesto dressing into the hot rice and pile into a warmed serving dish. Sprinkle with toasted pine kernels and garnish with basil sprigs. Serve with the garlic bread and a tomato and orange salad.

Rice with Black Beans

Any kind of bean cooking liquid is delicious for cooking rice – black beans are particularly good for their startling colour and earthy flavour.

NUTRITIONAL INFORMATION

Calories 252	Sugars 2g	
Protein 5g	Fat 8g	
Carbohydrate ...43g	Saturates 1g	

 15 mins   15 mins

SERVES 4

I N G R E D I E N T S

1 onion, roughly chopped

5 garlic cloves, roughly chopped

225 ml/8 fl oz vegetable stock

2 tbsp vegetable oil

175 g/ 6 oz long grain rice

225 ml/8 fl oz liquid from cooking black
    beans (including some black beans, too)

½ tsp ground cumin

salt and pepper

TO GARNISH

3–5 spring onions, thinly sliced

2 tbsp chopped fresh coriander leaves

VARIATION
Instead of black beans, use pinto beans or chick peas. Proceed as above and serve with any savoury spicy sauce and salad accompaniment.

1 Put the onion in a blender or food processor with the garlic and stock and process to a chunky sauce.

2 Heat the oil in a heavy-based pan. Add the rice and cook over a low heat, stirring constantly, until it is golden. Add the onion mixture, with the cooking liquid from the black beans (and any beans, too). Add the cumin and season with salt and pepper to taste.

3 Cover the pan and cook over a low heat for about 10 minutes or until the rice is just tender. The rice should be a greyish colour and taste delicious.

4 Fluff up the rice with a fork, re-cover and allow to rest for about 5 minutes.

5 Serve the rice hot, sprinkled with thinly sliced spring onions and chopped coriander leaves.

Rice with Lime

The tangy citrus taste of lime is marvellous with all sorts of rice dishes.
You could add wild rice to this dish, if desired.

NUTRITIONAL INFORMATION

Calories	227	Sugars	.........1g
Protein	.........4g	Fat	...........7g
Carbohydrate	...39g	Saturates	.......1g

5 mins   15 mins

SERVES 4

I N G R E D I E N T S

2 tbsp vegetable oil

1 small onion, finely chopped

3 garlic cloves, finely chopped

175 g/6 oz long grain rice

450 ml/16 fl oz vegetable stock

juice of 1 lime

1 tbsp chopped fresh coriander

1 Heat the oil in a heavy-based pan or flameproof casserole. Add the onion and garlic and cook gently, stirring occasionally, for 2 minutes.

2 Add the rice and cook for a further minute, stirring constantly. Pour in the stock, increase the heat and bring the rice to the boil. Reduce the heat to a very low simmer.

3 Cover and cook the rice for about 10 minutes or until it is just tender and the liquid is absorbed.

4 Sprinkle in the lime juice and fork the rice to fluff up and to mix the juice in. Sprinkle with the chopped coriander and serve immediately.

Vegetable Couscous

Made from semolina, couscous is very quick and easy to cook, and it makes a pleasant change from rice or pasta.

NUTRITIONAL INFORMATION

Calories 280	Sugars 13g
Protein 10g	Fat 7g
Carbohydrate ...47g	Saturates 1g

20 mins   40 mins

SERVES 4

INGREDIENTS

2 tbsp vegetable oil

1 large onion, roughly chopped

1 carrot, chopped

1 turnip, chopped

600 ml/1 pint vegetable stock

175 g/6 oz couscous

2 tomatoes, peeled and quartered

2 courgettes, chopped

1 red pepper, deseeded and chopped

125 g/4½ oz French beans, chopped

grated rind of 1 lemon

pinch of turmeric (optional)

1 tbsp finely chopped fresh coriander or parsley

fresh flat-leaved parsley sprigs, to garnish

1 Heat the oil in a large saucepan and fry the onion, carrot and turnip for 3–4 minutes. Add the stock, bring to the boil, cover and simmer for 20 minutes.

2 Meanwhile, put the couscous in a bowl and moisten with a little boiling water, stirring, until the grains have swollen and separated.

3 Add the tomatoes, courgettes, pepper and French beans to the saucepan.

4 Stir the lemon rind into the couscous, add the turmeric, if using, and mix thoroughly. Put the couscous in a steamer and position it over the saucepan of vegetables. Simmer the vegetables so that the couscous steams for 8–10 minutes.

5 Pile the couscous on to warmed serving plates. Ladle the vegetables over the top, together with some of their cooking liquid.

6 Scatter the vegetable couscous with the chopped coriander or parsley and serve at once, garnished with the flat-leaf parsley sprigs.

Risotto in Shells

An aubergine is halved and filled with a risotto mixture, topped with cheese and baked to make a snack or quick meal for two.

NUTRITIONAL INFORMATION

Calories	444	Sugars	........20g
Protein	........13g	Fat	..........23g
Carbohydrate	...50g	Saturates	.......8g

🕒 20 mins   🕐 55 mins

SERVES 2

I N G R E D I E N T S

60 g/2 oz mixed long grain and wild rice

1 aubergine, about 350 g/12 oz

1 tbsp olive oil

1 small onion, finely chopped

1 garlic clove, crushed

½ small red pepper, deseeded and chopped

2 tbsp water

25 g/1 oz raisins

25 g/1 oz cashew nuts, roughly chopped

½ tsp dried oregano

salt and pepper

40 g/1½ oz mature Cheddar
   or Parmesan cheese, grated

fresh oregano or parsley, to garnish

1 Cook the rice in boiling salted water for about 15 minutes, until just tender. Drain, rinse and drain again.

2 Bring a large saucepan of water to the boil. Cut the stem off the aubergine and cut the aubergine in half lengthways. Cut out the flesh from the centre carefully, leaving about a 1 cm/½ inch shell. Blanch the shells in the boiling water for 3–4 minutes. Drain thoroughly. Chop the aubergine flesh finely.

3 Heat the olive oil in a saucepan or frying pan. Add the onion and garlic and fry over a low heat until beginning to soften, then add the pepper and aubergine flesh and continue cooking for 2–3 minutes. Add the water to the pan and cook for a further 2–3 minutes.

4 Remove the pan from the heat, stir the raisins, chopped cashew nuts, dried oregano and cooked rice into the aubergine mixture, and season to taste with salt and pepper.

5 Place the aubergine shells in an ovenproof dish and spoon in the rice mixture, piling it up well. Cover and cook in a preheated oven, 190°C/375°F/Gas Mark 5, for 20 minutes.

6 Remove the lid and sprinkle the grated Cheddar or Parmesan cheese over the rice, covering it evenly. Place the dish under a preheated moderate grill and cook for 3–4 minutes, until golden brown and bubbling. Serve hot, garnished with oregano or parsley.

Special Fried Rice

In this simple recipe, cooked rice is fried with vegetables and cashew nuts. It can either be eaten on its own or served as an accompaniment.

NUTRITIONAL INFORMATION

Calories 355	Sugars 6g	
Protein 9g	Fat 15g	
Carbohydrate . . .48g	Saturates 3g	

10 mins   30 mins

SERVES 4

INGREDIENTS

175 g/6 oz long grain rice

60 g/2 oz cashew nuts

1 carrot

½ cucumber

1 yellow pepper

2 spring onions

2 tbsp vegetable oil

1 garlic clove, crushed

125 g/4½ oz frozen peas, thawed

1 tbsp soy sauce

1 tsp salt

fresh coriander leaves, to garnish

1 Bring a large pan of water to the boil. Add the rice to the pan and simmer for 15 minutes. Tip the rice into a sieve and rinse; drain thoroughly.

2 Heat a wok or large, heavy-based frying pan, add the cashew nuts and dry-fry until lightly browned. Remove and set aside.

3 Cut the carrot in half along the length, then slice thinly into semi-circles. Halve the cucumber lengthways and remove the seeds, using a teaspoon, then dice the flesh. Deseed and slice the pepper and chop the spring onions.

4 Heat the oil in a wok or large frying pan. Add the prepared vegetables and the garlic. Stir-fry for 3 minutes. Add the rice, peas, soy sauce and salt. Continue to stir-fry until the vegetables are just cooked and the rice is thoroughly heated.

5 Stir in the reserved cashew nuts. Transfer to a warmed serving dish, garnish with the coriander leaves and serve immediately.

COOK'S TIP

You can replace any of the vegetables in this recipe with others suitable for a stir-fry. Use leftover cooked rice for a perfect last-minute dish.

Spinach & Nut Pilau

Fragrant basmati rice is cooked with porcini mushrooms, spinach and pistachio nuts in this easy microwave recipe.

NUTRITIONAL INFORMATION

Calories	403	Sugars	........7g
Protein	........10g	Fat	..........15g
Carbohydrate	...62g	Saturates	.......2g

55 mins   15–20 mins

SERVES 4

I N G R E D I E N T S

10 g/⅓ oz dried porcini mushrooms

300 ml/½ pint hot water

1 onion, chopped

1 garlic clove, crushed

1 tsp grated root ginger

½ fresh green chilli, deseeded and chopped

2 tbsp oil

225 g/8 oz basmati rice

1 large carrot, grated

175 ml/6 fl oz vegetable stock

½ tsp ground cinnamon

4 cloves

½ tsp saffron strands

225 g/8 oz fresh spinach,
  long stalks removed

60 g/2 oz pistachio nuts

1 tbsp chopped fresh coriander

salt and pepper

fresh coriander leaves, to garnish

1 Place the porcini mushrooms in a small bowl. Pour over the hot water and leave to soak for 30 minutes.

2 Place the onion, garlic, ginger, chilli and oil in a large bowl. Cover and cook on HIGH power for 2 minutes. Rinse the rice, then stir it into the bowl, together with the carrot. Cover and cook on HIGH power for 1 minute.

3 Strain and coarsely chop the mushrooms. Add the mushroom soaking liquid to the stock to make 425 ml/¾ pint. Pour on to the rice.

4 Stir in the mushrooms, cinnamon, cloves, saffron and ½ teaspoon salt. Cover and cook on HIGH power for 10 minutes, stirring once. Leave the mixture to stand, covered, for 10 minutes.

5 Place the spinach in a large bowl. Cover and cook on HIGH power for 3½ minutes, stirring once. Drain well and chop the spinach coarsely.

6 Stir the spinach, pistachio nuts and chopped coriander into the rice.

7 Season to taste with salt and pepper and garnish with coriander leaves. Serve immediately.

Pilau Rice

Plain boiled rice is eaten by most people in India every day, but for entertaining, a more interesting rice dish, such as this, is served.

NUTRITIONAL INFORMATION

Calories	265	Sugars	.........0g
Protein	.........4g	Fat	..........10g
Carbohydrate	...43g	Saturates	.......6g

 5 mins   25 mins

SERVES 4

INGREDIENTS

200 g/7 oz basmati rice

2 tbsp ghee

3 green cardamoms

2 cloves

3 peppercorns

½ tsp salt

½ tsp saffron

400 ml/14 fl oz boiling water

1 Rinse the rice twice under running water and set aside until required.

2 Heat the ghee in a saucepan. Add the cardamoms, cloves and peppercorns to the pan and fry, stirring constantly, for about 1 minute.

3 Add the rice and stir-fry over a medium heat for a further 2 minutes.

4 Add the salt, saffron and water to the rice mixture and reduce the heat.

Cover the pan and simmer over a low heat until the water has been absorbed.

5 Transfer the pilau rice to a serving dish and serve hot.

COOK'S TIP

The most expensive of all spices, saffron strands are the stamens of a type of crocus. They give dishes a rich, golden colour, as well as adding a distinctive, slightly bitter taste. Saffron is sold as a powder or, more expensively, in strands.

Aubergine & Rice Rolls

Slices of aubergine are stuffed with a savoury rice and nut mixture, baked in a piquant tomato and wine sauce, and served cold.

NUTRITIONAL INFORMATION

Calories	142	Sugars	.........3g
Protein	.........6g	Fat	...........9g
Carbohydrate	....9g	Saturates	.......3g

30 mins · 1 hr 5 mins

SERVES 4

INGREDIENTS

3 aubergines (total weight about 750 g /1 lb 10 oz)

60 g/2 oz mixed long-grain and wild rice

4 spring onions, trimmed and thinly sliced

3 tbsp chopped cashew nuts or toasted chopped hazelnuts

2 tbsp capers, drained and rinsed

1 garlic clove, crushed

2 tbsp grated Parmesan cheese

1 egg, beaten

salt and pepper

1 tbsp olive oil, plus extra for greasing

1 tbsp balsamic vinegar

2 tbsp tomato purée

150 ml/¼ pint water

150 ml/¼ pint dry white wine

fresh coriander sprigs, to garnish

1 Using a sharp knife, cut off the stem end of each aubergine, then cut off and discard a strip of skin from alternate sides of each aubergine. Cut each aubergine into thin slices to give a total of 16 slices.

2 Blanch the aubergine slices in boiling water for 5 minutes, then drain on kitchen paper.

3 Cook the rice in boiling salted water for about 12 minutes or until just tender. Drain and place in a bowl. Add the spring onions, nuts, capers, garlic, cheese, egg and salt and pepper to taste, and stir well to combine.

4 Spread a thin layer of rice mixture over each slice of aubergine and roll up carefully, securing with a wooden cocktail stick. Place the rolls in a greased flameproof, ovenproof dish and brush each one with the olive oil.

5 Mix together the vinegar, tomato purée and water, and pour over the aubergine rolls. Cook in a preheated oven, at 180°C/350°F/Gas Mark 4, for about 40 minutes or until tender and most of the liquid has been absorbed. Transfer the rolls to a serving dish.

6 Add the wine to the pan juices and heat gently until the sediment loosens and then simmer gently for 2–3 minutes. Adjust the seasoning and strain the sauce over the aubergine rolls. Leave until cold and then chill thoroughly.

7 Garnish the aubergine rolls with sprigs of coriander and serve.

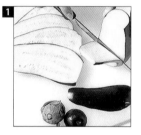  

Kitchouri

The traditional breakfast dish, kedgeree, reputedly has its roots in this Indian flavoured rice dish, adopted by English colonists.

NUTRITIONAL INFORMATION

Calories	.318	Sugars	.5g
Protein	.12g	Fat	.10g
Carbohydrate	.48g	Saturates	.6g

 10 mins   30 mins

SERVES 4

INGREDIENTS

2 tbsp ghee or butter

1 red onion, finely chopped

1 garlic clove, crushed

½ celery stick, finely chopped

1 tsp turmeric

½ tsp garam masala

1 green chilli, deseeded and finely chopped

½ tsp cumin seeds

1 tbsp chopped fresh coriander

125 g/4½ oz basmati rice, rinsed under cold water

125 g/4½ oz green lentils

300 ml/½ pint vegetable juice

600 ml/1 pint vegetable stock

1 Heat the ghee or butter in a large heavy-based saucepan. Add the onion, garlic and celery to the pan and cook for about 5 minutes, until soft.

2 Add the turmeric, garam masala, chopped green chilli, cumin seeds and coriander. Cook over a moderate heat, stirring constantly, for about 1 minute, until fragrant.

3 Add the rice and lentils and cook for 1 minute, until the rice is translucent.

4 Pour the vegetable juice and stock into the saucepan and bring to the boil over a medium heat. Cover the pan and simmer over a low heat, stirring occasionally, for about 20 minutes, or until the lentils are cooked (they should be tender when pressed between two fingers).

5 Transfer the kitchouri to a warmed serving dish and serve piping hot.

COOK'S TIP

This is a versatile dish, and can be served as a great-tasting and satisfying one-pot meal. It can also be served as a winter lunch dish with tomatoes and yogurt.

Green Rice

Based on the Mexican dish Arroz Verde, this recipe is perfect for pepper and chilli lovers. Serve with iced lemonade to quell the fire!

NUTRITIONAL INFORMATION

Calories 445	Sugars 6g
Protein 13g	Fat 12g
Carbohydrate ...76g	Saturates 2g

 25 mins   30 mins

SERVES 4

I N G R E D I E N T S

2 large green peppers

2 fresh green chillies

2 tbsp plus 1 tsp vegetable oil

1 large onion, finely chopped

1 garlic clove, crushed

1 tbsp ground coriander

300 g/10½ oz long grain rice

700 ml/1¼ pints vegetable stock

225 g/8 oz frozen peas

salt and pepper

6 tbsp chopped fresh coriander

1 egg, beaten

fresh coriander, to garnish

TO SERVE

tortilla chips

lime wedges

3 Stir in the ground coriander, rice, and stock. Bring to the boil, cover and simmer for 10 minutes. Add the peas, bring back to the boil, cover and simmer for a further 5 minutes, until the rice is tender. Remove from the heat and leave to stand, covered, for 10 minutes.

4 Season to taste with salt and pepper and add the fresh coriander. Pile into a warmed serving dish and keep warm.

5 Heat the remaining oil in a small omelette pan. Pour in the egg and cook over a medium heat for 1–2 minutes on each side, until set. Slide the omelette on to a plate, roll up and slice into thin rounds.

6 Arrange the omelette strips on top of the rice. Garnish with coriander and serve immediately with tortilla chips and lime wedges.

1 Halve, core and deseed the peppers. Cut the flesh into small cubes. Deseed and finely chop the chillies.

2 Heat 2 tablespoons of the oil in a saucepan and fry the onion, garlic, peppers and chillies for 5–6 minutes, until softened, but not browned.

Gnocchi Romana

This is a traditional Italian recipe, but if you prefer a less rich version, simply omit the eggs.

NUTRITIONAL INFORMATION

Calories	709	Sugars	9g
Protein	32g	Fat	41g
Carbohydrate	58g	Saturates	25g

 1¼ hrs   45 mins

SERVES 4

INGREDIENTS

700 ml/1¼ pints milk

pinch of freshly grated nutmeg

6 tbsp butter, plus extra for greasing

salt and pepper

225 g/8 oz semolina

125 g/4½ oz Parmesan cheese, freshly grated

2 eggs, beaten

55 g/2 oz Gruyère cheese, grated

fresh basil sprigs, to garnish

1 Pour the milk into a large pan and bring to the boil. Remove the pan from the heat and stir in the nutmeg, 2 tablespoons of the butter and salt and pepper to taste.

2 Gradually stir the semolina into the milk, whisking to prevent lumps from forming, and return the pan to a low heat. Simmer, stirring constantly, for about 10 minutes or until very thick.

3 Beat 55 g/2 oz of grated Parmesan cheese into the semolina mixture, then beat in the eggs. Continue beating the mixture until smooth. Set the mixture aside for a few minutes to cool slightly.

4 Spread out the cooled semolina mixture in an even layer on a sheet of baking paper or in a large, oiled baking tin, smoothing the surface with a damp spatula – it should be 1 cm/½ inch thick. Set aside to cool completely, then chill in the refrigerator for 1 hour.

5 Once chilled, cut out rounds of gnocchi, measuring about 4 cm/1½ inches in diameter, using a plain, greased pastry cutter.

6 Grease a shallow ovenproof dish or 4 individual ovenproof dishes. Arrange the gnocchi trimmings over the base of the dish or dishes and then cover them with the rounds of gnocchi, overlapping them slightly.

7 Melt the remaining butter and drizzle it over the gnocchi. Sprinkle over the remaining Parmesan cheese, then sprinkle the Gruyère cheese evenly over the top of the dish.

8 Bake in a preheated oven, 200°C/400°F/Gas Mark 6, for 25–30 minutes, until the top is crisp and golden brown. Serve hot, garnished with the basil.

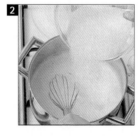

Spinach & Ricotta Gnocchi

Try not to handle the mixture too much when making gnocchi, as this will make the dough a little heavy.

NUTRITIONAL INFORMATION

Calories	712	Sugars	........15g
Protein	........29g	Fat	..........59g
Carbohydrate	...16g	Saturates	......33g

20 mins   15 mins

SERVES 4

INGREDIENTS

1 kg/2 lb 4 oz fresh spinach

350 g/12 oz ricotta cheese

125 g/4½ oz pecorino cheese, grated

3 eggs, beaten

¼ tsp freshly grated nutmeg

salt and pepper

plain flour, to mix

125 g/4½ oz unsalted butter, plus extra
for greasing

25 g/1 oz pine kernels

50 g/2 oz raisins

1 Wash and drain the spinach well and cook in a covered saucepan without any extra liquid until softened, about 8 minutes. Place the spinach in a colander and press well to remove as much liquid as possible. Either rub the spinach through a sieve or purée in a blender.

2 Combine the spinach purée with the ricotta, half of the pecorino, the eggs, nutmeg and seasoning to taste, mixing lightly but thoroughly. Work in enough flour, lightly and quickly, to make the mixture easy to handle.

3 Shape the dough quickly into small lozenge shapes, and dust lightly with a little flour.

4 Add a dash of oil to a large saucepan of salted water and bring to the boil. Add the gnocchi carefully and boil for about 2 minutes or until they float to the surface. Using a perforated spoon, transfer the gnocchi to a buttered ovenproof dish. Keep warm.

5 Melt the butter in a frying pan. Add the pine kernels and raisins and fry until the nuts start to brown slightly, but do not allow the butter to burn.

6 Pour the mixture over the gnocchi and serve sprinkled with the remaining grated pecorino.

Kidney Bean Risotto

The combination of brown rice and kidney beans provides a perfect nutritional balance, as well as tasting wonderful.

NUTRITIONAL INFORMATION

Calories	456	Sugars	.........9g
Protein	........14g	Fat	..........20g
Carbohydrate	...61g	Saturates	.......2g

  20 mins · 1 hr

SERVES 4

INGREDIENTS

4 tbsp olive oil

1 onion, chopped

2 garlic cloves, finely chopped

175 g/6 oz brown rice

600 ml/1 pint vegetable stock

1 red pepper, deseeded and chopped

2 celery sticks, sliced

225 g/8 oz chestnut mushrooms, thinly sliced

425 g/15 oz canned red kidney beans, drained and rinsed

3 tbsp chopped fresh parsley, plus extra to garnish

55 g/2 oz cashew nuts

salt and pepper

VARIATION
You could also make this dish with a mixture of long grain and wild rice. Follow the packet instructions for cooking.

1 Heat half the oil in a large, heavy-based saucepan. Add the onion and cook, stirring occasionally, for 5 minutes, until softened. Add half the garlic and cook, stirring frequently, for 2 minutes, then add the rice and stir for 1 minute until the grains are thoroughly coated with the oil. Add the vegetable stock and a pinch of salt and bring to the boil, stirring constantly. Lower the heat, cover and simmer for 35–40 minutes, until all the liquid has been absorbed.

2 Meanwhile, heat the remaining oil in a heavy-based frying pan. Add the red pepper and celery and cook, stirring frequently, for 5 minutes. Add the mushrooms and the remaining garlic and cook, stirring frequently, for 4–5 minutes.

3 Stir the rice into the frying pan and add the kidney beans, parsley and cashew nuts. Season to taste with salt and pepper and cook, stirring constantly, until the risotto is piping hot.

4 Transfer to a warm serving dish, sprinkle with extra parsley and serve.

Risotto alla Rustica

A proper risotto is thoroughly delicious, but it cannot be hurried if it is to acquire its characteristic creamy texture.

NUTRITIONAL INFORMATION

Calories 519	Sugars 6g
Protein 8g	Fat 16g
Carbohydrate . . .89g	Saturates 7g

5 mins   30 mins

SERVES 4

INGREDIENTS

850 ml/1½ pints vegetable stock

40 g/1½ oz butter

2 tbsp olive oil

1 onion, finely chopped

2 shallots, finely chopped

1 garlic clove, finely chopped

375 g/12 oz arborio rice

50 ml/2 fl oz dry white wine

4 plum tomatoes, skinned

1 fresh rosemary sprig, finely chopped

1 tbsp chopped fresh parsley

4 fresh basil leaves, torn

salt and pepper

2 tbsp single cream

1 Pour the stock into a large saucepan, bring to the boil, then lower the heat to a simmer and keep hot. Meanwhile, melt 25 g/1 oz of the butter with the olive oil in a large, heavy-based saucepan over a low heat. Add the onion, shallots and garlic and cook, stirring occasionally, for 5 minutes.

2 Add the rice and stir for about 1 minute to the coat the grains with the butter and oil. Pour in the wine, bring to the boil and cook, stirring, until almost all the liquid has evaporated. Add the tomatoes, breaking them up with a fork, and the rosemary, parsley and basil.

3 Add the hot stock, a large ladleful at a time, stirring until each addition is absorbed into the rice. Continue adding stock in this way, cooking until the rice is creamy, but the grains are still firm. This will take about 20 minutes.

4 Stir in the remaining butter and season to taste with salt and pepper. Stir in the cream and serve immediately.

Lemon Risotto

This is a stylish first course, with an aroma and fresh taste that stimulate the taste buds for the meal to follow.

NUTRITIONAL INFORMATION

Calories 442	Sugars 3g	
Protein 6g	Fat 15g	
Carbohydrate ...68g	Saturates 6g	

 10 mins   35 mins

SERVES 6–8

INGREDIENTS

2–3 lemons

2 tbsp olive oil

2 shallots, finely chopped

300 g/10½ oz arborio rice

125 ml/4 fl oz dry white vermouth

1 litre/1¾ pints vegetable stock, simmering

1 tbsp very finely chopped fresh
   flat-leaved parsley

2 tbsp butter

TO GARNISH

thin strips of pared lemon rind

fresh parsley sprigs

TO SERVE

Parmesan cheese shavings

avocado slices

1 Finely grate the rind from 2 lemons. Roll the rindless lemons backwards and forwards on a board, then squeeze 100 ml/3½ fl oz juice. If you don't have enough, squeeze another lemon. Set the rind and juice aside.

2 Heat the olive oil in a heavy-based pan. Add the shallots and fry, stirring, for about 3 minutes until soft. Add the rice and stir until all the grains are well coated.

3 Stir in the vermouth and cook until it evaporates. Lower the heat to medium–low. Add the lemon juice and a ladleful of simmering stock. Stir, then simmer, stirring occasionally, until all the liquid is absorbed.

4 Add another ladleful of stock and stir, then simmer until absorbed. Continue adding stock in this way, allowing it to be absorbed after each addition, until all the stock has been incorporated and the risotto is creamy.

5 Stir in the lemon rind and parsley. Add the butter, cover, remove from the heat and set aside for 5 minutes. Stir well and then garnish with lemon strips and parsley. Serve with Parmesan cheese and avocado slices.

Cumin Rice

Cumin seeds add a distinctive flavour to this colourful rice dish.
Serve as a side dish with any simple vegetable recipe.

NUTRITIONAL INFORMATION

Calories 258	Sugars 4g
Protein 5g	Fat 9g
Carbohydrate ...49g	Saturates 5g

 20 mins   20 mins

SERVES 4

INGREDIENTS

2 tbsp butter

1 tbsp vegetable oil

1 green pepper, deseeded and sliced

1 red pepper, deseeded and sliced

3 spring onions, thinly sliced

3–4 garlic cloves, finely chopped

175 g/6 oz long grain rice

1½ tsp cumin seeds

½ tsp dried oregano or marjoram, crushed

450 ml/16 fl oz vegetable stock

1 Heat the butter and vegetable oil in a heavy-based pan or flameproof casserole. Add the sliced green and red peppers and cook, stirring occasionally, until softened.

2 When the peppers have been softened, add the spring onions, garlic, rice and cumin seeds. Cook, stirring constantly, for about 5 minutes or until the rice turns slightly golden.

3 Add the oregano or marjoram and the stock to the pan or casserole, bring to the boil, then reduce the heat and simmer gently for 5–10 minutes until the rice is tender.

4 Cover with a clean tea towel and remove from the heat. Set aside for about 10 minutes to cool slightly. Fluff up the rice with a fork, transfer to a large serving dish and serve.

VARIATION
Fold through a portion or two of black beans for protein, and serve with a simple vegetable curry.

Baked Semolina Gnocchi

Semolina has a similar texture to polenta, but is slightly grainier. These gnocchi, which are flavoured with cheese and thyme, are easy to make.

NUTRITIONAL INFORMATION

Calories	259	Sugars	.........0g
Protein	.........9g	Fat	..........16g
Carbohydrate	...20g	Saturates	......10g

15 mins · 30 mins

SERVES 4

INGREDIENTS

425 ml/¾ pint vegetable stock

100 g/3½ oz semolina

1 tbsp fresh thyme, stalks removed

1 egg, beaten

salt and pepper

50 g/1¾ oz Parmesan cheese, grated

50 g/1¾ oz butter, plus extra for greasing

2 garlic cloves, crushed

1 Place the stock in a large saucepan and bring to the boil. Add the semolina in a steady trickle, stirring continuously. Keep stirring for 3–4 minutes until the mixture is thick enough to hold a spoon upright. Set aside and leave to cool slightly.

2 Add the thyme leaves, egg and half of the cheese to the semolina mixture, and season well to taste with salt and pepper.

3 Spread the semolina mixture on to a board to a thickness of about 1 cm/½ inch, and leave until it has cooled and set.

4 When the semolina is cold, cut it into 2.5 cm/1 inch squares, reserving any offcuts.

5 Grease an ovenproof dish, placing the reserved offcuts in the bottom. Arrange the semolina squares on top and sprinkle with the remaining cheese.

6 Melt the butter in a pan, add the garlic and season with pepper to taste. Pour the butter mixture over the gnocchi. Bake in a preheated oven, at 220°C/425°F/Gas Mark 7, for 15–20 minutes until the gnocchi are puffed up and golden. Serve hot.

VARIATION

Try adding ½ tablespoon of sun-dried tomato paste or 50 g/1¾ oz finely chopped mushrooms, fried in butter, to the semolina mixture in step 2. Follow Vegetable same cooking method.

Spiced Semolina

A south Indian savoury snack which is very quick and easy to prepare, this should be served warm. It has a really lovely aroma.

NUTRITIONAL INFORMATION

Calories 556   Sugars 2g
Protein ....9g   Fat 41g
Carbohydrate ...40g   Saturates 5g

 5 mins   15 mins

SERVES 4

INGREDIENTS

150 ml/¼ pint vegetable oil

1 tsp mixed onion and mustard seeds

4 dried red chillies

4 curry leaves (fresh or dried)

8 tbsp coarse semolina

50 g/1¾ oz cashew nuts

1 tsp salt

150 ml/¼ pint water

1 Heat the vegetable oil in a large, heavy-based frying pan over a fairly low heat.

2 Add the onion and mustard seeds, dried red chillies and curry leaves and fry, stirring constantly, for about 1 minute.

3 Reduce the heat to low and add the coarse semolina and the cashew nuts. Stir-fry for about 5 minutes, moving the mixture around the pan all the time to prevent it from catching and burning on the base.

4 Add the salt to the pan, mixing well, and continue to stir-fry over a low heat, keeping the mixture moving all the time.

5 Add the water and cook, stirring constantly, until the mixture is beginning to thicken.

6 Serve the spiced semolina warm as a delicious snack with Indian tea.

COOK'S TIP

Curry leaves are very similar in appearance to bay leaves but are very different in flavour. They can be bought both fresh and dried. They are mainly used to flavour lentil dishes and vegetable curries.

Chilli Polenta Chips

Polenta is used in Italy in the same way as potatoes and rice. It has little flavour, but combined with butter, garlic and herbs, it is transformed.

NUTRITIONAL INFORMATION

Calories 365   Sugars 1g
Protein ....8g   Fat 12g
Carbohydrate ...54g   Saturates 5g

5 mins   20 mins

SERVES 4

INGREDIENTS

350 g/12 oz instant polenta

2 tsp chilli powder

salt and pepper

1 tbsp olive oil or melted butter

150 ml/¼ pint soured cream

1 tbsp chopped fresh parsley

1 Place 1.5 litres/2¾ pints of water in a saucepan and bring to the boil. Add 2 teaspoons of salt, then add the polenta in a steady stream, stirring constantly.

2 Reduce the heat slightly and continue stirring for about 5 minutes. It is essential to stir the polenta, otherwise it will stick and burn. The polenta should have a thick consistency at this point and should be stiff enough to hold the spoon upright in the pan.

3 Add the chilli powder to the polenta mixture and stir well. Season to taste with a little salt and pepper.

4 Spread the polenta out on to a board or baking tray to about 4 cm/1½ inch thick. Leave to cool and set.

5 Cut the cooled polenta mixture into thin wedges.

6 Heat 1 tablespoon of oil in a pan. Add the polenta wedges and fry for 3–4 minutes on each side or until golden and crispy. Alternatively, brush with melted butter and grill for 6–7 minutes until golden. Drain the cooked polenta on kitchen paper.

7 Mix the soured cream with parsley and place in a bowl.

8 Serve the polenta with the soured cream and parsley dip.

COOK'S TIP

Easy-cook instant polenta is widely available in supermarkets and is quick to make. It will keep for up to 1 week in the refrigerator. The polenta can also be baked in a preheated oven, at 200°C/400°F/ Gas Mark 6, for 20 minutes.

Biryani with Onions

An assortment of vegetables cooked with tender rice, flavoured and coloured with bright yellow turmeric and other warming Indian spices.

NUTRITIONAL INFORMATION

Calories	223	Sugars	........18g
Protein	.........8g	Fat	..........4g
Carbohydrate	...42g	Saturates	......1g

 1¼ hrs   25 mins

SERVES 4

INGREDIENTS

175 g/6 oz basmati rice, rinsed

55 g/2 oz red lentils, rinsed

1 bay leaf

6 cardamom pods, split

1 tsp turmeric

6 cloves

1 tsp cumin seeds

1 cinnamon stick, broken

1 onion, chopped

225 g/8 oz cauliflower, broken into small florets

1 large carrot, diced

100 g/3½ oz frozen peas

55 g/2 oz sultanas

salt and pepper

600 ml/1 pint vegetable stock

naan bread, to serve

CARAMELIZED ONIONS

2 tsp vegetable oil

1 red onion, shredded

1 onion, shredded

2 tsp caster sugar

1 Place the rice, lentils, bay leaf, spices, onion, cauliflower, carrot, peas and sultanas in a large pan. Season with salt and pepper to taste and mix well.

2 Pour in the stock, bring to the boil, cover and simmer for 15 minutes, stirring occasionally, until the rice is tender. Remove from the heat and set aside, covered, for 10 minutes to allow the stock to be absorbed. Remove and discard the bay leaf, cardamom pods, cloves and cinnamon stick.

3 Heat the oil in a frying pan and add the onions. Fry them over a medium heat for about 3–4 minutes until they are just softened. Add the caster sugar, increase the heat and then cook, stirring constantly, for a further 2–3 minutes until the onions are golden.

4 Stir the rice and vegetables gently to combine and transfer to warm serving plates. Spoon over the caramelized onions and serve immediately with plain, warmed naan bread.

Curried Rice Patties

Substantial and flavourful, these patties are rich in protein and delicious. Leave the rice with a little bite to give extra texture.

NUTRITIONAL INFORMATION

Calories 311	Sugars 4g
Protein 7g	Fat 11g
Carbohydrate . . .50g	Saturates 2g

1¼ hrs   55 mins

SERVES 4–6

INGREDIENTS

70 g/2½ oz basmati rice

2 tbsp olive oil

1 red onion, finely chopped

2 garlic cloves, crushed

2 tsp curry powder

½ tsp crushed dried chilli flakes

1 small red pepper, deseeded and diced

115 g/4 oz frozen peas, thawed

1 small leek, finely chopped

1 tomato, peeled, deseeded and chopped

310 g/11 oz canned chick peas,
   rinsed and drained

85 g/3 oz fresh white breadcrumbs

1–2 tbsp chopped fresh coriander or mint

1 egg, lightly beaten

salt and pepper

vegetable oil, for frying

cucumber slices, to garnish

lime wedges, to serve

DRESSING

120 ml/4 fl oz tahini

2 garlic cloves, crushed

½ tsp ground cumin

pinch of cayenne pepper

5 tbsp lemon juice

drizzle of extra-virgin olive oil

1 To make the dressing, process the tahini, garlic, cumin, cayenne and lemon juice in a food processor until creamy. Slowly pour in the oil, then gradually add enough water to make a creamy dressing (about 125 ml/4 fl oz).

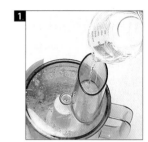

2 Bring a saucepan of water to the boil. Add ½ teaspoon of the salt and sprinkle in the rice; simmer for about 15–20 minutes, until the rice is just tender. Drain, rinse and set aside.

3 Heat the olive oil in a large pan. Add the onion and garlic and cook until beginning to soften. Stir in the curry powder and chilli flakes and cook for 2 minutes. Add the red pepper, peas, leek and tomato and cook gently for about 7 minutes until tender. Set aside.

4 Process the chick peas in a food processor until smooth. Add half the vegetables and process again. Transfer to a large bowl and add the remaining vegetable mixture, breadcrumbs, coriander and egg. Mix well. Stir in the rice and season to taste with salt and pepper. Chill for 1 hour in the refrigerator, then shape into 4–6 patties.

5 Fry the patties in oil for 6–8 minutes until golden. Garnish with cucumber slices and serve with the dressing and lime wedges.

Brown Rice Gratin

This dish is extremely versatile – it can be made with any vegetables that you have to hand, and basmati rice instead of brown.

NUTRITIONAL INFORMATION

Calories	321	Sugars	.........6g
Protein	........10g	Fat	.........18g
Carbohydrate	...32g	Saturates	.......9g

 15 mins   1 hr

SERVES 4

INGREDIENTS

100 g/3½ oz brown rice

2 tbsp butter or margarine, plus extra for greasing

1 red onion, chopped

2 garlic cloves, crushed

1 carrot, cut into thin batons

1 courgette, sliced

85 g/3 oz baby sweetcorn cobs, halved lengthways

2 tbsp sunflower seeds

3 tbsp chopped fresh mixed herbs

100 g/3½ oz grated mozzarella cheese

salt and pepper

2 tbsp wholemeal breadcrumbs

1 Cook the rice in a pan of lightly salted boiling water for 20 minutes until tender. Drain well.

2 Lightly grease an 850 ml/1½ pint ovenproof dish with butter.

3 Melt the butter in a frying pan. Cook the onion over a low heat, stirring constantly, for 2 minutes or until soft.

4 Add the garlic, carrot, courgette and baby sweetcorn cobs and cook,

stirring constantly, for a further 5 minutes until the vegetables are softened.

5 Combine the drained rice with the sunflower seeds and mixed herbs and stir into the pan. Stir in half of the mozzarella cheese and season with salt and pepper to taste.

6 Spoon the mixture into the prepared dish and top with the breadcrumbs and remaining cheese.

7 Cook in a preheated oven, 180°C/350°F/Gas Mark 4, for about 25–30 minutes or until the cheese has begun to turn golden. Serve immediately.

Egg Fried Rice

In this classic Chinese dish, boiled rice is fried with peas, spring onions and egg, and flavoured with soy sauce.

NUTRITIONAL INFORMATION

Calories 203   Sugars 1g
Protein ....9g   Fat 11g
Carbohydrate ...19g   Saturates 2g

 20 mins   10 mins

SERVES 4

INGREDIENTS

150 g/5½ oz long grain rice

3 eggs, beaten

2 tbsp vegetable oil

2 garlic cloves, crushed

4 spring onions, chopped

125 g/4½ oz cooked peas

1 tbsp light soy sauce

pinch of salt

shredded spring onion, to garnish

1 Cook the rice in a pan of boiling water for 10–12 minutes, until it is almost cooked but not soft. Drain well, rinse under cold water and drain again.

2 Place the beaten eggs in a saucepan and cook over a gentle heat, stirring until softly scrambled.

3 Heat the vegetable oil in a preheated wok or large frying pan, swirling the oil around the base of the wok until it is really hot.

4 Add the crushed garlic, spring onions and cooked peas and sauté, stirring occasionally, for 1–2 minutes. Stir the rice into the wok, mixing to combine.

5 Add the beaten eggs, the light soy sauce and a pinch of salt to the wok or frying pan and stir until the eggs are thoroughly mixed in.

6 When the eggs are cooked, transfer the egg fried rice to warmed serving dishes and serve garnished with the shredded spring onion.

COOK'S TIP

The rice is rinsed under cold water to wash out the starch and prevent it from sticking together.

Fried Spicy Rice

Ginger and garlic give this beautifully aromatic rice dish its lovely flavour. If desired, you can add a few peas to it for extra colour.

NUTRITIONAL INFORMATION

Calories . . . . .507 Sugars 2g
Protein . . . . .9g Fat 11g
Carbohydrate . . .99g Saturates 6g

10 mins   35 mins

SERVES 4

INGREDIENTS

500 g/1 lb 2 oz rice

1 onion

2 tbsp ghee

1 tsp finely chopped fresh root ginger

1 tsp crushed garlic

1 tsp salt

1 tsp black cumin seeds

3 whole cloves

3 whole green cardamoms

2 cinnamon sticks

4 black peppercorns

700 ml/1¼ pints water

1 Rinse the rice thoroughly under cold running water.

2 Using a sharp knife, cut the onion into thin slices.

3 Heat the ghee in a large saucepan. Add the onion and fry over a medium heat, stirring occasionally, until crisp and golden brown.

4 Add the ginger, garlic and salt to the onions in the pan, stirring to combine.

5 Remove half of the spicy onions from the saucepan and set aside.

6 Add the rice, black cumin seeds, cloves, cardamoms, cinnamon sticks and peppercorns to the pan and stir-fry for 3–5 minutes.

7 Add the water to the pan and bring to the boil over a medium heat. Reduce the heat, cover and simmer until steam

comes out through the lid. Check to see whether the rice is cooked and the liquid has been absorbed.

8 Transfer the fried spicy rice to a warmed serving dish and serve immediately garnished with the reserved fried onions.

Caribbean Rice and Peas

Depending on whether you are on an eastern or western Caribbean island, this dish is known as rice and peas or peas and rice!

NUTRITIONAL INFORMATION

Calories 349	Sugars 3g
Protein 11g	Fat 6g
Carbohydrate ...67g	Saturates 4g

 10 mins   1½ hrs

SERVES 4

INGREDIENTS

115 g/4 oz dried gunga peas, soaked overnight in cold water to cover

225 g/8 oz long grain rice

700 ml/1¼ pints water

55 g/2 oz creamed coconut

1 onion, chopped

2 garlic cloves, finely chopped

1 small red pepper, deseeded and chopped

1 tbsp fresh thyme leaves

1 bay leaf

½ tsp ground allspice

salt and pepper

COOK'S TIP

Dried gunga peas go by a variety of names, including pigeon, Congo and Jamaica peas. Fresh gunga peas, sometimes known as Cajun peas, also feature in Caribbean cooking.

1 Drain the gunga peas and put them in a large saucepan. Add enough cold water to cover them well. Bring to the boil, boil for 15 minutes, then simmer for about 45 minutes, until tender. Drain and return to the pan.

2 Add the rice, water, creamed coconut, onion, garlic, red pepper, thyme, bay leaf and allspice and season to taste with salt and pepper. Bring to the boil, stirring constantly, until the creamed coconut has melted, then lower the heat and simmer for 20 minutes.

3 Uncover the pan and continue to cook for about 5 minutes, until any excess liquid has evaporated. Gently fork through the rice to fluff up the grains, then serve it immediately.

Stuffed Peppers

Use a mixture of peppers for a colourful display at the supper table and serve with a mixed leaf salad.

NUTRITIONAL INFORMATION

Calories	480	Sugars	........15g
Protein	........14g	Fat	..........28g
Carbohydrate	...59g	Saturates	.......6g

🍧 🍧 🍧

🍲 25 mins, plus standing   🕐 20 mins

SERVES 4

INGREDIENTS

4 large red, yellow or orange peppers

450 ml/16 fl oz vegetable stock

200 g/7 oz long-grain rice

2 tbsp olive oil

1 onion, chopped

2 garlic cloves, finely chopped

115 g/4 oz chestnut mushrooms, chopped

4 tomatoes, skinned and chopped

1 carrot, diced

salt and pepper

1 tbsp chopped fresh parsley

100 g/3½ oz goat's cheese, crumbled

55 g/2 oz pine kernels

25 g/1 oz Parmesan cheese, freshly grated

1 Cut the peppers in half lengthways and deseed. Blanch them in a large saucepan of boiling water for 5 minutes, then remove from the pan with a slotted spoon and place upside down to drain.

2 Pour the stock into another saucepan, add the rice and bring to the boil. Lower the heat, cover and simmer for 15 minutes. Remove the pan from the heat and set aside, still covered, for 5 minutes.

3 Meanwhile, heat the olive oil in a large frying pan. Add the onion and cook, stirring occasionally, for 5 minutes, until softened. Add the garlic, mushrooms, tomatoes and carrot and season to taste with salt and pepper. Cover and cook for a further 5 minutes.

4 Stir the rice, parsley, crumbled goat's cheese and pine kernels into the vegetable mixture. Place the pepper halves, cut side up, in a roasting tin or ovenproof dish. Divide the rice and vegetable mixture among them.

5 Sprinkle the tops of the peppers with the grated Parmesan cheese and bake in a preheated oven, 190°C/375°F/Gas Mark 5, for about 20 minutes, until the cheese is golden brown and melted. Serve immediately, on warmed serving plates.

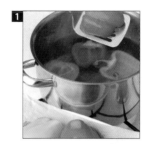

Lentil & Rice Casserole

This is a really hearty dish, perfect for cold days when a filling hot dish is just what you need to keep the winter out.

NUTRITIONAL INFORMATION

Calories 312	Sugars 9g
Protein 20g	Fat 2g
Carbohydrate . . .51g	Saturates 0.4g

15 mins   40 mins

SERVES 4

INGREDIENTS

225 g/8 oz split red lentils

55 g/2 oz long grain rice

1.2 litres/2 pints vegetable stock

1 leek, cut into chunks

3 garlic cloves, crushed

400 g/14 oz canned chopped tomatoes

1 tsp ground cumin

1 tsp chilli powder

1 tsp garam masala

1 red pepper, deseeded and sliced

100 g/3½ oz small broccoli florets

8 baby corn cobs, halved lengthways

55 g/2 oz French beans, halved

1 tbsp shredded fresh basil

salt and pepper

fresh basil sprigs, to garnish

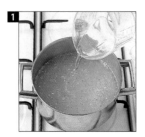

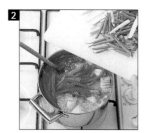

1 Place the lentils, rice and vegetable stock in a large flameproof casserole and cook over a low heat, stirring occasionally, for 20 minutes.

2 Add the leek, garlic, tomatoes and their can juice, ground cumin, chilli powder, garam masala, sliced pepper, broccoli, corn cobs and French beans to the pan.

3 Bring the mixture to the boil, reduce the heat, cover and simmer for a further 10–15 minutes or until the vegetables are tender.

4 Add the shredded basil and season with salt and pepper to taste.

5 Garnish with fresh basil sprigs and serve immediately.

VARIATION

You can vary the rice in this recipe – use brown or wild rice, if you prefer.

Stuffed Rice Pancakes

Dosas (pancakes) are widely eaten in southern India. The rice and urid dhal need to soak and ferment, so prepare well in advance.

NUTRITIONAL INFORMATION

Calories	748	Sugars 1g
Protein	........10g	Fat 47g
Carbohydrate	...76g	Saturates 5g

 15 mins 40–45 mins

SERVES 4

INGREDIENTS

200 g/7 oz rice and 50 g/1¾ oz urid dhal, or 200 g/7 oz ground rice and 50 g/1¾ oz urid dhal flour (ata)

425–600 ml/¾–1 pint water

1 tsp salt

4 tbsp vegetable oil

FILLING

900 g/2 lb potatoes, diced

3 fresh green chillies, deseeded and chopped

½ tsp turmeric

1 tsp salt

150 ml/5 fl oz vegetable oil

1 tsp mixed mustard and onion seeds

3 dried red chillies

4 curry leaves

2 tbsp lemon juice

1 To make the dosas, soak the rice and urid dhal for 3 hours. Grind the rice and urid dhal to a smooth consistency, adding water if necessary. Set aside for a further 3 hours to ferment. Alternatively, if you are using the ground rice and urid dhal flour (ata), mix together in a bowl. Add the water and salt and stir until a batter is formed.

2 Heat about 1 tablespoon of oil in a large, non-stick frying pan. Spoon a ladleful of batter into the frying pan. Tilt the frying pan to spread the mixture over the base. Cover and cook over a medium heat for about 2 minutes. Remove the lid and turn the dosa over very carefully. Pour a little oil around the edge, cover and cook for a further 2 minutes. Repeat with the remaining batter.

3 To make the filling, cook the potatoes in a pan of boiling water. Add the chillies, turmeric and salt and cook until the potatoes are just soft. Drain and mash lightly with a fork.

4 Heat the oil in a saucepan and fry the mustard and onion seeds, dried red chillies and curry leaves, stirring constantly, for about 1 minute. Pour the spice mixture over the mashed potatoes, sprinkle over the lemon juice and mix well. Spoon the potato filling on one half of each of the dosas and fold the other half over it. Serve hot on warmed plates.

Oriental-style Millet Pilau

Millet makes an interesting alternative to rice, which is the more traditional ingredient for a pilau. Serve with a crisp oriental salad.

NUTRITIONAL INFORMATION

Calories 660	Sugars 28g
Protein 15g	Fat 27g
Carbohydrate ...94g	Saturates 5g

🖐 🖐

 20 mins   30 mins

SERVES 4

INGREDIENTS

300 g/10½ oz millet grains

1 tbsp vegetable oil

1 bunch of spring onions, white and green parts, chopped

1 garlic clove, crushed

1 tsp grated fresh root ginger

1 orange pepper, deseeded and diced

600 ml/1 pint water

1 orange

salt and pepper

115 g/4 oz stoned dates, chopped

2 tsp sesame oil

115 g/4 oz dry-roasted cashew nuts

2 tbsp pumpkin seeds

oriental salad vegetables, to serve

1 Place the millet in a large pan and toast over a medium heat, shaking the pan occasionally, for 4–5 minutes, until the grains begin to crack and pop.

2 Heat the oil in another pan. Add the spring onions, garlic, ginger and pepper and cook over a medium heat, stirring frequently, for 2–3 minutes until just softened, but not browned. Add the millet and pour in the water.

3 Using a vegetable peeler, pare the rind from the orange and add the rind to the pan. Squeeze the juice from the orange into the pan. Season to taste with salt and pepper.

4 Bring to the boil, reduce the heat, cover and cook gently for 20 minutes until all the liquid has been absorbed.

Remove the pan from the heat, stir in the dates and sesame oil and set aside to stand for 10 minutes.

5 Remove and discard the orange rind and stir in the cashew nuts. Pile into a warmed serving dish, sprinkle with pumpkin seeds and serve immediately with oriental salad vegetables.

Green Herb & Coconut Rice

This is a deliciously different way to serve plain rice for a special occasion or to liven up a simple meal.

NUTRITIONAL INFORMATION

Calories 652	Sugars 9g
Protein 15g	Fat 17g
Carbohydrate . . .116g	Saturates 6g

1hr 10 mins   35 mins

SERVES 4

INGREDIENTS

2 tbsp olive oil

500 g/1 lb 2 oz basmati or Thai jasmine rice (see page 386), soaked for 1 hour, washed and drained

700 ml/1¼ pints coconut milk

1 tsp salt

1 bay leaf

2 tbsp chopped fresh coriander

2 tbsp chopped fresh mint

2 green chillies, deseeded and finely chopped

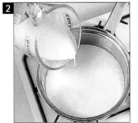

1 Heat the oil in a saucepan, add the rice and stir over a medium heat until it becomes translucent.

2 Add the coconut milk, salt and bay leaf. Bring to the boil and cook until all the liquid is absorbed.

3 Reduce the heat to very low, cover the saucepan tightly and cook for 10 minutes. Take great care that the rice does not catch and burn on the base of the saucepan.

4 Remove the bay leaf from the saucepan and stir in the chopped coriander, mint and green chillies. Fork through the rice gently to fluff up the grains. Transfer to a warm serving dish and serve immediately.

COOK'S TIP

The contrasting colours of this dish make it particularly attractive, and it can be made to look even more interesting with a carefully chosen garnish. Two segments of fresh lime complement the coriander perfectly.

Vegetable Pilau

This is a lovely way of cooking rice and vegetables together, and the saffron gives it a beautiful aroma. Serve this with any kebab.

NUTRITIONAL INFORMATION

Calories ....557 Sugars 9g
Protein ....11g Fat 14g
Carbohydrate ..104g Saturates 7g

20 mins   55 mins

SERVES 6

INGREDIENTS

4 tbsp ghee

450 g/1 lb potatoes, cut into 12 pieces

1 aubergine, cut into 6 pieces

2 carrots, sliced

50 g/1¾ oz French beans, chopped

2 onions, sliced

175 ml/6 fl oz natural yogurt

2 tsp finely chopped fresh root ginger

2 tsp crushed garlic

2 tsp garam masala

2 tsp black cumin seeds

½ tsp turmeric

3 black cardamom pods

3 cinnamon sticks

2 tsp salt

1 tsp chilli powder

½ tsp saffron strands

300 ml/½ pint milk

600 g/1 lb 5 oz basmati rice

5 tbsp lemon juice

TO GARNISH

4 fresh green chillies, chopped and deseeded

fresh coriander leaves, chopped

1 Have the prepared vegetables to hand. Heat the ghee in a pan. Add the potatoes, aubergine, carrots and beans and fry, turning frequently, until softened. Remove from the pan and set aside.

2 Add the onions and fry, stirring frequently, until soft. Add the yogurt, ginger, garlic, garam masala, 1 teaspoon black cumin seeds, the turmeric, 1 cardamom pod, 1 cinnamon stick, 1 teaspoon salt and the chilli powder and stir-fry for 3–5 minutes. Return the vegetables to the pan and fry for 4–5 minutes.

3 Put the saffron and milk in a saucepan and bring to the boil, stirring. Remove from the heat and set aside.

4 In a pan of boiling water, half-cook the rice with 1 teaspoon salt, 2 cinnamon sticks, 2 black cardamom pods and 1 teaspoon black cumin seeds. Drain the rice, leaving half in the pan, while transferring the other half to a bowl. Pour the vegetable mixture on top of the rice in the pan.

5 Pour half of the lemon juice and half of the saffron milk over the vegetables and rice, cover with the remaining rice and pour the remaining lemon juice and saffron milk over the top. Garnish with chillies and coriander, return to the heat and cover. Cook over a low heat for about 20 minutes. Serve while hot.

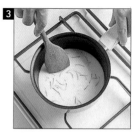

Refried Beans

The beans in this Mexican dish are cooked once and then literally refried to a delicious, thick purée, which tastes wonderful topped with cheese.

NUTRITIONAL INFORMATION

Calories 806	Sugars 7g
Protein 27g	Fat 57g
Carbohydrate ...50g	Saturates 20g

5–10 mins, plus soaking   3 hrs

Serves 4–6

I N G R E D I E N T S

1 quantity Mexican beans, with their cooking liquid (see page 449)

125 ml/4 fl oz vegetable oil

1–2 onions, chopped

½ tsp ground cumin

salt

250 g/9 oz Cheddar cheese, grated (optional)

1 Put two-thirds of the cooked beans, with their cooking liquid, in a food processor or blender and process to a purée. Stir in the remaining whole beans and set the mixture aside.

2 Heat the vegetable oil in a heavy-based frying pan. Add the onions and cook until they are very soft. Sprinkle with cumin and salt to taste.

3 Ladle in a cupful of the bean mixture, and cook, stirring, until the beans reduce down to a thick mixture; the beans will darken slightly as they cook.

4 Continue adding the bean mixture to the pan, a ladleful at a time, stirring and reducing down the liquid before adding the next ladleful. You should end up with a thick, chunky purée.

5 If you are using the grated Cheddar cheese, sprinkle it over the beans and cover tightly so that the heat in the pan melts the cheese. Alternatively, place the dish under a preheated grill until the cheese is melted and bubbling.

6 Serve the refried beans immediately on warmed serving plates. A crisp green salad goes well with this dish.

Polenta

Polenta is prepared and served in a variety of ways. This recipe gives a choice of two sauces to accompany it.

NUTRITIONAL INFORMATION

Calories 661	Sugars 5g	
Protein 15g	Fat 34g	
Carbohydrate . . .68g	Saturates 12g	

1¼ hrs   1 hr

SERVES 4

I N G R E D I E N T S

1.5 litres/2¾ pints water

1½ tsp salt

300 g/10½ oz polenta or cornmeal flour

2 eggs, beaten (optional)

125 g/4½ oz fresh fine white
  breadcrumbs (optional)

vegetable oil, for frying and oiling

2 quantities Basic Tomato Sauce
  (see page 7)

M U S H R O O M S A U C E

3 tbsp olive oil

250 g/8 oz mushrooms, sliced

2 garlic cloves, crushed

150 ml/¼ pint dry white wine

salt and pepper

4 tbsp double cream

2 tbsp chopped fresh mixed herbs

1 Bring the water and salt to the boil in a large pan and gradually sprinkle in the polenta or cornmeal flour, stirring all the time to prevent lumps forming. Simmer the mixture very gently, stirring frequently, until the polenta becomes very thick and starts to draw away from the sides of the pan, about 30–35 minutes. It is likely to splatter, in which case partially cover the pan with a lid.

2 Thoroughly oil a shallow tin, about 28 x 18 cm/11 x 7 inches, and spoon in the polenta. Spread out evenly, using a wet wooden spoon or spatula. Leave to cool, then leave to stand for a few hours at room temperature, if possible.

3 Cut the polenta into 30–36 squares. Heat the vegetable oil in a frying pan and fry the pieces, in batches, until golden brown all over, turning several times – this will take about 5 minutes. Alternatively, dip each piece of polenta in beaten egg and coat in breadcrumbs before frying in the hot vegetable oil.

4 To make the mushroom sauce, heat the olive oil in a pan and fry the mushrooms with the crushed garlic for 3–4 minutes. Add the wine, season well and simmer for 5 minutes. Add the cream and chopped herbs and simmer for 1–2 minutes.

5 Serve the polenta with either the tomato sauce or mushroom sauce.

Chana Dhal & Rice

Saffron is used to flavour this dish, which makes it rather special.
It is absolutely delicious served with any curry.

NUTRITIONAL INFORMATION

Calories 479	Sugars 7g	
Protein 12g	Fat 14g	
Carbohydrate ...80g	Saturates 8g	

 3¼ hrs   1 hr

SERVES 6

INGREDIENTS

100 g/3½ oz chana dhal (see page 453)

60 ml/4 tbsp ghee

2 onions, sliced

1 tsp finely chopped fresh root ginger

1 tsp crushed garlic

½ tsp turmeric

2 tsp salt

½ tsp chilli powder

1 tsp garam masala

5 tbsp natural yogurt

1.35 litres/2¼ pints water

150 ml/¼ pint milk

1 tsp saffron

3 tbsp lemon juice

2 fresh green chillies, deseeded
  and chopped

fresh coriander leaves

3 black cardamom pods

3 black cumin seeds

500 g/1 lb 2 oz basmati rice

1 Rinse and soak the chana dhal for 3 hours. Rinse the rice under running water and set aside.

2 Heat the ghee in a frying pan. Add the onion and fry until golden brown. Using a slotted spoon, remove half of the onion with a little of the ghee and set aside in a bowl.

3 Add the ginger, garlic, turmeric, 1 teaspoon of the salt, the chilli powder and the garam masala to the mixture remaining in the pan and stir-fry for 5 minutes. Stir in the yogurt and add the chana dhal and 150 ml/¼ pint of the water. Cook, covered, for 15 minutes. Set aside.

4 Meanwhile, boil the milk with the saffron, add the reserved fried onion, lemon juice, green chillies and coriander leaves, and set aside.

5 Boil the rest of the water and add the salt, black cardamoms, black cumin seeds and the rice, and cook, stirring, until the rice is half-cooked. Drain, and place half the milk and fried onion mixture on top of the chana dhal mixture. Place the rice on top of this and the rest of the milk and fried onion mixture on top of the rice.

6 Cover tightly with a lid and cook for 20 minutes over a very low heat. Mix with a slotted spoon before transferring to a warmed serving dish. Serve immediately.

Spiced Rice & Lentils

This is a lovely combination of rice and masoor dhal and is simple to cook. You can add a knob of unsalted butter before serving, if liked.

NUTRITIONAL INFORMATION

Calories 394	Sugars 3g	
Protein 14g	Fat 8g	
Carbohydrate ...70g	Saturates 1g	

 5 mins   30 mins

SERVES 4

INGREDIENTS

200 g/7 oz basmati rice

175 g/6 oz masoor dhal (see page 459)

2 tbsp ghee

1 small onion, sliced

1 tsp finely chopped fresh root ginger

1 tsp crushed garlic

½ tsp turmeric

600 ml/1 pint water

1 tsp salt

1 Combine the rice and dhal and rinse thoroughly in cold running water. Set aside until required.

2 Heat the ghee in a large saucepan. Add the onion and fry, stirring occasionally, for about 2 minutes.

3 Reduce the heat, add the ginger, garlic and turmeric to the pan and stir-fry for 1 minute.

4 Add the rice and dhal to the mixture in the pan and blend together, mixing gently, but thoroughly.

5 Add the water to the mixture in the pan and bring it to the boil over a medium heat. Reduce the heat, cover and cook for 20–25 minutes, until the rice is tender and the liquid is absorbed.

6 Just before serving, add the salt and mix to combine.

7 Transfer the spiced rice and lentils to a large warmed serving dish and serve immediately.

COOK'S TIP

Many Indian recipes specify using ghee as the cooking fat. This is because it is similar to clarified butter in that it can be heated to a very high temperature without burning. Ghee adds a nutty flavour to dishes and a glossy shine to sauces.

Vegballs with Chilli Sauce

These tasty, nutty morsels are delicious served with a fiery, tangy sauce that counteracts the richness of the peanuts.

NUTRITIONAL INFORMATION

Calories 615	Sugars 13g
Protein 23g	Fat 43g
Carbohydrate . . .37g	Saturates 8g

25 mins   30 mins

SERVES 4

I N G R E D I E N T S

3 tbsp groundnut oil

1 onion, finely chopped

1 celery stick, chopped

1 tsp dried mixed herbs

225 g/8 oz dry-roasted unsalted peanuts, ground

175 g/6 oz canned chick peas, drained and mashed

1 tsp yeast extract

60 g/2 oz fresh wholemeal breadcrumbs

1 egg yolk

25 g/1 oz plain flour

strips of fresh red chilli, to garnish

H O T   C H I L L I   S A U C E

2 tsp groundnut oil

1 large red chilli, deseeded and finely chopped

2 spring onions, finely chopped

2 tbsp red wine vinegar

200 g/7 oz canned chopped tomatoes

2 tbsp tomato purée

2 tsp caster sugar

salt and pepper

rice and green salad, to serve

1 Heat 1 tablespoon of the oil in a frying pan and gently fry the onion and celery for 3–4 minutes, until softened but not browned.

2 Place all the other ingredients, except the remaining oil and the flour, in a mixing bowl and add the onion and celery. Stir well to combine.

3 Divide the mixture into 12 portions and roll into small balls. Coat all over with the flour.

4 Heat the remaining oil in a frying pan. Add the chick pea and peanut balls and cook over a medium heat, turning frequently but carefully, for 15 minutes, until cooked through and golden. Drain well on absorbent kitchen paper.

5 Meanwhile, make the hot chilli sauce. Heat the groundnut oil in a small frying pan and gently fry the chilli and spring onions for 2–3 minutes. Stir in the remaining ingredients and season to taste with salt and pepper. Bring to the boil and simmer for 5 minutes.

6 Serve the chick pea and peanut balls with the hot chilli sauce, rice and a crisp green salad.

Red Bean Stew & Dumplings

There's nothing better on a cold day than a hearty dish topped with dumplings. This recipe is very quick and easy to prepare.

NUTRITIONAL INFORMATION

Calories 508	Sugars 15g
Protein 22g	Fat 12g
Carbohydrate ...83g	Saturates 4g

🕒 20 mins   🕐 40 mins

SERVES 4

INGREDIENTS

1 tbsp vegetable oil

1 red onion, sliced

2 celery sticks, chopped

850 ml/1½ pints vegetable stock

225 g/8 oz carrots, diced

225 g/8 oz potatoes, diced

225 g/8 oz courgettes, diced

4 tomatoes, peeled and chopped

125 g/4 oz split red lentils

400 g/14 oz canned kidney beans, rinsed and drained

1 tsp paprika

salt and pepper

DUMPLINGS

125 g/4½ oz plain flour

½ tsp salt

2 tsp baking powder

1 tsp paprika

1 tsp dried mixed herbs

25 g/1 oz vegetarian suet

7 tbsp water

sprigs of fresh flat-leaved parsley, to garnish

1 Heat the vegetable oil in a flameproof casserole or a large saucepan. Add the onion and celery and fry over a low heat, stirring frequently, for 3–4 minutes or until just softened.

2 Pour in the stock and stir in the carrots and potatoes. Bring to the boil, cover and cook for 5 minutes.

3 Stir in the courgettes, tomatoes, lentils, kidney beans, paprika and seasoning. Bring to the boil, cover and cook for 5 minutes.

4 Meanwhile, make the dumplings. Sift the flour, salt, baking powder and paprika into a bowl. Stir in the herbs and suet. Bind together with the water to form a soft dough. Divide into 8 portions and roll gently to form balls.

5 Uncover the stew, stir, then add the dumplings, pushing them slightly into the stew. Cover, reduce the heat so the stew simmers and cook for a further 15 minutes, until the dumplings have risen and are cooked through.

6 Serve immediately on warmed plates, garnished with flat leaf parsley.

Creamy Vegetable Curry

Vegetables are cooked in a mildly spiced curry sauce with yogurt and fresh coriander stirred in just before serving.

NUTRITIONAL INFORMATION

Calories 423	Sugars 24g	
Protein 16g	Fat 19g	
Carbohydrate ...50g	Saturates 7g	

 20 mins   25 mins

SERVES 4

I N G R E D I E N T S

2 tbsp sunflower oil

1 onion, sliced

2 tsp cumin seeds

2 tbsp ground coriander

1 tsp turmeric

2 tsp ground ginger

1 tsp chopped fresh red chilli

2 garlic cloves, chopped

400 g/14 oz canned chopped tomatoes

3 tbsp powdered coconut mixed with
   300 ml/½ pint boiling water

1 small cauliflower, broken into florets

2 courgettes, sliced

2 carrots, sliced

1 potato, diced

400 g/14 oz canned chick peas, drained
   and rinsed

salt and pepper

150 ml/¼ pint thick natural yogurt

2 tbsp mango chutney

3 tbsp chopped fresh coriander

fresh herbs, to garnish

1 Heat the oil in a saucepan and fry the onion until softened. Add the cumin, ground coriander, turmeric, ginger, chilli and garlic and fry for 1 minute.

2 Add the tomatoes and coconut mixture and mix well.

3 Add the cauliflower, courgettes, carrots, diced potato and chick peas

and season to taste with salt and pepper. Cover and simmer for 20 minutes, until the vegetables are tender.

4 Stir in the yogurt, mango chutney and fresh coriander and heat through gently, but do not boil.

5 Transfer to a warm serving dish, garnish and serve with rice.

Fragrant Chick Pea Curry

There are many different ways of cooking chick peas, but this version is probably one of the most delicious and popular.

NUTRITIONAL INFORMATION

Calories . . . . .313　Sugars 5g
Protein . . . . .8g　Fat 19g
Carbohydrate . . .29g　Saturates 2g

 10 mins　 20 mins

SERVES 4

INGREDIENTS

6 tbsp vegetable oil

2 onions, sliced

1 tsp finely chopped fresh root ginger

1 tsp ground cumin

1 tsp ground coriander

1 tsp crushed garlic

1 tsp chilli powder

2 fresh green chillies, deseeded and chopped

fresh coriander leaves

150 ml/¼ pint water

1 large potato

400 g/14 oz canned chick peas, drained

1 tbsp lemon juice

COOK'S TIP
Using canned chick peas saves time, but you can use dried chick peas if you prefer. Soak them for 10 minutes and simmer for 1–2 hours, or until soft.

1 Heat the vegetable oil in a large saucepan. Add the onions and fry over a medium heat, stirring occasionally, for 5–8 minutes, until golden brown.

2 Reduce the heat, add the ginger, ground cumin, ground coriander, garlic, chilli powder, fresh green chillies and coriander leaves to the pan and stir-fry for 2 minutes.

3 Add the water to the mixture in the pan and stir well to mix.

4 Using a sharp knife, cut the potato into small dice. Add the potato and the drained chick peas to the mixture in the pan. Lower the heat, cover and simmer, stirring occasionally, for 5–7 minutes.

5 Sprinkle the lemon juice over the curry and stir again.

6 Transfer the chick pea curry to warmed individual serving dishes and serve immediately. Warm naan breads go well with this dish.

Semolina Fritters

Based on a gnocchi recipe, these delicious cheese-flavoured fritters are accompanied by a fruity home-made apple relish.

NUTRITIONAL INFORMATION

Calories	682	Sugars	........40g
Protein	........19g	Fat	..........32g
Carbohydrate	...85g	Saturates	......11g

30 mins   40–45 mins

SERVES 4

INGREDIENTS

600 ml/1 pint milk

1 small onion

1 celery stick

1 bay leaf

2 cloves

125 g/4½ oz semolina

125 g/4½ oz mature Cheddar cheese, grated

½ tsp dried mustard powder

salt and pepper

2 tbsp plain flour

1 egg, beaten

60 g/2 oz dry white breadcrumbs

6 tbsp vegetable oil

celery leaves, to garnish

coleslaw, to serve

RELISH

2 celery sticks, chopped

2 small apples, cored and diced

90 g/3 oz sultanas

90 g/3 oz ready-to-eat dried apricots, chopped

6 tbsp cider vinegar

pinch of ground cloves

½ tsp ground cinnamon

1 Pour the milk into a saucepan and add the onion, celery, bay leaf and cloves. Bring to the boil, remove from the heat and allow to stand for 15 minutes.

2 Strain into another saucepan, bring to the boil and sprinkle in the semolina, stirring constantly. Reduce the heat and simmer for 5 minutes, until very thick, stirring occasionally to prevent it sticking.

3 Remove the pan from the heat. Beat in the cheese, mustard and seasoning. Place in a greased bowl and allow to cool.

4 To make the relish, put all the ingredients in a saucepan, bring to the boil, cover and simmer gently for 20 minutes, until tender. Allow to cool.

5 Put the flour, egg and breadcrumbs on separate plates. With floured hands, divide the cooled semolina mixture into 8 and press into 6 cm/2½ inch rounds.

6 Coat lightly in flour, then in egg and finally in breadcrumbs. Heat the oil in a large frying pan and gently fry the fritters for 3–4 minutes on each side, until golden. Drain on kitchen paper.

7 Garnish the fritters with celery leaves and serve immediately with the apple relish and coleslaw.

Fragrant Coconut Rice

This fragrant, sweet rice is delicious served with a variety of vegetable dishes as part of a Chinese menu.

NUTRITIONAL INFORMATION

Calories 306   Sugars 2g
Protein ....5g   Fat 6g
Carbohydrate ...61g   Saturates 4g

 5 mins   15 mins

SERVES 4

INGREDIENTS

275 g/9½ oz long grain white rice

600 ml/1 pint water

½ tsp salt

100 ml/3½ fl oz coconut milk

25 g/1 oz desiccated coconut

1 Rinse the rice thoroughly under cold running water until the water runs completely clear.

2 Drain the rice thoroughly in a sieve set over a large bowl. This is to remove some of the starch and to prevent the grains from sticking together.

3 Place the rice in a wok with the water. Add the salt and coconut milk to the wok and bring to the boil.

4 Cover the wok with a lid or a lid made of foil, curved into a domed shape and resting on the sides of the wok. Reduce the heat and leave to simmer for 10 minutes.

5 Remove the lid from the wok and fluff up the rice with a fork – all of the liquid should be absorbed and the

rice grains should be tender. If the rice is not quite cooked, add a little more water, replace the lid and continue to simmer for a few more minutes until all the liquid has been absorbed.

6 Spoon the rice into a warm serving bowl and scatter with the desiccated coconut. Serve immediately.

COOK'S TIP

Coconut milk is not the liquid found inside coconuts – that is called coconut water. Coconut milk is made from the white coconut flesh soaked in water and milk and then squeezed to extract all of the flavour. You can make your own or buy it in cans.

Midweek Curry Special

This easy curry is always enjoyed. Double the quantities for a great dish if you're cooking for a crowd.

NUTRITIONAL INFORMATION

Calories 403	Sugars 19g
Protein 19g	Fat 15g
Carbohydrate ...51g	Saturates 3g

20 mins   40–45 mins

SERVES 4

INGREDIENTS

2 tbsp vegetable oil

2 garlic cloves, crushed

1 large onion, chopped

1 large carrot, sliced

1 apple, cored and chopped

2 tbsp medium-hot curry powder

1 tsp finely grated root ginger

2 tsp paprika

850 ml/1½ pints vegetable stock

2 tbsp tomato purée

½ small cauliflower, broken into florets

425 g/15 oz canned chick peas, rinsed and drained

25 g/1 oz sultanas

2 tbsp cornflour

2 tbsp water

salt and pepper

4 hard-boiled eggs

paprika, to garnish

CUCUMBER DIP

7.5 cm/3 inch piece of cucumber, chopped

1 tbsp chopped fresh mint

150 ml/¼ pint natural yogurt

fresh mint sprigs, to garnish

1 Heat the vegetable oil in a large saucepan. Add the garlic, onion, carrot and apple and fry, stirring frequently, for 4–5 minutes, until softened.

2 Add the curry powder, ginger and paprika to the pan and fry for 1 minute. Stir in the vegetable stock and tomato purée.

3 Add the cauliflower, chick peas and sultanas. Bring to the boil, stirring, then reduce the heat, cover the pan and simmer for 25–30 minutes, or until all the vegetables are tender.

4 Blend the cornflour with the water to a smooth paste and add to the curry, stirring until thickened. Cook over a low heat for a further 2 minutes. Season to taste with salt and pepper.

5 To make the dip, mix together the cucumber, mint and yogurt in a small serving bowl.

6 Ladle the curry on to 4 warmed serving plates. Shell and quarter the eggs and arrange them on top of the curry. Sprinkle with a little paprika. Garnish the dip with mint and serve with the curry.

Lentil & Vegetable Biryani

A delicious mix of vegetables, basmati rice and green lentils produces a wholesome and nutritious dish.

NUTRITIONAL INFORMATION

Calories 516   Sugars 9g
Protein . . . . .20g   Fat 19g
Carbohydrate . . .72g   Saturates 3g

 20 mins   45 mins

SERVES 6

INGREDIENTS

125 g/4½ oz green lentils

4 tbsp ghee or oil

2 onions, quartered and sliced

2 garlic cloves, crushed

2.5 cm/1 inch piece fresh root ginger, chopped

1 tsp turmeric

½ tsp chilli powder

1 tsp ground coriander

2 tsp ground cumin

3 tomatoes, peeled and chopped

1 aubergine, trimmed and cut in 1 cm/½ inch pieces

1.75 litres/3 pints boiling vegetable stock

1 red or green pepper, deseeded and diced

350 g/12 oz basmati rice

125 g/4½ oz French beans, halved

225 g/8 oz cauliflower florets

125 g/4½ oz mushrooms, sliced or quartered

60 g/2 oz unsalted cashews

3 hard-boiled eggs, shelled, and fresh coriander sprigs, to garnish

1 Rinse the lentils under cold running water and drain. Heat the ghee or oil in a saucepan, add the onions and fry gently for 2 minutes. Stir in the garlic, ginger and spices and fry gently, stirring frequently, for 1 minute.

2 Add the lentils, tomatoes, aubergine and 600 ml/1 pint of the stock, mix well, then cover and simmer gently for 20 minutes.

3 Add the red or green pepper and cook for a further 10 minutes, or until the lentils are tender and all the liquid has been absorbed.

4 Meanwhile, rinse the rice under cold running water. Drain and place in another pan with the remaining stock. Bring to the boil, add the French beans, cauliflower and mushrooms, then cover and cook gently for 15 minutes, or until the rice and vegetables are tender. Remove from the heat and set aside, covered, for 10 minutes.

5 Add the lentil mixture and the cashews to the cooked rice and mix lightly together. Pile the biryani on to a warm serving platter and garnish with wedges of hard-boiled egg and coriander sprigs. Serve hot.

Dry Moong Dhal

This dhal has a baghaar (seasoned dressing) of butter, dried red chillies and white cumin seeds. It is simple to cook and tastes very good.

NUTRITIONAL INFORMATION

Calories 304	Sugars 1g
Protein 9g	Fat 21g
Carbohydrate ...21g	Saturates 14g

5 mins   30-35 mins

SERVES 4

I N G R E D I E N T S

150 g/5½ oz moong dhal

1 tsp finely chopped fresh root ginger

½ tsp ground cumin

½ tsp ground coriander

1 tsp crushed garlic

½ tsp chilli powder

600 ml/1 pint water

1 tsp salt

B A G H A A R

100 g/3½ oz unsalted butter

5 dried red chillies

1 tsp white cumin seeds

T O S E R V E

chapattis

vegetable curry

1 Rinse the lentils under cold running water and place them in a large saucepan. Add the ginger, ground cumin, ground coriander, garlic and chilli powder, and stir to mix well.

2 Pour in enough of the water to cover the lentil mixture. Cook over a medium heat, stirring frequently, until the lentils are soft but not mushy.

3 Stir in the salt, transfer to a serving dish and keep warm.

4 Meanwhile, make the baghaar. Melt the butter in a heavy-based saucepan over a fairly low heat. Add the dried red chillies and white cumin seeds and fry, stirring constantly, until they begin to pop and give off their aroma.

5 Pour the baghaar over the lentils and serve immediately with chapattis and a vegetable curry.

COOK'S TIP

Moong dhal are teardrop-shaped yellow split lentils, more popular in northern India than in the south. Dried red chillies are the quickest way to add heat to a dish.

Vegetable & Lentil Koftas

A mixture of vegetables, nuts and lentils is shaped into small balls and baked in the oven with a sprinkling of aromatic garam masala.

NUTRITIONAL INFORMATION

Calories	679	Sugars	.......20g
Protein	........29g	Fat	..........33g
Carbohydrate	...73g	Saturates	.......5g

 30 mins   50 mins

SERVES 4

INGREDIENTS

6 tbsp ghee or oil

1 onion, finely chopped

2 carrots, finely chopped

2 celery sticks, finely chopped

2 garlic cloves, crushed

1 fresh green chilli, deseeded and finely chopped

4½ tsp curry powder or paste

225 g/8 oz split red lentils

600 ml/1 pint vegetable stock

2 tbsp tomato purée

125 g/4½ oz fresh wholemeal breadcrumbs

90 g/3 oz unsalted cashews, finely chopped

2 tbsp chopped fresh coriander

1 egg, beaten

salt and pepper

garam masala, for sprinkling

YOGURT DRESSING

250 ml/9 fl oz natural yogurt

1–2 tbsp chopped fresh coriander

1–2 tbsp mango chutney, chopped if necessary

1 Heat 4 tablespoons of ghee or oil in a large saucepan and gently fry the onion, carrots, celery, garlic and chilli, stirring frequently, for 5 minutes. Add the curry powder or paste and the lentils and cook, stirring constantly, for 1 minute.

2 Add the stock and tomato purée and bring to the boil. Reduce the heat, cover and simmer for 20 minutes, or until the lentils are tender and all the liquid has been absorbed.

3 Remove from the heat and cool slightly. Add the breadcrumbs, nuts, coriander, egg and seasoning to taste. Mix well and leave to cool. Shape into rounds about the size of golf balls (use 2 spoons to help shape the rounds).

4 Place the balls on a greased baking tray, drizzle with the remaining oil and sprinkle with a little garam masala, to taste. Cook in a preheated oven, at 180°C/350°F/Gas Mark 4, for 15–20 minutes, or until piping hot and lightly golden in colour.

5 Meanwhile, to make the yogurt dressing mix all the ingredients together in a bowl. Serve the koftas hot with the yogurt dressing.

Spiced Black-eye Beans

This Indian dish is very good served with chapattis and a vegetable curry. The beans need to be soaked overnight so prepare well in advance.

NUTRITIONAL INFORMATION

Calories . . . . . . .757 Sugars 5g
Protein . . . . .10g Fat 69g
Carbohydrate . . .26g Saturates 7g

 15 mins, plus soaking   1 hr

SERVES 4

I N G R E D I E N T S

150 g/5½ oz black-eye beans

300 ml/½ pint vegetable oil

2 onions, sliced

1 tsp finely chopped fresh root ginger

1 tsp crushed garlic

1 tsp chilli powder

1½ tsp salt

1½ tsp ground coriander

1½ tsp ground cumin

150 ml/5 fl oz water

2 fresh green chillies, deseeded and finely chopped

fresh coriander leaves

1 tbsp lemon juice

1 Rinse the black-eye beans, place them in a bowl, cover with cold water and set aside to soak overnight.

2 Drain the beans, place in a pan and add water to cover. Bring slowly to the boil, boil for 15 minutes, then simmer gently for about 45 minutes. Drain thoroughly and set aside.

3 Heat the oil in a heavy-based pan. Add the onions and cook, stirring frequently, for 5–8 minutes, until golden brown. Add the ginger, garlic, chilli powder, salt, ground coriander and ground cumin and stir-fry the mixture over a low heat for 3–5 minutes. Add the water to the pan, cover and simmer until all of the water has completely evaporated.

4 Add the black-eye beans, green chillies and coriander leaves to the onions and stir-fry for 3–5 minutes.

5 Transfer the black-eye beans to a serving dish, sprinkle over the lemon juice and serve immediately. Alternatively, allow the beans to cool and serve cold.

COOK'S TIP

Black-eye beans are oval-shaped, grey or beige beans with a dark dot in the centre. They have a slightly smoky flavour. They are sold canned, as well as dried.

Midweek Medley

Canned chick peas are used in this dish, but you could use black-eye beans or red kidney beans, if preferred.

NUTRITIONAL INFORMATION

Calories 480	Sugars 8g	
Protein 11g	Fat 38g	
Carbohydrate ...25g	Saturates 13g	

15 mins

20-25 mins

SERVES 4

INGREDIENTS

1 large aubergine

2 courgettes

6 tbsp ghee or oil

1 large onion, quartered and sliced

2 garlic cloves, crushed

1–2 fresh green chillies, deseeded and chopped, or 1–2 tsp minced chilli

2 tsp ground coriander

2 tsp cumin seeds

1 tsp turmeric

1 tsp garam masala

400 g/14 oz canned chopped tomatoes

300 ml/½ pint vegetable stock or water

salt and pepper

400 g/14 oz canned chick peas, drained and rinsed

2 tbsp chopped fresh mint

150 ml/¼ pint double cream

rice or parathas, to serve

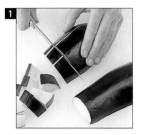

1 Trim the leaf end off the aubergine and cut it into cubes. Trim and slice the courgettes.

2 Heat the ghee or oil in a saucepan and fry the aubergine, courgettes, onion, garlic and chillies over a low heat, stirring frequently, for about 5 minutes, adding a little more oil to the pan, if necessary.

3 Stir in the spices and cook for 30 seconds. Add the tomatoes and stock and season with salt and pepper to taste. Cook for 10 minutes.

4 Add the drained chick peas to the pan and continue to cook for a further 5 minutes.

5 Stir in the mint and cream and reheat gently. Taste and adjust the seasoning, if necessary. Transfer to a warm serving dish and serve hot with plain or pilau rice, or with parathas, if preferred.

Aloo Chat

Aloo Chat is one of a variety of Indian foods served at any time of the day. The chick peas need to be soaked overnight.

NUTRITIONAL INFORMATION

Calories . . . . . . .262 Sugars 6g
Protein . . . . .13g Fat 4g
Carbohydrate . . .46g Saturates 0.5g

 35 mins   1 hr 5 mins

SERVES 4

I N G R E D I E N T S

125 g/4½ oz chick peas, soaked overnight in cold water and drained

1 dried red chilli

500 g/1 lb 2 oz waxy potatoes, boiled in their skins and peeled

1 tsp cumin seeds

2 tsp salt

1 tsp black peppercorns

½ tsp dried mint

½ tsp chilli powder

½ tsp ground ginger

2 tsp mango powder

125 ml/4 fl oz natural yogurt

oil, for deep frying

4 poppadoms

1 Boil the chick peas with the chilli in plenty of water for about 1 hour until tender, then drain.

2 Cut the potatoes into 2.5 cm/1 inch dice and mix into the chick peas while they are still warm. Set aside.

3 Grind together the cumin, salt and peppercorns in a spice grinder or with a pestle and mortar. Stir in the mint, chilli powder, ginger and mango powder.

4 Put a small saucepan or frying pan over a low heat and add the spice mix. Stir until the spices give off their aroma and then immediately remove the pan from the heat.

5 Stir half of the spice mix into the chick pea and potato mixture and stir the other half into the yogurt.

6 Cook the poppadoms according to the instructions on the packet. Drain on plenty of kitchen paper. Break into bite-size pieces and stir into the potatoes and chick peas, spoon over the spiced yogurt and serve immediately.

VARIATION

Instead of chick peas, diced tropical fruits can be stirred into the potatoes and spice mix; add a little lemon juice to balance the sweetness.

Vegetarian Paella

This recipe, full of Mediterranean vegetables, is one of the many different variations of this popular Spanish dish.

NUTRITIONAL INFORMATION

Calories	359	Sugars	.........8g
Protein	........10g	Fat	..........14g
Carbohydrate	...52g	Saturates	.......2g

 15 mins   40 mins

SERVES 6

I N G R E D I E N T S

¼ tsp saffron threads

3 tbsp hot water

6 tbsp olive oil

1 Spanish onion, sliced

3 garlic cloves, finely chopped

1 red pepper, deseeded and sliced

1 orange pepper, deseeded and sliced

1 large aubergine, cut into cubes

225 g/8 oz arborio rice

600 ml/1 pint vegetable stock

450 g/1 lb tomatoes, skinned and chopped

salt and pepper

115 g/4 oz mushrooms, sliced

115 g/4 oz French beans, halved

400 g/14 oz canned pinto beans or chick peas

COOK'S TIP

Arborio rice is rounder than long grain rice and can absorb a lot of liquid without becoming soggy. Spanish rice, which would be more authentic in this dish, is similar but is not so widely available.

1 Put the saffron and hot water in a small bowl and set aside. Meanwhile, heat the oil in a large, heavy-based frying pan or a paella pan. Add the onion and cook, stirring occasionally, for 5 minutes, until softened. Add the garlic, peppers and aubergine and cook, stirring occasionally, for 5 minutes more.

2 Add the rice and stir for about 1 minute, until the grains are coated in oil. Add the stock, tomatoes, saffron and soaking water to the pan and season to taste with salt and pepper. Bring to the boil, lower the heat and simmer, shaking the pan frequently and stirring the mixture occasionally, for 15 minutes.

3 Stir in the mushrooms, French beans and pinto beans or chick peas with their can juices. Cook for 10 minutes more, then serve.

Stuffed Cabbage Rolls

Bathed in a tomato sauce, these cabbage rolls are stuffed with a nutty filling of pearl barley and courgettes to make a satisfying main course.

NUTRITIONAL INFORMATION

Calories	224	Sugars	........19g
Protein	.........6g	Fat	...........5g
Carbohydrate	...43g	Saturates	.......1g

30 mins

1 hr 10 mins

SERVES 4

INGREDIENTS

8 large or 12 medium green
   cabbage leaves

1 litre/1¾ pints water

100 g/3½ oz pearl barley

2 tbsp chopped fresh parsley

2 garlic cloves, coarsely chopped

800 g/28 oz canned chopped tomatoes

4 tbsp red wine vinegar

1 tbsp sunflower or corn oil,
   plus extra for brushing

2 courgettes, diced

3 spring onions, sliced

salt and pepper

2 tbsp brown sugar

1 Cut out the thick stems from the cabbage leaves, then blanch the leaves in a large pan of boiling water for 1 minute. Drain the leaves well and spread out to dry. Bring the measured water to the boil in a large saucepan. Add the barley and half the chopped parsley, cover and simmer for about 45 minutes, until the liquid has been absorbed.

2 Meanwhile, put the garlic, half the tomatoes and the vinegar in a blender or food processor and process to a smooth purée. Scrape into a bowl and set aside.

Heat the oil in a large frying pan. Add the courgettes and the remaining parsley and cook, stirring frequently, for 3 minutes. Add the spring onions and cook briefly, then add the tomato purée mixture. Cook for about 10 minutes, until thickened, then transfer to a large bowl.

3 Add the cooked barley to the bowl, season to taste with salt and pepper and stir well. Lightly brush an ovenproof dish with oil. Place a spoonful of the barley mixture at the stem end of a cabbage leaf. Roll up, tucking in the sides, and place, seam side down, in the dish. Stuff and roll the remaining cabbage leaves in the same way, placing them in the dish in a single layer. Sprinkle the brown sugar over the cabbage rolls and pour the remaining tomatoes, with their can juice, on top. Cover with foil and bake in a preheated oven, 190°C/375°F/Gas Mark 5, for 30 minutes, or until tender. Serve straight from the dish.

Saucy Borlotti Beans

Fresh sage, a herb used frequently in Mediterranean cooking, adds a subtle flavour to these pink and white speckled beans.

NUTRITIONAL INFORMATION

Calories 84   Sugars 6g
Protein . . . . .4g   Fat 3g
Carbohydrate . . .10g   Saturates 0g

20 mins   30 mins

SERVES 4–6

I N G R E D I E N T S

600 g/1 lb 5 oz fresh borlotti beans

4 large fresh sage leaves, torn

1 tbsp olive oil

1 large onion, thinly sliced

300 ml/10 fl oz good-quality bottled or home-made tomato sauce (see page 269) for pasta

salt and pepper

shredded fresh sage leaves, to garnish

1 Shell the borlotti beans. Bring a saucepan of water to the boil, add the beans and torn sage leaves, bring back to the boil and simmer for about 12 minutes or until tender. Drain and set aside.

2 Heat the olive oil in a large, heavy-based frying pan over a medium heat. Add the onion and cook, stirring occasionally, for about 5 minutes until softened and translucent, but not browned. Stir the tomato sauce into the pan with the cooked borlotti beans and the torn sage leaves.

3 Increase the heat and bring to the boil, stirring. Lower the heat, partially cover and simmer for about 10 minutes or until the sauce has slightly reduced.

4 Adjust the seasoning, transfer to a serving bowl and serve hot, garnished with fresh sage leaves.

VARIATION

If fresh borlotti beans are unavailable, use 600 g/20 oz of canned beans instead. Drain and rinse, then add with the sage and tomato sauce in Step 2.

Mexican Beans

A pot of beans, bubbling away on the stove, is the basic everyday food of Mexico – delicious and healthy!

NUTRITIONAL INFORMATION

Calories	282	Sugars	.........1g
Protein	........18g	Fat	..........1g
Carbohydrate	...50g	Saturates	.......0g

 15 mins, plus soaking   2½ hrs

SERVES 4–6

I N G R E D I E N T S

500 g/1 lb 2 oz dried pinto or borlotti beans

fresh mint sprig

fresh thyme sprig

fresh flat leaf parsley sprig

1 onion, cut into chunks

salt

TO SERVE

warmed flour or corn tortillas

shreds of spring onion

1 Pick through the beans and remove any pieces of grit or stone. Put the beans in a bowl, cover with cold water and set aside to soak overnight. If you want to cut down on soaking time, bring the beans to the boil, boil for 5 minutes, then remove from the heat, cover and set aside for 2 hours.

2 Drain the beans, place in a pan and cover with fresh water. Add the mint, thyme and parsley sprigs. Bring to the boil, boil vigorously for 5 minutes, then reduce the heat to very low, cover and simmer gently for about 2 hours or until the beans are just tender.

3 Add the onion chunks and continue to cook until the onion and beans are very tender.

4 To serve as a side dish, drain, season with salt and serve in a bowl lined with warmed corn or flour tortillas, garnished with spring onion shreds.

COOK'S TIP
Beans cooked in this way, with their cooking liquid reserved, can be used for refried beans (see page 429).

Fruity Coconut Rice

The coconut, dried fruit, nuts, seeds and spices in this pale yellow rice make it a tasty accompaniment with a lovely texture.

NUTRITIONAL INFORMATION

Calories .... 578 Sugars 17g
Protein .... 8g Fat 31g
Carbohydrate .... 71g Saturates 15g

5 mins   35 mins

SERVES 4

INGREDIENTS

90 g/3 oz creamed coconut

700 ml/1¼ pints boiling water

1 tbsp sunflower oil (or olive oil for a stronger flavour)

1 onion, thinly sliced or chopped

250 g/9 oz long grain rice

¼ tsp turmeric

6 whole cloves

1 cinnamon stick

½ tsp salt

60–90 g/2–3 oz raisins or sultanas

60 g/2 oz walnut or pecan halves, roughly chopped

2 tbsp pumpkin seeds (optional)

1 Blend the creamed coconut with half the boiling water until smooth, then stir in the remainder until well blended.

2 Heat the oil in a preheated wok, add the onion and stir-fry gently for 3–4 minutes until the onion begins to soften.

3 Rinse the rice thoroughly under cold running water, drain well and add to the wok with the turmeric. Cook for 1–2 minutes, stirring all the time.

4 Add the coconut milk, cloves, cinnamon stick and salt to the wok and bring to the boil. Cover and cook very gently for 10 minutes.

5 Add the raisins, nuts and pumpkin seeds, if using, and mix well. Cover the wok again and continue to cook for a further 5–8 minutes or until all the liquid has been absorbed and the rice is tender. Remove from the heat and leave to stand, still tightly covered, for 5 minutes. Remove the cinnamon stick and serve.

COOK'S TIP

The addition of coconut milk gives the cooked rice a slightly sticky consistency and a special taste.

Lentils Simmered with Fruit

Although this might seem an unusual combination, when you taste this traditional Mexican dish you will discover just how delicious it is.

NUTRITIONAL INFORMATION

Calories	23	Sugars	........18g
Protein	........10g	Fat	..........7g
Carbohydrate	...36g	Saturates	.......1g

5 mins   45 mins

SERVES 4

INGREDIENTS

125 g/4½ oz brown or green lentils

about 1 litre/1¾ pints water

2 tbsp vegetable oil

3 small to medium onions, chopped

4 garlic cloves, roughly chopped

1 large Bramley apple, roughly chopped

about ¼ ripe pineapple, peeled and roughly chopped

2 tomatoes, deseeded and diced

1 almost ripe banana, cut into bite-size pieces

cayenne pepper

salt

fresh parsley sprig, to garnish

1 Put the lentils in a pan and add the water. Bring to the boil, then reduce the heat and simmer gently for about 40 minutes until the lentils are tender. Do not let them become mushy.

2 Meanwhile, heat the oil in a frying pan and fry the onions and garlic over a low heat for 10 minutes until lightly browned. Add the apple and continue to cook until golden. Add the pineapple, heat through, stirring, then add the tomatoes. Cook over a medium heat until thickened, stirring occasionally.

3 Drain the lentils, reserving 125 ml/ 4 fl oz of the cooking liquid. Add the drained lentils to the sauce, stirring in the reserved liquid if necessary. Heat the mixture through for a minute to allow the flavours to mingle.

4 Add the banana to the pan, then season to taste with cayenne pepper and salt. Garnish with the parsley sprig and serve immediately.

VARIATION
Instead of lentils, prepare the dish using cooked pinto or borlotti beans.

Egg & Lentil Curry

A nutritious meal that is easy and relatively quick to make. The curried lentil sauce would also be delicious served with cooked vegetables.

NUTRITIONAL INFORMATION

Calories ....298 Sugars 6g
Protein ....17g Fat 17g
Carbohydrate ...20g Saturates 4g

10 mins   35 mins

SERVES 4

INGREDIENTS

3 tbsp ghee or oil

1 large onion, chopped

2 garlic cloves, chopped

2.5 cm/1 inch piece of root ginger, chopped

½ tsp minced chilli or chilli powder

1 tsp ground coriander

1 tsp ground cumin

1 tsp paprika

90 g/3 oz split red lentils

425 ml/¾ pint vegetable stock

225 g/8 oz canned chopped tomatoes

6 eggs

50 ml/2 fl oz coconut milk

salt

2 tomatoes, cut into wedges, and fresh coriander sprigs, to garnish

parathas, chapattis or naan bread, to serve

1 Heat the ghee or oil in a saucepan, add the onion and fry gently for 3 minutes. Stir in the garlic, ginger, chilli and spices and cook gently, stirring frequently, for 1 minute. Stir in the lentils, stock and chopped tomatoes and bring to the boil. Reduce the heat, cover and simmer, stirring occasionally, for 30 minutes, until the lentils are tender.

2 Meanwhile, place the eggs in a saucepan of cold water and bring to the boil. Reduce the heat and simmer for 8 minutes. Drain and cover immediately with cold water.

3 Stir the coconut milk into the lentil mixture and season well with salt to taste. Process the mixture in a blender or food processor until smooth. Return to the pan and heat through.

4 Shell the hard-boiled eggs and cut them in half lengthways. Arrange 3 halves, in a petal design, on each of 4 warmed serving plates. Spoon the hot lentil sauce over the eggs, adding enough to flood the plate.

5 Arrange a tomato wedge and a coriander sprig between each halved egg. Serve the curry hot with parathas, chapattis or naan bread.

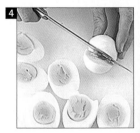

Spinach & Chana Dhal

An attractive-looking dish, this makes a good accompaniment to almost any dish. For a contrast in colour and taste, serve with a tomato curry.

NUTRITIONAL INFORMATION

Calories	175	Sugars	.........1g
Protein	.........6g	Fat	..........12g
Carbohydrate	...12g	Saturates	.......1g

5 mins, plus soaking   45 mins

SERVES 6

I N G R E D I E N T S

4 tbsp chana dhal

6 tbsp vegetable oil

1 tsp mixed onion and mustard seeds

4 dried red chillies

425 g/15 oz canned spinach, drained

1 tsp finely chopped fresh root ginger

1 tsp ground coriander

1 tsp ground cumin

1 tsp salt

1 tsp chilli powder

2 tbsp lemon juice

1 fresh green chilli, deseeded and finely chopped, to garnish

1 Soak the chana dhal in a bowl of warm water for at least 3 hours, or preferably overnight.

2 Drain the dhal, place in a saucepan, cover with water and bring to the boil. Lower the heat and simmer gently for 30 minutes, until tender. Drain well.

3 Heat the oil in another saucepan. Add the mixed onion and mustard seeds and dried red chillies and fry, stirring constantly, until they turn a shade darker.

4 Add the drained spinach to the pan, mixing gently. Add the ginger, ground coriander, ground cumin, salt and chilli powder. Reduce the heat and gently stir-fry the mixture for 7–10 minutes.

5 Add the drained dhal to the pan and blend into the spinach mixture well, stirring gently so that it does not break up.

6 Transfer the mixture to a warmed serving dish. Sprinkle over the lemon juice and garnish with the chopped green chilli. Serve immediately.

COOK'S TIP

Very similar in appearance to moong dhal – the yellow split peas – chana dhal have slightly less shiny grains.

Kabli Chana Sag

Pulses such as chick peas are widely used in India. They need to be soaked overnight so prepare well in advance.

NUTRITIONAL INFORMATION

Calories 217	Sugars 5g
Protein 12g	Fat 9g
Carbohydrate . . .25g	Saturates 1g

10 mins   1–2 hrs

SERVES 6

I N G R E D I E N T S

225 g/8 oz chick peas, soaked overnight and drained

5 cloves

2.5 cm/1 inch piece of cinnamon stick

2 garlic cloves

3 tbsp sunflower oil

1 small onion, sliced

3 tbsp lemon juice

1 tsp coriander seeds

2 tomatoes, peeled, deseeded and chopped

500 g/1 lb 2 oz fresh spinach, rinsed and any tough stems removed

1 tbsp chopped fresh coriander

T O   G A R N I S H

fresh coriander sprigs

lemon slices

1 Put the chick peas into a saucepan with enough water to cover. Add the cloves, cinnamon and 1 whole unpeeled garlic clove that has been lightly crushed with the back of a knife to release the juices. Bring to the boil, boil for 15

minutes, then simmer for 1–2 hours or until the chick peas are tender. Skim off any foam that comes to the surface.

2 Meanwhile, heat 1 tablespoon of the oil in a heavy-based pan. Crush the remaining garlic clove. Put it into the pan with the onion and cook over a moderate heat, stirring occasionally, for about 5 minutes.

3 Remove the cloves, cinnamon and garlic from the pan of chick peas and discard. Drain the chick peas. Place 85 g/3 oz of the chick peas in a food processor with the onion and garlic, the lemon juice and 1 tablespoon of the oil and process until smooth. Alternatively, blend together with a fork in a bowl. Stir this purée into the remaining chick peas.

4 Heat the remaining oil in a large frying pan, add the coriander seeds and stir for 1 minute until they give off their aroma. Add the tomatoes, stir and add the spinach. Cover and cook over a moderate heat for 1 minute. The spinach should be wilted, but not soggy. Stir in the chopped fresh coriander and remove the pan from the heat.

5 Transfer the chick peas to a warmed serving dish and spoon over the spinach mixture. Garnish with the coriander sprigs and slices of lemon and serve immediately.

Curried Rice with Tofu

Cooked rice is combined with marinated tofu, vegetables and peanuts to make this deliciously rich curry.

NUTRITIONAL INFORMATION

Calories	598	Sugars	.........2g
Protein	........16g	Fat	25
Carbohydrate	...81g	Saturates	.......4g

🌀 🌀

🧊 15 mins 🕐 15 mins

SERVES 4

INGREDIENTS

1 tsp coriander seeds

1 tsp cumin seeds

1 tsp ground cinnamon

1 tsp cloves

1 whole star anise

1 tsp cardamom pods

1 tsp white peppercorns

4 tbsp sunflower oil

6 shallots, roughly chopped

6 garlic cloves, roughly chopped

5 cm/2 inch piece lemongrass, sliced

4 fresh red chillies, deseeded and chopped

grated rind of 1 lime

1 tsp salt

250 g/9 oz marinated tofu, cut into
    2.5 cm/1 inch cubes

125 g/4½ oz French beans, cut into
    2.5 cm/1 inch lengths

1 kg/2 lb 4 oz cooked rice
    (300 g/10½ oz raw weight)

3 shallots, diced finely and deep-fried

1 spring onion, finely chopped

2 tbsp chopped dry-roasted peanuts

1 tbsp lime juice

1 To make the curry paste, grind together the seeds and spices in a pestle and mortar or spice grinder.

2 Heat 3 tablespoons of the sunflower oil in a preheated wok until it is really hot. Add the shallots, garlic and lemongrass and cook over a low heat until soft, about 5 minutes. Add the chillies and grind together with the dry spices. Stir in the lime rind and salt.

3 To make the curry, heat the remaining oil in a wok or large, heavy frying pan. Cook the tofu over a high heat for 2 minutes to seal. Stir in the curry paste and beans. Add the rice and stir over a high heat for about 3 minutes more.

4 Transfer to a warmed serving dish. Sprinkle with the deep-fried shallots, spring onion and peanuts, and squeeze over the lime juice. Serve hot.

Chinese Vegetable Rice

This tasty rice can either be served as a meal or as an accompaniment to other vegetable recipes.

NUTRITIONAL INFORMATION

Calories	228	Sugars	.........5g
Protein	.........5g	Fat	...........7g
Carbohydrate	...37g	Saturates	.......1g

🍳 🍳 🍳

🥔 5 mins   🕐 25 mins

SERVES 4

INGREDIENTS

350 g/12 oz long-grain white rice

1 tsp turmeric

salt

2 tbsp sunflower oil

225 g/8 oz courgettes, sliced

1 red pepper, deseeded and sliced

1 green pepper, deseeded and sliced

1 green chilli, deseeded and finely chopped

1 carrot, roughly grated

150 g/5½ oz beansprouts

6 spring onions, sliced, plus extra to garnish (optional)

2 tbsp soy sauce

1 Place the rice and turmeric in a pan of lightly salted water and bring to the boil. Reduce the heat and leave to simmer until the rice is just tender. Drain the rice thoroughly and press out any excess water with a sheet of absorbent kitchen paper. Set aside until required.

2 Heat the sunflower oil in a large preheated wok.

3 Add the courgettes to the wok and stir-fry for about 2 minutes.

4 Add the peppers and chilli to the wok and stir-fry for 2–3 minutes.

5 Add the cooked rice to the mixture in the wok, a little at a time, tossing well after each addition.

6 Add the carrots, beansprouts and spring onions to the wok and stir-fry for a further 2 minutes.

7 Drizzle with soy sauce and serve at once, garnished with extra spring onions, if desired.

COOK'S TIP

For real luxury, add a few saffron strands infused in boiling water instead of the turmeric.

Split Peas with Vegetables

Here is a simple yet nourishing and flavourful way of cooking yellow split peas. Vary the choice of vegetables and spices according to taste.

NUTRITIONAL INFORMATION

Calories	490	Sugars	.........8g
Protein	........21g	Fat	..........19g
Carbohydrate	...63g	Saturates	.......3g

🥣 15 mins, plus soaking 🕐 1 hr

SERVES 4

I N G R E D I E N T S

225 g/8 oz dried yellow split peas

1.2 litres/2 pints water

½ tsp turmeric (optional)

500g/1 lb 2 oz new potatoes

5 tbsp vegetable oil

2 onions, roughly chopped

175 g/6 oz button mushrooms

1 tsp ground coriander

1 tsp ground cumin

1 tsp chilli powder

1 tsp garam masala

salt and pepper

425 ml/15 fl oz vegetable stock

½ cauliflower, broken into florets

85 g/3 oz frozen peas

175 g/6 oz cherry tomatoes, halved

fresh mint sprigs, to garnish

1 Place the split peas in a bowl, add the water and set aside to soak for at least 4 hours or overnight.

2 Place the peas and the soaking liquid in a large saucepan, stir in the turmeric, if using, and bring to the boil. Skim off any scum that rises to the surface, half-cover the pan and simmer gently for 20 minutes or until the peas are tender and almost dry. Remove the pan from the heat and set aside.

3 Meanwhile, cut the potatoes into 5 mm/¼ inch thick slices. Heat the oil in a flameproof casserole, add the onions, potatoes and mushrooms and cook over a low heat, stirring frequently, for 5 minutes. Stir in the spices and fry, stirring frequently, for 1 minute, then season with salt and pepper to taste and add the stock and cauliflower florets.

4 Cover the pan and simmer, stirring occasionally, for 25 minutes or until the potatoes are tender. Add the split peas (and any of the cooking liquid) and the frozen peas. Bring to the boil, cover and continue cooking for 5 minutes.

5 Stir in the halved cherry tomatoes and cook for 2 minutes. Taste and adjust the seasoning, if necessary. Serve hot, garnished with mint sprigs.

VARIATION

Chana dhal (popular with vegetarians because of its high protein content) may be used instead of yellow split peas, if preferred. Chana dhal is similar to yellow split peas, although the grains are smaller and the flavour sweeter.

Toovar Dhal

Dried pulses and lentils can be cooked in similar ways, but the soaking and cooking times do vary, so check the pack for instructions.

NUTRITIONAL INFORMATION

Calories 195	Sugars 4g	
Protein 11g	Fat 5g	
Carbohydrate ...28g	Saturates 3g	

10 mins   50 mins

SERVES 6

INGREDIENTS

2 tbsp ghee

1 large onion, finely chopped

1 garlic clove, crushed

1 tbsp grated fresh root ginger

1 tbsp cumin seeds, ground

2 tsp coriander seeds, ground

1 dried red chilli, chopped

2.5 cm/1 inch piece of cinnamon stick

1 tsp salt

½ tsp turmeric

225 g/8 oz split yellow peas, soaked in cold water for 1 hour and drained

400 g/14 oz canned plum tomatoes

300 ml/½ pint water

2 tsp garam masala

COOK'S TIP

Use a non-stick saucepan if you have one, because the mixture is quite dense and does stick to the base of the pan occasionally. If the dhal is overstirred, the split peas will break up and the dish will not have much texture or bite.

1 Heat the ghee in a large saucepan, add the onion, garlic and ginger and fry for 3–4 minutes until the onion has softened slightly.

2 Add the cumin, coriander, chilli, cinnamon, salt and turmeric, then stir in the split peas until well mixed.

3 Add the tomatoes, with their can juices, breaking up the tomatoes slightly with the back of a spoon.

4 Add the water and bring to the boil. Reduce the heat to very low and simmer the dhal, uncovered, stirring occasionally, for about 40 minutes until most of the liquid has been absorbed and the split peas are tender. Skim the surface occasionally with a slotted spoon to remove any scum.

5 Gradually stir in the garam masala, tasting after each addition, until it is to your taste. Serve hot.

Onion Dhal

This dish is semi-dry, so is best served with a curry that has a sauce.
An ordinary onion can be used instead of spring onions.

NUTRITIONAL INFORMATION

Calories ....232 Sugars 1g
Protein ....6g Fat 17g
Carbohydrate ...15g Saturates 2g

5 mins   30 mins

SERVES 4

INGREDIENTS

100 g/3½ oz masoor dhal

6 tbsp vegetable oil

1 small bunch spring onions, chopped

1 tsp finely chopped fresh root ginger

1 tsp crushed garlic

½ tsp chilli powder

½ tsp turmeric

300 ml/½ pint water

1 tsp salt

1 fresh green chilli, deseeded and
   finely chopped

fresh coriander leaves

1 Rinse the lentils thoroughly and set aside until required.

2 Heat the oil in a heavy-based saucepan. Add the spring onions to the pan and fry over a medium heat, stirring frequently, until lightly browned.

3 Reduce the heat and add the ginger, garlic, chilli powder and turmeric. Briefly stir-fry the spring onions with the spices. Add the lentils and stir to blend.

4 Add the water to the lentil mixture, reduce the heat to low and cook for 20–25 minutes.

5 When the lentils are thoroughly cooked and tender, add the salt and stir gently to mix well.

6 Transfer the onion dhal to a serving dish. Garnish with the chopped green chillies and fresh coriander leaves and serve immediately.

COOK'S TIP
Masoor dhal are small, round, pale
orange split lentils. They turn a pale
yellow colour when cooked.

Murkha Dhal

In this dhal recipe, the garlic is intended to burn in the base of the pan, and this flavour permeates the dish.

NUTRITIONAL INFORMATION

Calories	372	Sugars 7g
Protein	........18g	Fat 16g
Carbohydrate	...42g	Saturates 10g

5 mins   55 mins

SERVES 4

I N G R E D I E N T S

60 g/2 oz butter

2 tsp black mustard seeds

1 onion, finely chopped

2 garlic cloves, finely chopped

1 tbsp grated fresh root ginger

1 tsp turmeric

2 green chillies, deseeded and finely chopped

225 g/8 oz red lentils

1 litre/1¾ pints water

300 ml/½ pint coconut milk

1 tsp salt

1 Melt the butter in a large heavy-based saucepan over a moderate heat. Add the mustard seeds and cover the pan. When you can hear the seeds popping, add the onion, garlic and grated ginger. Cook, uncovered, for about 7–8 minutes, until the onion is soft and the garlic is brown.

2 Stir in the turmeric and green chillies and cook for 1–2 minutes, until the chillies soften a little.

3 Add the lentils and cook, stirring frequently, for 2 minutes, until the lentils begin to turn translucent.

4 Stir in the water, coconut milk and salt. Bring to the boil, then reduce the heat and simmer for 40 minutes, or until the desired consistency is reached. However, if you intend to reheat the dhal later rather than eat it straight away, cook it for only 30 minutes to allow for reheating time.

5 Transfer the dhal to a warmed serving dish and serve immediately, while piping hot.

COOK'S TIP

There are many types of lentils used in India, but the two most common are red lentils and green or beige lentils. Red lentils are very useful, as they cook in a relatively short time to form a homogeneous mass. Green and beige lentils stay more separate when cooked.

Ghee-dressed Dhal

This dhal is given a baghaar (seasoned dressing) of ghee, onion and a combination of spicy seeds just before serving.

NUTRITIONAL INFORMATION

Calories ....173 Sugars 3g
Protein ....8g Fat 8g
Carbohydrate ...20g Saturates 5g

🐷 🐷

🧊 5 mins   🕐 30 mins

SERVES 4

INGREDIENTS

75 g/2¾ oz masoor dhal (see page 459)

50 g/1¾ oz moong dhal (see page 441)

425 ml/¾ pint water

1 tsp finely chopped fresh root ginger

1 tsp crushed garlic

2 red chillies, deseeded and chopped

1 tsp salt

BAGHAAR

2 tbsp ghee

1 onion, sliced

1 tsp mixed mustard and onion seeds

1 Rinse the dhal thoroughly and place in a large saucepan. Pour over the water, stirring. Add the ginger, garlic and red chillies and bring to a boil over a medium heat. Half-cover with a lid and simmer for about 15–20 minutes, until they are soft enough to be mashed.

2 Mash the lentils and add more water if necessary to form a thick sauce.

3 Add the salt to the lentil mixture and stir well. Transfer the lentils to a heatproof serving dish.

4 Just before serving, melt the ghee in a small saucepan. Add the onion and fry over a medium heat, stirring frequently, for about 5–8 minutes, until golden brown. Add the mustard and onion seeds and stir to mix well.

5 Pour the onion mixture over the lentils while it is still hot. Stir the mixture to combine thoroughly and serve the ghee-dressed dhal immediately.

COOK'S TIP
This dish makes a a very good accompaniment, especially for a dry curry. It also freezes well – simply re-heat it in a saucepan or covered in the oven.

Tarka Dhal

This is just one version of many dhals that are served throughout India; as many people are vegetarian, dhals form a staple part of the diet.

NUTRITIONAL INFORMATION

Calories	183	Sugars	.........4g
Protein	.........8g	Fat	...........8g
Carbohydrate	...22g	Saturates	.......5g

10 mins   25 mins

SERVES 4

INGREDIENTS

2 tbsp ghee

2 shallots, sliced

1 tsp yellow mustard seeds

2 garlic cloves, crushed

8 fenugreek seeds

1 tsp grated fresh root ginger

½ tsp salt

125 g/4½ oz red lentils

1 tbsp tomato purée

600 ml/1 pint water

2 tomatoes, peeled and chopped

1 tbsp lemon juice

4 tbsp chopped fresh coriander

½ tsp garam masala

½ tsp chilli powder

1 Heat half of the ghee in a large saucepan and add the shallots. Cook for 2–3 minutes over a high heat, then add the mustard seeds. Cover the pan until the seeds begin to pop.

2 Immediately remove the lid from the pan and add the garlic, fenugreek, ginger and salt.

3 Stir once and add the lentils, tomato purée and water. Bring to the boil, then lower the heat and simmer the mixture gently for 10 minutes.

4 Stir in the tomatoes, lemon juice, and chopped coriander and simmer for 4–5 minutes until the lentils are tender.

5 Transfer to a serving dish. Heat the remaining ghee in a pan. Remove from the heat and stir in the garam masala and chilli powder. Pour over the tarka dhal and serve.

COOK'S TIP

The flavours in a dhal can be altered to suit your particular taste; for example, for extra heat, add more chilli powder or chillies, or add fennel seeds for a pleasant aniseed flavour.

Risotto with Asparagus

Using the best asparagus available turns this simple recipe, an Italian classic, into a gourmet treat for lunch or supper.

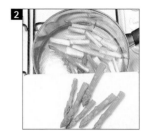

NUTRITIONAL INFORMATION

Calories 494	Sugars 3g	
Protein 15g	Fat 23g	
Carbohydrate 61g	Saturates 11g	

5–10 mins   30–35 mins

SERVES 6

I N G R E D I E N T S

900 g/2 lb fresh asparagus, washed

2 tbsp sunflower or other vegetable oil

6 tbsp unsalted butter

2 shallots or 1 small onion, chopped finely

400 g/14 oz arborio or carnaroli rice

1.5 litres/2¾ pints vegetable stock, simmering

85 g/3 oz Parmesan cheese, freshly grated

salt and pepper

Parmesan shavings, to garnish (optional)

1 Lightly peel the stems of the asparagus and trim off the woody ends. Cut the tips off each stalk and set them aside, then cut the remaining stems into 2.5 cm/1 inch pieces.

2 Add the asparagus stem pieces to a pan of boiling water and boil for 2 minutes. Add the asparagus tips and boil for about 1 minute, or until tender-crisp. Do not overcook. Rinse under cold running water and set aside.

3 Heat the oil with half the butter in a large heavy-based saucepan. Add the shallots and cook gently for 2 minutes until softened. Add the rice and cook, stirring frequently, for about 2 minutes, until the rice is translucent and well coated.

4 Add a ladleful of the simmering stock and cook, stirring constantly, until the stock is completely absorbed.

5 Continue adding the stock, about half a ladleful at a time, letting each addition be absorbed before adding the next. This should take about 20–25 minutes. The risotto should have a creamy consistency and the rice should be tender, but firm to the bite.

6 Heat the asparagus tips in the stock. Stir the stems into the risotto with the last ladleful of stock, the remaining butter and the grated Parmesan cheese. Remove from the heat, stir in the asparagus tips and season if necessary. Serve with Parmesan shavings, if wished.

Green Fried Rice

Spinach is used in this recipe to give the rice a wonderful green colouring. Tossed with the carrot strips, it is a really appealing dish.

NUTRITIONAL INFORMATION

Calories 139	Sugars 2g
Protein 3g	Fat 7g
Carbohydrate ...18g	Saturates 1g

5 mins   20 mins

SERVES 4

INGREDIENTS

150 g/5½ oz long grain rice

2 tbsp vegetable oil

2 garlic cloves, crushed

1 tsp grated fresh root ginger

1 carrot, cut into matchsticks

1 courgette, diced

225 g/8 oz baby spinach

2 tsp light soy sauce

2 tsp light brown sugar

1 Cook the rice in a saucepan of boiling water for about 15 minutes. Drain the rice well, rinse under cold running water and then rinse the rice thoroughly again. Set aside until required.

2 Heat the oil in a preheated wok or a large frying pan with a heavy base.

3 Add the crushed garlic and grated fresh root ginger to the wok or frying pan and stir-fry for about 30 seconds.

4 Add the carrot matchsticks and diced courgette to the mixture in the wok and stir-fry for about 2 minutes, so the vegetables still retain their crunch.

5 Add the baby spinach and stir-fry for 1 minute, until wilted.

6 Add the rice, soy sauce and sugar to the wok and mix together well.

7 Transfer the green fried rice to serving dishes and serve immediately.

COOK'S TIP

Light soy sauce has more flavour than the sweeter, dark soy sauce, which gives the food a rich, reddish colour.

Chatuchak Fried Rice

This is an excellent way to use up left-over rice. Pop it in the freezer as soon as it is cool, and it will be ready to reheat at any time.

NUTRITIONAL INFORMATION

Calories 241	Sugars 5g	
Protein 7g	Fat 5g	
Carbohydrate . . .46g	Saturates 1g	

 25 mins   15 mins

SERVES 4

I N G R E D I E N T S

1 tbsp sunflower oil

3 shallots, finely chopped

2 garlic cloves, crushed

1 red chilli, deseeded and finely chopped

2.5-cm/1-inch piece root ginger, finely shredded

½ green pepper, deseeded and finely sliced

150 g/5½ oz baby aubergines, quartered

90 g/3 oz sugar snap peas or mangetouts, trimmed and blanched

90 g/3 oz baby sweetcorn cobs, halved lengthways and blanched

1 tomato, cut into 8 pieces

90 g/3 oz beansprouts

500 g/1 lb 2 oz cooked jasmine rice

2 tbsp tomato ketchup

2 tbsp light soy sauce

TO GARNISH

fresh coriander leaves

lime wedges

1 Heat the oil in a wok or a large, heavy frying pan over a high heat.

2 Add the shallots, garlic, chilli and ginger to the wok or frying pan. Stir until the shallots have softened, then add the green pepper and quartered baby aubergines and stir well.

3 Add the sugar snap peas or the mangetouts, baby sweetcorn, tomato and beansprouts. Stir-fry for 3 minutes.

4 Add the cooked jasmine rice to the wok, and lift and stir with two spoons for about 4–5 minutes, until no more steam is released.

5 Stir the tomato ketchup and soy sauce into the mixture in the wok.

6 Serve the Chatuchak fried rice immediately on warmed plates, garnished with coriander leaves and lime wedges to squeeze over.

Fennel Risotto with Vodka

The alcohol in the vodka cooks out, but leaves a pleasant, tantalizing flavour which complements the cool sweetness of the fennel.

NUTRITIONAL INFORMATION

Calories	385	Sugars	4g
Protein	10g	Fat	10g
Carbohydrate	55g	Saturates	3g

5 mins   30–35 mins

SERVES 4–6

INGREDIENTS

2 large fennel bulbs

2 tbsp vegetable oil

6 tbsp unsalted butter

1 large onion, finely chopped

350 g/12 oz arborio or carnaroli rice

150 ml/5 fl oz vodka (or lemon-flavoured vodka, if you can find it)

1.3 litres/2¼ pints vegetable stock, simmering

55 g/2 oz Parmesan cheese, freshly grated

5–6 tbsp lemon juice

1 Trim the fennel, reserving the fronds for the garnish, if wished. Cut the bulbs in half lengthways, remove the V-shaped cores and roughly chop the flesh. (If you like, add any of the fennel trimmings to the stock for extra flavour.)

2 Heat the oil and half the butter in a large heavy-based saucepan over a medium heat. Add the onion and fennel and cook for about 2 minutes, stirring frequently, until the vegetables are softened. Add the rice and cook for about 2 minutes, stirring frequently, or until the rice is translucent and well coated.

3 Pour the vodka into the saucepan: it will bubble rapidly and evaporate almost immediately. Add a ladleful of the vegetable stock. Cook, stirring constantly with a spoon, until all of the stock is absorbed.

4 Continue stirring in the stock, about half a ladleful at a time, letting each addition be absorbed by the rice before adding the next. This should take about 20–25 minutes. The finished risotto should have a creamy consistency, and the rice grains should be just tender, but firm to the bite.

5 Stir in the remaining butter, with the grated Parmesan cheese and lemon juice. Remove from the heat, cover and leave to stand for 1 minute before serving. Garnish with a few of the reserved fennel fronds, if wished.

Fragrant Jasmine Rice

Jasmine rice has a delicate flavour and it can be served completely plain. This simple dish just has the light tang of lemon and soft scent of basil.

NUTRITIONAL INFORMATION

Calories ....384 Sugars 0g
Protein ....7g Fat 4g
Carbohydrate ...86g Saturates 1g

 15 mins   15 mins

SERVES 4

INGREDIENTS

400 g/14 oz jasmine rice

800 ml/28 fl oz water

rind of ½ lemon, finely grated

2 tbsp fresh sweet basil, chopped

1 Wash the rice in several changes of cold water until the water runs clear. Bring the water to the boil in a large pan, then add the rice.

2 Bring back to a rolling boil. Turn the heat to a low simmer, cover the pan and simmer for a further 12 minutes.

3 Remove the pan from the heat and set aside, covered, for 10 minutes. It is important to leave the pan tightly covered while the rice steams inside, so that the grains cook evenly and become fluffy and separate.

4 Fluff up the rice with a fork, then stir in the lemon rind. Serve sprinkled with basil leaves.

Vegetable Fried Rice

This dish can be served as part of a substantial meal for a number of people or as a meal in itself for four.

NUTRITIONAL INFORMATION

Calories 175	Sugars 3g
Protein 3g	Fat 10g
Carbohydrate ...20g	Saturates 2g

10 mins 20 mins

SERVES 4

INGREDIENTS

125 g/4½ oz long-grain white rice

3 tbsp peanut oil

2 garlic cloves, crushed

½ tsp Chinese five-spice powder

60 g/2 oz French beans

1 green pepper, deseeded and chopped

4 baby sweetcorn cobs, quartered lengthways

25 g/1 oz bamboo shoots, chopped

3 tomatoes, skinned, deseeded and chopped

60 g/2 oz cooked peas

1 tsp sesame oil

VARIATION

Use a selection of vegetables of your choice in this recipe, cutting them to a similar size in order to ensure that they cook in the same amount of time.

1 Bring a large saucepan of water to the boil. Add the long-grain white rice to the saucepan and cook for about 15 minutes. Drain the rice well, rinse under cold running water and drain thoroughly again.

2 Heat the peanut oil in a preheated wok or large frying pan. Add the garlic and Chinese five-spice and stir-fry for 30 seconds.

3 Add the French beans, chopped green pepper and quartered corn cobs to the wok or pan and continue to stir-fry for a further 2 minutes.

4 Stir the bamboo shoots, tomatoes, peas and rice into the mixture in the wok and stir-fry for 1 further minute.

5 Sprinkle with sesame oil and transfer to serving dishes. Serve immediately.

Risotto Primavera

This is a nice way to use those first green vegetables which signal the spring (*la primavera* in Italian). Feel free to add other vegetables.

NUTRITIONAL INFORMATION

Calories 381   Sugars 3g
Protein . . . . .13g   Fat 19g
Carbohydrate . . .43g   Saturates 8g

 15 mins   40 mins

SERVES 6–8

INGREDIENTS

225 g/8 oz fresh thin asparagus spears

4 tbsp olive oil

175 g/6 oz young French beans, cut into 2.5 cm/1 inch pieces

175 g/6 oz young courgettes, quartered and cut into 2.5 cm/1 inch lengths

225 g/8 oz fresh shelled peas

1 onion, finely chopped

1–2 garlic cloves, finely chopped

350 g/12 oz arborio or carnaroli rice

1.5 litres/2¾ pints vegetable stock, simmering, plus extra 2 tbsp

4 spring onions, cut into 2.5 cm/ 1 inch lengths

salt and pepper

4 tbsp unsalted butter

115 g/4 oz Parmesan cheese, freshly grated

2 tbsp chopped fresh chives

2 tbsp shredded fresh basil

spring onions, to garnish (optional)

1 Trim the woody ends of the asparagus and cut off the tips. Cut the stems into 2.5 cm/1 inch pieces and set aside with the tips.

2 Heat 2 tablespoons of the olive oil in a large frying pan over a high heat until very hot. Add the asparagus spears, French beans, courgettes and peas and stir-fry for 3–4 minutes until they are bright green and just beginning to soften. Set aside.

3 Heat the remaining olive oil in a large heavy-based pan over a medium heat. Add the onion and cook for about 1 minute until it begins to soften. Stir in the garlic and cook for 30 seconds. Add the rice and cook, stirring frequently, for 2 minutes until translucent and coated with oil.

4 Add a ladleful (about 225 ml/8 fl oz) of the hot stock; the stock will bubble rapidly. Cook, stirring constantly, until the stock is absorbed.

5 Continue adding the stock, about half a ladleful at a time, allowing each addition to be absorbed before adding the next – never allow the rice to cook 'dry'. This should take 20–25 minutes. The risotto should have a creamy consistency and the rice should be tender, but still firm to the bite.

6 Stir in the stir-fried vegetables and spring onions with a little more stock. Cook for 2 minutes, stirring frequently, then season with salt and pepper. Stir in the butter, Parmesan, chives and basil.

7 Remove the pan from the heat, cover and set aside for about 1 minute. Transfer the risotto to a warmed serving dish, garnish with spring onions, if wished, and serve immediately.

Stir-fries, Casseroles & Bakes

Stir-fries and sautés are simply wonderful! They take only a few minutes to prepare, they look gorgeous, they are endlessly adaptable and the ingredients retain all their goodness because they are cooked so quickly. They are also the ultimate in 'one-pot' cooking – the pot should ideally be a wok, as these are designed to distribute heat evenly and efficiently, but an ordinary, heavy-based frying pan is also fine. Casseroles are great for families and busy people – all the ingredients can go in one pot, and then you can put it in the oven and almost forget about it! Casseroles are great winter-warmers and are endlessly adaptable – you can use all kinds of vegetables and pulses to make a tasty dish.

Tofu with Peanut Sauce

This is a very sociable dish if served in the centre of the table where people can help themselves with cocktail sticks.

NUTRITIONAL INFORMATION

Calories	338	Sugars	.........9g
Protein	........16g	Fat	..........22g
Carbohydrate	...21g	Saturates	.......4g

 5 mins   20 mins

SERVES 4

INGREDIENTS

500 g/1 lb 2 oz marinated or plain tofu

2 tbsp rice vinegar

2 tbsp sugar

1 tsp salt

3 tbsp smooth peanut butter

½ tsp chilli flakes

3 tbsp barbecue sauce

1 litre/1¾ pints sunflower oil

2 tbsp sesame oil

BATTER

4 tbsp plain flour

2 eggs, beaten

4 tbsp milk

½ tsp baking powder

½ tsp chilli powder

COOK'S TIP

Tofu is made from puréed soya beans. It is white, with a soft cheese-like texture, and is sold in blocks, either fresh or vacuum-packed. Although it has a bland flavour, it blends well with other ingredients, and absorbs the flavours of spices and sauces.

1 Cut the tofu into 2.5 cm/1 inch triangles. Set aside until required.

2 Combine the rice vinegar, sugar and salt in a saucepan. Bring to the boil and then simmer for 2 minutes.

3 Remove the sauce from the heat and add the smooth peanut butter, chilli flakes and barbecue sauce, stirring well until thoroughly blended.

4 To make the batter, sift the plain flour into a bowl, make a well in the centre and add the eggs. Draw in the flour, adding the milk slowly. Stir in the baking powder and chilli powder.

5 Heat the sunflower oil and the sesame oil together in a deep-fryer or a large, heavy-based saucepan until a light haze appears on top.

6 Dip the tofu triangles into the batter and deep-fry until golden brown. You may need to do this in batches. Drain on absorbent kitchen paper.

7 Transfer the tofu triangles to a serving dish and serve with the peanut sauce.

Tofu with Mushrooms

Chunks of cucumber and smoked tofu are stir-fried with straw mushrooms, mangetouts and sweetcorn in a yellow bean sauce.

NUTRITIONAL INFORMATION

Calories	130	Sugars	.........2g
Protein	.........9g	Fat	...........9g
Carbohydrate	....3g	Saturates	.......1g

15 mins 10 mins

SERVES 4

INGREDIENTS

1 large cucumber

1 tsp salt

225 g/8 oz smoked tofu

2 tbsp vegetable oil

60 g/2 oz mangetouts

125 g/4½ oz baby sweetcorn cobs

1 celery stick, diagonally sliced

425 g/15 oz canned straw mushrooms, drained

2 spring onions, cut into strips

1 cm/½ inch piece ginger root, chopped

1 tbsp yellow bean sauce

1 tbsp light soy sauce

1 tbsp dry sherry

1 Halve the cucumber lengthways and remove the seeds, using a teaspoon or melon baller.

2 Cut the cucumber into cubes, place in a colander and sprinkle over the salt. Leave to drain for 10 minutes, then rinse thoroughly in cold water to remove the salt and drain thoroughly on absorbent kitchen paper.

3 Cut the smoked tofu into bite-sized cubes, using a very sharp knife to avoid squashing the tofu.

4 Heat the vegetable oil in a wok or large frying pan until smoking.

5 Add the tofu, mangetouts, baby sweetcorn and celery to the wok. Stir until the tofu is lightly browned. Add the straw mushrooms, spring onions and ginger, and stir-fry for a further minute.

6 Stir in the cucumber, yellow bean sauce, light soy sauce, dry sherry and 2 tbsp of water. Stir-fry for 1 minute and ensure that all the vegetables are coated in the sauces before serving.

COOK'S TIP

Straw mushrooms are available in cans from oriental suppliers and some supermarkets. If unavailable, substitute 250 g/ 9 oz baby button mushrooms.

Spicy Fried Tofu Triangles

Marinated tofu is ideal in this recipe for added flavour, although the spicy coating is very tasty with plain tofu.

NUTRITIONAL INFORMATION

Calories . . . . .224 Sugars 17g
Protein . . . . .10g Fat 13g
Carbohydrate . . .18g Saturates 2g

 1¼ hrs   ⊘ 10 mins

SERVES 4

I N G R E D I E N T S

1 tbsp sea salt

4½ tsp Chinese five-spice powder

3 tbsp light brown sugar

2 garlic cloves, crushed

1 tsp grated fresh root ginger

450 g/1 lb firm tofu

vegetable oil, for deep-frying

2 leeks, shredded and halved

shredded leek, to garnish

1 Mix together the salt, Chinese five-spice powder, sugar, garlic and ginger in a bowl and transfer to a plate.

COOK'S TIP

Fry the tofu in batches and keep each batch warm until all of the tofu has been fried and is ready to serve.

2 Cut the tofu cakes in half diagonally to form two triangles. Cut each triangle in half and then in half again to form 16 triangles.

3 Roll the tofu triangles in the spice mixture, turning them over until they are thoroughly coated on all sides. Set aside for 1 hour.

4 Heat the vegetable oil for deep-frying in a wok until it is almost smoking.

5 Reduce the heat slightly, add the tofu triangles and fry for 5 minutes, until golden brown. Remove from the wok with a slotted spoon, set aside and keep warm.

6 Add the leeks to the wok and stir-fry for 1 minute. Remove from the wok and drain on kitchen paper.

7 Arrange the leeks on a warm serving plate and place the fried tofu on top. Serve immediately, garnished with leek.

Vegetable & Nut Stir-fry

A colourful selection of vegetables are stir-fried in a creamy peanut sauce and sprinkled with nuts to serve.

NUTRITIONAL INFORMATION

Calories ....325 Sugars 6g
Protein ....11g Fat 21g
Carbohydrate ...26g Saturates 4g

🐷 🐷 🐷

🔔 10 mins   🕐 15 mins

SERVES 4

I N G R E D I E N T S

3 tbsp crunchy peanut butter

150 ml/¼ pint water

1 tbsp soy sauce

1 tsp sugar

1 carrot

½ red onion

4 baby courgettes

1 red pepper

250 g/9 oz dried thread egg noodles

25 g/1 oz peanuts, roughly chopped

2 tbsp vegetable oil

1 tsp sesame oil

1 small green chilli, deseeded and thinly
    sliced

1 garlic clove, thinly sliced

225 g/8 oz canned water chestnuts,
    drained and sliced

175 g/6 oz beansprouts

salt

1 Gradually blend the peanut butter with the water in a small bowl. Stir in the soy sauce and sugar. Set aside.

2 Cut the carrot into thin matchsticks and slice the red onion. Slice the courgettes on the diagonal and cut the pepper into chunks.

3 Bring a large pan of water to the boil and add the egg noodles. Remove from the heat immediately and leave to stand for 4 minutes, stirring occasionally to separate the noodles.

4 Heat a wok or large frying pan, add the peanuts and dry-fry them, stirring constantly, until they are beginning to brown. Remove with a perforated spoon and set aside until required.

5 Add the vegetable and sesame oils to the pan and heat. Add the carrot, onion, courgette, pepper, chilli and garlic, and stir-fry for 2–3 minutes. Add the water chestnuts, beansprouts and peanut sauce. Bring to the boil and heat thoroughly. Season with salt to taste.

6 Drain the noodles and serve with the vegetable and nut stir-fry. Sprinkle with the reserved peanuts.

Vegetable and Tofu Stir-fry

Tofu is a low-fat source of high-quality protein and, although it is naturally bland, it readily absorbs the flavours of other ingredients.

NUTRITIONAL INFORMATION

Calories 135   Sugars 5g
Protein ....11g   Fat 7g
Carbohydrate ....7g   Saturates 3g

10 mins, plus marinating   12 mins

SERVES 4

INGREDIENTS

225 g/8 oz firm tofu

1 tbsp groundnut or sunflower oil

2 spring onions, chopped

1 garlic clove, finely chopped

115 g/4 oz mangetouts

115 g/4 oz baby sweetcorn cobs, halved

115 g/4 oz shiitake mushrooms, thinly sliced

2 tbsp finely chopped coriander leaves

MARINADE

2 tbsp dark soy sauce

1 tbsp Chinese rice wine

2 tsp brown sugar

½ tsp Chinese five-spice powder

1 fresh red chilli, deseeded and finely chopped

2 spring onions, finely chopped

1 tbsp grated fresh root ginger

COOK'S TIP
Always use a sharp knife for cutting tofu – a blunt knife will squash it.

1 Combine all the marinade ingredients in a shallow, non-metallic dish, whisking well to mix. Cut the tofu into bite-size pieces, add to the marinade and turn to coat. Cover with clingfilm and set aside in the refrigerator to marinate for 2 hours, turning the tofu once or twice.

2 Drain the tofu and reserve the marinade. Heat the oil in a wok. Add the tofu and stir-fry for 2-3 minutes, until golden. Remove and set aside. Add the spring onions and garlic and stir-fry for 2 minutes, then add the corn cobs and stir-fry for 1 minute. Add the mangetouts and mushrooms and stir-fry for 2 minutes.

3 Return the tofu to the wok or frying pan and add the marinade. Cook gently for 1-2 minutes until heated through. Sprinkle with the chopped coriander and serve immediately.

Tofu with Peppers

Marinating tofu before cooking it is the best way to give it flavour.
Here it is given a delicious coating of soy sauce and sweet chilli sauce.

NUTRITIONAL INFORMATION

Calories 267   Sugars 2g
Protein ....9g   Fat 23g
Carbohydrate ....5g   Saturates 3g

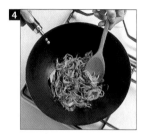

25 mins   15 mins

SERVES 4

INGREDIENTS

350 g/12 oz firm tofu

2 cloves garlic, crushed

4 tbsp soy sauce

1 tbsp sweet chilli sauce

6 tbsp sunflower oil

1 onion, sliced

1 green pepper, deseeded and diced

1 tbsp sesame oil

1 Using a sharp knife, cut the tofu into bite-sized pieces. Place the tofu in a shallow, non-metallic dish.

2 Mix together the garlic, soy sauce and sweet chilli sauce and drizzle over the tofu. Toss well to coat and leave to marinate for about 20 minutes.

3 Meanwhile, heat the sunflower oil in a large preheated wok.

4 Add the onion to the wok and stir-fry over a high heat until brown and crispy. Remove the onion with a slotted spoon and leave to drain on kitchen paper.

5 Add the tofu to the hot oil and stir-fry for about 5 minutes.

6 Remove all but 1 tablespoon of the sunflower oil from the wok. Add the pepper to the wok and stir-fry for 2–3 minutes, or until softened.

7 Return the tofu and onions to the wok until they are heated through, stirring occasionally.

8 Drizzle with sesame oil. Transfer to serving plates and serve immediately.

COOK'S TIP
If you are in a hurry, buy ready-marinated tofu from your supermarket.

French Bean Stir-fry

These beans are simply cooked in a spicy, hot sauce for an attractive, tasty and very easy recipe.

NUTRITIONAL INFORMATION

Calories . . . . .86 Sugars 4g
Protein . . . . .2g Fat 6g
Carbohydrates . . . .6g Saturates 1g

 5 mins   5 mins

SERVES 4

I N G R E D I E N T S

450 g/1 lb French beans

2 fresh red chillies

2 tbsp peanut oil

½ tsp ground star anise

1 garlic clove, crushed

2 tbsp light soy sauce

2 tsp clear honey

½ tsp sesame oil

1 Using a sharp knife, cut the French beans in half.

2 Slice the fresh chillies, removing the seeds first if you prefer a milder dish.

3 Heat the oil in a preheated wok or frying pan until it is almost smoking.

4 Lower the heat slightly, add the halved French beans to the wok and stir-fry for 1 minute.

5 Add the sliced red chillies, star anise and garlic to the wok and stir-fry for a further 30 seconds.

6 Mix together the soy sauce, honey and sesame oil in a small bowl.

7 Stir the sauce mixture into the wok. Cook for a further 2 minutes, tossing the beans to ensure that they are thoroughly coated in the sauce.

8 Transfer the mixture to a warm serving dish and serve immediately.

VARIATION

This recipe is surprisingly delicious made with Brussels sprouts instead of French beans. Trim the sprouts, then shred them finely. Stir-fry the sprouts in hot oil for 2 minutes, then proceed with the recipe from step 4.

Chinese Braised Vegetables

Quickly prepared and packed with flavour, this dish is stir-fried to begin with before the vegetables are briefly braised to finish them off.

NUTRITIONAL INFORMATION

Calories 150	Sugars 2g	
Protein 12g	Fat 13g	
Carbohydrates 7g	Saturates 4g	

 10 mins   10 mins

SERVES 4

INGREDIENTS

10 g/¼ oz Chinese dried mushrooms

3 tbsp groundnut or sunflower oil

225 g/8 oz firm tofu, cut into cubes

175 g/6 oz Chinese leaves, shredded

75 g/3 oz canned sliced bamboo shoots, drained and rinsed

75 g/3 oz straw mushrooms, halved

75 g/3 oz mangetouts

½ tsp muscovado sugar

1 tbsp dark soy sauce

dash of sesame oil

1 Put the dried mushrooms in a small bowl, cover with cold water and set aside for 20 minutes. Drain, then cut off and discard any hard stems.

2 Heat the groundnut or sunflower oil in a wok or frying-pan. Add the tofu and stir-fry for 2-4 minutes, until browned all over. Remove from the pan with a slotted spoon and set aside.

3 Add the Chinese mushrooms, Chinese leaves, bamboo shoots, straw mushrooms and mangetouts to the pan and stir-fry for 2 minutes.

4 Return the tofu to the pan and add the sugar and soy sauce. Stir for 1 minute, then cover and braise for 3 minutes. Sprinkle with a dash of sesame oil before serving.

COOK'S TIP
Firm, marinated and smoked tofu are all suitable for stir-frying.

Peppers with Chestnuts

This is a crisp and colourful recipe, topped with crisp, shredded leeks for both flavour and colour.

NUTRITIONAL INFORMATION

Calories 192   Sugars 5g
Protein . . . . .3g   Fat 14g
Carbohydrate . . .13g   Saturates 13g

 5 mins   15 mins

SERVES 4

I N G R E D I E N T S

225 g/8 oz leeks, to garnish

oil, for deep-frying

3 tbsp groundnut oil

1 yellow pepper, deseeded and diced

1 green pepper, deseeded and diced

1 red pepper, deseeded and diced

200 g/7 oz canned water chestnuts, drained and sliced

2 cloves garlic, crushed

3 tbsp light soy sauce

1 To make the garnish, finely shred the leeks into strips, using a sharp knife.

2 Heat the oil for deep-frying in a wok or large, heavy-based frying pan.

3 Add the shredded leeks to the wok or frying pan and cook them for 2–3 minutes, or until crispy. Set aside until they are required.

4 Heat the 3 tablespoons of groundnut oil in the wok or frying pan.

5 Add the diced yellow, green and red peppers to the wok and stir-fry over a high heat for about 5 minutes, or until

they are just beginning to brown at the edges and soften.

6 Add the sliced water chestnuts, garlic and light soy sauce to the wok and stir-fry all of the vegetables for a further 2–3 minutes.

7 Spoon the pepper stir-fry on to warm serving plates, garnish with the crispy leeks and serve.

COOK'S TIP

Add 1 tbsp of hoisin sauce with the soy sauce in step 6 for extra flavour and spice.

Stir-fried Greens

Eat your greens in this most delicious way – stir-fried, so that they retain all their colour, crunch and flavour.

NUTRITIONAL INFORMATION

Calories 116	Sugars 3g
Protein 5g	Fat 9g
Carbohydrate 5g	Saturates 1g

5 mins   10 mins

SERVES 4

INGREDIENTS

8 spring onions

2 celery sticks

125 g/4½ oz mooli (white radish)

125 g/4½ oz sugar snap peas or mangetouts

175 g/6 oz Chinese leaves

175 g/6 oz pak choi or spinach

2 tbsp vegetable oil

1 tbsp sesame oil

2 garlic cloves, finely chopped

3 tbsp light soy sauce

1 tsp finely grated fresh ginger root

pepper

1 Slice the spring onions and celery finely. Cut the mooli into matchstick strips. Trim the sugar snap peas or mangetouts. Shred the Chinese leaves and the pak choi or spinach.

2 Heat the vegetable oil and sesame oil together in a wok or large frying pan. Add the garlic and fry for about 1 minute.

3 Add the spring onions, celery, mooli and sugar snap peas or mangetouts to the wok or frying pan and stir-fry for about 2 minutes.

4 Add the shredded Chinese leaves and pak choi or spinach to the wok or frying pan, and continue to stir-fry for about 1 minute.

5 Stir the light soy sauce into the vegetables with the grated ginger. Cook for 1 minute. Season with pepper to taste, transfer to a warm serving dish and serve at once.

VARIATION
Any variety – and any amount – of fresh vegetables can be used in this dish. Just make sure that harder vegetables, such as carrots, are cut very finely so that they cook quickly.

Bamboo with Spinach

In this recipe, spinach is fried with spices and then braised in a soy-flavoured sauce with bamboo shoots for a rich, delicious dish.

NUTRITIONAL INFORMATION

Calories 105   Sugars 1g
Protein . . . . .3g   Fat 9g
Carbohydrate . . . .3g   Saturates 2g

     5 mins   10 mins

SERVES 4

INGREDIENTS

3 tbsp peanut oil

225 g/8 oz fresh spinach, chopped

175 g/6 oz canned bamboo shoots, drained and rinsed

1 garlic clove, crushed

2 fresh red chillies, deseeded and sliced

pinch of ground cinnamon

300 ml/½ pint vegetable stock

pinch of sugar

pinch of salt

1 tbsp light soy sauce

1 Heat the peanut oil in a preheated wok or large frying pan, swirling the oil around the base of the wok until it is really hot.

2 Add the spinach and bamboo shoots to the wok and stir-fry for 1 minute.

3 Add the garlic, chillies and cinnamon to the mixture in the wok and stir-fry for a further 30 seconds.

4 Stir in the stock, sugar, salt and light soy sauce, cover and cook over a medium heat for 5 minutes, or until the vegetables are cooked through and the sauce has reduced. If there is too much cooking liquid, blend a little cornflour with double the quantity of cold water and stir into the sauce.

5 Transfer the bamboo shoots and spinach to a serving dish and serve.

COOK'S TIP

Fresh bamboo shoots are rarely available in the West and, in any case, are extremely time-consuming to prepare. Canned bamboo shoots are quite satisfactory, as they are used to provide a crunchy texture, rather than for their flavour, which is fairly insipid.

Bamboo with Peppers

This dish has a wonderfully strong ginger flavour, which is integral to Chinese cooking. The mixed peppers give the dish a burst of colour.

NUTRITIONAL INFORMATION

Calories 101   Sugars 5g
Protein . . . . .3g   Fat 6g
Carbohydrate . . . .9g   Saturates 1g

 5 mins   🕐 15 mins

SERVES 4

INGREDIENTS

2 tbsp peanut oil

225 g/8 oz canned bamboo shoots, drained and rinsed

2 tbsp finely chopped fresh root ginger

1 small red pepper, deseeded and thinly sliced

1 small green pepper, deseeded and thinly sliced

1 small yellow pepper, deseeded and thinly sliced

1 leek, sliced

125 ml/4 fl oz vegetable stock

1 tbsp light soy sauce

2 tsp light brown sugar

2 tsp Chinese rice wine or dry sherry

1 tsp cornflour

2 tsp water

1 tsp sesame oil

1 Heat the peanut oil in a preheated wok or large frying pan, swirling the oil around the base until it is really hot.

2 Add the bamboo shoots, ginger, peppers and leek to the wok and stir-fry for 2–3 minutes.

3 Stir in the vegetable stock, the soy sauce, the light brown sugar and the Chinese rice wine or sherry and bring to the boil, stirring.

4 Reduce the heat to simmer and continue to cook the mixture for about 4–5 minutes, or until the vegetables begin to soften.

5 Blend the cornflour with the water to form a smooth paste, and stir the paste into the wok. Bring to the boil and cook, stirring constantly, until the sauce thickens and clears.

6 Sprinkle the sesame oil over the vegetables and cook for 1 minute. Serve immediately in a warm dish.

Gingered Broccoli

Ginger and broccoli are a perfect combination of flavours and make an exceptionally tasty side dish.

NUTRITIONAL INFORMATION

Calories 118	Sugars 3g
Protein 8g	Fat 7g
Carbohydrate 6g	Saturates 1g

5 mins   15 mins

SERVES 4

I N G R E D I E N T S

5 cm/2 inch piece fresh root ginger

2 tbsp peanut oil

1 garlic clove, crushed

675 g/1½ lb broccoli florets

1 leek, sliced

75 g/2¾ oz water chestnuts, halved

½ tsp caster sugar

125 ml/4 fl oz vegetable stock

1 tsp dark soy sauce

1 tsp cornflour

2 tsp water

1 Using a sharp knife, finely chop the ginger. (Alternatively, cut the ginger into larger strips, to be discarded later, for a slightly milder ginger flavour.)

2 Heat the peanut oil in a preheated wok. Add the garlic and ginger and stir-fry for 30 seconds.

3 Add the broccoli, leek and water chestnuts and stir-fry for a further 3–4 minutes.

4 Add the caster sugar, vegetable stock and dark soy sauce to the wok, reduce the heat and simmer for 4–5 minutes, or until the broccoli is almost cooked.

5 Blend the cornflour with the water to form a smooth paste and stir it into the wok. Bring to the boil and cook, stirring constantly, for 1 minute or until the mixture has thickened.

6 If you are using the larger strips of ginger, remove them from the wok and discard.

7 Transfer the vegetables to a serving dish and serve immediately.

VARIATION

Use spinach instead of the broccoli, if you prefer. Add the spinach leaves half way through step 3. Reduce the cooking time in step 4 to 3–4 minutes.

Bamboo with Cucumber

A simple stir-fried side dish of canned bamboo shoots and sliced cucumber is the perfect accompaniment to a Chinese main meal.

NUTRITIONAL INFORMATION

Calories . . . . .101 Sugars 0.2g
Protein . . . . .3g Fat 7g
Carbohydrate . . . .7g Saturates 1g

20 mins   10 mins

SERVES 4

INGREDIENTS

½ cucumber

salt

2 tbsp sesame oil

4 shallots, finely chopped

1 garlic clove, finely sliced

350 g/12 oz canned bamboo shoots, drained

1 tbsp dry sherry

1 tbsp soy sauce

2 tsp cornflour

1 tsp sesame seeds

TO GARNISH

2 red chilli flowers (see page 8)

sliced spring onions

1 Slice the cucumber thinly and sprinkle with salt. Leave for 10–15 minutes, then rinse with cold water. Prepare the chilli and spring onion garnish.

2 Heat the sesame oil in a wok or frying pan and add the shallots and garlic. Stir-fry for 2 minutes, until golden.

3 Add the bamboo shoots and the cucumber to the wok or frying pan and stir-fry for 2–3 minutes.

4 Blend together the dry sherry, soy sauce and cornflour. Add to the bamboo shoots and cucumber in the wok, stirring to combine.

5 Cook for 1–2 minutes to thicken slightly, then add the sesame seeds and stir through.

6 Transfer the vegetables to a warmed serving dish. Garnish with the chilli flowers and sliced spring onion and serve at once.

COOK'S TIP
Salting the cucumber before it is stir-fried draws out some of its moisture so that it stays crisp. Add some very finely sliced carrot to this dish to add some extra colour, if you like.

Lemon Chinese Leaves

These stir-fried Chinese leaves are served with a tangy sauce made of grated lemon rind, lemon juice and ginger.

NUTRITIONAL INFORMATION

Calories	120	Sugars	.........0g
Protein	.........5g	Fat	...........8g
Carbohydrate	....8g	Saturates	.......1g

 5 mins 10 mins

SERVES 4

I N G R E D I E N T S

500 g/1 lb 2 oz Chinese leaves

3 tbsp vegetable oil

1 cm/½ inch piece root ginger, grated

1 tsp salt

1 tsp sugar

125 ml/4 fl oz water or vegetable stock

1 tsp grated lemon rind

1 tbsp cornflour

1 tbsp lemon juice

1 Separate the Chinese leaves, wash and drain thoroughly. Pat dry with absorbent kitchen paper.

2 Cut the Chinese leaves into 5 cm/ 2 inch wide slices.

3 Heat the oil in a wok, add the grated ginger root followed by the Chinese leaves, and stir-fry for 2–3 minutes or until the leaves begin to wilt.

4 Add the salt and sugar, and mix well until the leaves soften. Remove the leaves with a slotted spoon and set aside.

5 Add the water or stock to the wok with the lemon rind. Bring to the boil.

6 Meanwhile, mix the cornflour to a smooth paste with the lemon juice, then add to the wok. Simmer, stirring constantly, for about 1 minute to make a smooth sauce.

7 Return the cooked Chinese leaves to the pan and mix thoroughly to coat the leaves in the lemon sauce. Arrange the leaves on a warm serving plate and serve them immediately.

COOK'S TIP

If Chinese leaves are unavailable, substitute slices of Savoy cabbage. Cook for 1 extra minute to soften the leaves.

Spicy Mushrooms

A mixture of mushrooms has been used in this recipe for a richly flavoured and textured dish.

NUTRITIONAL INFORMATION

Calories 103   Sugars 4g
Protein . . . . .3g   Fat 8g
Carbohydrate . . . .5g   Saturates 2g

5 mins   10 mins

SERVES 4

INGREDIENTS

2 tbsp peanut oil

2 garlic cloves, crushed

3 spring onions, chopped

300 g/10½ oz button mushrooms

2 large open-cap mushrooms, sliced

125 g/4½ oz oyster mushrooms

1 tsp chilli sauce

1 tbsp dark soy sauce

1 tbsp hoisin sauce

1 tbsp white wine vinegar

½ tsp ground Szechuan pepper

1 tbsp dark brown sugar

1 tsp sesame oil

chopped fresh parsley, to garnish

1 Heat the peanut oil in a preheated wok or large frying pan until it is almost smoking.

2 Reduce the heat slightly, add the garlic and spring onions to the wok or frying pan and stir-fry for 30 seconds.

3 Add all the mushrooms to the wok, together with the chilli sauce, dark soy sauce, hoisin sauce, wine vinegar, ground Szechuan pepper and dark brown sugar and stir-fry for 4–5 minutes, or until the mushrooms are cooked through. Stir constantly to prevent the mixture sticking to the base of the wok.

4 Sprinkle the sesame oil over the mixture in the wok. Transfer the spicy mushrooms to a warm serving dish, garnish with the chopped parsley and serve immediately.

COOK'S TIP

If Chinese dried mushrooms are available, add a small quantity to this dish for texture. 'Wood ears' are widely used and are available dried from Chinese food stores. They should be rinsed, soaked in warm water for 20 minutes and rinsed again before use.

Quorn & Vegetable Stir-fry

Quorn, like tofu, absorbs all of the flavours in a dish, making it ideal for this recipe, which is packed with classic Chinese flavourings.

NUTRITIONAL INFORMATION

Calories	167	Sugars 8g
Protein	........12g	Fat 9g
Carbohydrate	...10g	Saturates 1g

 30 mins   10 mins

SERVES 4

I N G R E D I E N T S

1 tbsp grated fresh root ginger

1 tsp ground ginger

1 tbsp tomato purée

2 tbsp sunflower oil

1 clove garlic, crushed

2 tbsp soy sauce

350 g/12 oz quorn or soya cubes

225 g/8 oz carrots, sliced

100 g/3½ oz French beans, sliced

4 celery sticks, sliced

1 red pepper, deseeded and sliced

boiled rice, to serve

COOK'S TIP

Ginger root will keep for several weeks in a cool, dry place. Ginger root can also be kept frozen – break off lumps as needed.

1 Place the grated fresh root ginger, ground ginger, tomato purée, 1 tablespoon of the sunflower oil, garlic, soy sauce and quorn or soya cubes in a large bowl. Mix well to combine, stirring carefully so that you don't break up the quorn or soya cubes. Cover the mixture and leave to marinate for 20 minutes.

2 Heat the remaining sunflower oil in a large preheated wok.

3 Add the marinated quorn mixture to the wok and stir-fry for about 2 minutes.

4 Add the carrots, French beans, celery and red pepper to the wok and stir-fry for a further 5 minutes.

5 Transfer the stir-fry to warm serving dishes and serve immediately with freshly cooked boiled rice.

Vegetables with Hoisin

This spicy vegetable stir-fry can be made using left-over brown rice. Serve as an accompaniment to a main dish, or with noodles.

NUTRITIONAL INFORMATION

Calories ....120 Sugars 6g
Protein ....4g Fat 6g
Carbohydrate ...12g Saturates 1g

20 mins   10 mins

SERVES 4

I N G R E D I E N T S

1 red onion

100 g/3½ oz carrots

1 yellow pepper

2 tbsp sunflower oil

50 g/1¾ oz cooked brown rice

175 g/6 oz mangetouts

175 g/6 oz beansprouts

4 tbsp hoisin sauce

1 tbsp snipped fresh chives

1 Using a sharp knife, thinly slice the red onion. Thinly slice the carrots. Seed and dice the yellow pepper.

2 Heat the sunflower oil in a large preheated wok or a frying pan with a heavy base.

3 Add the red onion slices, carrots and yellow pepper to the wok and stir-fry for about 3 minutes.

4 Add the cooked brown rice, mangetout and beansprouts to the mixture in the wok and stir-fry for a further 2 minutes. Stir briskly to ensure that the ingredients are well mixed and the rice grains are separated.

5 Stir the hoisin sauce into the vegetables and mix until combined and completely heated through.

6 Transfer the vegetable stir-fry to warm serving dishes and scatter with the chives. Serve immediately.

COOK'S TIP

Hoisin sauce is a dark reddish brown sauce made from soy beans, garlic, chilli and various other spices, and is commonly used in Chinese cookery. It may also be used as a dipping sauce.

Carrots with Pineapple

If you can use fresh pineapple, the flavour of this dish is even better and the texture crisper.

NUTRITIONAL INFORMATION

Calories 125   Sugars 17g
Protein . . . . .1g   Fat 6g
Carbohydrate . . .18g   Saturates 1g

 5 mins   15 mins

SERVES 4

INGREDIENTS

1 tbsp sunflower oil

1 tbsp olive oil

1 small onion, finely sliced

2.5 cm/1 inch piece ginger root, peeled and grated

1–2 garlic cloves, crushed

500 g/1 lb 2 oz carrots, thinly sliced

200 g/7 oz canned pineapple in natural juice, chopped, or 250 g/9 oz fresh pineapple, chopped

2–3 tbsp pineapple juice (from the can or fresh)

salt and black pepper

chopped fresh parsley or dill, to garnish

1 Heat the sunflower oil and the olive oil together in a wok. Add the onion, ginger and garlic to the wok and stir-fry briskly for 2–3 minutes.

2 Add the carrots and continue to stir-fry, lowering the heat a little, for about 5 minutes.

3 Add the pineapple and the pineapple juice to the wok with plenty of seasoning, and continue to stir-fry for about 5-6 minutes, or until the carrots are tender-crisp and the liquid has almost evaporated.

4 Adjust the seasoning, adding plenty of black pepper, and transfer the stir-fry to a warmed serving dish.

5 Sprinkle the stir-fry with the chopped fresh parsley or dill and serve as a vegetable accompaniment.

6 Alternatively, you can allow the carrots to cool and serve them as a delicious salad, tossed in 2-4 tablespoons of French dressing to taste.

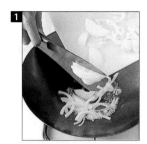

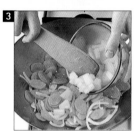

COOK'S TIP

If using canned pineapple, make sure it is in natural juice, not syrup: the sweet taste of the syrup will ruin the fresh flavour of this dish. Most fruits can now be bought canned in natural juice, which gives a much fresher, lighter taste.

Carrot & Orange Stir-fry

Carrots and oranges have long been combined in Oriental cooking, the orange juice bringing out the sweetness of the carrots.

NUTRITIONAL INFORMATION

Calories	341	Sugars	........26g
Protein	........10g	Fat	..........21g
Carbohydrate	...28g	Saturates	.......4g

10 mins　　10 mins

SERVES 4

INGREDIENTS

2 tbsp sunflower oil

450 g/1 lb carrots, grated

225 g/8 oz leeks, shredded

2 oranges, peeled and segmented

2 tbsp tomato ketchup

1 tbsp demerara sugar

2 tbsp light soy sauce

100 g/3½ oz chopped peanuts

1 Heat the sunflower oil in a large preheated wok.

2 Add the grated carrot and leeks to the wok and stir-fry for 2–3 minutes, or until the vegetables have just softened.

3 Add the orange segments to the wok and heat through gently, ensuring that you do not break up the orange segments as you stir the mixture.

4 Mix the tomato ketchup, demerara sugar and soy sauce together in a small bowl.

5 Add the tomato ketchup mixture to the wok and stir-fry for a further 2 minutes.

6 Transfer the stir-fry to warm serving bowls and scatter with the chopped peanuts. Serve immediately.

VARIATION
Cut the carrots into fine julienne strips to add a slightly crunchier texture to this dish.

Honey-fried Chinese Leaves

Chinese leaves are rather similar to lettuce in that the leaves are delicate with a sweet flavour.

NUTRITIONAL INFORMATION

Calories 121   Sugars 6g
Protein . . . . .5g   Fat 7g
Carbohydrate . . .10g   Saturates 1g

  5 mins   10 mins

SERVES 4

INGREDIENTS

450 g/1 lb Chinese leaves

1 tbsp peanut oil

1 tsp grated fresh root ginger

2 garlic cloves, crushed

1 fresh red chilli, deseeded and sliced

1 tbsp Chinese rice wine or dry sherry

4½ tsp light soy sauce

1 tbsp clear honey

125 ml/4 fl oz orange juice

1 tbsp sesame oil

2 tsp sesame seeds

orange rind, to garnish

COOK'S TIP

Single-flower honey has a better, more individual flavour than blended honey. Acacia honey is typically Chinese, but you could also try clover, lemon blossom, lime flower or orange blossom.

1 Separate the Chinese leaves and shred them finely, using a sharp knife.

2 Heat the peanut oil in a preheated wok. Add the ginger, garlic and chilli to the wok and stir-fry the mixture for about 30 seconds.

3 Add the Chinese leaves, Chinese rice wine or sherry, soy sauce, honey and orange juice to the wok. Reduce the heat and leave to simmer for 5 minutes.

4 Add the sesame oil to the wok, sprinkle the sesame seeds on top and mix to combine.

5 Transfer the stir-fry to a warm serving dish, garnish with the orange rind and serve immediately.

Stir-fried Spinach

This is an easy recipe to make as a quick accompaniment to a main course. The water chestnuts give a delicious crunch to the greens.

NUTRITIONAL INFORMATION

Calories 85   Sugars 2g
Protein ....4g   Fat 4g
Carbohydrate ....9g   Saturates 1g

5 mins   10 mins

SERVES 4

INGREDIENTS

1 tbsp sunflower oil

1 garlic clove, halved

2 spring onions, finely sliced

225 g/8 oz canned water chestnuts, drained and finely sliced

500 g/1 lb 2 oz fresh spinach, any tough stalks removed

1 tsp sherry vinegar

1 tsp light soy sauce

pepper

1 Heat the sunflower oil in a wok or large, heavy frying pan over a high heat, swirling the oil around the base of the wok until it is really hot.

2 Add the halved garlic clove and cook, stirring, for 1 minute. If the garlic should brown, remove it immediately.

3 Add the spring onions and water chestnuts and stir for 2–3 minutes.

4 Add the spinach leaves to the wok and stir to combine.

5 Add the sherry vinegar, soy sauce and a sprinkling of pepper. Cook, stirring, until the spinach is tender, then remove the garlic from the wok.

6 Using a slotted spoon, drain off the excess liquid from the wok and serve the stir-fried greens immediately.

COOK'S TIP
Several types of Oriental greens (for example, choi sam and pak choi) are widely available and any of these can be successfully substituted for the spinach.

Eight-jewel Vegetables

This recipe, as the title suggests, is a colourful mixture of eight vegetables, cooked in a black bean and soy sauce.

NUTRITIONAL INFORMATION

Calories 110   Sugars 3g
Protein ....4g   Fat 8g
Carbohydrate ....7g   Saturates 1g

 5 mins   10 mins

SERVES 4

INGREDIENTS

2 tbsp peanut oil

6 spring onions, sliced

3 garlic cloves, crushed

1 red pepper, deseeded and diced

1 green pepper, deseeded and diced

1 fresh red chilli, deseeded and sliced

2 tbsp chopped water chestnuts

1 courgette, chopped

125 g/4½ oz oyster mushrooms

3 tbsp black bean sauce

2 tsp Chinese rice wine or dry sherry

4 tbsp dark soy sauce

1 tsp dark brown sugar

2 tbsp water

1 tsp sesame oil

1 Heat the peanut oil in a preheated wok or large frying pan until it is almost smoking.

2 Lower the heat slightly, add the spring onions and garlic and stir-fry for about 30 seconds.

3 Add the red and green peppers, the fresh red chilli, water chestnuts and courgette to the wok or frying pan and stir-fry for 2–3 minutes, or until the vegetables are just beginning to soften.

4 Add the oyster mushrooms, black bean sauce, Chinese rice wine or dry sherry, dark soy sauce, dark brown sugar and water to the wok and stir-fry for a further 4 minutes.

5 Sprinkle the stir-fry with sesame oil and serve immediately.

COOK'S TIP

Eight jewels or treasures form a traditional part of the Chinese New Year celebrations, which start in the last week of the old year. The Kitchen God, an important figure, is sent to give a report to heaven, returning on New Year's Eve in time for the feasting.

Sherry & Soy Vegetables

This is a simple yet tasty side dish which also makes a delicious light snack or even a main course for two.

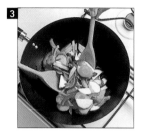

NUTRITIONAL INFORMATION

Calories 374   Sugars 10g
Protein ....14g   Fat 25g
Carbohydrate ...20g   Saturates 5g

 10 mins   15 mins

SERVES 4

INGREDIENTS

2 tbsp sunflower oil

1 red onion, sliced

175 g/6 oz carrots, thinly sliced

175 g/6 oz courgettes, diagonally sliced

1 red pepper, deseeded and sliced

1 small head Chinese leaves, shredded

150 g/5½ oz beansprouts

225 g/8 oz canned bamboo shoots, drained

150 g/5½ oz toasted cashew nuts

SAUCE

3 tbsp medium sherry

3 tbsp light soy sauce

1 tsp ground ginger

1 clove garlic, crushed

1 tsp cornflour

1 tbsp tomato purée

1 Heat the sunflower oil in a large preheated wok.

2 Add the red onion and stir-fry for 2–3 minutes or until softened.

3 Add the carrots, courgettes and pepper slices to the wok and stir-fry for a further 5 minutes.

4 Add the Chinese leaves, beansprouts and bamboo shoots and heat through for 2–3 minutes, or until the leaves begin to wilt. Stir in the cashews.

5 Combine the sherry, soy sauce, ginger, garlic, cornflour and tomato purée. Pour the sauce over the vegetables and toss well. Leave to simmer for about 2–3 minutes or until the juices start to thicken. Serve immediately.

VARIATION
Use any mixture of fresh vegetables that you have to hand in this very versatile dish.

Muttar Paneer

Paneer is a delicious fresh, soft cheese frequently used in Indian cooking. It is easily made at home, but must be made the day before it's required.

NUTRITIONAL INFORMATION

Calories	550	Sugars	.......25g
Protein	........19g	Fat	..........39g
Carbohydrate	...33g	Saturates	......12g

15 mins   25 mins

SERVES 6

INGREDIENTS

150 ml/¼ pint vegetable oil

2 onions, chopped

2 garlic cloves, crushed

2.5 cm/1 inch piece of root ginger, chopped

1 tsp garam masala

1 tsp turmeric

1 tsp chilli powder

500 g/1 lb 2 oz frozen peas

225 g/8 oz canned chopped tomatoes

125 ml/4 fl oz vegetable stock

salt and pepper

2 tbsp chopped fresh coriander

PANEER

2.5 litres/4½ pints full-cream milk

5 tbsp lemon juice

1 garlic clove, crushed (optional)

1 tbsp chopped fresh coriander (optional)

1 To make the paneer, bring the milk to a rolling boil in a large saucepan. Remove from the heat and stir in the lemon juice. Return to the heat for about 1 minute until the curds and whey separate. Remove from the heat. Line a colander with double thickness muslin and pour the mixture through the muslin, adding the garlic and coriander, if using. Squeeze all the liquid from the curds and leave to drain.

2 Transfer to a dish, cover with a plate and a heavy weight and leave overnight in the refrigerator.

3 Cut the pressed paneer into small cubes. Heat the oil in a large frying pan. Add the paneer and fry until golden on all sides. Remove from the pan and drain on kitchen paper.

4 Pour off some of the oil, leaving about 4 tablespoons in the pan. Add the onions, garlic and ginger and fry gently, stirring frequently, for 5 minutes. Stir in the spices and fry gently for 2 minutes. Add the peas, tomatoes and stock and season with salt and pepper. Cover and simmer, stirring occasionally, for 10 minutes, until the onion is tender.

5 Add the fried paneer cubes and cook for a further 5 minutes. Taste and adjust the seasoning, if necessary. Sprinkle with the coriander and serve at once.

Bubble & Squeak

Bubble and squeak is best known as fried mashed potato and left-over greens, served as an accompaniment. This version has tofu added.

NUTRITIONAL INFORMATION

Calories	301	Sugars	.........5g
Protein	.......11g	Fat	..........18g
Carbohydrate	...24g	Saturates	.......2g

15 mins   40 mins

SERVES 4

I N G R E D I E N T S

450 g/1 lb floury potatoes, diced

225 g/8 oz Savoy cabbage, shredded

5 tbsp vegetable oil

2 leeks, chopped

1 garlic clove, crushed

225 g/8 oz smoked tofu, cubed

salt and pepper

shredded cooked leek, to garnish

1 Cook the diced potatoes in a saucepan of lightly salted boiling water for 10 minutes, until tender. Drain and mash the potatoes.

2 Meanwhile, in a separate saucepan, blanch the cabbage in boiling water for 5 minutes. Drain well and add to the potato.

3 Heat the oil in a heavy-based frying pan. Add the leeks and garlic and fry gently for 2–3 minutes. Stir into the potato and cabbage mixture.

4 Add the smoked tofu and season well with salt and pepper. Cook over a moderate heat for 10 minutes.

5 Carefully turn the whole mixture over and continue to cook over a moderate heat for a further 5–7 minutes, until it is crispy underneath.

6 Serve immediately, garnished with shredded leek.

COOK'S TIP
This is a perfect main meal, because the smoked tofu cubes added to the basic bubble and squeak mixture make it very substantial and nourishing.

Tomato Curry

This vegetarian tomato curry is served topped with a few hard-boiled eggs. It is a lovely accompaniment to any Indian meal.

NUTRITIONAL INFORMATION

Calories 170	Sugars 3g	
Protein 6g	Fat 15g	
Carbohydrate 3g	Saturates 2g	

25 mins

15 mins

SERVES 4

INGREDIENTS

400 g/14 oz canned tomatoes

1 tsp finely chopped root ginger

1 tsp crushed garlic

1 tsp chilli powder

1 tsp salt

½ tsp ground coriander

½ tsp ground cumin

4 tbsp oil

½ tsp onion seeds

½ tsp mustard seeds

½ tsp fenugreek seeds

pinch of white cumin seeds

3 dried red chillies, deseeded and chopped

2 tbsp lemon juice

3 eggs, hard-boiled

fresh coriander leaves

1 Place the tomatoes in a large mixing bowl. Add the ginger, garlic, chilli powder, salt, ground coriander and ground cumin and blend well.

2 Heat the oil in a saucepan. Add the onion, mustard, fenugreek and white cumin seeds, and the dried red chillies, and stir-fry for about 1 minute, until they give off their aroma. Remove the pan from the heat.

3 Add the tomato mixture to the spicy oil mixture and return the pan to the heat. Stir-fry for about 3 minutes.

4 Reduce the heat and continue to cook, half covered with a lid, stirring frequently, for 7-10 minutes.

5 Sprinkle over 1 tablespoon of the lemon juice. Taste, and add the remaining lemon juice if required.

6 Transfer the tomato curry to a warmed serving dish and keep warm until required.

7 Shell the hard-boiled eggs and cut them into quarters. Add them to the tomato curry, pushing them in gently, yolk end downwards.

8 Garnish with the fresh coriander leaves and serve hot.

Potato & Cauliflower Curry

Potatoes and cauliflower go very well together. Served with a dhal and rice or bread, this dish makes a perfect vegetarian meal.

NUTRITIONAL INFORMATION

Calories ....426 Sugars 6g
Protein ....4g Fat 35g
Carbohydrate ...26g Saturates 4g

 10 mins   25 mins

SERVES 4

INGREDIENTS

150 ml/5 fl oz vegetable oil

½ tsp white cumin seeds

4 dried red chillies

2 onions, sliced

1 tsp finely chopped fresh root ginger

1 tsp crushed garlic

1 tsp chilli powder

1 tsp salt

pinch of turmeric

675/1½ lb potatoes, chopped

½ cauliflower, cut into small florets

2 fresh green chillies, chopped (optional)

1 tbsp fresh coriander leaves

150 ml/5 fl oz water

1 Heat the oil in a large, heavy-based saucepan. Add the white cumin seeds and the dried red chillies to the pan, stirring to mix.

2 Add the onions to the pan and fry them over a medium heat, stirring occasionally, for about 5–8 minutes, until golden brown.

3 Mix the ginger, garlic, chilli powder, salt and turmeric together. Add the spice mixture to the onions and stir-fry for about 2 minutes.

4 Add the potatoes and cauliflower to the pan and stir well to coat them thoroughly with the spice mixture. Reduce the heat and add the green chillies (if using), the coriander leaves and the water to the pan.

5 Cover the pan and simmer for about 10–15 minutes, until the vegetables are tender and cooked right through.

6 Transfer the potato and cauliflower curry to warmed serving plates and serve immediately.

COOK'S TIP
Ground ginger is no substitute for the fresh root. It has less aroma and flavour, and cannot be used in fried or sautéed dishes because it burns easily at the high temperatures required.

Green Curry with Tempeh

Green curry paste will keep for up to three weeks in the refrigerator. Serve the curry over rice or noodles.

NUTRITIONAL INFORMATION

Calories	237	Sugars	........4g
Protein	........16g	Fat	..........17g
Carbohydrate	....5g	Saturates	.......3g

20 mins   15–20 mins

SERVES 4

I N G R E D I E N T S

1 tbsp sunflower oil

175 g/6 oz marinated or plain tempeh, cut into diamonds

6 spring onions, cut into 2.5 cm/ 1 inch pieces

150 ml/¼ pint coconut milk

grated rind of 1 lime

15 g/½ oz fresh basil leaves

¼ tsp liquid seasoning, such as Maggi

GREEN CURRY PASTE

2 tsp coriander seeds

1 tsp cumin seeds

1 tsp black peppercorns

4 large fresh green chillies, deseeded

2 shallots, quartered

2 garlic cloves

2 tbsp chopped coriander

grated rind of 1 lime

1 tbsp roughly chopped galangal

1 tsp turmeric

salt

2 tbsp oil

TO GARNISH

fresh coriander leaves

2 fresh green chillies, deseeded and thinly sliced

1 To make the green curry paste, grind together the coriander and cumin seeds with the black peppercorns in a food processor or in a mortar with a pestle.

2 Process the remaining ingredients together in a blender and add the ground spice mixture. The curry paste can be stored in a clean, dry jar for up to 3 weeks in the refrigerator, or it can be frozen in a suitable container.

3 Heat the oil in a wok or large, heavy frying pan. Add the tempeh and stir over a high heat for about 2 minutes until sealed on all sides. Add the spring onions and stir-fry for 1 minute. Remove the tempeh and spring onions and reserve.

4 Put half the coconut milk into the wok or pan and bring to the boil. Add 6 tablespoons of the curry paste and the lime rind, and cook for 1 minute, until fragrant. Add the reserved tempeh and spring onions.

5 Add the remaining coconut milk and simmer for about 7–8 minutes. Stir in the fresh basil leaves and liquid seasoning. Leave the curry to simmer for a further minute before serving, garnished with coriander leaves and chillies.

French Bean & Potato Curry

You can use fresh or canned French beans for this semi-dry vegetable curry. Serve with dhaal for a good contrast of flavours and colours.

NUTRITIONAL INFORMATION

Calories	690	Sugars	........4g
Protein	.........3g	Fat	..........69g
Carbohydrate	...16g	Saturates	.......7g

15 mins   30 mins

SERVES 4

INGREDIENTS

300 ml/½ pint vegetable oil

1 tsp white cumin seeds

1 tsp mustard and onion seeds

4 dried red chillies

3 tomatoes, sliced

1 tsp salt

1 tsp finely chopped fresh root ginger

1 tsp crushed garlic

1 tsp chilli powder

200 g/7 oz French beans, chopped

450 g/1 lb potatoes, diced

300 ml/½ pint water

cooked rice, to serve

TO GARNISH

1 tbsp chopped fresh coriander

2 fresh green chillies, deseeded and finely chopped

1 Heat the vegetable oil in a large, heavy-based saucepan or flameproof casserole.

2 Add the white cumin seeds, the mustard and onion seeds and the dried red chillies to the pan, stirring well.

3 Add the tomatoes to the pan and fry the mixture for 3-5 minutes, stirring constantly.

4 Mix together the salt, ginger, garlic and chilli powder and sprinkle the mixture into the pan. Stir well to combine thoroughly.

5 Add the French beans and the diced potatoes to the pan and cook, stirring, for about 5 minutes.

6 Add the water to the pan, reduce the heat and leave to simmer for 10–15 minutes, stirring occasionally.

7 Garnish the French bean and potato curry with the chopped coriander leaves and green chillies.

8 Transfer the curry to warmed serving plates and serve hot, with cooked rice.

Spicy Mixed Vegetable Curry

You can vary the vegetables used in this recipe according to personal preferences – experiment!

NUTRITIONAL INFORMATION

Calories	408	Sugars	20
Protein	........11g	Fat	..........24g
Carbohydrate	...39g	Saturates	.......3g

 30 mins   45 mins

SERVES 4

I N G R E D I E N T S

225 g/8 oz turnips or swede, peeled

1 aubergine, leaf end trimmed

350 g/12 oz new potatoes

225 g/8 oz cauliflower

225 g/8 oz button mushrooms

1 large onion

225 g/8 oz carrots

6 tbsp ghee or vegetable oil

2 garlic cloves, crushed

5 cm/2 inch piece of ginger root, chopped

1–2 fresh green chillies, deseeded and chopped

1 tbsp paprika

2 tsp ground coriander

1 tbsp mild or medium curry powder or paste

450 ml/16 fl oz vegetable stock

400 g/14 oz canned chopped tomatoes

salt

1 green pepper, deseeded and sliced

1 tbsp cornflour

150 ml/¼ pint coconut milk

2–3 tbsp ground almonds

fresh coriander sprigs, to garnish

1 Using a sharp knife, cut the turnips or swede, aubergine and potatoes into 1 cm/½ inch cubes.

2 Divide the cauliflower into small florets. Leave the mushrooms whole, or slice thickly. Slice the onion and carrots.

3 Heat the ghee or oil in a large saucepan, add the onion, turnip, potato and cauliflower and cook gently for 3 minutes, stirring frequently.

4 Add the garlic, ginger, chilli and spices and cook for 1 minute, stirring.

5 Add the stock, tomatoes, aubergine and mushrooms and season with salt. Cover and simmer gently for about 30 minutes or until the vegetables are tender, stirring occasionally. Add the green pepper, cover and continue cooking for a further 5 minutes.

6 Blend the cornflour with the coconut milk to a smooth paste and stir into the mixture. Add the ground almonds and simmer for 2 minutes, stirring all the time. Taste and adjust the seasoning, if necessary. Serve hot, garnished with coriander sprigs.

Spinach & Cheese Curry

This simple curry is full of protein and iron. Paneer is a cheese that you can easily make at home the day before it is needed (see page 496).

NUTRITIONAL INFORMATION

Calories	578	Sugars	.........4g
Protein	........10g	Fat	..........58g
Carbohydrate	....4g	Saturates	.......7g

20–30 mins   25 mins

SERVES 4

INGREDIENTS

300 ml/½ pint vegetable oil

200 g/7 oz paneer, cubed (see page 496)

3 tomatoes, sliced

1 tsp ground cumin

1½ tsp ground chilli powder

1 tsp salt

400 g/14 oz fresh spinach

3 green chillies, deseeded and chopped

pooris or boiled rice, to serve

1 Heat the vegetable oil in a large, heavy-based frying pan. Add the cubed paneer and fry, stirring occasionally, until it is golden brown.

2 Add the tomatoes to the remaining oil in the pan and stir-fry, breaking them up with a spoon, for 5 minutes.

3 Add the ground cumin, the chilli powder and the salt to the pan and mix well to combine.

4 Add the spinach leaves to the pan and stir-fry over a low heat for about 7–10 minutes until wilted.

5 Add the green chillies and return the paneer to the pan. Cook, stirring constantly, for a further 2 minutes.

6 Transfer to warmed serving plates and serve immediately with pooris or plain boiled rice.

VARIATION

You could use frozen spinach in this recipe. It should be completely thawed and squeezed as dry as possible before using.

Potato Curry

Served hot with pooris, this curry makes an excellent brunch, with mango chutney as the perfect accompaniment.

NUTRITIONAL INFORMATION

Calories 390	Sugars 0.7g
Protein 2g	Fat 34g
Carbohydrate ...19g	Saturates 4g

 10 mins   🕐 25 mins

SERVES 4

INGREDIENTS

3 potatoes

150 ml/¼ pint vegetable oil

1 tsp onion seeds

½ tsp fennel seeds

4 curry leaves

1 tsp ground cumin

1 tsp ground coriander

1 tsp chilli powder

pinch of turmeric

1 tsp salt

1½ tsp dried mango powder

1 Peel the potatoes and rinse in cold water. Using a sharp knife, cut each potato into 6 slices.

2 Cook the potato slices in a saucepan of boiling water until they are just cooked, but not mushy (test with a sharp knife). Drain and set aside until required.

3 Heat the vegetable oil in a separate, heavy-based saucepan over a moderate heat. Reduce the heat and add the onion seeds, fennel seeds and curry leaves and stir thoroughly.

4 Remove the pan from the heat and add the ground cumin, coriander, chilli powder, turmeric, salt and dried mango powder, stirring well to combine.

5 Return the pan to a low heat and fry the mixture, stirring constantly, for about 1 minute.

6 Pour this mixture over the cooked potatoes, mix together and stir-fry over a low heat for about 5 minutes.

7 Transfer the potato curry to serving dishes and serve immediately.

COOK'S TIP

Traditionally, Semolina Dessert (see page 928) is served to follow Potato Curry.

Potato Stir-fry

In this sweet and sour dish, vegetables are simply stir-fried with spices and coconut milk, and flavoured with lime.

NUTRITIONAL INFORMATION

Calories ....138 Sugars 5g
Protein ....2g Fat 6g
Carbohydrate ...20g Saturates 1g

 10 mins   20 mins

SERVES 4

INGREDIENTS

4 waxy potatoes

2 tbsp vegetable oil

1 yellow pepper, diced

1 red pepper, diced

1 carrot, cut into matchstick strips

1 courgette, cut into matchstick strips

2 garlic cloves, crushed

1 red chilli, deseeded and sliced

1 bunch spring onions, halved lengthways

8 tbsp coconut milk

1 tsp chopped lemongrass

2 tsp lime juice

finely grated rind of 1 lime

1 tbsp chopped fresh coriander

1 Using a sharp knife, cut the potatoes into small dice.

2 Bring a large saucepan of water to the boil and cook the diced potatoes for 5 minutes. Drain thoroughly.

3 Heat the vegetable oil in a wok or large frying pan, swirling the oil around the base of the wok until it becomes really hot.

4 Add the potatoes, diced peppers, carrot, courgette, garlic and chilli to the wok and stir-fry the vegetables for about 2–3 minutes.

5 Stir in the spring onions, the coconut milk, the chopped lemongrass and the lime juice and stir-fry the mixture for a further 5 minutes.

6 Add the lime rind and coriander and stir-fry for 1 minute. Transfer to a warmed serving dish and serve hot.

COOK'S TIP
Check that the potatoes are not overcooked in step 2, otherwise the potato pieces will disintegrate when they are stir-fried in the wok.

Sweet & Sour Vegetables

Serve this dish with plain noodles or fluffy white rice for a filling and flavoursome oriental meal.

NUTRITIONAL INFORMATION

Calories 401	Sugars 16g
Protein 14g	Fat 9g
Carbohydrate . . .70g	Saturates 2g

 10 mins   15 mins

SERVES 4

INGREDIENTS

1 tbsp peanut oil

2 garlic cloves, crushed

1 tsp grated fresh root ginger

50 g/1¾ oz baby sweetcorn cobs

50 g/1¾ oz mangetouts

1 carrot, cut into matchstick sticks

1 green pepper, deseeded and cut into matchsticks

8 spring onions

50 g/1¾ oz canned bamboo shoots

225 g/8 oz marinated firm tofu, cubed

2 tbsp dry sherry or Chinese rice wine

1 tbsp cornflour, blended with 2 tbsp rice vinegar

2 tbsp clear honey

1 tbsp light soy sauce

150 ml/¼ pint vegetable stock

noodles or boiled rice, to serve

1 Heat the oil in a preheated wok until it is almost smoking. Add the garlic and the grated root ginger and cook over a medium heat, stirring frequently, for 30 seconds.

2 Add the baby sweetcorn cobs, the mangetouts, and the carrot and pepper matchsticks and stir-fry for about 5 minutes, or until the vegetables are tender, but still crisp.

3 Add the spring onions, bamboo shoots and tofu and cook for 2 minutes.

4 Stir in the sherry or Chinese rice wine, the cornflour and rice vinegar, honey, soy sauce and vegetable stock and bring to the boil. Reduce the heat and simmer for 2 minutes until heated through.

5 Transfer to warmed serving dishes and serve immediately.

Sweet & Sour Cauliflower

A sweet and sour sauce gives a wonderful flavour to vegetables, as in this tasty recipe.

NUTRITIONAL INFORMATION

Calories	154	Sugars	........16g
Protein	.........6g	Fat	..........7g
Carbohydrate	...17g	Saturates	.......1g

 5 mins   20 mins

SERVES 4

I N G R E D I E N T S

450 g/1 lb cauliflower florets

2 tbsp sunflower oil

1 onion, sliced

225 g/8 oz carrots, sliced

100 g/3½ oz mangetouts

1 ripe mango, sliced

100 g/3½ oz beansprouts

3 tbsp chopped fresh coriander

3 tbsp fresh lime juice

1 tbsp clear honey

6 tbsp coconut milk

1 Bring a large saucepan of water to the boil. Add the cauliflower to the pan and cook for 2 minutes. Drain the cauliflower thoroughly.

2 Heat the sunflower oil in a large preheated wok. Add the onion and carrots to the wok and stir-fry for about 5 minutes.

3 Add the drained cauliflower and mangetouts to the wok and stir-fry for 2–3 minutes.

4 Add the mango and beansprouts to the wok and stir-fry for about 2 minutes.

5 Mix together the coriander, lime juice, honey and coconut milk in a bowl.

6 Add the coriander and coconut mixture to the wok and stir-fry for about 2 minutes or until the juices are bubbling.

7 Transfer the sweet and sour cauliflower stir-fry to serving dishes and serve immediately.

VARIATION
Use broccoli instead of the cauliflower as an alternative, if you prefer.

Spiced Aubergine

This is a spicy and sweet dish, flavoured with mango chutney and heated up with chillies for a really wonderful combination of flavours.

NUTRITIONAL INFORMATION

Calories	208	Sugars	.......17g
Protein	.........1g	Fat	..........15g
Carbohydrate	...17g	Saturates	.......2g

 5 mins   25 mins

SERVES 4

I N G R E D I E N T S

3 tbsp groundnut oil

2 onions, sliced

2 cloves garlic, chopped

2 aubergines, diced

2 red chillies, deseeded and very finely chopped

2 tbsp demerara sugar

6 spring onions, sliced

3 tbsp mango chutney

oil, for deep-frying

2 cloves garlic, sliced, to garnish

1 Heat the groundnut oil in a large preheated wok or heavy-based frying pan, swirling the oil around the base of the wok until it is really hot.

2 Add the onions and chopped garlic to the wok, stirring well.

3 Add the diced aubergine and chillies to the wok and stir-fry for 5 minutes.

4 Add the demerara sugar, spring onions and mango chutney to the wok, stirring well.

5 Reduce the heat, cover and leave to simmer, stirring from time to time, for 15 minutes until the aubergine is tender.

6 Transfer the stir-fry to serving bowls and keep warm.

7 To prepare the garnish, heat the oil for deep-frying in the wok and quickly stir-fry the slices of garlic, until they brown slightly.

8 Garnish the stir-fry with the deep-fried garlic and serve immediately.

COOK'S TIP

The hotness of chillies varies enormously so always use with caution, but as a general guide the smaller they are the hotter they will be. The seeds are the hottest part and so are usually discarded.

Spinach with Mushrooms

For best results, use straw mushrooms, available in cans from Oriental shops. If these are unavailable, use button mushrooms instead.

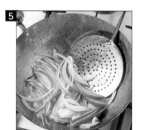

NUTRITIONAL INFORMATION

Calories 201	Sugars 8g	
Protein 7g	Fat 15g	
Carbohydrate . . .10g	Saturates 2g	

 5 mins 10 mins

SERVES 4

I N G R E D I E N T S

25 g/1 oz pine kernels

500 g/1 lb 2 oz fresh spinach leaves

1 red onion

2 garlic cloves

3 tbsp vegetable oil

425 g/15 oz canned straw mushrooms, drained

25 g/1 oz raisins

2 tbsp soy sauce

salt

1 Heat a wok or large, heavy-based frying pan.

2 Dry-fry the pine kernels in the wok until they are lightly browned. Remove with a perforated spoon and set aside until required.

3 Wash the spinach thoroughly, picking the leaves over and removing long stalks. Drain thoroughly and pat dry with absorbent kitchen paper.

4 Using a sharp knife, slice the red onion and the garlic.

5 Heat the vegetable oil in the wok or frying pan. Add the onion and garlic slices and stir-fry for 1 minute until slightly softened.

6 Add the spinach and mushrooms, and continue to stir-fry until the leaves have wilted. Drain off any excess liquid.

7 Stir in the raisins, reserved pine kernels and soy sauce. Stir-fry until thoroughly heated and all the ingredients are well combined.

8 Season to taste with salt, transfer to a warm serving dish and serve.

COOK'S TIP

Soak the raisins in 2 tablespoons dry sherry before using. This helps to plump them up as well as adding extra flavour to the stir-fry.

Vegetable Pasta Stir-fry

East meets West in this delicious dish. Prepare all the vegetables and cook the pasta in advance, then the dish can be cooked in a few minutes.

NUTRITIONAL INFORMATION

Calories	383	Sugars	........18g
Protein	........14g	Fat	.........23g
Carbohydrate	...32g	Saturates	.......8g

 20 mins   30 mins

SERVES 4

INGREDIENTS

400 g/14 oz dried wholewheat pasta shells, or other short pasta shapes

1 tbsp olive oil

2 carrots, thinly sliced

115 g/4 oz baby sweetcorn cobs

3 tbsp peanut oil

2.5 cm/1 inch piece fresh ginger root, thinly sliced

1 large onion, thinly sliced

1 garlic clove, thinly sliced

3 celery sticks, thinly sliced

1 small red pepper, deseeded and sliced into matchstick strips

1 small green pepper, deseeded and sliced into matchstick strips

salt

steamed mangetouts, to serve

SAUCE

1 tsp cornflour

2 tbsp water

3 tbsp soy sauce

3 tbsp dry sherry

1 tsp clear honey

dash of hot pepper sauce (optional)

1 Cook the pasta in a large pan of boiling, lightly salted water, adding the tablespoon of olive oil. When tender, but still firm to the bite, drain the pasta in a colander, return to the pan, cover and keep warm.

2 Cook the carrots and baby sweetcorn cobs in boiling, salted water for 2 minutes. Drain in a colander, plunge into cold water to prevent further cooking and drain again.

3 Heat the peanut oil in a large frying pan over medium heat. Add the ginger and stir-fry for 1 minute, to flavour the oil. Remove with a slotted spoon and discard.

4 Add the onion, garlic, celery and peppers to the oil and stir-fry over a medium heat for 2 minutes. Add the carrots and baby sweetcorn cobs, and stir-fry for a further 2 minutes, then stir in the reserved pasta.

5 Put the cornflour in a small bowl and mix to a smooth paste with the water. Stir in the soy sauce, the sherry and the honey.

6 Pour the sauce into the pan, stir well and cook for 2 minutes, stirring once or twice. Taste the sauce and season with hot pepper sauce if wished. Serve with a steamed green vegetable, such as mangetouts.

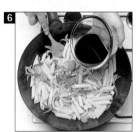

Winter Vegetable Stir-fry

Ordinary winter vegetables are given extraordinary treatment in this lively stir-fry, just the thing for perking up jaded palates.

NUTRITIONAL INFORMATION

Calories . . . . . . .175 Sugars 7g
Protein . . . . .6g Fat 13g
Carbohydrate . . . .9g Saturates 2g

 5 mins   10 mins

SERVES 4

INGREDIENTS

3 tbsp sesame oil

25 g/1 oz blanched almonds

1 large carrot, cut into thin strips

1 large turnip, cut into thin strips

1 onion, finely sliced

1 garlic clove, crushed

3 celery sticks, finely sliced

125 g/4½ oz Brussels sprouts, trimmed and halved

125 g/4½ oz cauliflower florets

125 g/4½ oz white cabbage, shredded

2 tsp sesame seeds

1 tsp grated fresh root ginger

½ tsp chilli powder

1 tbsp chopped fresh coriander

1 tbsp light soy sauce

salt and pepper

sprigs of fresh coriander, to garnish

2 Add all the vegetables to the wok or frying pan, except for the cabbage, and stir-fry the vegetables briskly for 3–4 minutes.

3 Add the cabbage, sesame seeds, ginger and chilli powder and cook, stirring, for 2 minutes.

1 Heat the oil in a wok or large frying pan. Stir-fry the almonds until lightly browned, then lift them out and drain on absorbent kitchen paper.

4 Stir in the chopped coriander, soy sauce and almonds. Season to taste. Serve the vegetables garnished with coriander sprigs.

COOK'S TIP

As well as adding protein, vitamins and useful fats to the diet, nuts and seeds add important flavour and texture to vegetarian meals. Sesame seeds are also a good source of vitamin E and calcium.

Vegetable Chop Suey

A classic Chinese dish found on all take-away menus, this recipe is quick to prepare and makes a tasty meal.

NUTRITIONAL INFORMATION

Calories	129	Sugars	........19g
Protein	.........5g	Fat	..........12g
Carbohydrate	...21g	Saturates	.......2g

10 mins   6 mins

SERVES 4

INGREDIENTS

2 tbsp peanut oil

1 onion, chopped

3 garlic cloves, chopped

1 green pepper, deseeded and diced

1 red pepper, deseeded and diced

75 g/2¾ oz broccoli florets

1 courgette, sliced

25 g/1 oz French beans

1 carrot, cut into matchsticks

100 g/3½ oz beansprouts

2 tsp light brown sugar

2 tbsp light soy sauce

125 ml/4 fl oz vegetable stock

salt and pepper

noodles, to serve

COOK'S TIP

The clever design of a wok, with its spherical base and high sloping sides, enables the food to be tossed so that it is cooked quickly and evenly. It is essential to heat the wok sufficiently before you add the ingredients to ensure quick and even cooking.

1 Heat the peanut oil in a preheated wok until it is almost smoking. Add the chopped onion and garlic to the wok and stir-fry for 30 seconds.

2 Add the diced peppers, the broccoli florets, the sliced courgette, the French beans and the carrot matchsticks to the pan and continue to stir-fry for a further 2–3 minutes.

3 Stir in the beansprouts, the light brown sugar, the soy sauce and the vegetable stock and toss to combine thoroughly. Season the mixture with salt and pepper to taste and continue to cook for a further 2 minutes.

4 Transfer the vegetables to warmed serving plates and serve immediately with noodles.

Braised Chinese Leaves

Shredded white cabbage can be used instead of the Chinese leaves for this delicious braised dish.

NUTRITIONAL INFORMATION

Calories 138	Sugars 4g	
Protein 6g	Fat 9g	
Carbohydrate ...10g	Saturates 1g	

5 mins   5 mins

SERVES 4

INGREDIENTS

500 g/1 lb 2 oz Chinese leaves or white cabbage

3 tbsp vegetable oil

½ tsp Szechuan red peppercorns

5–6 small dried red chillies, deseeded and chopped

½ tsp salt

1 tbsp sugar

1 tbsp light soy sauce

1 tbsp rice vinegar

a few drops sesame oil (optional)

1 Shred the Chinese leaves or white cabbage crosswise into thin pieces. (If Chinese leaves are unavailable, the best alternative to use in this recipe is a firm-packed white cabbage, not the dark green type of cabbage. Cut out the thick core of the cabbage with a sharp knife before you shred it.)

2 Heat the vegetable oil in a preheated wok or large frying pan, add the Szechuan red peppercorns and dried red chillies and stir for a few seconds.

3 Add the shredded Chinese leaves or white cabbage to the peppercorns and chillies and stir-fry them for about 1 minute.

4 Add the salt to the mixture in the wok or frying pan and continue stirring for another minute.

5 Add the sugar, light soy sauce and rice vinegar, blend well and braise for one more minute.

6 Finally, sprinkle on the sesame oil, if using. Serve the braised Chinese leaves hot or cold.

COOK'S TIP
Szechuan red peppercorns are not true peppers, but reddish-brown dry berries with a pungent, aromatic odour that distinguishes them from the hotter black peppercorns. Roast them briefly in the oven or dry-fry them. Grind them in a blender and store in a jar until needed.

Leeks with Bean Sauce

This is a simple side dish, cooked in a delicious yellow bean sauce, which is ideal with other main meal vegetarian dishes.

NUTRITIONAL INFORMATION

Calories	131	Sugars	.........3g
Protein	.........6g	Fat	...........9g
Carbohydrate	....7g	Saturates	.......2g

 5 mins   10 mins

SERVES 4

I N G R E D I E N T S

450 g/1 lb leeks

175 g/6 oz baby sweetcorn cobs

6 spring onions

3 tbsp groundnut oil

225 g/8 oz Chinese leaves, shredded

4 tbsp yellow bean sauce

1 Using a sharp knife, slice the leeks, halve the baby sweetcorn cobs and thinly slice the spring onions.

2 Heat the groundnut oil in a large, preheated wok or frying pan until it is smoking.

3 Add the leeks, shredded Chinese leaves and baby sweetcorn cobs to the wok or frying pan.

4 Stir-fry the vegetables over a high heat for about 5 minutes or until the edges of the vegetables are slightly brown.

5 Add the spring onions to the wok or frying pan, stirring to combine.

6 Add the yellow bean sauce to the wok or frying pan.

7 Continue to stir-fry the mixture in the wok for a further 2 minutes, or until the yellow bean sauce is heated through and the vegetables are thoroughly coated in the sauce.

8 Transfer the stir-fried vegetables and sauce to warm serving dishes and serve immediately.

COOK'S TIP

Yellow bean sauce adds an authentic Chinese flavour to stir-fries. It is made from crushed salted soya beans mixed with flour and spices to make a thick paste. It is mild in flavour and is excellent with a range of vegetables.

French & Black Bean Stir-fry

A terrific side dish, the variety of greens in this recipe make it as attractive as it is tasty.

NUTRITIONAL INFORMATION

Calories 88	Sugars 2g	
Protein 2g	Fat 7g	
Carbohydrate 4g	Saturates 4g	

 5 mins   10 mins

SERVES 4

INGREDIENTS

225 g/8 oz French beans, sliced

4 shallots, sliced

100 g/3½ oz shiitake mushrooms, thinly sliced

1 clove garlic, crushed

1 iceberg lettuce, shredded

1 tsp chilli oil

2 tbsp butter

4 tbsp black bean sauce

1 Using a sharp knife, slice the French beans, the shallots and the shiitake mushrooms. Crush the garlic in a pestle and mortar and shred the iceberg lettuce.

2 Heat the chilli oil and butter in a large, preheated wok or frying pan.

3 Add the French beans, shallots, garlic and mushrooms to the wok and stir-fry for 2–3 minutes.

4 Add the shredded lettuce to the wok or frying pan and stir-fry until the leaves have wilted.

5 Stir the black bean sauce into the mixture in the wok and heat through, tossing gently to mix thoroughly, until the sauce is bubbling.

6 Transfer the French and black bean stir-fry to a warm serving dish and serve immediately.

Stir-fried Beansprouts

Be sure to use fresh beansprouts, rather than the canned variety, for this crunchy-textured dish.

NUTRITIONAL INFORMATION

Calories 98	Sugars 2g	
Protein 2g	Fat 9g	
Carbohydrate 3g	Saturates 1g	

🔥 5 mins   🕐 5 mins

SERVES 4

INGREDIENTS

250 g/9 oz beansprouts

2–3 spring onions

1 red chilli pepper (optional)

3 tbsp vegetable oil

½ tsp salt

½ tsp sugar

1 tbsp light soy sauce

a few drops sesame oil (optional)

1 Rinse the beansprouts in cold water, discarding any husks or small pieces that float to the top.

2 Drain the beansprouts well on absorbent kitchen paper.

3 Using a sharp knife, cut the spring onions into short pieces.

4 Thinly shred the red chilli pepper, if using, discarding the seeds.

5 Heat the vegetable oil in a preheated wok, swirling the oil around the base of the wok until it is really hot.

6 Add the beansprouts, the spring onions and the chilli pepper, if using, to the wok, and stir-fry the mixture for about 2 minutes.

7 Add the salt, sugar, soy sauce and sesame oil, if using, to the mixture in the wok. Stir well to blend. Serve the bean sprouts hot or cold.

COOK'S TIP

The red chilli pepper gives a bite to this dish – leave the seeds in for an even hotter taste. If you prefer a milder, sweeter flavour, use red pepper instead of the chilli pepper. Core, seed and cut into strips in the same way.

Cabbage & Walnut Stir-fry

This is a really quick, one-pan dish using white and red cabbage for colour and flavour.

NUTRITIONAL INFORMATION

Calories 422   Sugars 9g
Protein ....13g   Fat 37g
Carbohydrate ...10g   Saturates 5g

10 mins   10 mins

SERVES 4

INGREDIENTS

350 g/12 oz white cabbage

350 g/12 oz red cabbage

4 tbsp peanut oil

1 tbsp walnut oil

2 garlic cloves, crushed

8 spring onions, trimmed

225 g/8 oz firm tofu, cubed

2 tbsp lemon juice

100 g/3½ oz walnut halves

2 tsp Dijon mustard

salt and pepper

2 tsp poppy seeds

1 Using a sharp knife, shred the white and red cabbages thinly and set aside until required.

2 Heat the peanut and walnut oils in a preheated wok. Add the garlic, cabbage, spring onions and tofu and cook for 5 minutes, stirring.

3 Add the lemon juice, walnuts and mustard to the wok and stir to combine thoroughly.

4 Season the mixture to taste with salt and pepper and cook for a further 5 minutes or until the cabbage is tender.

5 Transfer the stir-fry to a warm serving bowl, sprinkle with poppy seeds and serve immediately.

VARIATION
Sesame seeds could be used instead of the poppy seeds, and drizzle 1 tsp of sesame oil over the dish just before serving, if you wish.

Cauliflower with Greens

This is a delicious way to cook cauliflower with a lovely texture and flavour – even without the greens.

NUTRITIONAL INFORMATION

Calories	49	Sugars 2g
Protein	.........2g	Fat 3g
Carbohydrate	....3g	Saturates 0.5g

 5 mins   5 mins

SERVES 4

I N G R E D I E N T S

175 g/6 oz cauliflower, cut into florets

1 garlic clove

½ tsp turmeric

1 tbsp coriander root or stem

1 tbsp sunflower oil

2 spring onions, cut into 2.5 cm/
   1 inch pieces

125 g/4½ oz oriental greens, such as pak
   choi or mustard greens, tough stalks
   removed

1 tsp yellow mustard seeds

1 Blanch the cauliflower, rinse in cold running water and drain. Set aside until required.

2 Grind together the garlic, turmeric and coriander root or stem together in a pestle and mortar or spice grinder.

COOK'S TIP

Pestle and mortars are available in wood or stone. The stone mortar gives a finer grind than the wooden mortar. A coffee grinder can be used, but will need a thorough clean afterwards, as some of the spices used in Chinese cooking can be quite pungent!

3 Heat the sunflower oil in a wok or large, heavy frying pan.

4 Add the spring onions to the wok or frying pan and cook over a high heat for 2 minutes, stirring constantly.

5 Add the oriental greens and continue to stir-fry for 1 minute. Remove the mixture from the pan, keep warm and set aside until required.

6 Return the wok or frying pan to the heat and add the mustard seeds. Stir until the seeds start to pop.

7 Add the turmeric and coriander mixture and the blanched cauliflower to the pan, and stir until the cauliflower is thoroughly coated.

8 Serve the cauliflower with the greens on a warmed serving plate.

Butternut Squash Stir-fry

Butternut squash is, as its name suggests, deliciously buttery and nutty in flavour. If the squash is not in season, use sweet potatoes instead.

NUTRITIONAL INFORMATION

Calories 301	Sugars 4g
Protein 9g	Fat 22g
Carbohydrate . . .19g	Saturates 4g

 5 mins   25 mins

SERVES 4

I N G R E D I E N T S

1 kg/2 lb 4 oz butternut squash, peeled

3 tbsp groundnut oil

1 onion, sliced

2 cloves garlic, crushed

1 tsp coriander seeds

1 tsp cumin seeds

2 tbsp chopped fresh coriander

150 ml/5 fl oz coconut milk

100 ml/3½ fl oz water

100 g/3½ oz salted cashew nuts

T O   G A R N I S H

freshly grated lime rind

fresh coriander

lime wedges

1 Slice the butternut squash into small, bite-sized cubes, using a sharp knife.

2 Heat the groundnut oil in a large, preheated wok.

3 Add the butternut squash, the onion and the garlic to the wok and stir-fry for 5 minutes.

4 Stir in the coriander seeds, cumin seeds and fresh chopped coriander, and stir-fry for 1 minute.

5 Add the coconut milk and water to the wok and bring to the boil. Cover the wok and leave to simmer for 10–15 minutes, or until the squash is tender.

6 Add the cashew nuts and stir to combine thoroughly.

7 Transfer to warm serving dishes and garnish with freshly grated lime rind, fresh coriander and lime wedges. Serve hot and immediately.

COOK'S TIP
If you do not have coconut milk, grate some creamed coconut into the dish with a total of 225 ml/8 fl oz water in step 5.

Braised Vegetables

This colourful selection of braised vegetables makes a splendid light meal or an accompaniment to a main dish.

NUTRITIONAL INFORMATION

Calories	170	Sugars	........8g
Protein	.........7g	Fat	..........10g
Carbohydrate	...14g	Saturates	.......1g

 10 mins 10 mins

SERVES 4

INGREDIENTS

3 tbsp sunflower oil

1 garlic clove, crushed

1 Chinese cabbage, thickly shredded

2 onions, peeled and cut into wedges

250 g/9 oz broccoli florets

2 large carrots, peeled and cut into thin julienne strips

12 baby sweetcorn cobs, halved if large

60 g/2 oz mangetouts, halved

90 g/3 oz Chinese or oyster mushrooms, sliced

1 tbsp fresh ginger root, grated

175 ml/6 fl oz vegetable stock

2 tbsp light soy sauce

1 tbsp cornflour

pepper

½ tsp sugar

COOK'S TIP

This dish also makes an ideal vegetarian main meal. Double the quantities, to serve 4–6, and serve with noodles or Green Herb Rice (see page 427).

1 Heat the oil in a wok. Add the garlic, cabbage, onions, broccoli, carrots, corn, mangetouts, mushrooms and ginger and stir-fry for 2 minutes.

2 Add the vegetable stock, cover and cook for a further 2-3 minutes.

3 In a small bowl, blend together the cornflour and the soy sauce, and season to taste with pepper.

4 Remove the braised vegetables from the pan with a slotted spoon and keep warm. Add the soy sauce mixture to the pan juices, mixing well. Bring to the boil, stirring constantly, until the mixture thickens slightly. Stir in the sugar.

5 Return the vegetables to the pan and toss in the slightly thickened sauce. Cook gently to just heat through then serve immediately.

Vegetable Stir-fry with Eggs

Known as Gado Gado in Indonesia, this is a true classic which never fades from popularity – a delicious warm salad with a peanut sauce.

NUTRITIONAL INFORMATION

Calories	269	Sugars	........12g
Protein	........12g	Fat	.........19g
Carbohydrate	...14g	Saturates	.......3g

10 mins   15 mins

SERVES 4

INGREDIENTS

2 eggs

225 g/8 oz carrots

350 g/12 oz white cabbage

2 tbsp vegetable oil

1 red pepper, deseeded and thinly sliced

150 g/5½ oz beansprouts

1 tbsp tomato ketchup

2 tbsp soy sauce

75 g/2¾ oz salted peanuts, chopped

1 Bring a small saucepan of water to the boil. Add the eggs to the pan and cook for about 7 minutes. Remove the eggs from the pan and leave to cool under cold running water for 1 minute. Peel the shells from the eggs and then cut the eggs into quarters.

2 Peel the carrots and grate them on a coarse grater.

3 Remove any outer leaves from the white cabbage and cut out the stem, then shred the leaves very finely, either with a sharp knife or by using the fine slicing blade on a food processor.

4 Heat the vegetable oil in a large preheated wok or large frying pan.

5 Add the grated carrots, shredded white cabbage and sliced pepper to the wok and stir-fry for 3 minutes.

6 Add the beansprouts to the wok and stir-fry for 2 minutes.

7 Combine the tomato ketchup and soy sauce in a small bowl and add to the wok or frying pan.

8 Add the chopped peanuts to the wok and stir-fry for 1 minute.

9 Transfer the stir-fry to warm serving plates and garnish with the hard-boiled egg quarters. Serve immediately.

COOK'S TIP
The eggs are cooled in cold water immediately after cooking in order to prevent the egg yolk blackening around the edges.

Stir-fried Mixed Vegetables

The Chinese carefully select vegetables to achieve a harmonious balance of contrasting colours and textures.

NUTRITIONAL INFORMATION

Calories 534   Sugars 8g
Protein . . . . .14g   Fat 45g
Carbohydrate . . .19g   Saturates 5g

 5 mins   5 mins

SERVES 4

INGREDIENTS

60g/2 oz mangetouts

1 small carrot

125 g/4½ oz Chinese leaves

60 g/2 oz black or white mushrooms

60 g/2 oz canned bamboo shoots, rinsed and drained

3–4 tbsp vegetable oil

125 g/4½ oz beansprouts

1 tsp salt

1 tsp sugar

1 tbsp light soy sauce

a few drops sesame oil (optional)

dip sauce, to serve (optional)

1 Prepare the vegetables: top and tail the mangetouts, and cut the carrot, Chinese leaves, mushrooms and bamboo shoots into roughly the same shape and size as the mangetouts.

2 Heat the vegetable oil in a preheated wok or large frying pan and add the carrot. Stir-fry for a few seconds.

3 Add the mangetouts and the Chinese leaves to the wok or frying pan and stir-fry for a further minute.

4 Add the beansprouts, mushrooms and bamboo shoots to the other vegetables and continue to stir-fry for another minute.

5 Add the salt and sugar, continue stirring for another minute, then add the light soy sauce, blending well.

6 Sprinkle the vegetables with sesame oil (if using) and serve hot or cold, with a dip sauce, if liked, or with rice and toasted cashew nuts (see Cook's Tip).

COOK'S TIP

Put some rice on to cook while you are preparing the stir-fry. Serve the stir-fry on a bed of rice and scatter a few toasted cashew nuts on top for a perfectly balanced, and incredibly quick, nutritious meal.

Vegetable Sesame Stir-fry

Sesame seeds add a delicious flavour to any recipe and are particularly good with vegetables in this soy and rice wine or sherry sauce.

NUTRITIONAL INFORMATION

Calories	 118	Sugars	. . . . .2g
Protein	. . . . .3g	Fat	. . . . .9g
Carbohydrate	. . . .5g	Saturates	. . . . . . .1g

5 mins 10 mins

SERVES 4

INGREDIENTS

2 tbsp vegetable oil

3 garlic cloves, crushed

1 tbsp sesame seeds, plus extra to garnish

2 celery sticks, sliced

2 baby sweetcorn cobs, sliced

60 g/2 oz button mushrooms

1 leek, sliced

1 courgette, sliced

1 small red pepper, deseeded and sliced

1 fresh green chilli, deseeded and sliced

60 g/2 oz Chinese leaves, shredded

rice or noodles, to serve

SAUCE

½ tsp Chinese curry powder

2 tbsp light soy sauce

1 tbsp Chinese rice wine or dry sherry

1 tsp sesame oil

1 tsp cornflour

4 tbsp water

1 Heat the vegetable oil in a preheated wok or heavy-based frying pan, swirling the oil around the base of the wok until it is almost smoking.

2 Lower the heat slightly, add the garlic and sesame seeds to the wok or frying pan and stir-fry for 30 seconds.

3 Add the celery, baby sweetcorn cobs, mushrooms, leek, courgette, pepper, chilli and Chinese leaves and stir-fry for 4–5 minutes, until the vegetables are just beginning to soften.

4 To make the sauce, mix together the Chinese curry powder, light soy sauce,

Chinese rice wine or dry sherry, sesame oil, cornflour and water.

5 Add the sauce mixture to the wok and stir thoroughly to combine with the other ingredients.

6 Bring the mixture to the boil and cook, stirring constantly, until the sauce thickens and clears.

7 Cook the vegetables and sauce for 1 minute, spoon into a warm serving dish and garnish with sesame seeds.

8 Serve the vegetable sesame stir-fry immediately with rice or noodles.

Mixed Vegetable Balti

Any combination of vegetables or pulses can be used in this recipe. It would make a good dish for an informal vegetarian supper party.

NUTRITIONAL INFORMATION

Calories 207	Sugars 6g
Protein 8g	Fat 9g
Carbohydrate . . .24g	Saturates 1g

 10 mins   1 hr

SERVES 4

INGREDIENTS

225 g/8 oz split yellow peas

3 tbsp vegetable oil

1 tsp onion seeds

2 onions, sliced

115 g/4 oz courgettes, sliced

115 g/4 oz potatoes, cut into 1 cm/
    ½ inch cubes

115 g/4 oz carrots, sliced

1 small aubergine, sliced

225 g/8 oz tomatoes, chopped

300 ml/½ pint water

3 garlic cloves, chopped

1 tsp ground cumin

1 tsp ground coriander

1 tsp salt

2 fresh green chillies, deseeded and sliced

½ tsp garam masala

2 tbsp chopped fresh coriander

1 Put the split peas into a pan and cover with lightly salted water. Bring to the boil and simmer for 30 minutes. Drain the peas and keep warm.

2 Heat the oil in a special balti karahi or wok, add the onion seeds and fry until they start popping.

3 Add the onions and stir-fry over a medium heat until golden brown.

4 Add the courgettes, potatoes, carrots and aubergine to the pan. Stir-fry the vegetables for about 2 minutes.

5 Stir in the tomatoes, water, garlic, cumin, ground coriander, salt, chillies, garam masala and reserved split peas.

6 Bring to the boil, then lower the heat and simmer for 15 minutes until all the vegetables are tender.

7 Stir the fresh coriander into the vegetables. Transfer to a warmed serving dish and serve immediately.

Potato & Tomato Calzone

These pizza dough Italian pasties are best served hot with a salad for a delicious lunch or supper dish.

NUTRITIONAL INFORMATION

Calories	524	Sugars	.........8g
Protein	........17g	Fat	...........8g
Carbohydrate	..103g	Saturates	.......2g

1½ hrs   35 mins

SERVES 4

I N G R E D I E N T S

DOUGH

450 g/1 lb strong white bread flour

1 tsp easy-blend dried yeast

300 ml/10 fl oz vegetable stock

1 tbsp clear honey

1 tsp caraway seeds

skimmed milk, for glazing

vegetable oil, for greasing

FILLING

1 tbsp vegetable oil

225 g/8 oz waxy potatoes, diced

1 onion, halved and sliced

2 garlic cloves, crushed

40 g/1½ oz sun-dried tomatoes, chopped

2 tbsp chopped fresh basil

2 tbsp tomato purée

2 celery sticks, sliced

50 g/1¾ oz mozzarella cheese, grated

1 To make the dough, sift the flour into a large mixing bowl and stir in the yeast. Make a well in the centre of the mixture. Stir in the vegetable stock, honey and caraway seeds and bring the mixture together to form a dough.

2 Turn the dough out on to a lightly floured surface and knead for 8 minutes until smooth. Place the dough in a lightly oiled mixing bowl, cover and leave to rise in a warm place for 1 hour or until it has doubled in size.

3 Meanwhile, make the filling. Heat the oil in a frying pan and add all the remaining ingredients except for the cheese. Cook for about 5 minutes, stirring.

4 Divide the risen dough into 4 pieces. On a lightly floured surface, roll them out to form four 18 cm/7 inch circles. Spoon equal amounts of the filling on to one half of each circle. Sprinkle the cheese over the filling. Brush the edge of the dough with milk and fold the dough over to form 4 semi-circles, pressing to seal the edges.

5 Place on a non-stick baking tray and brush with milk. Cook in a preheated oven, 220°C/425°F/Gas Mark 7, for 30 minutes until golden and risen.

Apricot Slices

These vegan slices are ideal for children's lunches. They are full of flavour and made with healthy ingredients.

NUTRITIONAL INFORMATION

Calories	198	Sugars	........13g
Protein	.........4g	Fat	...........9g
Carbohydrate	...25g	Saturates	.......2g

50 mins · 1 hr

MAKES 12

I N G R E D I E N T S

PASTRY

100 g/3½ oz margarine, cut into
   small pieces, plus extra for greasing

225 g/8 oz wholemeal flour

55 g/2 oz finely ground mixed nuts

4 tbsp water

soya milk, to glaze

FILLING

225 g/8 oz dried apricots

grated rind of 1 orange

300 ml/10 fl oz apple juice

1 tsp ground cinnamon

55 g/2 oz raisins

1 Lightly grease a 23 cm/9 inch square cake tin. To make the pastry, place the flour and nuts in a mixing bowl and rub in the margarine with your fingers until the mixture resembles breadcrumbs. Stir in the water and bring together to form a dough. Wrap and set aside to chill in the refrigerator for 30 minutes.

2 To make the filling, place the apricots, orange rind and apple juice in a pan and bring to the boil. Simmer for 30 minutes until the apricots are mushy. Cool slightly, then process in a food processor or blender to a purée. Alternatively, press the mixture through a fine strainer. Stir in the cinnamon and raisins.

3 Divide the pastry in half, roll out 1 half and use to line the base of the tin. Spread the apricot purée over the top and brush the edges of the pastry with water. Roll out the rest of the dough to fit over the top of the apricot purée. Press down and seal the edges.

4 Prick the top of the pastry with a fork and brush with soya milk. Bake in a preheated oven, 200°C/400°F/Gas Mark 6, for 20–25 minutes until the pastry is golden. Set aside to cool slightly before cutting into 12 bars. Serve either warm or cold.

COOK'S TIP

These slices will keep in an airtight container for 3–4 days.

Cheese & Potato Plait

This bread has a delicious cheese and garlic flavour and is best eaten freshly baked, while it is still warm.

NUTRITIONAL INFORMATION

Calories	387	Sugars	.........1g
Protein	........13g	Fat	..........8g
Carbohydrate	...70g	Saturates	.......4g

 2½ hrs 55 mins

SERVES 8

INGREDIENTS

butter, for greasing

675 g/1½ lb strong white flour, plus extra for dusting

175 g/6 oz floury potatoes, diced

2 x 7 g sachets easy-blend dried yeast

450 ml/16 fl oz vegetable stock

2 garlic cloves, crushed

2 tbsp chopped fresh rosemary

115 g/4 oz Gruyère cheese, grated

1 tbsp vegetable oil

1 tbsp salt

1 Lightly grease and flour a baking sheet. Cook the potatoes in a pan of boiling water for 10 minutes or until soft. Drain well and mash.

2 Transfer the mashed potatoes to a large mixing bowl, stir in the yeast, flour and vegetable stock and mix to form a smooth dough. Add the garlic, chopped rosemary and 85 g/3 oz of the cheese and knead the dough for 5 minutes. Make a hollow in the dough, pour in the oil and knead the dough again.

3 Cover the dough and set it aside in a warm place for about 1½ hours or until doubled in size.

4 Knead the dough again and divide it into 3 equal portions. Roll each portion into a sausage shape about 35 cm/14 inches long.

5 Press one end of each of the sausage shapes firmly together, then carefully plait the dough, without breaking it, and fold the remaining ends under, sealing them together firmly.

6 Place the plait on the greased baking sheet, cover and set aside to rise for a further 30 minutes.

7 Sprinkle the remaining cheese over the top of the plait and bake in a preheated oven, 190°C/375°F/Gas Mark 5, for 40 minutes or until the base of the loaf sounds hollow when tapped. Serve while it is still warm.

  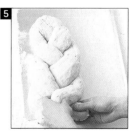

Cheese & Chive Scones

These tea-time classics have been given a healthy twist by the use of low-fat soft cheese and reduced-fat Cheddar cheese.

NUTRITIONAL INFORMATION

Calories 297	Sugars 3g	
Protein 13g	Fat 7g	
Carbohydrate ...49g	Saturates 4g	

   10 mins   20 mins

MAKES 10 SCONES

INGREDIENTS

225 g/8 oz self-raising flour

1 tsp powdered mustard

½ tsp cayenne pepper

½ tsp salt

100 g/3½ oz low-fat soft cheese with added herbs

2 tbsp fresh snipped chives, plus extra to garnish

100 ml/3½ fl oz skimmed milk, plus extra for brushing

55 g/2 oz reduced-fat mature Cheddar cheese, grated

low-fat soft cheese, to serve

1 Sift the flour, mustard, cayenne pepper and salt into a large mixing bowl.

2 Add the soft cheese to the mixture and mix together until well incorporated. Stir in the snipped chives.

3 Make a well in the centre of the ingredients and gradually pour in 100 ml/3½ fl oz milk, stirring as you pour, until the mixture forms a soft dough.

4 Turn the dough on to a floured surface and knead lightly. Roll out until 2 cm/¾ inch thick and use a 5 cm/2 inch plain pastry cutter to stamp out as many rounds as you can. Transfer the rounds to a baking sheet.

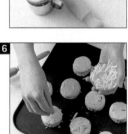

5 Re-knead the dough trimmings together and roll out again. Stamp out more rounds – you should be able to make 10 scones in total.

6 Brush the scones with milk and sprinkle with the grated cheese. Bake in a preheated oven, 200°C/400°F/Gas Mark 6, for 15–20 minutes until risen and golden. Transfer to a wire rack to cool.

7 Serve the scones warm with low-fat soft cheese, garnished with chives.

VARIATION

For sweet scones, omit the mustard, cayenne pepper, chives and grated cheese. Replace the flavoured soft cheese with plain low-fat soft cheese. Add 75 g/2¾ oz currants and 25 g/1 oz caster sugar. Serve with low-fat soft cheese and fruit spread.

Herb Focaccia

Rich with olive oil, this bread is so delicious it would turn a simple salad or bowl of soup into a positive feast.

NUTRITIONAL INFORMATION

Calories . . . . .210 Sugars 1g
Protein . . . . .6g Fat 5g
Carbohydrate . . . .5g Saturates 1g

 2 hrs   15 mins

MAKES 1 LOAF

I N G R E D I E N T S

400 g/14 oz unbleached strong white flour,
    plus extra for dusting

1 sachet easy-blend dried yeast

1½ tsp salt

½ tsp sugar

300 ml/½ pint hand-hot water

3 tbsp extra virgin olive oil, plus extra
    for greasing

4 tbsp finely chopped fresh herbs

polenta or cornmeal, for sprinkling

sea salt, for sprinkling

1 Combine the flour, yeast, salt and sugar in a bowl and make a well in the centre. Gradually stir in most of the water and 2 tablespoons of the olive oil to make a dough. Gradually add the remaining water, if necessary, drawing in all the flour.

2 Turn out on to a lightly floured surface and knead. Transfer to a bowl and lightly knead in the herbs for 10 minutes until soft but not sticky. Wash the bowl and lightly coat with olive oil.

3 Shape the dough into a ball, put it in the bowl and turn the dough over. Cover tightly with a tea towel or lightly greased clingfilm and set aside in a warm place to rise until the dough has doubled in volume. Meanwhile, sprinkle polenta over a baking sheet.

4 Turn the dough out on to a lightly floured surface and knead lightly. Cover with the upturned bowl and leave for 10 minutes.

5 Roll out and pat the dough into a 25 cm/10 inch circle, about 1 cm/½ inch thick, and carefully transfer it to the prepared baking sheet. Cover the dough with a tea towel and leave to rise again for 15 minutes.

6 Using a lightly oiled finger, poke indentations all over the surface of the loaf. Drizzle the remaining olive oil over and sprinkle lightly with sea salt. Bake in a preheated oven, 230°C/450°F/Gas Mark 8, for 15 minutes or until golden and the loaf sounds hollow when tapped on the bottom. Transfer the loaf to a wire rack to cool completely.

Garlic Bread

A perennial favourite, garlic bread is perfect with a range of barbecue meals, and works especially well with chargrilled vegetables.

NUTRITIONAL INFORMATION

Calories 261	Sugars 1g	
Protein 3g	Fat 22g	
Carbohydrate . . .15g	Saturates 14g	

 10 mins   15 mins

SERVES 4

INGREDIENTS

150 g/5½ oz butter, softened

3 cloves garlic, crushed

2 tbsp chopped fresh parsley

pepper

1 large or 2 small sticks of French bread

1 Mix together the butter, garlic and parsley in a bowl until well combined. Season with pepper to taste and mix well.

2 Cut the French bread into thick slices. Spread the garlic and parsley flavoured butter over one side of each slice and reassemble the loaf on a large sheet of thick kitchen foil.

3 Wrap the bread well in foil and barbecue over hot coals for about 10–15 minutes until the butter melts and the bread is piping hot.

4 Serve as an accompaniment to a wide range of dishes.

Mediterranean Bread

Many of the flavours of the Mediterranean are captured in this rustic loaf. It is a perfect accompaniment for pasta and vegetable dishes.

NUTRITIONAL INFORMATION

Calories 222   Sugars 1g
Protein . . . . .5g   Fat 12g
Carbohydrate . . .26g   Saturates 2g

🧀 🧀 🧀

🧊 25 mins, plus rising   🕐 40 mins

SERVES 4

I N G R E D I E N T S

400 g/14 oz plain flour, plus extra
for dusting

1 sachet easy-blend dried yeast

1 tsp salt

1 tbsp coriander seeds, lightly crushed

2 tsp dried oregano

200 ml/7 fl oz hand-hot water

3 tbsp olive oil, plus extra for greasing

150 g/5½ oz sun-dried tomatoes in oil,
drained, patted dry and chopped

85 g/3 oz feta cheese (drained weight),
patted dry and cubed

115 g/4 oz black olives, patted dry,
stoned and sliced

1 Combine the flour, yeast, salt, coriander seeds and oregano and make a well in the centre. Gradually add most of the water and the oil to make a dough. Gradually add the remaining water, if needed, drawing in all the flour.

2 Turn out on to a lightly floured surface and knead for 10 minutes. Knead in the tomatoes, cheese and olives. Wash the bowl and lightly coat it with oil.

3 Shape the dough into a ball, put it in the bowl and turn the dough over. Cover tightly and set aside the dough until it doubles in volume.

4 Turn the dough out on to a lightly floured surface. Knead lightly, then shape into a ball. Place on a lightly floured baking sheet. Cover and set aside to rise until it doubles in volume again.

5 Lightly sprinkle the top of the loaf with flour. Using a sharp knife, cut 3 shallow slashes in the top. Bake in a preheated oven, 230°C/450°F/Gas Mark 8, for 20 minutes. Lower the temperature to 200°C/400°F/Gas Mark 6 and bake for a further 20 minutes or until the loaf sounds hollow when you tap it on the bottom. Transfer to a wire rack to cool completely. This loaf keeps well for up to 3 days in an airtight container.

Fougasse

This distinctive-looking bread, with its herringbone slits, is baked daily throughout Provence. It is best eaten on the day it is baked.

NUTRITIONAL INFORMATION

Calories	161	Sugars	....1g
Protein	....5g	Fat	....0g
Carbohydrate	...36g	Saturates	....0g

1¾ hrs   25 mins

MAKES 2 LARGE LOAVES

I N G R E D I E N T S

750 g/1 lb 10 oz unbleached strong white flour, plus extra for dusting

1 sachet easy-blend dried yeast

2 tsp salt

1 tsp sugar

450 ml/16 fl oz hand-hot water

olive oil, for greasing

1 Combine the flour, yeast, salt and sugar in a bowl and make a well in the centre. Gradually stir in most of the water to make a dough. Gradually add the remaining water, if necessary, drawing in all the flour.

2 Turn out on to a lightly floured surface and knead for 10 minutes until smooth and elastic. Wash the bowl and lightly coat with olive oil.

3 Shape the dough into a ball, put it in the bowl and turn the dough over. Cover the bowl tightly with a tea towel or lightly oiled clingfilm and set aside in a warm place to rise until the dough has doubled in volume.

4 Knock back the dough and turn out on to a lightly floured surface. Knead lightly, then cover with the upturned bowl and leave for 10 minutes.

5 Put a roasting tin of water in the bottom of the oven while it preheats to 230°C/450°F/Gas Mark 8. Lightly flour a baking sheet.

6 Divide the dough into 2 pieces and roll each one into a 30 cm/12 inch oval, 1 cm/½ inch thick. Using a sharp knife, cut 5 x 7.5 cm/3 inch slices on an angle in a herringbone pattern on each of the dough ovals. Cut all the way through the dough, using the tip of the knife to open up the slits a little.

7 Spray the loaves with cold water. Bake for 20 minutes, turn upside down and continue baking for 5 minutes until the loaves sound hollow when tapped on the bottom. Transfer to wire racks to cool.

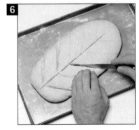

Olive Rolls

These country-style bread rolls depend on fruity olive oil and good-quality olives. You could use any of the Flavoured Olives (see page 845).

NUTRITIONAL INFORMATION

Calories 181   Sugars 1g
Protein . . . . .6g   Fat 3g
Carbohydrate . . .35g   Saturates 0.5g

 1¾ hrs   30 mins

MAKES 16 ROLLS

I N G R E D I E N T S

115 g/4 oz black or green olives in brine or oil, drained

750 g/1 lb 10 oz unbleached strong white flour, plus extra for dusting

1½ tsp salt

1 sachet easy-blend dried yeast

450 ml/16 fl oz hand-hot water

2 tbsp extra virgin olive oil, plus extra for brushing

4 tbsp finely chopped fresh oregano, parsley or thyme leaves, or 1 tbsp dried mixed herbs

1 Stone the olives with an olive or cherry pitter and finely chop them. Pat off the excess brine or oil with kitchen paper. Set aside.

2 Combine the flour, salt and yeast in a bowl and make a well in the centre. Gradually stir in most of the water and the olive oil to make a dough. Gradually add the remaining water, if necessary, drawing in all the flour.

3 Lightly knead in the chopped olives and herbs. Turn out the dough on to a lightly floured surface and knead for 10 minutes until smooth and elastic. Wash the bowl and lightly coat with oil.

4 Shape the dough into a ball, put it in the bowl and turn over so it is coated. Cover tightly with a tea towel or lightly oiled clingfilm and set aside to rise until it has doubled in volume. Dust a baking sheet with flour.

5 Turn out the dough on to a lightly floured surface and knead lightly. Roll the dough into 20 cm/8 inch ropes on a very lightly floured surface.

6 Cut the dough into 16 even pieces. Shape each piece into a ball and place on the prepared baking sheet. Cover and set aside to rise for 15 minutes.

7 Lightly brush the top of each roll with olive oil. Bake in a preheated oven, 220°C/425°F/Gas Mark 7 for about 25–30 minutes or until the rolls are golden brown. Transfer to a wire rack and set aside to cool completely.

Spicy Oven Bread

This is a Western-style bread with an Indian touch. It is very quick once the dough is made and is a quite rich and very tasty mix.

NUTRITIONAL INFORMATION

Calories 445	Sugars 1g
Protein 6g	Fat 26g
Carbohydrate ...49g	Saturates 17g

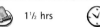

1½ hrs   10 mins

SERVES 8

I N G R E D I E N T S

½ tsp easy-blend dried yeast

300 ml/½ pint warm water

500 g/1 lb 2 oz strong white flour

1 tsp salt

225 g/8 oz butter, melted and cooled

½ tsp garam masala

½ tsp coriander seeds, ground

1 tsp cumin seeds, ground

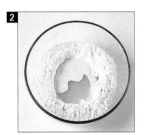

1 Mix the yeast with a little of the warm water until it starts to foam and is completely dissolved.

2 Put the flour and salt into a large bowl, make a well in the centre and add the yeast mixture, and 125 g/4½ oz of the melted butter. Blend the yeast and butter together before drawing in the flour and kneading lightly. Add the water gradually until a firm dough is obtained; you may not need it all.

3 Turn the dough out on to a floured surface and knead it for about 10 minutes, until smooth and elastic.

4 Put the dough into an oiled bowl and turn it over so that it is coated with the oil. Cover and leave in a warm place to rise for 30 minutes, until doubled in size.

Alternatively, leave the dough in the refrigerator overnight.

5 Knead the dough again and divide into 8 balls. Roll each one out to a 15 cm/6 inch round. Place on a floured baking sheet. Sprinkle with flour and leave for 20 minutes to rise.

6 Mix the spices together with the remaining melted butter.

7 Brush each bread with the spice and butter mixture and cover with foil. Place the baking sheet on the middle shelf of a preheated oven, 220°C/425°F/Gas Mark 7, for 5 minutes. Remove the foil, brush each bread with the spice and butter mixture once again and cook for a further 5 minutes.

8 Remove from the oven and wrap in a clean tea towel until ready to eat.

Sun-dried Tomato Loaf

This delicious tomato bread is great with cheese or soup or for making an unusual sandwich. This recipe makes one loaf.

NUTRITIONAL INFORMATION

Calories 403	Sugars 5g	
Protein 12g	Fat 2g	
Carbohydrate ...91g	Saturates 0.3g	

 1¾ hrs   35 mins

SERVES 4

INGREDIENTS

1½ tsp dried yeast

1 tsp granulated sugar

300 ml/½ pint hand-hot water

450 g/1 lb strong white flour

1 tsp salt

2 tsp dried basil

2 tbsp sun-dried tomato paste or tomato purée

margarine, for greasing

12 sun-dried tomatoes in oil, drained and cut into strips

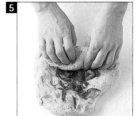

1 Place the yeast and sugar in a bowl and mix with 100 ml/3½ fl oz of the water. Leave to ferment in a warm place for 15 minutes.

2 Place the flour in a bowl and stir in the salt. Make a well in the dry ingredients and add the basil, yeast mixture, tomato paste and half of the remaining water. Using a wooden spoon, draw the flour into the liquid and mix to form a dough, adding the rest of the water a little at a time.

3 Turn out the dough on to a floured surface and knead for 5 minutes or until smooth. Cover with oiled clingfilm

and leave in a warm place to rise for about 30 minutes or until doubled in size.

4 Lightly grease a 900 g/2 lb loaf tin with a little margarine.

5 Remove the dough from the bowl and knead in the sun-dried tomatoes. Knead again for 2–3 minutes.

6 Place the dough in the prepared tin and leave to rise for 30–40 minutes or until it has doubled in size again. Bake in a preheated oven, 190°C/375°F/Gas

Mark 5, for 30–35 minutes or until golden and the base sounds hollow when tapped. Cool on a wire rack.

COOK'S TIP

You could make mini sun-dried tomato loaves for children. Divide the dough into 8 equal portions, leave to rise and bake in mini loaf tins for 20 minutes.

Roasted Pepper Bread

Peppers become marvellously sweet and mild when they are roasted and make this bread delicious.

NUTRITIONAL INFORMATION

Calories 426	Sugars 4g	
Protein 12g	Fat 4g	
Carbohydrate ...90g	Saturates 1g	

 1¾ hrs   1 hr 5 mins

SERVES 4

INGREDIENTS

margarine, for greasing

1 red pepper, halved and deseeded

1 yellow pepper, halved and deseeded

2 sprigs fresh rosemary

1 tbsp olive oil

1½ tsp dried yeast

1 tsp granulated sugar

300 ml/5 fl oz hand-hot water

450 g/1 lb strong white flour

1 tsp salt

1 Grease a 23 cm/9 inch deep round cake tin with margarine.

2 Place the peppers and rosemary in a shallow roasting tin. Pour over the oil and roast in a preheated oven, 200°C/400°F/Gas Mark 6, for 20 minutes or until slightly charred. Remove the skin from the peppers and cut the flesh into slices.

3 Place the yeast and sugar in a small bowl and mix with 100 ml/3½ fl oz of the hand-hot water. Leave to ferment in a warm place for 15 minutes.

4 Mix the flour and salt together in a large bowl. Stir in the yeast mixture and the remaining water and mix to form a smooth dough.

5 Knead the dough for about 5 minutes until smooth. Cover with oiled cling film and leave to rise for about 30 minutes or until doubled in size.

6 Cut the dough into 3 equal portions. Roll the portions into rounds slightly larger than the cake tin.

7 Place 1 round in the base of the tin so that it reaches up the sides of the tin by about 2 cm/¾ inch. Top with half of the pepper mixture.

8 Place the second round of dough on top, followed by the remaining pepper mixture. Place the last round of dough on top, gently pushing the edges of the dough down the sides of the tin to enclose the peppers completely.

9 Cover the dough with oiled clingfilm and leave to rise for 30–40 minutes. Bake for 45 minutes until golden or the base sounds hollow when lightly tapped. Transfer the bread to a wire rack to cool slightly and serve warm.

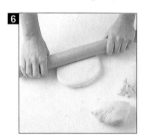

Roman Focaccia

Roman focaccia makes a delicious snack on its own or it can be served with soup, cheese and salad for a quick supper.

NUTRITIONAL INFORMATION

Calories	119	Sugars	2g
Protein	3g	Fat	2g
Carbohydrate	24g	Saturates	0.3g

  1 hr   45 mins

MAKES 16 SQUARES

INGREDIENTS

1½ tsp dried yeast

1 tsp granulated sugar

300 ml/½ pint hand-hot water

450 g/1 lb strong white flour

2 tsp salt

3 tbsp fresh rosemary, chopped

2 tbsp olive oil

450 g/1 lb mixed red and white onions, sliced into rings

4 garlic cloves, sliced

1 Place the yeast and sugar in a small bowl and mix with 100 ml/3½ fl oz of the water. Leave to ferment in a warm place for 15 minutes.

2 Mix the flour with the salt in a large bowl. Add the yeast mixture, half of the rosemary and the remaining water and mix to form a smooth dough. Knead the dough for 4 minutes. Cover the dough with oiled clingfilm and leave to rise for 30 minutes or until doubled in size.

3 Meanwhile, heat the oil in a large pan. Add the onions and garlic and fry over a low heat, stirring occasionally, for 5 minutes or until softened. Cover the pan and continue to cook for 7–8 minutes or until the onions are lightly caramelized.

4 Remove the dough from the bowl and knead it again for 1–2 minutes.

5 Roll the dough out to form a square shape. The dough should be no more than 5 mm/¼ inch thick because it will rise during cooking. Place the dough on a large baking tray, pushing out the edges to make a neat square.

6 Spread the mixed onion slices over the dough, and sprinkle with the remaining chopped rosemary.

7 Bake in a preheated oven, 200°C/ 400°F/Gas Mark 6, for 25–30 minutes or until a golden brown colour. Cool slightly, cut the focaccia into 16 squares and serve immediately.

Garlic & Sage Bread

This freshly made herb bread is an ideal accompaniment to salads and soups and is dairy-free.

NUTRITIONAL INFORMATION

Calories 207	Sugars 3g
Protein 9g	Fat 2g
Carbohydrate . . .42g	Saturates 0g

1¼ hrs   30 mins

SERVES 6

I N G R E D I E N T S

oil, for greasing

250 g/9 oz strong wholemeal bread flour

1 sachet easy-blend dried yeast

3 tbsp chopped fresh sage

2 tsp sea salt

3 garlic cloves, finely chopped

1 tsp clear honey

150 ml/5 fl oz hand-hot water

1 Grease a baking sheet. Sift the flour into a large mixing bowl and stir in the bran remaining in the sieve.

2 Stir in the easy-blend dried yeast, chopped fresh sage and half of the sea salt. Reserve 1 teaspoon of the chopped garlic for sprinkling and stir the remainder into the bowl. Add the honey and lukewarm water and mix together to form a dough.

3 Turn the dough out on to a lightly floured surface and knead it for about 5 minutes until smooth and elastic (alternatively, use an electric mixer with a dough hook).

4 Place the dough in a bowl greased with oil, cover with lightly oiled clingfilm and leave to rise in a warm place until doubled in size.

5 Knead the dough again for a few minutes. Roll it into a long sausage and then shape it into a ring. Place on the prepared baking sheet. Cover and leave to rise for 30 minutes or until springy to the touch. Sprinkle with the remaining sea salt and garlic.

6 Bake the loaf in a preheated oven, 200°C/400°F/Gas Mark 6, for 25–30 minutes. Transfer the bread to a wire rack to cool before serving.

COOK'S TIP

Other robust herbs may be used in this recipe, such as rosemary, marjoram or thyme.

Sweet Potato Bread

This is a great-tasting loaf, coloured light orange by the sweet potato.
Added sweetness from the honey is offset by the tangy orange rind.

NUTRITIONAL INFORMATION

Calories	267	Sugars	.........7g
Protein	.........4g	Fat	...........9g
Carbohydrate	...45g	Saturates	.......4g

 1½ hrs   1¼ hrs

SERVES 8

I N G R E D I E N T S

5 tbsp butter, plus extra for greasing

225 g/8 oz sweet potatoes, diced

150 ml/5 fl oz hand-hot water

2 tbsp clear honey

2 tbsp vegetable oil

3 tbsp orange juice

75 g/2¾ oz semolina

225 g/8 oz strong white bread flour

1 sachet easy-blend dried yeast

1 tsp ground cinnamon

grated rind of 1 orange

1 Lightly grease a 675 g/1½ lb loaf tin. Cook the diced sweet potatoes in a saucepan of boiling water for about 10 minutes or until soft. Drain well and mash until smooth.

2 Meanwhile, mix the water, honey, vegetable oil and orange juice together in a large mixing bowl.

3 Add the mashed sweet potatoes, semolina, three-quarters of the flour, the yeast, ground cinnamon and grated orange rind and mix thoroughly to form a dough. Set aside for about 10 minutes.

4 Dice the butter and knead it into the dough with the remaining flour. Knead for about 5 minutes until smooth.

5 Place the dough in the prepared loaf tin. Cover and set aside in a warm place for 1 hour or until doubled in size.

6 Bake the loaf in a preheated oven, 190°C/375°F/Gas Mark 5, for 45–60 minutes, or until the base sounds hollow when tapped.

7 Serve the bread while it is still warm, cut into slices.

Olive Oil Bread with Cheese

This flat cheese bread is very similar to Italian focaccia. It is delicious served with antipasto or simply on its own.

NUTRITIONAL INFORMATION

Calories	586	Sugars	.........3g
Protein	........22g	Fat	..........26g
Carbohydrate	...69g	Saturates	......12g

 1 hr   30 mins

SERVES 4

I N G R E D I E N T S

14 g/½ oz dried yeast

1 tsp sugar

250 ml/9 fl oz hand-hot water

350 g/12 oz strong white bread flour

1 tsp salt

3 tbsp olive oil

200 g/7 oz pecorino cheese, cubed

12 tbsp fennel seeds, lightly crushed

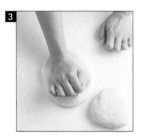

1 Mix the dried yeast with the sugar and 100 ml/3½ fl oz of the water. Leave to ferment in a warm place for about 15 minutes.

2 Mix the flour with the salt. Add 1 tablespoon of the oil, the yeast mixture and the remaining water to form a smooth dough. Knead the dough for 4 minutes.

3 Divide the dough into 2 equal portions. Roll out each portion to a form a round 5 mm/¼ inch thick. Place 1 round on a baking tray.

4 Scatter the cheese and half of the fennel seeds evenly over the round.

5 Place the second round on top and squeeze the edges together to seal so that the filling does not leak out during the cooking time.

6 Using a sharp knife, make a few slashes in the top of the dough and brush with the remaining olive oil.

7 Sprinkle with the remaining fennel seeds and leave the dough to rise for 20–30 minutes.

8 Bake in a preheated oven, 200°C/400°F/Gas Mark 6, for 30 minutes or until golden brown. Serve immediately while it is still hot.

COOK'S TIP

Pecorino is a hard, quite salty cheese, which is sold in most large supermarkets and Italian delicatessens. If you cannot obtain pecorino, use strong Cheddar or Parmesan cheese instead.

Italian Bruschetta

It is important to use a good quality olive oil for this recipe. Serve the bruschetta with vegetable kebabs for a really summery taste.

NUTRITIONAL INFORMATION

Calories	.415	Sugars	.2g
Protein	.8g	Fat	.24g
Carbohydrate	.45g	Saturates	.4g

10 mins　　10 mins

SERVES 4

INGREDIENTS

1 ciabatta loaf or small stick of
　French bread

1 plump garlic clove

extra virgin olive oil

fresh Parmesan cheese, grated (optional)

1 Slice the bread in half crossways and
again lengthways to give 4 portions.

2 Do not peel the garlic clove, but cut it
in half.

3 Barbecue the bread over hot coals for
2–3 minutes on both sides or until it
is golden brown.

4 Rub the garlic, cut side down, all over
the toasted surface of the bread.

5 Drizzle the olive oil over the bread
and serve hot as an accompaniment.

6 If using Parmesan cheese, sprinkle the
cheese over the bread.

7 Return the bread to the barbecue, cut
side up, for 1–2 minutes or until the
cheese just begins to melt. Serve hot.

COOK'S TIP

As ready-grated Parmesan
quickly loses its pungency and
'bite', it is better to buy small
quantities of the cheese in one piece
and grate it yourself as needed. Tightly
wrapped in clingfilm or foil, it will keep
in the refrigerator for several months.

Cheese and Tomato Bake

A juicy combination of vegetables concealed beneath a crisp topping needs only a mixed leaf salad to make a substantial family supper dish.

NUTRITIONAL INFORMATION

Calories 324	Sugars 11g	
Protein 14g	Fat 22g	
Carbohydrate ...19g	Saturates 11g	

 15 mins   40 mins

SERVES 4

INGREDIENTS

2 tbsp olive oil

2 onions, sliced

1 garlic clove, finely chopped

350 g/12 oz courgettes, sliced

1 tsp chopped fresh thyme

1 tbsp torn fresh basil leaves

salt and pepper

4 beef tomatoes, skinned and sliced

½ quantity cheese sauce (see page 304), made with Cheddar cheese

55 g/2 oz Cheddar cheese, grated

1 tbsp fresh breadcrumbs

1 Heat the oil in a frying pan. Add the onions and cook for 5 minutes, until softened. Add the garlic, courgettes, thyme and basil and season to taste with salt and pepper. Cook for 5 minutes.

2 Spoon half the onion and courgette mixture into a large ovenproof dish. Arrange the tomato slices on top and cover with the remaining onion and courgette mixture. Pour in the cheese sauce.

3 Combine the grated Cheddar and breadcrumbs in a small bowl, then sprinkle over the sauce. Bake in a preheated oven, 180°C/350°F/Gas Mark 4, for 30 minutes. Serve immediately.

Lentil and Mushroom Pie

This is a good dish for entertaining as it is tasty and filling and the filo topping looks hugely appetizing and attractive.

NUTRITIONAL INFORMATION

Calories	439	Sugars	.........2g
Protein	........18g	Fat	..........9g
Carbohydrate	...75g	Saturates	.......4g

25 mins, plus cooling

1½ hrs

SERVES 6

INGREDIENTS

175 g/6 oz Puy or green lentils

2 bay leaves

6 shallots, sliced

1.2 litres/2 pints vegetable stock

salt and pepper

25 g/1 oz butter

225 g/8 oz long grain rice

225 g/8 oz field mushrooms, sliced

2 tbsp chopped fresh parsley

2 tsp chopped fresh fennel or savory

1 egg, beaten

8 sheets filo pastry, thawed if frozen

melted butter, for brushing

3 hard-boiled eggs, sliced

1 Put the lentils, bay leaves and half the shallots in a large, heavy-based saucepan, add half the stock, bring to the boil and simmer for 25 minutes, until tender. Season to taste with salt and pepper and set aside to cool.

2 Melt the butter in a heavy-based saucepan. Add the remaining shallots to the pan and cook, stirring occasionally, for 5 minutes, until softened. Stir in the rice and cook, stirring constantly, for 1 minute, then add the remaining stock and the mushrooms. Season to taste and bring to the boil. Lower the heat, cover and simmer for 15 minutes. Remove the pan from the heat and set aside to cool.

3 Brush the inside of an ovenproof dish with melted butter and arrange the filo sheets in it with the sides overlapping, brushing each sheet with melted butter.

Stir the parsley and fennel or savory into the cooled rice mixture, then beat in the raw egg. Make layers of rice, hard-boiled egg, lentils and mushrooms in the dish, seasoning each layer with salt and pepper. Bring up the filo sheets and scrunch into folds on top of the pie. Brush with melted butter and chill for 15 minutes. Bake in a preheated oven, 190°C/375°F/Gas Mark 5, for 45 minutes. Leave the pie to stand for 10 minutes before serving.

Cheese, Herb & Onion Rolls

Great texture and flavour are achieved by mixing white and granary flours together with minced onion, grated cheese and fresh herbs.

NUTRITIONAL INFORMATION

Calories	529	Sugars	.........2g
Protein	........24g	Fat	..........7g
Carbohydrate	...98g	Saturates	......4g

 2 hrs   15 mins

SERVES 4

INGREDIENTS

225 g/8 oz strong white flour

1½ tsp salt

1 tsp mustard powder

good pinch of pepper

225 g/8 oz granary or malted wheat flour

2 tbsp chopped fresh mixed herbs

2 tbsp finely chopped spring onions

125–175 g/4½–6 oz mature low-fat Cheddar cheese, grated

15 g/½ oz fresh yeast; or 1½ tsp dried yeast plus 1 tsp caster sugar; or 1 sachet easy-blend yeast plus 1 tbsp oil

300 ml/½ pint warm water

1 Sift the white flour with the salt, mustard and pepper into a bowl. Mix in the granary flour, herbs, spring onions and most of the cheese.

2 Blend the fresh yeast with the warm water or, if using dried yeast, dissolve the sugar in the water, sprinkle the yeast on top and leave in a warm place for about 10 minutes until frothy. Add the yeast mixture of your choice to the dry ingredients and mix to form a firm dough, adding more flour if necessary.

3 Knead until smooth and elastic. Cover with an oiled polythene bag and leave in a warm place to rise for 1 hour or until doubled in size. Knock back and knead the dough until smooth. Divide into 10–12 pieces and shape into round or long rolls, coils or knots.

4 Alternatively, make one large plaited loaf. Divide the dough into 3 even pieces and roll each into a long thin sausage and join at one end. Beginning at the joined end, plait to the end and secure. Place on greased baking sheets, cover with an oiled sheet of polythene and leave to rise until doubled in size. Remove the polythene.

5 Sprinkle with the rest of the cheese. Bake in a preheated oven at 200°C/ 400°F/Gas Mark 6 for 15–20 minutes for the rolls, or 30–40 minutes for the loaf.

Olive Cake

This simple savoury cake makes a delicious snack to nibble with a chilled glass of sparkling wine. It keeps fresh for two days in an airtight tin.

NUTRITIONAL INFORMATION

Calories	214	Sugars	. . . . .2g
Protein	. . . . .5g	Fat	. . . . .13g
Carbohydrate	. . .21g	Saturates	. . . . . . .3g

5 mins   1 hr

MAKES 12–15 SLICES

I N G R E D I E N T S

250 g/9 oz stoned black or green olives, or a mixture

300 g/10½ oz self-raising flour

4 large eggs

1 tbsp caster sugar

125 ml/4 fl oz milk

125 ml/4 fl oz olive oil

butter, for greasing

salt and pepper

1 Lightly butter a 20 cm/8 inch cake tin, 5 cm/2 inches deep. Line the base with a piece of baking paper cut to fit. Put the olives in a small bowl and toss in 2 tablespoons of the measured flour.

2 Break the eggs into a bowl and lightly whisk. Stir in the sugar and season with salt and pepper to taste. Stir in the milk and olive oil.

3 Sift the remaining flour into the bowl, add the coated olives and stir together. Spoon the mixture into the prepared tin and smooth the surface.

4 Bake the olive cake in a preheated oven at 200°C/400°F/Gas Mark 6 for 45 minutes. Lower the oven temperature to 160°C/325°F/Gas Mark 3 and continue baking for 15 minutes until the cake is risen, golden and coming away from the side of the tin.

5 Remove from the oven and leave to cool in the tin on a wire rack for 20 minutes. Remove from the tin, peel off the lining paper and leave to cool completely. Store in an airtight container.

Mexican Chilli Corn Pie

This bake of sweetcorn and kidney beans, flavoured with chilli and fresh coriander, is topped with crispy cheese cornbread.

NUTRITIONAL INFORMATION

Calories . . . . .519 Sugars 17g
Protein . . . . .22g Fat 22g
Carbohydrate . . .61g Saturates 9g

25 mins   20 mins

SERVES 4

INGREDIENTS

1 tbsp corn oil

2 garlic cloves, crushed

1 red pepper, deseeded and diced

1 green pepper, deseeded and diced

1 celery stick, diced

1 tsp hot chilli powder

400 g/14 oz canned chopped tomatoes

325 g/11½ oz canned sweetcorn, drained

215 g/7½ oz canned kidney beans, drained and rinsed

salt and pepper

2 tbsp chopped fresh coriander

fresh coriander sprigs, to garnish

tomato and avocado salad, to serve

TOPPING

125 g/4½ oz cornmeal

1 tbsp plain flour

½ tsp salt

2 tsp baking powder

1 egg, beaten

6 tbsp milk

1 tbsp corn oil

125 g/4½ oz mature Cheddar cheese, grated

1 Heat the corn oil in a large frying pan and gently fry the garlic and the diced peppers and celery for 5–6 minutes until just softened.

2 Stir in the chilli powder, tomatoes, sweetcorn, beans and seasoning. Bring to the boil and simmer the mixture for 10 minutes. Stir in the coriander and spoon into an ovenproof dish.

3 To make the topping, mix together the cornmeal, flour, salt and baking powder. Make a well in the centre, add the egg, milk and oil and beat until a smooth batter is formed.

4 Spoon over the pepper and sweetcorn mixture and sprinkle with the cheese. Bake in a preheated oven, at 220°C/425°F/Gas Mark 7, for 25–30 minutes, until golden and firm.

5 Garnish with the coriander sprigs and serve the pie immediately with a tomato and avocado salad.

Vegetable Hotpot

In this recipe, a variety of vegetables are cooked under a layer of potatoes, topped with cheese and cooked until golden brown.

NUTRITIONAL INFORMATION

Calories	279	Sugars	........12g
Protein	........10g	Fat	...........11g
Carbohydrate	...34g	Saturates	.......4g

25 mins   1 hr

SERVES 4

I N G R E D I E N T S

600 g/1 lb 5 oz potatoes, thinly sliced

2 tbsp vegetable oil

1 red onion, halved and sliced

1 leek, sliced

2 garlic cloves, crushed

1 carrot, cut into chunks

100 g/3½ oz broccoli florets

100 g/3½ oz cauliflower florets

2 small turnips, quartered

1 tbsp plain flour

700 ml/1¼ pints vegetable stock

150 ml/5 fl oz dry cider

1 apple, cored and sliced

2 tbsp chopped fresh sage

pinch of cayenne pepper

salt and pepper

50 g/1¾ oz Cheddar cheese, grated

1 Cook the potato slices in a saucepan of boiling water for 10 minutes. Drain thoroughly and reserve.

2 Heat the vegetable oil in a flameproof casserole. Add the onion, leek and garlic to the oil and sauté, stirring occasionally, for 2–3 minutes.

3 Add the remaining vegetables and cook, stirring constantly, for a further 3–4 minutes.

4 Stir in the flour and cook for 1 minute. Gradually add the vegetable stock and cider and bring to the boil. Add the apple, sage and cayenne pepper and season well with salt and pepper.

5 Remove from the heat and transfer the vegetables to an ovenproof dish.

6 Arrange the potato slices on top of the vegetable mixture to cover.

7 Sprinkle the grated cheese on top of the potato slices and cook in a preheated oven, 190°C/375°F/Gas Mark 5, for about 30–35 minutes or until the potato is golden brown and beginning to crispen around the edges. Serve the vegetable hotpot immediately, straight from the dish.

Mushroom Tarts

Different varieties of mushrooms are becoming more widely available in supermarkets, so use this recipe to make the most of them.

NUTRITIONAL INFORMATION

Calories 494   Sugars 2g
Protein . . . . .9g   Fat 35g
Carbohydrate . . .38g   Saturates 18g

15 mins   20 mins

SERVES 4

INGREDIENTS

500 g/1 lb 2 oz filo pastry, thawed if frozen

115 g/4 oz butter, melted

1 tbsp hazelnut oil

4 tbsp pine kernels

350 g/12 oz mixed mushrooms, such as button, chestnut, oyster and shiitake, thickly sliced

2 tsp chopped fresh parsley

salt and pepper

225 g/8 oz soft goat's cheese

fresh parsley sprigs to garnish

lettuce, tomatoes, cucumber and spring onions, to serve

1 Cut the sheets of filo pastry into pieces about 10 cm/4 inches square and use them to line 4 individual tart tins, brushing each layer of pastry with melted butter. Line the tins with foil and baking beans. Bake in a preheated oven, 200°C/400°F/Gas Mark 6, for about 6–8 minutes or until light golden brown.

2 Remove the tarts from the oven and carefully take out the foil and baking beans. Reduce the oven temperature to 180°C/350°F/Gas Mark 4.

3 Put any remaining butter into a large pan with the hazelnut oil and fry the pine kernels until golden brown. Remove from the pan and drain on absorbent kitchen paper.

4 Add the mushrooms to the pan and cook gently, stirring frequently, for about 4–5 minutes. Add the parsley and season to taste with salt and pepper.

5 Spoon one-quarter of the goat's cheese into the base of each tart. Divide the mushrooms equally between them and sprinkle pine nuts over the top.

6 Return the tarts to the oven for about 5 minutes to heat through and then serve them, garnished with sprigs of parsley. Serve with lettuce, tomatoes, cucumber and spring onions.

Bean & Pasta Casserole

A satisfying winter dish, this hearty casserole with a crunchy topping is a slow-cooked, one-pot meal.

NUTRITIONAL INFORMATION

Calories	400	Sugars	.........2g
Protein	........26g	Fat	..........20g
Carbohydrate	...32g	Saturates	......10g

15 mins, plus soaking

3½ hrs

SERVES 4

INGREDIENTS

225 g/8 oz dried haricot beans, soaked overnight and drained

225 g/8 oz dried penne

6 tbsp olive oil

850 ml/1½ pints vegetable stock

2 large onions, sliced

2 garlic cloves, chopped

2 bay leaves

1 tsp dried oregano

1 tsp dried thyme

5 tbsp red wine

2 tbsp tomato purée

2 celery sticks, sliced

1 fennel bulb, sliced

115 g/4 oz mushrooms, sliced

250 g/8 oz tomatoes, sliced

salt and pepper

1 tsp dark muscovado sugar

4 tbsp dry white breadcrumbs

salad leaves and crusty bread, to serve

1 Put the haricot beans in a large saucepan and add sufficient cold water to cover. Bring to the boil and continue to boil vigorously for 20 minutes. Drain, set aside and keep warm.

2 Bring a large saucepan of lightly salted water to the boil. Add the penne and 1 tablespoon of the olive oil to the pan and cook for about 3 minutes. Drain the pasta and set aside, keeping it warm.

3 Put the beans in a large, flameproof casserole. Add the vegetable stock and stir in the remaining olive oil, the onions, garlic, bay leaves, dried oregano and thyme, red wine and tomato purée.

4 Bring to the boil, then cover and cook in a preheated oven at 180°C/350°F/Gas Mark 4 for 2 hours.

5 Add the penne, celery, fennel, mushrooms and tomatoes to the casserole and season to taste with salt and pepper. Stir in the muscovado sugar and sprinkle over the breadcrumbs. Cover the dish and cook in the oven for a further hour.

6 Serve the bean and pasta casserole hot with salad leaves and crusty bread.

Cold Weather Casserole

Heart-warming, comfort food on a chilly evening, this is a rich casserole of root vegetables, served with tasty parsley dumplings.

NUTRITIONAL INFORMATION

Calories	345	Sugars	.........7g
Protein	.........9g	Fat	..........17g
Carbohydrate	...43g	Saturates	......10g

 20 mins   1¼ hrs

SERVES 6

INGREDIENTS

55 g/2 oz butter or margarine

2 leeks, sliced

2 carrots, sliced

2 potatoes, cut into bite-size pieces

1 swede, cut into bite-size pieces

2 courgettes, sliced

1 fennel bulb, halved and sliced

2 tbsp plain flour

425 g/15 oz canned butter beans

600 ml/1 pint vegetable stock

2 tbsp tomato purée

1 tsp dried thyme

2 bay leaves

salt and pepper

PARSLEY DUMPLINGS

115 g/4 oz self-raising flour

55 g/2 oz vegetarian suet

2 tbsp chopped fresh parsley

about 4 tbsp water

1 Melt the butter in a large heavy-based saucepan. Add the leeks, carrots, potatoes, swede, courgettes and fennel and cook, stirring occasionally, for 10 minutes. Stir in the flour and cook, stirring constantly, for 1 minute. Stir in the can juice from the beans, the stock, tomato purée, thyme and bay leaves and season to taste with salt and pepper. Bring to the boil, stirring constantly, then cover and simmer for 10 minutes.

2 Meanwhile, make the dumplings. Sift the flour with a pinch of salt into a bowl. Stir in the suet and chopped parsley, then add enough water to bind to a soft dough. Divide the dough into 8 pieces and roll into balls.

3 Add the beans and the dumplings to the pan, then cover and simmer for a further 30 minutes. Remove and discard the bay leaf before serving.

Vegetable & Lentil Casserole

This easy, one-pot dish cooks slowly so that the flavours mingle deliciously. Use Puy lentils if possible for their superior flavour.

NUTRITIONAL INFORMATION

Calories 273   Sugars 10g
Protein . . . . .18g   Fat 2g
Carbohydrate . . . .5g   Saturates 0g

15 mins   2 hrs

SERVES 4

INGREDIENTS

1 onion

4 cloves

225 g/8 oz Puy or green lentils

1 bay leaf

1.5 litres/2¾ pints vegetable stock or water

2 leeks, sliced

2 potatoes, diced

2 carrots, chopped

3 courgettes, sliced

1 celery stick, chopped

1 red pepper, deseeded and chopped

salt and pepper

1 tbsp lemon juice

1 Stick the onion with the cloves. Put the lentils in a large casserole, add the onion and bay leaf and pour in the vegetable stock or water. Cover and bake in a preheated oven, 180°C/350°F/Gas Mark 4, for 1 hour.

2 Remove the casserole from the oven. Take out the onion and discard the cloves. Slice the onion and return it to the casserole with the leeks, potatoes, carrots, courgettes, celery and red pepper. Stir thoroughly and season to taste with salt and pepper. Cover and return to the oven for a further hour.

3 Remove and discard the bay leaf. Stir the lemon juice into the casserole and serve immediately, straight from the dish.

COOK'S TIP

Unlike other pulses, lentils do not require soaking before they are cooked.

Indian Curry Feast

This vegetable curry is quick and easy to prepare and it tastes superb.
A colourful Indian salad and mint raita make perfect accompaniments.

NUTRITIONAL INFORMATION

Calories	473	Sugars	........18g
Protein	........19g	Fat	..........9g
Carbohydrate	...84g	Saturates	.......1g

 25–30 mins   55 mins

SERVES 4

I N G R E D I E N T S

1 tbsp vegetable oil

2 garlic cloves, crushed

1 onion, chopped

3 celery sticks, sliced

1 apple, cored and chopped

1 tbsp medium-strength curry powder

1 tsp ground ginger

400 g/14 oz canned chick peas

125 g/4½ oz dwarf green beans, sliced

225 g/8 oz cauliflower florets

225 g/8 oz potatoes, diced

175 g/6 oz mushrooms, sliced

600 ml/1 pint vegetable stock

1 tbsp tomato purée

25 g/1 oz sultanas

175 g/6 oz basmati rice

1 tbsp garam masala

M I N T   R A I T A

150 ml/¼ pint natural yogurt

1 tbsp chopped mint

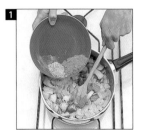

1 Heat the oil in a large saucepan. Add the garlic, onion, celery and apple to the pan and fry over a medium heat, stirring frequently, for 3–4 minutes. Add the curry powder and ginger, and cook gently for 1 more minute.

2 Drain the chick peas and add to the onion mixture, together with the dwarf green beans, cauliflower, potatoes, mushrooms, stock, tomato purée and sultanas.

3 Bring to the boil, reduce the heat, cover and simmer for 35–40 minutes.

4 Meanwhile, make the raita. Mix the yogurt and mint together. Transfer to a small serving bowl, then cover and chill in the refrigerator.

5 Cook the rice in a large saucepan of boiling, lightly salted water for about 12 minutes, or until just tender. Drain, rinse with boiling water and drain again.

6 Just before serving, stir the garam masala into the curry. Divide between four warmed serving plates and serve with the rice. Garnish the raita with fresh mint and hand the bowl separately.

Microwave Tofu Casserole

In this quick recipe, all the cooking is done in a microwave – there is not a wok in sight!

NUTRITIONAL INFORMATION

Calories . . . . . . .222 Sugars 3g
Protein . . . . .11g Fat 13g
Carbohydrate . . .16g Saturates 2g

1¼ hrs   15 mins

SERVES 4

INGREDIENTS

275 g/9½ oz smoked tofu, cubed

2 tbsp soy sauce

1 tbsp dry sherry

1 tsp sesame oil

4 dried Chinese mushrooms

250 g/9 oz dried egg noodles

1 carrot, cut into thin sticks

1 celery stick, cut into thin sticks

125 g/4½ oz baby sweetcorn cobs, halved lengthways

2 tbsp oil

1 courgette, sliced

4 spring onions, chopped

125 g/4½ oz mangetouts, each cut into 3 pieces

2 tbsp black bean sauce

1 tsp cornflour

salt and pepper

1 tbsp toasted sesame seeds, to garnish

1 Marinate the tofu in the soy sauce, sherry and sesame oil for 30 minutes.

2 Place the mushrooms in a small bowl and pour over boiling water to cover. Leave to soak for 20 minutes.

3 Place the egg noodles in a large bowl. Pour over enough boiling water to cover by 2.5 cm/1 inch. Add ½ teaspoon salt, cover the bowl and cook on HIGH power for 4 minutes.

4 Place the carrot, celery, sweetcorn and oil in a large bowl. Cover and cook on HIGH power for 1 minute.

5 Drain the mushrooms, reserving 1 tablespoon of the liquid. Squeeze out any excess water from the mushrooms and discard the hard stalks. Cut the mushrooms into thin slices.

6 Add the mushrooms to the bowl of vegetables with the courgette, spring onions and mangetouts. Mix well. Cover and cook on HIGH power for 4 minutes, stirring every minute. Add the black bean sauce to the vegetables, stirring to coat the vegetables in the sauce.

7 Mix the cornflour with the reserved mushroom water and stir into the vegetables with the tofu and marinade.

8 Cover and cook on HIGH power for 2–3 minutes until heated through and the sauce has thickened slightly.

9 Season with salt and pepper to taste. Drain the noodles, then garnish the vegetables with sesame seeds and serve with the noodles.

Chick Pea Hotpot

This is an economical and trouble-free dish that is packed with goodness and tastes simply wonderful.

NUTRITIONAL INFORMATION

Calories ....438 Sugars 14g
Protein ....19g Fat 13g
Carbohydrate ...66g Saturates 2g

15 mins   2½ hrs

SERVES 4

INGREDIENTS

225 g/8 oz dried chick peas, soaked
  overnight in water to cover

3 tbsp olive oil

1 large onion, sliced

2 garlic cloves, finely chopped

2 leeks, sliced

175 g/6 oz carrots, sliced

4 turnips, sliced

4 celery sticks, sliced

115 g/4 oz bulgur wheat

400 g/14 oz canned chopped tomatoes

2 tbsp snipped fresh chives,
  plus extra to garnish

salt and pepper

1 Drain the chick peas and place in a heavy-based saucepan. Add enough water to cover and bring to the boil. Boil for 15 minutes, then simmer for 1½ hours.

2 Meanwhile, heat the oil in a large saucepan. Add the onion and cook, stirring occasionally, for 5 minutes, until softened. Add the garlic, leeks, carrots, turnips and celery and cook, stirring occasionally, for 5 minutes.

3 Stir in the bulgur, tomatoes and chives, season to taste with salt and pepper and bring to the boil. Spoon the mixture into a heatproof pudding basin and cover with a lid or circle of foil.

4 When the chick peas have been cooking for 1½ hours, set a steamer over the saucepan. Place the basin in the steamer, cover tightly and cook for 40 minutes. Remove the basin from the steamer, drain the chick peas, then stir them into the vegetable and bulgur mixture. Transfer the hotpot to a warm serving dish and serve immediately, garnished with the extra chives.

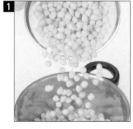  

COOK'S TIP

Remember to check the water level of the chick peas regularly and use boiling water to top up the saucepan as necessary.

Kenyan Dengu

This mildly spiced mung bean stew is economical, filling and easy to make – perfect for a midweek family supper.

NUTRITIONAL INFORMATION

Calories	254	Sugars	.........8g
Protein	........17g	Fat	...........6g
Carbohydrate	...34g	Saturates	.......1g

 15 mins   🕐 1 hr 40 mins

SERVES 4

INGREDIENTS

225 g/8 oz mung beans, soaked overnight in water to cover

2 tbsp sunflower oil

1 onion, chopped

2 garlic cloves, finely chopped

2 tbsp tomato purée

1 red pepper, deseeded and diced

1 green pepper, deseeded and diced

1 fresh red chilli, deseeded and finely chopped

300 ml/½ pint vegetable stock or water

1 Drain the mung beans, place in a saucepan and cover with water. Bring to the boil, boil for 15 minutes, then cover and simmer for 1 hour, or until tender. Drain well, return to the pan and mash thoroughly until smooth.

2 Heat the sunflower oil in another saucepan. Add the chopped onion and cook, stirring occasionally, for 10 minutes, until golden. Add the chopped garlic and cook for 2 minutes, then add the tomato purée and continue to cook, stirring constantly, for a further 3 minutes. Stir in the mashed beans.

3 Add the peppers, chilli and vegetable stock or water, stir well and simmer gently for 10 minutes. Transfer to a warm serving dish and serve immediately.

VARIATION
If you like, stir in 225 g/8 oz shredded spinach leaves 3–4 minutes before the end of cooking in step 3.

Potato & Lemon Casserole

This is based on a Moroccan dish in which potatoes are spiced with coriander and cumin and cooked in a lemon sauce.

NUTRITIONAL INFORMATION

Calories 338   Sugars 8g
Protein . . . . .5g   Fat 23g
Carbohydrate . . .29g   Saturates 2g

 15 mins   35 mins

SERVES 4

INGREDIENTS

100 ml/3½ fl oz olive oil

2 red onions, cut into 8 wedges

3 garlic cloves, crushed

2 tsp ground cumin

2 tsp ground coriander

pinch of cayenne pepper

1 carrot, thickly sliced

2 small turnips, quartered

1 courgette, sliced

500 g/1 lb 2 oz potatoes, thickly sliced

juice and rind of 2 large lemons

300 ml/10 fl oz vegetable stock

2 tbsp chopped fresh coriander

salt and pepper

COOK'S TIP
Check the vegetables while they are cooking, because they may begin to stick to the pan. Add a little more boiling water or stock if necessary.

1 Heat the olive oil in a flameproof casserole. Add the onion and sauté over a medium heat, stirring frequently, for 3 minutes.

2 Add the garlic and cook for 30 seconds. Stir in the cumin, ground coriander and cayenne and cook, stirring constantly, for 1 minute.

3 Add the carrot, turnips, courgette and potatoes and stir to coat in the oil.

4 Add the lemon juice and rind and the vegetable stock. Season to taste with salt and pepper. Cover and cook over a medium heat, stirring occasionally, for 20–30 minutes until tender.

5 Remove the lid, sprinkle in the chopped fresh coriander and stir well. Serve immediately.

Chinese Vegetable Casserole

This mixed vegetable casserole is very versatile and is delicious with any combination of vegetables of your choice.

NUTRITIONAL INFORMATION

Calories 218   Sugars 4g
Protein . . . . .7g   Fat 14g
Carbohydrate . . .12g   Saturates 2g

 5 mins   30 mins

SERVES 4

INGREDIENTS

4 tbsp vegetable oil

2 carrots, sliced

1 courgette, sliced

4 baby sweetcorn cobs, halved lengthways

125 g/4½ oz cauliflower florets

1 leek, sliced

125 g/4½ oz water chestnuts, halved

225 g/8 oz firm tofu, cubed

300 ml/½ pint vegetable stock

1 tsp salt

2 tsp dark brown sugar

2 tsp dark soy sauce

2 tbsp dry sherry

1 tbsp cornflour

2 tbsp water

1 tbsp chopped fresh coriander, to garnish

1 Heat the oil in a preheated wok until it is almost smoking. Lower the heat slightly, add the carrots, courgette, corn cobs, cauliflower and leek to the wok and stir-fry for 2–3 minutes.

2 Stir in the water chestnuts, cubed tofu, vegetable stock, salt, sugar, soy sauce and dry sherry and bring to the boil. Reduce the heat, cover the pan and simmer for 20 minutes.

3 Blend the cornflour with the water to form a smooth paste.

4 Stir the cornflour mixture into the wok. Bring the sauce to the boil and cook, stirring constantly, until it thickens and clears.

5 Transfer the casserole to a warm serving dish, sprinkle with chopped coriander and serve immediately.

COOK'S TIP

If there is too much liquid remaining, boil vigorously for 1 minute before adding the cornflour, to reduce it slightly.

Italian Vegetable Stew

In spite of the formidable list of ingredients, this flavoursome stew is very simple to make – simply put the ingredients in a pot, and cook!

NUTRITIONAL INFORMATION

Calories	307	Sugars	........15g
Protein	.........5g	Fat	..........24g
Carbohydrate	...20g	Saturates	.......3g

 30 mins   35–40 mins

SERVES 4

INGREDIENTS

1 red onion, sliced

2 leeks, sliced

4 garlic cloves, finely chopped

1 small acorn squash, diced

1 aubergine, sliced

1 small celeriac, diced

2 turnips, sliced

2 plum tomatoes, chopped

1 carrot, sliced

1 courgette, sliced

2 red peppers, deseeded and cut into strips

1 fennel bulb, sliced

175 g/6 oz chard or spinach beet, chopped

2 bay leaves

½ tsp fennel seeds

½ tsp chilli powder

pinch of dried thyme

pinch of dried oregano

pinch of sugar

125 ml/4 fl oz extra virgin olive oil

225 ml/8 fl oz vegetable stock

25 g/1 oz fresh basil leaves, torn

4 tbsp chopped fresh flat-leaved parsley

salt and pepper

2 tbsp freshly grated Parmesan cheese, to serve (optional)

1 Put the onion, leeks, garlic, squash, aubergine, celeriac, turnips, tomatoes, carrot, courgette, peppers, fennel, chard or spinach beet, bay leaves, fennel seeds, chilli powder, thyme, oregano, sugar, olive oil, vegetable stock and half the basil leaves in a large, heavy-based saucepan. Mix well and bring to the boil.

2 Lower the heat, cover the pan and simmer the vegetables for about 30 minutes, until tender.

3 Sprinkle in the remaining basil and the parsley and season to taste with salt and pepper. Serve immediately, sprinkled with the Parmesan, if you like.

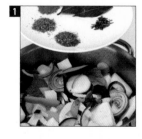

Black Bean Casserole

This colourful Chinese-style casserole is made with tofu and vegetables and flavoured with black bean sauce.

NUTRITIONAL INFORMATION

Calories 513	Sugars 5g
Protein 19g	Fat 25g
Carbohydrate . . .56g	Saturates 4g

  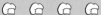

 30 mins   30 mins

SERVES 4

INGREDIENTS

6 Chinese dried mushrooms

275 g/9½ oz firm tofu

3 tbsp vegetable oil

1 carrot, cut into thin strips

125 g/4½ oz mangetouts

125 g/4½ oz baby sweetcorn cobs, halved lengthways

225 g/8 oz canned sliced bamboo shoots, drained

1 red pepper, deseeded and cut into chunks

125 g/4½ oz Chinese leaves, shredded

1 tbsp soy sauce

1 tbsp black bean sauce

1 tsp sugar

1 tsp cornflour

vegetable oil, for deep-frying

250 g/9 oz Chinese rice noodles

salt

1 Soak the dried mushrooms in a bowl of warm water for 20–25 minutes. Drain and squeeze out the excess water, reserving the liquid. Remove the tough centres and slice the mushrooms thinly.

2 Cut the tofu into cubes, then boil in a pan of lightly salted water for 2–3 minutes to firm up, and drain.

3 Heat half the vegetable oil in a saucepan. Add the tofu and fry until lightly browned. Remove and drain on kitchen paper.

4 Add the remaining vegetable oil and stir-fry the mushrooms, carrot, mangetouts, baby sweetcorn, bamboo shoots and pepper for 2–3 minutes. Add the Chinese leaves and tofu, and continue to stir-fry for a further 2 minutes.

5 Stir in the soy and black bean sauces and the sugar, and season with a little salt. Add 6 tablespoons of the reserved mushroom liquid mixed with the cornflour. Bring to the boil, reduce the heat, cover and braise for about 2–3 minutes, until the sauce thickens slightly.

6 Heat the oil for deep-frying in a large pan. Deep-fry the noodles, in batches, until puffed up and lightly golden. Drain and serve with the casserole.

Chinese Tofu Casserole

Tofu is ideal for absorbing all the other flavours in this dish. If marinated tofu is used, it will add a flavour of its own.

NUTRITIONAL INFORMATION

Calories 228	Sugars 3g
Protein 16g	Fat 15g
Carbohydrate 7g	Saturates 2g

 5 mins   15 mins

SERVES 4

INGREDIENTS

450 g/1 lb firm tofu

2 tbsp peanut oil

8 spring onions, cut into batons

2 celery sticks, sliced

125 g/4½ oz broccoli florets

125 g/4½ oz courgettes, sliced

2 garlic cloves, thinly sliced

450 g/1 lb baby spinach

rice, to serve

SAUCE

425 ml/15 fl oz vegetable stock

2 tbsp light soy sauce

3 tbsp hoisin sauce

½ tsp chilli powder

1 tbsp sesame oil

VARIATION

This recipe has a green vegetable theme, but you can alter the colour and flavour by adding your favourite vegetables. Add 75 g/2¾ oz fresh or canned and drained straw mushrooms with the vegetables in step 2.

1 Cut the tofu into 2.5 cm/1 inch cubes and set aside until required.

2 Heat the peanut oil in a preheated wok or large frying pan.

3 Add the spring onion batons, sliced celery, broccoli florets, courgette slices, garlic, baby spinach and tofu to the oil in the wok or frying pan and stir-fry for 3–4 minutes.

4 To make the sauce, mix together the vegetable stock, soy sauce, hoisin sauce, chilli powder and sesame oil in a flameproof casserole and bring to the boil.

5 Add the stir-fried vegetables and tofu to the saucepan, reduce the heat, cover and simmer for 10 minutes.

6 Transfer the tofu and vegetables to a warm serving dish and serve with rice.

Curry Pasties

These pasties are a delicious combination of vegetables and spices. They are just as delicious eaten either hot or cold.

NUTRITIONAL INFORMATION

Calories 455	Sugars 5g	
Protein 8g	Fat 27g	
Carbohydrate . . .48g	Saturates 5g	

20 mins,
plus chilling

1 hr

SERVES 4

I N G R E D I E N T S

225 g/8 oz wholemeal flour

100 g/3½ oz margarine,
   cut into small pieces

4 tbsp water

2 tbsp vegetable oil

225 g/8 oz diced root vegetables, such as
   potatoes, carrots and parsnips

1 small onion, chopped

2 garlic cloves, finely chopped

½ tsp curry powder

½ tsp turmeric

½ tsp ground cumin

½ tsp wholegrain mustard

5 tbsp vegetable stock

soya milk, to glaze

1 Place the flour in a mixing bowl and rub in the margarine with your fingertips until the mixture resembles fine breadcrumbs. Stir in the water and bring the mixture together to form a soft dough. Wrap and set aside to chill in the refrigerator for 30 minutes.

2 To make the filling, heat the oil in a large saucepan. Add the diced root vegetables and the chopped onion and garlic and fry, stirring occasionally, for 2 minutes. Stir in all of the spices, turning the vegetables to coat them thoroughly. Fry the vegetables, stirring constantly, for a further minute.

3 Add the stock to the pan and bring to the boil. Cover and simmer, stirring occasionally, for about 20 minutes, until the vegetables are tender and the liquid has been absorbed. Leave to cool.

4 Divide the pastry into four portions. Roll each portion into a 15 cm/ 6 inch round. Place the filling on one half of each round.

5 Brush the edges of each round with soya milk, then fold over and press the edges together to seal. Place on a baking tray. Bake in a preheated oven, 200°C/400°F/Gas Mark 6, for 25–30 minutes until golden brown.

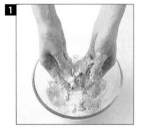  

Chick Pea Roast

This pastry case with a chick pea stuffing is delicious. Served with a sherry sauce and roast vegetables, it makes a tasty and impressive main dish.

NUTRITIONAL INFORMATION

Calories . . . . .795 Sugars 9g
Protein . . . . .24g Fat 48g
Carbohydrate . . .66g Saturates 3g

  20 mins, plus cooling 30 mins

SERVES 4

I N G R E D I E N T S

450 g/1 lb canned chick peas, drained

1 tsp yeast extract

150 g/5½ oz chopped walnuts

150 g/5½ oz fresh white breadcrumbs

1 onion, finely chopped

100 g/3½ oz mushrooms, sliced

50 g/1¾ oz canned sweetcorn, drained

2 garlic cloves, crushed

2 tbsp dry sherry

2 tbsp vegetable stock

1 tbsp chopped fresh coriander

salt and pepper

225 g/8 oz puff pastry

1 egg, beaten

2 tbsp milk

S A U C E

1 tbsp vegetable oil

1 leek, thinly sliced

4 tbsp dry sherry

150 ml/¼ pint vegetable stock

1 Blend the chick peas, yeast extract, nuts and breadcrumbs in a food processor for 30 seconds. In a frying pan, sauté the onion and mushrooms in their own juices for 3–4 minutes. Stir in the chick pea mixture, corn and garlic. Add the sherry, stock, coriander and seasoning and bind the mixture together. Remove from the heat and allow to cool.

2 Roll the pastry out on a floured surface to form a 35.5 x 30 cm/ 14 x 12 inch rectangle. Shape the chick pea mixture into a loaf shape and wrap the pastry around it, sealing the edges. Place seam-side down on a dampened baking tray and score the top in a criss-cross pattern. Mix the egg and milk and brush over the pastry. Cook in a preheated oven, 200°C/400°F/Gas Mark 6, for 25–30 minutes.

3 To make the sauce, heat the oil in a pan and sauté the leek for 5 minutes. Add the sherry and stock, bring to the boil and simmer for 5 minutes.

Layered Vegetable Gratin

In this tasty recipe an assortment of vegetables are cooked in a light nutmeg sauce with a potato and cheese topping.

NUTRITIONAL INFORMATION

Calories 236   Sugars 9g
Protein ....9g   Fat 9g
Carbohydrate ...31g   Saturates 3g

25 mins   1½ hrs

SERVES 6

INGREDIENTS

225 g/8 oz carrots

225 g/8 oz baby parsnips

1 fennel bulb

salt and pepper

500 g/1 lb 2 oz potatoes

90 g/3 oz low-fat spread

25 g/1 oz plain flour

300 ml/½ pint skimmed milk

½ tsp ground nutmeg

1 egg, beaten

25 g/1 oz Parmesan cheese, freshly grated

TO SERVE

crusty bread

tomato salad

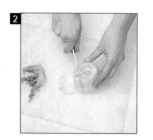
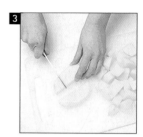

1 Cut the carrots and parsnips into thin strips lengthways. Cook in boiling water for 5 minutes. Drain well and transfer to an ovenproof baking dish.

2 Thinly slice the fennel and cook in boiling water for 2–3 minutes. Drain well and add to the carrots and parsnips. Season to taste with salt and pepper.

3 Peel and dice the potatoes into 2 cm/¾ inch cubes. Cook in boiling water for 6 minutes. Drain well.

4 Gently melt half the low-fat spread and stir in the flour. Remove from the heat and gradually mix in the milk.

5 Return to the heat and stir until thickened. Season and stir in the ground nutmeg. Cool for 10 minutes.

6 Beat in the egg and spoon over the vegetables. Arrange the potatoes on top and sprinkle over the cheese.

7 Dot the cheesy potatoes with the remaining low-fat spread. Bake the gratin in a preheated oven at 180°C/350°F/Gas Mark 4 for 1 hour until all the vegetables are tender and the topping is lightly golden.

8 Serve the vegetable gratin as a main meal with wedges of crusty bread and a tomato salad, or as an accompaniment to a light main course.

Mushroom & Spinach Puffs

These puff pastry parcels, filled with garlic, mushrooms and spinach, are easy to make and simply melt in the mouth.

NUTRITIONAL INFORMATION

Calories	467	Sugars	.........4g
Protein	.........8g	Fat	..........38g
Carbohydrate	...24g	Saturates	......18g

🥘 20 mins   🕐 30 mins

SERVES 4

I N G R E D I E N T S

25 g/1 oz butter

1 red onion, halved and sliced

2 garlic cloves, crushed

225 g/8 oz open-cap mushrooms, sliced

175 g/6 oz baby spinach

pinch of nutmeg

4 tbsp double cream

salt and pepper

225 g/8 oz puff pastry

1 egg, beaten

2 tsp poppy seeds

1 Melt the butter in a frying pan. Add the onion and garlic and sauté over a low heat, stirring, for 3–4 minutes, until the onion has softened.

2 Add the mushrooms, spinach and nutmeg and cook over a medium heat, stirring occasionally, for 2–3 minutes.

3 Stir in the double cream, stirring to combine thoroughly. Season with salt and pepper to taste and remove the pan from the heat.

4 Roll the pastry out on a lightly floured surface and cut into four 15 cm/6 inch rounds.

5 Put a quarter of the filling on to one half of each round and fold the pastry over to encase it.

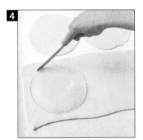

6 Press down to seal the edges and brush with the beaten egg. Sprinkle with the poppy seeds.

7 Place the parcels on a dampened baking tray and cook in a preheated oven, 200°C/400°F/Gas Mark 6, for 20 minutes, until risen and golden brown in colour.

8 Transfer the mushroom and spinach puffs to warmed serving plates and serve immediately.

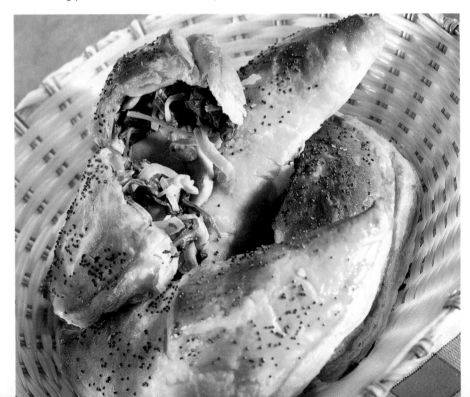

COOK'S TIP

The baking tray is dampened so that steam forms with the heat of the oven, which helps the pastry to rise and set.

Gratin of Mixed Vegetables

This gratin is very quick to make using canned artichoke and celery hearts. The Emmenthal and pecorino cheeses add an unusual touch.

NUTRITIONAL INFORMATION

Calories ....150 Sugars 3g
Protein ....7g Fat 12g
Carbohydrate ....8g Saturates 5g

 15 mins   1¼ hrs

SERVES 6

INGREDIENTS

2 parsnips, sliced

2 tbsp olive oil

1 aubergine, diced

1 garlic clove, finely chopped

2 tsp chopped fresh thyme

salt

10 g/¼ oz butter

2 shallots, chopped

4 canned artichoke hearts, drained

4 canned celery hearts, sliced

55 g/2 oz Emmenthal cheese, grated

55 g/2 oz pecorino cheese, freshly grated

1 Steam the parsnips over a pan of simmering water for about 4 minutes, until just tender. Set aside to cool.

2 Heat the oil in a heavy-based frying pan. Add the aubergine and cook, stirring frequently, for 5 minutes. Add the garlic and thyme, season to taste with salt and cook for 3 minutes. Using a slotted spoon, transfer the aubergine mixture to a dish. Add the butter to the pan. When it has melted, add the shallots and a pinch of salt and cook over a very low heat, stirring occasionally for 7–10 minutes.

3 Combine the shallots with the aubergine. Cut each artichoke heart into 8 pieces and add to the aubergine mixture with the parsnips, celery hearts, Emmenthal and half the pecorino. Mix well and spoon into an ovenproof dish. Sprinkle with the remaining pecorino and bake in a preheated oven, 180°C/350°F/Gas Mark 4, for 45 minutes. Serve at once.

COOK'S TIP

To chop garlic, place a clove on a chopping board, lay the flat side of a cook's knife on top and hit it with your fist. Remove the papery skin and chop the clove. Sprinkle a little salt on the garlic and work it into the clove with the flat side of the knife blade to release the juices.

Lentil & Vegetable Shells

These stuffed aubergines are delicious served hot or cold, topped with natural yogurt or cucumber raita.

NUTRITIONAL INFORMATION

Calories 386   Sugars 9g
Protein . . . . .14g   Fat 24g
Carbohydrate . . .30g   Saturates 3g

  25 mins   1 hr

SERVES 6

I N G R E D I E N T S

225 g/8 oz green lentils

850 ml/1½ pints water

2 garlic cloves, crushed

3 aubergines

150 ml/¼ pint vegetable oil, plus
   extra for brushing

salt and pepper

2 onions, chopped

4 tomatoes, chopped

2 tsp cumin seeds

1 tsp ground cinnamon

2 tbsp mild curry paste

1 tsp minced chilli

2 tbsp chopped fresh mint

natural yogurt and fresh mint sprigs,
   to serve

COOK'S TIP

Choose nice plump aubergines, rather than thin tapering ones, as they retain their shape better when filled and baked with a stuffing.

1 Rinse the lentils under cold running water. Drain them and place in a saucepan with the water and garlic. Cover and simmer for 30 minutes.

2 Cook the aubergines in a saucepan of boiling water for 5 minutes. Drain, then plunge into cold water for 5 minutes. Drain again, then cut the aubergines in half lengthways and scoop out most of the flesh and reserve, leaving a 1 cm/½ inch thick border to form a shell.

3 Place the aubergine shells in a shallow greased ovenproof dish, brush with a little oil and sprinkle with salt and pepper. Cook in a preheated oven, 190°C/375°F/ Gas Mark 5, for 10 minutes. Meanwhile, heat half the remaining oil in a frying pan, add the onions and tomatoes and fry gently for 5 minutes. Chop the reserved aubergine flesh, add to the pan with the spices and cook gently for 5 minutes. Season with salt.

4 Stir in the lentils, most of the remaining oil, reserving a little for later, and the chopped mint. Spoon the mixture into the shells. Drizzle with the remaining oil and bake for 15 minutes.

5 Serve hot or cold, topped with spoonfuls of natural yogurt and mint sprigs.

Potato & Aubergine Gratin

Similar to a simple moussaka, this recipe is made up of layers of aubergine, tomato and potato baked with a yogurt topping.

NUTRITIONAL INFORMATION

Calories	409	Sugars	.......17g
Protein	........28g	Fat	..........14g
Carbohydrate	...45g	Saturates	.......3g

 25 mins 1¼ hrs

SERVES 4

INGREDIENTS

500 g/1 lb 2 oz waxy potatoes, sliced

1 tbsp vegetable oil

1 onion, chopped

2 garlic cloves, crushed

500 g/1 lb 2 oz firm tofu, diced

2 tbsp tomato purée

2 tbsp plain flour

300 ml/½ pint vegetable stock

2 large tomatoes, sliced

1 aubergine, sliced

2 tbsp chopped fresh thyme

450 ml/16 fl oz natural yogurt

2 eggs, beaten

salt and pepper

salad, to serve

1 Cook the sliced potatoes in a saucepan of boiling water for about 10 minutes, until tender, but not breaking up. Drain and set aside.

2 Heat the oil in a frying pan. Add the onion and garlic and fry, stirring occasionally, for 2–3 minutes.

3 Add the tofu, tomato purée and flour and cook for 1 minute. Gradually stir in the stock and bring to the boil, stirring. Reduce the heat and simmer the mixture for 10 minutes.

4 Arrange a layer of the potato slices in the base of a deep ovenproof dish. Spoon the tofu mixture evenly on top. Layer the sliced tomatoes, then the aubergine and finally the remaining potato slices on top of the tofu mixture, making sure that it is completely covered. Sprinkle with thyme.

5 Mix the yogurt and beaten eggs together in a bowl and season to taste with salt and pepper. Spoon the yogurt topping over the sliced potatoes to cover them completely.

6 Bake in a preheated oven, 190°C/ 375°F/Gas Mark 5, for about 35–45 minutes or until the topping is browned. Serve with a crisp salad.

VARIATION

You can use marinated or smoked tofu for extra flavour, if you wish.

Vegetable Jalousie

This is a really easy dish to make, but looks impressive. The mixture of vegetables gives the dish a wonderful colour and flavour.

NUTRITIONAL INFORMATION

Calories 660   Sugars 7g
Protein ....11g   Fat 45g
Carbohydrate ...53g   Saturates 15g

 25 mins   45 mins

SERVES 4

INGREDIENTS

500 g/1 lb 2 oz puff pastry

1 egg, beaten

FILLING

2 tbsp butter or margarine

1 leek, shredded

2 garlic cloves, crushed

1 red pepper, deseeded and sliced

1 yellow pepper, deseeded and sliced

50 g/1¾ oz mushrooms, sliced

75 g/2¾ oz small asparagus spears

2 tbsp plain flour

6 tbsp vegetable stock

6 tbsp milk

4 tbsp dry white wine

1 tbsp chopped fresh oregano

salt and pepper

1 Melt the butter or margarine in a frying pan and sauté the leek and garlic, stirring frequently, for 2 minutes. Add the remaining vegetables and cook, stirring, for 3–4 minutes.

2 Add the flour and cook for 1 minute. Remove the pan from the heat and stir in the vegetable stock, milk and white wine. Return the pan to the heat and bring to the boil, stirring, until thickened.

Stir in the oregano and season with salt and pepper to taste.

3 Roll out half of the pastry on a lightly floured surface to form a rectangle 38 x 15 cm/15 x 6 inches.

4 Roll out the other half of the pastry to the same shape, but a little larger all round. Transfer the smaller rectangle to a baking tray lined with dampened baking paper.

5 Spoon the filling evenly on top of the smaller rectangle, leaving a 1 cm/½ inch clear margin around the edges.

6 Using a sharp knife, cut parallel diagonal slits across the larger rectangle to within 2.5 cm/1 inch of each of the long edges.

7 Brush the edges of the smaller rectangle with beaten egg and place the larger rectangle on top, pressing the edges firmly together to seal.

8 Brush the whole jalousie with egg to glaze and bake in a preheated oven, 200°C/400°F/Gas Mark 6, for about 30–35 minutes, until risen and golden. Transfer to a warmed serving dish and serve immediately.

 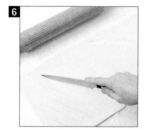 

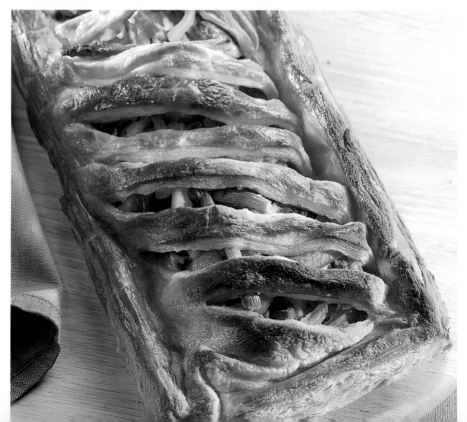

Italian Vegetable Tart

This mouth-wateringly attractive tart is full of Mediterranean flavours – spinach, red peppers, ricotta cheese and pine nuts.

NUTRITIONAL INFORMATION

Calories ....488 Sugars 7g
Protein ....13g Fat 40g
Carbohydrate ...21g Saturates 19g

 30 mins   30 mins

SERVES 6

I N G R E D I E N T S

225 g/8 oz frozen filo pastry, thawed

125 g/4½ oz butter, melted

350 g/12 oz frozen spinach, thawed

2 eggs

150 ml/¼ pint single cream

225 g/8 oz ricotta cheese

salt and pepper

1 red pepper, seeded and sliced into strips

60 g/2 oz pine kernels

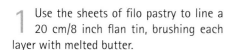

1 Use the sheets of filo pastry to line a 20 cm/8 inch flan tin, brushing each layer with melted butter.

2 Put the spinach into a strainer or colander and squeeze out the excess moisture with the back of a spoon or your hand. Form the spinach into 8–9 small balls and arrange them in the prepared flan tin.

3 Beat the eggs, cream and ricotta cheese together until thoroughly blended. Season to taste with salt and pepper and pour over the spinach.

4 Put the remaining butter into a saucepan. Add the red pepper strips and sauté them over a low heat, stirring frequently, for about 4–5 minutes, until softened. Arrange the strips on the flan.

5 Scatter the pine nuts over the surface and bake in a preheated oven at 190°C/375°F/Gas Mark 5 for about 20–25 minutes, until the filling has set and the pastry is golden brown. Serve immediately or allow to cool completely and serve at room temperature.

VARIATION

If you are not fond of peppers, you could use mushrooms instead. Wild mushrooms would be especially delicious. Add a few sliced sun-dried tomatoes for extra colour and flavour.

Potato-topped Lentil Bake

A wonderful mixture of red lentils, tofu and vegetables is cooked beneath a crunchy potato topping for a really hearty meal.

NUTRITIONAL INFORMATION

Calories 627	Sugars 7g	
Protein 26g	Fat 30g	
Carbohydrate ...66g	Saturates 13g	

 10 mins   1½ hrs

SERVES 4

INGREDIENTS

TOPPING

675 g/1½ lb floury potatoes, diced

25 g/1 oz butter

1 tbsp milk

50 g/1¾ oz pecan nuts, chopped

2 tbsp chopped fresh thyme

fresh thyme sprigs, to garnish

FILLING

225 g/8 oz red lentils

60 g/2 oz butter

1 leek, sliced

2 garlic cloves, crushed

1 celery stick, chopped

125 g/4½ oz broccoli florets

175 g/6 oz smoked tofu, cubed

2 tsp tomato purée

salt and pepper

1 To make the topping, cook the diced potatoes in a saucepan of boiling water for 10–15 minutes, or until cooked through. Drain well, add the butter and milk and mash thoroughly. Stir in the choped pecan nuts and the chopped thyme and set aside.

2 Cook the lentils in boiling water for 20–30 minutes, or until tender. Drain and set aside.

3 Melt the butter in a frying pan. Add the leek, garlic, celery and broccoli. Fry over a medium heat, stirring frequently, for 5 minutes, until softened.

4 Add the tofu cubes. Stir in the lentils, together with the tomato purée. Season with salt and pepper to taste, then turn the mixture into the base of a shallow ovenproof dish.

5 Spoon the mashed potato on top of the lentil mixture, spreading to cover it completely.

6 Cook the lentil bake in a preheated oven, 200°C/400°F/Gas Mark 6, for about 30–35 minutes, or until the topping is golden brown. Remove the bake from the oven, garnish with sprigs of fresh thyme and serve hot.

VARIATION

You can use almost any combination of your favourite vegetables in this dish.

Vegetable Crumble

Always a family favourite, the crisp, crunchy topping contrasts with the creamy mixture of vegetables beneath.

NUTRITIONAL INFORMATION

Calories	523	Sugars	........14g
Protein	........21g	Fat	.........30g
Carbohydrate	...45g	Saturates	......13g

 15 mins   40 mins

SERVES 4

INGREDIENTS

1 cauliflower, cut into florets

2 tbsp sunflower oil

25 g/1 oz plain flour

350 ml/12 fl oz milk

325 g/11½ oz canned sweetcorn kernels, drained

2 tbsp chopped fresh parsley

1 tsp chopped fresh thyme

140 g/5 oz Cheddar cheese, grated

salt and pepper

CRUMBLE TOPPING

55 g/2 oz wholemeal flour

25 g/1 oz butter

25 g/1 oz rolled oats

25 g/1 oz blanched almonds, chopped

1 Cook the cauliflower in a large saucepan of lightly salted boiling water for 5 minutes. Drain well, reserving the cooking water.

2 Heat the oil in a saucepan and stir in the flour. Cook, stirring constantly, for 1 minute. Remove the pan from the heat and gradually stir in the milk and 150 ml/ 5 fl oz of the reserved cooking water. Return the pan to the hear and bring to

the boil, stirring constantly. Cook, stirring constantly, for about 3 minutes, until thickened. Remove the pan from the heat.

3 Stir the sweetcorn, parsley, thyme and half the Cheddar into the sauce and season to taste with salt and pepper. Fold in the cauliflower, then spoon the mixture into an ovenproof dish.

4 To make the crumble topping, place the flour in a bowl and rub in the butter with your fingertips until the mixture resembles breadcrumbs. Stir in the oats, almonds and remaining Cheddar, then sprinkle the mixture evenly over the vegetables. Bake in a preheated oven, 190°C/375°F/Gas Mark 5, for 30 minutes. Serve immediately.

Lentil Roast

The perfect dish to serve for Sunday lunch. Roast vegetables make a succulent accompaniment.

NUTRITIONAL INFORMATION

Calories	400	Sugars	.........2g
Protein	........26g	Fat	..........20g
Carbohydrate	...32g	Saturates	......10g

15 mins   1 hr 20 mins

SERVES 6

INGREDIENTS

225 g/8 oz red lentils

450 ml/16 fl oz vegetable stock

1 bay leaf

15 g/½ oz butter or margarine, softened

2 tbsp dried wholemeal breadcrumbs

225 g/8 oz mature Cheddar cheese, grated

1 leek, finely chopped

125 g/4½ oz button mushrooms, finely chopped

90 g/3 oz fresh wholemeal breadcrumbs

2 tbsp chopped fresh parsley

1 tbsp lemon juice

2 eggs, lightly beaten

salt and pepper

fresh flat-leaved parsley sprigs, to garnish

mixed roast vegetables, to serve

1 Put the lentils, stock and bay leaf in a saucepan. Bring to the boil, cover and simmer gently for 15–20 minutes, until all the liquid is absorbed and the lentils have softened. Discard the bay leaf.

2 Base-line a 1 kg/2 lb 4 oz loaf tin with baking paper. Grease with the butter or margarine and sprinkle with the dried breadcrumbs.

3 Stir the grated cheese, chopped leek and mushrooms, breadcrumbs and parsley into the lentils.

4 Bind the mixture together with the lemon juice and eggs. Season with salt and pepper. Spoon into the prepared loaf tin and smooth the top.

5 Bake in a preheated oven, 190°C/375°F/Gas Mark 5, for about 1 hour, until golden.

6 Loosen the loaf with a palette knife and turn on to a warmed serving plate. Garnish with parsley and serve sliced, with roast vegetables.

Chilli Tofu Tortillas

A tasty Mexican-style dish with a melt-in-the-mouth combination of tofu and avocado served with a tangy tomato sauce.

NUTRITIONAL INFORMATION

Calories 806	Sugars 20g	
Protein 37g	Fat 54g	
Carbohydrate ...45g	Saturates 19g	

 30 mins   35 mins

SERVES 4

INGREDIENTS

½ tsp chilli powder

1 tsp paprika

2 tbsp plain flour

salt and pepper

225 g/8 oz firm tofu, cut into 1 cm/½ inch pieces

2 tbsp vegetable oil

1 onion, finely chopped

1 garlic clove, crushed

1 large red pepper, deseeded and finely chopped

1 large ripe avocado

1 tbsp lime juice

4 tomatoes, peeled, deseeded and chopped

125 g/4½ oz Cheddar cheese, grated

8 soft flour tortillas

150 ml/¼ pint soured cream

fresh coriander sprigs, to garnish

pickled green jalapeño chillies, to serve

SAUCE

850 ml/1½ pints sugocasa

3 tbsp chopped fresh parsley

3 tbsp chopped fresh coriander

1 Mix the chilli powder, paprika, flour and salt and pepper to taste on a plate and coat the tofu pieces.

2 Heat the oil in a frying pan and gently fry the tofu for 3–4 minutes, until golden. Remove with a slotted spoon, drain on kitchen paper and set aside.

3 Add the onion, garlic and pepper to the oil and fry for 2–3 minutes, until just softened. Drain and set aside.

4 Halve the avocado, peel and remove the stone. Slice lengthways, put in a bowl with the lime juice and toss to coat.

5 Add the tofu and onion mixture and gently stir in the chopped tomatoes and half the grated Cheddar cheese. Spoon one-eighth of the filling down the centre of each tortilla, top with soured cream and roll up.

6 Arrange the tortillas in a shallow ovenproof dish in a single layer.

7 To make the sauce, mix together all the ingredients. Spoon the sauce over the tortillas, sprinkle with the remaining grated cheese and bake in a preheated oven, 190°C/375°F/Gas Mark 5, for 25 minutes, until the cheese is golden brown and bubbling.

8 Garnish the chilli tofu tortillas with coriander sprigs and serve immediately with pickled jalapeño chillies.

Layered Pies

These individual pies of layered potato, aubergine and courgettes baked in a tomato sauce can be made in advance, so are good for entertaining.

NUTRITIONAL INFORMATION

Calories ....427 Sugars 8g
Protein ....22g Fat 21g
Carbohydrate ...41g Saturates 8g

40 mins   1 hr 20 mins

SERVES 4

INGREDIENTS

3 large waxy potatoes, thinly sliced

1 small aubergine, thinly sliced

1 courgette, sliced

3 tbsp vegetable oil

1 onion, diced

1 green pepper, deseeded and diced

1 tsp cumin seeds

2 tbsp chopped fresh basil

200 g/7 oz canned chopped tomatoes

salt and pepper

175 g/6 oz mozzarella cheese, sliced

225 g/8 oz firm tofu, sliced

55 g/2 oz fresh white breadcrumbs

2 tbsp grated Parmesan cheese

basil leaves, to garnish

1 Cook the sliced potatoes in a pan of boiling water for 5 minutes. Drain well and set aside.

2 Put the aubergine slices on a plate, sprinkle with salt and set aside for 20 minutes. Meanwhile, blanch the courgette in a pan of boiling water for 2–3 minutes. Drain and set aside.

3 Heat 2 tablespoons of the oil in a frying pan. Add the onion and cook over a low heat, stirring occasionally, for 2–3 minutes until softened. Add the green pepper, cumin seeds, basil and canned tomatoes. Season to taste with salt and pepper and simmer for 30 minutes.

4 Rinse the aubergine slices thoroughly under cold running water and pat dry with kitchen paper. Heat the remaining oil in a large frying pan. Add the aubergine slices and cook over a medium heat for 3–5 minutes, turning to brown both sides. Drain and set aside.

5 Arrange half of the potato slices in the base of 4 small loose-based flan tins. Cover with half of the courgette slices, half of the aubergine slices and half of the mozzarella slices. Lay the tofu on top and spoon over the tomato sauce. Repeat the layers of vegetables and cheese in the same order.

6 Mix the breadcrumbs and Parmesan together and sprinkle over the top. Cook in a preheated oven,190°C/375°F/Gas Mark 5, for 25–30 minutes or until golden. Garnish with fresh basil leaves and serve the pies immediately.

Provençal Bean Stew

Bursting with Mediterranean flavours, this colourful stew is delicious served with slices of warm garlic bread.

NUTRITIONAL INFORMATION

Calories	420	Sugars	........11g
Protein	........22g	Fat	...........9g
Carbohydrate	...64g	Saturates	.......1g

 20 mins   2½ hours

SERVES 4

INGREDIENTS

350 g/12 oz dried pinto beans, soaked overnight in water to cover

2 tbsp olive oil

2 onions, sliced

2 garlic cloves, finely chopped

1 red pepper, deseeded and sliced

1 yellow pepper, deseeded and sliced

400 g/14 oz canned chopped tomatoes

2 tbsp tomato purée

1 tbsp torn fresh basil leaves

2 tsp chopped fresh thyme

2 tsp chopped fresh rosemary

1 bay leaf

salt and pepper

55 g/2 oz black olives, stoned and halved

2 tbsp chopped fresh parsley, to garnish

1 Drain the beans and place in a large saucepan. Add cold water to cover and bring to the boil. Boil for 15 minutes, then cover and simmer for 1¼ hours, until almost tender. Drain, reserving 300 ml/10 fl oz of the cooking liquid.

2 Heat the olive oil in a heavy-based saucepan. Add the onions and cook, stirring occasionally, for 5 minutes, until softened. Add the garlic and peppers and cook, stirring frequently, for 10 minutes.

3 Add the tomatoes with their can juice, the tomato purée, basil, thyme, rosemary, bay leaf and beans and season to taste with salt and pepper. Cover and simmer for 40 minutes. Add the olives and simmer for 5 minutes more.

4 Transfer the stew to a warm serving dish, sprinkle with the parsley and serve immediately.

VARIATION
You could substitute other beans for the pinto beans in this recipe, such as borlotti, cannellini or haricot, or use a mixture of different types.

Mushroom Gougère

A gougère is a savoury round of choux pastry, usually flavoured with cheese. This dish is equally good served warm or cold.

NUTRITIONAL INFORMATION

Calories	490	Sugars	.........4g
Protein	........14g	Fat	..........39g
Carbohydrate	...21g	Saturates	......13g

 30 mins   1 hr

SERVES 4

INGREDIENTS

CHOUX PASTRY

70 g/2½ oz strong white flour

55 g/2 oz butter, plus extra for greasing

150 ml/5 fl oz water

2 eggs

55 g/2 oz Emmenthal cheese, grated

FILLING

2 tbsp olive oil

1 onion, chopped

225 g/8 oz chestnut mushrooms, sliced

2 garlic cloves, finely chopped

1 tbsp plain flour

150 ml/5 fl oz vegetable stock

85 g/3 oz walnuts, chopped

2 tbsp chopped fresh parsley

salt and pepper

1 To make the choux pastry, sift the flour with a pinch of salt on to a sheet of greaseproof paper. Heat the butter and water in a heavy-based saucepan until the butter melts, but do not let the water boil. Add the flour all at once and beat vigorously with a wooden spoon until the mixture is smooth and comes away from the sides of the pan. Remove the pan from the heat and leave to cool for 10 minutes, then gradually beat in the eggs until smooth and glossy. Beat in the cheese. Grease a round ovenproof dish with butter and spoon the choux pastry around the sides.

2 To make the filling, heat the oil in a large, heavy-based frying pan. Add the onion and cook, stirring occasionally, for 5 minutes, until softened. Add the mushrooms and garlic and cook for 2 minutes. Stir in the flour and cook, stirring, for 1 minute, then gradually stir in the stock. Bring to the boil, stirring constantly, and cook for 3 minutes, until thickened. Reserve 2 tablespoons of the walnuts and stir the remainder into the mushroom mixture with the parsley. Season to taste with salt and pepper.

3 Spoon the mushroom filling into the centre of the dish and sprinkle the reserved walnuts over it. Bake in a preheated oven, 200°C/400°F/Gas Mark 6, for about 40 minutes, until risen and golden brown. Serve immediately.

Green Vegetable Gougère

A tasty, simple supper dish of choux pastry and crisp green vegetables.
The choux pastry ring can be filled with all kinds of vegetables.

NUTRITIONAL INFORMATION

Calories . . . . . . .672 Sugars 6g
Protein . . . . .19g Fat 51g
Carbohydrate . . .36g Saturates 14g

 30 mins   40 mins

SERVES 4

I N G R E D I E N T S

150 g/5½ oz plain flour

125 g/4½ oz butter

300 ml/½ pint water

4 eggs, beaten

90 g/3 oz Gruyère cheese, grated

salt and pepper

1 tbsp milk

FILLING

2 tbsp garlic and herb butter or margarine

2 tsp olive oil

2 leeks, shredded

225 g/8 oz green cabbage, finely shredded

125 g/4½ oz beansprouts

½ tsp grated lime rind

1 tbsp lime juice

celery salt and pepper

lime slices, to garnish

1 Sift the flour on to a piece of baking paper. Cut the butter into dice and put in a saucepan with the water. Heat until the butter has melted.

2 Bring the butter and water to the boil, then tip in the flour all at once. Beat until the mixture becomes thick. Remove from the heat and continue to beat until the mixture is glossy and comes away from the sides of the saucepan.

3 Transfer to a mixing bowl and cool for 10 minutes. Gradually beat in the eggs, a little at a time, making sure they are thoroughly incorporated after each addition. Stir in 60 g/2 oz of the cheese and season with salt and pepper.

4 Place spoonfuls of the mixture in a 23 cm/9 inch circle on a dampened baking tray. Brush with milk and sprinkle with the remaining cheese.

5 Bake in a preheated oven, 220°C/425°F/Gas Mark 7, for 30–35 minutes, until golden and crisp. Transfer to a warmed serving plate.

6 Meanwhile, make the filling. Heat the butter or margarine and the olive oil in a large frying pan and stir-fry the leeks and cabbage for 2 minutes. Add the beansprouts, lime rind and juice and stir-fry for 1 minute. Season to taste.

7 Pile into the centre of the pastry ring. Garnish with lime slices and serve.

Vegetable & Tofu Strudels

These strudels look really impressive and are perfect for a casual supper or a more formal dinner party dish.

NUTRITIONAL INFORMATION

Calories 485   Sugars 5g
Protein ....16g   Fat 27g
Carbohydrate ...47g   Saturates 5g

25 mins   30 mins

SERVES 4

INGREDIENTS

FILLING

2 tbsp vegetable oil

2 tbsp butter

150 g/5½ oz potatoes, finely diced

1 leek, shredded

2 garlic cloves, crushed

1 tsp garam masala

½ tsp chilli powder

½ tsp turmeric

50 g/1¾ oz okra, sliced

100 g/3½ oz button mushrooms, sliced

2 tomatoes, diced

225 g/8 oz firm tofu, diced

salt and pepper

PASTRY CASES

350 g/12 oz (12 sheets) filo pastry

2 tbsp butter, melted

1 To make the filling, heat the oil and butter in a frying pan. Add the potatoes and leek and fry, stirring constantly, for 2–3 minutes.

2 Add the garlic and spices, okra, mushrooms, tomatoes and tofu and season to taste with salt and pepper. Cook, stirring, for 5–7 minutes, or until tender.

3 Lay the pastry out on a chopping board and brush each individual sheet with melted butter. Place 3 sheets on top of one another; repeat to make 4 stacks.

4 Spoon a quarter of the filling along the centre of each stack and brush the edges with melted butter. Fold the short edges in and roll up lengthways to form a cigar shape. Brush the outside with melted butter. Place the strudels on a greased baking tray.

5 Cook in a preheated oven, 190°C/ 375°F/Gas Mark 5, for 20 minutes, or until golden brown and crisp. Transfer the strudels to a warm serving dish and serve them immediately.

Bread & Butter Savoury

Quick, simple, nutritious and a pleasure to eat – what more could you ask for an inexpensive midweek meal?

NUTRITIONAL INFORMATION

Calories 472	Sugars 7g
Protein 22g	Fat 33g
Carbohydrate ...25g	Saturates 20g

 30 mins   45 mins

SERVES 4

INGREDIENTS

60 g/2 oz butter or margarine

1 bunch spring onions, sliced

6 slices of white or brown bread, crusts removed

175g/6 oz mature Cheddar cheese, grated

2 eggs

450 ml/16 fl oz milk

salt and pepper

fresh flat-leaved parsley sprigs, to garnish

1 Lightly grease a 1.5 litre/2½ pint ovenproof dish with a little of the butter or margarine.

2 Melt the remaining butter or margarine in a small saucepan. Add the spring onions and fry over a medium heat, stirring occasionally, until softened and golden.

3 Meanwhile, cut the bread into triangles and place half of them in the base of the dish. Cover with the sliced spring onions and top with half the grated Cheddar cheese.

4 Beat together the eggs and milk and season to taste with salt and pepper. Layer the remaining triangles of bread in the dish and carefully pour over the milk mixture. Leave to soak for 15–20 minutes.

5 Sprinkle the remaining cheese over the soaked bread. Bake in a preheated oven, 190°C/375°F/Gas Mark 5, for 35–40 minutes, until puffed up and golden brown. Garnish with flat-leaved parsley and serve immediately.

VARIATION
You can vary the vegetables used in this savoury bake, depending on what you have to hand. Shallots, mushrooms or tomatoes are all suitable.

Cheese & Potato Layer Bake

This is a quick dish to prepare and it can be left to cook in the oven without requiring any further attention.

NUTRITIONAL INFORMATION

Calories 766   Sugars 14g
Protein . . . . .44g   Fat 40g
Carbohydrate . . .60g   Saturates 23g

25 mins   45 mins

SERVES 4

INGREDIENTS

900 g/2 lb unpeeled waxy potatoes,
   cut into wedges

2 tbsp butter

1 red onion, halved and sliced

2 garlic cloves, crushed

2½ tbsp plain flour

600 ml/1 pint milk

400 g/14 oz canned artichoke hearts
   in brine, drained and halved

150 g/5½ oz frozen mixed vegetables,
   thawed

125 g/4½ oz Gruyère cheese, grated

125 g/4½ oz mature Cheddar cheese, grated

50 g/1¾ oz Gorgonzola cheese, crumbled

25 g/1 oz Parmesan cheese, freshly grated

225 g/8 oz firm tofu, sliced

2 tbsp chopped fresh thyme

salt and pepper

fresh thyme sprigs, to garnish

1 Cook the potato wedges in a saucepan of boiling water for 10 minutes, then drain thoroughly.

2 Meanwhile, melt the butter in a saucepan. Add the sliced onion and garlic and fry over a low heat, stirring frequently, for 2–3 minutes.

3 Stir the flour into the pan and cook for 1 minute. Gradually add the milk and bring to the boil, stirring constantly.

4 Reduce the heat and then add the artichoke hearts, mixed vegetables, half of each of the 4 cheeses and the sliced tofu to the pan, mixing well to combine thoroughly.

5 Stir in the chopped thyme and season with salt and pepper to taste.

6 Arrange a layer of parboiled potato wedges in the base of a shallow ovenproof dish. Spoon the vegetable mixture over the top and cover with the remaining potato wedges. Sprinkle the rest of the 4 cheeses over the top.

7 Cook in a preheated oven, 200°C/ 400°F/Gas Mark 6, for 30 minutes or until the potatoes are cooked and the top is golden brown. Serve the bake garnished with fresh thyme sprigs.

White Nut Filo Parcels

These crisp, buttery parcels, filled with nuts and pesto and served with cranberry sauce, would make a wonderful Sunday lunch.

NUTRITIONAL INFORMATION

Calories ....1100 Sugars 9g
Protein ....29g Fat 80g
Carbohydrate ...73g Saturates 15g

15 mins   25 mins

SERVES 4

INGREDIENTS

40 g/1½ oz butter or margarine

1 large onion, finely chopped

275 g/9½ oz mixed white nuts, such as pine kernels, unsalted cashew nuts, blanched almonds and unsalted peanuts, finely chopped

90 g/3 oz fresh white breadcrumbs

½ tsp ground mace

1 egg, beaten

salt and pepper

1 egg yolk

3 tbsp pesto sauce

2 tbsp chopped basil

125 g/4½ oz butter or margarine, melted

16 sheets filo pastry

fresh basil sprigs to garnish

TO SERVE

cranberry sauce

steamed vegetables

1 Melt the butter or margarine in a frying pan, add the onion and gently fry for 2–3 minutes, until just softened but not browned.

2 Remove from the heat and stir in the nuts, two-thirds of the breadcrumbs, the mace and beaten whole egg. Season to taste with salt and pepper. Set aside.

3 Place the remaining breadcrumbs in a bowl and stir in the egg yolk, pesto sauce, basil, and 1 tablespoon of the melted butter or margarine. Mix well.

4 Brush 1 sheet of filo pastry with melted butter or margarine. Fold in half and brush again. Repeat with a second sheet and lay it on top of the first one so that it forms a cross.

5 Put one-eighth of the nut mixture in the centre of the pastry. Top with one-eighth of the pesto mixture. Fold over the edges, brushing with more butter or margarine, to form a parcel. Brush the top with butter or margarine and transfer to a baking tray. Make eight parcels in the same way and brush with the remaining butter or margarine.

6 Bake in a preheated oven at 220°C/ 425°F/Gas Mark 7 for 15–20 minutes, until golden. Transfer to serving plates, garnish with basil sprigs and serve with cranberry sauce and steamed vegetables.

Green Easter Pie

This traditional Easter risotto pie is from the Piedmont region in northern Italy. Serve it warm or chilled in slices.

NUTRITIONAL INFORMATION

Calories ....392 Sugars 3g
Protein ....17g Fat 17g
Carbohydrate ...41g Saturates 5g

25 mins   50 mins

SERVES 4

INGREDIENTS

butter, for greasing

85 g/3 oz rocket leaves

2 tbsp olive oil

1 onion, chopped

2 garlic cloves, chopped

200 g/7 oz arborio rice

700 ml/1¼ pints hot vegetable stock

125 ml/4 fl oz dry white wine

55 g/2 oz Parmesan cheese,
   freshly grated

115 g/4 oz frozen peas, thawed

2 tomatoes, diced

4 eggs, beaten

3 tbsp fresh marjoram, chopped

salt and pepper

55 g/2 oz fresh breadcrumbs

1 Lightly grease a 23 cm/9 inch deep cake tin and line the base.

2 Using a sharp knife, roughly chop the rocket leaves.

3 Heat the oil in a frying pan and fry the onion and garlic over a low heat for 4–5 minutes or until softened.

4 Add the rice to the frying pan, mix well to combine, then begin adding the stock a ladleful at a time. Wait until each ladleful of stock has been absorbed before adding the next.

5 Continue to cook the mixture, adding the wine, until the rice is tender. This will take at least 15 minutes. Remove the pan from the heat.

6 Stir in the Parmesan cheese, peas, rocket leaves, tomatoes, eggs and 2 tablespoons of the marjoram. Season to taste with salt and pepper.

7 Spoon the risotto into the prepared tin and level the surface by pressing down with the back of a wooden spoon.

8 Top with the breadcrumbs and the remaining marjoram.

9 Bake in a preheated oven, 180°C/ 350°F/Gas Mark 4, for 30 minutes or until set. Cut into slices and serve.

Root Croustades

This colourful combination of grated root vegetables and mixed peppers would make a stunning dinner-party dish.

NUTRITIONAL INFORMATION

Calories ....304 Sugars 17g
Protein ....6g Fat 19g
Carbohydrate ...28g Saturates 3g

2½ hours   1¼ hours

SERVES 4

INGREDIENTS

1 orange pepper

1 red pepper

1 yellow pepper

3 tbsp olive oil

2 tbsp red wine vinegar

1 tsp French mustard

1 tsp clear honey

salt and pepper

fresh flat-leaved parsley sprigs, to garnish

green vegetables, to serve

CROUSTADES

225 g/8 oz potatoes, coarsely grated

225 g/8 oz carrots, coarsely grated

350 g/12 oz celeriac, coarsely grated

1 garlic clove, crushed

1 tbsp lemon juice

25 g/1 oz butter or margarine, melted

1 egg, beaten

salt and pepper

1 tbsp vegetable oil

1 Place the peppers on a baking tray and bake in a preheated oven, 190°C/375°F/Gas Mark 5, for 35 minutes, turning after 20 minutes.

2 Cover with a tea towel and leave to cool for 10 minutes.

3 Peel the skin from the cooked peppers; cut in half and discard the seeds. Thinly slice the flesh into strips and place in a shallow dish.

4 Put the oil, vinegar, mustard, honey and seasoning in a small screw-top jar and shake well to mix. Pour over the pepper strips, mix well and set aside to marinate for 2 hours.

5 To make the croustades, put the grated potatoes, carrots and celeriac in a mixing bowl and toss in the crushed garlic and lemon juice.

6 Mix in the melted butter or margarine and the egg. Season to taste with salt and pepper. Divide the mixture into 8 and pile on to 2 baking trays lined with baking paper, forming each into a 10 cm/4 inch round. Brush with oil.

7 Bake in a preheated oven, 220°C/425°F/Gas Mark 7, for 30–35 minutes, until the croustades are crisp around the edges and golden. Carefully transfer to a warmed serving dish.

8 Heat the peppers and the marinade for 2–3 minutes until warmed through. Spoon the peppers over the croustades, garnish with flat-leaved parsley and serve at once with green vegetables.

Spicy Potato & Nut Terrine

This delicious baked terrine has a base of mashed potato flavoured with nuts, cheese, herbs and spices.

NUTRITIONAL INFORMATION

Calories	1100	Sugars	........13g
Protein	........34g	Fat	..........93g
Carbohydrate	...31g	Saturates	......22g

15 mins   1 hr 20 mins

SERVES 4

INGREDIENTS

2 tbsp butter, plus extra for greasing

225 g/8 oz floury potatoes, diced

225 g/8 oz pecan nuts

225 g/8 oz unsalted cashew nuts

1 onion, finely chopped

2 garlic cloves, crushed

115 g/4 oz open-cap mushrooms, diced

2 tbsp chopped fresh mixed herbs

1 tsp paprika

1 tsp ground cumin

1 tsp ground coriander

4 eggs, beaten

115 g/4 oz full-fat soft cheese

55 g/2 oz Parmesan cheese, freshly grated

salt and pepper

SAUCE

3 large tomatoes, peeled, deseeded and chopped

2 tbsp tomato purée

5 tbsp red wine

1 tbsp red wine vinegar

pinch of caster sugar

1 Lightly grease a 900 g/2 lb loaf tin and line it with baking paper.

2 Cook the potatoes in a large pan of lightly salted boiling water for 10 minutes or until cooked through. Drain and mash thoroughly.

3 Finely chop the pecan and cashew nuts or process in a food processor or blender. Mix the nuts with the chopped onion and garlic and diced mushrooms. Melt the butter in a frying pan and cook the nut mixture for 5–7 minutes. Add the herbs and spices. Stir in the eggs, cheeses and potatoes and season to taste with salt and pepper.

4 Spoon the mixture into the prepared loaf tin, pressing it down quite firmly. Cook in a preheated oven, 190°C/375°F/Gas Mark 5, for 1 hour or until set.

5 To make the sauce, mix the tomatoes, tomato purée, wine, wine vinegar and sugar in a pan and bring to the boil, stirring constantly. Cook for 10 minutes, or until the tomatoes have reduced. Press the sauce through a sieve or process in a food processor or blender for 30 seconds.

6 Turn the terrine out of the tin on to a serving plate and cut into slices. Serve with the tomato sauce.

Roasted Pepper Terrine

Serve this terrine for Sunday lunch with Italian bread and a green salad.
You can use a hot grill instead of a barbecue to cook the vegetables.

NUTRITIONAL INFORMATION

Calories	196	Sugars 6g
Protein	.........6g	Fat 14g
Carbohydrate	...13g	Saturates 3g

30 mins   30 mins

SERVES 8

I N G R E D I E N T S

500 g/1 lb 2 oz broad beans

6 red peppers, halved and deseeded

3 small courgettes, sliced lengthways

1 aubergine, sliced lengthways

3 leeks, halved lengthways

6 tbsp olive oil, plus extra for greasing

salt and pepper

6 tbsp single cream

2 tbsp chopped fresh basil

1 Grease a 1.5 litre/2¾ pint terrine. Blanch the broad beans in boiling water for 1–2 minutes and pop them out of their skins. It is not essential to do this, but the effort is worthwhile as the beans taste a lot sweeter.

2 Roast the red peppers over a hot barbecue, turning until the skin is black – 10–15 minutes. Remove and put into a plastic bag. Seal and set aside.

3 Brush the courgette, aubergine and leeks with 5 tablespoons of the olive oil, and season with salt and pepper to taste. Cook over the hot barbecue until tender, about 8–10 minutes, turning once.

4 Meanwhile, purée the broad beans in a blender or food processor with 1 tablespoon of the olive oil, the cream and seasoning to taste.

5 Remove the red peppers from the bag and peel.

6 Open out the peppers to make flat pieces. Use to line the bottom and up the sides of the terrine.

7 Spread a third of the bean purée over the pepper. Cover with the aubergine slices and spread over half of the remaining bean purée.

8 Sprinkle over the basil. Top with courgettes and the remaining bean purée. Lay the leeks on top. Add any remaining pieces of red pepper. Put a piece of foil, folded 4 times, on the top and weigh down with tins.

9 Chill until required. Turn out on to a serving platter, slice and serve with Italian bread and a green salad.

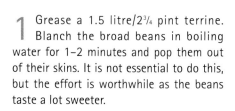

Mushroom & Nut Crumble

A filling, tasty dish that is ideal for a warming family supper. The crunchy topping is flavoured with three different types of nuts.

NUTRITIONAL INFORMATION

Calories	779	Sugars 5g
Protein	........16g	Fat 59g
Carbohydrate	...48g	Saturates 14g

 20 mins   55 mins

SERVES 4

INGREDIENTS

350 g/12 oz open-cap mushrooms, sliced

350 g/12 oz chestnut mushrooms, sliced

400 ml/14 fl oz vegetable stock

60 g/2 oz butter or margarine

1 large onion, finely chopped

1 garlic clove, crushed

60 g/2 oz plain flour

salt and pepper

4 tbsp double cream

2 tbsp chopped fresh parsley

fresh herbs, to garnish

CRUMBLE TOPPING

90 g/3 oz medium oatmeal

90 g/3 oz wholemeal flour

25 g/1 oz ground almonds

25 g/1 oz finely chopped walnuts

60 g/2 oz finely chopped unsalted shelled
    pistachio nuts

1 tsp dried thyme

salt and pepper

90 g/3 oz butter or margarine, softened

1 tbsp fennel seeds

1 Put the mushrooms and stock in a large saucepan, bring to the boil, cover and simmer for 15 minutes, until tender. Drain, reserving the stock.

2 In another saucepan, melt the butter or margarine and fry the onion and garlic for 2–3 minutes, until just soft. Stir in the flour and cook for 1 minute.

3 Remove from the heat and gradually stir in the reserved mushroom stock. Return to the heat and cook, stirring, until thickened. Add the mushrooms, seasoning, cream and parsley, stir to combine and spoon into a shallow ovenproof dish.

4 To make the topping, mix together in a bowl the medium oatmeal, flour, nuts, thyme and season with plenty of salt and pepper to taste.

5 Using a fork, mix in the butter or margarine until the topping resembles coarse breadcrumbs.

6 Sprinkle the topping evenly over the mushrooms and then sprinkle with the fennel seeds. Bake in a preheated oven, 190°C/375°F/Gas Mark 5, for about 25–30 minutes, or until the topping is golden and crisp. Garnish with fresh herbs and serve immediately.

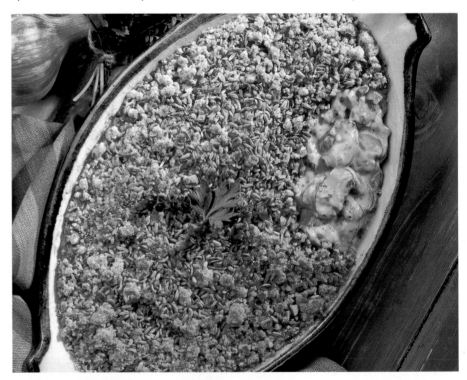

Vegetable Toad-in-the-hole

This dish can be cooked in a single large dish or in four individual Yorkshire pudding tins.

NUTRITIONAL INFORMATION

Calories 313	Sugars 9g	
Protein 9g	Fat 18g	
Carbohydrate . . .31g	Saturates 7g	

15 mins   55 mins

SERVES 4

INGREDIENTS

BATTER

100 g/3½ oz plain flour

salt

2 eggs, beaten

200 ml/7 fl oz milk

2 tbsp wholegrain mustard

2 tbsp vegetable oil

FILLING

25 g/1 oz butter

2 garlic cloves, crushed

1 onion, cut into eight

75 g/2¾ oz baby carrots, halved lengthways

50 g/1¾ oz French beans

50 g/1¾ oz canned sweetcorn, drained

2 tomatoes, deseeded and cut into chunks

1 tsp wholegrain mustard

1 tbsp chopped fresh mixed herbs

salt and pepper

1 To make the batter, sift the flour and a pinch of salt into a bowl. Beat in the eggs and milk to make a batter. Stir in the mustard and leave to stand.

2 Pour the oil into a shallow ovenproof dish and heat in a preheated oven, 200°C/400°F/ Gas Mark 6, for 10 minutes.

3 To make the filling, melt the butter in a frying pan and sauté the garlic and onion, stirring constantly, for 2 minutes. Cook the carrots and beans in a saucepan of boiling water for 7 minutes, or until tender. Drain well.

4 Add the sweetcorn and tomatoes to the frying pan with the mustard and chopped mixed herbs. Season well and add the carrots and beans.

5 Remove the heated dish from the oven and pour in the batter. Spoon the vegetables into the centre, return to the oven and cook for 30–35 minutes, until the batter has risen and set. Serve the vegetable toad-in-the-hole immediately.

Elizabethan Artichoke Pie

The filling of Jerusalem artichokes, grapes, onion, dates and hard-boiled eggs is an unusual but delicious blend of flavours.

NUTRITIONAL INFORMATION

Calories ....136 Sugars 8g
Protein ....6g Fat 6g
Carbohydrate ...16g Saturates 3g

1¼ hrs   55 mins

SERVES 6

INGREDIENTS

350 g/12 oz Jerusalem artichokes

25 g/1 oz butter or margarine

1 onion, chopped

1–2 garlic cloves, crushed

125 g/4½ oz white seedless grapes, halved

60 g/2 oz dates, roughly chopped

2 hard-boiled eggs, sliced

1 tbsp chopped fresh mixed herbs or
    1 tsp dried herbs

4–6 tbsp single cream or natural yogurt

SHORTCRUST PASTRY

350 g/12 oz plain flour

good pinch of salt

90 g/3 oz butter or margarine

90 g/3 oz white vegetable fat

4–6 tbsp cold water

beaten egg or milk, to glaze

1 To make the pastry, sift the flour and salt into a bowl, rub in the butter or margarine and vegetable fat until the mixture resembles fine breadcrumbs, then add sufficient water to mix to a pliable dough. Knead lightly. Wrap in foil or clingfilm and chill for 30 minutes.

2 Peel the artichokes, plunging them immediately into salted water to prevent discolouration. Drain, cover with fresh water, bring to the boil and simmer for 10–12 minutes until just tender. Drain.

3 Heat the butter or margarine in a pan and fry the onion and garlic until soft but not coloured. Remove from the heat and stir in the grapes and dates.

4 Roll out almost two-thirds of the pastry and use to line a 20 cm/8 inch pie dish. Slice the artichokes and arrange in the pie dish, then cover with slices of egg and then with the onion mixture, seasoning and herbs.

5 Roll out the remaining pastry, dampen the edges and use to cover the pie; press the edges firmly together, then trim and crimp. Roll out the trimmings and cut into narrow strips. Arrange a lattice over the top of the pie, dampening the strips to attach them.

6 Glaze with beaten egg or milk and make 2–3 holes in the lid. Bake in a preheated oven at 200°C/400°F/Gas Mark 6 for 40–50 minutes until golden. Gently heat the cream or yogurt and pour into the pie through the holes in the lid, then serve immediately.

Nutty Harvest Loaf

This attractive and nutritious loaf is also utterly delicious. Served with a fresh tomato sauce, it can be eaten hot or cold with salad.

NUTRITIONAL INFORMATION

Calories 554	Sugars 12g	
Protein 16g	Fat 37g	
Carbohydrate ...43g	Saturates 16g	

 20 mins   1½ hrs

SERVES 4

INGREDIENTS

2 tbsp butter, plus extra for greasing

450 g/1 lb floury potatoes, diced

1 onion, chopped

2 garlic cloves, crushed

115 g/4 oz unsalted peanuts

85 g/3 oz fresh white breadcrumbs

1 egg, beaten

2 tbsp chopped fresh coriander

150 ml/5 fl oz vegetable stock

85 g/3 oz mushrooms, sliced

55 g/2 oz sun-dried tomatoes in oil, drained and sliced

salt and pepper

SAUCE

150 ml/5 fl oz crème fraîche

2 tsp tomato purée

2 tsp clear honey

2 tbsp chopped fresh coriander

1 Grease a 450 g/1 lb loaf tin. Cook the potatoes in a saucepan of boiling water for 10 minutes, or until cooked through. Drain well, mash and set aside.

2 Melt half of the butter in a frying pan. Add the chopped onion and crushed garlic and fry gently for 2–3 minutes until soft. Finely chop the nuts or process them in a food processor or blender for 30 seconds with the breadcrumbs.

3 Mix the chopped nuts and the breadcrumbs into the potatoes with the egg, coriander and vegetable stock. Stir in the onion and garlic and season.

4 Melt the remaining butter in the frying pan, add the sliced mushrooms and cook for 2–3 minutes.

5 Press half of the potato mixture into the base of the loaf tin. Spoon the mushrooms on top and sprinkle with the sun-dried tomatoes. Spoon the remaining potato mixture on top and smooth the surface. Cover with foil and bake in a preheated oven, 190°C/375°F/Gas Mark 5, for 1 hour or until firm to the touch.

6 Meanwhile, mix the sauce ingredients together. Cut the nutty harvest loaf into slices and serve with the sauce.

Roast Pepper Tart

This tastes truly delicious, the flavour of roasted vegetables being entirely different from that of boiled or fried.

NUTRITIONAL INFORMATION

Calories 237   Sugars 3g
Protein ....6g   Fat 15g
Carbohydrate ...20g   Saturates 4g

 25 mins   40 mins

SERVES 8

INGREDIENTS

PASTRY

175 g/6 oz plain flour

pinch of salt

75 g/2¾ oz butter or margarine

2 tbsp green olives, stoned and finely chopped

3 tbsp cold water

FILLING

1 red pepper

1 green pepper

1 yellow pepper

2 garlic cloves, crushed

2 tbsp olive oil

100 g/3½ oz mozzarella cheese, grated

2 eggs

150 ml/¼ pint milk

1 tbsp chopped fresh basil

salt and pepper

1 To make the pastry, sift the flour and salt into a bowl. Rub in the butter or margarine until the mixture resembles breadcrumbs. Add the chopped olives and cold water, bringing the mixture together to form a dough.

2 Roll the dough out on a floured surface and use to line a 20 cm/8 inch loose-based flan tin. Prick the base with a fork and leave to chill.

3 Cut the peppers in half lengthways, deseed and place them, skin side uppermost, on a baking tray. Mix the garlic and oil and brush over the peppers. Cook in a preheated oven, 200°C/400°F/Gas Mark 6, for 20 minutes, or until beginning to char slightly.

4 Let the peppers cool slightly, then thinly slice them. Arrange the slices in the pastry case, layering with the grated mozzarella cheese.

5 Beat the eggs and milk and add the basil. Season and pour over the peppers. Put the tart on a baking tray and bake in the oven for 20 minutes, or until set. Serve hot or cold.

Spinach Roulade

A delicious savoury roll, stuffed with mozzarella and broccoli. Serve as a main course or as an appetizer, in which case it would easily serve six.

NUTRITIONAL INFORMATION

Calories	287	Sugars	.........8g
Protein	........23g	Fat	.........12g
Carbohydrate	....8g	Saturates	.......6g

 15 mins   25 mins

SERVES 4

INGREDIENTS

500 g/1 lb 2 oz small fresh spinach leaves

2 tbsp water

4 eggs, separated

salt and pepper

½ tsp ground nutmeg

300 ml/½ pint sugocasa, to serve

FILLING

175 g/6 oz small broccoli florets

25 g/1 oz Parmesan cheese, freshly grated

175 g/6 oz mozzarella cheese, grated

1 Wash the spinach and pack, still wet, into a large saucepan. Add the water. Cover the pan with a tight-fitting lid and cook the spinach over a high heat for 4–5 minutes, until reduced and soft. Drain thoroughly, squeezing out excess water. Chop finely and pat dry.

2 Mix the spinach with the egg yolks, seasoning and nutmeg. Whisk the egg whites until very frothy but not too stiff, and fold into the spinach mixture.

3 Grease and line a 32 x 23 cm/ 13 x 9 inch Swiss roll tin and line with baking paper to come 2.5 cm/1 inch above the sides of the tin. Spread the mixture in the tin and smooth the surface with a wet palette knife. Bake in a preheated oven, 220°C/425°F/Gas Mark 7, for about 12–15 minutes, until firm to the touch and golden.

4 Meanwhile, cook the broccoli florets in lightly salted boiling water for 4–5 minutes, until just tender. Drain and keep the florets warm.

5 Sprinkle Parmesan on a sheet of baking paper. Turn the base on to it and peel away the lining paper. Sprinkle with mozzarella and top with broccoli.

6 Hold one end of the paper and roll up the spinach base like a Swiss roll. Heat the sugocasa and spoon on to warmed serving plates. Slice the roulade and place on top of the sugocasa.

Cauliflower & Broccoli Flan

This really is a tasty flan. The delicious herb pastry case may be made in advance and frozen until required.

15 mins   50 mins

SERVES 4

INGREDIENTS

PASTRY

175 g/6 oz plain flour, plus extra for dusting

pinch of salt

½ tsp paprika

1 tsp dried thyme

6 tbsp margarine

3 tbsp water

FILLING

100 g/3½ oz cauliflower florets

100 g/3½ oz broccoli florets

1 onion, cut into 8 wedges

2 tbsp butter or margarine

1 tbsp plain flour

6 tbsp vegetable stock

125 ml/4 fl oz milk

85 g/3 oz Cheddar cheese, grated

salt and pepper

paprika, to garnish

1 To make the pastry, sift the flour and salt into a bowl. Add the paprika and thyme and rub in the margarine. Stir in the water and bind to form a dough.

2 Roll out the pastry on a floured surface and use to line an 18 cm/7 inch loose-based flan tin. Prick the base with a fork and line with baking paper. Fill with baking beans and bake in a preheated oven, 190°C/375°F/ Gas Mark 5, for 15 minutes. Remove the paper and beans and return the pastry case to the oven for 5 minutes.

3 To make the filling, cook the vegetables in a pan of lightly salted boiling water for 10–12 minutes until tender. Drain and reserve.

4 Melt the butter in a pan. Add the flour and cook, stirring constantly, for 1 minute. Remove from the heat, stir in the stock and milk and return to the heat. Bring to the boil, stirring constantly, and add 55 g/2 oz of the cheese. Season to taste with salt and pepper.

5 Spoon the cauliflower, broccoli and onion into the pastry case. Pour over the sauce and sprinkle with the remaining grated cheese. Return the flan to the oven for 10 minutes until the cheese is golden and bubbling. Garnish with paprika and serve immediately.

Cheese Enchiladas

Mole sauce makes a delicious enchilada – a good reason to make yourself a big pot of Mole Poblano (see page 853).

NUTRITIONAL INFORMATION

Calories ....668 Sugars 6g
Protein ....24g Fat 33g
Carbohydrate ...73g Saturates 13g

15 mins   30 mins

SERVES 4

I N G R E D I E N T S

8 corn tortillas

vegetable oil, for greasing

450 ml/16 fl oz mole sauce

about 225 g/8 oz grated cheese, such as Cheddar, mozzarella, Asiago or Mexican queso Oaxaco, one type or a mixture

225 ml/8 fl oz vegetable stock

5 spring onions, thinly sliced

2–3 tbsp chopped fresh coriander

handful of cos lettuce leaves, shredded

1 avocado, stoned, diced and tossed in lime juice

4 tbsp soured cream

salsa of your choice

1 Heat the tortillas in a lightly greased non-stick frying pan; wrap the heated tortillas in kitchen foil as you work to keep them warm.

2 Dip the tortillas into the mole sauce, and pile up on a plate. Fill the inside of the top sauced tortilla with a few spoonfuls of cheese. Roll up and place in a shallow ovenproof dish. Repeat this process with the remaining tortillas, reserving a handful of the cheese to sprinkle over the top.

3 Pour the rest of the mole sauce over the rolled tortillas, then pour the stock over the top. Sprinkle with the reserved grated cheese and cover the dish with kitchen foil.

4 Bake in a preheated oven, 190°C/ 375°F/Gas Mark 5, for about 30 minutes until the tortillas are very hot and the cheese filling has melted.

5 Arrange the sliced spring onions, fresh coriander, shredded lettuce, diced avocado and soured cream on top. Add the salsa of your choice to taste. Serve the enchiladas immediately.

Broccoli Enchiladas

These delicious and very nutritious enchiladas are served with a mild chilli sauce.

NUTRITIONAL INFORMATION

Calories ....605 Sugars 7g
Protein ....37g Fat 33g
Carbohydrate ...42g Saturates 18g

20 mins   30 mins

SERVES 4

INGREDIENTS

450 g/1 lb broccoli florets

225 g/8 oz ricotta cheese

1 garlic clove, chopped

½ tsp ground cumin

175–200 g/6–7 oz Cheddar cheese, grated

6–8 tbsp freshly grated Parmesan cheese

1 egg, lightly beaten

salt and pepper

4–6 flour tortillas

vegetable oil, for greasing

1 quantity Mild Red Chilli Sauce
   (see page 855)

225 ml/8 fl oz vegetable stock

½ onion, finely chopped

3–4 tbsp chopped fresh coriander

3 tomatoes, diced

hot salsa, to serve

1 Bring a pan of salted water to the boil, add the broccoli, bring back to the boil and blanch for 1 minute. Drain, refresh under cold running water, then drain again. Cut off the stems, peel and chop. Dice the heads.

2 Mix the broccoli with the ricotta cheese, garlic, cumin, and half the Cheddar and Parmesan in a bowl. Mix in the egg and season with salt and pepper.

3 Heat the tortillas in a lightly greased non-stick frying pan; then wrap in kitchen foil to keep warm.

4 Fill the tortillas with the broccoli mixture, rolling them up. Arrange the tortilla rolls in an ovenproof dish, then pour the Mild Red Chilli Sauce over the top. Pour over the stock.

5 Top with the remaining Cheddar and Parmesan cheeses and bake in a preheated oven at 190°C/375°F/Gas Mark 5 for about 30 minutes. Serve the enchiladas sprinkled with the chopped onion, fresh coriander and diced tomatoes. Serve with a hot salsa.

Potatoes with Goat's Cheese

This makes a really hearty and satisfying vegetarian main course.
Goat's cheese is a traditional food of Mexico.

NUTRITIONAL INFORMATION

Calories 725   Sugars 4g
Protein ....30g   Fat 43g
Carbohydrate ...56g   Saturates 28g

2 mins   35 mins

SERVES 4

INGREDIENTS

1.25 kg/2 lb 12 oz baking potatoes, peeled and cut into chunks

pinch of salt

pinch of sugar

200 ml/7 fl oz crème fraîche

125 ml/4 fl oz vegetable stock

3 garlic cloves, finely chopped

a few shakes of bottled chipotle salsa, or 1 dried chipotle, reconstituted, deseeded and thinly sliced

225 g/8 oz goat's cheese, sliced

175 g/6 oz mozzarella or Cheddar cheese, grated

55 g/2 oz Parmesan or pecorino cheese, grated

goat's cheese. Top with the remaining potatoes and sauce.

4 Sprinkle with the grated mozzarella or Cheddar cheese, then with the grated Parmesan or pecorino.

5 Bake in a preheated oven, 180°C/350°F/Gas Mark 4, for about 25 minutes, until the potatoes are tender and the cheese topping is lightly golden and has become crisp in places. Serve immediately, straight from the casserole.

1 Put the potatoes in a pan of water with the salt and sugar. Bring to the boil and cook for about 10 minutes until they are half cooked.

2 Combine the crème fraîche with the stock, garlic and chipotle salsa.

3 Arrange half the potatoes in a casserole. Pour half the crème fraîche sauce over the potatoes and cover with the

Spicy Black-eyed Beans

This is a hearty casserole of black-eyed beans in a rich, sweet tomato sauce flavoured with treacle and mustard.

NUTRITIONAL INFORMATION

Calories 233   Sugars 21g
Protein ....11g   Fat 4g
Carbohydrate ...42g   Saturates 1g

 15 mins   2 hrs

SERVES 4

I N G R E D I E N T S

350 g/12 oz dried black-eyed beans,
  soaked overnight in cold water

1 tbsp vegetable oil

2 onions, chopped

1 tbsp clear honey

2 tbsp treacle

4 tbsp dark soy sauce

1 tsp mustard powder

4 tbsp tomato purée

450 ml/16 fl oz vegetable stock

1 bay leaf

1 sprig each fresh rosemary, thyme and
  sage

1 small orange

pepper

1 tbsp cornflour

2 red peppers, deseeded and diced

2 tbsp chopped fresh flat-leaf parsley,
  to garnish

crusty bread, to serve

1 Rinse the beans and place in a saucepan. Cover with water, bring to the boil and boil rapidly for 5 minutes. Drain and place in a casserole.

2 Meanwhile, heat the oil in a frying pan. Add the onions and fry over a low heat, stirring occasionally, for 5 minutes. Stir in the honey, treacle, soy sauce, mustard and tomato purée. Pour in the vegetable stock, bring to the boil and pour over the beans in the casserole.

3 Tie the bay leaf and herbs together with a clean piece of string and add to the casserole. Using a vegetable peeler, pare off 3 pieces of orange rind and mix into the beans, along with plenty of pepper. Cover and cook in a preheated oven, 150°C/300°F/Gas Mark 2, for 1 hour.

4 Squeeze the juice from the orange and blend with the cornflour to form a smooth paste. Stir into the beans, together with the red peppers.

5 Cover the casserole and return to the oven for 1 hour, until the sauce is rich and thick and the beans are very tender. Remove and discard the herbs and the orange rind.

6 Garnish with chopped parsley and serve immediately with crusty bread.

Lentil & Red Pepper Flan

This savoury flan combines lentils and red peppers in a tasty wholemeal pastry case. This flan is suitable for vegans.

NUTRITIONAL INFORMATION

Calories 374	Sugars 5g	
Protein 13g	Fat 17g	
Carbohydrate ...44g	Saturates 7g	

15–20 mins   50 mins

SERVES 6

INGREDIENTS

PASTRY

225 g/8 oz wholemeal flour

100 g/3½ oz vegan margarine, cut into small pieces

4 tbsp water

FILLING

175 g/6 oz red lentils, rinsed

300 ml/½ pint vegetable stock

1 tbsp vegan margarine

1 onion, chopped

2 red peppers, deseeded and diced

1 tsp yeast extract

1 tbsp tomato purée

3 tbsp chopped fresh parsley

pepper

1 To make the pastry, sift the flour into a mixing bowl and tip in the bran remaining in the sieve. Add the vegan margarine and rub in with your fingertips until the mixture resembles fine breadcrumbs. Stir in the water and bring together to form a dough. Wrap and chill in the refrigerator for 30 minutes.

2 Meanwhile, make the filling. Put the lentils in a saucepan with the stock, bring to the boil and then simmer for 10 minutes until the lentils are tender and can be mashed to a purée.

3 Melt the margarine in a small pan, add the chopped onion and diced red peppers and fry until just soft.

4 Add the lentil purée, yeast extract, tomato purée and parsley. Season to taste with pepper. Mix until thoroughly combined.

5 On a lightly floured surface, roll out the dough and line a 24 cm/9½ inch loose-bottomed flan tin. Prick the base of the pastry with a fork and spoon the lentil mixture into the pastry case.

6 Bake in a preheated oven, 200°C/ 400°F/Gas Mark 6, for 30 minutes until the filling is firm.

VARIATION
Add sweetcorn kernels to the flan in step 4 for a colourful and tasty change, if you prefer.

Artichoke & Cheese Tart

Artichoke hearts are delicious to eat and are delicate in flavour and appearance. They are ideal for cooking in a cheese-flavoured pastry case.

NUTRITIONAL INFORMATION

Calories	276	Sugars	.........3g
Protein	........10g	Fat	..........19g
Carbohydrate	...18g	Saturates	......10g

 15 mins   30 mins

SERVES 8

INGREDIENTS

175 g/6 oz wholemeal flour, plus extra for dusting

pinch of salt

2 garlic cloves, crushed

6 tbsp butter or margarine

3 tbsp water

FILLING

2 tbsp olive oil

1 red onion, halved and sliced

10 canned artichoke hearts

100 g/3½ oz Cheddar cheese, grated

55 g/2 oz Gorgonzola cheese, crumbled

2 eggs, beaten

1 tbsp chopped fresh rosemary

150 ml/5 fl oz milk

salt and pepper

1 To make the pastry, sift the flour into a mixing bowl, add a pinch of salt and the crushed garlic. Rub in the butter or margarine with the fingertips until the mixture resembles fine breadcrumbs. Stir in the water and bring the mixture together to form a dough.

2 Roll out the pastry on a lightly floured surface to fit a 20 cm/8 inch flan tin. Prick the pastry with a fork.

3 Heat the oil in a frying pan. Add the onion and cook over a medium heat, stirring occasionally, for 3 minutes. Add the artichoke hearts and cook, stirring frequently, for a further 2 minutes.

4 Combine the Cheddar, Gorgonzola, beaten eggs, rosemary and milk in a large bowl. Remove the artichoke and onion mixture from the pan with a draining spoon and transfer to the cheese mixture, stirring gently. Season to taste with salt and pepper.

5 Spoon the artichoke and cheese mixture into the pastry case and cook in a preheated oven, 200°C/400°F/Gas Mark 6, for 25 minutes or until cooked and set. Remove the flan from the oven and serve hot or cold.

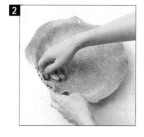

Mushroom Vol-au-Vent

A simple mixture of creamy, tender mushrooms filling a crisp, rich pastry case, this dish will make an impression at any dinner party.

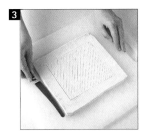
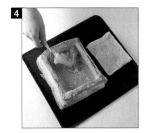

NUTRITIONAL INFORMATION

Calories 688	Sugars 2g
Protein 10g	Fat 52g
Carbohydrate ...45g	Saturates 22g

25 mins   50 mins

SERVES 4

INGREDIENTS

500 g/1 lb 2 oz puff pastry, thawed if frozen

1 egg, beaten, for glazing

FILLING

25 g/1 oz butter or margarine

750 g/1 lb 10 oz mixed mushrooms, such as open-cap, field, button, chestnut, shiitake, pied de mouton, sliced

6 tbsp dry white wine

4 tbsp double cream

2 tbsp chopped fresh chervil

salt and pepper

fresh chervil sprigs, to garnish

1 Roll out the puff pastry on a lightly floured surface to make a 20 cm/ 8 inch square.

2 Using a sharp knife, mark a square 2.5 cm/1 inch from the pastry edge, cutting halfway through the pastry.

3 Score the top in a diagonal pattern. Knock up the edges with a kitchen knife and put on a baking tray. Brush the top with beaten egg, taking care not to let the egg run into the cut. Bake in a preheated oven, 220°C/ 425°F/Gas Mark 7, for 35 minutes.

4 Cut out the central square. Discard the soft pastry inside the case, leaving the base intact. Return to the oven, with the square, for 10 minutes.

5 Meanwhile, make the filling. Melt the butter or margarine in a frying pan and stir-fry the sliced mushrooms over a high heat for 3 minutes.

6 Add the wine and cook, stirring occasionally, for 10 minutes, until the mushrooms have softened. Stir in the cream and chervil and season to taste with salt and pepper.

7 Pile into the pastry case. Top with the pastry square, garnish with sprigs of chervil and serve.

Spinach & Ricotta Pie

This puff pastry pie looks impressive, but it is actually fairly easy and quite quick to make. Serve it hot or cold.

NUTRITIONAL INFORMATION

Calories ....545 Sugars 3g
Protein ....19g Fat 42g
Carbohydrate ...25g Saturates 13g

25 mins   50 mins

SERVES 4

INGREDIENTS

225 g/8 oz fresh spinach

25 g/1 oz pine kernels

100 g/3½ oz ricotta cheese

2 large eggs, beaten

50 g/1¾ oz ground almonds

40 g/1½ oz Parmesan cheese,
  freshly grated

250 g/9 oz puff pastry, defrosted if frozen

1 small egg, beaten

1 Rinse the spinach, place in a large pan and cook with just the water clinging to the leaves for 4–5 minutes until wilted. Drain thoroughly. When the spinach is cool enough to handle, squeeze out the excess liquid.

2 Place the pine kernels on a baking tray and lightly toast under a preheated grill for 2–3 minutes or until golden brown.

3 Place the ricotta, spinach and eggs in a bowl and mix together. Add the pine kernels, beat well, then stir in the ground almonds and Parmesan cheese.

4 Roll out the puff pastry and make 2 squares, 20 cm/8 inches wide. Trim the edges, reserving the pastry trimmings.

5 Place 1 pastry square on a baking tray. Spoon over the spinach mixture

to within 1 cm/½ inch of the edge of the pastry. Brush the edges with beaten egg and place the second square over the top.

6 Using a round-bladed knife, press the pastry edges together by tapping along the sealed edge. Use the pastry trimmings to make a few leaves to decorate the pie.

7 Brush the pie with the beaten egg and bake in a preheated oven, 220°C/425°F/Gas Mark 8, for 10 minutes. Reduce the oven temperature to 190°C/375°F/Gas Mark 5 and bake for a further 25–30 minutes. Serve hot.

COOK'S TIP

Spinach must be washed very thoroughly in several changes of water to get rid of the grit and soil that can be trapped in it. Cut off any thick central ribs.

Cheese-topped Risotto Tart

Risotto, combined with spinach and cheese, makes a mouth-watering filling for this tart.

NUTRITIONAL INFORMATION

Calories	827	Sugars	.........4g
Protein	........29g	Fat	..........48g
Carbohydrate	...72g	Saturates	......30g

15 mins, plus chilling   35 mins

SERVES 6–8

INGREDIENTS

190 g/6½ oz plain flour

½ tsp salt

1 tsp caster sugar

115 g/4 oz unsalted butter, diced

1 egg yolk, beaten with 2 tbsp iced water

FILLING

1 quantity Basic Cheesy Rice with Parmesan (see page 9), still warm

250 g/9 oz fresh spinach, cooked, drained very well and chopped

2 tbsp double cream

225 g/8 oz mozzarella, preferably buffalo

85 g/3 oz Parmesan cheese, freshly grated

1 To make the shortcrust pastry, sift the flour, salt and sugar into a large bowl and sprinkle over the butter. Rub the butter into the flour until the mixture forms coarse crumbs. Sprinkle in the egg mixture and stir to make a dough.

2 Gather the dough into a ball, wrap in clingfilm and chill for at least 1 hour.

3 Gently roll out the pastry to a thickness of about 3 mm/⅛ inch, then use to line a lightly greased tart tin (23–25 cm/ 9–10 inch) with a removable base. Prick the bottom with a fork and chill for 1 hour.

4 Cover the tart case with baking paper and fill with baking beans. Bake blind in a preheated oven at 200°C/400°F/Gas Mark 6 for about 20 minutes until the pastry is set and the edge is golden. Remove the beans and paper and set aside. Reduce the oven temperature to 180°C/350°F/Gas Mark 4.

5 Put the cheesy rice in a bowl and stir in the spinach, cream, half the mozzarella and half the Parmesan. Spoon into the tart case and smooth the top. Sprinkle evenly with the remaining cheeses.

6 Bake for 12–15 minutes or until cooked through and golden. Remove the tart from the oven, cool slightly on a wire rack, then serve warm.

Basic Pizza Dough

Traditionally, pizza bases are made from bread dough; this recipe will give you a base similar to an Italian pizza.

NUTRITIONAL INFORMATION

Calories ....182 Sugars 2g
Protein ....5g Fat 3g
Carbohydrate ...36g Saturates 0.5g

🕐 1½ hrs   🕐 0 mins

SERVES 4

INGREDIENTS

15 g/½ oz fresh yeast or 1 tsp dried or
easy-blend yeast

6 tbsp lukewarm water

½ tsp sugar

1 tbsp olive oil

175 g/6 oz plain flour, plus extra for dusting

1 tsp salt

1 Combine the fresh yeast with the water and sugar in a bowl. If using dried yeast, sprinkle it over the surface of the water and whisk in until dissolved.

2 Set the yeast mixture aside in a warm place for 10–15 minutes until frothy on the surface. Stir in the olive oil.

3 Sift the flour and salt into a large bowl. If using easy-blend yeast, stir it in. Make a well in the centre and pour in the yeast liquid, or water and oil (without the sugar for easy-blend yeast).

4 Using either floured hands or a wooden spoon, mix together to form a dough. Turn out on to a floured work surface and knead for about 5 minutes or until smooth and elastic.

5 Place the dough in a large greased plastic bag and set aside in a warm place for about 1 hour or until doubled in size. An airing cupboard is often the best place for this process, as the temperature remains constant.

6 Turn out on to a lightly floured work surface and 'knock back' by punching the dough. This releases any trapped air bubbles which would make the pizza uneven. Knead 4 or 5 times. The dough is now ready to use.

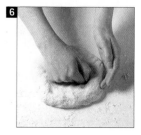

Scone Base

This is a quicker alternative to a bread dough base for pizza. If you do not have time to wait for bread dough to rise, a scone base is ideal.

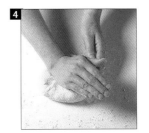

NUTRITIONAL INFORMATION

Calories 215	Sugars 3g	
Protein 5g	Fat 7g	
Carbohydrate . . .35g	Saturates 4g	

20 mins   0 mins

SERVES 4

INGREDIENTS

175 g/6 oz self-raising flour

½ tsp salt

25 g/1 oz butter

125 ml/4 fl oz milk

1 Sift the flour and salt into a large mixing bowl.

2 Rub in the butter with your fingertips until it resembles fine breadcrumbs.

3 Make a well in the centre of the flour and butter mixture and pour in nearly all of the milk at once. Mix in quickly with a knife. Add the remaining milk only if necessary to mix to a soft dough.

4 Turn the dough out on to a floured work surface and knead by turning and pressing with the heel of your hand 3 or 4 times.

5 Either roll out or press the dough into a 25 cm/10 inch circle on a lightly greased baking tray or pizza pan. Push up the edge slightly all round to form a ridge and use immediately.

Potato Base

This is an unusual pizza base made from mashed potatoes and flour and is a great way to use up any left-over boiled potatoes.

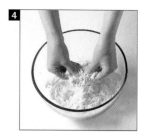

NUTRITIONAL INFORMATION

Calories 170	Sugars 1g	
Protein 4g	Fat 3g	
Carbohydrate . . .34g	Saturates 1g	

 15 mins   0 mins

SERVES 4

INGREDIENTS

225 g/8 oz boiled potatoes

60 g/2 oz butter or margarine

125 g/4½ oz self-raising flour

½ tsp salt

1 If the potatoes are hot, mash them, then stir in the butter until melted and distributed evenly throughout the potatoes. Leave to cool.

2 Sift the flour and salt together and stir into the mashed potato to form a soft dough.

3 If the potatoes are cold, mash them without adding the butter.

4 Sift the flour and salt into a bowl. Rub in the butter with your fingertips until the mixture resembles fine breadcrumbs, then stir the flour and butter mixture into the mashed potatoes to form a soft dough.

5 This potato base is rather tricky to lift before it is cooked, so it is better to roll it out directly on to the baking tray. Press the dough into a 25 cm/10 inch circle on a lightly greased baking tray or pizza pan, pushing up the edge slightly all round to form a ridge before adding the topping of your choice.

6 If the base is not required for cooking immediately, cover it with cling film and chill it for up to 2 hours.

Tomato Sauce

This is a basic topping sauce for pizzas. Using canned chopped tomatoes for this dish saves time.

NUTRITIONAL INFORMATION

Calories 41	Sugars 3g
Protein 1g	Fat 3g
Carbohydrate 3g	Saturates 0.4g

 5 mins 25 mins

SERVES 4

I N G R E D I E N T S

1 small onion, chopped

1 garlic clove, crushed

1 tbsp olive oil

200 g/7 oz canned chopped tomatoes

2 tsp tomato purée

½ tsp sugar

½ tsp dried oregano

1 bay leaf

salt and pepper

1 Fry the onion and garlic gently in the oil for 5 minutes or until softened but not browned.

2 Add the tomatoes, tomato purée, sugar, oregano, bay leaf and salt and pepper to taste. Stir well.

3 Bring the sauce to the boil, cover and leave to simmer gently for 20 minutes, stirring occasionally, until you have a thickish sauce.

4 Remove the bay leaf. Leave to cool completely before using. This sauce keeps well in a screw-top jar in the refrigerator for up to 1 week.

Special Tomato Sauce

This sauce is made with fresh tomatoes. Use the plum variety whenever available and always choose the ripest ones for the best flavour.

NUTRITIONAL INFORMATION

Calories	81	Sugars	.........6g
Protein	.........1g	Fat	...........6g
Carbohydrate	....6g	Saturates	.......1g

10 mins   35 mins

SERVES 4

INGREDIENTS

1 small onion, chopped

1 small red pepper, deseeded and chopped

1 garlic clove, crushed

2 tbsp olive oil

225 g/8 oz tomatoes

1 tbsp tomato purée

1 tsp soft brown sugar

2 tsp chopped fresh basil

½ tsp dried oregano

1 bay leaf

salt and pepper

4 Add the tomatoes to the onion mixture along with the tomato purée, sugar, herbs and seasoning to taste. Stir well. Bring to the boil, cover and leave to simmer gently for about 30 minutes, stirring occasionally, until you have a thickish sauce.

5 Remove the bay leaf and adjust the seasoning to taste. Leave to cool completely before using.

6 This sauce will keep well stored in a screw-top jar in the refrigerator for up to 1 week.

1 Fry the onion, pepper and garlic gently in the oil for 5 minutes until softened but not browned.

2 Cut a cross in the base of each tomato and place them in a bowl. Pour on boiling water and leave for about 45 seconds. Drain, and then plunge in cold water. The skins will slide off easily.

3 Chop the tomatoes, discarding any hard green cores.

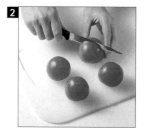

Pizza Margherita

Pizza means 'pie' in Italian. The fresh bread dough is not difficult to make but it does take a little time.

NUTRITIONAL INFORMATION

Calories 456	Sugars 7g	
Protein 16g	Fat 13g	
Carbohydrate ...74g	Saturates 5g	

1 hr   45 mins

SERVES 4

INGREDIENTS

PIZZA DOUGH

15 g/½ oz fresh yeast

½ tsp sugar

6 tbsp hand-hot water

1 tbsp olive oil

175 g/6 oz plain flour

1 tsp salt

TOPPING

400 g/14 oz canned chopped tomatoes

2 garlic cloves, crushed

2 tsp dried basil

1 tbsp olive oil

2 tbsp tomato purée

100 g/3½ oz mozzarella cheese, diced

35 g/1¼ oz Parmesan cheese, freshly grated

salt and pepper

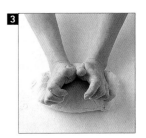

1 Mix together the yeast, sugar and 4 tablespoons of the water. Leave the yeast mixture in a warm place for 15 minutes or until frothy.

2 Mix the flour and salt and make a well in the centre. Add the oil, yeast mixture and remaining water. Mix to form a smooth dough.

3 Turn the dough out on to a floured surface and knead for 4–5 minutes or until smooth.

4 Return the dough to the bowl, cover with an oiled sheet of clingfilm and leave to rise for 30 minutes or until doubled in size.

5 Knead the dough for 2 minutes. Stretch the dough with your hands, then place it on an oiled baking tray, pushing out the edges until it forms an even circle. It should be no more than about 5 mm/¼ inch thick because it will rise during cooking.

6 To make the topping, place the chopped canned tomatoes, crushed garlic, dried basil and olive oil in a large, heavy-based frying pan and season to taste with salt and pepper. Simmer the mixture over a low heat for 20 minutes or until the sauce has thickened. Stir in the tomato purée, remove the pan from the heat and leave to cool slightly.

7 Spread the tomato topping evenly over the pizza base, almost to the rim. Top with the diced mozzarella and grated Parmesan cheese and bake in a preheated oven, 200°C/400°F/Gas Mark 6, for 20–25 minutes. Serve the pizza hot.

Mushroom Pizza

Juicy mushrooms and stringy mozzarella top this tomato-based pizza.
Use wild mushrooms or a combination of wild and cultivated mushrooms.

NUTRITIONAL INFORMATION

Calories 302	Sugars 7g	
Protein 10g	Fat 12g	
Carbohydrate . . .41g	Saturates 4g	

 1¼ hrs   45 mins

SERVES 4

INGREDIENTS

1 quantity Basic Pizza Dough
(see page 602)

TOPPING

200 g/7 oz mushrooms

400g/14 oz canned chopped tomatoes

2 garlic cloves, crushed

1 tsp dried basil

1 tbsp olive oil

salt and pepper

2 tbsp tomato purée

150 g/5½ oz mozzarella cheese, grated

fresh basil leaves, to garnish

1 Using a rolling pin, roll out the pizza dough to form an oval or a circular shape, then place it on a lightly oiled baking tray, pushing out the edges until even. The dough should be no more than about 5 mm/¼ inch thick because it will rise during cooking.

2 With a sharp knife, cut the mushrooms into fairly thin slices.

3 To make the topping, place the tomatoes, garlic, dried basil and olive oil in a large, heavy-based frying pan and season to taste with salt and pepper. Simmer over a low heat for 20 minutes or until the sauce has thickened. Stir in the tomato purée, remove the pan from the heat and leave to cool slightly.

4 Spread the sauce over the base of the pizza, top with the mushrooms and scatter over the mozzarella. Bake in a preheated oven, 200°C/400°F/Gas Mark 6, for 25 minutes. Garnish with basil leaves.

COOK'S TIP

An easy way to intensify the mushroom flavour is to add a few dried porcini that have been soaked in hot water to the topping. Although they are expensive, you need only a few as the flavour is very concentrated.

Gorgonzola & Pumpkin Pizza

A combination of blue Gorgonzola cheese, pumpkin and pears creates a colourful pizza. The wholemeal base adds a nutty flavour and texture.

NUTRITIONAL INFORMATION

Calories 470	Sugars 5g
Protein 17g	Fat 15g
Carbohydrate . . .72g	Saturates 6g

 1¼ hrs   35 mins

SERVES 4

INGREDIENTS

PIZZA DOUGH

7 g/¼ oz dried yeast

1 tsp sugar

250 ml/8 fl oz hand-hot water

175 g/6 oz strong plain wholemeal flour

175 g/6 oz strong plain white flour

1 tsp salt

1 tbsp olive oil

TOPPING

400 g/14 oz pumpkin or squash, peeled and cubed

1 tbsp olive oil

1 pear, cored, peeled and sliced

100 g/3½ oz Gorgonzola cheese

1 sprig fresh rosemary, to garnish

1 Place the dried yeast and sugar in a measuring jug and mix with 4 tablespoons of the water. Leave the yeast mixture in a warm place for about 15 minutes or until frothy.

2 Mix the wholemeal and plain flour together with the salt and make a well in the centre. Add the oil, the yeast mixture and the remaining water. Using a wooden spoon, mix to form a dough.

3 Turn the dough out on to a floured surface and knead it for about 4–5 minutes or until smooth.

4 Return the dough to the bowl, cover with an oiled sheet of clingfilm and leave to rise for 30 minutes or until doubled in size.

5 Remove the dough from the bowl. Knead the dough for 2 minutes. Using a rolling pin, roll out the dough to form a long oval shape, then place it on an oiled baking tray, pushing out the edges until even. The dough should be no more than 5 mm/¼ inch thick because it will rise during cooking.

6 To make the topping, place the pumpkin in a shallow roasting tin. Drizzle with the olive oil and cook under a preheated grill for 20 minutes or until soft and lightly golden.

7 Top the dough with the pear and the pumpkin, brushing with the oil from the tin. Crumble over the Gorgonzola. Bake in a preheated oven, 200°C/400°F/ Gas Mark 6, for 15 minutes or until the base is golden. Garnish with rosemary.

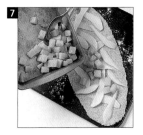

Roasted Vegetable Pizza

Wonderfully colourful vegetables are roasted in olive oil with thyme and garlic. The goat's cheese adds a nutty, piquant flavour.

NUTRITIONAL INFORMATION

Calories	387	Sugars	.........9g
Protein	........10g	Fat	..........21g
Carbohydrate	...42g	Saturates	.......5g

2½ hrs   40 mins

SERVES 4

INGREDIENTS

2 baby courgettes, halved lengthways

2 baby aubergines, quartered lengthways

½ red pepper, deseeded and cut into 4 strips

½ yellow pepper, deseeded and cut into 4 strips

1 small red onion, cut into wedges

2 garlic cloves, unpeeled

4 tbsp olive oil

1 tbsp red wine vinegar

1 tbsp chopped fresh thyme

salt and pepper

1 quantity Basic Pizza Dough (see page 602)

Tomato Sauce (see page 605)

90 g/3 oz goat's cheese

fresh basil leaves, to garnish

1 Place all of the prepared vegetables in a large roasting tin. Mix together the olive oil, vinegar, thyme and plenty of seasoning and pour over, coating well.

2 Roast the vegetables in a preheated oven, at 200°C/400°F/Gas Mark 6, for 15–20 minutes or until the skins have started to blacken in places, turning them over half-way through. Leave to rest for 5 minutes after roasting.

3 Carefully peel off the skins from the roast peppers and the garlic cloves. Slice the garlic.

4 Roll out or press the dough, using a rolling pin or your hands, into a 25 cm/10 inch circle on a lightly floured work surface. Place on a large greased baking tray or pizza pan and raise the edge a little to make a rim. Cover and leave for 10 minutes to rise slightly in a warm place. Spread with the tomato sauce almost to the edge.

5 Arrange the roasted vegetables on top and dot with the cheese. Drizzle the oil and juices from the roasting tin over the pizza and season.

6 Bake in a preheated oven, at 200°C/400°F/Gas Mark 6, for 18–20 minutes, or until the edge is crisp and golden. Serve immediately, garnished with basil leaves.

Pepper & Red Onion Pizza

The vibrant colours of the peppers and onion make this a delightful pizza.
Served cut into fingers, it is ideal for a party or buffet.

NUTRITIONAL INFORMATION

Calories 380   Sugars 19g
Protein . . . . .7g   Fat 17g
Carbohydrate . . .53g   Saturates 2g

25 mins   25 mins

SERVES 8

INGREDIENTS

1 quantity Basic Pizza Dough
(see page 602)

2 tbsp olive oil, plus extra for drizzling

½ red pepper, deseeded and thinly sliced

½ green pepper, deseeded and thinly sliced

½ yellow pepper, deseeded and
thinly sliced

1 small red onion, thinly sliced

1 garlic clove, crushed

Tomato Sauce (see page 605)

3 tbsp raisins

4 tbsp pine kernels

1 tbsp chopped fresh thyme

salt and pepper

1 Roll out or press the dough, using a rolling pin or your hands, on a lightly floured work surface to fit a 30 x 18 cm/ 12 x 7 inch greased Swiss roll tin. Place the dough in the tin and push up the edges slightly to make a rim.

2 Cover with clingfilm and set the dough aside in a warm place for about 10 minutes to rise slightly.

3 Heat the oil in a large frying pan. Add the peppers, onion and garlic and cook gently for 5 minutes until they have softened. Set aside to cool.

4 Spread the tomato sauce over the base of the pizza almost to the edge.

5 Sprinkle over the raisins and top with the cooled pepper mixture. Add the pine kernels and thyme. Drizzle with a little olive oil and season to taste with salt and pepper.

6 Bake in a preheated oven, 200°C/ 400°F/Gas Mark 6, for 18–20 minutes, or until the edges are crisp and golden. Cut into fingers and serve immediately.

Mushroom & Walnut Pizza

Wild mushrooms make a delicious pizza topping when mixed with walnuts and Roquefort cheese.

NUTRITIONAL INFORMATION

Calories 499   Sugars 9g
Protein . . . . .13g   Fat 32g
Carbohydrate . . .42g   Saturates 11g

 10 mins   25 mins

SERVES 4

I N G R E D I E N T S

1 quantity Basic Pizza Dough (see page 602) or 1 x 25 cm/10 inch pizza base

Tomato Sauce (see page 605)

115 g/4 oz soft cheese

1 tbsp chopped fresh mixed herbs, such as parsley, oregano and basil

225 g/8 oz wild mushrooms, such as oyster, shiitake or ceps, or 115 g/4 oz each wild and button mushrooms

2 tbsp olive oil, plus extra for drizzling

¼ tsp fennel seeds

4 tbsp roughly chopped walnuts

40 g/1½ oz blue cheese

salt and pepper

fresh flat-leaved parsley sprig, to garnish

1 Roll out or press the pizza dough, using a rolling pin or your hands, into a 25 cm/10 inch circle on a lightly floured work surface.

2 Place the pizza base on a large greased baking sheet or pizza pan and push up the edge a little with your fingers to form a rim.

3 Carefully spread the tomato sauce almost to the edge of the pizza base. Dot with the soft cheese and chopped fresh herbs.

4 Wipe and slice the mushrooms. Heat the oil in a large frying pan or wok and stir-fry the mushrooms and fennel seeds for 2–3 minutes. Spread over the pizza with the chopped walnuts.

5 Crumble the blue cheese over the pizza, drizzle with a little olive oil and season with salt and pepper to taste.

6 Bake in a preheated oven, 200°C/400°F/Gas Mark 6, for 18–20 minutes or until the edge is crisp and golden.

7 Serve the pizza immediately, garnished with a sprig of flat-leaved parsley.

Florentine Pizza

A pizza adaptation of Eggs Florentine – sliced hard-boiled eggs on freshly cooked spinach, with a crunchy almond topping.

NUTRITIONAL INFORMATION

Calories	474	Sugars	.........7g
Protein	........19g	Fat	..........26g
Carbohydrate	...43g	Saturates	.....7.5g

 20 mins   20 mins

SERVES 4

I N G R E D I E N T S

1 quantity Basic Pizza Dough (see page 602) or 1 x 25 cm/10 inch pizza base

3 tbsp olive oil, plus extra for drizzling

2 tbsp freshly grated Parmesan cheese

Tomato Sauce (see page 605)

175 g/6 oz fresh spinach

1 small red onion, thinly sliced

¼ tsp freshly grated nutmeg

2 hard-boiled eggs

15 g/½ oz fresh white breadcrumbs

55 g/2 oz Jarlsberg, Cheddar or Gruyère cheese, grated

2 tbsp flaked almonds

salt and pepper

1 Roll out or press the dough, using a rolling pin or your hands, into a 25 cm/10 inch circle on a lightly floured work surface. Brush with the olive oil and sprinkle with the Parmesan. Place on a large greased baking sheet or pizza pan and push up the edge slightly. Spread the tomato sauce almost to the edge.

2 Remove the stalks from the spinach and wash the leaves thoroughly in plenty of cold water. Drain well and pat off the excess water with kitchen paper.

3 Heat the remaining oil and cook the onion for 5 minutes until softened. Add the spinach and cook until just wilted. Drain off any excess liquid. Arrange on the pizza and sprinkle over the nutmeg.

4 Shell and slice the eggs. Arrange the slices of egg on top of the spinach.

5 Combine the breadcrumbs, cheese and almonds and sprinkle over. Drizzle with a little olive oil and season to taste.

6 Bake in a preheated oven, 200°C/ 400°F/Gas Mark 6, for 18–20 minutes, or until the edge is crisp and golden. Serve the pizza immediately.

Tomato & Ricotta Pizza

This is a traditional dish from the Calabrian Mountains in southern Italy, where it is made with naturally sun-dried tomatoes and ricotta cheese.

NUTRITIONAL INFORMATION

Calories . . . . . . .274 Sugars 4g
Protein . . . . .8g Fat 11g
Carbohydrate . . .38g Saturates 4g

 1¼ hrs   30 mins

SERVES 4

INGREDIENTS

1 quantity Basic Pizza Dough
(see page 602)

TOPPING

4 tbsp sun-dried tomato purée

150g/5½ oz ricotta cheese

10 sun-dried tomatoes bottled in
oil, drained

1 tbsp fresh thyme leaves

salt and pepper

COOK'S TIP

Sun-dried tomatoes are also available dried, in packets. Before using, soak them in hot water until they are soft. Keep the tomato-flavoured soaking water to use in soups or sauces.

1 Roll out the dough to form a circle, then transfer it to a lightly oiled baking tray, pushing out the edges until it forms an even circle. The dough should be no more than about 5 mm/¼ inch thick because it will rise during cooking.

2 Spread the sun-dried tomato purée evenly over the dough, then dot spoonfuls of ricotta cheese on top.

3 Cut the sun-dried tomatoes into thin strips and arrange these over the top of the pizza.

4 Finally, sprinkle the fresh thyme leaves over the top of the pizza and season with salt and pepper to taste. Bake in a preheated oven, 200°C/400°F/Gas Mark 6, for 30 minutes or until the crust is golden. Serve the pizza hot.

Giardiniera Pizza

As the name implies, this colourful pizza should be topped with fresh vegetables from the garden, especially in the summer months.

NUTRITIONAL INFORMATION

Calories	362	Sugars	........10g
Protein	........13g	Fat	..........15g
Carbohydrate	...48g	Saturates	.......5g

15 mins   20 mins

SERVES 4

INGREDIENTS

6 fresh spinach leaves

1 quantity Basic Pizza Dough (see page 602) or 1 x 25 cm/10 inch pizza base

Tomato Sauce (see page 605)

1 tomato, sliced

1 celery stick, thinly sliced

½ green pepper, deseeded and thinly sliced

1 baby courgette, sliced

25 g/1 oz asparagus tips

25 g/1 oz sweetcorn, thawed if frozen

4 tbsp peas, thawed if frozen

4 spring onions, trimmed and chopped

1 tbsp chopped fresh mixed herbs

55 g/2 oz mozzarella cheese, grated

2 tbsp freshly grated Parmesan cheese

1 canned artichoke heart

olive oil, for drizzling

salt and pepper

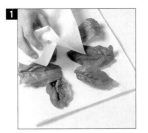

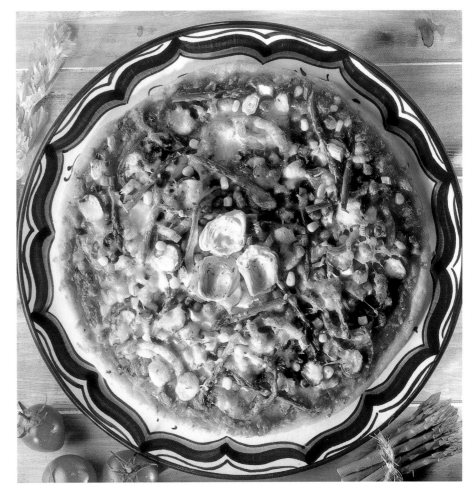

1 Remove any tough stalks from the spinach and wash the leaves in cold water. Pat dry with kitchen paper.

2 Roll out or press the pizza dough, using a rolling pin or your hands, into a 25 cm/10 inch circle on a lightly floured work surface. Place the round on a large greased baking sheet or pizza pan and push up the edge a little. Spread with the tomato sauce.

3 Arrange the spinach leaves on the sauce, followed by the tomato slices. Top with the remaining vegetables and the fresh mixed herbs.

4 Combine the cheeses and sprinkle over the pizza. Place the artichoke heart in the centre. Drizzle the pizza with a little olive oil and season to taste.

5 Bake the pizza in a preheated oven at 200°C/400°F/Gas Mark 6, for 18–20 minutes or until the edges are crisp and golden brown. Serve immediately.

Pizza Biancas

Simple, fresh flavours are the highlight of this thin pizza. For the best results, use buffalo mozzarella imported from Italy.

NUTRITIONAL INFORMATION

Calories 1191	Sugars 5g
Protein 60g	Fat 40g
Carbohydrate . .158g	Saturates 21g

🍳🍳🍳

🍲 1½ hrs   🕐 15 mins

MAKES TWO 23 CM/9 INCH PIZZAS

I N G R E D I E N T S

400 g/14 oz plain flour, plus extra
  for dusting

1 sachet easy-blend dried yeast

1 tsp salt

1 tbsp extra virgin olive oil, plus extra
  for greasing

T O P P I N G

2 courgettes

300 g/10½ oz buffalo mozzarella cheese

1½–2 tbsp finely chopped fresh rosemary,
  or ½ tbsp dried rosemary

1 To make the base, heat 225 ml/8 fl oz water in the microwave on HIGH power for 1 minute or until it reads 52°C/125°F on an instant-read thermometer. Alternatively, heat the water in a pan over a low heat until lukewarm.

2 Stir the flour, yeast and salt together and make a well in the centre. Stir in most of the water with the olive oil to make a dough. Add the remaining water, if necessary, to form a soft dough.

3 Turn out on to a lightly floured surface and knead for about 10 minutes until smooth but still soft. Wash the bowl and lightly coat with olive oil. Shape the dough into a ball, put in the bowl and turn the

dough over so it is coated. Cover and set aside until doubled in size.

4 Turn the dough out on to a lightly floured surface. Quickly knead a few times, then cover with the upturned bowl and set aside for 10 minutes.

5 Meanwhile, using a vegetable peeler, cut long, thin strips of courgettes. Drain and dice the mozzarella.

6 Divide the dough in half and shape each half into a ball. Cover 1 ball and roll out the other into a 23 cm/9 inch

round. Place the round on a lightly floured baking sheet.

7 Scatter half the mozzarella over the base. Add half the courgette strips and sprinkle with half the rosemary. Repeat with the remaining dough and topping ingredients.

8 Bake in a preheated oven, 220°C/ 425°F/Gas Mark 7, for 15 minutes or until crispy. Serve immediately.

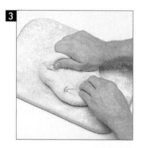
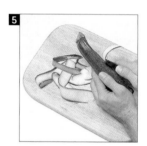

Ratatouille & Lentil Pizza

Ratatouille and lentils on a wholemeal bread base are topped with cheese and sunflower seeds for a really healthy pizza.

NUTRITIONAL INFORMATION

Calories 377   Sugars 6g
Protein . . . . .11g   Fat 19g
Carbohydrate . . .44g   Saturates 5g

2½ hrs   55 mins

SERVES 4

INGREDIENTS

60 g/2 oz green lentils

½ small aubergine, diced

1 small onion, sliced

1 garlic clove, crushed

3 tbsp olive oil

½ courgette, sliced

½ red pepper, deseeded and sliced

½ green pepper, deseeded and sliced

200 g/7 oz canned chopped tomatoes

1 tbsp chopped fresh oregano or 1 tsp dried

2 tbsp water

salt and pepper

1 quantity Basic Pizza Dough (see page 602), made with wholemeal flour

60 g/2 oz Cheddar, thinly sliced

1 tbsp sunflower seeds

olive oil, for drizzling

1 Soak the green lentils in hot water for 30 minutes. Drain and rinse; then cover with fresh water and simmer over a low heat for 10 minutes.

2 Place the aubergine in a colander, sprinkle with a little salt and leave the bitter juices to drain for about 20 minutes. Rinse well and pat dry with kitchen paper.

3 Fry the onion and garlic gently in the oil for 3 minutes. Add the courgette, peppers and aubergine. Cover and leave to cook over a low heat for about 5 minutes.

4 Add the chopped tomatoes, drained lentils, oregano, 2 tablespoons of water and seasoning. Cover and simmer for 15 minutes, stirring occasionally, adding more water if necessary.

5 Roll out or press the dough, using a rolling pin or your hands, into a 25 cm/10 inch circle on a lightly floured work surface. Place on a large greased baking tray or pizza pan and push up the edge slightly.

6 Cover and leave the dough to rise slightly for 10 minutes in a warm place.

7 Spread the ratatouille over the dough base almost to the edge. Arrange the cheese slices on top and sprinkle over the sunflower seeds. Drizzle with a little olive oil and season with a little salt and pepper to taste.

8 Bake in a preheated oven, at 200°C/400°F/Gas Mark 6, for 18–20 minutes, or until the edge is crisp and golden brown. Serve immediately.

Tofu & Corn Pizza

Chunks of tofu, marinated in ginger and soy sauce, impart something of an oriental flavour to this pizza.

NUTRITIONAL INFORMATION

Calories	596	Sugars	........17g
Protein	........33g	Fat	..........23g
Carbohydrate	...66g	Saturates	.......9g

1 hr   35 mins

SERVES 4

I N G R E D I E N T S

1 litre/1¾ pints milk

1 tsp salt

225 g/8 oz semolina

1 tbsp soy sauce

1 tbsp dry sherry

½ tsp grated fresh ginger root

250 g/9 oz tofu, cut into chunks

2 eggs

60 g/2 oz Parmesan cheese, grated

Tomato Sauce (see page 605)

25 g/1 oz baby sweetcorn, cut into 4

25 g/1 oz mangetouts, trimmed and
   cut into 4

4 spring onions, trimmed and cut into
   2.5 cm/1 inch strips

60 g/2 oz mozzarella, thinly sliced

2 tsp sesame oil

salt and pepper

2 Mix the soy sauce, sherry and ginger together in a bowl, add the tofu and stir gently to coat. Leave to marinate in a cool place for 20 minutes.

3 Beat the eggs with a little pepper. Add to the semolina with the Parmesan and mix well. Place on a large greased baking tray or pizza pan and pat into a 25 cm/10 inch round, using the back of a metal spoon. Spread the tomato sauce almost to the edge.

4 Blanch the sweetcorn and mangetouts in a saucepan of boiling water for 1 minute, drain thoroughly and place on the pizza with the drained tofu. Top with the spring onions and slices of cheese. Drizzle over the sesame oil and season with salt and pepper.

5 Bake in a preheated oven, at 200°C/ 400°F/Gas Mark 6, for 18–20 minutes, or until the edge is crisp and golden. Serve the pizza immediately.

1 Bring the milk to the boil with the salt. Sprinkle the semolina over the surface, stirring all the time. Cook for 10 minutes over a low heat, stirring occasionally, taking care not to let it burn. Remove from the heat and leave the mixture to cool until tepid.

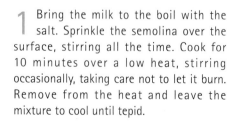

Tomato & Olive Pizzas

Halved ciabatta bread or baguettes are a ready-made pizza base.
The colours of the tomatoes and cheese contrast beautifully on top.

NUTRITIONAL INFORMATION

Calories 181	Sugars 4g
Protein 7g	Fat 10g
Carbohydrate . . .18g	Saturates 4g

45 mins   25 mins

SERVES 4

INGREDIENTS

2 loaves of ciabatta or 2 baguettes

Tomato Sauce (see page 605)

4 plum tomatoes, sliced thinly lengthways

150 g/5½ oz mozzarella cheese, thinly sliced

10 black olives, stoned and cut into rings

8 fresh basil leaves, shredded

olive oil, for drizzling

salt and pepper

1 Cut the bread in half lengthways and toast the cut side of the bread lightly. Carefully spread the toasted bread with the Tomato Sauce.

2 Arrange the tomato and mozzarella slices alternately along the length.

3 Top with the olive rings and half of the basil. Drizzle over a little olive oil and season with salt and pepper.

4 Either place under a preheated medium grill and cook until the cheese is melted and bubbling or bake in a preheated oven, 200°C/400°F/Gas Mark 6, for 15–20 minutes.

5 Sprinkle over the remaining basil and serve immediately.

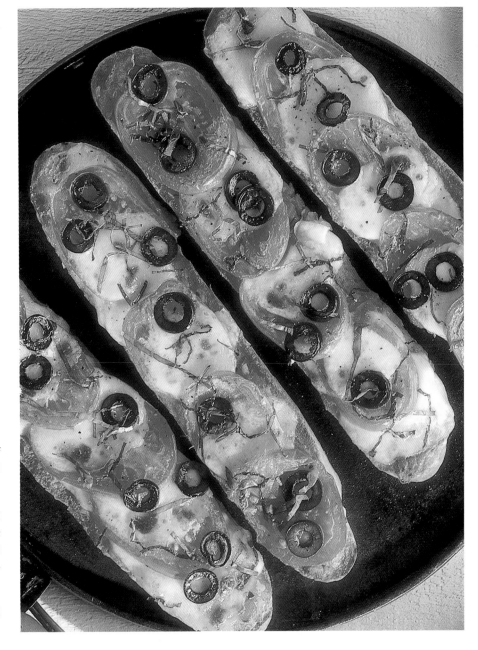

Tomato & Pepper Pizza

This pizza is made with a pastry base flavoured with cheese and topped with a delicious tomato sauce and roasted peppers.

NUTRITIONAL INFORMATION

Calories 611   Sugars 8g
Protein . . . . .14g   Fat 38g
Carbohydrate . . .56g   Saturates 21g

1½ hrs   55 mins

SERVES 4

I N G R E D I E N T S

225 g/8 oz plain flour

125 g/4½ oz butter, diced

½ tsp salt

35 g/1¼ oz dried grated Parmesan cheese

1 egg, beaten

2 tbsp cold water

2 tbsp olive oil

1 large onion, finely chopped

1 garlic clove, chopped

400 g/14 oz canned chopped tomatoes

4 tbsp tomato purée

1 red pepper, deseeded and halved

5 sprigs fresh thyme, stalks removed

6 black olives, stoned and halved

25 g/1 oz Parmesan cheese, freshly grated

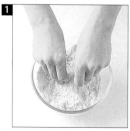

1 Sieve the flour into a bowl. Add the butter and rub in with the fingertips until the mixture resembles breadcrumbs. Stir in the salt and dried Parmesan. Add the egg and 1 tablespoon of the water and mix with a round-bladed knife. Add more water if necessary to make a soft dough. Form into a ball, cover with clingfilm and chill for 30 minutes.

2 Meanwhile, heat the oil in a frying pan and cook the onion and garlic for about 5 minutes or until golden. Add the tomatoes and cook for 8–10 minutes. Stir in the tomato purée.

3 Place the pepper, skin side up, on a baking tray and cook under a preheated grill for 15 minutes until charred. Place in a polythene bag and leave to sweat for 10 minutes. Peel off the skin and slice the flesh into thin strips.

4 Roll out the dough to fit a 23 cm/9 inch loose-bottomed fluted flan tin. Line with kitchen foil and bake in a preheated oven, 200°C/400°F/Gas Mark 6, for 10 minutes or until just set. Remove the kitchen foil and bake for a further 5 minutes until lightly golden. Leave to cool slightly.

5 Spoon the tomato sauce over the pastry base and top with the red pepper, thyme, black olives and fresh Parmesan. Return to the oven for 15 minutes or until the pastry is crisp. Serve warm or cold.

Garlic Mushroom Pizza

This pizza dough is flavoured with garlic and herbs and topped with mixed mushrooms and melting cheese for a really delicious pizza.

NUTRITIONAL INFORMATION

Calories 541   Sugars 5g
Protein . . . . .16g   Fat 15g
Carbohydrate . . .91g   Saturates 6g

45 mins   30 mins

SERVES 4

I N G R E D I E N T S

DOUGH

450 g/1 lb strong white flour, plus extra for dusting

2 tsp easy-blend dried yeast

2 garlic cloves, crushed

2 tbsp chopped fresh thyme

2 tbsp olive oil, plus extra for brushing

300 ml/10 fl oz lukewarm water

TOPPING

2 tbsp butter or margarine

350 g/12 oz mixed mushrooms, sliced

2 garlic cloves, crushed

2 tbsp chopped fresh parsley, plus extra to garnish

2 tbsp tomato purée

6 tbsp passata

salt and pepper

85 g/3 oz mozzarella cheese, grated

1 Put the flour, yeast, garlic and thyme in a bowl. Make a well in the centre and gradually stir in the oil and water. Bring together to form a soft dough.

2 Turn the dough on to a floured surface and knead for 5 minutes or until smooth. Roll into a 35 cm/14 inch round. Brush a baking sheet with a little oil and place the dough base on it. Set aside in a warm place for 20 minutes or until the dough puffs up.

3 Meanwhile, make the topping. Melt the margarine or butter in a frying pan and cook the mushrooms, garlic and parsley over a low heat for 5 minutes.

4 Combine the tomato purée and passata and spoon on to the pizza base, leaving a 1 cm/½ inch edge of dough. Spoon the mushroom mixture on top. Season to taste with salt and pepper and sprinkle the cheese on top.

5 Cook the pizza in a preheated oven, 190°C/375°F/ Gas Mark 5, for 20–25 minutes or until the base is crisp and the cheese has melted. Garnish with chopped parsley and serve immediately.

Barbecues

If you thought barbecues were strictly for the meat-eaters, this chapter will prove you wrong. Vegetables taste fantastic cooked over hot coals – if you've never tried barbecued corn-on-the-cob, you are really missing out, and vegetables skewers in a tasty marinade  are great served with rice or couscous, salad and garlic bread. Home-made vegetarian burgers and sausages work really well on the barbecue, too – cook them in a hinged rack so that you can turn them over easily. And for dessert, try Charcooked Pineapple, Stuffed Pears or Apple Skewers served with a toffee sauce – this one is perfect for Bonfire Night!

Tasty Barbecue Sauce

Just the thing for brushing on to vegetable kebabs and burgers, this sauce is easy and quick to make.

NUTRITIONAL INFORMATION

Calories 100	Sugars 9g	
Protein 1g	Fat 6g	
Carbohydrate . . .10g	Saturates 1g	

 5 mins 40 mins

SERVES 4

INGREDIENTS

25 g/1 oz butter or margarine

1 garlic clove, crushed

1 onion, finely chopped

400 g/14 oz canned chopped tomatoes

1 tbsp dark muscovado sugar

1 tsp hot chilli sauce

1–2 gherkins

1 tbsp capers, drained

salt and pepper

1 Melt the butter or margarine in a saucepan and fry the garlic and onion for 8–10 minutes, until well browned.

2 Add the chopped tomatoes, sugar and chilli sauce. Bring to the boil, then reduce the heat and simmer gently for 20–25 minutes, until thick and pulpy.

3 Chop the gherkins and capers finely. Add to the sauce, stirring to mix, and continue to cook the sauce over a low heat for 2 minutes.

4 Taste the sauce and season with a little salt and pepper.

5 Use this barbecue sauce as a baste for vegetarian kebabs and burgers, or as an accompaniment to other barbecued food such as vegetable kebabs.

COOK'S TIP

To make sure that the sauce has a good colour, it is important to brown the onions really well to begin with. When fresh tomatoes are cheap and plentiful, they can be used instead of canned ones. Peel and chop 500 g/1 lb 2 oz.

Citrus & Herb Marinades

Choose one of these marinades to give a marvellous flavour to barbecued food. The nutritional information is for Orange & Marjoram only.

NUTRITIONAL INFORMATION

Calories 269   Sugars 3g
Protein . . . . .0.4g   Fat 6g
Carbohydrate . . . .3g   Saturates 1g

 20 mins   0 mins

SERVES 4

INGREDIENTS

ORANGE & MARJORAM

1 orange

125 ml/4 fl oz olive oil

4 tbsp dry white wine

4 tbsp white wine vinegar

1 tbsp snipped fresh chives

1 tbsp chopped fresh marjoram

salt and pepper

THAI-SPICED LIME

1 lemongrass stalk

finely grated rind and juice of 1 lime

4 tbsp sesame oil

2 tbsp light soy sauce

pinch of ground ginger

1 tbsp chopped fresh coriander

salt and pepper

BASIL & LEMON

finely grated rind of 1 lemon

4 tbsp lemon juice

1 tbsp balsamic vinegar

2 tbsp red wine vinegar

2 tbsp virgin olive oil

1 tbsp chopped fresh oregano

1 tbsp chopped fresh basil

salt and pepper

1 To make the Orange & Marjoram marinade, remove the rind from the orange with a zester, or grate it finely, then squeeze the juice.

2 Mix the orange rind and juice with all the remaining ingredients in a small bowl, whisking together to combine. Season with salt and pepper.

3 To make the Thai-spiced Lime marinade, bruise the lemongrass by crushing it with a rolling pin. Mix the remaining ingredients together in a small bowl and add the lemongrass.

4 To make the Basil & Lemon marinade, whisk all the ingredients together in a small bowl. Season to taste with salt and pepper.

5 Keep the marinades covered with clingfilm or store them in screw-top jars, ready for using as marinades or bastes for vegetable kebabs, chargrilled vegetables and so on.

Three Favourite Dressings

You can rely on any of these dressings to bring out the best in your salads. The nutritional information is for the Mustard & Vinegar dressing.

NUTRITIONAL INFORMATION

Calories 245   Sugars 0.5g
Protein . . . . .0g   Fat 27g
Carbohydrate . . .0.5g   Saturates 4g

 45 mins   0 mins

SERVES 4

INGREDIENTS

WHOLEGRAIN MUSTARD & CIDER VINEGAR

125 ml/4 fl oz olive oil

4 tbsp cider vinegar

2 tsp wholegrain mustard

½ tsp caster sugar

salt and pepper

GARLIC & PARSLEY

1 small garlic clove

1 tbsp fresh parsley

150 ml/¼ pint single cream

4 tbsp natural yogurt

1 tsp lemon juice

pinch of caster sugar

salt and pepper

RASPBERRY & HAZELNUT

4 tbsp raspberry vinegar

4 tbsp light olive oil

4 tbsp hazelnut oil

½ tsp caster sugar

2 tsp chopped fresh chives

salt and pepper

1 To make the Wholegrain Mustard & Cider Vinegar dressing, whisk all the ingredients together in a small bowl.

2 To make the Garlic & Parsley dressing, crush the garlic clove and finely chop the fresh parsley.

3 Mix the garlic and parsley with the remaining ingredients, then whisk together until combined. Cover and chill for 30 minutes.

4 To make the Raspberry & Hazelnut vinaigrette, whisk all the ingredients together until combined.

5 Keep the dressings covered with cling film or sealed in screw-top jars. Chill until ready for use.

Mixed Vegetables

The wonderful aroma of vegetables as they are chargrilled over hot coals will set the tastebuds tingling.

NUTRITIONAL INFORMATION

Calories ....155 Sugars 6g
Protein ....2g Fat 12g
Carbohydrate ....7g Saturates 7g

10 mins   25 mins

SERVES 6

INGREDIENTS

8 baby aubergines

4 courgettes

2 red onions

4 tomatoes

salt and pepper

1 tsp balsamic vinegar, to serve

BASTE

75 g/2¾ oz butter

2 tsp walnut oil

2 garlic cloves, chopped

4 tbsp dry white wine or cider

1 To prepare the vegetables, cut the aubergines in half. Trim and cut the courgettes in half lengthways. Thickly slice the onion and halve the tomatoes.

2 Season all of the vegetables with salt and pepper to taste.

3 To make the baste, melt the butter with the oil in a saucepan. Add the garlic and cook gently for 1–2 minutes. Remove the pan from the heat and stir in the wine or cider.

4 Add the vegetables to the pan and toss them in the baste mixture. You may need to do this in several batches to ensure that all of the vegetables are coated thoroughly and evenly.

5 Remove the vegetables from the baste mixture, reserving any excess baste. Place the vegetables on an oiled rack over medium–hot coals. Barbecue the vegetables for 15–20 minutes, basting with the reserved baste mixture and turning once or twice during cooking.

6 Transfer the vegetables to warm serving plates and serve immediately, sprinkled with balsamic vinegar.

Cheeseburgers in Buns

Soya mince and seasonings combine to make these tasty vegetarian burgers, which are topped with cheese.

NUTRITIONAL INFORMATION

Calories 551   Sugars 4g
Protein . . . . .29g   Fat 24g
Carbohydrate . . .57g   Saturates 5g

1¼ hrs   10 mins

SERVES 4

I N G R E D I E N T S

150 g/5½ oz dehydrated soya mince

300 ml/½ pint vegetable stock

1 small onion, finely chopped

125 g/4½ oz plain flour

1 egg, beaten

1 tbsp chopped fresh herbs

1 tbsp mushroom ketchup or soy sauce

salt and pepper

2 tbsp vegetable oil

4 burger buns

4 cheese slices

B A R B E C U E   S A U C E

2 tbsp tomato ketchup

3 tbsp sweet chutney

1 tbsp vegetarian Worcestershire sauce

2 tsp Dijon mustard

1 tbsp white wine vinegar

2 tbsp fruity brown sauce

T O   G A R N I S H

dill pickle

tomato slices

T O   S E R V E

lettuce, cucumber and spring onion salad

1 Put the soya mince into a large bowl. Pour in the vegetable stock and set aside to soak for about 15 minutes until it has been absorbed.

2 Meanwhile, make the barbecue sauce. Combine the tomato ketchup, sweet chutney, vegetarian Worcestershire sauce and Dijon mustard in a small bowl. Stir in the white wine vinegar and fruity brown sauce, then cover and chill until required.

3 Add the onion, flour, beaten egg and chopped herbs to the soya mince and mix thoroughly. Stir in the mushroom ketchup or soy sauce and season to taste with salt and pepper, stirring to mix again.

4 Form the mixture into 8 burgers. Cover and chill until ready to cook.

5 Brush the burgers with oil and barbecue over hot coals, turning once. Allow about 5 minutes on each side. Alternatively, cook under a preheated grill.

6 Split the buns and top with a burger. Lay a cheese slice on top and garnish with barbecue sauce, dill pickle and tomato slices. Serve with a salad made with lettuce, spring onions and sliced cucumber.

Mushroom Burgers

Home-made veggie burgers are much tastier – and usually much healthier – than shop-bought ones.

NUTRITIONAL INFORMATION

Calories	164	Sugars	.........5g
Protein	.........7g	Fat	...........5g
Carbohydrate	...24g	Saturates	.......1g

 1 hr 20 mins 20 mins

SERVES 4

INGREDIENTS

2 tsp sunflower oil, plus extra for brushing

115 g/4 oz mushrooms, finely chopped

25 g/1 oz peanuts

1 carrot, chopped

1 onion, chopped

1 courgette, chopped

115 g/4 oz fresh white breadcrumbs

1 tbsp chopped fresh parsley

1 tsp yeast extract

1 tbsp plain flour

1 Prepare the vegetables. Heat the oil in a frying pan and cook the mushrooms, stirring constantly for about 8 minutes, until all the moisture has evaporated. Using a slotted spoon, transfer them to a bowl.

2 Put the peanuts, onion, courgette, and carrot in a food processor and process until finely chopped. Scrape into the bowl and stir in the breadcrumbs, parsley and yeast extract. Lightly flour your hands and shape the mixture into 4 patties. Place on plate, cover and chill in the refrigerator for at least 1 hour and up to 1 day.

3 Brush the mushroom burgers with the oil and cook on a hot barbecue for 8–10 minutes. Serve immediately.

Stuffed Tomatoes

These barbecued tomato cups are filled with a delicious Greek-style combination of herbs, nuts and raisins.

NUTRITIONAL INFORMATION

Calories 156	Sugars 10g
Protein 3g	Fat 7g
Carbohydrate ...22g	Saturates 0.7g

10 mins | 10 mins

SERVES 4

INGREDIENTS

4 beef tomatoes

salt and pepper

300 g/10½ oz cooked rice

8 spring onions, chopped

3 tbsp chopped fresh mint

2 tbsp chopped fresh parsley

3 tbsp pine kernels

3 tbsp raisins

2 tsp olive oil

1 Cut the tomatoes in half, then scoop out the seeds and discard.

2 Stand the tomatoes upside down on absorbent kitchen paper for a few moments to allow the juices to drain out, then turn the shells the right way up and sprinkle the insides with salt and pepper.

3 Mix together the rice, spring onions, mint, parsley, pine kernels and raisins.

4 Spoon the rice mixture into the tomato cups.

5 Drizzle a little olive oil over the stuffed tomatoes, then barbecue on an oiled rack over medium-hot coals for about 10 minutes until they are tender and cooked through.

6 Transfer the barbecued tomatoes to serving plates and serve immediately, while still hot. A crisp green salad and chunks of crusty bread go well with these.

COOK'S TIP

Tomatoes are a popular barbecue vegetable. Try grilling slices of beef tomato and slices of onion, brushed with a little oil and topped with sprigs of fresh herbs; or thread cherry tomatoes on to skewers and barbecue for 5–10 minutes.

Buttery Corn-on-the-cob

There are a number of ways of cooking corn-on-the-cob on a barbecue. Leaving on the husks protects the tender corn niblets.

NUTRITIONAL INFORMATION

Calories 79   Sugars 2g
Protein . . . . .3g   Fat 2g
Carbohydrate . . .14g   Saturates 0.2g

 10 mins   20–30 mins

SERVES 4

INGREDIENTS

4 sweetcorn cobs, with husks

100 g/3½ oz butter

1 tbsp chopped fresh parsley

1 tsp chopped fresh chives

1 tsp chopped fresh thyme

grated rind of 1 lemon

salt and pepper

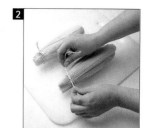

1 To prepare the cobs of sweetcorn, peel back the husks to the base and remove the silken hairs.

2 Fold back the husks and secure them in place with string if necessary.

3 Blanch the cobs in a large saucepan of boiling water for about 5 minutes. Remove with a perforated spoon and drain thoroughly.

4 Barbecue the cobs over medium–hot coals for 20–30 minutes, turning frequently to cook evenly.

5 Meanwhile, soften the butter and beat in the parsley, chives, thyme, lemon rind and salt and pepper to taste.

6 Transfer the cobs to serving plates, remove the string and pull back the husks. Serve with the herb butter.

COOK'S TIP
If you are unable to get fresh corn cobs, frozen cobs can be cooked on the barbecue. Spread some of the herb butter on to a sheet of double thickness foil. Wrap the cobs in the foil and barbecue among the coals for 20–30 minutes.

Turkish Kebabs

A spicy chick pea sauce is served with colourful, barbecued vegetable kebabs – perfect for a late Sunday lunch on a warm summer's day.

NUTRITIONAL INFORMATION

Calories	303	Sugars	........13g
Protein	........13g	Fat	..........15g
Carbohydrate	...30g	Saturates	.......2g

🥗 15 mins   🕐 15 mins

SERVES 4

INGREDIENTS

SAUCE

4 tbsp olive oil

3 garlic cloves, crushed

1 small onion, finely chopped

425 g/15 oz canned chick peas, rinsed and drained

300 ml/½ pint natural yogurt

1 tsp ground cumin

½ tsp chilli powder

lemon juice

salt and pepper

KEBABS

1 aubergine

1 red pepper, deseeded

1 green pepper, deseeded

4 plum tomatoes

1 lemon, cut into wedges

8 small bay leaves

olive oil, for brushing

1 To make the sauce, heat the olive oil in a small frying pan. Add the garlic and onion and cook over a medium heat, stirring occasionally, for about 5 minutes, until the onion is softened and has turned golden brown.

2 Put the chick peas and yogurt into a blender or food processor and add the cumin, chilli powder and onion mixture. Process for about 15 seconds until smooth. Alternatively, mash the chick peas with a potato masher and stir in the yogurt, ground cumin, chilli powder and onion mixture.

3 Scrape the puréed mixture into a bowl and season to taste with lemon juice, salt and pepper. Cover with clingfilm and chill in the refrigerator until ready to serve.

4 To prepare the kebabs, simply cut the vegetables into large chunks and thread them alternately on to 4 skewers, placing a bay leaf and lemon wedge at both ends of each kebab.

5 Brush the kebabs with olive oil and cook them on the barbecue, turning frequently, for 5–8 minutes. Alternatively, cook under a preheated grill.

6 While the kebabs are cooking, heat the spicy chick pea sauce and serve with the kebabs.

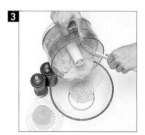

Vegetables with Pesto

These chargrilled Mediterranean vegetables are served with a very special creamy pesto sauce

NUTRITIONAL INFORMATION

Calories 313   Sugars 11g
Protein . . . . .10g   Fat 24g
Carbohydrate . . .15g   Saturates 6g

 30 mins   8 mins

SERVES 4

INGREDIENTS

1 red onion

1 fennel bulb

4 baby aubergines

4 baby courgettes

1 orange pepper

1 red pepper

2 beefsteak tomatoes, halved

2 tbsp olive oil

salt and pepper

CREAMY PESTO

55 g/2 oz fresh basil leaves

15 g/½ oz pine kernels

1 garlic clove

25 g/1 oz freshly grated Parmesan cheese

50 ml/2 fl oz extra virgin olive oil

150 ml/5 fl oz natural Greek yogurt

coarse sea salt

1 First, make the creamy pesto. Put the basil, pine kernels, garlic and a pinch of sea salt in a mortar and pound to a paste with a pestle. Gradually work in the Parmesan, then gradually stir in the oil. Place the yogurt in a small serving bowl and stir in 3–4 tablespoons of the pesto. Cover with clingfilm and chill in the refrigerator until required.

2 Cut the onion and fennel into wedges and halve and deseed the peppers.

3 Brush the onion, fennel, aubergines, courgettes, peppers and tomatoes with olive oil and season to taste with salt and pepper.

4 Cook the aubergines and peppers on a hot barbecue for 3 minutes, add the courgettes, onion and tomatoes, and cook, turning occasionally and brushing with more oil if necessary, for 5 minutes more. Serve immediately with the creamy pesto.

VARIATION
If baby vegetables are not available, cut 2 aubergines into slices and cut 2 courgettes in half lengthways instead.

Barbecued Bean Pot

Cook this tasty vegetable and Quorn casserole conventionally, then keep it piping hot over the barbecue – great for Bonfire Night.

NUTRITIONAL INFORMATION

Calories 381	Sugars 17g	
Protein 21g	Fat 19g	
Carbohydrate . . .34g	Saturates 3g	

🍲 10 mins   🕐 1 hr

SERVES 4

INGREDIENTS

4 tbsp butter or margarine

1 large onion, chopped

2 garlic cloves, crushed

2 carrots, sliced

2 celery sticks, sliced

1 tbsp paprika

2 tsp ground cumin

400 g/14 oz canned chopped tomatoes

425 g/15 oz canned mixed beans,
   rinsed and drained

150 ml/5 fl oz vegetable stock

1 tbsp muscovado sugar or black treacle

350 g/12 oz Quorn or soya cubes

salt and pepper

crusty French bread, to serve

1 Melt the butter or margarine in a large flameproof casserole and cook the chopped onion and crushed garlic over a medium heat, stirring occasionally, for about 5 minutes, until golden brown.

2 Add the sliced carrots and celery and cook, stirring occasionally, for a further 2 minutes, then stir in the paprika and ground cumin.

3 Add the tomatoes and beans. Pour in the vegetable stock and add the sugar or treacle. Bring to the boil, then reduce the heat and simmer, uncovered, stirring occasionally, for 30 minutes.

4 Add the Quorn or soya cubes to the casserole, cover and cook the mixture, stirring occasionally, for a further 20 minutes.

5 Season the bean pot to taste with salt and pepper, then transfer the casserole to the barbecue, setting it to one side to keep hot.

6 Ladle the bean pot on to plates and serve it immediately with crusty French bread.

VARIATION

If you prefer, cook the casserole in a preheated oven, 190°C/375°F/Gas Mark 5, from step 3, but keep the dish covered. Instead of mixed beans you could use just one type of canned beans.

Greek Vegetable Kebabs

A complete meal on a skewer, these tasty kebabs include vegetables, cheese and, perhaps surprisingly, nectarines in a colourful combination.

NUTRITIONAL INFORMATION

Calories	428	Sugars	........15g
Protein	........19g	Fat	..........23g
Carbohydrate	...40g	Saturates	.......4g

 45 mins 35 mins

SERVES 4

INGREDIENTS

8 new potatoes, washed but not peeled

2 onions, cut into wedges

1 aubergine, cut into 8 pieces

8 thick slices cucumber

1 red pepper, deseeded and cut into
  8 pieces

1 yellow pepper, deseeded and cut into
  8 pieces

225 g/8 oz halloumi cheese, cut into
  8 cubes

2 nectarines, stoned and cut into quarters

8 button mushrooms

2 tbsp olive oil

2 tsp chopped fresh thyme

2 tsp chopped fresh rosemary

salt

1 quantity Tsatziki (see page 147), to serve

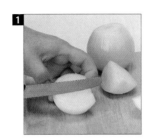

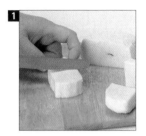

1 Prepare the ingredients. Cook the potatoes and onion wedges in a pan of lightly salted boiling water for about 20 minutes, until just tender. Drain and set aside to cool. Meanwhile, blanch the aubergine pieces in boiling water for 2 minutes, add the cucumber and simmer for 1 minute more. Add the peppers and simmer for 2 minutes, then drain and set all the vegetables aside to cool.

2 Place the cooled vegetables, cheese, nectarines and mushrooms in a bowl, add the olive oil and chopped herbs and toss to coat thoroughly. Thread the vegetables, cheese, nectarines and mushrooms on to skewers.

3 Cook the kebabs on a hot barbecue, turning frequently, for 15 minutes. Serve immediately with the tsatziki.

COOK'S TIP
Halloumi, a ewe's milk cheese, is perfect for barbecues because it softens and chars without melting.

Nutty Rice Burgers

Serve these burgers in toasted sesame seed baps. If you wish, add a slice of cheese to top the burger at the end of cooking.

NUTRITIONAL INFORMATION

Calories	517	Sugars	.........5g
Protein	........16g	Fat	..........26g
Carbohydrate	...59g	Saturates	.......6g

1¼ hrs   30 mins

SERVES 4

INGREDIENTS

1 tbsp sunflower oil

1 small onion, finely chopped

100 g/3½ oz mushrooms, finely chopped

350 g/12 oz cooked brown rice

100 g/3½ oz breadcrumbs

85 g/3 oz chopped walnuts

1 egg

2 tbsp brown fruity sauce

dash of Tabasco sauce

salt and pepper

vegetable oil, for basting

6 individual cheese slices (optional)

TO SERVE

onion slices

tomato slices

6 sesame seed baps

1 Heat the oil in a large pan and cook the onions for 3–4 minutes until they just begin to soften. Add the mushrooms and cook for a further 2 minutes.

2 Remove the pan from the heat. Transfer to a bowl and stir in the cooked rice, breadcrumbs, chopped walnuts, egg, and sauces to taste into the vegetables. Season to taste with salt and pepper and mix well.

3 Shape the mixture into 4 burgers, pressing the mixture together with your fingers. Set aside to chill in the refrigerator for at least 30 minutes.

4 Barbecue the burgers on an oiled rack over medium-hot coals for 5–6 minutes on each side, turning once and frequently basting with oil. Alternatively, cook under a preheated grill.

5 If liked, top the burgers with a slice of cheese 2 minutes before the end of the cooking time. Barbecue or grill the onion and tomato slices for 3–4 minutes until they are just beginning to colour.

6 Toast the sesame seed baps at the side of the barbecue. Serve the burgers in the baps, together with the barbecued onions and tomatoes.

Cajun Vegetables

These delicious slices of sweet potatoes and chunks of corn-on-the-cob are basted with butter and coated in cajun spice – a great side dish.

NUTRITIONAL INFORMATION

Calories 244	Sugars 7g
Protein 5g	Fat 8g
Carbohydrate . . .41g	Saturates 4g

10 mins   12–15 mins

SERVES 4

INGREDIENTS

4 corn cobs

2 sweet potatoes

25 g/1 oz butter, melted

CAJUN SPICE

2 tsp paprika

1 tsp ground cumin

1 tsp ground coriander

1 tsp ground black pepper

½–1 tsp chilli powder

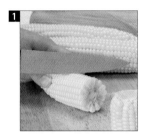

 Cut the corn cobs into quarters and slice the sweet potatoes thickly.

 To make the Cajun spice mix, combine all the spices in a small bowl.

3 Brush the corn cob quarters and sweet potato slices with melted butter and sprinkle with some of the Cajun spice mix.

4 Cook on a medium barbecue, turning frequently, for 12–15 minutes. Brush with more melted butter and sprinkle with more spice mixture during cooking.

COOK'S TIP
The flesh of sweet potatoes varies in colour from white to orange. Not only are the orange-flesh varieties more attractive, they also contain more nutrients.

Chargrilled Aubergines

The wonderful flavour and texture of chargrilled aubergines is hard to beat. Try serving the slices with pesto or minty cucumber sauce.

NUTRITIONAL INFORMATION

Calories	336	Sugars	.........6g
Protein	.........6g	Fat	..........32g
Carbohydrate	....6g	Saturates	.......5g

15 mins   10 mins

SERVES 4

INGREDIENTS

1 large aubergine

3 tbsp olive oil

1 tsp sesame oil

salt and pepper

PESTO

1 clove garlic

25 g/1 oz pine kernels

15 g/½ oz fresh basil leaves

2 tbsp freshly grated Parmesan cheese

6 tbsp olive oil

salt and pepper

CUCUMBER SAUCE

150 g/5½ oz natural yogurt

5 cm/2 inch piece cucumber

½ tsp mint sauce

1 Remove the stalk from the aubergine, then cut it lengthways with a sharp knife to make 8 thin slices.

2 Lay the slices on a plate or board and sprinkle them liberally with salt to remove the bitter juices. Leave to stand.

3 Meanwhile, prepare the baste. Combine the olive and sesame oils, season with pepper and set aside.

4 To make the pesto, put the garlic, pine kernels, basil and cheese in a food processor or blender until finely chopped. With the machine running, add the oil in a thin stream. Season to taste.

5 To make the minty cucumber sauce, place the yogurt in a mixing bowl. Remove the seeds from the cucumber and dice the flesh finely. Stir into the yogurt with the mint sauce.

6 Rinse the aubergine slices and pat them dry on absorbent kitchen paper.

7 Brush the aubergines with the oil mixture and barbecue over hot coals for about 10 minutes, turning once. The aubergine should be golden and tender.

8 Transfer the aubergine slices to serving plates and serve with either the cucumber sauce or the pesto.

Prune & Apricot Skewers

Try serving these unusual skewers as a starter, with a garnish of salad leaves and some fresh crusty bread to soak up any juices.

NUTRITIONAL INFORMATION

Calories	292	Sugars	........46g
Protein	.........5g	Fat	...........6g
Carbohydrate	...48g	Saturates	.......1g

🧊 15 mins   🕐 25 mins

SERVES 4

INGREDIENTS

175 g/6 oz prunes, stoned

225 g/8 oz dried apricots, stoned

5 cm/2 inch piece cinnamon stick

225 ml/8 fl oz white wine

2 tbsp chilli sauce

2 tbsp sunflower oil

500g/1 lb 2 oz baby onions, peeled and topped and tailed

1 Prepare the onions and fruit. Place the prunes, apricots, cinnamon stick and wine in a heavy-based saucepan and bring to the boil. Lower the heat and simmer for 5 minutes. Drain, reserving the cooking liquid, and set the fruit aside to cool.

2 Return the cooking liquid to the pan, bring back to the boil and boil until reduced by about half. Remove the pan from the heat and discard the cinnamon stick. Stir in the chilli sauce and oil.

3 Thread the prunes, apricots and onions on to skewers. Cook on a medium barbecue, turning and brushing frequently with the wine mixture, for 10 minutes. Serve immediately.

Indian Kebabs

Vegetables, fruit and cheese, brushed with a spicy glaze, need no more than a plate of salad to make a delicious vegetarian meal.

NUTRITIONAL INFORMATION

Calories	160	Sugars	........22g
Protein	.........7g	Fat	...........6g
Carbohydrate	...22g	Saturates	.......1g

15 mins   10–12 mins

SERVES 4

INGREDIENTS

8 cherry tomatoes

1 orange pepper, deseeded and cut into chunks

8 cauliflower florets

3 pineapple slices, cut into quarters

1 mango, peeled, stoned and cut into cubes

175 g/6 oz paneer, cut into cubes

salad and bread or rice, to serve

GLAZE

2 tbsp lime juice

2 tbsp chilli sauce

1 tbsp vegetable oil

1 tbsp clear honey

1 tbsp water

pinch of ground cumin

salt and pepper

COOK'S TIP

Paneer is a soft Indian cheese made by curdling milk with lemon juice, before straining and pressing flat. Most Indian cooks make their own, but it is available from Indian stores. Tofu could be used as a substitute.

1 Prepare the ingredients. Combine all the ingredients for the glaze in a small bowl, whisking until well mixed.

2 Thread the tomatoes, orange pepper chunks, cauliflower florets, pineapple pieces, mango cubes and paneer cubes on to 4 skewers.

3 Brush the kebabs with the glaze and cook on a medium barbecue, turning and brushing frequently with the glaze, for 10–12 minutes.

4 Serve the kebabs with a simple salad and either fresh crusty bread or some plain cooked rice.

Mixed Fruit Kebabs

You can use almost any firm-fleshed fruit to make these colourful, quick and easy kebabs.

NUTRITIONAL INFORMATION

Calories	185	Sugars	.......37g
Protein	.........3g	Fat	...........1g
Carbohydrate	...38g	Saturates	.......0g

1 hr 20 mins   5–7 mins

SERVES 4

INGREDIENTS

2 nectarines

1 mango, peeled, halved and stoned

2 kiwi fruit

4 red plums, halved and stoned

2 bananas, peeled and thickly sliced

8 strawberries, hulled

1 tbsp clear honey

3 tbsp Cointreau

1 Halve and stone the nectarines. Cut the nectarine pieces in half again and place on a large, shallow dish. Cut the mango flesh into chunks, peel and quarter the kiwi fruit and add to the dish with the plums, bananas and strawberries.

2 Combine the honey and Cointreau in a jug, mixing well. Pour the mixture over the fruit and toss lightly to coat. Cover with clingfilm and set aside to marinate for 1 hour.

3 Drain the fruit, reserving the honey and Cointreau marinade. Thread the fruit on to skewers and cook on a medium barbecue, turning and brushing frequently with the reserved marinade, for 5–7 minutes. Serve immediately.

Tropical Grilled Fruit

This delicious variation of a hot fruit salad includes wedges of tropical fruits, dusted with dark brown sugar and a pinch of spice before grilling.

NUTRITIONAL INFORMATION

Calories ...... 120 Sugars 20g
Protein .... 1g Fat 3g
Carbohydrate ... 21g Saturates 1g

15 mins, plus standing   5 mins

SERVES 4

INGREDIENTS

1 baby pineapple

1 ripe paw paw

1 ripe mango

2 kiwi fruit

4 apple bananas

4 tbsp dark rum

1 tsp ground allspice

2 tbsp lime juice

4 tbsp dark muscovado sugar

LIME 'BUTTER'

60 g/2 oz low-fat spread

½ tsp finely grated lime rind

1 tbsp icing sugar

1 Quarter the pineapple, trimming away most of the leaves, and place in a shallow dish. Peel the paw paw, cut it in half and scoop out the seeds. Cut the flesh into thick wedges and place with the pineapple.

2 Peel the mango, cut either side of the smooth, central flat stone and remove the stone. Slice the flesh into thick wedges. Peel the kiwi fruit and cut in half. Peel the bananas. Add all of these fruits to the dish.

3 Sprinkle over the rum, allspice and lime juice, cover and leave at room temperature for 30 minutes, turning occasionally, to allow the flavours to develop.

4 Meanwhile, make the lime 'butter'. Place the low-fat spread in a small bowl and beat in the finely grated lime rind and icing sugar until well mixed. Leave to chill until required.

5 Preheat the grill to hot. Drain the fruit, reserving the juices, and arrange in the grill pan. Sprinkle with the sugar and grill for 3–4 minutes until hot, bubbling and just beginning to char.

6 Transfer the fruit to a serving plate and spoon over the juices. Serve with the lime 'butter'.

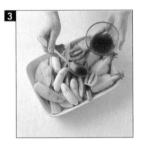

VARIATION

Serve with a light sauce of 300 ml/ ½ pint tropical fruit juice thickened with 2 tsp arrowroot.

Mini Kebabs

Cubes of smoked tofu are speared on bamboo satay sticks with crisp vegetables and marinated with lemon juice and olive oil.

NUTRITIONAL INFORMATION

Calories	322	Sugars	.........9g
Protein	........13g	Fat	..........24g
Carbohydrate	...13g	Saturates	.......7g

25 mins   15-20 mins

SERVES 6

I N G R E D I E N T S

300 g/10½ oz smoked tofu, cubed

1 large red pepper, deseeded and diced

1 large yellow pepper, deseeded and diced

175 g/6 oz button mushrooms

1 small courgette, sliced

finely grated rind and juice of 1 lemon

3 tbsp olive oil

1 tbsp chopped fresh parsley

1 tsp caster sugar

salt and pepper

fresh parsley sprigs, to garnish

S A U C E

115 g/4 oz cashew nuts

1 tbsp butter

1 garlic clove, crushed

1 shallot, finely chopped

1 tsp ground coriander

1 tsp ground cumin

1 tbsp caster sugar

1 tbsp desiccated coconut

150 ml/5 fl oz natural yogurt

1 Thread the tofu cubes, red and yellow peppers, mushrooms and courgettes on to bamboo satay sticks. Arrange them in a shallow dish.

2 Mix together the lemon rind and juice, olive oil, parsley and sugar. Season to taste with salt and pepper. Pour over the kebabs and brush them with the mixture. Set aside for 10 minutes.

3 To make the sauce, scatter the cashew nuts in a single layer on a baking sheet and toast them under a hot grill until lightly browned.

4 Melt the butter in a saucepan and sauté the garlic and shallot over a low heat until softened. Transfer to a blender or food processor and add the nuts, coriander, cumin, sugar, coconut and yogurt. Process for about 15 seconds or until combined. Alternatively, chop the nuts very finely and mix with the remaining ingredients.

5 Place the kebabs under a preheated grill and cook, turning and basting with the lemon juice mixture, until lightly browned. Garnish with sprigs of parsley and serve with the cashew nut sauce.

Colourful Kebabs

Brighten up a barbecue meal with these colourful vegetable kebabs. They are basted with an aromatic, flavoured oil.

NUTRITIONAL INFORMATION

Calories 131	Sugars 7g
Protein 2g	Fat 11g
Carbohydrate 8g	Saturates 2g

🥄 15 mins 🕐 15 mins

SERVES 4

INGREDIENTS

1 red pepper, deseeded

1 yellow pepper, deseeded

1 green pepper, deseeded

1 small onion

8 cherry tomatoes

100 g/3½ oz wild mushrooms

SEASONED OIL

6 tbsp olive oil

1 garlic clove, crushed

½ tsp mixed dried herbs or herbes de Provence

1 Cut the deseeded peppers into 2.5 cm/1 inch pieces.

2 Peel the onion and cut it into wedges, leaving the root end just intact to help keep the wedges together.

3 Thread the mixed pepper pieces, onion wedges, cherry tomatoes and mushrooms on to skewers, alternating the colours of the peppers.

4 To make the seasoned oil, mix together the olive oil, garlic and mixed herbs or herbes de Provence in a small bowl. Brush the mixture liberally over the kebabs.

5 Barbecue the kebabs over medium-hot coals for 10–15 minutes, brushing with the seasoned olive oil and turning the skewers frequently.

6 Transfer the vegetable kebabs on to warmed serving plates. Serve the kebabs immediately. If liked, accompany the kebabs with a rich walnut sauce (see Cook's Tip, left).

COOK'S TIP

To make walnut sauce, process 125 g/4½ oz walnuts in a food processor to a smooth paste. With the machine running, add 150 ml/5 fl oz double cream and 1 tablespoon of olive oil. Season to taste with salt and pepper.

Roast Leeks

Use a good-quality French or Italian olive oil for this deliciously simple yet sophisticated vegetable accompaniment.

NUTRITIONAL INFORMATION

Calories 71   Sugars 2g
Protein . . . . .2g   Fat 6g
Carbohydrate . . . .3g   Saturates 1g

5 mins   7 mins

SERVES 6

I N G R E D I E N T S

4 leeks

3 tbsp olive oil

2 tsp balsamic vinegar

sea salt and pepper

1 Cut the leeks in half lengthways, making sure that you hold the knife straight, so that the leek is held together by the root. Brush each leek liberally with the olive oil.

2 Cook the leeks over a hot barbecue for 6–7 minutes, turning once.

3 Remove the leeks from the barbecue and brush them lightly with the balsamic vinegar.

4 Season to taste with salt and pepper and serve hot or warm.

Grilled Corn-on-the-cob

Corn cobs are delicious grilled on the barbecue. They go particularly well with this creamy blue cheese dressing.

NUTRITIONAL INFORMATION

Calories 255   Sugars 4g
Protein . . . . .12g   Fat 14g
Carbohydrate . . .21g   Saturates 8g

 15 mins   15–20 mins

SERVES 6

INGREDIENTS

140 g/5 oz Danish blue cheese, crumbled

140 g/5 oz curd cheese

125 ml/4 fl oz natural Greek-style yogurt

salt and pepper

6 sweetcorn cobs in their husks

1 Crumble the Danish blue cheese with your fingers, place in a bowl and beat with a wooden spoon until creamy. Beat in the curd cheese until thoroughly combined. Gradually beat in the yogurt and season to taste with salt and pepper. Cover with clingfilm and chill in the refrigerator until required.

2 Fold back the husks on each corn cob and remove the silks. Smooth the husks back into place. Cut 6 pieces of foil, each large enough to enclose a corn cob. Wrap the corn cobs in the foil.

3 Cook the corn cobs on a hot barbecue, turning frequently, for 15–20 minutes. Unwrap the corn cobs and discard the foil. Peel back the husk on 1 side of each cob and trim off with a sharp knife or kitchen scissors. Serve immediately with the cheese dressing.

Stuffed Tomato Parcels

An unusual filling for stuffed tomatoes, spinach and cheese are given extra flavour with toasted sunflower seeds.

 15 mins, plus cooling   20 mins

SERVES 4

I N G R E D I E N T S

1 tbsp olive oil

2 tbsp sunflower seeds

1 onion, finely chopped

1 garlic clove, finely chopped

500 g/1 lb 2 oz spinach, thick stalks removed and leaves shredded

4 beef tomatoes

140 g/5 oz mozzarella cheese, diced

pinch of freshly grated nutmeg

salt and pepper

1 Heat the oil in a heavy-based saucepan. Add the sunflower seeds and cook, stirring constantly, for 2 minutes, until golden.

2 Add the onion and cook over a low heat, stirring occasionally, for 5 minutes, until softened but not brown. Add the garlic and spinach, cover and cook for a further 2–3 minutes until the spinach has wilted.

3 Remove from the heat and season to taste with nutmeg, salt and pepper. Set aside to cool.

4 Cut off and reserve a thin slice from the top of each tomato and scoop out the flesh with a teaspoon, taking care not to pierce the shell. Chop the flesh and stir it into the spinach mixture with the cheese.

5 Fill each of the tomato shells with some of the spinach and cheese mixture and replace the tops. Cut 4 squares of foil, each large enough to enclose a tomato. Place 1 tomato in the centre of each square and fold up the sides to enclose securely.

6 Cook the stuffed tomatoes on a hot barbecue, turning them occasionally, for 10 minutes. Serve immediately in the parcels.

Spicy Caribbean Kebabs

Bring a taste of the tropics to your barbecue with these sizzling vegetable kebabs in a spicy hot marinade.

NUTRITIONAL INFORMATION

Calories 250	Sugars 10g
Protein 5g	Fat 13g
Carbohydrate ...31g	Saturates 2g

3 hrs 20 mins — 15 mins

SERVES 4

INGREDIENTS

115 g/4 oz christophene, peeled, stoned and cut into 2.5 cm/1 inch cubes

1 plantain, peeled and cut into thick slices

1 corn cob, cut into 2.5 cm/1 inch thick slices

1 aubergine, cut into chunks

1 red pepper, deseeded and cut into chunks

1 green pepper, deseeded and cut into chunks

1 onion, cut into wedges

8 button mushrooms

4 cherry tomatoes

MARINADE

150 ml/5 fl oz tomato juice

4 tbsp sunflower oil

4 tbsp lime juice

3 tbsp dark soy sauce

1 shallot, finely chopped

2 garlic cloves, finely chopped

1 fresh green chilli, deseeded and finely chopped

½ tsp ground cinnamon

pepper

1 Prepare the vegetables. Blanch the christophene in boiling water for 2 minutes. Drain, refresh under cold water and drain again. Place it in a bowl with the plantain, corn cob, aubergine, peppers, onion, mushrooms and tomatoes.

2 Combine the tomato juice, sunflower oil, lime juice, soy sauce, shallot, garlic, chilli and cinnamon in a jug and season to taste with pepper. Pour the marinade over the vegetables, tossing to coat. Cover with clingfilm and set aside to marinate for 3 hours.

3 Drain the vegetables, reserving the marinade. Thread the vegetables on to skewers. Cook on a hot barbecue, turning and brushing frequently with the reserved marinade, for 10–15 minutes.

Potato Fans

These garlic-flavoured potatoes are baked in foil on the barbecue. They need plenty of time to cook, but otherwise they take care of themselves.

NUTRITIONAL INFORMATION

Calories 235	Sugars 2g	
Protein 6g	Fat 4g	
Carbohydrate ...46g	Saturates 1g	

5 mins   1 hr

SERVES 6

INGREDIENTS

6 large potatoes, scrubbed but not peeled

2 tbsp garlic-flavoured olive oil

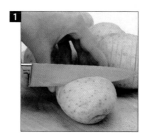

 Make a series of cuts across the potatoes almost all the way through. Cut out 6 squares of foil, each large enough to enclose a potato.

 Place a potato on each square of foil and brush generously with the garlic flavoured oil. Fold up the sides to enclose the potatoes entirely.

3 Cook on a hot barbecue, turning occasionally, for 1 hour. To serve, open the foil parcels and gently pinch the potatoes to open up the fans.

COOK'S TIP

If you do not have any garlic-flavoured oil, pour 2 tablespoons olive oil into a bowl, add 1 lightly crushed garlic clove, cover with clingfilm and set aside to 2 hours to infuse, then use as above.

Cheese & Red Onion Kebabs

Red onions have a mild, sweet flavour and retain their attractive colour when cooked. Here, they are barbecued with tart apples and salty cheese.

NUTRITIONAL INFORMATION

Calories ....449 Sugars 13g
Protein ....21g Fat 34g
Carbohydrate ...16g Saturates 2g

2 hrs 10 mins   10–15 mins

SERVES 4

I N G R E D I E N T S

3 red onions, cut into wedges

450g /1 lb halloumi cheese, cut into 2.5 cm/1 inch cubes

2 Bramley eating apples, cored and cut into wedges

4 tbsp olive oil

1 tbsp cider vinegar

1 tbsp Dijon mustard

1 garlic clove, finely chopped

1 tsp finely chopped sage

salt and pepper

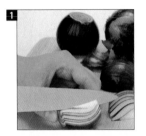
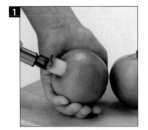

1 Prepare the ingredients. Place the onions, cheese and apples in a large, shallow, non-metallic dish. Combine the oil, cider, mustard, and the chopped garlic and sage in a jug and season to taste.

2 Pour the marinade over the onions, cheese and apples, tossing to coat. Cover with clingfilm and set aside to marinate for 2 hours.

3 Drain the marinated onions, cheese and apples, reserving the marinade for basting the skewers as they cook. Thread the onions, cheese and apples alternately on to skewers.

4 Cook the kebabs on a hot barbecue, turning and brushing frequently with the reserved marinade, for 10–15 minutes. Serve immediately.

COOK'S TIP

If you like, you could serve these kebabs with Mild Mustard Sauce (see page 8).

Apple Skewers

These fruit kebabs have a sticky toffee sauce. They are perfect for autumn barbecues such as Hallowe'en or Bonfire Night.

NUTRITIONAL INFORMATION

Calories 656   Sugars 48g
Protein . . . . .2g   Fat 52g
Carbohydrate . . .48g   Saturates 34g

10 mins   5 mins

SERVES 4

INGREDIENTS

2 dessert apples, cored and cut
    into wedges

2 firm pears, cored and cut into wedges

juice of ½ lemon

25 g/1 oz light muscovado sugar

¼ tsp ground allspice

TOFFEE SAUCE

25 g/1 oz unsalted butter, melted

125 g/4½ oz butter

100 g/3½ oz light muscovado sugar

6 tbsp double cream

1 Prepare the fruit and toss in lemon juice to prevent any discoloration.

2 Mix the sugar and allspice together and sprinkle over the fruit. Thread the fruit pieces on to skewers.

3 To make the toffee sauce, place the butter and sugar in a saucepan and heat, stirring gently, until the butter has melted and the sugar has dissolved.

4 Add the cream to the saucepan and bring to the boil. Boil for 1–2 minutes, then set aside to cool slightly

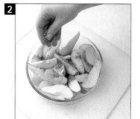

5 Meanwhile, place the fruit kebabs over the hot coals and barbecue them for about 5 minutes, turning and basting them frequently with the melted butter, until the fruit is just tender. Be careful turning the skewers as they get hot.

6 Transfer the fruit kebabs to warm serving plates and serve with the slightly cooled toffee sauce.

COOK'S TIP

Firm apples that will keep their shape are needed for this dish – varieties such as Golden Delicious, Granny Smith and Braeburn are a good choice. Soft apples and pears will become mushy as they cook.

Baked Bananas

The orange-flavoured cream can be prepared in advance but do not make up the banana parcels until just before you need to cook them.

NUTRITIONAL INFORMATION

Calories ....380 Sugars 40g
Protein ....2g Fat 18g
Carbohydrate ...43g Saturates 11g

30 mins   10 mins

SERVES 4

INGREDIENTS

4 bananas

2 passion fruit

4 tbsp orange juice

4 tbsp orange-flavoured liqueur

CREAM

150 ml/5 fl oz double cream

3 tbsp icing sugar

2 tbsp orange-flavoured liqueur

1 To make the orange-flavoured cream, pour the double cream into a mixing bowl and sprinkle over the icing sugar. Whisk the mixture until it is standing in soft peaks. Carefully fold in the orange-flavoured liqueur and chill in the refrigerator until required.

2 Peel the bananas and place each one on a sheet of kitchen foil.

3 Cut the passion fruit in half and squeeze the juice of each half over each banana. Spoon over the orange juice and liqueur.

4 Fold the kitchen foil over the top of the bananas so that they are completely enclosed.

5 Place the parcels on a baking sheet and bake the bananas in a preheated oven, 180°C/350°F/Gas Mark 4, for about 10 minutes or until they are just tender (test by inserting a cocktail stick).

6 Transfer the foil parcels to warm, individual serving plates. Open out the foil parcels at the table and then serve immediately with the chilled orange-flavoured cream.

VARIATION

Leave the bananas in their skins for a really quick dessert. Split the banana skins and pop in 1–2 squares of chocolate. Wrap the bananas in kitchen foil and bake for 10 minutes or until the chocolate has just melted.

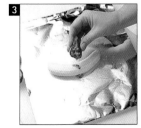

Exotic Fruit Parcels

Delicious pieces of exotic fruit are warmed through in a deliciously scented sauce to make a fabulous barbecue dessert.

NUTRITIONAL INFORMATION

Calories 43	Sugars 9g	
Protein 2g	Fat 0.3g	
Carbohydrate 9g	Saturates 0.1g	

🍳 🍳

🧊 10 mins, plus marinating   ⏰ 15–20 mins

SERVES 4

I N G R E D I E N T S

1 paw paw

1 mango

1 star fruit

1 tbsp grenadine

3 tbsp orange juice

single cream or low-fat natural yogurt, to serve

1 Cut the paw paw in half, scoop out the seeds and discard them. Peel the paw paw and cut the flesh into thick slices.

2 Prepare the mango by cutting it in half lengthways and cutting carefully away from the flat central stone.

3 Score each mango half in a criss-cross pattern. Push each mango half inside out to separate the cubes and cut them away from the peel.

4 Using a sharp knife, thickly slice the star fruit.

5 Place all of the fruit in a bowl and mix them together.

6 Mix the grenadine and orange juice together and pour over the fruit. Leave to marinate for at least 30 minutes.

7 Divide the fruit among 4 double thickness squares of kitchen foil and gather up the edges to form a parcel that encloses the fruit.

8 Place the foil parcel on a rack set over warm coals and barbecue the fruit for 15–20 minutes.

9 Serve the fruit in the parcel, with the low-fat natural yogurt.

COOK'S TIP

Grenadine is a sweet syrup made from pomegranates. If you prefer you could use pomegranate juice instead. To extract the juice, cut the pomegranate in half and squeeze gently with a lemon squeezer – do not press too hard or the juice may become bitter.

Fruit with Maple Syrup

Slices of juicy fruit are coated in a rich maple syrup sauce as they cook in little parcels on the barbecue.

NUTRITIONAL INFORMATION

Calories	383	Sugars	........33g
Protein	.........2g	Fat	..........24g
Carbohydrate	...42g	Saturates	......16g

 20 mins   🕐 10 mins

SERVES 4

INGREDIENTS

1 paw paw

2 bananas

2 peaches, peeled and stoned

1 ogen melon, halved and seeded

1 mango

115 g/4 oz unsalted butter, diced

4 tbsp maple syrup

pinch of ground allspice

1 Cut out 4 large squares of foil. Halve and seed the paw paw, cut into thick slices and peel off the skin. Peel the bananas and cut in half lengthways. Slice the peach halves. Cut the melon halves into thin wedges, then cut the flesh away from the rind. Peel, stone and slice the mango. Divide the fruit among the foil squares and set aside.

2 Dice the unsalted butter, put in a food processor with the maple syrup and process until thoroughly combined and smooth. Divide the flavoured butter between the piles of fruit and sprinkle with a little allspice. Fold up the sides of the foil to enclose the fruit securely.

3 Cook the fruit parcels over a medium barbecue, turning occasionally, for 10 minutes. Serve immediately.

Stuffed Pears

It has long been known that sprinkling strawberries with pepper brings out their flavour, and this is just as effective with other fruit.

NUTRITIONAL INFORMATION

Calories 184	Sugars 42g
Protein 1g	Fat 3g
Carbohydrate ...42g	Saturates 2g

20 mins | 20 mins

SERVES 4

INGREDIENTS

2 tsp unsalted butter

4 firm dessert pears

2 tbsp lemon juice

4 tbsp rosehip syrup

1 tsp green peppercorns, lightly crushed

140 g/5 oz redcurrants

4 tbsp caster sugar

vanilla ice cream, to serve

1 Cut 4 squares of foil, each large enough to enclose the pears, and grease with the butter. Halve and core the pears, but do not peel them. Brush the cut surfaces with lemon juice. Place 2 pear halves on each of the foil squares, brush them with the rosehip syrup and sprinkle with the pepper.

2 Put the redcurrants in a bowl and sprinkle with the sugar. Spoon the redcurrant mixture into the cavities of the pears. Fold up the sides of the foil to enclose the pears securely.

3 Cook the pears on a hot barbecue for 20 minutes. Serve with ice cream.

VARIATION
Substitute your own favourite soft fruit, such as blackcurrants or blueberries, for the redcurrants.

Banana Sizzles

Bananas are particularly sweet and delicious when grilled – and conveniently come with their own protective wrapping.

NUTRITIONAL INFORMATION

Calories 284	Sugars 37g
Protein 2g	Fat 12g
Carbohydrate . . .41g	Saturates 8g

 10 mins   6–8 mins

SERVES 4

INGREDIENTS

3 tbsp butter, softened

2 tbsp dark rum

1 tbsp orange juice

4 tbsp muscovado sugar

pinch of ground cinnamon

4 bananas

1 Beat the butter with the rum, orange, sugar and cinnamon in a small bowl until thoroughly combined and smooth.

2 Place the bananas, without peeling, on a hot barbecue and cook, turning frequently, for 6–8 minutes, until the skins are blackened.

3 Transfer the bananas to serving plates, slit the skins and cut partially through the flesh lengthways. Divide the flavoured butter between the bananas and serve.

VARIATION

You can also cook the bananas wrapped in foil. Cut them in half lengthways without peeling. Spread the flavoured butter on the cut surfaces and reassemble the bananas. Wrap in foil parcels and cook on a medium barbecue for 5–10 minutes.

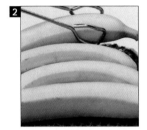
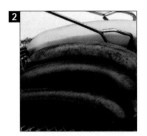

Courgette & Cheese Parcels

These delicately flavoured, melt-in-the mouth stuffed courgettes are cooked in the barbecue embers and need no attention.

NUTRITIONAL INFORMATION

Calories ....172 Sugars 6g
Protein ....9g Fat 12g
Carbohydrate ....8g Saturates 1g

 10 mins   30 mins

SERVES 4

INGREDIENTS

8 courgettes

1 tbsp olive oil, plus extra for brushing

1 tbsp fresh mint

155 g/4 oz feta cheese (drained weight), cut into strips

ground black pepper

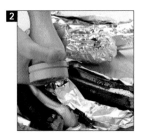

1 Cut 8 rectangles of foil, each large enough to enclose a courgette, and brush lightly with oil. Cut a slit along the length of each courgette and place them on the foil rectangles.

2 Finely chop the fresh mint. Insert strips of feta into the courgette slits, drizzle with the olive oil, sprinkle with the mint and season to taste with pepper. Fold in the sides of the foil securely to enclose the courgettes.

3 Bake in the barbecue embers for 30 minutes. Unwrap and serve.

VARIATION
Substitute mozzarella or fontina for the feta cheese.

Chargrilled Vegetables

This medley of peppers, courgettes, aubergine and red onion can be served on its own or as an unusual side dish.

NUTRITIONAL INFORMATION

Calories	66	Sugars	.........7g
Protein	.........2g	Fat	...........3g
Carbohydrate	....7g	Saturates	.....0.5g

15 mins   15 mins

SERVES 4

INGREDIENTS

1 large red pepper

1 large green pepper

1 large orange pepper

1 large courgette

4 baby aubergines

2 red onions

2 tbsp lemon juice

1 tbsp olive oil

1 garlic clove, crushed

1 tbsp chopped fresh rosemary or
   1 tsp dried rosemary

salt and pepper

TO SERVE

cracked wheat, cooked

tomato and olive relish

1 Halve and deseed the peppers and cut into even-size pieces, about 2.5 cm/ 1 inch wide.

2 Trim the courgettes, cut in half lengthways and slice into 2.5 cm/ 1 inch pieces. Place the peppers and courgettes in a large bowl.

3 Trim the aubergines and quarter them lengthways. Peel the onions, then cut each of them into 8 even-size wedges.

Add the aubergines and onions to the peppers and courgettes.

4 In a small bowl, whisk the lemon juice with the olive oil, garlic and rosemary. Season to taste with salt and pepper. Pour the mixture over the vegetables and stir to coat them evenly.

5 Thread the vegetables on to 8 metal or pre-soaked wooden skewers. Cook on a barbecue over hot coals, turning

frequently, for about 8–10 minutes until softened and beginning to char. Alternatively, arrange the kebabs on the grill rack and cook under a preheated grill, turning frequently, for about 10–12 minutes until the vegetables are lightly charred and just softened.

6 Drain the vegetable kebabs and serve them immediately on a bed of cracked wheat accompanied by a tomato and olive relish.

Vegetable Platter

Chargrilling is a popular way of cooking vegetables in the Mediterranean because it intensifies the flavour of the sun-ripened produce.

NUTRITIONAL INFORMATION

Calories 157	Sugars 6g	
Protein 5g	Fat 10g	
Carbohydrate ...15g	Saturates 2g	

 10 mins   🕐 15–20 mins

SERVES 4–6

INGREDIENTS

2 kg/4 lb 8 oz mixed fresh vegetables, such as aubergines, chicory, courgettes, fennel, peppers, spring onions

garlic-flavoured olive oil

salt and pepper

fresh basil leaves, to garnish

1 Prepare the vegetables as necessary. Top and tail the aubergines and cut into 5 mm/¼ inch slices. Cut each head of chicory in half lengthways.

2 Top and tail the courgettes and cut into 5 mm/¼ inch slices. Remove the fronds from the fennel and slice thickly across the grain.

3 Cut the peppers into quarters, then remove the cores and seeds. Trim the top green part of the spring onions, and cut in half lengthways if large.

4 As each vegetable is prepared, put it in a large bowl, drizzle with the garlic oil and season lightly with salt and pepper. Using your hands, toss the vegetables together so they are just lightly coated with oil; the vegetables should not be dripping in oil.

5 Heat a large, ridged cast-iron frying pan over a high heat. Lightly brush with oil. Add a batch of vegetables – enough to fit in the pan in a single layer. Cook the vegetables on one side over medium–high heat until they are starting to turn limp.

6 Brush the half-cooked vegetables with a little more oil, then turn them.

Continue cooking until they are tender – the exact cooking times will depend on the age and thickness of the vegetables.

7 Transfer to a large platter and repeat with the remaining vegetables.

8 While still hot, sprinkle the vegetables with salt and pepper. Garnish with basil leaves and serve.

Fruit Parcels

Cooking fruit in a parcel is a good idea for dessert as it avoids any contamination from earlier courses.

NUTRITIONAL INFORMATION

Calories . . . . .112 Sugars 29g
Protein . . . . .2g Fat 0g
Carbohydrate . . .28g Saturates 0g

15 mins   4 mins

SERVES 4

I N G R E D I E N T S

2 oranges

2 dessert apples

juice of 1 lemon

2 pears

4 tsp muscovado sugar

1 Peel the oranges, carefully removing all the pith. Cut each horizontally into 6 slices. Core the apples, but do not peel. Cut each horizontally into 6 slices. Brush the slices with lemon juice. Peel and core the pears, then cut each of them horizontally into 6 slices. Brush the slices with lemon juice.

2 Cut out 4 large squares of foil. Divide the fruit slices equally among the squares and sprinkle each pile with 1 teaspoon of the sugar. Fold up the sides of the squares to enclose the fruit securely.

3 Cook the parcels on a medium barbecue for about 4 minutes. Serve immediately.

  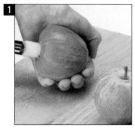

Charcooked Pineapple

Fresh pineapple slices are cooked on the barbecue, and brushed with a buttery fresh ginger and brown sugar baste.

NUTRITIONAL INFORMATION

Calories 461	Sugars 44g
Protein 5g	Fat 30g
Carbohydrate . . .45g	Saturates 20g

🗂 10 mins   🕑 10 mins

SERVES 4

INGREDIENTS

1 pineapple

BUTTER

125 g/4½ oz butter

90 g/3 oz light muscovado sugar

1 tsp finely grated fresh root ginger

TOPPING

225 g/8 oz natural fromage frais

½ tsp ground cinnamon

1 tbsp light muscovado sugar

1 Prepare the pineapple by cutting off the spiky top. Peel the pineapple with a sharp knife, remove the 'eyes', and cut the flesh into thick slices.

2 To make the ginger-flavoured butter, put the butter, sugar and ginger into a small saucepan and heat gently until melted. Transfer to a heatproof bowl and keep warm at the side of the barbecue, ready for basting the fruit.

3 To prepare the topping, mix together the fromage frais, cinnamon and sugar. Cover and chill until ready to serve.

4 Barbecue the pineapple slices, brushing them well with the ginger butter baste, for about 2 minutes on each side.

5 Serve the charcooked pineapple with a little extra ginger butter sauce poured over. Top with a spoonful of the spiced fromage frais.

VARIATION

If you prefer, substitute ½ teaspoon ground ginger for the grated root ginger. Light muscovado sugar gives the best flavour, but you can use ordinary soft brown sugar instead.

Vine Leaf Parcels

A wonderful combination of soft cheese, chopped dates, ground almonds and lightly fried nuts is encased in vine leaves.

NUTRITIONAL INFORMATION

Calories 459   Sugars 8g
Protein . . . . .12g   Fat 42g
Carbohydrate . . . .9g   Saturates 20g

25 mins   15 mins

SERVES 4

INGREDIENTS

300 g/10½ oz full-fat soft cheese

55 g/2 oz ground almonds

2 tbsp chopped stoned dates

salt and pepper

2 tbsp butter

4 tbsp flaked almonds

12–16 vine leaves

barbecued baby sweetcorn cobs, to serve

TO GARNISH

fresh rosemary sprigs

tomato wedges

1 Beat the soft cheese in a large bowl until smooth. Add the ground almonds and chopped dates and mix together thoroughly. Season to taste with salt and pepper.

2 Melt the butter in a small frying pan. Add the flaked almonds and fry over a very low heat, stirring constantly, for 2–3 minutes, until golden brown. Remove from the heat and set aside to cool for a few minutes.

3 Mix the fried almonds into the soft cheese mixture, stirring well to combine thoroughly.

4 Soak the vine leaves in water, if specified on the packet. Drain them, lay them out on a work surface and spoon an equal amount of the soft cheese mixture on to each. Fold over the leaves to enclose the filling.

5 Wrap the vine leaf parcels in foil, 1 or 2 per foil package. Place over the barbecue to heat through for about 8–10 minutes, turning once. Serve with barbecued baby corn and garnish with sprigs of rosemary and tomato wedges.

Garlic Potato Wedges

Serve this tasty barbecued potato dish with vegetable kebabs, bean burgers or vegetarian sausages.

NUTRITIONAL INFORMATION

Calories ....257 Sugars 1g
Protein ....3g Fat 16g
Carbohydrate ...26g Saturates 5g

10 mins   30–35 mins

SERVES 4

INGREDIENTS

3 large baking potatoes, scrubbed

4 tbsp olive oil

2 tbsp butter

2 garlic cloves, chopped

1 tbsp chopped fresh rosemary

1 tbsp chopped fresh parsley

1 tbsp chopped fresh thyme

salt and pepper

Barbecue Sauce (see page 624) or
mayonnaise, to serve

1 Bring a large pan of water to the boil, add the potatoes and parboil them for 10 minutes. Drain the potatoes, refresh under cold water, then drain them again.

2 Transfer the potatoes to a chopping board. When the potatoes are cold enough to handle, cut them into thick wedges, but do not peel.

3 Heat the oil and butter in a small pan together with the garlic. Cook gently until the garlic begins to brown, then remove the pan from the heat.

4 Stir the herbs and seasoning into the mixture in the pan.

5 Brush the herb and butter mixture all over the potato wedges.

6 Barbecue the potatoes over hot coals, brushing liberally with any of the remaining herb and butter mixture, for 10–15 minutes or until the potato wedges are just tender.

7 Transfer the potato wedges to a warm serving plate and serve as a starter or as a side dish, accompanied by barbecue sauce or mayonnaise, if desired.

COOK'S TIP
You may find it easier to barbecue these potatoes in a hinged rack or in a specially designed barbecue roasting tray.

Cheese & Onion Baguettes

Part-baked baguettes are split and filled with a tasty cheese and onion mixture, then wrapped in foil and cooked over the barbecue.

NUTRITIONAL INFORMATION

Calories 715   Sugars 5g
Protein . . . . .21g   Fat 41g
Carbohydrate . . .70g   Saturates 25g

15 mins   20 mins

SERVES 4

INGREDIENTS

4 part-baked baguettes

2 tbsp tomato relish

60 g/2 oz butter

8 spring onions, finely chopped

125 g/4½ oz cream cheese

125 g/4½ oz Cheddar cheese, grated

1 tsp snipped fresh chives

pepper

TO SERVE

mixed salad leaves

herbs

1 Split the part-baked baguettes in half lengthways, without cutting right through. Spread a little tomato relish on each split baguette.

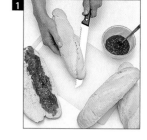

2 Melt the butter in a frying pan and add the chopped spring onions. Fry them over a medium heat, stirring frequently, for 5 minutes, until softened and golden. Remove from the heat and set aside to cool slightly.

3 Beat the cream cheese in a mixing bowl to soften it. Mix in the spring onions, with any remaining butter. Add the grated cheese and snipped chives and mix well. Season to taste with pepper.

4 Divide the cheese mixture between the baguettes, spread it over the cut surfaces and sandwich the baguettes together again. Wrap each baguette tightly in kitchen foil.

5 Heat the baguettes over the barbecue for about 10–15 minutes, turning them occasionally. Peel back the foil to check that they are cooked and if the cheese mixture has melted.

6 Serve the baguettes with salad leaves and garnished with fresh herbs.

COOK'S TIP

If there's no room on the barbecue, and you want to eat these at the same time as the rest of the food, bake them in a preheated oven, at 200°C/400°F/ Gas Mark 6, for 15 minutes.

Sidekick Vegetables

Colourful vegetables are barbecued over hot coals to make this unusual hot salad, which is served with a spicy chilli sauce on the side.

NUTRITIONAL INFORMATION

Calories	224	Sugars	........14g
Protein	.........4g	Fat	..........15g
Carbohydrate	...21g	Saturates	.......2g

🍶 15 mins   🕐 30 mins

SERVES 4

INGREDIENTS

1 red pepper, deseeded

1 orange or yellow pepper, deseeded

2 courgettes

2 corn cobs

1 aubergine

olive oil, for brushing

salt and pepper

handful of chopped fresh thyme, rosemary and parsley

lime or lemon wedges, to serve

DRESSING

2 tbsp olive oil

1 tbsp sesame oil

1 garlic clove, crushed

1 small onion, finely chopped

1 celery stick, finely chopped

1 small fresh green chilli, deseeded and chopped

4 tomatoes, chopped

5 cm/2 inch piece of cucumber, chopped

1 tbsp tomato purée

1 tbsp lime or lemon juice

salt and pepper

1 To make the dressing, heat the olive and sesame oils together in a saucepan or frying pan. Add the garlic and onion, and cook over a low heat for about 3 minutes until softened.

2 Add the celery, chilli and tomatoes to the pan and cook, stirring frequently, for 5 minutes.

3 Stir in the cucumber, tomato purée and lime or lemon juice, and simmer over a low heat for 8–10 minutes until thick and pulpy. Season to taste with salt and pepper.

4 Cut the vegetables into thick slices and brush with a little olive oil.

5 Cook the vegetables over the hot coals of the barbecue for about 5–8 minutes, sprinkling them with salt and pepper and fresh herbs as they cook, and turning once.

6 Divide the vegetables between 4 serving plates and spoon some of the dressing on to the side. Serve immediately, sprinkled with a few more chopped herbs and accompanied by the lime or lemon wedges.

Marinated Brochettes

These tofu and mushroom brochettes are marinated in a lemon, garlic and herb mixture so that they soak up a delicious flavour.

NUTRITIONAL INFORMATION

Calories 192   Sugars 0.5g
Protein ....11g   Fat 16g
Carbohydrate ....1g   Saturates 2g

15 mins, plus marinating   6 mins

SERVES 4

INGREDIENTS

1 lemon

1 garlic clove, crushed

4 tbsp olive oil

4 tbsp white wine vinegar

1 tbsp chopped fresh herbs, such as rosemary, parsley and thyme

salt and pepper

300 g/10½ oz smoked tofu

350 g/12 oz mushrooms

fresh herbs, to garnish

TO SERVE

mixed salad leaves

cherry tomatoes, halved

1 Finely grate the rind from the lemon and squeeze out the juice.

2 Add the garlic, olive oil, vinegar and chopped herbs and mix well. Season to taste with salt and pepper.

3 Slice the tofu into large chunks with a sharp knife. Thread the pieces on to metal or wooden skewers, alternating them with the mushrooms.

4 Place the brochettes in a shallow, non-metallic dish and pour over the marinade. Cover with clingfilm and chill in the refrigerator for 1–2 hours, turning the brochettes in the marinade occasionally.

5 Remove the brochettes from the dish, reserving the marinade. Cook on a medium-hot barbecue, brushing them frequently with the marinade and turning often, for 6 minutes until cooked through and golden brown. Alternatively, cook under a preheated grill, turning frequently and brushing with the reserved marinade.

6 Transfer to warmed serving plates, garnish with fresh herbs and serve immediately with mixed salad leaves and cherry tomatoes.

Aubergine & Potato Rolls

Partially cooked in advance, these attractive little aubergine rolls with a tasty sweet-potato filling are baked in foil parcels.

NUTRITIONAL INFORMATION

Calories 452	Sugars 14g
Protein 17g	Fat 27g
Carbohydrate . . .39g	Saturates 11g

🕒 30 mins   🕐 45–50 mins

SERVES 4–6

I N G R E D I E N T S

450 g/1 lb sweet potatoes

4 spring onions, chopped

175 g/6 oz Gruyère cheese, diced

1 red pepper, deseeded and chopped

1 garlic clove, crushed

1 tsp chopped fresh thyme

salt and pepper

25 g/1 oz plain flour

1½ tsp paprika

1½ tsp curry powder

1½ tsp celery salt

1 tsp caster sugar

1 tbsp garlic granules

4 large aubergines

3 tbsp olive oil, plus extra for brushing

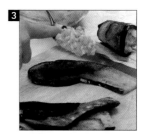

1 Cook the sweet potatoes in a large pan of lightly salted water for 20 minutes, or until tender. Drain and leave until cool enough to handle. Peel and mash in a large bowl until smooth. Add the spring onions, cheese, red pepper, garlic and thyme and season to taste with salt and pepper.

2 Place the flour on a plate and stir in the paprika, curry powder, celery salt, sugar and garlic granules. Slice each aubergine lengthways into quarters and dust with the seasoned flour. Heat half the oil in a large, heavy-based frying pan. Add the aubergine slices, in batches, and cook until just golden brown, adding more oil as necessary. Remove with a slotted spoon and leave to cool.

3 Place a spoonful of the sweet potato mixture on each aubergine slice and roll up. Cut out 4 x 30 cm/12 inch squares of foil and brush each one with oil. Place 4 aubergine rolls on each square and fold up the sides to enclose the rolls. Cook on a medium–hot barbecue, turning occasionally, for 25-30 minutes. Unwrap the parcels and transfer the rolls to a serving dish.

COOK'S TIP

Salting the aubergines helps to prevent them soaking up so much oil during frying. Place the slices in a colander, sprinkling each layer liberally with salt, and leave to drain for 30 minutes. Rinse thoroughly and pat dry with kitchen paper before coating with seasoned flour.

Aubergines with Tsatziki

This makes a delicious appetizer for a barbecue party or can be served as part of a vegetarian barbecue meze.

NUTRITIONAL INFORMATION

Calories ....137 Sugars 4g
Protein ....5g Fat 11g
Carbohydrate ....5g Saturates 4g

15 mins   10 mins

SERVES 4

INGREDIENTS

200 ml/7 fl oz natural Greek yogurt

½ cucumber

4 spring onions, finely chopped

1 garlic clove, finely chopped

3 tbsp chopped fresh mint

salt and pepper

2 tbsp olive oil

2 aubergines, thinly sliced

1 First, make the tsatziki. Dice the cucumber. Place the yogurt in a bowl and beat well until smooth. Stir in the cucumber, spring onions, garlic and mint. Season to taste with salt and pepper. Transfer to a serving bowl, cover with clingfilm and chill in the refrigerator until required.

VARIATION

An alternative dip to serve with the aubergine slices can be made very quickly by combining 300 ml/½ pint soured cream with 2 very finely chopped garlic cloves. Season to taste with salt and pepper and chill before serving.

2 Season the olive oil to taste with plenty of salt and pepper, then brush the aubergine slices generously with the seasoned oil.

3 Cook the aubergines on a hot barbecue for 5 minutes on each side, brushing with more oil, if necessary. Serve immediately with the tsatziki.

Pumpkin Parcels

This spicy side dish is perfect for a Hallowe'en or Bonfire Night barbecue party, although it is equally delicious on a summer evening, too.

NUTRITIONAL INFORMATION

Energy 118	Sugar 3g
Protein 1g	Fat 11g
Carbohydrates 4g	Saturates 4g

 10 mins   25–30 mins

SERVES 4

INGREDIENTS

700 g/1 lb 9 oz pumpkin or squash

2 tbsp sunflower oil

25 g/1 oz butter

½ tsp chilli sauce

grated rind of 1 lime

2 tsp lime juice

1 Halve the pumpkin or squash and scoop out the seeds. Rinse the seeds and reserve. Cut the pumpkin into thin wedges and peel.

2 Heat the oil and butter together in a large saucepan, stirring constantly, until melted. Stir in the chilli sauce, lime rind and juice.

3 Add the pumpkin or squash and seeds to the pan and toss to coat all over in the flavoured butter.

4 Divide the mixture between 4 double thickness sheets of kitchen foil. Fold over the kitchen foil to enclose the pumpkin or squash mixture completely.

5 Barbecue the foil parcels over hot coals for 15–25 minutes, or until the pumpkin or squash is tender.

6 Transfer the foil parcels to warm serving plates. Open the parcels at the table and serve at once.

VARIATION
Add 2 teaspoons of curry paste to the oil instead of the lime and chilli. Use butternut squash when pumpkin is not available.

Spicy Sweet Potato Slices

Serve these as an accompaniment to other barbecue dishes or with a spicy dip as nibbles while the main dishes are being cooked.

NUTRITIONAL INFORMATION

Calories 178	Sugars 0.8g	
Protein 2g	Fat 6g	
Carbohydrate ...32g	Saturates 0.7g	

10 mins   25 mins

SERVES 4

INGREDIENTS

450 g/1 lb sweet potatoes

2 tbsp sunflower oil

1 tsp chilli sauce

salt and pepper

1 Bring a large pan of water to the boil, add the unpeeled sweet potatoes and parboil them for 10 minutes. Drain the potatoes thoroughly and transfer to a chopping board.

2 Peel the potatoes and cut them into thick slices.

3 Mix together the sunflower oil, chilli sauce and salt and pepper to taste in a small bowl.

4 Brush the spicy mixture liberally over one side of the potatoes. Place the potatoes, oil side down, over medium–hot coals and barbecue for 5–6 minutes.

5 Lightly brush the tops of the potatoes with the spiced oil, then turn them over and continue to barbecue for a further 5 minutes or until the potatoes are crisp and golden.

6 Transfer the potatoes to a warm serving dish and serve at once.

COOK'S TIP

For a simple spicy dip, combine 150 ml/5 fl oz soured cream with ½ teaspoon of sugar, ½ teaspoon of Dijon mustard and salt and pepper to taste. Leave to chill until required.

Barbecue Mushrooms

Large mushrooms have more flavour than the smaller button mushrooms. Serve these mushrooms as part of a vegetarian barbecue.

NUTRITIONAL INFORMATION

Calories 148	Sugars 1g
Protein 11g	Fat 7g
Carbohydrate 11g	Saturates 3g

🔥 🔥

🍲 10 mins   🕐 15 mins

SERVES 4

INGREDIENTS

12 open-cap mushrooms

4 tsp olive oil

4 spring onions, chopped

100 g/3½ oz fresh brown breadcrumbs

1 tsp chopped fresh oregano

100 g/3½ oz low-fat mature
   Cheddar cheese

1 Remove the stalks from the mushrooms, reserving the caps. Chop the stalks finely.

2 Heat half the oil in a frying pan. Add the mushroom stalks and spring onions and cook over a low heat, stirring occasionally, for 5 minutes.

3 Transfer the mushroom stalks and spring onions to a large bowl with a draining spoon and add the breadcrumbs and oregano. Mix well.

4 Crumble the cheese into small pieces in a small bowl. Add the cheese to the breadcrumb mixture and mix well. Carefully spoon the stuffing mixture into the mushroom caps.

5 Drizzle the remaining oil over the stuffed mushrooms. Cook the mushrooms on an oiled rack over medium–hot coals for 10 minutes or until cooked through. Alternatively, arrange on a baking sheet and bake in a preheated oven, 180°C/350°F/Gas Mark 4 for about 20 minutes or until cooked through.

6 Transfer the mushrooms to serving plates and serve hot.

VARIATION
For a change, replace the cheese with chopped hard-boiled eggs or chopped olives. Mop up the juices with some crusty bread.

Vegetarian Sausages

The delicious cheese flavour will make these sausages a hit with vegetarians, who need not feel left out when it comes to a barbecue.

NUTRITIONAL INFORMATION

Calories 213	Sugars 4g
Protein 8g	Fat 12g
Carbohydrate . . .19g	Saturates 4g

50 mins   25 mins

MAKES 8

I N G R E D I E N T S

1 tbsp sunflower oil

1 small onion, finely chopped

55 g/2 oz mushrooms, finely chopped

½ red pepper, deseeded and finely chopped

400 g/14 oz canned cannellini beans, rinsed
   and drained

100 g/3½ oz fresh breadcrumbs

100 g/3½ oz Cheddar cheese, grated

1 tsp dried mixed herbs

1 egg yolk

seasoned plain flour

vegetable oil, to baste

TO SERVE

bread rolls

slices of fried onion

1 Heat the oil in a pan. Add the onion, mushrooms and red pepper and cook over a low heat, stirring frequently, for 5 minutes or until softened.

2 Mash the cannellini beans in a large mixing bowl with a potato masher. Add the onion, mushroom and pepper mixture, the breadcrumbs, grated Cheddar, herbs and egg yolk and mix together well.

3 Press the mixture together with your fingers and shape into 8 sausages. Roll each sausage in the seasoned flour to coat evenly.

4 Set the sausages aside to chill in the refrigerator for at least 30 minutes.

5 Barbecue the sausages on a sheet of oiled foil set over medium–hot coals for 15–20 minutes, turning and basting frequently with oil, until golden. Alternatively, cook under a preheated grill, basting frequently with the oil.

6 Split a bread roll down the middle lengthways and insert a layer of fried onion slices. Place a sausage in the roll and serve immediately.

Summer Vegetable Parcels

You can use any baby vegetables you like – patty pan squash, sweetcorn and plum tomatoes look attractive and add colour.

NUTRITIONAL INFORMATION

Calories 299	Sugars 8g
Protein 3g	Fat 25g
Carbohydrate ...17g	Saturates 16g

15 mins   25–30 mins

SERVES 4

I N G R E D I E N T S

1 kg/2 lb 4 oz mixed baby vegetables, such as carrots, patty pan squash, sweetcorn cobs, plum tomatoes, leeks, courgettes and onions

115 g/4 oz unsalted butter

3 tbsp chopped mixed fresh herbs, such as parsley, thyme and chervil

2 garlic cloves

grated rind and juice of 1 lemon

salt and pepper

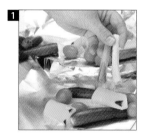

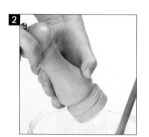

1 Cut out 4 x 30 cm/12 inch squares of foil and divide the vegetables equally among them.

2 Zest the lemon. Put the butter, herbs, garlic and lemon rind in a food processor and process until blended, then season to taste with salt and pepper. Alternatively, beat in a bowl until blended.

3 Divide the butter equally between the vegetables, dotting it on top. Fold up the sides of the foil to enclose the vegetables, sealing securely. Cook on a medium–hot barbecue, turning occasionally, for 25–30 minutes. Open the parcels, sprinkle with the lemon juice and serve.

COOK'S TIP
Use a double thickness of foil to make parcels for cooking on the barbecue so that they don't tear when you turn them.

Barbecue Bean Burgers

These tasty patties are ideal for a barbecue in the summer, but they are equally delicious cooked indoors at any time of year.

NUTRITIONAL INFORMATION

Calories 443   Sugars 12g
Protein ....17g   Fat 14g
Carbohydrate ...68g   Saturates 2g

🍲 15 mins   🕐 1 hr 5 mins

SERVES 6

INGREDIENTS

125 g/4½ oz dried aduki beans

125 g/4½ oz dried black-eyed beans

6 tbsp vegetable oil

1 large onion, finely chopped

1 tsp yeast extract

125 g/4½ oz grated carrot

90 g/3 oz fresh wholemeal breadcrumbs

2 tbsp wholemeal flour

salt and pepper

BARBECUE SAUCE

½ tsp chilli powder

1 tsp celery salt

2 tbsp light muscovado sugar

2 tbsp red wine vinegar

2 tbsp vegetarian Worcestershire sauce

3 tbsp tomato purée

dash of Tabasco sauce

TO SERVE

6 wholemeal baps, toasted

mixed salad

jacket potato fries

1 Place the beans in separate pans, cover with water and bring to the boil, then boil for 15 minutes. Cover and simmer the aduki beans for 25 minutes and the black-eyed beans for 35 minutes, until tender. Drain and rinse well.

2 Transfer to a mixing bowl and lightly mash together with a potato masher or fork. Set aside.

3 Heat 1 tablespoon of the oil in a frying pan and gently fry the onion for 3–4 minutes, until softened. Mix into the beans with the yeast extract, grated carrot, breadcrumbs and seasoning. Bind the mixture together well.

4 With wet hands, divide the mixture into 6 and form into burgers 8 cm/ 3½ inches in diameter. Put the flour on a plate and use to coat the burgers.

5 To make the barbecue sauce, mix all the ingredients together until they are well blended.

6 Cook the burgers on a medium-hot barbecue for 3–4 minutes on each side, brushing with the remaining oil from time to time.

7 Serve the burgers in the toasted baps with a mixed salad, jacket potato fries and a spoonful of the barbecue sauce.

Vegetarian Brochettes

In this lovely colourful recipe, the tofu absorbs the flavour of the mustard and honey glaze.

NUTRITIONAL INFORMATION

Calories 174	Sugars 9g
Protein 10g	Fat 10g
Carbohydrate 11g	Saturates 3g

20 mins   8–10 mins

SERVES 4

I N G R E D I E N T S

2 courgettes

1 yellow pepper, deseeded and cut into quarters

225 g/8 oz firm tofu, cut into 2.5 cm/1 inch cubes

4 cherry tomatoes

4 baby onions

8 button mushrooms

MUSTARD AND HONEY GLAZE

2 tbsp olive oil

1 tbsp Meaux mustard

1 tbsp clear honey

salt and pepper

1 Peel off strips of skin along the length of the courgettes to leave alternate yellow and green stripes, then cut each courgette into 8 thick slices. Cut each of the yellow pepper quarters in half. Slice the tofu.

2 Thread the pieces of pepper, courgette slices, tofu cubes, cherry tomatoes, baby onions and button mushrooms on to 4 skewers.

 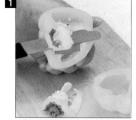 

3 Combine the olive oil, mustard and honey in a jug and season with salt and pepper.

4 Brush the brochettes with the honey mixture and cook on a medium–hot barbecue, turning and brushing frequently with the honey mixture, for 8–10 minutes. Serve the brochettes immediately.

Tofu Skewers

Although tofu is rather bland on its own, it develops a fabulous flavour when it is marinated in garlic and herbs.

NUTRITIONAL INFORMATION

Calories 149	Sugars 5g
Protein 13g	Fat 9g
Carbohydrate 5g	Saturates 1g

🦪 40 mins   🕐 15 mins

SERVES 4

INGREDIENTS

350 g/12 oz firm tofu

1 red pepper

1 yellow pepper

2 courgettes

8 button mushrooms

lemon slices, to garnish

MARINADE

grated rind and juice of ½ lemon

1 garlic clove, crushed

½ tsp chopped fresh rosemary

½ tsp chopped fresh thyme

1 tbsp walnut oil

1 To make the marinade, combine the lemon rind and juice, garlic, rosemary, thyme and oil in a shallow dish.

2 Drain the tofu, pat it dry on kitchen paper and cut it into squares with a sharp knife. Add to the marinade and toss to coat. Cover and set aside to marinate for 20–30 minutes.

3 Meanwhile, deseed and cut the peppers into 2.5 cm/1 inch pieces. Blanch in boiling water for 4 minutes, refresh in cold water and drain.

4 Using a canelle knife or potato peeler, remove strips of peel from the courgettes. Cut the courgette into 2.5 cm/ 1 inch chunks.

5 Remove the tofu from the marinade, reserving the liquid. Thread it on to 8 skewers, alternating with the peppers, courgette and button mushrooms.

6 Barbecue the skewers over medium–hot coals for about 6 minutes, turning and basting with the reserved marinade. Alternatively, cook under a preheated grill. Transfer the skewers to warmed individual serving plates, garnish with slices of lemon and serve.

Barbecued Baked Apples

When they are wrapped in kitchen foil, apples bake to perfection on the barbecue and make a delightful finale to any meal.

NUTRITIONAL INFORMATION

Calories	 294	Sugars 30g
Protein	.... 3g	Fat 18g
Carbohydrate	... 31g	Saturates 7g

🍧 15 mins   🕐 25–30 mins

SERVES 4

INGREDIENTS

4 Bramley apples

4 tbsp chopped walnuts

4 tbsp ground almonds

25 g/1 oz light muscovado sugar

25 g/1 oz cherries, chopped

25 g/1 oz stem ginger, chopped

1 tbsp Amaretto liqueur (optional)

2 tbsp butter

single cream or thick natural yogurt, to serve

1 Core the apples and, using a knife, score each around the middle to prevent the skins from splitting during barbecuing.

2 To make the filling, combine the walnuts, almonds, sugar, cherries, ginger and amaretto liqueur, if using, in a small bowl.

3 Spoon the filling mixture into each apple, pushing it down into the hollowed-out core. Mound a little of the filling mixture on top of each apple.

4 Place each apple on a large square of double thickness kitchen foil and generously dot all over with the butter. Wrap up the foil so that each apple is completely enclosed.

5 Barbecue the foil parcels over hot coals for 25–30 minutes or until the apples are tender.

6 Transfer the apples to warm, individual serving plates. Serve immediately with lashings of single cream or thick natural yogurt.

COOK'S TIP

If the coals are dying down, place the kitchen foil parcels directly on them, raking them up around the apples. Barbecue for 25–30 minutes.

Coconut Apples

This is a variation of the popular dessert of baked apples, but instead of being filled with dried fruit, they are layered with jam and coconut.

NUTRITIONAL INFORMATION

Calories 312   Sugars 32g
Protein . . . . .2g   Fat 20g
Carbohydrate . . .32g   Saturates 17g

10 mins   15–20 mins

SERVES 4

INGREDIENTS

2 tsp unsalted butter

4 tbsp ginger and apple jam

115 g/4 oz desiccated coconut

pinch of ground cinnamon

4 Bramley apples

double cream or vanilla ice cream, to serve (optional)

1 Cut 4 squares of foil, each large enough to enclose 1 apple, and lightly grease with the butter. Combine the jam and coconut in a small bowl and stir in cinnamon to taste.

2 Core the apples, but don't peel them. Cut each apple horizontally into 3 slices. Spread the mixture between the apple slices and reassemble the apples. Place 1 apple on each sheet of foil and fold up the sides to enclose securely.

3 Cook the apples on a hot barbecue for 15–20 minutes. Serve immediately with cream or ice cream, if you like.

VARIATION
Substitute large, firm pears for the apples.

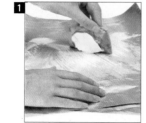  

Caramelised Fruit

Strawberries work surprisingly well in a chargrilled fruit salad. Choose large, ripe berries, don't hull them and turn frequently while cooking.

NUTRITIONAL INFORMATION

Calories	234	Sugars	........49g
Protein	.........2g	Fat	...........0g
Carbohydrate	...49g	Saturates	.......0g

1 hr 15 mins   5 mins

SERVES 4

INGREDIENTS

150 ml/5 fl oz medium sherry

115 g/4 oz caster sugar

1 ogen melon, halved and deseeded

4 peaches

225 g/8 oz strawberries

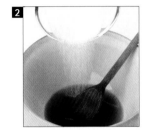

1 To peel peaches, make a tiny nick in the skin with the point of a sharp knife. Place them in a bowl and cover with boiling water. Leave for 15-30 seconds, then remove with a slotted spoon. Peel off the skin.

2 Combine the sherry with the sugar in a large bowl, stirring until the sugar has dissolved.

3 Cut the melon halves into wedges and cut the flesh away from the skin. Add the melon wedges, peach halves and strawberries to the bowl, tossing gently to coat. Cover with clingfilm and set aside to marinate for 1 hour.

4 Drain the fruit, and reserve the marinade. Cook the melon and peaches on a hot barbecue for 3 minutes, then add the strawberries and cook for 2 minutes more. Turn the fruit and brush frequently with the reserved marinade.

Totally Tropical Pineapple

The delicious aroma of fresh pineapple and rum as this succulent dessert is cooking will transport your imagination to a Caribbean beach.

NUTRITIONAL INFORMATION

Calories 206	Sugars 20g
Protein 1g	Fat 12g
Carbohydrate ...20g	Saturates 7g

15 mins

6–8 mins

SERVES 4

INGREDIENTS

1 pineapple

3 tbsp dark rum

2 tbsp muscovado sugar

1 tsp ground ginger

4 tbsp melted unsalted butter

1 Using a sharp knife, cut off the crown of the pineapple, then cut the fruit into 2 cm/¾ inch thick slices. Cut away the peel from each slice and flick out the 'eyes' with the point of the knife. Stamp out the cores with an apple corer or small pastry cutter.

2 Combine the rum, sugar, ginger and butter in a jug, stirring until the sugar has dissolved. Brush the pineapple rings with the mixture.

3 Cook the pineapple rings on a hot barbecue for about 3–4 minutes on each side.

4 Serve the pineapple rings immediately with the remaining rum mixture poured over them.

VARIATION

If you prefer, you can cut the pineapple into cubes or quarter slices and thread on skewers before brushing with the rum mixture and cooking.

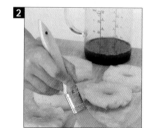

Panettone with Strawberries

Panettone is a sweet Italian bread. It is delicious toasted on the barbecue and topped with mascarpone and marinated strawberries.

NUTRITIONAL INFORMATION

Calories ....475 Sugars 20g
Protein ....7g Fat 31g
Carbohydrate ...36g Saturates 19g

5 mins, plus chilling

2 mins

SERVES 4

INGREDIENTS

225 g/8 oz strawberries

25 g/1 oz caster sugar

6 tbsp Marsala wine

½ tsp ground cinnamon

4 slices panettone

4 tbsp mascarpone cheese

1 Hull and slice the strawberries top to bottom, and place them in a bowl. Add the sugar, Marsala wine and ground cinnamon to the strawberries.

2 Toss the strawberries in the sugar and cinnamon mixture until they are well coated. Leave to chill in the refrigerator for at least 30 minutes.

3 When ready to serve, transfer the slices of panettone to a rack set over medium–hot coals. Barbecue the panettone for about 1 minute on each side or until golden brown.

4 Remove the panettone from the barbecue and transfer to serving plates. Top the panettone with the mascarpone cheese and the marinated strawberries. Serve immediately.

COOK'S TIP
Mascarpone is an Italian soft cheese with a rich, creamy texture, which tastes like very thick cream. It will melt into the panettone, making it quite delicious. If mascarpone is unavailable, clotted cream would be a good alternative.

Mincemeat-stuffed Pears

Pears quickly go soft and lose their shape when they are cooked, so choose fruit with good firm flesh for this recipe.

NUTRITIONAL INFORMATION

Calories 187	Sugars 29g
Protein 1g	Fat 7g
Carbohydrate ...31g	Saturates 3g

 10 mins 25–30 mins

SERVES 4

INGREDIENTS

4 firm pears

1 tsp lemon juice

2 tbsp vegetarian mincemeat

5 tbsp cake crumbs or 4 amaretti biscuits, crushed

15 g/½ oz butter

vanilla ice cream, to serve

1 Using a sharp knife, cut the pears in half. Using a teaspoon, scoop out the core and discard.

2 Brush the cut surface of each of the pear halves with a little lemon juice to prevent discoloration.

3 Mix together the vegetarian mincemeat and cake crumbs or crushed amaretti biscuits.

VARIATION

Use vegetarian mincemeat to stuff apples instead of pears and bake them on the barbecue in the same way.

4 Divide the mixture among the pear halves, spooning it into a mound where the core has been removed.

5 Place 2 pear halves on a large square of double thickness kitchen foil and generously dot all over with the butter.

6 Wrap up the foil around the pears so that they are completely enclosed.

7 Transfer the foil parcels to a rack set over hot coals. Barbecue for 25–30 minutes or until the pears are hot and just tender.

8 Transfer the cooked pears to individual serving plates.

9 Serve the pears with 2 scoops of ice cream per serving.

Special Peach Melba

The elegant simplicity of this dessert makes it the perfect end to a special occasion barbecue party.

NUTRITIONAL INFORMATION

Calories	480	Sugars	........79g
Protein	.........8g	Fat	..........15g
Carbohydrate	...83g	Saturates	......10g

🧊 1 hr 15 mins   ⏱ 3-5 mins

SERVES 4

I N G R E D I E N T S

2 large peaches, peeled, halved and stoned

1 tbsp light brown sugar

1 tbsp Amaretto liqueur

450 g/1 lb raspberries

115 g/4 oz icing sugar

600 ml/1 pint vanilla ice cream

1 Put the peach halves in a large, shallow dish and sprinkle with the brown sugar. Pour the Amaretto over them, cover with clingfilm and set aside for 1 hour.

2 Meanwhile, using the back of a spoon, press the raspberries through a fine sieve set over a bowl. Discard the contents of the sieve. Stir the icing sugar into the raspberry purée. Cover the bowl with clingfilm and chill in the refrigerator until required.

3 Drain the peach halves, reserving the marinade. Cook on a hot barbecue, turning and brushing frequently with the reserved marinade, for 3–5 minutes. To serve the peaches, put 2 scoops of ice cream in each of 4 sundae glasses, top with a peach half and spoon the raspberry sauce over it.

Salads
& Side Dishes

Forget limp lettuce leaves and dull vegetables
– this chapter has some wonderful ideas for
really unusual salads and side dishes. Salads
are often served as an accompaniment, but
put together the right ingredients and a salad
can be a meal in itself. Salads are also perfect

to serve as part of a summer buffet lunch or picnic, or for
a healthy packed lunch, and even to satisfy your midwinter need for a warming dish. And try accompanying
your entrée with a really different side dish – cauliflower
and broccoli in a lemony cheese sauce, spiced up with
ginger and cilantro, or a spicy Mexican sauce garnished
with chocolate!

Tropical Rice Salad

Rice salads are always popular and this colourful, fruity mixture is perfect as part of a summer buffet lunch or on a picnic.

NUTRITIONAL INFORMATION

Calories 300	Sugars 26g
Protein 5g	Fat 7g
Carbohydrate ...57g	Saturates 0g

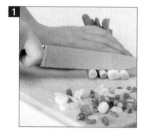

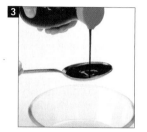

20 mins   15 mins

SERVES 4

INGREDIENTS

115 g/4 oz long-grain rice, rinsed

225 g/8 oz canned pineapple pieces in natural juice

200 g/7 oz canned sweetcorn, kernels drained

2 red peppers, deseeded and diced

4 spring onions, thinly sliced

3 tbsp sultanas

salt and pepper

DRESSING

1 tbsp groundnut oil

1 tbsp hazelnut oil

1 tbsp light soy sauce

1 garlic clove, finely chopped

1 tsp chopped fresh root ginger

1 Prepare the vegetables. Cook the rice in a saucepan of lightly salted boiling water for 15 minutes. Drain and rinse with cold water. Place the rice in a serving bowl.

2 Drain the pineapple pieces, reserving the juice in a jug. Add the pineapple, sweetcorn, red peppers, spring onions and sultanas to the rice and mix lightly.

3 Add all the dressing ingredients to the fruit juice, whisking well, and season to taste with salt and pepper. Pour the dressing over the salad and toss to coat.

Red & Green Salad

Beetroot and orange is a classic combination and here they are combined with tender, baby spinach leaves to make a dramatic warm salad.

NUTRITIONAL INFORMATION

Calories	173	Sugars	........19g
Protein	.........5g	Fat	...........9g
Carbohydrate	...20g	Saturates	.......1g

10 mins   5 mins

SERVES 4

I N G R E D I E N T S

3 tbsp extra virgin olive oil

juice of 1 orange

1 tsp caster sugar

1 tsp fennel seeds

650 g/1 lb 7 oz cooked beetroot

115 g/4 oz fresh baby spinach leaves

salt and pepper

1 Cut the beetroot into bite-sized cubes. Heat the olive oil in a small, heavy-based saucepan. Add the orange juice, sugar and fennel seeds and season to taste with salt and pepper. Stir until the sugar has dissolved.

2 Add the beetroot to the pan and stir gently to coat with the dressing. Remove the pan from the heat.

3 Arrange the spinach leaves in a salad bowl. Spoon the warm beetroot on top and serve.

COOK'S TIP

To cook raw beetroot, trim the tops, leaving about 5 cm/2 inches, and rinse under cold running water. Do not trim or peel the root. Simmer in a pan of lightly salted water for about 1 hour, until tender. Drain and cool, then rub off the skin and trim the leaves and root.

Sweet Potato & Nut Salad

Pecan nuts, with their slightly bitter flavour, are mixed with sweet potatoes to make a sweet and sour salad with an interesting texture.

NUTRITIONAL INFORMATION

Calories 330   Sugars 5g
Protein ....4g   Fat 20g
Carbohydrate ...36g   Saturates 2g

 25 mins   10 mins

SERVES 4

INGREDIENTS

500 g/1 lb 2 oz sweet potatoes, diced

2 celery sticks, sliced

125 g/4½ oz celeriac, grated

2 spring onions, sliced

50 g/1¾ oz pecan nuts, chopped

2 heads chicory, separated

1 tsp lemon juice

fresh thyme sprigs, to garnish

DRESSING

4 tbsp vegetable oil

1 tbsp garlic wine vinegar

1 tsp soft light brown sugar

2 tsp chopped fresh thyme

COOK'S TIP

Sweet potatoes do not store as well as ordinary potatoes. It is best to store them in a cool, dark place (not the refrigerator) and use within 1 week of purchase.

1 Cook the sweet potatoes in a large saucepan of boiling water for 10–15 minutes, until tender. Drain thoroughly and set aside to cool.

2 When the potatoes have cooled, stir in the celery, celeriac, spring onions and pecan nuts.

3 Line a salad plate with the chicory leaves and sprinkle with lemon juice.

4 Spoon the sweet potato mixture into the centre of the leaves.

5 In a small bowl, whisk together the vegetable oil, garlic wine vinegar, soft light brown sugar and chopped fresh thyme leaves.

6 Pour the dressing over the salad and serve at once, garnished with fresh thyme sprigs.

Three-bean Salad

Fresh French beans are combined with soya beans and red kidney beans in a chive and tomato dressing to make a tasty salad.

NUTRITIONAL INFORMATION

Calories	276	Sugars	.........7g
Protein	........18g	Fat	..........15g
Carbohydrate	...18g	Saturates	......4g

10 mins   5 mins

SERVES 6

INGREDIENTS

3 tbsp olive oil

1 tbsp lemon juice

1 tbsp tomato purée

1 tbsp light malt vinegar

1 tbsp snipped fresh chives, plus extra
   to garnish

175g/6 oz French beans

400 g/14 oz canned soya beans,
   rinsed and drained

400 g/14 oz canned red kidney beans,
   rinsed and drained

2 tomatoes, chopped

4 spring onions, trimmed and chopped

125 g/4½ oz feta cheese (drained weight),
   cut into cubes

salt and pepper

mixed salad leaves, to serve

1 Put the olive oil, lemon juice, tomato purée, light malt vinegar and snipped fresh chives into a large bowl and mix thoroughly. Set aside until required.

2 Cook the French beans in a small pan of lightly salted boiling water for 4–5 minutes. Drain, refresh under cold water to prevent any further cooking and drain well again. Pat dry with absorbent kitchen paper.

3 Add all the beans to the dressing, stirring well to mix.

4 Add the tomatoes, spring onions and feta cheese to the bean mixture, tossing gently to coat in the dressing. Season to taste with salt and pepper.

5 Arrange the salad leaves on serving plates. Pile the bean salad on top, garnish with extra chives and serve.

COOK'S TIP
For a more substantial light meal, top the salad with 2–3 sliced hard-boiled eggs and serve with crusty bread to mop up the juices.

Multi-coloured Salad

The beetroot adds a rich colour to this dish, tinting the potato an appealing pink. Mixed with cucumber, it is a really vibrant salad.

NUTRITIONAL INFORMATION

Calories 174	Sugars 8g
Protein 4g	Fat 6g
Carbohydrate ...27g	Saturates 1g

15–20 mins   20 mins

SERVES 4

INGREDIENTS

500 g/1 lb 2 oz waxy potatoes, diced

4 small cooked beetroot, sliced

½ small cucumber, thinly sliced

2 large dill pickles, sliced

1 red onion, halved and sliced

fresh dill sprigs, to garnish

DRESSING

1 garlic clove, crushed

2 tbsp olive oil

2 tbsp red wine vinegar

2 tbsp chopped fresh dill

salt and pepper

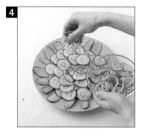

1 Cook the diced potatoes in a saucepan of boiling water for about 15 minutes, or until just tender. Drain and set aside to cool.

2 When cool, mix the diced potato and beetroot together gently in a bowl and set aside.

3 To make the dressing, whisk together the garlic, olive oil, vinegar and dill and season to taste with salt and pepper.

4 When you are ready to serve the salad, line a large serving platter with the slices of cucumber, the sliced dill pickles and the sliced red onion.

5 Spoon the potato and beetroot mixture on top of the other vegetables in the centre of the platter.

6 Pour the dressing over the salad and serve immediately, garnished with fresh dill sprigs.

VARIATION

Line the salad platter with 2 heads of chicory, separated into leaves, and arrange the cucumber, dill pickle and red onion slices on top of the leaves.

Three-way Potato Salad

New potatoes are served warm in a delicious dressing. The nutritional information is for the potato salad with the curry dressing only.

NUTRITIONAL INFORMATION

Calories 310	Sugars 12g
Protein 6g	Fat 19g
Carbohydrate . . .31g	Saturates 4g

🍃 10–20 mins   🕐 20 mins

SERVES 4

I N G R E D I E N T S

500 g/1 lb 2 oz new potatoes for
  each dressing

fresh herbs, to garnish

LIGHT CURRY DRESSING

1 tbsp vegetable oil

1 tbsp medium curry paste

1 small onion, chopped

1 tbsp mango chutney, chopped

6 tbsp natural yogurt

3 tbsp single cream

2 tbsp mayonnaise

salt and pepper

1 tbsp single cream, to garnish

VINAIGRETTE DRESSING

6 tbsp hazelnut oil

3 tbsp cider vinegar

1 tsp wholegrain mustard

1 tsp caster sugar

a few fresh basil leaves, torn

salt and pepper

PARSLEY CREAM

3 tbsp low-fat mayonnaise

150 ml/5 fl oz soured cream

4 spring onions, finely chopped

1 tbsp chopped fresh parsley

salt and pepper

1 To make the Light Curry Dressing, heat the vegetable oil in a saucepan, add the curry paste and onion and fry, stirring frequently, until the onion is soft. Remove from the heat and set aside to cool slightly.

2 Mix together the mango chutney, yogurt, cream and mayonnaise. Add the curry mixture and blend together. Season with salt and pepper.

3 To make the Vinaigrette Dressing, whisk the oil, vinegar, mustard, sugar and basil together in a small jug or bowl. Season with salt and pepper.

4 To make the Parsley Cream, combine the mayonnaise, soured cream, spring onions and parsley, mixing well. Season with salt and pepper.

5 Cook the new potatoes in lightly salted boiling water until they are just tender. Drain well and set aside to cool for 5 minutes, then add the chosen dressing, tossing to coat the potatoes thoroughly.

6 Serve the potato salad garnished with a sprinkling of chopped fresh herbs – basil or parsley, as appropriate. If you have used the light curry dressing, drizzle a little single cream over the potatoes to garnish.

Hot Lentil Salad

A robust vinaigrette dressing is served with this warm salad. If you prefer, you can serve the salad cold.

NUTRITIONAL INFORMATION

Calories	...125	Sugars	...3g
Protein	...6g	Fat	...6g
Carbohydrate	...12g	Saturates	...1g

10 mins   50 mins

SERVES 6-8

I N G R E D I E N T S

175 g/6 oz Puy lentils, cooked

4 tbsp olive oil

1 small onion, sliced

4 sticks celery, sliced

2 cloves garlic, crushed

2 courgettes, trimmed and diced

125 g/4½ oz French beans, trimmed and cut into short lengths

½ red pepper, deseeded and diced

½ yellow pepper, deseeded and diced

1 tsp Dijon mustard

1 tbsp balsamic vinegar

salt and pepper

1 Place the lentils in a large mixing or serving bowl. The lentils can still be warm, if wished.

2 Heat the oil in a saucepan and fry the onion and celery for 2–3 minutes until softened but not browned.

3 Stir the garlic, courgettes and green beans into the pan and cook for a further 2 minutes.

4 Add the peppers to the pan and cook for 1 minute.

5 Stir the mustard and the balsamic vinegar into the pan and mix until warm and well combined.

6 Pour the warm mixture over the lentils and toss together to mix well. Season with salt and pepper to taste and serve immediately.

COOK'S TIP

To cook the lentils, rinse them well and place in a large saucepan. Cover with plenty of cold water and bring to the boil. Reduce the heat and simmer for 45 minutes until the lentils are tender. Drain well.

Sweet Potato Salad

This hot fruity salad combines sweet potato and fried bananas with colourful mixed peppers, tossed in a honey-based dressing.

NUTRITIONAL INFORMATION

Calories 424	Sugars 29g	
Protein 5g	Fat 17g	
Carbohydrate ...68g	Saturates 8g	

15 mins   20 mins

SERVES 4

INGREDIENTS

500 g/1 lb 2 oz sweet potatoes, diced

4 tbsp butter

1 tbsp lemon juice

1 garlic clove, crushed

1 red pepper, deseeded and diced

1 green pepper, deseeded and diced

2 bananas, thickly sliced

2 thick slices white bread,
   crusts removed, diced

DRESSING

2 tbsp clear honey

2 tbsp chopped chives

2 tbsp lemon juice

2 tbsp olive oil

1 Cook the sweet potatoes in a pan of boiling water for 10–15 minutes, until tender. Drain thoroughly and reserve.

2 Meanwhile, melt the butter in a frying pan. Add the lemon juice, garlic and peppers and cook, stirring constantly for 3 minutes.

3 Add the banana slices to the pan and cook for 1 minute. Remove the bananas from the pan with a slotted spoon and stir into the potatoes.

4 Add the bread cubes to the frying pan and cook, stirring frequently, for 2 minutes, until golden brown on all sides.

5 Mix the dressing ingredients together in a small saucepan and heat until the honey is runny.

6 Spoon the potato mixture into a serving dish and season to taste. Pour over the honey dressing and sprinkle the croûtons over the top. Serve immediately.

COOK'S TIP

Use firm, slightly underripe bananas in this recipe as they won't turn soft and mushy when they are fried.

Goat's Cheese Salad

A delicious hot salad of melting goat's cheese over sliced tomato and basil on a base of hot ciabatta bread.

NUTRITIONAL INFORMATION

Calories 379	Sugars 3g
Protein 15g	Fat 23g
Carbohydrate ...30g	Saturates 10g

 10 mins   6 mins

SERVES 4

INGREDIENTS

3 tbsp olive oil

1 tbsp white wine vinegar

1 tsp black olive paste

1 garlic clove, crushed

1 tsp chopped fresh thyme

1 ciabatta loaf

4 small tomatoes

12 fresh basil leaves

2 x 125 g/4½ oz logs goat's cheese

TO SERVE

mixed salad leaves, including rocket and radicchio

COOK'S TIP

Many French goat's cheeses are widely available. Those labelled chèvre or pur chèvre must be made purely from goat's milk. The goat's milk in mi-chèvre cheeses is mixed with up to 75 percent cow's milk.

1 Mix the olive oil, white wine vinegar, black olive paste, garlic and chopped thyme together in a screw-top jar and shake vigorously.

2 Cut the ciabatta loaf in half horizontally then in half again vertically to make 4 pieces.

3 Drizzle some of the dressing over the bread, then arrange the tomatoes and basil leaves on the top.

4 Cut each roll of goat's cheese into 6 slices and place 3 slices on each piece of ciabatta.

5 Brush with some of the dressing and bake in a preheated oven, 230°C/450°F/Gas Mark 8, for 5–6 minutes until turning brown at the edges.

6 Pour the remaining dressing over the mixed salad leaves and serve with the baked ciabatta bread.

Cheese, Nut & Pasta Salad

Use colourful salad leaves to provide visual contrast to match the contrasts of taste and texture.

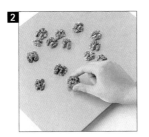

NUTRITIONAL INFORMATION

Calories	694	Sugars	1g
Protein	22g	Fat	57g
Carbohydrate	24g	Saturates	15g

 15 mins   15–20 mins

SERVES 4

INGREDIENTS

225 g/8 oz dried pasta shells

1 tbsp olive oil

115 g/4 oz shelled and halved walnuts

mixed salad leaves, such as radicchio, escarole, rocket, lamb's lettuce and frisée

225 g/8 oz dolcelatte cheese, crumbled

salt

DRESSING

2 tbsp walnut oil

4 tbsp extra virgin olive oil

2 tbsp red wine vinegar

salt and pepper

1 Boil a large pan of lightly salted water. Add the pasta shells and olive oil and cook for 8–10 minutes or until tender but *al dente*. Drain the pasta, refresh under cold running water, drain again, and set aside.

2 Spread out the shelled walnut halves on to a baking tray and toast under a preheated grill for 2–3 minutes. Set aside to cool while you make the dressing.

3 To make the dressing, whisk together the walnut oil, olive oil and vinegar in a small bowl, and season to taste.

4 To make up the salad, arrange the salad leaves in a serving bowl. Pile the cooled pasta in the middle of the salad leaves and sprinkle over the dolcelatte cheese. Just before serving, pour the dressing over the pasta salad, scatter the walnut halves on top, and toss together to coat with dressing. Serve immediately.

COOK'S TIP

Dolcelatte is a semi-soft, blue-veined cheese from Italy. Its texture is creamy and smooth and the flavour is delicate, but piquant. You could use Roquefort instead. It is essential that whatever cheese you choose, it is of the best quality and in peak condition.

Carrot & Nut Coleslaw

This simple salad has a dressing made from poppy seeds pan-fried in sesame oil to bring out their flavour and aroma.

NUTRITIONAL INFORMATION

Calories	220	Sugars	.........7g
Protein	.........4g	Fat	..........19g
Carbohydrate	...10g	Saturates	.......3g

 15 mins   5–10 mins

SERVES 4

I N G R E D I E N T S

1 large carrot, grated

1 small onion, finely chopped

2 celery sticks, chopped

¼ small hard white cabbage, shredded

1 tbsp chopped fresh parsley

salt and pepper

4 tbsp sesame oil

½ tsp poppy seeds

55 g/2 oz cashew nuts

2 tbsp white wine vinegar or cider vinegar

fresh parsley sprigs, to garnish

1 In a large salad bowl, combine the grated carrot, chopped onion and celery and the shredded white cabbage. Stir in the chopped fresh parsley and season to taste with salt and pepper.

2 Heat the sesame oil in a saucepan with a lid. Add the poppy seeds and cover the pan. Cook over a medium-high heat until the seeds start to make a popping sound. Remove from the heat and set aside to cool.

3 Spread out the cashew nuts in a single layer on a baking sheet. Place them under a preheated medium-hot grill and toast until lightly browned, turning occasionally. Be careful not to burn them. Remove from the heat and set aside to cool.

4 Add the wine or cider vinegar to the sesame oil and poppy seed mixture, then pour the poppy seed dressing over the vegetable mixture.

5 Add the cooled cashew nuts to the vegetable mixture and toss together to coat all the ingredients thoroughly in the dressing.

6 Garnish the salad with the sprigs of fresh parsley and serve immediately.

Hot Salad

This quickly-made dish is ideal for a cold winter's night. Serve with crusty bread, freshly made rolls or garlic bread.

NUTRITIONAL INFORMATION

Calories 154   Sugars 13g
Protein ....4g   Fat 9g
Carbohydrate ...14g   Saturates 6g

10 mins   10 mins

SERVES 4

INGREDIENTS

½ cauliflower

1 green pepper

1 red pepper

½ cucumber

4 carrots

2 tbsp butter

salt and pepper

crusty bread, rolls or garlic bread, to serve

DRESSING

3 tbsp olive oil

1 tbsp white wine vinegar

1 tbsp light soy sauce

1 tsp caster sugar

salt and pepper

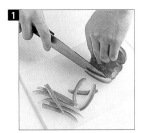

1 Cut the cauliflower into small florets, using a sharp knife. Deseed the peppers and cut the flesh into thin slices. Cut the cucumber into thin slices. Thinly slice the carrots lengthways.

2 Melt the butter in a large, heavy-based saucepan. Add the cauliflower florets, peppers, cucumber and carrots and fry over a medium heat, stirring constantly, for 5–7 minutes, until tender, but still firm to the bite. Season with salt and pepper. Lower the heat, cover with a lid, and simmer for 3 minutes.

3 Meanwhile, make the dressing. Whisk together all the ingredients until thoroughly combined.

4 Transfer the vegetables to a serving dish, pour over the dressing, toss to mix well and serve immediately.

VARIATION
You can replace the vegetables in this recipe with any of your choice, such as broccoli, spring onions and courgettes.

Green & White Salad

This potato, rocket and apple salad is flavoured with creamy, salty goat's cheese – perfect with salad leaves.

NUTRITIONAL INFORMATION

Calories ....282 Sugars 10g
Protein ....8g Fat 17g
Carbohydrate ...26g Saturates 5g

  15 mins   20 mins

SERVES 4

INGREDIENTS

2 large potatoes, unpeeled and sliced

2 green apples, diced

1 tsp lemon juice

25 g/1 oz walnut pieces

125 g/4½ oz goat's cheese, cubed

150 g/5½ oz rocket leaves

salt and pepper

DRESSING

2 tbsp olive oil

1 tbsp red wine vinegar

1 tsp clear honey

1 tsp fennel seeds

1 Cook the potato slices in a pan of lightly salted boiling water for about 15 minutes, or until just tender. Drain and set aside to cool. Transfer the cooled potatoes to a serving bowl.

2 Toss the diced apples in the lemon juice, then drain them, add them to the bowl with the cold potatoes and stir gently to mix.

3 Add the walnut pieces, the cubed goat's cheese and the rocket leaves to the potatoes and apples, then toss the salad to mix.

4 In a small bowl, whisk the olive oil, red wine vinegar, clear honey and fennel seeds together until well combined. Pour the dressing over the salad, and serve immediately.

COOK'S TIP

Serve this salad immediately to prevent the apple from discolouring. Alternatively, prepare all of the other ingredients in advance and add the apple at the last minute.

Moroccan Salad

Couscous is a type of semolina made from durum wheat. It is wonderful in salads, as it readily takes up the flavour of the dressing.

NUTRITIONAL INFORMATION

Calories 195	Sugars 15g
Protein 8g	Fat 2g
Carbohydrate ...40g	Saturates 0.3g

30-35 mins   0 mins

SERVES 6

INGREDIENTS

175 g/6 oz couscous

1 bunch spring onions, finely chopped

1 small green pepper, deseeded and chopped

10 cm/4 inch piece of cucumber, chopped

175 g/6 oz canned chick peas, rinsed and drained

60 g/2 oz sultanas or raisins

salt and pepper

2 oranges

fresh mint sprigs, to garnish

lettuce leaves, to serve

DRESSING

finely grated rind of 1 orange

1 tbsp chopped fresh mint

150 ml/¼ pint natural yogurt

2 Add the spring onions, green pepper, cucumber, chick peas and sultanas or raisins to the couscous, stirring to combine. Season with salt and pepper.

4 Using a sharp serrated knife, remove the peel and pith from the oranges. Cut the flesh into segments, removing all the membrane.

1 Put the couscous into a bowl and cover with boiling water. Leave it to soak for about 15 minutes to swell the grains, then stir gently with a fork to separate them.

3 To make the dressing, place the orange rind, mint and yogurt in a bowl and mix together until well combined. Pour over the couscous mixture and stir to mix well.

5 Arrange the lettuce leaves on 6 serving plates. Divide the couscous mixture between the plates and arrange the orange segments on top. Garnish with sprigs of fresh mint and serve.

Grapefruit & Coconut Salad

This salad is quite deceptive – it is, in fact, surprisingly filling, even though it looks very light.

NUTRITIONAL INFORMATION

Calories	201	Sugars	........13g
Protein	.........3g	Fat	..........15g
Carbohydrate	...14g	Saturates	.......9g

🍳 10 mins   🕐 10 mins

SERVES 4

INGREDIENTS

125 g/4½ oz grated coconut

2 tsp light soy sauce

2 tbsp lime juice

2 tbsp water

2 tsp sunflower oil

1 garlic clove, halved

1 onion, finely chopped

2 large ruby grapefruits, peeled and segmented

90 g/3 oz alfalfa sprouts

COOK'S TIP

Alfalfa sprouts can be bought in trays or packets from most supermarkets, but it is very easy to grow your own, and you will have a constant and cheap supply.

1 Toast the grated coconut in a dry frying pan over a low heat, stirring constantly, for about 3 minutes, or until it is golden brown. Transfer the toasted coconut to a bowl.

2 Add the light soy sauce, lime juice and water to the toasted coconut and mix together well.

3 Heat the oil in a saucepan and fry the garlic and onion until soft. Stir the onion into the coconut mixture. Remove and discard the garlic.

4 Divide the grapefruit segments between 4 plates. Sprinkle each with a quarter of the alfalfa sprouts and spoon over a quarter of the coconut mixture.

Aubergine Salad

A salad with a difference from Sicily. It has a real bite, both from the sweet-sour sauce, and from the texture of the celery.

NUTRITIONAL INFORMATION

Calories 390	Sugars 15g	
Protein 8g	Fat 33g	
Carbohydrate ...16g	Saturates 5g	

  1½ hrs 25 mins

SERVES 4

INGREDIENTS

2 large aubergines, about 1 kg/2 lb 4 oz

6 tbsp olive oil

1 small onion, finely chopped

2 garlic cloves, crushed

6–8 celery sticks, cut into 1 cm/½ inch slices

2 tbsp capers, drained

12–16 green olives, stoned and sliced

2 tbsp pine kernels

25 g/1 oz bitter or dark chocolate, grated

4 tbsp white wine vinegar

1 tbsp brown sugar

salt and pepper

2 hard-boiled eggs, sliced, to serve

celery leaves or curly endive, to garnish

2 Heat most of the oil in a frying pan and fry the aubergine cubes until golden brown all over. Drain on kitchen paper then put in a large bowl.

3 Add the onion and garlic to the pan with the remaining oil and fry very gently until just soft.

4 Add the celery to the pan and fry for a few minutes, stirring frequently, until lightly coloured but still crisp. Add the celery to the aubergines with the capers, olives and pine kernels and mix together lightly.

5 Add the chocolate, vinegar and sugar to the residue in the pan. Heat gently until melted, then bring to the boil. Season with salt and pepper to taste. Pour over the salad and mix lightly. Cover, leave until cold and then chill thoroughly.

6 Serve the aubergine salad with sliced hard-boiled eggs and garnish with celery leaves or curly endive.

1 Cut the aubergine into 2.5 cm/1 inch cubes and sprinkle liberally with 2–3 tablespoons of salt. Leave to stand for 1 hour to extract the bitter juices, then rinse off the salt thoroughly under cold water, drain and dry on paper towels.

Mixed Bean & Apple Salad

Use any mixture of beans you have to hand in this recipe, but the wider the variety, the more colourful the salad.

NUTRITIONAL INFORMATION

Calories	183	Sugars	.........8g
Protein	.........6g	Fat	...........7g
Carbohydrate	...26g	Saturates	.......1g

 20 mins   20 mins

SERVES 4

INGREDIENTS

225 g/8 oz new potatoes, scrubbed and quartered

225 g/8 oz mixed canned beans, such as red kidney beans, flageolet and borlotti beans, drained and rinsed

1 red apple, diced and tossed in 1 tbsp lemon juice

1 yellow pepper, deseeded and diced

1 shallot, sliced

½ fennel bulb, sliced

oakleaf lettuce leaves

DRESSING

1 tbsp red wine vinegar

2 tbsp olive oil

1½ tsp American mustard

1 garlic clove, crushed

2 tsp chopped fresh thyme

salt and pepper, to taste

VARIATION

Use Dijon or wholegrain mustard in place of American mustard for a different flavour.

1 Cook the quartered potatoes in a saucepan of boiling water for 15 minutes until tender. Drain and transfer to a large bowl.

2 Add the mixed beans to the potatoes, with the apple, yellow pepper, shallot and fennel. Mix well, taking care not to break up the cooked potatoes.

3 To make the dressing, whisk all the dressing ingredients together until thoroughly combined, then pour it over the potato salad.

4 Line a serving plate or salad bowl with the oakleaf lettuce leaves and spoon the potato mixture into the centre. Serve the salad immediately.

Quick Bean Salad

This attractive-looking chick pea salad makes a delicious light but satisfying meal in summer.

NUTRITIONAL INFORMATION

Calories 139   Sugars 5g
Protein ....8g   Fat 3g
Carbohydrate ...21g   Saturates 0.4g

 10 mins   0 mins

SERVES 4

INGREDIENTS

400 g/14 oz canned chick peas

4 carrots

1 bunch spring onions

1 cucumber

½ tsp salt

½ tsp pepper

3 tbsp lemon juice

1 red pepper, deseeded

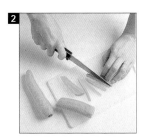

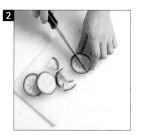

1 Drain the chick peas thoroughly and place them in a salad bowl.

2 Using a sharp knife, peel and slice the carrots, cut the spring onions into small pieces and cut the cucumber into thick slices and quarter.

3 Add the carrots, spring onions and cucumber to the chick peas and mix. Season with the salt and pepper and sprinkle with the lemon juice.

4 Toss the salad ingredients together gently using 2 serving spoons.

5 Using a sharp knife, slice the red pepper thinly.

6 Arrange the slices of red pepper on top of the chick pea salad.

7 Serve the salad immediately or chill in the refrigerator until required.

COOK'S TIP

Using canned chick peas rather than the dried ones speeds up the cooking time.

Salad with Garlic Dressing

This is a very quick and refreshing salad using a whole range of colourful ingredients which make it look as good as it tastes.

NUTRITIONAL INFORMATION

Calories ....82 Sugars 5g
Protein ....2g Fat 6g
Carbohydrate ....5g Saturates 1g

 10 mins   0 mins

SERVES 4

INGREDIENTS

85 g/3 oz cucumber, cut into batons

6 spring onions, halved

2 tomatoes, deseeded and cut into 8 wedges

1 yellow pepper, deseeded and cut into strips

2 celery sticks, cut into strips

4 radishes, quartered

85 g/3 oz rocket

1 tbsp chopped fresh mint, to garnish

DRESSING

2 tbsp lemon juice

1 garlic clove, crushed

150 ml/5 fl oz low-fat natural yogurt

2 tbsp olive oil

salt and pepper

1 To make the salad, gently mix the cucumber batons, spring onions, tomato wedges, yellow pepper strips, celery strips, radishes and rocket in a large serving bowl.

2 To make the dressing, stir the lemon juice, garlic, natural yogurt and olive oil together in a small bowl until thoroughly combined. Season with salt and pepper to taste.

3 Spoon the dressing over the salad and toss gently to coat all the ingredients thoroughly. Sprinkle the salad with chopped mint and serve immediately.

COOK'S TIP

Rocket has a distinctive warm, peppery flavour which is ideal in green salads. If rocket is unavailable, lamb's lettuce makes a good substitute.

Italian Pasta Salad

All the ingredients of pesto sauce are included in this salad, which has a fabulous summery taste, perfect for al fresco eating.

NUTRITIONAL INFORMATION

Calories	432	Sugars	.........3g
Protein	........14g	Fat	..........29g
Carbohydrate	...30g	Saturates	.......6g

25 mins   15 mins

SERVES 4

INGREDIENTS

225 g/8 oz dried fusilli

4 tomatoes

50 g/1¾ oz black olives

25 g/1 oz sun-dried tomatoes in oil

2 tbsp pine kernels

2 tbsp grated Parmesan cheese

fresh basil, to garnish

VINAIGRETTE

15 g/½ oz fresh basil leaves

1 clove garlic

2 tbsp grated Parmesan cheese

4 tbsp extra virgin olive oil

2 tbsp lemon juice

salt and pepper

1 Cook the pasta in a saucepan of lightly salted boiling water for 8–10 minutes or until just tender. Drain the pasta, rinse under cold water, then drain again thoroughly. Transfer the pasta to a large bowl.

2 To make the vinaigrette, place the basil leaves, garlic, cheese, oil and lemon juice in a food processor or blender and season to taste. Process until the leaves are well chopped and the ingredients are combined. Alternatively, finely chop the basil leaves by hand and combine with the other ingredients. Pour the vinaigrette over the pasta and toss to coat.

3 Cut the tomatoes into wedges. Stone and halve the olives. Slice the sun-dried tomatoes. Toast the pine kernels on a baking tray under the grill until golden.

4 Add the fresh and sun-dried tomatoes and the olives to the pasta and mix.

5 Transfer the pasta to a serving dish, scatter over the Parmesan and pine kernels and garnish with basil leaves.

COOK'S TIP

Sun-dried tomatoes have a strong, intense flavour. They are most frequently found packed in oil with herbs and garlic. Do not waste the oil, which has an excellent flavour – use it in salad dressings.

Tomato & Basil Salad

These extra-large tomatoes make an excellent salad, especially when combined with basil, garlic, kiwi fruit, onion rings and new potatoes.

NUTRITIONAL INFORMATION

Calories 167   Sugars 4g
Protein ....2g   Fat 11g
Carbohydrate ...16g   Saturates 2g

🥗 35 mins   🕐 15 mins

SERVES 8

I N G R E D I E N T S

500 g/1 lb 2 oz tiny new or salad
  potatoes, scrubbed

4–5 tomatoes

2 kiwi fruit

1 onion, sliced very thinly

2 tbsp roughly chopped fresh basil leaves

fresh basil leaves, to garnish

D R E S S I N G

4 tbsp virgin olive oil

2 tbsp balsamic vinegar

1 garlic clove, crushed

salt and pepper

2 tbsp mayonnaise or soured cream

1 Cook the potatoes in their skins in a saucepan of salted water for about 10–15 minutes or until just tender. Drain the potatoes thoroughly.

2 To make the dressing, whisk together the oil, vinegar, garlic and salt and pepper to taste until completely emulsified. Transfer half of the dressing to another bowl and whisk in the mayonnaise or soured cream.

3 Add the creamy dressing to the warm potatoes and toss thoroughly, then leave until cold.

4 Wipe the tomatoes and slice thinly. Peel the kiwi fruit and cut into thin slices. Layer the tomatoes with the kiwi fruit, slices of onion and chopped basil in a fairly shallow dish, leaving a space in the centre for the potatoes.

5 Spoon the potatoes in their dressing into the centre of the tomato salad.

6 Drizzle a little of the dressing over the tomatoes, or serve separately in a bowl or jug. Garnish the salad with fresh basil leaves. Cover the dish with cling film and chill until ready to serve.

COOK'S TIP
Ordinary tomatoes can be used for this salad, but make sure they are firm and bright red. You will need 8–10 ordinary-sized tomatoes.

Coconut Couscous Salad

The nutty taste of toasted coconut really stands out in this delicious dish. It's perfect for picnics or for a healthy packed lunch.

NUTRITIONAL INFORMATION

Calories 330   Sugars 18g
Protein ....7g   Fat 7g
Carbohydrate ...63g   Saturates 3g

1½ hrs   15 mins

SERVES 4

INGREDIENTS

350 g/12 oz couscous

175 g/6 oz no-need-to-soak dried apricots

1 small bunch fresh chives

2 tbsp unsweetened desiccated coconut

1 tsp ground cinnamon

salt and pepper

shredded fresh mint leaves, to garnish

DRESSING

1 tbsp olive oil

2 tbsp unsweetened orange juice

½ tsp finely grated orange rind

1 tsp wholegrain mustard

1 tsp clear honey

2 tbsp chopped fresh mint leaves

salt and pepper

1 Soak the couscous according to the instructions on the packet. Bring a large saucepan of water to the boil. Transfer the couscous to a steamer or large sieve lined with muslin and place over the water. Cover and steam as directed. Remove from the heat, place in a heatproof bowl and set aside to cool.

2 Slice the apricots into thin strips and place in a small bowl. Using scissors, snip the chives over the apricots.

3 When the couscous is cool, mix in the apricots, chives, coconut and cinnamon. Season well.

4 To make the dressing, mix all the ingredients together and season. Pour over the couscous and mix until well combined. Cover and leave to chill for 1 hour to allow the flavours to develop. Serve the salad garnished with shredded mint leaves.

VARIATION
To serve this salad hot, when the couscous has been steamed, mix in the apricots, chives, coconut, cinnamon and seasoning along with 1 tbsp olive oil. Transfer to a warmed serving bowl and serve.

Red-hot Slaw

As well as being an exciting side dish, this colourful salad makes an unusual filling for jacket potatoes.

NUTRITIONAL INFORMATION

Calories . . . . . . .169 Sugars 16g
Protein . . . . .11g Fat 7g
Carbohydrate . . .17g Saturates 3g

1 hr   0 mins

SERVES 4

INGREDIENTS

½ small red cabbage

1 large carrot

2 red apples

1 tbsp lemon juice

1 red onion

100 g/3½ oz reduced-fat Cheddar cheese, grated

TO GARNISH

fresh red chilli strips

carrot strips

DRESSING

3 tbsp reduced-calorie mayonnaise

3 tbsp low-fat natural yogurt

1 garlic clove, crushed

1 tsp paprika

1–2 tsp chilli powder

pinch of cayenne pepper (optional)

salt and pepper

1 Cut the red cabbage in half and remove the central core. Finely shred the leaves and place in a large bowl. Peel and coarsely grate or finely shred the carrot and mix it into the cabbage.

2 Core the apples and finely dice, leaving on the skins. Place in another bowl and toss in the lemon juice to help prevent the apple from browning. Mix the apple into the cabbage and carrot.

3 Peel and finely shred or grate the onion. Stir into the other vegetables with the cheese and mix together.

4 To make the dressing, mix together the mayonnaise, yogurt, garlic and paprika in a small bowl. Add 1 or 2 tsp chilli powder, according to taste, and the cayenne pepper, if using – remember this will add more spice to the dressing. Season to taste with salt and pepper.

5 Add the dressing to the vegetables and toss well to mix. Cover and leave to chill in the refrigerator for 1 hour to allow the flavours to develop.

6 Serve garnished with strips of fresh red chilli and carrot.

Potato & Tomato Salad

Potato salad is always a favourite, but it is even more delicious with the addition of sun-dried tomatoes and fresh parsley.

NUTRITIONAL INFORMATION

Calories	425	Sugars	.........6g
Protein	.........6g	Fat	..........27g
Carbohydrate	...43g	Saturates	.......5g

 10 mins, plus chilling   12 mins

SERVES 4

INGREDIENTS

450g/1 lb baby potatoes, unpeeled, or larger potatoes, halved

8 sun-dried tomatoes

4 tbsp natural yogurt

4 tbsp mayonnaise

salt and pepper

2 tbsp chopped fresh flat-leaved parsley

1 Rinse and clean the potatoes and place them in a large pan of water. Bring to the boil and then cook for 8–12 minutes, or until just tender. (The cooking time will vary according to the size of your potatoes.)

2 Meanwhile, using a sharp knife, thinly slice the sun-dried tomatoes.

3 To make the dressing, mix together the yogurt and mayonnaise in a bowl and season to taste with a little salt and pepper. Stir in the sun-dried tomato slices and the chopped flat-leaved parsley.

4 Remove the potatoes with a perforated spoon, drain them thoroughly and then set them aside to cool. If you are using larger potatoes, cut them into 5 cm/2 inch chunks.

5 Pour the dressing over the potatoes and toss to mix.

6 Leave the potato salad to chill in the refrigerator for about 20 minutes, then serve either as a starter or as an accompaniment to a main meal.

COOK'S TIP
It is easier to cut the larger potatoes once they are cooked. Although smaller pieces of potato will cook more quickly, they tend to disintegrate and become mushy.

Roast Pepper Salad

Serve chilled as an antipasto with cold meats, or warm as a side dish. Garlic bread makes a delicious accompaniment.

NUTRITIONAL INFORMATION

Calories 141   Sugars 8g
Protein . . . . .1g   Fat 11g
Carbohydrate . . . .9g   Saturates 2g

20 mins   20 mins

SERVES

I N G R E D I E N T S

4 large mixed red, green and yellow peppers

4 tbsp olive oil

1 large red onion, sliced

2 garlic cloves, crushed

4 tomatoes, peeled and chopped

pinch of sugar

1 tsp lemon juice

salt and pepper

1 Trim and halve the peppers and remove the seeds.

2 Place the peppers, skin side up, under a preheated hot grill. Cook until the skins char. Rinse under cold water and remove the skins.

3 Trim off any thick membranes and slice thinly.

4 Heat the oil and fry the onion and garlic until softened. Then add the peppers and tomatoes and fry over a low heat for 10 minutes.

5 Remove from the heat, add the sugar and lemon juice, and season to taste. Serve immediately or leave to cool (the flavours will develop as the salad cools).

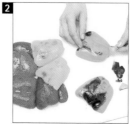

Orange & Fennel Salad

Fresh, juicy oranges and the sharp aniseed flavour of fennel combine to make this refreshing Spanish salad.

NUTRITIONAL INFORMATION

Calories	136	Sugars	........19g
Protein	.........3g	Fat	...........6g
Carbohydrate	...19g	Saturates	.......1g

 30 mins   0 mins

SERVES 4

INGREDIENTS

4 large oranges

1 large bulb fennel

2 tsp fennel seeds

2 tbsp extra virgin olive oil

freshly squeezed orange juice, to taste

finely chopped fresh parsley, to garnish

1 Using a small serrated knife, remove the rind and pith from 1 orange, cutting carefully from the top to the bottom of the orange so it retains its shape. Work over a small bowl to catch the juices.

2 Peel the remaining oranges the same way, reserving all the juices. Cut the oranges horizontally into 5 mm/¼ inch slices and arrange in an attractive serving bowl; reserve the juices.

3 Cut the fronds from the fennel bulb, cut the bulb in half lengthways and then into quarters. Cut crossways into the very thin slices. Immediately place in the bowl of oranges and toss with a little of the reserved juice to prevent browning.

4 Sprinkle the fennel seeds over the oranges and fennel.

5 Whisk the oil with the remaining orange juice, plus extra fresh orange juice to taste. Pour over the oranges and fennel and toss gently. Cover with clingfilm and chill until ready to serve.

6 Just before serving, remove from the refrigerator and sprinkle with parsley.

VARIATION
Replace the fennel with a finely sliced onion or a large bunch of spring onions, finely chopped. This version is from Spain, where orange-coloured oranges would be used, but in Sicily the dish is made with blood-red oranges.

Hot & Spicy Rice Salad

Serve this spicy Indian-style dish with a low-fat natural yogurt raita for a delightfully refreshing contrast.

NUTRITIONAL INFORMATION

Calories ....329 Sugars 27g
Protein ....8g Fat 8g
Carbohydrate ...59g Saturates 1g

30 mins   25 mins

SERVES 4

INGREDIENTS

2 tsp vegetable oil

1 onion, finely chopped

1 fresh red chilli, deseeded and finely chopped

8 cardamom pods

1 tsp turmeric

1 tsp garam masala

350 g/12 oz basmati rice, rinsed

700 ml/1¼ pints boiling water

1 orange pepper, deseeded and chopped

225 g/8 oz cauliflower florets, divided into small florets

salt and pepper

4 ripe tomatoes, peeled, deseeded and chopped

125 g/4½ oz seedless raisins

25 g/1 oz toasted flaked almonds

raita of low-fat natural yogurt, onion, cucumber and mint, to serve

1 Heat the vegetable oil in a large, non-stick saucepan. Add the onion, chilli, cardamom pods, turmeric and garam masala to the pan and fry over a low heat for 2–3 minutes until the vegetables are just softened.

2 Stir in the rice, boiling water, orange pepper and cauliflower. Season to taste with salt and pepper.

3 Cover the pan with a tight-fitting lid and bring the mixture to the boil. Lower the heat and simmer for 15 minutes without lifting the lid.

4 Uncover the pan and fork through the rice. Stir in the tomatoes and raisins.

5 Cover the pan again, turn off the heat and leave for a further 15 minutes. Discard the cardamom pods.

6 Pile the salad on to a warmed serving platter and garnish with a sprinkling of the toasted flaked almonds.

7 Serve the rice salad immediately with a separate bowl of the yogurt raita as an accompaniment.

Cool Cucumber Salad

This cooling salad is another good foil for a highly spiced meal. Omit the green chilli, if preferred.

NUTRITIONAL INFORMATION

Calories 11   Sugars 2g
Protein . . . . .0.4g   Fat 0g
Carbohydrate . . . .2g   Saturates 0g

 1¼ hrs   0 mins

SERVES 4

INGREDIENTS

225 g/8 oz cucumber

1 fresh green chilli (optional)

fresh coriander leaves, finely chopped

2 tbsp lemon juice

½ tsp salt

1 tsp sugar

fresh mint leaves and red pepper strips, to garnish

1 Using a sharp knife, slice the cucumber thinly. Arrange the cucumber slices on a round serving plate.

2 Using a sharp knife, deseed and chop the green chilli (if using). Scatter the chopped chilli over the cucumber.

3 To make the dressing, mix together the chopped coriander, lemon juice, salt and sugar.

4 Place the cucumber in the refrigerator and leave to chill for at least 1 hour, or until required.

5 When ready to serve, transfer the cucumber to a serving dish. Pour the salad dressing over the cucumber just before serving and garnish with fresh mint and red pepper.

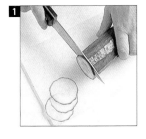

Indian Potato Salad

There are many hot, spicy, Indian potato dishes that are served with curry, but this fruity salad is delicious chilled.

NUTRITIONAL INFORMATION

Calories	175	Sugars	.........8g
Protein	.........6g	Fat	...........1g
Carbohydrate	...38g	Saturates	.....0.3g

25 mins   20 mins

SERVES 4

INGREDIENTS

900 g/2 lb floury potatoes, diced

75 g/2¾ oz small broccoli florets

1 small mango, diced

4 spring onions, sliced

salt and pepper

small cooked spiced poppadoms, to serve

DRESSING

½ tsp ground cumin

½ tsp ground coriander

1 tbsp mango chutney

150 ml/5 fl oz low-fat natural yogurt

1 tsp chopped fresh root ginger

2 tbsp chopped fresh coriander

1 Cook the potatoes in a saucepan of boiling water for 10 minutes or until tender. Drain and place in a mixing bowl.

2 Meanwhile, blanch the broccoli florets in a separate saucepan of boiling water for 2 minutes. Drain the broccoli well and add the florets to the potatoes in the bowl.

3 When the potatoes and broccoli have cooled, add the mango and spring onions. Season to taste with salt and pepper and mix well to combine.

4 In a small bowl, stir all of the dressing ingredients together.

5 Spoon the dressing over the potato mixture and mix together carefully, taking care not to break up the potatoes and broccoli.

6 Serve the potato salad immediately, accompanied by the poppadoms.

COOK'S TIP

Mix the dressing ingredients together in advance and leave to chill in the refrigerator for a few hours to allow the flavour to develop.

Sweet Potato Salad

This unusual and filling salad, with its peppery yogurt dressing and lovely mix of textures, is best served warm.

NUTRITIONAL INFORMATION

Calories 192   Sugars 23g
Protein . . . . .7g   Fat 4g
Carbohydrate . . .33g   Saturates 1g

   10 mins   15 mins

SERVES 4

I N G R E D I E N T S

1 sweet potato, peeled and diced

2 carrots, sliced

3 tomatoes, deseeded and chopped

85 g/3 oz canned chick peas, drained

8 iceberg lettuce leaves

1 tbsp sultanas

1 tbsp chopped walnuts

1 small onion, thinly sliced into rings

D R E S S I N G

6 tbsp natural yogurt

1 tbsp clear honey

1 tsp coarsely ground black pepper

salt

1 Cook the diced sweet potato in a large pan of boiling water for 10 minutes. Add the carrots and cook for a further 3–5 minutes until the sweet potato is tender, but still firm to the bite. Drain well and place in a bowl.

2 Add the tomatoes and chick peas to the sweet potato and carrots and mix thoroughly.

3 Line a salad bowl with the lettuce leaves and spoon the vegetable mixture into the centre. Sprinkle with the sultanas, walnuts and onion rings.

4 To make the dressing, combine the yogurt, honey and black pepper in a small serving bowl, whisking thoroughly with a fork. Season to taste with salt.

5 Serve the salad warm and hand the yogurt and honey dressing separately.

Fruity Coleslaw

Home-made coleslaw tastes so much better than the sort you buy.
This recipe has a lovely olive oil, cider vinegar and honey dressing.

NUTRITIONAL INFORMATION

Calories	234	Sugars	........30g
Protein	.........3g	Fat	..........12g
Carbohydrate	...30g	Saturates	.......2g

 10 mins   0 mins

SERVES 6

INGREDIENTS

½ small red cabbage, thinly shredded

½ small white cabbage, thinly shredded

175/6 oz dried dates, stoned and chopped

1 red dessert apple

2 green dessert apples

4 tbsp lemon juice

25 g/1 oz pine kernels, toasted

DRESSING

5 tbsp olive oil

2 tbsp cider vinegar

1 tsp clear honey

salt and pepper

1 Put the shredded red and white cabbage and the dates into a salad bowl and toss well to mix.

COOK'S TIP

A good way to mix salad dressings is to put all the ingredients into a screw-top jar, put on the lid and shake vigorously to combine.

2 Core the apples, but do not peel them. Thinly slice them and place in another bowl. Add the lemon juice and toss well to coat to prevent the apples from turning brown. Add them to the salad bowl.

3 To make the dressing, whisk together the olive oil, vinegar and honey in a small bowl and season to taste with salt and pepper. Pour the dressing over the salad and toss. Sprinkle with the pine kernels, toss lightly and serve.

Coleslaw

This home-made coleslaw has a creamy low-fat dressing. If you make it in advance, add the sunflower seeds just before serving.

NUTRITIONAL INFORMATION

Calories . . . . . . .224 Sugars 8g
Protein . . . . .3g Fat 20g
Carbohydrate . . . .8g Saturates 3g

10 mins   5 mins

SERVES 4

INGREDIENTS

1 white cabbage

4 carrots

1 green pepper

2 tbsp sunflower seeds

DRESSING

150 ml/5 fl oz low-fat mayonnaise

150 ml/5 fl oz low-fat natural yogurt

dash of Tabasco sauce

salt and pepper

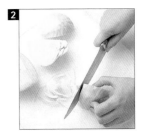

1 To make the dressing, combine the mayonnaise, yogurt, Tabasco sauce and salt and pepper to taste in a small bowl. Leave to chill until required.

2 Cut the cabbage in half and then into quarters. Remove and discard the tough centre stalk. Shred the cabbage leaves finely. Wash the leaves and dry them thoroughly.

3 Peel the carrots and shred using a food processor or a mandolin. Alternatively, coarsely grate the carrot.

4 Quarter and deseed the pepper and cut the flesh into thin strips.

5 Combine the vegetables in a large bowl and toss to mix. Pour over the dressing and toss until the vegetables are coated. Chill until required.

6 Just before serving, place the sunflower seeds on a baking tray and toast them in the oven or under the grill until golden brown. Transfer the salad to a large serving dish, scatter with the sunflower seeds and serve.

VARIATION
To give the coleslaw a slightly different flavour and texture, try adding one or more of the following ingredients: raisins, grapes, grated apple, chopped walnuts, cubes of cheese or dry-roasted peanuts.

Mango & Wild Rice Salad

The very slight edge that counteracts the sweetness of the fruit makes a juicy ripe mango the perfect choice for a summery salad.

NUTRITIONAL INFORMATION

Calories	320	Sugars	........10g
Protein	.........6g	Fat	..........20g
Carbohydrate	...30g	Saturates	......2g

15 mins   1¼ hrs

SERVES 4

INGREDIENTS

85 g/3 oz wild rice

150 g/5½ oz basmati rice

3 tbsp hazelnut oil

1 tbsp sherry vinegar

salt and pepper

1 ripe mango

3 celery sticks

85 g/3 oz ready-to-eat dried apricots, chopped

55 g/2 oz flaked almonds, toasted

2 tbsp chopped fresh coriander or mint

fresh coriander or mint sprigs, to garnish

1 Cook the wild rice and basmati rice in separate saucepans of lightly salted boiling water. Cook the wild rice for 45–50 minutes and the basmati rice for 10–12 minutes. Drain, rinse well and drain again. Place both rices in a large bowl.

2 Whisk together the oil and vinegar and season to taste with salt and pepper. Pour over the rice and toss well.

3 Cut the mango in half lengthways, as close to the stone as possible. Remove and discard the stone.

4 Peel the skin from the mango and cut the flesh into slices.

5 Thinly slice the celery and add to the cooled rice with the mango, apricots, almonds and chopped herbs. Toss together and transfer to a serving dish.

6 Garnish the salad with coriander or mint sprigs and serve.

COOK'S TIP

To toast almonds, place them on a baking sheet in a preheated oven, 180°C/350°F/Gas Mark 4, for 5–10 minutes. Alternatively, toast them under the grill, turning frequently and keeping a close eye on them because they will quickly burn.

Mixed Leaf Salad

Make this green leafy salad with as many varieties of salad leaves and edible flowers as you can find to give an unusual effect.

NUTRITIONAL INFORMATION

Calories . . . . .51 Sugars 0.1g
Protein . . . . .0.1g Fat 6g
Carbohydrate . . . .1g Saturates 1g

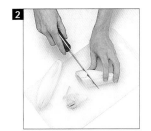

5 mins   0 mins

SERVES 4

INGREDIENTS

½ head frisée

½ head oakleaf lettuce or quattro stagione

few leaves of radicchio

1 head chicory

25 g/1 oz rocket leaves

few fresh basil or flat-leaved parsley sprigs

edible flowers, to garnish (optional)

FRENCH DRESSING

1 tbsp white wine vinegar

pinch of sugar

½ tsp Dijon mustard

3 tbsp extra virgin olive oil

salt and pepper

1 Tear the frisée, oakleaf lettuce and radicchio into pieces. Place the salad leaves in a large serving bowl or individual bowls if you prefer.

2 Cut the chicory into diagonal slices and add to the bowl with the rocket leaves and basil or parsley.

3 To make the dressing, beat the white wine vinegar, sugar and mustard together in a small bowl until the sugar has dissolved. Gradually beat in the olive oil until the dressing is creamy and thoroughly mixed. Season to taste with salt and pepper.

4 Pour the dressing over the salad and toss thoroughly. Sprinkle a mixture of edible flowers over the top and serve.

COOK'S TIP

Violas, hardy geraniums, nasturtiums, chive flowers and pot marigolds add vibrant colours and a sweet flavour to this salad. Use it as a centrepiece at a dinner party, or to liven up a simple everyday meal.

Beetroot Salad

This simple salad has a delicate, subtle flavour that will not overpower the main dish. The beetroot looks wonderful with lamb's lettuce leaves.

NUTRITIONAL INFORMATION

Calories 339	Sugars 6g
Protein 3g	Fat 33g
Carbohydrate 7g	Saturates 7g

  10 mins — 0 mins

SERVES 4

INGREDIENTS

175 g/6 oz lamb's lettuce

4 small beetroot, cooked and diced

2 tbsp chopped walnuts

DRESSING

2 tbsp lemon juice

2 garlic cloves, finely chopped

1 tbsp Dijon mustard

pinch of sugar

salt and pepper

125 ml/4 fl oz sunflower oil

125 ml/4 fl oz soured cream

1 To make the soured cream dressing, combine the lemon juice, garlic, mustard and sugar in a bowl and season to taste with salt and pepper. Gradually whisk in the sunflower oil. Lightly beat the soured cream, then whisk it into the dressing.

2 Put the lamb's lettuce in a bowl and pour about one-third of the dressing over it. Toss to coat, then divide the lettuce among 4 plates.

3 Top each portion of lamb's lettuce with the diced beetroot and drizzle over the remaining dressing.

4 Garnish the salad with a sprinkling of chopped walnuts and serve immediately.

COOK'S TIP
You can prepare the dressing in advance, but do not pour it on to the salad until you are ready to serve because the lamb's lettuce will become soggy.

Egg & Fennel Salad

This is a very refreshing salad. The subtle liquorice flavour of fennel combines well with the cucumber and mint.

NUTRITIONAL INFORMATION

Calories	90	Sugars	.........7g
Protein	.........4g	Fat	...........5g
Carbohydrate	....7g	Saturates	.......1g

 10 mins   0 mins

SERVES 4

I N G R E D I E N T S

1 fennel bulb

lemon juice

2 small oranges

1 small or ½ large cucumber

1 tbsp chopped fresh mint

1 tbsp virgin olive oil

2 eggs, hard boiled

  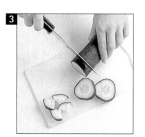

1 Using a sharp knife, trim the outer leaves from the fennel. Slice the fennel bulb thinly then quickly place in a bowl of water and sprinkle with lemon juice (see Cook's Tip).

2 Grate the rind of the oranges over a bowl. Using a sharp knife, pare away the orange peel, then segment the orange by carefully slicing between each line of pith. Do this over the bowl in order to retain the juice.

3 Using a sharp knife, cut the cucumber into 12 mm/½ inch rounds, then cut each round into quarters. Drain the sliced fennel, mix with the orange segments and juice, add the sliced cucumber and the chopped mint and mix gently to combine.

4 Pour the olive oil over the fennel and cucumber salad and toss well.

5 Peel and quarter the hard-boiled eggs and use these to decorate the salad. Serve at once.

COOK'S TIP
Fennel will discolour if it is left for any length of time without a dressing. To prevent any discoloration, place it in a bowl of water and sprinkle with lemon juice.

Spinach & Garlic Salad

This robust salad goes especially well with pasta dishes. Roasting garlic gives it a deliciously sweet flavour.

NUTRITIONAL INFORMATION

Calories . . . . . . .228 Sugars 2g
Protein . . . . .6g Fat 21g
Carbohydrate . . . .3g Saturates 2g

5 mins   15 mins

SERVES 4

INGREDIENTS

12 garlic cloves

4 tbsp olive oil

450 g/1 lb baby spinach leaves

55 g/2 oz chopped walnuts or pine kernels

2 tbsp lemon juice

salt and ground black pepper

1 Do not peel the garlic. Place the cloves in an ovenproof dish, add 2 tablespoons of the olive oil and toss well to coat. Roast in a preheated oven, 190°C/375°F/Gas Mark 5, for 15 minutes.

2 Transfer the garlic and oil to a salad bowl. Add the spinach, walnuts or pine kernels, lemon juice and remaining oil. Toss well to coat and season to taste with salt and pepper.

3 Serve the salad immediately while the garlic is still warm – the diners squeeze the softened garlic out of the skins at the table.

VARIATION

Substitute young sorrel leaves for the spinach for a delicious lemony flavour.

Beansprouts & Pepper Salad

This is a very light dish and is ideal on its own for a summer meal or as a starter.

NUTRITIONAL INFORMATION

Calories 70   Sugars 5g
Protein . . . . .4g   Fat 3g
Carbohydrate . . . .7g   Saturates 0.5g

10 mins   1 min

SERVES 4

INGREDIENTS

350 g/12 oz beansprouts

1 small cucumber

1 green pepper, deseeded and cut into matchsticks

1 carrot, cut into matchsticks

2 tomatoes, finely chopped

1 celery stick, cut into matchsticks

1 garlic clove, crushed

dash of chilli sauce

2 tbsp light soy sauce

1 tsp wine vinegar

2 tsp sesame oil

16 fresh chives

1 Blanch the beansprouts in boiling water for 1 minute. Drain well and rinse under cold water. Drain thoroughly again.

2 Cut the cucumber in half lengthways. Scoop out the seeds with a teaspoon and discard. Cut the flesh into matchsticks and mix with the beansprouts, green pepper, carrot, tomatoes and celery.

3 Mix together the garlic, chilli sauce, soy sauce, vinegar and sesame oil. Pour the dressing over the vegetables, tossing well to coat. Spoon on to 4 individual serving plates. Garnish with fresh chives and serve.

VARIATION
You could substitute 350 g/ 12 oz cooked, cooled French beans or mangetouts for the cucumber. Vary the beansprouts for a different flavour. Try aduki bean or alfalfa sprouts, as well as the better-known mung and soya bean sprouts.

Coronation Salad

The curried mayonnaise dressing for this dish is based on one invented for the coronation of Queen Elizabeth II.

NUTRITIONAL INFORMATION

Calories	236	Sugars	........24g
Protein	.........7g	Fat	...........5g
Carbohydrate	...43g	Saturates	......1g

 25 mins   0 mins

SERVES 4

INGREDIENTS

1 red pepper

60 g/2 oz sultanas

1 celery stick, sliced

125 g/4½ oz canned sweetcorn
  kernels, drained

1 Granny Smith apple, diced

125 g/4½ oz white seedless grapes,
  washed and halved

250 g/9 oz cooked basmati rice

1 cos lettuce, washed and drained

1 tsp paprika to garnish

DRESSING

4 tbsp low-fat mayonnaise

2 tsp mild curry powder

1 tsp lemon juice

1 tsp paprika

pinch of salt

1 Deseed and chop the red pepper, then combine with the sultanas, celery, sweetcorn, apple and grapes in a large bowl. Stir in the cooked rice and mix well.

2 To make the dressing, put the mayonnaise, curry powder, lemon juice, paprika and salt into a small bowl and mix well to combine.

3 Pour the dressing over the salad and gently mix until evenly coated.

4 Line the serving plate with cos lettuce leaves and spoon on the salad. Sprinkle over the paprika and serve.

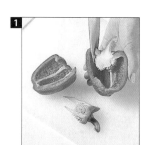

COOK'S TIP

Mayonnaise can be bought in varying thicknesses, from the type that you spoon out of the jar to the pouring variety. If you need to thin down mayonnaise for a dressing, simply add water little by little until the desired consistency is reached.

Cool Bean Salad

This is ideal for serving at a barbecue, for accompanying one of the hotter Indian curries, or for serving as part of a salad buffet at parties.

NUTRITIONAL INFORMATION

Calories 98	Sugars 5g
Protein 9g	Fat 1g
Carbohydrate . . .14g	Saturates 0.3g

 15 mins   15 mins

SERVES 4

INGREDIENTS

1 red onion, thinly sliced

350 g/12 oz broad beans, fresh or frozen

150 ml/5 fl oz natural yogurt

1 tbsp chopped fresh mint

1½ tsp lemon juice

1 garlic clove, halved

salt and ground white pepper

½ cucumber, peeled, halved and sliced

1 Rinse the red onion slices briefly under cold running water, then drain them thoroughly.

2 Cook the broad beans in a small pan of boiling water and until tender: about 8–10 minutes for fresh beans, or 5–6 minutes for frozen.

3 Drain, rinse under cold running water and drain again.

4 If you wish, shell the beans from their white outer shells to leave only the sweet green bean.

5 Place the yogurt, mint, lemon juice, garlic and seasoning in a bowl and stir well to combine.

6 Combine the onion, cucumber and broad beans. Toss them in the yogurt dressing until well coated. Remove and discard the garlic halves.

7 Spoon the salad on to a serving plate and serve immediately.

COOK'S TIP

Rinsing the onion under cold running water takes the edge off the raw taste, as it washes away some of the juices. The same technique can be used on other pungent vegetables and salad ingredients, such as spring onions, bitter cucumbers and chillies.

Caesar Salad

Caesar Cardini, not Caesar Augustus, created this salad in the United States in the 1920s, and it is now regarded as a classic.

NUTRITIONAL INFORMATION

Calories 280	Sugars 2g
Protein 11g	Fat 21g
Carbohydrate ...14g	Saturates 5g

15 mins, plus cooling   20 mins

SERVES 4

INGREDIENTS

1 garlic clove, halved

1 lettuce

55 g/2 oz Parmesan cheese, coarsely grated

GARLIC CROÛTONS

3 tbsp olive oil

1 large garlic clove, halved

4 slices wholemeal bread, crusts removed, diced

DRESSING

1 egg

1 tsp vegetarian Worcestershire sauce

2 tbsp lemon juice

2 tsp Dijon mustard

2 tbsp olive oil

salt and pepper

VARIATION

Some people, such as the elderly, the very young, invalids and pregnant women, should avoid raw or lightly cooked eggs because of the risk of salmonella. As an alternative, omit the softly boiled egg from the dressing and add quartered hard-boiled eggs to the salad.

1 First make the garlic croûtons. Pour the olive oil into a small saucepan and add the garlic. Heat gently for 5 minutes. Remove and discard the garlic. Place the cubes of bread in a bowl and pour in the oil. Toss well, then spread out on a baking sheet. Bake in a preheated oven, 190°C/375°F/Gas Mark 5, for 10 minutes until crisp. Remove from the oven and set aside to cool.

2 To make the dressing, boil the egg for 1 minute. Crack it into a bowl and scoop out any remaining egg white from the shell. Whisk in the Worcestershire sauce, lemon juice, mustard and oil and season to taste with salt and pepper.

3 Rub the inside of a salad bowl with the garlic halves, then discard them.

4 Arrange the lettuce leaves in the salad bowl and sprinkle with the Parmesan. Drizzle the dressing over the salad and sprinkle the garlic croûtons on top. Toss the salad at the table and serve at once.

Potatoes in Italian Dressing

The warm potatoes quickly absorb the wonderful flavours of olives, tomatoes and olive oil. This salad is good served warm or cold.

NUTRITIONAL INFORMATION

Calories 239	Sugars 2g
Protein 4g	Fat 10g
Carbohydrate ...36g	Saturates 1g

15 mins · 15 mins

SERVES 4

INGREDIENTS

750 g/1 lb 10 oz waxy potatoes

1 shallot

2 tomatoes

1 tbsp chopped fresh basil

salt

ITALIAN DRESSING

1 tomato, skinned and finely chopped

4 black olives, pitted and finely chopped

4 tbsp olive oil

1 tbsp wine vinegar

1 garlic clove, crushed

salt and pepper

1 Cook the potatoes in a saucepan of boiling salted water for 15 minutes or until they are tender.

2 Drain the potatoes well, chop roughly and put into a bowl.

3 Chop the shallot. Cut the tomatoes into wedges and add the shallot and tomatoes to the potatoes.

4 To make the Italian dressing, put all the ingredients into a screw-top jar and mix together thoroughly.

5 Pour the Italian dressing over the potato mixture and toss thoroughly to coat the vegetables.

6 Transfer the salad to a serving dish and sprinkle with the basil.

COOK'S TIP

Be sure to use a really good quality extra virgin olive oil for the Italian dressing to give a really fruity flavour to the potatoes.

Sicilian Aubergine Salad

This colourful cooked salad from Sicily, with its Mediterranean flavours, was first brought to Italy by the Moors.

NUTRITIONAL INFORMATION

Calories 217   Sugars 12g
Protein . . . . .2g   Fat 18g
Carbohydrate . . .13g   Saturates 3g

10 mins

25 mins

SERVES 4

INGREDIENTS

6 tbsp olive oil

1 onion, chopped

2 garlic cloves, chopped

2 celery sticks, chopped

450 g/1 lb aubergines

400 g/14 oz canned chopped tomatoes

50 g/1¾ oz green olives, stoned and
   chopped

25 g/1 oz granulated sugar

100 ml/3½ fl oz red wine vinegar

25 g/1 oz capers, drained and rinsed

salt and pepper

1 tbsp fresh flat-leaved parsley, roughly
   chopped, to garnish

1 Heat 2 tablespoons of the olive oil in a large frying pan. Add the prepared onions, garlic and celery to the frying pan and cook, stirring, for 3–4 minutes.

COOK'S TIP

This salad is best served cold the day after it is made, which allows the flavours to mingle and be fully absorbed.

2 Using a sharp knife, slice the aubergines into thick rounds, then cut each round into 4 pieces.

3 Add the aubergine pieces to the frying pan with the remaining olive oil and fry for 5 minutes, or until golden.

4 Add the tomatoes, olives and sugar to the pan, stirring constantly until the sugar has dissolved.

5 Add the red wine vinegar, then reduce the heat and leave the mixture to simmer for 10–15 minutes, until the sauce is thick and the aubergines are tender.

6 While the pan is still on the heat, stir in the capers. Season to taste with salt and pepper. Leave to get cold.

7 Transfer to serving plates and garnish with the parsley just before serving.

Gazpacho Rice Salad

All the flavours of a zesty Spanish gazpacho – garlic, tomatoes, peppers and cucumber combined with rice make a great summer salad.

NUTRITIONAL INFORMATION

Calories	253	Sugars	........15g
Protein	.........7g	Fat	...........5g
Carbohydrate	...46g	Saturates	.......1g

 30 mins   35 mins

SERVES 4

INGREDIENTS

7 tbsp extra virgin olive oil

1 onion, finely chopped

4 garlic cloves, finely chopped

200 g/7 oz long grain white rice

350 ml/12 fl oz vegetable stock or water

1½ tsp dried thyme

3 tbsp sherry vinegar

1 tsp Dijon mustard

1 tsp clear honey

salt and pepper

1 red pepper, deseeded and chopped

½ yellow pepper, deseeded and chopped

½ green pepper, deseeded and chopped

1 red onion, finely chopped

½ cucumber, peeled, deseeded and chopped (optional)

3 tomatoes, deseeded and chopped

2–3 tbsp chopped fresh flat-leaved parsley

TO SERVE

12 cherry tomatoes, halved

12 black olives, stoned and roughly chopped

1 tbsp flaked almonds, toasted

1 Heat 2 tablespoons of the olive oil in a large saucepan. Add the onion and cook, stirring frequently, for 2 minutes until beginning to soften. Stir in half the garlic and cook for a further minute.

2 Add the rice, stir to coat and cook for about 2 minutes until translucent. Stir in the stock and half the thyme and bring to the boil. Season to taste.

3 Cover the pan and simmer gently for about 20 minutes until tender. Stand, still covered, for about 15 minutes; uncover and cool the rice completely.

4 Whisk the sherry vinegar with the remaining garlic and thyme, the mustard, honey and salt and pepper in a large bowl. Gradually whisk in the remaining olive oil. Using a fork, gently fluff the rice into the vinaigrette.

5 Add the peppers, red onion, cucumber, tomatoes and parsley to the rice, then toss to combine and adjust the seasoning if necessary.

6 Transfer the rice salad to a warm serving bowl and garnish with the halved cherry tomatoes, the chopped black olives and the toasted almonds. Serve the salad while it is still warm.

Potato Salad

You can use left-over cold potatoes, cut into bite-size pieces, for this salad, but tiny new potatoes are best for maximum flavour.

NUTRITIONAL INFORMATION

Calories	275	Sugars	........8g
Protein	.........5g	Fat	.........13g
Carbohydrate	...38g	Saturates	......2g

20 mins   20 mins

SERVES 4

INGREDIENTS

700 g/1 lb 9 oz tiny new potatoes

8 spring onions

1 hard-boiled egg (optional)

250 ml/9 fl oz low-fat mayonnaise

1 tsp paprika

salt and pepper

TO GARNISH

2 tbsp snipped chives

pinch of paprika

1 Bring a large pan of lightly salted water to the boil. Add the potatoes and cook for 10–15 minutes or until they are just tender.

2 Drain the potatoes in a colander and rinse them under cold running water until they are completely cold. Drain them again thoroughly. Transfer to a mixing bowl and set aside until required.

3 Trim and slice the spring onions thinly on the diagonal.

4 Shell and chop the hard-boiled egg into bite-sized pieces, if using.

5 Mix together the mayonnaise, paprika and salt and pepper to taste in a bowl until well blended. Pour the mixture over the potatoes.

6 Add the sliced spring onions and the chopped egg, if using, and toss together gently.

7 Transfer the potato salad to a serving bowl, sprinkle with snipped chives and a pinch of paprika. Cover and chill in the refrigerator until required.

COOK'S TIP

To make a lighter dressing, use a mixture of half mayonnaise and half natural yogurt.

Pesto Risotto-rice Salad

This is a cross between a risotto and a rice salad – using Italian arborio rice produces a slightly heavier, stickier result.

NUTRITIONAL INFORMATION

Calories 406	Sugars 5g	
Protein 7g	Fat 28g	
Carbohydrate ...34g	Saturates 5g	

45 mins   30 mins

SERVES 4–6

INGREDIENTS

3 tbsp extra virgin olive oil, plus extra for drizzling

1 onion, finely chopped

200 g/7 oz arborio rice

450 ml/16 fl oz boiling water

6 sun-dried tomatoes in oil, drained and cut into thin slivers

½ small red onion, very thinly sliced

3 tbsp lemon juice

PESTO

55 g/2 oz fresh basil leaves

2 garlic cloves, finely chopped

2 tbsp pine kernels, lightly toasted

125 ml/4 fl oz extra virgin olive oil

55 g/2 oz Parmesan cheese, freshly grated

salt and pepper

TO GARNISH

fresh basil leaves

Parmesan shavings

1 To make the pesto, put the basil, garlic and pine kernels in a food processor and process for 30 seconds. With the motor running, gradually add the olive oil through the feeder tube until a smooth paste forms. Add the cheese and pulse until blended, but still with texture. Scrape into a bowl and season to taste.

2 Heat 1 tablespoon of the oil in a saucepan and fry the chopped onion until softened. Stir in the rice and cook, stirring occasionally, for 2 minutes. Stir in the water and season. Cover and simmer for 20 minutes until the rice is tender and the water absorbed. Cool slightly.

3 Put the sun-dried tomatoes and sliced onion in a bowl, add the lemon juice and 2 tablespoons of oil. Fork in the hot rice and stir in the pesto. Toss to combine. Adjust the seasoning if necessary. Cover and cool to room temperature.

4 Fork the rice mixture into a shallow serving bowl. Drizzle with some olive oil and garnish with basil leaves and Parmesan shavings. Serve the salad at room temperature, not chilled.

Mexican Potato Salad

The flavours of Mexico are echoed in this dish where potato slices are topped with tomatoes and chillies, and served with guacamole.

NUTRITIONAL INFORMATION

Calories 260	Sugars 6g
Protein 6g	Fat 9g
Carbohydrate ...41g	Saturates 2g

 20 mins   20 mins

SERVES 4

INGREDIENTS

1.25 kg/2 lb 12 oz waxy potatoes, sliced

1 ripe avocado

1 tsp olive oil

1 tsp lemon juice

1 garlic clove, crushed

1 onion, chopped

2 large tomatoes, sliced

1 green chilli, deseeded and chopped

1 yellow pepper, deseeded and sliced

2 tbsp chopped fresh coriander

salt and pepper

lemon wedges, to garnish

VARIATION

You can omit the green chilli from this salad if you do not like really hot dishes.

1 Cook the potato slices in a saucepan of boiling water for 10–15 minutes, or until tender. Drain and set aside to cool.

2 Cut the avocado in half and remove the stone. Mash the avocado flesh in a bowl with a fork, then add the olive oil, lemon juice, garlic and onion and stir to mix. Cover the bowl with clingfilm, to minimize discoloration, and set aside.

3 Mix the tomatoes, chilli and yellow pepper together and transfer to a salad bowl with the potato slices.

4 Arrange the avocado mixture on top of the salad and sprinkle with the chopped coriander.

5 Season to taste and serve garnished with the lemon wedges.

Potato & Apple Salad

Baby new potatoes are perfect for salads, as they look tempting and have a wonderful nutty flavour and texture.

NUTRITIONAL INFORMATION

Calories	219	Sugars	. . . . .6g
Protein	. . . . .4g	Fat	. . . . .11g
Carbohydrate	. . .29g	Saturates	. . . . . . .2g

10 mins   15 mins

SERVES 6

I N G R E D I E N T S

900 g/2 lb baby new potatoes

2 green dessert apples

4 spring onions, chopped

4 celery sticks, chopped

150 ml/5 fl oz Mayonnaise (see page 8)

salt and pepper

1 Cook the unpeeled potatoes in a large saucepan of lightly salted boiling water for 15 minutes, until tender. Drain well and place in a salad bowl.

2 Core and chop the apples and add them to the salad bowl with the spring onions and celery.

3 Add the mayonnaise to the potato and apple mixture and season to taste with salt and pepper.

4 Stir well to mix, then set aside to cool and allow the flavours to develop. Serve the salad at room temperature.

VARIATION
Stir 1 tablespoon snipped fresh chives into the mayonnaise before adding it to the salad in step 3.

Roast Vegetable Salad

A colourful collection of Mediterranean vegetables makes a wonderful salad for a hot summer day. Serve at room temperature or just warm.

NUTRITIONAL INFORMATION

Calories	249	Sugars	........13g
Protein	.........3g	Fat	..........19g
Carbohydrate	...17g	Saturates	.......3g

 25 mins   35 mins

SERVES 6

INGREDIENTS

6 tbsp olive oil

2 aubergines

1 yellow pepper, deseeded and quartered

1 red pepper, deseeded and quartered

1 orange pepper, deseeded and quartered

6 shallots

3 red onions, quartered

6 plum tomatoes, quartered

6 fresh basil leaves

DRESSING

4 tbsp olive oil

1 tbsp red wine vinegar

1 clove garlic, crushed

salt and pepper

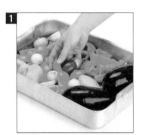

1 Pour the oil into a large roasting tin. Add the vegetables and toss well to coat. Roast in a preheated oven, 230°C/450°F/Gas Mark 8, for 20 minutes, turning occasionally. Using a slotted spoon, transfer the peppers, shallots, onions and tomatoes to a serving platter.

2 Return the aubergines to the oven and continue to roast, turning once, for 15 minutes more. Remove from the oven and set aside until cool enough to handle. Cut the aubergines into bite-size pieces and add to the vegetable platter.

3 To make the dressing, combine the oil, vinegar and garlic, whisking well with a fork. Season to taste with salt and pepper and pour the dressing over the vegetables. Sprinkle the salad with the basil and serve.

Mixed Bean Salad

You can use a mixture of any canned beans to make this crunchy, colourful and very filling salad.

NUTRITIONAL INFORMATION

Calories 198	Sugars 6g
Protein 10g	Fat 6g
Carbohydrate ...26g	Saturates 1g

 30 mins   15–20 mins

SERVES 8

I N G R E D I E N T S

400 g/14 oz canned flageolet beans, drained

400 g/14 oz canned red kidney beans, drained

400 g/14 oz canned butter beans, drained

1 small red onion, thinly sliced

175 g/6 oz French beans, topped and tailed

1 red pepper, halved and deseeded

salt

D R E S S I N G

4 tbsp olive oil

2 tbsp sherry vinegar

2 tbsp lemon juice

1 tsp light muscovado sugar

1 tsp chilli sauce (optional)

1 Put the canned beans in a large mixing bowl. Add the sliced onion and mix together.

2 Cut the French beans in half and cook them in lightly salted boiling water for about 8 minutes until just tender. Refresh under cold water and drain again. Add to the mixed beans and onions.

3 Place the pepper halves, cut side down, on a grill rack and cook until the skin blackens and chars. Leave the peppers to cool slightly then pop them into a plastic bag for about 10 minutes. Peel away the skin from the peppers and discard. Roughly chop the pepper flesh and add it to the beans.

4 To make the dressing, place the oil, sherry vinegar, lemon juice, sugar and chilli sauce (if using) in a screw-top jar and shake vigorously.

5 Pour the dressing over the mixed bean salad and toss well. Leave to chill in the refrigerator until required.

VARIATION
Use any combination of beans in this salad. For a distinctive flavour, add 1 teaspoon of curry paste instead of the chilli sauce.

Chinese Hot Salad

This salad can also be eaten cold – add 3-4 tablespoons French dressing as the vegetables cool, toss well and serve cold or chilled.

NUTRITIONAL INFORMATION

Calories 192   Sugars 13g
Protein . . . . .5g   Fat 9g
Carbohydrate . . .20g   Saturates 1g

 5 mins   10 mins

SERVES 4

INGREDIENTS

1 tbsp dark soy sauce

1½–2 tsp bottled sweet chilli sauce

2 tbsp sherry

1 tbsp brown sugar

1 tbsp wine vinegar

salt and pepper

2 tbsp sunflower oil

1 garlic clove, crushed

4 spring onions, thinly sliced diagonally

250 g/9 oz courgettes, cut into julienne strips about 4 cm/1½ inches long

250 g/9 oz carrots, cut into julienne strips about 4 cm/1½ inches long

1 red or green pepper, deseeded and thinly sliced

400 g/14 oz canned bean sprouts, well drained

125 g/4½ oz French or fine beans, cut into 5 cm/2 inch lengths

1 tbsp sesame oil

1–2 tsp sesame seeds, to garnish

1 In a small bowl, combine the soy sauce, chilli sauce, sherry, sugar, vinegar and seasoning in a small bowl.

2 Heat the 2 tablespoons of sunflower oil in a wok or large, heavy-based frying pan, swirling it around until it is really hot.

3 Add the garlic and spring onions to the wok and stir-fry for 1–2 minutes.

4 Add the courgettes, carrots and peppers and stir-fry for 1–2 minutes,

then add the soy sauce mixture and bring to the boil.

5 Add the bean sprouts and French beans and stir-fry for 1–2 minutes, making sure all the vegetables are thoroughly coated with the sauce.

6 Drizzle the sesame oil over the vegetables in the wok and stir-fry for about 30 seconds.

7 Serve the salad hot, sprinkled with sesame seeds.

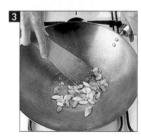

Courgette & Mint Salad

This salad uses lots of green-coloured ingredients which look and taste wonderful with the minty yogurt dressing.

NUTRITIONAL INFORMATION

Calories 49   Sugars 5g
Protein . . . . .4g   Fat 1g
Carbohydrate . . . .6g   Saturates 0g

   30 mins   7–8 mins

SERVES 4

I N G R E D I E N T S

2 courgettes, cut into batons

100 g/3½ oz French beans, cut into thirds

1 green pepper, deseeded and cut
  into strips

2 celery sticks, sliced

1 bunch of watercress

D R E S S I N G

200 ml/7 fl oz natural yogurt

1 garlic clove, crushed

2 tbsp chopped fresh mint

pepper

1 Cook the courgette batons and beans in a saucepan of lightly salted boiling water for 7–8 minutes. Drain, rinse under cold running water and drain again. Set aside to cool completely.

2 Mix the courgettes and beans with the green pepper strips, celery and watercress in a large serving bowl.

3 To make the dressing, combine the natural yogurt, garlic and chopped mint in a small bowl. Season the dressing with pepper to taste.

4 Spoon the dressing on to the salad and serve immediately.

COOK'S TIP
The salad must be served as soon as the yogurt dressing has been added – the dressing will start to separate if it is kept for any length of time.

Mushroom Salad

This easy salad is a useful, year-round accompaniment that goes well with a wide variety of main courses.

NUTRITIONAL INFORMATION

Calories	74	Sugars	.........4g
Protein	.........2g	Fat	...........6g
Carbohydrate	....4g	Saturates	.......1g

🥗 40 mins, plus marinating 🕐 0 mins

SERVES 4

INGREDIENTS

½ cucumber, cut into chunks

115 g/4 oz button mushrooms, thinly sliced

1 small lettuce, torn

4 tomatoes, sliced

1 tbsp chopped fresh coriander

DRESSING

2 tbsp olive oil

1 tbsp white wine vinegar

1 bay leaf

1 garlic clove, finely chopped

1 fresh tarragon sprig

1 fresh rosemary sprig

salt and pepper

1 First make the dressing. Combine the oil, vinegar, bay leaf, garlic, tarragon and rosemary in a large bowl, whisking well. Season to taste with salt and pepper.

2 Add the cucumber and mushrooms to the dressing, tossing well to mix. Cover with clingfilm and set aside to marinate for 30 minutes.

3 Place the lettuce in a salad bowl. Using a slotted spoon, transfer the mushrooms and cucumber to the salad bowl and add the tomatoes. Sprinkle with the coriander.

4 Strain the dressing and discard the contents of the sieve. Pour the dressing over the salad and serve at once.

COOK'S TIP

To clean mushrooms, wipe with damp kitchen paper or brush with a small vegetable brush. Never immerse them in water.

Cheesy Pasta Salad

This delicious salad, packed with carbohydrate, protein and vitamins, is hearty enough to be served as a main meal.

NUTRITIONAL INFORMATION

Calories	759	Sugars	.........3g
Protein	........17g	Fat	..........56g
Carbohydrate	...43g	Saturates	......17g

 15 mins   8-10 mins

SERVES 4

INGREDIENTS

225 g/8 oz dried fusilli

100g/3½ oz mixed salad leaves, such as oakleaf lettuce, radina, baby spinach, rocket and lamb's lettuce

225 g/8 oz dolcelatte cheese

4 tbsp sunflower oil

2 tbsp walnut oil

2 tbsp red wine vinegar

115 g/4 oz walnut halves

salt and pepper

1 Cook the pasta in a large saucepan of lightly salted boiling water for 8-10 minutes, until it is tender but still firm to the bite. Drain, rinse with cold water and drain again.

2 Cube the cheese. Place the salad leaves in a serving bowl and add the pasta. Scatter the cheese on top.

3 Combine the sunflower oil, walnut oil and wine vinegar in a jug and season.

4 Lightly toast the walnut halves. Pour the dressing over the salad, toss lightly to coat the ingredients, then top with the walnuts.

VARIATION
You can substitute another piquant cheese for the dolcelatte, such as Stilton, goat's cheese or feta.

Fruity Wild Rice Salsa

Wild rice has a nutty flavour and a good texture, ideal for salsas and salads, and goes well with the black beans in this dish.

NUTRITIONAL INFORMATION

Calories . . . . .467 Sugars 15g
Protein . . . . .10g Fat 20g
Carbohydrate . . .49g Saturates 4g

2¼ hrs   1 hr

SERVES 4–6

INGREDIENTS

150 g/5½ oz small black beans, soaked overnight in cold water

1 onion, studded with 4 cloves

150 g/5½ oz wild rice

2 garlic cloves

450 ml/16 fl oz boiling water

1 red onion, finely chopped

2 fresh red chillies, deseeded and thinly sliced

1 large red pepper, deseeded and chopped

1 small mango or pawpaw, peeled and diced

2 oranges, segments removed and juice reserved

4 passion fruit, pulp and juice

juice of 3–4 limes

½ tsp ground cumin

1 tbsp maple syrup or light brown sugar

150 ml/5 fl oz extra virgin olive oil

1 small bunch of fresh coriander, leaves stripped from stems and chopped

lime slices, to garnish

1 Drain the beans and put in a large pan with the clove-studded onion. Cover well with cold water. Bring to the boil, lower the heat and boil for 15 minutes, then simmer for 45 minutes until the beans are tender. Discard the onion, rinse the beans under cold running water and drain.

2 Meanwhile, put the wild rice and garlic in a pan and pour in the boiling water. Cover and simmer over a low heat for 30–50 minutes. Cool slightly and discard the garlic cloves.

3 Put the beans in a large bowl and fork in the wild rice. Add the onion, chillies, pepper, mango, orange segments and their juice and the passion fruit pulp and juice. Toss well together.

4 Combine the lime juice, cumin and maple syrup or sugar. Whisk in the olive oil and half the coriander, then pour over the rice mixture and toss well. Cover and set aside for up to 2 hours.

5 Spoon into a serving bowl, sprinkle with the remaining coriander and serve garnished with lime slices.

Red Rice Salad

This hearty salad is made with red rice from the French Camargue. It has an earthy flavour, which goes well with the other robust ingredients.

NUTRITIONAL INFORMATION

Calories	192	Sugars	.........5g
Protein	.........6g	Fat	...........5g
Carbohydrate	...33g	Saturates	.......1g

1½ hrs   30 mins

SERVES 6–8

I N G R E D I E N T S

1 tbsp olive oil

200 g/7 oz red rice

600 ml/1 pint water

400 g/14 oz canned red kidney beans, drained and rinsed

1 small red pepper, deseeded and diced

1 small red onion, finely chopped

2 small cooked beetroots (not in vinegar), peeled and diced

6–8 red radishes, thinly sliced

2–3 tbsp chopped fresh chives

salt and pepper

fresh chives, to garnish

HOT DRESSING

2 tbsp creamed horseradish

1 tbsp Dijon mustard

1 tsp sugar

50 ml/2 fl oz red wine vinegar

125 ml/4 fl oz extra virgin olive oil

1 Put the olive oil and red rice in a heavy-based saucepan and place over a medium heat. Add the water and 1 teaspoon of salt. Bring to the boil, reduce the heat, cover and simmer gently until the rice is tender and all the water has been absorbed. (There are several varieties, all differing in cooking times, so follow the packet instructions.) Remove the pan from the heat and set aside to cool to room temperature.

2 To make the dressing, put the creamed horseradish, Dijon mustard and sugar into a small bowl and whisk thoroughly to combine. Whisk in the red wine vinegar, then gradually whisk in the oil to form a smooth dressing.

3 In a large bowl, combine the kidney beans, red pepper, onion, beetroot, radishes and chives and toss together. Season with salt and pepper to taste.

4 Using a fork, fluff the rice into the bowl with the vegetables. Pour over the dressing and toss well. Cover and leave the salad to stand for about 1 hour. Spoon into a large shallow serving bowl, garnish with fresh chives and serve immediately.

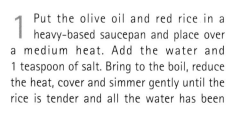

Mango Chutney

Everyone's favourite chutney, this has a sweet and sour taste. It is best made well in advance and stored for at least 2 weeks before use.

NUTRITIONAL INFORMATION

Calories 2819	Sugars 731g
Protein 12g	Fat 2g
Carbohydrate . .734g	Saturates 1g

 10-15 mins 1 hr 5 mins

MAKES 1 QUANTITY

INGREDIENTS

1 kg/2 lb 4 oz mangoes

4 tbsp salt

600 ml/1 pint water

500 g/1 lb 2 oz sugar

450 ml/16 fl oz vinegar

2 tsp finely chopped fresh root ginger

2 tsp crushed garlic

2 tsp chilli powder

2 cinnamon sticks

75 g/2¾ oz raisins

100 g/3½ oz dates, stoned

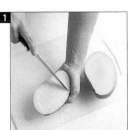

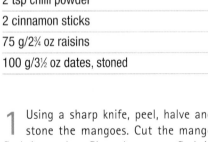

COOK'S TIP

When choosing mangoes, select ones that are shiny with unblemished skins. To test if they are ripe, gently cup the mango in your hand and squeeze – it will give slightly to the touch if it is ready for eating.

1 Using a sharp knife, peel, halve and stone the mangoes. Cut the mango flesh into cubes. Place the mango flesh in a large bowl. Add the salt and water and leave overnight. Drain the liquid from the mangoes and set aside.

2 Bring the sugar and vinegar to the boil in a large saucepan over a low heat, stirring constantly.

3 Gradually add the mango cubes, stirring to coat them in the mixture.

4 Add the ginger, garlic, chilli powder, cinnamon sticks, raisins and dates, and bring the mixture to the boil again, stirring occasionally. Reduce the heat and cook for about 1 hour, or until the mixture thickens. Remove from the heat and set aside to cool.

5 Remove the cinnamon sticks from the chutney and discard.

6 Spoon the chutney into clean dry jars and cover tightly with lids. Leave in a cool place for the flavours to develop fully.

Tamarind Chutney

A mouth-watering chutney which is extremely popular all over India and is served with various vegetarian snacks, particularly with samosas.

NUTRITIONAL INFORMATION

Calories 8	Sugars 1g
Protein 0.3g	Fat 0.3g
Carbohydrate 1g	Saturates 0g

 10 mins   0 mins

SERVES 6

INGREDIENTS

2 tbsp tamarind paste

5 tbsp water

1 tsp chilli powder

½ tsp ground ginger

½ tsp salt

1 tsp sugar

finely chopped fresh coriander leaves,
   to garnish

1 Place the tamarind paste in a medium-sized mixing bowl.

2 Gradually add the water to the tamarind paste, gently whisking with a fork to form a smooth, runny paste.

3 Add the chilli powder, ginger, salt and sugar to the mixture and blend well.

4 Transfer the chutney to a serving dish and garnish with the coriander.

COOK'S TIP

Vegetable dishes are often given a sharp, sour flavour with the addition of tamarind. This is made from the semi-dried, compressed pulp of the tamarind fruit. You can buy bars of the pungent-smelling pulp in Indian and oriental grocery stores.

Mixed Pepper Pooris

These pooris are easy to make and so good to eat served with a scrumptious topping of spicy mixed peppers and yogurt.

NUTRITIONAL INFORMATION

Calories 386   Sugars 6g
Protein . . . . .5g   Fat 32g
Carbohydrate . . .21g   Saturates 4g

55 mins   15 mins

SERVES 6

INGREDIENTS

POORIS

125 g/4½ oz plain wholemeal flour

1 tbsp ghee or vegetable oil

pinch of salt

5 tbsp hot water

vegetable oil, for shallow frying

fresh coriander sprigs, to garnish

natural yogurt, to serve

TOPPING

4 tbsp ghee or oil

1 large onion, quartered and thinly sliced

½ red pepper, deseeded and thinly sliced

½ green pepper, deseeded and thinly sliced

¼ aubergine, cut lengthways into 6 wedges and thinly sliced

1 garlic clove, crushed

2.5 cm/1 inch piece of fresh root ginger, chopped

½–1 tsp minced chilli

2 tsp mild or medium curry paste

225 g/8 oz canned chopped tomatoes

salt

1 Put the flour in a bowl with the ghee or oil and salt. Add the hot water and mix to form a fairly soft dough. Knead gently, cover with a damp cloth and leave for 30 minutes.

2 Meanwhile, prepare the topping. Heat the ghee or oil in a large saucepan. Add the onion, peppers, aubergine, garlic, ginger, chilli and curry paste and fry gently for 5 minutes. Stir in the tomatoes and salt to taste and simmer gently, uncovered, for 5 minutes, stirring occasionally until the sauce thickens. Remove from the heat.

3 Knead the dough on a floured surface and divide into 6. Roll each piece to a round about 15 cm/6 inches in diameter. Cover each one as you finish rolling to prevent drying out.

4 Heat about 1 cm/½ inch of vegetable oil in a large frying pan. Add the pooris, one at a time, and fry them for about 15 seconds on each side, until puffed and golden, turning frequently. Drain on absorbent kitchen paper and keep warm while you are cooking the remainder in the same way.

5 Reheat the vegetable mixture. Place a poori on each serving plate and top with the vegetable mixture. Add a spoonful of yogurt to each, garnish with the coriander sprigs and serve.

Peshwari Naan

A tandoor oven throws out a ferocious heat; this bread is traditionally cooked on its side wall, where the heat is slightly less intense.

NUTRITIONAL INFORMATION

Calories	420	Sugars	........13g
Protein	........11g	Fat	...........9g
Carbohydrate	...77g	Saturates	.......3g

3¾ hrs   30 mins

SERVES 6

INGREDIENTS

50 ml/2 fl oz hand-hot water

pinch of sugar

½ tsp easy-blend dried yeast

500 g/1 lb 2 oz strong white flour, plus extra for dusting

½ tsp salt

50 ml/2 fl oz natural yogurt

2 Bramley apples, peeled, cored and diced

vegetable oil, for brushing

55 g/2 oz sultanas

55 g/2 oz flaked almonds

1 tbsp fresh coriander leaves

2 tbsp grated coconut

1 Combine the water and sugar in a bowl and sprinkle over the yeast. Set aside for 5–10 minutes, until the yeast has dissolved and the mixture is foamy.

2 Put the flour and salt into a bowl and make a well in the centre. Add the yeast mixture and yogurt. Draw in the flour until it is all incorporated. Mix thoroughly, adding enough hand-hot water to form a soft dough. Turn out on to a floured board and knead for 10 minutes until smooth. Put into an oiled bowl, cover and set aside for 3 hours in a warm place.

3 Meanwhile, line the grill pan with foil, with the shiny side facing up.

4 Put the apples into a saucepan with a little water. Bring to the boil, mash them down, reduce the heat and simmer for 20 minutes, mashing occasionally.

5 Divide the dough into 4 pieces and roll each piece out to a 20 cm/8 inch oval. Pull one end out into a teardrop shape, about 5 mm/¼ inch thick. Lay on a floured surface and prick the dough all over with a fork.

6 Brush both sides of the bread with vegetable oil. Place 1 oval under a preheated grill at the highest setting. Cook for 3 minutes, turn the bread over, using tongs, and cook for a further 3 minutes. It should have dark brown spots all over.

7 Spread a teaspoonful of the apple purée all over the bread, then sprinkle over a quarter of the sultanas, flaked almonds, coriander leaves and the coconut. Grill the remaining 3 ovals of dough and spread with the apple purée and flavourings in the same way.

Gram Flour Bread

This filling bread goes well with any vegetarian curry and lime pickle. Store the gram flour in a cool, dark place in an airtight container.

NUTRITIONAL INFORMATION

Calories 112	Sugars 1g
Protein 3g	Fat 2g
Carbohydrate . . .21g	Saturates 0g

30 mins   15 mins

SERVES 4–6

INGREDIENTS

100 g/3½ oz wholemeal flour (ata or chapatti flour), plus extra for dusting

85 g/3 oz gram flour

½ tsp salt

1 small onion

fresh coriander leaves, very finely chopped

2 fresh green chillies, deseeded and very finely chopped

150 ml/5 fl oz water

2 tsp ghee

1 Sift the wholemeal and gram flours together into a large mixing bowl. Add the salt to the flours and mix together thoroughly.

2 Chop the onion very finely. Stir the onion, coriander and chillies into the flour mixture and stir to blend.

3 Add the water and mix to form a soft dough. Cover the dough with a clean tea towel or clingfilm and set aside for about 15 minutes.

4 Turn out the dough and knead thoroughly for 5–7 minutes. Divide the dough into 8 equal portions.

5 Roll out the dough portions to rounds about 18 cm/7 inches in diameter on a lightly floured surface.

6 Place the dough rounds individually in a frying pan and cook over a medium heat, turning them over three times and lightly greasing each side with the ghee each time.

7 Transfer the gram flour bread to serving plates and serve hot.

COOK'S TIP

In Indian kitchens, gram flour is used to make breads, bhajis and batters, to thicken sauces and to stabilise yogurt when it is added to hot dishes.

Chapattis

This Indian bread contains no fat, but some people like to brush the chapattis with a little melted butter before serving.

NUTRITIONAL INFORMATION

Calories	61	Sugars	0.5g
Protein	2g	Fat	0.3g
Carbohydrate	13g	Saturates	0g

40 mins | 25 mins

MAKES 10–12

INGREDIENTS

225 g/8 oz wholemeal flour (ata or chapatti flour)

½ tsp salt

200 ml/⅓ pint water

1 Place the flour in a large mixing bowl. Add the salt and mix to combine.

2 Make a well in the middle of the flour and gradually pour in the water, mixing well with your fingers to form a supple dough.

3 Knead the dough for about 7–10 minutes. Ideally, set the dough aside and allow to stand for 15–20 minutes, but if time is short, roll it out straight away. Divide the dough into 10–12 equal portions. Roll out each piece to form a round on a well-floured surface.

4 Place a heavy-based frying pan over a high heat. When steam starts to rise from the pan, lower the heat to medium.

5 Place a chapatti in the frying pan and when it starts to bubble turn it over. Carefully press down on the chapatti with a clean tea towel or a flat spoon, and turn it over once again.

6 Remove the chapatti from the pan, set aside and keep warm while you make the others. Repeat the process until all of the chapattis are cooked. If possible, serve immediately (see Cook's Tip).

COOK'S TIP

Ideally, chapattis should be eaten as they come out of the frying pan, but if that is not practical keep them warm after cooking by wrapping them up in foil. In India, chapattis are sometimes cooked on a naked flame, which makes them puff up.

Naan Bread

There are many ways of making naan bread, but this recipe is very easy to follow. Naan bread should be served immediately after cooking.

NUTRITIONAL INFORMATION

Calories 152   Sugars 1g
Protein ....3g   Fat 7g
Carbohydrate ...20g   Saturates 4g

2¼ hrs   10 mins

SERVES 8

INGREDIENTS

1 tsp sugar

1 tsp fresh yeast

150 ml/¼ pint warm water

200 g/7 oz plain flour

1 tbsp ghee

1 tsp salt

50 g/1¾ oz unsalted butter

1 tsp poppy seeds

1 Put the sugar, yeast and warm water in a small bowl or jug, and mix thoroughly until the yeast has completely dissolved. Set aside for 10–15 minutes, or until the mixture is frothy.

2 Place the flour in a large mixing bowl. Make a well in the centre of the flour, add the ghee and salt and pour in the yeast mixture. Mix thoroughly to form a dough, using your hands and adding more water if required.

3 Turn the dough out on to a floured work surface and knead for about 5 minutes, or until smooth.

4 Return the dough to the bowl, cover and set aside to rise in a warm place for 1½ hours, or until doubled in size.

5 Turn the dough out on to a floured surface and knead for a further 2 minutes. Break off small balls with your hand and pat into rounds about 12 cm/ 5 inches in diameter and 1 cm/½ inch thick.

6 Place the dough rounds on a greased sheet of foil and grill under a very hot preheated grill for about 7–10 minutes, turning them over twice and brushing with the butter and sprinkling with the poppy seeds.

7 Serve warm immediately, or keep wrapped in foil until required.

Pooris

Although pooris are deep-fried, they are very light. The nutritional information supplied is for each poori.

NUTRITIONAL INFORMATION

Calories	165	Sugars	.......0.7g
Protein	.........3g	Fat	.........10g
Carbohydrate	...17g	Saturates	.......1g

🐘 🐘 🐘

🍲 35 mins   ⏲ 15-20 mins

MAKES 10

I N G R E D I E N T S

225 g/8 oz wholemeal flour (ata or chapatti flour)

½ tsp salt

150 ml/¼ pint water

600 ml/1 pint vegetable oil

1 Place the flour and salt in a large mixing bowl and stir to combine.

2 Make a well in the centre of the flour. Gradually pour in the water and mix together to form a dough, adding more water if necessary.

3 Knead the dough until it is smooth and elastic and set aside in a warm place to rise for about 15 minutes.

4 Divide the dough into about 10 equal portions and with lightly oiled or floured hands pat each into a smooth ball.

5 On a lightly oiled or floured work surface, roll out each ball to form a thin round.

6 Heat the vegetable oil in a deep frying pan. Deep-fry the rounds, in batches, turning once, until they are golden brown in colour.

7 Remove the pooris from the pan and drain. Serve hot.

COOK'S TIP
You can serve pooris either piled one on top of the other or spread out in a layer on a large serving platter so that they remain puffed up.

Parathas

These triangular shaped breads are so easy to make and are the perfect addition to most Indian meals. Serve hot, spread with a little butter.

NUTRITIONAL INFORMATION

Calories	127	Sugars	.......0.5g
Protein	.........3g	Fat	...........4g
Carbohydrate	...22g	Saturates	.....0.4g

 50 mins   10 mins

SERVES 6

I N G R E D I E N T S

90 g/3 oz wholemeal flour

90 g/3 oz plain flour

pinch of salt

1 tbsp vegetable oil, plus extra for greasing

75 ml/3 fl oz tepid water

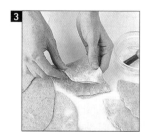

1 Place the flours and the salt in a bowl. Drizzle 1 tablespoon of oil over the flour, add the tepid water and mix to form a soft dough, adding a little more water, if necessary. Knead on a lightly floured surface until smooth, then cover and leave for 30 minutes.

2 Knead the dough on a floured surface and divide into 6 equal pieces. Shape each one into a ball. Roll out on a floured surface to a 15 cm/6 inch round and brush very lightly with oil.

3 Fold in half, and then in half again to form a triangle. Roll out to form an 18 cm/7 inch triangle (when measured from point to centre top), dusting with extra flour as necessary.

4 Brush a large, heavy-based frying pan with a little oil and heat until hot, then add one or two parathas and cook for about 1–1½ minutes. Brush the surfaces very lightly with oil, then turn and cook the other sides for 1½ minutes until completely cooked through.

5 Place the cooked parathas on a plate and cover with foil, or place between the folds of a clean tea towel to keep warm, while you are cooking the remainder in the same way, greasing the pan between cooking each batch.

VARIATION

For added flavour, try brushing the parathas with a garlic- or chilli-flavoured oil as they are cooking.

Spinach Poori

These little nibbles are very satisfying to make and they will still be little puffballs when you get to the table.

NUTRITIONAL INFORMATION

Calories . . . . . . .368 Sugars 3g
Protein . . . . .6g Fat 25g
Carbohydrate . . .33g Saturates 3g

🥄 1 hr   🕐 10 mins

SERVES 6

INGREDIENTS

125 g/4½ oz wholemeal flour

125 g/4½ oz plain flour

½ tsp salt

2 tbsp vegetable oil

125 g/4½ oz fresh or frozen spinach, chopped, blanched, puréed and all excess water squeezed out

50 ml/2 fl oz water

oil, for deep-frying

RELISH

2 tbsp chopped fresh mint

2 tbsp natural yogurt

½ red onion, sliced and rinsed

½ tsp cayenne pepper

1 Sift the flours and salt together into a bowl. Drizzle over the oil and rub in with the fingertips until the mixture resembles fine breadcrumbs.

2 Add the spinach and water, and stir in to make a stiff dough. Turn out and knead for 10 minutes until smooth. Form the dough into a ball. Put into an oiled bowl, turn to coat, cover with clear film and set aside for 30 minutes.

3 Meanwhile make the relish. Combine the mint, yogurt and onion, transfer to a serving bowl and sift the cayenne over the top.

4 Knead the dough again and divide into 12 small balls. Remove 1 ball and keep the rest covered. Roll this ball out into a 12 cm/5 inch circle.

5 Put the oil for deep frying into a wok or wide frying pan to a depth of 2.5 cm/1 inch. Heat the oil until a haze appears – it must be very hot.

6 Have ready a plate lined with absorbent kitchen paper. Put 1 poori on the surface of the oil – if it sinks, it should rise up immediately and sizzle; if it doesn't, the oil isn't hot enough. Keep the poori submerged in the oil, using the back of a slotted spoon. The poori will puff up immediately. Turn it over and cook the other side for 5–10 seconds.

7 As soon as the poori is cooked, remove and drain on kitchen paper. Repeat with the remaining balls of dough, and serve immediately.

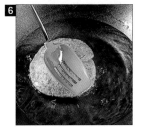

Baby Cauliflowers

Whole baby cauliflowers coated with a red Leicester cheese and poppy seed sauce are cooked to perfection in the microwave oven.

NUTRITIONAL INFORMATION

Calories 173	Sugars 6g
Protein 8g	Fat 11g
Carbohydrate ...10g	Saturates 6g

30 mins   15 mins

SERVES 4

INGREDIENTS

4 cloves

½ onion

½ carrot

1 bouquet garni

250 ml/9 fl oz milk

4 baby cauliflowers

3 tbsp water

15 g/½ oz butter

15 g/½ oz plain flour

60 g/2 oz red Leicester cheese, grated

1 tbsp poppy seeds

pinch of paprika

salt and pepper

fresh parsley, to garnish

1 Stick the cloves into the onion. Place in a bowl with the carrot, bouquet garni and milk. Heat on HIGH power for 2½–3 minutes. Leave the milk to stand for 20 minutes to allow the flavours to infuse.

2 Trim the base and leaves from the cauliflowers and scoop out the stem using a small sharp knife, leaving the cauliflowers intact. Place the cauliflowers upside down in a large dish. Add the water, cover and cook on HIGH power for 5 minutes, until just tender. Leave to stand for 2–3 minutes.

3 Put the butter in a bowl and cook on HIGH power for 30 seconds, until melted. Stir in the flour. Cook on HIGH power for 30 seconds.

4 Strain the milk into a jug, discarding the vegetables. Gradually add to the flour and butter, beating well between each addition. Cover and cook on HIGH power for 3 minutes, stirring every 30 seconds after the first minute, until the sauce has thickened.

5 Stir the cheese and poppy seeds into the sauce and season with salt and pepper to taste. Cover and cook on HIGH power for 30 seconds.

6 Drain the cauliflowers and arrange on a plate or in a shallow dish. Pour over the sauce and sprinkle with a little paprika. Cook on HIGH power for 1 minute to reheat. Serve garnished with fresh parsley.

Dry Split Okra

This is an unusual way of cooking this delicious vegetable. The dish is dry when cooked, and should be served hot with chapattis and a dhal.

NUTRITIONAL INFORMATION

Calories 190   Sugars 4g
Protein . . . . .3g   Fat 18g
Carbohydrate . . . .5g   Saturates 2g

🍲 10 mins   🕐 20 mins

SERVES 4

I N G R E D I E N T S

500 g/1 lb 2 oz okra

150 ml/¼ pint vegetable oil

100 g/3½ oz dried onions

2 tsp dried mango powder

1 tsp ground cumin

1 tsp chilli powder

1 tsp salt

1 Prepare the okra by cutting the ends off and discarding them. Carefully split the okra down the middle without cutting through completely.

2 Heat the oil in a large saucepan. Add the dried onions and fry until crisp.

3 Remove the onions from the pan with a slotted spoon and drain thoroughly on kitchen paper. When cool enough to handle, roughly tear the dried onions and place in a large bowl.

4 Add the dried mango powder, ground cumin, chilli powder and salt to the dried onions and blend well together.

5 Spoon the onion and spice mixture into the split okra.

6 Reheat the oil in the saucepan. Gently add the okra to the hot oil and cook over a low heat for about 10–12 minutes.

7 Transfer the cooked okra to a serving dish and serve immediately.

COOK'S TIP
Ground cumin has a warm, pungent aromatic flavour and is used extensively in Indian cooking. It is a good storecupboard standby.

Herby Potatoes & Onion

Fried potatoes are a classic favourite; here they are given extra flavour by frying them in butter with onion, garlic and herbs.

NUTRITIONAL INFORMATION

Calories 413   Sugars 4g
Protein . . . . .5g   Fat 26g
Carbohydrate . . .42g   Saturates 17g

 10 mins   50 mins

SERVES 4

INGREDIENTS

900 g/2 lb waxy potatoes, cut into cubes

125 g/4½ oz butter

1 red onion, cut into 8 wedges

2 garlic cloves, crushed

1 tsp lemon juice

2 tbsp chopped fresh thyme

salt and pepper

1 Cook the cubed potatoes in a saucepan of boiling salted water for 10 minutes. Drain thoroughly.

2 Melt the butter in a large, heavy-based frying pan and add the red onion wedges, garlic and lemon juice. Cook, stirring constantly for 2–3 minutes.

3 Add the potatoes to the pan and mix well to coat in the butter mixture.

4 Reduce the heat, cover and cook for 25–30 minutes, or until the potatoes are golden brown and tender.

5 Sprinkle the chopped thyme over the top of the potatoes and season to taste with salt and pepper.

6 Transfer to a warm serving dish and serve immediately.

COOK'S TIP

Keep checking the potatoes and stirring throughout the cooking time to ensure that they do not burn or stick to the base of the frying pan.

Sweet Hot Carrots & Beans

Take care not to overcook the vegetables in this tasty dish – they are definitely at their best served tender-crisp.

NUTRITIONAL INFORMATION

Calories	268	Sugars	........16g
Protein	.........5g	Fat	........19g
Carbohydrate	...19g	Saturates	.......3g

10 mins   15 mins

SERVES 4

INGREDIENTS

500 g/1 lb 2 oz young carrots

225 g/8 oz French beans

1 bunch spring onions

4 tbsp ghee or vegetable oil

1 tsp ground cumin

1 tsp ground coriander

3 cardamom pods, split and seeds removed

2 dried red chillies

2 garlic cloves, crushed

1–2 tsp clear honey

1 tsp lemon or lime juice

55 g/2 oz unsalted cashews, toasted

1 tbsp chopped fresh coriander or parsley

salt and pepper

TO GARNISH

slices of lime or lemon

fresh coriander sprigs

1 Cut the carrots lengthways into quarters and then in half crossways if very long. Trim the beans. Cut the spring onions into 5 cm/2 inch pieces.

2 Cook the carrots and beans in a saucepan of lightly salted boiling water for 5–6 minutes until they are tender-crisp. Drain well.

3 Heat the ghee or oil in a large frying pan, add the spring onions, carrots, beans, ground cumin and coriander, cardamom seeds and whole dried chillies. Cook over a low heat, stirring frequently, for 2 minutes.

4 Stir in the garlic, honey and lemon or lime juice and continue cooking, stirring occasionally, for a further 2 minutes. Season to taste with salt and pepper. Remove and discard the chillies.

5 Sprinkle the vegetables with the cashews and chopped coriander and mix together lightly. Serve immediately, garnished with lime or lemon slices and coriander sprigs.

Spicy Potatoes & Onions

Masala aloo are potatoes cooked semi-dry in a spicy mixture and dressed with a baghaar. They make an excellent accompaniment to a curry.

NUTRITIONAL INFORMATION

Calories 313	Sugars 5g
Protein 2g	Fat 25g
Carbohydrate . . .21g	Saturates 3g

10–15 mins   10 mins

SERVES 4

INGREDIENTS

6 tbsp vegetable oil

2 onions, finely chopped

1 tsp finely chopped fresh root ginger

1 tsp crushed garlic

1 tsp chilli powder

1½ tsp ground cumin

1½ tsp ground coriander

1 tsp salt

400 g/14 oz canned new potatoes

1 tbsp lemon juice

BAGHAAR

3 tbsp oil

3 dried red chillies, finely chopped

½ tsp onion seeds

½ tsp mustard seeds

½ tsp fenugreek seeds

TO GARNISH

fresh coriander leaves

1 green chilli, deseeded and finely chopped

1 Heat the oil in a large, heavy-based saucepan. Add the onions and fry, stirring, until golden brown. Reduce the heat, add the ginger, garlic, chilli powder, ground cumin, ground coriander and salt and stir-fry for about 1 minute. Remove the pan from the heat and set aside until required.

2 Drain the water from the potatoes. Add the potatoes to the onion and spice mixture and heat through. Sprinkle over the lemon juice and mix well.

3 To make the baghaar, heat the oil in a separate pan. Add the red chillies, onion seeds, mustard seeds and fenugreek seeds and fry until the seeds turn a shade darker. Remove the pan from the heat and pour the baghaar over the potatoes.

4 Garnish with coriander leaves and chillies, then serve.

Pommes Anna

This is a classic potato dish, which may be left to cook unattended while the remainder of the meal is being prepared.

NUTRITIONAL INFORMATION

Calories	237	Sugars	.........1g
Protein	.........4g	Fat	..........13g
Carbohydrate	...29g	Saturates	.......8g

15 mins · 2 hrs

SERVES 4

INGREDIENTS

5 tbsp butter, melted

675 g/1½ lb waxy potatoes

4 tbsp chopped fresh mixed herbs

salt and pepper

chopped fresh herbs, to garnish

1 Brush a shallow 1 litre/1¾ pint ovenproof dish with a little of the melted butter.

2 Slice the potatoes very thinly and pat dry with kitchen paper.

3 Arrange a layer of potato slices in the prepared dish until the base is covered. Brush with a little butter and sprinkle with a quarter of the chopped mixed herbs. Season to taste.

4 Continue layering the potato slices, brushing each layer with melted butter and sprinkling with herbs, until they are all used up.

5 Brush the top layer of potato slices with butter, cover the dish and cook in a preheated oven, 190°C/375°F/Gas Mark 5, for 1½ hours.

6 Turn the potatoes out on to a warm, ovenproof platter and return them to the oven for a further 25–30 minutes, until golden brown. Serve the Pommes Anna at once, garnished with the chopped fresh herbs.

COOK'S TIP
Make sure that the potatoes are sliced very thinly so that they are almost transparent. This will ensure that they cook thoroughly.

Boston Beans

These are the original baked beans and you will find that they are much tastier than the canned variety.

NUTRITIONAL INFORMATION

Calories	217	Sugars	........11g
Protein	........14g	Fat	...........11g
Carbohydrate	...40g	Saturates	.......0g

 10 mins   5½ hrs

SERVES 8

INGREDIENTS

500 kg/1 lb 2 oz dried haricot beans,
  soaked overnight in cold water to cover

2 onions, chopped

2 large tomatoes, skinned and chopped

2 tsp American mustard

2 tbsp treacle

salt and pepper

COOK'S TIP

Serve these beans with chunks of wholemeal bread or toast for a perfectly balanced light lunch or supper dish.

1 Drain the beans and place in a large saucepan. Add enough cold water to cover, bring to the boil and boil for 15 minutes. Drain, reserving 300 ml/10 fl oz of the cooking liquid. Transfer the beans to a large casserole and add the onions.

2 Return the reserved cooking liquid to the pan and add the tomatoes. Bring to the boil and simmer for 10 minutes. Remove the pan from the heat, stir in the mustard and treacle and season to taste with salt and pepper.

3 Pour the tomato mixture into the casserole and bake in a preheated oven, 140°C/275°F/Gas Mark 1, for 5 hours. Serve immediately.

Broad Beans with Savory

This is a traditional combination – summer savory is often grown with broad beans to protect them against black fly.

NUTRITIONAL INFORMATION

Calories	180	Sugars	.........2g
Protein	.........8g	Fat	..........13g
Carbohydrate	...10g	Saturates	.......8g

15 mins   20 mins

SERVES 4

I N G R E D I E N T S

900 g/2 lb broad beans

1 fresh summer savory sprig

55 g/2 oz butter or margarine

1 tbsp lemon juice

salt and pepper

1 tbsp chopped fresh summer savory

1 Reserve 1 pod and shell the remaining beans. Bring a large saucepan of lightly salted water to the boil and add the beans, the reserved pod and the sprig of summer savory. Cover and simmer for 10–15 minutes, until the beans are tender.

2 Drain the beans and discard the pod and sprig of summer savory.

3 Melt the butter or margarine in the saucepan, add the lemon juice and beans and season to taste with pepper. Toss the beans gently to coat.

4 Transfer the beans to a warm serving dish. Sprinkle them with the chopped summer savory and serve immediately.

COOK'S TIP

If using mature broad beans, skin them before tossing them in the melted butter or margarine.

Kashmiri Spinach

This is an imaginative way to serve spinach, which adds a little zip to it. It is a very simple dish, which will complement almost any curry.

NUTRITIONAL INFORMATION

Calories 81   Sugars 2g
Protein . . . . .4g   Fat 7g
Carbohydrate . . . .2g   Saturates 1g

5 mins   25 mins

SERVES 4

I N G R E D I E N T S

500 g/1 lb 2 oz spinach, Swiss chard or baby leaf spinach

2 tbsp mustard oil

¼ tsp garam masala

1 tsp yellow mustard seeds

2 spring onions, sliced

1 Remove any tough stalks from the spinach, and rinse it several times in cold running water.

2 Heat the mustard oil in a preheated wok or large heavy-based frying pan until it smokes.

3 Add the garam masala and mustard seeds to the oil. Cover the pan quickly – you will hear the mustard seeds popping inside.

4 When the popping has ceased, remove the cover and add the spring onions and spinach. Cook, stirring constantly, until the spinach has wilted.

5 Continue cooking the spinach, uncovered, over a medium heat for 10–15 minutes, until most of the water has evaporated. If using frozen spinach, it will not need to cook for so long – cook it until most of the water has evaporated.

6 Remove the spinach and spring onions with a slotted spoon, draining off any remaining liquid. (This dish is pleasanter to eat when it is served as dry as possible.)

7 Transfer the Kashmiri spinach to a warmed serving dish and serve immediately, while it is still piping hot.

COOK'S TIP

Mustard oil is made from mustard seeds and is very fiery when raw. However, when it is heated to this smoking stage, it loses a lot of the fire and takes on a delightful sweet quality.

Seasonal Vegetables

These vegetables are ideal for a special occasion, such as Christmas Day. The glazed carrots and spiced cabbage take little time to cook.

NUTRITIONAL INFORMATION

Calories 434   Sugars 20g
Protein . . . . .7g   Fat 19g
Carbohydrate . . .62g   Saturates 5g

 20 mins   1 hr 40 mins

SERVES 8

INGREDIENTS

CRISPY ROAST POTATOES

2 kg/4 lb 8 oz potatoes

vegetable oil, for roasting

salt

HONEY-GLAZED CARROTS

1 kg/2 lb 4 oz carrots

1 tbsp clear honey

25 g/1 oz butter

2 tsp sesame seeds, toasted

SPICED WINTER CABBAGE

1 white cabbage

2 dessert apples, peeled, cored and chopped

few drops of lemon juice

salt

25 g/1 oz butter

freshly grated nutmeg

1 To make Crispy Roast Potatoes, peel the potatoes and cut them into large, even-sized chunks. Put them into a saucepan of cold water with ½ teaspoon salt. Bring to the boil, and then reduce the heat. Cover and simmer for about 8–10 minutes to parboil them. Drain thoroughly.

2 Heat about 150 ml/¼ pint vegetable oil in a large roasting tin until very hot. Add the potatoes, basting thoroughly. Roast in a preheated oven, 200°C/400°F/Gas Mark 6, for about 1 hour, basting occasionally, until crisp and golden brown.

3 To make Honey-glazed Carrots, put the carrots into a saucepan and barely cover with water. Add the honey and butter. Cook, uncovered, for about 15 minutes, until the liquid has just evaporated and the carrots are glazed.

Serve in a warmed dish, sprinkled with toasted sesame seeds.

4 To maked Spiced Winter Cabbage, shred the cabbage just before cooking it to retain the vitamins. Add the chopped apples and lemon juice, and cook in a small amount of water in a covered saucepan over a medium heat for about 6 minutes. Drain thoroughly. Season to taste with salt and add the butter, tossing to melt. Transfer to a warmed serving dish, sprinkle with freshly grated nutmeg and serve immediately.

Sweet & Sour Vegetables

This is a dish of Persian origin, not Chinese as it sounds. Aubergines are fried and mixed with tomatoes, mint, sugar and vinegar.

NUTRITIONAL INFORMATION

Calories	218	Sugars	.......12g
Protein	.........3g	Fat	..........17g
Carbohydrate	...14g	Saturates	.......3g

45 mins   30 mins

SERVES 4

INGREDIENTS

2 large aubergines

6 tbsp olive oil

4 garlic cloves, crushed

1 onion, cut into 8 wedges

4 large tomatoes, deseeded and chopped

3 tbsp chopped fresh mint

150 ml/¼ pint vegetable stock

4 tsp brown sugar

2 tbsp red wine vinegar

1 tsp chilli flakes

salt and pepper

fresh mint sprigs, to garnish

1 Using a sharp knife, cut the aubergines into cubes. Put them in a colander, sprinkle with plenty of salt and leave to stand for 30 minutes. Rinse well under cold running water to remove all traces of the salt and drain thoroughly. This process removes all the bitter juices from the aubergines. Pat dry with absorbent kitchen paper.

2 Heat the oil in a large, heavy-based frying pan.

3 Add the aubergine and sauté over a medium heat, stirring, for about 1–2 minutes, until beginning to colour.

4 Stir in the garlic and onion wedges and cook, stirring constantly, for a further 2–3 minutes.

5 Stir in the chopped tomatoes and mint and the vegetable stock. Lower the heat, cover the pan with a lid and simmer for about 15–20 minutes, or until the aubergines are tender.

6 Add the brown sugar, red wine vinegar and chilli flakes, then season with salt and pepper according to taste and cook for a further 2–3 minutes, stirring constantly.

7 Transfer to a warmed serving dish, garnish the aubergines with fresh mint sprigs and serve immediately.

Chilli Roast Potatoes

Small new potatoes are scrubbed and boiled in their skins, before being coated in a chilli mixture and roasted to perfection in the oven.

NUTRITIONAL INFORMATION

Calories ....178 Sugars 2g
Protein ....2g Fat 11g
Carbohydrate ...18g Saturates 1g

5–10 mins   30 mins

SERVES 4

INGREDIENTS

500 g/1 lb 2 oz small new potatoes, scrubbed

150 ml/5 fl oz vegetable oil

1 tsp chilli powder

½ tsp caraway seeds

1 tsp salt

1 tbsp chopped fresh basil

1 Cook the potatoes in a saucepan of boiling water for 10 minutes, then drain thoroughly.

2 Pour a little of the oil into a shallow roasting tin to coat the base. Heat the oil in a preheated oven, 200°C/400°F/Gas Mark 6, for 10 minutes. Add the potatoes to the tin and brush them with the hot oil.

3 In a small bowl, mix together the chilli powder, caraway seeds and salt. Sprinkle the mixture over the potatoes, turning to coat them all over.

4 Add the remaining oil to the tin and roast the potatoes in the oven for about 15 minutes, or until cooked through.

5 Using a slotted spoon, remove the potatoes from the the oil, draining them well, and transfer them to a warmed serving dish.

6 Sprinkle the chopped basil over the top and serve immediately.

VARIATION

Use any other spice of your choice, such as curry powder or paprika, for a variation in flavour.

Potatoes Dauphinois

This is a classic potato dish of layered potatoes, cream, garlic, onion and cheese. Serve it as an accompaniment to a simple main dish.

NUTRITIONAL INFORMATION

Calories 580	Sugars 5g
Protein 10g	Fat 46g
Carbohydrate . . .34g	Saturates 28g

 25 mins   🕐 1½ hrs

SERVES 4

INGREDIENTS

1 tbsp butter

675 g/1½ lb waxy potatoes, sliced

2 garlic cloves, crushed

1 red onion, sliced

85 g/3 oz Gruyère cheese, grated

salt and pepper

300 ml/½ pint double cream

1 Lightly grease a 1 litre/1¾ pint shallow ovenproof dish with butter.

2 Arrange a single layer of potato slices in the base of the prepared dish.

3 Top the potato slices with half the garlic, half the sliced red onion and one-third of the grated Gruyère cheese. Season to taste with a little salt and some pepper.

4 Repeat the layers in exactly the same order, finishing with a layer of potatoes topped with grated cheese.

5 Pour the cream over the top of the potatoes and cook in a preheated oven, 180°C/350°F/Gas Mark 4, for 1½ hours, or until the potatoes are cooked through and the top is browned and crispy. Serve the potatoes at once, straight from the dish.

COOK'S TIP

There are many versions of this classic potato dish, but the recipes always contain double cream, making it a rich and very filling side dish or accompaniment. This recipe must be cooked in a shallow dish to ensure there is plenty of crispy topping.

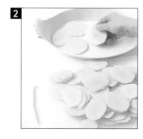

Aubergines in Saffron Sauce

Here is a quick and simple, delicately spiced and delicious way to cook aubergines and onion.

NUTRITIONAL INFORMATION

Calories	350	Sugars	........14g
Protein	.........3g	Fat	..........31g
Carbohydrate	...15g	Saturates	......14g

25 mins   20 mins

SERVES 4

INGREDIENTS

a good pinch of saffron strands, finely crushed

1 tbsp boiling water

1 large aubergine

3 tbsp vegetable oil

1 large onion, roughly chopped

2 garlic cloves, crushed

2.5 cm/1 inch piece of fresh root ginger, chopped

1½ tbsp mild or medium curry paste

1 tsp cumin seeds

150 ml/¼ pint double cream

150 ml/¼ pint Greek-style yogurt

2 tbsp mango chutney, chopped if necessary

salt and pepper

1 Place the saffron in a small bowl, add the boiling water and set aside to infuse for 5 minutes. Cut the aubergine lengthways into quarters, then into 1 cm/½ inch thick slices.

2 Heat the oil in a large frying pan, add the onion and cook gently for 3 minutes. Stir in the aubergine, garlic, ginger, curry paste and cumin and cook gently for 3 minutes.

3 Stir in the saffron water, cream, yogurt and chutney and cook, stirring frequently, for 8-10 minutes, until the aubergine is tender.

4 Season with salt and pepper to taste and serve hot.

COOK'S TIP

Yogurt adds a creamy texture and pleasant tartness to this sauce. If you are worried about it curdling on heating, add a tablespoonful at a time and stir it in well before adding another.

Brindil Bhaji

This is one of the most delicious – and easiest – of the Indian bhaji dishes and has a wonderful sweet and spicy flavour.

NUTRITIONAL INFORMATION

Calories 117	Sugars 8g
Protein 3g	Fat 8g
Carbohydrate 9g	Saturates 5g

20 mins   20 mins

SERVES 4

INGREDIENTS

500 g/1 lb 2 oz aubergines, sliced

2 tbsp ghee

1 onion, thinly sliced

2 garlic cloves, sliced

2.5 cm/1 inch piece of fresh root ginger, grated

½ tsp turmeric

1 dried red chilli, finely chopped

½ tsp salt

400 g/14 oz canned tomatoes

1 tsp garam masala

fresh coriander sprigs, to garnish

1 Cut the aubergine slices into finger-width strips.

2 Heat the ghee in a heavy-based pan. Add the onion and cook over a medium heat, stirring constantly, for 7–8 minutes, until very soft and just beginning to colour.

3 Add the garlic and aubergine strips, increase the heat and cook, stirring constantly, for 2 minutes. Stir in the ginger, turmeric, chilli, salt and tomatoes, with their can juices. Use the back of a wooden spoon to break up the tomatoes. Lower the heat and simmer the mixture, uncovered, for 15–20 minutes, until the aubergines are very soft.

4 Stir in the garam masala and simmer for a further 4–5 minutes.

5 Transfer the brindil bhaji to a warmed serving plate, garnish with fresh coriander sprigs and serve immediately.

VARIATION

Other vegetables can be used instead of the aubergines. Try courgettes, potatoes or peppers, or any combination of these vegetables, using the same sauce.

Curried Okra

Okra, also known as bhindi and lady's fingers, are a favourite Indian vegetable. They are now sold in many of the larger supermarkets.

NUTRITIONAL INFORMATION

Calories	156	Sugars	.........5g
Protein	.........5g	Fat	..........12g
Carbohydrate	....6g	Saturates	.......2g

🕙 10 mins   ⏲ 20 mins

SERVES 4

INGREDIENTS

500 g/1 lb 2 oz fresh okra

4 tbsp ghee or oil

1 bunch spring onions, sliced

2 garlic cloves, crushed

5 cm/2 inch piece fresh root ginger, chopped

1 tsp minced chilli

1½ tsp ground cumin

1 tsp ground coriander

1 tsp turmeric

225 g/8 oz canned chopped tomatoes

150 ml/¼ pint vegetable stock

salt and pepper

1 tsp garam masala

chopped fresh coriander, to garnish

1 Wash the okra, trim off the stalks and pat dry (see Cook's Tip). Heat the ghee or oil in a large pan, add the spring onions, garlic, ginger and chilli and fry over a low heat, stirring frequently, for 1 minute.

2 Stir in the spices and fry gently for 30 seconds, then add the tomatoes, stock and okra. Season with salt and pepper to taste and simmer, stirring and turning the mixture occasionally, for about 15 minutes, until the okra is cooked, but still a little crisp.

3 Sprinkle with the garam masala, taste and adjust the seasoning, if necessary.

4 Transfer the curried okra to a warm serving dish, garnish with the chopped coriander and serve hot.

COOK'S TIP

If preferred, slice the okra into rings, add to the mixture (step 2), cover and cook until tender-crisp, stirring occasionally. When you buy fresh okra, make sure that the pods are not shrivelled and do not have any brown spots.

Gingered Potatoes

This simple spicy dish is ideal with a plain main course. The cashew nuts and celery add extra crunch.

NUTRITIONAL INFORMATION

Calories ....325 Sugars 1g
Protein ....5g Fat 21g
Carbohydrate ...30g Saturates 9g

20 mins   30 mins

SERVES 4

INGREDIENTS

675 g/1½ lb waxy potatoes, cubed

2 tbsp vegetable oil

4 tsp grated fresh root ginger

1 fresh green chilli, deseeded and chopped

1 celery stick, chopped

25 g/1 oz cashew nuts

few strands of saffron

3 tbsp boiling water

5 tbsp butter

celery leaves, to garnish

1 Cook the potatoes in a saucepan of boiling water for 10 minutes, then drain thoroughly.

2 Heat the oil in a heavy-based frying pan and add the potatoes. Cook over a medium heat, stirring constantly, for about 3–4 minutes.

COOK'S TIP

Use a non-stick, heavy-based frying pan because the potato mixture is fairly dry and may stick to an ordinary pan.

3 Add the grated ginger, the chopped chilli and celery and the cashew nuts and cook for another minute.

4 Meanwhile, place the saffron strands in a small bowl. Add the boiling water and set aside to soak for 5 minutes.

5 Add the butter to the pan, lower the heat and stir in the saffron mixture. Cook over a low heat for 10 minutes, or until the potatoes are tender.

6 Transfer to a warm dish, garnish with celery leaves and serve at once.

Sesame Stir-fry

This wonderfully quick and easy stir-fry can be served either as part of a Chinese meal or as a simple vegetable accompaniment.

NUTRITIONAL INFORMATION

Calories ....165 Sugars 2g
Protein ....6g Fat 13g
Carbohydrate ....6g Saturates 2g

🕐 10 mins 🕐 12 mins

SERVES 4

INGREDIENTS

3 tbsp groundnut or sunflower oil

1 tbsp sesame oil

12 garlic cloves, finely chopped

225 g/8 oz broccoli florets

115 g/4 oz mangetouts or sugar snap peas

1 head Chinese leaves

6 spring onions, chopped

2 tbsp dark soy sauce

2 tbsp Chinese rice wine

3 tbsp water

1 tbsp sesame seeds, toasted, to garnish

1 Heat both oils in a large, heavy-based frying pan or wok. Add the garlic and stir-fry for 30 seconds. Add the broccoli and stir-fry for 3 minutes.

2 Add the mangetouts or sugar snaps and stir-fry for 2 minutes.

3 Add the Chinese leaves and spring onions and continue to stir-fry for a further 2 minutes.

4 Stir in the soy sauce and Chinese rice wine and cook, stirring constantly, for 3–4 minutes.

5 Transfer the stir-fry to a warm serving dish, sprinkle with the toasted sesame seeds and serve immediately.

VARIATION

Use only half the Chinese leaves and add 115 g/4 oz thinly sliced carrots and 115 g/4 oz baby sweetcorn cobs with the broccoli in step 1.

Potato Crumble

This is a delicious way to liven up mashed potato by topping it with a crumble mixture flavoured with herbs, mustard and onion.

NUTRITIONAL INFORMATION

Calories	451	Sugars	. . . . .5g
Protein	. . . . .13g	Fat	. . . . .19g
Carbohydrate	. . .60g	Saturates	. . . . . .12g

 25 mins   30 mins

SERVES 4

INGREDIENTS

900 g/2 lb floury potatoes, diced

25 g/1 oz butter

2 tbsp milk

50 g/1¾ oz mature Cheddar cheese or blue cheese, grated

CRUMBLE TOPPING

40 g/1½ oz butter

1 onion, cut into chunks

1 garlic clove, crushed

1 tbsp wholegrain mustard

175 g/6 oz fresh wholemeal breadcrumbs

2 tbsp chopped fresh parsley

salt and pepper

1 Cook the potatoes in a pan of lightly salted boiling water for 10 minutes, or until cooked through.

2 Meanwhile, make the crumble topping. Melt the butter in a frying pan. Add the onion, garlic and mustard and fry over a medium heat, stirring constantly, for 5 minutes, until the onion has softened.

3 Put the breadcrumbs in a mixing bowl and stir in the fried onion mixture and chopped parsley. Season to taste with salt and pepper.

4 Drain the potatoes thoroughly and place them in another mixing bowl. Add the butter and milk, then mash until smooth. Stir in the grated cheese while the potato is still hot.

5 Spoon the mashed potato into a shallow ovenproof dish and sprinkle with the crumble topping.

6 Cook the potato crumble in a preheated oven, 200°C/400°F/Gas Mark 6, for 10–15 minutes, until the topping is golden brown and crunchy. Serve immediately.

COOK'S TIP

For extra crunch, add freshly cooked vegetables, such as celery and peppers, to the mashed potato in step 4.

Fried Cauliflower

A dry dish flavoured with a few herbs, this is a very versatile accompaniment to curries and rice dishes.

NUTRITIONAL INFORMATION

Calories 135	Sugars 3g
Protein 4g	Fat 12g
Carbohydrate 4g	Saturates 1g

 5 mins   20 mins

SERVES 4

I N G R E D I E N T S

4 tbsp vegetable oil

½ tsp onion seeds

½ tsp mustard seeds

½ tsp fenugreek seeds

4 dried red chillies, finely chopped

1 small cauliflower, cut into small florets

1 tsp salt

1 green pepper, deseeded and diced

1 Heat the oil in a large, heavy-based saucepan over a moderate heat.

2 Add the onion seeds, mustard seeds, fenugreek seeds and the dried red chillies to the pan, stirring to mix.

3 Reduce the heat and gradually add the cauliflower florets and the salt to the pan. Stir-fry the mixture for 7–10 minutes, thoroughly coating the cauliflower in the spices.

4 Add the diced green pepper to the pan and stir-fry the over a low heat for 3–5 minutes.

5 Transfer the spicy fried cauliflower to a warmed serving dish and serve hot.

Lemon Beans

Use a variety of beans if possible, although this recipe is perfectly acceptable with just one type of bean.

NUTRITIONAL INFORMATION

Calories 285	Sugars 6g
Protein 9g	Fat 19g
Carbohydrate . . .18g	Saturates 6g

  5 mins   20 mins

SERVES 4

INGREDIENTS

900 g/2 lb mixed green beans, such as broad beans, French beans, runner beans

75 g/2½ oz butter or margarine

4 tsp plain flour

300 ml/½ pint vegetable stock

5 tbsp dry white wine

6 tbsp single cream

3 tbsp chopped fresh mixed herbs

grated rind of 1 lemon

2 tbsp lemon juice

salt and pepper

1 Cook the beans in a saucepan of boiling salted water for 10 minutes, or until tender. Drain and place in a warmed serving dish.

VARIATION

Use lime rind and juice instead of lemon for an alternative citrus flavour. Replace the single cream with natural yogurt for a healthier version of this dish.

2 Meanwhile, melt the butter in a saucepan. Add the flour and cook, stirring constantly, for 1 minute. Remove the pan from the heat and gradually stir in the stock and wine. Return the pan to the heat and bring to the boil, stirring.

3 Remove the pan from the heat once again and stir in the single cream, mixed herbs, lemon juice and rind. Season with salt and pepper to taste. Pour the sauce over the beans, mixing well to coat thoroughly. Serve immediately.

Spanish Potatoes

This type of dish is usually served as a part of Spanish tapas and is delicious with salad or a simply cooked main course dish.

NUTRITIONAL INFORMATION

Calories	176	Sugars	.........9g
Protein	.........5g	Fat	..........6g
Carbohydrate	...27g	Saturates	.......1g

 20 mins   35 mins

SERVES 4

I N G R E D I E N T S

2 tbsp olive oil

500 g/1 lb 2 oz small new potatoes, halved

1 onion, halved and sliced

1 green pepper, deseeded and cut into strips

1 tsp chilli powder

1 tsp mustard

300 ml/½ pint passata

300 ml/½ pint vegetable stock

salt and pepper

chopped fresh parsley, to garnish

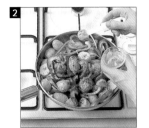

1 Heat the olive oil in a large heavy-based frying pan. Add the new potatoes and onion and cook, stirring frequently, for 4–5 minutes, until the onion slices are soft and translucent.

2 Add the green pepper strips, chilli powder and mustard to the pan and cook for a further 2–3 minutes.

3 Stir the passata and the vegetable stock into the pan and bring to the boil. Reduce the heat and simmer for about 25 minutes, or until the potatoes are tender. Season to taste.

4 Transfer the potatoes to a warmed serving dish. Sprinkle the parsley over the top and serve immediately.

5 Alternatively, leave the Spanish potatoes to cool completely and serve cold, at room temperature.

COOK'S TIP
In Spain, tapas are traditionally served with a glass of chilled sherry or some other aperitif.

Italian Courgettes

This tasty method of cooking courgettes, in a vegetable stock with a touch of fresh marjoram, really brings out their full flavour.

NUTRITIONAL INFORMATION

Calories 10	Sugars 3g
Protein 3g	Fat 6g
Carbohydrate . . .10g	Saturates 1g

10 mins   20 mins

SERVES 4

INGREDIENTS

2 tbsp olive oil

1 large onion, chopped

1 garlic clove, finely chopped

5 courgettes, sliced

150 ml/5 fl oz vegetable stock

1 tsp chopped fresh marjoram

salt and pepper

1 tbsp chopped fresh flat-leaved parsley, to garnish

1 Heat the olive oil in a large, heavy-based frying pan. Add the onion and garlic and cook, stirring occasionally, for 5 minutes, until softened.

2 Add the courgettes and cook, stirring frequently, for 3–4 minutes, until they are just beginning to brown.

3 Add the stock and marjoram and season to taste with salt and pepper. Simmer for about 10 minutes, until almost all the liquid has evaporated. Transfer to a warm serving dish, sprinkle with the parsley and serve immediately.

Cauliflower Fritters

This makes an unusual accompaniment to bakes or gratins and could also be served as an appetizer with a dipping sauce.

NUTRITIONAL INFORMATION

Calories 253	Sugars 3g	
Protein 10g	Fat 13g	
Carbohydrate . . .26g	Saturates 2g	

15 mins   15 mins

SERVES 4

I N G R E D I E N T S

1 large cauliflower, cut into florets

115 g/4 oz plain flour

pinch of dried thyme

2 eggs, separated

150 ml/5 fl oz water

4 tbsp milk

sunflower or corn oil, for deep-frying

salt

1 Blanch the cauliflower in a large saucepan of boiling water for 5 minutes. Drain well and pat dry with kitchen paper.

2 Sift the flour with a pinch of salt into a bowl and add the thyme, egg yolks and water. Beat well with a wooden spoon until smooth. Beat in the milk.

3 In a separate, grease-free bowl, whisk the egg whites until stiff peaks form.

Gently fold a little of the egg white into the batter, then fold in the rest.

4 Heat the oil in a deep-fryer or pan to 180°C/350°F or until a cube of bread browns in 30 seconds. Dip the cauliflower florets in the batter to coat, then fry, in batches, until golden brown.

5 Drain the cauliflower fritters on kitchen paper and serve immediately.

COOK'S TIP
Reheat the oil between batches, as the temperature will drop during cooking.

Okra Bhaji

This is a very mild-tasting, rich curry, which would be an ideal accompaniment to a tomato-based main-course curry.

NUTRITIONAL INFORMATION

Calories ....173 Sugars 11g
Protein ....6g Fat 11g
Carbohydrate ...13g Saturates 5g

 25 mins   🕐 35 mins

SERVES 4

INGREDIENTS

1 tbsp sunflower oil

1 tsp black mustard seeds

1 tsp cumin seeds

1 tsp ground coriander

½ tsp turmeric

1 green chilli, deseeded and finely chopped

1 red onion, finely sliced

2 garlic cloves, crushed

1 orange pepper, deseeded and thinly sliced

500 g/1 lb 2 oz okra, trimmed and blanched

250 ml/9 fl oz vegetable juice

150 ml/¼ pint single cream

1 tbsp lemon juice

salt

1 Heat the oil in a preheated wok or large heavy-based frying pan. Add the mustard seeds and cover the pan until they start to pop.

2 Stir in the cumin seeds, ground coriander, turmeric and chilli. Stir constantly for 1 minute, until the spices are giving off their aroma.

3 Add the onion, garlic and pepper, and cook, stirring frequently, for about 5 minutes, until soft.

4 Add the blanched okra to the pan and stir to combine all the ingredients thoroughly.

5 Pour in the vegetable juice, bring to the boil and cook over a high heat, stirring occasionally, for 5 minutes.

6 When most of the liquid has evaporated, check the seasoning and add salt if necessary.

7 Add the cream, bring to the boil again and continue to cook the mixture over a high heat for about 12 minutes, until it is almost dry.

8 Sprinkle the lemon juice over the okra bhaji, transfer to a warmed serving dish and serve immediately.

COOK'S TIP

Okra, or lady's fingers, have a unique glutinous quality which, when they are added to curries and casseroles, disperses in the sauce and thickens it wonderfully – and naturally!

Carrot & Orange Bake

Poppy seeds add texture and flavour to this recipe and counteract the slightly sweet flavour of the carrots.

NUTRITIONAL INFORMATION

Calories	138	Sugars	........31g
Protein	.........2g	Fat	...........1g
Carbohydrate	...32g	Saturates	.....0.2g

20 mins   40 mins

SERVES 4

INGREDIENTS

675 g/1½ lb carrots, cut into thin strips

1 leek, sliced

300 ml/½ pint fresh orange juice

2 tbsp clear honey

1 garlic clove, crushed

1 tsp mixed spice

2 tsp chopped thyme

1 tbsp poppy seeds

salt and pepper

fresh thyme sprigs and orange rind, to garnish

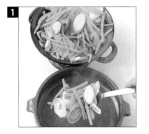

1 Cook the carrots and leek in a saucepan of boiling lightly salted water for 5–6 minutes. Drain well and transfer to a shallow ovenproof dish until required.

2 Mix together the orange juice, honey, garlic, mixed spice and thyme and pour the mixture over the vegetables. Season with salt and pepper to taste.

3 Cover the dish and cook in a preheated oven, 180°C/350°F/Gas Mark 4, for 30 minutes, or until the vegetables are tender.

4 Remove the lid and sprinkle with poppy seeds. Transfer the bake to a warmed serving dish, garnish with the fresh thyme sprigs and orange rind and serve immediately.

COOK'S TIP
Lemon or lime juice could be used instead of the orange juice, if you prefer. Garnish with lemon or lime rind.

Palak Paneer

Paneer, curd cheese, figures widely on Indian menus. It is combined with all sorts of ingredients, but most popularly with spinach and vegetables.

NUTRITIONAL INFORMATION

Calories	287	Sugars	.........7g
Protein	........12g	Fat	..........18g
Carbohydrate	...22g	Saturates	......11g

 20 mins   40 mins

SERVES 6

INGREDIENTS

2 tbsp ghee

1 onion, sliced

1 garlic clove, crushed

1 dried red chilli, finely chopped

1 tsp turmeric

500 g/1 lb 2 oz waxy potatoes, cut into
   2.5 cm/1 inch cubes

400 g/14 oz canned tomatoes, drained

150 ml/¼ pint water

225 g/8 oz fresh spinach

500 g/1 lb 2 oz curd cheese, cut into
   2.5 cm/1 inch cubes

1 tsp garam masala

1 tbsp chopped fresh coriander

1 tbsp chopped fresh parsley

salt and pepper

naan bread, to serve

1 Heat the ghee in a saucepan. Add the onion and cook over a low heat, stirring frequently, for 10 minutes, until very soft. Add the garlic and chilli and cook for a further 5 minutes.

2 Add the turmeric, a little salt, potatoes, canned tomatoes and water to the pan and bring to the boil.

3 Simmer for 10–15 minutes, until the potatoes are cooked.

4 Stir in the spinach, cheese cubes, garam masala and chopped coriander and parsley.

5 Simmer for a further 5 minutes and season well. Serve with naan bread.

VARIATION

Fresh Italian pecorino cheese can be used as a substitute for Indian paneer.

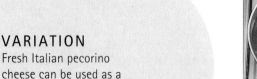

Mixed Vegetables

This is a very popular vegetarian recipe. You can make it with any vegetables you choose, but the combination below is ideal.

NUTRITIONAL INFORMATION

Calories . . . . . . .669 Sugars 17g
Protein . . . . .7g Fat 57g
Carbohydrate . . .36g Saturates 8g

🥄 🥄

5 mins   45 mins

SERVES 4

I N G R E D I E N T S

300 ml/½ pint vegetable oil

1 tsp mustard seeds

1 tsp onion seeds

½ tsp white cumin seeds

3–4 curry leaves, chopped

450 g/1 lb onions, finely chopped

3 tomatoes, chopped

½ red and ½ green pepper, deseeded and sliced

1 tsp finely chopped fresh root ginger

1 tsp fresh garlic, crushed

1 tsp chilli powder

¼ tsp turmeric

1 tsp salt

425 ml/¾ pint water

450 g/1 lb potatoes, cut into pieces

½ cauliflower, cut into small florets

4 carrots, peeled and sliced

3 fresh green chillies, deseeded and finely chopped

1 tbsp fresh coriander leaves

1 tbsp lemon juice

1 Heat the oil in a large saucepan. Add the mustard, onion and white cumin seeds along with the curry leaves and fry until the mixture turns a shade darker.

2 Add the onions to the pan and fry them over a medium heat until they turn golden brown.

3 Add the tomatoes and peppers and stir-fry for approximately 5 minutes.

4 Add the ginger, garlic, chilli powder, turmeric and salt and mix well.

5 Add 300 ml/½ pint of the water, cover the pan and leave to simmer for 10–12 minutes, stirring occasionally.

6 Add the potatoes, cauliflower florets, carrots, green chillies and fresh coriander leaves and cook, stirring, for about 5 minutes.

7 Add the remaining water and the lemon juice to the pan, stirring to combine. Cover the pan and leave the mixture to simmer for about 15 minutes, stirring occasionally.

8 Transfer the mixed vegetables to serving plates and serve immediately.

Cheese & Potato Layer Bake

This really is a great side dish, perfect for serving alongside main meals cooked in the oven.

NUTRITIONAL INFORMATION

Calories	295	Sugars	.........5g
Protein	........13g	Fat	..........17g
Carbohydrate	...24g	Saturates	......11g

 15 mins   1½ hrs

SERVES 4

I N G R E D I E N T S

500 g/1 lb 2 oz potatoes

1 leek, sliced

3 garlic cloves, crushed

50 g/1¾ oz Cheddar cheese, grated

50 g/1¾ oz mozzarella cheese, grated

25 g/1 oz Parmesan cheese, freshly grated

2 tbsp chopped fresh parsley

salt and pepper

150 ml/5 fl oz single cream

150 ml/5 fl oz milk

chopped fresh flat-leaved parsley,
    to garnish

1 Cook the potatoes in a saucepan of boiling salted water for 10 minutes. Drain well.

2 Cut the potatoes into thin slices. Arrange a layer of potatoes in the base of an ovenproof dish. Layer with a little of the sliced leek, crushed garlic, grated cheeses and chopped parsley. Season to taste with salt and pepper.

3 Repeat the layers until all of the ingredients have been used, finishing with a layer of cheese.

4 Mix the cream and milk together, season with salt and pepper to taste and pour over the potato layers.

5 Cook the cheese and potato bake in a preheated oven, 160°C/ 325°F/Gas Mark 3, for 1–1¼ hours, or until the cheese is golden brown and bubbling and the potatoes are cooked through and tender.

6 Garnish the bake with chopped fresh flat-leaved parsley and serve immediately.

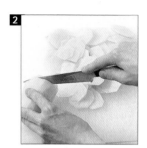

COOK'S TIP

Potatoes make a very good basis for a vegetable accompaniment. They are a good source of complex carbohydrate and contain a number of vitamins. From the point of view of flavour, they combine well with a vast range of other ingredients.

Steamed Vegetable Parcels

Baby vegetables are cooked whole so that they lose none of their flavour, colour, texture or goodness. Serve them still wrapped in their parcels.

NUTRITIONAL INFORMATION

Calories 170	Sugars 9g
Protein 3g	Fat 12g
Carbohydrate 11g	Saturates 8g

🍳 15 mins   ⏱ 8–10 mins

SERVES 4

I N G R E D I E N T S

115 g/4 oz French beans

55 g/2 oz mangetouts

12 baby carrots

8 baby onions or shallots

12 baby turnips

8 radishes

salt and pepper

55 g/2 oz unsalted butter or margarine

4 thinly pared strips of lemon rind

4 tsp finely chopped fresh chervil

4 tbsp dry white wine

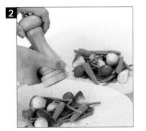

1 Cut out 4 double thickness rounds of greaseproof paper about 30 cm/ 12 inches in diameter.

2 Divide the French beans, mangetouts, carrots, onions or shallots, turnips and radishes among the rounds, placing them on one half. Season to taste with salt and pepper and dot with the butter. Add a strip of lemon rind to each. Sprinkle with the chervil and drizzle with the wine. Fold over the double layer of paper, twisting the edges together to seal.

3 Bring a large pan of water to the boil and place a steamer on top. Put the parcels in the steamer, cover tightly and steam for 8–10 minutes. Serve the parcels immediately, to be unwrapped at table.

VARIATION
Substitute 4 tbsp olive oil for the butter or margarine, chopped fresh mint for the chervil and cherry tomatoes for the radishes.

Spiced Lentils with Spinach

This dish is a good accompaniment to a main dish, or can be eaten as a complete meal in itself, with a tomato and onion side salad.

NUTRITIONAL INFORMATION

Calories 179	Sugars 3g
Protein 11g	Fat 5g
Carbohydrate ...24g	Saturates 1g

  15 mins   🕐 35 mins

SERVES 4–6

INGREDIENTS

2 tbsp olive oil

1 large onion, finely chopped

1 large garlic clove, crushed

½ tbsp ground cumin

½ tsp ground ginger

250 g/9 oz Puy lentils

about 600 ml/1 pint vegetable stock

100 g/3½ oz baby spinach leaves

2 tbsp fresh mint leaves

1 tbsp fresh coriander leaves

1 tbsp fresh flat-leaved parsley

lemon juice

salt and pepper

strips of lemon rind, to garnish

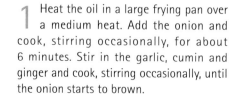

COOK'S TIP

This recipe uses green lentils from Puy in France because they are good at keeping their shape, even after long cooking. You can, however, also use orange or brown lentils but it is necessary to watch them while they cook or they will quickly turn to a mush.

1 Heat the oil in a large frying pan over a medium heat. Add the onion and cook, stirring occasionally, for about 6 minutes. Stir in the garlic, cumin and ginger and cook, stirring occasionally, until the onion starts to brown.

2 Stir in the lentils. Pour in enough stock to cover the lentils by 2.5 cm/ 1 inch and bring to the boil. Lower the heat and simmer for 20–30 minutes until the lentils are tender.

3 Meanwhile, rinse the spinach leaves in several changes of cold water and shake dry. Finely chop the mint, coriander and parsley leaves.

4 If there isn't any stock left in the pan, add a little extra. Add the spinach and stir through until it just wilts. Stir in the mint, coriander and parsley. Adjust the seasoning, adding lemon juice and salt and pepper. Transfer to a serving bowl and serve, garnished with lemon rind.

Ratatouille Vegetable Grill

Ratatouille is a classic dish of vegetables cooked in a tomato and herb sauce. Here it is topped with diced potatoes and cheese.

NUTRITIONAL INFORMATION

Calories 287	Sugars 13g	
Protein 14g	Fat 4g	
Carbohydrate ...53g	Saturates 2g	

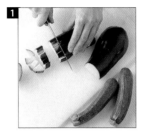
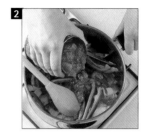

15 mins   25 mins

SERVES 4

INGREDIENTS

2 onions

1 garlic clove

1 red pepper

1 green pepper

1 aubergine

2 courgettes

800 g/1 lb 12 oz canned chopped tomatoes

1 bouquet garni

2 tbsp tomato purée

900 g/2 lb potatoes

75 g/2¾ oz reduced-fat mature Cheddar cheese, grated

salt and pepper

2 tbsp snipped fresh chives, to garnish

1 Peel and finely chop the onions and garlic. Deseed and slice the peppers. Trim the aubergine and cut into small dice. Trim and thinly slice the courgettes.

2 Place the onion, garlic and peppers in a large saucepan. Add the tomatoes, and stir in the bouquet garni, tomato purée and salt and pepper to taste. Bring to the boil, cover and simmer for 10 minutes, stirring half-way through. Stir in the prepared aubergine and courgettes and cook the vegetables, uncovered, for a further 10 minutes, stirring occasionally.

3 Peel the potatoes and cut them into 2.5 cm/1 inch cubes. Place in another saucepan and cover with water. Bring to the boil and cook for 10–12 minutes until tender. Drain and set aside.

4 Transfer the aubergine mixture to a heatproof gratin dish. Arrange the potatoes evenly over the vegetables.

5 Preheat the grill to medium. Sprinkle the cheese over the potatoes and grill for 5 minutes until golden, bubbling and hot. Serve garnished with snipped chives.

VARIATION
You can vary the vegetables in this dish depending on seasonal availability and personal preference. Try broccoli, carrots or sweetcorn, if you prefer.

Gnocchi with Herb Sauce

These potato dumplings are a traditional Italian starter or side dish. They can also make a substantial main course if served with a salad and bread.

NUTRITIONAL INFORMATION

Calories 619   Sugars 3g
Protein . . . . .11g   Fat 30g
Carbohydrate . . .81g   Saturates 9g

  30 mins   30 mins

SERVES 6

I N G R E D I E N T S

1 kg/2 lb 4 oz floury potatoes, cut into
   1 cm/½ inch pieces

salt

60 g/2 oz butter or margarine

1 egg, beaten

300 g/10½ oz plain flour

H E R B   S A U C E

125 ml/4 fl oz olive oil

2 garlic cloves, very finely chopped

salt and pepper

1 tbsp chopped fresh oregano

1 tbsp chopped fresh basil

T O   S E R V E   (O P T I O N A L)

freshly grated Parmesan cheese

mixed salad

warm ciabatta bread

1 Cook the potatoes in a saucepan of boiling salted water for about 10 minutes or until tender. Drain well.

2 Press the hot potatoes through a sieve into a large bowl. Add 1 teaspoon of salt, the butter or margarine, the egg and 150 g/5½ oz of the flour. Stir the mixture well to bind together.

3 Turn on to a lightly floured surface and knead, gradually adding the remaining flour, until a smooth, soft, slightly sticky dough is formed.

4 Flour the hands and roll the dough into 2 cm/¾ inch thick rolls. Cut each roll into 1 cm/½ inch pieces. Press the top of each piece with the floured prongs of a fork and spread out on a floured tea towel.

5 Bring a large saucepan of salted water to a gentle simmer. Add the gnocchi and cook them in batches for about 2–3 minutes, or until they rise to the surface.

6 Remove the gnocchi with a perforated spoon and put in a warmed, greased serving dish. Cover and keep warm.

7 To make the sauce, put the oil, garlic and seasoning in a pan and cook, stirring, for 3–4 minutes until the garlic is golden. Remove from the heat and stir in the herbs. Pour over the gnocchi and serve, sprinkled with Parmesan, and accompanied by salad and warm ciabatta, if desired.

Potato & Spinach Gnocchi

These small potato dumplings are flavoured with spinach, cooked in boiling water and served with a simple tomato sauce.

NUTRITIONAL INFORMATION

Calories 315	Sugars 7g	
Protein 8g	Fat 8g	
Carbohydrate . . .56g	Saturates 1g	

20 mins   30 mins

SERVES 4

I N G R E D I E N T S

300 g/10½ oz floury potatoes, diced

175 g/6 oz fresh spinach

1 egg yolk

1 tsp olive oil

salt and pepper

125 g/4½ oz plain flour

fresh spinach leaves, to garnish

S A U C E

1 tbsp olive oil

2 shallots, chopped

1 garlic clove, crushed

300 ml/10 fl oz passata

2 tsp soft light brown sugar

1 Cook the diced potatoes in a saucepan of boiling water for 10 minutes or until cooked through. Drain and mash the potatoes.

2 Meanwhile, in a separate pan, blanch the spinach in a little boiling water for 1–2 minutes. Drain the spinach and shred the leaves.

3 Transfer the mashed potato to a lightly floured chopping board and make a well in the centre. Add the egg yolk, olive oil, spinach, salt and pepper and a little of the flour and quickly mix the

ingredients into the potato, adding more flour as you go, until you have a firm, workable dough. Divide the mixture into very small dumplings.

4 Cook the gnocchi, in batches, in a saucepan of boiling salted water for about 5 minutes or until they rise to the surface.

5 Meanwhile, make the sauce. Put the oil, shallots, garlic, passata and sugar into a saucepan and cook over a low heat for 10–15 minutes or until the sauce has reduced and thickened.

6 Drain the gnocchi using a perforated spoon and transfer to warm serving dishes. Spoon the sauce over the gnocchi and garnish with the fresh spinach leaves.

VARIATION
Add chopped fresh herbs and cheese to the gnocchi dough instead of the spinach, if you prefer.

Potatoes with Almonds

This oven-cooked dish has a subtle, creamy almond flavour and the turmeric gives it a lovely pale yellow colour.

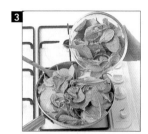

NUTRITIONAL INFORMATION

Calories . . . . .531 Sugars 6g
Protein . . . . .7g Fat 46g
Carbohydrate . . .24g Saturates 23g

 5 mins   40–45 mins

SERVES 4

INGREDIENTS

600 g/1 lb 5 oz potatoes,
  unpeeled and sliced

1 tbsp vegetable oil

1 red onion, halved and sliced

1 garlic clove, crushed

50 g/2 oz flaked almonds

½ tsp turmeric

125 g/4 oz rocket leaves

300ml/½ pint double cream

salt and pepper

1 Cook the sliced potatoes in a saucepan of boiling water for 10 minutes. Drain thoroughly.

2 Heat the vegetable oil in a heavy-based frying pan. Add the onion and garlic and fry over a medium heat, stirring frequently, for 3–4 minutes.

3 Add the almonds, turmeric and potato slices to the frying pan and cook, stirring constantly, for 2–3 minutes. Stir in the rocket.

4 Transfer the potato and almond mixture to a shallow ovenproof dish.

5 Pour the double cream over the top and season with salt and pepper.

6 Cook in a preheated oven, 190°C/ 375°F/Gas Mark 5, for 20 minutes, or until the potatoes are cooked through. Transfer to a warmed serving dish and serve immediately.

Greek Beans

This dish contains many Greek flavours such as lemon, garlic, oregano and olives, for a really flavourful recipe.

NUTRITIONAL INFORMATION

Calories	115	Sugars	4g
Protein	6g	Fat	4g
Carbohydrate	15g	Saturates	0.6g

 5 mins   1 hr

SERVES 4

INGREDIENTS

400 g/14 oz canned haricot beans, drained

1 tbsp olive oil

3 garlic cloves, crushed

425 ml/¾ pint vegetable stock

1 bay leaf

2 sprigs fresh oregano

1 tbsp tomato purée

juice of 1 lemon

1 small red onion, chopped

25 g/1 oz black olives, stoned and halved

salt and pepper

1 Put the haricot beans in a flameproof casserole dish.

2 Add the olive oil and crushed garlic and cook over a gentle heat, stirring occasionally, for 4–5 minutes.

3 Add the stock, bay leaf, oregano, tomato purée, lemon juice and red onion. Cover and simmer for about 1 hour or until the sauce has thickened.

4 Stir in the black olives, then season the beans with salt and pepper to taste. The beans are delicious served either warm or cold.

VARIATION

You can substitute other canned beans for the haricot beans – try cannellini or black-eyed beans or chick peas instead. Drain and rinse them before use as canned beans often have sugar or salt added.

Potato Hash

This recipe is a variation of a hearty American dish, which was served to seagoing New Englanders.

NUTRITIONAL INFORMATION

Calories 302   Sugars 5g
Protein . . . . .15g   Fat 10g
Carbohydrate . . .40g   Saturates 4g

🍠 10 mins   🕑 30 mins

SERVES 4

INGREDIENTS

2 tbsp butter

1 red onion, halved and sliced

1 carrot, diced

25 g/1 oz French beans, halved

900 g/2 lb waxy potatoes, diced

2 tbsp plain flour

600 ml/1 pint vegetable stock

225 g/8 oz firm tofu, diced

salt and pepper

chopped fresh parsley, to garnish

1 Melt the butter in a large, heavy-based frying pan. Add the onion, carrot, French beans and potatoes and fry over a fairly low heat, stirring constantly, for about 5–7 minutes, or until the vegetables begin to turn golden brown.

2 Add the flour to the frying pan and cook, stirring constantly, for 1 minute. Gradually pour in the vegetable stock, still stirring constantly.

3 Reduce the heat to low and simmer for about 15 minutes, or until the potatoes are tender.

4 Add the diced tofu to the pan and cook for a further 5 minutes. Season to taste with salt and pepper.

5 Sprinkle the chopped fresh parsley over the top of the potato hash to garnish and then serve hot, straight from the frying pan.

COOK'S TIP

Hash is an American term meaning to chop food into small pieces. Therefore a traditional hash dish is made from chopped fresh ingredients, such as peppers, onion and celery.

Spinach & Cauliflower Bhaji

This excellent vegetable dish goes well with most Indian food – and it is simple and quick-cooking, too.

NUTRITIONAL INFORMATION

Calories 212	Sugars 12g
Protein 10g	Fat 13g
Carbohydrate . . .14g	Saturates 2g

 10 mins   25 mins

SERVES 4

INGREDIENTS

1 cauliflower

500 g/1 lb 2 oz fresh spinach, washed, or 225 g/8 oz frozen spinach, thawed

4 tbsp ghee or vegetable oil

2 large onions, roughly chopped

2 garlic cloves, crushed

2.5 cm/1 inch piece of fresh root ginger, chopped

1¼ tsp cayenne pepper, or to taste

1 tsp ground cumin

1 tsp turmeric

2 tsp ground coriander

400 g/14 oz canned chopped tomatoes

300 ml/½ pint vegetable stock

salt and pepper

1 Divide the cauliflower into small florets, discarding the hard central stalk. Trim the stalks from the spinach leaves. Heat the ghee or oil in a large saucepan, add the onions and cauliflower florets and fry over a low heat, stirring frequently, for about 3 minutes.

2 Add the garlic, ginger and spices and cook gently, stirring occasionally, for 1 minute. Stir in the tomatoes and the vegetable stock and season to taste with salt and pepper. Bring to the boil, cover the pan, reduce the heat and simmer gently for 8 minutes.

3 Add the spinach to the pan, stirring and turning to wilt the leaves. Cover and simmer gently, stirring frequently, for about 8–10 minutes, until the spinach and the cauliflower are tender. Transfer to a warmed serving dish and serve hot.

COOK'S TIP
When buying cauliflower, look for firm, white curds with no discoloration or signs of wilting.

Long Beans with Tomatoes

Indian meals often need some green vegetables to complement the spicy dishes and to off-set the richly flavoured sauces.

NUTRITIONAL INFORMATION

Calories	76	Sugars 3g
Protein	........2g	Fat 6g
Carbohydrate	....4g	Saturates 3g

15 mins

25 mins

SERVES 6

INGREDIENTS

500 g/1 lb 2 oz French beans, cut into 5 cm/2 inch lengths

2 tbsp ghee

2.5 cm/1 inch piece of fresh root ginger, grated

1 garlic clove, crushed

1 tsp turmeric

½ tsp cayenne pepper

1 tsp ground coriander

4 tomatoes, peeled, deseeded and diced

150 ml/5 fl oz vegetable stock

1 Blanch the beans briefly in boiling water, drain, refresh under cold running water and drain again.

2 Melt the ghee in a wok or a large frying pan over a moderate heat. Add the grated ginger and crushed garlic, stir and add the turmeric, cayenne and ground coriander. Stir over a low heat for about 1 minute until fragrant.

3 Add the diced tomatoes to the pan, tossing until they are thoroughly coated in the spice mix.

4 Add the vegetable stock to the pan, bring to the boil and simmer over a medium-high heat, stirring occasionally, for about 10 minutes until the sauce has reduced and thickened.

5 Add the beans, reduce the heat to moderate and heat through, stirring constantly, for 5 minutes.

6 Transfer to a warmed serving dish and serve immediately.

COOK'S TIP

A ginger grater is an invaluable piece of equipment to have when cooking Indian food. These small, flat graters, made of either bamboo or china, can be held directly over the pan while you grate.

Souffléd Cheesy Potato Fries

These small potato chunks are coated in a creamy cheese sauce and fried in oil until deliciously golden brown.

NUTRITIONAL INFORMATION

Calories	614	Sugars	.........2g
Protein	........12g	Fat	..........46g
Carbohydrate	...40g	Saturates	......18g

 20 mins   25 mins

SERVES 4

INGREDIENTS

900 g/2 lb potatoes, cut into chunks

150 ml/5 fl oz double cream

75 g/3 oz Gruyère cheese, grated

pinch of cayenne pepper

salt and pepper

2 egg whites

vegetable oil, for deep-frying

TO GARNISH

chopped fresh flat-leaved parsley

grated cheese

1 Cook the potatoes in a saucepan of lightly salted boiling water for about 10 minutes. Drain thoroughly and pat dry with absorbent kitchen paper. Set aside until required.

2 Mix the double cream and Gruyère cheese in a large bowl. Stir in the cayenne pepper and season with salt and pepper to taste.

3 Whisk the egg whites until stiff peaks form. Gently fold into the cheese mixture until fully incorporated.

4 Add the cooked potatoes, turning to coat thoroughly in the mixture.

5 Heat the oil for deep-frying to 180°C/350°F or until a cube of bread browns in 30 seconds. Lift the coated potatoes from the cheese mixture with a slotted spoon and cook in the oil, in batches if necessary, for 3–4 minutes, or until golden.

6 Transfer the potatoes to a warmed serving dish and garnish with parsley and grated cheese. Serve immediately.

VARIATION
Add other flavourings, such as grated nutmeg or curry powder, to the cream and cheese.

Easy Cauliflower & Broccoli

Whole baby cauliflowers are used in this recipe. Try to find them if you can, but if not use large bunches of florets instead.

NUTRITIONAL INFORMATION

Calories	433	Sugars	.........2g
Protein	.........8g	Fat	..........44g
Carbohydrate	....3g	Saturates	.......9g

10 mins   20 mins

SERVES 4

INGREDIENTS

2 baby cauliflowers

225 g/8 oz broccoli

salt and pepper

SAUCE

8 tbsp olive oil

4 tbsp butter or margarine

2 tsp grated fresh root ginger

juice and rind of 2 lemons

5 tbsp chopped fresh coriander

5 tbsp grated Cheddar cheese

1 Using a sharp knife, cut the cauliflowers in half and the broccoli into very large florets.

2 Cook the cauliflower and broccoli in a saucepan of boiling salted water for 10 minutes. Drain well, transfer to a shallow ovenproof dish and keep warm until required.

3 To make the sauce, put the oil and butter or margarine in a pan and heat gently until the butter melts.

4 Add the grated root ginger, lemon juice, lemon rind and chopped coriander and simmer for 2–3 minutes, stirring occasionally.

5 Season the sauce with salt and pepper to taste, then pour over the vegetables in the dish and sprinkle the cheese on top.

6 Cook under a preheated hot grill for 2–3 minutes, or until the cheese is bubbling and golden brown. Leave to cool for 1–2 minutes and then serve.

COOK'S TIP

Lime or orange could be used instead of the lemon for a fruity and refreshing sauce.

Saffron-flavoured Potatoes

Saffron strands are the dried stigma of the saffron crocus. They are very expensive, but only a very small amount is needed.

NUTRITIONAL INFORMATION

Calories 197	Sugars 4g	
Protein 4g	Fat 6g	
Carbohydrate . . .30g	Saturates 1g	

 20 mins   40 mins

SERVES 4

I N G R E D I E N T S

a good pinch of saffron strands

6 tbsp boiling water

675 g/1½ lb waxy potatoes, unpeeled and cut into wedges

1 red onion, cut into 8 wedges

2 garlic cloves, crushed

1 tbsp white wine vinegar

2 tbsp olive oil

1 tbsp wholegrain mustard

5 tbsp vegetable stock

5 tbsp dry white wine

2 tsp chopped fresh rosemary

salt and pepper

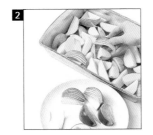

1 Place the saffron strands in a small bowl and pour over the boiling water. Set aside to soak for about 10 minutes.

2 Place the potatoes in a roasting tin, together with the wedges of red onion and the garlic.

3 Add the white wine vinegar, olive oil, mustard, vegetable stock, white wine, rosemary and the saffron and its water to the potatoes and onion in the tin. Season to taste with salt and pepper.

4 Cover the roasting tin with kitchen foil and bake in a preheated oven, 200°C/400°F/Gas Mark 6, for 30 minutes.

5 Remove the foil and continue to cook the potatoes for a further 10 minutes until they are crisp, browned and cooked through. Serve hot.

COOK'S TIP
Turmeric may be used instead of saffron to provide the yellow colour in this recipe. How ever, it is worth using saffron, if possible, for the lovely nutty flavour it gives a dish.

Aubergine Bhaji

The panch poran spice mix used here is one of many traditional spice mixes used in Indian cooking and originated in the Bengal state.

NUTRITIONAL INFORMATION

Calories . . . . 170 Sugars 4g
Protein . . . . 2g Fat 17g
Carbohydrate . . . . 4g Saturates 2g

 5 mins   25 mins

SERVES 4

I N G R E D I E N T S

2 tbsp mustard oil

4 tbsp sunflower oil

1 tsp panch poran spice mix (see Cook's Tip on page 800)

6 baby aubergines, quartered, or 2 aubergines, cut into 2.5 cm/ 1 inch cubes

¼ tsp cayenne

1 tsp coriander seeds, ground

½ tsp turmeric

200 g/7 oz canned chopped tomatoes

½ tsp sugar

salt

2 tsp lime juice

1 Heat the mustard oil in a wok or large frying pan until it just starts to smoke. Reduce the heat and add the sunflower oil. Add the panch poran mix to the pan, stir once and then add the aubergine pieces.

2 Add the cayenne, coriander and turmeric to the pan and stir over a high heat for 2–3 minutes, until the aubergine is sealed on all sides.

3 Add the chopped tomatoes, together with their can juices, to the pan and bring to the boil.

4 Simmer for 15 minutes, or until the bhaji is nearly dry. Stir once or twice. Remove from the heat and stir in the sugar, a pinch of salt and the lime juice.

5 Transfer to a warmed serving dish, and serve immediately.

COOK'S TIP

Most Asian cooks do not salt aubergines. The aubergines available for most of the year are so fresh that they do not have any bitter juices, especially the plump, shiny ones that have been left on the plant until they are sweet.

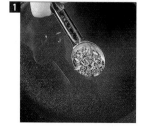

Candied Sweet Potatoes

A taste of the Caribbean is introduced in this recipe, where sweet potatoes are cooked with sugar and lime with a dash of brandy.

NUTRITIONAL INFORMATION

Calories	348	Sugars	........21g
Protein	.........3g	Fat	...........9g
Carbohydrate	...67g	Saturates	.......6g

 15 mins   25 mins

SERVES 4

I N G R E D I E N T S

675 g/1½ lb sweet potatoes, sliced

3 tbsp butter

1 tbsp lime juice

75 g/2¾ oz soft dark brown sugar

1 tbsp brandy

grated rind of 1 lime

lime wedges, to garnish

1 Cook the sweet potatoes in a saucepan of boiling water for about 5 minutes. Test that the potatoes have softened by pricking with a fork. Remove the sweet potatoes with a perforated spoon and drain thoroughly.

2 Melt the butter in a large frying pan. Add the lime juice and the brown sugar and heat gently, stirring, until the sugar has dissolved.

3 Stir the sweet potatoes and the brandy into the sugar and lime juice mixture. Cook over a low heat for about 10 minutes or until the potato slices are cooked through.

4 Sprinkle the grated lime rind over the top of the sweet potatoes and stir well to combine.

5 Transfer the candied sweet potatoes to a serving plate. Garnish with lime wedges and serve at once.

COOK'S TIP
Sweet potatoes have a pinkish skin and either white, yellow or orange flesh. It doesn't matter which type is used for this dish.

Indian Potatoes & Peas

This quick and easy-to-prepare Indian dish can be served either as an accompaniment or on its own with chapatis.

NUTRITIONAL INFORMATION

Calories 434	Sugars 6g
Protein 5g	Fat 35g
Carbohydrate . . .28g	Saturates 4g

 15 mins   25 mins

SERVES 4

INGREDIENTS

150 ml/¼ pint vegetable oil

3 onions, sliced

1 tsp crushed garlic

1 tsp finely chopped fresh root ginger

1 tsp chilli powder

½ tsp turmeric

1 tsp salt

2 fresh green chillies, deseeded and finely chopped

300 ml/½ pint water

675 g/1½ lb potatoes

100 g/4 oz shelled peas

TO GARNISH

chopped red chillies

fresh coriander leaves

COOK'S TIP

Turmeric is an aromatic root that is dried and ground to produce the distinctive bright yellow-orange powder used in many Indian dishes. It has a warm, aromatic smell and a full, somewhat musty taste.

1 Heat the oil in a large, heavy-based frying pan. Add the onions to the frying pan and fry, stirring occasionally, until the onions are golden brown.

2 Mix together the garlic, ginger, chilli powder, turmeric, salt and fresh green chillies. Add the spice mixture to the onions in the pan.

3 Stir in 150 ml/5 fl oz of the water, cover and cook until the onions are cooked through.

4 Meanwhile, cut the potatoes into six slices each, using a sharp knife.

5 Add the potato slices to the mixture in the pan and stir-fry for 5 minutes.

6 Add the peas and the remaining water to the pan, cover and cook for 7–10 minutes.

7 Transfer the potatoes and peas to serving plates and serve, garnished with chopped red chillies and coriander leaves.

Spicy Corn

This dish is an ideal accompaniment to a wide range of Indian dishes and would also go well with a casserole.

NUTRITIONAL INFORMATION

Calories	162	Sugars	.........6g
Protein	.........2g	Fat	...........11g
Carbohydrate	...15g	Saturates	.......7g

 10 mins   10 mins

SERVES 4

INGREDIENTS

200 g/7 oz frozen or canned
   sweetcorn kernels

1 tsp ground cumin

1 tsp crushed garlic

1 tsp ground coriander

1 tsp salt

2 fresh green chillies, deseeded

1 onion, finely chopped

3 tbsp unsalted butter

4 dried red chillies, crushed

½ tsp lemon juice

1 tbsp fresh coriander leaves, plus extra
   to garnish

1 Thaw frozen sweetcorn, if using, or drain canned corn, and set aside.

2 Place the cumin, garlic, coriander, salt, 1 green chilli and the onion in a mortar or a food processor and grind to form a smooth paste.

3 Heat the butter in a large frying pan. Add the onion and spice mixture to the pan and fry over a medium heat, stirring occasionally, for 5–7 minutes.

4 Add the crushed dried red chillies to the mixture in the pan and stir to combine thoroughly.

5 Add the sweetcorn to the pan and stir-fry for a further 2 minutes.

6 Add the remaining green chilli, finely chopped, the lemon juice and the fresh coriander leaves to the pan, stirring to combine.

7 Transfer the spicy sweetcorn mixture to a warmed serving dish. Garnish with the fresh coriander leaves and serve hot.

COOK'S TIP
Coriander is available ground or as seeds and is one of the essential ingredients in Indian cooking. Coriander seeds are often dry roasted before use to develop their flavour.

Spiced Potatoes & Spinach

This is a classic Indian accompaniment for many different curries or plainer main vegetable dishes. It is very quick to cook.

NUTRITIONAL INFORMATION

Calories 176   Sugars 4g
Protein . . . . .6g   Fat 9g
Carbohydrate . . .18g   Saturates 1g

 10 mins   20 mins

SERVES 4

INGREDIENTS

3 tbsp vegetable oil

1 red onion, sliced

2 garlic cloves, crushed

½ tsp chilli powder

2 tsp ground coriander

1 tsp ground cumin

150 ml/5 fl oz vegetable stock

300 g/10½ oz potatoes, diced

500 g/1 lb 2 oz baby spinach

salt and pepper

1 red chilli, deseeded and sliced

1 Heat the oil in a heavy-based frying pan. Add the onion and garlic and sauté over a medium heat, stirring occasionally, for 2–3 minutes.

2 Stir in the chilli powder and the ground coriander and cumin and cook, stirring constantly, for a further 30 seconds.

3 Add the vegetable stock, potatoes and spinach and bring to the boil. Reduce the heat, cover the frying pan and simmer for about 10 minutes, or until the potatoes are cooked through and tender.

4 Uncover the pan, season the vegetables to taste with salt and pepper, add the chilli and cook for a further 2–3 minutes. Transfer to a warmed serving dish and serve immediately.

COOK'S TIP

Besides adding extra colour to a dish, red onions have a sweeter, less pungent flavour than other varieties.

Curried Roast Potatoes

This is the kind of Indian-inspired dish that would fit easily into any vegetarian menu, or could be served with a curry in place of rice.

NUTRITIONAL INFORMATION

Calories 297   Sugars 2g
Protein ....3g   Fat 19g
Carbohydrate ...30g   Saturates 12g

5 mins   30-35 mins

SERVES 4

INGREDIENTS

2 tsp cumin seeds

2 tsp coriander seeds

90 g/3 oz butter

1 tsp turmeric

1 tsp black mustard seeds

2 garlic cloves, crushed

2 dried red chillies, finely chopped

750 g/1 lb 10 oz baby new potatoes

1 Grind the cumin and coriander seeds together in a mortar with a pestle or spice grinder. Grinding them fresh like this captures all of the flavour before it has a chance to dry out.

2 Melt the butter gently in a roasting tin and add the turmeric, mustard seeds, garlic and chillies and the ground cumin and coriander seeds. Stir well to combine evenly. Place in a preheated oven at 200°C/400°F/Gas Mark 6 for 5 minutes.

3 Remove the tin from the oven – the spices should be very fragrant at this stage – and add the potatoes. Stir well so that the butter and spice mix coats the potatoes completely.

4 Return to the oven and bake for 20–25 minutes. Stir occasionally to ensure that the potatoes are coated evenly. Test the potatoes with a skewer – if they drop off the end of the skewer when lifted, they are done. Transfer to a serving dish and serve immediately.

COOK'S TIP

Baby new potatoes are now available all year round from supermarkets. However, they are not essential for this recipe. Red or white old potatoes can be substituted, cut into 2.5 cm/1 inch cubes.

Bombay Potatoes

Although virtually unknown in India, this dish is a very popular item on Indian restaurant menus in other parts of the world.

NUTRITIONAL INFORMATION

Calories 307	Sugars 9g	
Protein 9g	Fat 9g	
Carbohydrate . . .51g	Saturates 5g	

 5 mins   1 hr 10 mins

SERVES 4

INGREDIENTS

1 kg/2 lb 4 oz waxy potatoes

2 tbsp ghee

1 tsp panch poran spice mix (see Cook's Tip)

3 tsp ground turmeric

2 tbsp tomato purée

300 ml/½ pint natural yogurt

salt

chopped fresh coriander, to garnish

1 Put the whole potatoes into a large saucepan of salted cold water, bring to the boil, then simmer until the potatoes are just cooked, but not tender; the time depends on the size of the potato, but an average-sized one should take about 15 minutes.

2 Heat the ghee in a saucepan over a medium heat and add the panch poran, turmeric, tomato purée, yogurt and salt to taste. Bring to the boil and simmer the mixture, uncovered, for 5 minutes.

3 Drain the potatoes and cut each one into 4 pieces. Add the potatoes to the pan, cover and cook briefly.

4 Transfer to an ovenproof casserole, cover and cook in a preheated oven, 180°C/350°F/Gas Mark 4, for about 40 minutes, or until the potatoes are tender and the sauce has thickened a little.

5 Sprinkle the potatoes with the chopped fresh coriander and serve immediately.

COOK'S TIP

Panch poran spice mix can be bought from Asian or Indian grocery stores, or make your own from equal quantities of cumin seeds, fennel seeds, mustard seeds, nigella seeds and fenugreek seeds.

Colcannon

This is an old Irish recipe that is delicious served with a main course – although you may be tempted to eat it just as it is!

NUTRITIONAL INFORMATION

Calories 102	Sugars 4g
Protein 4g	Fat 4g
Carbohydrate . . .14g	Saturates 2g

20 mins   20 mins

SERVES 4

I N G R E D I E N T S

225 g/8 oz green cabbage, shredded

5 tbsp milk

225 g/8 oz floury potatoes, diced

1 large leek, chopped

pinch of freshly grated nutmeg

1 tbsp butter, melted

salt and pepper

1 Cook the shredded cabbage in a saucepan of boiling salted water for 7–10 minutes. Drain thoroughly and set aside.

2 Meanwhile, in a separate saucepan, bring the milk to the boil and add the potatoes and leek. Reduce the heat and simmer for 15–20 minutes, or until they are cooked through.

3 Remove from the heat, stir in the freshly grated nutmeg and thoroughly mash the potatoes and leek together.

4 Add the drained cabbage to the mashed potato and leek mixture, season to taste and mix together well.

5 Spoon the mixture into a warmed serving dish, making a hollow in the centre with the back of a spoon.

6 Pour the melted butter into the hollow and serve the colcannon at once, while it is still hot.

COOK'S TIP

There are many different varieties of cabbage, which produce hearts at varying times of year, so you can be sure of being able to make this delicious cabbage dish all year round.

Aubergine Bake

This is an unusual 'back-to-front' dish, in that the aubergine is first baked in the oven, then cooked in a saucepan.

NUTRITIONAL INFORMATION

Calories	140	Sugars	.........5g
Protein	.........3g	Fat	..........12g
Carbohydrate	....6g	Saturates	.......1g

 10 mins 55 mins

SERVES 4

INGREDIENTS

2 aubergines

4 tbsp vegetable oil

1 onion, sliced

1 tsp white cumin seeds

1 tsp chilli powder

1 tsp salt

3 tbsp natural yogurt

½ tsp mint sauce

fresh mint leaves, to garnish

1 Rinse the aubergines under cold running water and pat thoroughly dry with absorbent kitchen paper.

2 Place the aubergines side by side in an ovenproof dish or roasting tin. Bake in a preheated oven,160°C/325°F/ Gas Mark 3, for 45 minutes. Remove the baked aubergines from the oven and set aside to cool.

3 Using a teaspoon, scoop out the aubergine flesh and set aside.

4 Heat the vegetable oil in a heavy-based saucepan over a low heat. Add the sliced onion and the white cumin seeds to the pan and fry, stirring constantly, for 1-2 minutes.

5 Add the chilli powder, salt, natural yogurt and mint sauce to the pan and stir well to mix.

6 Add the aubergine flesh to the onion and yogurt mixture and continue to fry over a medium heat, stirring constantly, for about 5–7 minutes, or until all of the liquid has been absorbed and the mixture is quite dry.

7 Transfer the aubergine and yogurt mixture to a warmed serving dish.

8 Serve the aubergine bake immediately, garnished with the fresh mint leaves.

Potatoes Lyonnaise

In this classic French recipe, sliced potatoes are cooked with onions to make a delicious accompaniment to a main meal.

NUTRITIONAL INFORMATION

Calories 277	Sugars 4g	
Protein 5g	Fat 12g	
Carbohydrate . . .40g	Saturates 4g	

 10 mins   25 mins

SERVES 6

INGREDIENTS

1.25 kg/2 lb 12 oz potatoes

4 tbsp olive oil

2 tbsp butter

2 onions, sliced

2–3 garlic cloves, crushed (optional)

salt and pepper

chopped fresh parsley, to garnish

1 Cut the potatoes into 5 mm/¼ inch slices. Put in a large saucepan of lightly salted water and bring to the boil. Cover and simmer gently for about 10–12 minutes, until just tender. Avoid boiling too rapidly or the potatoes will break up and lose their shape. When the potatoes are cooked, drain well.

2 While the potatoes are cooking, heat the oil and butter in a very large frying pan. Add the onions and garlic, if using, and fry over a medium heat, stirring frequently, until the onions are softened.

3 Add the cooked potato to the frying pan and cook with the onions, stirring occasionally, for about 5–8 minutes until the potatoes are well browned.

4 Season to taste with salt and pepper and sprinkle over the chopped parsley to serve. If necessary, the potatoes and onions can be transferred to a large ovenproof dish and kept warm in a low oven until you are ready to serve them.

COOK'S TIP

If the potatoes blacken slightly as they are boiling, add a spoonful of lemon juice to the cooking water.

Braised Chicory

Chicory is a much underrated vegetable. It looks very attractive and provides a refreshing, slightly bitter contrast to a rich main course.

NUTRITIONAL INFORMATION

Calories	40	Sugars 2g
Protein	. . . . .1g	Fat 3g
Carbohydrate	. . . .4g	Saturates 2g

🍲 🍲

🧊 15 mins   🕐 50 mins

SERVES 6

I N G R E D I E N T S

500 ml/18 fl oz vegetable stock

1 bay leaf

6 fresh parsley sprigs

2 fresh thyme sprigs

12 heads chicory

4 tbsp lemon juice

6 tbsp fresh parsley leaves

5 tbsp single cream

salt and pepper

1 Pour the stock into a large saucepan and bring to the boil. Tie the bay leaf, parsley and thyme together, add to the pan, cover and simmer for 10 minutes. Add the chicory and lemon juice, re-cover and simmer for 20-25 minutes, until the chicory is tender.

2 Transfer the chicory to a warm serving dish and keep warm. Remove and discard the herbs. Bring the liquid back to the boil and continue to boil, uncovered, for about 15 minutes, until reduced to about 150 ml/5 fl oz.

3 Meanwhile, blanch the parsley leaves in boiling water for 1 minute, then drain and put in a food processor. Process until very finely chopped. With the motor running, gradually add the cooking liquid.

4 Transfer to a small saucepan, stir in the cream and season to taste with salt and pepper. Heat through gently, but do not allow the sauce to boil. Pour the sauce over the chicory and serve at once.

COOK'S TIP
To prepare chicory, remove the core at the base with a sharp knife and cut off any wilted or damaged leaves.

Caramelized New Potatoes

This simple recipe is best served with a plainly cooked main course, because it is fairly sweet and has delicious juices.

NUTRITIONAL INFORMATION

Calories	289	Sugars	........18g
Protein	.........3g	Fat	..........13g
Carbohydrate	...43g	Saturates	.......8g

 5 mins   20 mins

SERVES 4

INGREDIENTS

675 g/1½ lb new potatoes, scrubbed

4 tbsp dark brown sugar

60 g/2 oz butter

1 tbsp orange juice

1 tbsp chopped fresh parsley or coriander

salt and pepper

orange rind curls, to garnish

1 Cook the new potatoes in a saucepan of boiling water for 10 minutes, or until almost tender. Drain thoroughly.

2 Melt the sugar in a large, heavy-based frying pan over a low heat, stirring constantly.

3 Add the butter and orange juice to the pan, and continue to stir the mixture constantly as the butter melts.

4 Add the potatoes to the orange and butter mixture and continue to cook, turning the potatoes frequently until they are completely coated in the caramel.

5 Sprinkle the chopped fresh parsley or coriander over the potatoes and season according to taste with salt and pepper.

6 Transfer the caramelized new potatoes to a serving dish and garnish with the orange rind. Serve immediately.

VARIATION
Lemon or lime juices may be used instead of the orange juice, if preferred. In addition, garnish the finished dish with pared lemon or lime rind, if desired.

Garlic Mash

A delicious change from plain mash, serve this garlic mash with stuffed vegetables, casseroles and stews.

NUTRITIONAL INFORMATION

Calories	..... .347	Sugars 3g
Protein	.... .6g	Fat .... .18g
Carbohydrate	...41g	Saturates 12g

 15 mins   30 mins

SERVES 4

INGREDIENTS

900 g/2 lb floury potatoes, cut into chunks

8 garlic cloves, crushed

150 ml/5 fl oz milk

85 g/3 oz butter

pinch of freshly grated nutmeg

salt and pepper

1   Put the potatoes in a large saucepan. Add enough cold water to cover and a pinch of salt. Bring to the boil and cook for 10 minutes. Add the garlic and cook for 10 minutes more, until the potatoes are tender.

2   Drain the potatoes and garlic thoroughly, reserving 3 tablespoons of the cooking liquid.

3   Return the reserved liquid to the pan, add the milk and bring to simmering point. Add the butter and return the potatoes and garlic to the pan. Mash thoroughly with a potato masher.

4   Season to taste with nutmeg, salt and pepper and beat the potato mixture with a wooden spoon until light and fluffy. Serve immediately.

VARIATION

Substitute single cream for the milk and 8 tablespoons extra virgin olive oil for the butter.

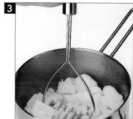

Fried Spiced Potatoes

Deliciously good and a super accompaniment to almost any main course dish, although rather high in calories!

NUTRITIONAL INFORMATION

Calories .... .430	Sugars 7g	
Protein 4g	Fat .... .35g	
Carbohydrate ...26g	Saturates ...... .11g	

15 mins   30 mins

SERVES 6

INGREDIENTS

2 onions, quartered

5 cm/2 inch piece of fresh root ginger, finely chopped

2 garlic cloves

2–3 tbsp mild or medium curry paste

4 tbsp water

750 g/1 lb 10 oz new potatoes

vegetable oil, for deep frying

3 tbsp ghee or oil

150 ml/¼ pint Greek-style yogurt

150 ml/¼ pint double cream

3 tbsp chopped fresh mint

salt and pepper

½ bunch spring onions, chopped, to garnish

1 Place the onions, ginger, garlic, curry paste and water in a blender or food processor and process until smooth.

2 Cut the potatoes into quarters and pat dry with kitchen paper. Heat the oil in a deep fryer to 180°C/350°F, or until a cube of bread browns in 30 seconds, and fry the potatoes, in batches, for about 5 minutes or until golden brown, turning frequently. Remove from the pan and drain on kitchen paper.

3 Heat the ghee or oil in a large frying pan, add the curry and onion mixture and fry gently, stirring constantly, for 2 minutes. Add the yogurt, cream and 2 tablespoons of mint and mix well.

4 Add the fried potatoes and stir until coated in the sauce. Cook, stirring frequently, for 5–7 minutes, or until heated through and sauce has thickened.

5 Season with salt and pepper to taste and sprinkle with the remaining mint and sliced spring onions. Serve at once.

COOK'S TIP
When buying new potatoes, look for the freshest you can find. The skin should be beginning to rub off. Cook them as soon after purchase as possible, but if you have to store them, keep them in a cool, dark, well-ventilated place.

Chinese Potato Sticks

These potato sticks are a variation of the great Western favourite, flavoured with soy sauce and chilli.

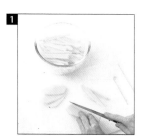

NUTRITIONAL INFORMATION

Calories . . . . . . .326 Sugars 1g
Protein . . . . .4g Fat 22g
Carbohydrate . . .29g Saturates 3g

10 mins   15 mins

SERVES 4

INGREDIENTS

650 g/1 lb 7 oz potatoes

125 ml/4 fl oz vegetable oil

1 fresh red chilli, deseeded and halved

1 small onion, quartered

2 garlic cloves, halved

2 tbsp soy sauce

pinch of salt

1 tsp wine vinegar

1 tbsp sea salt

pinch of chilli powder

1 Peel the potatoes and cut into thin slices lengthways. Cut the slices into matchsticks.

2 Bring a saucepan of water to the boil and blanch the potato sticks for 2 minutes, drain, rinse under cold water and drain well again. Pat the potato sticks thoroughly dry with sheets of absorbent kitchen paper.

3 Heat the oil in a preheated wok until it is almost smoking. Add the chilli, onion and garlic and stir-fry for 30 seconds. Remove and discard the chilli, onion and garlic.

4 Add the potato sticks to the oil and fry for 3–4 minutes, or until golden.

5 Add the soy sauce, salt and wine vinegar to the wok, reduce the heat and fry for about 1 minute, or until the potatoes are crisp.

6 Remove the potatoes with a slotted spoon and leave to drain on absorbent kitchen paper.

7 Transfer the potato sticks to a serving dish, sprinkle with the sea salt and chilli powder and serve.

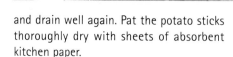

VARIATION
Sprinkle other flavourings over the cooked potato sticks, such as curry powder, or serve with a chilli dip.

Spicy Indian Potatoes

In Indian cooking there are many variations of spicy potatoes. In this recipe, spinach is added for both colour and flavour.

NUTRITIONAL INFORMATION

Calories	65	Sugars	. . . . . . .1.9g
Protein	. . . . .2.5g	Fat	. . . . .3.4g
Carbohydrate	. . .6.5g	Saturates	. . . . .0.4g

 10 mins 40 mins

SERVES 4

I N G R E D I E N T S

½ tsp coriander seeds

1 tsp cumin seeds

4 tbsp vegetable oil

2 cardamom pods

1 tsp grated fresh root ginger

1 red chilli, deseeded and chopped

1 onion, chopped

2 garlic cloves, crushed

450 g/1 lb new potatoes, quartered

150 ml/5 fl oz vegetable stock

675 g/1½ lb spinach, chopped

4 tbsp natural yogurt

salt and pepper

1 Grind the coriander and cumin seeds using a pestle and mortar.

2 Heat the oil in a frying pan. Add the coriander and cumin seeds to the pan, together with the cardamom pods and ginger, and cook for about 2 minutes.

3 Add the chilli, onion and garlic to the pan. Cook for a further 2 minutes, stirring frequently.

4 Add the potatoes to the pan together with the vegetable stock. Cook gently for 30 minutes or until the potatoes are cooked through, stirring occasionally.

5 Add the spinach to the pan and cook for a further 5 minutes.

6 Remove the pan from the heat and stir in the yogurt. Season with salt and pepper to taste. Transfer the potatoes and spinach to a warmed serving dish and serve immediately.

VARIATION
Use frozen spinach instead of fresh, if you prefer. Defrost the frozen spinach and drain it thoroughly before adding it to the dish, otherwise it will turn soggy.

Vegetable Medley

Serve this crisp and colourful vegetable dish as an accompaniment or as a main dish with pitta bread, chapattis or naan.

NUTRITIONAL INFORMATION

Calories 190	Sugars 17g
Protein 7g	Fat 7g
Carbohydrate . . .27g	Saturates 1g

 10 mins 20 mins

SERVES 4

I N G R E D I E N T S

150 g/5½ oz young, tender French beans

8 baby carrots

6 baby turnips

½ small cauliflower

2 tbsp vegetable oil

2 large onions, sliced

2 garlic cloves, finely chopped

300 ml/½ pint low-fat natural yogurt

1 tbsp cornflour

2 tbsp tomato purée

large pinch of chilli powder

salt

1 Top and tail the beans and snap them in half. Cut the carrots in half and the turnips in quarters. Divide the cauliflower into florets, discarding the thickest part of the stalk. Steam the vegetables over boiling, salted water for 3 minutes, then turn them into a colander and plunge them at once in a large bowl of cold water to prevent further cooking.

2 Heat the vegetable oil in a frying pan and fry the onions until they are translucent. Stir in the garlic and cook for 1 further minute.

3 Mix together the yogurt, cornflour and tomato purée to form a smooth paste. Stir this paste into the onions in the pan and cook for 1–2 minutes until the sauce is well blended.

4 Drain the vegetables well, then gradually stir them into the sauce, taking care not to break them up. Season with salt and chilli powder to taste, cover and simmer gently for 5 minutes, until the vegetables are just tender. Taste and adjust the seasoning if necessary. Serve immediately.

Peas with Baby Onions

This is a delightful dish with a subtle creamy flavour, and is perfect made with the first fresh peas of the season.

NUTRITIONAL INFORMATION

Calories	...317	Sugars	...6g
Protein	...8g	Fat	...23g
Carbohydrate	...22g	Saturates	...14g

 20 mins   25 mins

SERVES 4

INGREDIENTS

15 g/½ oz unsalted butter

175 g/6 oz baby onions

900 g/2 lb fresh peas, shelled

125 ml/4 fl oz water

2 tbsp plain flour

150 ml/5 fl oz double cream

1 tbsp chopped fresh parsley

salt and pepper

1 tbsp lemon juice

1 Melt the butter in a large, heavy-based saucepan. Add the whole baby onions and cook, stirring occasionally, for 5 minutes. Add the peas and cook, stirring constantly, for a further 3 minutes, then add the measured water and bring to the boil. Lower the heat, partially cover and simmer for 10 minutes.

2 Beat the flour into the cream. Remove the pan from the heat and stir in the cream mixture and parsley and season to taste with salt and pepper.

3 Return the pan to the heat and cook, stirring gently but constantly, for about 3 minutes, until thickened.

4 Stir the lemon juice into the sauce and serve the peas immediately.

VARIATION
Substitute 2 kg/2 lb 8 oz young broad beans for the peas and cook as above.

Casseroled Potatoes

This potato dish is cooked in the oven with leeks and wine. It is very quick and simple to prepare and tastes superb.

NUTRITIONAL INFORMATION

Calories 187	Sugars 2g
Protein 4g	Fat 3g
Carbohydrate ...31g	Saturates 2g

 10 mins   45 mins

SERVES 4

INGREDIENTS

675 g/1½ lb waxy potatoes, cut into chunks

1 tbsp butter

2 leeks, thickly sliced

150 ml/5 fl oz dry white wine

150 ml/5 fl oz vegetable stock

1 tbsp lemon juice

2 tbsp chopped mixed fresh herbs

salt and pepper

TO GARNISH

grated lemon rind

chopped mixed fresh herbs (optional)

1 Cook the potato chunks in a large saucepan of boiling water for 5 minutes. Drain thoroughly.

2 Meanwhile, melt the butter in a frying pan and cook the leeks for 5 minutes or until they have softened.

3 Spoon the partly cooked potatoes and leeks into an ovenproof dish.

4 Combine the white wine, vegetable stock, lemon juice and chopped mixed herbs in a jug. Season to taste with salt and pepper, then pour the mixture over the potatoes.

5 Cook in a preheated oven, 190°C/375°F/Gas Mark 5, for 35 minutes or until the potatoes are tender.

6 Garnish the potato casserole with lemon rind and fresh herbs, if using, and serve as an accompaniment to a casserole or vegetable bake.

COOK'S TIP

Cover the ovenproof dish halfway through cooking if the leeks start to brown on the top.

Lemony & Herby Potatoes

Choose from these two tasty recipes for new potatoes. To check if new potatoes are fresh, rub the skin; the skin will come off easily if fresh.

NUTRITIONAL INFORMATION

Calories	226	Sugars	.........2g
Protein	.........5g	Fat	..........5g
Carbohydrate	...42g	Saturates	......3g

20 mins   35 mins

SERVES 4

INGREDIENTS

LEMONY NEW POTATOES

1 kg/2 lb 4 oz new potatoes

25 g/1 oz butter

1 tbsp finely grated lemon rind

2 tbsp lemon juice

1 tbsp chopped fresh dill or chives

salt and pepper

extra chopped fresh dill or chives,
   to garnish

HERBY NEW POTATOES

1 kg/2 lb 4 oz new potatoes

3 tbsp light olive oil

1 tbsp white wine vinegar

pinch of mustard powder

pinch of caster sugar

salt and pepper

2 tbsp chopped mixed fresh herbs,
   such as parsley, chives, marjoram,
   basil and rosemary

extra chopped fresh mixed herbs, to garnish

1 For the lemony potatoes, either scrub the potatoes well or remove the skins by scraping them off with a sharp knife. Cook the potatoes in plenty of lightly salted boiling water for about 15 minutes until just tender.

2 While the potatoes are cooking, melt the butter over a low heat. Add the lemon rind, juice and herbs. Season with salt and pepper.

3 Drain the cooked potatoes and transfer to a serving bowl.

4 Pour over the lemony butter mixture and stir gently to mix. Garnish with extra herbs and serve hot or warm.

5 For the herby potatoes, prepare and cook the potatoes as described in step 1. Whisk the olive oil, vinegar, mustard, caster sugar and seasoning together in a small bowl. Add the chopped herbs and mix well.

6 Drain the potatoes and pour over the oil and vinegar mixture, stirring to coat evenly. Garnish with extra fresh herbs and serve warm or cold.

Potatoes en Papillotes

New potatoes are perfect for this recipe. The potatoes and vegetables are wrapped in greaseproof paper, sealed, and steamed in the oven.

NUTRITIONAL INFORMATION

Calories	.85	Sugars	.4g
Protein	.2g	Fat	.0.5g
Carbohydrate	.15g	Saturates	.0.1g

 10 mins   35 mins

SERVES 4

I N G R E D I E N T S

450 g/1 lb small new potatoes

1 carrot, cut into matchstick

1 fennel bulb, sliced

75 g/2¾ oz French beans

1 yellow pepper, deseeded and cut into strips

240 ml/8½ fl oz dry white wine

4 fresh rosemary sprigs

salt and pepper

fresh rosemary sprigs, to garnish

1 Cut 4 squares of greaseproof paper measuring approximately 25 cm/ 10 inches in size.

2 Divide the vegetables equally among the 4 paper squares, placing them in the centre.

3 Bring up the edges of the paper and scrunch them together to encase the vegetables, leaving the top open.

4 Place the parcels in a shallow roasting tin and spoon 4 tablespoons of white wine into each parcel. Add a rosemary sprig, and season.

5 Fold the top of each parcel over to seal it. Cook in a preheated oven, 190°C/375°F/Gas Mark 5, for 30–35 minutes or until the vegetables are tender.

6 Transfer the sealed parcels to four individual serving plates and garnish with rosemary sprigs.

7 Open the parcels at the table so that the full aroma of the vegetables may be appreciated.

COOK'S TIP

If small new potatoes are unavailable, use larger potatoes and halve or quarter them to ensure that they cook through in the specified cooking time.

Trio of Potato Purées

These small moulds filled with layers of flavoured potato look very impressive. They are ideal with a vegetable casserole.

15 mins   1¼ hrs

SERVES 4

INGREDIENTS

1 tbsp butter, plus extra for greasing

300 g/10½ oz floury potatoes, chopped

125 g/4½ oz swede, diced

1 carrot, chopped

450 g/1 lb spinach

1 tbsp skimmed milk

2½ tbsp plain flour

1 egg

½ tsp ground cinnamon

salt and pepper

1 tbsp orange juice

¼ tsp grated nutmeg

carrot batons, to garnish

1 Lightly grease 4 x 150 ml/5 fl oz ramekins with a little butter.

2 Cook the potatoes in a saucepan of boiling water for 10 minutes. In separate pans cook the swede and carrot in boiling water for 10 minutes. Blanch the spinach in boiling water for 5 minutes. Drain the vegetables. Add the milk and butter to the potatoes and mash until smooth. Stir in the flour and egg.

3 Divide the potato mixture between 3 bowls. Spoon the swede into 1 bowl

and mix well. Spoon the carrot into the second bowl and mix well. Spoon the spinach into the third bowl and mix well.

4 Add the cinnamon to the swede and potato mixture and season to taste. Stir the orange juice into the carrot and potato mixture. Stir the nutmeg into the spinach and potato mixture.

5 Spoon a layer of the swede and potato mixture into each of the

ramekins and smooth the surface. Cover each with a layer of spinach and potato mixture, then top with the carrot and potato mixture. Cover the ramekins with kitchen foil and place in a roasting tin. Half-fill the tin with boiling water and cook in a preheated oven, 180°C/350°F/Gas Mark 4, for 40 minutes or until set.

6 Turn out on to warmed serving plates, garnish with the carrot batons and serve immediately.

Glazed Baby Onions

These onions are bathed in a rich, intensely flavoured glaze, making them a good accompaniment to a nut roast.

NUTRITIONAL INFORMATION

Calories 81	Sugars 8g
Protein 1g	Fat 4g
Carbohydrate 11g	Saturates 1g

  10 mins   25 mins

SERVES 4–6

INGREDIENTS

500 g/1 lb 2 oz baby onions

2 tbsp olive oil

2 large garlic cloves, crushed

300 ml/½ pint vegetable stock

1 tbsp fresh thyme leaves

1 tbsp light brown sugar

2 tbsp red wine vinegar

about 1½ tsp balsamic vinegar

salt and pepper

fresh thyme sprigs, to garnish

1 Put the baby onions in a large heatproof bowl, pour over enough boiling water to cover and set aside for 2 minutes. Drain well.

2 Using a small knife and your fingers, peel off the skins, which should slip off easily.

3 Heat the olive oil in a large frying pan over a medium heat. Add the onions and cook, stirring constantly, for about 8 minutes until they are golden all over.

4 Add the crushed garlic and cook, stirring, for 2 minutes. Add the stock, thyme leaves, sugar and wine vinegar, stirring until the sugar has dissolved.

5 Bring to the boil, then lower the heat and simmer gently for 10 minutes or until the onions are tender when you pierce them with the tip of a sharp knife and the cooking liquid is reduced to a syrupy glaze.

6 Stir in the balsamic vinegar. Season the glazed onions to taste with salt and pepper and add extra balsamic vinegar, if desired.

7 Transfer to a serving dish and serve the onions either hot or cold, garnished with fresh thyme sprigs.

VARIATION

For extra texture, stir in 2 tbsp toasted pine nuts just before serving. Do not add them earlier or they will become soft.

Vegetables à la Grecque

'A la Grecque' is the French term for cooked vegetables left to cool in their highly flavoured cooking liquid and then served cold.

NUTRITIONAL INFORMATION

Calories 67   Sugars 4g
Protein . . . . .2g   Fat 4g
Carbohydrate . . . .6g   Saturates 1g

 15 mins, plus chilling   35–40 mins

SERVES 4–6

I N G R E D I E N T S

250 g/9 oz small pickling onions

250 g/9 oz mushrooms

250 g/9 oz courgettes

450 ml/16 fl oz water

5 tbsp olive oil

2 tbsp lemon juice

2 strips lemon rind

2 large garlic cloves, thinly sliced

½ Spanish onion, finely chopped

1 bay leaf

15 black peppercorns, lightly crushed

10 coriander seeds, lightly crushed

pinch of dried oregano

finely chopped fresh flat-leaved parsley or
    coriander, to garnish

focaccia, to serve

1 Put the small pickling onions in a heatproof bowl and pour over boiling water to cover. Set aside for 2 minutes, then drain. Peel and set aside.

2 Trim the mushroom stems. Cut the mushrooms into halves or quarters, if they are large, or leave whole if small. Trim the courgettes, cut off strips of the peel for a decorative finish, then cut into 5 mm/ ¼ inch slices. Set both the mushrooms and courgettes aside.

3 Put the water, olive oil, lemon juice and rind, garlic, Spanish onion, bay leaf, peppercorns, coriander seeds and oregano in a saucepan over a high heat and bring to the boil. Lower the heat and simmer for 15 minutes.

4 Add the small onions and continue to simmer for 5 minutes. Add the mushrooms and courgettes and simmer for a further 2 minutes.

5 Using a draining spoon, transfer all the vegetables to a heatproof dish.

6 Return the liquid to the boil and boil until reduced to about 6 tablespoons. Pour the liquid over the vegetables and set aside to cool completely.

7 Cover with clingfilm and chill for at least 12 hours.

8 To serve, put the vegetables and cooking liquid in a serving dish and sprinkle the fresh herbs over them. Serve with chunks of focaccia.

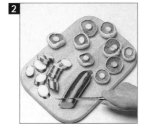

Chinese Fried Vegetables

The Chinese are known for their colourful, crisp vegetables, quickly stir-fried. In this recipe, they are tossed in a tasty soy and hoisin sauce.

NUTRITIONAL INFORMATION

Calories	137	Sugars	.........7g
Protein	.........8g	Fat	...........7g
Carbohydrate	...10g	Saturates	......11g

5 mins   10 mins

SERVES 4

INGREDIENTS

2 tbsp peanut oil

350 g/12 oz broccoli florets

1 tbsp chopped fresh root ginger

2 onions, cut into 8 pieces

3 celery sticks, sliced

175 g/6 oz baby spinach

125 g/4½ oz mangetouts

6 spring onions, quartered

2 garlic cloves, crushed

2 tbsp light soy sauce

2 tsp caster sugar

2 tbsp dry sherry

1 tbsp hoisin sauce

150 ml/5 fl oz vegetable stock

1 Heat the peanut oil in a preheated wok until it is almost smoking.

2 Add the broccoli florets, chopped root ginger, onions and celery to the wok and stir-fry for 1 minute.

3 Add the spinach, mangetouts, spring onions and garlic and stir-fry for 3–4 minutes.

4 Mix together the soy sauce, caster sugar, sherry, hoisin sauce and vegetable stock.

5 Pour the stock mixture into the wok, mixing well to coat the vegetables.

6 Cover the wok and cook over a medium heat for 2–3 minutes, or until the vegetables are cooked through, but still crisp.

7 Transfer the Chinese fried vegetables to a warm serving dish and serve immediately.

COOK'S TIP

You could use this mixture to fill Chinese pancakes. They are available from Chinese food stores and can be reheated in a steamer in 2–3 minutes.

Deep-fried Courgettes

These crisp courgette slices are so irresistible that you should always make more than you think you will need – they disappear very quickly!

NUTRITIONAL INFORMATION

Calories	299	Sugars	........4g
Protein	.........4g	Fat	..........18g
Carbohydrate	...33g	Saturates	.......2g

5 mins, plus standing   5 mins

SERVES 4

I N G R E D I E N T S

5 tbsp cornflour

1 tsp salt

pinch of cayenne pepper, or to taste

150 ml/5 fl oz water

900 g/2 lb courgettes

vegetable oil, for frying

sea salt, to serve

fresh herb sprigs, such as basil, flat-leaved parsley or sage, to garnish

1 Sift the cornflour, salt and cayenne pepper into a large mixing bowl and make a well in the centre. Pour in the water and beat until just blended to make a thin batter. The batter may have a few lumps but this does not matter. Set aside for 20 minutes.

2 Meanwhile, cut the courgettes into 5 mm/¼ inch slices. Heat the oil in a deep frying pan or deep-fat fryer to 190°C/375°F or until a cube of bread browns in 20 seconds.

3 Stir the batter. Working in batches, put some courgette slices in the batter and stir around until coated. Using a slotted spoon, remove the slices from the batter, shaking off the excess.

4 Drop the coated courgette slices into the hot oil, working in batches, and fry for about 45–60 seconds, or until they are just golden brown on each side. Immediately remove from the oil and drain well on crumpled kitchen paper. Sprinkle with sea salt and keep warm while you cook the rest of the slices.

5 Repeat the process with the remaining courgette slices. You can serve them garnished with a variety of herbs, according to what is available.

VARIATION
Fry red onion rings coated with the batter.

Saffron Rice

This is the classic way to serve rice, paired with saffron, so that each brings out the best in the other.

NUTRITIONAL INFORMATION

Calories 63   Sugars 0.1g
Protein . . . . .1.4g   Fat 2g
Carbohydrate . . . .11g   Saturates 0.2g

15 mins   25 mins

SERVES 8

INGREDIENTS

12 saffron threads, crushed lightly

2 tbsp warm water

400 ml/14 fl oz water

225 g/8 oz basmati rice

1 tbsp toasted flaked almonds

1 Put the saffron threads into a bowl with the warm water and leave for 10 minutes. They need to be crushed before soaking to ensure that the maximum flavour and colour is extracted at this stage.

2 Put the water and rice into a medium saucepan and set it over the heat to boil. Add the saffron and saffron water and stir.

3 Bring back to a gentle boil, stir again and let the rice simmer, uncovered, for about 10 minutes, until all the water has been absorbed.

4 Cover the pan tightly, reduce the heat as much as possible and leave for 10 minutes. Do not remove the lid. This ensures that the grains separate and that the rice is not soggy.

5 Alternatively, you can soak the rice overnight and drain thoroughly before cooking. Follow the cooking instructions in steps 2, 3 and 4, but reduce the cooking time by 3–4 minutes to compensate for the presoaking.

6 Remove the rice from the heat and transfer to a warmed serving dish. Fork through the rice gently and sprinkle over the toasted almonds before serving.

COOK'S TIP

Saffron, grown in Europe and the Middle East, is the most ancient of spices and continues to be the most expensive – literally worth its weight in gold. It is still harvested and sorted by hand and is a treasured commodity.

Ratatouille

This slow-cooked Provençal vegetable stew makes a delicious side dish, and is also lovely served with crusty bread to mop up the juices.

NUTRITIONAL INFORMATION

Calories	157	Sugars	........11g
Protein	.........4g	Fat	...........9g
Carbohydrate	...14g	Saturates	.......1g

 40 mins   45 mins

SERVES 4–6

INGREDIENTS

1 large aubergine, about 300 g/10½ oz

5 tbsp olive oil

2 large onions, thinly sliced

2 large garlic cloves, crushed

4 courgettes, sliced

800 g/1 lb 12 oz canned chopped tomatoes

1 tsp sugar

1 bouquet garni of 2 fresh thyme sprigs,
    2 large fresh parsley sprigs, 1 fresh basil
    sprig and 1 bay leaf, tied in a 7.5 cm/
    3 inch piece of celery

salt and pepper

fresh basil leaves, to garnish

1 Coarsely chop the aubergine, then place in a colander. Sprinkle with salt and set aside for 30 minutes to drain. Rinse well under cold running water to remove all traces of the salt and pat dry with kitchen paper.

2 Heat the oil in a large, heavy-based flameproof casserole over a medium heat. Add the onions, lower the heat and cook, stirring occasionally, for 10 minutes until softened and light golden brown.

3 Add the garlic and continue to fry for 2 minutes until the onions are tender.

4 Add the aubergine, courgettes, tomatoes, with their can juices, sugar and bouquet garni. Season with salt and pepper to taste. Bring to the boil, then lower the heat to very low, cover and simmer for 30 minutes.

5 Taste and adjust the seasoning if necessary. Remove and discard the bouquet garni. Garnish the vegetable stew with basil leaves and serve immediately.

COOK'S TIP
This is equally good served hot, at room temperature or chilled. As an alternative to bread, serve it with couscous.

Tofu Sandwiches

Slices of tofu are sandwiched together with a cucumber and cream cheese filling and coated in batter.

NUTRITIONAL INFORMATION

Calories	398	Sugars 8g
Protein	........13g	Fat 24g
Carbohydrate	...35g	Saturates 7g

40 mins   15 mins

MAKES 28

INGREDIENTS

4 Chinese dried mushrooms (if unavailable, use thinly sliced open-cup mushrooms)

275 g/9½ oz firm tofu

½ cucumber, grated

1 cm/½ inch piece fresh root ginger, grated

60 g/2 oz cream cheese

salt and pepper

BATTER

125 g/4½ oz plain flour

1 egg, beaten

125 ml/4 fl oz water

½ tsp salt

2 tbsp sesame seeds

vegetable oil, for deep-frying

SAUCE

150 ml/¼ pint natural yogurt

2 tsp honey

2 tbsp chopped fresh mint

1 Place the dried mushrooms in a small bowl and cover with warm water. Leave to soak for 20–25 minutes.

2 Drain the mushrooms, squeezing out the excess water. Remove the tough centres and chop the mushrooms.

3 Drain the tofu thoroughly and slice it thinly, then cut the slices to make 2.5 cm/1 inch squares.

4 Squeeze the excess liquid from the grated cucumber and then mix the cucumber with the mushrooms, grated ginger and cream cheese. Season well with salt and pepper. Use as a filling to sandwich slices of tofu together, making about 28 sandwiches.

5 To make the batter, sift the flour into a bowl. Beat in the egg, water and salt to make a thick batter. Stir in the sesame seeds. Heat the oil in a wok. Coat the sandwiches in the batter and deep-fry in batches until golden. Remove and drain on absorbent kitchen paper.

6 To make the dipping sauce, combine the yogurt, honey and mint. Serve with the tofu sandwiches.

Creamed Coconut Potatoes

A colourful way to serve potatoes that is quick and easy to make.
Serve it with a spicy curry and a cool, crisp green salad.

NUTRITIONAL INFORMATION

Calories 93   Sugars 1.5g
Protein . . . . .2.8g   Fat 4.8g
Carbohydrate . .10.3g   Saturates 4.0g

10 mins   15 mins

SERVES 4

I N G R E D I E N T S

600 g/1½ lb potatoes

1 onion, thinly sliced

2 fresh red bird-eye chillies, deseeded and
  finely chopped

½ tsp salt

½ tsp black pepper

85 g/3 oz creamed coconut

350 ml/12 fl oz vegetable stock

chopped fresh coriander or basil, to garnish

1 Peel the potatoes thinly. Use a sharp knife to cut into 2 cm/¾ inch chunks.

2 Place the potatoes in a pan with the onion, chillies, salt, pepper and creamed coconut. Stir in the stock.

3 Bring to the boil, stirring, then lower the heat, cover the pan and simmer gently, stirring occasionally, until the potatoes are tender.

4 Adjust the seasoning to taste, then sprinkle with chopped coriander or basil. Serve immediately while hot.

COOK'S TIP

If the potatoes are thin-skinned, or a new variety, simply wash or scrub to remove any dirt and cook with the skins on. This adds extra dietary fibre and nutrients to the finished dish and cuts down on the preparation time. Baby new potatoes can be cooked whole.

Indonesian Onions

This is Indonesia's most popular garnish, but it also makes a tasty accompaniment to many vegetarian dishes.

NUTRITIONAL INFORMATION

Calories 76	Sugars 4g
Protein 1g	Fat 6g
Carbohydrate 6g	Saturates 1g

10 mins, plus drying

20 mins

SERVES 6

INGREDIENTS

450 g/1 lb small onions

groundnut or sunflower oil, for deep-frying

1 Using a sharp knife, slice the onions as thinly and evenly as possible. Spread out the slices on kitchen paper in a well-ventilated place and leave for up to 2 hours to dry out.

2 Heat the oil in a wok or deep-fryer to 180°C/350°F or until a cube of bread browns in 30 seconds. Add the dried onion slices, in batches, and fry until crisp and golden.

3 Remove the onions with a slotted spoon and drain them on kitchen paper. Cook the remaining onion slices in the same way.

COOK'S TIP

It is important that the onions are well dried before frying or they will not become crisp. Small onions tend to be less watery than large ones.

Pesto Potatoes

Pesto sauce is more commonly used as a pasta sauce but is also delicious served over potatoes.

NUTRITIONAL INFORMATION

Calories	531	Sugars	3g
Protein	13g	Fat	38g
Carbohydrate	36g	Saturates	8g

15 mins   15 mins

SERVES 4

INGREDIENTS

900 g/2 lb small new potatoes

75 g/2¾ oz fresh basil

2 tbsp pine kernels

3 garlic cloves, crushed

100 ml/3½ fl oz olive oil

75 g/2¾ oz mixed Parmesan and pecorino cheeses, grated

salt and pepper

fresh basil sprigs, to garnish

1 Cook the potatoes in a saucepan of boiling salted water for 15 minutes or until tender. Drain well, transfer to a warm serving dish and keep warm until required.

2 Meanwhile, put the fresh basil, pine kernels, crushed garlic and a little salt and pepper to taste in a food processor. Blend for 30 seconds, adding the oil gradually, until smooth.

3 Remove the mixture from the food processor and transfer it to a mixing bowl. Stir in the grated Parmesan and pecorino cheeses.

4 Spoon the pesto sauce over the potatoes and mix well. Garnish with fresh basil sprigs and serve immediately.

Pepperonata

This is a delicious mixture of peppers and onions, cooked with tomatoes and herbs for a rich side dish.

NUTRITIONAL INFORMATION

Calories 206	Sugars 19g
Protein 5g	Fat 12g
Carbohydrate . . .21g	Saturates 2g

15 mins   40 mins

SERVES 4

INGREDIENTS

4 tbsp olive oil

1 onion, halved and finely sliced

2 red peppers, deseeded and cut into strips

2 green peppers, deseeded and cut into strips

2 yellow peppers, deseeded and cut into strips

2 garlic cloves, crushed

800 g/1 lb 12 oz canned chopped tomatoes, drained

2 tbsp chopped coriander

salt and pepper

2 tbsp chopped stoned black olives

COOK'S TIP

Stir the vegetables occasionally during the 30 minutes' cooking time to prevent them sticking to the bottom of the pan. If the liquid has not evaporated by the end of the cooking time, remove the lid and boil rapidly until the dish is dry.

1 Heat the olive oil in a large frying pan. Add the sliced onion and sauté for 5 minutes, stirring constantly, until just beginning to colour.

2 Add the red, green and yellow pepper strips and the crushed garlic to the pan and cook for a further 3–4 minutes.

3 Stir in the tomatoes and chopped coriander and season to taste with salt and pepper. Cover the pan and cook the vegetables gently for about 30 minutes or until the mixture is dry.

4 Stir in the pitted black olives and serve the pepperonata immediately.

Roasted Green Chillies

Mild chillies are cooked in a delicious garlic- and cumin-flavoured cream sauce in this unusual side dish.

NUTRITIONAL INFORMATION

Calories	150	Sugars	.........5g
Protein	.........5g	Fat	..........12g
Carbohydrate	....6g	Saturates	.......7g

 5 mins, plus standing 30 mins

SERVES 4–6

INGREDIENTS

4 large fresh mild green chillies, such as anaheim or poblano, or a combination of 4 green peppers and 2 jalapeños

2 tbsp butter

1 onion, finely chopped

3 garlic cloves, finely chopped

¼ tsp ground cumin

salt and pepper

225 ml/8 fl oz single cream

225 ml/8 fl oz vegetable stock

1 lime, halved, to serve

1 Roast the fresh mild chillies, or the combination of green peppers and jalapeños, in a heavy-based ungreased frying pan or under a preheated grill until the skins are charred. Place in a polythene bag, twist to seal well and set aside for 20 minutes to allow the skins to loosen.

2 Remove the seeds from the chillies and peppers, if using, and peel off the skins. Slice the flesh, and set aside.

3 Melt the butter in a large frying pan, add the onion and garlic and sauté for about 3 minutes or until softened.

Sprinkle with the cumin and season with salt and pepper to your taste.

4 Stir in the sliced chillies and pour in the cream and stock. Cook over a medium heat, stirring, until the liquid reduces in volume and forms a richly flavoured creamy sauce.

5 Transfer to a serving dish and serve warm, squeezing over lime juice at the last minute.

VARIATION
Add an equal amount of sweetcorn with the chillies – they add a delicious sweetness to the dish.

Potatoes in Green Sauce

Earthy potatoes, served in a tangy spicy tomatillo sauce and topped with spring onions and soured cream, are delicious.

NUTRITIONAL INFORMATION

Calories . . . . .61 Sugars 1.4g
Protein . . . . .2g Fat 1.4g
Carbohydrate . .10.6g Saturates 0.2g

5 mins   25 mins

SERVES 5

INGREDIENTS

1 kg/2 lb 4 oz small waxy potatoes

1 onion, halved and unpeeled

8 garlic cloves, unpeeled

1 fresh green chilli

8 tomatillos, outer husks removed, or small
    tart tomatoes

225 ml/8 fl oz vegetable stock

1 tsp ground cumin

1 fresh thyme sprig or a generous pinch of
    dried thyme

1 fresh oregano sprig or a generous
    pinch of dried

2 tbsp vegetable or extra virgin olive oil

1 courgette, roughly chopped

1 bunch of fresh coriander, chopped

salt

1 Put the potatoes in a pan of lightly salted water. Bring to the boil and cook for about 15 minutes or until almost tender. Be careful not to over-cook them. Drain and set aside.

2 Meanwhile lightly char the onion, garlic, chilli and the tomatillos or tomatoes in a heavy-based, ungreased frying pan. Set aside, and when cool enough to handle, peel and chop the onion, garlic and chilli. Chop the tomatillos or tomatoes. Put in a blender or food processor with half the stock and process to form a purée. Add the cumin, thyme and oregano.

3 Heat the oil in the heavy-based frying pan. Add the purée and cook over a medium heat, stirring constantly, for about 5 minutes to reduce slightly and concentrate the flavours.

4 Add the potatoes and courgette to the purée and pour in the remaining stock. Add about half of the chopped coriander and cook for a further 5 minutes or until the courgette is tender.

5 Transfer to a serving bowl and serve sprinkled with the remaining chopped coriander to garnish.

Puff Potato Pie

This pie, with its rich filling, is a great alternative to plain potatoes as a side dish with any meal. Alternatively, serve with salad for a light lunch.

NUTRITIONAL INFORMATION

Calories	198	Sugars	.......1.4g
Protein	........3.7g	Fat	.........12.4g
Carbohydrate	..19.8g	Saturates	.....2.9g

5–10 mins   50 mins

SERVES 6

INGREDIENTS

700 g/1 lb 9 oz potatoes, thinly sliced

2 spring onions, finely chopped

1 red onion, finely chopped

150 ml/5 fl oz double cream

salt and pepper

500 g/1 lb 2 oz puff pastry

2 eggs, beaten

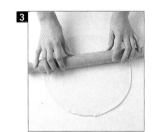

1 Lightly grease a baking tray. Bring a saucepan of water to the boil, add the sliced potatoes, bring back to the boil and then simmer for a few minutes. Drain the potato slices and leave to cool. Dry off any excess moisture with kitchen paper.

2 In a bowl, mix together the spring onions, red onion and the cooled potato slices. Stir in 2 tablespoons of the cream and plenty of seasoning.

3 Divide the pastry in half and roll out one piece to a 23 cm/9 inch round. Roll the remaining pastry to a 25 cm/ 10 inch round.

4 Place the smaller circle on to the baking tray and top with the potato mixture, leaving a 2.5 cm/1 inch border. Brush this border with a little of the beaten egg.

5 Top with the larger circle of pastry, seal well and crimp the edges of the pastry. Cut a steam vent in the middle of the pastry and, using the back of a knife, mark with a pattern. Brush with the

beaten egg and bake in a preheated oven, 200°C/400°F/Gas Mark 6, for 30 minutes.

6 Mix the remaining beaten egg with the rest of the double cream and pour slowly into the pie through the steam vent. Return the potato pie to the oven for 15 minutes, then remove it and leave it to cool for 30 minutes. Transfer to a serving plate and serve warm or cold.

Two Classic Salsas

A Mexican meal is not complete without an accompanying salsa.
These two salsas are ideal for seasoning any traditional dish.

NUTRITIONAL INFORMATION

Calories 21	Sugars 3g
Protein 1g	Fat 0g
Carbohydrate 4g	Saturates 0g

 5 mins   0 mins

SERVES 4–6

I N G R E D I E N T S

J A L A P E Ñ O   S A L S A

1 onion, finely chopped

2–3 garlic cloves, finely chopped

4–6 tbsp roughly chopped pickled
jalapeño chillies

juice of ½ lemon

about ¼ tsp ground cumin

salt

S A L S A   C R U D A

6–8 ripe tomatoes, finely chopped

about 100 ml/3½ fl oz tomato juice

3–4 garlic cloves, finely chopped

½–1 bunch fresh coriander leaves,
roughly chopped

pinch of sugar

3–4 fresh green chillies, such as jalapeño
or serrano, deseeded and finely chopped

½–1 tsp ground cumin

3–4 spring onions, finely chopped

salt

1 To make the Jalapeño Salsa, put the onion in a bowl with the chopped garlic, jalapeños, lemon juice and cumin. Season to taste with salt and stir together. Cover with clingfilm and chill in the refrigerator until required.

2 To make a chunky-textured Salsa Cruda, stir all the ingredients together in a bowl and season with salt to taste. Cover with clingfilm and chill in the refrigerator until required.

3 To make a smoother-textured salsa, process the ingredients in a blender or food processor, scraping down the sides if necessary. Transfer to a bowl, cover and chill as above.

Orange and White Coulis

Steaming is a healthy way to cook and is ideally suited to vegetables, as it helps to preserve valuable vitamins and minerals.

NUTRITIONAL INFORMATION

Calories 99	Sugars 12g	
Protein 3g	Fat 3g	
Carbohydrate ...16g	Saturates 1g	

 15 mins   10 mins

SERVES 4

I N G R E D I E N T S

ORANGE COULIS

150 ml/5 fl oz freshly squeezed
orange juice

225 g/8 oz carrots, thinly sliced

55 g/2 oz fromage frais or ricotta cheese

pinch of ground coriander

1 tsp lemon juice

salt and ground white pepper

WHITE COULIS

150 ml/¼ pint vegetable stock

225 g/8 oz parsnips, thinly sliced

55 g/2 oz fromage frais or ricotta cheese

pinch of freshly grated nutmeg

1 tsp lemon juice

salt and ground white pepper

1 To make the Orange Coulis, pour the orange juice into a small saucepan and bring to the boil. Place the carrots in a steamer on top of the pan, cover tightly and steam for 10 minutes.

2 To make the White Coulis, place the vegetable stock in a small saucepan and bring to the boil. Place the parsnips in a steamer on top of the pan, cover tightly and steam for 10 minutes.

3 Transfer the carrots and orange juice to a blender or food processor and process to a smooth purée. Scrape into a bowl and stir in the fromage frais or ricotta cheese, coriander and lemon juice and season to taste with salt and pepper. Keep warm.

4 Transfer the parsnips and vegetable stock to a blender or food processor and process to a smooth purée. Scrape into a bowl and stir in the fromage frais or ricotta cheese, nutmeg and lemon juice and season to taste with salt and pepper.

5 Spoon the coulis decoratively on to serving plates and serve immediately.

VARIATION

To make a green coulis, steam a green vegetable, such as shredded cabbage or Brussels sprouts, over 150 ml/5 fl oz vegetable stock, then process and combine with fromage frais, 1 tbsp chopped fresh mint and lemon juice, as above.

Chargrilled Vegetables

You can cook this colourful collection of vegetables under the grill or on the barbecue. They look fabulous served with salsa verde.

NUTRITIONAL INFORMATION

Calories ....172 Sugars 6g
Protein ....2g Fat 12g
Carbohydrate ...15g Saturates 2g

20 mins, plus cooling   15 mins

SERVES 6

INGREDIENTS

2 sweet potatoes, sliced

3 courgettes, halved lengthways

3 red peppers, deseeded and
   cut into quarters

olive oil, for brushing

salt

SALSA VERDE

2 fresh green chillies, halved and deseeded

8 spring onions, roughly chopped

2 garlic cloves, roughly chopped

1 tbsp capers (see Cook's Tip)

bunch of fresh parsley, roughly chopped

grated rind and juice of 1 lime

4 tbsp lemon juice

6 tbsp olive oil

1 tbsp green Tabasco sauce

pepper

COOK'S TIP

If using capers bottled in vinegar, rinse them before using. If using salted capers, simply brush them with your fingertips to remove some of the salt.

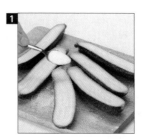  

1 Cook the sweet potato slices in boiling water for 5 minutes. Drain and set aside to cool. Sprinkle the courgettes with salt and set aside for 30 minutes. Rinse and pat dry with kitchen paper.

2 Meanwhile, make the salsa verde. Put the chillies, spring onions and garlic in a food processor and process briefly. Add the capers and parsley and pulse until finely chopped. Transfer the mixture to a serving bowl.

3 Stir in the lime rind and juice, lemon juice, olive oil and Tabasco. Season to taste with pepper, cover with clingfilm and chill in the refrigerator until required.

4 Brush the sweet potato slices, courgettes and peppers with olive oil and spread out on a grill rack or barbecue. Grill, turning once and brushing with more olive oil, for 8–10 minutes, until tender and lightly charred. Serve the vegetables immediately with the salsa verde.

Vegetables in Coconut Milk

This is a deliciously crunchy way to prepare a mixture of raw vegetables and would be ideal as a buffet dish for a party.

NUTRITIONAL INFORMATION

Calories 201   Sugars 10g
Protein . . . . .9g   Fat 13g
Carbohydrate . . .13g   Saturates 3g

5 mins   5 mins

SERVES 4

I N G R E D I E N T S

1 fresh red chilli, deseeded and chopped

1 tsp coriander seeds

1 tsp cumin seeds

2 garlic cloves, crushed

juice of 1 lime

250 ml/9 fl oz coconut milk

115 g/4 oz beansprouts

115 g/4 oz white cabbage, shredded

115 g/4 oz mangetouts, trimmed

115 g/4 oz carrots, thinly sliced

115 g/4 oz cauliflower florets

3 tbsp peanut butter

grated or shaved coconut, to serve

1 Grind the red chilli, the coriander and cumin seeds, the crushed garlic and the lime juice in a mortar with a pestle, or blend in a food processor, until a smooth paste is formed.

2 Put the spice paste into a medium pan and heat gently for about 1 minute or until fragrant. Add the coconut milk and stir constantly until it is just about to boil.

3 Combine the beansprouts, shredded white cabbage, mangetouts, sliced carrots and cauliflower florets in a large mixing bowl.

4 Stir the peanut butter into the coconut mixture until well blended and then pour into the bowl, stirring to coat the vegetables thoroughly. Serve garnished with a sprinkling of the grated or shaved coconut.

COOK'S TIP

If you prefer, the cauliflower, carrots and mangetouts may be blanched first for less bite.

Lightly Fried Bread

This is perfect with egg dishes and vegetable curries. Allow two portions of bread per person. The nutritional information is for each portion.

NUTRITIONAL INFORMATION

Calories . . . . . . .133 Sugars 1g
Protein . . . . .3g Fat 7g
Carbohydrate . . .17g Saturates 4g

 35 mins   20-25 mins

MAKES 10

INGREDIENTS

225 g/8 oz wholemeal (ata or
  chapatti) flour

½ tsp salt

1 tbsp ghee

300 ml/½ pint water

1 Place the flour and the salt in a large mixing bowl and mix to combine.

2 Make a well in the centre of the flour. Add the ghee and rub in well. Gradually pour in the water and work until a soft dough is formed. Set the dough aside to rise for 10–15 minutes.

3 Carefully knead the dough for about 5–7 minutes. Divide the dough into about 10 equal portions.

4 On a lightly floured surface, roll out each dough portion to form a flat pancake shape.

5 Using a sharp knife, lightly draw lines in a criss-cross pattern on each rolled-out dough portion.

6 Heat a heavy-based frying pan. Gently place the dough portions, one by one, into the pan.

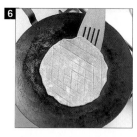

7 Cook the bread for about 1 minute, then turn over and spread with 1 teaspoon of ghee. Turn the bread over again and fry gently, moving it around the pan with a spatula, until golden brown. Turn the bread over once again, then remove from the pan and keep warm while you cook the remaining batches.

COOK'S TIP

In India, breads are cooked on a tava, a traditional flat griddle. A large frying pan makes an adequate substitute.

Italian-style Potato Wedges

These oven-cooked potato wedges use classic pizza ingredients and are delicious served with a simple vegetable dish or with a dip.

NUTRITIONAL INFORMATION

Calories	115	Sugars	.........4g
Protein	.........6g	Fat	...........5g
Carbohydrate	...13g	Saturates	.......3g

15 mins   35 mins

SERVES 4

I N G R E D I E N T S

2 large waxy potatoes, unpeeled

4 large ripe tomatoes, peeled and deseeded

150 ml/5 fl oz vegetable stock

2 tbsp tomato purée

1 small yellow pepper, deseeded and cut into strips

125 g/4½ oz button mushrooms, quartered

1 tbsp chopped fresh basil

salt and pepper

55 g/2 oz Cheddar cheese, grated

1 Cut each of the potatoes into 8 equal wedges. Parboil the potatoes in a pan of boiling water for 15 minutes. Drain well and place in a shallow ovenproof dish.

2 Chop the tomatoes and add to the dish. Combine the vegetable stock and tomato purée, then pour the mixture over the potatoes and tomatoes.

3 Add the yellow pepper strips, mushrooms and basil. Season well with salt and pepper.

4 Sprinkle the grated cheese over the top and cook in a preheated oven, 190°C/375°F/Gas Mark 5, for about 15–20 minutes until the topping is golden brown. Serve at once.

Sauté of Summer Vegetables

The freshness of lightly cooked summer vegetables is enhanced by the aromatic flavour of a tarragon and white wine dressing.

NUTRITIONAL INFORMATION

Calories 217	Sugars 8g
Protein 2g	Fat 18g
Carbohydrate 9g	Saturates 9g

 10 mins   10–15 mins

SERVES 4

INGREDIENTS

225 g/8 oz baby carrots, scrubbed

125 g/4½ oz runner beans

2 courgettes, trimmed

1 bunch of large spring onions

1 bunch of radishes

4 tbsp butter

2 tbsp light olive oil

2 tbsp white wine vinegar

4 tbsp dry white wine

1 tsp caster sugar

1 tbsp chopped fresh tarragon

salt and pepper

fresh tarragon sprigs, to garnish

1 Cut the carrots in half lengthways, slice the runner beans and courgettes, and halve the spring onions and radishes, so that all the vegetables are cut into even-sized pieces.

2 Melt the butter in a large, heavy-based frying pan or wok. Add all the vegetables and fry them over a medium heat, stirring frequently, until they are tender, but still crisp and firm to the bite.

3 Meanwhile, pour the olive oil, vinegar, and white wine into a small saucepan and add the sugar. Place over a low heat, stirring constantly until the sugar has dissolved. Remove the pan from the heat and add the chopped tarragon.

4 When the vegetables are just cooked, pour over the 'dressing'. Stir through, tossing the vegetables well to coat. Season to taste with salt and pepper and then transfer to a warmed serving dish.

5 Garnish with sprigs of fresh tarragon and serve the sauté immediately.

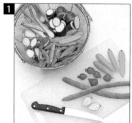

Rösti

This popular Swiss dish is a kind of crispy potato pancake and is a great favourite with children – serve with vegetarian sausages and a salad.

NUTRITIONAL INFORMATION

Calories 267   Sugars 1g

Protein . . . . .5g   Fat 11g

Carbohydrate . . .38g   Saturates 6g

15 mins, plus cooling and chilling   30 mins

SERVES 4

I N G R E D I E N T S

900 g/2 lb potatoes

25–55 g/1–2 oz unsalted butter or margarine

1–2 tbsp olive oil

salt and pepper

 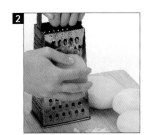 

1 Cook the unpeeled potatoes in a large saucepan of water for 10 minutes. Drain and leave to cool. Transfer the potatoes to a plate and chill in the refrigerator for 30 minutes or longer.

2 Peel and coarsely grate the potatoes. Melt 25 g/1 oz of the unsalted butter or margarine with 1 tablespoon of the olive oil in a heavy-based 23 cm/9 inch frying pan over a medium heat. Spread out the grated potato evenly in the pan, lower the heat and cook for 10 minutes.

3 Cover the pan with a plate and invert the pan and the plate. Slide the potato back into the pan to cook the second side. Cook for 10 minutes more, adding more butter and olive oil if necessary. Season to taste with salt and pepper and serve immediately.

COOK'S TIP

Chilling the parboiled potatoes is not essential, but it makes it much easier to grate them.

Honey-fried Spinach

This stir-fry is the perfect accompaniment to tofu dishes and it is wonderfully quick and simple to make.

NUTRITIONAL INFORMATION

Calories . . . . . . .146 Sugars 9g
Protein . . . . .4g Fat 9g
Carbohydrate . . .10g Saturates 2g

 5 mins 15 mins

SERVES 4

INGREDIENTS

4 spring onions

3 tbsp groundnut oil

350 g/12 oz shiitake mushrooms, sliced

2 garlic cloves, crushed

350 g/12 oz fresh baby leaf spinach

2 tbsp dry sherry

2 tbsp clear honey

1 Using a sharp knife, thickly slice the spring onions on the diagonal.

2 Heat the groundnut oil in a large preheated wok or frying pan with a heavy base.

3 Add the shiitake mushrooms to the wok or pan and stir-fry for about 5 minutes or until they have softened.

4 Stir the crushed garlic into the wok or frying pan. Add the baby leaf spinach and continue to stir-fry for a further 2–3 minutes or until the spinach leaves have just begun to wilt.

5 Mix together the dry sherry and the clear honey in a small bowl until thoroughly combined. Drizzle the sherry and honey mixture over the spinach and heat through, stirring to coat the spinach leaves thoroughly in the mixture.

6 Transfer the stir-fry to warm serving dishes, scatter with the sliced spring onions and serve immediately.

COOK'S TIP

Single-flower honey has a better, more individual flavour than blended honey. Acacia honey is typically Chinese, but you could also try clover, lemon blossom, lime flower or orange blossom.

Broccoli & Black Bean Sauce

Broccoli works well with black bean sauce and Chinese leaves in this recipe, while the almonds add extra crunch and flavour.

NUTRITIONAL INFORMATION

Calories 139   Sugars 3g
Protein . . . . .7g   Fat 10g
Carbohydrate . . . .5g   Saturates 1g

5 mins   15 mins

SERVES 4

INGREDIENTS

450 g/1 lb broccoli florets

2 tbsp sunflower oil

1 onion, sliced

2 garlic cloves, thinly sliced

25 g/1 oz flaked almonds

1 head Chinese leaves, shredded

4 tbsp black bean sauce

1 Bring a large saucepan of water to the boil. Add the broccoli florets to the pan and cook for 1 minute. Drain, rinse in cold water to prevent any further cooking and drain thoroughly again.

2 Meanwhile, heat the sunflower oil in a large preheated wok.

3 Add the onion and garlic slices to the wok and stir-fry until they are just beginning to brown.

4 Add the drained broccoli florets and the flaked almonds and stir-fry for a further 2–3 minutes.

5 Add the shredded Chinese leaves to the wok and continue to stir-fry for a further 2 minutes.

6 Stir the black bean sauce into the vegetables, tossing to coat them thoroughly, and cook until the juices are just beginning to bubble.

7 Transfer the vegetables to warm serving bowls and serve immediately.

VARIATION
Use unsalted cashew nuts instead of the almonds, if preferred.

Crisp Pickled Vegetables

The fresh red chillies in this recipe ensure that these crisp pickled vegetables have a kick as well as a bite!

NUTRITIONAL INFORMATION

Calories 108	Sugars 5g	
Protein 3g	Fat 7g	
Carbohydrate 5g	Saturates 1g	

🥄 20 mins   🕐 10 mins

SERVES 6–8

I N G R E D I E N T S

½ small cauliflower

½ cucumber

2 carrots, peeled

200 g/7 oz French beans

½ small Chinese cabbage

500 ml/18 fl oz rice vinegar

1 tbsp caster sugar

1 tsp salt

3 garlic cloves

3 shallots

3 fresh red bird's-eye chillies

5 tbsp groundnut oil

COOK'S TIP
To make simple carrot flowers, peel the carrot thinly, then use a canelle knife or small sharp knife to cut narrow 'channels' down the length of it at regular intervals. Slice the carrot and the slices will resemble flowers.

1 Trim the cauliflower. Peel and deseed the cucumber. Peel the carrots. Top and tail the beans. Trim the cabbage, then cut all the vegetables into bite-size pieces. If you have time, cut the carrots into flower shapes.

2 Place the rice vinegar, sugar and salt in a large pan and bring almost to the boil. Add the vegetables, lower the heat and simmer for 3–4 minutes until they are just tender, but still crisp inside. Remove from the heat and leave the vegetables to cool in the liquid in the pan.

3 Peel the garlic and shallots and deseed the chillies. Place in a mortar and grind with a pestle until a smooth paste is formed.

4 Heat the oil in a frying pan and stir-fry the spice paste gently for 1–2 minutes. Add the vegetables, along with the rice vinegar, and cook for a further 2 minutes to reduce the liquid slightly. Remove from the heat and set aside to cool completely.

5 Serve the pickles cold, or pack into jars and store in the refrigerator for up to 2 weeks.

Chipotle Salsa

This garlicky chipotle and tomato salsa is incredibly quick to prepare, so if possible leave it until the last minute and serve it freshly made.

NUTRITIONAL INFORMATION

Calories 34	Sugars 5g
Protein 2g	Fat 0.5g
Carbohydrate 6g	Saturates 0g

 10 mins   0 mins

MAKES ABOUT 450 ml/16 fl oz

I N G R E D I E N T S

450 g/1 lb ripe juicy tomatoes, diced

3–5 garlic cloves, finely chopped

½ bunch fresh coriander leaves, roughly chopped

1 small onion, chopped

1–2 tsp adobo marinade from canned chipotle chillies (see Cook's Tip)

½–1 tsp sugar

lime juice, to taste

salt

pinch of cinnamon (optional)

pinch of ground allspice (optional)

pinch of ground cumin (optional)

1 Put the diced tomatoes and the chopped garlic and coriander in a blender or food processor.

2 Process the mixture until it is smooth, then add the onion, adobo marinade, and the sugar.

3 Squeeze in lime juice to taste. Season with salt to taste, then add the cinnamon, allspice or cumin, if wished.

4 Serve at once, or cover and chill until ready to serve. Salsa, however, is at its best when it is served freshly made.

COOK'S TIP
To simplify preparation, the fresh tomatoes can be replaced with 400 g/14 oz canned chopped tomatoes. Canned chipotle chillies are available from specialist Mexican stores.

Fennel with Tomatoes

Full of Italian flavours, this simple-to-prepare dish makes an excellent accompaniment for an extra special meal.

NUTRITIONAL INFORMATION

Calories	43	Sugars	........3g
Protein	........1g	Fat	..........3g
Carbohydrate	....4g	Saturates	.......0g

10 mins   25 mins

SERVES 6

INGREDIENTS

2 fennel bulbs

1 tbsp olive oil

1 onion, thinly sliced

2 tomatoes, skinned and chopped

55 g/2 oz black olives, stoned

2 tbsp torn fresh basil leaves

pepper

1 Cut off and chop the fennel fronds. Cut the bulbs in half lengthways, then slice thinly.

2 Heat the oil in a heavy-based frying pan. Add the onion to the pan and cook over a low heat, stirring occasionally, for 5 minutes, until softened.

3 Add the fennel slices and cook, stirring occasionally, for a further 10 minutes.

4 Increase the heat and add the tomatoes and olives. Cook, stirring frequently, for 10 minutes, then stir in the basil and season to taste with pepper.

5 Transfer the vegetables to a warm serving dish, garnish with the fennel fronds and serve immediately.

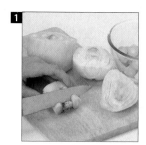

COOK'S TIP

Do not slice the fennel too much in advance, as the cut surfaces discolour on exposure to air. Alternatively, put the slices in a bowl of water acidulated with 2 tablespoons lemon juice and drain before using.

Braised Red Cabbage

A delicious sharp-sweet taste and an eye-catching colour make this a vegetable accompaniment with attitude.

NUTRITIONAL INFORMATION

Calories 170   Sugars 28g
Protein . . . . .3g   Fat 4g
Carbohydrate . . .29g   Saturates 0g

 10 mins   55 mins

SERVES 6

I N G R E D I E N T S

2 tbsp sunflower oil

2 onions, thinly sliced

2 apples, peeled, cored and
 thinly sliced

900 g/2 lb red cabbage, cored and shredded

4 tbsp red wine vinegar

2 tbsp sugar

¼ tsp ground cloves

55 g/2 oz raisins

125 ml/4 fl oz red wine

salt and pepper

2 tbsp redcurrant jelly

1 Heat the oil in a large, heavy-based saucepan. Add the onions and cook, stirring occasionally, for 10 minutes, until softened and golden. Stir in the apples and cook for 3 minutes.

2 Add the cabbage, vinegar, sugar, cloves, raisins and red wine and season to taste with salt and pepper. Bring to the boil, stirring occasionally. Lower the heat, cover and cook, stirring occasionally, for 40 minutes, until the cabbage is tender and most of the liquid has been absorbed.

3 Stir in the redcurrant jelly, transfer the red cabbage to a warm serving dish and serve immediately.

COOK'S TIP
You can also braise the cabbage, in a preheated oven, 180°C/350°F/ Gas Mark 4, for about 1 hour.

Oven-dried Tomatoes

The name may not have quite the same enticing ring to it as 'sun-dried tomatoes', but the result is excellent!

NUTRITIONAL INFORMATION

Calories . . . . .81 Sugars 2g
Protein . . . . .0.5g Fat 8g
Carbohydrate . . . .2g Saturates 1g

15 mins   2½ hrs

MAKES 1 x 250 ml/9 fl oz JAR

I N G R E D I E N T S

1 kg/2 lb 4 oz large, juicy,
    full-flavoured tomatoes

sea salt

extra-virgin olive oil

1 Using a sharp knife, cut each of the tomatoes into quarters.

2 Using a teaspoon, scoop out the seeds and discard. If the tomatoes are large, cut each quarter in half lengthways again.

3 Sprinkle sea salt in a roasting tin and arrange the tomato slices, skin side down, on top. Roast in a preheated oven at 120°C/250°F/Gas Mark ½ for 2½ hours,

or until the edges are just starting to look charred and the flesh is dry but still pliable. The exact roasting time and yield will depend on the size and juiciness of the tomatoes. Check the tomatoes at 30 minute intervals after 1½ hours.

4 Remove the dried tomatoes from the pan and leave to cool completely. Put into a 250 ml/9 fl oz preserving jar and pour over enough olive oil to cover. Seal the jar tightly and store in the refrigerator, where it will keep for up to 2 weeks.

COOK'S TIP

Serve these oven-dried tomatoes with slices of buffalo mozzarella: drizzle with olive oil and sprinkle with coarsely ground pepper and finely torn basil leaves.

Flavoured Olives

You are sure to find Mediterranean stalls selling all kinds of flavoured olives. This nutritional analysis is based on a portion of 3 Provençal olives.

NUTRITIONAL INFORMATION

Calories	53	Sugars	........0g
Protein	.........0g	Fat	..........6g
Carbohydrate	....0g	Saturates	.......1g

10–15 mins · 0 mins

MAKES 3 x 500 ml/18 fl oz JARS

I N G R E D I E N T S

fresh herb sprigs, to serve

P R O V E N C A L   O L I V E S

3 dried red chillies

1 tsp black peppercorns

300 g/10½ oz black Niçoise olives in brine

2 lemon slices

1 tsp black mustard seeds

1 tbsp garlic-flavoured olive oil

fruity extra virgin olive oil

C A T A L A N   O L I V E S

½ grilled red or orange pepper

150 g/5½ oz black olives in brine

150 g/5½ oz pimento-stuffed olives in brine

1 tbsp capers in brine, drained and rinsed

pinch of dried chilli flakes

4 tbsp chopped fresh coriander leaves

1 bay leaf

fruity extra virgin olive oil

G R E E K   O L I V E S

½ large lemon

300 g/10½ oz kalamata olives in brine

4 fresh thyme sprigs

1 shallot, very finely chopped

1 tbsp fennel seeds, lightly crushed

1 tsp dried dill

fruity extra virgin olive oil

1 To make the Provençal olives, place the dried red chillies and black peppercorns in a mortar and lightly crush. Drain and rinse the olives, then pat dry with kitchen paper. Put all the ingredients in a 500 ml/18 fl oz preserving jar, pouring in enough olive oil to cover.

2 Seal the jar and leave for at least 10 days before serving, shaking the jar daily.

3 To make the Catalan olives, finely chop the pepper. Drain and rinse both types of olives, then pat dry with kitchen paper. Put all the ingredients into a 500 ml/18 fl oz preserving jar, pouring in enough olive oil to cover. Seal and marinate as in Step 2.

4 To make the Greek olives, cut the lemon into 4 slices, then cut each slice into wedges. Drain and rinse the olives, then pat dry with kitchen paper.

5 Slice each olive lengthways on one side down to the stone. Put all the ingredients in a 500 ml/18 fl oz preserving jar, pouring in olive oil to cover. Seal and marinate as in Step 2.

6 To serve, spoon the olives into a bowl and garnish with fresh herbs.

Rouille

This is a great way to use up the remains of a good, rustic loaf – sliced white bread just won't give the same result.

10 mins   0 mins

MAKES ABOUT 175 g/ 6 oz

I N G R E D I E N T S

60 g/2¼ oz day-old country-style white bread

2 large garlic cloves

2 small red chillies, deseeded

pinch of salt

3 tbsp extra-virgin olive oil

1 tbsp tomato purée

cayenne pepper (optional)

pepper

soup and croûtes, to serve

1 Cut the crusts off the bread. Put the bread in a bowl, pour over enough water to cover and leave to soak for 30 seconds, or until soft. Squeeze the bread dry, reserving 2 tablespoons of the soaking liquid.

2 Coarsely chop the garlic and chillies. Put them in a mortar with a pinch of salt and pound until they form a paste.

3 Add the paste to the squeezed bread, then continue working in the mortar until the ingredients blend together. Transfer to a bowl and slowly add the olive oil, beating constantly. If the mixture begins to separate, add a little of the reserved soaking liquid.

4 Add the tomato purée and cayenne pepper to taste. Adjust seasoning. Spread on croûtes and use to float on the surface of soup.

COOK'S TIP

If the sauce appears to be separating after it has been standing for a while, stir in 1 tbsp hot water. If it appears too thin to spread on croûtes, beat in a little extra soaked bread.

Greek Strained Yogurt

Genuine Greek or Greek-style strained yogurt is readily available in supermarkets, but it is much cheaper and more fun to make your own.

NUTRITIONAL INFORMATION

Calories 56	Sugars 6g	
Protein 4g	Fat 2g	
Carbohydrate 6g	Saturates 1g	

15 mins, plus draining and standing   0 mins

MAKES ABOUT 500 g/ 1 lb 2 oz

INGREDIENTS

1 kg/2 lb 4 oz natural yogurt

½ tsp salt, or to taste

OPTIONAL TOPPINGS

fruity extra-virgin olive oil

orange-blossom or lavender-flavoured honey

finely grated lemon rind

coriander seeds, crushed

powdered paprika

very finely chopped fresh mint or coriander

1 Place a 125 x 75 cm/50 x 30 inch piece of muslin in a saucepan, cover with water and bring to the boil to sterilize. Remove the pan from the heat and, using a wooden spoon, lift out the muslin. Wearing clean rubber gloves, wring the cloth dry.

2 Fold the cloth into a double layer and use it to line a colander or sieve set over a large bowl. Put the yogurt in a bowl and stir in the salt. Spoon the yogurt into the centre of the cloth.

3 Tie the cloth so it is suspended above the bowl. If your sink is deep enough, gather up the corners of the cloth and tie it to the tap. If not, lay a broom handle across 2 chairs and put the bowl between the chairs. Tie the cloth to the broom handle, then remove the colander or sieve and leave the yogurt to drain into the bowl for at least 12 hours.

4 Transfer the thickened drained yogurt to a nylon sieve, sitting it over a bowl. Cover lightly with clingfilm and keep in the refrigerator for another 24 hours until soft and creamy. This yogurt will keep refrigerated for up to 5 days.

5 To serve, taste and add extra salt if needed. Spoon the yogurt into a bowl and garnish as desired.

Chipotle Salsa

Unusually, this salsa is cooked. It uses dried chipotle chillies – be sure to read the warning in the Cook's Tip before you embark on this recipe!

NUTRITIONAL INFORMATION

Calories . . . . .102 Sugars 17g
Protein . . . . .2g Fat 3g
Carbohydrate . . .19g Saturates 0.5g

 5 mins   30 mins

MAKES ABOUT 450 ml/16 fl oz

INGREDIENTS

3 dried chipotle chillies

1 onion, finely chopped

400 g/14 oz canned tomatoes, including their juices

2–3 tbsp dark brown sugar

2–3 garlic cloves, finely chopped

pinch of ground cinnamon

pinch of ground cloves or allspice

large pinch of ground cumin

juice of ½ lemon

1 tbsp extra virgin olive oil

salt

lemon rind strips, to garnish

1 Place the chillies in a pan with enough water to cover. Protecting your face against fumes and making sure the kitchen is well ventilated, bring the chillies and water to the boil. Cook for about 5 minutes, then remove from heat, cover and let stand until softened.

2 Remove the chillies from the water with a slotted spoon. Cut away and discard the stem and seeds, then either scrape the flesh from the skins or chop up the whole chillies.

3 Put the onion in a pan with the tomatoes and sugar and cook over a medium heat, stirring, until thickened.

4 Remove from the heat and add the garlic, cinnamon, cloves, cumin, lemon juice, olive oil and prepared chipotle chillies. Season with salt to taste and allow to cool. Serve garnished with the lemon rind strips.

COOK'S TIP

Do not inhale the fumes given off during the boiling process as they can irritate your lungs. This salsa freezes extremely well. Freeze in an ice-cube tray, then pop the cubes out and store in a plastic bag, ready to use for individual portions.

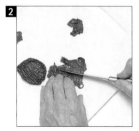

Hot Mexican Salsas

These salsas capture the inimitable tangy, spicy flavour of Mexico. Choose from a fresh minty fruit salsa, charred chilli salsa or a spicy 'green' salsa.

NUTRITIONAL INFORMATION

Calories ....59 Sugars 12g
Protein ....1g Fat 0g
Carbohydrate ...12g Saturates 0g

10 mins   5 mins

SERVES 4–6

INGREDIENTS

TROPICAL FRUIT SALSA

½–1 fresh green chilli

½–1 fresh red chilli

½ pineapple, peeled, cored and diced

1 mango, peeled, stoned and diced

½ red onion, chopped

1 tbsp sugar

juice of 1 lime

3 tbsp chopped fresh mint

salt

CHARRED CHILLI SALSA

2–3 fresh green chillies

1 green pepper

2 garlic cloves, finely chopped

juice of ½ lime

1 tsp salt

2–3 tbsp extra virgin olive oil

pinch each dried oregano and ground cumin

SALSA VERDE

450 g/1 lb oz canned tomatillos, drained

1–2 fresh green chillies

1 green pepper, deseeded and chopped

1 small onion, chopped

1 bunch fresh coriander, finely chopped

½ tsp ground cumin

salt

1 To make the Tropical Fruit Salsa, deseed the green chilli and chop both chillies. Combine all the ingredients in a large bowl and season with salt to taste. Cover the bowl with clingfilm and chill in the refrigerator until required.

2 For the Charred Chilli Salsa, char the chillies and green pepper in an ungreased frying pan. Cool, deseed, skin and chop. Combine the chillies and green pepper with the garlic, lime juice, salt and oil in a bowl. Top with oregano and cumin.

3 For the Salsa Verde, drain and chop the tomatillos. Deseed and finely chop the chillies and deseed and chop the green pepper. Combine all the ingredients in a bowl and season with salt to taste. If a smoother sauce is preferred, blend the ingredients in a food processor, then spoon into a bowl to serve.

Marinated Chipotle Salsa

This fiery, spicy salsa will add a kick to all sorts of vegetarian dishes, and is of course perfect to serve as part of a Mexican menu.

NUTRITIONAL INFORMATION

Calories	84	Sugars	........13g
Protein	.........2g	Fat	..........2g
Carbohydrate	...15g	Saturates	.....0.5g

10 mins   35 mins

SERVES 4–6

INGREDIENTS

6 dried chipotle chillies

6 tbsp tomato ketchup

350 g/12 oz ripe tomatoes, diced

1 large onion, chopped

5 garlic cloves, chopped

2 tbsp cider vinegar

300 ml/½ pint water

1 tbsp extra virgin olive oil

2 tbsp sugar, preferably
  molasses sugar

pinch of salt

¼ tsp ground allspice

¼ tsp ground cloves

¼ tsp ground cinnamon

¼ tsp ground cumin

3–4 tbsp lime juice or combination of
  pineapple and lemon juice

pepper

1 Place the dried chipotle chillies in a medium-sized saucepan with enough water to cover. Bring to the boil, taking care not to inhale the fumes given off as they can irritate your lungs. Cover the saucepan and simmer the chillies for about 20 minutes, then remove from the heat and let cool.

2 Remove the chillies from the water. Cut away and discard the stem and seeds, then either scrape the flesh from the skins or chop up the whole chillies.

3 Place the tomato ketchup and tomatoes in a pan with the onion, chillies, garlic, vinegar, water, olive oil, sugar, salt, allspice, cloves, cinnamon and cumin. Bring to the boil. Reduce the heat and simmer for about 15 minutes until the mixture has thickened.

4 Season with salt and pepper to taste, then stir in the fruit juice and use the salsa as required.

Fresh Pineapple Salsa

This sweet fruity salsa is fresh and fragrant, a wonderful foil to spicy dishes, and is perfect with food cooked on the barbecue.

NUTRITIONAL INFORMATION

Calories 37   Sugars 08
Protein . . . . .1g   Fat 0.5g
Carbohydrate . . . .8g   Saturates 0g

15 mins   0 mins

SERVES 4

I N G R E D I E N T S

½ ripe pineapple

juice of 1 lime or lemon

1 garlic clove, finely chopped

1 spring onion, thinly sliced

½–1 fresh green or red chilli, deseeded and
   finely chopped

½ red pepper, deseeded and chopped

3 tbsp chopped fresh mint

3 tbsp chopped fresh coriander

pinch of salt

pinch of sugar

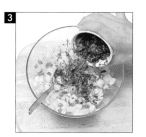

1 Using a long, sharp knife, cut off the top and bottom of the pineapple. Place the pineapple upright on a chopping board, then slice off the skin, cutting downwards. If any 'eyes' still remain in the flesh, cut them out with a small, pointed knife.

2 Cut the pineapple flesh into slices about 1 cm/½ inch thick, halve the slices and remove the cores. Dice the flesh.

Reserve any juice that accumulates as you cut the pineapple.

3 Place the pineapple and any juice in a bowl and stir in the lime juice, garlic, spring onion, chilli and red pepper. Stir in the chopped fresh mint and coriander. Add the salt and sugar and stir well to combine all the ingredients. Cover the bowl with clingfilm and chill until ready to serve.

COOK'S TIP
A fresh pineapple is ripe if it has a sweet aroma. The flesh will still be fairly firm to touch. Fresh-looking leaves are a sign of good condition.

Mole Verde

This gorgeous Mexican sauce is based on toasted pumpkin seeds, so it is as nutritious as it is tasty.

NUTRITIONAL INFORMATION

Calories 319   Sugars 6g
Protein . . . . .12g   Fat 25g
Carbohydrate . . .12g   Saturates 4g

 10 mins   20 mins

SERVES 4

INGREDIENTS

250 g/9 oz toasted pumpkin seeds

1 litre/1¾ pints vegetable stock

several pinches of ground cloves

8–10 tomatillos, diced, or 225 ml/8 fl oz
   mild tomatillo salsa

½ onion, chopped

½ fresh green chilli, deseeded and diced

3 garlic cloves, chopped

½ tsp fresh thyme leaves

½ tsp fresh marjoram leaves

3 tbsp vegetable oil

3 bay leaves

4 tbsp chopped fresh coriander

salt and pepper

fresh green chilli slices, to garnish

VARIATION
Make a tamale dough and
poach in the mole as dumplings,
making a filling snack.

1 Grind the toasted pumpkin seeds in a food processor. Add half the vegetable stock, the cloves, tomatillos, onion, chilli, garlic, thyme and marjoram and blend to a purée.

2 Heat the vegetable oil in a heavy-based frying pan and add the puréed pumpkin seed mixture, together with the bay leaves. Cook over a medium-high heat for about 5 minutes until the mixture has began to thicken.

3 Remove from the heat and add the rest of the vegetable stock and the coriander. Return the pan to the heat and cook until the sauce thickens, then remove from the heat.

4 Remove the bay leaves and process the sauce until completely smooth again. Add salt and pepper to taste.

5 Transfer the sauce to a bowl, garnish with chilli and serve.

Mole Poblano

This great Mexican celebration dish, with its combination of chillies and chocolate, is ladled out at fiestas, baptisms and weddings.

NUTRITIONAL INFORMATION

Calories	152	Sugars	........10g
Protein	.........4g	Fat	...........8g
Carbohydrate	...17g	Saturates	.......1g

  20 mins, plus standing   15 mins

SERVES 4

INGREDIENTS

3 mulato chillies

3 mild ancho chillies

5–6 New Mexico or California chillies

1 onion, chopped

5 garlic cloves, chopped

450 g/1 lb ripe tomatoes

2 tortillas, preferably stale, cut into small pieces

pinch of cloves

pinch of fennel seeds

⅛ tsp each ground cinnamon, coriander and cumin

3 tbsp lightly toasted sesame seeds or tahini

3 tbsp flaked or coarsely ground blanched almonds

2 tbsp raisins

1 tbsp peanut butter, optional

475 ml/16 fl oz vegetable stock

3–4 tbsp grated dark chocolate, plus extra for garnishing

2 tbsp mild chilli powder

3 tbsp vegetable oil

salt and pepper

about 1 tbsp lime juice

1 Using metal tongs, toast each chilli over an open flame for a few seconds until the colour darkens. Alternatively, roast in an ungreased frying pan over a medium heat, turning constantly, for about 30 seconds.

2 Place the toasted chillies in a bowl or a pan and pour boiling water over to cover. Cover with a lid and leave to soften for at least 1 hour or overnight. Once or twice lift the lid and rearrange the chillies so that they soak evenly.

3 Remove with a slotted spoon. Discard the stems and seeds and cut the flesh into pieces. Place in a blender.

4 Add the onion, garlic, tomatoes, tortillas, cloves, fennel seeds, cinnamon, coriander, cumin, sesame seeds, almonds, raisins and peanut butter if using, then process to combine. With the motor running, add enough stock through the feed tube to make a smooth paste. Stir in the remaining stock, chocolate and chilli powder.

5 Heat the oil in a heavy-based pan until it is smoking, then pour in the mole mixture. It will splatter and pop as it hits the oil. Cook for 10 minutes, stirring occasionally.

6 Season with salt, pepper and lime juice, garnish with grated chocolate and serve.

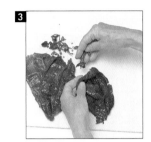

Hot Sauce of Dried Chillies

Preserved in an attractive bottle, this hot sauce would make an excellent gift for a chilli-loving friend.

NUTRITIONAL INFORMATION

Calories	9	Sugars	.........1g
Protein	.........5g	Fat	...........5g
Carbohydrate	....1g	Saturates	.......0g

5 mins, plus cooling

5 mins

MAKES ABOUT 225 ml/8 fl oz

I N G R E D I E N T S

10 dried arbol chillies, stems removed (see Cook's Tip)

225 ml/8 fl oz cider or white wine vinegar

½ tsp salt

1 Place the dried arbol chillies in a mortar and crush finely with a pestle.

2 Put the cider or white wine vinegar in a pan and add the crushed chillies and salt. Stir to combine, then bring the liquid to the boil.

3 Remove from the heat and set aside to cool completely to let the flavours infuse. Pour into a bowl and serve. The sauce will keep for up to a month, if covered and kept in the refrigerator.

COOK'S TIP

Arbol are dried long hot red chillies, with a dusty heat that is reminiscent of the Mexican desert. If arbol chillies are not available, use any hot dried chilli, or chilli flakes, such as cayenne.

Mild Red Chilli Sauce

In this delicious recipe, the chillies are first roasted, either over a naked flame or under a grill, to give them a delicious smoky flavour.

NUTRITIONAL INFORMATION

Calories 24	Sugars 0.5g	
Protein 2g	Fat 1g	
Carbohydrate 2g	Saturates 0g	

10 mins, plus cooling   15 mins

MAKES ABOUT 350 ml/12 fl oz

INGREDIENTS

5 large fresh mild chillies, such as New Mexico or ancho

450 ml/16 fl oz vegetable stock

1 tbsp masa harina or 1 crumbled corn tortilla, puréed with enough water to make a thin paste

large pinch of ground cumin

1–2 garlic cloves, finely chopped

juice of 1 lime

salt

1 Using metal tongs, roast each chilli over an open flame until the colour darkens on all sides. Alternatively, place the chillies under a preheated grill, turning them frequently.

2 Put the chillies in a bowl and pour boiling water over them. Cover and leave the chillies to cool.

3 Meanwhile, put the stock in a pan and bring to a simmer.

4 When the chillies have cooled and are swelled up and softened, remove from the water with a slotted spoon. Remove the seeds from the chillies, then cut or tear the flesh into pieces and place in a blender or food processor. Process to form a purée, then mix in the hot stock.

5 Put the chilli and stock mixture in a pan. Add the masa harina or puréed tortilla, cumin, garlic and lime juice. Bring to the boil and cook for a few minutes, stirring, until the sauce has thickened. Adjust the seasoning and serve.

Hot Tomato Sauce

This fresh green chilli and tomato sauce is an unusual accompaniment, but it is also good served as an appetiser with corn chips.

NUTRITIONAL INFORMATION

Calories 17	Sugars 2g
Protein 1g	Fat 0.5g
Carbohydrate 3g	Saturates 0g

5 mins   0 mins

SERVES 4

I N G R E D I E N T S

2–3 fresh green chillies, such as jalapeño
  or serrano

225 g/8 oz canned chopped tomatoes

1 spring onion, thinly sliced

2 garlic cloves, chopped

2–3 tbsp cider vinegar

50–80 ml/2–3 fl oz water

large pinch of dried oregano

large pinch of ground cumin

large pinch of sugar

large pinch of salt

1 Slice the chillies open, remove the seeds if wished, then chop.

2 Put the chillies in a blender or food processor together with the tomatoes, sliced spring onion, chopped garlic, cider vinegar, water, oregano, cumin, sugar and salt. Process until smooth.

3 Adjust the seasoning and chill until ready to serve. The sauce will keep for up to a week, covered, in the refrigerator.

COOK'S TIP

If you have sensitive skin, it may be advisable to wear rubber gloves when preparing chillies, as the oil in the seeds and flesh can cause irritation. Make sure that you do not touch your eyes when handling cut chillies.

Quick Tomato Sauce

This tomato sauce is very quick and very versatile – it can be served over pasta or form the basis for spicy bean casseroles.

NUTRITIONAL INFORMATION

Calories	58	Sugars	.........3g
Protein	.........1g	Fat	..........6g
Carbohydrate	....5g	Saturates	.....0.5g

  5 mins   🕐 15 mins

SERVES 4–6

I N G R E D I E N T S

2 tbsp vegetable or olive oil

1 onion, thinly sliced

5 garlic cloves, thinly sliced

400 g/14 oz canned tomatoes, diced, plus their juices, or 600 g/1 lb 5 oz fresh tomatoes, diced

several shakes of mild chilli powder

350 ml/12 fl oz vegetable stock

salt and pepper

pinch of sugar (optional)

1 Heat the oil in a large frying pan. Add the sliced onion and garlic and cook, stirring, until just softened.

2 Add the tomatoes, chilli powder to taste and the vegetable stock. Cook over a medium-high heat for about 10 minutes or until the tomatoes have reduced slightly and the flavour of the sauce is more concentrated.

3 Season the sauce with salt and pepper to taste, add a pinch of sugar if liked, and serve the dish warm.

VARIATION
For a hotter kick, add ½ tsp of finely chopped fresh chilli with the onion.

Sesame Seed Chutney

This chutney is delicious served with spiced rice dishes and also makes an unusual filling to spread in sandwiches.

NUTRITIONAL INFORMATION

Calories	120	Sugars	.........0g
Protein	.........4g	Fat	..........12g
Carbohydrate	...0.2g	Saturates	......2g

   10 mins   5 mins

SERVES 4

INGREDIENTS

8 tbsp sesame seeds

2 tbsp water

½ bunch of fresh coriander

3 fresh green chillies, deseeded and chopped

1 tsp salt

2 tsp lemon juice

chopped fresh red chilli, to garnish

1 Place the sesame seeds in a large, heavy-based saucepan and dry roast them, stirring constantly. Remove from the heat and set aside to cool.

2 Once cooled, place the sesame seeds in a mortar or food processor and grind well to form a fine powder.

3 Add the water to the ground sesame seeds and mix thoroughly to form a smooth paste.

4 Finely chop the coriander. Add the chillies and coriander to the sesame seed paste and grind again.

5 Add the salt and the lemon juice to the mixture and grind once again.

6 Remove the mixture from the food processor or mortar and transfer to a serving dish. Garnish with chopped red chilli and serve.

COOK'S TIP

Dry roasting brings out the flavour of spices and takes just a few minutes. You will be able to tell when the spices are ready because of the wonderful fragrance that develops. Stir the spices constantly to ensure that they do not burn.

Fried Aubergines

This makes a good alternative to a raita. The aubergines are fried until crisp, then given a baghaar, or seasoned oil dressing.

NUTRITIONAL INFORMATION

Calories 215   Sugars 4g
Protein . . . . .3g   Fat 21g
Carbohydrate . . . .5g   Saturates 2g

5 mins   15 mins

SERVES 4

I N G R E D I E N T S

200 ml/7 fl oz natural yogurt

5 tbsp water

1 tsp salt

1 aubergine

150 ml/¼ pint oil

1 tsp white cumin seeds

6 dried red chillies

1 Place the yogurt in a bowl and beat with a fork. Add the water and salt to the yogurt and mix well.

2 Using a sharp knife, slice the aubergine thinly.

3 Heat the oil in a large, heavy-based frying pan. Add the aubergine slices and fry, in batches if necessary, over a medium heat, turning occasionally, until they begin to turn crisp. Remove from the pan, drain on kitchen paper, transfer to a serving plate and keep warm.

4 When all of the aubergine slices have been fried, lower the heat, and add the white cumin seeds and the dried red chillies to the frying pan. Cook, stirring constantly, for 1 minute, then remove from the heat.

5 Spoon the thinned yogurt on top of the fried aubergine slices, then pour over the white cumin and red chilli mixture. Serve immediately.

COOK'S TIP
Rich in protein and calcium, yogurt plays an important part in Indian cooking. It is used as a marinade, as a creamy flavouring in curries and sauces and as a cooling accompaniment to hot dishes.

Raitas

Raitas are easy to prepare, very versatile and have a cooling effect which will be appreciated if you are serving hot, spicy dishes.

NUTRITIONAL INFORMATION

Calories 33	Sugars 5g
Protein 3g	Fat 0.4g
Carbohydrate 5g	Saturates 0.3g

 10 mins 20 mins

SERVES 4

INGREDIENTS

MINT RAITA

200 ml/7 fl oz low-fat natural yogurt

50 ml/2 fl oz water

1 small onion, finely chopped

½ tsp mint sauce

½ tsp salt

3 fresh mint leaves, to garnish

CUCUMBER RAITA

225 g/8 oz cucumber

1 onion

½ tsp salt

½ tsp mint sauce

300 ml/10 fl oz low-fat natural yogurt

150 ml/5 fl oz water

fresh mint leaves, to garnish

AUBERGINE RAITA

1 aubergine

1 tsp salt

1 small onion, finely chopped

2 fresh green chillies, deseeded and finely chopped

200 ml/7 fl oz low-fat natural yogurt

3 tbsp water

1 To make the mint raita, place the yogurt in a bowl and whisk with a fork. Gradually whisk in the water. Add the onion, mint sauce and salt and blend together. Garnish with mint leaves.

2 To make the cucumber raita, peel and slice the cucumber. Chop the onion finely. Place the cucumber and onion in a large bowl, then add the salt and the mint sauce. Add the yogurt and the water, place the mixture in a blender and blend well. Serve garnished with mint leaves.

3 To make the aubergine raita, remove the top end of the aubergine and chop the rest into small pieces. Boil in a pan of water for 20 minutes, until softened, then drain and mash. Add the salt, onion and green chillies, mixing well. Whisk the yogurt with the water, add to the mixture and mix thoroughly.

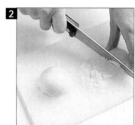

Tomato Salsa

This salad is used extensively in Mexican cooking and served as a dip or a relish, and is eaten as an accompaniment to almost any dish.

NUTRITIONAL INFORMATION

Calories 10	Sugars 2g
Protein 0.4g	Fat 0.1g
Carbohydrate 2g	Saturates 0g

 10 mins   0 mins

SERVES 4

INGREDIENTS

4 tomatoes

1 red onion or 6 spring onions

1–2 garlic cloves, crushed (optional)

2 tbsp chopped fresh coriander

½ red or green chilli (optional)

finely grated rind of ½–1 lemon or lime

1–2 tbsp lemon or lime juice

pepper

1 Chop the tomatoes fairly finely and evenly, and put into a bowl. They must be firm and a good strong red colour for the best results, but if preferred, they may be peeled by placing them in boiling water for about 20 seconds and then plunging into cold water. The skins should then slip off easily when they are nicked with a knife.

2 Peel and slice the red onion thinly, or trim the spring onions and cut into thin slanting slices; add to the chopped tomatoes with the garlic and coriander and mix lightly.

3 Remove the seeds from the red or green chilli, chop the flesh very finely and add to the salad. Treat the chillies with care; do not touch your eyes or face after handling them until you have washed your hands thoroughly. Chilli juices can burn.

4 Add the lemon or lime rind and juice to the salsa, and mix well. Transfer to a serving bowl and sprinkle with pepper.

COOK'S TIP
If you don't like the distinctive flavour of fresh coriander, you can replace it with flat-leaved parsley instead.

Desserts

As long as you are happy to include dairy

foods in your vegetarian diet, the sky is the

limit as far as desserts are concerned. In fact,

many of the sumptuous desserts in this

chapter are made from fresh and dried fruits,

nuts, eggs, yogurt – good, wholesome foods,

in fact, transformed into wonderful treats for when you

have the urge for something indulgent. If you still have

half a mind on your health, choose unrefined, organic

ingredients where possible. These are all readily available

in supermarkets – even chocolate! But whether you choose

a healthy Creamy Fruit Parfait or a hearty Spiced Steamed

Pudding – just enjoy it!

Mango Ice Cream

This delicious ice cream with its refreshing tang of mango and lime makes the perfect ending to a hot and spicy meal.

NUTRITIONAL INFORMATION

Calories	275	Sugars	........25g
Protein	.........2g	Fat	..........19g
Carbohydrate	...26g	Saturates	......11g

 5¾ hrs   5 mins

SERVES 6

INGREDIENTS

150 ml/¼ pint single cream

2 egg yolks

½ tsp cornflour

1 tsp water

800 g/1 lb 12 oz canned mango slices in syrup, drained

1 tbsp lime or lemon juice

150 ml/¼ pint double cream

fresh mint sprigs, to decorate

COOK'S TIP

Use the drained mango syrup for adding to fruit salads or for mixing into drinks.

1 Heat the single cream in a saucepan until hot (but do not allow it to boil). Place the egg yolks in a bowl with the cornflour and water and mix together until smooth. Pour the hot cream on to the egg yolk mixture, stirring all the time.

2 Return the mixture to the pan and place over a very low heat, whisking or stirring all the time until the mixture thickens and coats the back of a wooden spoon. (Do not try and hurry this process or the mixture will overcook and spoil.) Pour into a bowl.

3 Process the mango slices in a blender or food processor until smooth. Mix with the custard and stir in the lime juice. Whip the double cream until softly peaking and fold into the mango mixture until thoroughly combined.

4 Transfer the mixture to a loaf tin or shallow freezerproof container. Cover and freeze for 2–3 hours, or until half-frozen and still mushy in the centre. Turn the mixture into a bowl and mash well with a fork until smooth. Return to the container, cover and freeze until firm.

5 Transfer the container of ice cream to the main compartment of the refrigerator for about 30 minutes before serving to allow it to soften slightly. Scoop or spoon the ice cream into serving dishes and decorate with mint sprigs.

Ricotta Ice Cream

The ricotta cheese adds a creamy flavour, while the nuts add a crunchy texture. This ice cream needs to be frozen in the freezer overnight.

NUTRITIONAL INFORMATION

Calories . . . . . . .438 Sugars 39g
Protein . . . . .13g Fat 25g
Carbohydrate . . .40g Saturates 9g

20 mins   0 mins

SERVES 6

INGREDIENTS

25 g/1 oz pistachio nuts

25 g/1 oz walnuts or pecan nuts

25 g/1 oz toasted chopped hazelnuts

grated rind of 1 orange

grated rind of 1 lemon

25 g/1 oz crystallized or stem ginger

25 g/1 oz glacé cherries

25 g/1 oz dried apricots

25 g/1 oz raisins

500 g/1 lb 2 oz ricotta cheese

2 tbsp Maraschino, Amaretto or brandy

1 tsp vanilla essence

4 egg yolks

125 g/4½ oz caster sugar

TO DECORATE

whipped cream

a few glacé cherries, pistachio nuts or fresh mint leaves

3 Stir the ricotta evenly through the fruit mixture, then beat in the liqueur and vanilla essence.

4 Put the egg yolks and sugar in a bowl and whisk hard until very thick and creamy. Use an electric hand whisk if you have one, otherwise whisking over a pan of gently simmering water speeds up the process. Leave to cool if necessary.

5 Carefully fold the ricotta mixture evenly through the beaten eggs and sugar until smooth.

6 Line an 18 x 12 cm/7 x 5 inch loaf tin with a double layer of clingfilm or baking paper. Pour in the ricotta mixture, level the top, cover with more clingfilm or baking paper and chill in the freezer until firm – at least overnight.

7 To serve, remove the ice cream from the tin and peel off the paper.

8 Transfer the ice cream to a serving dish and decorate with whipped cream, glacé cherries, pistachio nuts and/or mint leaves. Serve in slices.

1 Roughly chop the pistachio nuts and walnuts and mix with the toasted hazelnuts, orange and lemon rind.

2 Finely chop the crystallized or stem ginger, cherries, apricots and raisins, and add them to the bowl.

Potato & Nutmeg Scones

Making these scones with mashed potato gives them a slightly different texture from traditional scones, but they are just as delicious.

NUTRITIONAL INFORMATION

Calories 135	Sugars 6g
Protein 3g	Fat 4g
Carbohydrate ...23g	Saturates 2g

 5 mins   25 mins

SERVES 8

INGREDIENTS

225 g/8 oz floury potatoes, diced

125 g/4½ oz plain flour

1½ tsp baking powder

½ tsp freshly grated nutmeg

50 g/1¾ oz sultanas

1 egg, beaten

3 tbsp double cream

2 tsp soft light brown sugar

1 Line and grease a flat baking sheet or Swiss roll tin.

2 Cook the diced potatoes in a saucepan of unsalted boiling water for 10 minutes or until soft. Drain well and mash the potatoes.

3 Transfer the mashed potatoes to a large mixing bowl and stir in the plain flour, baking powder and freshly grated nutmeg, mixing well to combine the ingredients thoroughly.

4 Stir in the sultanas, egg and double cream and beat the mixture with a wooden spoon until smooth.

5 Shape the mixture into 8 rounds, approximately 2 cm/¾ inch thick, and place on the baking tray.

6 Cook in a preheated oven, 200°C/400°F/Gas Mark 6, for 15 minutes or until the scones have risen and are golden. Sprinkle the scones with sugar and serve warm, spread with butter.

COOK'S TIP

For extra convenience, make a batch of scones in advance and freeze them. Thaw thoroughly and warm in a moderate oven when ready to serve.

Pear Tart

Pears are a very popular fruit in Italy. In this recipe from Trentino they are flavoured with almonds, cinnamon, raisins and apricot jam.

NUTRITIONAL INFORMATION

Calories 629   Sugars 70g
Protein ....7g   Fat 21g
Carbohydrate ..109g   Saturates 13g

1½ hrs   50 mins

SERVES 6

I N G R E D I E N T S

275 g/9½ oz plain flour

pinch of salt

125 g/4½ oz caster sugar

125 g/4½ oz butter, diced

1 egg

1 egg yolk

few drops of vanilla essence

2–3 tsp water

sifted icing sugar, for sprinkling

F I L L I N G

4 tbsp apricot jam

60 g/2 oz amaretti or ratafia biscuits, crumbled

1 kg/2 lb 4 oz pears, peeled and cored

1 tsp ground cinnamon

90 g/3 oz raisins

60 g/2 oz soft brown or demerara sugar

2 Using your fingers, gradually work the flour into the other ingredients to give a smooth dough, adding more water if necessary. Wrap in clingfilm and chill for 1 hour or until firm. Alternatively, put all the ingredients into a food processor or blender and process until the dough forms a smooth ball around the blade.

3 Roll out three-quarters of the dough and use to line a shallow 25 cm/ 10 inch cake tin or deep flan tin. Spread the jam over the base and sprinkle with the crushed biscuits.

4 Slice the pears very thinly. Arrange over the biscuits in the pastry case.

Sprinkle with cinnamon, then with raisins, and finally with brown sugar.

5 Roll out a thin sausage shape using one-third of the remaining pastry dough, and place around the edge of the pie. Roll the remainder of the pastry dough into thin sausages and arrange in a lattice over the pie, 4 or 5 strips in each direction, attaching them to the strip around the edge.

6 Cook in a preheated oven, at 200°C/ 400°F/Gas Mark 6, for 50 minutes until golden brown and cooked through. Leave to cool, then serve warm or chilled, sprinkled with sifted icing sugar.

1 Sift the flour and salt on to a flat surface, make a well in the centre and add the sugar, butter, egg, egg yolk, vanilla essence and most of the water.

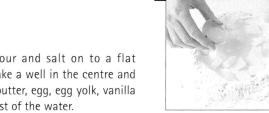

Eggless Sponge

This is a healthy and extremely tasty variation of the classic Victoria sponge cake. The sunflower oil gives the cake a lovely moist texture.

NUTRITIONAL INFORMATION

Calories	273	Sugars	........27g
Protein	.........3g	Fat	...........9g
Carbohydrate	...49g	Saturates	......1g

1¼ hrs   30 mins

MAKES 1 X 8" CAKE

INGREDIENTS

margarine, for greasing

225 g/8 oz self-raising wholemeal flour

2 tsp baking powder

175 g/6 oz caster sugar

6 tbsp sunflower oil

250 ml/8 fl oz water

1 tsp vanilla essence

4 tbsp strawberry or raspberry reduced-sugar spread

caster sugar, for dusting

1 Grease 2 x 20 cm/8 inch sandwich cake tins and line the bases with circles of baking paper.

2 Sift the self-raising flour and baking powder into a large mixing bowl, stirring in any bran remaining in the sieve. Stir in the caster sugar.

3 Pour in the sunflower oil, water and vanilla essence. Mix well with a wooden spoon for about 1 minute until the mixture is smooth, then divide between the prepared tins.

4 Bake in a preheated oven, 180°C/350°F/Gas Mark 4, for 25–30 minutes until just firm to the touch.

5 Leave the sponges to cool in the tins before turning out and transferring to a wire rack.

6 To serve, peel off the baking paper and place one of the sponges on a serving plate. Cover with the strawberry or raspberry spread and place the other sponge on top.

7 Dust the eggless sponge cake with a little caster sugar before serving.

VARIATION

To make a chocolate sponge, replace 15 g/½ oz of the flour with sifted cocoa powder. To make a citrus sponge, add the grated rind of ½ a lemon or orange to the flour in step 2. To make a coffee sponge, replace 2 teaspoons of the flour with instant coffee powder.

Scottish Shortbread

Many recipes for shortbread contain rice flour; combined with plain flour, it produces a delicate, crisp shortbread biscuit.

NUTRITIONAL INFORMATION

Calories 164	Sugars 6g	
Protein 2g	Fat 9g	
Carbohydrate . . .20g	Saturates 6g	

10 mins   50–60 mins

MAKES 16 WEDGES

I N G R E D I E N T S

225 g/8 oz plain flour

60 g/2 oz rice flour

¼ tsp salt

175 g/6 oz unsalted butter,
   at room temperature

60 g/2 oz caster sugar

25 g/1 oz icing sugar, sifted

1/4 tsp vanilla essence (optional)

sugar, for sprinkling

2 Using an electric mixer, beat the butter for about 1 minute in a large bowl until creamy. Add the sugars and continue beating for 1–2 minutes until very light and fluffy. If using, beat in the vanilla.

3 Using a wooden spoon, stir the flour mixture into the unsalted butter and caster sugar until well blended. Turn on to a lightly floured surface and knead lightly to blend completely.

4 Divide the dough evenly between the 2 tins, smoothing the surface. Using a fork, press 2 cm/³⁄₄ inch radiating lines around the edge of the dough. Lightly sprinkle the surfaces with a little sugar, then prick the surface lightly with the fork.

5 Using a sharp knife, mark each dough round into 8 wedges. Bake in a preheated oven at 120°C/250°F/Gas Mark ¹⁄₂ for 50–60 minutes until pale golden and crisp. Cool in the tins on a wire rack for about 5 minutes.

6 Carefully remove the side of each tin and slide the bottoms on to a heatproof surface. Using the knife marks as a guide, cut each shortbread into 8 wedges while still warm. Cool completely on the wire rack, then store in an airtight container.

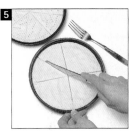

1 Lightly grease two 20–23 cm/ 8–9 inch cake or tart tins with removable bases. Sift the plain flour, rice flour and salt into a bowl; set aside.

Yogurt Scones

Yogurt is a suitable alternative to buttermilk, providing just the acidity needed to produce perfect scones.

NUTRITIONAL INFORMATION

Calories 109   Sugars 5g
Protein . . . . .3g   Fat 4g
Carbohydrate . . .17g   Saturates 2g

15 mins   10 mins

MAKES 16 SCONES

INGREDIENTS

225 g/8 oz plain flour, plus extra for dusting

1 tsp salt

1 tbsp baking powder

60 g/2 oz unsalted butter, chilled, plus extra for greasing

60 g/2 oz sugar

1 egg

6 tbsp low-fat natural yogurt

1 Sift together the flour, salt and baking powder. Cut the butter into small pieces, and rub it into the dry ingredients until the mixture resembles fine breadcrumbs. Stir in the sugar.

2 Beat together the egg and yogurt and stir it quickly into the dry ingredients.

Mix to form a thick dough and knead until it is smooth and free from cracks.

3 Lightly flour a pastry board or work top and rolling pin and roll out the dough to a thickness of 2 cm/¾ inch.

4 Cut out rounds with a 5 cm/2 inch pastry cutter, gather up the trimmings and roll them out again. Cut out as many more rounds as possible.

5 Grease a baking tray lightly with butter and heat it in the oven. Transfer the dough rounds to the tray and dust lightly with flour.

6 Bake the scones in the oven for 10 minutes, 180°C/350°F/Gas Mark 4, or until they are risen and golden brown.

7 Transfer the scones to a wire rack to cool, but serve while still warm.

VARIATION

For spiced scones add up to 1½ tsp ground ginger or cinnamon to the flour. For savoury scones, omit the sugar. At the end of step 1, stir in up to 45g/1½ oz grated mature Cheddar.

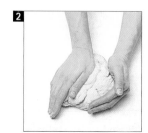

Carrot & Ginger Cake

This melt-in-the-mouth version of a favourite cake has a fraction of the fat of the traditional cake.

NUTRITIONAL INFORMATION

Calories 249   Sugars 28g
Protein . . . . .7g   Fat 6g
Carbohydrate . . .46g   Saturates 1g

15 mins   1¼ hrs

SERVES 10

INGREDIENTS

butter, for greasing

225 g/8 oz plain flour

1 tsp baking powder

1 tsp bicarbonate of soda

2 tsp ground ginger

½ tsp salt

175 g/6 oz light muscovado sugar

225 g/8 oz carrots, grated

2 pieces chopped stem ginger

25 g/1 oz grated fresh root ginger

60 g/2 oz seedless raisins

2 eggs, beaten

3 tbsp corn oil

juice of 1 orange

FROSTING

225 g/8 oz low-fat soft cheese

4 tbsp icing sugar

1 tsp vanilla essence

TO DECORATE

grated carrot

finely chopped stem ginger

ground ginger

1 Preheat the oven to 180°C/350°F/Gas Mark 4. Grease and line a 20 cm/ 8 inch round cake tin with baking paper.

2 Sift the flour, baking powder, bicarbonate of soda, ground ginger and salt into a bowl. Stir in the sugar, carrots, stem ginger, fresh root ginger and raisins. Beat together the eggs, oil and orange juice, then pour into the bowl. Mix the ingredients together well.

3 Spoon the mixture into the tin and bake in the oven for 1–1¼ hours until firm to the touch or until a fine skewer inserted into the centre of the cake comes out clean.

4 To make the frosting, place the soft cheese in a bowl and beat to soften. Sift in the icing sugar and add the vanilla essence. Mix well.

5 Remove the cake from the tin and cool. Smooth the frosting over the top. Decorate the cake and serve.

Fruity Muffins

The perfect choice for people on a low-fat diet, these little cakes contain no butter, just a little corn oil.

NUTRITIONAL INFORMATION

Calories 162	Sugars 11g
Protein 4g	Fat 4g
Carbohydrate ...28g	Saturates 1g

 10 mins 30 mins

MAKES 10 MUFFINS

INGREDIENTS

225 g/8 oz self-raising wholemeal flour

2 tsp baking powder

25 g/1 oz light muscovado sugar

100 g/3½ oz no-need-to-soak dried apricots, finely chopped

1 banana, mashed with 1 tbsp orange juice

1 tsp finely grated orange rind

300 ml/½ pint skimmed milk

1 egg, beaten

3 tbsp corn oil

2 tbsp rolled oats

fruit spread, honey or maple syrup, to serve

1 Place 10 paper muffin cases in a deep patty tin. Sift the flour and baking powder into a mixing bowl, adding any bran that remains in the sieve. Stir in the sugar and chopped apricots.

2 Make a well in the centre and add the banana, orange rind, milk, beaten egg and oil. Mix together well to form a thick batter. Divide the batter evenly among the 10 paper cases.

3 Sprinkle a few rolled oats on top of the muffins and bake in a preheated oven, 200°C/400°F/Gas Mark 6, for about 25–30 minutes until well risen and firm to the touch or until a skewer inserted into the centre comes out clean.

4 Transfer the muffins to a wire rack and leave them to cool slightly. Serve the muffins while they are still warm with a little reduced-sugar fruit spread, honey or maple syrup.

VARIATION

If you like dried figs, they make a deliciously crunchy alternative to the apricots; they also go very well with the flavour of orange. Other no-need-to-soak dried fruits, chopped finely, can be used as well.

Chocolate & Pineapple Cake

Decorated with thick yogurt and canned pineapple, this is a low-fat cake, but it is by no means lacking in flavour.

NUTRITIONAL INFORMATION

Calories 199   Sugars 19g
Protein . . . . .5g   Fat 9g
Carbohydrate . . .28g   Saturates 3g

10 mins   25 mins

SERVES 9

I N G R E D I E N T S

150 g/5½ oz low-fat spread, plus extra for greasing

125 g/4½ oz caster sugar

100 g/3½ oz self-raising flour, sifted

3 tbsp cocoa powder, sifted

1½ tsp baking powder

2 eggs

225g/8 oz canned pineapple pieces in natural juice

125 ml/4 fl oz low-fat thick natural yogurt

about 1 tbsp icing sugar

grated chocolate, to decorate

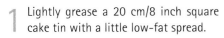

1 Lightly grease a 20 cm/8 inch square cake tin with a little low-fat spread.

2 Place the low-fat spread, caster sugar, self-raising flour, cocoa powder, baking powder and eggs in a large mixing bowl. Beat with a wooden spoon or electric hand whisk until smooth.

3 Pour the cake mixture into the prepared tin and level the surface. Bake in a preheated oven, 190°C/325°F/Gas Mark 5, for 20–25 minutes or until

springy to the touch. Set aside to cool slightly in the tin before transferring to a wire rack to cool completely.

4 Drain the pineapple, chop the pineapple pieces and drain again. Reserve a little pineapple for decoration, then stir the remainder into the yogurt and sweeten to taste with icing sugar.

5 Spread the pineapple and yogurt mixture over the cake and decorate with the reserved pineapple pieces. Sprinkle with the grated chocolate.

Coconut Bananas

This elaborate dessert is the perfect finale for a Chinese banquet.
Bananas are fried in a citrus-flavoured butter and served with coconut.

NUTRITIONAL INFORMATION

Calories 514	Sugars 70g
Protein 4g	Fat 21g
Carbohydrate . . .75g	Saturates 14g

10 mins

10 mins

SERVES 4

INGREDIENTS

3 tbsp shredded fresh coconut

60 g/2 oz unsalted butter

1 tbsp grated root ginger

grated rind of 1 orange

60 g/2 oz caster sugar

4 tbsp fresh lime juice

6 bananas

6 tbsp orange liqueur (Cointreau or Grand
    Marnier, for example)

3 tsp toasted sesame seeds

lime slices, to decorate

ice cream, to serve (optional)

1 Heat a small, non-stick frying pan until hot. Add the shredded coconut and cook, stirring constantly, for 1 minute until lightly coloured. Remove from the pan and allow to cool.

2 Melt the butter in a large frying pan and add the ginger, orange rind, sugar and lime juice. Mix well.

3 Peel and slice the bananas in half lengthways (and halve them again if they are very large).

4 Place the bananas, cut-side down, in the butter mixture and cook for 1–2 minutes or until the sauce mixture starts to become sticky. Turn the bananas to coat thoroughly in the sauce.

5 Remove the bananas and sauce and place on heated serving plates. Keep warm.

6 Return the pan to the heat and add the orange liqueur, blending well. Ignite with a taper, allow the flames to die down, then pour the liqueur over the bananas.

7 Sprinkle with the reserved coconut and sesame seeds and serve at once, decorated with slices of lime.

COOK'S TIP

For a very special treat try serving
this with a flavoured ice-cream
such as coconut, ginger or praline.

Banana & Lime Cake

A low-fat cake that is ideal served for tea. The mashed bananas help to keep the cake moist and the lime icing gives it extra zing and zest.

NUTRITIONAL INFORMATION

Calories 235   Sugars 31g
Protein . . . . .5g   Fat 1g
Carbohydrate . . .55g   Saturates 0.3g

35 mins   45 mins

SERVES 10

INGREDIENTS

butter, for greasing

300 g/10½ oz plain flour

1 tsp salt

1½ tsp baking powder

175 g/6 oz light muscovado sugar

1 tsp lime rind, grated

1 egg, beaten

1 banana, mashed with 1 tbsp lime juice

150 ml/5 fl oz low-fat natural fromage frais

115 g/4 oz sultanas

TOPPING

115 g/4 oz icing sugar

1–2 tsp lime juice

½ tsp finely grated lime rind

TO DECORATE

banana chips

finely grated lime rind

1 Grease and line a deep 18 cm/7 inch round cake tin with baking paper.

2 Sift the flour, salt and baking powder into a mixing bowl and stir in the sugar and lime rind.

3 Make a well in the centre of the dry ingredients and add the egg, banana, fromage frais and sultanas. Mix well until thoroughly incorporated.

4 Spoon the mixture into the tin and smooth the surface. Bake in a preheated oven, 180°C/350°F/Gas Mark 4, for 40–45 minutes until firm to the touch or until a skewer inserted in the centre comes out clean.

5 Leave the cake to cool for 10 minutes, then turn out on to a wire rack.

6 To make the topping, sift the icing sugar into a small bowl and mix with the lime juice to form a soft, but not too runny icing. Stir in the grated lime rind. Drizzle the icing over the cake, letting it run down the sides.

7 Decorate the cake with banana chips and lime rind. Let the cake stand for 15 minutes so that the icing sets.

VARIATION

For a delicious alternative, replace the lime rind and juice with orange and the sultanas with chopped apricots.

White Chocolate Florentines

These attractive jewelled biscuits are coated with white chocolate to give them a delicious flavour.

NUTRITIONAL INFORMATION

Calories 235   Sugars 20g
Protein . . . . .3g   Fat 17g
Carbohydrate . . .20g   Saturates 7g

20 mins   15 mins

MAKES 20

I N G R E D I E N T S

200 g/7 oz butter

225 g/8 oz caster sugar

125 g/4½ oz walnuts, chopped

125 g/4½ oz almonds, chopped

60 g/2 oz sultanas, chopped

25 g/1 oz glacé cherries, chopped

25 g/1 oz mixed candied peel,
    finely chopped

2 tbsp single cream

225 g/8 oz white chocolate

1 Line 3–4 baking trays with non-stick baking paper.

2 Melt the butter over a low heat and then add the sugar, stirring until it has dissolved. Boil the mixture for exactly 1 minute. Remove from the heat.

3 Add the chopped walnuts, almonds, sultanas, glacé cherries and mixed peel and the single cream to the saucepan, stirring well to mix.

4 Drop heaped teaspoonfuls of the mixture on to the baking trays, allowing plenty of room for them to spread while cooking. Bake in a preheated oven, at 180°C/350°F/Gas Mark 4, for 10 minutes or until golden brown.

5 Remove the biscuits from the oven and neaten the edges with a knife while they are still warm. Leave the biscuits to cool slightly, and then transfer them to a wire rack to cool completely.

6 Melt the chocolate in a bowl placed over a pan of gently simmering water. Spread the underside of the biscuits with chocolate and use a fork to make wavy lines across the surface.

7 Leave the Florentines on the wire rack until the chocolate has cooled completely, then store them in an airtight tin, kept in a cool place.

COOK'S TIP

A combination of white and dark chocolate Florentines looks very attractive, especially if you are making them as gifts. Pack them in pretty boxes, lined with tissue paper and tied with some ribbon.

Florentine Twists

These famous and delicious Florentine biscuits are twisted into curls or cones and then just the ends are dipped in chocolate.

NUTRITIONAL INFORMATION

Calories 28	Sugars 15g
Protein 1g	Fat 7g
Carbohydrate . . .15g	Saturates 4g

20 mins   20 mins

MAKES 20

INGREDIENTS

90 g/3 oz butter

125 g/4½ oz caster sugar

60 g/2 oz blanched or flaked almonds, roughly chopped

25 g/1 oz raisins, chopped

45 g/1½ oz chopped mixed peel

45 g/1½ oz glacé cherries, chopped

25 g/1 oz dried apricots, finely chopped

finely grated rind of ½ lemon or ½ small orange

about 125 g/4½ oz dark or white chocolate

1 Line 2–3 baking trays with non-stick baking paper; then grease 4–6 cream horn tins, or a fairly thin rolling pin, or wooden spoon handles.

2 Melt the butter and sugar together gently in a saucepan and then bring to the boil for 1 minute. Remove the pan from the heat and stir in all the remaining ingredients, except for the chocolate. Leave the mixture to cool.

3 Put heaped teaspoonfuls of the mixture on to the baking sheets, keeping them well apart, only 3–4 per sheet, and flatten slightly.

4 Bake in a preheated oven, at 180°C/ 350°F/Gas Mark 4, for 10–12 minutes, or until golden. Leave to cool until they begin to firm up. As they cool, press the edges back to form a neat shape. Remove each one with a palette knife and wrap quickly around a cream horn tin, or lay over the rolling pin or spoon handles. If they become too firm to bend, return to the oven briefly to soften.

5 Leave until cold and crisp and then slip carefully off the horn tins or remove from the rolling pin or spoons.

6 Melt the chocolate in a heatproof bowl over a saucepan of hot water, or in a microwave oven set on HIGH power for about 45 seconds, and stir until smooth.

7 Either dip the end of each Florentine twist into the chocolate or, using a pastry brush, paint chocolate to come about halfway up the twist. As the chocolate sets, it can be marked into wavy lines with a fork. Leave to set completely.

Chocolate Brownies

You really can have a low-fat chocolate treat. These moist bars contain a dried fruit purée, which enables you to bake without adding any fat.

NUTRITIONAL INFORMATION

Calories	283	Sugars	........49g
Protein	.........5g	Fat	..........4g
Carbohydrate	...61g	Saturates	.......2g

 1¼ hrs   35–40 mins

MAKES 12

I N G R E D I E N T S

60 g/2 oz unsweetened stoned
  dates, chopped

60 g/2 oz no-soak dried prunes, chopped

6 tbsp unsweetened apple juice

4 eggs, beaten

300 g/10½ oz dark muscovado sugar

1 tsp vanilla essence

4 tbsp low-fat drinking chocolate powder,
  plus extra for dusting

2 tbsp cocoa powder

175 g/6 oz plain flour

60 g/2 oz dark chocolate chips

I C I N G

125 g/4½ oz icing sugar

1–2 tsp water

1 tsp vanilla essence

COOK'S TIP

Make double the amount, cut one
of the cakes into bars and freeze,
then store in plastic bags.
Take out pieces of cake as and
when you need them – they'll
take no time at all to defrost.

1 Preheat the oven to 180°C/350°F/ Gas Mark 4. Grease and line an 18 x 28 cm/7 x 11 inch cake tin with baking paper. Place the dates and prunes in a small saucepan and add the apple juice. Bring to the boil, cover and simmer for 10 minutes until soft. Beat to form a smooth paste, then set aside to cool.

2 Place the cooled fruit in a mixing bowl and stir in the eggs, sugar and vanilla essence. Sift in the drinking chocolate, the cocoa and the flour, and fold in along with the chocolate chips until well incorporated.

3 Spoon the mixture into the prepared tin and smooth over the top. Bake for 25–30 minutes until firm to the touch or until a skewer inserted into the centre comes out clean. Cut into 12 bars and leave to cool in the tin for 10 minutes. Transfer to a wire rack to cool completely.

4 Sift the icing sugar into a bowl and mix with water and vanilla essence to form a soft, but not too runny, icing.

5 Drizzle the icing over the chocolate brownies and allow to set. Dust with the extra chocolate powder before serving.

Rice Muffins

Italian rice gives these delicate muffins an interesting texture. They are delicious – and very indulgent – served with a swirl of Amaretto butter.

NUTRITIONAL INFORMATION

Calories	203	Sugars	.........6g
Protein	.........3g	Fat	..........12g
Carbohydrate	...20g	Saturates	.......7g

15 mins   15 mins

MAKES 12 MUFFINS

INGREDIENTS

140 g/5 oz plain flour

1 tbsp baking powder

½ tsp bicarbonate of soda

½ tsp salt

1 egg

50 ml/2 fl oz honey

125 ml/4 fl oz milk

2 tbsp sunflower oil

½ tsp almond essence

60 g/2¼ oz cooked arborio rice

2–3 amaretti biscuits, roughly crushed

AMARETTO BUTTER

115 g/4 oz unsalted butter,
  at room temperature

1 tbsp honey

1–2 tbsp Amaretto liqueur

1–2 tbsp mascarpone cheese

1 Sift the plain flour, baking powder, bicarbonate of soda and salt into a large bowl and stir to combine. Make a well in the centre.

2 In another bowl, beat the egg, honey, milk, oil and almond essence with an electric mixer for about 2 minutes until light and foamy. Gradually beat in the rice.

Pour into the well and, using a fork, stir lightly until just combined. Do not over-beat; the mixture can be slightly lumpy.

3 Spoon the batter into a lightly greased 12-cup muffin pan or two 6-cup pans. Sprinkle each muffin with some of the amaretti crumbs and bake in a preheated oven at 200°C/400°F/Gas Mark 6 for about 15 minutes until risen and golden; the tops should spring back lightly when pressed.

4 Cool in the pans on a wire rack for about 1 minute. Carefully remove the muffins and cool slightly.

5 To make the Amaretto butter, put the butter and honey in a bowl and beat until creamy. Add the Amaretto and mascarpone and beat together. Spoon into a serving bowl and serve with the muffins.

COOK'S TIP

Use paper liners to line the muffin pan cups to avoid sticking.

Christmas Shortbread

Make this wonderful shortbread and then give it the Christmas touch by cutting it into shapes with seasonal biscuit cutters.

NUTRITIONAL INFORMATION

Calories 162   Sugars 10g
Protein ....1g   Fat 9g
Carbohydrate ...21g   Saturates 6g

 45 mins   15 mins

MAKES 24

INGREDIENTS

125 g/4½ oz caster sugar

225 g/8 oz butter

350 g/12 oz plain flour, sifted

pinch of salt

TO DECORATE

60 g/2 oz icing sugar

silver balls

chopped glacé cherries

chopped angelica

1 Beat the sugar and butter together in a large bowl until they are combined (thorough creaming is not necessary).

2 Sift in the flour and salt and work together to form a stiff dough. Turn out on to a lightly floured surface. Knead lightly for a few moments until smooth, but avoid overhandling. Chill in the refrigerator for 10–15 minutes.

3 Roll out the shortbread dough on a lightly floured work surface and cut into shapes with small Christmas cutters, such as bells, stars and angels. Place on greased baking trays.

4 Bake the biscuits in a preheated oven, 180°C/350°F/Gas Mark 4, for 10–15 minutes, until pale golden brown. Leave on the baking trays for 10 minutes, then transfer to wire racks to cool completely.

5 Sift the icing sugar, mix it with a little water to make a glacé icing, and use to ice the biscuits.

6 Decorate the iced biscuits with silver balls and tiny pieces of glacé cherries and angelica.

7 Store in an airtight container or wrap the biscuits individually in cellophane, tie them with coloured ribbon or string and then hang them on the Christmas tree as edible decorations.

Christmas Tree Clusters

Popcorn is the perfect nibble to have around at Christmas. If wrapped in cellophane, these clusters make ideal decorations for the Christmas tree.

NUTRITIONAL INFORMATION

Calories 94	Sugars 14g	
Protein 1g	Fat 4g	
Carbohydrate ...15g	Saturates 0.3g	

10 mins
10 mins

MAKES 16

INGREDIENTS

1 tbsp vegetable oil

25 g/1 oz popcorn kernels

25 g/1 oz butter

60 g/2 oz light brown sugar

4 tbsp golden syrup

25 g/1 oz glacé cherries, chopped

60 g/2 oz sultanas or raisins

25 g/1 oz ground almonds

15 g/½ oz nibbed almonds

½ tsp mixed spice

1 To pop the corn, heat the vegetable oil in a large saucepan or in a popcorn pan. The oil is hot enough when a kernel spins around in the pan. Add the popcorn kernels, cover tightly and pop the corn over a medium–high heat, shaking the pan frequently.

2 Remove the pan from the heat but do not remove the lid until the popping sound subsides.

3 Put the butter, sugar and syrup into a large saucepan and heat gently, stirring frequently, to dissolve the sugar. Do not allow the mixture to boil. Remove from the heat once the sugar is dissolved.

4 Add the popped corn, glacé cherries, sultanas or raisins, ground almonds and nibbed almonds and mixed spice to the syrup mixture, stirring well to coat the ingredients thoroughly. Set aside to cool for a few minutes.

5 Shape the mixture into small balls. Set the balls aside to cool completely, then wrap them in cellophane and tie with coloured ribbon or string and hang from the Christmas tree.

VARIATION
Omit the cherries, sultanas, ground almonds and mixed spice and replace with 60 g/2 oz roughly chopped pecan nuts and ½ tsp ground cinnamon to make Pecan Nut Clusters.

Christmas Rice Pancakes

These delicious pancakes are almost like little rice puddings scented with Christmas mincemeat. Serve them with a rum-flavoured custard.

NUTRITIONAL INFORMATION

Calories . . . . .121 Sugars 13g
Protein . . . . .2g Fat 5g
Carbohydrate . . .18g Saturates 2g

  15 mins, plus cooling 45 mins

MAKES ABOUT 24 PANCAKES

INGREDIENTS

700 ml/1¼ pints milk

salt

100 g/3½ oz long grain white rice

1 cinnamon stick

60 g/2¼oz sugar

40 g/1½oz plain flour

1 tsp baking powder

¾ tsp bicarbonate of soda

2 eggs, beaten

125 ml/4 fl oz soured cream

2 tbsp dark rum

1 tsp vanilla essence

½ tsp almond essence

2 tbsp butter, melted

350 g/12 oz homemade or bought vegetarian mincemeat

melted butter, for frying

ground cinnamon, for dusting

1 Bring the milk to the boil in a saucepan. Add a pinch of salt and sprinkle in the rice. Add the cinnamon stick and simmer gently for 35 minutes or until the rice is tender and the milk is almost absorbed.

2 Remove from the heat, add the sugar and stir until dissolved. Discard the cinnamon stick and pour into a large bowl. Cool, stirring occasionally, for about 30 minutes.

3 Combine the flour, baking powder, bicarbonate of soda and a pinch of salt and set aside. Beat the eggs with the soured cream, rum, vanilla and almond essences and the melted butter.

4 Whisk the egg mixture into the rice, then stir in the flour mixture until just blended; do not over-mix. Fold in the vegetarian mincemeat.

5 Heat a large frying pan or griddle, and brush with butter. Stir the batter and drop 2–3 tablespoons on to the pan. Cook for about 2 minutes until the undersides are golden and the tops covered with bubbles that burst open. Gently turn, cook for another minute. Keep warm.

6 Dust the pancakes lightly with cinnamon and serve on a warmed serving plate.

Chocolate Fudge Pudding

This fabulous steamed pudding, served with a rich chocolate fudge sauce, is perfect for cold winter days.

NUTRITIONAL INFORMATION

Calories 646	Sugars 43g	
Protein 10g	Fat 42g	
Carbohydrate ...62g	Saturates 16g	

10 mins 35–40 mins

SERVES 6

INGREDIENTS

150 g/5½ oz soft margarine

150 g/5½ oz self-raising flour

150 g/5½ oz golden syrup

3 eggs

25 g/1 oz cocoa powder

CHOCOLATE FUDGE SAUCE

100 g/3½ oz dark chocolate

125 ml/4 fl oz condensed milk

4 tbsp double cream

1 Lightly grease a 1.2 litre/2 pint pudding basin.

2 Place the ingredients for the sponge in a mixing bowl and beat until well combined and smooth.

3 Spoon into the prepared basin and level the top. Cover with a disc of baking paper and tie a pleated sheet of foil over the basin. Steam the pudding for 1½–2 hours until it is cooked through and springy to the touch.

4 To make the chocolate fudge sauce, break the chocolate into small pieces and place them in a small pan with the condensed milk. Heat gently, stirring, until the chocolate melts.

5 Remove the pan from the heat and stir in the double cream.

6 To serve the pudding, turn it out on to a warm serving plate and pour over a little of the chocolate fudge sauce to decorate. Serve the pudding warm, with the remaining sauce.

Coconut Cream Moulds

Smooth, creamy and refreshing – these tempting little custards are made with an unusual combination of coconut milk, cream and eggs.

NUTRITIONAL INFORMATION

Calories	288	Sugar	........24g
Protein	.........4g	Fat	..........20g
Carbohydrate	...25g	Saturates	......14g

 10 mins   45 mins

SERVES 8

INGREDIENTS

CARAMEL

125 g/4½ oz granulated sugar

150 ml/¼ pint water

CUSTARD

300 ml/½ pint water

90g/3 oz creamed coconut, chopped

2 eggs

2 egg yolks

1½ tbsp caster sugar

300 ml/½ pint single cream

sliced banana or slivers of fresh pineapple

1–2 tbsp freshly grated or desiccated coconut

1 Have ready 8 small ovenproof dishes about 150 ml/¼ pint capacity. To make the caramel, place the granulated sugar and water in a saucepan and heat gently to dissolve the sugar, then boil rapidly, without stirring, until the mixture turns a rich golden brown.

2 Immediately remove the pan from the heat and dip the base into a bowl of cold water to prevent the caramel cooking further. Quickly but carefully divide the caramel among the ovenproof dishes to coat the bases.

3 To make the custard, place the water in the same saucepan as you used for the caramel, add the coconut and heat, stirring constantly, until the coconut dissolves. Place the eggs, egg yolks and caster sugar in a bowl and beat well with a fork. Add the hot coconut milk and stir well to dissolve the sugar. Stir in the cream and strain the mixture into a jug.

4 Arrange the dishes in a roasting tin and fill with enough cold water to come halfway up the sides of the dishes.

Pour the custard mixture into the caramel-lined dishes, cover with greaseproof paper or foil and cook in a preheated oven, 150°C/300°F/Gas Mark 2, for about 40 minutes, or until set.

5 Remove the dishes, set aside to cool and then chill overnight. To serve, run a knife around the edge of each dish and turn out on to a serving plate. Serve with slices of banana or slivers of fresh pineapple sprinkled with freshly grated or desiccated coconut.

Raspberry Fool

This dish is very easy to make and can be prepared in advance and stored in the refrigerator until required.

NUTRITIONAL INFORMATION

Calories	288	Sugars	........19g
Protein	.........4g	Fat	.........22g
Carbohydrate	...19g	Saturates	......14g

1¼ hrs   0 mins

SERVES 4

I N G R E D I E N T S

300 g/10½ oz fresh raspberries

50 g/1¾ oz icing sugar

300 ml/½ pint crème fraîche

½ tsp vanilla essence

2 egg whites

fresh raspberries and lemon balm leaves,
  to decorate

1 Put the raspberries and icing sugar in a food processor or blender and process until smooth. Alternatively, press through a sieve with the back of a spoon.

2 Reserve 4 tablespoons of crème fraîche for decorating.

3 Put the vanilla essence and remaining crème fraîche in a bowl and stir in the raspberry mixture.

4 Whisk the egg whites in a separate mixing bowl until stiff peaks form. Gently fold the egg whites into the raspberry mixture using a metal spoon, until fully incorporated.

5 Spoon the raspberry fool into individual serving dishes and chill for at least 1 hour. Decorate with the reserved crème fraîche, raspberries and lemon balm leaves and serve.

COOK'S TIP
Although this dessert is best made with fresh raspberries in season, an acceptable result can be achieved with frozen raspberries, which are available from most supermarkets.

Cinnamon Pears

These spicy sweet pears are accompanied by a delicious melt-in-the-mouth cream, which is relatively low in fat.

NUTRITIONAL INFORMATION

Calories	190	Sugars	.......28g
Protein	.........6g	Fat	...........7g
Carbohydrate	...28g	Saturates	.......4g

10 mins   25 mins

SERVES 4

INGREDIENTS

1 lemon

4 firm ripe pears

300 ml/½ pint dry cider or
  unsweetened apple juice

1 cinnamon stick, broken in half

fresh mint leaves, to decorate

MAPLE RICOTTA CREAM

125 g/4½ oz ricotta cheese

125 g/4½ oz natural fromage frais

½ tsp ground cinnamon

½ tsp grated lemon rind

1 tbsp maple syrup

lemon rind, to decorate

1 Using a swivel vegetable peeler, remove the lemon rind and put it in a non-stick frying pan. Squeeze the lemon and pour the juice into a shallow bowl.

2 Peel, halve and core the pears. Toss them in the lemon juice to prevent them from discolouring. Add them to the frying pan and pour over the lemon juice remaining in the bowl.

3 Add the cider or apple juice and the cinnamon stick. Gently bring to the boil, then lower the heat and simmer for 10 minutes. Carefully remove the pears using a slotted spoon, and reserve the cooking juice. Put the pears in a warm heatproof serving dish, cover with foil and keep warm in a low oven.

4 Return the pan to the heat, bring to the boil, then simmer for about 8–10 minutes, until reduced by half. Spoon over the pears.

5 To make the maple ricotta cream, mix together all the ingredients. Decorate with lemon rind and serve with the pears.

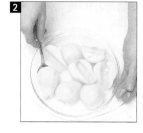

Poached Allspice Pears

These pears are moist and delicious after poaching in a sugar and allspice mixture. They are wonderful served hot or cold.

NUTRITIONAL INFORMATION

Calories	157	Sugars	........17g
Protein	.........5g	Fat	..........19g
Carbohydrate	...17g	Saturates	......12g

5 mins   15 mins

SERVES 4

INGREDIENTS

4 large ripe pears

300 ml/½ pint orange juice

2 tsp ground allspice

60 g/2 oz raisins

2 tbsp light brown sugar

grated orange rind, to decorate

1 Using an apple corer, core the pears. Using a sharp knife, peel the pears and cut them in half.

2 Place the pear halves in a large saucepan.

3 Add the orange juice, allspice, raisins and sugar to the pan and heat gently, stirring, until the sugar has dissolved. Bring the mixture to the boil for 1 minute.

4 Reduce the heat to low and leave to simmer for about 10 minutes, or until the pears are cooked, but still fairly firm – test them by inserting the tip of a small, sharp knife.

5 Remove the cooked pears from the saucepan with a slotted spoon and transfer to serving plates. Decorate with the grated orange rind and serve hot with the syrup.

COOK'S TIP

The Chinese do not usually have desserts to finish off a meal, except at banquets and special occasions. Sweet dishes are usually served in between main meals as snacks, but fruit is refreshing at the end of a big meal.

Panforte di Siena

This famous Tuscan honey and nut cake is a Christmas speciality. In Italy it is sold in pretty boxes, and served in very thin slices.

NUTRITIONAL INFORMATION

Calories 257	Sugars 29g	
Protein 5g	Fat 13g	
Carbohydrate ...33g	Saturates 1g	

10 mins   1¼ hrs

SERVES 12

INGREDIENTS

125 g/4½ oz almonds, halved

125 g/4½ oz hazelnuts

90 g/3 oz chopped mixed peel

60 g/2 oz no-soak dried apricots

60 g/2 oz glacé or crystallized pineapple

grated rind of 1 large orange

60 g/2 oz plain flour

2 tbsp cocoa powder

2 tsp ground cinnamon

125 g/4½ oz caster sugar

175 g/6 oz honey

icing sugar, for dredging

1 Toast the almonds under the grill until lightly browned, and place in a bowl.

2 Toast the hazelnuts until the skins split. Place on a dry tea towel and rub off the skins. Roughly chop the hazelnuts and add them to the almonds along with the mixed peel.

3 Chop the apricots and pineapple fairly finely, add to the nuts with the orange rind and mix well.

4 Sift the flour with the cocoa and cinnamon, add to the nut mixture; mix.

5 Line a round 20 cm/8 inch cake tin or deep loose-based flan tin with non-stick baking paper.

6 Put the sugar and honey into a saucepan and heat until the sugar dissolves, then boil gently for about 5 minutes or until the mixture thickens and begins to turn a deeper shade of brown. Quickly add to the nut mixture and stir well to mix evenly. Turn into the prepared tin and level the top using the back of a damp spoon.

7 Cook the cake in a preheated oven, at 150°C/300°F/Gas Mark 2, for 1 hour. Remove from the oven and leave in the tin until completely cold. Take out of the tin and carefully peel off the paper. Before serving, dredge the Panforte di Siena heavily with sifted icing sugar. Serve in very thin slices.

Steamed Coffee Sponge

This sponge pudding is very light and is delicious served with a coffee or chocolate sauce.

NUTRITIONAL INFORMATION

Calories 343   Sugars 21g
Protein . . . . .9g   Fat 12g
Carbohydrate . . .54g   Saturates 4g

 10 mins   1–1¼ hrs

SERVES 4

INGREDIENTS

2 tbsp margarine

2 tbsp soft brown sugar

2 eggs

5½ tbsp plain flour

¾ tsp baking powder

6 tbsp milk

1 tsp coffee essence

SAUCE

300 ml/½ pint milk

1 tbsp soft brown sugar

1 tsp cocoa powder

2 tbsp cornflour

4 tbsp cold water

1 Lightly grease a 600 ml/1 pint pudding basin. Cream the margarine and sugar until light and fluffy, then beat in the eggs.

2 Gradually stir in the flour and baking powder, then stir in the milk and coffee essence to make a smooth batter.

3 Spoon the mixture into the pudding basin and cover with a pleated piece of baking paper and then a pleated piece of foil, securing around the bowl with tightly tied string.

4 Place in a steamer or large pan half full of boiling water. Cover and steam for 1–1¼ hours or until the pudding is cooked through.

5 To make the sauce, put the milk, sugar and cocoa powder in a pan and heat until the sugar dissolves. Blend the cornflour with 4 tablespoons of cold water to a paste and stir into the pan. Bring the sauce to the boil, stirring until thickened. Cook over a gentle heat for 1 minute.

6 Turn the pudding out on to a warmed serving plate and spoon the sauce over the top. Serve immediately.

Rice & Banana Brûlée

Take a can of rice pudding, flavour it with orange rind, stem ginger, raisins and sliced bananas, and top with a brown sugar glaze.

NUTRITIONAL INFORMATION

Calories 509	Sugars 98g
Protein 9g	Fat 6g
Carbohydrate ...112g	Saturates 4g

🍈 🍈

🧊 50 mins   🕐 2–3 mins

SERVES 2

INGREDIENTS

400 g/14 oz canned creamed rice pudding

grated rind of ½ orange

2 pieces of stem ginger, finely chopped

2 tsp ginger syrup from the jar

40 g/1½ oz raisins

1–2 bananas

1–2 tsp lemon juice

4–5 tbsp demerara sugar

1 Empty the can of rice pudding into a bowl and stir in the grated orange rind, ginger, ginger syrup and raisins.

2 Cut the bananas diagonally into slices, toss them in the lemon juice to prevent them from discolouring, then drain and divide the slices between 2 individual flameproof dishes.

3 Spoon the rice mixture in an even layer over the bananas so that the dishes are almost full.

4 Sprinkle an even layer of sugar over the rice in each dish.

5 Place the dishes under a preheated moderate grill and heat until the sugar melts, watching carefully that the sugar does not burn.

6 Set aside to cool until the caramel sets, then chill in the refrigerator until ready to serve. Tap the caramel with the back of a spoon to break it.

COOK'S TIP

Canned rice pudding is very versatile and is delicious heated with orange segments and grated apples added. Try it served cold with grated chocolate and mixed chopped nuts stirred through it.

Indian Bread Pudding

This, the Indian equivalent of the English bread and butter pudding, is rather a special dessert, usually cooked for special occasions.

NUTRITIONAL INFORMATION

Calories	445	Sugars	........43g
Protein	........10g	Fat	..........20g
Carbohydrate	...60g	Saturates	......11g

20 mins   25 mins

SERVES 6

INGREDIENTS

6 slices white bread

5 tbsp ghee (preferably pure)

150 g/5½ oz sugar

300 ml/½ pint water

3 green cardamoms, without husks

600 ml/1 pint milk

175 ml/6 fl oz evaporated milk or
 khoya (see Cook's Tip)

good pinch saffron strands

double cream, to serve (optional)

TO DECORATE

8 pistachio nuts, soaked, peeled
 and chopped

chopped almonds

2 leaves varq (edible silver leaf, see page
 912) (optional)

1 Cut the bread slices into quarters. Heat the ghee in a large, heavy-based frying-pan. Add the bread slices and fry, turning once, until a crisp golden brown colour. Place the fried bread in the base of a heatproof dish and set aside.

2 To make a syrup, place the sugar, water and cardamom seeds in a saucepan and bring the mixture to the boil over a medium heat, stirring constantly, until the sugar has dissolved. Boil until the syrup thickens, then pour over the bread.

3 Put the milk, evaporated milk or khoya (see Cook's Tip) and the saffron in a separate saucepan and bring to the boil over a low heat. Simmer until it has halved in volume. Pour the mixture over the syrup-coated bread.

4 Decorate the pudding with the pistachios, chopped almonds and varq (if using). Serve the bread pudding with double cream, if liked.

COOK'S TIP

To make khoya, bring 900 ml/ 1½ pints milk to the boil in a large, heavy saucepan. Reduce the heat and boil, stirring occasionally, for 35–40 minutes, until reduced to a quarter of its volume and resembling a sticky dough.

Apple Fritters

These apple fritters are coated in a light, spiced batter and deep-fried until crisp and golden. Serve warm with an unusual almond sauce.

NUTRITIONAL INFORMATION

Calories ....438 Sugars 15g
Protein ....6g Fat 32g
Carbohydrate ...35g Saturates 4g

15 mins   15 mins

SERVES 4

INGREDIENTS

100 g/4 oz plain flour

pinch of salt

½ tsp ground cinnamon

175 ml/6 fl oz warm water

4 tsp vegetable oil

2 egg whites

2 dessert apples, peeled

vegetable or sunflower oil,
   for deep-frying

caster sugar and cinnamon,
   to decorate

SAUCE

150 ml/¼ pint natural yogurt

½ tsp almond essence

2 tsp clear honey

1 Sift the flour and salt together into a large mixing bowl.

2 Add the cinnamon and mix well. Stir in the warm water and vegetable oil to make a smooth batter.

3 Whisk the egg whites until stiff peaks form and fold into the batter.

4 Using a sharp knife, cut the apples into chunks and dip the pieces of apple into the batter to coat.

5 Heat the oil for deep-frying to 180°C/350°F or until a cube of bread browns in 30 seconds. Fry the apple pieces, in batches if necessary, for about 3–4 minutes until they are light golden brown and puffy.

6 Remove the apple fritters from the oil with a slotted spoon and drain on absorbent kitchen paper.

7 Mix together the caster sugar and the cinnamon and sprinkle over the warm fritters.

8 Mix the sauce ingredients in a serving bowl and serve with the fritters.

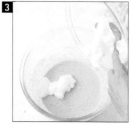

Fruit Crumble

Any fruits in season can be used in this wholesome pudding. It is suitable for vegans as it contains no dairy produce.

NUTRITIONAL INFORMATION

Calories	426	Sugars	........37g
Protein	.........8g	Fat	..........16g
Carbohydrate	...67g	Saturates	.......4g

 10 mins   30 mins

SERVES 6

I N G R E D I E N T S

vegan margarine, for greasing

6 pears, peeled, cored, quartered and sliced

1 tbsp chopped stem ginger

1 tbsp dark muscovado sugar

2 tbsp orange juice

T O P P I N G

175 g/6 oz plain flour

75 g/2¾ oz vegan margarine, cut into small pieces

25 g/1 oz flaked almonds

25 g/1 oz porridge oats

50 g/1¾ oz dark muscovado sugar

soya custard, to serve

1 Lightly grease a 1 litre/2 pint ovenproof dish with vegan margarine.

2 Mix together the pears, ginger, muscovado sugar and orange juice in a large bowl. Spoon the mixture into the prepared dish.

3 To make the crumble topping, sift the flour into a mixing bowl. Add the margarine and rub in with your fingertips until the mixture resembles fine breadcrumbs. Stir in the flaked almonds, porridge oats and muscovado sugar. Mix until well combined.

4 Sprinkle the crumble topping evenly over the pear and ginger mixture in the dish.

5 Bake in a preheated oven, 190°C/ 375°F/Gas Mark 5, for 30 minutes, until the topping is golden and the fruit tender. Serve with soya custard, if using.

VARIATION

Stir 1 tsp ground mixed spice into the crumble mixture in step 3 for added flavour, if you prefer.

Baked Coconut Rice Pudding

A wonderful baked rice pudding cooked with flavoursome coconut milk and a little lime rind. Serve hot or chilled with fresh or stewed fruit.

NUTRITIONAL INFORMATION

Calories	.211	Sugars	.27g
Protein	.5g	Fat	.2g
Carbohydrate	.46g	Saturates	.1g

 5 mins   2½ hrs

SERVES 4–6

INGREDIENTS

90 g/3 oz short or round-grain pudding rice

600 ml/1 pint coconut milk

300 ml/½ pint milk

1 large strip lime rind

60 g/2 oz caster sugar

knob of butter

pinch of ground star anise (optional)

fresh or stewed fruit, to serve

1 Lightly grease a 1.5 litre/2½ pint shallow ovenproof dish.

2 Mix the pudding rice with the coconut milk, milk, lime rind and caster sugar until all the ingredients are well blended.

3 Pour the rice mixture into the greased ovenproof dish and dot the surface with a little butter. Bake in the oven for about 30 minutes.

4 Remove the dish from the oven. Remove and discard the strip of lime from the rice pudding.

5 Stir the pudding well, add the pinch of ground star anise, if using, return to the oven and cook for a further 1–2 hours or until almost all the milk has been absorbed and a golden brown skin has baked on the top of the pudding. Cover the top of the pudding with foil if it starts to brown too much towards the end of the cooking time.

6 Serve the baked coconut rice pudding warm, or chilled if you prefer, with fresh or stewed fruit.

Chocolate Mousse

This is a light and fluffy mousse with a subtle hint of orange. It is wickedly delicious served with a fresh fruit sauce.

NUTRITIONAL INFORMATION

Calories 164   Sugars 24g
Protein ....5g   Fat 5g
Carbohydrate ...25g   Saturates 3g

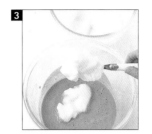

2¼ hrs   5 mins

SERVES 8

INGREDIENTS

100 g/3½ oz plain chocolate, melted

300 ml/10 fl oz natural yogurt

150 ml/5 fl oz quark

4 tbsp caster sugar

1 tbsp orange juice

1 tbsp brandy

1½ tsp gelozone (vegetarian gelatine)

9 tbsp cold water

2 large egg whites

TO DECORATE

roughly grated dark and white chocolate

orange rind

1 Put the melted chocolate, yogurt, quark, sugar, orange juice and brandy in a food processor or blender and process for 30 seconds. Transfer the mixture to a large bowl.

2 Sprinkle the gelozone over the water and stir until dissolved, then bring the mixture to the boil for 2 minutes. Cool slightly, then stir the gelozone into the chocolate mixture.

3 Whisk the egg whites until stiff peaks form and fold into the chocolate mixture using a metal spoon.

4 Line a 500 g/1 lb loaf tin with clingfilm. Spoon the mousse into the tin and chill in the refrigerator for 2 hours until set. When you are ready to serve the mousse, turn it out carefully on to a serving plate and decorate with the grated chocolate and orange rind.

COOK'S TIP

For a quick fruit sauce, process a can of mandarin segments in natural juice in a food processor and press through a strainer. Stir in 1 tablespoon clear honey and serve with the mousse.

Quick Syrup Sponge

You won't believe your eyes when you see just how quickly this light-as-air sponge pudding cooks in the microwave oven!

NUTRITIONAL INFORMATION

Calories 650	Sugars 60g
Protein 10g	Fat 31g
Carbohydrate ...89g	Saturates 7g

 15 mins 🕐 5 mins

SERVES 4

INGREDIENTS

125 g/4½ oz butter or margarine

4 tbsp golden syrup

90 g/3 oz caster sugar

2 eggs

125 g/4½ oz self-raising flour

1 tsp baking powder

about 2 tbsp warm water

custard, to serve

1 Grease a 1.5 litre/2½ pint pudding basin with a small amount of the butter or margarine. Spoon the syrup into the basin.

2 Cream the remaining butter or margarine with the sugar until light and fluffy. Gradually add the eggs, beating well after each addition.

3 Sift the flour and baking powder together, then fold into the creamed mixture using a large metal spoon. Add enough water to give a soft, dropping consistency. Spoon into the pudding basin and level the surface.

4 Cover with microwave-safe film, leaving a small space to allow air to escape. Microwave on HIGH power for 4 minutes, then remove the pudding from the microwave and allow it to stand for 5 minutes, while it continues to cook.

5 Turn the pudding out on to a warm serving plate. Serve with custard.

COOK'S TIP

If you don't have a microwave, this pudding can be steamed. Cover the basin with a piece of pleated baking paper and a piece of pleated foil. Place in a saucepan, add boiling water and steam for 1½ hours.

Mixed Fruit Crumble

In this crumble, tropical fruits are flavoured with ginger and coconut, for something a little different and very tasty.

NUTRITIONAL INFORMATION

Calories	602	Sugars	........51g
Protein	.........6g	Fat	..........29g
Carbohydrate	...84g	Saturates	......11g

10 mins   50 mins

SERVES 4

INGREDIENTS

2 mangoes, sliced

1 pawpaw, seeded and sliced

225 g/8 oz fresh pineapple, cubed

1½ tsp ground ginger

100 g/3½ oz margarine

100 g/3½ oz light brown sugar

175 g/6 oz plain flour

55 g/2 oz desiccated coconut, plus extra
   to decorate

1 Place the fruit in a pan with ½ teaspoon of the ground ginger, 2 tablespoons of the margarine and 4 tablespoons of the sugar. Cook over a low heat for 10 minutes until the fruit softens. Spoon the fruit into the base of a shallow ovenproof dish.

2 Combine the flour and remaining ginger. Rub in the remaining margarine until the mixture resembles fine breadcrumbs. Stir in the remaining sugar and the coconut and spoon over the fruit to cover completely.

3 Cook the crumble in a preheated oven, 180°C/350°F/Gas Mark 4, for about 40 minutes or until the top is crisp. Decorate with a sprinkling of desiccated coconut and serve.

Saffron-spiced Rice Pudding

This rich pudding is cooked in milk delicately flavoured with saffron, then mixed with dried fruit, almonds and cream before baking.

NUTRITIONAL INFORMATION

Calories	339	Sugars	........28g
Protein	.........9g	Fat	..........16g
Carbohydrate	...41g	Saturates	.......9g

    5 mins   1 hr

SERVES 4

INGREDIENTS

600 ml/1 pint creamy milk

several pinches of saffron strands,
   finely crushed (see Cook's Tip)

60 g/2 oz pudding rice

1 cinnamon stick or piece of cassia bark

40 g/1½ oz sugar

25 g/1 oz seedless raisins or sultanas

25 g/1 oz ready-to-eat dried
   apricots, chopped

1 egg, beaten

5 tbsp single cream

15 g/½ oz butter, diced

15 g/½ oz flaked almonds

freshly grated nutmeg, for sprinkling

cream, for serving (optional)

1 Place the milk and crushed saffron in a non-stick saucepan and bring to the boil. Stir in the rice and cinnamon stick, reduce the heat and simmer very gently, uncovered, stirring frequently, for 25 minutes, until tender.

2 Remove the pan from the heat. Remove and discard the cinnamon stick from the rice mixture. Stir in the sugar, the raisins or sultanas and the dried apricots, then beat in the egg, cream and diced butter.

3 Transfer the mixture to a greased ovenproof pie or flan dish and sprinkle with the flaked almonds and freshly grated nutmeg to taste. Cook in a preheated oven, 180°C/350°F/Gas Mark 4, for about 25–30 minutes, until the mixture is set and lightly golden. Serve the pudding hot with extra cream, if wished.

COOK'S TIP

For a slightly stronger flavour, place the saffron strands on a small piece of kitchen foil and toast them lightly under a hot grill for a few moments and then crush between your fingers and thumb.

Passion Cake

Decorating this moist, rich carrot cake with sugared flowers lifts it into the celebration class. It is a perfect choice for Easter.

NUTRITIONAL INFORMATION

Calories	...506	Sugars	...40g
Protein	...10g	Fat	...27g
Carbohydrate	...60g	Saturates	...4g

 15 mins 1½ hrs

SERVES 10

I N G R E D I E N T S

150 ml/¼ pint corn oil

175 g/6 oz golden caster sugar

4 tbsp natural yogurt

3 eggs, plus 1 extra yolk

1 tsp vanilla essence

125 g/4 oz walnut pieces, chopped

175 g/6 oz carrots, grated

1 banana, mashed

175 g/6 oz plain flour

90 g/3 oz fine oatmeal

1 tsp bicarbonate of soda

1 tsp baking powder

1 tsp ground cinnamon

½ tsp salt

F R O S T I N G

150 g/5½ oz soft cheese

4 tbsp natural yogurt

90 g/3 oz icing sugar

1 tsp grated lemon rind

2 tsp lemon juice

D E C O R A T I O N

primroses and violets

1 egg white, lightly beaten

40 g/1½ oz caster sugar

1 **Grease and line** a 23 cm/9 inch round cake tin. Beat together the oil, sugar, yogurt, eggs, egg yolk and vanilla essence. Beat in the chopped walnuts, grated carrot and banana.

2 **Sift together** the remaining cake ingredients and gradually beat into the mixture.

3 **Pour the mixture** into the tin and level the surface. Bake in a preheated oven, 180°C/350°F/Gas Mark 4, for 1½ hours, or until the cake is firm. Leave to cool in the tin for 15 minutes, then turn out on to a wire rack.

4 **To make the frosting,** beat together the soft cheese and the yogurt. Sift in the icing sugar and stir in the lemon rind and juice. Spread the frosting over the top and sides of the cake.

5 **To prepare** the decoration, dip the flowers quickly in the beaten egg white, then sprinkle with caster sugar to cover the surface completely. Place well apart on baking parchment.

6 **Leave the flowers** in a warm, dry place for several hours until they are dry and crisp, then arrange them in a pattern on top of the cake.

Indian Vermicelli Pudding

Indian vermicelli, which is very fine, is delicious cooked in milk and ghee. Muslims make this for a religious festival called Eid.

NUTRITIONAL INFORMATION

Calories	397	Sugars	........42g
Protein	........11g	Fat	..........17g
Carbohydrate	...54g	Saturates	.......8g

5 mins   20 mins

SERVES 6

I N G R E D I E N T S

25 g/1 oz pistachio nuts (optional)

25 g/1 oz flaked almonds

3 tbsp ghee

100 g/3½ oz seviyan (Indian vermicelli)

850 ml/1½ pints milk

175 ml/6 fl oz evaporated milk

8 tbsp sugar

6 dried dates, pitted

1 Soak the pistachio nuts (if using) in a bowl of water for at least 3 hours. Peel the pistachios and mix them with the flaked slivered almonds. Chop the nuts finely and set aside.

2 Melt the ghee in a large saucepan and lightly fry the seviyan. Reduce the heat immediately (the seviyan will turn golden very quickly so be careful not to burn it), and if necessary remove the pan from the heat (do not worry if some bits are a little darker than others).

3 Add the milk to the seviyan and bring to the boil over a low heat, taking care that it does not boil over.

4 Add the evaporated milk, sugar and dates to the mixture in the pan. Simmer over a low heat, uncovered, stirring occasionally, for about 10 minutes. When the consistency starts to thicken, pour the pudding into a warmed serving bowl.

5 Decorate the pudding with the chopped pistachio nuts (if using) and the flaked almonds.

COOK'S TIP

You will find seviyan (Indian vermicelli) in Indian foodstores. This dessert can be served warm or cold.

Bread & Butter Pudding

Everyone has their own favourite recipe for this dish. This one has added marmalade and grated apples for a really rich and unique taste.

NUTRITIONAL INFORMATION

Calories 427   Sugars 63g
Protein . . . . .9g   Fat 13g
Carbohydrate . . .74g   Saturates 7g

45 mins   1 hr

SERVES 6

INGREDIENTS

5 tbsp butter, softened

4–5 slices of white or brown bread

4 tbsp chunky orange marmalade

grated rind of 1 lemon

85–125 g/3–4½ oz raisins or sultanas

40 g/1½ oz chopped mixed peel

1 tsp ground cinnamon or mixed spice

1 Bramley apple, peeled, cored and
    coarsely grated

85 g/3 oz light brown sugar

3 eggs

500 ml/18 fl oz milk

2 tbsp demerara sugar

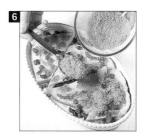

1 Use the butter to grease an ovenproof dish lightly and to spread on the slices of bread, then spread the bread with the marmalade.

2 Place a layer of bread in the base of the dish and sprinkle with the lemon rind, half the raisins or sultanas, half the mixed peel, half the spice, all of the apple and half the light brown sugar.

3 Add another layer of bread, cutting the slices so that they fit the dish.

4 Sprinkle over most of the remaining raisins or sultanas and the remaining peel, spice and light brown sugar, sprinkling it evenly over the bread. Top with a final layer of bread, again cutting to fit the dish.

5 Lightly beat together the eggs and milk and then carefully strain the mixture over the bread in the dish. If you have enough time to spare, set the pudding aside to stand for 20–30 minutes.

6 Sprinkle the top of the pudding with the demerara sugar and scatter over the remaining raisins or sultanas. Cook in a preheated oven, 200°C/400°F/Gas Mark 6, for 50–60 minutes, until risen and golden.

7 Serve immediately if serving hot or cool completely and serve cold.

Apricot Brûlée

Serve this melt-in-the-mouth dessert with crisp-baked meringues for an extra-special occasion.

NUTRITIONAL INFORMATION

Calories . . . . .307 Sugars 38g
Protein . . . . .5g Fat 16g
Carbohydrate . . .38g Saturates 9g

2¼ hrs   35 mins

SERVES 6

INGREDIENTS

125 g/4½ oz unsulphured dried apricots

150 ml/¼ pint orange juice

4 egg yolks

2 tbsp caster sugar

150 ml/¼ pint natural yogurt

150 ml/¼ pint double cream

1 tsp vanilla essence

90 g/3 oz demerara sugar

meringues, to serve (optional)

1 Place the apricots and orange juice in a bowl and set aside to soak for at least 1 hour. Pour into a small pan, bring slowly to the boil and simmer for 20 minutes. Process in a blender or food processor or chop very finely and push through a sieve.

2 Beat together the egg yolks and sugar until the mixture is light and fluffy. Place the yogurt in a small pan, add the cream and vanilla and bring to the boil over a low heat.

3 Pour the yogurt mixture over the eggs, beating all the time, then transfer to the top of a double boiler or place the bowl over a pan of simmering water. Stir until the custard thickens. Transfer the apricot mixture into 6 ramekins and carefully pour on the custard. Cool, then chill in the refrigerator at least 1 hour.

4 Sprinkle the demerara sugar evenly over the custard and place under a preheated grill until the sugar caramelizes. Set aside to cool. To serve the brûlée, crack the hard caramel topping with the back of a tablespoon.

Spiced Steamed Pudding

Steamed puddings are irresistible on a winter's day, but the texture of this pudding is so light it can be served throughout the year.

NUTRITIONAL INFORMATION

Calories	488	Sugars	........56g
Protein	.........5g	Fat	..........19g
Carbohydrate	...78g	Saturates	.......4g

 15 mins   1½ hrs

SERVES 6

INGREDIENTS

2 tbsp golden syrup, plus extra to serve

125 g/4½ oz butter or margarine

125 g/4½ oz caster or light brown sugar

2 eggs

175 g/6 oz self-raising flour

¾ tsp ground cinnamon or mixed spice

grated rind of 1 orange

1 tbsp orange juice

90 g/3 oz sultanas

40 g/1½ oz stem ginger, finely chopped

1 eating apple, peeled, cored and
    coarsely grated

1 Thoroughly grease a 850 ml/1½ pint pudding basin. Put the golden syrup into the basin.

2 Cream the butter or margarine and sugar together until very light and fluffy and pale in colour. Beat in the eggs, one at a time, following each with a spoonful of the flour.

3 Sift the remaining flour with the cinnamon or mixed spice and fold into the mixture, followed by the orange rind and juice. Fold in the sultanas, then the ginger and apple.

4 Turn the mixture into the pudding basin and level the top. Cover with a piece of pleated, greased baking paper, tucking the edges under the rim of the basin.

5 Cover with a sheet of pleated foil. Tie securely in place with string, with a piece of string tied over the top of the basin for a handle to make it easy to lift out of the saucepan.

6 Put the pudding basin into a saucepan half-filled with boiling water, cover and steam for 1½ hours, adding more boiling water to the pan as necessary during cooking.

7 To serve the spiced steamed pudding, remove the foil and the baking paper, turn the pudding out on to a warmed serving plate, and serve at once in slices with extra golden syrup.

Pistachio Dessert

Rather an attractive-looking dessert, especially when decorated with mint leaves, this is a dish that can be prepared in advance.

NUTRITIONAL INFORMATION

Calories ....676　Sugars 98g
Protein ....15g　Fat 27g
Carbohydrate ...98g　Saturates 9g

 15 mins　 10 mins

SERVES 6

INGREDIENTS

850 ml/1½ pints water

225 g/8 oz pistachio nuts

225 g/8 oz powdered milk

500 g/1 lb 2 oz sugar

2 cardamom pods, with seeds removed and crushed

2 tbsp rosewater

a few strands of saffron

TO DECORATE

fresh mint leaves

1 Put about 1 pint/600 ml water in a saucepan and bring to the boil. Remove the pan from the heat and soak the pistachios in this water for about 5 minutes. Drain the pistachios thoroughly and remove the skins.

COOK'S TIP

It is best to buy whole pistachio nuts and grind them yourself, rather than using packets of ready-ground nuts. Freshly ground nuts have the best flavour, as grinding releases their natural oils.

2 Process the pistachios in a food processor or grind them in a mortar with a pestle.

3 Add the powdered milk to the ground pistachios and mix well.

4 To make the syrup, place the remaining water and the sugar in a pan and heat gently. When the liquid begins to thicken, add the cardamom seeds, rosewater and saffron.

5 Add the syrup to the pistachio mixture and cook, stirring constantly, for about 5 minutes, until the mixture thickens. Set the mixture aside to cool slightly.

6 Once the mixture is cool enough to handle, roll it into balls in the palms of your hands.

7 Decorate with the fresh mint leaves and leave to set before serving.

Upside-down Cake

Margarine and oil are used instead of butter and eggs in this recipe for a classic favourite – and the result is every bit as delicious.

NUTRITIONAL INFORMATION

Calories	354	Sugars	........31g
Protein	.........3g	Fat	..........15g
Carbohydrate	...56g	Saturates	.......2g

 15 mins   50 mins

SERVES 4

INGREDIENTS

4 tbsp margarine, cut into small pieces, plus extra for greasing

425 g/15 oz canned unsweetened pineapple pieces in fruit juice, drained, with the juice reserved

4 tsp cornflour

50 g/2 oz soft brown sugar

125 ml/4 fl oz water

rind of 1 lemon

SPONGE

3½ tbsp sunflower oil

75 g/2¾ oz soft brown sugar

150 ml/5 fl oz water

150 g/5½ oz plain flour

2 tsp baking powder

1 tsp ground cinnamon

1 Grease a deep 18 cm/7 inch cake tin. Mix the reserved juice from the pineapple with the cornflour until it forms a smooth paste. Put the paste in a saucepan with the sugar, margarine and water and stir over a low heat until the sugar has dissolved. Bring to the boil and simmer for 2–3 minutes until thickened. Set aside to cool slightly.

2 To make the sponge, place the oil, sugar and water in a saucepan. Heat gently until the sugar has dissolved, but do not allow it to boil. Remove from the heat and leave to cool. Sift the flour, baking powder and ground cinnamon into a mixing bowl. Pour over the cooled sugar syrup and beat well to form a batter.

3 Arrange the pineapple pieces and the lemon rind on the base of the prepared tin and pour over 4 tablespoons of the pineapple syrup. Spoon the sponge batter on top.

4 Bake in a preheated oven, 180°C/ 350°F/Gas Mark 4, for 35–40 minutes until set and a fine metal skewer inserted into the centre comes out clean. Invert on to a plate, leave to stand for 5 minutes, then remove the tin. Serve the pudding with the remaining syrup.

Caramelized Oranges

The secret of these oranges is to allow them to marinate in the syrup for at least 24 hours, so the flavours amalgamate.

NUTRITIONAL INFORMATION

Calories	235	Sugars	.......59g
Protein	.........2g	Fat	..........0.2g
Carbohydrate	...59g	Saturates	.......0g

3¼ hrs   20 mins

SERVES 6

INGREDIENTS

6 large oranges

225 g/8 oz sugar

250 ml/9 fl oz water

6 whole cloves (optional)

2–4 tbsp orange-flavoured liqueur
  or brandy

1 Using a citrus zester or potato peeler, pare the rind from 2 of the oranges in narrow strips without any white pith attached. If using a potato peeler, cut the peel into very thin strips.

2 Put the strips into a small saucepan and barely cover with water. Bring to the boil and simmer for 5 minutes. Drain the strips and reserve the water.

3 Cut away all the white pith and peel from the remaining oranges using a very sharp knife. Then cut horizontally into 4 slices. Reassemble the oranges and hold in place with wooden cocktail sticks. Stand in a heatproof dish.

4 Put the sugar and water into a heavy-based saucepan with the cloves, if using. Bring to the boil and simmer gently until the sugar has dissolved, then boil hard without stirring until the syrup thickens and begins to colour. Continue to cook until a light golden brown, then remove from the heat and carefully pour in the reserved orange rind liquid.

5 Place over a gentle heat until the caramel has fully dissolved again, then remove from the heat and add the liqueur or brandy. Pour over the oranges.

6 Sprinkle the orange strips over the oranges, cover with cling film and leave until cold. Chill for at least 3 hours and preferably for 24–48 hours before serving. If time allows, spoon the syrup over the oranges several times while they are marinating. Discard the cocktail stick before serving the oranges.

Cherry Clafoutis

This is a hot dessert that is simple and quick to put together. Try the batter with other fruits. Apricots and plums are particularly delicious.

NUTRITIONAL INFORMATION

Calories 261   Sugars 24g
Protein . . . . .10g   Fat 6g
Carbohydrate . . .40g   Saturates 3g

🍽 10 mins   🕐 40 mins

SERVES 6

INGREDIENTS

125 g/4½ oz plain flour

4 eggs, lightly beaten

2 tbsp caster sugar

pinch of salt

600 ml/1 pint milk

butter, for greasing

500 g/1 lb 2 oz black cherries, fresh or canned, stoned

3 tbsp brandy

1 tbsp sugar, to decorate

3 Thoroughly grease a 1.75 litre/3 pint ovenproof serving dish with butter and pour in about half of the batter.

4 Spoon over the cherries and pour the remaining batter over the top. Sprinkle the brandy over the batter.

5 Bake in a preheated oven, 180°C/350°F/Gas Mark 4, for 40 minutes, until risen and golden.

6 Remove from the oven and sprinkle over the sugar just before serving. Serve the clafoutis warm.

1 Sift the plain flour into a large mixing bowl. Make a well in the centre and add the eggs, sugar and salt. Gradually draw in the flour from around the edges and whisk.

2 Pour in the milk and whisk the batter thoroughly until very smooth.

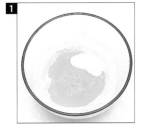

Sweet Saffron Rice

This exotic dessert, which is quick and easy to make, looks very impressive decorated with pistachio nuts and edible silver.

NUTRITIONAL INFORMATION

Calories 460	Sugars 57g
Protein 4g	Fat 9g
Carbohydrate ...97g	Saturates 5g

5 mins   35 mins

SERVES 4

INGREDIENTS

200 g/7 oz basmati rice

200 g/7 oz sugar

1 pinch saffron strands

300 ml/½ pint water

2 tbsp vegetable ghee

3 cloves

3 cardamom pods

25 g/1 oz sultanas

TO DECORATE

a few pistachio nuts (optional)

varq (edible silver leaf, see page 912) (optional)

1 Rinse the rice twice and bring to the boil in a saucepan of water, stirring constantly. Remove the pan from the heat when the rice is half-cooked, drain the rice thoroughly and set aside.

2 In a separate saucepan, boil the sugar and saffron in the water, stirring constantly, until the syrup thickens. Set the syrup aside until required.

3 In another saucepan, heat the ghee with the cloves and cardamoms, stirring occasionally. Remove the pan from the heat.

4 Return the rice to a low heat and stir in the sultanas.

5 Pour the syrup over the rice mixture and stir to mix.

6 Pour the ghee mixture over the rice and simmer over a low heat for about 10–15 minutes. Check to see whether the rice is cooked. If it is not, add a little boiling water, cover and continue to simmer until tender.

7 Serve warm, decorated with pistachio nuts and varq (silver leaf), if desired.

COOK'S TIP

Basmati rice is the 'prince of rices' and comes from the foothills of the Himalayas. Basmati means 'fragrant' and this rice has a superb texture and flavour.

Traditional Apple Pie

This apple pie has a double crust and can be served either hot or cold.
The apples can be flavoured with other spices or grated citrus rind.

NUTRITIONAL INFORMATION

Calories 577   Sugars 36g
Protein . . . . .6g   Fat 28g
Carbohydrate . . .80g   Saturates 9g

 55 mins   50 mins

SERVES 6

I N G R E D I E N T S

750 g–1 kg/1 lb 10 oz–2 lb 4 oz Bramley
apples, peeled, cored and sliced

about 125 g/4½ oz brown or white sugar,
plus extra for sprinkling

½–1 tsp ground cinnamon, mixed spice
or ground ginger

1–2 tbsp water

S H O R T C R U S T   P A S T R Y

350 g/12 oz plain flour

pinch of salt

90 g/3 oz butter or margarine

90 g/3 oz white vegetable fat

about 6 tbsp cold water

beaten egg or milk, for glazing

1 To make the pastry, sift the plain flour and salt into a large mixing bowl. Add the butter or margarine and white vegetable fat and rub in with the fingertips until the mixture resembles fine breadcrumbs. Add the water to the mixture and gather the ingredients together into a dough. Wrap the dough in kitchen foil and chill for around 30 minutes.

2 Roll out almost two-thirds of the pastry thinly and use it to line a 20–23 cm/8–9 inch deep pie plate or shallow pie tin.

3 Mix the cooking apples with the brown or white sugar and spice in a mixing bowl and pack into the pastry case; the filling can come up above the rim of the pastry in the pie plate. Add the water if liked, particularly if the cooking apples are a dry variety.

4 Roll out the remaining pastry to form a lid for the pie. Dampen the edges of the pie rim with water and position the lid, pressing the edges firmly together with your fingers. Trim the edges and crimp them decoratively.

5 Use the trimmings to cut out leaves or other shapes to decorate the top of the pie, dampen and attach. Glaze the top of the pie with beaten egg or milk, make 1–2 slits in the top and put the pie on a baking sheet.

6 Bake in a preheated oven, 220°C/ 425°F/Gas Mark 7, for 20 minutes, then reduce the temperature to 180°C/ 350°F/Gas Mark 4 and cook for about 30 minutes, until the pastry is a light golden brown. Serve the pie hot or cold, sprinkled with sugar.

Lemon & Lime Syllabub

This dessert is rich but absolutely delicious. It is not, however, for the calorie conscious as it contains a high proportion of cream.

NUTRITIONAL INFORMATION

Calories	403	Sugars	........16g
Protein	.........2g	Fat	..........36g
Carbohydrate	...16g	Saturates	......22g

 4¼ hrs   0 mins

SERVES 4

INGREDIENTS

50 g/1¾ oz caster sugar

grated rind and juice of 1 small lemon

grated rind and juice of 1 small lime

50 ml/2 fl oz Marsala or medium sherry

300 ml/½ pint double cream

lime and lemon rind, to decorate

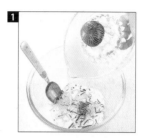

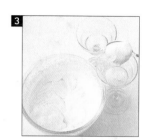

1 Put the caster sugar, the lemon juice and rind, the lime juice and rind and the Marsala or sherry in a bowl, mix well and set aside to infuse for 2 hours.

2 Add the double cream to the fruit juice mixture and whisk until it just holds its shape.

3 Spoon the mixture into 4 tall serving glasses and chill in the refrigerator for at least 2 hours.

4 Decorate the syllabub with lime and lemon rind and serve.

Fruity Pancake Bundles

These unusual pancakes are filled with a sweet cream flavoured with ginger, nuts and apricots and served with a raspberry and orange sauce.

NUTRITIONAL INFORMATION

Calories	610	Sugars	. . . . .60g
Protein	. . . . .19g	Fat	. . . . .20g
Carbohydrate	. . .94g	Saturates	. . . . . . .5g

15 mins   35 mins

SERVES 2

I N G R E D I E N T S

B A T T E R

55 g/2 oz plain flour

pinch of salt

¼ tsp ground cinnamon

1 egg

135 ml/4½ fl oz milk

white vegetable fat, for frying

F I L L I N G

1½ tsp plain flour, sifted

1½ tsp cornflour

1 tbsp caster sugar

1 egg

150 ml/5 fl oz milk

4 tbsp chopped nuts

40 g/1½ oz ready-to-eat dried apricots, chopped

1 piece of stem or crystallised ginger, finely chopped

S A U C E

3 tbsp raspberry preserve

5 tsp orange juice

finely grated rind of ¼ orange

1 To make the batter, sift the flour, salt and cinnamon into a bowl and make a well in the centre. Add the egg and milk and gradually beat in until smooth.

2 Melt a little fat in a medium frying pan. Pour in half the batter. Cook for 2 minutes until golden, then turn and cook the other side for about 1 minute until browned. Set aside and make a second pancake.

3 For the filling, beat the flour with the cornflour, sugar and egg. Gently heat the milk in a pan, then beat 2 tablespoons of it into the flour mixture. Transfer to the pan and cook gently, stirring constantly until thick. Remove from the heat, cover with baking paper to prevent a skin from forming and set aside to cool.

4 Beat the chopped nuts, apricots and ginger into the cooled mixture and put a heaped tablespoonful in the centre of each pancake. Gather and squeeze the edges together to make a bundle. Place in an ovenproof dish and bake in a preheated oven, 180°C/350°F/Gas Mark 4, for about 15–20 minutes until the pancakes are hot but not too brown.

5 To make the sauce, melt the preserve gently with the orange juice, then strain. Return to a clean pan with the orange rind and heat through. Serve with the pancakes.

Rice Pudding

Indian rice pudding is cooked in a saucepan over a low heat, rather than in the oven like the British version.

NUTRITIONAL INFORMATION

Calories 152   Sugars 23g
Protein ....5g   Fat 3g
Carbohydrate ...29g   Saturates 1g

10 mins   30 mins

SERVES 10

INGREDIENTS

75 g/2¾ oz basmati rice

1.2 litres/2 pints milk

8 tbsp sugar

varq (edible silver leaf) or chopped pistachio nuts, to decorate

1 Rinse the rice and place in a large saucepan. Add 600 ml/1 pint of the milk and bring to the boil over a very low heat.

2 Cook, stirring occasionally, until the milk has been completely absorbed by the rice.

3 Remove the pan from the heat. Mash the rice, making swift, round movements in the pan, for at least 5 minutes, until all of the lumps have been removed.

4 Gradually add the remaining 600 ml/1 pint milk. Bring to the boil again over a low heat, stirring occasionally.

5 Add the sugar and continue to cook, stirring constantly, for about 7–10 minutes, or until the mixture is quite thick in consistency.

6 Transfer the rice pudding to a heatproof serving bowl. Decorate with varq (edible silver leaf) or chopped pistachio nuts and serve on its own or with pooris.

COOK'S TIP

Varq is edible silver that is used to decorate elaborate dishes prepared for special occasions and celebrations in India. It is pure silver that has been beaten until it is wafer thin. It comes with a backing paper that is peeled off as the varq is laid on the cooked food.

Chocolate Tofu Cheesecake

This cheesecake takes a little time to prepare and cook but is well worth the effort. It is quite rich and is good served with a little fresh fruit.

NUTRITIONAL INFORMATION

Calories 471
Sugars 20g
Protein 10g
Fat 33g
Carbohydrate . . .28g
Saturates 5g

 1¼ hrs   1–1¼ hrs

SERVES 12

INGREDIENTS

100 g/3½ oz plain flour

100 g/3½ oz ground almonds

200 g/7 oz muscovado sugar

150 g/5½ oz margarine

675 g/1 lb 8 oz firm tofu

175 ml/6 fl oz vegetable oil

125 ml/4 fl oz orange juice

175 ml/6 fl oz brandy

6 tbsp cocoa powder, plus extra to decorate

2 tsp almond essence

TO DECORATE

icing sugar

Cape gooseberries

1 Put the flour, ground almonds and 1 tablespoon of the sugar in a bowl and mix well. Rub the margarine into the mixture to form a dough.

2 Lightly grease and line the base of a 23 cm/9 inch springform tin. Press the dough into the base of the tin to cover, pushing the dough right up to the edge of the tin.

3 Roughly chop the tofu and put in a food processor with the vegetable oil, orange juice, brandy, cocoa powder,

almond essence and remaining sugar, and process until smooth and creamy. Pour over the base in the tin and cook in a preheated oven, 160°C/325°F/Gas Mark 3, for about 1–1¼ hours or until set.

4 Leave to cool in the tin for 5 minutes, then remove from the tin and chill in the refrigerator. Dust with icing sugar and cocoa powder. Decorate with Cape gooseberries and serve.

COOK'S TIP
Cape gooseberries make an attractive decoration for many desserts.

Stuffed Pooris

This is a very old family recipe from India. The pooris freeze well, so it pays to make a large quantity and re-heat them in the oven.

NUTRITIONAL INFORMATION

Calories 429	Sugars 22g	
Protein 9g	Fat 21g	
Carbohydrate . . .54g	Saturates 7g	

6½ hrs   1 hr

MAKES 10

INGREDIENTS

POORIS

200 g/7 oz coarse semolina

100 g/3½ oz plain flour

½ tsp salt

4½ tsp ghee, plus extra for frying

150 ml/¼ pint milk

FILLING

8 tbsp chana dhal

850 ml/1½ pints water

5 tbsp ghee

2 green cardamom pods, husks removed

4 cloves

8 tbsp sugar

2 tbsp ground almonds

½ tsp saffron strands

50 g/1¾ oz sultanas

1 To make the pooris, place the semolina, flour and salt in a bowl and mix. Add the ghee and rub in with your fingertips. Add the milk and mix to form a dough. Knead the dough for 5 minutes, cover and set aside for about 3 hours to prove. Knead the dough on a floured surface for 15 minutes.

2 Roll out the dough until it measures 25 cm/10 inches and divide into 10 portions. Roll out each of these into 12.5 cm/5 inch rounds and set aside.

3 Soak the chana dhal for at least 3 hours. Place the dhal in a pan and add 750 ml/1¼ pints of the water. Bring to the boil over a medium heat and simmer until all of the water has evaporated and the dhal is soft. Add more water only if needed. Mash into a paste.

4 Meanwhile, heat the ghee. Add the cardamom seeds and cloves. Lower the heat, add the dhal paste and stir for 5–7 minutes.

5 Fold in the sugar and almonds and cook, stirring constantly, for 10 minutes. Add the saffron and sultanas and blend until thickened. Cook, stirring constantly, for 5 minutes.

6 Spoon the filling on to one half of each pastry round. Dampen the edges with water and fold the other half over, pressing to seal.

7 Heat the ghee in a pan and fry the filled pooris, in batches, over a low heat until golden. Drain on kitchen paper and serve immediately.

Summer Puddings

A wonderful mixture of summer fruits encased in slices of white bread which soak up all the deep red, flavoursome juices.

NUTRITIONAL INFORMATION

Calories	250	Sugars	........41g
Protein	.........4g	Fat	...........4g
Carbohydrate	...53g	Saturates	.......2g

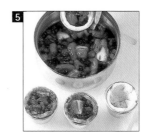

10 mins

10 mins

SERVES 6

INGREDIENTS

vegetable oil or butter, for greasing

6–8 thin slices white bread, crusts removed

175 g/6 oz caster sugar

300 ml/½ pint water

225 g/8 oz strawberries

500 g/1 lb 2 oz raspberries

175 g/6 oz blackcurrants and/or redcurrants

175 g/6 oz blackberries or loganberries

fresh mint sprigs, to decorate

pouring cream, to serve

1 Grease 6 x 150 ml/¼ pint moulds with butter or oil.

2 Line the moulds with the bread, cutting it so it fits snugly.

3 Place the sugar in a saucepan with the water and heat gently, stirring frequently until dissolved, then bring to the boil and boil for 2 minutes.

4 Reserve 6 large strawberries for decoration. Add half the raspberries and the rest of the fruits to the syrup, cutting the strawberries in half if large, and simmer gently for a few minutes, until they are beginning to soften but still retain their shape.

5 Spoon the fruits and some of the liquid into moulds. Cover with more slices of bread. Spoon a little juice around the sides of the moulds so the bread is well soaked. Cover with a saucer and a heavy weight, leave to cool, then chill thoroughly, preferably overnight.

6 Process the remaining raspberries in a food processor or blender, or press through a non-metallic sieve. Add enough of the liquid from the fruits to give a coating consistency.

7 Turn on to serving plates and spoon the raspberry sauce over. Decorate with the mint sprigs and reserved strawberries and serve with cream.

Meringue-topped Rice

This dessert is really two in one – a rice pudding base with a melt-in-the-mouth meringue topping. Double heaven!

NUTRITIONAL INFORMATION

Calories	358	Sugars	........56g
Protein	........10g	Fat	...........5g
Carbohydrate	...72g	Saturates	.......2g

 10 mins 1½ hours

SERVES 6–8

INGREDIENTS

125 ml/4 fl oz water

1.2 litres/2 pints milk

100 g/3½ oz long grain white rice

2–3 strips of lemon rind

1 cinnamon stick

1 vanilla pod, split

115 g/4 oz sugar

3 tbsp cornflour

4 egg yolks

MERINGUE

6 egg whites

¼ tsp cream of tartar

225 g/8 oz caster sugar

1 Bring the water and 225 ml/8 fl oz of the milk to the boil in a large heavy-based saucepan. Add the rice, lemon rind, cinnamon stick and vanilla pod and reduce the heat to low. Cover the saucepan and simmer for about 20 minutes until the rice is tender and all the liquid is absorbed. Remove the lemon rind, cinnamon stick and vanilla pod from the pan and add the remaining milk; return the saucepan to the boil.

2 Stir together the sugar and the cornflour. Stir in a little of the hot rice-milk to make a paste, then stir into the pan of rice. Cook, stirring constantly, until the mixture boils and thickens. Boil for 1 minute, then remove from the heat to cool slightly.

3 Beat the egg yolks in a glass bowl until smooth. Stir a large spoonful of the hot rice mixture into the yolks, beating until well blended, then stir into the rice mixture. Pour into a 3 litre/5¼ pint baking dish.

4 To make the meringue, whisk the egg whites with the cream of tartar in a large bowl to form stiff peaks. Add the sugar, 2 tablespoons at a time, whisking well after each addition, until the mixture is stiff and glossy.

5 Gently spoon the meringue over the top of the rice pudding, spreading evenly. Make decorative swirls with the back of a spoon.

6 Bake in a preheated oven at 150°C/300°F/Gas Mark 2 for about 1 hour until the top is golden and set. Turn off the oven, open the door and let the pudding cool in the oven. Serve warm, at room temperature, or cold.

Pancakes with Apples

The sharpness of the apples contrasts with the sweetness of the butterscotch sauce in this mouthwatering pancake recipe.

NUTRITIONAL INFORMATION

Calories	.543	Sugars	.55g
Protein	.8g	Fat	.24g
Carbohydrate	.78g	Saturates	.14g

 15 mins   45 mins

SERVES 4

INGREDIENTS

125 g/4½ oz plain flour

pinch of salt

1 tsp finely grated lemon rind

1 egg

300 ml/½ pint milk

1–2 tbsp vegetable oil, plus extra
 for greasing

pared lemon rind, to garnish

FILLING

225 g/8 oz Bramley apples, peeled,
 cored and sliced

2 tbsp sultanas

SAUCE

85 g/3 oz butter

3 tbsp golden syrup

85 g/3 oz light muscovado sugar

1 tbsp rum or brandy (optional)

1 tbsp lemon juice

1 Sift the flour and salt into a bowl. Add the lemon rind, egg and milk and whisk to make a smooth batter.

2 Heat a little oil in a heavy-based frying pan. Make 8 thin pancakes, using extra oil as required. Stack the cooked pancakes, layering them with kitchen paper.

3 To make the filling, cook the apples with the sultanas in a little water until soft. Divide the mixture evenly between the pancakes and roll up or fold into triangles. Brush an ovenproof dish with a little oil and arrange the pancakes in it. Bake in a preheated oven, 160°C/325°F/Gas Mark 3, for 15 minutes until the pancakes are warmed through.

4 To make the sauce, melt the butter, syrup and sugar together in a pan, stirring well. Add the rum or brandy, if using, and the lemon juice. Do not allow the mixture to boil.

5 Serve the pancakes on warm plates, with a little sauce poured over and garnished with lemon rind.

Portuguese Rice Pudding

This buttery, spicy, egg-rich rice pudding is quite irresistible – and even more so when served with a topping of thick cream.

NUTRITIONAL INFORMATION

Calories	365	Sugars	........22g
Protein	.........7g	Fat	..........19g
Carbohydrate	...43g	Saturates	......10g

10 mins   50 mins

SERVES 6–8

INGREDIENTS

200 g/7 oz valencia, arborio or pudding rice

pinch salt

1 lemon

450 ml/16 fl oz milk

150 ml/5 fl oz single cream

1 cinnamon stick

85 g/3 oz butter

140 g/5 oz sugar (or to taste)

8 egg yolks

ground cinnamon, for dusting

thick or double cream, to serve

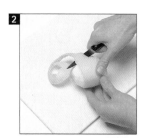

1 Bring a saucepan of water to the boil. Sprinkle in the rice and salt and return to the boil; reduce the heat and simmer until just tender. Drain, rinse under cold water and drain again.

2 Using a small sharp knife or swivel-bladed vegetable peeler, and working in a circular motion, try to peel the rind off the lemon in one curly piece; this will make it easier to remove from the pudding later. Alternatively, peel off in strips.

3 Bring the milk and cream to a simmer over a medium heat. Add the rice, cinnamon stick, butter and the lemon rind 'curl' or strips. Reduce the heat to low and simmer gently for about 20 minutes until thick and creamy. Remove from the heat; remove and discard the cinnamon stick and the lemon rind. Add the sugar, stirring until it has dissolved.

4 In a large bowl, beat the egg yolks until well blended. Gradually beat in the rice mixture until thick and smooth. Continue to stir frequently to prevent the eggs curdling, until slightly cooled, then pour into a bowl or 6–8 individual glasses. Dust with cinnamon and serve with cream.

Florentine Rice Pudding

This very sophisticated rice pudding from Florence is like a cross between a mousse and a soufflé, and is best served warm.

NUTRITIONAL INFORMATION

Calories	836	Sugars	.......127g
Protein	........14g	Fat	.........25g
Carbohydrate	..148g	Saturates	......14g

 15 mins   1 hr

SERVES 6

I N G R E D I E N T S

150 g/5½ oz long grain white rice or
   arborio rice

pinch of salt

1 litre/1¾ pints milk

5 eggs

400 g/14 oz sugar or 450 g/1 lb honey, or
   a mixture

115 g/4 oz butter, melted
   and cooled

2 tbsp orange flower water or 4 tbsp
   orange-flavoured liqueur

225 g/8 oz diced candied orange peel

225 g/8 oz orange marmalade

2–3 tablespoons water

icing sugar, for dusting

1 Put the rice and salt in a large heavy-bottomed saucepan. Add the milk and bring to the boil, stirring occasionally. Reduce the heat to low and simmer gently for about 25 minutes until the rice is tender and creamy. Remove the saucepan from the heat.

2 Pass the cooked rice through a food mill into a large bowl, or process in a food processor for about 30 seconds until smooth. Set aside. Stir from time to time to prevent a skin forming.

3 Meanwhile, using an electric mixer, beat the eggs with the sugar in a large bowl for about 4 minutes until very light and creamy. Gently fold into the rice with the melted butter. Stir in half the orange flower water, then stir in the candied orange peel.

4 Turn into a well-buttered 2 litre/3½ pint soufflé dish or charlotte mould. Place the dish in a roasting tin and pour in enough boiling water to come 4 cm/1½ inches up the side of the dish.

5 Bake in a preheated oven, at 180°C/350°F/Gas Mark 4, for about 25 minutes until the pudding is puffed and lightly set. Transfer the dish to a wire rack to cool slightly.

6 Heat the marmalade with the water, stirring until it has dissolved and become smooth. Stir in the remaining orange flower water and pour into a sauceboat. Dust the top of the pudding with the icing sugar and serve warm with the marmalade sauce.

Rhubarb & Apple Crumble

A mixture of rhubarb and apples is flavoured with orange rind, brown sugar and spices and topped with a crunchy crumble topping.

NUTRITIONAL INFORMATION

Calories	.516	Sugars	.45g
Protein	.6g	Fat	.22g
Carbohydrate	.77g	Saturates	.4g

 15 mins   45 mins

SERVES 6

I N G R E D I E N T S

500 g/1 lb 2 oz rhubarb

500 g/1 lb 2 oz Bramley apples

grated rind and juice of 1 orange

½–1 tsp ground cinnamon

about 90 g/3 oz light soft brown sugar

C R U M B L E

225 g/8 oz plain flour

125 g/4½ oz butter or margarine

125 g/4½ oz light soft brown sugar

40–60 g/1½–2 oz toasted chopped hazelnuts

2 tbsp demerara sugar (optional)

1 Cut the rhubarb into 2.5 cm/1 inch lengths and place in a large saucepan.

2 Peel, core and slice the apples and add to the rhubarb, together with the grated orange rind and juice.

3 Bring to the boil, lower the heat and simmer for 2–3 minutes, until the fruit begins to soften.

4 Add the cinnamon and sugar to taste and turn the mixture into an ovenproof dish. Make sure that the dish is not more than two-thirds full.

5 Sift the flour into a bowl and rub in the butter or margarine until the mixture resembles fine breadcrumbs (this can be done by hand or in a food processor). Stir in the sugar, followed by the nuts.

6 Spoon the crumble mixture evenly over the fruit in the dish and level the top. Sprinkle with the demerara sugar, if liked.

7 Cook in a preheated oven, 200°C/400°F/Gas Mark 6, for 30–40 minutes, until the topping is browned. Serve the crumble hot or cold.

VARIATION

Other flavourings, such as 60 g/ 2 oz chopped stem ginger, can be added either to the fruit or the crumb mixture. Any fruit, or mixtures of fruits can be topped with crumble.

Traditional Tiramisu

This favourite Italian dessert is flavoured with coffee and Amaretto. You could replace the Amaretto with brandy or Marsala.

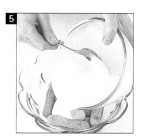

NUTRITIONAL INFORMATION

Calories	569	Sugars	........28g
Protein	........12g	Fat	..........43g
Carbohydrate	...34g	Saturates	......22g

 2¼ hrs   5 mins

SERVES 6

INGREDIENTS

20–24 sponge fingers, about 150 g/5½ oz

2 tbsp cold black coffee

2 tbsp coffee essence

2 tbsp Amaretto

4 egg yolks

90 g/3 oz caster sugar

few drops of vanilla essence

grated rind of ½ lemon

350 g/12 oz mascarpone cheese

2 tsp lemon juice

250 ml/9 fl oz double cream

1 tbsp milk

25 g/1 oz flaked almonds, lightly toasted

2 tbsp cocoa powder

1 tbsp icing sugar

1 Arrange almost half of the sponge fingers in the base of a glass bowl or serving dish.

2 Combine the black coffee, coffee essence and Amaretto together and sprinkle a little more than half of the mixture over the sponge fingers.

3 Put the egg yolks into a heatproof bowl with the sugar, vanilla essence and lemon rind. Stand the bowl over a saucepan of gently simmering water and whisk the mixture until very thick and creamy and the whisk leaves a very heavy trail when lifted from the bowl.

4 Put the mascarpone in a separate bowl with the lemon juice and beat until smooth.

5 Combine the egg and mascarpone cheese mixtures and when evenly blended pour half over the sponge fingers and spread out evenly.

6 Add another layer of sponge fingers, sprinkle with the remaining coffee and Amaretto mixture, then cover with the rest of the cheese and egg mixture. Chill the tiramisu for at least 2 hours and preferably longer, or overnight.

7 To serve, whip the cream and milk together until fairly stiff and spread or pipe over the dessert. Sprinkle with the flaked almonds and then sift an even layer of cocoa powder so the top is completely covered. Finally, sift a light layer of icing sugar over the cocoa.

Pink Syllabubs

The pretty pink colour of this dessert is achieved by adding blackcurrant liqueur to the wine and cream before whipping.

NUTRITIONAL INFORMATION

Calories	536	Sugars	........17g
Protein	.........2g	Fat	..........48g
Carbohydrate	...17g	Saturates	......30g

 45 mins   0 mins

SERVES 2

INGREDIENTS

5 tbsp white wine

2–3 tsp blackcurrant liqueur

finely grated rind of ½ lemon or orange

1 tbsp caster sugar

200 ml/7 fl oz double cream

4 boudoir biscuits (optional)

TO DECORATE

fresh fruit, such as strawberries, raspberries or redcurrants, or pecan or walnut halves

fresh mint sprigs

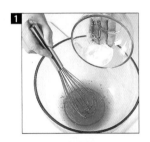

COOK'S TIP

These syllabubs will keep in the refrigerator for 48 hours, so it is worth making more than you need, and keeping the extra for another day.

1 Mix together the white wine, blackcurrant liqueur, grated lemon or orange rind and caster sugar in a bowl and set aside for at least 30 minutes.

2 Add the cream to the wine mixture and whip until the mixture has thickened enough to stand in soft peaks.

3 If you are using the boudoir biscuits, break them up roughly and divide them between 2 glasses.

4 For a decorative effect, put the mixture into a piping bag fitted with a large star or plain nozzle and pipe it over the biscuits. Alternatively, simply pour the syllabub over the biscuits. Chill until ready to serve.

5 Before serving, decorate each syllabub with slices or small pieces of fresh soft fruit or nuts, and sprigs of mint.

Berry Cheesecake

Use a mixture of berries, such as blueberries, blackberries, raspberries and strawberries, for a really fruity cheesecake.

NUTRITIONAL INFORMATION

Calories	478	Sugars	........28g
Protein	........10g	Fat	.........32g
Carbohydrate	...40g	Saturates	......15g

2¼ hrs   5 mins

SERVES 8

INGREDIENTS

BASE

75 g/2¾ oz margarine

175 g/6 oz oatmeal biscuits

50 g/1¾ oz desiccated coconut

TOPPING

1½ tsp gelozone (vegetarian gelatine)

9 tbsp cold water

125 ml/4 fl oz evaporated milk

1 egg

6 tbsp light brown sugar

450 g/1 lb soft cream cheese

350 g/12 oz mixed berries

2 tbsp clear honey

1 Put the margarine in a saucepan and heat until melted. Put the biscuits in a food processor and process until thoroughly crushed or crush finely with a rolling pin. Stir the crumbs into the margarine, together with the coconut.

2 Press the mixture evenly into a base-lined 20 cm/ 8 inch springform tin and set aside to chill in the refrigerator while you are preparing the filling.

3 To make the topping, sprinkle the gelozone over the water and stir to dissolve. Bring to the boil and boil for 2 minutes. Let cool slightly.

4 Put the milk, egg, sugar and soft cream cheese in a large mixing bowl and beat until smooth. Stir in 50 g/ 2 oz of the berries. Add the gelozone in a stream, stirring constantly.

5 Spoon the mixture on to the biscuit base and return to the refrigerator to chill for 2 hours, or until set.

6 Remove the cheesecake carefully from the tin and transfer to a serving plate.

7 Arrange the remaining berries on top of the cheesecake and drizzle the honey over the top. Serve.

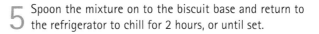

Sweet Fruit Wontons

These sweet wontons are very adaptable and may be filled with whole, small fruits or a spicy chopped mixture as here.

NUTRITIONAL INFORMATION

Calories 244   Sugars 25g
Protein ....2g   Fat 12g
Carbohydrate ...35g   Saturates 3g

10 mins   15 mins

SERVES 4

INGREDIENTS

12 wonton wrappers

2 tsp cornflour

6 tsp cold water

oil, for deep-frying

2 tbsp clear honey

selection of fresh fruit (such as kiwi fruit, limes, oranges, mango and apples), sliced, to serve

FILLING

175 g/6 oz dried stoned dates, chopped

2 tsp dark brown sugar

½ tsp ground cinnamon

1 To make the filling, mix together the dates, sugar and cinnamon in a bowl.

2 Spread out the wonton wrappers on a chopping board and spoon a little of the filling into the centre of each wrapper.

3 Blend the cornflour and water and brush this mixture around the edges of the wrappers.

4 Fold the wrappers over the filling, bringing the edges together, then bring the two corners together, sealing with the cornflour mixture.

5 Heat the oil for deep-frying in a wok to 180°C/350°F, or until a cube of bread browns in 30 seconds. Fry the wontons, in batches, for 2-3 minutes, until golden. Remove the wontons from the oil with a slotted spoon and leave to drain on absorbent kitchen paper.

6 Place the clear honey in a bowl and stand it in warm water, to soften it slightly. Drizzle the honey over the sweet fruit wontons and serve with a selection of fresh fruit.

COOK'S TIP

Wonton wrappers may be found in Chinese supermarkets. Alternatively, use half the quantity of the dough made for Wonton Soup (page 113).

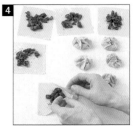

Boston Chocolate Pie

This lighter version of the popular chocolate cream pie is made with yogurt and crème fraîche.

NUTRITIONAL INFORMATION

Calories 795	Sugars 73g	
Protein 13g	Fat 40g	
Carbohydrate . . .99g	Saturates 21g	

 25 mins   35 mins

SERVES 6

INGREDIENTS

225 g/8 oz shortcrust pastry

CHOCOLATE CARAQUE

225 g/8 oz dark chocolate, broken into squares

FILLING

3 eggs

125 g/4½ oz caster sugar

60 g/2 oz flour, plus extra for dusting

1 tbsp icing sugar

pinch of salt

1 tsp vanilla essence

400 ml/14 fl oz milk

150 ml/¼ pint natural yogurt

150 g/5½ oz dark chocolate, broken into pieces

2 tbsp kirsch

TOPPING

150 ml/¼ pint crème fraîche

1 Roll out the pastry and use to line a 23 cm/9 inch loose-based flan tin. Prick the base with a fork, line with baking paper and fill with dried beans. Bake blind for 20 minutes. Remove the beans and paper and return to the oven for 5 minutes. Remove from the oven and place the tin on a wire rack to cool.

2 To make the chocolate caraque, put squares of dark chocolate on a heatproof plate over a pan of simmering water until melted. Spread on a cool surface with a palette knife. When cool, scrape it into curls with a sharp knife.

3 To make the filling, whisk the eggs and sugar until fluffy. Sift in the flour, icing sugar and salt. Stir in the vanilla essence. Bring the milk and yogurt to the boil in a small pan and strain on to the egg mixture. Pour into a double boiler or set over a pan of simmering water. Stir until it coats the back of a spoon.

4 Gently heat the chocolate and kirsch in a small pan until melted. Stir into the custard. Remove from the heat and stand the double boiler or bowl in cold water. Leave it to cool. Pour the chocolate mixture into the pastry case. Spread the crème fraîche over the chocolate, and arrange the caraque rolls on top.

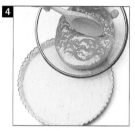

Fresh Fruit Compôte

Elderflower cordial is used in the syrup for this refreshing fruit compôte, giving it a delightfully summery flavour.

NUTRITIONAL INFORMATION

Calories 255   Sugars 61g
Protein ....4g   Fat 1g
Carbohydrate ...61g   Saturates 0.2g

20 mins   15 mins

SERVES 4

INGREDIENTS

1 lemon

60 g/2 oz caster sugar

4 tbsp elderflower cordial

300 ml/½ pint water

4 dessert apples

225 g/8 oz blackberries

2 fresh figs

TOPPING

150 g/5½ oz Greek yogurt

2 tbsp clear honey

1 Thinly pare the rind from the lemon using a swivel vegetable peeler. Squeeze the juice. Put the lemon rind and juice into a saucepan, together with the sugar, elderflower cordial and water. Set over a low heat and simmer, uncovered, for 10 minutes.

2 Core and slice the apples. Add the apples to the saucepan. Simmer gently for about 4–5 minutes, until just tender. Remove the pan from the heat and set aside to cool.

3 When cold, transfer the apples and syrup to a serving bowl and add the blackberries. Slice and add the figs. Stir gently to mix. Cover and chill in the refrigerator until ready to serve.

4 Spoon the yogurt into a small serving bowl and drizzle the honey over the top. Cover and chill before serving.

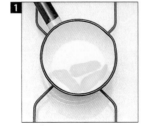

COOK'S TIP

Greek-style yogurt may be made from cow's or ewe's milk. The former is often strained to make it more concentrated and has a high fat content, which perfectly counterbalances the sharpness and acidity of fruit.

Autumn Fruit Bread Pudding

This is like a summer pudding, but it uses fruits which appear later in the year. This dessert requires chilling overnight so prepare in advance.

NUTRITIONAL INFORMATION

Calories	177	Sugars	........29g
Protein	.........3g	Fat	...........1g
Carbohydrate	...42g	Saturates	.....0.1g

  10 mins, plus chilling   15 mins

SERVES 8

I N G R E D I E N T S

900 g/2 lb mixed blackberries, chopped apples and chopped pears

150 g/5½ oz soft light brown sugar

1 tsp cinnamon

225 g/8 oz white bread, thinly sliced, crusts removed (about 12 slices)

1 Place the fruit in a large saucepan with the soft light brown sugar, cinnamon and 7 tablespoons of water, stir and bring to the boil. Reduce the heat and simmer for 5–10 minutes so that the fruits soften but still hold their shape.

2 Meanwhile, line the base and sides of a 900 ml/1½ pint pudding basin with the bread slices, ensuring that there are no gaps between the pieces of bread.

3 Spoon the fruit into the centre of the bread-lined bowl and cover the fruit with the remaining bread.

4 Place a saucer on top of the bread pudding and place a heavy weight on. Chill the pudding in the refrigerator overnight.

5 Turn the pudding out on to a serving plate and serve immediately.

COOK'S TIP

This pudding would be delicious served with vanilla ice cream to counteract the tartness of the blackberries. Stand the pudding on a plate when chilling to catch any juices that run down the sides of the basin.

Semolina Dessert

This dish is eaten with pooris and potato curry for breakfast in northern India, but you can serve it with fresh cream for a delicious dessert.

NUTRITIONAL INFORMATION

Calories ....676 Sugars 66g

Protein ....10g Fat 31g

Carbohydrate ...96g Saturates 19g

 5 mins   10 mins

SERVES 4

INGREDIENTS

6 tbsp pure ghee

3 whole cloves

3 whole cardamom pods

8 tbsp coarse semolina

½ tsp saffron

50 g/1¾ oz sultanas

10 tbsp sugar

300 ml/½ pint water

300 ml/½ pint milk

cream, to serve

TO DECORATE

25 g/1 oz desiccated coconut, toasted

25 g/1 oz chopped almonds

25 g/1 oz pistachio nuts, soaked and chopped (optional)

1 Place the ghee in a saucepan and melt over a medium heat.

2 Add the cloves and the whole cardamoms to the melted butter and reduce the heat, stirring to mix.

3 Add the semolina to the mixture in the pan and stir-fry until it turns a little darker.

4 Add the saffron, sultanas and sugar to the semolina mixture, stirring to combine thoroughly.

5 Pour in the water and milk and cook, stirring the mixture continuously until the semolina has softened. Add a little more water if required.

6 Remove the pan from the heat and transfer the semolina to a warmed serving dish.

7 Decorate the semolina dessert with the toasted coconut, flaked almonds and pistachios. Serve with a little cream drizzled over the top.

Coconut Sweet

Quick and easy to make, this sweet is very similar to coconut ice.
Pink food colouring may be added towards the end if desired.

NUTRITIONAL INFORMATION

Calories 338	Sugars 5g	
Protein 4g	Fat 34g	
Carbohydrate 5g	Saturates 26g	

1¼ hrs   15 mins

SERVES 6

INGREDIENTS

75 g/2¾ oz butter

200 g/7 oz desiccated coconut

175 ml/6 fl oz condensed milk

a few drops of pink food colouring (optional)

1 Place the butter in a heavy-based saucepan and melt over a low heat, stirring constantly so that the butter doesn't burn on the base of the pan.

2 Add the desiccated coconut to the melted butter, stirring to mix.

3 Stir in the condensed milk and the pink food colouring (if using) and mix continuously for 7–10 minutes.

4 Remove the saucepan from the heat, set aside and leave the coconut mixture to cool slightly.

5 Once cool enough to handle, shape the coconut mixture into long blocks and cut into equal-sized rectangles. Leave to set for about 1 hour, then serve.

VARIATION

If you prefer, you could divide the coconut mixture in step 2, and add the pink food colouring to only one half of the mixture. This way, you will have an attractive combination of pink and white coconut sweets.

Sweet Carrot Halva

This nutritious dessert is flavoured with spices, nuts and raisins. The nutritional information does not include cream for serving.

NUTRITIONAL INFORMATION

Calories 284	Sugars 33g
Protein 7g	Fat 14g
Carbohydrate ...34g	Saturates 3g

10 mins   55 mins

SERVES 6

INGREDIENTS

750 g/1 lb 10 oz carrots, grated

700 ml/1¼ pints milk

1 cinnamon stick or piece of cassia
    bark (optional)

4 tbsp ghee or oil

60 g/2 oz granulated sugar

25 g/1 oz unsalted pistachio nuts, chopped

25–50 g/1–1¾ oz blanched almonds,
    flaked or chopped

60 g/2 oz seedless raisins

8 cardamom pods, split and seeds removed
    and crushed

thick cream, to serve

1 Put the grated carrots, milk and cinnamon or cassia, if using, into a large, heavy-based saucepan and bring to the boil. Reduce the heat to very low and simmer, uncovered, for 35–40 minutes, or until the mixture is thick (with no milk remaining). Stir the mixture frequently during cooking to prevent it from sticking.

2 Remove and discard the cinnamon or cassia. Heat the ghee or oil in a non-stick frying pan, add the carrot mixture and stir-fry over a medium heat for about 5 minutes, or until the carrots take on a glossy sheen.

3 Add the sugar, pistachios, almonds, raisins and crushed cardamom seeds, mix thoroughly and continue frying for a further 3–4 minutes, stirring frequently. Serve warm or cold with thick cream.

COOK'S TIP

The quickest and easiest way to grate this quantity of carrots is by using a food processor fitted with the appropriate blade.

Satsuma & Pecan Pavlova

Make this spectacular dessert for the perfect way to round off a special occasion. You can make the meringue base well in advance.

NUTRITIONAL INFORMATION

Calories	339	Sugars	........36g
Protein	.........3g	Fat	..........21g
Carbohydrate	...37g	Saturates	......10g

 2½ hrs   3 hrs

SERVES 8

INGREDIENTS

4 egg whites

225 g/8 oz light muscovado sugar

300 ml/½ pint double or whipping cream

60 g/2 oz pecan nuts

4 satsumas, peeled

1 passion fruit or pomegranate

2 Whip the egg whites in a large grease-free bowl until stiff. Add the sugar gradually, continuing to beat until the mixture is very glossy.

3 Pipe or spoon a layer of meringue mixture on to the circle marked on the baking paper; then pipe large rosettes or place spoonfuls on top of the meringue's outer edge. Pipe any remaining meringue mixture in tiny rosettes on the second baking sheet.

4 Bake in a preheated oven, 140°C/275°F/Gas Mark 1 for 2–3 hours, making sure that the oven is well-ventilated by using a folded tea towel to keep the door slightly open. Remove from the oven and leave to cool completely. When cold, peel off the baking paper carefully.

5 Whip the double or whipping cream in a large chilled bowl until thick. Spoon about one-third into a piping bag, fitted with a star nozzle. Reserve a few pecan nuts and 1 satsuma for decoration. Chop the remaining nuts and fruit, and fold into the remaining cream.

6 Pile on top of the meringue base and decorate with the tiny meringue rosettes, piped cream, satsuma segments and pecan nuts. Scoop the seeds from the passion fruit or pomegranate with a teaspoon and sprinkle them on top.

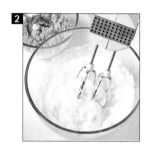

1 Line 2 baking sheets with non-stick baking paper or greaseproof paper. Draw a 23 cm/9 inch circle on one of the sheets.

Baked Tofu Cheesecake

This cheesecake has a rich creamy texture, but contains no dairy produce, as it is made with tofu.

NUTRITIONAL INFORMATION

Calories 282   Sugars 17g
Protein ....9g   Fat 15g
Carbohydrate ...29g   Saturates 4g

2¼ hrs   45 mins

SERVES 6

I N G R E D I E N T S

margarine, for greasing

125 g/4½ oz digestive biscuits, crushed

4 tbsp margarine, melted

50 g/1¾ oz dates, stoned and chopped

4 tbsp lemon juice

rind of 1 lemon

3 tbsp water

350 g/12 oz firm tofu

150 ml/5 fl oz apple juice

1 banana, mashed

1 tsp vanilla essence

1 mango, peeled, stoned and chopped

1 Lightly grease an 18 cm/7 inch round loose-bottomed cake tin.

2 Mix together the digestive biscuit crumbs and melted margarine in a bowl. Press the mixture into the base of the prepared tin.

3 Put the chopped dates, lemon juice, lemon rind and water into a saucepan and bring to the boil. Simmer for 5 minutes until the dates are soft, then mash them roughly with a fork.

4 Place the mixture in a blender or food processor, together with the tofu, apple juice, mashed banana and vanilla essence, and process until the mixture is a thick, smooth purée.

5 Pour the tofu purée on to the prepared biscuit crumb base and gently smooth the surface.

6 Bake the cheesecake in a preheated oven, 180°C/350°F/Gas Mark 4, for about 30–40 minutes until the surface is lightly golden. Leave the cheesecake to cool completely in the tin, then chill thoroughly before serving.

7 Place the chopped mango in a blender and process until smooth. Serve it as a sauce with the cheesecake.

VARIATION

Silken tofu may be substituted for the firm tofu to give a softer texture; it will take 40–50 minutes to set.

Cherry Pancakes

This dish can be made with either fresh stoned cherries or, if time is short, with canned cherries for extra speed.

NUTRITIONAL INFORMATION

Calories	345	Sugars	........25g
Protein	.........8g	Fat	...........11g
Carbohydrate	...56g	Saturates	.......2g

 10 mins   15 mins

SERVES 4

INGREDIENTS

FILLING

400 g/14 oz canned stoned cherries

½ tsp almond essence

½ tsp mixed spice

2 tbsp cornflour

PANCAKES

100 g/3½ oz plain flour

pinch of salt

2 tbsp chopped fresh mint

1 egg

300 ml/½ pint milk

vegetable oil, for frying

icing sugar and toasted flaked almonds,
to decorate

1 Put the cherries and 300 ml/½ pint of the can juice in a pan with the almond essence and mixed spice. Stir in the cornflour and bring to the boil, stirring until thickened and clear. Set aside.

2 To make the pancakes, sift the flour into a bowl with the salt. Add the chopped mint and make a well in the centre. Gradually beat in the egg and milk to make a smooth batter.

3 Heat 1 tablespoon of oil in an 18 cm/ 7 inch frying pan; pour off the oil when hot. Add just enough batter to coat the base of the frying pan and cook for

1–2 minutes, or until the underside is cooked. Flip the pancake over and cook for 1 minute. Remove from the pan and keep warm. Repeat to use up all the batter.

4 Spoon a quarter of the cherry filling on to a quarter of each pancake and fold the pancake into a cone shape. Dust with icing sugar and sprinkle the flaked almonds over the top. Serve immediately.

Almond & Pistachio Dessert

Rich and mouth-watering, this dessert can be prepared well in advance of the meal. It is best served cold.

NUTRITIONAL INFORMATION

Calories	565	Sugars	........37g
Protein	........8g	Fat	.........43g
Carbohydrate	...38g	Saturates	......16g

 1¼ hrs   🕐 15 mins

SERVES 6

INGREDIENTS

75 g/2¾ oz unsalted butter

200 g/7 oz ground almonds

150 ml/¼ pint single cream

200 g/7 oz sugar

8 almonds, chopped

10 pistachio nuts, chopped

1 Place the butter in a medium-sized saucepan, preferably non-stick. Melt the butter, stirring well.

2 Add the ground almonds, cream and sugar to the melted butter in the pan, stirring to combine. Reduce the heat and stir constantly for 10-12 minutes, scraping the base of the pan.

3 Increase the heat until the mixture turns a little darker in colour.

4 Transfer the almond mixture to a shallow serving dish and smooth the top with the back of a spoon.

5 Decorate the top of the dessert with the chopped almonds and pistachios.

6 Leave the dessert to set for about 1 hour, then cut into diamond shapes and serve cold.

COOK'S TIP

This almond dessert can be made in advance and stored in an airtight container in the refrigerator for several days. You could use a variety of shaped pastry cutters, to cut the dessert into different shapes, rather than diamonds, if you prefer.

Mocha Swirl Mousse

A combination of feather-light yet rich chocolate and coffee mousses, whipped and attractively presented in serving glasses.

NUTRITIONAL INFORMATION

Calories . . . . . . .542 Sugars 12g
Protein . . . . .5g Fat 6g
Carbohydrate . . .13g Saturates 4g

1¼ hrs   0 mins

SERVES 4

INGREDIENTS

1 tbsp coffee and chicory essence

2 tsp cocoa powder, plus extra for dusting

1 tsp low-fat drinking chocolate powder

150 ml/5 fl oz low-fat crème fraîche, plus 4 tsp to serve

2 tsp powdered gelozone (vegetarian gelatine)

2 tbsp boiling water

2 large egg whites

2 tbsp caster sugar

4 chocolate coffee beans, to serve

1 Place the coffee and chicory essence in one bowl, and 2 teaspoons cocoa powder and the drinking chocolate in another bowl. Divide the crème fraîche between the 2 bowls and mix both well.

2 Dissolve the gelozone in the boiling water and set aside. In a grease-free bowl, whisk the egg whites and sugar until stiff and divide this evenly between the two mixtures.

3 Divide the dissolved gelozone between the 2 mixtures and, using a large metal spoon, gently fold until well mixed.

4 Spoon small amounts of the 2 mousses alternately into 4 serving glasses and swirl together gently. Place in the refrigerator and chill for about 1 hour or until set.

5 To serve, top each mousse with a teaspoonful of reserved crème fraîche, a chocolate coffee bean and a light dusting of cocoa powder. Serve immediately.

COOK'S TIP
The vegetarian equivalent of gelatine, called gelozone, is available from healthfood shops.

Brown Sugar Pavlovas

This simple combination of fudgey meringue topped with fromage frais and raspberries is the perfect finale to any meal.

NUTRITIONAL INFORMATION

Calories	155	Sugars	.......34g
Protein	.........5g	Fat	.........0.2g
Carbohydrate	...35g	Saturates	......0g

 1 hr   1 hr

SERVES 4

INGREDIENTS

2 large egg whites

1 tsp cornflour

1 tsp raspberry vinegar

100 g/3½ oz light muscovado sugar,
    crushed free of lumps

2 tbsp redcurrant jelly

2 tbsp unsweetened orange juice

150 ml/5 fl oz low-fat fromage frais

175 g/6 oz raspberries, defrosted if frozen

rose-scented geranium leaves,
    to decorate (optional)

1 Line a large baking tray with baking paper. Whisk the egg whites until very stiff and dry. Gently fold in the cornflour and vinegar.

2 Gradually whisk in the sugar, a spoonful at a time, until the mixture is thick and glossy.

3 Divide the mixture into 4 and spoon on to the baking tray, spaced well apart. Smooth each portion into a round about 10 cm/4 inches across.

4 Bake in a preheated oven, 150°C/300°C/Gas Mark 2, for 40–45 minutes until lightly browned and crisp. Remove from the oven and leave to cool on the baking tray.

5 Place the redcurrant jelly and orange juice in a small pan and heat, stirring, until the redcurrant jelly has melted. Leave to cool for 10 minutes.

6 Using a palette knife, carefully remove each pavlova from the baking paper and transfer to a serving plate. Top with the fromage frais and the raspberries.

7 Brush the raspberries with the redcurrant and orange glaze, and decorate with the rose-scented geranium leaves, if using.

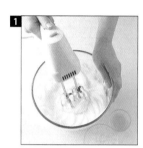

COOK'S TIP
Make a large pavlova by forming the meringue into a single round, measuring 18 cm/7 inches across, on a lined baking tray and bake for 1 hour.

Almond Cheesecakes

These creamy cheese desserts are so delicious that it's hard to believe that they are low in fat.

NUTRITIONAL INFORMATION

Calories 361	Sugars 29g	
Protein 16g	Fat 15g	
Carbohydrate . . .43g	Saturates 4g	

1¼ hrs   10 mins

SERVES 4

INGREDIENTS

12 amaretti biscuits

1 egg white, lightly beaten

225 g/8 oz skimmed-milk soft cheese

½ tsp almond essence

½ tsp finely grated lime rind

25 g/1 oz ground almonds

25 g/1 oz caster sugar

55 g/2 oz sultanas

2 tsp powdered gelozone (vegetarian gelatine)

2 tbsp boiling water

2 tbsp lime juice

TO DECORATE

25 g/1 oz flaked toasted almonds

strips of lime rind

1 Place the biscuits in a clean plastic bag, seal the bag and, using a rolling pin, crush them into small pieces.

2 Place the crumbs in a bowl and bind together with the egg white.

3 Arrange 4 non-stick pastry rings or poached egg rings, 9 cm/3½ inches across, on a baking tray lined with baking paper. Divide the biscuit mixture into 4 equal portions and spoon it into the rings, pressing down well. Bake in a preheated oven, 180°C/350°F/Gas Mark 4, for 10 minutes until crisp. Remove from the oven and leave to cool in the rings.

4 Beat the soft cheese, then beat in the almond essence, lime rind, ground almonds, sugar and sultanas until thoroughly combined.

5 Dissolve the gelozone in the boiling water and stir in the lime juice. Fold into the cheese mixture and spoon over the biscuit bases. Smooth over the tops and chill for 1 hour or until set.

6 Loosen the cheesecakes from the tins using a small palette knife or spatula and transfer to serving plates. Decorate with flaked toasted almonds and strips of lime rind, and serve.

Pavlova

This delicious dessert originated in Australia. Serve it with sharp fruits to balance the sweetness of the meringue.

NUTRITIONAL INFORMATION

Calories 354   Sugars 34g
Protein ....3g   Fat 24g
Carbohydrate ...34g   Saturates 15g

1 hr 10 mins   1¼ hrs

MAKES 6

INGREDIENTS

3 egg whites

salt

175 g/6 oz caster sugar

300 ml/½ pint double cream, lightly whipped

fresh fruit of your choice (raspberries, strawberries, peaches, passion fruit, or Cape gooseberries)

1 Line a baking sheet with a sheet of baking paper.

2 Whisk the egg whites with a pinch of salt in a large bowl until they form soft peaks.

3 Whisk in the sugar, a little at a time, whisking well after each addition until all the sugar has been incorporated.

4 Spoon three-quarters of the meringue on to the baking sheet, forming a round 20 cm/8 inches in diameter.

5 Place spoonfuls of the remaining meringue all around the edge of the round to form a rim, creating a nest shape.

6 Bake in a preheated oven, 140°C/275°F/Gas Mark 1, for 1¼ hours.

7 Turn the heat off, but leave the pavlova in the oven until it is completely cold.

8 To serve, place the pavlova on a serving dish. Spread with the lightly whipped cream, then arrange the fresh fruit on top.

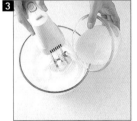

COOK'S TIP

Do not decorate the pavlova too far in advance of serving it, or it will be soggy instead of crisp.

Baked Apples with Berries

This winter dessert is a classic dish. Large, fluffy apples are hollowed out and filled with spices, almonds and blackberries.

NUTRITIONAL INFORMATION

Calories	228	Sugars	........31g
Protein	.........1g	Fat	..........2g
Carbohydrate	...31g	Saturates	.....0.2g

10 mins

45 mins

SERVES 4

INGREDIENTS

4 Bramley apples

1 tbsp lemon juice

100 g/3½ oz prepared blackberries, defrosted if frozen

15 g/½ oz flaked almonds

½ tsp ground allspice

½ tsp finely grated lemon rind

2 tbsp demerara sugar

300 ml/½ pint ruby port

1 cinnamon stick, broken

2 tsp cornflour blended with 2 tbsp cold water

low-fat custard, to serve

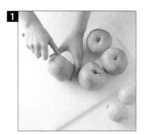

1 Wash and dry the apples. Using a small sharp knife, make a shallow cut through the skin around the middle of each apple – this will prevent the apples from bursting during cooking.

2 Core the apples, brush the centres with the lemon juice to prevent them from browning and stand them in an ovenproof dish.

3 In a bowl, mix together the blackberries, almonds, allspice, lemon rind and sugar. Using a teaspoon, spoon the mixture into the centre of each apple.

4 Pour the port into the dish around the apples, add the cinnamon stick and bake the apples in a preheated oven, 200°C/400°F/Gas Mark 6, for about 35–40 minutes or until tender and soft.

5 Drain the cooking juices into a pan and keep the apples warm.

6 Discard the cinnamon and add the cornflour mixture to the cooking juices. Cook over a medium heat, stirring constantly, until thickened.

7 Heat the custard until piping hot. To serve, pour the sauce over the apples and hand round the custard separately.

Mixed Fruit Brûlées

Traditionally a rich mixture made with cream, this fruit-based version is just as tempting using low-fat smetana and fromage frais as a topping.

NUTRITIONAL INFORMATION

Calories ....165 Sugars 21g
Protein ....5g Fat 7g
Carbohydrate ...21g Saturates 5g

🥗 5 mins   🕐 5 mins

SERVES 4

INGREDIENTS

450 g/1 lb prepared assorted summer fruits, such as strawberries, raspberries, blackcurrants, redcurrants and cherries, thawed if frozen

150 ml/5 fl oz smetana (buttermilk)

150 ml/5 fl oz low-fat natural fromage frais

1 tsp vanilla essence

4 tbsp demerara sugar

1 Divide the prepared summer fruits evenly among 4 small heat-proof ramekin dishes.

2 Combine the smetana, fromage frais and vanilla essence.

3 Spoon the mixture over the fruit, to cover it completely.

4 Top each serving with 1 tablespoon demerara sugar and place the desserts under a preheated grill for 2–3 minutes until the sugar melts completely and begins to caramelise. Set the mixed fruit brûlées aside for a couple of minutes before serving.

COOK'S TIP

Vegetarians should read the labels carefully when buying low-fat products such as fromage frais, as some brands are thickened with non-vegetarian additives.

New Age Spotted Dick

This is a deliciously moist low-fat pudding. The sauce is in the centre of the pudding, and will spill out when the pudding is cut.

NUTRITIONAL INFORMATION

Calories	529	Sugars	........41g
Protein	.........9g	Fat	.........31g
Carbohydrate	...58g	Saturates	......4g

25 mins   1¼ hrs

SERVES 6–8

INGREDIENTS

125 g/4 oz raisins

125 ml/4 fl oz corn oil,
  plus a little for brushing

125 g/4 oz caster sugar

25 g/1 oz ground almonds

2 eggs, lightly beaten

175 g/6 oz self-raising flour

SAUCE

60 g/2 oz walnuts, chopped

60 g/2 oz ground almonds

300 ml/½ pint semi-skimmed milk

4 tbsp granulated sugar

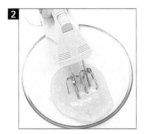

1 Put the raisins in a saucepan with 125 ml/4 fl oz water. Bring to the boil, then remove from the heat. Leave to steep for 10 minutes, then drain.

2 Whisk together the oil, sugar and ground almonds until thick and syrupy; this will take about 8 minutes of beating if using an electric whisk on medium speed.

3 Add the eggs, one at a time, beating well after each addition. Combine the flour and raisins. Stir into the mixture.

4 Brush a 1 litre/1¾ pint pudding basin with oil, or line with baking paper.

5 Put all the sauce ingredients into a saucepan. Bring to the boil, stir and simmer for 10 minutes.

6 Transfer the sponge mixture to the greased basin and pour on the hot sauce. Place on a baking tray.

7 Bake in a preheated oven at 170°C/340°F/Gas Mark 3½ for about 1 hour. Lay a piece of baking paper across the top if it starts to brown too fast.

8 Leave to cool for 2–3 minutes in the basin before turning out on to a serving plate.

COOK'S TIP
Always soak raisins before baking them, as they retain their moisture nicely and you taste the flavour of them instead of biting on a dried-out raisin.

Summer Fruit Clafoutis

Serve this mouthwatering French-style fruit-in-batter pudding hot or cold with low-fat fromage frais or yogurt.

NUTRITIONAL INFORMATION

Calories	228	Sugars	........26g
Protein	.........9g	Fat	..........2g
Carbohydrate	...42g	Saturates	......1g

  1¾ hrs | 50 mins

SERVES 4

INGREDIENTS

500 g/1 lb 2 oz prepared fresh assorted soft fruits, such as blackberries, raspberries, strawberries, blueberries, gooseberries, redcurrants, blackcurrants

4 tbsp soft fruit liqueur such as crème de cassis, kirsch or framboise

4 tbsp skimmed milk powder

115 g/4 oz plain flour

pinch of salt

55 g/2 oz caster sugar

2 eggs, beaten

300 ml/½ pint skimmed milk

1 tsp vanilla essence

2 tsp caster sugar, for dusting

TO SERVE

assorted soft fruits

low-fat yogurt or natural fromage frais

1 Place the assorted soft fruits in a mixing bowl and spoon over the fruit liqueur. Cover and chill for 1 hour for the fruit to macerate.

2 In a large bowl, combine the skimmed milk powder, flour, salt and sugar.

Make a well in the centre and gradually whisk in the eggs, milk and vanilla essence, using a balloon whisk, until smooth. Transfer to a jug and set aside for 30 minutes.

3 Line the base of a 23 cm/9 inch round ovenproof dish with baking paper, and spoon in the fruits and juices.

4 Whisk the batter again and pour it over the fruits, stand the dish on a baking sheet and bake in a preheated oven, 200°C/400°F/Gas Mark 6, for 50 minutes until firm, risen and golden brown.

5 Dust with caster sugar. Serve immediately with extra fruits, low-fat natural yogurt or fromage frais.

Orange Syllabub

A zesty, creamy whip made from yogurt and milk with a hint of orange, served with light and luscious sweet sponge cakes.

NUTRITIONAL INFORMATION

Calories 464	Sugars 74g	
Protein 22g	Fat 5g	
Carbohydrate ...89g	Saturates 2g	

 1½ hrs   10 mins

SERVES 4

I N G R E D I E N T S

4 oranges

600 ml/1 pint low-fat natural yogurt

6 tbsp skimmed milk powder

4 tbsp caster sugar

1 tbsp grated orange rind, plus extra
   to decorate

4 tbsp orange juice

2 egg whites

S P O N G E   H E A R T S

2 eggs, size 2

90 g/3 oz caster sugar

40 g/1½ oz plain flour

40 g/1½ oz wholemeal flour

1 tbsp hot water

1 tsp icing sugar

1 Slice off the tops and bottoms of the oranges and the skin. Then cut out the segments, removing the rind and membranes between each one. Divide the orange segments between 4 dessert glasses, then chill.

2 In a mixing bowl, combine the yogurt, milk powder, sugar, orange rind and juice. Cover and chill for 1 hour. Whisk the egg whites until stiff, then fold into the yogurt mixture. Pile on to the orange slices and chill for an hour. Decorate with fresh orange rind.

3 To make the sponge hearts, line a 15 x 25 cm/6 x 10 inch baking tin with baking paper. Whisk the eggs and caster sugar together until thick and pale. Sift, then fold in the flours using a large metal spoon, adding the hot water at the same time.

4 Pour into the tin and bake in a preheated oven at 220°C/425°F/Gas Mark 7 for 9–10 minutes until golden and firm to the touch.

5 Turn the sponge out on to a sheet of baking parchment. Using a 5 cm/ 2 inch heart-shaped cutter, stamp out hearts. Transfer to a wire rack to cool. Lightly dust with icing sugar before serving with the syllabub.

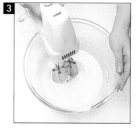

Chinese Fruit Salad

The syrup for this colourful and unusual fruit salad is filled with Chinese flavours for a refreshing dessert.

NUTRITIONAL INFORMATION

Calories	405	Sugars 81g
Protein	.........3g	Fat 6g
Carbohydrate	...83g	Saturates 1g

1¾ hrs   10 mins

SERVES 4

INGREDIENTS

75 ml/3 fl oz Chinese rice wine or dry sherry

rind and juice of 1 lemon

850 ml/1½ pints water

225 g/8 oz caster sugar

2 cloves

2.5 cm/1 inch piece cinnamon stick, bruised

1 vanilla pod

pinch of mixed spice

1 star anise pod

2.5 cm/1 inch piece fresh ginger root, sliced

50 g/1¾ oz unsalted cashew nuts

2 kiwi fruits

1 star fruit

115 g/4 oz strawberries

400 g/14 oz canned lychees in syrup, drained

1 piece stem ginger, drained and sliced

chopped fresh mint, to decorate

 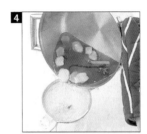 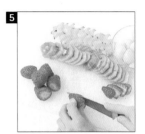

1 Put the Chinese rice wine or sherry in a saucepan together with the lemon rind and juice and the water.

2 Add the caster sugar, cloves, bruised cinnamon stick, vanilla pod, mixed spice, star anise and fresh ginger root to the saucepan.

3 Heat the mixture in the pan gently over a low heat, stirring constantly, until the sugar has dissolved, and then bring it to the boil. Reduce the heat and simmer the mixture for 5 minutes. Set aside to cool completely.

4 Strain the syrup into a bowl or jug, discarding the flavourings. Stir in the cashew nuts, cover with clingfilm and chill in the refrigerator.

5 Meanwhile, prepare the fruits: halve and slice the kiwi fruit, slice the star fruit, and hull and slice the strawberries.

6 Spoon the prepared fruit into a dish with the lychees and ginger. Stir through gently to mix.

7 Pour the syrup over the fruit, decorate with chopped mint and serve.

Exotic Fruit Salad

This is a sophisticated fruit salad that makes use of some of the exotic fruits that can now be seen in the supermarket.

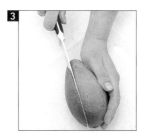

NUTRITIONAL INFORMATION

Calories	149	Sugars	........39g
Protein	.........1g	Fat	...........0.1g
Carbohydrate	...39g	Saturates	.......0g

10 mins   15 mins

SERVES 6

I N G R E D I E N T S

3 passion fruit

125 g/4 oz caster sugar

150 ml/¼ pint water

1 mango

10 lychees, canned or fresh

1 star fruit

1 Halve the passion fruit and press the flesh through a sieve into a saucepan.

2 Add the sugar and water to the pan and bring to a gentle boil, stirring.

3 Put the mango on a chopping board and cut a thick slice from either side, cutting as near to the stone as possible. Cut away as much flesh as possible in large chunks from the stone section.

4 Take the 2 side slices and make 3 cuts through the flesh but not the skin, and 3 more at right angles to make a lattice pattern.

5 Push the mango skin inside out so that the cubed flesh is exposed and you can easily cut it off.

6 Peel and stone the lychees and cut the star fruit into 12 slices.

7 Add all the mango flesh, the lychees and the star fruit to the passion-fruit syrup and poach gently for 5 minutes. Remove the fruit with a perforated spoon.

8 Bring the syrup to the boil and cook for 5 minutes until it thickens slightly.

9 To serve, transfer all the fruit to individual serving glasses, pour over the sugar syrup and serve warm.

COOK'S TIP

A delicious accompaniment to any exotic fruit dish is cardamom cream. Crush the seeds from 2 cardamom pods, add 300 ml/½ pint whipping cream and whip until soft peaks form.

Tropical Fruit Salad

Pawpaws are ready to eat when they yield to gentle pressure.
Serve in the shells of baby pineapples for a stunning effect.

NUTRITIONAL INFORMATION

Calories	69	Sugars	........13g
Protein	.........1g	Fat	..........0.3g
Carbohydrate	...14g	Saturates	......0g

 10 mins　　 0 mins

SERVES 8

INGREDIENTS

1 pawpaw

2 tbsp fresh orange juice

3 tbsp rum

2 bananas

2 guavas

1 small pineapple or 2 baby pineapples

2 passion fruit

pineapple leaves, to decorate

1 Cut the pawpaw in half and remove the seeds. Peel and slice the flesh into a bowl. Pour over the orange juice together with the rum.

2 Peel and slice the bananas and the guavas, and add both to the bowl.

COOK'S TIP

Guavas have a heavenly smell when ripe – their scent will fill a whole room. They should give to gentle pressure when ripe, and their skins should be yellow. The canned varieties are very good and have a pink tinge to the flesh.

3 Cut the top and base from the pineapple, then cut off the skin.

4 Slice the pineapple flesh, discard the core, then cut the flesh into pieces and add to the bowl.

5 Halve the passion fruit, scoop out the flesh with a teaspoon, add to the bowl and stir well to mix.

6 Spoon the salad into glass bowls and decorate with pineapple leaves.

Mango & Passion Fruit Salad

The rich mascarpone cream that accompanies the exotic fruit salad gives this Chinese dessert an Italian twist.

NUTRITIONAL INFORMATION

Calories	211	Sugars	........18g
Protein	.........6g	Fat	..........10g
Carbohydrate	...18g	Saturates	.......6g

1¼ hrs   0 mins

SERVES 4

INGREDIENTS

1 large mango

2 oranges

4 passion fruit

2 tbsp orange-flavoured liqueur, such as Grand Marnier

fresh mint or geranium leaves, to decorate

MASCARPONE CREAM

125 g/4½ oz mascarpone cheese

1 tbsp clear honey

4 tbsp Greek yogurt

few drops vanilla essence

1 Using a sharp knife, cut the mango in half lengthways as close to the stone as possible. Remove the stone, using a sharp knife.

2 Peel off the mango skin, cut the flesh into slices and place in a large bowl.

3 Peel the oranges, removing all the pith, and cut into segments. Add to the bowl with any juices.

4 Halve the passion fruit, scoop out the flesh and add to the bowl with the orange-flavoured liqueur. Mix together all the ingredients in the bowl.

5 Cover the bowl with clingfilm and chill in the refrigerator for 1 hour. Turn into individual glass serving dishes.

6 To make the mascarpone cream, blend the mascarpone cheese and honey together. Add the natural yogurt and the vanilla essence and stir until thoroughly blended.

7 Serve the fruit salad with the mascarpone cream, decorated with mint or geranium leaves.

COOK'S TIP
Passion fruit are ready to eat when their skins are well dimpled. They are most readily available in the summer. Substitute guava or pineapple for the passion fruit, if you prefer.

Aromatic Fruit Salad

The fruits in this salad are arranged attractively on serving plates with a spicy syrup spooned over.

NUTRITIONAL INFORMATION

Calories ....125 Sugars 29g
Protein ....3g Fat 1g
Carbohydrate ...29g Saturates 0.2g

25 mins   5 mins

SERVES 6

INGREDIENTS

60 g/2 oz granulated sugar

150 ml/¼ pint water

1 cinnamon stick or large piece of cassia bark

4 cardamom pods, crushed

1 clove

juice of 1 orange

juice of 1 lime

½ honeydew melon

a good-sized wedge of watermelon

2 ripe guavas

3 ripe nectarines

about 18 strawberries

a little toasted shredded coconut, for sprinkling

sprigs of fresh mint or rose petals, to decorate

strained low-fat Greek yogurt, for serving

1 First prepare the syrup. Put the sugar, water, cinnamon, cardamom pods and cloves into a pan and bring to the boil, stirring to dissolve the sugar. Simmer for 2 minutes, then remove from the heat.

2 Add the orange and lime juices to the syrup and leave to cool and infuse while preparing the fruits.

3 Peel and remove the seeds from the honeydew melon and watermelon and cut the flesh into neat slices.

4 Cut the guavas in half, scoop out the seeds, then peel carefully and slice the flesh neatly.

5 Cut the nectarines into slices and hull and slice the strawberries.

6 Arrange the slices of fruit attractively on 6 serving plates.

7 Strain the prepared cooled syrup and spoon over the sliced fruits.

8 Sprinkle the fruit salad with a little toasted coconut. Decorate each serving with sprigs of mint or rose petals and serve with yogurt.

Tropical Fruit Fool

Fruit fools are always popular, and this light, tangy version will be no exception. You can use your favourite fruits in this recipe.

NUTRITIONAL INFORMATION

Calories 149	Sugars 25g	
Protein 6g	Fat 0.4g	
Carbohydrate ...32g	Saturates 0.2g	

🍧 35 mins 🕐 0 mins

SERVES 4

INGREDIENTS

1 mango

2 kiwi fruit

1 banana

2 tbsp lime juice

½ tsp finely grated lime rind, plus extra to decorate

2 egg whites

425 g/15 oz canned low-fat custard

½ tsp vanilla essence

2 passion fruit

1 Peel the mango, then slice either side of the smooth, flat central stone. Roughly chop the flesh and process the fruit in a food processor or blender until smooth. Alternatively, mash with a fork.

2 Peel the kiwi fruit, chop the flesh into small pieces and place in a bowl. Peel and chop the banana and add to the bowl. Toss the fruit in the lime juice and rind and mix well.

3 In a grease-free bowl, whisk the egg whites until stiff and then gently fold in the custard and vanilla essence until thoroughly mixed.

4 In 4 tall glasses, alternately layer the chopped fruit, mango purée and custard mixture, finishing with the custard on top. Set aside to chill in the refrigerator for 20 minutes.

5 Halve the passion fruits, scoop out the seeds and spoon the passion fruit over the fruit fools. Decorate each serving of tropical fruit fool with the extra lime rind and serve.

VARIATION
Other tropical fruits to try include pawpaw purée, with chopped pineapple and dates or pomegranate seeds to decorate.

Melon & Kiwi Salad

A refreshing fruit salad, ideal to serve after a rich meal. This recipe uses Galia melon, but Charentais or Cantaloupe melons are also good.

NUTRITIONAL INFORMATION

Calories 88	Sugars 17g
Protein 1g	Fat 0.2g
Carbohydrate ...17g	Saturates 0g

1¼ hrs   0 mins

SERVES 4

INGREDIENTS

½ Galia melon

2 kiwi fruits

125 g/4½ oz white seedless grapes

1 pawpaw, halved

3 tbsp orange-flavoured liqueur, such as Cointreau

1 tbsp chopped fresh lemon verbena, lemon balm or mint

sprigs of fresh lemon verbena or Cape gooseberries, to decorate

1 Remove the seeds from the melon, cut it into 4 slices and carefully cut away the skin. Cut the flesh into cubes and put into a bowl.

COOK'S TIP

Lemon balm or sweet balm is a fragrant lemon-scented plant with slightly hairy serrated leaves and a pronounced lemon flavour. Lemon verbena can also be used – this has an even stronger lemon flavour and smooth elongated leaves.

2 Peel the kiwi fruits and cut across into slices. Add to the melon with the white grapes.

3 Remove the seeds from the pawpaw and cut off the skin. Slice the flesh thickly and cut into diagonal pieces. Add to the fruit bowl and mix well.

4 Mix together the liqueur and the chopped lemon verbena, pour over the fruit and leave to macerate for 1 hour, stirring occasionally.

5 Spoon the fruit salad into glasses, pour over the juices and decorate with lemon verbena sprigs or Cape gooseberries.

Summer Fruit Salad

A mixture of soft summer fruits in an orange-flavoured syrup with a dash of port, served with low-fat fromage frais.

NUTRITIONAL INFORMATION

Calories . . . . .110 Sugars 26g
Protein . . . . .1g Fat 0.1g
Carbohydrate . . .26g Saturates 0g

 5 mins   10 mins

SERVES 6

I N G R E D I E N T S

85 g/3 oz caster sugar

5 tbsp water

grated rind and juice of 1 small orange

250 g/9 oz redcurrants, stripped from their stalks

2 tsp arrowroot

2 tbsp port

115 g/4 oz blackberries

115 g/4 oz blueberries

115 g/4 oz strawberries

225 g/8 oz raspberries

low-fat fromage frais, to serve

1 Put the sugar, water and grated orange rind into a heavy-based pan and heat gently, stirring until the sugar has dissolved.

2 Add the redcurrants and orange juice, bring to the boil and simmer gently for 2–3 minutes.

3 Strain the fruit, reserving the syrup, and put into a bowl.

4 Blend the arrowroot with a little water. Return the syrup to the pan, add the arrowroot and bring to the boil, stirring constantly until thickened.

5 Add the port and mix together well. Then pour the syrup over the redcurrants in the bowl.

6 Add the blackberries, blueberries, strawberries and raspberries to the bowl. Mix the fruit together and set aside to cool until required.

7 Serve in individual glass dishes with low-fat fromage frais.

COOK'S TIP

This salad is best made with fresh fruits in season. However, you can achieve an acceptable result with frozen fruit, perhaps with the exception of strawberries. You can buy frozen fruits of the forest, which would be ideal, in most supermarkets.

Chocolate Cheese Pots

These super-light desserts are just the thing if you have a craving for chocolate. Serve on their own or with a selection of fruits.

NUTRITIONAL INFORMATION

Calories 117   Sugars 17g
Protein . . . . .9g   Fat 1g
Carbohydrate . . .18g   Saturates 1g

 40 mins   0 mins

SERVES 4

INGREDIENTS

300 ml/½ pint low-fat natural fromage frais

150 ml/5 fl oz low-fat natural yogurt

2 tbsp icing sugar

4 tsp low-fat drinking chocolate powder

4 tsp cocoa powder

1 tsp vanilla essence

2 tbsp dark rum, optional

2 egg whites

4 chocolate cake decorations

TO SERVE

pieces of kiwi fruit, orange and banana

strawberries and raspberries

1 Combine the fromage frais and low-fat yogurt in a bowl. Sift in the icing sugar, drinking chocolate and cocoa powder and mix well. Add the vanilla essence and rum, if using.

2 In a clean bowl, whisk the egg whites until stiff. Using a metal spoon, gently fold the egg whites into the chocolate mixture.

3 Spoon the fromage frais and chocolate mixture into 4 small china dessert pots and set aside in the refrigerator to chill for about 30 minutes.

4 Decorate each chocolate cheese pot with a chocolate decoration and serve with an assortment of fresh fruit, such as kiwi fruit, orange, banana, strawberries and raspberries.

COOK'S TIP

This mixture would make an excellent filling for a cheesecake. Make the base out of crushed amaretti biscuits and egg white, and set the filling with 2 tbsp gelozone dissolved in 2 tbsp of boiling water.

Tropical Fruit Rice Mould

A rice pudding with a twist – light flakes of rice with a tang of pineapple and lime. You can serve it with any selection of your favourite fruits.

NUTRITIONAL INFORMATION

Calories	145	Sugars	........18g
Protein	.........7g	Fat	...........1g
Carbohydrate	...30g	Saturates	.....0.3g

 4¼ hrs   25 mins

SERVES 8

I N G R E D I E N T S

225 g/8 oz short-grain or pudding
    rice, rinsed

850 ml/1½ pints skimmed milk

1 tbsp caster sugar

4 tbsp white rum with coconut, or
    unsweetened pineapple juice

175 ml/6 fl oz low-fat natural yogurt

400 g/14 oz canned pineapple pieces in
    natural juice, drained and chopped

1 tsp grated lime rind

1 tbsp lime juice

2 tsp powdered gelozone (vegetarian
    gelatine) dissolved in 3 tbsp boiling water

lime wedges, to decorate

mixed tropical fruits, such as
    passion fruit, baby pineapple, pawpaw,
    mango, star fruit, to serve

1 Place the rice and milk in a saucepan. Bring to the boil, then simmer gently, uncovered, for 20 minutes until the rice is soft and the milk is absorbed. Stir the mixture occasionally and keep the heat low to prevent sticking.

2 Transfer the mixture to a mixing bowl and leave to cool.

3 Stir the sugar, white rum with coconut or pineapple juice, yogurt, pineapple pieces, lime rind and juice into the rice. Fold in the gelozone mixture.

4 Rinse a 1.5 litre/2½ pint non-stick ring mould or ring cake tin with water and spoon in the rice mixture. Press down well, level the top with the back of a spoon and chill for 2 hours until firm.

5 To serve, gently loosen the rice from the mould with a small palette knife and invert it carefully onto a serving plate.

6 Decorate with lime wedges and fill the centre with assorted tropical fruits.

COOK'S TIP

Try serving this dessert with a light sauce made from 300 ml/½ pint tropical fruit or pineapple juice thickened with 2 tsp arrowroot.

Blackberry Pudding

A delicious dessert to make when blackberries are in abundance.
If blackberries are unavailable, try using currants or gooseberries.

NUTRITIONAL INFORMATION

Calories 455   Sugars 47g
Protein ....7g   Fat 18g
Carbohydrate ...70g   Saturates 11g

15–20 mins   30 mins

SERVES 4

INGREDIENTS

butter, for greasing

450 g/1 lb blackberries

75 g/2¾ oz caster sugar

1 egg

75 g/2¾ oz soft brown sugar

6 tbsp butter, melted

8 tbsp milk

125 g/4½ oz self-raising flour

sugar, for sprinkling

1 Lightly grease a large 900-ml/1½-pint ovenproof dish with butter.

2 In a large mixing bowl, gently mix together the blackberries and caster sugar until well combined.

3 Transfer the blackberry and sugar mixture to the prepared dish.

4 Beat the egg and soft brown sugar in a separate mixing bowl. Stir in the melted butter and milk.

5 Sift the flour into the egg and butter mixture and fold together lightly with a figure-of-eight movement to form a smooth batter.

6 Carefully spread the batter over the blackberry and sugar mixture in the ovenproof dish.

7 Bake the pudding in a preheated oven, 180°C/350°F/Gas Mark 4, for about 25–30 minutes until the topping is firm and golden.

8 Sprinkle the pudding with a little sugar and serve hot.

VARIATION

You can add 2 tablespoons of cocoa powder to the batter in step 5, if you prefer a chocolate flavour.

Sticky Sesame Bananas

These tasty morsels are a real treat. Pieces of banana are drizzled with caramel and then sprinkled with a few sesame seeds.

NUTRITIONAL INFORMATION

Calories 215   Sugars 38g
Protein . . . . .6g   Fat 3g
Carbohydrate . . .41g   Saturates 1g

10 mins   20 mins

SERVES 4

I N G R E D I E N T S

4 ripe bananas

3 tbsp lemon juice

115 g/4 oz caster sugar

4 tbsp cold water

2 tbsp sesame seeds

150 ml/5 fl oz low-fat natural fromage frais

1 tbsp icing sugar

1 tsp vanilla essence

T O   D E C O R A T E

grated lemon rind

grated lime rind

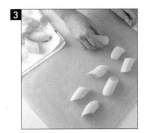

1 Peel the bananas and cut into 5 cm/ 2 inch pieces. Place the banana pieces in a bowl, spoon over the lemon juice and stir well to coat – this will help prevent the bananas from discolouring.

2 Place the sugar and water in a small pan and heat gently, stirring constantly, until the sugar dissolves. Bring to the boil and cook for 5–6 minutes until the mixture turns golden brown.

3 Meanwhile, drain the bananas and blot with kitchen paper to dry. Line a baking sheet or board with baking paper and arrange the bananas, well spaced apart, on top.

4 When the caramel is ready, drizzle it over the bananas, working quickly because the caramel sets almost instantly. Sprinkle the sesame seeds over the caramelised bananas and set aside to cool for 10 minutes.

5 Mix the fromage frais with the icing sugar and vanilla essence.

6 Peel the bananas away from the paper and arrange on serving plates.

7 Serve the sweetened fromage frais as a dip, decorated with the grated lemon and lime rind.

Apricot & Orange Jellies

These bright, fruity little desserts are really easy to make. Serve them with low-fat ice cream and be transported back to childhood!

NUTRITIONAL INFORMATION

Calories 206   Sugars 36g
Protein . . . . .8g   Fat 5g
Carbohydrate . . .36g   Saturates 3g

 4¼ hrs   25 mins

SERVES 4

I N G R E D I E N T S

225 g/8 oz no-need-to-soak dried apricots

300 ml/½ pint unsweetened orange juice

2 tbsp lemon juice

2–3 tsp clear honey

1 tbsp powdered gelozone (vegetarian gelatine)

4 tbsp boiling water

TO DECORATE

orange segments

sprigs of fresh mint

CINNAMON 'CREAM'

125 g/4½ oz medium-fat ricotta cheese

125 g/4½ oz low-fat natural fromage frais

1 tsp ground cinnamon

1 tbsp clear honey

1 Place the apricots in a saucepan and pour in the orange juice. Bring to the boil, cover and simmer for 15–20 minutes until the apricots are plump and soft. Leave to cool for 10 minutes.

2 Transfer the mixture to a blender or food processor and blend until smooth. Stir in the lemon juice and add the honey. Pour the mixture into a measuring jug and make up to 600 ml/ 1 pint with cold water.

3 Dissolve the gelozone in the boiling water and then stir it into the apricot mixture in the jug.

4 Pour the mixture into 4 individual moulds, each 150 ml/5 fl oz, or into 1 large mould, 600 ml/1 pint. Leave to chill until set.

5 Meanwhile, make the cinnamon 'cream'. Mix all the ingredients together and place in a small bowl. Cover the mixture and leave to chill until needed.

6 To turn out the jellies, dip the moulds in hot water for a few seconds and invert on to serving plates.

7 Decorate the jellies with the orange segments and sprigs of mint. Serve with the cinnamon 'cream', dusted with a little extra cinnamon.

Lime Mousse with Mango

Lime-flavoured cream moulds, served with a fresh mango and lime sauce, make a stunning dessert.

NUTRITIONAL INFORMATION

Calories .... .254	Sugars 17g
Protein 5g	Fat 19g
Carbohydrate ...17g	Saturates 12g

10 mins

0 mins

SERVES 4

INGREDIENTS

250 g/9 oz fromage frais

grated rind of 1 lime

1 tbsp caster sugar

125 ml/4 fl oz double cream

MANGO SAUCE

1 mango

juice of 1 lime

4 tsp caster sugar

TO DECORATE

4 Cape gooseberries

strips of lime rind

1 Put the fromage frais, lime rind and sugar in a bowl and mix together.

2 Whisk the double cream in a separate bowl and fold into the fromage frais.

3 Line 4 decorative moulds or ramekin dishes with muslin or clingfilm and divide the mixture evenly between them. Fold the muslin or clingfilm over the top and press down firmly.

4 To make the sauce, slice through the mango on each side of the large flat stone, then cut the flesh from the stone. Remove the skin.

5 Cut off 12 thin slices and set aside. Chop the remaining mango and put in a food processor with the lime juice and sugar. Blend until smooth. Alternatively, push the mango through a sieve, then mix with the lime juice and sugar.

6 Turn out the moulds on to serving plates. Arrange 3 slices of mango on each plate, pour some sauce around, decorate and serve.

COOK'S TIP
Cape gooseberries have a tart and mildly scented flavour and make an excellent decoration for many desserts. Peel back the papery husks to expose the bright orange fruits.

Raspberry Risotto

Why shouldn't risotto be served as a dessert? If you think about it, most risottos are really savoury rice puddings. This is really delicious – try it.

NUTRITIONAL INFORMATION

Calories ....595 Sugars 54g
Protein ....8g Fat 26g
Carbohydrate ...81g Saturates 16g

 15 mins   30 mins

SERVES 4–6

INGREDIENTS

450 ml/16 fl oz milk

450 ml/16 fl oz canned unsweetened coconut milk

pinch of salt

1 vanilla pod, split

2–3 strips lemon rind

2 tbsp unsalted butter

125 g/4½ oz arborio rice

50 ml/2 fl oz dry white vermouth

100 g/3½ oz sugar

125 ml/4 fl oz double or whipping cream

2–3 tbsp raspberry-flavoured liqueur

350 g/12 oz fresh raspberries

2 tbsp good-quality raspberry jam or preserve

squeeze of lemon juice

toasted flaked almonds, to decorate (optional)

1 Heat the milk in a heavy-based saucepan with the coconut milk, salt, vanilla pod and lemon rind until bubbles begin to form around the edge of the pan. Reduce the heat to low and keep the milk mixture hot, stirring occasionally.

2 Heat the butter in another large heavy-based pan over a medium heat until foaming. Add the rice and cook, stirring, for 2 minutes to coat well.

3 Add the vermouth; it will bubble and steam rapidly. Cook, stirring, until the wine is completely absorbed. Gradually add the hot milk, about 125 ml/4 fl oz at a time, allowing each addition of milk to be absorbed completely before adding the next.

4 When half the milk has been added, stir in the sugar until dissolved. Continue stirring and adding the milk until the rice is tender, but still firm to the bite: this should take about 25 minutes. Remove the pan from the heat and remove the vanilla pod and lemon strips. Stir in half the cream, the liqueur and half the fresh raspberries; cover.

5 Heat the raspberry jam with the lemon juice and 1–2 tablespoons water, stirring until smooth. Remove from the heat, add the remaining raspberries and mix. Stir the remaining cream into the risotto and serve with the glazed raspberries. Decorate with almonds if wished.

Strawberry Roulade

Serve this moist, light sponge rolled up with an almond and strawberry fromage frais filling for a delicious tea-time treat.

NUTRITIONAL INFORMATION

Calories 166	Sugars 19g	
Protein 6g	Fat 3g	
Carbohydrate . . .30g	Saturates 1g	

 30 mins   10 mins

SERVES 8

INGREDIENTS

3 large eggs

125 g/4½ oz caster sugar

125 g/4½ oz plain flour

1 tbsp hot water

FILLING

200 ml/7 fl oz low-fat fromage frais

1 tsp almond essence

225 g/8 oz small strawberries

TO DECORATE

1 tbsp flaked almonds, toasted

1 tsp icing sugar

1 Line a 35 x 25 cm/14 x 10 inch Swiss roll tin with baking paper. Put the eggs in a mixing bowl with the caster sugar. Place the bowl over a pan of hot, but not boiling, water and whisk until the mixture is pale and thick.

2 Remove the bowl from the pan. Sift in the flour and fold into the eggs with the hot water. Pour the mixture into the tin and bake in a preheated oven, 220°C/425°F/Gas Mark 7, for about 8–10 minutes, until golden and set.

3 Turn the sponge onto a fresh sheet of baking paper. Peel off the lining paper and roll up the sponge tightly, using the baking paper to help roll. Wrap in a tea towel and set aside to cool.

4 Mix together the fromage frais and the almond essence. Reserving a few strawberries for decoration, wash, hull and slice the remainder. Leave the fromage frais mixture and strawberries to chill in the refrigerator until required.

5 Unroll the sponge, spread the fromage frais mixture over the sponge and sprinkle with the sliced strawberries. Roll the sponge up again and transfer to a serving plate.

6 Sprinkle the strawberry roulade with the flaked almonds and lightly dust with the icing sugar. Decorate with the reserved strawberries.

Ricotta Lemon Cheesecake

Italian bakers pride themselves on their baked ricotta cheesecakes, studded with fruit soaked in spirits.

NUTRITIONAL INFORMATION

Calories ....188 Sugars 21g
Protein ....6g Fat 8g
Carbohydrate ...23g Saturates 4g

  3¾ hrs 30–40 mins

SERVES 6–8

INGREDIENTS

55 g/2 oz sultanas

3 tbsp Marsala or grappa

butter, for greasing

2 tbsp semolina, plus extra for dusting

350 g/12 oz ricotta cheese, drained

3 large egg yolks, beaten

100 g/3½ oz caster sugar

3 tbsp lemon juice

2 tbsp candied orange peel, finely chopped

finely grated rind of 2 large lemons

TO DECORATE

icing sugar

fresh mint sprigs

redcurrants or berries (optional)

1 Soak the sultanas in the Marsala or grappa in a small bowl for about 30 minutes or until the liquid has been absorbed and the fruit is swollen.

2 Meanwhile, cut out a circle of baking paper to fit a loose-based 20 cm/8 inch round cake tin, about 5 cm/2 inches deep. Grease and base-line the tin. Lightly dust with semolina and tip out the excess.

3 Using a wooden spoon, press the ricotta cheese though a nylon sieve into a bowl. Add the egg yolks, sugar, semolina and lemon juice and beat well until blended.

4 Fold in the sultanas, candied orange peel and lemon rind. Pour into the tin and smooth the surface.

5 Bake the cheesecake in the centre of a preheated oven, 180°C/350°F/Gas Mark 4 for 30–40 minutes until firm when you press the top and coming away slightly from the side of the tin.

6 Turn off the oven and open the door. Leave the cheesecake to cool in the oven for 2–3 hours. To serve, remove from the pan and transfer to a plate. Sift over a layer of icing sugar to dust the top and sides lightly. Decorate with mint and redcurrants, if wished.

Balsamic Strawberries

Generations of Italian cooks have known that the unlikely combination of freshly ground black pepper and ripe, juicy strawberries is fantastic.

NUTRITIONAL INFORMATION

Calories ....132 Sugars 5g
Protein ....1g Fat 12g
Carbohydrate ....5g Saturates 7g

10 mins, plus chilling   0 mins

SERVES 4–6

I N G R E D I E N T S

450 g/1 lb fresh strawberries

2–3 tbsp balsamic vinegar

fresh mint leaves, torn, plus extra to decorate (optional)

115–175 g/4–6 oz mascarpone cheese

pepper

1 Wipe the strawberries with a damp cloth, rather than rinsing them, so they do not become soggy. Using a paring knife, cut off the stalks at the top and then use the tip to remove the core.

2 Cut each strawberry in half or into quarters if large. Transfer to a bowl.

3 Add ½ tablespoon of the vinegar per person. Add several twists of ground black pepper, then gently stir together. Cover with clingfilm and chill for 4 hours.

4 Just before serving, stir in the mint leaves to taste. Spoon the mascarpone into bowls and spoon the berries on top.

5 Decorate the balsamic strawberries with a few mint leaves, if wished. Sprinkle with extra pepper to taste.

COOK'S TIP
This is most enjoyable when it is made with the best-quality balsamic vinegar, one that has aged slowly and has turned thick and syrupy. Unfortunately, the genuine mixture is always expensive – cheaper versions are artificially sweetened and coloured.

Piña Colada Pineapple

The flavours of pineapple and coconut blend as well together on the barbecue as they do in the well-known cocktail.

NUTRITIONAL INFORMATION

Calories 231   Sugars 22g
Protein . . . . .1g   Fat 15g
Carbohydrate . . .22g   Saturates 11g

15 mins   25 mins

SERVES 4

INGREDIENTS

1 small pineapple

2 tbsp unsalted butter

25 g/1 oz light muscovado sugar

55 g/2 oz fresh coconut, grated

2 tbsp coconut-flavoured liqueur or rum

1 Using a very sharp knife, cut the pineapple into quarters and then remove the tough core from the centre, leaving the leaves attached.

2 Carefully cut the pineapple flesh away from the skin. Remove any 'eyes' with small sharp knife. Make horizontal cuts across the flesh of the pineapple quarters.

3 Gently heat the butter in a pan until melted, stirring constantly. Brush the melted butter over the pineapple and sprinkle with the sugar.

4 Cover the pineapple leaves with kitchen foil to prevent them from burning, and transfer the pineapple quarters to a rack set over hot coals.

5 Barbecue the pineapple for about 10 minutes.

6 Sprinkle the coconut over the pineapple and barbecue, cut side up, for a further 5–10 minutes or until the pineapple is piping hot.

7 Transfer the pineapple to serving plates and remove the foil from the leaves. Spoon a little coconut-flavoured liqueur or rum over the pineapple and serve immediately.

COOK'S TIP

Fresh coconut has the best flavour for this dish. If you prefer, however, you can use desiccated coconut.

Fruit Salad & Ginger Syrup

This is a very special fruit salad made from the most exotic and colourful fruits, soaked in a syrup made with fresh ginger and ginger wine.

NUTRITIONAL INFORMATION

Calories 225	Sugars 45g
Protein 2g	Fat 4g
Carbohydrate ...45g	Saturates 3g

4½ hrs   5 mins

SERVES 4

INGREDIENTS

2.5 cm/1 inch piece fresh root ginger, peeled and chopped

60 g/2 oz caster sugar

150 ml/¼ pint water

grated rind and juice of 1 lime

4 tbsp ginger wine

1 pineapple, peeled, cored and cut into bite-sized pieces

2 mangoes, peeled, stoned and diced

4 kiwi fruit, peeled and sliced

1 pawpaw, peeled, seeded and diced

2 passion fruit, halved and flesh removed

350 g/12 oz lychees, peeled and stoned

¼ fresh coconut, grated

60 g/2 oz Cape gooseberries, to decorate (optional)

coconut ice cream, to serve (optional)

1 Place the ginger, sugar, water and lime juice in a pan and bring slowly to the boil. Simmer for 1 minute, remove from the heat and allow to cool slightly.

2 Sieve the syrup, add the ginger wine and mix well. Cool completely.

3 Place the prepared fruit in a serving bowl. Add the cold syrup and mix well. Cover and chill the fruit in the refrigerator for 2–4 hours.

4 Just before serving, add half of the grated coconut to the salad and mix well. Sprinkle the remainder on top.

5 If using Cape gooseberries to decorate the salad, peel back each calyx to form a flower. Wipe the berries clean, then arrange them around the side of the fruit salad before serving.

COOK'S TIP
Cape gooseberries are golden in colour and in appearance resemble ground cherries, rather than gooseberries. They make a delightful decoration to many fruit-based desserts.

Thai Rice Pudding

This Thai-style version of rice pudding is mildly spiced and creamy, with a rich custard topping. It is excellent served warm or cold.

NUTRITIONAL INFORMATION

Calories 351	Sugars 16g
Protein 7g	Fat 21g
Carbohydrate . . .37g	Saturates 16g

🍶 10 mins   🕐 1–1¼ hrs

SERVES 4

INGREDIENTS

100 g/3½ oz short grain rice

2 tbsp palm sugar

1 cardamom pod, split

300 ml/½ pint coconut milk

150 ml/5 fl oz water

3 eggs

200 ml/7 fl oz coconut cream

1½ tbsp caster sugar

sweetened coconut flakes, to decorate

fresh fruit, to serve

1 Place the rice and palm sugar in a pan. Crush the seeds from the cardamom pod in a mortar with a pestle and add to the pan. Stir in the coconut milk and water.

2 Bring to the boil, stirring to dissolve the sugar. Lower the heat and simmer, uncovered, stirring occasionally, for about 20 minutes until the rice is tender and most of the liquid is absorbed.

3 Spoon the rice into 4 individual ovenproof dishes and spread evenly. Place the dishes in a wide roasting tin and pour in enough water to come about halfway up the sides.

4 Beat the eggs with the coconut cream and caster sugar and spoon over the rice. Cover with foil and bake in a preheated oven, 180°C/350°F/Gas Mark 4, for about 45–50 minutes or until the custard sets.

5 Serve the rice puddings warm or cold, decorated with sweetened coconut flakes and a portion of the fresh fruit of your choice.

COOK'S TIP

Cardamom is quite a powerful spice, so if you find it too strong, it can be left out altogether or replaced with a little ground cinnamon.

Kesari Kheer

This is a classic Indian milk pudding, full of exotic spices. This version contains saffron, which gives it a lovely deep-yellow colour.

NUTRITIONAL INFORMATION

Calories	470	Sugars	........42g
Protein	........11g	Fat	.........25g
Carbohydrate	...53g	Saturates	......13g

5 mins, plus chilling

1 hr

SERVES 4–6

INGREDIENTS

2 tbsp clarified butter or ghee

85 g/3 oz basmati rice, washed and well drained

1.5 litres/2¾ pints milk

115 g/4 oz sugar or to taste

10–12 green cardamom pods, crushed to remove the black seeds (pods discarded)

70 g/2½ oz sultanas or raisins

large pinch saffron threads, about ½ tsp, soaked in 2–3 tbsp milk

60 g/2¼ oz green pistachios, lightly toasted

150 ml/5 fl oz double cream, whipped (optional)

ground cinnamon, for dusting

varq (edible silver foil, see page 912), to decorate (optional)

1 Melt the butter in a large, heavy-based saucepan over a medium heat. Pour in the rice and cook, stirring almost constantly, for about 6 minutes until the rice grains are translucent and a deep golden brown.

2 Pour in the milk and bring to the boil over a high heat. Reduce the heat to medium-high and simmer for about 30 minutes, stirring occasionally, until the milk has reduced by about half.

3 Add the sugar, cardamom seeds and sultanas and cook for about a further 20 minutes until reduced and thick. Stir in the saffron-milk mixture and simmer over a low heat until as thick as possible, stirring almost constantly. Remove from the heat and stir in half the pistachios.

4 Place the saucepan in a larger pan of iced water and stir until cool. If using, stir in the cream, then spoon into a serving bowl and chill.

5 To serve, dust the top of the pudding with ground cinnamon. Sprinkle with the remaining pistachios and, if using, decorate with pieces of varq.

COOK'S TIP
Using the whipped double cream in this recipe is not authentic, but it does make the pudding very light.

Aztec Oranges

Simplicity itself, this refreshing orange dessert is hard to beat and is the perfect follow-up to a hearty, spiced main course dish.

NUTRITIONAL INFORMATION

Calories 98   Sugars 20g
Protein . . . . .2g   Fat 0g
Carbohydrate . . .20g   Saturates 0g

45 mins   0 mins

SERVES 4–6

I N G R E D I E N T S

6 oranges

1 lime

2 tbsp tequila

2 tbsp orange-flavoured liqueur

dark soft brown sugar, to taste

fine lime rind strips, to decorate
   (see Cook's Tip)

1 Using a sharp knife, cut a slice off the top and bottom of the oranges, then remove the peel and pith, cutting downwards and taking care to retain the shape of the oranges.

2 Holding the oranges on their side, cut them horizontally into slices.

3 Place the oranges in a bowl. Cut the lime in half and squeeze over the oranges. Sprinkle with the tequila and liqueur, then sprinkle over sugar to taste.

4 Cover with clingfilm and chill in the refrigerator until ready to serve, then transfer to a serving dish and garnish with lime strips.

COOK'S TIP

To make the decoration, finely pare the rind from a lime using a vegetable peeler, then cut into thin strips. Blanch in boiling water for 2 minutes. Drain and rinse under cold running water. Drain again and pat dry with kitchen paper.

Italian Lemon Rice Cake

This lemony cake should have a crisp crust with a soft, moist centre.
Soaking the currants in rum brings out their fruitiness.

NUTRITIONAL INFORMATION

Calories	283	Sugars	........24g
Protein	.........7g	Fat	..........10g
Carbohydrate	...41g	Saturates	.......6g

1¼ hrs   1¼ hrs

SERVES 8–10

INGREDIENTS

1 litre/1¾ pints milk

pinch of salt

200 g/7 oz arborio or pudding rice

1 vanilla pod, split

55 g/2 oz currants

50 ml/2 fl oz rum or water

2 tsp melted butter, for greasing

cornmeal or polenta, for dusting

140 g/5 oz sugar

grated rind of 1 large lemon

4 tbsp butter, diced

3 eggs

2–3 tbsp lemon juice (optional)

icing sugar

TO SERVE

175 g/6 oz mascarpone cheese

2 tbsp rum

2 tbsp whipping cream

1 Bring the milk to the boil. Sprinkle in the salt and rice and bring back to the boil. Add the vanilla pod and seeds. Lower the heat and simmer, stirring occasionally, for 30 minutes.

2 Meanwhile, bring the currants and rum to the boil, then set aside.

3 Brush the base and side of a 25 cm/ 10 inch loose-based cake tin with butter. Dust with 2–3 tablespoons of cornmeal and shake out any excess.

4 Remove the rice from the heat and remove the vanilla pod. Stir in all but 1 tablespoon of sugar, with the lemon rind and butter, until the sugar is dissolved. Place in iced water to cool. Stir in the soaked currants and remaining rum.

5 Using an electric mixer, beat the eggs for about 2 minutes until light and foamy. Gradually beat in about half the rice mixture, then stir in the rest. If using, stir in the lemon juice.

6 Pour into the prepared tin and smooth the top. Sprinkle with the reserved sugar and bake in a preheated oven, 160°C/325°F/Gas Mark 3 for about 40 minutes until risen and golden and slightly firm. Cool in the tin on a wire rack.

7 Remove the side of the tin and slide the cake off the base onto a serving plate. Dust the top with icing sugar. Whisk the mascarpone with the rum and cream and serve with the cake.

Ginger & Apricot Alaskas

No ice cream in this Alaska but a mixture of apples and apricots poached in orange juice and enclosed in meringue.

NUTRITIONAL INFORMATION

Calories ....442 Sugars 77g
Protein ....7g Fat 9g
Carbohydrate ...83g Saturates 3g

15 mins   10 mins

SERVES 2

INGREDIENTS

2 slices rich, dark ginger cake, about
  2 cm/¾ inch thick

1–2 tbsp ginger wine or rum

1 apple

6 ready-to-eat dried apricots, chopped

4 tbsp orange juice or water

15 g/½ oz flaked almonds

2 small egg whites

100 g/3½ oz caster sugar

1 Place each slice of ginger cake on an ovenproof plate and sprinkle with the ginger wine or rum.

2 Quarter, core and slice the apple into a small saucepan. Add the chopped apricots and orange juice or water, and simmer the mixture over a low heat for about 5 minutes, or until tender.

3 Stir the flaked almonds into the cooked fruit and spoon the mixture equally over the slices of soaked cake, piling it up in the centre.

4 Whisk the egg whites until very stiff and dry, then whisk in the sugar, a little at a time, making sure the meringue has become stiff again before adding the next quantity of sugar.

5 Either pipe or spread the meringue over the fruit and cake, making sure that both are completely covered.

6 Place in a preheated oven, 200°C/ 400°F/Gas Mark 6, for 4–5 minutes, until golden brown. Serve hot.

VARIATION

A slice of vanilla, coffee or chocolate ice cream can be placed on the fruit before adding the meringue, but this must be done at the last minute and the dessert must be eaten immediately after it is removed from the oven.

Eve's Pudding

This is a popular family favourite pudding with soft apples on the bottom and a light buttery sponge on top.

NUTRITIONAL INFORMATION

Calories 365   Sugars 40g
Protein ....5g   Fat 14g
Carbohydrate ...58g   Saturates 7g

 15 mins   45 mins

SERVES 4

INGREDIENTS

6 tbsp butter, plus extra for greasing

450 g/1 lb Bramley apples, peeled, cored and sliced

85 g/3 oz granulated sugar

1 tbsp lemon juice

55 g/2 oz sultanas

85 g/3 oz caster sugar

1 egg, beaten

150 g/5½ oz self-raising flour

3 tbsp milk

25 g/1 oz flaked almonds

custard or double cream, to serve

1 Grease a 900 ml/1½ pint ovenproof dish with butter.

2 Mix the apples with the granulated sugar, lemon juice and sultanas. Spoon the mixture into the prepared dish.

3 In a mixing bowl, cream the butter and caster sugar together until pale. Add the beaten egg, a little at a time.

4 Carefully fold in the self-raising flour and stir in the milk to give a soft, dropping consistency.

5 Spread the sponge mixture evenly over the apples and sprinkle with the flaked almonds.

6 Bake in a preheated oven, 180°C/350°F/Gas Mark 4, for 40–45 minutes until the sponge is golden brown.

7 Serve the pudding piping hot, accompanied by home-made custard or double cream.

COOK'S TIP
To increase the almond flavour of this pudding, add 25 g/1 oz ground almonds with the flour in step 4.

Raspberry Shortcake

For this lovely summery dessert, two crisp rounds of shortbread are sandwiched together with fresh raspberries and lightly whipped cream.

NUTRITIONAL INFORMATION

Calories 496   Sugars 14g
Protein ....4g   Fat 41g
Carbohydrate ...30g   Saturates 26g

 40 mins   15 mins

SERVES 8

INGREDIENTS

100 g/3½ oz butter, cut into cubes, plus extra for greasing

175 g/6 oz self-raising flour

85 g/3 oz caster sugar

1 egg yolk

1 tbsp rosewater

600 ml/1 pint whipping cream, lightly whipped

225 g/8 oz raspberries, plus a few extra for decoration

TO DECORATE

icing sugar

fresh mint leaves

1 Lightly grease 2 baking sheets with a little butter.

2 To make the shortcake, sift the self-raising flour into a bowl. Add the butter and rub it into the flour with your fingertips until the mixture resembles fine breadcrumbs.

3 Stir the caster sugar, egg yolk and rose water into the mixture and bring together with your fingers to form a soft dough. Divide the dough in half.

4 Roll out each piece of dough to a 20 cm/8 inch round on a lightly floured surface. Carefully lift each one with the rolling pin on to the prepared baking sheets. Gently crimp the edges of the dough with your finger.

5 Bake in a preheated oven, 190°C/375°F/Gas Mark 5, for 15 minutes until lightly golden brown. Transfer the shortcakes to a wire rack and leave them to cool completely.

6 Mix the lightly whipped cream with the raspberries and spoon the mixture on top of one of the shortcakes, spreading it out evenly to cover completely. Place with the other shortcake round on top. Dust the raspberry shortcake with a little icing sugar and decorate with the extra raspberries and mint leaves.

COOK'S TIP

The shortcake can be made a few days in advance and stored in an airtight container until required.

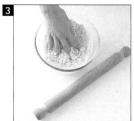

Peaches & Mascarpone

If you prepare these in advance, all you have to do is pop the peaches on the barbecue when you are ready to serve them.

NUTRITIONAL INFORMATION

Calories 301	Sugars 24g	
Protein 6g	Fat 20g	
Carbohydrate . . .24g	Saturates 9g	

 10 mins   🕐 10 mins

SERVES 4

INGREDIENTS

4 peaches

175 g/6 oz mascarpone cheese

40 g/1½ oz pecan or walnuts, chopped

1 tsp sunflower oil

4 tbsp maple syrup

1 Cut the peaches in half and remove the stones. If you are preparing this recipe in advance, press the peach halves together and wrap them in clingfilm.

2 Combine the mascarpone and pecans or walnuts in a small bowl. Set aside to chill in the refrigerator until required.

3 To grill, brush the peaches with a little sunflower oil and place on a rack set over medium-hot coals. Barbecue the peaches for 5–10 minutes, turning once, until hot.

4 Transfer the peaches to a serving dish and top them with the mascarpone cheese and nut mixture.

5 Drizzle the maple syrup over the peaches and mascarpone filling and serve immediately.

VARIATION

You can use nectarines instead of peaches for this recipe. Remember to choose ripe but firm fruit which won't go soft and mushy when it is barbecued. Prepare the nectarines in the same way as the peaches and barbecue for 5–10 minutes.

Green Fruit Salad

This delightfully refreshing fruit salad is the perfect finale for a Chinese meal. It has a lovely light syrup made with fresh mint and honey.

NUTRITIONAL INFORMATION

Calories ....157 Sugars 34g
Protein ....1g Fat 0.2g
Carbohydrate ...34g Saturates 0g

30 mins   15 mins

SERVES 4

INGREDIENTS

1 small Charentais or honeydew melon

2 green apples

2 kiwi fruit

115 g/4 oz seedless white grapes

fresh mint sprigs, to decorate

SYRUP

1 orange

150 ml/5 fl oz white wine

150 ml/5 fl oz water

4 tbsp clear honey

fresh mint sprigs

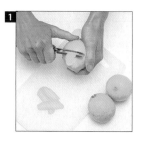  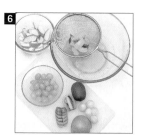

1 To make the syrup, pare the rind from the orange using a potato peeler.

2 Put the orange rind in a pan with the white wine, water and clear honey.

Bring the mixture to the boil, then simmer gently for 10 minutes.

3 Remove the syrup from the heat. Add the mint sprigs and set aside to cool.

4 To prepare the fruit, first slice the melon in half and scoop out the seeds. Use a melon baller or a teaspoon to make melon balls.

5 Core and chop the apples. Peel and slice the kiwi fruit.

6 Strain the cooled syrup into a serving bowl, removing and reserving the orange rind and discarding the mint sprigs.

7 Add the apple, grapes, kiwi fruit and melon to the serving bowl. Stir through gently to mix and coat all the ingredients with syrup.

8 Serve the fruit salad, decorated with sprigs of fresh mint and some of the reserved orange rind.

COOK'S TIP

Single-flower honey has a better, more individual flavour than blended honey. Acacia honey is typically Chinese, but you could also try clove, lemon blossom, lime flower or orange blossom.

Chocolate Meringues

The Mexican name for these delicate meringues is 'suspiros', meaning 'sighs' – supposedly the contented sighs of the nuns who created them.

NUTRITIONAL INFORMATION

Calories	55	Sugars	........11g
Protein	.........1g	Fat	...........1g
Carbohydrate	....11g	Saturates	.......1g

1¼ hrs   2 hrs

SERVES 4

INGREDIENTS

4–5 egg whites, at room temperature

pinch of salt

¼ tsp cream of tartar

¼–½ tsp vanilla essence

175–200 g/6–7 oz caster sugar

⅛–¼ tsp ground cinnamon

115 g/4 oz bitter or dark chocolate, grated

TO SERVE

ground cinnamon

115 g/4 oz strawberries

chocolate-flavoured cream (see Cook's Tip)

1 Whisk the egg whites until they are foamy, then add the salt and cream of tartar and whisk until very stiff. Whisk in the vanilla, then slowly whisk in the sugar, a small amount at a time, until the meringue is shiny and stiff. This should take about 3 minutes by hand, and less than a minute with an electric whisk.

2 Whisk in the cinnamon and grated chocolate. Spoon or pipe mounds of about 2 tablespoons, well apart, on to an ungreased non-stick baking sheet.

3 Place in a preheated oven at 150°C/300°F/Gas Mark 2 and cook for 2 hours until set and dry.

4 Carefully remove the meringues from the baking sheet with a palette knife. If the meringues are still too moist and soft, return them to the oven to firm up and dry out a little more. Allow to cool completely on a wire rack.

5 Serve the meringues dusted with a sprinkling of cinnamon and accompanied by strawberries and chocolate-flavoured cream.

COOK'S TIP
To make the flavoured cream, simply stir half-melted chocolate pieces into stiffly whipped cream, then chill until solid.

Toasted Tropical Fruit

Spear some chunks of exotic tropical fruits on to kebab sticks, sear them over the barbecue and serve with this amazing chocolate dip.

NUTRITIONAL INFORMATION

Calories ....435 Sugars 60g
Protein ....6g Fat 11g
Carbohydrate ...68g Saturates 6g

45 mins   5 mins

SERVES 4

INGREDIENTS

DIP

125 g/4½ oz plain chocolate,
    broken into pieces

2 tbsp golden syrup

1 tbsp cocoa powder

1 tbsp cornflour

200 ml/7 fl oz milk

KEBABS

1 mango

1 pawpaw

2 kiwi fruit

½ small pineapple

1 large banana

2 tbsp lemon juice

150 ml/¼ pint white rum

1 Put all the ingredients for the chocolate dip into a heavy-based saucepan. Heat over the barbecue or over a low heat, stirring constantly, until thickened and smooth. Keep warm at the edge of the barbecue.

2 Slice the mango on each side of its large, flat stone. Cut the flesh into chunks, removing the peel. Halve the

papaya, remove the seeds with a spoon and cut it into chunks. Peel the kiwi fruit and slice it into chunks. Peel and cut the pineapple into chunks. Peel and slice the banana and dip the pieces in the lemon juice to prevent them from discolouring.

3 Thread the pieces of fruit alternately on to 4 wooden skewers. Place them in a shallow dish and pour over the rum. Leave the fruit to soak up the flavour of the rum for at least 30 minutes, until ready to barbecue.

4 Cook the kebabs over the hot coals, turning frequently, for about 2 minutes, until the fruit is seared. Serve, accompanied by the hot chocolate dip.

Bunuelo Stars

These delicious, crisp little stars, coated in cinnamon sugar, are a Mexican treat, and are very simple to make.

NUTRITIONAL INFORMATION

Calories 299	Sugars 32g
Protein 4g	Fat 6g
Carbohydrate ...61g	Saturates 1g

 5 mins   5 mins

SERVES 4

INGREDIENTS

4 flour tortillas

3 tbsp ground cinnamon

6–8 tbsp caster sugar

vegetable oil, for frying

chocolate ice cream, to serve

fine orange rind strips, to decorate

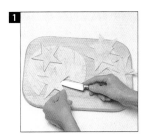

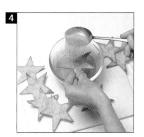

1 Using a sharp knife or kitchen scissors, cut each tortilla into star shapes.

2 Mix the cinnamon and sugar together and set aside.

3 Heat the vegetable oil in a shallow, wide frying pan until it is hot enough to brown a cube of bread in 30 seconds. Working one at a time, fry the star-shaped tortillas until one side is golden, then turn and cook until golden on the other side. Remove from the hot oil with a slotted spoon and drain on kitchen paper.

4 Sprinkle the stars generously with the cinnamon and sugar mixture. Serve with chocolate ice cream, sprinkled with orange rind strips.

COOK'S TIP

These star-shaped bunuelos make an attractive decoration for an ice cream sundae with Mexican flavours: caramel, cinnamon, coffee and chocolate.

Deep-Fried Sweetmeats

This is one of the most popular Indian sweetmeats. The flavour and beautiful aroma come from the rosewater in the syrup.

NUTRITIONAL INFORMATION

Calories 325   Sugars 25g
Protein . . . . .3g   Fat 24g
Carbohydrate . . .25g   Saturates 12g

20 mins   20 mins

SERVES 6-8

INGREDIENTS

5 tbsp powdered milk

1½ tbsp plain flour

1 tsp baking powder

1½ tbsp unsalted butter

1 egg

1 tsp milk to mix (if required)

10 tbsp ghee

SYRUP

750 ml/1¼ pints water

8 tbsp sugar

2 green cardamom pods, peeled, with
  seeds crushed

1 large pinch saffron strands

2 tbsp rosewater

1 Place the powdered milk ,flour and baking powder in a bowl.

2 Place the unsalted butter in a pan and heat, stirring, until melted.

3 Whisk the egg in a bowl. Add the melted butter and whisked egg to the dry ingredients and blend together with a fork (and add the 1 teaspoon extra milk at this stage if necessary) to form a soft dough.

4 Break the dough into about 12 small pieces and shape, in the palms of your hands, into small, smooth balls.

5 Heat the ghee in a deep frying-pan. Reduce the heat and start frying the dough balls, about 3–4 at a time, tossing and turning gently with a perforated spoon until a dark golden brown colour. Remove the sweetmeats from the pan and set aside in a deep serving bowl.

6 To make the syrup, boil the water and sugar in a pan for 7–10 minutes. Add the crushed cardamom seeds and saffron, and pour over the sweetmeats.

7 Pour the rosewater sparingly over the top. Leave to soak for about 10 minutes for the sweetmeats to soak up some of the syrup. Serve hot or cold.

Oranges in Spiced Caramel

Unusually, some of the spice in this delicious and impressive orange dessert is provided by the addition of black pepper to the caramel!

NUTRITIONAL INFORMATION

Calories	257	Sugars 56g
Protein	.........3g	Fat 4g
Carbohydrate	...56g	Saturates 0.5g

15 mins   10 mins

SERVES 4

I N G R E D I E N T S

4 large juicy oranges

4–6 tbsp shelled pistachio nuts, chopped, to decorate

S P I C E D   C A R A M E L

250 g/9 oz caster sugar

5 black peppercorns, lightly crushed

4 cloves

1 green cardamom pod, lightly crushed

300 ml/½ pint water

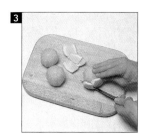

1 To make the spiced caramel, put the sugar, peppercorns, cloves, cardamom pod and 150 ml/¼ pint of the water in a pan and stir to dissolve the sugar over a medium heat. When the sugar has dissolved, turn up the heat and boil, without stirring, until the syrup thickens and turns a deep caramel colour. Use a wet pastry brush to brush down the side of the pan if necessary.

2 Very carefully, pour in another 150 ml/¼ pint water, standing back because it will splatter. Remove from the heat and, using a long-handled wooden spoon, stir until all the caramel has dissolved. Set aside to cool.

3 Pare off the orange rind and pith, cutting carefully so the oranges retain their shape. Either leave the oranges whole, or, working over a bowl, cut them into segments, cutting the flesh away from the membranes.

4 Pour the caramel syrup with the spices over the oranges and stir together gently. Cover and chill until ready to serve. Serve in individual bowls with chopped pistachio nuts sprinkled over the tops at the last minute.

VARIATION
Turn this Spanish dessert into a Sicilian-style one by using the blood-red oranges that grow in great profusion on the island.

Baked Sweet Ravioli

These scrumptious little parcels are the perfect dessert for anyone with a really sweet tooth and a fancy for something unusual.

NUTRITIONAL INFORMATION

Calories ....765 Sugars 56g
Protein ....16g Fat 30g
Carbohydrate ...114g Saturates 15g

1½ hrs   20 mins

SERVES 4

I N G R E D I E N T S

SWEET PASTA DOUGH

425 g/15 oz plain flour

140 g/5 oz butter, plus extra for greasing

140 g/5 oz caster sugar

4 eggs

25 g/1 oz fresh yeast

125 ml/4 fl oz warm milk

FILLING

175 g/6 oz chestnut purée

55 g/2 oz cocoa powder

55 g/2 oz caster sugar

55 g/2 oz chopped almonds

55 g/2 oz crushed amaretti biscuits

175 g/6 oz orange marmalade

1 To make the sweet pasta dough, sieve the flour into a mixing bowl, then mix in the butter, sugar and 3 of the eggs.

2 Mix together the yeast and warm milk in a small bowl and when thoroughly combined, mix into the dough.

3 Knead the dough for 20 minutes, cover with a clean cloth and set aside in a warm place for 1 hour to rise.

4 Mix together the chestnut purée, cocoa powder, sugar, almonds, crushed amaretti biscuits and orange marmalade in a separate bowl.

5 Generously grease a baking tray with some butter.

6 Lightly flour the work surface. Roll out the sweet pasta dough into a thin sheet and cut into 5 cm/2 inch rounds with a plain pastry cutter.

7 Put a spoonful of the filling mixture on to one half of each pasta round and then fold over the other half, pressing the edges firmly together to seal. Transfer the ravioli to the prepared baking tray, spacing them out well.

8 Beat the remaining egg and brush all over the ravioli to glaze. Bake in a preheated oven, 180°C/350°F/Gas Mark 4, for 20 minutes. If necessary, bake the ravioli in batches. Serve hot.

Honey & Nut Nests

Pistachio nuts and honey are combined with crisp cooked angel hair pasta in this unusual and scrumptious dessert.

NUTRITIONAL INFORMATION

Calories . . . . . . .802 Sugars 53g
Protein . . . . .13g Fat 48g
Carbohydrate . . .85g Saturates 16g

 10 mins   1 hr

SERVES 4

I N G R E D I E N T S

225 g/8 oz dried angel hair pasta

115 g/4 oz butter

175 g/6 oz shelled pistachio nuts, chopped

115 g/4 oz sugar

115 g/4 oz clear honey

150 ml/5 fl oz water

2 tsp lemon juice

salt

Greek-style yogurt, to serve

1 Bring a large saucepan of lightly salted water to the boil. Add the angel-hair pasta, bring back to the boil and cook for 8–10 minutes or until tender, but still firm to the bite. Drain the pasta and return to the pan. Add the butter and toss to coat the pasta thoroughly. Set aside to cool completely.

2 Arrange 4 small flan or poaching rings on a baking tray. Divide the angel-hair pasta into 8 equal quantities and spoon 4 of them into the rings. Press down lightly. Top the pasta with half of the nuts, then add the remaining pasta.

3 Bake in a preheated oven, 180°C/ 350°F/Gas Mark 4, for 45 minutes or until golden brown.

4 Meanwhile, put the sugar, honey and water in a saucepan and bring to the boil over a low heat, stirring constantly until the sugar has dissolved completely. Simmer for 10 minutes, add the lemon juice and simmer for 5 minutes.

5 Using a spatula or fish slice, carefully transfer the angel-hair nests to a serving dish. Pour over the honey syrup, sprinkle over the remaining nuts and set aside to cool completely before serving. Hand the Greek-style yogurt separately.

COOK'S TIP
Angel hair pasta is also known as capelli d'Angelo. Long and very fine, it is usually sold in small bunches that already resemble nests.

Raspberry Almond Spirals

This is the ultimate in self-indulgence — a truly delicious dessert that tastes every bit as good as it looks.

NUTRITIONAL INFORMATION

Calories	235	Sugars	.......20g
Protein	.........7g	Fat	...........7g
Carbohydrate	...36g	Saturates	.......1g

 5 mins   20 mins

SERVES 4

INGREDIENTS

175 g/6 oz dried fusilli

700g/1 lb 9 oz raspberries

2 tbsp caster sugar

1 tbsp lemon juice

4 tbsp flaked almonds

3 tbsp raspberry liqueur

1 Bring a large pan of lightly salted water to the boil. Add the fusilli and cook until tender, but still firm to the bite. Drain the fusilli thoroughly, return to the pan and set aside to cool.

2 Using the back of a spoon, firmly press 225 g/8 oz of the raspberries through a sieve set over a large mixing bowl to form a smooth purée.

3 Put the raspberry purée and sugar in a small saucepan and simmer over a low heat, stirring occasionally, for 5 minutes. Stir in the lemon juice and set the sauce aside until required.

4 Add the remaining raspberries to the fusilli in the pan and mix together well. Transfer the raspberry and fusilli mixture to a serving dish.

5 Spread the almonds out on a baking tray and toast under the grill until golden brown. Remove and set aside to cool slightly.

6 Stir the raspberry liqueur into the reserved raspberry sauce and mix together well until very smooth. Pour the raspberry sauce over the fusilli, generously sprinkle over the toasted almonds and serve.

COOK'S TIP

You could use almost any sweet, really ripe berry for making this dessert. Strawberries and blackberries are especially suitable, combined with the correspondingly flavoured liqueur.

Zabaglione

This well-known dish is a light but rich mousse flavoured with Marsala.
It will not keep, so make it fresh and serve immediately.

NUTRITIONAL INFORMATION

Calories ....158 Sugars 29g
Protein ....1g Fat 1g
Carbohydrate ...29g Saturates 0.2g

15 mins   0 mins

SERVES 4

INGREDIENTS

5 egg yolks

100 g/3½ oz caster sugar

150 ml/5 fl oz Marsala or sweet sherry

amaretti biscuits, to serve (optional)

1 Place the egg yolks in a large mixing bowl.

2 Add the caster sugar to the egg yolks and whisk them together until the mixture is thick and very pale and has doubled in volume.

3 Place the bowl containing the whisked egg yolks and sugar over a saucepan of gently simmering water.

4 Add the Marsala or sweet sherry to the egg yolk and sugar mixture and continue whisking until the foam mixture becomes warm. This process may take as long as 10 minutes.

5 Pour the mixture, which should be frothy and light, into 4 wine glasses.

6 Serve the zabaglione warm with fresh fruit or amaretti biscuits.

COOK'S TIP

Any other type of liqueur may be used instead of the Marsala, or sweet sherry, if you prefer. Serve soft fruits such as strawberries or raspberries with the zabaglione – to make a delicious combination.

Marinated Peaches

A very simple but incredibly pleasing dessert, which is especially good for a dinner party on a hot summer day.

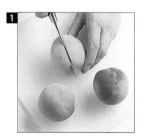

NUTRITIONAL INFORMATION

Calories	89	Sugars	........14g
Protein	.........1g	Fat	...........0g
Carbohydrate	...14g	Saturates	.......0g

10 mins, plus chilling

0 mins

SERVES 4

INGREDIENTS

4 large peaches

2 tbsp icing sugar, sifted

1 orange

200 ml/7 fl oz medium or sweet white wine, chilled

1　Using a sharp knife, halve the peaches, remove the stones and discard them. Peel the peaches, if you prefer. Slice into thin wedges.

2　Place the peach wedges in a glass serving bowl and sprinkle over the icing sugar.

3　Using a sharp knife, pare the rind from the orange. Cut the orange rind into matchsticks, place them in a bowl of cold water and set aside.

4　Squeeze the juice from the orange and pour over the peaches, together with the chilled white wine.

5　Place the bowl in the refrigerator for at least 1 hour to allow the peaches to marinate and chill.

6　Remove the orange rind matchsticks from the water and pat them dry with kitchen paper.

7　Garnish the chilled marinated peaches with the strips of orange rind and serve immediately.

COOK'S TIP

There is absolutely no need to use expensive wine in this recipe, so it can be quite economical to make.

Steamed Coconut Cake

This steamed coconut cake, steeped in a syrup of lime and ginger, is typical of Thai desserts and sweets. It has a distinctly Chinese influence.

NUTRITIONAL INFORMATION

Calories 243	Sugars 17g
Protein 4g	Fat 12g
Carbohydrate ...31g	Saturates 8g

15 mins

30 mins

SERVES 8

INGREDIENTS

2 large eggs, separated

pinch of salt

100 g/3½ oz caster sugar

75 g/2¾ oz butter, melted and cooled

5 tbsp coconut milk

150 g/5½ oz self-raising flour

½ tsp baking powder

3 tbsp desiccated coconut

4 tbsp stem ginger syrup

3 tbsp lime juice

TO DECORATE

3 pieces stem ginger, diced

curls of freshly grated coconut

strips of lime rind

1 Cut a 28 cm/11 inch round of non-stick paper and press into an 18 cm/7 inch steamer basket to line it.

2 Whisk the egg whites with the salt until stiff. Gradually whisk in the sugar, 1 tablespoon at a time, whisking hard after each addition until the mixture stands in stiff peaks.

3 Whisk in the yolks, then quickly stir in the butter and coconut milk. Sift the flour and baking powder over the mixture, then fold in lightly and evenly with a large metal spoon. Fold in the coconut.

4 Spoon the mixture into the steamer basket and tuck the spare paper over the top. Place the basket over boiling water, cover and steam for 30 minutes.

5 Turn the cake onto a plate, remove the paper and cool slightly. Mix the ginger syrup and lime juice together and spoon over the cake. Cut into squares and top with ginger, coconut and lime rind.

COOK'S TIP
Coconuts grow on tropical beaches all around the world, but probably originated in South-East Asia, and it is here that coconut is most important in cooking.

Sticky Rice Shapes

The gluten in the rice is sufficient to hold these attractive, delicately coloured balls together – definitely a recipe for a sweet tooth!

NUTRITIONAL INFORMATION

Calories	762	Sugars	.......131g
Protein	.........6g	Fat	..........01g
Carbohydrate	..187g	Saturates	.......0g

15 mins, plus soaking

35 mins

SERVES 4

INGREDIENTS

300 g/10½ oz glutinous rice

500 g/1 lb 2oz granulated sugar

300 ml/10 fl oz water

pink and green food colourings

rose petals or jasmine flowers, to decorate

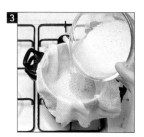

1 Place the rice in a bowl and add enough cold water to cover. Leave to soak for 3 hours or overnight.

2 Drain the rice and rinse thoroughly in cold water.

3 Line the top part of a steamer with muslin and tip the rice into it. Place the steamer over boiling water, cover and steam the rice for 30 minutes. Remove and set aside to cool.

4 Heat the sugar, water and essences gently until the sugar dissolves. Bring to the boil for 4–5 minutes to reduce to a thin syrup. Remove the pan from the heat.

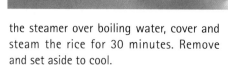

5 Divide the rice in half and colour one half pale pink, the other half pale green. Shape into small balls.

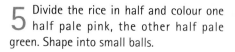

6 Using 2 forks, dip the rice balls into the syrup. Drain off the excess syrup and pile on to a dish. Scatter with rose petals or jasmine flowers to decorate.

COOK'S TIP

If you prefer, the rice can be shaped in small sweet moulds or piled into small castle or turret shapes, like dariole moulds.

Caramel Apple Wedges

Crisp apple slices are deep-fried in a sesame seed batter and given a delicious caramel coat – a wonderful Bonfire Night treat.

NUTRITIONAL INFORMATION

Calories	345	Sugars	........12g
Protein	.........4g	Fat	..........21g
Carbohydrate	...35g	Saturates	.......2g

15 mins   15 mins

SERVES 4

INGREDIENTS

115 g/4 oz flour

1 egg

125 ml/4 fl oz water

4 crisp dessert apples

2½ tbsp sesame seeds

250 g/9 oz caster sugar

2 tbsp vegetable oil, plus extra for deep-frying

1 Place the flour, egg and water in a bowl and whisk well until a smooth, thick batter forms.

2 Core the apples and cut each into 8 wedges. Drop into the batter and stir in the sesame seeds.

3 Put the sugar and 2 tablespoons of oil in a heavy-based pan and heat, stirring, until the sugar dissolves. Continue until the syrup begins to turn golden. Remove from the heat but keep warm.

4 Heat the oil for frying in a wok or deep pan to 180°C/350°F or until a cube of bread turns golden in 30 seconds. Lift the apple pieces one by one from the batter, using tongs or chopsticks, and lower into the hot oil. Fry for 2–3 minutes until golden brown and crisp.

5 Remove with a perforated spoon and dip very quickly into the sugar mixture. Dip the apple wedges briefly into iced water and drain on non-stick paper. Serve immediately.

COOK'S TIP
Take care not to overheat the sugar syrup or it will become difficult to handle and burn. If it begins to set before you have finished dipping the apple pieces, warm it slightly over the heat until it becomes liquid again.

Banana Fritters

These wonderful little fritters are fried in a coconut batter for a special flavour. Rice flour makes the batter especially crisp.

NUTRITIONAL INFORMATION

Calories	345	Sugars	........31g
Protein	.........6g	Fat	..........12g
Carbohydrate	...55g	Saturates	.......2g

 10 mins   10 mins

SERVES 4

INGREDIENTS

70 g/2½ oz plain flour

2 tbsp rice flour

1 tbsp caster sugar

1 egg, separated

150 ml/5 fl oz coconut milk

4 large bananas

sunflower oil, for deep-frying

TO DECORATE

1 tsp icing sugar

1 tsp ground cinnamon

lime wedges

1 Sift the plain flour, the rice flour and the sugar into a mixing bowl and make a well in the centre. Add the egg yolk and coconut milk.

2 Beat the mixture until a smooth, thick batter forms. Whisk the egg white in a clean, dry bowl until it is stiff enough to hold soft peaks. Fold it into the batter lightly and evenly.

3 Heat a 6 cm/2½ inch depth of oil in a large pan to 180°C/350°F or until a cube of bread browns in 30 seconds. Cut the bananas in half crossways, then dip them quickly into the batter to coat them.

4 Drop the bananas carefully into the hot oil and fry them, in batches, for 2–3 minutes until they are golden brown, turning once.

5 Drain on kitchen paper. Sprinkle with icing sugar and cinnamon and serve immediately, with lime wedges for squeezing juice as desired.

COOK'S TIP

If you can buy the baby finger bananas that are popular in this dish in the East, leave them whole for coating and frying.

Coconut Custard Squares

A delicious variation of baked custard, these squares are made with coconut milk. The light brown sugar gives the squares a rich colour.

NUTRITIONAL INFORMATION

Calories 324	Sugars 49g	
Protein 12g	Fat 11g	
Carbohydrate ...49g	Saturates 4g	

10 mins   40 mins

SERVES 4

INGREDIENTS

1 tsp butter, melted

6 eggs

400 ml/14 fl oz coconut milk

175 g/6 oz soft light brown sugar

salt

fruit slices, to serve

TO DECORATE

shreds of coconut

lime rind

1 Brush the butter over the inside of a 18 cm/7 inch square ovenproof dish or tin, about 4 cm/1½ inch in depth.

2 Beat the eggs together in a large, heatproof bowl and then beat in the coconut milk, light brown sugar and a pinch of salt.

3 Place the bowl over a pan of gently simmering water and stir the mixture with a wooden spoon for 15 minutes or until it begins to thicken. Pour into the prepared dish or tin.

4 Bake the custard in a preheated oven, 180°C/350°F/Gas Mark 4, for 20–25 minutes until just set. Remove from the oven and allow to cool completely.

5 Turn the custard out of the dish or tin and cut it into squares.

6 Serve the custard squares decorated with coconut shreds and strips of lime rind together with fruit slices.

COOK'S TIP
Keep an eye on the custard as it bakes, as, if it overcooks, the texture will be spoiled. When it comes out of the oven, it should be barely set and still slightly wobbly in the centre, but it will firm up slightly as it cools.

Summer Fruit Dessert

A sweet cream cheese dessert that complements the tartness of fresh summer fruits rather well.

NUTRITIONAL INFORMATION

Calories 725   Sugars 36g
Protein ....10g   Fat 59g
Carbohydrate ...36g   Saturates 36g

 5 mins, plus chilling   0 mins

SERVES 4

INGREDIENTS

450 g/1 lb mascarpone cheese

4 egg yolks

100 g/3½ oz caster sugar

400 g/14 oz frozen summer fruits, such as raspberries and redcurrants, kept frozen

redcurrants, to decorate

amaretti biscuits, to serve

1 Place the mascarpone cheese in a large mixing bowl. Using a wooden spoon, beat the cheese until smooth.

2 Stir the egg yolks and sugar into the mascarpone cheese, mixing well. Leave the mixture to chill in the refrigerator for about 1 hour.

3 Spoon a layer of the mascarpone mixture into 4 individual serving dishes. Spoon a layer of the frozen summer fruits on top. Repeat the layers in the same order, reserving some of the mascarpone mixture for the top.

4 Leave the mousses to chill in the refrigerator for about 20 minutes. The fruits should still be slightly frozen.

5 Serve the mousses with amaretti biscuits and topped with redcurrants.

VARIATION
Try adding 3 tablespoons of your favourite liqueur to the mascarpone cheese in step 1, if you like.

Mascarpone Cheesecake

Lemon and mascarpone give this baked cheesecake a wonderfully tangy flavour. Ricotta cheese could be used as an alternative.

NUTRITIONAL INFORMATION

Calories	327	Sugars	25g
Protein	9g	Fat	18g
Carbohydrate	33g	Saturates	11g

15 mins   50 mins

SERVES 4

INGREDIENTS

1½ tbsp unsalted butter, plus extra for greasing

150 g/5½ oz ginger biscuits, crushed

25 g/1 oz stem ginger, chopped

500 g/1 lb 2 oz mascarpone cheese

finely grated rind and juice of 2 lemons

100 g/3½ oz caster sugar

2 large eggs, separated

fruit coulis (see Cook's Tip), to serve

1 Grease a 25 cm/10 inch springform cake tin or loose-bottomed tin and paper line the base with baking paper.

2 Melt the butter in a pan and stir in the crushed biscuits and chopped ginger. Use the mixture to line the tin, pressing the mixture about 5 mm/¼ inch up the sides.

3 Beat together the cheese, lemon rind and juice, sugar and egg yolks until quite smooth.

4 Whisk the egg whites until they are stiff and fold into the cheese and lemon mixture.

5 Pour the mixture into the prepared tin and bake in a preheated oven, 180°C/350°F/Gas Mark 4, for 35–45 minutes until it is just set. Don't worry if it cracks or sinks – this is quite normal.

6 Leave the cheesecake in the tin to cool completely.

7 Serve the cheesecake with a fruit coulis (see Cook's Tip).

COOK'S TIP
Make a delicious fruit coulis by cooking 400 g/14 oz fruit, such as blueberries, for 5 minutes with 2 tbsp water. Sieve the mixture, then stir in 1 tbsp (or more to taste) of sifted icing sugar. Leave to cool before serving.

Tiramisu Layers

This is a rather unusual presentation of the well-known and very traditional chocolate dessert from Italy.

NUTRITIONAL INFORMATION

Calories 990	Sugars 69g
Protein 11g	Fat 75g
Carbohydrate ...84g	Saturates 42g

1 hr 25 mins   5 mins

SERVES 4

INGREDIENTS

150 ml/5 fl oz double cream

400 g/14 oz mascarpone cheese

300 g/10½ oz dark chocolate

400 ml/14 fl oz black coffee with 4 tbsp caster sugar, cooled

6 tbsp dark rum or brandy

36 sponge fingers, about 400 g/14 oz

cocoa powder, to dust

1 Whip the cream until it just holds its shape and stir it into the mascarpone to combine. Melt the chocolate in a bowl set over a saucepan of simmering water, stirring occasionally. Leave the chocolate to cool slightly, then stir it into the mascarpone and cream.

2 Mix the coffee and rum together in a bowl. Dip the sponge fingers into the mixture very briefly so that they absorb the coffee and rum liquid but do not become soggy.

3 Place 3 sponge fingers, spaced a little apart, on 4 serving plates.

4 Spoon a layer of the mascarpone, cream and chocolate mixture over the sponge fingers.

5 Place 3 more sponge fingers, at right angles to the first layer, on top of the mascarpone layer. Spread another layer of the mascarpone and chocolate mixture and top with 3 more sponge fingers.

6 Leave the tiramisu to chill in the refrigerator for at least 1 hour. Dust all over with a little cocoa powder just before serving.

VARIATION

Try adding 50 g/1¾ oz toasted, chopped hazelnuts to the chocolate cream mixture in step 1, if you prefer.

Tuscan Pudding

These baked mini ricotta puddings are delicious served warm or chilled and will keep in the refrigerator for up to four days.

NUTRITIONAL INFORMATION

Calories	293	Sugars	........28g
Protein	.........9g	Fat	..........17g
Carbohydrate	...28g	Saturates	.......9g

 20 mins   15 mins

SERVES 4

I N G R E D I E N T S

1 tbsp butter

75 g/2¾ oz mixed dried fruit

250 g/9 oz ricotta cheese

3 egg yolks

50 g/1¾ oz caster sugar

1 tsp cinnamon

finely grated rind of 1 orange, plus extra to decorate

crème fraîche, to serve

1 Lightly grease 4 mini pudding basins or ramekin dishes with the butter.

2 Put the dried fruit in a bowl and cover with warm water. Set aside to soak for 10 minutes.

3 Beat the ricotta cheese with the egg yolks in a bowl. Stir in the caster sugar, cinnamon and orange rind and mix to combine thoroughly.

4 Drain the dried fruit in a sieve set over a bowl. Mix the drained fruit with the ricotta cheese mixture.

5 Spoon the mixture into the basins or ramekin dishes.

6 Bake in a preheated oven, 180°C/ 350°F/Gas Mark 4, for 15 minutes. The tops should be firm to the touch but should not have turned brown.

7 Decorate the puddings with grated orange rind. Serve warm or chilled with a spoonful of crème fraîche, if liked.

COOK'S TIP
Crème fraîche has a slightly sour, nutty taste and is very thick. It is suitable for cooking, but has the same fat content as double cream. It can be made by stirring cultured buttermilk into double cream and refrigerating overnight.

Orange Crème à Catalanas

This delectable, orange-flavoured custard is thoroughly chilled before being finished with a caramelized sugar topping.

NUTRITIONAL INFORMATION

Calories	265	Sugars	........33g
Protein	.........8g	Fat	...........9g
Carbohydrate	...41g	Saturates	.......3g

25 mins, plus cooling   30 mins

SERVES 8

INGREDIENTS

1 litre/1¾ pints milk

finely grated rind of 6 large oranges

9 large egg yolks

200 g/7 oz caster sugar, plus extra for the topping

3 tbsp cornflour

2 Return the milk to the heat and simmer for 10 minutes. Put the egg yolks and sugar in a large heatproof bowl over a saucepan of boiling water. Whisk until the mixture is creamy and the sugar dissolved.

3 Add 5 tablespoons of the flavoured milk to the cornflour, stirring until smooth. Stir into the milk. Strain the milk into the eggs, whisking until blended.

4 Rinse out the pan and put a layer of water in the bottom. Put the bowl on top of the pan, making sure the base does not touch the water. Simmer over a medium heat, whisking, until the custard is thick enough to coat the back of a wooden spoon, which can take as long as 20 minutes. Do not boil.

5 Pour into eight 150 ml/5 fl oz ramekins and leave to cool. Cover each with a piece of cling film and put in the refrigerator to chill for at least 6 hours.

6 When ready to serve, sprinkle the top of each ramekin with a layer of sugar. Use a kitchen blowtorch to melt and caramelize the sugar (see Cook's Tip). Allow to stand for a few minutes until the caramel hardens, then serve at once. Do not return to the refrigerator or the topping will become soft.

1 Put the milk and orange rind in a saucepan over a medium–high heat. Bring to the boil, then remove from the heat, cover and leave to cool for 2 hours.

COOK'S TIP

A kitchen blowtorch is the best way to melt the sugar quickly and guarantee a crisp topping. These are sold at good kitchen-supply shops. Alternatively, you can melt the sugar under a preheated hot grill.

Spanish Flan

This gorgeous 'flan' is a version of crème caramel. It needs to be served well chilled, so is a great dessert to make in advance for a dinner party.

NUTRITIONAL INFORMATION

Calories	215	Sugars	.......35g
Protein	.........7g	Fat	..........6g
Carbohydrate	...35g	Saturates	.......3g

10 mins, plus chilling   1¼–1½ hrs

SERVES 4–6

INGREDIENTS

butter, for greasing

175 g/6 oz caster sugar

4 tbsp water

juice of ½ lemon

500 ml/18 fl oz milk

1 vanilla pod

2 large eggs

2 large egg yolks

1 Lightly butter a 1.2 litre/ 2 pint soufflé dish. To make the caramel, put 75 g/2¾ oz sugar with the water in a pan over a medium–high heat and cook, stirring constantly, until the sugar dissolves. Boil until the syrup turns a deep golden brown.

2 Immediately remove from the heat and add a few drops of lemon juice. Pour into the soufflé dish and swirl around. Set aside.

3 Pour the milk into a pan. Slit the vanilla pod lengthways and add it to the milk. Bring to the boil, remove the pan from the heat and stir in the remaining sugar, stirring until it dissolves. Set aside.

4 Beat the eggs and egg yolks together in a bowl. Pour the milk mixture over them, whisking. Remove the vanilla pod. Strain the egg mixture into a bowl, then transfer to the soufflé dish.

5 Place the dish in a roasting tin filled with enough boiling water to come two-thirds up the side.

6 Bake in a preheated oven at 160°C/325°F/Gas Mark 3 for 1¼–1½ hours until a knife inserted in the centre comes out clean. Leave to cool completely. Cover with clingfilm and refrigerate for at least 24 hours.

7 Run a round-bladed knife around the edge of the dish. Place an upturned, rimmed serving plate on top, then invert the plate and dish, giving a sharp shake half-way over. Lift off the dish and serve.

COOK'S TIP
The lemon juice is added to the caramel in Step 2 to stop the cooking process, to prevent it from burning.

Pear Cake

This is a really moist cake, deliciously flavoured with chopped pears and cinnamon and drizzled with honey.

NUTRITIONAL INFORMATION

Calories 119	Sugars 16g
Protein 2g	Fat 0.3g
Carbohydrate . . .29g	Saturates 0g

  1 hr   🕐 1½ hrs

SERVES 12

INGREDIENTS

margarine, for greasing

4 pears, peeled and cored

2 tbsp water

200 g/7 oz plain flour

2 tsp baking powder

100 g/3½ oz soft light brown sugar

4 tbsp milk

2 tbsp clear honey, plus extra for drizzling

2 tsp ground cinnamon

2 egg whites

1 Grease and line the base of a 20 cm/ 8 inch cake tin.

2 Put 1 pear in a food processor or blender with the water and process until almost smooth. Transfer to a mixing bowl.

3 Sift in the flour and baking powder into a large bowl. Beat in the sugar, milk, honey and cinnamon.

4 Chop 2 of the remaining pears and add to the mixture.

5 Whisk the egg whites until peaks form and gently fold into the mixture until fully blended.

6 Slice the remaining pear and arrange it decoratively in a fan pattern on the base of the prepared tin.

7 Spoon the cake mixture into the tin and cook in a preheated oven, 150°C/ 300°F/Gas Mark 2, for 1¼–1½ hours or until cooked through.

8 Remove the cake from the oven and set aside to cool in the tin for 10 minutes. Turn the cake out on to a wire cooling rack and drizzle honey over the pear topping.

9 Set the cake aside to cool completely, then transfer to a serving plate and cut into slices to serve.

COOK'S TIP

To test if the cake is cooked through, insert a skewer into the centre – if it comes out clean, the cake is cooked. If not, return the cake to the oven and test at frequent intervals.

Oat & Raisin Biscuits

These oaty, fruity biscuits couldn't be easier to make and are delicious served with a creamy rum and raisin ice cream.

NUTRITIONAL INFORMATION

Calories 227   Sugars 22g
Protein ....4g   Fat 7g
Carbohydrate ...39g   Saturates 3g

 50 mins   15 mins

SERVES 4

INGREDIENTS

4 tbsp butter, plus extra for greasing

125 g/4½ oz caster sugar

1 egg, beaten

50 g/1¾ plain flour

½ tsp salt

½ tsp baking powder

175 g/6 oz rolled oats

125 g/4½ oz raisins

2 tbsp sesame seeds

1 Lightly grease 2 baking sheets with a little butter.

2 In a large mixing bowl, cream together the butter and sugar until light and fluffy.

3 Gradually add the beaten egg, beating well after each addition, until thoroughly combined.

4 Sift the flour, salt and baking powder into the creamed mixture. Mix gently to combine. Add the rolled oats, raisins and sesame seeds and mix together until thoroughly combined.

5 Place spoonfuls of the mixture, spaced well apart, on the prepared baking sheets to allow room to expand during cooking, and flatten them slightly with the back of a spoon.

6 Bake the biscuits in a preheated oven, 180°C/350°F/Gas Mark 4, for 15 minutes, until golden.

7 Leave the biscuits to cool slightly on the baking sheets.

8 Carefully transfer the biscuits to a wire rack and leave to cool and firm up completely before serving.

COOK'S TIP
To enjoy these biscuits at their best, store them in an airtight container.

Vanilla Tea Cake

This really is a gorgeous cake to serve with afternoon tea – light and delicious. Using vanilla sugar adds a very special taste and aroma.

NUTRITIONAL INFORMATION

Calories	260	Sugars	........23g
Protein	.........4g	Fat	..........14g
Carbohydrate	...31g	Saturates	.......7g

15 mins   1½ hrs

MAKES 12–15 SLICES

INGREDIENTS

225 g/8 oz quality glacé fruit, such as cherries and orange, lemon and lime peels, or candied citrus peel

85 g/3 oz ground almonds

finely grated rind of ½ lemon

85 g/3 oz plain flour

175 g/6 oz butter, softened, plus extra for greasing

175 g/6 oz vanilla-flavoured sugar (see Cook's Tip)

½ tsp vanilla essence

3 large eggs, lightly beaten

85 g/3 oz self-raising flour

pinch of salt

glacé fruit, to decorate

COOK'S TIP

Make your own vanilla-flavoured sugar by storing a sliced vanilla pod in a closed jar of caster sugar.

1 Grease a 22 x 12 x 5 cm/8½ x 4½ x 2 inch loaf tin and line the base with a piece of baking paper.

2 Chop the fruit into small pieces, reserving a few larger slices for the top. Combine with the ground almonds, lemon rind and 2 tablespoons of the measured plain flour. Set aside.

3 Beat the butter and sugar together until creamy. Beat in the vanilla essence and eggs, a little at a time.

4 Sift both flours and the salt into the creamed mixture, then fold in. Fold in the fruit and ground almonds.

5 Spoon the mixture into the tin and smooth the surface. Arrange the reserved fruit slices on the top. Loosely cover the tin with foil, making sure it does not touch the cake.

6 Bake the cake in a preheated oven at 180°C/350°F/Gas Mark 4 for about 1½ hours until risen and a skewer inserted into the centre comes out clean.

7 Cool the cake in the tin on a wire rack for 5 minutes. Turn out, remove the bake parchment and cool completely. Wrap the cake in foil and store in an airtight container for up to 4 days. Serve decorated with glacé fruit.

Almond Biscuits

These mouth-wateringly crisp Mediterranean biscuits are lovely with coffee, and are also a perfect accompaniment for creamy desserts.

NUTRITIONAL INFORMATION

Calories	125	Sugars	.........4g
Protein	.........2g	Fat	..........8g
Carbohydrate	....11g	Saturates	.......4g

15 mins   25 mins

MAKES ABOUT 32 BISCUITS

I N G R E D I E N T S

150 g/5½ oz unblanched almonds

225 g/8 oz butter, softened

6 tbsp icing sugar, plus extra for sifting

275 g/9½ oz plain flour

2 tsp vanilla essence

½ tsp almond essence

1 Line 2 baking sheets with baking paper. Using a cook's knife, finely chop the almonds, or process them in a small food processor, taking care not to let them turn into a paste. Set aside.

2 Put the softened butter in a bowl and beat with an electric mixer until smooth. Sift in the icing sugar and continue beating until the mixture is creamed and smooth.

3 Sift in the flour, holding the sieve high above the bowl, and gently beat it in until blended. Add the vanilla and almond essences and beat again to form a soft dough. Stir in the chopped almonds.

4 Using a teaspoon, shape the dough into 32 round balls about the size of walnuts. Place on the prepared baking sheets, spacing them well apart. Bake in a preheated oven, 180°C/350°F/Gas Mark 4, for 20–25 minutes until the biscuits are set and just starting to turn brown.

5 Leave the biscuits to stand on the baking sheets for 2 minutes to firm up. Sift a thick layer of icing sugar over them. Transfer to a wire rack and leave to cool completely.

6 Lightly dust with more icing sugar, just before serving. Store the biscuits in an airtight container.

VARIATION
Although not a true Mediterranean ingredient, pecan nuts can be used instead of the almonds. Alternatively, add 2 teaspoons finely grated orange rind to the dough in Step 3.

Rich Chocolate Loaf

Another rich chocolate dessert, this loaf is very simple to make and can be served as a tea-time treat as well.

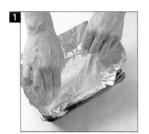

NUTRITIONAL INFORMATION

Calories	118	Sugars	........16g
Protein	.........3g	Fat	..........12g
Carbohydrate	...18g	Saturates .:.....6g	

🕐 1 hr 20 mins ⏱ 5 mins

MAKES 16 SLICES

INGREDIENTS

150 g/5 oz dark chocolate

6 tbsp unsalted butter

200 ml/7 fl oz condensed milk

2 tsp cinnamon

75 g/3 oz almonds

75 g/3 oz amaretti biscuits, broken

50 g/2 oz dried no-soak apricots, roughly chopped

1 Line a 675 g/1½ lb loaf tin with a sheet of kitchen foil.

2 Using a sharp knife, roughly chop the almonds.

COOK'S TIP
To melt chocolate, first break it into manageable pieces. The smaller the pieces, the quicker it will melt.

3 Place the dark chocolate, butter, condensed milk and cinnamon in a heavy-based saucepan.

4 Heat the chocolate mixture over a low heat for about 3–4 minutes, stirring constantly with a wooden spoon, until the chocolate has melted. Beat the mixture well.

5 Stir the chopped almonds, broken biscuits and chopped apricots into the chocolate mixture, stirring with a wooden spoon, until well mixed.

6 Pour the mixture into the prepared tin and leave to chill in the refrigerator for about 1 hour or until set. Cut the rich chocolate loaf into slices to serve.

Sweet Risotto Cake

Served with your favourite summer berries and a scented mascarpone cream, this baked sweet risotto makes an unusual dessert.

NUTRITIONAL INFORMATION

Calories	444	Sugars	.......21g
Protein	.........9g	Fat	.........21g
Carbohydrate	...54g	Saturates	......13g

20 mins

45 mins

SERVES 6–8

INGREDIENTS

90 g/3¼ oz arborio rice

350 ml/12 fl oz milk

3–4 tbsp sugar

½ tsp freshly grated nutmeg

salt

190 g/6½ oz plain flour

1½ tsp baking powder

1 tsp bicarbonate of soda

1–2 tbsp caster sugar

1 egg

175 ml/6 fl oz milk

125 ml/4 fl oz soured cream or yogurt

1 tbsp butter, melted

2 tbsp honey

½ tsp almond essence

2 tbsp flaked almonds, toasted

1 tbsp butter, melted

icing sugar, for dusting (optional)

MUSCAT BERRIES

450 g/1 lb mixed summer berries

50 ml/2 fl oz Muscat wine

1–2 tbsp sugar

MASCARPONE CREAM

2 tbsp Muscat wine

1 tbsp honey

½ tsp almond essence

225 ml/8 fl oz mascarpone cheese

1 Put the rice, milk, sugar, nutmeg and ½ teaspoon of salt in a heavy-based saucepan. Bring to the boil, reduce the heat slightly and cook, stirring constantly, until the rice is tender and the milk has almost been absorbed. Cool.

2 Combine the flour, baking powder, bicarbonate of soda, pinch of salt and the sugar. In a bowl, beat the egg, milk, soured cream, butter, honey and almond essence with an electric mixer until smooth. Gradually beat in the rice. Stir in the flour mixture and the almonds.

3 Gently spoon the mixture into a 23–25 cm/9–10 inch well-greased cake tin with removable bottom, smoothing the top evenly. Bake in a preheated oven at 160°C/325°F/Gas Mark 3 for about 20 minutes until golden. Cool in the tin on a wire rack.

4 Put the mixed berries in a bowl and add the wine and sugar. To make the mascarpone cream, stir all the ingredients together and chill.

5 Remove the sides of the tin and slide the cake on to a serving plate. Dust with icing sugar and serve the cake warm with the Muscat berries and mascarpone cream (the cream can be piped on top of the cake for a decorative finish, if liked).

Torta de Cielo

'Cielo' is the Mexican word for 'heaven', and this cake really is heavenly – and very easy to make for a tea-time treat or dessert.

NUTRITIONAL INFORMATION

Calories	753	Sugars	........41g
Protein	........13g	Fat	..........51g
Carbohydrate	...64g	Saturates	......23g

 10 mins   40–50 mins

SERVES 4–6

I N G R E D I E N T S

175 g/6 oz unblanched almonds, in their skins

225 g/8 oz unsalted butter, at room temperature

225 g/8 oz sugar

3 eggs, lightly beaten

1 tsp almond essence

1 tsp vanilla essence

9 tbsp plain flour

a pinch of salt

butter, for greasing

TO SERVE

icing sugar, for dusting

flaked almonds, toasted

1 Lightly butter a 20 cm/8 inch round or square cake tin and line the tin with baking paper.

2 Put the almonds in a food processor to form a 'mealy' mixture. Set aside.

3 Beat together the butter and sugar in a bowl until smooth and fluffy. Add the eggs, the almonds and both the almond and vanilla essences and beat until the mixture is well blended.

4 Add the flour and salt and mix briefly, until the flour is just incorporated.

5 Pour or spoon the batter into the greased tin and smooth the surface.

6 Bake in a preheated oven at 180°C/350°F/Gas Mark 4 for 40–50 minutes or until the cake feels spongy when gently pressed.

7 Remove from the oven, and leave to stand on a wire rack to cool.

8 To serve the torta, dust with icing sugar and decorate with toasted almonds.

Churros

Another Mexican treat, these are like crisp little doughnuts, but with a delicious lemon and spice flavour.

NUTRITIONAL INFORMATION

Calories	439	Sugars	.......0.5g
Protein	.........9g	Fat	..........35g
Carbohydrate	...24g	Saturates	......15g

15 mins   15 mins

SERVES 4

INGREDIENTS

225 ml/8 fl oz water

grated rind of 1 lemon

6 tbsp butter

⅛ tsp salt

125 g/4½ oz plain flour

¼ tsp ground cinnamon, plus extra for dusting

½–1 tsp vanilla essence

3 eggs

vegetable oil, for frying

caster sugar, for dusting

1 Place the water with the lemon rind in a heavy-based saucepan. Bring to the boil, add the butter and salt and cook the mixture for a few moments until the butter melts.

2 Add the flour all at once, with the cinnamon and vanilla, then remove the pan from the heat and stir rapidly until the mixture forms the consistency of mashed potatoes.

3 Beat in the eggs, one at a time, using a wooden spoon; if you find it difficult incorporating the eggs to a smooth mixture, use a potato masher, then when it is mixed, return to a wooden spoon and mix until smooth.

4 Heat 2.5 cm/1 inch oil in a deep frying pan until it is hot enough to brown a cube of bread in 30 seconds.

5 Place the batter in a pastry tube with a wide nozzle, then squeeze out 12 cm/5 inch lengths directly into the hot oil, making sure that the churros are about 8–10 cm/3–4 inches apart, as they will puff up as they cook. You may need to fry them in 2 or 3 batches.

6 Cook the churros in the hot oil for about 2 minutes on each side, until they are golden brown. Remove with a slotted spoon and drain on kitchen paper.

7 Dust generously with sugar and sprinkle with cinnamon to taste. Serve either hot or at room temperature.

Banana & Cranberry Loaf

The addition of chopped nuts, mixed peel, fresh orange juice and dried cranberries makes this a rich, moist tea bread.

NUTRITIONAL INFORMATION

Calories	388	Sugars	.......40g
Protein	.........5g	Fat	..........17g
Carbohydrate	...57g	Saturates	.......2g

 45 mins   1 hr

SERVES 8

INGREDIENTS

butter, for greasing

175 g/6 oz self-raising flour

½ tsp baking powder

150 g/5½ oz soft brown sugar

2 bananas, mashed

55 g/2 oz chopped mixed peel

25 g/1 oz chopped mixed nuts

55 g/2 oz dried cranberries

5–6 tbsp orange juice

2 eggs, beaten

150 ml/5 fl oz sunflower oil

85 g/3 oz icing sugar, sifted

grated rind of 1 orange

COOK'S TIP

This tea bread will keep for a couple of days. Wrap it carefully and store in a cool, dry place.

1 Grease a 900 g/2 lb loaf tin and line the base with baking paper.

2 Sift the flour and baking powder into a mixing bowl. Stir in the brown sugar, bananas, chopped mixed peel, nuts and dried cranberries.

3 Stir the orange juice, eggs and sunflower oil together until well combined. Add the mixture to the dry ingredients and mix until thoroughly blended. Spoon the mixture into the prepared loaf tin and use a palette knife to smooth the top.

4 Bake in a preheated oven, 180°C/350°F/Gas Mark 4, for about 1 hour until firm to the touch or until a fine skewer inserted into the centre of the loaf comes out clean.

5 Turn out the loaf and leave it to cool on a wire rack.

6 Mix the icing sugar with a little water and drizzle the icing over the loaf. Sprinkle the orange rind over the top.

7 Leave the icing to set before serving the loaf in slices.

Tarte au Citron

Although this classic French lemon tart is quite rich, it is also incredibly refreshing, making an ideal dessert to follow a hearty main course.

NUTRITIONAL INFORMATION

Calories	369	Sugars	........14g
Protein	.........7g	Fat	..........25g
Carbohydrate	...31g	Saturates	......14g

15 mins, plus chilling   35 mins

SERVES 6–8

INGREDIENTS

grated rind of 2–3 large lemons

150 ml/5 fl oz lemon juice

100 g/3½ oz caster sugar

125 ml/4 fl oz double cream or
  crème fraîche

3 large eggs

3 large egg yolks

icing sugar, for dusting

PASTRY

175 g/6 oz plain flour

½ tsp salt

115 g/4 oz cold unsalted butter, diced

1 egg yolk, beaten with
  2 tbsp ice-cold water

1 To make the pastry, sift the flour and salt into a bowl. Using your fingertips, rub the butter into the flour until the mixture resembles fine breadcrumbs. Add the egg yolk and water to the flour and stir to make a dough.

2 Gather the dough into a ball, wrap in clingfilm and refrigerate for at least 1 hour. Roll out on a lightly floured work surface and use to line a 23–25 cm/9–10 inch fluted tart tin with a removable base. Prick the base all over with a fork and line with a sheet of baking paper. Cover the base with baking beans.

3 Bake in a preheated oven at 200°C/400°F/Gas Mark 6 for 15 minutes until the pastry looks set. Remove the paper and beans. Reduce the oven temperature to 190°C/375°F/Gas Mark 5.

4 Beat the lemon rind, lemon juice and sugar together until blended. Slowly beat in the cream, then beat in the eggs and yolks, one by one.

5 Set the pastry case on a baking sheet and pour in the filling. Transfer to the preheated oven and bake the dessert for 20 minutes until the filling is set.

6 Leave to cool completely on a wire rack. Dust the tart with icing sugar. Serve garnished with candied citrus peel.

Pine Kernel Tartlets

Pine kernels and orange rind are popular ingredients in Mediterranean dishes – here they add a twist of flavour to luscious chocolate tartlets.

NUTRITIONAL INFORMATION

Calories ....654 Sugars 61g
Protein ....11g Fat 33g
Carbohydrate ...85g Saturates 14g

1 hr 40 mins   45 mins

SERVES 4

INGREDIENTS

60 g/2 oz dark chocolate, with at least 70% cocoa solids

5 tbsp unsalted butter

175 g/6 oz plus 2 tbsp caster sugar

6 tbsp light brown sugar

6 tbsp milk

3½ tbsp golden syrup

finely grated rind of 2 large oranges and 2 tbsp freshly squeezed juice

1 tsp vanilla essence

3 large eggs, lightly beaten

100 g/3½ oz pine kernels

PASTRY

250 g/9 oz plain flour

pinch of salt

100 g/3½ oz butter

115 g/4 oz icing sugar

1 large egg and 2 large egg yolks

1 To make the pastry, sift the flour and a pinch of salt into a bowl. Make a well in the centre and add the butter, icing sugar, whole egg and egg yolks. Using your fingertips, mix the ingredients in the well into a paste.

2 Gradually incorporate the flour to make a soft dough. Quickly and lightly knead the dough. Shape into a ball, wrap in clingfilm and chill for at least 1 hour.

3 Roll the pastry into 8 circles, each 15 cm/6 inch across. Use to line 8 loose-bottomed 10 cm/4 inch tartlet tins. Line each with baking paper to fit and fill with baking beans. Chill for 10 minutes.

4 Bake in a preheated oven, 200°C/400°F/Gas Mark 6 for 5 minutes. Remove the paper and beans and bake for a further 8 minutes. Leave to cool on a wire rack. Reduce the oven temperature to 180°C/350°F/Gas Mark 4.

5 Meanwhile, break the chocolate into a saucepan over medium heat. Add the butter and stir until blended.

6 Stir in the remaining ingredients. Spoon the filling into the tartlet cases on a baking tray. Bake for 25–30 minutes, or until the tops puff up, crack and feel set. Cover with foil for the last 5 minutes if the pastry is browning too much.

7 Transfer the tarts to a wire rack and leave to cool for at least 15 minutes before unmoulding. Serve warm or at room temperature.

Lavender Hearts

If you've never thought of using lavender to flavour your baking, these beautiful little heart-shaped biscuits will soon convert you!

NUTRITIONAL INFORMATION

Calories	36	Sugars	........2g
Protein	.........1g	Fat	...........1g
Carbohydrate	....5g	Saturates	.......1g

  20 mins 10 mins

MAKES ABOUT 48 BISCUITS

I N G R E D I E N T S

225 g/8 oz plain flour, plus extra for dusting

75 g/2¾ oz chilled butter, diced

75 g/2¾ oz lavender sugar (see page 1014), or ordinary caster sugar

1 large egg

1 tbsp dried lavender flowers, very finely chopped

TO DECORATE

about 4 tbsp icing sugar

about 1 tsp water

about 2 tbsp fresh lavender flowers

with the dried lavender flowers. Stir the mixture until a stiff paste is formed.

3 Turn out the dough on to a lightly floured work surface and roll out until about 5 mm/¼ inch thick.

4 Using a 5 cm/2 inch heart-shaped biscuit cutter, press out 48 biscuits, occasionally dipping the cutter into extra flour, and re-rolling the trimmings as necessary. Transfer the pastry hearts to the baking sheets.

5 Prick the surface of each heart with a fork. Bake in a preheated oven at 180°C/350°F/Gas Mark 4 for 10 minutes, or until lightly browned. Transfer to a wire rack set over a sheet of baking parchment to cool.

6 Sift the icing sugar into a bowl. Add 1 teaspoon cold water and stir until a thin, smooth icing forms, adding a little extra water if necessary.

7 Drizzle the icing from the tip of the spoon over the cooled biscuits in a random pattern. Immediately sprinkle with the fresh lavender flowers while the icing is still soft so that they stick in place. Leave for at least 15 minutes until the icing has set. Store the biscuits for up to 4 days in an airtight container.

1 Line 2 baking sheets with baking paper. Put the flour in a bowl, add the butter and lightly rub in with your fingertips until the mixture resembles fine crumbs. Stir in the lavender sugar.

2 Lightly beat the egg, then add it to the flour and butter mixture along

Cannoli

No Sicilian celebration is complete without cannoli. If you can't find the moulds, use large dried pasta tubes, covered with foil, shiny side out.

NUTRITIONAL INFORMATION

Calories 171	Sugars 8g
Protein 5g	Fat 9g
Carbohydrate . . .18g	Saturates 4g

1¾ hrs   15–20 mins

MAKES 20

INGREDIENTS

3 tbsp lemon juice

3 tbsp water

1 large egg

250 g/9 oz plain flour

1 tbsp caster sugar

1 tsp mixed spice

pinch of salt

2 tbsp butter, softened

sunflower oil, for deep frying

1 small egg white, lightly beaten

icing sugar

FILLING

750 g/1 lb 10 oz ricotta cheese, drained

4 tbsp icing sugar

1 tsp vanilla essence

finely grated rind of 1 large orange

4 tbsp very finely chopped glacé fruit

50 g/1¾ oz dark chocolate, grated

pinch of ground cinnamon

2 tbsp Marsala or orange juice

1 Combine the lemon juice, water and egg. Put the flour, sugar, spice and salt in a food processor and process. Add the butter and, with the motor running, pour the egg mixture through the feed tube. Process until the mixture forms a dough.

2 Turn the dough out on to a lightly floured surface and knead lightly. Wrap in clingfilm and chill for 1 hour.

3 Meanwhile, make the filling. Beat the ricotta cheese until smooth. Sift in the icing sugar, then beat in the remaining ingredients. Cover and chill until required.

4 Roll out the dough on a floured surface until 1.5 mm/¹⁄₁₆ inch thick. Using a ruler, cut out 8.5 x 7.5 cm/3½ x 3 inch pieces, re-rolling and cutting the trimmings, making about 20 pieces in all.

5 Heat 5 cm/2 inches of oil in a pan to 190°C/375°F. Roll a piece of pastry

around a greased cannoli mould, to just overlap the edge. Seal with egg white, pressing firmly. Repeat with all the moulds you have. Fry 2 or 3 moulds until the cannoli are golden, crisp and bubbly.

6 Remove with a slotted spoon and drain on kitchen paper. Leave until cool, then carefully slide off the moulds. Repeat with the remaining cannoli.

7 Store the cannoli unfilled in an airtight container for up to 2 days. Pipe in the ricotta filling no more than 30 minutes before serving to prevent the pastry becoming soggy. Sift icing sugar over and serve.

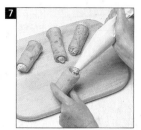

Baklava

This traditional Greek pastry is truly delectable. It is also very rich and highly calorific, so serve it in very small pieces.

NUTRITIONAL INFORMATION

Calories	406	Sugars	........30g
Protein	.........6g	Fat	..........28g
Carbohydrate	...36g	Saturates	.......8g

20 mins   1¼ hrs

MAKES 25 PIECES

I N G R E D I E N T S

300 g/10 oz walnut halves

200 g/7 oz shelled pistachio nuts

100 g/3½ oz blanched almonds

4 tbsp pine kernels, finely chopped

finely grated rind of 2 large oranges

6 tbsp sesame seeds

1 tbsp sugar

½ tsp ground cinnamon

½ tsp ground mixed spice

about 300 g/10½ oz butter, melted

23 sheets filo pastry, each 25 cm/10 inches square, defrosted if frozen

S Y R U P

600 g/1 lb 5 oz caster sugar

500 ml/18 fl oz water

5 tbsp honey

3 cloves

2 large strips lemon rind

1 To make the filling, put the walnuts, pistachio nuts, almonds and pine kernels in a food processor and pulse until finely chopped but not ground. Transfer to a bowl and stir in the orange rind, sesame seeds, sugar, cinnamon and mixed spice.

2 Butter a 25 cm/10 inch square, 5 cm/2 inch deep ovenproof dish.

Cut the stacked sheets of filo pastry to size, using a ruler. Keep them covered with a damp tea towel.

3 Place a sheet of filo on the bottom of the dish and brush with melted butter. Top with 7 more sheets, brushing with butter between each layer.

4 Sprinkle with 125 g/4½ oz of the filling. Top with 3 more sheets of filo, brushing each one with butter. Continue layering until all the filo and filling are used, ending with a top layer of 3 sheets of filo. Brush with butter.

5 Using a very sharp knife cut the baklava into twenty-five 5 cm/2 inch squares. Brush again with butter. Bake in a preheated oven at 160°C/325°F/Gas Mark 3 for 1 hour.

6 Meanwhile, place all of the syrup ingredients in a saucepan, stirring to dissolve the sugar. Bring to the boil, then simmer for 15 minutes, without stirring, until a thin syrup forms. Leave to cool.

7 Remove the baklava from the oven and pour the syrup over the top. Leave to set in the dish.

Creamy Fruit Parfait

On the tiny Greek island of Kythera, this luscious combination of summer fruits and yogurt is served at tavernas as well as in homes.

NUTRITIONAL INFORMATION

Calories	261	Sugars	......17g
Protein	......10g	Fat	......18g
Carbohydrate	...17g	Saturates	......7g

 15 mins 0 mins

SERVES 4–6

INGREDIENTS

225 g/8 oz cherries

2 large peaches

2 large apricots

700 ml/1¼ pints Greek Strained Yogurt (see page 847), or natural thick yogurt

55 g/2 oz walnut halves

2 tbsp flower-scented honey

fresh redcurrants or berries, to decorate (optional)

1 To prepare the fruit, use a cherry or olive stoner to remove the cherry stones. Cut each cherry in half. Cut the peaches and apricots in half from top to bottom and remove the stones, then finely chop the flesh of all the fruit.

2 Place the finely chopped cherries, peaches and apricots in a bowl and gently stir together.

3 Spoon one-third of the yogurt into an attractive glass serving bowl. Top with half the fruit mixture.

4 Repeat with another layer of yogurt and fruit and, finally, top with the remaining yogurt.

5 Place the walnuts in a small food processor and pulse until they are chopped into quite small pieces, but not finely ground. Alternatively, chop them with a sharp knife. Sprinkle the walnuts over the top of the yogurt.

6 Drizzle the honey over the nuts and yogurt. Cover the bowl with clingfilm and chill in the refrigerator for at least 1 hour. Decorate the bowl with a small bunch of fresh redcurrants, if using, just before serving.

Espresso Granita

Enjoy this crunchy granita as a cooling mid-morning snack or as a light dessert at the end of an al fresco supper.

NUTRITIONAL INFORMATION

Calories ....133 Sugars 35g

Protein ....0g Fat 0g

Carbohydrate ...35g Saturates 0g

4 hrs   5 mins

SERVES 4–6

INGREDIENTS

200 g/7 oz caster sugar

600 ml/1 pint water

½ tsp vanilla essence

600 ml/1 pint very strong espresso
coffee, chilled

fresh mint, to garnish

1 Put the sugar in a pan with the water and stir over a low heat to dissolve the sugar. Increase the heat and boil for 4 minutes, without stirring. Use a wet pastry brush to brush down any spatters on the side of the pan.

2 Remove the pan from the heat and pour the syrup into a heatproof non-metallic bowl. Sit the bowl in the kitchen sink filled with iced water to speed up the cooling process. Stir in the vanilla and coffee and leave until completely cool.

3 Transfer to a shallow metal container, cover and freeze for up to 3 months.

4 Thirty minutes before serving, place individual serving bowls in the refrigerator to chill.

5 To serve, invert the container on to a chopping board. Rinse a cloth in very hot water, wring it out then rub on the bottom of the container for 15 seconds. Give the container a sharp shake and the mixture should fall out.

6 Break up the granita with a knife and transfer to a food processor. Process until it becomes grainy and crunchy. Serve in the chilled bowls, decorated with mint.

COOK'S TIP

A very dark, fruity-flavoured espresso is the only choice for this Italian speciality, or the flavour will be marred by the freezing.

Rich Vanilla Ice Cream

Italy is synonymous with ice cream. This home-made version of real vanilla ice cream is absolutely delicious and so easy to make.

NUTRITIONAL INFORMATION

Calories 652   Sugars 33g
Protein . . . . .8g   Fat 55g
Carbohydrate . . .33g   Saturates 32g

 5 mins, plus cooling   10 mins

SERVES 4–6

INGREDIENTS

600 ml/1 pint double cream

1 vanilla pod

pared rind of 1 lemon

4 eggs, beaten

2 egg yolks

175 g/6 oz caster sugar

1 Place the cream in a heavy-based saucepan and heat gently, whisking. Add the vanilla pod, lemon rind, eggs and egg yolks and heat until the mixture reaches just below boiling point.

2 Reduce the heat and cook for 8–10 minutes, whisking the mixture continuously, until thickened.

3 Stir the sugar into the cream mixture, set aside and leave to cool.

4 Strain the cream mixture into a bowl through a sieve.

5 Slit open the vanilla pod, scoop out the tiny black seeds and stir them into the cream.

6 Pour the ice cream mixture into a shallow freezing container with a lid and freeze overnight until set. The ice cream can be stored in the freezer until required, but remove it to the refrigerator just before serving to soften slightly.

COOK'S TIP

Ice cream is one of the traditional dishes of Italy. Everyone eats it and there are numerous gelato stalls selling a wide variety of flavours, usually in a cone. It is also served in scoops, and even sliced!

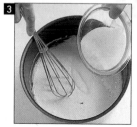

Lemon & Coffee Granitas

A delightful end to a meal, granitas are made from slushy ice rather than frozen solid, so they need to be served very quickly.

NUTRITIONAL INFORMATION

Calories	159	Sugars	........38g
Protein	.........1g	Fat	...........0g
Carbohydrate	...38g	Saturates	.......0g

10 mins, plus freezing

6 mins

SERVES 4

I N G R E D I E N T S

LEMON GRANITA

3 lemons

200 ml/7 fl oz lemon juice

100 g/3½ oz caster sugar

500 ml/18 fl oz cold water

COFFEE GRANITA

2 tbsp instant coffee

2 tbsp sugar

2 tbsp hot water

600 ml/1 pint cold water

2 tbsp rum or brandy

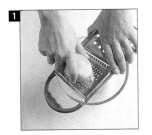  

1 To make lemon granita, finely grate the lemon rind. Place the rind, juice and caster sugar in a pan. Bring to the boil and leave to simmer for 5-6 minutes or until thick and syrupy. Leave to cool.

2 Once cooled, stir in the cold water and pour into a shallow freezer container with a lid. Freeze the granita for 4-5 hours, stirring occasionally to break up the ice. Serve as a palate cleanser between dinner courses.

3 To make coffee granita, place the coffee and sugar in a bowl and pour over the hot water, stirring until dissolved.

4 Stir in the cold water together with the rum or brandy.

5 Pour the mixture into a shallow freezer container with a lid. Freeze for at least 6 hours, stirring every 1–2 hours in order to create a grainy texture. Serve with cream, if you wish.

VARIATION

If you would prefer a non-alcoholic version of the coffee granita, simply omit the rum or brandy and add extra instant coffee instead.

Frozen Citrus Soufflés

These delicious desserts are a refreshing way to end a meal. They can be made in advance and kept in the freezer until required.

NUTRITIONAL INFORMATION

Calories 364   Sugars 27g
Protein ....11g   Fat 24g
Carbohydrate ...27g   Saturates 14g

35 mins   0 mins

SERVES 4

INGREDIENTS

1 tbsp gelozone (vegetarian gelatine)

6 tbsp very hot water

3 eggs, separated

90 g/3 oz caster sugar

finely grated rind and juice of 1 lemon,
    ½ lime and ½ orange

150 ml/¼ pint double cream

125 g/4½ oz plain fromage frais

thin lemon, lime and orange slices,
    to decorate

1 Tie greaseproof paper collars around 4 individual soufflé or ramekin dishes or around 1 large (15 cm/6 inch diameter) soufflé dish.

2 Sprinkle the gelozone into the very hot water, stirring well to disperse. Leave the mixture to stand for 2–3 minutes, stirring occasionally, to give a completely clear liquid. Leave to cool for 10–15 minutes.

3 Meanwhile, whisk the egg yolks and sugar, using a hand-held electric mixer or wire whisk, until very pale and light in texture. Add the rind and juice from the fruits, mixing well. Stir in the cooled gelozone liquid, making sure that it is thoroughly incorporated.

4 Put the cream in a large chilled bowl and whip until it holds its shape. Stir the fromage frais and then add it to the cream, mixing it in gently. Fold the cream mixture into the citrus mixture, using a large metal spoon.

5 Using a clean whisk, beat the egg whites in a clean bowl until stiff and then gently fold them into the citrus mixture, using a metal spoon.

6 Pour the mixture into the prepared dishes, almost to the top of their collars. Allow some room for the mixture to expand on freezing. Transfer the dishes to the freezer and open-freeze for about 2 hours, until frozen.

7 Remove from the freezer 10 minutes before serving. Peel away the paper collars carefully and decorate with the slices of lemon, lime and orange.

Chocolate Cookie Ice Cream

This marvellous frozen dessert offers the best of both worlds, delicious chocolate chip cookies and a rich dairy-flavoured ice.

NUTRITIONAL INFORMATION

Calories 238	Sugars 23g
Protein 9g	Fat 10g
Carbohydrate . . .30g	Saturates 4g

6 hrs   5 mins

SERVES 6

INGREDIENTS

300 ml/½ pint milk

1 vanilla pod

2 eggs

2 egg yolks

60 g/2 oz caster sugar

300 ml/½ pint natural yogurt

125 g/4½ oz chocolate chip cookies, broken into small pieces

1 Pour the milk into a small pan, add the vanilla pod and bring to the boil over a low heat. Remove from the heat, cover the pan and set aside to cool.

2 Beat the eggs and egg yolks in a double boiler or in a bowl set over a pan of simmering water. Add the sugar and continue beating until the mixture is pale and creamy.

3 Reheat the milk to simmering point and strain it over the egg mixture. Stir continuously until the custard is thick enough to coat the back of a spoon. Remove the custard from the heat and stand the pan or bowl in cold water to prevent any further cooking. Wash and dry the vanilla pod for future use.

4 Stir the yogurt into the cooled custard and beat until it is well blended. When the mixture is thoroughly cold, stir in the broken cookies.

5 Transfer the mixture to a chilled metal cake tin or plastic container, cover and freeze for 4 hours. Remove from the freezer every hour, transfer to a chilled bowl and beat vigorously to prevent ice crystals from forming, then return to the freezer. Alternatively, freeze the mixture in an ice-cream maker, following the manufacturer's instructions.

6 An hour before you are ready to serve the ice cream, transfer it to the main part of the refrigerator to soften slightly. Serve scoops of the ice cream in individual glass bowls.

Lavender Ice Cream

This delicious ice cream, flavoured with lavender flowers, has the wonderful scent of a summer garden.

NUTRITIONAL INFORMATION

Calories	294	Sugars	........24g
Protein	.........5g	Fat	..........21g
Carbohydrate	...24g	Saturates	......11g

35 mins, plus freezing | 0 mins

SERVES 6–8

INGREDIENTS

flowers from 10–12 large sprigs fresh lavender, plus extra to decorate

6 large egg yolks

150 g/5½ oz caster sugar, or lavender sugar (see Cook's Tip)

500 ml/18 fl oz milk

250 ml/9 fl oz double cream

1 tsp vanilla essence

1 Strip the small flowers from the stems, discarding any brown or green bits. Place them in a small sieve and rinse, then pat dry with kitchen paper. Set aside.

2 Put the egg yolks and sugar in a heatproof bowl that will sit over a saucepan with plenty of room underneath. Using an electric mixer, beat the eggs and sugar together until they are thick.

3 Put the milk, cream and vanilla essence in a saucepan over a low heat and bring to a simmer, stirring. Pour the hot milk over the egg mixture, whisking constantly. Rinse the pan and place 2.5 cm/1 inch water in the bottom. Place the bowl on top, making sure the base of the bowl does not touch the water. Turn the heat to medium–high.

4 Cook the mixture, stirring, until it is thick enough to coat the back of the wooden spoon.

5 Remove the custard from the heat and stir in the flowers. Cool, then cover and set aside to infuse for 2 hours, chilling for the last 30 minutes. Strain the mixture through a nylon sieve to remove all the lavender flowers.

6 Churn the ice cream in an ice-cream maker, following the manufacturer's instructions. Alternatively, freeze and whisk as in step 5 of Rich Vanilla Ice Cream (see page 1010).

7 Transfer to a freezerproof bowl, smooth the top and cover with cling film or foil. Freeze for up to 3 months.

8 Soften slightly in the refrigerator for 20 minutes before serving. Decorate with fresh lavender flowers.

COOK'S TIP

To make lavender sugar, put 500g/1lb 2 oz sugar in a food processor, add 125 g/4½ oz lavender flowers, and blend. Leave in a sealed container for 10 days. Sift out the flower bits and store the sugar in a sealed jar.

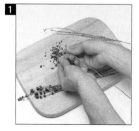

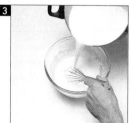

Mint & Chocolate Gelato

Rich, creamy gelati, or ice creams, are one of the great Italian culinary contributions to the world. This version is made with fresh mint.

NUTRITIONAL INFORMATION

Calories	575	Sugars	........53g
Protein	........17g	Fat	..........34g
Carbohydrate	...54g	Saturates	......18g

5–6 hrs   20 mins

SERVES 4

INGREDIENTS

6 large eggs

150 g/5½ oz caster sugar

300 ml/½ pint milk

150 ml/5 fl oz double cream

large handful fresh mint leaves, rinsed and dried

2 drops green food colouring, optional

60 g/2 oz dark chocolate, finely chopped

1 Put the eggs and sugar in a heatproof bowl that will sit over a saucepan with plenty of room underneath. Using an electric mixer, beat the eggs and sugar together until thick and creamy.

2 Put the milk and cream in the saucepan and bring to a simmer, stirring. Pour on to the eggs, whisking constantly. Rinse the pan and put 2.5 cm/1 inch of water in the bottom. Place the bowl on top, making sure the base does not touch the water. Turn the heat to medium–high.

3 Transfer the mixture to a pan and cook the mixture, stirring constantly, until it is thick enough to coat the back of the wooden spoon and leave a mark when you pull your finger across it.

4 Tear the mint leaves and stir them into the custard. Remove the custard from the heat. Leave to cool, then cover and infuse for at least 2 hours, chilling for the last 30 minutes.

5 Strain the mixture through a small nylon sieve, to remove the pieces of mint. Stir in the green food colouring, if using. Transfer the mixture to a freezer container and freeze for 1–2 hours until it is frozen 2.5 cm/1 inch in from the sides.

6 Scrape into a bowl and beat again until smooth. Stir in the chocolate pieces, smooth the top and cover with clingfilm or kitchen foil. Freeze until it is set, and store for up to 3 months.

7 Soften slightly in the refrigerator for 20 minutes before serving.

Orange & Bitters Sorbet

Made from a distinctive Italian drink and freshly squeezed orange juice, this smooth, pale-pink sorbet is a cooling dessert with a refreshing tang.

NUTRITIONAL INFORMATION

Calories 212   Sugars 52g
Protein . . . . .2g   Fat 0g
Carbohydrate . . .52g   Saturates 0g

3 hrs   3–5 mins

SERVES 4–6

INGREDIENTS

3–4 large oranges

225 g/8 oz caster sugar

600 ml/1 pint water

3 tbsp red Italian bitters, such as Campari

2 large egg whites

TO DECORATE

fresh mint leaves

candied citrus peel (optional)

3 Remove the pan from the heat and pour into a heatproof non-metallic bowl. Add the orange rind and infuse while the mixture cools to room temperature.

4 Roll the pared oranges back and forth on the work surface, pressing down firmly. Cut them in half and squeeze 125 ml/4½ fl oz juice. If you need more juice, squeeze the extra orange.

5 When the syrup is cool, stir in the orange juice and bitters. Strain the mixture into a container, cover and chill for at least 30 minutes.

6 Put the mixture in an ice-cream maker and churn for about 15 minutes. Alternatively, follow the instructions on page 1010. Whisk the egg whites in a clean, grease-free bowl until stiff peaks form.

7 Add the egg whites to the ice-cream maker and continue churning for 5 minutes or according to the manufacturer's instructions. Transfer to a shallow, freezerproof container, cover and freeze for up to 2 months.

8 About 15 minutes before serving, put the ice cream in the refrigerator to soften. Scoop into bowls and serve decorated with mint leaves and candied citrus peel.

1 Working over a bowl to catch any juice, pare the rind from 3 of the oranges, without removing the bitter white pith. If some of the pith does come off with the rind, use the knife to scrape it off.

2 Put the sugar and water in a pan and stir over a low heat until dissolved. Increase the heat and boil for 2 minutes, without stirring. Using a wet pastry brush, brush any crystals down the side of the pan, if necessary.

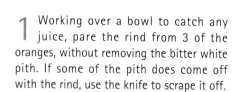

Italian Rice Ice Cream

It stands to reason that a nation which thinks of risotto as its national dish should produce a rice ice cream – and this one is excellent.

NUTRITIONAL INFORMATION

Calories 570	Sugars 51g	
Protein 10g	Fat 31g	
Carbohydrate . . .44g	Saturates 16g	

15 mins, plus freezing

25 mins

MAKES ABOUT 1.2 LITRES/2 PINTS

I N G R E D I E N T S

100 g/3 ½ oz short-grain pudding rice

500 ml/18 fl oz milk

85 g/3 oz sugar

85 g/3 oz good-quality honey

½ tsp lemon essence

1 tsp vanilla essence

175 g/6 oz good-quality lemon curd

500 ml/18 fl oz double or whipping cream

grated rind and juice of 1 large lemon

1 Put the rice and milk in a large heavy-based saucepan and bring to a gentle simmer, stirring occasionally; do not let it boil. Reduce the heat to low, cover and simmer very gently for about 25 minutes, stirring occasionally, until the rice is just tender and the liquid absorbed.

2 Remove from the heat and stir in the sugar, honey, and the lemon and vanilla essences, stirring until the sugar is dissolved. Pour into a food processor or blender and pulse 3 or 4 times. The mixture should be thick and creamy, but it should not be completely smooth.

3 Put the lemon curd in a bowl and gradually beat in about 225 ml/8 fl oz of the cream. Stir in the rice mixture with the lemon rind and juice until blended.

Lightly whip the remaining cream until it just begins to hold its shape, then fold into the lemon-rice mixture. Chill.

4 Stir the rice mixture and pour into an ice-cream machine. Churn according to the manufacturer's instructions for 15–20 minutes. Transfer to a freezerproof container and freeze for 6–8 hours or overnight. Transfer to the refrigerator about 1 hour before serving.

COOK'S TIP

If you do not have an ice-cream machine, transfer the chilled rice mixture to a freezerproof container. Freeze for 1 hour until slightly slushy, then whisk to break up any crystals; refreeze. Repeat twice more.

Italian Drowned Ice Cream

A classic vanilla ice cream is topped with steaming coffee to make a wonderful instant dessert. Remember to serve in heatproof bowls.

NUTRITIONAL INFORMATION

Calories 646	Sugars 48g
Protein 10g	Fat 47g
Carbohydrate ...48g	Saturates 26g

7½ hrs   10 mins

SERVES 4

INGREDIENTS

about 475 ml/16 fl oz freshly made espresso coffee

chocolate-covered coffee beans, to decorate

VANILLA ICE CREAM

1 vanilla pod

6 large egg yolks

150 g/5½ oz caster sugar, or vanilla-flavoured sugar (sugar that has been stored with a vanilla pod)

500 ml/17 fl oz milk

250 ml/8 fl oz plus 2 tbsp double cream

1 To make the ice cream, slit the vanilla pod lengthways and scrape out the tiny brown seeds. Set aside.

2 Put the yolks and sugar in a heatproof bowl that will sit over a saucepan with plenty of room underneath it. Beat the eggs and sugar together until the mixture is thick and creamy.

3 Put the milk, cream and vanilla seeds in the pan over a low heat and bring to a simmer. Pour the milk over the egg mixture, whisking. Pour 2.5 cm/1 inch of water in the bottom of a pan. Place the bowl on top, making sure that the base

does not touch the water. Turn the heat to medium–high.

4 Cook the mixture, stirring constantly, until it is thick enough to coat the back of the spoon. Remove from the heat, transfer to a bowl and leave to cool.

5 Churn the mixture in an ice-cream maker, following the manufacturer's instructions. Alternatively, place it in a freezerproof container and freeze for 1 hour, turn out into a bowl and whisk to

break up the ice crystals, then return to the freezer, repeating the process 4 times at 30 minute intervals.

6 Transfer the frozen ice cream to a freezerproof container, smooth the top and cover with clingfilm or foil. Freeze for up to 3 months.

7 Soften in the refrigerator 20 minutes before serving. Place scoops of ice cream in each bowl. Pour over the coffee and sprinkle with coffee beans.

Mango & Lime Sorbet

A refreshing sorbet is the perfect way to round off a spicy Thai meal, and mangoes make a deliciously smooth-textured, velvety sorbet.

NUTRITIONAL INFORMATION

Calories 158	Sugars 34g	
Protein 1g	Fat 3g	
Carbohydrate ...34g	Saturates 2g	

4 hrs   4 mins

SERVES 4

INGREDIENTS

6 tbsp caster sugar

100 ml/3½ fl oz water

rind of 3 limes, finely grated

2 tbsp coconut cream

2 large, ripe mangoes

135 ml/4½ fl oz lime juice

curls of fresh coconut, toasted, to decorate

1 Place the sugar, water and lime rind in a small pan and heat gently, stirring constantly, until the sugar dissolves. Boil rapidly for 2 minutes to reduce slightly, then remove from the heat and strain into a bowl or jug. Stir in the coconut cream and set aside to cool.

2 Halve the mangoes, remove the stones and peel thinly. Chop the flesh roughly and place in a food processor or blender with the lime juice. Process to a smooth purée and transfer to a small bowl.

3 Pour the cooled syrup into the mango purée, mixing evenly. Tip into a freezer container and freeze for 1 hour, or until slushy in texture. (Alternatively, use an electric ice-cream maker.)

4 Remove the container from the freezer and beat with an electric mixer to break up the ice crystals. Refreeze for a further hour, then remove from the freezer and beat the contents again until smooth.

5 Cover the container, return to the freezer and freeze until firm. To serve, remove from the freezer and leave at room temperature for about 15 minutes to soften slightly before scooping. Sprinkle with curls of toasted coconut to serve.

Citrus Meringue Crush

This is an excellent way to use up left-over meringue shells and is very simple to prepare. Serve with a spoonful of tangy fruit sauce.

NUTRITIONAL INFORMATION

Calories 165   Sugars 32g
Protein ....5g   Fat 1g
Carbohydrate ...37g   Saturates 0.4g

2 hrs   10 mins

SERVES 4

I N G R E D I E N T S

8 ready-made meringue nests

300 ml/½ pint low-fat natural yogurt

½ tsp finely grated orange rind

½ tsp finely grated lemon rind

½ tsp finely grated lime rind

2 tbsp orange liqueur or orange juice

TO DECORATE

sliced kumquat

grated lime rind

SAUCE

55 g/2 oz kumquats

8 tbsp orange juice

2 tbsp lemon juice

2 tbsp lime juice

2 tbsp water

2–3 tsp caster sugar

1 tsp cornflour mixed with 1 tbsp water

1 Place the meringues in a plastic bag and, with a rolling pin, crush into small pieces. Place in a mixing bowl.

2 Stir in the yogurt, grated citrus rinds and the liqueur or juice. Spoon the mixture into 4 mini-basins and freeze for 1½–2 hours until firm.

3 Thinly slice the kumquats for the sauce and place them in a small pan with the fruit juices and water. Bring the water gently to the boil and then simmer over a low heat for 3–4 minutes until the kumquats soften.

4 Sweeten with sugar to taste, stir in the cornflour mixture and cook, stirring, until thickened.

5 Pour into a small bowl, cover the surface with clingfilm and set aside to cool – the film will help prevent a skin from forming. Chill in the refrigerator until required.

6 To serve, dip the meringue basins in hot water for 5 seconds, or until they loosen, and turn on to serving plates. Spoon over a little sauce, decorate with slices of kumquat and lime rind and serve.

Brown Bread Ice Cream

Although it sounds unusual, this yogurt-based recipe is delicious.
It contains no cream and is ideal for a low-fat diet.

NUTRITIONAL INFORMATION

Calories 264	Sugars 25g	
Protein 12g	Fat 6g	
Carbohydrate ...43g	Saturates 1g	

2¼ hrs   5 mins

SERVES 4

INGREDIENTS

175 g/6 oz fresh wholemeal breadcrumbs

25 g/1 oz finely chopped walnuts

60 g/2 oz caster sugar

½ tsp ground nutmeg

1 tsp finely grated orange rind

450 ml/16 fl oz low-fat natural yogurt

2 large egg whites

TO DECORATE

walnut halves

orange slices

fresh mint

1 Preheat the grill to medium. Mix the breadcrumbs, walnuts and sugar and spread over a sheet of foil in the grill pan.

2 Grill, stirring frequently, for 5 minutes until crisp and evenly browned (take care that the sugar does not burn). Remove from the heat and leave to cool.

3 When cool, transfer to a mixing bowl and mix in the nutmeg, orange rind and yogurt. In another bowl, whisk the egg whites until stiff. Gently fold into the breadcrumb mixture, using a metal spoon.

4 Spoon the mixture into 4 mini basins, smooth over the tops and freeze for 1½–2 hours until firm.

5 To serve, hold the bases of the moulds in hot water for a few seconds, then immediately turn the ice cream out on to serving plates.

6 Serve at once, decorated with the walnuts, oranges and fresh mint.

COOK'S TIP
If you don't have mini basins, use ramekins or teacups or, if you prefer, use one large bowl. Alternatively, spoon the mixture into a large freezing container to freeze and serve the ice cream in scoops.

Index